The Solicitor's Handbook 2019

THE SOLICITOR'S HANDBOOK 2019

By

Gregory Treverton-Jones QC, Nigel West, Susanna Heley and Robert Forman

© The Law Society 2019

ISBN 978-1-78446-101-0

Crown copyright material in the Appendices is reproduced with the permission of the Controller of Her Majesty's Stationery Office.

First edition published in 2008
Second edition published in 2009
Third edition published in 2011
Fourth edition published in 2012
Fifth edition published in 2013
Sixth edition published in 2014
Seventh edition published in 2016

This eighth edition published in 2019 by the Law Society
113 Chancery Lane, London WC2A 1PL

Typeset by Columns Design XML Ltd, Reading
Printed and bound in the UK by Hobbs the Printers Ltd, Totton, Hants

The paper used for the text pages of this book is FSC certified. FSC (The Forest Stewardship Council) is an international network to promote responsible management of the world's forests.

Contents

Foreword to the 2008 edition

The authors have asked me to write a short foreword to this book. I am delighted to do so because I entirely agree with the views expressed in the Preface. Although I quite understand that it may be necessary to use the Internet in order for practitioners to be fully up to date at any given moment, many people (and not only the very old like me) like to have a book which sets out the basic principles and which they can readily consult. *The Solicitor's Handbook* is precisely that. It concisely sets out the relevant position under a number of different headings and is very user friendly.

The authors express the hope that the book will prove to be a valuable resource for regulator and regulated alike and that it will contribute to good regulation by identifying and explaining areas of particular concern and risk, especially where practitioners have, in the past, made innocent mistakes which have nevertheless had serious consequences.

I know that hope springs eternal, but in this case I am confident that the authors' hopes will be fulfilled. I wish it well.

Sir Anthony Clarke

Master of the Rolls
Royal Courts of Justice
October 2007

Preface to the 2008 edition

For generations of solicitors *The Guide to the Professional Conduct of Solicitors* (first published in 1960 and always provided free of charge) was the source of all knowledge in relation to the rules that controlled the profession. If you could not find it in the Guide, or if the available published guidance still left you in a quandary, you could always 'ring Redditch' – the Law Society's ethics helpline. Looking it up in the Guide and seeking the Law Society's advice was a total solution. After all; how could you be criticised for following the Law Society's own advice?

The Guide is no more. The eighth edition, published in 1999, was the last. We have moved into the modern era; the paperless age. The Solicitors' Code of Conduct 2007 (which henceforth we will refer to as 'the Code') appears on the website of the Solicitors Regulation Authority (SRA); so do the Solicitors' Accounts Rules 1998, and the Financial Services Rules and other rules. Diligent searching on the Law Society website will reveal much in the way of published guidance, pronunciations and edicts. Information about how clients can complain about you, and what will happen when they do, can be found on the website of the Legal Complaints Service (LCS).

Only in the two thick volumes of the mighty *Cordery on Solicitors* will practitioners find in written form all the law and professional rules relating to solicitors.

But the paperless age and rapidly changing regulatory rules carry with them real dangers for practitioners who may find it difficult or impossible to discover what rules were in force when they did things which later become the subject of regulatory concern. This Handbook, which will be updated annually, seeks to remove those problems.

This Handbook brings together all the professional rules governing the conduct and regulation of solicitors in a manner that is convenient and inexpensive. We hope that we have added much more of value, by drawing upon our professional experience to explain how the rules and the regulatory machinery work in practice.

We have addressed our book to 'you' the practitioner: it has been written from the perspective of the practitioner, to whom it is intended to provide information and guidance. We have included material that we consider relevant and important to the practitioner but which is not included within the formal rules (for example, how money laundering, mortgage fraud and investment scams work), so that independently of the published guidance you can spot problems before they develop into loss to clients and others, damage to reputation, and regulatory interest.

We have included guidance on the workings of the Solicitors Disciplinary Tribunal, on the powers of intervention available to the SRA and the regime for the imposition of conditions on practising certificates.

And we have included a section on where you can obtain further specialist advice and help if all else fails.

It is unlikely that any practitioner currently feels that the profession is under-regulated; the weight of regulation, and dealings with the SRA, can be daunting. The Solicitors' Practice Rules 1936 (made by virtue of section 1 of the Solicitors Act 1933) comprised seven rules (in reality only four) and could be printed on one page.[1] The latest Code, if printed on A4, occupies 253 pages (and 190 pages of this book). We also live in a rapidly changing regulatory environment. The Code came into force on 1 July 2007: one month later it was amended for the first time. An updated version of the Accounts Rules to be incorporated into the Code by amendment is already in contemplation. We now have two regulators – the LCS, dealing with client complaints and redress for poor service, and the SRA, dealing with everything else. Under the previous system, if a complaint engaged both conduct and service issues it was a 'hybrid' and both aspects were dealt with together. Now, all consumer complaints and redress will be dealt with first by the LCS and if any conduct issues are considered to arise they will be referred to the SRA to be dealt with subsequently (although, if very serious concerns are raised and the interests of the public require it, more urgent action will no doubt be taken).

You can still 'ring Redditch' for advice on issues of professional conduct, but the official and published position of the SRA is that for the purpose of any investigation or adjudication it is 'not bound' by any opinion or advice given by its own staff on the ethics helpline. In other words, you can follow the advice of the regulator, but – in theory at least – the regulator can nevertheless find you guilty of misconduct and impose sanctions. It is also not clear to what extent, if at all, information provided for the purposes of seeking such advice will be regarded as confidential, as opposed to being useful intelligence for regulatory purposes about the person making the enquiry.

The Legal Services Act 2007 maintains the division between conduct and service, hiving off consumer complaints and redress to the independent Office for Legal Complaints, which will succeed the LCS. The Act grants significant new powers to the SRA (which we have touched upon in Chapter 2) and sweeps away significant parts of the current statutory regime, for example in relation to conditions on practising certificates. Where changes will occur, we explain what the future holds.

We hope that this book will prove to be a valuable resource for regulator and regulated alike, and that it will contribute to good regulation in identifying and explaining areas of particular concern and risk – especially where practitioners have in the past made innocent mistakes that have nevertheless had serious consequences.

We would welcome feedback from practitioners, and particularly any requests and recommendations for the inclusion of material in areas we have not covered in this first edition.

We are grateful to the following for their drafting and other suggestions: Euros Jones of James Saunders & Co., who conducted extensive research and provided consider-able input for the money laundering chapter; Mike Calvert of the SRA and Che Odlum of the Law Society, who shared their practical experience of money laundering and investment fraud issues; Iain Miller of Bevan Brittan for his substantial contributions to the chapter on the Code; and Geoffrey Williams QC for reviewing and suggesting amendments to Chapter 14. Many other members of the SRA and SDT, notably Sue Elson and Liz Aldred, answered our queries construc-tively and with unfailing courtesy. All provided invaluable assistance, although the responsibility for any errors and omissions is ours alone. Others deserve particular thanks. Michael Hoyle was the inspiration for Andrew Hopper's original interest in solicitors' regulatory law and practice. When legal complications arose after we finished the writing, we received matchless assistance from Nick Gardner and David Mayhew at Herbert Smith, and valuable advice from Tony Grabiner at 1 Essex Court, and Sean Wilken and Ben Williams at 39 Essex Street. Finally, we are both deeply grateful to our respective wives, Ros and Tamsin, for their support and forbearance while their otherwise apparently sane husbands buried themselves in some of the more esoteric material contained in this book.

1   In brief – Rule 1: no touting; Rule 2: no charging under the published scale fees; Rule 3: no fee sharing; Rule 4: no association with ambulance chasers; Rule 5: provision for waivers; Rule 6: definitions; Rule 7: commencement.

Preface to the 2019 edition

The writing of this edition, the eighth since the first edition in 2008, has been tinged with great sadness. I wrote the first seven editions with Andrew Hopper QC, and together we had planned to write this one too. However, it was not to be: Andrew was diagnosed with cancer in July 2017, and died at home almost exactly a year later. He is, and will continue to be, greatly missed by innumerable former colleagues and clients. An obituary which was published in the Law Society's *Gazette* shortly after his death, is on page xiii of this book. This edition is dedicated to Andrew's memory.

After it became clear that he would be too ill to contribute significantly to the writing of this edition, Andrew and I were able to discuss, and agree upon, a succession plan. We invited Nigel West and Susanna Heley of RadcliffesLeBrasseur (joint authors of *The Solicitors' Disciplinary Tribunal* published in 2016 by the Law Society), and Robert Forman of Messrs Murdochs (who had previously contributed to the chapter on Intervention in earlier editions of *The Solicitor's Handbook*), to join me in the writing of this edition. Fortunately, they accepted.

During the two years since the last edition of this book, there has been a torrent of new rules and regulations. Pride of place goes to the new Principles and the two new Codes of Conduct which come into force in November 2019. This represents the third major rewrite of those fundamental provisions in the last 12 years. The vast Code of Conduct 2007 lasted for a mere four years, before the advent of outcomes-focused regulation as enshrined in the 2011 Principles and Code of Conduct. Now, a mere eight years later, those documents have been rewritten, and solicitors now have to face two Codes of Conduct (which we have described as the 'Code for Individuals' and the 'Code for Firms') rather than one. After the 'rules' set out in the 2007 Code, solicitors had to learn to live with 'outcomes' and 'indicative behaviours': now, under the two 2019 Codes, they must familiarise themselves with 'standards'. We have analysed and summarised these new provisions. The most important, and controversial, change is that regulated solicitors will be able to carry out reserved legal activities in unregulated entities. But there is a plethora of changes in the small print of the new Principles and Codes, and solicitors will have to navigate their way through that. We hope that this edition will assist in that task. The Accounts Rules have been significantly rewritten, as have rules and regulations concerning money laundering and professional indemnity insurance.

In the courts, the Supreme Court in *Ivey* altered the twin subjective/objective test for dishonesty which had held sway in disciplinary tribunals for more than a decade, and important Court of Appeal judgments have been handed down concerning the meaning of lack of integrity (*Wingate and Evans*), and challenges to interventions (*Neumans*). The Divisional Court has recently provided new guidance on the meaning of exceptional circumstances in dishonesty cases (*James, MacGregor and Naylor*). The highest profile case in the last two years was the unsuccessful SRA prosecution of two partners and a former assistant solicitor in Leigh Day, and the firm itself. The SRA's appeal to the High Court against the acquittals on all charges failed (*Day and others*): the profession has been left to pick up a substantial bill as a result.

In order to accommodate the changes noted above, we have expanded the number of chapters. The new Principles and Codes of Conduct are dealt with in three separate chapters. There is a new chapter on data protection. Chapter 19, on the nature of professional misconduct, has been greatly expanded to include sections on dishonesty, lack of integrity and manifest incompetence. Many other chapters have been radically rewritten to encompass the new provisions. The work involved has dwarfed that needed for any of the previous editions, save for the first, and I owe Nigel, Susanna and Robert my heartfelt thanks for taking on the amount of work which has been required of them, and for their constant cheerfulness in carrying it out.

As ever, we express our thanks to our publishers for their rapid and efficient work in producing this edition, which has been every bit as challenging for them to produce as it has been for us to write. Particular thanks are owed to Simon Hamlet and Sarah Kent. Errors and omissions are our responsibility alone.

The law is stated as at 26 August 2019. Although the book will be published in September 2019, and most of the new rules will not come into force until 25 November 2019, we have written it on the basis that more or less all of the new principles, codes and rules are actually in force.

GT-J   *QC*

Andrew Hopper QC: obituary

Andrew Hopper, who died at home in South Wales on 25 July 2018, was, without question, the country's foremost solicitor in the field of the regulation of legal professionals. For many years he was the first and last port of call for solicitors facing regulatory or disciplinary investigations or proceedings. He helped many hundreds of fellow solicitors through what can be the most frightening and stressful period of any solicitor's professional career. As a result, he built up a devoted following: his clients loved him, and, with a few exceptions, he loved them back. In him they knew that they had found someone who would fearlessly and unflinchingly fight their corner against a powerful and often unsympathetic regulator.

Andrew was born in Swansea. His father died when Andrew was eleven, and the family then pooled its resources and purchased Talygarn House in the Vale of Glamorgan, just outside Pontyclun. He remained at that house for the rest of his life, both before and after his marriage to Ros. They enjoyed a long and happy marriage. He was admitted to the Roll in 1972. After a stint at a Cardiff firm, Adams and Black, he struck out on his own, working from home as a sole practitioner. By then he had started to specialise in solicitors' regulatory work.

From the late 1970s until early 2002 the bulk of his instructions came from the regulatory arm of the Law Society, known variously as the Solicitors Complaints Bureau, the Office for Supervision of Solicitors, and, since 2007, the Solicitors Regulation Authority. For many years, he was the principal prosecutor instructed by the regulator. He acquired rights of audience in the High Court, and impressed the late Lord Bingham of Cornhill, and other members of the senior judiciary. In those days most regulatory and disciplinary appeals by solicitors against decisions of the Law Society or the Solicitors' Disciplinary Tribunal were heard by the Master of the Rolls (regulatory appeals) and the Lord Chief Justice or his deputy (disciplinary appeals). He was appointed Queen's Counsel in 2001, only the fifth solicitor, and the first outside the City of London, to achieve that distinction.

I first came across Andrew in about 1990, when I started to receive instructions from the Law Society. He was, to put it mildly, a little different from the average instructing solicitor. His swept back fair hair was longish. He rarely wore a suit unless he had to. If a Judge asked me a question to which I did not know the answer, Andrew would supply it in a stage whisper loud enough for the Judge to hear. If he felt that the Judge was being a little slow on the uptake, that too would be conveyed in the same loud stage whisper, a rather uncomfortable experience for the young barrister who was supposed to be presenting the case and getting on the right side of the Judge.

In 2002 he decided no longer to accept instructions from the Law Society due to what he perceived to be increasing unfairness by the regulator against those it was regulating. Thereafter he devoted his time to assisting solicitors who were in regulatory difficulties. It was this last period which was, I have no doubt, much the most enjoyable and fulfilling of his professional life. Although there are a small number of 'rotten apples' in the profession, Andrew did not attract that sort of client. The overwhelming majority of his clients comprised decent men and women under investigation or facing disciplinary action by their regulator, or those seeking advice as to whether they could make business decisions that are compliant with their regulatory obligations. He was a constant beacon of hope to countless solicitors under investigation. He helped many hundreds of men and women, often without financial reward (he reckoned to have advised/represented approximately one thousand in the post-2002 period).

Advising and representing solicitors in regulatory and/or disciplinary matters against the SRA can often be a difficult and thankless task. As can be easily imagined, the scales in regulatory proceedings are loaded fairly heavily in favour of the regulator. But Andrew advised and represented a series of Davids against Goliath with distinction and success, skill and integrity. In 2006, I switched to the 'defence' side also, and worked closely with him for the next 11 years. I saw at first hand the supreme quality of his work, even if correspondence which he drafted was from time to time unnecessarily abrasive in its criticism of the regulator.

His contribution was far wider than that, however. He put his unique store of knowledge and experience at the disposal of the profession. He was an editor of *The Guide to the Professional Conduct of Solicitors* (*Guide*), published by the Law Society, and distributed free of charge to the profession until 1999. He was an editor of *Cordery on Solicitors*, published by LexisNexis (now re-branded as *Cordery on Legal Services*) for many years.

In 2007, Andrew and I conceived the idea of *The Solicitor's Handbook*, a publication to take over from the defunct *Guide*: the first edition was published by the Law Society in 2008, followed by six subsequent editions over eight years. We decided to write it because there was nowhere convenient for solicitors to turn when they came up against a regulatory or disciplinary problem. Andrew wrote the lion's share of each edition. Likewise, when the SRA created outcomes-focused regulation, in 2011, our publishers turned to Andrew and I to write about it: the result was *Outcomes-Focused Regulation: A Practical Guide*, published again by the Law Society in August 2011.

For many years Andrew possessed the only searchable database of decisions of the Solicitors Disciplinary Tribunal (SDT): he made that resource readily available to those who asked, only rarely charging for the research he carried out. When the SDT created its own searchable database, it turned to Andrew to help set it up. He contributed hours of his time to help to create that resource, which is now available to all who consult the SDT website.

In recent years Andrew was recruited by the Law Society to sit on its Regulatory Affairs Board. He was also chair of the Regulatory Processes Committee – effectively the sharp end of representation of the profession in dealing with SRA, its rules and processes. He was a member of the Legal Ombudsman's Stakeholder Advisory Panel, selected personally (not as a Law Society representative) by the Legal Ombudsman, to provide advice and feedback on its systems and processes. For several years, he sat as a respondent's representative on the users' group established by the SDT to enable a forum for debate to ensure efficiency and fairness in its procedures. All of this was unpaid, and all of it was done for the benefit, not of himself, but of the profession.

One of Andrew's defining characteristics was his generosity. He was generous to his clients, always working hard, often for no financial reward. He was also generous to other lawyers, always dealing rapidly with queries sent to him by those who needed to know the answer to a knotty regulatory issue. He was seen by other solicitors as an oracle and received many such requests for advice. He always responded. And he was astonishingly generous to me in many different ways.

In case anything that I have written above should lead the reader to believe that Andrew was a paragon of virtue, he would, I know, wish me to correct that inaccurate impression. He could be rude and waspish, usually in the direction of the SRA. He loved gossip, the more salacious the better. Although he loved tennis and badminton, he developed an irrational dislike of Andy Murray. He had very little time for vegetables or salads but adored red wine and cheese. Within the profession he was seen as something of a maverick and was able to live life in his own way and on his own terms.

The cancer, when it came, was brutal and relentless. He was diagnosed almost exactly a year before he died, and although the initial surgery seemed to have been successful, the cancer spread, and became inoperable. In April 2018, he was told that he had only a limited time left. He did not plan to rage against the dying of the light. He regarded himself as having lived a charmed life and wanted only to celebrate with Ros and carefully selected friends at a series of parties. The disease progressed too rapidly for that, and it was not to be. I saw him two days before he died, and by then, I think, he was ready to let go.

Professional life without Andrew will seem very empty for me and many others. His regular clients will, I know, have been devastated. But he was right in saying that he had led a charmed life, and he was able to use a large part of that good fortune for the benefit of others. He leaves behind a wonderful legacy of memories. All of us who came along for parts of the ride are the richer for it.

Greg Treverton-Jones QC

Table of cases

Table of statutes

Paragraph references printed in **bold type** indicate where the enactment is set out in part or in full.

Table of statutory instruments

Paragraph references printed in **bold type** indicate where the enactment is set out in part or in full.

Table of European legislation and other international materials

Table of other enactments

Paragraph references printed in **bold** type indicate where the enactment is set out in part or in full.

PART I
Overview

CHAPTER I

The regulatory and disciplinary landscape

1.1

In the earliest times only the courts exercised disciplinary jurisdiction over solicitors, as officers of the court. When Mr Brounsall was struck off the roll of attorneys in 1778, having been convicted of stealing a guinea, for which he had been sentenced 'to be branded on the hand, and to be confined to the house of correction for nine months' the question was raised as to whether the striking off would amount to a second, and unlawful, penalty. Lord Mansfield announced that as this raised issues concerning the dignity of the profession, 'a solemn opinion should be given' and that the matter should be mentioned 'to all the judges'. On 27 June 1778, a Saturday, Lord Mansfield announced:

> 'We have consulted all the judges upon this case, and they are unanimously of opinion, that the defendant's having been burnt in the hand, is no objection to his being struck off the roll. And it is on this principle; that he is an unfit person to practise as an attorney.'[1]

The nineteenth century saw a move towards control of the profession by its own professional body. The Law Society was formed in 1823, as a successor to the Society of Gentleman Practisers, and incorporated by Royal Charter in 1831. By virtue of the Solicitors Act 1888, complaints of misconduct against solicitors were made to a Committee of the Incorporated Law Society, whose members were appointed by the Master of the Rolls. The Committee made findings which were embodied in a report to the court, but the court continued to exercise the disciplinary jurisdiction. No report from the Society's Committee was necessary however; the court could still act on its own motion.[2]

1   *Ex parte Brounsall* [1778] 2 Cowp 829.
2   Sections 12, 13 and 19 of the Solicitors Act 1888; and see *Re Weare* [1893] 2 QB 439, CA.

1.2

The Solicitors Act 1919 granted the powers of the court, to strike solicitors from the roll and to impose other penalties, to the Disciplinary Committee of the Law Society, but preserved the court's inherent jurisdiction. The Disciplinary Committee was not a committee of the Council of the Law Society, but a separate statutory body whose members continued to be appointed by the Master of the Rolls. The Disciplinary Committee was replaced by the Solicitors Disciplinary Tribunal (the Tribunal or SDT) in 1975, by the Solicitors Act (SA) 1974. The members continued (and still continue) to be appointed by the Master of the Rolls. Section 50 of SA 1974 preserves the court's parallel and inherent jurisdiction. The functions of the investigator and prosecutor have remained with the Law Society throughout, as they still do (in the sense that although the Solicitors Regulation Authority (SRA) operates independently of the Society through its own Board, it has no separate legal existence).

1.3

In January 2007 the Law Society split into three organisations:

(1)   the Society itself, based in Chancery Lane, which remains the representative body for solicitors; their 'trade union' – though not in the fullest sense of that phrase; the Society represents solicitors as a membership organisation whether they are employers or employees. It also remains impossible, for example, for the Law Society to assist directly in the defence of any individual solicitor in dealings with the SRA;

(2)   the SRA, which since October 2012 is based in Birmingham, with a satellite City of London office, and which is the regulator; and

(3)   the now defunct Legal Complaints Service (LCS) which between 2007 and October 2010 dealt with client complaints.

The functions of the LCS were brought to an end in respect of all complaints made on and after 6 October 2010 and it ceased to exist. Consumer or client complaints were removed by the Legal Services Act (LSA) 2007 from the existing regulators altogether[1] and vested in the Office for Legal Complaints (which uses the title of Legal Ombudsman). Part 6 of LSA 2007 established a comprehensive ombudsman scheme for the handling of complaints by consumers. For the Legal Ombudsman see **CHAPTER 14.**

The SRA is run by its own Board. As the statutory powers remain vested in the Council of the Law Society, under SA 1974 as amended, those powers are delegated by the Council to and through the SRA Board, to enable the SRA to operate independently of the Law Society.

1   Section 157 of LSA 2007.

1.4

Under LSA 2007, the Legal Services Board (LSB) is established to promote and maintain regulatory objectives relating to the provision of legal services, namely:

(1)   protecting and promoting public interest;

(2)   supporting the constitutional principle of the rule of law;

(3)   improving access to justice;

(4)   protecting and promoting the interests of consumers;

(5)   promoting competition in the provision of legal services;

(6)   encouraging an independent, strong, diverse and effective legal profession;

(7)   increasing public understanding of the citizen's legal rights and duties; and

(8)   promoting and maintaining adherence to professional principles.[1]

The professional principles are:

(1)   acting with independence and integrity;

(2)   maintaining proper standards of work;

(3)   acting in the best interests of clients;

(4)   complying with the duty to the court to act with independence in the interests of justice in relation to litigation and advocacy; and

(5)   keeping the affairs of clients confidential.[2]

The LSB regulates the regulators, delegating the primary role to approved regulators (including the Law Society/SRA) but maintaining oversight. A detailed consideration of the Board's powers is outside the parameters of this book.

1   Section 1(1) of LSA 2007.
2   Section 1(3).

1.5

Part 5 of LSA 2007 is concerned with alternative business structures (ABSs) – the licensing of bodies, not owned or controlled by lawyers, to provide legal services. The Council for Licensed Conveyancers began licensing ABSs from 6 October 2011, providing legal services restricted to conveyancing and probate, and the SRA began taking applications in January 2012.

In order to ensure that the existing suite of rules was appropriate for the changed landscape that would exist when ABSs became licensed, the SRA undertook the mammoth task of amending it. The result was the SRA Handbook 2011, which brought together a new set of Principles and a new Code of Conduct, Accounts Rules, the various rules covering authorisation and practising requirements, client protection (insurance and compensation), discipline and costs recovery, and specialist services. The SRA Handbook is made available in hard copy but is updated more regularly online. It has been regularly amended and version 21 was issued in December 2018, while the SRA continued work on a new regulatory regime to replace the 2011 Handbook.

In November 2015 the SRA announced plans to reduce the 600-page Handbook to about 50 pages, and to replace prescriptive rules with principles. That process is now substantially complete following various consultations on new regulatory arrangements, which dealt with a new Code of Conduct in two parts (one for individuals and one for entities), new Accounts Rules and proposals for changes in regulation for individual solicitors. These consultations presaged the wholesale abandonment of the SRA Practice Framework Rules, which will be replaced with new SRA Authorisation of Individuals Regulations and SRA Authorisation of Firms Rules (see **CHAPTER 2**). The entire 2011 Handbook will be replaced on 25 November 2019.

Duties of approved regulators

1.6

Under section 28 of LSA 2007, approved regulators are under a statutory duty to act in a way that is compatible with the regulatory objectives (see **1.4**) and in a way most appropriate for the purpose of meeting those objectives. Those objectives require, of course, regulation in the public interest, but a strong and independent profession is in the view of Parliament an essential requirement in the public interest. It is therefore part of the function of the SRA to work towards improving access to justice, promoting competition in the provision of legal services, encouraging an independent, strong, diverse and effective legal profession, and increasing public understanding of the citizen's legal rights and duties, all of which involve support for the profession.

Approved regulators must also have regard to the principles under which regulatory activities should be transparent, accountable, proportionate, consistent and targeted only at cases in which action is needed.[1] It has not always been the case (so it has seemed to informed commentators and so it may have seemed to the profession following encounters with the SRA) that these principles have been rigorously applied in practice, although they are officially adopted as SRA policy.

In April 2014 the Better Regulation Delivery Office of the Department for Business, Innovation and Skills issued a 'Regulators' Code' (see **APPENDIX 12**), which sets out six principles each with accompanying detailed requirements. The general principles are:

(1)   Regulators should carry out their activities in a way that supports those they regulate to comply and grow.

(2)   Regulators should provide simple and straightforward ways to engage with those they regulate and hear their views.

(3)   Regulators should base their regulatory activities on risk.

(4)   Regulators should share information about compliance and risk.

(5)   Regulators should ensure clear information, guidance and advice is available to help those they regulate meet their responsibilities to comply.

(6)   Regulators should ensure that their approach to their regulatory activities is transparent.

The Regulators' Code is not fully applicable to the SRA but does apply to the LSB and is likely to be adopted in principle by the SRA or to be imposed on all the approved regulators by the LSB.

---

1   Section 28(3) of LSA 2007.

CHAPTER 2

The regulation and authorisation of business entities

Entity or firm-based regulation

2.1

The year 2009 saw the beginning of a series of substantial changes in the way that the profession is regulated. The Solicitors Regulation Authority (SRA) moved to firm-based regulation, although the first signs of this happening in practice did not emerge until the third quarter of 2010. The intention was that the focus of investigation and regulatory action would more frequently be the business within which solicitors practise, rather than individual practitioners. Explanations were to be sought from the firm, in relation to matters perceived to have gone wrong, and less from individual solicitors. The business entity became liable to rebukes, fines and controls on the way it is permitted to operate, although individual solicitors, or other managers or employees of the business, may also be targeted. In practice, through 21 editions of the SRA Handbook 2011, the emphasis remained for the most part on individual responsibility. The introduction of separate codes for firms and individuals in the 2019 regulatory arrangements acknowledges the need for clearer dividing lines. For a consideration of the practical consequences of this, see **15.8**.

Secondly, the Legal Services Act (LSA) 2007 created an environment in which businesses that provide legal services may have a choice as to which of the available approved regulators is to regulate the firm. For example, the Council for Licensed Conveyancers (CLC) regulates those who supply conveyancing and probate services; the Institute of Chartered Accountants of England and Wales (ICAEW) regulates the supply of probate (at present). The regulatory arm of the Chartered Institute of Legal Executives, CILEx Regulation, authorises and regulates firms, and grants individual practising rights (litigation, advocacy, conveyancing, probate and immigration).

Since 31 March 2009, firms of solicitors have been able to become legal disciplinary partnerships and, if they limit the services they provide to conveyancing and probate, may choose to be regulated by the CLC in place of the SRA. With the approval of the Bar Standards Board (BSB) and CILEx Regulation as licensing authorities (regulators able to license alternative business structures to provide legal services), the number of potential regulators is growing.

2.2

In consequence, individual solicitors may find themselves subject to two different regulatory regimes simultaneously. For example, the business by which they are employed may be an entity regulated by the BSB, CLC, CILEx Regulation or ICAEW, while the solicitors as individuals may be regulated by the SRA. LSA 2007 provides[1] that if a conflict arises between the regulations that apply to the entity and those that apply to an employee or manager of the entity, the regulations applying to the entity prevail. Thus, a solicitor who is a manager of or employed by a business regulated by the CLC must comply with the rules of the CLC in relation to, for example, referral fees and deposit interest. However, the SRA Principles apply to a solicitor who is practising as such, whether or not the entity through which the individual practises is subject to the Principles.[2] The SRA Code of Conduct for Solicitors, RELs and RFLs 2019 (the 'Code for Individuals') will also apply to individuals irrespective of the entity through which they may practise, although the extent of the obligations varies when individuals are not providing services to the public as set out in that Code. Solicitors are also subject to the requirement to have a practising certificate issued by the SRA, even if employed by a legal services provider regulated by another regulator, or if they are managers of such a body, if the solicitor's involvement in the firm, or the work undertaken, depends on the individual being a solicitor, or the individual is employed or held out explicitly or implicitly as a solicitor.[3] A publication concerned with the regulation of solicitors can no longer focus exclusively on the rules promulgated by the SRA. Therefore, a brief consideration of the CLC rules is contained in **CHAPTER 13** and the CLC Code of Conduct is reproduced at **APPENDIX 10**.

One of the principal changes introduced by the 2019 regulatory arrangements is to permit solicitors, as individuals, to provide unregulated legal services through unregulated businesses. It was considered anomalous, for example, that the effect of the SRA Practice Framework Rules 2011 (see **2.25**) was that a solicitor may not work, using the title of solicitor, in an unregulated will-writing business.

The effect of this is that in-house solicitors are no longer restricted to acting for their employers only (with limited exceptions as formerly set out in rule 4 of the Practice Framework Rules). Solicitors may (for example) provide legal advice to anyone, not just to their employers, because legal advice is not a reserved legal activity. The restrictions on in-house solicitors providing reserved legal activities for persons other than their employer remain. If the employer wishes to provide reserved legal services to the general public, or a sector of the public, it will have to be regulated as an entity. This is a natural consequence of the general requirement that persons providing reserved legal activities must be authorised to do so.[4]

Solicitors may (using their title as solicitors) set up businesses which are unregulated to provide advice and any other legal service provided they are not undertaking reserved legal activities. They will be regulated as solicitors in terms of their personal conduct, but the business will not have to comply with the regulatory burdens of an SRA-authorised firm. For example, there will be no compulsory insurance, no compliance officer for legal practice (COLP) or compliance officer for finance and administration (COFA), no Compensation Fund contributions. However, clients will have less protection and dealings may not be covered by legal professional privilege. Solicitors must make clear to clients the extent of the regulatory protections available to them under paragraph 8.11 of the Code for Individuals.[5]

Existing law firms will be able to hive off non-reserved legal services into such new unregulated businesses, provided that clients are properly informed.[6]

1 Section 52(4) of LSA 2007.
2 SRA Principles – Introduction.
3 This is the natural consequence of sections 1 and 21 of the Solicitors Act (SA) 1974, although there are no longer any express provisions in SRA regulations explaining this.
4 Section 14 of LSA 2007.
5 See **CHAPTER 4**.

Authorisation

2.3

'Authorisation' is one of the three strands of regulation covered by the SRA
regulations, the other two being supervision and enforcement.

Authorisation as an area of regulation covers the processes whereby individuals may
be permitted to provide legal services, including the process of being admitted as a
solicitor, and thus includes the SRA Authorisation of Firms Rules 2019, SRA
Authorisation of Individuals Regulations 2019 (as amended), SRA Education,
Training and Assessment Provider Regulations 2019 and the SRA Assessment of
Character and Suitability Rules 2019 which, as well as being relevant to the
enrolment of students and admission to the roll, is applicable in relation to the
approval of non-lawyer managers of law firms (within legal disciplinary partnerships
and alternative business structures), of COLPs and COFAs (see **CHAPTER 7**), and of
non-lawyers who own a material interest in a law firm.

Authorisation also encompasses the procedures regulating firms and individuals in
the manner in which they provide legal services, through the SRA Authorisation of
Firms Rules 2019 and the SRA Authorisation of Individuals Regulations 2019 (as
amended).

SRA Authorisation Rules

2.4

These rules are the core of the SRA's control mechanism for all forms of practice.
They comprise the SRA Authorisation of Firms Rules 2019 and the SRA
Authorisation of Individuals Regulations 2019. We will refer to the rules collectively
as the 'Authorisation Rules' and individually as the 'Firm Rules' and the 'Individual
Rules'.

The Firm Rules apply to alternative business structures (ABSs) ('licensable bodies' or
'licensed bodies' depending on the context) and to all other more traditional forms
of practice ('legal services bodies' or 'recognised bodies'), including legal disciplinary
partnerships. From 1 November 2015, sole practitioners (who had previously been
regulated separately through 'sole practitioner recognition' are regulated in the same
way as any other recognised body.

There are two key elements to the Firm Rules:

● the process of authorisation, including applications and conditions; and

● the approval process for managers, owners and compliance officers.

There are also provisions relating to the duration, suspension and revocation of
authorisation; the effect of unforeseen breaches in relation to the requirements for
authorisation; appeals and transitional arrangements.

'Authorisation' is used to describe the recognition process for recognised bodies, *and* the licensing process for ABSs. Once authorised a firm, including a sole practice, will not need to renew its authorisation (recognition or licence); it will continue in force until withdrawn or revoked, although there will be a requirement to make annual returns with specified information and to pay annual fees.

Applications

2.5

The SRA must make a decision on an application that has been duly made, using the correct form and accompanied by all the required information, within six months unless an extension notice is served, which may be done only once, so as to bring the maximum period for any decision to nine months.[1] This is plainly intended to provide for the most complex ABS authorisation applications which require extensive investigation. More routine applications are dealt with far faster. This is an area in which the SRA has improved very considerably and genuinely urgent applications, such as the grant of a new ABS licence to enable an existing ABS to acquire the shares in a failing business as a 'rescue', can be processed very quickly indeed.

The SRA may only grant an application for authorisation if the applicant satisfies, in terms of the business structure, the statutory requirements for a legal services body (non-ABS) or a licensable body (ABS). The body must have at least one practising address in England and Wales.[2]

The applicant will also have to: satisfy the requirements as to the appointment of compliance officers, and obtain the SRA's approval; demonstrate that all managers and owners of the business are approved as necessary, and not disqualified (for example, as a result of having been struck off); and comply with rule 9.4 of the Firm Rules as to supervision of regulated work by a lawyer of England and Wales who has practised as such for a minimum of three years.

The SRA will refuse an application even though these conditions are satisfied:

- if it is not satisfied that the applicant body's managers, interest holders or management and governance arrangements are suitable to operate or control a business providing regulated legal services;

- if it is not satisfied that, if the authorisation is granted, the applicant body will comply with the SRA's regulatory arrangements; or

- if for any other reason, the SRA considers that it would be against the public interest or otherwise incompatible with the regulatory objectives to grant authorisation.[3]

---

1   Rules 1.5 and 1.6 of the SRA Application, Notice, Review and Appeal Rules 2019.
2   Rule 1.3(b) of the Firm Rules.
3   Rule 2.2 of the Firm Rules.

Conditions

2.6

All authorisations will be subject to standard conditions (under rules 6–11 of the Firm Rules) as well as any specific conditions the SRA decides to impose (under rule 3). These conditions are designed to protect the public, ensure compliance with regulatory arrangements and promote the regulatory objectives.

The standard conditions impose duties as to regulatory compliance; as to making suitable arrangements to ensure compliance; as to the payment of periodical fees; as to any limits on the activities that may be carried out; as to the appointment of compliance officers; as to those permitted to have management responsibilities and control; and as to the provision of information by means of an annual return.[1]

1   Rules 6–11 of the Firm Rules.

2.7

The Firm Rules should be read in conjunction with the Code for Firms, which requires that all managers of a firm are jointly and severally responsible for compliance with that Code and that compliance officers must take all reasonable steps to ensure compliance with the SRA's regulatory arrangements (see **CHAPTER 5**).

Managers and COLPs should be particularly aware of the ongoing compliance requirements embodied in the Firm Rules.

Rule 5.3 specifies that an authorised body may only carry on a regulated activity if that is done through a person (a body or an individual) who is authorised to carry on that activity.

Rule 7.1 requires that every authorised body must pay to the SRA the prescribed periodical fees by the prescribed date. In the case of merger or demerger, an authorised body is required to provide notice to the SRA within 28 days if it wishes the change to be taken into account in the calculation of the fee (see rule 16.1).

Rule 9.1 requires that an authorised body must ensure that any manager or owner of the authorised body, or any manager of a body corporate which is a manager or owner of the authorised body, has been approved by the SRA. Solicitors with a current practising certificate and existing authorised bodies are deemed to be approved in the absence of any regulatory or disciplinary investigations or adverse findings by the SRA, the Solicitors Disciplinary Tribunal (the Tribunal or SDT), or other regulatory body.[1] No manager of a licensed body may be a person who is disqualified from being a manager.[2] An authorised body (or manager or employee of such a body) and a recognised body (or manager or employee) must not employ or remunerate a person without the written permission of the SRA if they are in certain categories, for example, struck off or suspended solicitors or persons subject to an order under section 43 of SA 1974. Nor may such a person be permitted to be a manager or owner of the body.

Rule 9.4 requires that an authorised body must have at least one manager or employee, or must procure the services of an individual who is a lawyer of England and Wales (and has practised as such for a minimum of three years) who supervises the work undertaken by the authorised body in so far as it is regulated by the SRA. This requirement replaces the requirement that a firm have an individual who is 'qualified to supervise'. The requirement should be read in conjunction with the supervision requirements of the Codes of Conduct (see **4.37** and **5.40**).

Rule 14.1 deals with the matters that must be addressed by, respectively, partnerships, recognised bodies and licensed bodies where the last remaining individual whose presence ensures that there is a valid partnership, or that a recognised body meets the requirements for a legal services body, or that a licensed body remains a licensable body, ceases to be able to fulfil that role, through imprisonment, illness, loss of mental capacity, abandonment or the imposition of regulatory conditions. In any such case the body must inform the SRA within seven days and must within 28 days ensure that the body regularises the position or (in the case of a recognised body or licensed body) ceases to practise.

1   Rule 13.2 of the Firm Rules.
2   Rule 10.1(d) of the Firm Rules.

Additional conditions and modifications

2.8

Under rule 3.1 of the Firm Rules the SRA may at any time impose further conditions.

3.1   The *SRA* may at any time, whether on grant of an application for authorisation or otherwise, impose such conditions on a body's authorisation (whether indefinite or for a specified period), where it considers it appropriate in the public interest to do so and in accordance with rules 3.2 and 3.3.

3.2   The *SRA* may impose conditions under rule 3.1 if it is satisfied that the *authorised body*, or a *manager, compliance officer, employee, owner,* or *interest holder* of the *authorised body*:

(a)   is unsuitable to undertake certain activities or engage in certain business or practising arrangements;

(b)   is putting or is likely to put at risk the interests of *clients*, third parties or the public;

(c)   will not comply with the *SRA's regulatory arrangements*, or requires monitoring of compliance with the *SRA's regulatory arrangements*; or

(d)   should take specified steps conducive to the *regulatory objectives*.

3.3   The conditions imposed by the *SRA* under rule 3.1 may:

(a)   specify certain requirements that must be met or steps that must be taken;

(b)   restrict the carrying on of particular activities or holding of particular roles; or

(c)   prohibit the taking of specified steps without its approval.

A condition imposed under rule 3.1 takes effect from the date on which the condition is imposed unless otherwise specified by the SRA.

Under rule 12.1 the SRA may at any time extend, revoke or vary any terms or conditions on a body's authorisation, imposed in accordance with rule 3 or otherwise, either on the application of the body or on its own initiative.

Approval

2.9

As part of the authorisation process express approval is required by the SRA of an authorised body's managers, owners and compliance officers. Solicitors who hold a current practising certificate and existing authorised bodies will be deemed to be approved to be owners or managers of an authorised body, provided that there are no practising certificate conditions or conditions on the body's authorisation which would be inconsistent with approval, and provided that the SRA has been notified that the person or body should be a manager or owner, and has not withdrawn approval.[1]

It should be noted that the deeming provisions in relation to the appointment of compliance officers are not the same and in particular only apply to authorised bodies with a turnover of no more than £600,000.[2] The position of COLPs and COFAs is considered in more detail in **CHAPTER 7**.

1   Rules 13.3, 13.4 and 13.10 of the Firm Rules.
2   See rule 13.5.

SRA Assessment of Character and Suitability Rules 2019

2.10

Those who are not deemed to be approved for their roles must be expressly approved by the SRA which will apply its Assessment of Character and Suitability Rules 2019 (the 'Suitability Rules'). These are largely designed to exclude those who have been convicted of criminal offences of varying degrees of seriousness, and those with other serious lapses in their history.

Those with a conviction for an offence for which they received a custodial or suspended sentence; or which involved dishonesty, fraud, perjury and/or bribery; or which was of a violent or sexual nature; or which was associated with obstructing the course of justice; or which demonstrated behaviour showing signs of discrimination towards others; or which was associated with terrorism; those who have been convicted by a court of more than one criminal offence; those who have accepted a caution from the police for an offence involving dishonesty, violence or discrimination, or a sexual offence; and those included on the Violent and Sex Offender Register are all likely to be refused approval.

This test has been relaxed slightly from the requirements of the former Suitability Test, which was found to be too rigid in its approach.

An application may still fail, but has some prospect of success, if the applicant has received a local warning from the police; accepted a caution from the police for an offence not involving dishonesty; received a Penalty Notice for Disorder from the police; received a final warning or reprimand from the police (youths only); and/or received a referral order from the courts (youths only).

The onus is very firmly on individuals to provide to the SRA all material information regarding their character and suitability. Any failure to disclose any material information may be taken into consideration by the SRA when making a determination (rule 6.7). The express suggestion in the former Suitability Test that a failure to disclose will be treated as prima facie evidence of dishonesty has been removed, replaced with the more generic provision allowing the SRA greater flexibility. However, historically the SRA has regarded a failure to make full and proper disclosure of previous brushes with the criminal law as being almost as serious as the criminal offences themselves, and this is unlikely to change.

2.11

It is not only criminal convictions that are relevant. A raft of other issues may be taken into account, as set out in rule 4.1; however, there is no longer any automatic outcome associated with the listed factors. While it can reasonably be predicted that, in practice, there will still be no approval for those who have been responsible for behaviour which is dishonest or violent; or where there is evidence of discrimination towards others; or where the individual has misused his or her position to obtain pecuniary advantage; or abused a position of trust in relation to vulnerable people; or been responsible for other forms of behaviour which demonstrate that he or she could not be relied upon to comply with regulatory responsibilities, it is no longer an express requirement that there be exceptional circumstances. Instead, these are matters which must be assessed and taken into account as seems appropriate in any particular case.

Similarly, those who have committed or have been adjudged by an education establishment to have committed a deliberate assessment offence which amounts to plagiarism or cheating to gain an advantage, whether for the individual or others, will face extreme difficulty in securing approval.

Past financial failings are relevant. The SRA will take into account evidence that finances have not been managed properly and carefully; or evidence that the applicant has deliberately sought to avoid responsibility for his or her debts, particularly if there is evidence of dishonesty in relation to the management of finances.

2.12

A poor regulatory history is relevant. The SRA will take into account any serious disciplinary finding, sanction or action by a regulatory body and/or any court or other body hearing appeals in relation to disciplinary or regulatory findings; or any failure to disclose information to a regulatory body when required to do so; or who has provided false or misleading information or significantly breached the requirements of a regulatory body; or who has been refused registration by a regulatory body; or who has failed to comply with the reasonable requests of a regulatory body.

The SRA will also take into account a disqualification as a charity trustee or a company director and any offences under the Companies Act 2006, as well as any case in which the applicant has been rebuked, reprimanded or received a warning about his or her conduct by a regulatory body.

2.13

All the above considerations apply to those seeking to be admitted as a solicitor and those seeking approval for any role covered by the Authorisation Rules: that is, any COLP, COFA, owner or manager.

The new approach to assessing character as set out in the Suitability Rules is (in keeping with the SRA's new approach generally) more streamlined. The abandonment of rigid requirements enables the test simply to list relevant factors without prescribing outcomes if those factors are present. Instead, the SRA lists aggravating and mitigating factors. Despite this attempt to relax the overly prescriptive requirements of the old Suitability Test, it remains likely that little will change in practice.

The SRA is obliged by LSA 2007 to consider the associates of those to be approved as owners of material interests in ABSs,[1] and has extended the same requirement to all covered by the Authorisation Rules. Applications for approval may be refused if the SRA has evidence reflecting on the honesty and integrity of a person the applicant is related to, affiliated with, or acts together with, where there is reason to believe that the person may have an influence over the way in which the applicant will exercise his, her or its authorised role.

1   Paragraph 6 of Schedule 13 to LSA 2007.

2.14

It is important to bear in mind that the onus is on applicants to satisfy the regulator. There is no entitlement to an appointment. The law and the relevant tests to be applied are considered in the context of appeals to the Tribunal in relation to licensing matters; see **23.15.**

Withdrawal of approval

2.15

The SRA may withdraw approval where approval, including deemed approval, has been granted if it is not satisfied that the person is fit and proper to undertake the designated role.[1] Fitness and propriety are determined in accordance with the Suitability Rules.

Where withdrawal of approval relates to a director of a company, the SRA may set separate dates for that individual ceasing to be a director and disposing of his or her shares.[2]

1   Rule 13.9 of the Firm Rules.
2   Rule 13.12 of the Firm Rules.

Revocation and suspension of authorisation

2.16

The SRA may revoke or suspend a body's authorisation where, in the case of an authorised body (that is, any practice that the SRA has authorised, ABS or non-ABS):

15

- authorisation was granted as a result of error, misleading or inaccurate information, or fraud;

- the body is or becomes ineligible to be authorised in accordance with the criteria set out in the Firm Rules;

- the body has failed to provide any information reasonably requested by the SRA;

- the body has failed to pay any prescribed fee to the SRA;

- a relevant insolvency event[1] has occurred in relation to the body;

- the body makes an application to the SRA for its authorisation to be revoked or suspended but the SRA may refuse the application if the applicant is subject to any proceedings, investigation or consideration of their conduct or practice by the SRA or the Tribunal;

- the SRA has decided to exercise its intervention powers;

- the body has failed to comply with any obligation under the SRA's regulatory arrangements;

- in the case of a licensed body (applicable to ABSs alone), the body fails to comply with the prohibition on appointing disqualified managers; or in the case of any authorised body, the body fails to comply with the prohibition on employing disqualified persons (struck off solicitors and the like) if the manager or employee concerned was disqualified as a result of breach of the duties imposed upon the manager or employee by sections 176 or 90 of LSA 2007 (the general duties imposed to comply with all regulatory arrangements for ABSs);

- for any other reason it is in the public interest.

A 'relevant insolvency event' is defined as occurring when:

'(a)   a resolution for a voluntary winding up of the body is passed without a declaration of solvency under section 89 of the Insolvency Act 1986;

(b)   the body enters administration within the meaning of paragraph 1(2)(b) of Schedule B1 to that Act;

(c)   an administrative receiver within the meaning of section 251 of that Act is appointed;

(d)   a meeting of creditors is held in relation to the body under section 95 of that Act (creditors' meeting which has the effect of converting a members' voluntary winding up into a creditors' voluntary winding up);

(e)   an order for the winding up of the body is made;

(f)   all of the managers in a body which is unincorporated have been adjudicated bankrupt; or

(g)   the body is an overseas company or a societas Europaea registered outside England, Wales, Scotland and Northern Ireland and the body is subject to an event in its country of incorporation analogous to an event as set out in paragraphs (a) to (f) above.'

The SRA may also revoke or suspend a body's authorisation where, in the case of a *licensed* body (applicable to ABSs alone), a non-authorised person holds an interest in the licensed body:

- as a result of the person taking a step in circumstances where that constitutes an offence under paragraph 24(1) of Schedule 13 to LSA 2007 (whether or not the person is charged with or convicted of an offence under that paragraph) – this is failing to give notice as to the proposed or actual acquisition of a material interest in an ABS;

- in breach of conditions imposed on the owners of material interests in the ABS; or

- the person's holding of which is subject to an objection by the licensing authority.

2.17

Before the SRA can revoke or suspend an authorisation it must first give the authorised body an opportunity to make representations to it on the issues that have led the SRA to consider this course, and it must also give at least 28 days' notice of its intention to make the decision to revoke or suspend.[1]

Guidance notes to rule 22 of the SRA Authorisation Rules 2011 emphasised that the SRA was unlikely to revoke or suspend authorisation if to do so would present any risk to clients, the public, the protection of public money or to any SRA investigation. This guidance has not been reissued but the approach would be consistent with the proper exercise of the SRA's duty and is likely to be maintained in practice.

1   Rule 4.5 of the Firm Rules.

Unforeseen temporary breach

2.18

Rule 14.1 of the Firm Rules provides for a variety of situations in which authorised bodies (ABSs and non-ABSs) could cease to be eligible to be authorised; for example, if an ABS no longer has a manager who is a qualified lawyer, or a recognised body no longer has one manager who is a solicitor. The body has seven days to notify the SRA of the event and must remedy the situation within 28 days or cease to carry on reserved legal activities and to hold itself out as an authorised body.

Partnership changes and temporary emergency authorisation

2.19

The express provisions of rule 24.2 of the Authorisation Rules 2011 have not survived the reform of the SRA's regulatory arrangements. The express provisions dealing with changes in the composition of an authorised body have been replaced by the generic and unhelpful rule 14.2 of the Firm Rules, which provides:

14.2   Subject to any *prescribed* application requirements, the *SRA* may:

(a)   transfer a body's authorisation to another body where the first body

> ceases to exist and the second body succeeds to the whole or substantially the whole of its business;
>
> (b) substitute a body's authorisation for another type of authorisation where it is satisfied that the body is materially carrying on the same practice, notwithstanding a change in its management or control; and
>
> (c) permit any *person* previously approved as a *manager, owner,* or *compliance officer* of the body to continue to act in their designated role, notwithstanding the transfer or substitution.

While this omission is unlikely to trouble incorporated practices which have separate legal identities, it may require traditional partnerships to consider their position more carefully upon a change in the composition of the partnership – particularly if there is no partnership agreement in place.

Under the Authorisation Rules 2011, a change in composition of a partnership did not generally affect the firm's authorisation. However, if the change in composition resulted in there being no individual who was a partner after the change who was also a partner before the change, that was not a change in composition at all, but the cessation of one firm and the creation of another. The new firm could not adopt the authorisation of the old firm.[1]

It may be suggested that any change in composition which does not result in a complete loss of eligibility does not require an application to be made for authorisation of the changed entity – however, the position is unclear under the Firm Rules. Rule 4.2, for example, provides that authorisation ceases to have effect when a body ceases to exist, subject to the limited savings in rules 14 and 15, essentially permitting the SRA to continue authorisation by allowing firms a short period to rectify unforeseen problems through the temporary emergency recognition process.

It is implicit under rule 15.1 that a change in management or control of an authorised body can bring into being a new unauthorised body. That is one of the grounds upon which an application for temporary emergency recognition can be made. What is not clear is *when* a change in management and control *can* bring into being a new unauthorised entity and, in the absence of any express provision, it must be assumed that the general law will apply.

1   Rule 24.2(a) of the Authorisation Rules 2011 (now superseded).

Review and appeals

2.20

The SRA reserves to itself the right to review any decision made by a decision-maker. Historically, this power has been used in disciplinary investigations when adjudicators have made decisions which the SRA staff had not expected or did not agree with (see **20.15**). A review may be undertaken on the SRA's own initiative or on the application of the person affected by the decision.[1]

1   Rules 3.1(b) and 3.2 of the SRA Application, Notice, Review and Appeal Rules 2019.

2.21

The appeal provisions vary depending on whether the authorised body is or is not an ABS, because the licensing and appeal decisions for an ABS are dictated by LSA 2007.

An ABS may appeal to the Tribunal against a refusal of authorisation, a decision to impose a condition on an authorisation, a decision to revoke or suspend an authorisation, a refusal to approve a step which under a condition requires prior approval, a decision to modify, or to refuse to modify the conditions of an authorisation.[1]

An ABS or the person affected may appeal to the Tribunal against a refusal to approve a person as a manager or compliance officer, a decision to impose conditions on an approval or to withdraw approval, a decision to grant approval or conditional approval of the holding of a material interest in an ABS and a decision to withdraw approval of a manager, an owner or a compliance officer of an ABS.[2]

There are also ABS-specific provisions concerning financial penalties, disqualification and ownership issues, dealt with in **CHAPTERS 25** and **26**.

1 Rule 5.1 of and Annex 2 to the SRA Application, Notice, Review and Appeal Rules 2019.
2 Ibid.

2.22

Traditional firms (legal services bodies/recognised bodies) do not have any right of appeal to the Tribunal, nor do individuals within them affected by authorisation or approval decisions. The statutory background to the process of approval of recognised bodies is the Administration of Justice Act 1985 as amended by LSA 2007, and under Schedule 2 to that statute[1] appeal lies where relevant to the High Court.

A legal services body may appeal to the High Court against a refusal of authorisation, a decision to impose a condition on an authorisation, or a decision to revoke or suspend an authorisation.[2]

A legal services body or the person affected may appeal to the High Court against the withdrawal of approval for the roles of COLP, COFA, manager or owner of a recognised body.[3]

If the body is not an ABS, but a legal services body/recognised body, there is no external right of appeal at all, and only the prospect of an appeal to a different decision-maker in the SRA[4] in relation to decisions:

- to refuse to approve a person to be an owner of the body;[5]

- to refuse to approve a person as a compliance officer – COLP or COFA;

- to approve a manager, owner or compliance officer subject to conditions;

- to modify or to refuse to modify terms and conditions of authorisation.

1 See **APPENDIX 18**.
2 Annex 3 to the SRA Application, Notice, Review and Appeal Rules 2019.
3 Annex 3 to the SRA Application, Notice, Review and Appeal Rules 2019.
4 Annex 1 to the SRA Application, Notice, Review and Appeal Rules 2019. This would not prevent an application for judicial review in appropriate cases.

5   If a non-authorised person has an interest in a regulated firm that is equivalent to 10 per cent or more the firm is licensable as an ABS and the interest holder must be expressly approved (see **25.1** and **25.3**). If a non-authorised person has an interest that is less than 10 per cent, the body does not qualify as an ABS but the SRA still has to be satisfied that the body's managers and interest holders are suitable, as a group, to operate or control a business providing regulated legal services; see rule 2.2(a) of the Firm Rules.

2.23

The SRA's decision to adopt the same authorisation principles for all practices regardless of the statutory background has therefore created serious anomalies. A decision, for example, to impose conditions on a manager or to refuse approval of a compliance officer where the individual's role is in an ABS may be subject to an internal review process but is also subject to external review by the Tribunal, potentially with costs consequences if the SRA got it wrong.

Exactly the same decisions, made under the same rules applying the same principles and the same procedures, but where the individual's role is within an authorised practice that is not an ABS, can only be appealed internally. If the SRA decision-maker on appeal endorses the decision of the SRA first instance decision-maker there is no further right of appeal, leaving only the unsatisfactory remedy of judicial review.

2.24

The time limit for internal review is 28 days from notification of the decision and reasons. The SRA specifies that unless otherwise provided in rules of the High Court or the Tribunal appeals to the court or Tribunal must be made within 28 days.[1] Appeals to the High Court are governed by Part 52 of the Civil Procedure Rules and should be entered in the Administrative Court within 21 days of the decision, or of receipt of the reasons for the decision if later.[2] The Tribunal has set the time for appeal as 28 days from receipt of the decision in all cases; see **23.6**.

1   Rule 5.1 of the SRA Application, Notice, Review and Appeal Rules 2019.
2   CPR rule 52.4; Part 52 Practice Direction 52D, paragraphs 3.3A and 27.1.

The SRA Authorisation of Individuals Regulations 2019

2.25

The SRA Authorisation of Individuals Regulations 2019 (the 'Individual Rules') deal with the requirements for seeking admission to the roll, the admission of qualified lawyers, the formalities of obtaining practising certificates and explain what authorisation entitles you to do.

The lists of the various ways in which solicitors, registered European lawyers (RELs), registered foreign lawyers (RFLs) and authorised bodies could practise when regulated by the SRA, which characterised the now defunct Practice Framework Rules 2011, have been abandoned.

Matters considered likely to be relevant in everyday practice are in part considered elsewhere in this book; for RELs and RFLs see **CHAPTER 12**; for in-house and overseas practice see **CHAPTER 10**.

Two particularly relevant and important issues are dealt with in these rules – the circumstances in which practising certificates are required and the rules permitting solicitors to act as a solicitor through an unregulated entity.

All solicitors require practising certificates (unless they are in the privileged group exempted by section 88 of SA 1974, such as those employed in central government) if:

- they provide reserved legal activities;[1]
- they act as a solicitor within the meaning of section 20 of SA 1974; or
- the individual is held out explicitly or implicitly as a practising solicitor within the meaning of section 21 of SA 1974; or
- section 1A of SA 1974 applies.

Section 1A of SA 1974 states that a person who has been admitted as a solicitor and whose name is on the roll shall be taken to be acting as a solicitor (if this would not otherwise be so) if he or she is employed in connection with the provision of any legal services by any person who is qualified to act as a solicitor, by a partnership at least one member of which is qualified to act as a solicitor, by a recognised body, or by any other person or body who is authorised under LSA 2007 to provide reserved legal services.

Thus by section 1A any solicitor employed in what may be loosely termed private practice must always have a practising certificate. Solicitors employed by other bodies, for example, in industry or local government or by charities, will need to consider whether their employment depends on them being solicitors, whether they are employed on that basis, or whether they are held out as practising solicitors.[2]

1 Section 14 of LSA 2007.
2 See SRA Ethics guidance, 'When do I need a practising certificate?', issued 4 July 2019.

2.26

In 2019, it is possible for the first time for solicitors to describe themselves as solicitors and to provide certain legal services to the public through an unregulated entity. This proposal generated significant resistance from the Law Society and from the Legal Services Consumer Panel due to perceived consumer detriment and potential damage to the reputation of solicitors.

The SRA's approach to this issue has been that it is better for consumers to have some regulatory protection than none.

Solicitors who intend to call themselves a solicitor will need a practising certificate to comply with SA 1974, irrespective of the entity through which they may practise. All solicitors will be subject to the requirements of the Code for Individuals and should pay particular attention to the information requirements set out at paragraphs 8.10 and 8.11 of the Code.

Solicitors who intend to practise other than through an authorised body, including a recognised sole practice, may provide reserved legal activities in the extremely limited circumstances set out at regulation 10.2(b) of the Individual Rules, which provides:

(b) any *reserved legal activities* you carry on are provided through an *authorised body* or an *authorised non-SRA firm*, or in circumstances in which you:

    (i) have practised as a *solicitor* or an *REL* for a minimum of three years since admission or registration;

    (ii) are self-employed and practise in your own name, and not through a trading name or service company;

    (iii) do not employ anyone in connection with the services that you provide;

    (iv) are engaged directly by the *client* with your *fees* payable directly to you;

    (v) have a practising address in the *UK*;

    (vi) take out and maintain indemnity insurance that provides adequate and appropriate cover in respect of the services that you provide, whether or not they comprise *reserved legal activities*; and

    (vii) do not hold *client money*, save that you may hold money which falls within the category of *client money* set out in rule 2.1(d) of the SRA Accounts Rules so long as:

        (A) any money held for *disbursements* relates to costs or expenses incurred by you on behalf of your *client* and for which you are liable; and

        (B) you have informed your *client* in advance of where and how the money will be held,

and you choose for your practice not to be authorised as a *recognised sole practice*.

It is not possible to provide reserved legal services through an unauthorised body. Such services can only be provided directly and in person and with the benefit of professional indemnity insurance.[1] Solicitors practising within the limits of regulation 10.2(b) will be described as independent solicitors.[2]

It is not permissible to provide regulated immigration services in this way as regulation 9.5 of the Individual Rules requires that such services be provided through an authorised body. Similar considerations apply to claims management services (regulation 9.8) and financial services (regulation 9.9).

Solicitors wishing to provide unreserved legal services to members of the public may do so through an unregulated entity. They may not provide reserved legal services, immigration services, claims management services or financial services unless the entity is duly regulated to enable the provision of such services. Solicitors practising in this way may not hold client money.[3]

[1] This does not have to comply with the SRA Minimum Terms; however the SRA has published guidance on what information must be provided to clients. See 'Unregulated organsiations – giving information to clients', issued 23 July 2019, at www.sra.org.uk.

[2] SRA Ethics guidance, 'Preparing to become a sole practitioner or an SRA-regulated freelance solicitor', issued 4 July.

[3] Regulation 9.1 of the Individual Rules, incorporating the restrictions in regulation 10.2(b) listed above.

PART 2

The SRA Principles and Codes

CHAPTER 3

Overview of the Principles and the Codes

Introduction

3.1

The rather modest regulatory impact of the 1936 Solicitors' Practice Rules has been mentioned in the Preface to the 2008 edition of this book. The Practice Rules changed very little in subsequent decades. A new rule was made in 1967, requiring that only solicitors with practising certificates should be listed on notepaper and the office nameplate. Rule 2 (which prohibited the sin of charging less than scale fees) was replaced in 1972 with a rule against acting for both parties in conveyancing transactions subject to specified exceptions. A comprehensive new set of Rules was made in 1987, which are recognisably the precursor to the Solicitors' Practice Rules 1990 and very little different from the 1990 Rules in their original form. The 1990 Rules were amended and supplemented extensively after they were implemented; not all the changes were readily accessible.

The Law Society embarked on the preparation of a new comprehensive set of rules in and before 2004, and the resulting Solicitors' Code of Conduct 2007 (2007 Code) came into force on 1 July 2007. The 2007 Code abandoned the historical approach of relatively narrow practice rules and wider but non-exclusive (official and published) guidance. Instead, it created a comprehensive regulatory framework for all aspects of a solicitor's conduct. The 2007 Code comprised 25 individual rules and was supplemented by guidance produced by the Solicitors Regulation Authority (SRA) which amplified and explained its provisions. The guidance was not mandatory and did not form part of the 2007 Code; however, the SRA added a note to the preamble to the 2007 Code with effect from 31 March 2009 to the effect that if solicitors did not follow the guidance they could be required to demonstrate (ie prove) how they nevertheless complied with the rules.

The 2007 Code's life was short. Because of its all-encompassing nature, the 2007 Code and the guidance associated with each rule had to be amended regularly, which caused problems for solicitors who found it difficult to pinpoint what rule or guidance was in force at a given time. This was accompanied by an approach to regulation by the SRA which appeared to concentrate on minutiae – for example, precisely what needed to be said to clients about referral arrangements, and when it had to be said, about which it was not difficult to make mistakes, even when solicitors were doing what they thought was entirely proper.

3.2

The passing of the Legal Services Act (LSA) 2007, the inevitable need to create a regulatory environment which would work for both traditional law firms and alternative business structures (ABSs) and strong guidance from the Legal Services

Board, created the need to move to a different basis and style of regulation. Principles-based regulation had been pioneered by the financial services profession, and was then introduced to the legal profession in October 2011 under the title 'outcomes-focused regulation' (OFR). Instead of professionals being bound, and often hamstrung, by a prescriptive set of rules, the onus shifted to the regulated individual or entity to deliver satisfactory outcomes for consumers based upon an overarching set of ethical principles. The regulated individual, the solicitor, is (or should be) trusted to think for him- or herself in order to achieve satisfactory outcomes for clients.

OFR was designed to move away, both in the form of rules and by the way in which they were policed, from the tick-box, strict liability, 'every breach is a breach' approach described above, which had seriously damaged the relationship between the profession and the regulator. The problem with that former approach was that it was too easy to hit the wrong target – the solicitor trying to get it right but making mistakes, as opposed to the one who does not care, or deliberately breaks the rules.

3.3

During the consultation process before the introduction of the SRA Code of Conduct 2011 (2011 Code), the SRA announced that:

> 'We know that the current rule book is too prescriptive. OFR will give firms the flexibility to do new and better things for consumers. It will lead to a more grown-up relationship between the SRA and the regulated community.'

and:

> 'The introduction of OFR will give a simplified rulebook and freedom to practise innovatively, which will be good for consumers and providers of legal services alike. OFR is risk-based regulation; firms will have to comply with broad principles rather than detailed rules. Firms will be able to comply with the principles in the ways which best suit their businesses. Formal rules will still apply in important areas including accounts and indemnity, where they are necessary. ...
>
> The SRA's enforcement of OFR will be effective, fair and proportionate. We will focus on the things which really matter to consumers; for example risks which may lead to a loss of their money, justice, or social or economic wellbeing.'[1]

That, as an announcement, was welcome as it stated an intention to turn the clock back to a time when the consequence of something going wrong – whether there was in fact any mischief or prejudice caused, as opposed to being a 'bare breach' – was an important if not determinative factor in how the regulator could be expected to treat the solicitor concerned.

Accordingly, we anticipated that we would see a refreshingly different approach to enforcement of the 2011 Code by the SRA. The experience of practitioners after October 2011 was mixed. Many found the relationship with their regulator easier than it had been in the past, but others reported that little had changed, with all the 'old' tendencies towards disproportionate reaction and judgement by hindsight.

There was also a tendency to move back towards a prescriptive approach to the rules. That can be demonstrated by the use of indicative behaviours in the 2011 Code. When the indicative behaviours were introduced in 2011, it was stated that they were not mandatory and were designed to specify the kind of behaviour which may establish compliance with, or contravention of, the Code. There was always a fear in the profession that they would gradually acquire the status of rules, despite an absolute disavowal that they had that force. By 2016 it was common for the SRA to send disciplinary letters to practitioners informing them that they had breached indicative behaviours.

1   'Freedom in practice: better outcomes for consumers. A passport to regulatory reform' issued by the SRA in April 2010.

3.4

In June 2016 the SRA announced a decision to change the profession's rules again. The new rules were submitted to the Legal Services Board for approval in August 2018. The announcements made at that time by the SRA were very similar to the announcements made before the introduction of the 2011 Code:

> 'In developing our new rules, we have sought to reduce unnecessary regulation – we have removed prescriptive drafting to produce requirements that:
>
> ● are clearer and more accessible, with duplication removed
>
> ● are easier to understand in terms of purpose and effect
>
> ● are targeted at the issues that really matter
>
> ● operate at a higher level, and so are less detailed and less prescriptive, providing flexibility to apply to changing circumstances ...'

and:

> 'We are removing restrictions we cannot justify and will allow more freedom for those we regulate to innovate and provide services to meet consumers' needs ...
>
> Our current Handbook is long and complex. We have therefore reviewed all our rules to create a shorter, sharper, clearer set of regulatory arrangements ...
>
> Many we regulate agree and consider that the current Handbook duplicates other legislative and regulatory obligations, is too prescriptive and needs changing too often ...
>
> [The new codes] allow more flexibility for individuals and firms to decide how best to comply with our rules than is provided under our current prescriptive rulebook.'[1]

1   'Application for the approval of regulatory arrangements', issued by the SRA in August 2018, paras 12–26.

3.5

On indicative behaviours, the SRA said it was removing them because some had started to give them the status of rules. It announced that the new regulatory arrangements will instead be supported by new guidance to help those it regulates, that the guidance will not have the force of rules and is there to help support solicitors in the judgements they make.[1] It remains to be seen whether a departure from the guidance will in the future be relied on per se as evidence of a breach of the rules.

1 'Application for the approval of regulatory arrangements', issued by the SRA in August 2018, para 61.

3.6

In this edition we will consider substantively only the 2019 Principles and Codes, because they govern all acts and omissions occurring after the 2019 regulatory arrangements came into force. The 2011 rules will continue to be relevant to disciplinary proceedings relating to acts and omissions that occurred before the introduction of the 2019 regulatory arrangements, and detailed commentary on the 2011 rules can be found in *The Solicitor's Handbook 2017*.

3.7

Taking an overview of the history, from 1936 when nearly all the 'rules' were unwritten but clearly understood, through successive Guides to Professional Conduct and changes in the Solicitors' Practice Rules, and the succession of Codes of Conduct from 2007 onwards, little has really changed, because the standards of behaviour required of solicitors have largely remained constant. There cannot be any solicitors who do not know that they have to behave honestly, or that they have to keep their clients' affairs confidential, or that they cannot ordinarily act where there is a conflict of interest. The moves from Rules to Codes, from rules to outcomes, and from outcomes to new regulatory arrangements have been costly, as firms need to ensure that their internal arrangements comply with each set of new rules, but have not, in our view, caused any changes in behaviour, nor would they be expected to.

Arguably, what needs to change is not a matter of drafting, though simplification of the rule book is welcome, but an approach to enforcement which is reliably consistent and proportionate, and in accordance with the Regulators' Code (see **APPENDIX 12**).

The SRA Principles 2019

3.8

The SRA Principles 2019 apply, as did their predecessors, to every person and body regulated by the SRA: solicitors of course, but also registered European lawyers, registered foreign lawyers (RELs and RFLs), the business entity itself; partnerships, limited liability partnerships (LLPs), limited liability companies, recognised sole practitioners, legal disciplinary practices, and the managers and employees of those entities and licensed bodies. That is subject to one exception: regulated individuals who are practising overseas and are subject to the Overseas Principles must comply with those Overseas Principles rather than the SRA Principles 2019.[1] In the case of licensed bodies the Principles apply to the individuals and the part of the body (where applicable) involved in delivering the regulated service under the terms of the licence. Although this book is written principally for solicitors, the reach of regulation should not be overlooked.

1   See the SRA Overseas and Cross-border Practice Rules 2019 (the 'Overseas Rules' or 'OCB Rules') and **4.8**. The Overseas Principles are set out in rule 2.1 of the Overseas Rules.

The seven Principles

3.9

There are seven mandatory Principles which apply to all those regulated by the SRA (apart from those who are practising overseas and are subject to the Overseas Principles).[1]

You act:

1. in a way that upholds the constitutional principle of the rule of law, and the proper administration of justice.

2. in a way that upholds public trust and confidence in the *solicitors'* profession and in legal services provided by *authorised persons*.

3. with independence.

4. with honesty.

5. with integrity.

6. in a way that encourages equality, diversity and inclusion.

7. in the best interests of each *client*.

1   See **3.8** and **4.8**.

3.10

Solicitors, RELs and RFLs must comply with the Principles in relation to activities which fall outside their legal practices, including activities conducted in a private, as well as a business, capacity. In practice, the Principles which apply to an individual's private life are principles 1, 2, 4, 5 and 6.

General guidance on the application of the Principles is set out in the introduction to the SRA Principles 2019 in the following terms:

> 'The SRA Principles comprise the fundamental tenets of ethical behaviour that we expect all those that we regulate to uphold …
>
> Should the Principles come into conflict, those which safeguard the wider public interest (such as the rule of law, and public confidence in a trustworthy solicitors' profession and a safe and effective market for regulated legal services) take precedence over an individual client's interests. You should, where relevant, inform your client of the circumstances in which your duty to the Court and other professional obligations will outweigh your duty to them.'

The introduction also states that the Principles and Codes are underpinned by the SRA's Enforcement Strategy, which explains in more detail the SRA's approach to taking regulatory action in the public interest.

3.11

The emphasis placed by the regulatory arrangements on different core duties has varied from time to time over the past 30 years. The Solicitors' Practice Rules 1987 identified five principles, which were the solicitor's independence and integrity, the client's freedom of choice, the best interests of the client, the good repute of the solicitor and the profession, and the solicitor's proper standard of work. The Solicitors' Practice Rules (SPR) 1990 added, importantly, the solicitor's duty to the court. Rule 1 of the 2007 Code identified six core duties: justice and the rule of law; integrity; independence; the best interests of the client; the solicitor's good standard of service; and public confidence in the profession. Those six core duties were virtually identical to principles 1 to 6 of the ten principles in the SRA Principles 2011. Principles 7 to 10 of the SRA Principles 2011 added a further four principles: compliance with legal and regulatory obligations; sound management; encouraging equality of opportunity and respect for diversity; and protecting client money and assets.

It should be noted that four of the SRA's 2011 Principles have been entirely jettisoned, namely:

- principle 5 – you must provide a proper standard of service to your client;

- principle 7 – you must comply with your legal and regulatory obligations and deal with your regulators and ombudsmen in an open, timely and co-operative manner;

- principle 8 – you must run your business or carry out your role in the business effectively and in accordance with proper governance and sound financial and risk management principles;

- principle 10 – you must protect client money and assets.

The four principles which were removed have been placed in the Codes.[1] The new principle is the requirement to act honestly. It is questionable whether that really needed to be expressly provided for, but other regulators do make such a requirement of those they regulate, and it may be that the SRA considered that it should fall into line.

1   See in particular paragraph 3.2 of the SRA Code of Conduct for Solicitors, RELs and RFLs 2019 (the 'Code for Individuals') (proper standard of service), paragraph 7.1 of the Code for Individuals (compliance with legal and regulatory obligations), paragraphs 2.4 and 2.5 of the SRA Code of Conduct for Firms (the 'Code for Firms') (sound management) and paragraph 4.2 of the Code for Individuals (protecting client money and assets).

Principle 1 – the constitutional principle of the rule of law and the proper administration of justice

3.12

Somehow, along the way, the solicitor's duty to the court has become rephrased as a duty to 'uphold the administration of justice'. Upholding the administration of justice could be said to equate to a duty to the court, but could also be said to be wider than that. The duty to the court is one of the 'professional principles' set out in section 1(3)(d) of LSA 2007, and is reinforced by section 188 of LSA 2007, which states that a person who exercises a right of audience or conducts litigation has a duty to the court to act with independence in the interests of justice. It is also reinforced by section 2 of the 'Code for Individuals' which sets out specific conduct obligations relating to proceedings before courts, tribunals and inquiries (see **4.14**).

Upholding 'the constitutional principle of the rule of law' may be more controversial, and possibly a mistake. Upholding the rule of law is not the same as upholding the law or complying with the law (as it occasionally seems to be suggested in proceedings before the Solicitors Disciplinary Tribunal; see for example *SRA v Olujinmi*).[1] The rule of law is a constitutional principle (see section 1(1)(b) of LSA 2007) the basic concept of which is:

> 'that all persons and authorities within the state, whether public or private, should be bound by and entitled to the benefit of laws publicly made, taking effect (generally) in the future and publicly administered in the courts.'[2]

That is primarily an obligation of the state, not of individuals. However, principle 1 will be interpreted by the SRA as a principle which imposes an obligation on every regulated person to comply with the law in their practice and their personal lives, and also on every regulated entity to comply with the law.

1 11442–2015, SDT.
2 Tom Bingham, *The Rule of Law*, Penguin Books, 2010.

Principle 2 – public trust and confidence

3.13

Principle 2 relates to preserving the reputation of, and public confidence in, the regulated legal profession.[1] A comparable core duty was set out in rule 1(d) of SPR 1990, rule 1.06 of the 2007 Code, and the 2011 Principles. The principle relates to standards of behaviour in a solicitor's private life, as well as behaviour within the context of professional practice. The SRA has stated that it is required to act on any report of conduct outside practice that may damage public confidence or suggest that the solicitor might present a risk while in practice (such as a report of a lack of financial probity).[2]

1 See *SRA v Wingate* [2018] EWCA Civ 366 at [105], on the comparable provision in the 2011 Principles.
2 'Application for the approval of regulatory arrangements', issued by the SRA in August 2018, para 94.

Principle 3 – independence

3.14

The duty to act with independence is one of the professional principles enshrined in section 1(3) of LSA 2007. It is a core duty which was also included in rule 1(a) of

SPR 1990, rule 1.03 of the 2007 Code, and the 2011 Principles. It encompasses obligations such as the duties to avoid conflicts of interest and to not take unfair advantage of a client.

Principle 4 – honesty

3.15

The SRA Principles 2011 included a duty to act with integrity but did not include a duty to act with honesty. In 2017 Mostyn J stated that the SRA Principles did not additionally include honesty because honesty and integrity were the same thing.[1] That decision was overruled by the Court of Appeal, which held that honesty and integrity are different concepts,[2] and the addition of a new principle of honesty reinforces the fact that the two principles are different. Integrity is a broader concept than honesty[3] and encompasses conduct such as sexual harassment and reckless misconduct, which can involve a lack of integrity even if the conduct is not dishonest.

In *Ivey* the Supreme Court said that the test for dishonesty is objective, although the mindset of the individual is highly relevant to the fact-finding process. Lord Hughes set out the test as follows:

> 'When dishonesty is in question the fact-finding tribunal must first ascertain (subjectively) the actual state of the individual's knowledge or belief as to the facts. The reasonableness or otherwise of his belief is a matter of evidence (often in practice determinative) going to whether he held the belief, but it is not an additional requirement that his belief must be reasonable; the question is whether it is genuinely held. When once his actual state of mind as to knowledge or belief as to facts is established, the question whether his conduct was honest or dishonest is to be determined by the fact-finder by applying the (objective) standards of ordinary decent people. There is no requirement that the defendant must appreciate that what he has done is, by those standards, dishonest.'[4]

1 *Malins v SRA* [2017] EWHC 835 (Admin) at [30].
2 *SRA v Wingate* [2018] EWCA Civ 366 at [95].
3 Ibid.
4 *Ivey v Genting Casinos (UK) Ltd* [2017] UKSC 67 at [74]. For application of the *Ivey* test in Tribunal proceedings, see *Zivancevic v SRA* [2019] EWHC 1950 (Admin) at [19]; see also **19.2**.

Principle 5 – integrity

3.16

The duty to act with integrity is one of the professional principles enshrined in section 1(3) of LSA 2007. It is a core duty which was also included in rule 1(a) of SPR 1990, rule 1.02 of the 2007 Code and the 2011 Principles.

In *Wingate*, Jackson LJ said:

> 'In professional codes of conduct, the term "integrity" is a useful shorthand to express the higher standards which society expects from professional persons and which the professions expect from their own members ... The

underlying rationale is that the professions have a privileged and trusted role in society. In return they are required to live up to their own professional standards ...

Integrity connotes adherence to the ethical standards of one's own profession ...

The duty of integrity does not require professional people to be paragons of virtue. In every instance, professional integrity is linked to the manner in which that particular profession professes to serve the public ...'[1]

In *Newell-Austin* Morris J observed that the test for lack of integrity is objective but an individual's state of knowledge of, and intentions relating to, the underlying facts are relevant to determining whether they have acted without integrity.[2] It is submitted that this is plainly correct: a deliberate or reckless breach of rules or standards of professional conduct may demonstrate a lack of integrity, whereas an inadvertent or negligent breach may not.[3] (See also **3.16** and **19.5**.)

1   *SRA v Wingate* [2018] EWCA Civ 366 at [97]–[102].
2   *Newell-Austin v SRA* [2017] EWHC 411 (Admin) at [48]–[50].
3   For examples of lack of integrity see SRA Ethics guidance, 'Acting with Integrity', issued 23 July 2019.

Principle 6 – equality, diversity and inclusion

3.17

The importance that the SRA attaches to equality, diversity and inclusion is emphasised by the fact that it is treated as a core principle and not a standard.

Equality and diversity were first made the subject of regulatory requirements by the Solicitors' Anti-Discrimination Rules 2004. These were replaced by rule 6 of the 2007 Code, which simply imposed obligations not to discriminate in a way that would be unlawful, and to have a written policy. The language in the 2011 Code wholly changed. Principle 9 of the 2011 Code stated you must 'run your business or carry out your role in the business in a way that encourages equality of opportunity and respect for diversity'. That was supplemented by Chapter 2 of the 2011 Code, which concerned equality and diversity, and the introduction to Chapter 2 of the 2011 Code stated that it 'is about encouraging equality of opportunity and respect for diversity, and preventing unlawful discrimination'.

The emphasis on 'encouragement' has been carried forward into the 2019 Principles and widened in scope: principle 6 states that you must act 'in a way that encourages equality, diversity and inclusion'. That goes beyond the statutory requirements in the Equality Act 2010, which prohibit direct and indirect discrimination, harassment and victimisation in relation to a protected characteristic. There are provisions in the Equality Act 2010 which contemplate positive action, such as the duty to make reasonable adjustments for disabled persons,[1] the public sector duty to advance equality of opportunity[2] and the ability of service providers, public bodies and other associations to take positive action in recruitment and promotion.[3] However, those provisions do not impose a general obligation on businesses to encourage equality, diversity and inclusion.

The protected characteristics under the Equality Act 2010 are age, disability, gender reassignment, marriage and civil partnership, pregnancy and maternity, race, religion or belief, and sex or sexual orientation. The SRA intends that all regulated individuals and entities should contribute to compliance with the protections afforded to those characteristics by embedding appropriate values in the workplace and by challenging inappropriate behaviour and processes. The individual's responsibility for embedding these values will vary depending on the role in the organisation. The managers of the firm, the compliance officer for legal practice (COLP) and the firm have a wider responsibility to ensure that appropriate policies and procedures are in place. It is plainly intended that principle 6 should supplement rather than merely restate the general law. However, the extent to which the SRA expects firms to go beyond their statutory obligations is unclear.

On 23 July 2019 the SRA published an Ethics guidance note on principle 6[4] which describes equality, diversity and inclusion (EDI) in the following manner:

'1. Equality is about making sure there is a level playing field and people are treated fairly.

2. Diversity is about encouraging and valuing people with a broad range of different backgrounds, knowledge, skills, and experiences.

3. Inclusion is about accepting people for who they are and encouraging everyone to participate and contribute.'

The guidance note states that, while legislation sets minimum legal obligations, a solicitor's regulatory obligations extend beyond strict compliance with the law. Those obligations extend to how solicitors run their firms and provide services, how they interact with people they work with, including employees and how they meet the diverse needs of clients and others. Firms are encouraged to produce a policy statement which articulates support for EDI, and to monitor and analyse the diversity of staff and clients. Senior leaders have a responsibility to encourage EDI and identify and remove barriers in recruitment, promotion and progression, and all solicitors, whether they are managers or employees, have a role to play in implementing EDI policies and procedures.

The word 'encourage' is probably to be treated as a regulatory obligation to approach issues of equality, diversity and inclusion in a positive frame of mind; to be alive to opportunities and, in a manner falling short of positive discrimination, seek to ensure that issues of equality, diversity and inclusion remain at the forefront when decisions are made.

In short, principle 6 is about having the right attitude of mind.

1   Section 20 of the Equality Act 2010.
2   Section 149 of the Equality Act 2010.
3   Sections 158 and 159 of the Equality Act 2010.
4   SRA, 'Guidance on the SRA's approach to equality, diversity and inclusion', issued 23 July 2019.

3.18

More positive assistance is available from the Law Society, which promotes a Diversity and Inclusion Charter, the signatories to which make a commitment to:

'Strive to achieve best practice in our recruitment, retention and career progression practices as employers.

Support the development of good diversity practice by collecting and sharing examples of practical activities that contribute to progress with other signatories.

Assign responsibility for meeting our charter commitments to a named, senior level individual.

Work together to develop and adopt future protocols that support the practical implementation of the aims of this charter.

Annually publish the diversity profile of our UK employees and details of our work on equality, diversity and inclusion.

Publish a joint annual report on the basis of a monitoring exercise to measure the impact of this charter and its protocols. These reports will form the basis of regular dialogue with stakeholders, employees and clients.'

The Law Society makes available, free of charge to those who commit to the Charter, its Diversity and Inclusion Standards, accompanied by best practice guidance designed to help the legal profession to promote successfully and implement best practice in equality, diversity and inclusion – as employers, as providers of legal services, as purchasers of goods and services and in its wider role in society.

For further details visit www.lawsociety.org.uk/support-services/practice-management/Diversity-inclusion.

3.19

In the SRA's Risk Outlook for 2018/19, the SRA said that to improve diversity and inclusion, firms can:

- create a culture where people feel able to talk about diversity and staff feel included and valued;

- offer mentoring schemes, which can improve access to the profession and diversity at management levels;

- use the SRA's law firm diversity tool to benchmark their diversity, and encourage all staff to respond to all questions;

- carry out pay audits to identify any pay gaps between different groups of people;

- consider unconscious biases and help staff overcome these to make objective decisions about recruitment and selection;

- offer flexible working, such as home working, to help the work–life balance of all staff, particularly those with caring responsibilities;

- ask senior managers to lead by example, such as challenging any offensive behaviour in the workplace;

- support different routes to the profession, including apprentices, paralegals and legal executives, so talented people from all backgrounds can access the profession;

- consider the wellbeing of staff and help staff manage stress levels.[1]

1   SRA Risk Outlook 2018/19, 'Diversity in the profession', issued by the SRA in July 2018.

3.20

Principle 6 applies to solicitors in their private and professional lives. A solicitor who, for example, carries on a separate business unrelated to legal activities, could face disciplinary proceedings if the separate business does not encourage equality, diversity and inclusion. Similarly, a solicitor who expresses personal views on social media platforms which are incompatible with the principles of equality, diversity and inclusion would breach principle 6.

Principle 7 – best interests of the client

3.21

The duty to act in the best interests of clients arises out of the solicitor's status as a fiduciary, and is one of the professional principles enshrined in section 1(3) of LSA 2007. It is a core duty which was also included in rule 1(c) of SPR 1990, rule 1.04 of the 2007 Code, and the 2011 Principles. It encompasses obligations such as the duty of confidentiality, the obligation to avoid conflicts of interest and the obligation not to take unfair advantage of a client.

CHAPTER 4

The SRA Code of Conduct for Solicitors, RELs and RFLs

Introduction

4.1

There have been four different sets of conduct rules within a space of 12 years.

Until 1 July 2007, solicitors were governed by the Solicitors' Practice Rules 1990 as amended from time to time, and wider non-codified provisions which might be described as the common law of conduct. The Law Society periodically issued *The Guide to the Professional Conduct of Solicitors*, free of charge to the profession. The final edition, the eighth, was published in 1999, and so was considerably out of date by July 2007, although attempts had been made to keep it current by postings on the Solicitors Regulation Authority (SRA) website under the style of the 'Guide Online'.

The Solicitors' Code of Conduct 2007 (2007 Code) came into force on 1 July 2007, but both the rules and the associated guidance were regularly amended thereafter.

The SRA Code of Conduct 2011 (2011 Code) came into force on 6 October 2011. The 2011 Code was also regularly amended and, by the time of the 2019 Codes, the 2011 Code had been amended 21 times.

4.2

There are now two codes of conduct: one for individuals (solicitors, registered European lawyers (RELs) and registered foreign lawyers (RFLs)), and one for regulated firms, including their managers, compliance officers and employees.

The SRA Code of Conduct for Solicitors, RELs and RFLs 2019 (the 'Code for Individuals') sets out the 'standards of professionalism' that are expected and 'comprise a framework for ethical and competent practice'.

The SRA Code of Conduct for Firms 2019 (the 'Code for Firms') sets out the 'standards and business controls' that are expected and which 'aim to create and maintain the right culture and environment for the delivery of competent and ethical legal services'.

Although the separation of the 2011 Code into two is a radical change in the presentation of the conduct rules, the SRA has said that 'firms and individuals who do not want to make changes to their current arrangements will in the main not have, or need, to do so'.[1]

---

1   'Application for the approval of regulatory arrangements', issued by the SRA in August 2018, para 96.

4.3

The main changes affecting the 2011 Principles and Code have been summarised by the SRA as changes in two broad areas:

> 'a.   The implementation of a set of drafting principles to restructure and clarify the SRA Principles and Code of Conduct 2011 … and
>
> b.   The proposed policy changes about where solicitors can practise'.[1]

The change in drafting approach is designed to lead to a shorter and less prescriptive code which introduces 'more flexibility to require those to whom the Codes apply to use their own judgment when applying the Code to their practice and conduct'.[2]

There are two policy changes about where solicitors can practise. Solicitors can now provide unreserved legal services to the public while working in businesses not regulated by the Legal Services Act (LSA) 2007 and using their solicitor title. Individual solicitors working on their own can in some circumstances practise without applying for authorisation as a recognised sole practitioner. Those changes have led to some new provisions in the Code for Individuals (such as the provision of information to clients in paragraph 8.10).

1   'Looking to the future – flexibility and public protection', issued by the SRA in June 2016, Annex 5, p 15.
2   'Looking to the future – flexibility and public protection', issued by the SRA in June 2016, Annex 4, p 13.

4.4

In addition to those main changes, some new provisions have been added to the Codes. The Code for Individuals includes new provisions relating to litigation (paragraphs 2.4 and 2.5), continuing competence (paragraph 3.3), supervision (paragraph 3.5), keeping up to date with the law (paragraph 7.1), identification of clients (paragraphs 3.1 and 8.1) and alternative dispute resolution (ADR) in complaints handling (paragraph 8.4).

4.5

In this chapter, we examine the Code for Individuals section by section, making practical suggestions as to how solicitors can best achieve compliance with the standards.

Solicitors will continue to be prosecuted for breaches of the 2011 Principles and Code, as some of the alleged misconduct brought before the Solicitors Disciplinary Tribunal (the Tribunal or SDT) occurs over a significant period of time. If a commentary on the 2011 Principles and Code is needed, it can found in *The Solicitor's Handbook 2017*.

4.6

The introduction to the Code for Individuals is as follows:

Introduction

The Code of Conduct describes the standards of professionalism that we, the SRA, and the public expect of individuals (solicitors, registered European lawyers and registered foreign lawyers) authorised by us to provide legal services.

They apply to conduct and behaviour relating to your practice, and comprise a framework for ethical and competent practice which applies irrespective of your role or the environment or organisation in which you work (subject to the Overseas Rules which apply to your practice overseas); although paragraphs 8.1 to 8.11 apply only when you are providing your services to the public or a section of the public.

You must exercise your judgement in applying these standards to the situations you are in and deciding on a course of action, bearing in mind your role and responsibilities, areas of practice, and the nature of your clients (which in an in house context will generally include your employer and may include other persons or groups within or outside your employer organisation).

You are personally accountable for compliance with this Code – and our other regulatory requirements that apply to you – and must always be prepared to justify your decisions and actions.

A serious failure to meet our standards or a serious breach of our regulatory requirements may result in our taking regulatory action against you. A failure or breach may be serious either in isolation or because it comprises a persistent or concerning pattern of behaviour. In addition to the regulatory requirements set by us in our Codes, Principles and our rules and regulations, we directly monitor and enforce the requirements relating to referral fees set out in section 56 of the Legal Aid, Sentencing and Punishment of Offenders Act 2012, and provisions relating to anti money laundering and counter terrorist financing, as set out in regulations made by the Treasury as in force from time to time [Link].

All these requirements are underpinned by our Enforcement Strategy. That strategy explains in more detail our views about the issues we consider to be serious, and our approach to taking regulatory action in the public interest.

4.7

The introduction to the Code for Individuals states that the code applies to 'conduct and behaviour relating to your practice'. That can be contrasted with the 2019 Principles, which apply to an individual's conduct in private life as well as in practice.

4.8

The Code for Individuals does not apply to solicitors and other regulated individuals who are practising overseas, unless the practice predominantly comprises the provision of legal services to clients within England and Wales, or in relation to assets located in England and Wales.[1] A solicitor who is practising overseas, and whose practice does not fall within that exception, must instead comply with the SRA

Overseas and Cross-border Practice Rules 2019. The SRA Glossary defines 'practising overseas' in relation to a solicitor to mean 'a practice ... of a solicitor established outside England and Wales for the purpose of providing legal services in an overseas jurisdiction', and 'overseas' means outside England and Wales.

1   Rules 1.1(a) and 1.3 of the SRA Overseas and Cross-border Practice Rules 2019.

Maintaining trust and acting fairly

4.9

1.1   You do not unfairly discriminate by allowing your personal views to affect your professional relationships and the way in which you provide your services.

1.2   You do not abuse your position by taking unfair advantage of *clients* or others.

1.3   You perform all *undertakings* given by you, and do so within an agreed timescale or if no timescale has been agreed then within a reasonable amount of time.

1.4   You do not mislead or attempt to mislead your *clients*, the *court* or others, either by your own acts or omissions or allowing or being complicit in the acts or omissions of others (including your *client*).

Discrimination

4.10

It is probably no coincidence that the first standards in the Code for Individuals and the Code for Firms relate to discrimination. The SRA is committed to encouraging equality, diversity and inclusion and preventing discrimination.

The SRA intends that everyone should contribute to compliance with those requirements by embedding appropriate values in the workplace and by challenging inappropriate behaviour and processes. The responsibility falls on the individual as well as the firm.

Under the Equality Act 2010, the protected characteristics are age, disability, gender reassignment, marriage and civil partnership, pregnancy and maternity, race, religion or belief, and sex or sexual orientation.[1]

Direct discrimination is defined in the Equality Act 2010 as follows: 'A person (A) discriminates against another (B) if, because of a protected characteristic, A treats B less favourably than A treats or would treat others'. There are detailed statutory provisions in the Equality Act 2010 which qualify or extend the statutory definition in differing ways for differing protected characteristics. For example, in relation to age, direct discrimination can be justified if it is a proportionate means of achieving a legitimate aim. Direct discrimination also covers a situation where someone is treated less favourably than another person because they are thought to have a protected characteristic or because they associate with someone who has a protected characteristic.[2]

Paragraph 1.1 goes hand in hand with principle 6 (you must act in a way that encourages equality, diversity and inclusion). See the commentary on principle 6 at **3.17**.

Paragraph 1.1 also prohibits indirect discrimination. For indirect discrimination see the commentary on paragraph 1.1 of the Code for Firms at **5.12**.

The use of the phrase 'unfairly discriminate' rather than 'unlawfully discriminate' in paragraph 1.1 could extend the standard to behaviour beyond the discrimination prohibited by the Equality Act 2010.

1 Section 4 of the Equality Act 2010.
2 See sections 13 to 18 of the Equality Act 2010.

Taking unfair advantage

4.11

Paragraph 1.2 reflects a long-standing rule of professional conduct, previously contained in outcome 11.1 of the 2011 Code and rule 10.01 of the 2007 Code, that solicitors must not take unfair advantage of anyone.

The introduction to the Code for Individuals states that the standards apply to conduct and behaviour relating to the solicitor's practice. That is a departure from the 2011 Code, which stated that solicitors should not take unfair advantage of third parties in their professional or personal capacity. However, if a solicitor uses his or her status as a solicitor to gain an unfair advantage when acting in a personal capacity, there will be a breach of principle 2 (upholding public trust and confidence in the profession) and possibly also principle 5 (integrity) of the SRA Principles 2019.

Paragraph 1.2 could be breached if, for example, a solicitor communicates with a third party after becoming aware that the third party has instructed another solicitor; or takes advantage of an opposing party's lack of legal knowledge where they have not instructed a lawyer; or knowingly makes a demand in litigation for a remedy which is not legally recoverable, such as a demand for a debtor to pay the cost of a letter of claim when it cannot be said at that stage that the cost is legally recoverable.

Undertakings

4.12

Paragraph 1.3 is concerned with undertakings. An undertaking is defined in the SRA Glossary to mean:

> 'a statement, given orally or in writing, whether or not it includes the word "undertake" or "undertaking", to someone who reasonably places reliance on it, that you or a third party will do something or cause something to be done, or refrain from doing something.'

Misleading others

4.13

If a solicitor deliberately misleads others (whether clients, third parties, or the court), or attempts to do so, he is at risk of being struck off for dishonesty. For commentary on paragraph 1.4 in relation to the courts see **4.17**.

Dispute resolution and proceedings before courts, tribunals and inquiries

4.14

2.1   You do not misuse or tamper with evidence or attempt to do so.

2.2   You do not seek to influence the substance of evidence, including generating false evidence or persuading witnesses to change their evidence.

2.3   You do not provide or offer to provide any benefit to witnesses dependent upon the nature of their evidence or the outcome of the case.

2.4   You only make assertions or put forward statements, representations or submissions to the *court* or others which are properly arguable.

2.5   You do not place yourself in contempt of *court*, and you comply with *court* orders which place obligations on you.

2.6   You do not waste the *court's* time.

2.7   You draw the *court's* attention to relevant cases and statutory provisions, or procedural irregularities of which you are aware, and which are likely to have a material effect on the outcome of the proceedings.

4.15

There is nothing unusual in the requirements of section 2 and any practitioner familiar with the proper standards of behaviour of litigators and advocates need have no concern that section 2 presents any traps or creates obligations that have not hitherto been owed. Section 2 is supplemented by paragraph 1.4 (you do not mislead or attempt to mislead your clients, the court or others), which is contained in section 1 of the Code as its scope is not limited to the courts. Paragraph 1.4 is wider than its predecessors and the effect of the standard needs to be considered carefully (see **4.17**).

Paragraph 1.4 and section 2 are not an exhaustive list of the professional obligations relating to the court. Every solicitor is an officer of the court, and owes duties to the court under case law, statute and procedural rules. Outcome 5.6 of the 2011 Code contained an express provision that solicitors must comply with their duties to the court. That express provision has been removed from the 2019 Codes but the professional obligation to comply with the duties owed to the court remains; it falls within the general obligation under paragraph 7.1 of the Code for Individuals to follow the law governing the way solicitors work. If a solicitor breaches any of the duties owed to a senior court it is open to the court either to admonish the solicitor under the court's inherent jurisdiction or to refer the matter to the SRA as professional misconduct.[1] Inferior courts are restricted to referring the matter to the SRA. In practice the matter would normally be referred to the SRA, as the inherent jurisdiction is rarely invoked.[2]

1   *Sathivel v Secretary of State for the Home Department* [2018] EWHC 913 (Admin) at [2].
2   See **CHAPTER 24**.

4.16

LSA 2007 imposes statutory duties on litigators. Section 1(3) of LSA 2007 states that one of the five professional principles is that persons who exercise before any court a right of audience, or conduct litigation in relation to proceedings in any court, by virtue of being authorised persons should comply with their duty to the court to act with independence in the interests of justice. Sections 176(1) and 188(3) of LSA 2007 impose a duty on regulated persons to comply with their conduct rules relating to the exercise of a right of audience and the conduct of litigation. Any conflict between those statutory duties and other professional duties (such as the duty to act in the best interests of the client) is governed by section 188(3) of LSA 2007, which provides that the duties to act with independence in the interests of justice, and to comply with the relevant conduct rules, override any obligations which the person who is conducting the litigation or exercising a right of audience may have (otherwise than under the criminal law) if they are inconsistent with them.

In March 2015 the SRA published a Risk Resource paper on the need to balance the duty fearlessly to advance a client's case with the duties owed to the court and third parties.[1] The paper highlighted instances in which litigators unduly prioritise clients' interests by using the threat of litigation in unmeritorious cases to obtain settlement, mislead the court by knowingly or recklessly permitting false information to be given to the court and use the litigation process for purposes that are not directly connected to resolving a specific dispute. Cases in that third category include immigration cases in which last-minute applications are made for injunctions as a strategy to defeat removal proceedings.[2]

1   'Walking the line: the balancing of duties in litigation', issued by the SRA in March 2015.
2   See *R (Hamid) v Secretary of State for the Home Department* [2012] EWHC 3070 (Admin) and *Sathivel v Secretary of State for the Home Department* [2018] EWHC 913 (Admin).

4.17

Paragraph 1.4 has its origins in rule 11 of the 2007 Code and Chapter 5 of the 2011 Code. Both rule 11 of the 2007 Code and the first drafts of Chapter 5 of the 2011 Code included references to the court being misled by others: in rule 11: 'You must never … knowingly allow the court to be misled' and in the draft Chapter 5: 'You do not knowingly allow another person to deceive or mislead … the court'.

Both could have been interpreted to mean that in the well-known situation in which, in the criminal courts, the prosecution fails to identify that the defendant had previous convictions, a defence advocate would have been under a regulatory obligation to correct the misunderstanding. The 2007 rule was never interpreted in that way because it was well understood that in this respect the 2007 Code served to codify existing principles and guidance and not to change them. The 2011 Code was different and was intended to be interpreted as it stands without assistance from the legislative background, because it was part of a complete new regulatory system. An outcome which required defence advocates to prevent the court being innocently misled by the prosecution would, among other things, have required different standards to be applied by barristers and solicitors.

In the House of Lords in *Ali v Sydney Mitchell & Co* Lord Diplock set out the law as follows:

> 'A barrister must not wilfully mislead the court as to the law nor may he actively mislead the court as to the facts; although, consistently with the rule that the prosecution must prove its case, he may passively stand by and watch the court being misled by reason of its failure to ascertain facts that are within the barrister's knowledge.'[1]

The draftsman changed Chapter 5 so that outcome 5.2 prohibited a solicitor from being 'complicit' in another person misleading the court, and that change maintained the status quo.

Paragraph 1.4 of the Code for Individuals states: 'You do not mislead or attempt to mislead your clients, the court or others, either by your own acts or omissions or allowing or being complicit in the acts or omissions of others (including your client)'. Again the retention of the word 'complicit' is indicative of a lack of intention to change the legal position, but the use of the word 'allowing' leaves room for doubt, and raises the question of whether the standard is inconsistent with the duty set out by the House of Lords.

1   *Saif Ali v Sydney Mitchell & Co* [1980] AC 198, HL per Lord Diplock at 220.

4.18

Rule 11 of the 2007 Code replaced the Law Society's Code for Advocacy and those principles that were previously contained in Chapter 21 of *The Guide to the Professional Conduct of Solicitors 1999* (8th edn). Rule 11 imposed on all solicitors who conduct litigation some of the obligations that had previously been imposed only on advocates – including a provision in rule 11.01(3)(a) that a solicitor could not draft documents containing any allegation that he or she did not consider properly arguable. Rule 11 was considered by the Court of Appeal in *Richard Buxton (Solicitors) v Mills-Owens*[1] in which it was held that solicitors could lawfully determine their retainer when required by a client to advance an argument which they considered to be untenable. Rule 11.01(3)(a) was included in the 2011 Code as indicative behaviour 5.7 and an abbreviated version of the rule is now found in paragraph 2.4 of the Code for Individuals.

1   [2010] EWCA Civ 122.

Solicitor advocates

4.19

For solicitors who appear as advocates, it is worth repeating some of the contents of rule 11 of the 2007 Code, which were included in earlier editions of *The Solicitor's Handbook* but which have not found their way into the Code for Individuals, as there can be no doubt that they still hold good. Rule 11.05 provided that:

> 'If you are appearing as an advocate:

(a) you must not say anything which is merely scandalous or intended only to insult a witness or any other person;

(b) you must avoid naming in open court any third party whose character would thereby be called into question, unless it is necessary for the proper conduct of the case;

(c) you must not call into question the character of a witness you have cross-examined unless the witness has had the opportunity to answer the allegations during cross-examination; and

(d) you must not suggest that any person is guilty of a crime, fraud or misconduct unless such allegations:

> (i) go to a matter in issue which is material to your client's case; and
>
> (ii) appear to you to be supported by reasonable grounds.'

Rule 11.08 provided that:

'If you are acting in the defence or prosecution of an accused and you have in your possession a copy of an audio or video recording of a child witness which has been identified as having been prepared to be admitted in evidence at a criminal trial in accordance with the relevant provisions of the Criminal Justice Act 1991 or the Youth Justice and Criminal Evidence Act 1999, you must:

(a) not make or permit any person to make a copy of the recording;

(b) not release the recording to the accused;

(c) not make or permit any disclosure of the recording or its contents to any person except when, in your opinion, it is necessary in the course of preparing the prosecution, defence or appeal against conviction and/or sentence;

(d) ensure that the recording is always kept in a locked, secure container when not in use; and

(e) return the recording when you are no longer instructed in the matter.'

The solicitor as potential witness

4.20

The rule relating to cases in which solicitors are potential witnesses has not been included in the Code for Individuals. The principle has caused difficulties in the past because it has not always seemed to be wholly logical. It was first expressed as guidance in successive editions of *The Guide to the Professional Conduct of Solicitors*, and appeared in the 1999 edition as principle 21.12. There the principle was:

'A solicitor must not accept instructions to act as advocate for a client if it is clear that he or she or a member of the firm will be called as a witness on behalf of the client, unless the evidence is purely formal.'

It will be noted that the focus is not only on advocacy, but on the sequence of events. The question was whether a solicitor could 'accept instructions to act' – in other words the mischief at which the principle is aimed is a situation in which it is *already* clear that the solicitor is or is likely to be a material witness. One can well see that if the solicitor had, for example, been a witness to a road accident and one of the drivers or passengers subsequently instructed that solicitor's firm, professional issues would be likely to arise.

The 2007 Code went further than the earlier principle 21.12. The guidance notes to rule 11.06 of the 2007 Code provided that it would be 'extremely rare' for it to be proper for a solicitor to act in litigation where that solicitor is also a witness.

That rule had far less logical application as it extended to situations in which the solicitor acts for the client perfectly properly, and then something arises as a result of the solicitor/client relationship which makes it appropriate or necessary for the solicitor to give supportive evidence. It is commonplace for solicitors to give evidence for their clients about matters arising in the course of the retainer, for example, on procedural matters and as to dealings with opposing solicitors in civil proceedings, and in criminal proceedings where, for instance, evidence may be needed to explain that the defendant exercised his right of silence on advice. The proposition that, in this situation, the solicitor would be obliged to cease to act would make little sense.

The rule 11.06 provisions were dropped from the 2011 Code. Indicative behaviour 5.6 of the 2011 Code provided that a solicitor should not appear as an advocate, or act in litigation, if it is clear that the solicitor, or anyone in the firm, will be called as a witness in the matter unless the solicitor is satisfied that it would not prejudice his independence as an advocate, or litigator, or the interests of clients or the interests of justice. That indicative behaviour moved away from rule 11.06 towards the former principle 21.12, by shifting the focus from the giving of evidence, per se, to whether giving evidence would offend any of the Principles requiring independence, the interests of the client and the interests of justice to be considered. No such concerns tend to arise in the everyday situations in which most solicitors find themselves giving evidence.

In our view the primary historical concern which lay behind the previous rules was the situation in which a solicitor who is a material witness to matters unrelated to the solicitor/client relationship is subsequently asked to act in the case.

Service and competence

4.21

> 3.1   You only act for *clients* on instructions from the *client*, or from someone properly authorised to provide instructions on their behalf. If you have reason to suspect that the instructions do not represent your *client's* wishes, you do not act unless you have satisfied yourself that they do. However, in circumstances where you have legal authority to act notwithstanding that it is not possible to obtain or ascertain the instructions of your *client*, then you are subject to the overriding obligation to protect your *client's* best interests.
>
> 3.2   You ensure that the service you provide to *clients* is competent and delivered in a timely manner.

3.3 You maintain your competence to carry out your role and keep your professional knowledge and skills up to date.

3.4 You consider and take account of your *client's* attributes, needs and circumstances.

3.5 Where you supervise or manage others providing legal services:

(a) you remain accountable for the work carried out through them; and

(b) you effectively supervise work being done for *clients*.

3.6 You ensure that the individuals you manage are competent to carry out their role, and keep their professional knowledge and skills, as well as understanding of their legal, ethical and regulatory obligations, up to date.

Paragraph 3.1: Client instructions

4.22

Paragraph 3.1 contains new provisions which were not included in the 2011 Code. In a 2016 consultation paper on the new codes, the SRA stated that new requirements relating to confirmation of a client's identity were being added because of the increase in theft, fraud and cybercrime.[1] Similarly, in the 2018 application to the Legal Services Board (LSB) for approval of the new regulatory arrangements, the SRA stated that a small number of new requirements, such as the obligations on obtaining instructions (paragraph 3.1) and identifying your client (paragraph 8.1) had been added where the SRA considered that 'protections were lacking, or that requirements were not as clear as they should be'.[2]

1 'Looking to the future – flexibility and public protection', issued by the SRA in June 2016.
2 'Application for the approval of regulatory arrangements', issued by the SRA in August 2018, para 88.

4.23

When a solicitor is acting on the basis that instructions are to be provided directly by a client, the solicitor needs to ensure that the instructions are in fact being provided by the client, and not by a fraudster. That involves standard identification checks under the firm's anti-money laundering (AML) procedures, but solicitors also need to be aware of the particular risks in their area of work. In conveyancing, for example, there have been cases in which properties have been sold on the basis of instructions from fraudsters masquerading as the owner. A growing risk is email modification fraud, where a fraudster breaks into a client's email account and intercepts and falsifies emails between the client and the firm on conveyancing matters, in order to divert completion monies to the fraudster's bank account. Most of these frauds take place on Fridays just before a property completion, and a property lawyer receiving an email of that type shortly before completion would have good reason to suspect that the instructions do not represent the client's wishes, and that the completion monies should not be sent to the bank account without speaking to the client. The growing prevalence of cybercrime means that it is advisable for every solicitor to read the SRA's Risk Outlook, which is published on an annual basis and highlights risks of all types identified by the SRA, including cybercrime. Given the fast changing nature of cybercrime, it is also advisable to periodically check the SRA website for any additional warnings. For cybercrime, see also **5.43**.

4.24

Where instructions are provided by a third party, paragraph 3.1 imposes an obligation on the solicitor to ensure that the third party is properly authorised to provide the instructions. The Code for Individuals does not specify what steps should be taken, and that is a matter for the solicitor to decide in the circumstances of the case. For example, in the case of a manager below board level providing instructions on behalf of a corporate client, it may require written confirmation from the directors at board level that the manager has authority to provide the instructions. In the case of a relative providing instructions on behalf of an individual, it may require a direct discussion with the individual and written confirmation of the authorisation. In the case of joint clients, where the instructions are provided by one of the joint clients, it may again require written confirmation of the authorisation from the other joint client(s). The obligation continues throughout the retainer. If there is reason at any time to suspect that instructions do not represent the client's wishes, the solicitor must satisfy himself or herself that they do, and that is likely to involve the need to take instructions directly from the client.

4.25

When deciding whether to take instructions from a third party, the solicitor needs to consider whether the client is vulnerable, whether the client is giving informed consent, whether it is in the best interests of the client to take instructions from the third party and whether there are any conflicts of interest between the third party and the client. It may also be necessary to warn the client that the third party will be sharing confidential information, which carries with it an inherent risk of subsequent misuse of the confidential information. In litigation matters, the solicitor also needs to consider whether certain steps require the direct authorisation of the client such as certification of a statement of truth in a pleading and confirmation that proper disclosure of documents has been made.

4.26

The obligation to act in the best interests of the client means that the solicitor should consider whether significant steps require direct authorisation from the client despite a general authorisation relating to third party instructions (such as decisions in litigation to issue proceedings or settle claims), whether the client should be kept directly informed of events and whether the authorisation instructions need to be reviewed directly with the client during the course of the retainer.

4.27

If a solicitor acts without proper authority there is a risk of civil claims, such as negligence, by the underlying client, as well as disciplinary action. In court proceedings, the proceedings could be an abuse of process. There could be a risk of a wasted costs order and possibly also in extreme cases a finding of contempt of court.

4.28

In March 2016 the SRA published a warning notice on personal injury claims, which stated that the role of referral organisations in the sector meant that solicitors should be particularly cautious in ensuring that they are acting on valid instructions. It also warned that they are likely to have to take instructions from, or check them directly with, the client throughout the course of the case, particularly in relation to significant decisions such as whether to settle and, if so, for how much.[1]

1   'Risk factors in personal injury claims: warning notice', issued by the SRA on 21 March 2016, updated December 2017.

4.29

By paragraph 3.1, in circumstances where a solicitor has legal authority to act notwithstanding that it is not possible to obtain or ascertain the instructions of the client, the solicitor is subject to an overriding obligation to protect the client's best interests. The provision is limited to circumstances in which the solicitor has legal authority to act. A general instruction to act on a matter may not give the solicitor legal or contractual authority take a step which requires a specific decision by the client on a matter which has significant consequences, without specific instructions from the client.

Paragraph 3.2: The service provided to clients

4.30

Solicitors are generally free to decide whether or not to accept instructions, but must refuse to act or cease to act when acting for the client would involve a breach of the law or professional rules, or when the solicitor has insufficient resources or competence.

4.31

Chapter 1 of the 2011 Code contained a number of outcomes and indicative behaviours relating to the level of service to be provided to clients. Those have not been carried into the 2019 Codes, and that is consistent with the SRA's overall approach of allowing more flexibility for individuals and firms to decide how best to comply with the rules of professional practice.[1]

The SRA has stated that most complaints regarding the standard of service relate to conveyancing, criminal advocacy and immigration. Identified shortcomings relate to a failure to give clear, concise and accessible information throughout the work about the cost (which should be updated when the cost is likely to change), the legal work required, the progress of the work, and complaints processes.[2]

1   See 'Application for approval of regulatory arrangements', issued by the SRA in August 2018, para 26.
2   SRA Risk Outlook 2018/19, 'Standards of service'.

4.32

In general, matters of poor service are investigated or considered by the Legal Ombudsman or the courts, rather than the SRA. Mere negligence is not professional misconduct. In *Preiss v GDC*, the Privy Council said that gross negligence can amount to professional misconduct but, for the opprobrium which attaches to a disciplinary offence, something more is required than the degree of negligence which gives rise to civil liability.[1] In *Re a Solicitor* (1972) Lord Denning said that negligence can amount to professional misconduct if it is inexcusable and such as to be regarded as deplorable by the profession.[2]

In February 2019 the SRA published a guidance note on competence and standard of service which confirmed that mere negligence will not be regarded as a disciplinary matter, but stated that the SRA would 'investigate competence or service issues where these are particularly grave or suggest multiple failures or repeat or persistent poor conduct'. Aggravating features include circumstances in which a firm or an individual knowingly or recklessly acts outside their competence or fails to take reasonable steps to update their knowledge and skills or fails to properly supervise work.[3]

1   *Preiss v GDC* [2001] UKPC 36 at [28].
2   *Re a Solicitor* [1972] 1 WLR 869, CA; see also **19.12**.
3   'SRA Topic Guide: Competence and standard of service', 7 February 2019.

4.33

The question of whether solicitors can cease to act when it transpires they have insufficient resources or lack the competence to deal with a matter was considered by the Court of Appeal in *R v Ulcay*.[1] In a criminal trial the judge had refused an adjournment for the amount of time requested by defence counsel and solicitors who had been instructed in place of the original defence team at the end of the prosecution case. The new solicitors had withdrawn on the basis that the time allowed did not enable them to prepare their client's case to the necessary standard. It was held that they were wrong to do so and that the rule did not allow a solicitor to refuse to act or to cease to act where an order of the court creates difficulties and makes it harder for him to discharge his professional duties. Those difficulties arose because of the judge's ruling, and not as a result of the absence of appropriate resources or competence.

1   [2007] EWCA Crim 2379.

4.34

The common law position that solicitors must not cease acting for a client except for good cause and on reasonable notice was considered in *Richard Buxton (Solicitors) v Mills-Owens*[1] in a situation in which the client was persisting in a course that his solicitors and counsel considered unwise. He insisted on points being advanced and argued on his behalf that his lawyers considered to be wholly unarguable. They considered their position to be untenable, obtained supportive advice to this effect from the Law Society and ceased to act on reasonable notice. It was held at first instance that they were not entitled to do so (at [21]):

> 'if a client who is prepared to pay for a case to be advanced, and who wants the claim advanced on a particular basis, which does not involve impropri-ety on the part of the solicitor or counsel, then it is no answer for the solicitor to say that he believes it is bound to fail therefore he will not do it.'

In consequence, a claim for costs by the solicitor for the work done up to the date the retainer was terminated was disallowed on the basis that he was required to complete the retainer: to carry on the action to the end. This was (fortunately) reversed by the Court of Appeal[2] which held that the solicitors had good reason to terminate the retainer, and were entitled to be paid their costs to date. The Law Society intervened in the appeal in support of the firm. The court noted (at [32]) that rule 11.01(3) of the 2007 Code provided:[3]

'you must not construct facts supporting your client's case or draft any documents relating to any proceedings containing … any contention which you do not consider to be properly arguable.'

Dyson LJ (with whom Sir Mark Potter P and Maurice Kay LJ agreed) stated (at [41]):

'There is no comprehensive definition of what amounts to a good reason to terminate in the Solicitors' Practice Rules or the Code of Conduct (although examples are given in both documents), or in any of the authorities that have been cited to us. That is not surprising, since whether there is a good reason to terminate is a fact-sensitive question. I accept the submission of Mr Drabble [for the Law Society] that it is wrong to restrict the circumstances in which a solicitor can lawfully terminate his retainer to those in which he is instructed to do something improper.'

And at [43]:

'I am in no doubt that even before the point was spelt out in the 2007 Code, it would have been understood by all solicitors that, as officers of the court, they were under a professional duty (i) not to include in the court documents that they drafted any contention which they did not consider to be properly arguable and (ii) not to instruct counsel to advance contentions which they did not consider to be properly arguable. That duty was reinforced by CPR 1.3.'

1 [2008] EWHC 1831 (QB).
2 [2010] EWCA Civ 122.
3 See also indicative behaviour 5.7 of the 2011 Code.

Paragraph 3.3: Keeping knowledge and skills up to date

4.35

On 1 November 2016 the SRA replaced the continuing professional development (CPD) programme with continuing competence. Under continuing competence, every solicitor with a practising certificate should reflect on their practice to identify learning needs, plan how to address those needs, complete the planned activities, record the process and make an annual declaration when applying for renewal of their practising certificate that they have reflected on their practice and addressed any identified learning and development needs. The SRA's guidance note on competence and standards of service states that a failure to consider or address training needs will be treated as an aggravating feature in professional issues relating to standard of service.[1]

1 'SRA Topic Guide: Competence and standard of service', issued in August 2018.

Paragraph 3.4: The client's attributes, needs and circumstances

4.36

The SRA places particular emphasis on the requirement to recognise the needs of vulnerable clients. The SRA Enforcement Strategy categorises vulnerable clients to include those facing barriers preventing access to legal services for cost or geographical reasons, those involved in sensitive family matters, those facing loss of personal liberty or deportation and those with health or learning disabilities. Vulnerability could be short term or permanent, and does not only result from the client's personal circumstances. It could result from the structure of the market or the nature of legal services and could mean that corporate clients are vulnerable in some circumstances. The Enforcement Strategy states that the SRA will consider a breach of the standards to be particularly serious where the client's vulnerability is relevant to the culpable behaviour.[1]

1 SRA Enforcement Strategy, issued in February 2019, p 11. See www.sra.org.uk/sra/strategy-2017-2020/sub-strategies/sra-enforcement-strategy

Paragraphs 3.5 and 3.6: Supervision and management

4.37

Under the 2011 Code, the primary responsibility for supervision and training fell on managers rather than individual solicitors below the management level. Paragraphs 3.5 and 3.6 place responsibilities for supervision and training relating to matters that affect client work on all solicitors who supervise or manage others, regardless of their seniority within the firm.

The standards apply to solicitors working in firms which are not regulated, as well as solicitors working in firms regulated by the SRA. In guidance for solicitors working in firms which are not regulated, the SRA has stated 'you will remain responsible for the work of those you supervise as far as we are concerned ... the Legal Ombudsman may also accept a complaint where it is clear that this has been supervised by a solicitor'.[1]

1 'Giving information to clients of businesses that are not authorised by a legal services regulator', issued by the SRA in August 2018. See also 'SRA standards and regulations guidance for the not for profit sector', 23 July 2019, para 7.6.2.

Client money and assets

4.38

4.1 You properly account to *clients* for any *financial benefit* you receive as a result of their instructions, except where they have agreed otherwise.

4.2 You safeguard money and *assets* entrusted to you by *clients* and others.

4.3 You do not personally hold *client money* save as permitted under regulation 10.2(b)(vii) of the Authorisation of Individuals Regulations, unless you work in an *authorised body*, or in an organisation of a kind *prescribed* under this rule on any terms that may be *prescribed* accordingly.

Commissions and financial benefits

4.39

The SRA Glossary states that 'financial benefit includes any commission, discount or rebate, but does not include your fees or interest earned on any client account'. The paragraph 4.1 requirement relating to financial benefits is comparable to the general law. Under the general law, a solicitor must not make a secret profit, or obtain any secret advantage, and must disclose to the client any interest in the transaction for which the solicitor is retained. The general law is satisfied if the fiduciary obtains the informed consent of the client at the outset of the retainer to retention of a financial benefit.

The 2007 Code, and its predecessors for many years, only imposed a professional duty to account in respect of commissions of £20 or more. The distinction between a commission and other benefits such as discounts and rebates caused difficulty in practice and led to the introduction of the wider phrase 'financial benefit' in the 2011 Code.[1] The £20 *de minimis* exception was not reproduced in the 2011 Code, and no longer exists; a secret profit is a secret profit, whether of £20 or £20 million, and it is arguable as a matter of legal principle that the Law Society should never have created the *de minimis* exception in the first place.

In the 2011 Code indicative behaviour 1.20 referred to a solicitor 'keeping [a financial benefit] only where you can justify keeping it, you have told the client the amount of the benefit … and the client has agreed that you can keep it'. There was no explanation as to how a solicitor might 'justify' retaining the benefit, and it was unclear whether the SRA was saying that the client's informed consent was not enough, and there had to be some additional justification, or whether indicative behaviour 1.20 was poorly worded. Indicative behaviour 1.20 has not been replicated in the 2019 Code.

Under paragraph 4.1, and the general law on fiduciaries and secret profits, solicitors can justify keeping a financial benefit including commission whenever they have been transparent from the outset about receipt of that sum, and the client has provided informed consent to its retention. A fiduciary is under no obligation in law to account for benefits which he is authorised to take under the terms of the agreement under which he acts as a fiduciary.[2]

Commissions and payments for introductions are a normal part of business life. Clients are generally, in our experience, unconcerned with the business arrangements solicitors make with third parties provided that they are transparent and cause no prejudice to the clients. The fact that solicitors may take a commission raises no eyebrows.

1 See *Law Society v Adcock and Mocroft* [2006] EWHC 3212 (Admin), [2007] 1 WLR 1096.
2 The liability to account arises if there is no such authority: 'If the person in a fiduciary position does gain or receive any financial benefit arising out of the use of the property of the beneficiary he cannot keep it unless he can show such authority', *Brown v Inland Revenue Commissioners* [1965] AC 244, HL per Lord Reid at 256G.

4.40

Solicitors should be aware that financial benefits received from third parties in the course of personal injury work may be prohibited under section 56(2) of the Legal Aid, Sentencing and Punishment of Offenders Act (LASPO) 2012, which provides that a regulated person is in breach of section 56 if, while providing legal services in the course of prescribed legal business, the regulated person arranges for a third party to provide services to the client and is paid or has been paid for making that arrangement. This is likely to be relevant, for example, where the solicitor arranges for the client to be examined by a medical practitioner who is on the books of a medical agency, and/or helps the client obtain after-the-event insurance, and/or helps to arrange car hire for the injured claimant following a road traffic accident. Such arrangements are caught by the referral fee ban, and outlawed if the solicitor is paid for the referral, or if there is any other consideration for the referral.[1]

1 See also paragraphs 5.1 and 5.2 of the Code for Individuals and **4.45**.

Client money and assets

4.41

The requirement in paragraph 4.2 to safeguard money and assets was formerly found in principle 10 of the 2011 Principles (which stated that you must protect client money and assets) and the protection has been extended to third parties as well as clients. Since 2017 the SRA has often asserted in disciplinary proceedings that there has been a breach of the obligation to protect client money when a shortfall arises on client account. Managers of a practice are strictly liable for shortfalls under the SRA Accounts Rules.[1] Human error and shortfalls can arise in the best run firms. An extension of the SRA Accounts Rules principle of strict liability to a rule in a code of conduct would be a departure from the principle that there has to be a culpable act or omission to act for there to be a breach of a code setting out standards of professional behaviour.

1 Rule 6.1 of the SRA Accounts Rules 2011 and rule 1.2 of the SRA Accounts Rules 2019.

4.42

Client money can only be held by solicitors working in authorised bodies unless one of the two exceptions in paragraph 4.3 applies. The 'authorised bodies' are recognised sole practices, recognised bodies (including traditional firms) and licensed bodies.[1] The first exception relates to sole solicitors who practise on their own without being authorised as a recognised sole practice and who are entitled to carry out reserved legal activities.[2] They are entitled to hold client money on account of fees and unpaid disbursements provided that (a) the client is told in advance where the money will be held and (b) any money held for disbursements relates to expenses which the sole solicitor has incurred on the client's behalf and is personally liable to pay.[3] The money need not be held in a client account.[4] As the expenses have to be incurred before the money on account can be obtained, the sole solicitor is at risk of personal liability for the incurred expenses (such as counsel's and expert's fees) until the money is obtained on account. The second exception relates to prescribed organisations. As at the date of this edition, no organisations have been prescribed.

1 See the SRA Glossary.
2 The conditions which sole solicitors need to meet to carry out reserved legal activities are set out in regulation 10.2(b) of the SRA Authorisation of Individuals Regulations 2019.
3 Regulation 10.2(b)(vii) of the SRA Authorisation of Individuals Regulations 2019.
4 Rule 2.2 of the SRA Accounts Rules 2019.

4.43

See **5.43** for steps which can be taken by a firm to protect client money from cybercrime.

Business requirements

Referrals, introductions and separate businesses

4.44

5.1   In respect of any referral of a *client* by you to another *person*, or of any third party who introduces business to you or with whom you share your *fees*, you ensure that:

(a)   *clients* are informed of any financial or other interest which you or your business or employer has in referring the *client* to another *person* or which an *introducer* has in referring the *client* to you;

(b)   *clients* are informed of any fee sharing arrangement that is relevant to their matter;

(c)   the fee sharing agreement is in writing;

(d)   you do not receive payments relating to a referral or make payments to an *introducer* in respect of *clients* who are the subject of criminal proceedings; and

(e)   any *client* referred by an *introducer* has not been acquired in a way which would breach the *SRA's regulatory arrangements* if the *person* acquiring the *client* were regulated by the *SRA*.

5.2   Where it appears to the *SRA* that you have made or received a *referral fee*, the payment will be treated as a *referral fee* unless you show that the payment was not made as such.

5.3   You only:

(a)   refer, recommend or introduce a *client* to a *separate business*; or

(b)   divide, or allow to be divided, a *client's* matter between you and a *separate business*;

where the *client* has given informed consent to your doing so.

Referral fees: introduction

4.45

No subject has been more controversial for solicitors than the payment of referral fees by solicitors to introducers. The profession itself has been sharply divided over the issue. One part regards the whole idea of buying work, and thereby increasing the basic overhead cost of conducting a client's case, to be distasteful, and damaging in tending to increase costs. The other maintains that solicitors' practices are businesses, that the payment of commissions for the introduction of work is a common and inevitable feature of business life, and that a return to more restrictive practices would defy the marketplace, which never really works, and in any event it would probably be unlawful as being anti-competitive. From 2004 until the passing of LASPO 2012, this liberal attitude prevailed. However, LASPO 2012 turned the clock back and, with effect from 1 April 2013, the profession again had to come to terms with the fact that in personal injury cases, solicitors cannot pay referral fees.

In his *Review of Civil Litigation Costs: Final Report* (published in 2010), Lord Justice Jackson recommended the abolition of referral fees, alternatively their capping at £200. The Government issued a Green Paper late in 2010, and consultation upon it closed at the end of February 2011. The Green Paper did not make any recommendation as to the future of referral fees: the Government was apparently awaiting the Report of the LSB before making its decision. That Report emerged in May 2011 and concluded that the purely regulatory case for a general ban in the legal services market had not been made out. This was because sufficient evidence of consumer detriment, which would have been needed to merit a ban, had not been found.

During the summer of 2011, a number of politicians called publicly for the banning of referral fees. They had become concerned both by the so-called 'compensation culture' that had grown over the previous decade leading to some spurious or exaggerated claims, and by the aggressive, often unscrupulous, and on occasions fraudulent activities of those who sought, for commercial gain, to incite personal injury victims to make legal claims in respect of the injuries they had sustained. This political campaign proved to be very successful, and the necessary provisions were somewhat hastily inserted into the Bill that was making its way through Parliament.

4.46

Other than arrangements caught by sections 56 to 60 of LASPO 2012, there is no inhibition against the payment by solicitors of referral fees in the general law.

As for agreements between introducers and their clients entered into before the client is introduced to the solicitor, solicitors may need to consider the doctrine of unconscionable bargain. In *Strydom v Vendside Limited*,[1] an attempt was made to set aside an agreement with a claims handling company associated with the Union of Democratic Mineworkers. Blair J, on appeal from the county court judge's decision, summarised the law on unconscionable bargains as follows (at [36]):

> 'before the court will consider setting a contract aside as an unconscionable bargain, one party has to have been disadvantaged in some relevant way as regards the other party, that other party must have exploited that disadvantage in some morally culpable manner, and the resulting transaction must be overreaching and oppressive. No single one of these factors is sufficient – all three elements must be proved, otherwise the enforceability of contracts is undermined (see the reasoning in Goff & Jones, *The Law of Restitution*, 7th edition, para 12–006). Where all these requirements are met, the burden then passes to the other party to satisfy the court that the transaction was fair, just and reasonable (*Snell's Equity*, 31st edition, para 8–47).'

1   [2009] EWHC 2130 (QB).

The referral fee ban in personal injury cases: sections 56 to 60 of LASPO 2012

4.47

LASPO 2012[1] received Royal Assent on 1 May 2012, and sections 56 to 60, which contain the referral fee ban, came into force in April 2013. In March 2013, the SRA published guidance to enable practitioners to plan for the forthcoming changes with a reasonably clear view of what the regulator regarded as acceptable and unacceptable arrangements. This was particularly helpful in explaining the SRA's interpretation of the statute, what was prohibited and, constructively, what in the SRA's interpretation was not prohibited.

In October 2013, just six months after the referral fee ban came into force, the SRA issued a warning notice to practitioners who have arrangements with introducers in connection with personal injury work. The full text of the warning notice is at **APPENDIX 9**. The reason for issuing the warning notice was explained thus:

> 'We know that the ban on referral fees has raised difficult issues in relation to its application and interpretation. We are also aware that, because of the wording of LASPO [alternative abbreviation of LASPO 2012], it is possible for firms to have arrangements that involve the introduction of personal injury work without being in breach of LASPO. We are concerned, however, that in setting up arrangements in a way that does not breach LASPO, firms are failing to consider their wider duties to their clients and others, and in doing so may be breaching the Principles or failing to achieve the Outcomes. Examples include:
>
> - agreeing with an introducer to deduct money from clients' damages;
>
> - inappropriate outsourcing of work to introducers;
>
> - referrals to other service providers which are not in the best interests of clients;
>
> - failure to properly advise clients about the costs and how their claim should be funded; and
>
> - lack of transparency about the arrangement.'[2]

This guidance was rather less helpful and in many respects caused some confusion. For example, because LASPO 2012 removed the principal source of income of many introducers including claims management companies, it would be expected that where a genuine service was provided such companies would charge for it. Further, Parliament had expressly sanctioned this because the Damages-Based Agreements Regulations 2013[3] provided for permissible damages-based agreements (DBAs) with claims management companies. By regulation 1(2) of those regulations a representative with whom a DBA could be entered into is defined as: 'the person providing the advocacy services, litigation services or claims management services to which the damages-based agreement relates'.

It was therefore illogical for the SRA to object, in principle, to any deduction from damages arising from such authorised and regulated activity, and no solicitor could realistically be expected to fail to obtain any necessary client consent.

The overall impression given by this guidance was that it reflected certain extremes of behaviour which the SRA encountered, the details of which were not disclosed, and that it was likely to be unhelpful and confusing to those who were trying to get it right (the kind of people who would read warnings from the SRA).

---

1   LASPO 2012 currently only affects the relationship between introducers and law firms in relation to claims for personal injury or death.
2   SRA warning notice, 'Referral fees, LASPO and the SRA principles', 11 October 2013.
3   SI 2013/609.

Mechanism of the ban

4.48

By section 56(1) and (2), a regulated person is in breach of the section if he refers prescribed legal business to another and is paid for the referral; or if the regulated person pays or has paid for the referral of prescribed legal business. Regulated persons are defined in section 59, and in simple terms are persons regulated by the Financial Conduct Authority, the Ministry of Justice, the Law Society and the Bar Council, in other words barristers, solicitors, claims management companies and insurers. The definition of prescribed legal business is complex and requires consideration of section 56(4) and (6) of LASPO 2012, and section 12(3) of LSA 2007. To date, the ban has been restricted to legal services relating to claims for personal injury and death: other areas of legal work where referral fees are commonplace, such as conveyancing and non-personal injury claims, e g damage-only accidents, and claims arising out of allegedly missold payment protection insurance, are untouched. However, the Lord Chancellor has power to make regulations to widen the definition of prescribed legal business.[1]

1   See section 56(4)(c) of LASPO 2012.

4.49

A referral is defined in section 56(5): there is a referral if a person (not the client) provides information to another person and it is information that a solicitor would need to make an offer to act for a client. Thus in the typical scenario of a claims management company and a solicitor, the introducer will pass on the details of the prospective client: the solicitor will then make contact with the client. Such a situation is clearly caught by the legislation if a payment is made. Where, however, the flow of information is in a different direction, e g where the introducer gives information about the solicitor to the prospective client, and the client is then left to contact the solicitor if he or she so chooses, this would not be a referral within the meaning of the Act.

The following extract from the March 2013 guidance published by the SRA confirms the correctness of this analysis:

'**14.** We consider that the communication of a client's name and contact details to or by a regulated person would amount to a referral, as this information would enable the recipient to make an offer to the client to provide relevant services.

15. Example: An insurance company has an agreement with a firm of solicitors for the referral of clients. The insurance company is contacted by the claimant who notifies the insurer of a claim involving personal injury. The client's details are provided to the firm, who write to the claimant/client offering their services. The firm pays a fee for each email sent from the website. We would regard this as a referral because the insurer has passed to the firm information which will enable the firm to offer to act for the claimant.

16. Example: A website offers to find a suitable firm of solicitors for members of the public. The potential client is required to input their postcode and the area of law in which they need help. They then receive an email providing contact details of a suitable firm in their area.

17. We do not consider that this amounts to a referral within the terms of LASPO as the potential client's details are not being provided to the firm. (However, the transparency requirements set out in Chapter 9 of the SRA Code of Conduct 2011 would still apply.)'[1]

1   SRA, 'The prohibition of referral fees in the Legal Aid, Sentencing and Punishing of Offenders Act 2012 (LASPO) sections 56–60', 25 March 2013, paras 14–17.

4.50

By section 56(8), payment includes any form of consideration (whether the benefit is received by the solicitor or a third party) but excludes the provision of reasonable hospitality.

Enforcing the ban

4.51

Parliament has thrown the responsibility for monitoring and enforcing the referral fee ban upon the regulators, who must ensure that they have appropriate arrangements in place and may make rules for this purpose.[1] As a result, the SRA amended the 2011 Code with effect from 1 April 2013 to add outcome 6.4 (you must not be paid a prohibited referral fee), outcome 9.8 (you must not pay a prohibited referral fee) and indicative behaviour 9.8 (ensure payments for services do not amount to payment of a prohibited referral fee). Those express provisions have been removed from the 2019 Codes, which is consistent with the SRA's intention to streamline the 2019 Codes.[2] LASPO 2012 can be enforced by the general requirement of paragraph 7.1 to follow the law and regulation governing the way you work and by the requirement of principle 1 to uphold the principle of the rule of law.[3] The introduction to the Code for Individuals states:

> 'In addition to the regulatory requirements set by us in our Codes, Principles and our rules and regulations, we directly monitor and enforce the requirements relating to referral fees set out in section 56 of [LASPO 2012]'.

1   See section 57(1)–(3) of LASPO 2012.
2   The only provision in the 2019 Codes which expressly refers to prohibited referral fees is paragraph 5.2 of the Code for Individuals. Paragraph 7.1(b) of the Code for Firms incorporates that standard into the Code for Firms.
3   But see **3.12** on principle 1.

4.52

LASPO 2012 provides that a breach of section 56 does not make the perpetrator guilty of a criminal offence, nor does it give rise to an action for breach of statutory duty.[1] A breach of section 56 does not make anything void or unenforceable, but a contract to make or pay for a referral or arrangement in breach of that section is unenforceable.[2]

1   See section 57(5) of LASPO 2012.
2   See section 57(6).

Anti-avoidance provisions

4.53

The pre-2004 ban was widely circumvented by solicitors. Instead of paying referral fees per se, solicitors paid 'administration fees' or 'marketing fees' for services allegedly provided of such description. As a result section 57 of LASPO 2012 includes within it some important anti-avoidance provisions.

4.54

Section 57(7) provides in substance from a solicitor's perspective that where a referral is made to a solicitor and it appears to the SRA that payment by the solicitor may be a referral fee, subsection (8) will apply. That subsection provides that rules under section 57(2) may provide for the payment to be treated as a referral fee unless the solicitor shows that the payment was made (a) as consideration for the provision of services, or (b) for another reason, and not as a referral fee. Paragraph 5.2 of the Code for Individuals contains a rule to that effect. The sting is in section 57(9), which provides that a payment which would otherwise be regarded as consideration for the provision of services of any description may be treated as a referral fee if it exceeds the amount specified in relation to services of that description in regulations made by the Lord Chancellor.

4.55

Some commentators have expressed the view that these subsections permit a kind of pre-2004 device, ie payments being made for 'services' to avoid the ban, but it is submitted that this is plainly not so. Regulations made under section 57(2) could not have the effect of changing the definition of what is prohibited by virtue of section 56. Rather, a statutory mechanism has been created in deliberately vague terms (to cater for business ingenuity) to enable regulators to identify arrangements which on the surface would not offend section 56, but avoid the legislative intent. In reality, section 56 may be so effective in its terms that these anti-avoidance provisions may prove to be unnecessary. If it becomes necessary to deploy them it is unclear precisely how the Lord Chancellor will decide upon an approved fee or cost for a particular kind of service.

The referral fee ban and ABSs

4.56

Although the creation of alternative business structures (ABSs) under LSA 2007 was unconnected with the new referral fee ban, on the face of it introducers and solicitors should be able to surmount the difficulties caused by the ban by joining forces in an ABS. As soon as solicitor and introducer are under the same legal roof as part of the same legal entity there can no longer be a 'referral', which requires information flowing from one legal person to another. In its discussion paper, the SRA recognised this:

> 'Concern has been expressed that businesses may become ABSs in order to circumvent the ban. For example, a claims management company might join forces with a firm of solicitors to form an ABS, which would do all of the work previously carried out by the two different businesses within one

entity. There would be no need for referrals, and therefore no referral fees would be paid. We believe that provided that all of the requirements for authorisation are met and the ABS complies with all of its regulatory obligations, we cannot seek to prevent such arrangements simply because they are set up to avoid being caught by the ban. An ABS is a legitimate form of business, supported by a strong statutory and regulatory framework.'

The referral fee ban and collective advertising by solicitors

4.57

There have been a number of successful schemes under which solicitors have pooled resources and created a third party organisation such as Injury Lawyers 4U, and National Accident Helpline, to carry out advertising and marketing on behalf of the firms, and then to refer claims generated by such activities to the solicitors on their panels. On the face of it, these collective schemes have the potential to be caught by the referral fee ban. However, where enforcement of the ban has been delegated by Parliament to the regulators, the view of the latter will be of decisive importance. The SRA's March 2013 guidance contained the following:

'**21.** Our view is that where there is a referral of a matter to or by a regulated person, or an arrangement for another person to provide services, a payment will be prohibited to the extent that it is being paid for the referral or arrangement. Where a payment is for the provision of other services of for another reason, the payment would not be in breach of LASPO.

22. This may cause difficulties where a third party refers clients to a firm of solicitors in addition to or in the course of providing other services such as marketing.

23. Example: a company carries out marketing for a group of firms. Enquiries are made to a call centre, details of potential clients are passed to member firms on a rota basis and each firm pays an equal share of the costs of advertising and operating the scheme. There has been a referral within the terms of LASPO because the details of potential clients have been passed to firms by the company carrying out the marketing. The firms involved will need to be satisfied that any payments they make to the marketing company are for the marketing and not for the referral of clients. If a payment is made for each "lead" or the payment varies according to the number of referrals made, this is likely to suggest that the payment is for the referrals rather than for the marketing. Even if there is no specific number of leads guaranteed the solicitor would need to be satisfied that the payment they are making is reasonable in view of the services being provided.

24. If it appears to us that a payment may have been made for a referral or for making an arrangement, we will treat that as a prohibited referral fee for the purposes of LASPO, unless the regulated person can show that the payment was made for services or for another reason and not as a referral fee. Where you advertise jointly and pay only for that service, you are unlikely to breach the provisions of LASPO – however, you will need to be satisfied that the arrangement does not contain a referral fee element.

25. Example: A CMC advertises in local newspapers in its own name and has a panel of firms to which they refer cases. When a potential client contacts the CMC, the CMC takes brief details and asks a standard set of questions to ensure the claim is not time barred. The client is told that a solicitor will contact them within the next 24 hours. Firms pay a fixed fee in respect of each client referred. The CMC says that the payments are for advertising, operating the call centre and vetting potential claims.

26. A firm in this situation would need to show that the payments were genuinely for the services described. In this case the vetting would appear to be minimal and it is difficult to see how the payment for advertising could be genuine as it is being paid "per client" rather than reflecting the actual cost of advertising. It is therefore likely that the payment would include a referral fee element.

27. When determining whether referral fees are being paid, we will take into account all of the circumstances but the following factors may indicate a prohibited referral fee:

- payment for services appear to be excessive;

- an arrangement where receipt of referrals is conditional upon payment;

- payments that are made per referral or which are otherwise linked to the number of referrals;

- no evidence that a genuine service is being provided.

28. Where it appears to us that a referral fee may have been paid, the onus will be on the regulated person to demonstrate that the payment was not for the referral (reference section 57(7) of LASPO). Firms should therefore fully investigate all relevant matters before making or receiving referrals of prescribed legal business.'[1]

1   SRA, 'The prohibition of referral fees in the Legal Aid, Sentencing and Punishing of Offenders Act 2012 (LASPO) sections 56–60', 25 March 2013, paras 21–28.

Paragraph 5.1: Referral arrangements and fee sharing in the Code for Individuals

4.58

It should be stressed that the LASPO referral fee ban currently applies only to personal injury and fatal accident cases. In most other areas of practice[1] solicitors may pay referral fees to introducers, and the solicitor's conduct is governed by the Principles and the provisions of the Code for Individuals.

1   There is a prohibition against referral fees in criminal proceedings – see paragraph 5.1(d).

4.59

Paragraphs 5.1(a) and (b) centre upon transparency and financial arrangements. The section 1 standards are also relevant to referrals: the client must be treated fairly. Principles 3 and 7 should also be taken into account as the solicitor should maintain his independence and act in the best interests of the client.

The 2011 Code expressly included the obligations to maintain independence and act in the best interests of clients in the chapter on referral arrangements. Outcome 9.1 stated that a solicitor's independence and professional judgement must not be prejudiced by virtue of any arrangement with another person. Outcome 9.2 stated that clients' interests must be protected regardless of the interests of an introducer or the solicitor's interest in receiving referrals. Outcome 9.3 required that clients should be in a position to make informed decisions about how to pursue their case. Indicative behaviour 9.2 stated that the solicitor might have to advise a client that an arrangement with an introducer is not in the client's best interests. All of those points are encapsulated by the 2019 Principles and continue to apply to referral agreements.

4.60

Although paragraphs 5.1(a) and (b) require that clients are informed of any financial or other interest which an introducer has in referring the client to the solicitor, and of any fee sharing arrangement, the provision does not mandate when this has to be done. There were similar provisions in the 2011 Code (outcomes 9.3, 9.4 and 9.5) which again did not mandate when the information had to be supplied. The nearest that the SRA came to giving guidance on the relevant outcomes was in a series of 'Q and As' on its website. The answer to the question 'When do I have to give this information to clients?' was:

> 'The outcomes do not specify when the information should be provided. However, in order to achieve outcome 9.3, you will need to consider whether you need to give the information before the client has committed themselves to instructing your firm i.e. at the outset of the matter. The nature of the referral arrangement may affect the client's decision to instruct your firm.'

It would however be equally logical, and much easier in pragmatic terms, if solicitors used the medium of routine client care documents to provide this information, provided there is no detriment or prejudice to clients or potential clients if they were to decide to terminate the retainer in the light of the disclosure of a referral arrangement.

4.61

Paragraphs 5.1(a) and (b) do not state whether the information to be supplied to clients should be in writing. Principle 7 (acting in the best interests of clients) is likely to mean in most circumstances that the information should be clear and in writing, so that the client can make an informed decision.

The 2011 Code contained an indicative behaviour on written information: indicative behaviour 9.6 stated that 'where information needs to be given to a client, ensuring the information is clear and in writing, or in a form appropriate to the client's needs' would tend to show compliance with the 2011 Code and Principles.

4.62

Paragraph 5.1(c) states that 'in respect of any referral of a client by you to another person, or of any third party who introduces business to you or with whom you share your fees, you ensure that ... the agreement is in writing'.

Read literally, that standard is difficult to understand. It is presumably not intended to cover referrals made between solicitors on a one-off basis to overcome a conflict of interest where there is no underlying agreement to pay a fee. It appears to require a written document for any agreement or arrangement for referrals, introductions or fee sharing.

4.63

Paragraph 5.1(d) outlaws referral fees in respect of clients who are the subject of criminal proceedings.

4.64

The 2007 Code imposed obligations on the solicitor to require the introducer to provide information to the client. In the absence of any specific rule to that effect in subsequent Codes, solicitors can safely abandon that obligation. The obligation was onerous and difficult to perform, and it was not missed.

4.65

By paragraph 5.1(e) solicitors must ensure that the introducers have not referred clients who have been acquired in a way which would breach the SRA's regulatory arrangements if the person acquiring the client were regulated by the SRA. The phrase 'SRA regulatory arrangements' has a very wide meaning. The SRA Glossary states it 'has the meaning given to it by section 21 of the LSA'. Section 21 of LSA 2007 defines 'regulatory arrangements' to include all authorisation arrangements, practice rules, conduct rules, qualification regulations and indemnification arrangements. The standard places a potentially onerous burden on solicitors, and it may be impossible to ensure that introducers have not breached such a wide-ranging requirement.

The comparable provisions in the 2011 Code were indicative behaviours which identified specific types of conduct. The 2011 Code included indicative behaviours which suggested that acting in the following ways would tend to show that solicitors had complied with the 2011 Code and Principles:

- only entering into arrangements with reputable third parties (indicative behaviour 9.1);

- in any case where a client has entered into, or is proposing to enter into, an arrangement with an introducer in connection with their matter which is not in their best interest, advising the client that this is the case (indicative behaviour 9.2);

- being satisfied that any client referred by the introducer has not acquired the client as a result of marketing or other activities which if done by a person regulated by the SRA would be contrary to the Principles or any requirements of the Code (indicative behaviour 9.4).

The indicative behaviours also provided that acting in the following way would tend to show that the solicitor had not complied with the 2011 Code and Principles:

- accepting referrals where you have reason to believe that clients have been pressurised or misled into instructing you (indicative behaviour 9.12).

Adopting those indicative behaviours as guidelines, it can be said that, under paragraph 5.1(e), solicitors should not accept referrals from introducers if there has been marketing such as cold calling, or there is reason to believe that clients have been pressurised or misled into instructing the introducer, or the introducer is entering into unfair agreements with clients relating to, for example, payment of disproportionate fees.[1] However, the standard is wider than that, and in practice it may often be impossible to ensure that the introducer complies with all applicable regulatory arrangements.

Paragraph 5.1(e) does not exclude introducers subject to other regulatory regimes. Claims management companies are regulated by the Financial Conduct Authority and are subject to their own suite of regulatory rules. By paragraph 5.1(e) a solicitor is required to ensure claims management companies do not offend the SRA regulations, despite that regulation by the FCA.[2]

1 See **4.67**.
2 Claims management services have been regulated by the FCA under the Financial Services and Markets Act 2002 since 1 April 2019. Before that date they were regulated by the Claims Management Regulation Unit of the Ministry of Justice under the Competition Act 2006.

4.66

The referral provisions in section 5 of the Code for Individuals apply to referrals between lawyers. Referral agreements need to be in writing. Any referral fees or fee sharing arrangements need to be disclosed to the client under paragraphs 5.1(a) and (b).

Pre-retainer arrangements between clients and introducers

4.67

The question of whether solicitors should advise their clients on pre-retainer arrangements between the client and an introducer, when those arrangements are not in the client's best interests, requires special mention.

Until recent years, it has not been suggested that solicitors are under any duty to advise their clients as to the wisdom or otherwise of contractual arrangements that they (the clients) may have made before instructing the solicitor. Indeed the imposition of such a duty in the general law is fraught with danger, and the courts have consistently pointed out the limits of a solicitor's retainer. In the words of Lord Jauncey in *Clark Boyce v Mouat*:[1]

> 'When a client in full command of his faculties and apparently aware of what he is doing seeks the assistance of a solicitor in the carrying out of a particular transaction, that solicitor is under no duty whether before or after accepting instructions to go beyond those instructions by proffering unsought advice on the wisdom of the transaction. To hold otherwise could impose intolerable burdens on solicitors.'

However, in some of the disciplinary prosecutions arising out of the miners' compensation cases, and later in disciplinary prosecutions arising out of the activities of an organisation known as Justice Direct, the Tribunal held that solicitors should have advised clients about agreements with introducers entered into before instruction of the solicitors, by which the client agreed to yield up a proportion of their compensation to the introducer.

1   [1994] 1 AC 428, PC at 437D.

4.68

The extent of the obligation is difficult to define. For instance, what is the solicitor to do where the client is introduced by an estate agent who charges significantly more than its competitors, with no apparent added value for the client? Is the solicitor to advise the new client that he or she is paying far too much to the estate agency which has introduced the client to the solicitor? In the judgment in the *Beresford* appeal[1] the Divisional Court discussed this issue at some length ([61]–[80] inclusive) but declined to decide it; observing that:

> 'It would for instance be a distraction to set about determining whether the Vendside agreements were indeed unenforceable in law. They were certainly questionable, as Beresfords knew or ought to have known. Vendside were not providing the services for which the fee was stated to be payable.'

The court appeared to take the view that there was an obligation to advise that the agreement was 'questionable' (at [75]). There remains uncertainty. In the *Beresford* case itself, the Tribunal provided some guidance as to what was expected of solicitors acting for claimants in the miners' compensation cases:

> 'The Tribunal had no doubt that it was part of Beresfords' retainer for them to read the agreement and comment on it to ensure that the miners fully understood what they had agreed to and to indicate to them that there was some uncertainty about the agreement and therefore about the deductions from their compensation.'[2]

1   *Beresford and Smith v SRA* [2009] EWHC 3155 (Admin).
2   9666–2007, SDT at para 156.

4.69

After its success in the *Beresford* case, the SRA prosecuted four separate sole practitioner solicitors who had accepted work from Justice Direct, an organisation that charged a hefty slice of a client's damages for doing little more than finding a solicitor for the client. All four admitted the allegations, and the Tribunal followed its approach in *Beresford* by agreeing that the failure to alert the clients to the disadvantageous nature of the Justice Direct contract amounted to professional misconduct. In the first such case, *Tilbury*,[1] the Tribunal stated:

> 'The Tribunal was satisfied that by entering into the agreement with Justice Direct, the Respondent effectively disabled himself from advising his clients as to the desirability of the client becoming liable to pay 25% of any recoverable damages to Justice Direct in return for an introduction to the solicitor. The benefits to the client of entering into the Purchase Order were claimed to be some initial screening of the claim and introduction of a suitably qualified solicitor. Neither in the Tribunal's view could justify the payment to Justice Direct of so disproportionate a share of the damages awarded to the client and the Tribunal considered that no competent

solicitor rendering advice in the best interests of the client could recommend the client to enter into such an agreement.'

Both the Justice Direct cases and *Beresford* are therefore consistent with a duty to advise in relation to a pre-existing contract, if on the facts there is something obviously inaccurate or uncertain, or a fee that is apparently wholly unreasonable and disproportionate. The question remains open as to what, in the case of a lawful contract, which is unreasonable and unfair, but not unconscionable and liable to be set aside, solicitors are expected to advise. They may find themselves in an unenviable position, in breach of regulatory duty if they stay silent, and at risk of committing the tort of inducing a breach of contract, or being informed by the client that the cost of the advice is outside the scope of the retainer, if they advise in detail. It may not be very constructive, but it would be compliant, for solicitors to 'advise' that the client would have been better not to have entered into the agreement, but that nothing can now be done about it.

If a solicitor enters into or continues an arrangement with an introducer in order to generate fee income, in circumstances where he is aware that the introducer is entering into unfair agreements with the clients, he or she is at risk of allegations of lack of integrity and a breach of paragraph 5.1(e).

1   9880–2008, SDT.

Involvement of the introducer after the case has been referred to the solicitor

4.70

One of the legitimate concerns of the SRA in policing referral fee arrangements is that solicitors may develop an unhealthy dependence upon a flow of work from a particular introducer, and then permit the introducer an inappropriate degree of control over how the solicitor carries out the work. An introducer has a legitimate interest in ensuring that the chosen solicitor carries out the work to a reasonable standard, as the introducer has entrusted the client to the solicitor. It is commonplace to see agreements between solicitors and introducers by which the introducer has the right to audit the work of the solicitor. However, unless dealt with in the agreement between introducer and client and/or the retainer letter between solicitor and client, such a right of audit may cut across the confidentiality that is owed by the solicitor to the client. Appropriate contractual provisions can reduce or eliminate any regulatory concern on that front, but solicitors should be aware that the SRA remains very concerned at the ability of introducers to weaken the independence of solicitors' advice to their clients.

Fee sharing

4.71

The rule against solicitors fee sharing with non-solicitors was traditionally based upon the risk of a non-solicitor having an inappropriate amount of influence over a solicitor in the handling of a claim for a client. It was steadily eroded over the years. Historically, there was an absolute prohibition, but that was relaxed in March 2004 to permit fee sharing with those who introduced capital or services into a firm.

Rule 8.02 of the 2007 Code maintained this exception. Because the former Practice Rules (and therefore the Code for Individuals) had the effect of subordinate legislation enacted for the protection of the public,[1] the rule against fee sharing with non-solicitors rendered an agreement to share fees in breach of the rule illegal and unenforceable.[2]

The advent of ABSs meant that the old objection to fee sharing between solicitors and non-solicitors had fallen away. The whole purpose of the reforms was to permit non-lawyers to share profits with solicitors. Fee sharing is inevitable where, for instance, a company merges with a firm of solicitors to create an ABS, or sets up an SRA-regulated subsidiary to provide legal services to existing clients. As fee sharing is permissible *within* one overall corporate structure, there is no logical reason why fee sharing *between* two independent corporate structures should be outlawed.

1   *Swain v Law Society* [1983] 1 AC 598, HL.
2   *Mohamed v Alaga & Co (a firm)* [1999] 3 All ER 699, CA; *Westlaw Services Limited and anor v Boddy* [2010] EWCA Civ 929.

4.72

In the 2011 Code there were a number of specific references to fee sharing (in Chapter 1: indicative behaviour 1.4, 'explaining any arrangements, such as fee sharing or referral arrangements, which are relevant to the client's instructions'; and in Chapter 9: particularly outcome 9.2 and indicative behaviours 9.3 and 9.11). Those references made it clear that fee sharing was no longer outlawed. Equally, the references to fee sharing in paragraph 5.1 of the Code for Individuals show that fee sharing is no longer outlawed.

In a nutshell, solicitors simply have to (a) be transparent to clients about arrangements with fee sharers; (b) ensure that the fee sharing agreement is in writing; (c) ensure that there is no sacrifice of their independence (ie permitting the fee sharer inappropriate influence); and (d) ensure that the best interests of clients remain paramount.

Referrals to financial advisers

4.73

Chapter 6 of the 2011 Code contained a series of outcomes and indicative behaviours relating to referrals to financial advisers. Those rules had in turn derived from rule 9.03 and rule 19.01(1)(a) of the 2007 Code. They have not been retained in the 2019 Codes. That is consistent with the SRA's aim of producing regulatory arrangements which are less prescriptive and focus on overarching values and behaviours.[1] On any referral to any third party solicitors should have regard to principle 3 (acting with independence) and principle 7 (acting in the best interests of each client).

1   For the SRA's approach to the 2019 Codes see, for example, 'Application for the approval of regulatory arrangements', issued by the SRA in August 2018, paras 12–26.

Paragraph 5.2

4.74

Paragraph 5.2 relates to LASPO 2012. The SRA Glossary states that 'referral fee' means 'a referral fee as defined within section 57(7) of [LASPO] 2012'. The definition in section 57(7) of LASPO 2012 relates to referral fees for legal services concerning a claim or potential claim for damages for personal injury or death, or for other prescribed legal business.[1]

By section 57(8) of LASPO 2012, the SRA may make rules which provide that, where it appears to the SRA that a payment made to or by a regulated person may be a referral fee prohibited by LASPO 2012, the payment is to be treated as a referral fee unless the regulated person shows that the payment was made (a) as consideration for the provision of services or (b) for another reason, and not as a referral fee. Paragraph 5.2 is a rule made by the SRA pursuant to section 57(8) of LASPO 2012.

1   At present there is no other prescribed legal business; other prescribed legal business is 'business of a description specified in regulations made by the Lord Chancellor' (section 56(4) of LASPO 2012) and no regulations have been made.

Paragraph 5.3

4.75

Since 1 November 2015 solicitors have been permitted to own and/or actively participate in a separate unregulated business which provided legal services of all kinds except for reserved legal activities.[1]

If a solicitor owns or actively participates in a separate business[2] which is not authorised by the SRA or another approved regulator, and if the solicitor wishes to refer the client or part of the client's work to the separate business, the client's informed consent is needed. Clients should in particular be informed that their work is no longer being carried out by a solicitors' firm in a regulated environment. It makes sense that, if the client decides to instruct a regulated firm, and is then encouraged to instruct the unregulated firm, the transfer should only be done on the basis of informed consent.

On 21 October 2015 the SRA published guidance on the information to supply to clients who instruct a solicitors' firm and a separate business.[3] Although part of the guidance is now obsolete, it continues to be of assistance on the information to be supplied on the regulatory protection obtained by instructing a solicitors' firm as well as factors to take into account when deciding on the amount of information to provide on the division of work between regulated and unregulated businesses. For further information on the guidance see **4.124**.

1   The rules were introduced into Chapter 12 of the 2011 Code and were called the separate business rules. There were separate business rules before 1 November 2015 which allowed solicitors to have interests in businesses which did not provide legal services, but the earlier separate business rules prevented solicitors from hiving off unreserved legal services.
2   The SRA Glossary states that separate business
    'means where you own, manage or are employed by an authorised body, a separate business:
    (a)   which you own;
    (b)   which you are owned by;

(c) where you actively participate in the provision of its services, including where you have any direct control over the business or any indirect control over the business through another person, or

(d) which you are connected with,

and which is not an authorised body, an authorised non-SRA firm or an overseas practice'.

3 See www.sra.org.uk/solicitors/guidance/guidance.page 'Chapter 12 of the SRA Code of Conduct 2011 – the separate business rule (SBR)' issued 21 October 2015.

Other business requirements

4.76

5.4 You must not be a *manager, employee, member* or *interest holder* of a business that:

(a) has a name which includes the word 'solicitors'; or

(b) describes its work in a way that suggests it is a *solicitors'* firm; unless it is an *authorised body*.

5.5 If you are a *solicitor* who holds a practising certificate, an *REL* or *RFL*, you must complete and deliver to the *SRA* an annual return in the *prescribed* form.

5.6 If you are a *solicitor* or an *REL* carrying on *reserved legal activities* in a *non-commercial body*, you must ensure that the body takes out and maintains indemnity insurance that provides adequate and appropriate cover in respect of the services that you provide, whether or not they comprise *reserved legal activities*.

4.77

Paragraphs 5.4 and 5.5 speak for themselves.

A 'non-commercial body' is defined by the SRA Glossary to mean 'a body which falls within section 23(2) of the LSA'. The bodies falling within section 23(2) of LSA 2007 are: (a) a not for profit body; (b) a community interest body; and (c) an independent trade union. Those bodies are entitled to carry out reserved legal activities despite the fact that they are not regulated by an approved regulator.[1] A solicitor conducting litigation in, for example, a trade union must ensure that the trade union has professional indemnity cover for all of the solicitor's work.

1 By section 23(3) of LSA 2007, the right to carry out the reserved legal activities continues during a transitional period from the date on which the relevant part of LSA 2007 relating to reserved legal activities came into force to a date to be appointed by the Lord Chancellor.

Conflict, confidentiality and disclosure

Conflict of interests

4.78

6.1 You do not act if there is an *own interest conflict* or a significant risk of such a conflict.

6.2   You do not act in relation to a matter or particular aspect of it if you have a *conflict of interest* or a significant risk of such a conflict in relation to that matter or aspect of it, unless:

(a)   the *clients* have a *substantially common interest* in relation to the matter or the aspect of it, as appropriate; or

(b)   the *clients* are *competing for the same objective*,

and the conditions below are met, namely that:

(i)   all the *clients* have given informed consent, given or evidenced in writing, to you acting;

(ii)   where appropriate, you put in place effective safeguards to protect your *clients'* confidential information; and

(iii)   you are satisfied it is reasonable for you to act for all the *clients*.

Own interest conflict

4.79

An 'own interest conflict' is defined in the SRA Glossary to mean 'any situation where your duty to act in the best interests of any client in relation to a matter conflicts, or there is a significant risk that it may conflict, with your own interests in relation to that or a related matter'.

The prohibition on acting in an 'own interest conflict' is absolute. While it could be said that this has always been so, there has also always been an understanding that not every dealing between solicitor and client which has the potential for conflict, in fact involves a conflict or a significant risk of one. Examples are an unsecured interest-free loan from solicitor to client, as an act of humanity; or bridging finance on standard terms; or a modest gift to a solicitor by a client in a will, as distinct from a gift which is 'significant'.

Guidance to the equivalent rule in the 2007 Code made it clear that solicitors could take security for their costs by a charge over the client's property, and that independent legal advice 'would not normally be essential unless the terms of the proposed charge are particularly onerous or would give you some unusual benefit or profit'. So was that not a conflict, or was it a conflict that was exceptionally permitted? It would be difficult to argue that it was not, strictly speaking, a conflict of interests (what were the terms of the legal charge to be?).

Similarly, rule 3.04 of the 2007 Code made it clear that a solicitor could accept a lifetime gift or a gift on death from a client who was not a family member without requiring the client to take independent advice unless the gift was 'significant' either in itself or having regard to the size of the client's estate and the reasonable expectations of prospective beneficiaries.

Are these historic indications still valid? In our view they are. The SRA's position may be gauged from its policy statements. In relation to the 2011 Code the SRA said:[1]

'The position under OFR is that we now expect firms to exercise their own judgement as to whether it would be proper to act in a particular situation, rather than the Handbook specifying the circumstances where it is appropriate to do so.'

In relation to the 2019 Codes the SRA said:

'Our new approach is to describe the standards to be achieved and give flexibility as to how these apply in any given situation. In doing so, we recognise that what is appropriate ... will depend on the circumstances and will, as a rule, best be judged by the solicitor or firm involved'.[2]

That suggests not a change in 'the rules', as such, but a change in the form of regulation, placing the onus on practitioners, in effect, to think and make judgements. That is indeed the outcomes-focused regulation approach, and in our view in the situations described above by way of historic example there would be no failure to comply with the 2019 Codes, because there would be perceived to be no genuine 'own interest conflict'.

Where, however, there is a genuine 'own interest conflict', the prohibition against a solicitor acting where his or her personal interests actually conflict with those of a client is absolute. Many solicitors continue to believe that merely informing a client that independent advice should be taken is sufficient to discharge their duties to the client. This is not so and normally, if the client does not in fact take independent advice, the solicitor must not proceed with the transaction (whether it be the purchase of an asset from the client, the drafting of a will containing a significant bequest in favour of the solicitor, etc).

Solicitors providing services to the public as an employee of an unregulated organisation need to take account of conflicts between the interests of their clients and their employer. In a guidance note dated 23 July 2019, the SRA has said that it will normally assume that where a client's interests conflict with an employer's interests, then they will also conflict with the solicitor's interests, and the solicitor should not therefore act. That is because there will be a clash between the potential pressure on the solicitor in terms of his or her employment contract and the duty to act in the client's best interests.[3]

1   SRA, 'Policy statement on our October 2010 Consultation', March 2011, para 75.
2   'Application for approval of regulatory arrangements', issued by the SRA in August 2018, para 82.
3   SRA Ethics guidance, 'Unregulated organisations – conflict and confidentiality,' 23 July 2019.

Client conflict

4.80

A 'conflict of interest' is defined in the SRA Glossary to mean 'a situation where your separate duties to act in the best interests of two or more clients conflict'.

As to 'client conflicts', *The Guide to the Professional Conduct of Solicitors 1999* (8th edn) contained a valuable commentary which remains valid and the substance of which is reproduced here: where a solicitor is acting for two or more clients, whether they are husband and wife, business partners or companies embarking on a joint venture, the solicitor always owes a duty to each individual person or body and he or she must advise each individual in accordance with that individual's interests. A practical initial test to apply to assist in identifying whether a conflict exists is to ask: what would occur if the solicitor was only acting for one of the parties? In particular, would any advice be different?

A conflict between clients must involve current retainers from two or more relevant clients.

Paragraph 6.2 does not prohibit a solicitor from acting for a client against a former client. In this situation, paragraph 6.3 will be in play in relation to any confidential information that may be held about the former client. Paragraph 6.2 does not permit a client to consent to a solicitor acting in a conflict of interests situation unless one of the specified exceptions applies. It is not possible to erect an information barrier (or Chinese wall) to 'cure' a client conflict unless one of the exceptions applies.

4.81

The exceptions in paragraph 6.2 enabling solicitors to act despite a client conflict reflect the provisions of the 2011 Code, expressed rather more economically. The phrase 'substantially common interest' is defined in the SRA Glossary:

> 'a situation where there is a clear common purpose between the clients and a strong consensus on how it is to be achieved.'

The phrase 'competing for the same objective' is also defined in the SRA Glossary:

> 'any situation in which two or more clients are competing for an "objective" which, if attained by one client, will make that "objective" unattainable to the other client or clients and "objective" means an asset, contract or business opportunity which two or more clients are seeking to acquire or recover through a liquidation (or some other form of insolvency process) or by means of an auction or tender process or a bid or offer but not a public takeover.'

In a guidance note dated 23 July 2019 the SRA has stated that, if clients are competing for the same objective, the clients are likely to need to keep at least some information confidential from each other. That in turn means that the exception can normally only be relied on if separate lawyers (or teams) act for each bidder and there are effective safeguards in place to protect confidential information.[1] The test for an effective information barrier is high and requires an established structural separation within the firm (see **4.93** to **4.95**).

When deciding whether it is reasonable to rely on one of the exceptions in paragraph 6.2, factors to take into account include any particular benefits to the clients (such as niche specialist knowledge, speed, convenience and lower cost) and (in the case of the common interest exception), the respective knowledge and bargaining power of the clients, the extent to which there will need to be negotiations between the clients and whether a client who is vulnerable needs independent advice.[2]

1   SRA Ethics guidance, 'Unregulated organisations – conflict and confidentiality', 23 July 2019.
2   See the examples in SRA Ethics guidance, 'Unregulated organisations – conflict and confidentiality', 23 July 2019.

The importance of making a judgement

4.82

As noted above, the 2019 Codes challenge solicitors to make judgements, rather than setting out in prescriptive rules how they must behave. The exercise of judgement is nowhere more important than in a solicitor's assessment of whether it is proper to act in a situation where there may be a conflict of interests. If the matter is properly and conscientiously addressed by the solicitor, an error of judgement will not amount to professional misconduct.[1] However, this does not mean that a solicitor's professional obligations are discharged merely by giving careful thought to the matter. If a solicitor does not honestly and genuinely address the matter, he may be guilty of a disciplinary offence. And if his decision is one that no reasonably competent solicitor could have made, it may be inferred that he had not (or could not have) properly addressed the issue. This inference may well be appropriate where the reason given for the solicitor's professional decision is manifestly unsustainable.

1   See *Connolly v Law Society* [2007] EWHC 1175 (Admin) at [62].

Conveyancing

4.83

The 2019 Codes do not contain any conflict rules which specifically relate to conveyancing. The SRA has stated that it intends to publish guidance on the 2019 Codes, but as at the date of this edition, no guidance has been published on conflicts in conveyancing. There were a number of indicative behaviours in the 2011 Code which related to conveyancing, and provided guidance, but no indicative behaviours have been included in the 2019 Codes. The SRA has given the following reason for excluding indicative behaviours:

> 'The new codes no longer include Indicative Behaviours. Early feedback from stakeholders suggested that many individuals and firms find their status confusing, with many interpreting them as rigid requirements rather than indicators of ways in which they could achieve or evidence compliance with the Outcomes'.[1]

As they were excluded because they were misinterpreted as rigid requirements rather than indicators, and as the substantive rules on conflicts have not changed from those in the 2011 Code, the 2011 indicative behaviours on conveyancing conflicts do provide some guidance on the SRA's expectations. They are set out below:

> 'Acting in the following way(s) may tend to show that you have achieved these outcomes and therefore complied with the *Principles*:
>
> **IB(3.3)** declining to act for *clients* where you may need to negotiate on matters of substance on their behalf, for example negotiating on price between a buyer and seller of a property;
>
> **IB(3.4)** declining to act where there is unequal bargaining power between the *clients*, for example acting for a seller and buyer where a builder is selling to a non-commercial *client*;

IB(3.5) declining to act for *clients* under Outcome 3.6 (*substantially common interest*) or Outcome 3.7 (*competing for the same objective*) where the *clients* cannot be represented even-handedly, or will be prejudiced by lack of separate representation;

IB(3.6) acting for *clients* under Outcome 3.7 (*competing for the same objective*) only where the *clients* are sophisticated users of legal services;

IB(3.7) acting for *clients* who are the lender and borrower on the grant of a mortgage of land only where:

   (a)   the mortgage is a standard mortgage (i.e. one provided in the normal course of the lender's activities, where a significant part of the lender's activities consists of lending and the mortgage is on standard terms) of property to be used as the borrower's private residence;

   (b)   you are satisfied that it is reasonable and in the *clients'* best interests for you to act; and

   (c)   the certificate of title required by the lender is in the form approved by the *Society* and the Council of Mortgage Lenders.

Acting in the following way(s) may tend to show that you have not achieved these outcomes and therefore not complied with the *Principles*:

IB(3.8) in a personal capacity, selling to or buying from, lending to or borrowing from a *client*, unless the *client* has obtained independent legal advice;

IB(3.9) advising a *client* to invest in a business, in which you have an interest which affects your ability to provide impartial advice;

IB(3.10) where you hold a power of attorney for a *client,* using that power to gain a benefit for youyrself which in your professional capacity you would not hae been prepared to allow to a third party;

IB(3.11) acting for two or more *clients* in a *conflict of interests* under Outcome 3.6 (*substantially common interest*) where the *clients'* interests in the end result are not the same, for example one partner buying out the interest of the other partner in their joint business or a seller transferring a property to a buyer;

IB(3.12) acting for two or more *clients* in a *conflict of interests* under Outcome 3.6 (*substantially common interest*) where it is unreasonable to act because there is unequal bargaining power;

IB(3.13) acting for two buyers where there is a *conflict of interests* under Outcome 3.7 (*competing for the same objective*), for example where two buyers are competing for a residential property;

IB(3.14) acting for a buyer (including a lessee) and seller (including a lessor) in a transaction relating to the transfer of land for value, the grant or assignment of a lease or some other interest in land for value.'

1   'Application for the approval of regulatory arrangements', issued by the SRA in August 2018, para 91.

4.84

Before 2011, much of the 2007 Code was concerned with domestic conveyancing, and the circumstances in which a firm could act for both buyer and seller, as well as for lender and borrower. Rule 3.07 of the 2011 Code and its many predecessors, imposed limitations on the ability of a firm to act for both parties, even if no conflict of interests existed. In other words, it was accepted that there was no inherent conflict of interests in acting for buyer and seller, but by regulation going beyond the requirements of the common law, solicitors were prevented from acting for both parties in most circumstances, even when there was no conflict. Solicitors were permitted to act for both parties, by exception to the general rule, in limited circumstances (for example, where both were established clients and gave written consent), but the exceptions did not apply if there was a conflict of interests.

A rule having this effect was first made in 1972 but the earliest commentary on the subject, in the 1960 *Guide to the Professional Conduct and Etiquette of Solicitors*, stated firmly:[1]

> 'there are a good many conveyancing transactions in which the possibility of a conflict of interest between vendor and purchaser is remote and is rarely experienced in practice. There is thus nothing inherently improper in a solicitor acting for both vendor and purchaser ... The complete cessation of the practice of acting for both parties would cause hardship and inconvenience to the public, particularly where both parties are already established clients of the same solicitor.'

The 2011 Code signposted a new approach to conveyancing and to acting for buyer and seller, which was readily seen from indicative behaviour 3.14, which provided that acting for seller and buyer 'may tend to show that you have not achieved' the outcomes. This reflected the view of the SRA that the traditional approach was no longer correct. In its policy statement on its October 2010 consultation the SRA stated its view in diametrically opposite terms:[2]

> 'the circumstances in which either there is no conflict of interests nor a significant risk of a conflict of interests as between buyer and seller must be extremely limited ... There may, of course, be some conveyancing situations where there are no conflicts of interests, although, for example, as between a seller and a buyer we expect that these will be rare. Our intention was not to prohibit acting in such cases, but rather to put the onus on firms to make the assessment as to whether a conflict exists.'

It may be noted that the Council for Licensed Conveyancers does not take the same view, and those it regulates may act for both parties in circumstances broadly comparable with rule 3 of the 2007 Code, though the CLC rules are somewhat less restrictive. The SRA has not explained why and on what evidential basis it came to the conclusion that something that had always in the past been thought not to involve an inherent or overwhelmingly likely conflict, now did.

The SRA's change of stance in the 2011 Code had a profound effect on conveyancing practice, the extent of which depended on the attitude of firms to regulatory risk. Many decided that indicative behaviour 3.14 was in effect a rule against acting for buyer and seller bearing in mind that it was unqualified in terms. Such firms will have also noted the assertions by the SRA quoted above that:

'the circumstances in which either there is no conflict of interests nor a significant risk of a conflict of interests as between buyer and seller must be extremely limited ... There may, of course, be some conveyancing situations where there are no conflicts of interests, although, for example, as between a seller and a buyer we expect that these will be rare'

and may have decided that the SRA's use of 'extremely limited' and 'rare' was a pretty broad hint that the regulator would need a great deal of persuading that it was proper for a firm to act, ever, for buyer and seller and that its 'default' position was that it cannot be done.

The rest of the quotation however may also be noted:

'Our intention was not to prohibit acting in such cases, but rather to put the onus on firms to make the assessment as to whether a conflict exists.'

That intention – that the firm should exercise its own judgement depending on the circumstances – is replicated in the SRA's approach to the 2019 Codes. As quoted above, the SRA has stated:

'Our new approach is to describe the standards to be achieved and give flexibility as to how these apply in any given situation. In doing so, we recognise that what is appropriate ... will depend on the circumstances and will, as a rule, best be judged by the solicitor or firm involved'.[3]

1   At p 114.
2   At paras 74 and 75.
3   'Application for the approval of regulatory arrangements', issued by the SRA in August 2018, para 82.

Practical suggestions

4.85

There is nothing in the 2019 Codes which says that the changes introduced by the 2011 Code on acting for buyer and seller in conveyancing transactions have been altered. Property lawyers, and firms, can take the safest line and simply cease to act rather than carry out a risk assessment for each case; or can decide that cases will be assessed individually. If the latter course is taken and the solicitor decides to act on both sides of the transaction, he or she will be well advised to make a contemporaneous documentary record of why that decision was taken.

One of the pre-2011 factors relevant to a firm's decision to act for both parties continues to be relevant to an assessment of risk and the identification of a conflict: that the transaction is not at arm's length. Others are plainly not relevant at all. The fact that both parties are established clients or that they are represented by two separate offices of the firm cannot be relevant to the presence or the absence of a conflict of interests or a risk thereof.

Another problem is that because the SRA's 'default position' is that only rarely will there not be a conflict of interests, a property lawyer who genuinely believes that in a particular case there is no conflict, but that there is nothing out of the ordinary about the transaction, may struggle to convince the SRA that it is in the narrow category where it is proper to act. The SRA has developed a written 'supervision and enforcement strategy' for conveyancing which stresses the risks of conflicts of interests in conveyancing. The primary risks are: removal from lender panels; economic downturn; competition caused by financial instability; property-related fraud and money laundering; conflicts of interests; costs information (including publicity about fees); and referral arrangements.

Regard must also be had to the Code for Firms: firms of all sizes must be able to demonstrate appropriate systems and controls, including staff training, to identify and assess potential conflicts.

4.86

Confidentiality and disclosure

6.3   You keep the affairs of current and former *clients* confidential unless disclosure is required or permitted by law or the *client* consents.

6.4   Where you are acting for a *client* on a matter, you make the *client* aware of all information material to the matter of which you have knowledge, except when:

(a)   the disclosure of the information is prohibited by legal restrictions imposed in the interests of national security or the prevention of crime;

(b)   your *client* gives informed consent, given or evidenced in writing, to the information not being disclosed to them;

(c)   you have reason to believe that serious physical or mental injury will be caused to your *client* or another if the information is disclosed; or

(d)   the information is contained in a privileged document that you have knowledge of only because it has been mistakenly disclosed.

6.5   You do not act for a *client* in a matter where that *client* has an interest adverse to the interest of another current or former *client* of you or your business or employer, for whom you or your business or employer holds confidential information which is material to that matter, unless:

(a)   effective measures have been taken which result in there being no real risk of disclosure of the confidential information; or

(b)   the current or former *client* whose information your business or employer holds has given informed consent, given or evidenced in writing, to you acting, including to any measures taken to protect their information.

4.87

Paragraphs 6.3 to 6.5 are the successors to the outcomes in Chapter 4 of the 2011 Code on the duties of disclosure and confidentiality; these have had some changes, although the underlying philosophy is unaltered.[1]

The fiduciary relationship between a solicitor and client gives rise to a number of duties including a duty not to disclose confidential information to others unless there is a clear obligation or principle overriding that duty, such as fraud on the part of the client or disciplinary proceedings.[2] The duty of confidentiality continues beyond the end of the retainer, and is owed to former clients as well as current clients.

The duty to disclose information material to a retainer is also fiduciary in nature. In *Hilton v Barker Booth & Eastwood* Lord Scott observed that the duty was 'both contractual and fiduciary, the content of the contractual duty of full disclosure being rooted in the fiduciary relationship between solicitor and client'.[3]

The SRA Glossary defines client to mean 'the person for whom you act and, where the context permits, includes prospective and former clients'.

In practice, if a confidentiality issue arises in relation to two or more *current* clients, the principles on conflicts of interest in paragraph 6.2 are also likely to be applicable.

1 The regulatory duty of confidentiality can be traced back to the introduction of rule 16E of the Solicitors' Practice Rules 1990 on 25 April 2006. Before that there was no specific practice rule dealing with the duty of confidentiality – although the duty had long been recognised by the courts and in the guidance provided by the Law Society.
2 See *Finers v Miro* [1991] 1 WLR 35 and *Parry-Jones v Law Society* [1968] Ch 195.
3 *Hilton v Barker Booth and Eastwood* [2005] UKHL 8.

4.88

Outcome 4.3 of the 2011 Code provided that, where a duty of confidentiality to one client comes into conflict with a duty of disclosure to another client, the duty of confidentiality takes precedence. That outcome has not found its way into the 2019 Code. A solicitor facing the conflicting duties may have to cease acting on the grounds of a conflict of interest (see paragraphs 6.1 and 6.2) and may be liable to compensate a client who is not supplied with information.[1]

A decision not to supply a client with information, on the ground that the information is confidential to another current or former client, could also lead to a professional complaint. In a guidance note dated 23 July 2019, the SRA has stated:

'[You could] find yourself in a position where your duty of confidentiality to another current or former client (A) prevents you from disclosing evidence that you obtained in relation to A's case to your new client (B). The fact that you cannot meet your obligations to B because of your obligation to A will be no defence in those circumstances either to a claim against you by B or in relation to a breach of your obligations under paragraph 6.4.'[2]

It is therefore important to consider whether the duty of disclosure owed to a new client could lead to a conflict between the competing duties of disclosure and confidentiality before agreeing to take on the new work.[3] Once the work is taken on, it may be too late to prevent a civil claim or a professional complaint.

1 See *Hilton v Barker Booth & Eastwood* [2005] UKHL 8.
2 SRA Ethics guidance, 'Unregulated organisations – conflict and confidentiality', 23 July 2019. Although the guidance note relates to solicitors working in unregulated organisations, the risk of conflict between the competing duties of disclosure and confidentiality applies to all solicitors.
3 The competing duties could be resolved by information barriers and informed consent – see **4.90**.

Inadvertent disclosure of privileged material

4.89

Privileged documents inadvertently disclosed in civil proceedings will in some circumstances have to be returned to the opponent, and not disclosed to the client. The test for deciding whether the documents have to be returned is set out in *Al-Fayed v Commissioner of Police for the Metropolis*:

> 'The court may grant an injunction if the documents have been made available for inspection as a result of an obvious mistake. A mistake is likely to be held to be obvious ... where the documents are received by a solicitor and (a) the solicitor appreciates that a mistake has been made before making some use of the documents or (b) it would be obvious to a reasonable solicitor in his position that a mistake has been made; and in either case there are no other circumstances which would make it unjust or inequitable to grant relief.'[1]

Where a mistake is obvious, lawyers on both sides should co-operate to resolve the matter as soon as possible. Both parties are subject to a duty of honesty and it should not be necessary to involve the court.[2]

1 *Al-Fayed v Commissioner of Police of the Metropolis* [2002] EWCA Civ 780.
2 *Atlantisrealm Ltd v Intelligent Land Investments (Renewable Energy) Ltd* [2017] EWCA Civ 1029.

Informed consent and information barriers

4.90

There are exceptional circumstances in which it is possible to act for one client, to whom a duty would be owed to disclose material information, when there is a contemporaneous duty of confidentiality to a second client (or former client) which would prevent such disclosure. It is possible to continue to act, provided that (a) effective measures have been taken which result in there being no real risk of disclosure of confidential information or (b) the client or former client has given informed consent, given or evidenced in writing, to the solicitor acting, and to any measures taken to protect the information. It is important to recognise that this is an exception to the normal absolute rule that continuing to act in these circumstances would be bound to put a solicitor, the managers or the firm in breach of duties owed to one or other of the clients, and therefore impossible.[1]

If the matter relates to two clients, and there is a conflict of interest, the solicitor must also comply with paragraph 6.2.

1 See e.g. *Hilton v Barker Booth & Eastwood (a firm)* [2005] UKHL 8, [2005] 1 WLR. 567.

4.91

As for informed consent from the client or former client entitled to confidentiality, solicitors will need to justify their approach should questions be raised by the SRA or the courts. A detailed written record of all aspects of the matter relating to obtaining the informed consent will therefore be all but essential. Particular caution should be exercised where the clients or former clients are not sophisticated users of legal services.

In its guidance note dated 23 July 2019, the SRA has stated that, for there to be informed consent, a client or former client must have an understanding of any possible prejudice which could occur. That means that the person seeking the consent must be different to the person proposing to carry out the work for the new client, as knowledge of the confidential information is needed to ensure the client or former client understands the possible prejudice.[1]

1   SRA Ethics guidance, 'Uunregulated organisations – conflict and confidentiality', 23 July 2019.

4.92

Paragraph 6.5 does not contain an express requirement to obtain infomed consent to an information barrier from the client to whom the duty of disclosure is owed. Practitioners should consider whether there is an underlying fiduciary obligation giving rise to a firm's need for consent, even if that is not required under the 2019 Codes.[1] See **4.95**.

1   Outcome 4.4(a) of the 2011 Code included a requirement to obtain informed consent from the client to whom the duty of disclosure is owed, but that has been removed from the 2019 Codes. Under paragraph 6.4 of the Code for Individuals and paragraph 6.4 of the Code for Firms, there is an obligation on the individual acting for that client to make the client aware of all information material to the matter of which the individual has knowledge. That would include the existence of the information barrier.

4.93

To set up information barriers (which are also known as Chinese walls or ethical walls) an understanding of the law is required. The leading case, which relates to an information barrier between a client and a former client, is *Bolkiah v KPMG*,[1] particularly the speech of Lord Millett. The principles are helpfully extracted and summarised in *Koch Shipping Inc v Richards Butler*,[2] in the following terms (at [24]):[3]

'(1)   The Court's jurisdiction to intervene is founded on the right of the former client to the protection of his confidential information (per Lord Millett at p.234).

(2)   The only duty to the former client which survives the termination of the client relationship is a continuing duty to preserve the confidentiality of information imparted during its subsistence (per Lord Millett at p.235).

(3)   The duty to preserve confidentiality is unqualified. It is a duty to keep the information confidential, not merely to take all reasonable steps to do so (per Lord Millett at p.235).

(4)   The former client cannot be protected completely from accidental or inadvertent disclosure, but he is entitled to prevent his former solicitor from exposing him to any avoidable risk. This includes the increased risk of the use of the information to his prejudice arising from the acceptance of instructions to act for another client with an adverse interest in a matter to which the information may be relevant (per Lord Millett at pp.235–236).

(5)   The former client must establish that the defendant solicitors possess confidential information which is or might be relevant to the matter and to the disclosure of which he has not consented (per Lord Millett at pp.234–235).

(6)   The burden then passes to the defendant solicitors to show that there is *no risk* of disclosure. The court should intervene unless it is satisfied that there is no risk of disclosure. The risk must be a real one, and not merely fanciful or theoretical, but it need not be substantial (per Lord Millett at p.237).

(7)   It is wrong in principle to conduct a balancing exercise. If the former client establishes the facts in (5) above, the former client is entitled to an injunction unless the defendant solicitors show that there is no risk of disclosure.

(8)   In considering whether the solicitors have shown that there is no risk of disclosure, the starting point must be that, unless special measures are taken, information moves within a firm (per Lord Millett at p.237). However, that is only the starting point. The Prince Jefri case does not establish a rule of law that special measures have to be taken to prevent the information passing within a firm: see also *Young v Robson Rhodes* [1999] 3 All ER 524, per Laddie J at p.538. On the other hand, the courts should restrain the solicitors from acting unless satisfied on the basis of clear and convincing evidence that all effective measures have been taken to ensure that no disclosure will occur (per Lord Millett at pp.237–238, where he adapted the test identified by Sopinka J in *MacDonald Estate v Martin* (1991) 77 DLR (4th) 249 at p.269). This is a heavy burden (per Lord Millett at p.239).'

And at [25]:

'It is to my mind important to emphasise that each case turns on its own facts.'

In *Gus Consulting GmbH v LeBoeuf Lamb Greene & Macrae* (a case involving a current client and a former client) the 'ethical wall' involved three main steps: software preventing access to any electronic documents relating to restricted matters; allocation of a matter number used in archive management software to prevent given lawyers from being able to retrieve any files; and the files were physically stamped as being restricted. In addition, instructions were disseminated internally to draw attention to the importance of the confidential material not coming to the attention of anybody, particularly those in the team working on the arbitration. The sensitive material related to transactions which had taken place and been concluded some years previously. It was only upon the basis of these arrangements and the undertakings that the court was persuaded not to restrain the firm from acting by injunction.[4]

In *Georgian American Alloys Inc v White & Case* (a case involving two current clients) the firm used industry standard software to build an electronic 'ethical screen' between the teams of individuals on the opposite sides. The software automatically added a fee earner and his or her secretary to one side of the ethical screen as soon as any relevant documents relating to that side of the ethical screen were accessed, and the individuals on one side of the ethical screen could not access documents which related to the client on the other side of the ethical screen. The High Court granted an injunction restraining White & Case from continuing to act in circumstances where the ethical screen was not put in place until ten months after the work started, the firm had not produced evidence to show that all the fee earners, including those who had left, had not accessed confidential information from the other side of the ethical screen and the ethical screen did not prevent disclosure by telephone or on a face-to-face basis in circumstances where some members of the opposing side shared the same office or could meet for events organised by the firm.[5]

1   [1999] 2 AC 222, HL. See also *Marks & Spencer plc v Freshfields* [2004] EWCA Civ 741.
2   [2002] EWCA Civ 1280, [2003] PNLR 11.
3   A useful example of the practical measures necessary to be taken can be seen from the undertakings given by the solicitors in *Gus Consulting GmbH v LeBoeuf Lamb Greene & Macrae* [2006] EWCA Civ 683, [2006] PNLR 32 at [20].
4   *Gus Consulting GmbH v LeBoeuf, Lamb, Gren & Macrae* [2006] EWCA Civ 369.
5   *Georgian American Alloys Inc v White & Case LLP* [2014] EWHC 94 (Comm).

4.94

It follows that every case will remain fact sensitive, and unless the arrangements are effective, it would not be lawful for a firm to continue acting, unless it were to be possible – on the basis of informed consent by the affected client – to impose safeguards which were less than is required by the common law.

In its guidance note dated 23 July 2019, the SRA states:

> "Examples of effective measures ... could ... include a combination of:
>
> ● Systems that identify the potential confidentiality issue
>
> ● Separate departments handling the cases
>
> ● Separate servers so that information cannot be cross accessed
>
> ● Information being encrypted, and password protected
>
> ● Relevant individuals in the firm being aware of the "information barrier" and knowing not to cross it
>
> ● Appropriate organisational policies and training for staff ...'[1]

The 2011 Code contained the following note which continues to be relevant:

> '(i)   The protection of confidential information may be at particular risk where:
>
> (a)   two or more firms merge;
>
> (b)   when you leave one firm and join another, such as if you join a firm acting against one of your former clients.
>
> (ii)   The following circumstances may make it difficult to implement effective safeguards and information barriers:
>
> (a)   you are a small firm;
>
> (b)   the physical structure or layout of the firm means that it will be difficult to preserve confidentiality; or
>
> (c)   the clients are not sophisticated users of legal services'.[2]

It is unsurprising that the note emphasises the difficulty of implementing effective safeguards and information barriers if the firm is small; if the physical structure or layout of the firm means that it will be difficult to preserve confidentiality; or if the clients are not sophisticated users of legal services. While this is not a 'City firm only' rule or '20+ partner only' rule, in reality it is unlikely in the extreme that any small firm would be able to achieve an effective barrier.

1   SRA Ethics guidance, 'Uunregulated organisations – conflict and confidentiality', 23 July 2019. Although the guidance note relates to solicitors working in unregulated organisations, the standards for effective safeguards are required as a matter of law and the same high standards apply to all organisations whether they are regulated or unregulated.
2   SRA Code of Conduct 2011, note to Chapter 4.

A practical checklist

4.95

The 2019 Codes do not address the obligations owed to the new client for whom the firm will act if the information barrier is put in place. If a solicitor wishes to use the exception provided by paragraph 6.5(a) the following checklist may assist (where A is a new client who would be interested in receiving information, and B is a client or former client whose right to confidentiality is in play):

• Would it be reasonable, in principle, for the firm to act for A if effective safeguards to protect B could be put in place? Would this be in A's interests? One could envisage a situation in which those acting for A within the firm might have been compromised by learning of the confidential information so that, as a minimum, a new team would have to take over immediately, and it might on balance be better if A instructs a different firm. There may also be situations in which there is a risk that B will apply for an injunction against the firm and obtain an order restraining the firm from continuing to act. If so, is it in A's interest for that risk to be taken? If the answers to those questions are yes:

• A must give informed consent; that is, A must be informed that the firm has information of potential value that it cannot disclose. The firm would almost certainly not be in a position to identify B as the source of that information or to say anything more about it, although, for example, as a result of a protest by B, A may otherwise learn something of this. A must be content, without knowing more, for the firm to continue acting on the basis that the information will never be disclosed. This would require a sophisticated thought process and an enlightened individual or body, well able to understand among other things that there will be 'no cheating'. A should also be warned of the risk of an application for an injunction, and the consequences of an injunction, if there is such a risk. If A does give informed consent, either:

• B is consulted, agrees that the firm may continue to act and agrees the safeguards to be put in place to protect the confidential information, which could be to a standard sufficient to meet the common law requirements, or something less; or

• In the absence of B's informed consent, effective barriers are put in place to meet the firm's obligations under the 2019 Codes and at law.

Cooperation and accountability

4.96

> 7.1   You keep up to date with and follow the law and regulation governing the way you work.

7.2 You are able to justify your decisions and actions in order to demonstrate compliance with your obligations under the *SRA's regulatory arrangements*.

7.3 You cooperate with the *SRA*, other regulators, ombudsmen, and those bodies with a role overseeing and supervising the delivery of, or investigating concerns in relation to, legal services.

7.4 You respond promptly to the *SRA* and:

(a) provide full and accurate explanations, information and documents in response to any request or requirement; and

(b) ensure that relevant information which is held by you, or by third parties carrying out functions on your behalf which are critical to the delivery of your legal services, is available for inspection by the *SRA*.

7.5 You do not attempt to prevent anyone from providing information to the *SRA* or any other body exercising regulatory, supervisory, investigatory or prosecutory functions in the public interest.

7.6 You notify the *SRA* promptly if:

(a) you are subject to any criminal charge, conviction or caution, subject to the Rehabilitation of Offenders Act 1974;

(b) a *relevant insolvency event* occurs in relation to you; or

(c) if you become aware:

(i) of any material changes to information previously provided to the *SRA*, by you or on your behalf, about you or your practice, including any change to information recorded in the *register*; and

(ii) that information provided to the *SRA*, by you or on your behalf, about you or your practice is or may be false, misleading, incomplete or inaccurate.

7.7 You report promptly to the SRA or another *approved regulator*, as appropriate, any facts or matters that you reasonably believe are capable of amounting to a serious breach of their regulatory arrangements by any *person* regulated by them (including you).

7.8 Notwithstanding paragraph 7.7, you inform the *SRA* promptly of any facts or matters that you reasonably believe should be brought to its attention in order that it may investigate whether a serious breach of its *regulatory arrangements* has occurred or otherwise exercise its regulatory powers.

7.9 You do not subject any *person* to detrimental treatment for making or proposing to make a report or providing or proposing to provide information based on a reasonably held belief under paragraph 7.7 or 7.8 above, or paragraph 3.9, 3.10, 9.1(d) or (e) or 9.2(b) or (c) of the SRA Code of Conduct for Firms, irrespective of whether the *SRA* or another *approved regulator* subsequently investigates or takes any action in relation to the facts or matters in question.

7.10 You act promptly to take any remedial action requested by the *SRA*. If requested to do so by the *SRA* you investigate whether there are any serious breaches that should be reported to the *SRA*.

> 7.11   You are honest and open with *clients* if things go wrong, and if a *client* suffers loss or harm as a result you put matters right (if possible) and explain fully and promptly what has happened and the likely impact. If requested to do so by the *SRA* you investigate whether anyone may have a claim against you, provide the *SRA* with a report on the outcome of your investigation, and notify relevant persons that they may have such a claim, accordingly.
>
> 7.12   Any obligation under this section or otherwise to notify, or provide information to, the *SRA* will be satisfied if you provide information to your firm's *COLP* or *COFA*, as and where appropriate, on the understanding that they will do so.

4.97

Section 7[1] appears to represent a retention of the type of prescriptive rule-making which has been abandoned elsewhere in the Codes since 2011. The clear message for solicitors is that all of those regulated by the SRA must co-operate in all respects with their regulator.

For the most part, the contents of section 7 speak for themselves.

1   Section 7 was amended by the SRA Regulatory Arrangements (Reporting Concerns) (Amendment) Rules 2019 which were approved by the LSB on 9 May 2019.

4.98

The SRA has stated that paragraph 7.1 was introduced so that there is a provision 'requiring solicitors or authorised firms (or their managers and employees) to stay up to date with legal developments and the regulatory framework linked to their area of work which reflects the principles of continuing competence'.[1]

1   'Looking to the future – flexibility and public protection', issued by the SRA in June 2016, Annex 4, p 11.

Information held by third parties

4.99

By paragraph 7.4(b) a solicitor must ensure that information held by third parties carrying out functions on behalf of the solicitor which are critical to the delivery of legal services is available for inspection by the SRA. Paragraph 7.4(b) may have its origins in provisions about outsourcing in the 2011 Code: outcome 7.10(b) provided that 'where you outsource legal activities or any operational functions that are critical to the delivery of any legal activities, you ensure such outsourcing ... (b) is subject to contractual arrangements that enable the SRA or its agent to obtain information from, inspect the records (including electronic records) of, or enter the premises of, the third party, in relation to the outsourced activities or functions'.

In order to be able to comply with paragraph 7.4, it is advisable to include a term in contracts with third parties which requires the third party to produce records and other information on demand, coupled with a provision that the term continues after termination of the services supplied under the contract.

The 2011 Code also required solicitors to produce documents under their control and to provide any necessary permission for information to be verified by clients, staff, banks, building societies and other financial institutions.[1] This provision too has been swept up into paragraph 7.4(b).

1   Outcomes 10.9 and 10.10 of the SRA Code of Conduct 2011.

Non-disclosure agreements

4.100

By paragraph 7.5 a solicitor must not attempt to prevent anyone from providing information to anybody exercising a regulatory, supervisory, investigatory or prosecutorial function in the public interest. The comparable provision in the 2011 Code was limited to information supplied to the SRA and the Legal Ombudsman.[1] The mischief targeted by the 2011 Code was the solicitor who attempted to prevent a client or member of staff from reporting the solicitor's misconduct to the SRA under the terms of a settlement agreement. Paragraph 7.5 is far wider than that.

In July 2018 the Women and Equalities Committee (WESC) published a report on the prevalence of sexual harassment in the workplace, which was critical of solicitors who improperly use settlement agreements to silence victims of sexual harassment.[2] The new paragraph 7.5 prevents managers in law firms who are dealing with internal complaints of sexual harassment from entering into non-disclosure agreements (NDAs) which prevent victims from reporting the matter to the police as well as the SRA. It also prevents employment lawyers dealing with sexual harassment cases for employers in any sector from imposing similar NDAs on victims. In sexual harassment cases, paragraph 7.5 should be considered in conjunction with an SRA warning notice on NDAs which recognises that NDAs can be used to protect commercial interests but makes it clear that the confidentiality clause in an NDA must have exceptions permitting the victim to report the matter to regulators and law enforcement agencies.[3]

1   Outcome 10.7 of the SRA Code of Conduct 2011.
2   'Sexual harassment in the workplace', issued by the Women and Equalities Committee on 25 July 2018.
3   'Use of non-disclosure agreements: Warning notice', issued by the SRA on 12 March 2018.

Criminal charges, convictions and cautions

4.101

Under paragraph 7.6(a) a solicitor has to notify the SRA of any criminal charge, conviction or caution (subject to the Rehabilitation of Offenders Act 1974). The requirement to notify the SRA of any charge, conviction or caution is expressly wider than the former provisions under the 2011 regulations. By rules 3.1 and 15.1 of the SRA Practising Regulations 2011 a solicitor was only required to notify the SRA if the solicitor was charged or convicted of an indictable offence, or convicted of an offence under specified statutes relating to the provision of legal services. Cautions and other charges and convictions were only reportable if they amounted to serious misconduct or material changes of relevant information held by the SRA under outcomes 10.3 and 10.4 of the 2011 Code.

As regards the new, wider reporting regime, the SRA's Enforcement Strategy states that the SRA will always investigate criminal convictions or cautions, whether or not they relate to the individual's practice. The regulator is unlikely to be concerned about behaviour which is low level in terms of seriousness, such as minor motoring offences, but will take seriously convictions for drink driving, assault and other offences against the person, and property offences.[1] The initial guidance notes published by the SRA relating to the 2019 Codes included a Topic Guide on drink driving convictions and a Topic Guide on criminal offences. The Topic Guide on drink driving states that one-off offences with good mitigation are likely to result in a warning, whereas serious cases with, for example, a history of drink driving will be referred to the Tribunal.[2] The Topic Guide on criminal convictions states that the SRA will not generally look behind a criminal conviction and points out that a person who accepts a caution admits that an offence has been committed.[3]

1   SRA Enforcement Strategy, issued in February 2019.
2   'SRA Topic Guide: Driving with excess alcohol convictions', 7 February 2019.
3   'SRA Topic Guide: Criminal offences outside of practice', 7 February 2019.

Financial difficulty

4.102

Paragraph 7.6(a) requires a solicitor to notify the SRA when a 'relevant insolvency event' occurs in relation to the solicitor. The definition of 'relevant insolvency event' in the SRA Glossary relates to insolvency events concerning the firm or regulated entity, and not the individual. That may have been unintentional, as personal insolvency is relevant to questions of whether an individual should act as a manager and hold client money.

There is a strong emphasis on informing the SRA when financial difficulties arise in a regulated entity (see **5.32**).

Self-reporting and reporting others

4.103

Paragraphs 7.7 and 7.8 impose reporting obligations relating to a 'serious' breach of the regulatory arrangements. The 2019 Codes and the SRA Glossary do not define a 'serious' breach. There was a similar lacuna in the 2011 Code, and that led to widespread uncertainty and confusion in the profession as to what should be reported.

The reporting obligations under paragraphs 7.7 and 7.8 are wide. Paragraph 7.7 requires a solicitor to report any facts or matters which the solicitor reasonably believes are capable of amounting to a serious breach by any regulated person (including the solicitor) of their regulatory arrangements to that person's approved regulator.[1] For example, a serious breach by a chartered legal executive would have to be reported to CILEx. A solicitor who is also a notary would have to self-report a serious breach to the Master of Faculties as well as the SRA.

Paragraph 7.8 requires a solicitor to report to the SRA any facts or matters which the solicitor reasonably believes should be brought to the SRA's attention so that it may investigate whether a serious breach of the SRA's regulatory arrangements has occurred. Paragraph 7.8 also requires a solicitor to report to the SRA any facts or matters which should be brought to its attention in order that it may otherwise exercise its regulatory powers. The SRA's regulatory powers include intervention, the imposition of conditions on a firm's authorisation, the withdrawal of approval of the compliance officer for legal practice (COLP) or compliance officer for finance and administration (COFA) and the imposition of conditions on practising certificates.

The requirement in paragraphs 7.7 and 7.8 to report facts or matters which could comprise a serious breach was introduced into the 2019 Codes by a late amendment to the regulatory arrangements approved by the LSB on 9 May 2019. When applying for approval for the amendments, the SRA said that some solicitors thought they only had to make a report if they had carried out an investigation which conclusively proved that there was a serious breach. The amendment is designed to ensure that reports are made at an earlier stage.[2]

The SRA has stated that the test for making a report combines a subjective element (what the person making a report believes) with an objective element (the belief was reasonable bearing in mind the circumstances, information and evidence available to the decision-maker). That serves to avoid a reporting of mere allegations and suspicions and provides a balance on the spectrum between that on the one hand and fully investigated findings on the other.[3]

Paragraph 7.9 prohibits the detrimental treatment of persons who make reports. The SRA has stated that paragraph 7.9 is designed to ensure that those who make reports are supported in making what can sometimes be difficult decisions, and that solicitors are clear that they should not subject anyone making or intending to make a report to detrimental treatment for doing so.[4]

Paragraph 7.12 states that an obligation to report to the SRA is satisfied if the information is provided to the firm's COLP or COFA on the understanding that they will then make a report to the SRA. That relates only to the SRA; the solicitor still has to personally make a direct report to any other approved regulator.

1   The SRA Glossary defines 'approved regulator' to mean 'any body listed as an approved regulator in paragraph 1 of Schedule 4 to the LSA or designated as an approved regulator under paragraph 17 of that Schedule'. In shorthand, that means the regulators approved by the LSB.
2   See the LSB final decision notice dated 9 May 2019.
3   See SRA application to the LSB dated 18 April 2019 for the approval of amendments to introduce new SRA Regulatory Arrangements (Reporting Concerns) (Amendment) Rules, and paragraph 7 of the LSB final decision notice dated 9 May 2019.
4   As above, see SRA application to the LSB dated 18 April 2019 and paragraph 7 of the LSB final decision notice dated 9 May 2019.

Schemes of redress

4.104

Paragraph 7.11 effectively permits the SRA to require solicitors to *investigate* whether any person may have a claim for redress; to *report* the outcome of the investigation; and to *notify* persons that they may have a right of redress. The standard also requires the solicitor to 'put matters right (if possible)' if 'things go wrong' and a client suffers loss or harm.

However, solicitors should have in mind section 157(1) of LSA 2007, which provides:

> 'The regulatory arrangements of an approved regulator must not include any provision relating to redress.'

Section 158 provides, so far as relevant:

> '(1) Section 157 does not prohibit the regulatory arrangements of an approved regulator from making provision requiring, or authorising the approved regulator to require, a relevant authorised person –
>
>> (a)   to investigate whether there are any persons who may have a claim against the relevant authorised person in relation to a matter specified by the approved regulator;
>>
>> (b)   to provide the approved regulator with a report on the outcome of the investigation;
>>
>> (c)   to identify persons ("affected persons") who may have such a claim;
>>
>> (d)   to notify affected persons that they may have such a claim;'

LSA 2007 does not authorise the SRA to require solicitors to write letters in a particular form drafted by the SRA, or to require solicitors to provide redress, as happened prior to LSA 2007 in, for example, the miners' compensation cases. The clear legislative intention is that regulators should *not* be involved in the provision of redress. The role of the regulator, as circumscribed by Parliament, is simply to require solicitors to carry out investigations, identify potential claimants, and then to notify potential claimants that they may have a claim. It is no longer part of the regulator's function effectively to organise a widespread compensation scheme for a solicitor's former clients. That is the function, if appropriate, of the Legal Ombudsman.

When you are providing services to the public or a section of the public

4.105

Client identification

8.1   You identify who you are acting for in relation to any matter.

Complaints handling

8.2   You ensure that, as appropriate in the circumstances, you either establish and maintain, or participate in, a procedure for handling complaints in relation to the legal services you provide.

8.3   You ensure that *clients* are informed in writing at the time of engagement about:

(a)   their right to complain to you about your services and your charges;

(b)   how a complaint can be made and to whom; and

(c)   any right they have to make a complaint to the *Legal Ombudsman* and when they can make any such complaint.

8.4   You ensure that when *clients* have made a complaint to you, if this has not been resolved to the *client's* satisfaction within 8 weeks following the making of a complaint they are informed, in writing:

(a)   of any right they have to complain to the *Legal Ombudsman*, the time frame for doing so and full details of how to contact the *Legal Ombudsman*; and

(b)   if a complaint has been brought and your complaints procedure has been exhausted:

    (i)   that you cannot settle the complaint;

    (ii)   of the name and website address of an alternative dispute resolution (ADR) approved body which would be competent to deal with the complaint; and

    (iii)   whether you agree to use the scheme operated by that body.

8.5   You ensure that complaints are dealt with promptly, fairly, and free of charge.

Client information and publicity

8.6   You give *clients* information in a way they can understand. You ensure they are in a position to make informed decisions about the services they need, how their matter will be handled and the options available to them.

8.7   You ensure that *clients* receive the best possible information about how their matter will be priced and, both at the time of engagement and when appropriate as their matter progresses, about the likely overall cost of the matter and any *costs* incurred.

8.8   You ensure that any *publicity* in relation to your practice is accurate and not misleading, including that relating to your charges and the circumstances in which *interest* is payable by or to *clients*.

8.9   You do not make unsolicited approaches to members of the public, with the exception of current or former *clients*, in order to advertise legal services provided by you, or your business or employer.

8.10   You ensure that *clients* understand whether and how the services you provide are regulated. This includes:

(a)   explaining which activities will be carried out by you, as an *authorised person*;

(b)   explaining which services provided by you, your business or employer, and any *separate business* are regulated by an *approved regulator*; and

(c)   ensuring that you do not represent any business or employer which is not authorised by the *SRA*, including any *separate business*, as being regulated by the *SRA*.

8.11   You ensure that *clients* understand the regulatory protections available to them.

Client identification

4.106

Paragraph 8.1 is a new standard which was not included in the 2011 Code. The requirement to properly identify clients has been added because of the increase in identity theft, fraud and cybercrime affecting legal businesses.[1] See also paragraph 3.1 and **4.21**.

1   'Looking to the future – flexibility and public protection', issued by the SRA in June 2016.

Complaints handling

4.107

Paragraphs 8.2 to 8.4 relate to the requirement for a complaints handling procedure, and for information to be supplied to clients about complaints procedures. The obligation to set up or participate in a complaints system applies to all solicitors including solicitors working in unauthorised bodies.[1]

Paragraph 8.3 imposes a requirement that all clients are informed at the time of engagement, in writing, of their right to complain to the solicitor about their services and charges and how to do so, and of any right to complain to the Legal Ombudsman (LeO) and when to do so. In the 2007 Code practitioners could elect not to provide some or all of the information under the general heading of 'client care' if it could be demonstrated that it was inappropriate in the circumstances to do so;[2] in other words, if there were repeat clients or sophisticated clients who evidently knew their rights and did not need to be informed or reminded at the time of each engagement, it was possible to avoid providing basic client care information relating to complaints. This is no longer the case. However, the compulsory elements are limited to the information set out in paragraph 8.3, and so to be compliant, the relevant section of a client care letter could be very limited.

Firms need to adapt their standard documentation to match their client base and the specific needs of clients. Many clients have no right to complain to LeO. In general terms, only individuals and small businesses may do so. Larger corporate clients have no such remedy.[3] In some cases it might be that solicitors would not know at the outset, or even at the conclusion of the retainer, whether a business client is able to complain to LeO, because this is a question determined by the number of staff, turnover, balance sheet value, net asset value or annual income. In those cases it will be necessary to inform the client of the possibility of the existence of a right to complain to LeO, with the relevant time limits and contact details, subject to the client being within the Legal Ombudsman Scheme Rules.

Paragraph 8.3 includes a requirement to inform clients about their statutory rights to challenge bills.

Paragraph 8.4(b) is a new requirement added to the 2019 Codes to take account of the EU Directive on consumer alternative dispute resolution.[4] The EU Directive is intended to improve consumer access to ADR in the EU. If a client makes a complaint to a firm which cannot be settled to the client's satisfaction within eight weeks under the complaints handling procedure, the solicitor must inform the client in writing not only of (a) any right to complain to LeO but also (b) the name of an

ADR approved body which would be competent to deal with the complaint, and whether the solicitor agrees to use the scheme operated by that body.

1   Solicitors working in unauthorised bodies are also required to inform clients of their right to complain to LeO about the service the solicitor, but not the employer, is providing – see SRA guidance 'Giving information to clients of businesses that are not authorised by a legal services regulator', issued in August 2018.
2   Rules 2.03(7) and 2.05(2) of the 2007 Code.
3   See rules 2.1–2.5 of the Legal Ombudsman Scheme Rules (**APPENDIX 13**), and **CHAPTER 14**.
4   EU Directive on Consumer Alternative Dispute Resolution (2013/11/EU), implemented by the Alternative Dispute Resolution for Consumer Disputes (Competent Authorities and Information) Regulations 2015 (SI 2015/542). See also the SRA document 'Looking to the future – flexibility and public protection', issued in June 2016, p 12.

Client information and client care letters

4.108

There is no express provision in the 2019 Codes which requires a solicitor to send the client a 'client care letter'. However, paragraphs 8.1–8.11 contain a number of rules on information which must be provided to clients and it makes sense to provide a client with all the relevant information in one letter.

The following provisions in paragraph 8 refer to information which is relevant to client care letters:

•   information about the complaints handling procedure (paragraph 8.2);

•   the client's right to complain about services and charges (paragraph 8.3(a));

•   how a complaint can be made and to whom (paragraph 8.3(b));

•   any right to make a complaint to LeO and when such a complaint can be made (paragraph 8.3(c);

•   information on how the matter will be handled (paragraph 8.6);

•   the best possible information about how the matter will be priced and the likely overall cost of the matter (paragraph 8.7);

•   explanation as to which activities will be carried ot by the solicitor as an authorised person (paragraph 8.10(a));

•   explanation as to which services are regulated by an approved regulator (paragraph 8.10(b));

•   ensuring any separate business is not represented as being regulated by the SRA (paragraph 8.10(c));

•   ensuring clients understand the regulatory protections available to them (paragraph 8.11).

The regulatory protections available to clients instructing SRA authorised firms vary according to the type of client and the services supplied by the firm. Typical regulatory protections include PI cover, resort to the Compensation Fund, the right to complain to LeO, the right to complain to the ICO, the right to use other available regulatory redress schemes such as OISC and the FCA, and the right to assessment of costs under Part III of the Solicitors Act 1974.[1]

Other information which can be included in a client care letter varies according to the type of client and the services supplied by the firm. Practitioners dealing with consumers should consider in particular the Consumer Contracts (Information, Cancellation and Additional Charges) Regulations 2013, whch require legal services providers to give consumers[2] prescribed information including the main chracteristics of the service, the firm's name, geographical address and telephone number, the best possible information about the likely overall cost of the matter, the length of the contract, or if it is of indeterminate duration the conditions for cancelling it, and (in the case of contracts entered into off-premises) the cancellation rights during a 14-day cancellation period.

Practitioners should also consider whether to include an a client care letter information which must be provided to recipients of services under the Provision of Services Regulations 2009. See **4.114**.

An SRA guidance note on client care letters states that it is important that the client care letter is easy to understand and that one of the most common complaints is about a lack of clarity on costs.[3]

It is relevant to note that LeO has reported that costs are the single largest reason for client dissatisfaction, an indication that the profession could do much more to keep clients informed, particularly as the matter progresses and circumstances change, so that initial information needs to be updated. Most firms are well organised in giving adequate information at the outset; it is much more difficult to manage the situation and to keep clients informed about changes in costs estimates as matters proceed, frequently at a fast pace.

1   For information to be provided to clients by solicitors working in unregulated organisations see SRA Ethics guidance, 'Unregulated organisations – giving information to clients', 23 July 2019. See also **4.120**.
2   A 'consumer' is defined as 'an individual acting for purposes which are wholly or mainly outside that individual's trade, business, craft or profession' by regulation 4 of the Consumer Contracts (Information, Cancellation and Additional Charges) Regulations 2013.
3   SRA Ethics guidance, 'Client care letters', 23 July 2019.

Costs – contingency fees

4.109

There is no reference in the 2019 Codes, at all, to contingency fees, either in relation to the solicitor/client retainer, or in relation to associations with other organisations who charge such fees. The closest provision is paragraph 8.6: 'You ensure [clients] are in a position to make informed decisions about the services they need, how their matter will be handled and the options available to them.' In other words, to the extent that contingency fees are lawful, they no longer raise any regulatory concern per se (but suitability and the best interests of the client need still to be considered).

The provisions of the 2019 Codes follow the law without any 'add-on' obligation or constraint. The relevant law can be summarised as follows.

Contingency fees in non-contentious work

4.110

It has always been lawful for solicitors to charge contingency fees in non-contentious work. This is currently enshrined in section 57 of the Solicitors Act (SA) 1974.[1] Solicitors can (and always have been able to) enter into a retainer in respect of non-contentious business whereby the solicitor can be remunerated by way of a cut of any spoils, or conditional on the result. To be enforceable a non-contentious business agreement must be in writing and signed by the person to be bound by it 'or his agent in that behalf' (section 57(3)). Section 87 of SA 1974 defines contentious business:

> ' "contentious business" means business done, whether as solicitor or advocate, in or for the purposes of proceedings begun before a court or before an arbitrator, not being business which falls within the definition of non-contentious or common form probate business contained in section 128 of the Senior Courts Act 1981.'

Any business that is not within that definition is non-contentious. In order to fall within the definition, proceedings must actually have been commenced before a court or an arbitrator. Thus, work undertaken in relation to a claim which might be litigated, but which is in fact resolved without the issue of proceedings, remains outside the definition of contentious business.

Similarly, in 'proceedings' which bear all the attributes of contentious work, such as those in employment tribunals, but which are not proceedings before a court or an arbitrator, solicitors have been able to charge clients on a contingency fee basis. Contingency fee agreements in relation to employment and other matters are now subject to express regulation.[2]

Otherwise there is no statutory or regulatory limit on what a solicitor may charge by way of a contingency fee in non-contentious work. The Principles and paragraph 7.1 of course require not only that the fee agreement is legal, but also that it takes account of the client's best interests. It has, in short, to be fair.

Paragraph 8.3 requires that clients are informed about their right to challenge or complain about bills, and, where applicable, their right to complain to the Legal Ombudsman (LeO). Costs due under a non-contentious business agreement are liable to detailed assessment and the costs judge/officer may enquire into the facts and if appropriate certify for the court that the agreement should be set aside or the amount payable reduced, and the court may so order.[3]

Solicitors need also to have one eye on the doctrine of unconscionable bargain,[4] although there is no reported example of a contingency fee agreement in non-contentious work between solicitor and client being struck down as unconscionable. If such an agreement were found to be an unconscionable bargain, not only would the agreement be unenforceable, but the solicitor would be at risk of a finding of a breach of principle 2, which requires him or her to act 'in a way that upholds public trust and confidence in the solicitors' profession and in legal services provided by authorised persons'.

1   '(1) Whether or not any order is in force under section 56, a solicitor and his client may, before or after or in the course of the transaction of any non-contentious business by the solicitor, make an agreement as to his remuneration in respect of that business. (2) The agreement may provide for the remuneration of the solicitor by a gross sum or by reference to an hourly rate, or by a commission or percentage, or by a salary, or otherwise ...'
2   Section 58AA of the Courts and Legal Services Act 1990 (introduced into that Act by section 154 of the Coroners and Justice Act 2009) and the Damages-Based Agreements Regulations 2013 (SI 2013/609).
3   Section 57(5) of SA 1974.
4   See **4.46**.

Contingency fees in contentious work: CFAs and DBAs

4.111

For centuries, contingency fees in contentious work were outlawed on public policy grounds as offending the rule against champerty. The scope of the law of champerty has become attenuated in the light of shifting public policy perceptions.[1] The funding revolution of the 1990s brought an end to the absolute prohibition by permitting conditional fee agreements (CFAs), and CFAs are now permitted in all types of proceedings save for family and criminal proceedings,[2] provided that they comply with formalities imposed by delegated legislation.

Following the coming into force of the relevant provisions of LASPO 2012 on 1 April 2013, the law relating to CFAs fundamentally changed again. Thenceforth, the success fee was no longer recoverable from the losing party, and a cap was imposed upon the amount of the success fee that the client would have to yield up to the solicitor out of damages in personal injury cases. At the same time, damages-based agreements (DBAs) became lawful in a wide range of cases (hitherto, they had been restricted to employment law cases). These are true contingency fees, the solicitor's remuneration ordinarily being calculated as a percentage of the client's damages, subject to statutory maxima.

A detailed consideration of the legal framework for CFAs and DBAs is beyond the scope of this book, and that framework is not affected by changes in the SRA's rules.

1   See *R v Secretary of State for Transport, ex p Factortame* [2003] QB 381, CA. The issue of contingency fees and the reach of the modern law on champerty was revisited by the Court of Appeal in *Sibthorpe and Morris v Southwark LBC* [2011] EWCA Civ 25.
2   For the proceedings which cannot be subject to an enforceable CFA, see section 58A of the Courts and Legal Services Act 1990.

Introducers operating on a contingency fee basis

4.112

This issue is now largely historical, in that the 2011 Code abolished a rule that had caused difficulty and controversy for many years. Rule 9.04 of the 2007 Code re-enacted Rule 9 of the Solicitors' Practice Rules 1990 and provided that:

'You must not, in respect of any claim arising as a result of death or personal injury, either: (a) enter into an arrangement for the referral of clients with; or (b) act in association with, any person whose business, or any part of whose business, is to make, support or prosecute (whether by action or otherwise, and whether by a solicitor or agent or otherwise) claims arising as a result of death or personal injury, and who, in the course of such business, solicits or receives contingency fees in respect of such claims.'

The controversy arose from the fact that the 2007 Code, in all its draft forms up to the beginning of 2007, did not contain any such provision. The policy decision had been made to abolish the rule, not least because claims management companies were to become regulated under the Compensation Act 2006. In the event, the provision was saved, and became rule 9.01(4) of the 2007 Code.

Many solicitors have found themselves before the SDT as a result of arrangements made with introducers who have charged on a contingency fee basis in both contentious and non-contentious work. A large number of solicitors handling miners' compensation cases under the claims handling agreements relating to vibration white finger and pulmonary disease claims were disciplined between 2006 and 2010 because introducers (whether commercial entities or trades unions) had agreed to take a slice of the miners' compensation. The courts eventually ruled that these were contentious proceedings.[1] There was also a handful of successful prosecutions arising out of solicitors' arrangements with an organisation known as Justice Direct, which introduced employment tribunal and personal injury claims to solicitors in return for a 'broker's fee' calculated as 25 per cent of any sum recovered plus a percentage of the fees charged by its panel solicitors.[2]

Finally, in 2011, the rule was abolished. That is not the end of the matter, however. The focus now is upon whether the solicitor can properly maintain independence if he or she has an arrangement with an introducer who operates on a contingency fee basis, and whether the agreement between the introducer and the client by which the client agrees to yield up a slice of the damages is in the client's best interests. The Tribunal decision in *Tilbury* remains highly relevant, and solicitors must ask themselves when taking on a new client whether a contingency fee arrangement between the client and the introducer was an unconscionable bargain or otherwise not in the best interests of the new client. This is considered in greater detail in relation to the requirements of section 5 of the Code for Individuals and paragraph 5.1(e); see **4.67** to **4.69**.

1   *Beresford and Smith v SRA* [2009] EWHC 3155 (Admin).
2   *Tilbury*, 9880–2008, SDT; *Kelsall*, 10352–2009, SDT.

Information on disbursements

4.113

In 2008 there were widespread problems over the misdescription of telegraphic transfer fees, now likely to be only of historical interest as firms should long since have reacted to the publicity associated with this issue. The (hopefully past) problem was that firms developed a practice of making a charge for undertaking routine telegraphic transfers in conveyancing. There was nothing wrong with that, but what tended to happen was that if the bank charged the firm, say, £10, the firm would make a charge to the client of £20 – but still describe the fee as a disbursement, as if it had all been paid to the bank. The mischief was neither in passing on the bank's charge, nor in charging a fee for the work entailed, but rather in misdescribing a charge as a disbursement. This misled the client and hid the fact that the firm was making an extra modest profit. A similar principle applies to charges for internal photocopying, which should not normally be described as a disbursement.

Provision of Services Regulations 2009

4.114

It is convenient to deal with the Provision of Services Regulations 2009[1] at this point because they require certain information to be provided to clients, but these requirements go beyond what is required by the 2019 Codes: specifically, the firm's VAT number, details of compulsory professional indemnity insurance cover, details as to how to access the professional rules and detailed information on complaint resolution procedures, and measures to avoid conflicts of interest.[2]

Not all the information has to be provided in the same way. The VAT number and insurance information – which must include the contact details of the insurers and the territorial coverage of the insurance – may optionally be given in writing at the outset, in a client care letter or terms of business, or made easily accessible to clients in hard copy at the firm's offices or on the firm's website.

Information about professional rules, which requires a reference to the professional rules and how to access them and details of the SRA Codes of Conduct and the address at which those codes may be consulted by electronic means must be provided on request. Information on other activities undertaken by the firm which are directly linked to the service in question and on the measures taken to avoid conflicts of interest must be included in any information document in which the firm gives a detailed description of the service and must also be provided on request.[3]

Information about complaint resolution procedures involves telling clients about the role of LeO and where further information can be obtained. This must be provided in a clear and unambiguous manner in good time before the conclusion of the contract or, if there is no written contract, before the service is provided, but must also be provided in any information document in which the firm gives a detailed description of the service provided. This could therefore also be provided through a website and/or the client care letter. However, LeO provides a service only to individuals and small businesses (see **CHAPTER 14**), so that telling all clients including large corporate clients that there is a complaint resolution service through LeO when they will not, in fact, be able to take advantage of it, would be misleading and unhelpful.

---

1   SI 2009/2999.
2   Regulation 8(1)(g) covers VAT; 8(1)(n), insurance; 9(1)(c), conflicts of interest; 9(1)(d), professional rules; 10, complaint resolution; and 11, manner of providing information. The Provision of Services Regulations 2009 also prescribe other information to be made available to recipients of services including information on the price and main features of the service and the provider's name, legal status, geographic address, and general terms and conditions, including any terms concerning competent courts and applicable law.
3   Regulations 9(1)(c) and 9(2).

Publicity

4.115

In the 2011 Code, the SRA stated that its overriding concern about publicity is that it is not misleading. Paragraph 8.8 shows that is still the case. Paragraph 8.9 retains the ban on unsolicited approaches to members of the public apart from current and former clients (ie cold calling).

In the SRA Glossary, publicity is comprehensively defined as including:

> 'all promotional material and activity, including the name or description of your firm, stationery, advertisements, brochures, websites, directory entries, media appearances, promotional press releases, and direct approaches to potential clients and other persons, whether conducted in person, in writing, or in electronic form, but does not include press releases prepared on behalf of a client.'

The Transparency Rules

4.116

On 1 December 2018 the SRA introduced the SRA Transparency Rules 2018, which relate to costs, complaints and regulatory information. The rules apply to all regulated firms and the information must be published in a prominent location on the firm's website. If there is no website the information must be made available to any member of the public on request.

Costs information must be publicised for specified categories of work carried out for individuals and businesses. For individuals, costs information is required for residential conveyancing (including remortgages), uncontested probate, immigration applications and Tribunal appeals (excluding asylum cases), summary only road traffic offences and Employment Tribunal claims for unfair and wrongful dismissal. For businesses, costs information is required for Employment Tribunal claims for unfair and wrongful dismissal, debt recovery up to £100,000 and licensing applications. There are detailed requirements on the content of the published costs information (see the SRA Transparency Rules at **APPENDIX 5**). Those details include information on the fee earners carrying out and supervising the work, the basis of their charges and the total cost for the service (or, where that is not practicable, the average costs or range of costs).

The website must also include the firm's SRA number, the SRA's digital badge and details of the firm's complaints handling procedure (including details of how and when complaints can be made to LeO and the SRA).

The SRA Transparency Rules also state that the firm's letterhead and emails must contain the firm's SRA number and the words 'authorised and regulated by the Solicitors Regulation Authority'.[1]

The SRA Transparency Rules contain provisions for solicitors who are not working in authorised bodies to give clients information on the availability of any professional indemnity (PI) cover and any inability to make claims against the Compensation Fund; see **4.121**.

1 Rule 4.2 of the SRA Transparency Rules 2018.

Information on regulated services, unregulated organisations and separate businesses

4.117

A working knowledge of the provisions of LSA 2007 relating to reserved legal activities is needed in order to understand the different practice models permitted by the 2019 regulatory arrangements, and in turn the information which needs to be supplied to clients on the regulatory protections available under each different practice model.

Under LSA 2007, subject to a small number of exceptions,[1] a person (or entity) is only entitled to carry on a reserved legal activity if that person is authorised to do so by an approved regulator or licensing authority.[2] The approved regulators are the Law Society (acting through the SRA), the Bar Council (through the Bar Standards Board), the Chartered Institute of Legal Executives (CILEx), the Council for Licensed Conveyancers (CLC), the Chartered Institute of Patent Attorneys (CIPA), the Chartered Institute of Trade Mark Attorneys (CITMA), the Association of Costs Lawyers (ACL), the Institute of Chartered Accountants of England and Wales (ICAEW), the Association of Chartered Certified Accountants (ACCA) and the Master of Faculties. Some of those approved regulators, such as the Law Society (acting through the SRA), are also licensing authorities, which means that they can license ABSs that provide reserved legal activities.

The reserved legal activities are listed in section 12(1) of LSA 2007 as follows:

'(a) the exercise of a right of audience

(b) the conduct of litigation

(c) reserved instrument activities

(d) probate activities

(e) notarial activities

(f) the administration of oaths.'

Schedule 2 to LSA 2007 (see **APPENDIX 20**) contains detailed provisions about what constitutes each of the reserved legal activities. A significant feature of the provisions is that the scope of the reserved instrument activities and the probate activities is very limited. For example, 'probate activities' means 'preparing any probate papers … [relating to England and Wales] … on which to found or oppose a grant of probate or a grant of letters of administration'. In consequence, a person who is not authorised under LSA 2007 can provide legal services relating to the administration of an estate, apart from the application for the grant.

None of the approved regulators has power to authorise all of the reserved legal activities. For example, the Master of Faculties is the only approved regulator with power to authorise notarial activities. The Law Society (acting through the SRA) has power to authorise all of the reserved legal activities apart from notarial activities. The Institute of Chartered Accountants of England and Wales (ICAEW) and the Association of Chartered Certified Accountants (ACCA) only have power to authorise probate activities.

1   The main exceptions relate to the provision of immigration services under the Immigration and Asylum Act 1999 and to the exemptions specified in Schedules 3 and 5 to LSA 2007.
2   Section 13(2) of LSA 2007.

4.118

Under the 2011 Code, at the time of its introduction, solicitors providing any type of legal services to members of the public generally had to provide the services within an authorised entity, regardless of whether the legal service was a reserved legal activity or an unreserved legal service. There were exceptions, such as solicitors practising in law centres and in-house solicitors permitted to provide pro bono work to third parties, but those exceptions were limited.

On 1 November 2015 the SRA introduced new rules on separate businesses, known as the 'separate business rules', which permitted solicitors to own and/or actively participate in a separate unregulated business which provided legal services of all kinds except for reserved legal activities.[1] That was a significant deregulatory measure because the categories of reserved legal activities are comparatively narrow and it allowed solicitors to manage or work in legal businesses which were not regulated by the SRA. The separate business rules were, however, restrictive in the sense that the solicitor could not hold himself out as practising as a solicitor in the separate business.

The 2019 regulatory arrangements relax the old rules even further, and allow solicitors to work as solicitors in legal businesses which are not regulated by any approved regulator. The SRA has explained the rationale for the change as follows:

> 'Our key aim is to allow bodies that previously would not have done so to employ solicitors to provide services to the public. While there are many individuals who qualified as solicitors working for non-LSA regulated businesses currently, they must give up their practising certificate and therefore regulation to do so, or act as an in-house solicitor and supervise or advise others. On the other hand, individuals without any qualifications are permitted to provide this service. We no longer think that these restrictions ... can be justified ... nearly any body but solicitors can deliver unreserved services outside of LSA regulated firms. ...
>
> The removal in 2015 of the restrictions on solicitors owning or participating in separate businesses that are not regulated under the LSA ... was a first step towards allowing solicitors to practise in a non-LSA regulated business ...'[2]

At the same time, under the 2019 regulatory arrangements, the SRA has relaxed the rules on authorisation of sole practitioners to permit some individuals working on their own ('freelance lawyers') to carry out unreserved legal activities and, subject to certain conditions, reserved legal activities. The rationale for that change has been explained by the SRA as follows:

'We will allow individual self-employed solicitors and RELs that are working alone as freelancers to provide reserved legal services to the public under their individual authorisation. They would not be required to have their practice authorised as a recognised sole practice … These freelance solicitors would have to:

- act as an individual; without any employees or partners and not work through a service company

- be engaged directly by the client

- not hold client money (except for payments on account of costs and disbursements for which the freelancer is responsible).

… we recognised that by not allowing … freelance lawyers, we might be unnecessarily restricting models of practice …'[3]

1   Chapter 12 of the 2011 Code. There were separate business rules before 1 November 2015 which allowed solicitors to have interests in business which did not provide legal services, but the earlier separate business rules prevented solicitors from hiving off unreserved legal services.
2   'Application for the approval of regulatory arrangements', issued by the SRA in August 2018, paras 117–125.
3   'Application for the approval of regulatory arrangements', issued by the SRA in August 2018, paras 199–204.

4.119

The changes to models of practice introduced under the 2019 regulatory arrangements mean that there are risks that consumers will not have a clear understanding of the differing services which can be provided by differing business models or the regulatory protections (such as PI cover) available under the business model. For example, a consumer instructing a solicitor working in a non-authorised firm may assume incorrectly that the solicitor can conduct litigation or apply for a grant of probate. Equally, the consumer may assume incorrectly that the non-authorised firm must have compulsory insurance cover.

To avoid confusion of that type, paragraphs 8.10 and 8.11 require solicitors to ensure that clients understand how the services are regulated and what the regulatory protections are. The SRA has explained the rationale for the standards as follows:

'We are introducing very clear mandatory information requirements that will apply to all solicitors. We will require solicitors working in businesses that are not regulated by us, or another legal regulator, to be clear with prospective service users about the protections in place. That means that before they begin working with a client, they will need to explain their insurance arrangements position and be clear that their client will not be eligible to submit a claim to the SRA Compensation Fund if things go wrong …

… Our Code … will place responsibility on the solicitor to explain to clients which services are provided by the solicitor as an authorised person and which are provided by others, and whether those persons are authorised or not … This will help to mitigate the risk of consumer confusion under the new regulatory arrangements and also address the current position where consumers do not know what protections come with different types of providers including solicitors'.[1]

1   'Application for the approval of regulatory arrangements', issued by the SRA in August 2018, paras 145–146.

4.120

From a regulatory point of view, the main protections which would be available to clients instructing a solicitor who is practising in an SRA authorised firm are:

- compulsory PI cover;

- resort to the Compensation Fund;

- the right to complain to LeO;

- money on account of costs held on client account subject to the SRA Accounts Rules;

- legal professional privilege.

Not all of those protections are available to a client who instructs a solicitor who is practising under a different business model. For example, if a client instructs a solicitor working in a non-authorised firm:

- neither the solicitor nor the firm are required to have compulsory PI cover;

- clients cannot make a claim on the Compensation Fund;

- the client can complain to LeO but only about the work provided by the solicitor;

- there is no regulated client account;

- there are arguments that legal professional privilege does not apply.

4.121

On the introduction of the 2019 regulatory arrangements, the SRA Transparency Rules 2018 were amended to include new rules 4.3 and 4.4 relating to information on PI cover and the Compensation Fund, which must be provided to clients in many circumstances by solicitors who are not working in authorised firms.

By rule 4.3 of the SRA Transparency Rules 2018, a solicitor who is providing legal services to the public or a section of the public other than through a firm that is regulated by the SRA must (a) where they are not required to have compulsory PI cover inform all clients of that fact before engagement and specify that alternative insurance arrangements are in place if that is the case (together with information about the cover provided if requested) and (b) where applicable inform the client that they will not be eligible to apply for a grant from the SRA Compensation Fund.

By rule 4.4 of the SRA Transparency Rules 2018, rule 4.3 does not apply to a solicitor working in an authorised non-SRA firm (such as a firm authorised by the ACCA) or a 'non-commercial body'.[1]

1   Section 23(2) of LSA 2007 and the SRA Glossary define non-commercial body to mean an independent trade union, a not-for-profit body or a community interest company.

4.122

In February 2019 the SRA produced a guidance note for solicitors working in unauthorised firms on information to supply to clients.[1] The guidance note includes the following:

'•   you will be providing [a] service on behalf of an employer that is not authorised and regulated to provide legal services and it will be important for clients to understand this

•   Compliance with paragraphs 8.10 and 8.11 will include explaining to the client which services are provided by you as ... a solicitor ... and which are provided by others ... [and] the consequences of this in terms of the different protections available if activities are subject to our jurisdiction and that of the Legal Ombudsman

•   The client [needs to be told] who will be carrying out the work on their behalf. It may be the case ... that they chose to instruct the firm because they particularly wanted to use your services as a solicitor

•   [you should explain] that we require the firms that we regulate to have compulsory minimum levels of insurance to protect clients in case something goes wrong and what these are ... but that these arrangements do not apply to the firm you are in because it is not regulated by the SRA ... [and] if your work is covered by [other] professional indemnity insurance ... [then you should also inform the client of that fact]

•   [You should tell clients] that they will not be able to make a claim on the SRA Compensation Fund

•   You must set up or participate in a complaints system and give clients information about how to complain under that system

•   Rules 8.3 and 8.4 set out your obligations to inform clients of their right to complain to the Legal Ombudsman

•   You should make sure that clients understand that while they ... have ... [a] ... right to complain to [LeO and the SRA about you] ... they will have no such rights in relation to your employer.'

1   SRA Ethics guidance, 'Unregulated organisations – giving information to clients', 23 July 2019.

4.123

When providing information to clients, the solicitor working in an unauthorised organisation should bear in mind the SRA Principles, and consider whether it is in the client's best interests to instruct an organisation without regulatory protection. The solicitor should also bear in mind the standards in the Code for Individuals including, for example, the obligation to ensure that clients receive proper information on referrals (paragraph 5.1) and costs (paragraph 8.7).

4.124

As regards clients who instruct a solicitors firm and a separate business, the SRA published guidance on 21 October 2015 on the information to supply to the clients.[1] Although part of the guidance is now obsolete, the following extracts remain helpful in setting out factors to take into account when deciding on the amount of information to provide on the division of work between regulated and unregulated businesses:

'5. You will always be responsible for your own services and publicity to clients and for the extent to which you refer clients to separate business or divide cases with them, and you must always act in the client's best interests. There may be some circumstances where it would be appropriate for you to consider terminating your links with the separate business altogether as it may be impossible otherwise for you to comply with your obligations; for example where you consider that the separate business lacks integrity or lacks competence to deal with the cases that it is taking on. [...]

7. The extent of the information to be provided ... will depend on the likelihood of the confusion arising.

8. The more obviously "separate" the business, and the further away its activities are from legal activities that consumers might expect to be provided by a lawyer, then the less detail will need to be provided.

[...]

15. If a matter is divided with a separate business or the referral is for the primary purpose of the separate business carrying on legal activity, then it is important for the client to be made aware of the differences in regulatory protection and of redress between the two businesses. The concept of informed consent includes the client understanding the consequences of these differences, not just the facts of them. [...]

16. In these circumstances, the information will need to be at an appropriate level of detail and it is likely to be necessary to explicitly draw it to the client's attention, for example in a client care letter, rather than the information just being contained in terms and conditions of engagement.

17. The starting point is that clients should be informed that the work carried out by the separate business will not be regulated by the SRA and that:

- there will be no right to complain to the Legal Ombudsman,

- there will be no right to apply for a grant to be made out of the Compensation Fund,

- the work will not be covered by compulsory professional indemnity insurance (PII) (you may explain what insurance arrangements the separate business has in place),

- the work will not be covered by legal professional privilege,

- the protections in the SRA Accounts Rules 2011 in relation to client money will not apply.

18. This is only a starting point – the test is whether the client has actual understanding of the differences in regulation and redress and the potential consequences and it is your responsibility to ensure that this is the case.

19. Where there are factors increasing vulnerability, it may well be

necessary to explain these issues in more detail to ensure that the client understands the potential consequences.'

1   See www.sra.org.uk/solicitors/guidance/guidance.page, 'Chapter 12 of the SRA Code of Conduct 2011 – the separate business rule (SBR)' issued on 21 October 2015.

CHAPTER 5

The SRA Code of Conduct for Firms

Introduction

5.1

The 2019 regulatory arrangements contain two codes: the SRA Code of Conduct for Solicitors, RELs and RFLs 2019 (the 'Code for Individuals') and the SRA Code of Conduct for Firms 2019 (the 'Code for Firms'). This is the first time that there has been a separate code for entities. In the application to the Legal Services Board (LSB) for approval of the two codes, the SRA explained its reasoning for two separate codes as follows:

> 'By introducing two separate codes, we will make the distinction clearer between what is expected of an individual solicitor and SRA regulated firms (and by extension, to their managers and employees and compliance officers). Separate codes will ensure that enforcement is similarly targeted. By adopting a structure that distinguishes between individual and firm regulation, we have also significantly reduced the overall requirements on firms and individuals ...

> We have sought to differentiate as clearly as possible between the two codes – the systems and procedures that a firm would need to have in place, and the ethical and behavioural standards required of individual solicitors, RELs and RFLs.'[1]

The distinction between individual and firm obligations is drawn out in the introductions to the two codes. The introduction to the Code for Individuals states that the Code for Individuals sets out the 'standards of professionalism' that are expected from individuals and comprises 'a framework for ethical and competent practice'. In contrast the introduction to the Code for Firms (which is set out in full below) sets out the 'standards and business controls' that are expected in firms, and which 'aim to create and maintain the right culture and environment for the delivery of competent and ethical legal services'.

1 'Application for the approval of regulatory arrangements', issued by the SRA in August 2018, paras 87 and 92.

5.2

Although the 2019 regulatory arrangements have two codes, there are in fact five categories of persons or entities facing obligations under the 2019 Codes (individual lawyers, firms, managers, employees and compliance officers) and the Code for Firms contains the obligations imposed on the managers and compliance officers as well as employees in the firm. The managers and compliance officers are responsible for a firm's systems and controls, and it is readily understandable why their responsibilities are included in the Code for Firms. The employees, however, are not directly responsible for the firm's systems and controls and the inclusion of obligations on employees in the Code for Firms blurs the distinction between the two codes, and sometimes makes it difficult to understand which obligations are imposed on the employees.

5.3

In this chapter, we examine the 2019 Code for Firms section by section.

Firms will continue to be prosecuted for breaches of the 2011 Principles and Code, as some of the alleged misconduct brought before the Solicitors Disciplinary Tribunal (the Tribunal or SDT) occurs over a significant period of time. If a commentary on the 2011 Principles and Code is needed, it can found in *The Solicitor's Handbook 2017*.

5.4

The introduction to the Code for Firms is as follows:

This Code of Conduct describes the standards and business controls that we, the SRA, and the public expect of firms (including sole practices) authorised by us to provide legal services. These aim to create and maintain the right culture and environment for the delivery of competent and ethical legal services to clients. These apply in the context of your practice: the way you run your business and all your professional activities (subject, if you are a licensed body, to any terms of your licence).

Paragraphs 8.1 and 9.1 to 9.2 set out the requirements of managers and compliance officers in those firms, respectively.

A serious failure to meet our standards or a serious breach of our regulatory requirements may lead to our taking regulatory action against the firm itself as an entity, or its managers or compliance officers, who each have responsibilities for ensuring that the standards and requirements are met. We may also take action against employees working within the firm for any breaches for which they are responsible. A failure or breach may be serious either in isolation or because it comprises a persistent or concerning pattern of behaviour.

In addition to the regulatory requirements set by us in our Codes, Principles and our rules and regulations, we directly monitor and enforce the requirements relating to referral fees set out in section 56 of the Legal Aid, Sentencing and Punishment of Offenders Act 2012, and provisions relating to anti money laundering and counter terrorist financing, as set out in regulations made by the Treasury as in force from time to time [Link].

All of these requirements are underpinned by our Enforcement Strategy, which explains in more detail our views about the issues we consider to be serious, and our approach to taking regulatory action in the public interest.

5.5

The Code for Firms applies to all entities authorised by the Solicitors Regulation Authority (SRA), including alternative business structures (ABSs), LLPs, limited companies, traditional firms and recognised sole practices. It does not apply to separate businesses,[1] freelance solicitors providing legal services under their individual authorisation, firms which employ solicitors but are 'authorised non-SRA firms'[2] or businesses which employ solicitors but are not authorised by a legal services regulator.[3]

The Code for Firms also applies to managers and compliance officers of entities authorised by the SRA and employees of regulated entities.[4]

1   The SRA Glossary states that separate business
     'means where you own, manage or are employed by an authorised body,
     a separate business
     (a)   which you own;
     (b)   which you are owned by;
     (c)   where you actively participate in the provision of its services, including where you have any
            direct control over the business or any indirect control over the business through another
            person, or
     (d)   which you are connected with,
     and which is not an authorised body, an authorised non-SRA firm, or an overseas practice'.
2   The SRA Glossary defines an authorised non-SRA firm to mean 'a firm which is authorised to carry
     on legal activities as defined by section 12 of the LSA by an approved regulator other than the SRA'.
3   The SRA has produced guidance for businesses which employ solicitors but are not authorised by an
     approved regulator. See SRA Guidance note, 'Unregulated organisations – for employers of SRA
     regulated lawyers', 23 July 2019.
4   See paragraphs 8.1, 9.1 and 9.2. See also **5.2** and **5.6**.

5.6

The Code for Firms also applies to employees, as the introduction states that the SRA may take action against employees working within the firm, including employees who are not solicitors, for any breaches for which they are responsible. If an employee who is not a solicitor breaches the Code for Firms, the SRA has a range of disciplinary and regulatory powers which can be levelled against the employee. The main powers include a power to make an order under section 43 of the Solicitors Act (SA) 1974 prohibiting any firm from employing the employee except with the permission of the SRA (a 'section 43 order'), powers to fine employees[1] and power to refer employees to the Solicitors Disciplinary Tribunal, so that the Tribunal can then fine the employee or impose an order under section 43 of SA 1974.[2] The power to fine is rarely used in practice against employees, apart from a power to fine senior managers of ABSs, and the SRA normally seeks to control the conduct of an employee by obtaining a section 43 order. See **CHAPTER 18**.

1   See section 44D of SA 1974 and section 95 of the Legal Services Act (LSA) 2007.
2   Sections 34A(2) and 47(2E) of SA 1974.

5.7

The introduction to the SRA Principles states that the Principles apply to all those regulated by the SRA, including firms. It is difficult to see how principles which are based on a state of mind, such as the duty to act with honesty, apply to firms.[1] However, other principles can clearly apply to firms, including in particular principle 6, which is the duty to act in a way which encourages equality, diversity and inclusion. Care needs to be taken to ensure that proper systems are in place to comply with that duty.[2]

1   It is also difficult to see how a corporate entity can behave with a lack of integrity, although this has been conceded in the Solicitors Disciplinary Tribunal on at least one occasion; see *SRA v Locke Lord*, 11717–2017.
2   See **3.17** for commentary on principle 6.

5.8

When applying for LSB approval of the 2019 Codes, the SRA said that it intended to shorten the rules and remove duplication. For that reason the SRA also said that, when the same standards applied to firms and individuals, it would set out the standards in the Code for Individuals and simply include cross-references to those standards in the Code for Firms.[1] That has happened to a certain extent, as there are cross-references in the Code for Firms to the standards in the Code for Individuals relating to the courts, referrals and (loosely speaking) 'client care'.[2] However, somewhere along the way, the idea of removing all the duplication was dropped, and there are a number of standards in the Code for Firms which simply replicate the matching standard in the Code for Individuals.

In this edition, when standards in the Code for Firms are simply replicated in the Code for Individuals, cross-references are provided for the commentary on the matching standards in the Code for Individuals.

1   'Looking to the future – flexibility and public protection', issued by the SRA in June 2016, Annex 4, pp 3 and 9.
2   See paragraph 7.1 of the Code for Firms.

Businesses which employ solicitors and are not authorised by a legal services regulator

5.9

Businesses that employ solicitors and are not authorised by a legal services regulator are not under an obligation to comply with the Code for Firms, or any other regulatory arrangements of the SRA.

The managers of the business need to ensure that the business does not breach any of the provisions of LSA 2007 or other statutes regulating legal services. In particular, the business should not be held out to be regulated by the SRA, or any other approved regulator, and should not supply legal services to external clients which fall within the categories of reserved legal activities,[1] immigration work (unless authorised by the Office of the Immigration Services Commissioner) and claims management services (unless authorised by the Financial Conduct Authority (FCA)).

The solicitors who are employed by the businesses are under an obligation to comply with the SRA Principles, the Code for Individuals and all other regulatory arrangements which apply to them. In practice, the managers of the business will therefore need to be satisfied that suitable arrangements are in place to ensure that the employed solicitors can comply with their regulatory obligations. Important factors to take into account include the rules that the solicitor should hold a practising certificate, should not hold client money in his or her own name, must act with independence and in the best interests of clients, owes a duty of confidentiality to the client and must establish, maintain or participate in a complaints service.[2]

The retainer with the client may need contractual provisions which permit the solicitor to comply with his or her professional obligations and which also permit the business to comply with SRA requests for information. If the SRA decides to investigate the conduct of a solicitor relating to a client matter, the SRA is likely to ask for production of the client file, and can apply to the High Court for an order for a third party to produce the file under section 44BB of SA 1974. If the retainer does not permit the business to produce the client file, the business may owe a contractual duty of confidentiality to the client which prevents it from complying with the SRA request unless the client consents or the SRA takes court proceedings against the business and obtains a production order.

1   See the commentary on paragraph 8.10 at **4.119**.
2   See also the SRA Ethics guidance, 'Unregulated organisations – for employers of SRA regulated lawyers', 23 July 2019.

Maintaining trust and acting fairly

5.10

1.1   You do not unfairly discriminate by allowing your personal views to affect your professional relationships and the way in which you provide your services.

1.2   You do not abuse your position by taking unfair advantage of *clients* or others.

1.3   You perform all *undertakings* given by you and do so within an agreed timescale or if no timescale has been agreed then within a reasonable amount of time.

1.4   You do not mislead or attempt to mislead your *clients*, the *court* or others, either by your own acts or omissions or allowing or being complicit in the acts or omissions of others (including your *client*).

1.5   You monitor, report and publish workforce diversity data, as *prescribed*.

5.11

Paragraphs 1.1 to 1.4 are identical to paragraphs 1.1 to 1.4 of the Code for Individuals. For general commentary on those standards see **4.9–4.13**.

5.12

Paragraph 1.1 prohibits unfair discrimination. Under the Equality Act (EqA) 2010, discrimination can be direct or indirect, and the protected characteristics are age, disability, gender reassignment, marriage and civil partnership, pregnancy and maternity, race, religion or belief, and sex or sexual orientation.[1]

Direct discrimination is defined in EqA 2010 as follows: 'A person (A) discriminates against another (B) if, because of a protected characteristic, A treats B less favourably than A treats or would treat others'. There are detailed statutory provisions in EqA 2010 which qualify or extend the statutory definition in differing ways for differing protected characteristics. For example, in relation to age, direct discrimination can be justified if it is a proportionate means of achieving a legitimate aim. Direct discrimination also covers a situation where someone is treated less favourably than another person because they are thought to have a protected characteristic or because they associate with someone who has a protected characteristic.[2]

Indirect discrimination under EqA 2010 is defined as follows: 'A person (A) discriminates against another (B) if A applies to B a provision, criterion or practice which is discriminatory in relation to a relevant protected characteristic of B's.' Indirect discrimination can only be justified if it can be shown that the policy, criterion or practice is a proportionate means of achieving a legitimate aim. Indirect discrimination does not apply to pregnancy or maternity.[3]

The use of the phrase 'unfairly discriminate' rather than 'unlawfully discriminate' in paragraph 1.1 could extend the standard to behaviour beyond the discrimination prohibited by EqA 2010.

1   Section 4 of EqA 2010.
2   See sections 13 to 18 of EqA 2010.
3   Section 19 of the Equality Act 2010.

5.13

Paragraph 1.5 imposes a specific obligation on firms to monitor, report and publish workforce diversity data 'as prescribed'. The SRA Glossary states that 'prescribed' means 'prescribed by the SRA'. At the date of this edition, the SRA has not prescribed any rules. Principle 6 of the SRA Principles states that you must act in a way which encourages equality, diversity and inclusion, and paragraphs 1.5 (workforce diversity data) and 1.1 (unfair discrimination) are facets of principle 6. For commentary on principle 6 see **3.17**.

5.14

The SRA published a case study on discrimination in August 2018 to supplement the 2019 Codes. The case study makes it clear that the SRA regards discrimination as a serious matter which undermines the public trust and confidence in the profession. If the SRA receives a compliance officer for legal practice (COLP) report on discrimination by an employee, the SRA may look at the firm's systems and controls relating to equality, diversity and inclusion to see whether they were effective, and may also expect the firm to implement additional training for everyone in the firm.[1]

1   'Case study – Discrimination', issued by the SRA in August 2018.

5.15

Section 1 signposts a firm's need for appropriate policies and records for undertakings and policies and procedures relating to equality, diversity and inclusion.[1]

1   For policies on equality diversity and inclusion, see the SRA Ethics guidance 'Guidance on the SRA's approach to equality, diversity and inclusion', 23 July 2019.

Compliance and business systems

5.16

2.1   You have effective governance structures, arrangements, systems and controls in place that ensure:

(a)   you comply with all the *SRA's regulatory arrangements*, as well as with other regulatory and legislative requirements, which apply to you;

(b)   your *managers* and employees comply with the *SRA's regulatory arrangements* which apply to them;

(c)   your *managers* and *interest holders* and those you employ or contract with do not cause or substantially contribute to a breach of the *SRA's regulatory arrangements* by you or your *managers* or employees;

(d)   your *compliance officers* are able to discharge their duties under paragraphs 9.1 and 9.2 below.

2.2   You keep and maintain records to demonstrate compliance with your obligations under the *SRA's regulatory arrangements*.

2.3   You remain accountable for compliance with the *SRA's regulatory arrangements* where your work is carried out through others, including your *managers* and those you employ or contract with.

2.4   You actively monitor your financial stability and business viability. Once you are aware that you will cease to operate, you effect the orderly wind-down of your activities.

2.5   You identify, monitor and manage all material risks to your business, including those which may arise from your *connected practices*.

5.17

The responsibility for the management of the business in the broadest sense rests with the managers. The managers should determine what arrangements are appropriate to comply with legislation and the SRA's rules, to manage all material risks to the business, and to monitor financial stability and business viability.

5.18

Whereas paragraphs 2.1 to 2.3 require systems that are designed to ensure compliance, paragraphs 2.4 and 2.5 require firms to identify and monitor 'all material risks' to the business including risks to compliance and financial stability, and to take steps to manage and address issues identified.

There were similar obligations under the 2011 Code and a standard question post-2011 from the SRA to a firm might be: 'What are the major risks to compliance and the financial viability of your firm that you have identified, and what steps have you taken to address them?'.

This question would obviously cover the relatively traditional matters – the risk of misappropriation of funds by accounts staff, and the checks and balances established to minimise those risks – but would also relate to larger issues, such as an over-dependence on work of a particular kind, which could dry up or be lost to competition, or an over-dependence on one or a small number of sources of work the withdrawal of which would threaten the viability of the business.

The SRA publishes a Risk Outlook on an annual basis which identifies risks regarded by the SRA to be of central importance to the profession. The business risks identified in the Risk Outlook for 2018/19 included cyber security, lack of diversity in the profession, information security, money laundering and misuse of client money. The main risks in specific areas of work were dubious investment schemes and the management of litigation claims relating to personal injury, holiday sickness and payment protection insurance.[1]

1   SRA Risk Outlook 2018/19.

5.19

Section 2 cannot be considered in isolation, in terms of the responsibilities associated with running a business authorised by the SRA. Paragraph 8.1 imposes an obligation on all managers to ensure compliance with the Code for Firms, including all the obligations in section 2. There is a fundamental obligation on all firms including recognised sole practitioners to have a compliance officer for legal practice (COLP) and a compliance officer for finance and administration (COFA) who must be approved in these roles by the SRA, and are under a duty to ensure compliance with the regulatory arrangements.[1] In small firms the same individual may perform both roles, and a sole practitioner may be his or her own COLP and COFA, provided approval is obtained.

For a full review of the relevant rules and the responsibilities of the COLP and COFA see **Chapter 7**.

1   See paragraphs 9.1(b) and 9.2(a) of the Code for Firms.

Financial stability

5.20

The recession which followed the financial crisis in 2008 had a substantial impact upon the legal profession. The financial stability of many firms was called into question, and there were a number of high-profile failures of law firms. Much of the SRA's focus and resources during 2012–13 were devoted to this issue, demonstrating the central importance that financial management now has in the regulation of the profession.

It is in this area of regulation that the greatest impact of outcomes-focused regulation has been felt, because of its focus on risk and risk avoidance. For example, a firm in which no partner or employee has ever been guilty of misconduct in the traditional sense, which has complied meticulously with the Accounts Rules and to whom any breach of the rules of conduct would be anathema, may nevertheless feel the full force of regulatory interest and supervision if it constantly struggles to stay within its overdraft limit, and to pay the VAT, PAYE and rent on time. For these are indications that the firm may not be viable, or that the partners are imprudent in terms of the level of drawings.

Not long ago, if the question were to be asked: 'Is it professional misconduct to fail to pay the office rent?' the answer would have been that the regulator was not a debt collection agency and business debts did not raise issues of conduct, although this might trigger a precautionary inspection of the firm's accounts because of the enhanced risk that money might be 'borrowed' from the client account in such circumstances.

The modern view is that the same facts could amount to a breach of paragraph 2.5 – which requires a firm to manage all risks including financial stability.

5.21

The SRA has published a non-exhaustive list of 'poor behaviours' and 'good behaviours' drawn from its experience of firms that have suffered severe financial difficulties.

The 'poor behaviours' are:

- drawings exceeding net profits;
- high borrowing to net asset ratios;
- increasing firm indebtedness by maintaining drawing levels;
- firms controlled by an inner circle of senior management;
- key financial information not shared with rank and file partners;
- payments made to partners irrespective of cash at the bank figure;
- all net profits drawn with no reserve capital pot retained;
- short-term borrowings to fund partners' tax bills;
- VAT receipts used as cash received;
- partners out of touch with office bank account balances;
- heavy dependence on high overdraft borrowings.

The 'good behaviours' are:

- all partners regularly receive full financial information including office account bank balances;
- drawings are linked to cash collection targets and do not exceed profits;
- provision is made to fund partners' tax from income received;
- a capital element is retained from profit, and a capital reserve account built up;
- premises costs are contained;
- profitability levels are tested and unprofitable work is (properly) dropped.

5.22

If a firm reports serious financial difficulties to the SRA, the firm is likely to be assigned to a member of the SRA's supervision team, who will assess the difficulties and consider the matter from a regulatory perspective. The SRA has stated that its concern is to protect clients and the wider public interest.[1] Financial advice is not provided. A firm might be required to demonstrate the steps that are being taken to deal with the situation, including redundancy programmes, a freeze on drawings, capital injection, or an acceptance that the business has become unviable and that a plan for the orderly closure of the practice is required, under the SRA's supervision.

1   'Financial stability – what we're doing', SRA Update, issue 31, April 2013.

Outsourcing

5.23

Paragraph 2.3 states that the firm remains accountable for compliance with the regulatory arrangements where work is carried out through others, and paragraph 2.1(c) requires the firm to have effective arrangements in place to ensure that third parties contracted by the firm do not cause or substantially contribute to a breach of the regulatory arrangements.

5.24

Traditionally, firms have always outsourced work to specialists who can provide assistance on client matters such as counsel, medical experts, tax and accountancy experts, costs lawyers and process servers. Over the past ten years, outsourcing has increased and it now embraces a wide range of other activities.

In 2011, the SRA published a non-exhaustive list of other activities that are outsourced:

- activities which would normally be conducted by a paralegal;

- initial drafting of contracts;

- legal secretarial services – digital dictation to an outsourced secretarial service for word processing or typing;

- proofreading;

- research;

- document review;

- Companies House filing;

- due diligence (for example, in connection with the purchase of a company);

- IT functions which support the delivery of legal activities;

- business process outsourcing.[1]

1   'Q&A – Outsourcing', SRA, 10 October 2011.

5.25

In practice, those who provide traditional specialist services, such as counsel and experts instructed in litigation, are ordinarily aware of a solicitor's regulatory obligations affecting the service they provide, and are often regulated themselves, so that it is not normally necessary for any formal arrangements to be put in place to protect matters such as client confidentiality.

In the 2011 Code, the SRA introduced a new rule (outcome 7.10) which specifically dealt with outsourcing for the first time. Outcome 7.10(a) stated that 'where you outsource legal activities or any operational functions that are critical to the delivery of any legal activities, you ensure such outsourcing … does not adversely affect your ability to comply with, or the SRA's ability to monitor your compliance with, your obligations in the Handbook'. Outcome 7.10(b) went far further and stated that the firm should ensure that the third party is subject to contractual arrangements which permit the SRA to enter the premises of the third party and inspect their records.[1] Shortly after publication of the 2011 Code the SRA issued a Q&A web page on outsourcing which stated that 'the outsourcing provisions in the Code … do not apply when you use a specialist service to assist with the provision of legal services to a client, for example instructing counsel, medical experts'.[2] That web page reflects the fact that the risks arising from outsourcing do not relate to traditional suppliers of specialist services, and that to achieve the outcomes or the new standards, the firm needs to concentrate on outsourcing arrangements with other third parties.

However, when instructing a specialist such as counsel, the firm cannot ignore its responsibilities for ensuring the client is provided with a competent service. The firm would remain 'responsible' for the service overall, including the choice of counsel, and would (perhaps jointly) be liable for any mistakes in the sense that counsel's advice or drafts could not be uncritically passed on.[3]

Reserved legal activities should not be outsourced to a person who is not authorised to conduct such activities (since to conduct unauthorised reserved legal activities is unlawful).[4]

1   Outcome 7.10(b) has not been retained in the 2019 Codes.
2   'Q&A – Outsourcing', SRA, 10 October 2011.
3   See *Davy-Chiesman v Davy-Chiesman* [1984] 2 WLR 291, CA per May LJ at 303: 'a solicitor is in general entitled to rely on the advice of counsel properly instructed. However, this does not operate so as to give a solicitor an immunity in every such case. A solicitor is highly trained and rightly expected to be experienced in his particular legal fields. He is under a duty at all times to exercise that degree of care, to both client and the court, that can be expected of a reasonably prudent solicitor. He is not entitled to rely blindly and with no mind of his own on counsel's views'.
4   Section 14 of LSA 2007. For a summary of the reserved legal activities see **4.117**.

5.26

The SRA appears to have two main aims on outsourcing, again as apparent from its website: 'It is important that when firms outsource work this does not affect our ability to regulate the firm's activities and that clients remain fully protected'.[1] So in part this element of regulation is intended to ensure that outsourcing does not take matters outside the ability of the SRA to regulate, as well as stating what might be described as the basic requirement that any practitioner would appreciate: protection of the clients' interests.

When deciding which services to outsource, and to whom, the firm should in particular bear in mind the duties to act transparently (paragraph 6.4); act in the clients' best interests (principle 7); provide a competent service (paragraph 4.2); protect client confidentiality (paragraph 6.3); protect data (see paragraphs 3.1 and 5.2); and avoid conflicts of interest (paragraphs 6.1 and 6.2). The firm should also take account of the obligation to identify, monitor and manage all material risks to a business (paragraph 2.5); the need to maintain records to demonstrate compliance with the regulatory arrangements (paragraph 2.2); and the requirement for arrangements that ensure third parties do not cause or substantially contribute to a breach of the regulatory arrangements (paragraph 2.1(c)), as well as the fact that the firm remains accountable to the SRA for work carried out through others (paragraph 2.3).

Despite the multiplicity of standards which need to be considered, outsourcing should not be regarded as something to be avoided at all costs. In relation to IT innovation, which almost inevitably involves outsourcing, the SRA has said: 'We are committed to helping solicitors and law firms develop their businesses in new ways. An innovative legal sector is essential for delivering the efficient, affordable services the public needs'.[2]

1   'Q&A – Outsourcing', SRA, 10 October 2011.
2   'IT and innovation', issued by the SRA in March 2016.

5.27

The Principles and standards should be taken into account when deciding whether to outsource an activity, including the questions of whether outsourcing is in the client's interest and what risks the firm faces if the activity is outsourced.

Once a decision has been made to outsource, the first issue is the repute of the outsourcing company. This is a growth field and new entrants to the market are to be expected. It is necessary to investigate the background of the company and to establish reputation by suitable enquiry, including the taking of references if necessary, review of the company's systems for security of data, the control of conflicts, and the protection of client confidentiality. Assurances are required as to the qualifications and competence of those who will be undertaking the work and their supervision, and also as to their ethical standards which can vary by reference to local *mores*. The supplier's data protection policies need to be aligned with the firm's policies. There need to be systems for review of the quality of the work undertaken; how problems are rectified and disputes resolved; and what records the outsourcing company is required to keep.

There should be a written contract to control, where appropriate, matters such as the protection of data; the protection of client confidentiality; the ability to audit and check the quality of the supplier's work; the supply of records to the firm and, if necessary, the SRA; and the delivery up of data and confidential information on insolvency of the supplier or termination of the contract.

5.28

When outsourcing a service, the firm needs to consider whether clients need to be informed that the service is being outsourced and whether the client's consent is needed for the supply of confidential information or data to a third party. It is difficult to see how confidential information can be passed to a third party without the client's informed consent.

If outsourcing is driven by clients, particularly sophisticated clients who may themselves be outsourcing business processes, the clients may demand reduced legal costs on the basis of similar efficiencies. The clients need to be informed of any enhanced risks arising from outsourcing. There should also be openness in charging. There is no reason why a firm cannot take a profit from outsourcing, just as it takes a profit from the product of its own employees.[1] There is no obligation to charge clients for the outsourced services at cost, any more than there is an obligation to charge for the work of employed staff at no more than their overhead cost to the firm, but equally clients will expect savings to be made and that charging policies are clear and fair.

1   See e g *Crane v Canons Leisure Centre* [2008] 1 WLR 2549, CA.

5.29

The SRA has published a report on cloud computing (which is the storing, accessing and processing of information on a network of remote servers managed by a third party and accessed over the internet). That is a form of outsourcing.

The report recognises that there are advantages of cloud computing, including cost and flexibility (it is easy to scale cloud computing resources up or down to meet requirements) and mobility (it is easy to access facilities when out of the office). However, the report also states that there are risks which must be managed:

- it is hard for the firm to see whether the outsourcer is acting compliantly;

- firms must meet their legal obligations including data protection duties, and it is important to ensure the chosen provider can meet those requirements;

- no IT system is guaranteed to work all the time and the firm should check the provider's service level agreement, contingency plans and reliability;

- firms should be sure they know what will happen if the supplier becomes insolvent;

- firms should be sure of the exit terms, including how they retrieve their data;

- firms should check the security of access arrangements;

- sending data to an outsourcer does not remove the duty of confidentiality – it is reasonable to expect the highest standards from IT providers.[1]

1   'IT security: keeping information and money safe', issued by the SRA in December 2016.

Cooperation and accountability

5.30

3.1   You keep up to date with and follow the law and regulation governing the way you work.

3.2   You cooperate with the *SRA*, other regulators, ombudsmen and those bodies with a role overseeing and supervising the delivery of, or investigating concerns in relation to, legal services.

3.3   You respond promptly to the *SRA* and:

(a)   provide full and accurate explanations, information and documentation in response to any requests or requirements;

(b)   ensure that relevant information which is held by you, or by third parties carrying out functions on your behalf which are critical to the delivery of your legal services, is available for inspection by the *SRA*.

3.4   You act promptly to take any remedial action requested by the *SRA*.

3.5   You are honest and open with *clients* if things go wrong, and if a *client* suffers loss or harm as a result you put matters right (if possible) and explain fully and promptly what has happened and the likely impact. If requested to do so by the *SRA* you investigate whether anyone may have a claim against you, provide the *SRA* with a report on the outcome of your investigation, and notify relevant persons that they may have such a claim, accordingly.

3.6   You notify the *SRA* promptly:

(a)   of any indicators of serious financial difficulty relating to you;

(b)   if a *relevant insolvency event* occurs in relation to you;

(c)   if you intend to, or become aware that you will, cease operating as a legal business;

      (d)   of any change to information recorded in the *register*.

3.7   You provide to the *SRA* an information report on an annual basis or such other period as specified by the *SRA* in the *prescribed* form and by the *prescribed* date.

3.8   You notify the *SRA* promptly if you become aware:

      (a)   of any material changes to information previously provided to the *SRA*, by you or on your behalf, about you or your *managers*, *owners* or *compliance officers*; and

      (b)   that information provided to the *SRA*, by you or on your behalf, about you or your *managers*, *owners* or *compliance officers* is or may be false, misleading, incomplete or inaccurate.

3.9   You report promptly to the *SRA* or another *approved regulator*, as appropriate, any facts or matters that you reasonably believe are capable of amounting to a serious breach of their *regulatory arrangements* by any *person* regulated by them (including you). If requested to do so by the *SRA* you investigate whether there have been any serious breaches that should be reported to the *SRA*.

3.10   Notwithstanding paragraph 3.9, you inform the *SRA* promptly of any facts ot matters that you reasonably believe should be brought to its attention in order that it may investigate whether a serious breach of its *regulatory arrangements* has occurred or otherwise exercise its regulatory powers.

3.11   You do not attempt to prevent anyone from providing information to the *SRA* or any other body exercising regulatory, supervisory, investigatory or prosecutory functions in the public interest.

3.12   You do not subject any *person* to detrimental treatment for making or proposing to make a report or providing, or proposing to provide, information based on a reasonably held belief under paragraph 3.9 or 3.10 above or 9.1 (d) or (e) or 9.2 (b) or (c) below, or under paragraph 7.7 or 7.8 of the Code of Conduct for Solicitors, RFLs and RELs, irrespective of whether the *SRA* or another *approved regulator* subsequently investigates or takes any action in relation to the facts or matters in question.

5.31

All of the standards in section 3 are comparable to standards in section 7 of the Code for Individuals apart from paragraphs 3.6 to 3.8. For commentary on the comparable standards see **4.97** to **4.104**.[1]

1   Sections 3 and 9 of the Code for Firms and section 7 of the Code for Individuals were amended by the SRA Regulatory Arrangements (Reporting Concerns) (Amendment) Rules 2019, which were approved by the LSB on 9 May 2019.

5.32

Paragraphs 3.6(a) and (b) impose requirements on firms to notify the SRA when firms are in financial difficulty. There is a strong emphasis on informing the SRA when financial difficulties arise in a regulated entity. This was a direct result of the recession and the difficult trading conditions faced by solicitors after 2008. It can also be seen as a corollary of the obligations concerning the management of the business, and the identification and management of the risks to financial stability. The SRA is anxious to ensure the orderly wind-down of law firms where the business is failing, so as to avoid the financial costs and human distress of an intervention. The sooner that the SRA is informed about an entity's financial problems, the greater will be the opportunity to avoid an intervention. Costs of interventions tend to be very high, and to fall for the most part upon the profession rather than the intervened-upon solicitor, who rarely has the funds to discharge the obligation to pay those costs.[1]

The SRA Glossary states (in summary) that a 'relevant insolvency event' occurs in relation to an entity if there is a resolution for voluntary winding up without a declaration of solvency, the body enters into administration, an administrative receiver is appointed, a meeting of creditors is held under section 95 of the Insolvency Act 1986, a court order is made for winding up, all of the managers of an unincorporated body are made bankrupt or the body is an overseas company subject to an analogous event. The SRA Glossary does not define what is meant by 'indicators of serious financial difficulty'. The difficulty would have to relate to the firm rather than any individual in the firm, and paragraph 8.1 imposes the responsibility for deciding whether such an event has occurred on all the managers, as well as the relevant compliance officer.

The 2011 rules imposed a joint obligation on the COLP and COFA to maintain and make reports in relation to the financial stability of the firm. That position has changed under the 2019 regulatory arrangements. The COFA's responsibilities are now limited to the SRA Accounts Rules and the COLP is responsible for reports relating to financial stability (see paragraph 9.1 of the Code for Firms and see **CHAPTER 7** on COLPs and COFAs).

1 The costs of an intervention are recoverable from an intervened-upon solicitor as a debt by virtue of para 13 of Schedule 1 to SA 1974, and the costs of an intervention into a firm can be recoverable by court order from managers of the firm under Schedule 2 to the Administration of Justice Act 1985 and Schedule 14 to LSA 2007.

5.33

Paragraph 3.6(c) imposes an obligation to notify the SRA promptly if the firm intends to cease operating as a legal business, or managers become aware that it will cease operating. The former obligation in the 2011 Code under outcome 10.13 required solicitors to notify the SRA 'before the firm closes'. The new standard therefore emphasises the need for early notification as soon as managers know the firm will close. The notification obligation relates to mergers and other business transfers, as well as situations in which the business is closed down. The SRA's primary concern relates to disorderly business closures rather than transfers. The SRA may appoint a supervisor to oversee and advise on closure issues and ensure that suitable arrangements are in place for matters such as storage and return of client files, transfer of current cases, closure of the client account and run-off cover. If proper arrangements are not put in place and clients' interests are at risk, the SRA may intervene. See **CHAPTER 17** on intervention and orderly closure.

5.34

The reporting requirements in paragraphs 3.6(d) to 3.8 are comparable to reporting requirements under the 2011 rules. The SRA Glossary definition of 'register' states 'register includes the roll and the register of solicitors with practising certificates kept under Part I of the SA, the register of European lawyers, the register of foreign lawyers and the register of authorised bodies kept under the AJA and the LSA'.

Service and competence

5.35

4.1 You only act for *clients* on instructions from the *client*, or from someone properly authorised to provide instructions on their behalf. If you have reason to suspect that the instructions do not represent your *client's* wishes, you do not act unless you have satisfied yourself that they do. However, in circumstances where you have legal authority to act notwithstanding that it is not possible to obtain or ascertain the instructions of your *client*, then you are subject to the overriding obligation to protect your *client's* best interests.

4.2 You ensure that the service you provide to *clients* is competent and delivered in a timely manner, and takes account of your *client's* attributes, needs and circumstances.

4.3 You ensure that your *managers* and employees are competent to carry out their role, and keep their professional knowledge and skills, as well as understanding of their legal, ethical and regulatory obligations, up to date.

4.4 You have an effective system for supervising *clients'* matters.

5.36

Section 4 of the Code for Firms is comparable to section 3 of the Code for Individuals. Paragraphs 4.1 and 4.2 contain similar provisions to paragraphs 3.1, 3.2 and 3.4 of the Code for Individuals. For general commentary on those standards see **4.22–4.34 AND 4.36**.

5.37

In the 2018 application to the LSB for approval of the new regulatory arrangements, the SRA stated that the obligations in the Code for Firms on obtaining instructions (paragraph 4.1) and identifying your client (paragraph 7.1(c)) have been added because of the reported increase in identity theft, fraud and cybercrime.[1]

In relation to cybercrime, the SRA has said that the most commonly reported issue on fraudulent instructions is email modification fraud where a rogue hacks a client's email account and sends an email to the firm diverting completion monies to the rogue's bank account.[2] For the type of action the SRA recommends that firms should take to combat cybercrime see **5.43**.

1   'Looking to the future – flexibility and public protection', issued by the SRA in June 2016, Annex 4, p 11.
2   'IT security: keeping information and money safe', issued by the SRA in December 2016.

5.38

Firms carrying out claimant personal injury work should take account of the SRA warning notice of March 2016 on personal injury claims when deciding what systems are needed to comply with paragraph 4.1. The warning notice states that the role of referral organisations in the sector means that solicitors should take extra caution to ensure that they are acting on valid instructions and that they are likely to have to take instructions from, or check them directly with, the client throughout the course of the case, particularly in relation to significant decisions such as whether to settle and, if so, for how much.[1]

1   'Risk factors in personal injury claims: warning notice', issued by the SRA on 21 March 2016, updated in December 2017.

5.39

Paragraph 4.3 was not in the 2011 Code. It is a new standard introduced to take account of continuing competence. On 1 November 2016 the SRA replaced the continuing professional development (CPD) programme with continuing competence. Under continuing competence, every solicitor with a practising certificate should reflect on their practice to identify learning needs, plan how to address those needs, complete the planned activities, record the process and make an annual declaration when applying for renewal of their practising certificate that they have reflected on their practice and addressed any identified learning and development needs. The SRA's guidance note on competence and standards of service states that a failure to consider or address training needs will be treated as an aggravating feature in professional issues relating to standard of service.[1]

1   'SRA Topic Guide: Competence and standard of service', issued in August 2018.

5.40

Paragraph 4.4 states that a firm must have an effective system for supervising client matters. The general nature of that obligation is consistent with the SRA's aim of moving away from prescriptive drafting and introducing more flexibility, so that managers of firms can use their own judgement when applying the Code for Firms to their practice.[1] The 2011 Code required firms to ensure that supervision included the regular checking of the quality of the work by suitably competent and experienced people[2] and those two factors are likely to be core requirements of any system whenever supervision is needed.

Rule 9.4 of the SRA Authorisation of Firms Rules 2019 states that an authorised body must have at least one manager or employee, or must procure the services of an individual who is a lawyer of England and Wales and has practised as such for a minimum of three years and who supervises the work undertaken by the authorised body (or if the body is a licensed body, the work undertaken by the body that is regulated by the SRA).

LSA 2007 has provisions relating to supervision which affect firms. If a firm carries out reserved legal activities, employees who are not authorised to carry out reserved legal activities (such as trainees and legal executives) can only carry out reserved instrument activities and probate activities at the direction of and under the supervision of a person who is entitled to carry out the activity (such as a solicitor). An employee can exercise a right of audience in proceedings heard in chambers (apart from reserved family proceedings), provided the employee's work includes assisting in the conduct of litigation and the employee is assisting under instructions given by the solicitor and under the supervision of the solicitor.[3] The employee cannot, however, conduct the litigation. If the employee carries out the permitted reserved legal activities without supervision, or if the employee conducts the litigation, the firm could commit an offence.[4] The Immigration and Asylum Act 1999 also has provisions requiring an unauthorised employee who provides immigration advice or immigration services to be supervised by a person who is qualified to provide the immigration advice and services.[5]

1   'Looking to the future – flexibility and public protection', issued by the SRA in June 2016, Annex 4, p 13.
2   Outcome 7.8 of the 2011 Code.
3   See section 13(2)(b) of and Schedule 3 to LSA 2007.
4   Section 16(2) of LSA 2007.
5   Section 84 of the Immigration and Asylum Act 1999.

Client money and assets

5.41

> 5.1   You properly account to *clients* for any *financial benefit* you receive as a result of their instructions, except where they have agreed otherwise.
>
> 5.2   You safeguard money and *assets* entrusted to you by *clients* and others.

5.42

Section 5 of the Code for Firms is comparable to section 4 of the Code for Individuals. Paragraphs 5.1 and 5.2 are identical to paragraphs 4.1 and 4.2 of the Code for Individuals. For general commentary on those standards see **4.39–4.41**.

Cybercrime

5.43

The SRA has said that cybercrime is a priority risk and that firms should have robust procedures in place to combat it.[1]

In December 2016 the SRA published a report on cybercrime which stated that emails are the medium of choice for cybercriminals and that the majority of cybercrimes reported to the SRA are email modification scams. In a typical email modification scam a rogue hacks into a client's email system and sends an email to a conveyancing solicitor which appears to be from the client but redirects the completion funds to the rogue's bank.[2] Other scams have included bogus law firms impersonating genuine law firms in an attempt to steal mortgage redemption monies,[3] and the 'CEO fraud' in which a rogue impersonates a senior partner or director and instructs a junior staff member to transfer money. Ransomware programs can be introduced into a firm's system by attachments to emails which when opened encrypt files and demand a ransom in return for decrypting the files.[4] In 2016 and 2017 there was a series of frauds in which fraudsters impersonated members of a bank's fraud department in order to obtain firms' pin codes for electronic transfers. The pin codes were then used to withdraw money from the client accounts.

The SRA has stated that it is important for a firm to take protective steps in relation to the IT system, which need not be complex, such as using an up-to-date antivirus system, using encryption on mobile devices, backing up files on a regular basis and setting up access controls. Backups can, for example, defeat most ransomware attacks provided the backup is not routinely connected to the main system.[5] It is also important to ensure only approved staff can transfer money. Most cybercrimes target people rather than systems and the best defence is staff training, including training to recognise common scams such as CEO fraud and email modification fraud, to not open unsolicited emails, to avoid using unapproved connection devices such as personal USBs, and to ensure passwords are not used in public spaces and are changed regularly. There should also be a robust process to confirm any requests to change bank details for payments to clients or third parties.[6] Firms should also have procedures to deal with attacks when they occur, such as knowing in advance whom to contact at the bank to try to stop payments going through.[7] It may also be necessary to report an attack to the firm's insurer, the SRA and the police. Firms should also consider whether their standard PI policy covers all loss from client account and whether additional insurance is needed to cover the firm's own losses from cybercrime.

1   'Cybercrime issues continue', SRA news release, 28 March 2017.
2   'IT security: keeping information and money safe', SRA risk publication, December 2016.
3   See 'Bogus law firms and identity theft: warning notice', SRA, 26 March 2012.
4   SRA Risk Outlook 2018/19.
5   See 'IT and innovation', SRA risk publication, March 2016, p.12.
6   'IT security: keeping information and money safe', SRA risk publication, December 2016.
7   'Cybercrime issues continue', SRA news release, 28 March 2017.

5.44

For the firm's obligations relating to data protection see **CHAPTER 29**.

Conflict, confidentiality and disclosure

5.45

Conflict of interests

6.1   You do not act if there is an *own interest conflict* or a significant risk of such a conflict.

6.2   You do not act in relation to a matter or a particular aspect of it if you have a *conflict of interest* or a significant risk of such a conflict in relation to that matter or aspect of it, unless:

(a)   the *clients* have a *substantially common interest* in relation to the matter or the aspect of it, as appropriate; or

(b)   the *clients* are *competing for the same objective*, and the conditions below are met, namely that:

(i)   all the *clients* have given informed consent, given or evidenced in writing, to you acting;

(ii)   where appropriate, you put in place effective safeguards to protect your *clients'* confidential information; and

(iii)   you are satisfied it is reasonable for you to act for all the *clients*.

Confidentiality and disclosure

6.3   You keep the affairs of current and former *clients* confidential unless disclosure is required or permitted by law or the *client* consents.

6.4   Any individual who is acting for a *client* on a matter makes the *client* aware
of all information material to the matter of which the individual has
knowledge except when:

(a)   the disclosure of the information is prohibited by legal restrictions
imposed in the interests of national security or the prevention of
crime;

(b)   the *client* gives informed consent, given or evidenced in writing, to
the information not being disclosed to them;

(c)   the individual has reason to believe that serious physical or mental
injury will be caused to the *client* or another if the information is
disclosed; or

(d)   the information is contained in a privileged document that the
individual has knowledge of only because it has been mistakenly
disclosed.

6.5   You do not act for a *client* in a matter where that *client* has an interest
adverse to the interest of another current or former *client* for whom you
hold confidential information which is material to that matter, unless:

(a)   effective measures have been taken which result in there being no real
risk of disclosure of the confidential information; or

(b)   the current or former *client* whose information you hold has given
informed consent, given or evidenced in writing, to you acting,
including to any measures taken to protect their information.

5.46

Section 6 of the Code for Firms is comparable to section 6 of the Code for
Individuals. The standards in both codes are virtually identical and there are no
significant differences. For commentary on the standards see **4.79–4.95**.

Applicable standards in the SRA Code of
Conduct for Solicitors, RELs and RFLs

5.47

7.1   The following paragraphs in the SRA Code of Conduct for Solicitors,
RELs and RFLs apply to you in their entirety as though references to 'you'
were references to you as a firm:

(a)   dispute resolution and proceedings before courts, tribunals and
inquiries (2.1 to 2.7);

(b)   referrals, introductions and *separate businesses* (5.1 to 5.3); and

(c)   standards which apply when providing services to the public or a
section of the public, namely client identification (8.1), complaints
handling (8.2 to 8.5), and client information and publicity (8.6 to
8.11).

5.48

For commentary see the following paragraphs of CHAPTER 4:

(a)   dispute resolution and proceedings: **4.15–4.20**;

(b)   referrals introductions and separate businesses: **4.45–4.75**;

(c)   client identification, client care and publicity: **4.106–4.115**.

Managers in SRA authorised firms

5.49

> 8.1   If you are a *manager*, you are responsible for compliance by your firm with this Code. This responsibility is joint and several if you share management responsibility with other *managers* of the firm.

5.50

Standard 8.1 imposes a responsibility on every partner (or manager[1]) of a firm to ensure that the firm's obligations are complied with. In almost all firms, different responsibilities have to be delegated to different partners, as client work cannot be carried out effectively without delegation. However, under paragraph 8.1 delegation by one partner does not absolve the other partners of their responsibilities to ensure the standards are achieved. The SRA has not produced any guidance on the steps the other partners should take properly to delegate managerial functions. The other partners should at least satisfy themselves that the delegatee is suitably qualified to carry out the role and that the delegatee's work is subject to appropriate oversight, review and reports. In practice the SRA and the SDT have historically expected a greater degree of direct oversight in small firms than in large ones, and have expected a partner in a two-partner firm to have far greater knowledge and control over the managerial activities of the co-partner than that expected from a partner in a larger firm.

1   The SRA Glossary defines manager to mean 'the sole principal in a recognised sole practice, a member of a LLP, a director of a company, a partner in a partnership or in relation to any other body a member of its governing body'.

Compliance officers

5.51

> 9.1   If you are a *COLP* you must take all reasonable steps to:
>
> (a)   ensure compliance with the terms and conditions of your firm's authorisation;
>
> (b)   ensure compliance by your firm and its *managers*, employees or *interest holders* with the *SRA's regulatory arrangements* which apply to them;
>
> (c)   ensure that your firm's *managers* and *interest holders* and those they employ or contract with do not cause or substantially contribute to a breach of the *SRA's regulatory arrangements*;

(d)   ensure that a prompt report is made to the *SRA* of any facts or matters that you reasonably believe are capable of amounting to a serious breach of the terms and conditions of your firm's authorisation, or the *SRA's regulatory arrangements* which apply to your firm, *managers* or employees;

(e)   notwithstanding paragraph (d), you ensure the SRA is informed promptly of any facts ot matters that you reasonably believe should be brought to its attention in order that it may investigate whether a serious breach of its *regulatory arrangements* has occurred or otherwise exercise its regulatory powers.

save in relation to the matters which are the responsibility of the *COFA* as set out in paragraph 9.2 below.

9.2   If you are a *COFA* you must take all reasonable steps to:

(a)   ensure that your firm and its *managers* and employees comply with any obligations imposed upon them under the SRA Accounts Rules;

(b)   ensure that a prompt report is made to the *SRA* of any facts or matters that you reasonably believe are capable of amounting to a serious breach of the SRA Accounts Rules which apply to them;

(c)   notwithstanding paragraph (b), you ensure the *SRA* is informed promptly of any facts ot matters that you reasonably believe should be brought to its attention in order that it may investigate whether a serious breach of its *regulatory arrangements* has occurred or otherwise exercise its regulatory powers.

5.52

For the responsibilities of COLPs and COFAs see **CHAPTER 7**.[1]

---

1   Sections 3 and 9 of the Code for Firms and section 7 of the Code for Individuals were amended by the SRA Regulatory Arrangements (Reporting Concerns) (Amendment) Rules 2019, which were approved by the LSB on 9 May 2019.

PART 3
Other rules

CHAPTER 6

The SRA Accounts Rules 2019

The new rules

6.1

The SRA Accounts Rules 2019 are much shorter than their predecessors, reduced from 70 pages to little over six pages.

The Solicitors Regulation Authority (SRA) has stated that there are three main changes:

- the rules are simpler (and shorter) and easier to understand;
- they provide the option for firms to hold limited types of client money outside client account;
- they provide an alternative to the holding of client money through the use of third party managed accounts (TPMAs).

The SRA's explanation for the changes is that the old Accounts Rules, which had not changed significantly for many years, were prescriptive and restrictive, that many firms were finding themselves in technical breach of the Accounts Rules when there was no real risk to client money, and that the complexity and resultant technical breaches were resulting in confusion, cost and non-compliance rather than good practice.[1]

1   'Application for the approval of regulatory arrangements', SRA, August 2018, pages 56–57.

6.2

The SRA has also stated that the changes to the Accounts Rules do not mean that firms have to change their accounts systems:

> 'We expect that many firms, at least at first, will continue to operate as they do under the current rules and in doing so will remain compliant with the new Accounts Rules.'[1]

That reflects the fact that, despite the radical reduction in length, the following underlying principles remain the same, are straightforward, and are well known to all practitioners – even if they may not be familiar with all the detail:

- keep other people's money in a client account, and separate from your own money;
- use only each client's or trust's money for that client's or trust's matters;
- have a proper accounts system and proper internal controls over it;
- keep accounting records to show money held for each client or trust;

- pay interest when appropriate;
- co-operate with regulatory checks and inspections by the SRA; and
- obtain an annual accountant's report when appropriate.

1 'Application for the approval of regulatory arrangements', issued by the SRA in August 2018, paragraph 255.

6.3

When submitting the application to the Legal Services Board (LSB) for approval of the new Accounts Rules, the SRA said that the new Accounts Rules would be supplemented by guidance. In addition to an updated warning notice on banking facilities (**APPENDIX 9**), in July 2019 the SRA posted to its website a range of further or updated 'Ethics guidance', effective from 25 November 2019.[1] Historically, some SRA guidance on Accounts Rules has acquired the status of prescriptive rules over time, and the eventual status and effect of any new guidance could for that reason be uncertain to the profession for a number of years.[2]

There is also scope for uncertainty arising from the substitution of words such as 'promptly', 'fair' and 'appropriate' in place of prescriptive time limits and other requirements found in the SRA Accounts Rules 2011. Those words are intended to give practitioners more flexibility, but it is unclear whether the SRA will take a restrictive approach to interpretation of those provisions over time.

1 See www.sra.org.uk and **APPENDIX 21** for a list of guidance topics, which include: 'Accountant's report and the exemption to obtain one', issued 1 August 2017 and updated 4 July 2019; 'Do I need to operate a client account?', issued 4 July 2019; 'Helping you keep accurate client accounting records', issued 4 July 2019; 'Joint accounts and record keeping', issued 4 July 2019; 'Planning for and completing an accountant's report', issued 1 August 2017, updated June 2019; 'Third-party managed accounts', issued 6 December 2017, updated 4 July 2019.
2 In 2017 the SRA prosecuted a number of solicitors for breach of guidance note (ix) to rule 15 of the Solicitors' Accounts Rules 1998. The note provided guidance on use of a client account as a banking facility before the introduction of a rule against banking facilities in the SRA Accounts Rules 2011 – see *Langford, Howard Kennedy and others*, 11686–2017.

6.4

The SRA Accounts Rules 2019 comprise an introduction and a further four parts:

- Part 1 (rules 1.1 to 1.3) is concerned with to whom the rules apply and who has responsibility for them.
- Part 2 (rules 2.1 to 8.4) concerns the definition of client money, its proper handling, the correct operation of client account, interest, and accounts systems and controls.
- Part 3 (rules 9.1 to 11.2) concerns dealing with other money belonging to clients or third parties not held in a firm's client account.
- Part 4 (rules 12.1 to 13.1) is concerned with accountants' reports and the retention of accounting records.

6.5

The SRA Accounts Rules 2011, which came into force on 6 October 2011, will continue to apply to compliance obligations for accounting transactions and entries during the period from the date the SRA Accounts Rules 2011 came into force

(6 October 2011) to the date of introduction of the SRA Accounts Rules 2019. The SRA Accounts Rules 2011 will therefore continue to be relevant to any SRA investigation relating to that period. The SRA Accounts Rules 2011, and commentary on them, can be found in *The Solicitor's Handbook 2017*.

Introduction and rule I

6.6

Introduction

These rules set out our requirements for when firms (including sole practices) authorised by us receive or deal with money belonging to clients, including trust money or money held on behalf of third parties. The rules apply to all firms we regulate, including all those who manage or work within such firms.

Firms will need to have systems and controls in place to ensure compliance with these rules and the nature of those systems must be appropriate to the nature and volumes of client transactions dealt with and the amount of client money held or received.

PART I: GENERAL

Application section

1.1   These rules apply to *authorised bodies*, their *managers* and employees and references to 'you' in these rules should be read accordingly.

1.2   The *authorised body's managers* are jointly and severally responsible for compliance by the *authorised body*, its *managers* and employees with these rules.

1.3   In relation to a *licensed body*, the rules apply only in respect of activities regulated by the *SRA* in accordance with the terms of its licence.

Application and scope of the Accounts Rules

6.7

The SRA Accounts Rules 2019 apply to authorised bodies, their managers and employees. The SRA Glossary defines 'authorised body' to mean '(a) a body that has been authorised by the SRA to practise as a licensed body or a recognised body, or (b) a sole practitioner's practice that has been authorised by the SRA as a recognised sole practice'. Traditional firms and LLPs are recognised bodies. Alternative business structures (ABSs) are licensed bodies.

In the case of an ABS or a licensed body, the SRA Accounts Rules 2019 only apply in respect of activities regulated by the SRA in accordance with the terms of its licence.[1] ABSs may be supplying both regulated and unregulated services (through multi-disciplinary practices (MDPs)). In relation to MDPs the rules apply only in respect of those activities for which the practice is regulated by the SRA, and are concerned only with money handled by the practice which relates to those regulated activities.

1 Rule 1.3 of the SRA Accounts Rules 2019.

6.8

The introduction to the SRA Accounts Rules 2019 and rule 1.1 provide that the Accounts Rules apply to all employees of authorised bodies, including employees who are not solicitors. If an employee who is not a solicitor breaches the SRA Accounts Rules 2019, the SRA has a range of disciplinary and regulatory powers which can be applied against the employee. The main powers include a power to make an order under section 43 of the Solicitors Act (SA) 1974 prohibiting any firm from employing the employee except with the permission of the SRA (a 'section 43 order'), powers to rebuke and fine employees[1] and a power to refer an employee of a recognised body to the Solicitors Disciplinary Tribunal (the Tribunal or SDT), so that the Tribunal can then fine the employee.[2] The fining powers are rarely used in practice against employees, apart from senior managers of ABSs, and the SRA normally seeks to control the conduct of an employee by obtaining a section 43 order.

1 See section 44D of SA 1974 and section 95 of the Legal Services Act (LSA) 2007.
2 Sections 34A(2) and 47(2E) of SA 1974.

6.9

The SRA Accounts Rules 2019 do not apply to solicitors who practise outside an authorised body. These include traditional in-house solicitors, freelance solicitors, solicitors practising in authorised non-SRA firms (such as firms regulated by the Council for Licensed Conveyancers) and solicitors practising in firms which are not authorised by a legal services regulator.

The circumstances in which a solicitor practising outside an authorised body can hold client account money are governed by paragraph 4.3 of the SRA Code of Conduct for Solicitors, RELs and RFLs 2019 (the 'Code for Individuals'). By paragraph 4.3 a solicitor must not personally hold client money unless:

- the solicitor works in an authorised body; or

- the solicitor works in a 'prescribed' organisation; or

- the solicitor is a 'freelance solicitor' permitted to hold client money under regulation 10.2(b)(vii) of the SRA Authorisation of Individuals Regulations 2019.

At the date of this edition, there are no 'prescribed' organisations in which solicitors can personally hold client money.

Under regulation 10.2(b)(vii) of the SRA Authorisation of Individuals Regulations 2019, an individual self-employed solicitor working alone whose practice is not authorised as a recognised sole practice (a 'freelance solicitor') is permitted to hold client money on account of fees and unpaid disbursements before delivery of a bill,[1] provided that (a) any money held for disbursements relates to costs or expenses incurred by the solicitor on behalf of the client and for which the solicitor is liable and (b) the solicitor has informed the client in advance of where and how the money is to be held.

In summary, a freelance solicitor holding client money on account of costs and disbursements under rule 10.2(b)(vii) does not have to comply with the SRA Accounts Rules 2019.

1   That is client money falling within rule 2.1(d) of the SRA Accounts Rules 2019.

Systems and controls

6.10

The introductory sections of the SRA Accounts Rules 2011 set out lengthy lists of principles and outcomes which related to client accounts and had to be achieved. In contrast the introduction to the SRA Accounts Rules 2019 simply states that

> 'Firms will need to have systems and controls in place to ensure compliance with these rules and the nature of those systems must be appropriate to the nature and volumes of client transactions dealt with and the amount of client money.'

While it may be comforting to smaller firms to read that the SRA's expectations of the systems employed will be proportionate to the client work and money handled, in practice, if a breach occurs, and if the breach is investigated by the SRA, the onus will rest with the firm to demonstrate that its systems were appropriate, which is often difficult.

However, the SRA has said that the new regulatory arrangements will be targeted at cases where action is needed. The new rules remove unnecessary prescription to focus on the most important aspects of client money.[1] The SRA has also commented upon the 2019 regulatory arrangements:

> 'It is our view that we need to put more trust in solicitors' professional judgement. We do not need pages and pages of prescriptive rules for a solicitor or firms to do the right thing and maintain professional standards … For instance, all good solicitors know that they should not steal money belonging to their clients. We do not think they need – or benefit – from more than 40 pages of detailed Accounts Rules setting out how to avoid stealing.'[2]

For commentary on systems and controls and the requirement for five-weekly reconciliations, see **6.44–6.46**.

1   'Application for the approval of regulatory arrangements', SRA August 2018, page 76.
2   'Our response to consultation: Accounts Rules review', SRA, June 2017.

6.11

Paragraph 9.2 of the SRA Code of Conduct for Firms (the 'Code for Firms') requires the compliance officer for finance and administration (COFA) to take all reasonable steps to ensure that the firm and its managers and employees comply with any obligations imposed on them under the SRA Accounts Rules 2019. That places an obligation on the COFA to ensure that proper accounting systems and controls are in place.

The responsibilities are not limited to the COFA. Under the Code for Firms, the firm must have effective arrangements in place to ensure that compliance officers can discharge their duties,[1] and the firm is also required to have effective systems and controls in place to ensure that the firm complies with all of the regulatory arrangements.[2] By paragraph 8.1 of the Code for Firms, all of the partners in a firm are responsible for ensuring that the firm complies with those obligations.

1   Paragraph 2.1(d) of the Code for Firms.
2   Paragraph 2.1(a) of the Code for Firms.

Liability for breaches

6.12

Rule 1.2 provides that the managers of a firm are jointly and severally responsible for compliance by the firm, its managers and employees. The word 'managers' is defined by the SRA Glossary to include all members of an LLP and all partners in a firm (and not simply those partners and members closely involved in the day-to-day management of the firm).

The comparable provision in the SRA Accounts Rules 2011 stated that all principals of the firm 'must ensure compliance with the rules by the principals themselves and by everyone employed in the firm'.[1] That provision was treated as a rule imposing strict liability on the principals for all breaches. It remains to be seen whether the SRA and the Tribunal will say that the new wording (which has changed from 'principals ... must ensure compliance' to 'managers ... are ... responsible for compliance') also imposes strict liability on all managers.

It is commonplace for solicitors to be unaware that breaches have occurred until well after the event (because the accounts function is usually delegated to non-solicitors), but the managers will still be responsible for compliance. The lack of knowledge or complicity on the part of the ignorant individual does not mean that a breach could not have occurred: he or she is responsible for compliance. That is why robust systems and hands-on involvement and oversight at partnership or management level are essential.

Failure to comply with any of the SRA Accounts Rules 2019 may be the subject of a complaint to the SDT[2] or an internal SRA disciplinary finding and sanction. Whether a breach results in an SRA finding, sanction, or referral to the SDT, and the severity of any sanction applied, will depend on factors such as the seriousness of the breach and the systems and controls adopted to avoid it.[3]

1   Rule 6.1 of the SRA Accounts Rules 2011.
2   Section 32(3) of SA 1974.
3   In the period of June 2012 to December 2013, more than 4,500 firms delivered a qualified accountant's report and yet only 179 were referred for consideration for further regulatory action – see 'Application for the approval of regulatory arrangements', issued by the SRA in August 2018.

6.13

Under the SRA Accounts Rules 2011, the COFA was under a duty to ensure compliance with the Accounts Rules. That has changed under the SRA Accounts Rules 2019, as the new Accounts Rules do not impose any obligations on the COFA. The SRA has made the following comment on that change:

'We reflected on feedback that ... [making] ... the COFA directly responsible for compliance with the rules ... would place an unreasonable burden on the COFA ... [Rule 1.2] now emphasises that the Accounts Rules create obligations on the firm and its managers, not on the COFA. The COFA's obligations ... under the Code of Conduct to take all reasonable steps to ensure compliance with the Accounts Rules ... will still apply.'[1]

1   'Application for the approval of regulatory arrangements', issued by the SRA in August 2018, page 60.

6.14

The Codes of Conduct also impose obligations on individual solicitors and the firm to safeguard client money. Paragraph 4.2 of the Code for Individuals provides that 'You safeguard money and assets entrusted to you by clients and others' and there is an identical provision in paragraph 5.2 of the Code for Firms.

Rule 2: Client money

6.15

Client money

2.1   '*Client money*' is money held or received by you:

(a)   relating to *regulated services* delivered by you to a *client*;

(b)   on behalf of a third party in relation to *regulated services* delivered by you (such as money held as agent, stakeholder or held to the sender's order);

(c)   as a trustee or as the holder of a specified office or appointment, such as donee of a power of attorney, Court of Protection deputy or trustee of an occupational pension scheme;

(d)   in respect of your *fees* and any unpaid *disbursements* if held or received prior to delivery of a bill for the same.

2.2   In circumstances where the only *client money* you hold or receive falls within rule 2.1(d) above, and:

(a)   any money held for *disbursements* relates to costs or expenses incurred by you on behalf of your *client* and for which you are liable; and

(b)   you do not for any other reason maintain a *client account*; you are not required to hold this money in a *client account* if you have informed your *client* in advance of where and how the money will be held. Rules 2.3, 2.4, 4.1, 7, 8.1(b) and (c) and 12 do not apply to *client money* held outside of a *client account* in accordance with this rule.

2.3   You ensure that *client money* is paid promptly into a *client account* unless:

(a)   in relation to money falling within 2.1(c), to do so would conflict with your obligations under rules or regulations relating to your specified office or appointment;

(b)   the *client money* represents payments received from the Legal Aid Agency for your *costs*; or

(c)   you agree in the individual circumstances an alternative arrangement in writing with the *client*, or the third party, for whom the money is held.

2.4   You ensure that *client money* is available on demand unless you agree an alternative arrangement in writing with the *client*, or the third party for whom the money is held.

2.5   You ensure that *client money* is returned promptly to the *client*, or the third party for whom the money is held, as soon as there is no longer any proper reason to hold those funds.

Client money or office money?

6.16

Keeping your own money and that of other people separate should create no problems of interpretation, but solicitors still have problems with this issue from time to time. All money held or received in the course of practice is 'client money' (held or received for a client or as trustee) or 'office money' (which belongs to the practice).

The simplest approach is to ask the question: does this money belong, now, unconditionally and exclusively, to the firm? If the answer is 'yes', the money is office money and must be paid into office account. If the answer is 'no', it is client money.

The word 'unconditionally' is used to emphasise the fact that if a condition has to be satisfied in order for the firm to be entitled (such as the delivery of a bill), it is client money. The word 'exclusively' is used to emphasise that if someone else has an interest in the money, it is client money.

Regulated services

6.17

The SRA Glossary defines 'regulated services' to mean 'the legal and other professional services that you provide that are regulated by the SRA and includes, where appropriate, acting as a trustee or as the holder of a specified office or appointment'. That is a very wide definition, which ensures that all money received in the course of practice falls within the definition of 'client money' under rule 2.1 if it does not belong to the firm.[1]

---

1   The first draft of the SRA Accounts Rules 2019 used the phrase 'legal services'. That was changed following the consultation process to 'regulated services' to avoid the possibility that money received

from a client might not fall within the definition of client money if the service supplied to the client was not a legal service. See 'Application for the approval of regulatory arrangements', SRA, August 2018, para 250.

Partners' money

6.18

Under rules 12.1 and 12.8 of the SRA Accounts Rules 2011, money which belonged to a partner in a firm was always office money, even if the partner was a client of the firm. If the firm was acting for a partner purchasing a property, and received a deposit in preparation for exchange, the deposit had to be paid into office account. The position under the new Accounts Rules is different. If the firm is acting for a partner, the partner is a client[1] and the money held or received relating to the service supplied to the partner is client money under rule 2.1.

1   The SRA Glossary defines 'client' to mean 'the person for whom you act and, where the context permits, includes prospective and former clients'.

Costs

6.19

When a firm is paid on account of costs for work that has not yet been billed, that money still belongs to the client and must be paid into client account.

Firms may legitimately transfer money held on account of costs from client account to office account for the payment of their fees, but only if a bill or other written notification of costs has been sent to the client.

There may be thought to be an inconsistency in the new Accounts Rules between rule 2.1(d) and rule 4.3(a). Rule 2.1(d) states that money held on account of costs is client money while it is held 'prior to delivery of a bill'. Rule 4.3(a) provides that money held on client account on account of costs can be transferred after 'you … give a bill of costs, or other written notification of the costs incurred, to the client or the paying party'. It is submitted that rule 4.3(a) prevails, as that specifically relates to transfers of costs, and that money on account of costs can be transferred after giving written notification of costs, even if the bill has not yet been delivered. That practice is consistent with the position under the SRA Accounts Rules 2011 (rule 17.2 of the SRA Accounts Rules 2011 permitted transfers after written notification of costs).

For commentary on payment of costs out of money which is not expressly held on account of costs, see **6.35**.

The Tribunal's records are packed with cases involving solicitors who transferred money to which they considered they were fully entitled, because they had done the work, but where they had 'not got around to sending a bill'. Similar numbers of cases have involved 'tidying up the accounts' by sweeping old and small balances from client to office account on the basis of 'dummy bills' or 'accounts only bills' (meaning pieces of paper that were never intended to be delivered to the clients whose money was being taken).

Agreed fees

6.20

Under rule 17.5 of the SRA Accounts Rules 2011, a payment for an 'agreed fee' had to be paid into office account. For the purpose of rule 17.5, an 'agreed fee' was narrowly defined to be one that was fixed, which could not be varied upwards or downwards, was not dependent on the transaction being completed and was evidenced in writing. The narrow definition led to confusion, as some practitioners mistakenly thought that all agreed fees could be paid into office account. The rule has now gone. Under rule 2.1(d) of the SRA Accounts Rules 2019, all money received in respect of fees is client money prior to delivery of a bill.

Professional disbursements

6.21

It is common and proper to bill a client for costs and disbursements, including counsels' fees that have been incurred but are yet to be paid (which should be marked on the bill as unpaid[1]). It is permissible to pay the whole sum received in payment of such a bill into office account before the firm discharges its liability to pay the amount due to third parties in respect of the disbursements.

Rule 17.1(b) of the SRA Accounts Rules 2011 provided that the element relating to unpaid professional disbursements had to be paid to the professionals entitled to the money by the end of the second working day following receipt. That rule has now gone, and there is no rule in the SRA Accounts Rules 2019 governing the timing of the firm's payment of professional disbursements out of office account.

It is a well-known but wholly improper practice to withhold payment of unpaid professional disbursements for a lengthy period of time so that the office overdraft is reduced by the amount owed to counsel and others, possibly many thousands or tens of thousands of pounds. A slightly more sophisticated version of this practice is to write cheques to those entitled, which when entered on the accounts appear to show prompt payment, but the cheques are not sent and, rather, accumulate in the top left-hand drawer of the principal's or bookkeeper's desk, or comparable location. This would be regarded very seriously.[2]

Under the 2019 regulatory arrangements, improper delays in payment of professional disbursements, such as counsel's fees after the client has paid the amount due to the firm, could be treated as a breach of principle 2 (not upholding public trust and confidence in the profession) and paragraph 1.2 of the Code for Firms (taking unfair advantage of others). A serious case could lead to an allegation of breach of principle 5 (lack of integrity).

---

1   Section 67 of SA 1974.
2   See, for example, *SRA v Wingate* [2016] EWHC 3455 (Admin), per Holman J at [133]–[139]; this part of the decision was not affected by the subsequent appeal to the Court of Appeal.

Rule 2.2 payments on account of costs which do not have to be placed in client account

6.22

Under rule 2.2 payments on account of costs do not have to be placed in a client account if:

(1)   the only client money the firm holds or receives is money held or received for fees and unpaid disbursements prior to delivery of a bill;

(2)   any money held for disbursements relates to costs or expenses incurred by the firm on behalf of the client for which the firm is liable;

(3)   the firm does not maintain a client account for any other reason; and

(4)   the firm has informed the client in advance of where and how the money will be held.

If a firm relies on the rule 2.2 exemption, the money held on account of costs can be paid into the firm's office account. It is not subject to rule 2.3 (pay money promptly into a client account), rule 2.4 (ensure client money is available on demand), rule 4.1 (keep client money separate from office money), rule 7 (account for interest on client money), rule 8.1(b) and (c) (maintain a running total of all client ledger balances and a cash book showing a running total of all transactions through client account), and rule 12 (accountants' reports).

The other rules which relate to 'client money' (as opposed to the 'client account') will continue to apply to the money held on account of costs. In particular, there is a continuing obligation to return the money promptly to the client if there is no longer any reason to hold the funds (rule 2.5), to provide a bill of costs or other notification of costs (rule 4.3), to keep a client ledger recording receipts, payments and bills of costs (rule 8.1(a)), to obtain bank statements for the business account holding the money at least every five weeks (rule 8.2), to keep a central record of bills and notifications of costs (rule 8.4), and to keep the accounting records for at least six years (rule 13.1).

Firms relying on the rule 2.2 exemption will continue to need a COFA, who will be responsible for ensuring compliance with the obligations in the SRA Accounts Rules 2019 that apply if payments on account of costs are placed in an office account. The COFA will also be responsible for checking whether there is a need to operate a client account for any other reason (which would mean that the right to rely on the rule 2.2 exemption is then lost).

The partners in the firm will be under an obligation to comply with the Principles and the Code for Firms. The partners will have to ensure that clients are in a position to make informed decisions about the options available to them and the regulatory protections arising from use of a client account (paragraph 7.1(c) of the Code for Firms). If there is any risk of insolvency, and if money on account of costs is placed into office account, the partners are at risk of allegations that they have breached principle 3 (act with independence), principle 5 (act with integrity), principle 7 (act in the best interests of each client) and paragraph 5.2 (safeguard money entrusted to you by clients).

The SRA has commented that 'clients should be clearly informed that the money is not being held in a client account and agree to this in the knowledge of what it means'.[1] Whether this can be achieved using a client care letter alone will perhaps depend on the sophistication of the client and how clear the reference is. The SRA has also said:

> 'Where a firm does not operate a client account (because they intend to rely on the exemption) they will need to ensure that the client is given sufficient information to make an informed decision. A key risk that will need to [be] identified and properly understood by consumers is what happens in the event of insolvency as the money would not be separated ... However ... the client would ... be able to make a claim on the Compensation Fund'.[2]

It should not be overlooked that the Compensation Fund is a discretionary fund of last resort, and solicitors would be unwise to provide over much reassurance to clients (particularly corporate clients) that the Fund would automatically respond in an insolvency situation.

The rule 2.2 exemption applies to disbursements only if the expense has been incurred by the firm on behalf of the client and if the firm is liable for the expense. That appears to have been added to prevent firms from obtaining payments on account for payment of stamp duty land tax and placing them in office account under rule 2.2.[3] However, it also means firms cannot rely on rule 2.2 if money is obtained on account for payment of counsel's fees before counsel is instructed.

The SRA Glossary definition of disbursements needs to be borne in mind. 'Disbursements' are defined to mean 'any costs or expenses paid or to be paid to a third party on behalf of the client or trust (including any VAT element) save for office expenses such as postage and courier fees'. A firm wishing to rely on the rule 2.2 exemption cannot obtain money on account for courier fees (or postage).

It is open to a firm to combine the rule 2.2 exemption with the use of a third party managed account (TPMA) or an agreement with a client under rule 2.3(c) for an alternative arrangement for client money. A TPMA could enable a firm, for example, to carry out property work without the need to operate a client account. In the application to the LSB for approval of the SRA Accounts Rules 2019, the SRA said:

> '[The rule 2.2 exemption] ... does not enable firms to hold other types of client money (such as a house deposit or stamp duty) outside of client account. Firms that handle these categories of client money will still be required to hold the money in client account or a TPMA unless otherwise agreed with the client (as is currently permitted for all firms).'[4]

The rule 2.2 exemption has been included to avoid the need for firms who do not hold other categories of client money from operating a client account. The expressed aim is to reduce overheads. There will be no need to invest in client account software, to employ cashiers to operate the client account or to pay for reporting accountants to prepare an accountant's report. The professional indemnity insurance premium may also be cheaper.

It is important to note that firms are not permitted to adopt a 'pick and mix' approach to payments on account of costs; if a firm operates a client account for any other reason, it will need to keep this category of client money in client account, and not, for example, use it to keep office account within an overdraft limit. For that reason, the SRA has said:

> 'All fees and disbursements paid in advance are considered client money until the point at which they are billed. These payments must therefore be held in a client account, unless they are the only categories of client money held by the firm and the firm takes advantage of the exemption (in new rule 2.2).'[5]

1 'Our response to consultation: Accounts Rules review', SRA June 2017.
2 'Application for the approval of regulatory arrangements', SRA, August 2018, paras 278–279.
3 'Application for the approval of regulatory arrangements', SRA, August 2018, para 271.
4 'Application for the approval of regulatory arrangements', SRA, August 2018, para 271.
5 'Application for the approval of regulatory arrangements', SRA, August 2018, para 272.

Legal aid

6.23

The power to receive Legal Aid Agency (LAA) payments for costs into office account is retained by rule 2.3(b). Costs are defined by the SRA Glossary as fees and disbursements. There is no longer a requirement, after a specified time period, to transfer sums representing unpaid disbursements to client account, but practitioners should be particularly careful not to delay the payment of such disbursements, otherwise they risk being accused of propping up the office account. A failure to pay within a reasonable time could lead to allegations of breach of principle 2 (upholding public trust and confidence in the profession), principle 5 (integrity) and paragraph 1.2 of the Code for Firms (not taking unfair advantage of others).

Alternative arrangements – rule 2.3(c)

6.24

Alternative arrangements agreed under rule 2.3(c) should be adopted cautiously, and only where the client's interests are better served by such an alternative arrangement.

The SRA Glossary states that 'client account' has 'the meaning given to it in the SRA Accounts Rules'. The SRA Accounts Rules 2019 do not define 'client account', but rule 3.1 restricts client accounts to accounts at a branch or the head office of a bank or building society in England and Wales. Rule 2.3(c) allows firms to make arrangements for holding client money outside accounts of that type.

The power is not in fact new. Rule 2.3(c) effectively replaces rule 15.1 of the SRA Accounts Rules 2011. Rule 15.1 gave the following examples of appropriate circumstances in which alternative arrangements might be agreed: retaining money in the firm's safe in the form of cash;[1] placing money in an account in the firm's name which is not a client account, such as an account outside England and Wales; placing the money in a bank, building society or other financial institution opened in the name of the client or of a person designated by the client.

None of the other provisions of SRA Accounts Rules 2019 relating to client money are excluded if an alternative arrangement is agreed under rule 2.3. That means, for example, that the client money must be kept separate from the firm's money (rule 4.1) and there are obligations to account for interest (rule 7), to keep accounting records to the extent that they relate to client money rather than the client account (rule 8) and to obtain accountants' reports when appropriate (rule 12).

Similarly, none of the provisions of the Code for Firms are excluded, such as the obligation to safeguard client money (paragraph 5.2), and the partners in the firm continue to hold the client money subject to the Principles, including the duty to act in the client's best interests (principle 7).

1   The handling of some cash such as small amounts of foreign currency travel money received at the start of the administration of an estate would not lead to a risk of breaching the anti-money laundering (AML) legislation.

Designated deposit accounts

6.25

Rule 2.4 permits firms to reach an agreement with clients that client money should not be available on demand. That enables client funds to be placed in designated deposit accounts paying a higher rate of interest. The arrangement has to be agreed in writing, and that would presumably be satisfied by an exchange of emails on the terms of the deposit account.

Dormant balances

6.26

Rules have been in force since 14 July 2008 to deal with the substantial problem caused by dormant accounts or 'residual balances'. The problem is now addressed by rule 2.5. There is an obligation to return funds to the client or other person entitled promptly, as soon as there is no longer any proper reason to retain them.

The SRA Accounts Rules 2011 contained a detailed rule relating to deposits held in property transactions and other retentions, which required firms to give written notice to the client, or other beneficiary of the funds, on an annual basis after the substantial conclusion of a matter of the amount held and the reason for the retention.[1] That rule has now gone. However, it makes sense for firms to retain a procedure for periodically reminding clients of retentions and obtaining confirmation that the retention is still needed. If a firm does not have such a procedure there is a risk that the firm will not know when there is no longer a proper reason for the retention.

The SRA Accounts Rules 2011 also contained rules permitting firms to dispose of minor residual balances not exceeding £500 to charity without obtaining the specific consent of the SRA and to dispose of larger residual balances with the permission of the SRA.[2]

The SRA Accounts Rules 2019 do not include a parallel provision for disposal of minor residual balances not exceeding £500, but rule 5.1(c) states that withdrawals can be made with the SRA's prior written authorisation or in prescribed circumstances. 'Prescribed' means prescribed by the SRA.[3] At the date of this edition, the

SRA has not prescribed any rules for disposing of minor residual balances without the need for written authorisation from the SRA.

1   Rule 14.4 of the SRA Accounts Rules 2011.
2   Rules 20.1 and 20.2 of the SRA Accounts Rules 2011.
3   See the SRA Glossary.

Rule 3: Client account

6.27

Client account

3.1   You only maintain a *client account* at a branch (or the head office) of a *bank* or a *building society* in England and Wales.

3.2   You ensure that the name of any *client account* includes:

(a)   the name of the *authorised body*; and

(b)   the word 'client' to distinguish it from any other type of account held or operated by the *authorised body*.

3.3   You must not use a *client account* to provide banking facilities to *clients* or third parties. Payments into, and transfers or withdrawals from a *client account* must be in respect of the delivery by you of *regulated services*.

6.28

Rules 3.1 and 3.2 are self explanatory.

For commentary on holding client money outside a bank or building society account in England and Wales, see **6.24**.

Banking facilities

6.29

Since 2011, the SRA has focused increasingly on concerns that firms should not provide a 'banking facility' for clients or third parties, and has prosecuted solicitors for alleged breaches of some antiquity.[1]

The rule against banking facilities first appeared in the Accounts Rules in 2011, as rule 14.5 of the SRA Accounts Rules 2011.[2] The wording of the current rule is different from the wording of the former rule 14.5, and it is worthwhile comparing the two rules.

Rule 14.5 of the SRA Accounts Rules 2011 provided:

'*You* must not provide banking facilities through a *client account*. Payments into, and transfers or withdrawals from, a *client account* must be in respect of instructions relating to an underlying transaction (and the funds arising therefrom) or to a service forming part of *your* normal regulated activities.'

In contrast rule 3.3 of the SRA Accounts Rules 2019 provides:

'You must not use a *client account* to provide banking facilities to *clients* or third parties. Payments into, and transfers or withdrawals from a *client account* must be in respect of the delivery by you of *regulated services*.'

The main difference is in the second sentence. The references to 'underlying transaction' and 'normal regulated activities' have been removed, and replaced by a rule that client account transactions must be 'in respect of the delivery by you of regulated services'. The SRA Glossary defines 'regulated services' to mean:

'the legal and other professional services that you provide that are regulated by the SRA and includes, where appropriate, acting as a trustee or as the holder of a specified office or appointment.'

The change in the wording has removed a number of difficulties which arose on the interpretation of rule 14.5. It was, for example, unclear from rule 14.5 whether a client account transaction had to be connected to underlying legal work carried out by the firm, or whether the existence somewhere else of an underlying transaction was enough. The uncertainties led to two High Court cases which involved disputes on the construction of rule 14.5,[3] and the profession did not have any very clear idea of how the SRA interpreted rule 14.5 until a warning notice was published in December 2014, more than three years after introduction of the rule.

The new rule 3.3 is consistent with the interpretation set out in the warning notice, and it is safe to say that the new rule assists in understanding the SRA's prohibition against banking facilities (as it removes some of the interpretation difficulties) but does not change the prohibition.

The warning notice was updated on 6 August 2018, and a copy of the updated warning notice is at **APPENDIX 9**.[4]

The warning notice includes the following guidance on the purpose of the rule:

'It is not a proper part of a solicitor's everyday business or practice to operate a banking facility for third parties, whether they are clients of the firm or not …

… The rule is not intended to prevent usual practice in traditional work undertaken by solicitors such as conveyancing, company acquisitions, the administration of estates or dealing with formal trusts. So it does not affect your ability to make usual and proper payments from client account when they are related to the transaction (such as the payment of estate agents' fees in a conveyancing transaction) …'

The warning notice and an SRA Case Studies web page include the following examples of cases which breach the rule and cases which do not:

- 'Historically, some solicitors have held funds for clients to enable them to pay the client's routine outgoings. This has been mainly for the clients' convenience such as where they are long term private clients or based abroad. In view of technological change, such as the ease of internet and telephone banking, we consider that allowing client account to be used in this way is no longer justifiable and a breach of rule 14.5'

- 'Banks commonly withdraw facilities when told that there has been a winding up petition. If a law firm allows its client account to be used in an insolvency situation to receive and process money, the client will improperly obtain a banking service'

- 'We have also seen firms making multiple transfers of money between the ledgers of different clients or companies without evidence of the purpose or legal basis for the transfers (such as Board resolutions or contracts). Transfers in such circumstances will be a breach of rule 14.5, particularly if they are simply carried out on request'

- 'A law firm has been instructed by a client to advise on a transaction involving government bonds in a foreign jurisdiction. The lead solicitor has advised the client that the firm will need to instruct lawyers in the foreign jurisdiction to provide specialist advice. The client has asked the firm to project manage the transaction and proposed that money could be paid to the firm so that it can pay the foreign lawyers' fees …we do not consider that this scenario gives rise to a breach …'

- 'A law firm acts for a developer who intends to enter into a development agreement with a buyer of land. The buyer is to make payments in instalments, but it has a weak covenant strength. Buyer and seller have agreed that the total price will be paid up front to the buyer's solicitors and held by the firm. Instalments will be released when they are payable … the firm will [advise] on the interpretation of the payment provisions in the agreement as the development progresses … this scenario is unlikely to [be a] breach'

- 'A law firm acted for a property development company. The original retainer related to a redevelopment of a block of flats, the creation of separate leasehold interests and sale of the individual leases. When the flats were sold, the client asked the firm to retain the proceeds in the firm's client account. The company then asked the firm to make a series of payments from client account, using the proceeds of sale from the first development to pay a building contractor, architect and council tax in relation to another development site, and to pay … a consultant for his services as a sales agent … the firm was not instructed to provide legal advice about the second development … there is a clear risk here that … the firm would be in breach …'

- 'Where the solicitors are acting as trustees … they will be providing a regulated professional service. In this situation, receiving trust income into client account and making payments out of it, would not give rise to a breach … The situation is different when the law firm acts for trustees, rather than as trustees. Here the firm's role is more limited to undertaking routine trust administration services, such as collecting income, preparing accounts and possibly checking the terms of the trust arrangement. On the basis that this type of work is part of the normal and longstanding regulated activities of law firms, we do not consider that this type of work [is a] breach'

- 'A law firm is instructed by the landlord of a new development of commercial properties to prepare the lease agreements. The firm is also instructed to receive, and hold in client account, the rental deposits that are paid by the tenants. These will be held [until] the lease comes to an end and any conditions e g dilapidations are met. The receipt and holding of commercial rent deposits in client account would not, in itself, [be a] breach …'

- 'Where solicitors are acting as attorney under an LPA … they act on the instructions of the donor and in the specific circumstances set out in the power of attorney. In this situation receiving or holding the donor's money into client account and making payments out of it, would not give rise to a breach …'[5]

Receipts and payments from and to clients and third parties should be scrutinised carefully to ensure that rule 3.3 is not offended. The warning notice recommends that throughout the retainer solicitors should ask themselves why they are being asked to receive funds and for what purpose. They should also always ask themselves why they are being asked to make a payment and why the client cannot make or receive payment directly itself.

If a solicitor allows a client account to be used as a banking facility, there is an additional risk that the solicitor is assisting money laundering. The original warning notice of December 2014 stated that risk factors of money laundering included the payment of substantial sums to others, including family members, or to corporate entities, particularly overseas, since there is no reason why the client could not receive the money into its own account and transfer it from there.

In a publication, 'Solicitors and investment fraud' of December 2016, the SRA notified the profession of its concern that use of a client account as a banking facility may be a hallmark of fraudulent or otherwise dubious investment schemes. Similarly, in a 2017 warning notice on investment schemes, the SRA warned that breaches of the rule prohibiting banking facilities can provide fraudsters with credibility and the facility to transfer investors' money through a bank account.[6] Solicitors have received significant fines at the SDT for agreeing to act as facilitator to dubious schemes.

In a nutshell, practices which were unremarkable a decade or two ago (e g the use of client account to settle commercial debts owed by the client to third parties) may well now fall foul of the rule. Practitioners should prudently repay client funds as soon as possible following completion of a retainer, and consider whether to do so during a hiatus in instructions. A delay in returning funds promptly could be a breach of rule 3.3 as well as a breach of the rule 2.5 requirement for prompt payment out of client money at the end of a case. Likewise, solicitors should be very cautious about paying client money out of client account to anyone other than the client, and, if in doubt, should take specialist advice as the risks in this area are considerable.

---

1   See, for example, *Langford, Howard Kennedy and others*, 11686–2017.
2   The Solicitors' Accounts Rules 1998, which continued in force until October 2011, contained no original provision about a 'banking facility'. In 2004 in *SRA v Wood and Burdett* the SDT imposed severe sanctions on the two partners in a firm that was using its client account to offer a cheque-cashing service to all and sundry in Merseyside, clients and non-clients, to 'diversify' the business. In consequence, within a short time a guidance note was added to the 1998 Rules making express reference to *Wood and Burdett* and stating for the first time that: 'Solicitors should not … provide banking facilities through a client account'. The 1998 Rules were to be 'interpreted in the light of the notes' so there remained no specific rule until October 2011. The reference to *Wood and Burdett* meant that the facts which might be regarded by practitioners to involve the provision of a banking facility were fairly extreme.
3   *Patel v SRA* [2012] EWHC 3373 (Admin) and *Fuglers v SRA* [2014] EWHC 179 (Admin).
4   The updated warning notice was listed in Annex B to the SRA's August 2018 application to the LSB for approval of the new regulatory arrangements. It was included as guidance, which is applicable to the new regulatory arrangements.
5   See SRA warning notice, 'Improper use of client account as a banking facility', SRA, 18 December 2014, updated 6 August 2018 (at **APPENDIX 9**) and 'Case studies: Improper use of client account as a banking facility', SRA, 6 August 2018. The examples in the case studies and warning notice are fact specific and should be read in full before making any decisions on rule 3.3 on the basis of comparisons with them. See also *Fuglers v SRA* [2014] EWHC 179 (Admin).
6   'Investment schemes (including conveyancing): warning notice', SRA, 23 June 2017.

Rule 4: Client money must be kept separate

6.30

Client money must be kept separate

4.1 You keep *client money* separate from money belonging to the *authorised body*.

4.2 You ensure that you allocate promptly any funds from *mixed payments* you receive to the correct *client account* or business account.

4.3 Where you are holding *client money* and some or all of that money will be used to pay your *costs*:

(a) you must give a bill of *costs*, or other written notification of the *costs* incurred, to the *client* or the paying party;

(b) this must be done before you transfer any *client money* from a *client account* to make the payment; and

(c) any such payment must be for the specific sum identified in the bill of *costs*, or other written notification of the *costs* incurred, and covered by the amount held for the particular *client* or third party.

Keeping office and client money separate

6.31

The rule 4.1 requirement to keep office and client money in separate accounts does not apply if the only client money which a firm holds is money on account of costs and the firm relies on the exception in rule 2.2. For commentary on rule 2.2 see **6.22**.

Mixed payments

6.32

The SRA Glossary defines a 'mixed payment' as 'a payment that includes both client money and non-client money'.

By rule 4.2, the detailed requirements on initial allocation of, and time limits for separation of, mixed payments previously seen in rules 17 and 18 of the SRA Accounts Rules 2011 are removed and are replaced with: 'you allocate promptly ... to the correct client account or business account'.

Rule 4.2 does not prevent mixed payments from initially being placed in an office account. In the application to the LSB for approval of the new regulatory arrangements, the SRA said:

'We did receive objections to this proposal, which were concerned about this being an unnecessary removal of client protection and about the risk that firms will use client funds to manipulate their cash position. However we were not persuaded. If a firm were to use client money to manipulate its cash position, it is likely it would be in breach of our rules. Firms will still be required to move money between accounts promptly and comply with all our other rules. This includes the requirement to act in a client's best interest to not retain funds for longer than necessary and to act with honesty and integrity.'[1]

Under the Solicitors' Accounts Rules 1998, some legal aid practitioners faced disciplinary proceedings in circumstances where the firm operated its office account beyond an agreed overdraft limit. LAA payments for costs including counsel's fees had to be paid into office account under those rules, and the bank enforced the overdraft limit after receipt of the LAA costs and refused to permit the practitioners to pay counsel's fees. The SRA then prosecuted the solicitors for failure to pay counsel's fees.[2] A similar problem could occur under rule 4.2. If a firm operates its office account beyond an agreed overdraft limit, and places a mixed payment into office account, there is always a risk that the bank will enforce the overdraft limit and refuse to transfer the whole of the client element of a mixed payment out of the overdrawn office account. In such circumstances, a decision to place a mixed payment in office account could not be in the client's best interests, and would carry the risk of disciplinary proceedings.

1 'Application for the approval of regulatory arrangements', SRA, August 2018, para 244.
2 See for example *SRA v Dhaliwal*, 9397–2005.

Payment of costs out of client account

6.33

By rule 4.3 it is obligatory to deliver a bill of costs or other written notification of costs incurred before transferring money from client account to office account in respect of costs.

As noted earlier,[1] there is an inconsistency between the rule 2.1 definition of client money (which provides that money held on account of costs is client money until delivery of a bill) and the rule 4.3 right to transfer money held on account of costs after written notification of the costs (and before delivery of a bill). It is submitted that rule 4.3 can be followed, and costs transferred from client to office account, after giving written notification of costs, even if a bill has not yet been delivered. However, the position is unclear. For commentary on the issue, see **6.19**.

Rule 4.3(c) provides that a firm may only transfer 'the specific sum identified in the bill' and 'covered by the amount held for the particular client or third party'. That appears to suggest that the firm can only transfer the exact sum due as identified in the bill, and not a lesser sum, even if the firm holds some funds that could be applied towards payment. In light of the SRA's expressed intention to provide flexibility, that cannot have been intended. In view of the reference to 'other written notification of the costs incurred' it should be acceptable to make a part payment after giving the client advance written notification of a part payment out of the costs incurred. However, the position is again unclear.

The words 'covered by the amount held' mean that sufficient funds must be held for the client, and that the funds are held for the purposes of payment of costs. Costs cannot be paid out of client money held for a specific purpose unrelated to a firm's costs.

It is not uncommon for solicitors to face disciplinary proceedings for making 'round sum transfers' from client account to office account at month end to pay salaries, in the hope that the round sum transfer can then be allocated to month end bills which are in the course of being issued, or bills which could be issued at some time in the future to cover the amount transferred. Rule 4.3 makes it clear that this practice is unacceptable, and that any transfer must directly correlate to a specific sum payable by a specific client after the client has received notice of the amount payable.

When transferring costs, rule 5.1 must be taken into account. Rule 5.1 states that a firm can only withdraw client money from a client account 'for the purpose for which it is being held', or following receipt of instructions or receipt of SRA authorisation, or in prescribed circumstances (of which there are presently none). It is possible that a number of different types of client receipts which have traditionally been used to pay costs, such as completion monies on a property sale and damages obtained on a settlement, are not (in the client's eyes at least) held for the purpose of payment of costs. It may be advisable for firms to include a term in retainer letters which permits payment of costs out of any monies held unless there is an express agreement that the funds will be held for a different purpose.

The SRA Accounts Rules 2019 do not contain any specific rules on the timing of costs transfers from client account to office account after delivery of a bill. That contrasts with the SRA Accounts Rules 2011, which contained a mandatory requirement that money earmarked for costs had to be transferred out of client account within 14 days.[2] The removal of that mandatory 14-day period does not mean that there can be delays in making transfers. Money held for costs ceases to be client money (and becomes office money) after a bill has been delivered (see rule 2.1(d)), and money belonging to the firm must be kept separate from client money (see rule 4.1). In a busy office with a large number of month end bills it can be a time-consuming task for cashiers to have to identify quickly the bills which have to be paid out of money held on account, and in a large office the COFA needs to ensure cashiers have sufficient time to carry out that task. The removal of the 14-day time period means that it is now uncertain how quickly the task needs to be carried out.

For delays in payment of counsel's fees after the fees have been transferred to the office account, see the commentary at **6.21**.

1   See **6.19**.
2   Rule 17.3 of the SRA Accounts Rules 2011.

Rule 5:Withdrawals from client account

6.34

Withdrawals from client account

5.1   You only withdraw *client money* from a *client account*:

(a)   for the purpose for which it is being held;

(b)   following receipt of instructions from the *client*, or the third party for whom the money is held; or

(c)   on the *SRA's* prior written authorisation or in *prescribed* circumstances.

5.2   You appropriately authorise and supervise all withdrawals made from a *client account*.

5.3   You only withdraw *client money* from a *client account* if sufficient funds are held on behalf of that specific *client* or third party to make the payment.

Authorisation for withdrawals

6.35

Rule 5.1 sets out the circumstances in which money can be withdrawn from client account.

The SRA Glossary defines 'prescribed' to mean 'prescribed by the SRA from time to time', and the reference in rule 5.1(c) to withdrawals permitted in 'prescribed circumstances' is therefore a reference to withdrawals permitted in circumstances prescribed by the SRA. At the date of this edition, there are no prescribed circumstances.

For commentary on the entitlement to pay costs out of client account see **6.33**. For commentary on clearing dormant balances see **6.26**.

Internal procedures for withdrawals from client account

6.36

Rule 5.2 requires firms to authorise and supervise appropriately all withdrawals from client account. That is a brief rule which is consistent with the SRA's aim of providing firms with the flexibility to manage their accounts systems in a manner which is suitable for the firm's particular practice. All responsible firms will already have addressed these issues in detail, and decided who is best suited and qualified to authorise and supervise withdrawals from client account.

The SRA Accounts Rules 2011 contained some (limited) guidance notes on factors which should be taken into account when deciding who should have authority to make withdrawals. The guidance, which was at note (i) to rule 21 of the SRA Accounts Rules 2011, is of general application and provides useful groundwork for any system:

'A firm should select suitable people to authorise withdrawals from the client account. Firms will wish to consider whether any employee should be able to sign on client account, and whether signing rights should be given to all managers of the practice or limited to those managers directly involved in providing legal services. Someone who has no day-to-day involvement in the business of the practice is unlikely to be regarded as a suitable signatory because of the lack of proximity to client matters. An appropriate understanding of the requirements of the rules is essential ...'

When considering withdrawal authorisations, firms should remember that cyber-crime needs to be borne in mind. The SRA has issued a series of notices warning firms that cybercrime is a priority risk, that the problem is increasing and that new scams are emerging all the time.[1] It is advisable for firms to review their systems for client account withdrawals periodically, taking account of the publications issued by the SRA and the Law Society highlighting the cybercrime risks faced by the profession. Staff training is also an important part of the authorisation system. In a publication on IT security and keeping money safe, the SRA stated that most cybercrimes target people rather than systems and that the best defence is to learn, and to train staff to recognise common scams.[2]

All of the partners (as well as the firm) are responsible for ensuring that appropriate systems are in place (see rule 1.2) and the COFA must take all reasonable steps to ensure the partners and the firm comply with that obligation.[3]

1   See, for example, 'SRA news: cybercrime issues continue', 28 March 2017, and SRA Risk Outlook 2018/19.
2   'IT security: keeping information and money safe', SRA, December 2016.
3   Paragraph 9.2 of the Code for Firms.

Teeming and lading – rule 5.3

6.37

Using a client's money only for that client's purposes is a fundamental requirement. The Tribunal's caseload is materially increased by those solicitors who, when something goes wrong (either by miscalculation or through a transactional problem), and more money is needed for the client than is available, simply overdraw that client's individual ledger, using the substantial balance available in the general client bank account. This invariably means that the funds of one or more clients are being used, without their knowledge, for someone else's benefit. Effecting transfers between the clients' ledgers in these circumstances to 'cover' the shortage is a breach of rule 5.3. This is teeming and lading – robbing Peter to pay Paul. It does not overcome the fundamental problem – that there is an overall shortage of client funds. It is not uncommon to see this practice begin on a small scale before being repeated at ever reducing intervals such that it becomes very difficult to keep accurate books of account and remedy the issues. The client account shortfall tends to increase. Using client money in this way may lead to allegations of acting without integrity or dishonesty, intervention by the SRA, and amount to a criminal offence.

Rule 30 of the Solicitors' Accounts Rules 1998 (replaced by rule 27 of the SRA Accounts Rules 2011) was introduced in an attempt to inhibit this practice: it was not permissible to make a private (ie non-institutional) loan of one client's funds to another, even by means of a paper transfer between ledgers, except with the prior written authority of both clients. That rule has now gone.

Although the rule has been removed, it would be prudent to ensure that, before any private loan is made of one client's funds to another, there is prior written authority from both clients, that both clients have first taken independent legal advice and that the independent advice is documented. It would also be prudent to consider whether a client-to-client transfer in respect of the loan would breach rule 3.3 relating to banking facilities.[1]

1   For rule 3.3 and banking facilities see **6.29**.

Rule 6: Duty to correct breaches upon discovery

6.38

Duty to correct breaches upon discovery

6.1 You correct any breaches of these rules promptly upon discovery. Any money improperly withheld or withdrawn from a *client account* must be immediately paid into the account or replaced as appropriate.

6.39

Rule 6.1 upgrades the previous rule 7 of the SRA Accounts Rules 2011, by requiring client account shortfalls to be remedied immediately, rather than promptly. Any other breach of the Rules must be remedied promptly upon discovery.

The rule requires the replacement of effectively any client account shortfall howsoever caused, using a partner's own money if necessary. This duty falls on all partners in the practice, and not just on the individual causing the breach or who was, for example, the partner responsible for supervising the person at fault.

For this reason, the Accounts Rules effectively require all partners to know what is going on in their own accounts department; they will be personally responsible for putting right any problem, with their own money. While accounting functions are invariably delegated to non-solicitors in all but the tiniest practices, the Accounts Rules require effective oversight at management level, for example, in checking client balances; that the five-weekly (monthly in practice) reconciliation has been carried out, and is understood; and that any information given by it which prompts action is acted upon. In practice, the larger the firm, the less likely it is that the SRA will, upon discovery of a sanctionable breach, take regulatory action against all of its partners, preferring instead to sanction the firm and those that it deems are most culpable.

Rule 7: Payment of interest

6.40

Payment of interest

7.1 You account to *clients* or third parties for a fair sum of *interest* on any *client money* held by you on their behalf.

7.2 You may by a written agreement come to a different arrangement with the *client* or the third party for whom the money is held as to the payment of *interest*, but you must provide sufficient information to enable them to give informed consent.

6.41

Rule 7.1 imposes a general requirement to account to clients and third parties for a fair sum of interest on money held on client account.

Rule 7.2 enables a firm to agree with its client not to account for interest, but the client must have sufficient information to give informed consent and the agreement must be in writing. When entering into such an agreement, the managers must have regard to the Principles, including the duties to act with independence (principle 3) and in the client's best interests (principle 7). As regards the informed consent, the SRA has stated:

> 'The level of information that will be sufficient will depend on the circumstances. It is for a firm to satisfy themselves that they have given the client the opportunity to give informed consent. The prominence and the ease of access to the information will be important in determining this.'[1]

1   'Application for the approval of regulatory arrangements', SRA, August 2018, para 246.

6.42

The SRA Accounts Rules 2011 required a firm to have a policy for payment of interest. Rule 22.3 of the SRA Accounts Rules 2011 provided:

> '*You* must have a written policy on the payment of *interest*, which seeks to provide a fair outcome. The terms of the policy must be drawn to the attention of the *client* at the outset of a retainer, unless it is inappropriate to do so in the circumstances.'

That rule has been removed from the SRA Accounts Rules 2019. However, that does not mean that there is no longer a requirement for an interest policy. Paragraph 8.8 of the Code for Individuals and paragraph 7.1(c) of the Code for Firms require publicity relating to circumstances in which interest is payable to clients to be accurate and not misleading. Although it is not apparent from the wording of those rules, SRA commentary assumes that the rules impose an obligation to have a clear interest policy. The SRA has said:

> 'We have removed the requirement [in the Accounts Rules] to have a published interest policy. This duplicates with the new standard 8.8 in the code for individuals and does not comprise a change in policy. Firms are still required to have a clear interest policy in place. The requirement to have an interest policy also applies to firms through rule 7.1(c) in the Code of Conduct for Firms'.[1]

Rules 24 and 25 of the Solicitors' Accounts Rules 1998 contained detailed provisions on the circumstances in which interest should be paid, and the amount of the interest, including a £20 *de minimis* provision.[2] There is no reason why firms should not adopt a policy which bears a close resemblance to those rules if that is fair having regard to the nature of the practice.

1   'Application for the approval of regulatory arrangements', SRA, August 2018, para 245.
2   The Solicitors' Accounts Rules 1998 are available on the internet.

Rule 8: Client accounting systems and controls

6.43

Client accounting systems and controls

8.1 You keep and maintain accurate, contemporaneous, and chronological records to:

(a) record in client ledgers identified by the *client's* name and an appropriate description of the matter to which they relate:

(i) all receipts and payments which *client money* on the client side of the client ledger account;

(ii) all receipts and payments which are not *client money* and bills of *costs* including transactions through the *authorised body's* accounts on the business side of the client ledger account;

(b) maintain a list of all the balances shown by the client ledger accounts of the liabilities to *clients* (and third parties), with a running total of the balances; and

(c) provide a cash book showing a running total of all transactions through *client accounts* held or operated by you.

8.2 You obtain, at least every five weeks, statements from *banks, building societies* and other financial institutions for all *client accounts* and business accounts held or operated by you.

8.3 You complete at least every five weeks, for all *client accounts* held or operated by you, a reconciliation of the *bank* or *building society* statement balance with the cash book balance and the client ledger total, a record of which must be signed off by the *COFA* or a *manager* of the firm. You should promptly investigate and resolve any differences shown by the reconciliation.

8.4 You keep readily accessible a central record of all bills or other written notifications of *costs* given by you.

6.44

The obligation to have and to maintain proper accounting systems generally needs no explanation. Firms should periodically review their systems, engaging external support where necessary. External support, for example, in the development and maintenance of systems may help to demonstrate compliance, or at least avoid a finding of culpability.

The general obligation is not expressly referred to in the Accounts Rules. It is set out in paragraph 2.1 of the Code for Firms, which requires the firm to have effective governance structures, arrangements, systems and controls in place to ensure that the firm complies with all the regulatory arrangements including the Accounts Rules. It is also reflected in the obligation on the COFA under paragraph 9.2 of the Code for Firms to take all reasonable steps to ensure that the firm, its managers and employees comply with the obligations imposed on them by the Accounts Rules. The general obligation is also referred to in the introduction to the SRA Accounts Rules 2019.

It is important not to overlook the requirement for internal controls. Firms should periodically audit compliance with their systems, not only examining the firm's books of account, but additionally checking that staff are following procedures. Evidence of such audits being carried out should be retained to demonstrate to the SRA that controls are in place to limit the risk of systemic breaches.

6.45

One issue, which is both a requirement of the SRA Accounts Rules 2019 and a matter of business management, deserves special mention: it is accepted that errors will occur in the best ordered systems and one of the most effective controls in ensuring that mistakes are identified is a bank reconciliation that satisfies rule 8.3. This compares the total of all individual client ledger balances with the client cashbook and the amount shown on the bank statement or statements, shows any difference between any one of those three components and any other, and reconciles that difference. If this is done properly, most significant errors will be identified – certainly most types of client account shortage should be immediately spotted. The bank reconciliation is important; it is not a tedious bureaucratic requirement, but an essential management tool designed to enable principals who are not concerned with the day-to-day minutiae of the accounts to be informed of any serious underlying problems.

Managers should check reconciliation statements and their supporting documents carefully,[1] investigating any references to 'balancing items' or to a 'suspense account'.[2] If unexplained differences cannot be reconciled swiftly, a protective payment into client account may be necessary, along with an entry in the firm's risk register, and a self-report to the SRA.

Perhaps surprisingly, it is not uncommon during an SRA forensic investigation to discover that reconciliations are not being performed correctly. Some reporting accountants appear to believe that they are doing firms a favour by not pointing out errors. Errors can and will occur; the key to avoiding regulatory action is spotting them swiftly and taking appropriate remedial action.

The SRA Accounts Rules 2019 continue to require regular reconciliations and the importance of this is emphasised by a new provision (rule 8.3) that every reconciliation must be 'signed off' by a manager or the COFA.

The importance of the monthly reconciliations is also emphasised by the SRA's explanation for retaining the rule in the Accounts Rules, despite the drive to simplify them and reduce their length:

> 'We have retained the requirement to obtain bank statements and do reconciliations every five weeks (at a minimum) as we consider that both are important mechanisms to ensure firms, their reporting accountants and our supervisory and enforcement functions can check compliance'.[3]

1   The firm must maintain a list of all individual client ledger balances under rule 8.1(b). The individual balances, which will be included in the supporting documents, as well as the running total, need to be checked. It is not permissible to offset a credit balance (money held) for one client against a debit balance (money owed) for another client.
2   Temporary use of a suspense account is acceptable, and is required to record unidentified receipts, but it would be imprudent to retain unallocated items on a suspense account for successive reconciliation periods unless exceptional circumstances apply and are documented.
3   'Application for the approval of regulatory arrangements', SRA, August 2018, para 242.

6.46

Rule 8.1 introduces a new phrase which states the firm's records must be 'accurate, contemporaneous and chronological'. The SRA has not offered guidance to smaller firms on how often postings should be updated. The greater the level of transactions passing through client account, the more likely it will be deemed that records should be updated daily.

Rules 9 to 11: Operation of joint accounts, operation of a client's own account and TPMAs

6.47

PART 3: DEALINGS WITH OTHER MONEY BELONGING TO CLIENTS OR THIRD PARTIES

Operation of joint accounts

9.1   If, when acting in a *client's* matter, you hold or receive money jointly with the *client* or a third party, Part 2 of these rules does not apply save for:

(a) rule 8.2 – statements from *banks, building societies* and other financial institutions;

(b) rule 8.4 – bills and notifications of *costs*.

Operation of a client's own account

10.1   If, in the course of practice, you operate a *client's* own account as signatory, Part 2 of these rules does not apply save for:

(a) rule 8.2 – statements from *banks, building societies* and other financial institutions;

(b) rule 8.3 – reconciliations;

(c) rule 8.4 – bills and notifications of *costs*.

Third party managed accounts

11.1   You may enter into arrangements with a *client* to use a *third party managed account* for the purpose of receiving payments from or on behalf of, or making payments to or on behalf of, the *client* in respect of *regulated services* delivered by you to the *client*, only if:

(a)   use of the account does not result in you receiving or holding the *client's* money; and

(b)   you take reasonable steps to ensure, before accepting instructions, that the *client* is informed of and understands:

(i)   the terms of the contractual arrangements relating to the use of

> the *third party managed account*, and in particular how any *fees* for use of the *third party managed account* will be paid and who will bear them; and
>
> (ii) the *client's* right to terminate the agreement and dispute payment requests made by you.
>
> 11.2 You obtain regular statements from the provider of the *third party managed account* and ensure that these accurately reflect all transactions on the account.

Rules 9 and 10

6.48

Rules 9 and 10 are self explanatory.

Third party managed accounts

6.49

The SRA has defined a third party managed account (TPMA) as follows: 'We define a TPMA as an account where a third party (a payment service[s] provider) holds money … [for] two … transacting parties, … a law firm and their client'.[1] In conveyancing (for example), on the purchase of a property, the payment services provider would open an account for the client, receive the purchase monies from the client (or the client's mortgagee), obtain authority from the client to operate the account on the basis of the solicitor's instructions and pay the deposit and completion monies to the vendor when directed to do so by the solicitor.

A TPMA provides an opportunity to carry out work such as conveyancing without the need to operate a client account. That would reduce the firm's overheads and avoid the regulatory risks of operating a client account. If a client account is not operated, a firm could rely on the rule 2.2 exemption to pay money on account of costs into office account.[2]

During the consultation for the SRA Accounts Rules 2019, a number of respondents said they were concerned a TPMA would not provide the firm with the level of control over funds needed for a transaction. Some others said they would wait to see what products the market develops before deciding whether the TPMA is a viable option.[3]

1 'Application for the approval of regulatory arrangements', SRA, August 2018, para 293.
2 For the rule 2.2 exemption relating to money on account, see **6.22**.
3 'Application for the approval of regulatory arrangements', SRA, August 2018, paras 294–295.

6.50

There was nothing in the 2011 rules to prevent the use of a TPMA and, as money placed by a client into a TPMA operated by a payment services provider is not client money, there were no professional rules directly controlling the use of TPMAs. The SRA produced an Ethics guidance note in December 2017, updated in July 2019, on the use of TPMAs and rule 11 has been introduced to control the manner in which firms use TPMAs.

6.51

The Ethics guidance note states that the solicitor should make sure the payment services provider who operates the TPMA is regulated by the Financial Conduct Authority (FCA) either as an authorised/EEA authorised payment institution or as a small payment institution. The TPMA must be an account held at a bank or building society operated as an escrow account (the third party receives and disburses money on your and your client's behalf). The solicitor should take reasonable steps to make sure that the client understands the arrangement with the payment services provider before it is entered into, including in particular how their money will be held and how the transaction will work,[1] their right to terminate the agreement[2] and dispute payment requests by the solicitor, responsibility for the costs associated with the agreement,[3] the fact that complaints should be made to the FCA in accordance with their complaints procedure, and that the regulatory protections that apply to TPMAs are different from those that apply to client money held in a firm's client account.[4] The solicitor should also comply with the obligations to safeguard client money and have suitable arrangements in place for the use and monitoring of TPMAs, including monitoring the transactions on the account and keeing appropriate records. The SRA expects to be notified when a firm enters into an arrangement with, or ceases to use a TPMA provider, and has produced a form for this purpose, current 'FA9' a link to which is provided in the Ethics guidance note.[5]

1   Paragraph 8.6 of the Code for Individuals.
2   Rule 11.1(b)(ii) of the Accounts Rules.
3   Rule 11.1(b)(i) of the Accounts Rules.
4   Paragraph 8.11 of the Code for Indivduals.
5   SRA Ethics guidance, 'Third-party-managed accounts', issued 6 December 2017, updated 4 July 2019.

6.52

Rules 11.1 and 11.2 impose regulations on the use of TPMAs which replicate the core advice in the Ethics guidance note by requiring the solicitor to take reasonable steps to ensure the client understands the contractual arrangements with the payment services provider, to obtain statements on the TPMA and to ensure the statements reflect the transactions on the account.

Rule 11.1 does not expressly state that the payment services provider must be regulated by the FCA as an authorised/EEA authorised payment institution or a small payment institution. Rule 11.1 is instead permissive. It states that the firm may use a third party managed account; 'third party managed account' is defined in the SRA Glossary as 'an account held at a bank or building society in the name of a third party which is an authorised payment institution, [or] a small payment institution that has chosen to implement safeguarding arrangement[s] in accordance with the Payment Services Regulations or an EEA authorised payment institution (as each [is] defined in the Payment Services Regulations) regulated by the FCA, in which monies are owned beneficially by the third party, and which is operated upon terms agreed between the third party, you and your client as an escrow payment service'.

Despite the permissive nature of rule 11.1, the SRA has made the following comments on rule 11, which make it clear that the SRA expects firms to only use TPMAs which fall within the Glossary definition:

'Our approach is to allow firms to use a TPMA if:

- The TPMA is either an authorised payment institution ... and, as a result has mandatory safeguarding arrangement[s], or is a small payment institution ... which has adopted voluntary safeguarding arrangements

- The firm can demonstrate that it has suitable arrangements for the implementation, use and monitoring of TPMAs. For example that appropriate information is provided to clients and appropriate internal controls are in place ...

... We will restrict the use of TPMAs to those operated by payment services providers that are regulated by the FCA under the Payment Services Regulations 2017'.[1]

The SRA has also stated that it does not intend to restrict the type of legal services which can be carried out with TPMAs but that it expects firms to carry out an assessment of the suitability of the provider's product for the client in the circumstances of the case.[2]

1   'Application for the approval of regulatory arrangements', SRA, August 2018, paras 300 and 303.
2   'Application for the approval of regulatory arrangements', SRA, August 2018, para 311.

Rule 12: Obtaining and delivery of accountants' reports

6.53

PART 4: ACCOUNTANTS' REPORTS AND STORAGE AND RETENTION OF ACCOUNTING RECORDS

Obtaining and delivery of accountants' reports

12.1   If you have, at any time during an *accounting period*, held or received *client money*, or operated a joint account or a *client's* own account as signatory, you must:

(a)   obtain an accountant's report for that *accounting period* within six months of the end of the period; and

(b)   deliver it to the *SRA* within six months of the end of the *accounting period* if the accountant's report is qualified to show a failure to comply with these rules, such that money belonging to *clients* or third parties is, or has been, or is likely to be placed, at risk.

12.2   You are not required to obtain an accountant's report if:

(a)   all of the *client money* held or received during an *accounting period* is money received from the Legal Aid Agency; or

(b)   in the *accounting period*, the statement or passbook balance of *client money* you have held or received does not exceed:

(i)   an average of £10,000; and

(ii)   a maximum of £250,000,

or the equivalent in foreign currency.

12.3   In rule 12.2 above a 'statement or passbook balance' is the total balance of:

(a)   all *client accounts* held or operated by you; and

(b)   any joint accounts and *clients'* own accounts operated by you,

as shown by the statements obtained under rule 8.2.

12.4   The *SRA* may require you to obtain or deliver an accountant's report to the *SRA* on reasonable notice if you cease to operate as an *authorised body* and to hold or operate a *client account*, or the *SRA* considers that it is otherwise in the public interest to do so.

12.5   You ensure that any report obtained under this rule is prepared and signed by an accountant who is a member of one of the *chartered accountancy bodies* and who is, or works for, a registered auditor.

12.6   The *SRA* may disqualify an accountant from preparing a report for the purposes of this rule if:

(a)   the accountant has been found guilty by their professional body of professional misconduct or equivalent; or

(b)   the *SRA* is satisfied that the accountant has failed to exercise due care and skill in the preparation of a report under these rules.

12.7   The *SRA* may specify from time to time matters that you must ensure are incorporated into the terms on which an accountant is engaged.

12.8   You must provide to an accountant preparing a report under these rules:

(a)   details of all accounts held or operated by you in connection with your practice at any *bank*, *building society* or other financial institution at any time during the *accounting period* to which the report relates; and

(b)   all other information and documentation that the accountant requires to enable completion of their report.

12.9   The accountant must complete and sign their report in the *prescribed* form.

6.54

Rules 12.1 to 12.3 set out the circumstances in which a firm must obtain an accountant's report, and if necessary deliver it to the SRA. The requirements are more or less unchanged from the latest version of the SRA Accounts Rules 2011, save in relation to the type of qualified reports which need to be delivered to the SRA. Under the SRA Accounts Rules 2011, all qualified reports were required to be delivered to the SRA. In contrast, by rule 12.1(b) of the SRA Accounts Rules 2019, firms are only required to deliver qualified reports which 'show a failure to comply with these rules, such that money belonging to clients or third parties is, or has been, or is likely to be placed, at risk'.

The new rule avoids the need to deliver qualified reports on minor breaches but it calls for a difficult value judgement as to when third party monies were, or were likely to be, at risk.

The SRA produced an Ethics guidance note in August 2017, updated in June 2019, on planning for and completing an accountant's report. The note indicates that the guidance is designed to help 'assess what factors might lead the accountant to decide that the report should be qualified and therefore submitted to use for further consideration of the risks posed', but indicates that reporting accountants should exercise their professional judgement when deciding whether a report needs to be qualified.[1]

The accountant is under a statutory duty to make an immediate report to the SRA if the accountant discovers evidence of fraud or theft in relation to the client account or another account operated by the firm, or if the accountant obtains information which is likely to be of material significance in determining whether a solicitor is a fit and proper person to hold client money.[2]

Subject to the statutory duty, the SRA has issued the following guidance on when it expects a report to be qualified and delivered:[3]

- It only expects reports to be qualified where there has been a significant breach of the Accounts Rules, such that money belonging to clients or third parties is, has been or may be placed at risk.

- Breaches from administrative errors are not likely to be significant, but still could be if they are persistent, derive from a lack of controls or breakdown of existing controls, and have put client money at risk.

- If the reporting accountant consider that their work has been limited in scope to the extent that they feel unable to make the declarations required on the accountant's report form, then they should qualify the report on that basis and make a report.

- When exercising their professional judgment, the accountant's assessment should be based on an understanding of the seriousness of all the risks posed in the context of the firm's size and complexity, areas of work, systems and controls, compliance histort and the likely impact on the firm and its clients if money were to be misused or not accounted for.

- The presence of one or more serious factors is likely to lead to a qualification, including, a significant and/or unreplaced shortfall, evidence of disregard for the safety of client money and assets, actual or suspected fraud or dishonesty by the managers or employees of the firm that may impact upon the safety of money belonging to clients or third parties, accounting records unavailable or significantly deficient, bank accounts/ledgers failing to include reference to a client, failing to provide documentation requested by the accountant, client account bank reconciliations not carried out, client account improperly used as a banking facility and any other significant breaches not already reported to the SRA by firms and their compliance officers.

- The presence of one or more moderate factors may lead to a qualification depending upon context, including, a significant, fully replaced client money shortfall, actual or suspected fraud by third parties that have impacted or may impact on the safety of client money, unreported serious breaches, accounting records that are insufficient, unreliable or not retained for six years, poor control environment, inadequate performance or review of client account bank reconciliations, longstanding residual balances due to clients and improper use of suspense accounts.

The SRA's guidance note also schedules a large number of 'key risk areas' for checking by the reporting accountants.

When deciding whether to deliver a qualified report, it would be prudent to err on the side of caution, and, if in doubt, to deliver.

Firms should ensure that any qualifications noted on an accountant's report are investigated swiftly, and any breaches remedied.

The SRA also expects reporting accountants to report to them the termination of an accountant's appointment where this is based on their intention to issue a qualified accountant's report.[4]

1   SRA Ethics guidance, 'Planning for and completing an accountant's report', issued 1 August 2017, updated June 2019.
2   Section 34(9) of SA 1974.
3   SRA Ethics guidance, 'Planning for and completing an accountant's report', issued 1 August 2017, updated June 2019.
4   Ibid.

6.55

There is no longer a positive requirement to deliver an accountant's report on ceasing to hold client money.[1] However, rule 12.4 empowers the SRA to require a firm to deliver an accountant's report on reasonable notice if a firm ceases to operate as an authorised body and to hold or operate a client account, or the SRA considers that it is otherwise in the public interest to do so.

The 'cease to hold' rule was changed because the old rule unnecessarily required a firm to file a cease to hold accountant's report when the firm changed its legal status from one form to another without cessation of the provision of legal services. It is not yet known whether the SRA will routinely ask for cease to hold reports whenever the underlying business is closed down. The SRA has commented that it will require a cease to hold report for client money if it believes it 'necessary', and has given the example of *'when a firm shuts down and closes its client account on a case-by-case basis'*.[2]

1   Rule 33.5 of the SRA Accounts Rules 2011 required 'cease to hold' reports.
2   Application for the approval of regulatory arrangements', SRA, August 2018, para 254.

6.56

The SRA Accounts Rules 2011 contained guidance notes with examples of circumstances when the SRA is likely to consider it in the public interest to require an accountant's report. The following examples continue to be relevant:

- when no report has been delivered but the SRA has reason to believe that a report should have been delivered;

- when a report has been delivered but the SRA has reason to believe that it may be inaccurate;

- when the conduct of the solicitor gives the SRA reason to believe that it would be appropriate to require delivery of a report;

- when the conduct of the solicitor gives the SRA reason to believe that it would be appropriate to require frequent delivery of reports (eg every six months).[1]

1   Note (iii) to rule 32A.2 of the SRA Accounts Rules 2011.

6.57

Rule 12.5 restricts those who may prepare reports to members of various accountants' professional bodies who are also registered auditors, or their employees.

Before engaging an accountant, a firm can check with the SRA whether the accountant has been disqualified from preparing a report. Rule 12.6 empowers the SRA to disqualify an accountant from preparing a report in certain circumstances. If the SRA is aware of a firm which has recently obtained an accountant's report from an accountant who is disqualified, there is a risk that the SRA will require delivery of an accountant's report under rule 12.4 and that the firm undergoes an SRA forensic investigation.

6.58

The stringent provisions of rule 12.8 govern the information and documents the firm must provide, including details of all accounts held at banks, building societies and other financial institutions operated by the firm during the relevant accounting period, and any other information the accountant requires for completion of the report.

Rule 13: Storage and retention of accounting records

6.59

13.1 You must store all *accounting records* securely and retain these for at least six years.

6.60

The SRA Glossary defines 'accounting records' to mean 'all reconciliations, bank and building society statements (paper or electronic), original passbooks, signed letters of engagement with reporting accountants, the accountants' reports (whether qualified or not), any client's written instructions to hold client money other than in accordance with these rules, records and documents, including electronic records, relating to any third party managed accounts and any other records or documents necessary to show compliance with the SRA Accounts Rules'.

CHAPTER 7

Compliance officers (COLPs and COFAs)

7.1

Compliance officers for legal practice (COLPs) and compliance officers for finance and administration (COFAs) have their origins in the Legal Services Act (LSA) 2007 which requires alternative business structures (ABSs) licensed under Part 5 of that Act to have individuals to fulfil the roles and to perform the duties of Head of Legal Practice (HOLP) and Head of Finance and Administration (HOFA).[1]

The Solicitors Regulation Authority (SRA) elected to extend the concept to all firms, and to create the roles of COLP and COFA with effect from 1 January 2013. Since then all SRA regulated practices, whether licensed as an ABS or not, must have a COLP and a COFA (who may be the same person, and a sole practitioner may fulfil both the roles him- or herself).

1 Sections 91 and 92 of LSA 2007.

The appointment of compliance officers

The business organisations which need compliance officers

7.2

The requirement to appoint compliance officers is set out in rule 8.1 of the SRA Authorisation of Firms Rules 2019 (the 'Firm Rules'). Rule 8.1 states:

'8.1 An *authorised body* must at all times have an individual who is designated as its *COLP* and an individual who is designated as its *COFA*, and whose designations the *SRA* has approved.'

The SRA Glossary defines 'authorised body' to mean '(a) a body that has been authorised by the SRA to practise as a licensed body or a recognised body or (b) a sole practitioner's practice that has been authorised by the SRA as a recognised sole practice'.

A recognised sole practitioner must therefore have a COLP and a COFA (and the same individual could hold both roles). In contrast a 'freelance solicitor' who practises on his own without applying for entity authorisation does not need to appoint a COLP or a COFA.[1] Equally, a solicitor who practises in a business which is not authorised by the SRA does not need to appoint a COLP or COFA.

1 For a solicitor's right to practise on his own without authorisation, see regulation 10.2 of the SRA Authorisation of Individuals Regulations 2019.

Who is eligible to be appointed?

7.3

The requirement for a COFA is that he or she:

(1) should not be disqualified from acting as a HOLP or HOFA under section 99 of LSA 2007;[1]

(2) has consented to act;

(3) is approved by the SRA; and

(4) is either:

    (a) a manager or an employee of the authorised body; or

    (b) a current compliance officer and manager or employee of a related authorised body.

Two authorised bodies are related if they have a common manager or owner.[2] The COLP must fulfil those requirements and must also be either a solicitor, or another individual who is authorised to carry on reserved legal activities by an approved regulator.[3]

1 For HOLPs and HOFAs see **7.1** and **7.12**.
2 Rule 8.3 of the Firm Rules.
3 Rule 8.2(d) of the Firm Rules.

Selection of compliance officers by the firm

7.4

In small firms, and sole practices in particular, one person may fulfil all roles, and there is no requirement that it should be otherwise. Small firms, however, must bear in mind that it is compulsory to have compliance officers at all times and they must be expressly approved by the SRA. If there is no COLP or COFA the firm cannot maintain its authorisation, and would have to close.

Larger firms will face difficult questions: should the COLP be the managing partner, or would that create an unmanageable conflict for someone with the primary role of driving the business? Or should it be the general counsel, but would that not create a conflict with that person's role in being able to give advice in privileged circumstances?

If the compliance officer is not in the top echelon in the firm, what protections, beyond those provided in the Codes of Conduct, will it be necessary to provide to someone who may have the role of a whistle-blower, against the wishes of senior partners or managers?[1]

What level of access to information, at board level for example, must a compliance officer have? The likely inference and position of the SRA is that he/she must have access to everything. Will that mean that a COLP will have to be a partner/manager, or is the situation capable of being regulated by contract?

SRA guidance maintained on its website states that 'Whilst some senior or managing partners might wish to take on these roles, firms, particularly larger firms, need to consider whether senior or managing partners will be able to devote the time necessary to the role'.[2]

At the same time, the firm should take into account rule 2.3 of the SRA Assessment of Character and Suitability Rules 2019 (the 'Suitability Rules'). Rule 2.3 states that, when assessing suitability, the SRA will consider whether the applicant is of sufficient seniority and in a position of sufficient responsibility to fulfil the requirements of the role.

None of these issues are easy to resolve and we do not make the attempt. It is understandable at the simplest level that the SRA should want to have one or two people with the primary responsibility to deal with the regulator, but the SRA must, it seems to us, be sensitive to the problems inherent in requiring compliance officers to be primarily responsible for increasing regulatory responsibilities and the firm's internal policemen. The danger is that it may become increasingly difficult to recruit and retain managers prepared to fulfil the role.

On the whole, the selection process has not proven to be particularly burdensome for firms. There is a sense that in a small number of firms, the role is viewed as a poisoned chalice, and that salaried partners without sufficient seniority or responsibility (or skills and experience) have been appointed. Managers remain responsible for compliance and such an approach is unlikely to avoid regulatory action for the managers in the event of serious breach. Changes seen in the new Codes and the Accounts Rules emphasise the continuing nature of the managers' responsibilities.

1   Paragraphs 3.11 and 3.12 of the SRA Code of Conduct for Firms 2019 (the 'Code for Firms'); paragraph 7.9 of the SRA Code of Conduct for Solicitors, RELs and RFLs 2019 (the 'Code for Individuals').
2   SRA, 'Question of ethics: nominating your COLP and COFA', May 2012.

Making the application for appointment

7.5

The approval of compliance officers for new entities is part of the authorisation process, and any application for authorisation as an ABS, or as a new non-ABS practice, must therefore name the proposed compliance officers whenever the application is first made.

Applications for appointment of new compliance officers in existing firms are made online by completing an SRA application form, which is available on the SRA website, unless the new nominee is automatically appointed under the deeming provisions. For the procedure if the deeming provisions apply see **7.7**.

Temporary emergency applications

7.6

If a firm (traditional or ABS) ceases to have a compliance officer of either class it must notify the SRA promptly.[1]

An application can be made for temporary emergency approval of a new compliance officer within seven days of the former compliance officer ceasing to act. The SRA will only grant a temporary approval if the SRA is satisfied that a substantive application could not reasonably have been commenced in advance, and the SRA has no reason to believe that the new appointee in not a fit and proper person to act as a compliance officer.[2]

A grant of temporary approval will be for an initial period of 28 days. It may be granted effective from the date when the former compliance officer ceased to act, so that the firm is not in default, but the temporary approval does not guarantee that a substantive application for approval will be granted, or granted without conditions. The temporary approval can be granted subject to such conditions as the SRA considers appropriate in the public interest. The initial 28-day period can be extended for such period as the SRA thinks fit, and will be extended pending determination of a substantive application if the substantive application is made within the initial 28-day period. The temporary approval, and any extension, may be revoked if the SRA considers it appropriate to do so in the public interest.[3]

1   Paragraph 3.8(a) of the Code for Firms.
2   Rule 15.2 and 15.3 of the Firm Rules.
3   Rule 15.4 of the Firm Rules.

SRA approval

7.7

The SRA may approve an individual to act as a compliance officer if it is satisfied that the individual is fit and proper to undertake the role.[1]

An individual is deemed to be fit and proper to act as a compliance officer if: (1) the individual is a lawyer and a manager of the authorised body; (2) the authorised body has an annual turnover of no more than £600,000; (3) the individual is not a compliance officer of any other authorised body; and (4) the individual is not subject to a regulatory or disciplinary investigation or adverse finding or decision of the SRA, the Solicitors Disciplinary Tribunal (the Tribunal or SDT) or another regulatory body. If those deeming provisions apply, the authorised body must notify the SRA promptly on a prescribed form of the identity of the compliance officer and the SRA will then approve the appointment.[2]

If the deeming provisions do not apply, the SRA will make a decision whether the individual is fit and proper to undertake the role on the basis of the Suitability Rules.

Under the Suitability Rules, the SRA will consider whether the applicant is of sufficient seniority and in a position of sufficient responsibility to fulfil the requirements of the role. The SRA will also consider past conduct and behaviour, including criminal convictions, cautions, regulatory and disciplinary findings, any evidence of insolvency or financial mismanagement and any other available information relating to the applicant's character and suitability for the role. The applicant will be under a duty to disclose all relevant matters and must provide a certificate from the Disclosure and Barring Service and any further information the SRA may request. When making the decision the SRA will take into account the need to protect the public and maintain trust and confidence in the provision of legal services.[3]

Approval takes effect from the date of the decision, unless otherwise stated. It remains effective only if the individual takes up the role within the period specified in the notice of approval, or one year if no period is specified. The approval expires when the individual ceases to act as a compliance officer.[4]

The roles of COLP and COFA are not interchangeable. Someone already approved as a COLP cannot step into the role of a COFA without going through a further process of approval. Equally someone approved as a COLP for one entity cannot automatically step into the role of COLP for another entity.

1 Rule 13.1 of the Firm Rules.
2 Rules 13.5 and 13.6 of the Firm Rules.
3 See the Suitability Rules.
4 Rule 13.7 of the Firm Rules.

Conditions

7.8

When granting approval the SRA has power to impose conditions on the individual's approval if it considers that there are risks to the public or the public interest which can be addressed by the imposition of condtions.[1] The SRA also has the power to impose conditions on the firm's authorisation if it is in the public interest to do so and if the SRA is satisfied that a compliance officer, or the authorised body, its managers, employees, owners, or interest holders, is unsuitable to engage in certain practising arrangements, is likely to put the interests of clients or third parties at risk, requires monitoring of compliance with the regulatory arrangements or should take steps conducive to the regulatory objectives.[2]

1 Rule 2.4 of the Suitability Rules.
2 Rules 3.1 and 3.2 of the Firm Rules.

Notification obligations

7.9

After appointment a compliance officer is under a duty to notify the SRA promptly of any information concerning the compliance officer which would be relevant to an assessment of the individual's fitness and propriety to act. The SRA can require a compliance officer to make a self-declaration as to their continuing fitness and propriety to act.[1]

A compliance officer whose appointment is based on an SRA assessment under the Suitability Rules (rather than the deeming provisions)[2] also has an ongoing obligation under the Suitability Rules to tell the SRA promptly about anything which raises a question as to his or her suitability and character, or any change to information which has previously been disclosed to the SRA in support of the application for approval.[3]

Those reporting obligations place compliance officers in a position where they will need to report to the SRA if they are unable to fulfil their roles, whether as a result of lack of time or ability, or lack of assistance from the firm.

The firm has an obligation to notify the SRA promptly if it becomes aware that information provided to the SRA by or on behalf of the firm about its compliance officers may be false, misleading, incomplete or inaccurate, or if there have been any material changes to any such information,[4] or if it becomes aware of any facts or matters that it reasonably believes are capable of amounting to a serious breach [by the compliance officer] of their regulatory arrangements.[5]

1   Rule 13.10 of the Firm Rules.
2   See **7.7**.
3   Rule 6.5 of the Suitability Rules.
4   Paragraph 3.8 of the Code for Firms.
5   Paragraphs 3.9 and 3.10 of the Code for Firms – see **7.27** for further commentary.

Withdrawal of approval

7.10

Under rule 13.9 of the Firm Rules, the SRA may withdraw approval of a compliance officer at any time if it is not satisfied that he or she is fit and proper to undertake the designated role.

Withdrawal of approval of a COLP or COFA could be terminal for a practice. If for any reason a firm ceases to have an approved COLP and COFA it must notify the SRA promptly and designate a replacement and ensure an application is made for the replacement; temporary emergency approval, if sought within seven days, may be granted pending determination of the substantive application (see **7.6**).

Larger firms may find it desirable to have more than one potential compliance officer of each class in a position to take over the role in the event of unforeseen circumstances, although as things stand there is no mechanism by which approval can be sought other than by the formal process of approval of the appointment (there is no process whereby one can obtain approval of someone with a view to later appointment).

The powers of the SRA to disqualify a HOLP or HOFA of an ABS are considered in **CHAPTER 26**.

Reviews and appeals

7.11

An individual has a right to apply for an internal review of an SRA decision to refuse approval of the person's designation as a compliance officer, or an SRA decision to withdraw approval of the person's designation as a compliance officer. The application must be made within 28 days from notice being given of the decision, and the review is decided on the papers.[1]

In the case of COLPs and COFAs of ABSs, the individual affected has a right of appeal to the Tribunal against the SRA's refusal of an application for approval and a decision to withdraw approval. The appeal must be made within 28 days of the decision taking effect. If there has been a prior on-time application for review, that 28-day period runs from the date the review is determined. For appeals to the Tribunal see **CHAPTER 23**.

Where a COLP or COFA is appointed within a non-ABS authorised practice, such as a traditional firm, there is no right of appeal to the Tribunal. There is a right to appeal a decision to withdraw the individual's designation as compliance officer to the High Court, but there is no right of appeal to the High Court in respect of a decision to refuse approval of an individual's designation as a compliance officer.

Because every practice must have an approved COLP and COFA, and a refusal to approve the appointment of a particular individual could mean that a practice has to close, it is not entirely satisfactory that one kind of authorised practice has a right of appeal to the Tribunal, with possible costs consequences if the SRA got it wrong, and another kind of authorised practice bound by exactly the same set of SRA rules has no external right of appeal, so that the only remedy is litigation, by judicial review. Judicial review does not generally entail a full review of the merits of the original decision and is consequently an unsatisfactory remedy.

1   The rights of internal review and external appeal are contained in the SRA Application, Notice, Review and Appeal Rules 2019.

Disqualification

7.12

Within the ABS regime, the licensing authority has the power under section 99 of LSA 2007 to disqualify a person from being a HOLP, a HOFA, or a manager, or employee of any licensed body, so that a COLP or COFA of an ABS may face the near equivalent of being struck off by the SRA as licensing authority (someone disqualified in these circumstances is likely to be unemployable in the regulated legal community).

For these powers and associated rights of appeal see **CHAPTERS 26** and **23** respectively.

These are powers which are specific to ABSs and do not apply to COLPs and COFAs of other kinds of authorised practices.

Duties of a COLP and COFA

Paragraph 9 of the Code for Firms

7.13

The compliance officers' duties are set out in paragraphs 9.1 and 9.2 of the Code for Firms, which are reproduced below.[1]

> 9.1   If you are a *COLP* you must take all reasonable steps to:
>
> (a)   ensure compliance with the terms and conditions of your firm's authorisation;
>
> (b)   ensure compliance by your firm and its *managers*, employees or *interest holders* with the *SRA's regulatory arrangements* which apply to them;
>
> (c)   ensure that your firm's *managers* and *interest holders* and those they

employ or contract with do not cause or substantially contribute to a breach of the *SRA's regulatory arrangements*;

(d)   ensure that a prompt report is made to the *SRA* of [any facts or matters that you reasonably believe are capable of amounting to a] serious breach of the terms and conditions of your firm's authorisation, or the *SRA's regulatory arrangements* which apply to your firm, *managers* or employees;

[(e)   notwithstanding sub-paragraph (d), you ensure that the *SRA* is informed promptly of any facts or matters that you reasonably believe should be brought to its attention in order that it may investigate whether a serious breach of its *regulatory arrangements* has occurred or otherwise exercise its regulatory powers],

save in relation to the matters which are the responsibility of the *COFA* as set out in paragraph 9.2 below.

9.2   If you are a *COFA* you must take all reasonable steps to:

(a)   ensure that your firm and its *managers* and employees comply with any obligations imposed upon them under the SRA Accounts Rules;

(b)   ensure that a prompt report is made to the *SRA* of any [facts or matters that you reasonably believe are capable of amounting to a] serious breach of the SRA Accounts Rules which apply to them;

[(c)   notwithstanding sub-paragraph (b), you ensure that the *SRA* is informed promptly of any facts or matters that you reasonably believe should be brought to its attention in order that it may investigate whether a serious breach of its *regulatory arrangements* has occurred or otherwise exercise its regulatory powers.]

---

1   Paragraphs 9.1(d) and (e) and 9.2(b) and (c) [in square brackets] added by the SRA Regulatory Arrangements (Reporting Concerns) (Amendment) Rules 2019, approved by the LSB on 9 May 2019.

The COFA's duties

7.14

The COFA's duties under paragraph 9.2 of the Code for Firms are limited to two duties: (1) a duty to take all reasonable steps to ensure compliance with the Accounts Rules, that is to ensure appropriate systems and controls are in place; and (2) a duty to report (for the duty to report see **7.27**).

The COFA's duties relating to accounts under the Code for Firms are narrower than the duties imposed on the COFA under the 2011 rules because there have been the following three changes:

- Under the 2011 rules, the COLP and COFA were both under a duty to monitor and control the firm's financial stability. That duty now falls on the COLP alone.

- Under the 2011 rules, the COFA was directly responsible for breaches of the SRA Accounts Rules (as well as the systems and controls relating to the Accounts Rules). That direct responsibility for breaches has gone.

• There is no longer an express duty to record failures to comply with the SRA Accounts Rules and make the records available to the SRA on request (but see below).

Those changes are considered in further detail in the next three sections.

7.15

As regards financial stability, the COFA's duties are now in line with the duties of a HOFA under LSA 2007. When originally envisaged the role of the COFA was expected to be quite narrow. Despite the title and the references to 'finance' and 'administration' the origins of the role are found in section 92(1) of LSA 2007 in relation to ABSs:

'The Head of Finance and Administration of a licensed body must take all reasonable steps to ensure compliance with licensing rules made under paragraph 20 of Schedule 11 (accounts)'

and in the quoted paragraph of Schedule 11:

'The licensing rules must make provision as to the treatment of money ... and the keeping of accounts in respect of such money.'

The 'money' in question is 'money (including money held on trust) which is received, held or dealt with by the licensed body, its managers and employees for clients or other persons'. Thus the role of the HOFA under LSA 2007 is very specific: responsibility for the correct treatment of client and trust money and the keeping of accounts. It does not entail any wider responsibility for running the business.

There was a considerable amount of 'regulatory creep' under the SRA's 2011 rules. The SRA Authorisation Rules 2011 required the COFA to take all reasonable steps to ensure the firm complied with the Accounts Rules. Rule 1.2 of the SRA Accounts Rules 2011 said: 'You must comply with the Principles set out in the Handbook, and the outcomes in Chapter 7 of the SRA Code of Conduct in relation to the effective financial management of the firm ...'. Chapter 7 included the obligation to 'maintain systems and controls for monitoring the financial stability of your firm and risks to money and assets entrusted to you by clients and others, and ... take steps to address issues identified' (outcome 7.4). By that means the SRA asserted that the COFA had a role in relation to financial stability. The COLP also had a direct responsibility to take all reasonable steps to ensure that the firm complied with outcome 7.4, and the COLP and the COFA therefore had overlapping responsibilities relating to financial stability.

The overlapping responsibility has now gone, and the COLP alone has responsibilities in relation to financial stability, as the SRA Accounts Rules 2019 do not include any obligations relating to financial stability of the firm.

7.16

As regards direct responsibility for compliance with the Accounts Rules, rule 6.1 of the SRA Accounts Rules 2011 stated that the COFA and all principals in the firm must ensure compliance with the rules. In contrast, rule 1.2 of the SRA Accounts Rules 2019 (the comparable provision in the SRA Accounts Rules 2019) states that the authorised body's managers are jointly and severally responsible for compliance with the Accounts Rules. The SRA has said that wording which makes the COFA directly responsible for compliance with the Accounts Rules 'would place an unreasonable burden on the COFA', and that:

> 'The rule now emphasises that the Accounts Rules create obligations on the firm and its managers, not on the COFA. The COFA's obligations under the Code of Conduct to take all reasonable steps to ensure compliance with the Accounts Rules and report any concerns from a position of independence will still apply'.[1]

1   'Application for the approval of regulatory arrangements', SRA, August 2018, para 249.

7.17

As regards record keeping, rule 8.5(e)(i)(B) of the SRA Authorisation Rules 2011 stated that the COFA must take all reasonable steps to record any failure to comply with any obligations imposed under the SRA Accounts Rules, and make such records available on request to the SRA. That express duty has been removed from the 2019 regulatory arrangements (see paragraph 9.2 of the Code for Firms at **7.13**). However that does not mean that record keeping can be abandoned. The SRA has frequently said that records of breaches are needed to monitor a firm's systems and to identify any patterns of breaches which, when viewed cumulatively, constitute a material or serious reportable breach. In other words, record keeping is an integral part of the firm's systems and controls, as well as the reporting obligations, and the COFA needs to keep records of breaches of the SRA Accounts Rules 2019 to comply with paragraph 9.2 of the Code for Firms.

The records which the COFA needs to keep under paragraph 9.2 of the Code for Firms are less extensive than the records which had to be kept under the 2011 rules because there is no longer a need for the COFA to keep any records relating to financial stability.

The COLP's duties

7.18

The role of the COLP under paragraph 9.1(a) to (c) of the Code for Firms is very wide indeed.

There is an obligation to 'take all reasonable steps' to ensure that the firm, its managers, employees and interest holders comply with all of their obligations under the SRA's regulatory arrangements (except for the obligations under the Accounts Rules) and that they do not 'cause or substantially contribute to' any breaches of those obligations.

There is also an obligation to take all reasonable steps to ensure that those whom the firm's managers or interest holders contract with do not cause or substantially contribute to a breach of the SRA's regulatory arrangements.

The SRA Glossary states 'regulatory arrangements' has 'the meaning given to it by section 21 of the LSA'. Section 21 of LSA 2007 defines 'regulatory arrangements' as including all rules, regulations and arrangements which apply in relation to a regulated person.

The COLP's obligations therefore extend to all of the rules in the SRA regulatory arrangements and all legislation which has to be complied with under those rules, apart from the Accounts Rules.

The next seven sections comment on changes introduced by the Code for Firms to the scope of the COLP's obligations relating to: (1) control of the firm's work; (2) solicitors' conduct in their private lives; (3) contracts with third parties; (4) training; (5) client instructions; (6) financial stability; and (7) record keeping.

7.19

Rule 6.1 of the Firm Rules places a duty on COLPs to monitor and control the scope of a firm's business, including the scope of the fee earning and other income producing work.

> 6.1 If you are a recognised body or *recognised sole practice*, your business may consist only of the provision of:
>
> (a) professional services of the sort provided by individuals practising as *solicitors* and/or *lawyers* of other jurisdictions; and
>
> (b) the services set out in annex 2 (whether or not they are also included in paragraph (a)),
>
> and if you have a notary public as a *manager* or *employee*, then professional services of the sort provided by notaries public.

Annex 2 to the Firm Rules lists 12 categories of business which can be carried on, ranging from alternative dispute resolution (ADR) and company secretarial services to estate agency, authorship and publishing. The COLP will have to take reasonable steps to ensure that the firm's business activities fall within the scope of rule 6.1 and Annex 2.

Rule 6.1 does not apply to ABSs. The scope of work carried out by an ABS is defined by its licence and any conditions or waivers attached to the licence. The COLP of an ABS was under a duty to take all reasonable steps to ensure that the ABS complies with the terms of its authorisation under the 2011 rules[1] and that duty has been carried into the 2019 arrangements by paragraph 9.1(a) of the Code for Firms.

1 Rule 8.5(c)(i)(A) of the SRA Authorisation Rules 2011.

7.20

Paragraph 9.1(b) of the Code for Firms places COLPs under a duty to take reasonable steps to ensure managers and employees do not breach any of the regulatory arrangements relating to them. Managers and employees who are solicitors are under a duty to adhere to the Principles which extend to an individual's private life. The guidance published by the SRA in August 2018 to accompany the new regulatory arrangements included Topic Guides on criminal offences outside practice (including fixed penalty notices), driving with excess alcohol convictions and the use of offensive comments on social media. The extent of the COLP's duty to control adherence to the Principles in private life is unclear. It may, for example, require new provisions in employment contracts and firm manuals on behaviour outside the office.

7.21

Paragraph 9.1(c) of the Code for Firms places an obligation on COLPs to monitor contractual arrangements with third parties to ensure they do not cause or substantially contribute to a breach of the SRA's regulatory arrangements.

The obligation in paragraph 9.1(c) relates to third parties with whom the managers and interest holders contract. It is not immediately clear why the obligation relates to contracts with the managers and interest holders rather than with the firm. It is possible that the provision is intended, or will be interpreted by the SRA, so as to regulate the relationship between corporate managers and interest holders and those they employ or contract with. Alternatively, it may be construed as referring to the firm's contracts with third parties (on the basis that the managers can be said to be contracting on behalf of the firm) and the standard emphasises the need to set up systems to monitor outsourcing arrangements, as well as arrangements with, for example, claims management companies and medical agencies in personal injury work.[1] The monitoring may need to cover issues such as data protection, confidentiality, and cold calling.

1   For outsourcing see **5.23**.

7.22

Paragraph 7.1 of the Code for Individuals introduced a new standard requiring solicitors to keep up to date with the law. An identical provision has been added to the Code for Firms (paragraph 3.1), and the inclusion of that standard in the Code for Firms shows that the SRA expects firms to ensure that individual solicitors in the firm keep up to date with the law. That may require COLPs to introduce new systems to monitor continuing competence.

7.23

Paragraph 3.1 of the Code for Individuals introduced a new standard requiring solicitors only to act on instructions from the client, or someone with authority to provide instructions on the client's behalf. An identical standard has been added to the Code for Firms. The SRA introduced those standards to combat the increasing prevalence of identity frauds and cybercrime.[1] The new standards may require COLPs to introduce systems to keep up to date with reports on new cybercrime scams affecting law firms and to review the firm's systems on a frequent basis to keep up to date with the ever-changing nature of cybercrime fraud.

1   'Application for the approval of regulatory arrangements', SRA, August 2018, para 104.

7.24

Under the Code for Firms, the compliance officer duties relating to financial stability now fall on the COLP alone. Under the 2011 rules, the COLP and COFA were both responsible for financial stability. See **7.15**.

7.25

The express duty on the COLP under the 2011 rules to keep records of breaches has not been carried over to the new rules. However the COLP should continue to keep records. See **7.17**.

The responsibilities of the managers

7.26

It is important to appreciate the distinction between the responsibilities of compliance officers and managers. The COLPs and COFAs are responsible for *systems*, and for recording and reporting compliance failings. The obligation to 'ensure compliance' does not mean, in our view, that the compliance officer is personally liable if there is non-compliance. He or she can expect to face disciplinary consequences if there are no adequate systems in place to minimise risks or to monitor the effectiveness of controls, or if there is a failure to keep adequate records, or a failure to report to the SRA when it was appropriate to do so.

In contrast, the managers can be responsible for specific breaches. Paragraph 8.1 of the Code for Firms states that the managers are responsible for compliance with the Code for Firms by the firm, and rule 1.2 of the SRA Accounts Rules states that the managers are jointly and severally responsible for compliance with the Accounts Rules by the firm, its managers and employees.

The managers are also responsible for ensuring that the firm has effective governance structures, arrangements, systems and controls in place to ensure that compliance officers are able to discharge their duties.[1] There can be expected to be consequential tensions between COLPs and COFAs and managers. If a compliance officer is not provided with adequate facilities and resources that will be the responsibility of the managers, but that in itself will be a failure of compliance which is likely to mean that the compliance officer cannot carry out his/her duties, which would trigger an obligation for the compliance officer to report.

1   Paragraph 2.1(d) of the Code for Firms.

Reports – when to report to the SRA

7.27

The Code for Firms requires COLPs and COFAs to:

- report to the SRA promptly any facts or matters they reasonably believe are capable of amounting to a serious breach of:
    - for COLPs, the terms and conditions of the firm's authorisation, or the SRA's regulatory arrangements that apply to the firm, managers or employees, excluding potential breaches of the SRA Accounts Rules 2019;[1] and
    - for COFAs, the SRA Accounts Rules 2019 that apply to the firm;[2] and
- inform the SRA promptly of any facts or matters they reasonably believe should be brought to its attention in order that it may investigate whether a serious breach of its regulatory arrangements has occurred, or otherwise exercise its regulatory powers.[3]

This represents a significant change from the 2011 rules, which required COLPs and COFAs to report breaches by the firm or its personnel of rules, deemed to be 'material'. While there is no practical difference between a 'material' breach and a 'serious' breach, the reporting threshold has been lowered in a number of respects:

- Compliance officers are no longer required to determine whether a breach by the firm is serious; there is an obligation is to report facts or matters *capable* of amounting to a serious breach by the firm.

- There is an obligation on both COLPs and COFAs to report facts and matters, whether relating to the firm or not, which warrant *an investigation* whether a serious breach has occurred.

- There is an obligation on both COLPs and COFAs to report facts or matters, whether relating to the firm or not, which should be brought to the SRA's attention so that it may otherwise exercise its regulatory powers. Matters that might otherwise warrant the exercise of regulatory powers could include knowledge of other regulated entities' and persons' dealings that could lead to, for example, intervention, or a decision not to approve a compliance officer or to impose conditions on a practising certificate.

One of the most vexing problems faced by compliance officers on a daily basis is whether to report.

The SRA has indicated that it will be producing supporting guidance and case studies, available by the summer of 2019. As at the time of writing, Topic Guides are available for competence and standard of service, criminal offences outside practice, driving with excess alcohol convictions, the SRA Transparency Rules 2018 and use of social media and offensive communications.

Further guidance is available in the Codes of Conduct and the SRA Enforcement Strategy.

In the introduction to each Code of Conduct it is stated that 'A failure or breach may be serious either in isolation or because it comprises a persistent or concerning pattern of behaviour.' The SRA has also expressed its view that: 'A mere breach is not in and of itself reportable: it must be "serious".'[4]

The new SRA Enforcement Strategy[5] indicates that 'if you are unsure about whether to make a report, you should err on the side of caution and do so' and signposts users to its Professional Ethics helpline for help in reaching a decision. The SRA Enforcement Strategy sets out the factors which affect the SRA's view of seriousness, including:[6]

(a)   Past behaviour.

(b)   Future risk – taking into account expressions of apology and remorse, and whether the conduct has been repeated.

(c)   The systems in place and environment in which the events took place – eg assessing whether stressful circumstances and ill health might have affected the solicitor's judgement.

(d)   The responsibility or control the individual had over the matters in question.

(e)   The nature of the allegation. Allegations of abuse of trust, taking unfair advantage of clients or others, the misuse of client money, sexual and violent misconduct, dishonest and criminal behaviour will be treated as inherently more serious. Information security breaches may also be treated as being serious.

(f)   Intent/motivation. Questions to be asked under this head include: Was the conduct planned or premeditated, persistent, repeated or concealed? Was an advantage gained? What remedial action been taken? Was there a deliberate or reckless disregard for obligations?

(g)   Competence. Serious or persistently poor levels of competence – aggravated if the solicitor knowingly acted outside his or her competence or failed to update knowledge and skills. Genuine mistakes will not generally result in action (and thus not be serious) unless the failure arises from a lack of knowledge which the individual could reasonably be expected to have acquired, or there is a concerning lack of judgment.

(h)   Harm and impact – including potential harm even if not materialised.

(i)   Vulnerability of the client.

(j)   Role, experience and seniority of the solicitor.

SRA warning notices can also provide assistance in deciding whether a breach is serious. Generally speaking, warning notices are only issued to address perceived serious misconduct, and warning notices can contain examples of the type of conduct which is permitted and the type of misconduct which is serious.

1   Paragraph 9.1(d) of the Code for Firms.
2   Paragraph 9.2(b).
3   Paragraphs 9.1(e) and 9.2(c).
4   SRA, 'Reporting concerns: our post-consultation position', January 2019.
5   7 February 2019.
6   Paragraph 2.2.

General guidance on COLP and COFA duties

7.28

The SRA Authorisation Rules 2011 contained guidance notes on systems and controls which are not replicated in the new rules. However, they might prudently be used as a guide towards achieving compliance. The relevant guidance notes are reproduced below.

'(vi) The roles of COLP and COFA are a fundamental part of a firm's compliance and governance arrangements. COLPs' and COFAs' ability to take the steps they need to ensure compliance is dependent on the firm having suitable arrangements in place … The firm must therefore ensure that any person designated as its COLP or COFA is of sufficient seniority, in a position of sufficient power and responsibility and has clear reporting lines to enable them to have access to all management systems and arrangements and all other relevant information including client files and business information. The existence of compliance officers in a firm and the requirements on them to ensure that the firm, as well as its managers and employees, are complying with the regulatory arrangements (COLP) and the SRA Accounts Rules (COFA) is not a substitute for the firm's and managers' responsibilities and their obligations to comply with …[the rules]. Firms and managers need to take care not to obstruct, whether intentionally or unwittingly, a COLP or COFA in fulfilling their role.

(vii) COLPs and COFAs are responsible for ensuring that the firm has systems and controls in place to enable the firm, as well as its managers and employees and anyone who owns any interest in the firm, to comply with the requirements on them. The firm and its managers are not absolved from any of their own obligations and remain fully responsible for compliance ...

(viii)... How ... breaches are ... monitored is a matter for firms to decide as part of their compliance plan, bearing in mind that it is necessary for a firm to be able to detect patterns of non-material breaches which, when taken together, amount to material non-compliance which the firm is required to report ...

(ix) Those designated as COLP will need to be in a position to be able to discharge the role. They will need to consider whether they are in a position to, for example:

    (a) take all reasonable steps to ensure compliance with the terms of the firm's authorisation; compliance with the SRA's regulatory arrangements by the firm, its employees and managers; and with relevant statutory obligations e.g.

        (A) that non-authorised persons comply with the duty imposed by section 90 of the LSA (duty not to do anything which causes or substantially contributes to a breach of the SRA's regulatory arrangements by an authorised body or its employee or manager);

        (B) that authorised persons and other managers and employees comply with the duty imposed by section 176 of the LSA (duty to comply with the SRA's regulatory arrangements);

        (C) under the LSA, AJA and the SA in respect of practice matters;

    [...]

(x) Those designated as COFA will need to be in a position to be able to discharge the role. They will need to consider whether they are in a position to, for example:

    (a) ensure that they have access to all accounting records;

    (b) carry out regular checks on the accounting systems;

    (c) carry out file and ledger reviews;

    (d) ensure that the reporting accountant has prompt access to all the information needed to complete the accountant's report;

    (e) take steps to ensure that breaches of the SRA Accounts Rules are remedied promptly;

    (f) monitor, review and manage risks to compliance with the SRA Accounts Rules;

    (g) in the case of a licensed body, as soon as reasonably practicable report to the SRA any failure to comply with the SRA Accounts Rules. Where such failure is material, either on its own or because it forms part of a pattern, the immediacy of the report will depend on the circumstances and seriousness of the breach. ...

(h)   in the case of a recognised body or recognised sole practice, as soon as reasonably practicable, report to the SRA any material failure to comply with the SRA Accounts Rules, whether such failure is material either on its own or because it forms part of a pattern of non-compliance. The immediacy of the report will depend on the circumstances and seriousness of the breach.

[…]

(xii) In developing their governance and administrative arrangements firms will need to consider how they approach unexpected risks such as the absence of key staff, including COLP and COFA, and whether the nature of the absence will trigger the need to notify the SRA … and to obtain approval for a replacement.'[1]

---

1   SRA Authorisation Rules 2011, guidance notes to rule 8.

CHAPTER 8

Financial services regulation

8.1

The statutory framework for financial services regulation is provided by the Financial Services and Markets Act (FSMA) 2000. Section 19(1) of FSMA 2000 provides that no person may carry on a regulated activity in the United Kingdom or purport to do so unless he is (a) an authorised person or (b) an exempt person. This is referred to as the general prohibition. A breach of this requirement is a criminal offence with a maximum penalty of two years' imprisonment.

Regulated activities are defined by the Financial Services and Markets Act 2000 (Regulated Activities) Order 2001 (RAO 2001).[1] Activities are regulated if an *activity* of a specified kind is carried on *by way of business* in relation to an *investment* of a specified kind. The Financial Services and Markets Act 2000 (Carrying on Regulated Activities by Way of Business) Order 2001[2] makes provision as to when a person is or is not to be regarded as carrying on a regulated activity by way of business. We are dealing with solicitors acting in the course of their professional practice and will assume that this requirement will be met.

1 SI 2001/544.
2 SI 2001/1177.

'Activities'

8.2

The specified *activities* are:

- accepting deposits;[1]

- issuing electronic money;

- effecting and carrying out contracts of insurance;

- dealing or arranging deals in investments;

- credit broking;

- operating an electronic system in relation to lending;

- managing investments;

- assisting in the administration and performance of a contract of insurance;

- activities in relation to debt: debt adjusting, debt counselling, debt collection and debt administration;

- safeguarding and administering investments;

- sending dematerialised instructions;[2]

- specified involvement in collective investment schemes;

- the like involvement in pension schemes;

- providing basic advice on stakeholder products;

- advising on investments;

- various forms of activity at Lloyd's;

- providing funeral plan contracts; and

- specified involvement in regulated credit agreements, regulated consumer hire agreements, regulated mortgage contracts, regulated home reversion plans, regulated home purchase plans and regulated sale and rent back agreements.

There are exclusions applicable to the various categories of activity.

With effect from 1 April 2014 consumer credit activity was added as a new category of regulated activity.[3] It was formerly regulated by being licensed by the Office of Fair Trading, and the solicitors' profession enjoyed the benefits of a group licence. The consequences are considered in further detail below.

1   A sum is not a deposit for these purposes if it is received by a practising solicitor acting in the course of his profession: article 7 of RAO 2001. A 'practising solicitor' includes recognised bodies, registered European lawyers and registered foreign lawyers.
2   See the Uncertificated Securities Regulations 2001 (SI 2001/3755) – essentially the process whereby shares and other investments can be held in electronic form on computer systems.
3   Financial Services and Markets Act 2000 (Regulated Activities) (Amendment) (No 2) Order 2013 (SI 2013/1881).

'Investments'

8.3

The specified *investments* are:

- deposits;

- electronic money;

- rights under a contract of insurance;

- shares;

- debt instruments (debentures, loan stock, bonds, certificates of deposit);

- alternative finance investment bonds;

- government and public securities (gilts);

- warrants and other instruments giving entitlement to investments;

- certificates representing certain securities (conferring contractual or property rights in shares, debentures, etc);

- units in a collective investment scheme;

- rights under a pension scheme;

- emission allowances;

- options;

- futures;

- contracts for differences (for example, trading on the expected performance of a share or other index);

- Lloyd's syndicate capacity and syndicate membership;

- rights under a funeral plan contract, regulated mortgage contract, regulated home reversion plan or regulated home purchase plan, regulated sale and rent back agreements;

- credit agreements;

- consumer hire agreements; and

- rights to or interests in investments.

8.4

This book does not attempt to deal with the requirements imposed by the Financial Conduct Authority (FCA) on those authorised and regulated by that Authority. Solicitors and their practices may become involved in mainstream investment business and be required to be authorised by the FCA, but the vast majority of the profession take advantage of Part XX of FSMA 2000 which allows persons who are regulated by designated professional bodies (of which the Law Society/Solicitors Regulation Authority (SRA) is one) to undertake regulated activities without being authorised by the FCA, provided that they comply with rules made by their own professional body. Solicitors and others regulated by the SRA complying with their own professional rules will be carrying on 'exempt regulated activities'.[1]

The rules applicable to solicitors and their practices; any form of 'authorised body', traditional firm, legal disciplinary partnership, alternative business structures or authorised sole practitioner, are the SRA Financial Services (Scope) Rules 2019[2] and the SRA Financial Services (Conduct of Business) Rules 2019,[3] which in this chapter will be referred to as the 'Scope Rules' and the 'COB Rules'.

The Scope Rules specify the regulated activities which solicitors and others regulated by the SRA may and may not undertake if they are to take advantage of the Part XX exemption, and the conditions that must be satisfied. The COB Rules regulate the manner in which exempt regulated activities may be carried on by solicitors and their practices.

1 Section 327 of FSMA 2000.
2 Formerly the SRA Financial Services (Scope) Rules 2001.
3 Formerly the SRA Financial Services (Conduct of Business) Rules 2001.

The Scope Rules

8.5

The Scope Rules, read with section 327 of FSMA 2000, require that certain basic conditions be met. These are primarily:

(1) that the regulated activities arise out of, or are complementary to, the provision of a particular professional service to a particular client;[1]

(2) that the provision of any service relating to regulated activities is incidental to the provision of professional services (this would, for example, therefore cover

the arrangement of after the event insurance which is incidental to the main purpose of the retainer, ie the pursuit of a claim for damages);[2]

(3) that the firm accounts to the client for any pecuniary reward or other advantage which the firm receives from a third party;[3] and

(4) that the firm does not carry on or hold itself out as carrying on any regulated activity that is not permitted under the Scope Rules.[4]

As to whether the regulated activity is incidental, it is necessary to consider the scale of regulated activity in proportion to other professional services provided; whether and to what extent activities that are regulated activities are held out as separate services; and the impression given as to how the firm provides regulated activities, for example, through its advertising of its services.

As to accounting for commission and other financial benefits see paragraph 4.1 of the SRA Code of Conduct for Solicitors, RELs and RFLs 2019, paragraph 5.1 of the SRA Code of Conduct for Firms 2019,[5] and the commentary in **CHAPTER 4** (see **4.39**). Notes to the former version of the Scope Rules also encouraged practitioners at the outset, in advance of the arrangement or the provision of the financial service, to inform clients of their rights to any commission; to inform clients that the arrangement and/or provision of the service is not dependent on their agreement to waive their right to any commission; and to seek and to record client agreement as to whether any commission should be passed to the client, retained by the firm to offset fees, or retained by the firm with the client waiving their right to it. While these notes have not survived into the 2019 Scope Rules, the requirement to account for any commission remains, and providing clear advance information to clients regarding the issue remains an obviously prudent course.

This is consistent with the FCA guidance to the Council for Licensed Conveyancers on the same subject; see **13.8**.

1   Rule 2.1(b).
2   Section 327(4) of FSMA 2000.
3   Section 327(3) of FSMA 2000.
4   Section 327(5) of FSMA 2000.
5   Previously outcome 1.15 of the SRA Code of Conduct 2011.

Prohibited activities

8.6

Activities from which solicitors are prohibited under the Scope Rules may be divided into two parts.

8.6.1 Those prohibited by orders made under section 327(6) of FSMA 2000:[1]

- accepting deposits;

- issuing electronic money;

- buying, selling, subscribing for or underwriting securities or contractually based investments (other than investments specified by article 87 or article 89 of RAO 2001) as principal;

- dealing in investments as agent or arranging deals in investments in so far as it relates to a transaction for the sale or purchase of rights under a contract of insurance and is carried on by a person not included in the record of insurance intermediaries;

- managing investments in so far as it consists of buying or subscribing for a security, contractually based investment or structured deposit;[2]

- advising on investments where such advice falls within article 6 of the Financial Services and Markets Act 2000 (Professions) (Non-Exempt Activities) Order;

- establishing, operating or winding up a stakeholder pension scheme or a personal pension scheme;

- providing basic advice on stakeholder products;

- effecting and carrying out contracts of insurance as principal;

- assisting in the administration and performance of a contract of insurance if it is carried on by a person who is not included in the record of insurance intermediaries;

- bidding in emissions auctions;

- specified activities in relation to collective investment schemes;

- managing the underwriting capacity of a syndicate as a managing agent at Lloyd's;

- advising a person to become a member of a particular Lloyd's syndicate;

- entering as provider into a funeral plan contract;

- administering a benchmark;

- advising on regulated mortgage contracts where such advice consists of a recommendation to an individual to enter into a regulated mortgage contract as borrower and, by doing so, that person would be carrying on an activity specified in article 61 of RAO 2001;[3]

- advising on regulated home reversion plans where such advice consists of a recommendation to an individual to enter into a regulated home reversion plan with a particular person and, by doing so, that person would be carrying on an activity specified in article 63B(1) of RAO 2001;[4]

- advising on regulated home purchase plans where such advice consists of a recommendation to an individual to enter into a regulated home purchase plan with a particular person and, by doing so, that person would be carrying on an activity specified in article 63F(1) of RAO 2001;[5]

- advising on regulated sale and rent back agreements where such advice consists of a recommendation to an individual to enter into a sale and rent back agreement with a particular person and, by doing so, that person would be carrying on an activity specified in article 63J(1) of RAO 2001;[6]

- entering into:
    - a regulated mortgage contract as lender or administering a regulated mortgage contract;

- – a regulated home purchase plan as a provider or administering a regulated home purchase plan;

- – a regulated home reversion plan as a provider or administering a regulated home reversion plan; and

- – a regulated sale and rent back agreement as an agreement provider or administering a regulated sale and rent back agreement,

unless in the firm's capacity as a trustee or personal representative and the borrower, home purchaser, reversion seller or agreement seller is a beneficiary of the trust, will or intestacy.

8.6.2 Those directly prohibited by the Scope Rules:[7]

- entering into a regulated credit agreement as lender except where the regulated credit agreement relates exclusively to the payment of disbursements or professional fees due to you;

- exercising, or having the right to exercise, the lender's rights and duties under a regulated credit agreement except where the regulated credit agreement relates exclusively to the payment of disbursements or professional fees due to you;

- entering into a regulated consumer hire agreement as owner;

- exercising, or having the right to exercise, the owner's rights and duties under a regulated consumer hire agreement;

- operating an electronic system in relation to lending within the meaning of article 36H of RAO 2001;

- providing credit references within the meaning of article 89B of RAO 2001;

- insurance distribution activities in relation to insurance-based investment products; or

- creating, developing, designing or underwriting a contract of insurance.

All relevant definitions are contained in the SRA Glossary or RAO 2001.

1 Financial Services and Markets Act 2000 (Professions) (Non-Exempt Activities) Order 2001 (SI 2001/1227).
2 See article 5(2) of SI 2001/1227 for limitations.
3 See article 6A of SI 2001/1227. Note that endorsing the recommendation of an authorised or exempt person is not caught (see article 6A(3)).
4 See article 6C of SI 2001/1227. Note that endorsing the recommendation of an authorised or exempt person is not caught (see article 6C(3)).
5 See article 6C of SI 2001/1227. Note that endorsing the recommendation of an authorised or exempt person is not caught (see article 6E(3)).
6 See article 6C of SI 2001/1227. Note that endorsing the recommendation of an authorised or exempt person is not caught (see article 6G(3)).
7 Rule 3.1 of the Scope Rules.

8.7

There are other restrictions relating to corporate finance. Firms must not act as a sponsor to an issue of securities to be admitted for dealing on the London Stock Exchange or as nominated adviser to an issue of securities to be admitted for dealing on the Alternative Investment Market of the London Stock Exchange or as corporate adviser to an issue in respect of securities to be admitted for dealing on the PLUS Market.[1]

1   Rule 4.1 of the Scope Rules.

Insurance distribution activities

8.8

Firms may only carry on insurance distribution activities as an ancillary insurance intermediary.[1] Firms must not carry on any insurance distribution activities unless they are registered in the FCA Financial Services register and have appointed an insurance distribution officer who will be responsible for those activities.[2]

The 2019 rules have been updated to abandon (for the most part) the phrase 'insurance mediation' which caused much confusion, not least because of the use of the word 'mediation'. The term now used in the Scope Rules is 'insurance distribution' as defined in the FCA Handbook. 'Insurance distribution activity' is defined in the SRA Glossary and involves dealing as an agent in contracts of insurance and/or rights to or interests in a life policy, arranging deals in contracts of insurance and/or rights to or interests in a life policy, making arrangements with a view to a person entering into a contract of insurance and/or involving rights to or interests in a life policy, assisting in the administration or performance of a contract of insurance and/or rights to or interests in a life policy, advising on the merits of buying or selling a contract of insurance and/or rights to or interests in a life policy, or agreeing to do any of the above.

Most insurance contracts are now regulated investments, including life and pension policies, defective title and missing beneficiary indemnity policies, household and building insurance, long-term care insurance and after the event legal expenses insurance.

In practice, therefore, most of the profession will be likely to become involved in insurance distribution activities, even if only by advising on or arranging a title indemnity policy or after the event insurance. The process of being registered with the FCA for these purposes is arranged through the SRA (usually by completing the question on the annual application for practising certificates or recognition renewal to confirm that the firm does carry out this activity) or by informing the SRA separately if this has not been done or if the circumstances have changed since certificates or recognitions were renewed.

It seems that many firms have made mistakes in this respect. All that is required is that the person filling in the firm's annual application forms does not appreciate that 'insurance distribution' has a special meaning and ticks the box for 'No' as to whether the firm engages in that activity. In consequence the firm will not be registered with the FCA and there will be criminal offences committed every time the firm arranges an after the event legal expenses policy or title indemnity insurance. In addition, all managers and the firm's COLP may be in breach of requirements in the SRA Codes of Conduct if such a mistake arises due to a lack of understanding of legal, ethical or regulatory obligations such as to amount to a breach of the requirement at paragraph 4.3 of the SRA Code of Conduct for Firms 2019.

1   Rule 5.1 of the Scope Rules.
2   Rule 5.2 of the Scope Rules.

Regulated mortgages and other property plans

8.9

Firms must not recommend that a client enters into a regulated mortgage contract as a borrower, but can endorse a recommendation given by a person who is regulated by the FCA for this purpose or who is exempt from the general prohibition.[1]

A regulated mortgage contract is one where the borrower is an individual or trust, the lender takes a first legal charge over property in the United Kingdom and at least 40 per cent of the property is occupied or intended to be occupied by the borrower as a dwelling or, in the case of a trust, by a beneficiary, or (in either case) by that person's spouse (or someone, whether or not of the opposite sex, whose relationship with the borrower or beneficiary has the characteristics of the relationship between husband and wife) or that person's parent, brother, sister, child, grandparent or grandchild (article 61(3) of RAO 2001).

Firms must not recommend that a client, as a purchaser, enters into a regulated home purchase plan or a regulated home reversion plan or, as a seller, a regulated sale and rent back agreement with a particular person but can endorse a recommendation given by a person who is regulated by the FCA or who is exempt from the general prohibition.[2]

A regulated home purchase plan is an arrangement under which a 'home purchase provider' buys all or part of a freehold or leasehold interest which provides for a home purchaser to buy the provider's interest during the course of or at the end of a specified period and the purchaser or a related person is entitled to occupy at least 40 per cent of the land as a dwelling and intends to do so (article 63F(3) of RAO 2001).

A regulated home reversion plan is an arrangement whereby a person, the reversion provider, buys all or part of a freehold or leasehold interest from an individual or trustees (the reversion occupier), and the reversion occupier or a related person is entitled to occupy at least 40 per cent of the land as a dwelling and intends to do so, and the arrangement specifies that the entitlement to occupy will end in specified circumstances (article 63B(3) of RAO 2001).

A regulated sale and rent back agreement is an arrangement whereby a provider buys all or part of a freehold or leasehold interest on terms that the seller or a related person is entitled to occupy at least 40 per cent of the land as a dwelling and intends to do so, but which is not a home reversion plan (article 63J(3)(a) of RAO 2001).

1   Article 6A of the Financial Services and Markets Act 2000 (Professions) (Non-Exempt Activities) Order 2001 (SI 2001/1227).
2   Articles 6C, 6E and 6G of SI 2001/1227.

Consumer credit activity

8.10

On 1 April 2014 consumer credit activity became a mainstream financial services activity regulated by the FCA. The categories of activity listed in rule 3.1(c)–(h) of the Scope Rules and set out at **8.6.2** are prohibited consumer credit activities. Solicitors may only carry out consumer credit activities:

- if they are fully FCA-authorised, or had previously been granted interim permission to continue to do so, for which application had to be made by 31 March 2014 (and which will not therefore be considered);

- if they have the benefit of the Part XX exemption (see **8.4**) though this may be more problematic in its application than in relation to other regulated activities; or

- if they are acting in the course of contentious business as defined in section 87 of the Solicitors Act 1974 (which must involve proceedings before a court or arbitrator, excluding non-contentious probate business). It is important to note that this therefore only applies where proceedings have been commenced, and not to any activity carried out before proceedings have been issued.[1]

Regulated consumer credit activities include:

- credit broking;
- operating an electronic system in relation to lending;
- debt adjusting;
- debt-counselling;
- debt-collecting;
- debt administration;
- entering into a regulated credit agreement as lender;
- exercising or having the right to exercise lender's rights under a regulated consumer credit agreement;
- entering into a regulated consumer hire agreement as owner;
- exercising or having the right to exercise owner's rights under a regulated consumer hire agreement;
- providing credit information services;
- providing credit references;
- agreeing to carry on any of the above.

Each of the listed activities has exemptions specific to the relevant activity and those firms likely to be undertaking these activities as a mainstream activity (to which this book is not addressed) need to consider RAO 2001 in detail, as amended by the Financial Services and Markets Act 2000 (Regulated Activities) (Amendment) (No 2) Order 2013.[2]

Of greater relevance to most solicitors' firms will be the Part XX exemption, which is available where the activity arises out of, or is complementary to, the provision of a particular professional service to a particular client; the manner of the provision of any service in the course of carrying on the activities is incidental to the provision of professional services; the firm accounts to a client for any pecuniary reward or other advantage which the firm receives from a third party; and the firm does not carry on any activities regulated by the FCA other than those permitted under Part XX of FSMA 2000, or in relation to which the firm is an exempt person.

The 'incidental' test must be applied on a case-by-case basis and it is unlikely that firms specialising in debt collection to any substantial extent would be able to avoid being regulated by the FCA.

Rule 6 of the Scope Rules sets out the relevant limitations:

Credit-related regulated financial services activities

6.1   You must not enter into any transaction with a *client* in which you:

(a)   provide the *client* with credit card cheques, a credit or store card, *credit tokens, running account credit,* a current account or *high-cost short-term credit;*

(b)   hold a *continuous payment authority* over the client's account; or

(c)   take any article from the *client* in *pledge* or *pawn* as security for the transaction.

6.2   You must not:

(a)   enter into a *regulated credit agreement* as lender; or

(b)   exercise, or have the right to exercise, the lender's rights and duties under a *regulated credit agreement,*

which is secured on land by a *legal or equitable mortgage.*

6.3   You must not:

(a)   enter into a *regulated credit agreement* as lender; or

(b)   exercise, or have the right to exercise, the lender's rights and duties under a *regulated credit agreement,*

which includes a variable rate of interest.

6.4   You must not provide a *debt management plan* to a *client.*

6.5   You must not charge a separate fee for, or attribute any element of your fees to, *credit broking* services.

1   For example articles 36F(1)(b) and 39K(1)(b) of RAO 2001 as amended.
2   SI 2013/1881.

The COB Rules

8.11

As explained above, the COB Rules govern the manner in which solicitors' firms may carry out regulated activities that they are permitted to carry out under the Scope Rules. The Rules apply to licensed bodies (alternative business structures,

ABSs) only in respect of that part of their business which is regulated under the Legal Services Act 2007: in other words, to the provision of legal services as opposed to any other services that the business may be providing (such as funeral services). They apply, with one exception, to firms that are not regulated by the FCA and to firms that are regulated by the FCA but only in relation to non-mainstream regulated activities and to managers and employees of those firms.

Status disclosure

8.12

The exception is rule 2, which relates to status disclosure and which applies only to firms that are *not* regulated by the FCA. Before such a firm provides any service which includes a regulated financial services activity it must give the client the following information in writing, in a manner that is clear, fair and not misleading:

- a statement that the firm is not authorised by the FCA;

- the name and practising address of the firm;

- the nature of the regulated financial services activities carried on by the firm and the fact that they are limited in scope;

- a statement that the firm is authorised and regulated by the SRA; and

- a statement explaining that complaints and redress mechanisms are provided through the SRA and the Legal Ombudsman (LeO).[1]

The following words are not compulsory but are in an acceptable form when combined with the other specific requirements listed above:

'The Law Society is a designated professional body for the purposes of the Financial Services and Markets Act 2000 but responsibility for regulation and complaints handling has been separated from the Law Society's representative functions. The Solicitors Regulation Authority is the independent regulatory body of the Law Society.'

Where you are providing services which include the carrying on of insurance distribution activity, the following specific written disclosure must be provided to the client in good time before the conclusion of a contract of insurance, along with confirmation that you are an ancillary insurance intermediary:

'[This firm is] [We are] not authorised by the Financial Conduct Authority. However, we are included on the register maintained by the Financial Conduct Authority so that we can carry on insurance distribution activity, which is broadly the advising on, selling and administration of insurance contracts. This part of our business, including arrangements for complaints or redress if something goes wrong, is regulated by the Solicitors Regulation Authority. The register can be accessed via the Financial Conduct Authority website at www.fca.org.uk/firms/financial-services-register.'

There is no reason why the required disclosures cannot be incorporated in the firm's standard client care material, but they can be provided separately. It is not necessary to tailor the disclosure to the needs of the specific client, although the 2019 Rules require that the disclosure be provided in a way which is clear, fair and not misleading.[2] Since LeO's service is available not to all clients, but only to individuals and small businesses (see **CHAPTER 14**), care should be used in making reference to the availability of a redress mechanism in the very generic terms required by the SRA.

1   Rule 2.1 of the COB Rules.
2   Rule 2.2 of the COB Rules, and associated guidance notes.

Other requirements

8.13

Firms must ensure that when it has been decided or agreed to effect a transaction they do so as soon as possible, unless it is reasonably believed that it is not in the best interests of the client to do so.[1]

The COB Rules contain provisions requiring specified records to be kept of transactions, commissions received, how the firm accounted for commission to the client, and as to the safekeeping of clients' investments.[2] As to the principles involved in accounting for commission, see **8.5**.

If a firm arranges any transaction for a client involving a retail investment product on an execution-only basis, the firm must send written confirmation to the client that, as the case may be, no advice had been sought from or given by the firm, or advice had been given but the client nevertheless persisted in requiring the transaction to be effected – and in either case that the transaction is effected on express instructions.[3]

There are additional detailed requirements where firms engage in insurance distribution activities. These are primarily concerned with the disclosure of information and the extent to which a comparative market analysis has been carried out, with the need to establish by reasonable steps that the recommended policy is suitable for the client's demands and needs, and with the obligation to provide a 'demands and needs statement' before the contract is finalised (among other things explaining any recommendation made). Specific rules also govern the use of intermediaries, remuneration and fee disclosure, cross-selling requirements where insurance is the ancillary product and organisation requirements, including the obligation to ensure that the firm and its employees possess appropriate knowledge and ability in order to complete their tasks and perform duties adequately and all managers and persons directly involved in insurance distribution activities are of good repute. 'Good repute' essentially involves not being convicted of crimes involving property or financial activities and not being bankrupt – in either case, unless rehabilitated.[4] In practice, it is the latter which is most likely to be of concern to firms. Should any manager of a firm be declared bankrupt, this may have an impact on the firm's ability to lawfully conduct insurance distribution activity.[5]

1   Rule 3.1 of the COB Rules.
2   Rules 4, 5 and 6 of the COB Rules.
3   Rule 7 of the COB Rules.
4   Rule 20.2 of the COB Rules.
5   Part 3 of the COB Rules.

8.14

In relation to consumer credit activities firms must comply with Part 4 of the COB Rules:

Disclosure of information

23.1 Where you undertake *credit-related regulated financial services activities* for a *client*, you must ensure that information in connection with such activities and any agreements to which they relate are communicated to the *client* in a way that is clear, fair and not misleading.

23.2 Where you carry on the activity of *credit broking*, you must indicate in any advertising and documentation intended for consumers or *clients* the extent and scope of your *credit broking* activities, in particular whether you work exclusively with one or more lenders or as an independent broker.

Regulated credit agreements

24.1 Where you carry on a credit-related regulated financial services activity involving a proposed *regulated credit agreement*, you must;

(a) provide adequate explanations to the *client* in order to enable the *client* to assess whether the proposed *regulated credit agreement* is suitable to the *client's* needs and financial situation; and

(b) when providing such explanations, comply with the requirements of Article 5(6) of the Directive 2008/48/EC on credit agreements for consumers.

24.2 Before entering into a *regulated credit agreement* as lender, you must assess the *client's* creditworthiness on the basis of sufficient information to enable you to make the assessment, where appropriate such information will be obtained from the *client* and, where necessary, from a credit reference agency.

24.3 After entering into a *regulated credit agreement* where you are the lender, if the parties agree to change the total amount of credit, you must update the financial information you hold concerning the *client* and assess the *client's* creditworthiness before any significant increase in the total amount of credit.

24.4 In the event of you assigning to a third party your rights as lender in relation to a *regulated credit agreement*, you must inform the *client* of the assignment.

Appropriation of payments

25.1 Where you are entitled to payments from the same *client* in respect of two or more *regulated credit agreements*, you must allow the *client* to put any payments made, in respect of those agreements, towards the satisfaction of the sum due under any one or more of the agreements in such proportions as the *client* thinks fit.

Consumer credit guidance

26.1 Where you undertake *credit-related regulated financial services activities*, you must have regard to any guidance issued by the *SRA* from time to time relating to such activities.

Financial promotions

8.15

There is a second separate strand of regulation under FSMA 2000 of which practitioners should be aware. Under section 21 of FSMA 2000, you are prohibited from, in the course of business, communicating an invitation or inducement to engage in investment activity unless this is done by an authorised person, or the content of the communication is approved by an authorised person. Solicitors' practices are not authorised persons but can take advantage of an exemption to undertake exempt regulated activities as explained above, for the purposes of RAO 2001. This regime does not, however, apply to financial promotions, which are covered by the Financial Services and Markets Act 2000 (Financial Promotion) Order 2005 (FPO 2005).[1] Regulated activities for the purposes of RAO 2001 are not precisely the same as (though are very similar to) controlled activities for the purposes of FPO 2005.

If a firm, therefore, does communicate invitations or inducements to engage in an investment activity, it must, if it is regulated by the SRA rather than the FCA, be able to rely on an exemption within FPO 2005. Fortunately, there are exemptions specifically in favour of members of professions. Under article 55 of FPO 2005, the financial promotion restriction does not apply to a real time communication (whether solicited or unsolicited) which is made by a person who carries on a regulated activity to which the general prohibition does not apply by virtue of section 327 of FSMA 2000 (in other words those carrying out exempt regulated activities and who are regulated by their own professional body); and which is made to a recipient who has, prior to the communication being made, engaged that person to provide professional services, and where the activity to which the communication relates is (in short) for the purposes of, and incidental to, the provision of professional services to or at the request of the recipient.

A real time communication is any communication made in the course of a personal visit, telephone conversation or other interactive dialogue.[2] Note that this exemption applies to communications with existing clients, but can be solicited or unsolicited.

The article 55 exemption does not apply to non-real time communications, including letters, emails and material in a publication such as a brochure. Article 55A provides an exemption for members of a profession in relation to non-real time communications if the stated conditions are satisfied. The financial promotion restriction does not apply to a non-real time communication which is made by a person who carries on Part XX activities (that is, again, those who are carrying out exempt regulated activities and who are regulated by their own professional body) and which is limited to a communication expressly provided for in article 55A: that is, one that promotes an activity that is within Part XX of FSMA 2000 (in other words, one that is not prohibited by the Scope Rules). The communication must contain the following:

'This [firm/company] is not authorised under the Financial Services and Markets Act 2000 but we are able in certain circumstances to offer a limited range of investment and consumer credit-related and claims management-related services to clients because we are members of [relevant designated professional body]. We can provide these investment and consumer credit-related services if they are an incidental part of the professional services we have been engaged to provide.'[3]

Note that this is similar to but not identical with the notice that is required by the COB Rules for insurance mediation activities (see **8.12**).

Firms can therefore communicate an invitation or inducement in writing provided the promoted activities fall within the scope of exempt regulated activities and the invitation or inducement is accompanied by the specified notice.

1   SI 2005/1529.
2   Article 7 of FPO 2005.
3   Article 55A(2) of FPO 2005.

CHAPTER 9

Property selling

9.1

The Property Selling Rules were a part of the 2011 Handbook. They were relatively prescriptive in that they were required to mirror the statutory provisions of the Estate Agents Act 1979. The SRA's approach in the 2019 regulatory arrangements is to not include specific provisions which are adequately covered by statute or more generic requirements. There is no replacement for the Property Selling Rules 2011 in the 2019 arrangements.

Firms engaged in property selling should ensure compliance with the information requirements at section 8 of the SRA Code of Conduct for Solicitors, RELs and RFLs 2019 (the 'Code for Individuals') discussed at **4.105** to **4.115**.

Solicitors engaged in property selling should pay particular attention to the requirement of paragraph 8.6 of the Code for Individuals: to ensure that clients are in a position to make informed decisions about the services they need, how their matter will be handled and the options available to them. While there are no longer any express requirements relating to property selling in the 2019 regulatory arrangements, any failure to provide information which would be required pursuant to the Estate Agents Act 1979 could well amount to a breach of this requirement.

CHAPTER 10

Overseas and European cross-border practice

10.1

Overseas and European cross-border practice is governed by the SRA Overseas and Cross-border Practice Rules 2019 (the 'OCB Rules'). The OCB Rules disapply the SRA Principles and the Codes of Conduct and replace them with modified requirements for the purposes of regulating practice outside England and Wales. Individual solicitors practising outside England and Wales may nevertheless be subject to the SRA Principles and SRA Code of Conduct for Solicitors, RELs and RFLs 2019 if their practice predominantly comprises the provision of legal services to clients in England and Wales or in relation to assets located in England and Wales.[1] This provision is intended to ensure that solicitors do not seek to circumvent regulation by the Solicitors Regulation Authority (SRA) by physically moving out of the jurisdiction but conducting their practice remotely.

Overseas practice involves a branch office, subsidiary company or undertaking or entity otherwise owned or managed in fact and law by an authorised body established outside England and Wales and providing legal services as well as an individual so established acting as a representative of an authorised body, or sole principal so established whose business management or ownership is controlled in fact or law by an authorised body.

The OCB Rules modify the SRA Principles very slightly to make it clear that it is the administration of justice in England and Wales and public trust in the profession in England and Wales which are within the ambit of principles 1 and 2 respectively and to constrain the requirement to encourage equality, diversity and inclusion (principle 6) by reference to the legal, regulatory and cultural contexts where your practice is located.

Other requirements for cross-border practice are designed to ensure proper stewardship of client funds[2] and to ensure proper co-operation with the SRA and regulatory bodies (including the Legal Ombudsman).[3] The reporting requirements are less onerous than those imposed in respect of practice in England and Wales but nevertheless require full and accurate explanations, information and documentation to be provided in response to any request made by the SRA.[4]

The OCB Rules are very short and little is added by commenting in further detail.

European cross-border practice involves professional activity regulated by the SRA in a CCBE state (see **10.2**) other than the United Kingdom, whether or not the practitioner or firm is physically present in that state, and any professional contact of a kind that is regulated by the SRA with a lawyer of a CCBE state other than the United Kingdom. Contacts and activities within a firm or in-house legal department are not within the definition.[5]

1   Rule 1.3 of the OCB Rules.
2   Rule 3.1 of the OCB Rules.
3   Rule 4.1 of the OCB Rules.
4   Rule 4.4(a) of the OCB Rules.
5   See the SRA Glossary.

10.2

CCBE is the recognised abbreviation for the Council of the Bars and Law Societies of Europe and was originally the Commission Consultative des Barreaux d'Europe. Its correct current French title is 'Conseil des Barreaux Européens'. The Council's principal object is to study all questions affecting the legal profession in the member states of the European Union and the European Economic Area and to formulate solutions designed to co-ordinate and harmonise professional practice. It has set up a Council for Advice and Arbitration to assist in resolving complaints between lawyers in different member states.

The CCBE has published a Code of Conduct for Lawyers in the European Community (in October 1988; most recently updated in May 2006) for the purposes of regulating the conduct of lawyers within the Community concerned in cross-border activities.

There are 32 full member states of the CCBE, three associated members and ten observer members. The CCBE Code of Conduct applies to all of them without distinction.

The full members are:

Austria	Greece	Poland
Belgium	Hungary	Portugal
Bulgaria	Iceland	Romania
Croatia	Ireland	Slovak Republic
Cyprus	Italy	Slovenia
Czech Republic	Latvia	Spain
Denmark	Liechtenstein	Sweden
Estonia	Lithuania	Switzerland
Finland	Luxembourg	The Netherlands
France	Malta	United Kingdom
Germany	Norway	

The associated members are:

Montenegro
Serbia
Turkey

The observer members are:

Albania	Former	San Marino
Andorra	Yugoslav Republic	Ukraine
Armenia	of Macedonia	
Bosnia and Herzegovina	Moldova	
Georgia	Russia	

10.3

The sole requirement of the provisions in the OCB Rules relating to European cross-border practice is that solicitors engaged in European cross-border practice comply with the CCBE Code of Conduct for Lawyers in the European Community. The CCBE Code is included at **APPENDIX 6**.

10.4

There are some aspects of the CCBE Code which may be sufficiently dissimilar to requirements applicable in England and Wales to warrant mention and which were formerly mentioned expressly in the SRA European Cross-Border Practice Rules 2011:

- occupations considered incompatible with legal practice, which is an issue to be determined by reference to the rules of the CCBE state in question (rule 2.5 of the CCBE Code);

- fee sharing with non-lawyers (rule 3.6 of the CCBE Code);

- co-operation between lawyers of different CCBE states (rule 5.2 of the CCBE Code);

- considerations arising from correspondence between lawyers of different CCBE states, because 'confidential' and 'without prejudice' may be interpreted differently (rule 5.3 of the CCBE Code);

- a prohibition on payment of referral fees to non-lawyers (rule 5.4 of the CCBE Code);

- the proper procedure in the event of a dispute between lawyers (rule 5.9 of the CCBE Code); and

- obligations in relation to fees when other lawyers are instructed (rule 5.7 of the CCBE Code).

10.5

Rule 2.5 provides that if you act in legal proceedings or proceedings before public authorities in a CCBE state other than the United Kingdom, you must, in that state, comply with any rules regarding occupations incompatible with the practice of law, as if you were a lawyer of that state, whether or not you are based at an office in that state; and if you are a solicitor based at an office in a CCBE state other than the United Kingdom, you must respect any rules regarding participation in commercial or other activities not connected with the practice of law, as they are applied to lawyers of that state.

Rule 3.6 provides that whether you are practising in a CCBE state other than the United Kingdom, or in the United Kingdom, you must not share your fees with a non-lawyer in a CCBE state (other than the United Kingdom) except within the firm as permitted by the SRA, or with retired partners, members, etc or their dependants.

Rule 5.2 imposes an obligation to provide reasonable co-operation to other lawyers. It requires that if you are approached by a lawyer of a CCBE state other than the United Kingdom to undertake work which you are not competent to undertake, you must assist that lawyer to obtain the information necessary to find and instruct a lawyer capable of providing the service requested. When co-operating with a lawyer of a CCBE state other than the United Kingdom you must take into account the differences which may exist between the respective legal systems and the professional organisations, competencies and obligations of lawyers in their respective states.

10.6

Rule 5.3 seeks to avoid misunderstandings in professional correspondence when communications are intended to be 'confidential' or 'without prejudice'. Before sending the communication you must clearly express your intention in order to avoid misunderstanding, and ask if the lawyer is able to accept the communication on the intended basis. When you send the communication you must express your intention clearly at the head of the communication or in a covering letter. If you are the intended recipient of a communication from a lawyer in another CCBE state which is stated to be 'confidential' or 'without prejudice', but which you are unable to accept on the basis intended by that lawyer, you must inform the sender accordingly without delay. If the communication has already been sent you must return it unread without revealing the contents to others. If you have already read the communication and you are under a professional duty to reveal it to your client you must inform the sender immediately.

10.7

Under rule 5.4 the payment of referral fees to non-lawyers is prohibited if the non-lawyer is situated in a CCBE state other than the United Kingdom or if you are practising from an office in a CCBE state other than the United Kingdom, whether or not you are physically present at that office. The rule applies to any fee, commission or any other compensation as a consideration for referring a client.

Under rule 5.7, unless agreed to the contrary, you are under a professional obligation to pay the fees of a lawyer or legal business in another CCBE state instructed by you even if the underlying client becomes insolvent or unable to pay you, subject to specified exceptions including an express disclaimer. This does not apply where your involvement goes no further than a recommendation to instruct the lawyer or legal business.

By virtue of rule 5.9, if you consider that a lawyer in a CCBE state other than the United Kingdom has acted in breach of a rule of professional conduct you must draw the breach to the other lawyer's attention and, before commencing any form of proceedings against the other lawyer, you must inform the Law Society and the other lawyer's bar or law society in order to allow them an opportunity to assist in resolving the matter.

CHAPTER 11

Professional indemnity insurance

11.1

The compulsory requirement that solicitors should be insured against professional risks dates from 1976, when the Law Society made indemnity rules under the powers provided by section 37 of the Solicitors Act 1974. From then until 1987 the Law Society negotiated the terms of a master policy with the insurance industry year by year. In 1987 the Solicitors Indemnity Fund (SIF) was established to replace the master policy scheme.

In 2000 the requirement that all solicitors be insured through the SIF was abolished and solicitors became free to negotiate their professional indemnity insurance on the open market.

Save for three recent exceptions,[1] since 2000 there have been two stipulations within what is otherwise a free market:

(1)   the insurer must be a participating insurer, that is an authorised insurer (essentially any insurer authorised to carry out that class of business under the Financial Services and Markets Act 2000)[2] which has entered into a participating insurers agreement with the Solicitors Regulation Authority (SRA)[3] which remains in force for the purposes of underwriting new business at the date of the insurance contract; and

(2)   the terms of the insurance cover must meet the 'minimum terms and conditions' set by the current indemnity insurance rules.[4]

Qualifying insurance may be underwritten by more than one insurer provided that, collectively, the minimum terms and conditions are satisfied and that one insurer is identified as the lead insurer.[5] A list of participating insurers can be found on the SRA website.

Until 30 September 2013 all insurance policies ran for one year from 1 October in each year. Since 1 October 2013 insurers have been free to issue policies with variable renewal dates. Policies may be for periods of any length.

The obligation to effect insurance and ancillary rules are:

●   for SRA authorised firms, set out in the SRA Indemnity Insurance Rules (SIIR) 2019;

●   for freelance solicitors, set out in the SRA Authorisation of Individuals Regulations 2019;[6]

●   for solicitors providing reserved legal services from non-commercial bodies, set out in the SRA Code of Conduct for Solicitors, RELs and RFLs 2019 (the 'Code for Individuals').[7]

The SIIR 2019 have been approved by the Legal Services Board (LSB),[8] but at the time of writing have not been uploaded to the SRA website, perhaps because at least one further amendment is expected in relation to the minimum level of cover requirements – see **11.3** below. This chapter assumes that the rules will be implemented.

Further sweeping and controversial changes to the rules are still being considered by the SRA. In June 2018 the SRA closed a consultation on proposed changes, the most controversial of which were not included in SIIR 2019. The SRA has indicated that the proposals remain under consideration.

SIIR 2019 are addressed below at **11.2–11.10**, the obligations of non-SRA firms, freelance solicitors and solicitors practising in non-commercial bodies at **11.11**, and commentary on the further changes being considered by the SRA is provided at **11.13**.

1   The SRA Indemnity Insurance Rules 2019 do not apply to solicitors providing unreserved legal services from a non-SRA firm, freelance solicitors, or solicitors providing reserved legal services through a non-commercial body: see **11.11**.
2   See the Participating Insurers Agreement 2018, being the latest available at the time of writing.
3   Formerly with the Law Society.
4   Annex 1 to SIIR 2019.
5   Clause 2.6 of Annex 1 to SIIR 2019.
6   Regulation 10.2(b)(vi).
7   Paragraph 5.6.
8   Decision made 31 May 2019.

11.2

The SIF remains relevant to current regulatory requirements in that it will provide run-off cover for new claims against principals who retired before 1 September 2000 in circumstances where there is no successor practice, and will also provide run-off cover for claims where the run-off cover provided by qualifying insurers has expired. Qualifying insurers provide run-off cover for a period of six years under the minimum terms and conditions. The SIF will provide cover between 1 September 2007 and 1 September 2020 for claims notified within that period after the six-year period of commercial run-off cover has expired (and has arranged reinsurance in respect of those risks). At present there is no cover available for run-off for affected firms beyond 2020. Consequently, firms will need to consider their insurance arrangements carefully when planning closure, succession and merger.

Solicitors are currently subject to four sets of indemnity rules – the SRA Indemnity Rules 2012, which regulate the relationship between the profession and the SIF, SIIR 2019, which set out the requirements for SRA authorised firms to obtain qualifying insurance on the open market, the SRA Authorisation of Individuals Regulations 2019,[1] and the SRA Code of Conduct for Solicitors, RELs and RFLs (the 'Code for Individuals'),[2] the latter two of which set out the requirement for freelance solicitors and solicitors providing reserved legal services in non-commercial bodes to obtain 'adequate and appropriate' insurance.

With the closure of the SIF looming, it is expected that the SRA Indemnity Rules 2012 will only be relevant in practice to the mechanisms for dealing with an increasingly small number of potential claims capable of being indemnified under the run-off arrangements. These issues are likely to be of minimal significance and will therefore not be considered.

1   Regulation 10.2(b)(vi).
2   Paragraph 5.6.

The SRA Indemnity Insurance Rules 2019 – the basic requirements

11.3

The rules only apply to SRA authorised firms[1] and their principals[2] and thus do not apply to solicitors providing unreserved legal services from a body that is not authorised by the SRA, freelance solicitors – whether providing reserved legal services or not, or solicitors providing reserved legal services from a non-commercial body (see **11.11**).

Every SRA authorised firm must arrange insurance with one or more qualifying insurers that must comply with the minimum terms and conditions set out in Annex 1 to SIIR 2019; the obligation is imposed both on the firm and on every principal.[3] Licensed bodies (alternative business structures, ABSs) must have qualifying insurance in relation to their regulated activities, where they undertake both regulated and unregulated activities, and SIIR 2019 apply to licensed bodies generally only in relation to their regulated activities.

SIIR 2019 enable the SRA to require the production of information and evidence that qualifying insurance is in place.[4]

The rules do not apply to overseas practice.

SIIR 2019, as approved by the SRA Board and submitted to the LSB for approval, set the minimum level of cover at £2 million, or £3 million if the firm is a recognised body or licensed body (ABS).[5] On its face this appears to be a significant change from SIIR 2013, which only required 'relevant' recognised and licensed bodies to procure £3 million cover. In SIIR 2013, the definition of a 'relevant recognised body' excluded, in most cases, conventional (unincorporated) partnerships. SIIR 2019, as submitted to the LSB for approval in March 2019, do not exclude conventional partnerships from the requirement to procure a minimum £3 million of cover. However, having brought this to the attention of the SRA, the authors are advised that such a change was unintended, and consequently the SRA intends to amend or add to the SRA Glossary, such that the minimum cover obligation on conventional partnerships will remain at £2 million. Firms should check the position carefully.

In any event, firms are obligated to effect a higher level of cover if the minimum level fails to provide 'adequate and appropriate cover'.[6] Thus, if a firm regularly conducts transactions of a value exceeding the compulsory layer, if it fails to provide adequate cover for claims that might arise, the firm and its senior managers lay themselves open to allegations of professional misconduct.

Firms must take into account current and past practice, as well as any alternative arrangements the firm or its clients make.[7] Past practice is relevant, as cover is provided on a 'claims made' basis, that is, cover is provided by the insurer, subject to the terms for the insurance period in which a claim is first made (unless a 'circumstance' has been notified to an insurer in an earlier period) and which, for example, may relate to a negligent act in earlier years. The 'adequate and appropriate cover' rule necessitates careful consideration, and communication with a firm's insurer, before the acquisition of another firm is completed. Any excess layer above and beyond that complying with the minimum terms and conditions need not be with participating insurers, but the terms of cover will need to be adequate and appropriate.

The SRA has indicated that it expects firms to carry out an assessment to consider whether the minimum level of cover is sufficient.[8]

Even if it is not required to satisfy the 'adequate and appropriate cover' rule, firms are free to arrange cover in excess of the minimum levels and may do so with insurers which are not participating insurers.

Firms and insurers are free to negotiate the level of any excess which the firm may elect to meet in respect of claims – see **11.5**.

Firms must ensure that clients have the benefit of the indemnity insurance required by the rules, and must not exclude or attempt to exclude liability below the minimum level of cover required under these rules.[9] The SRA may intend that firms cannot limit liability below the level of 'adequate and appropriate cover', as required by the rules, if that is higher than the minimum level of cover requirement.

A minimum of six years' run-off cover is required if the firm ceases to practise during an indemnity period. Run-off cover is not required if there is a successor practice. In that event the qualifying insurance will be that of the successor practice.

Version 19 of the SRA Handbook, released on 1 October 2017, amended the minimum terms and conditions to remove the obligation on firms which transfer between regulators to obtain run-off cover, as opposed to arranging insurance meeting the requirements of the other regulator. It had been a significant barrier for conveyancing firms wishing to be regulated by the Council for Licensed Conveyancers that the SRA has formerly treated the firm as 'closing', triggering the need for run-off cover. The removal of the obligation to obtain run-off cover in these circumstances is conditional upon the firm becoming an authorised non-SRA firm, as now defined in the SRA Glossary, and the authorised non-SRA regulator being a signatory to a protocol on terms agreed by the SRA which relates to switching between approved regulators.[10]

The SRA has withdrawn its power to direct an insurer, in the event of a coverage dispute, to conduct a claim, advance defence costs and compromise and pay a claim. This power[11] was an important safeguard for small firms, unable to finance a claim against a large commercial insurer following a declinature, and thus its omission is regrettable. The SRA has decided to withdraw this power despite acknowledging in its consultation that the positions taken by insurers can be controversial.

1   Licensed bodies, recognised bodies and recognised sole practices.
2   Rule 1.1 of SIIR 2019.
3   Rule 4.1.
4   Rule 6.1.
5   Clause 2.1 of Annex 1 to SIIR 2019.
6   Rule 3.1.
7   Rule 3.1.
8   Application to the LSB for approval of changes to regulatory arrangements relating to the SRA's professional indemnity insurance requirements, 5 March 2019.
9   Rule 3.2.

10 Clause 5.7 of Annex 1 to SIIR 2019.
11 Previously clause 4.10 of Appendix 1 to SIIR 2013.

The extended policy period and the cessation period

11.4

Until 30 September 2013 there was an expensive safety net for firms which were unable to acquire insurance in the open market: the Assigned Risks Pool (ARP). For an analysis of this system see Chapter 10 of the *Solicitor's Handbook 2013*. From 1 October 2013 the ARP was abolished save in respect of run-off cover. From that date, if a firm is unable to renew its existing policy or to obtain insurance from another participating insurer on or by the renewal date it has 30 days within which to obtain cover, during which its existing insurer will continue to insure (the 'extended policy period', formerly known as the 'extended indemnity period'). If no qualifying insurance is found in that period the firm must cease practice promptly, and in any event no later than a further 60 days (the 'cessation period'), unless qualifying insurance can be found within the cessation period which will be effective from the renewal date. The existing insurer will also provide cover during the cessation period.[1]

During the cessation period (after the extended policy period has expired) the firm and every principal must ensure that the firm, every principal and every employee undertakes no work in relation to private legal practice and accepts no instructions, save to the extent that the work or the instructions are necessary to discharge obligations within the scope of the firm's existing instructions.[2]

In short, from the date of renewal, the firm has 30 days to find cover during which it may continue to work normally, but from that point on, although it may still try to find insurance for a further 60 days, it is obliged to work towards an orderly close down, accepting no new work.

The insurer providing cover for the previous insurance period must extend cover for the whole of the 90 days, unless another participating insurer steps in.

The minimum terms and conditions permit insurers to require reimbursement, to the extent that it is just or equitable having regard to the prejudice caused to the insurer's interests, where the firm undertakes work in the cessation period contrary to rule 5.2 of SIIR 2019.[3]

The circumstances in which firms were able to continue in practice without being able to obtain insurance on the open market and without (in many cases) paying the ARP premium has been brought to an end.

If the insurer suffers an insolvency event, then, subject to any waiver granted by the SRA, the firm and its principals must ensure that alternative qualifying insurance is arranged within four weeks of the insolvency event.[4]

1 Rule 2.4 of SIIR 2019.
2 Rule 4.2.
3 Clause 7.2(b) of Annex 1 to SIIR 2019.
4 Rule 5.1.

The minimum terms and conditions

11.5

The minimum terms and conditions (MTC) are set out in Annex 1 to SIIR 2019. Some aspects have already been mentioned, namely the minimum level of cover at £2 million or £3 million for recognised bodies or licensed bodies for each claim.[1]

The insurance must indemnify against civil liability to the extent that it arises from private legal practice[2] in connection with the insured firm's practice, on a 'claims made' basis; that is, claims are covered if made:

- within the period of insurance; or

- after the period of insurance, if arising from 'circumstances' first notified during the period of insurance.

The insurance must indemnify against any amount paid or payable in accordance with the recommendation of the Office for Legal Complaints (including the Legal Ombudsman) or any other regulatory authority to the same extent as it indemnifies the insured against civil liability, but not in respect of any determination requiring the firm to refund fees.[3]

Defence costs must also be covered without limit.[4] Where a claim exceeds the sum insured, the insurer may limit its liability for costs to the proportion that the sum insured bears to the total amount paid or payable to dispose of the claim.[5]

The insurance may make provision as to the meaning of 'one claim' for the purposes of determining the limit of indemnity and, in particular, may provide that all claims against any one or more insured will be regarded as one claim when arising from:

(a)   one act or omission;

(b)   one series of related acts or omissions;

(c)   the same act or omission in a series of related matters or transactions; or

(d)   similar acts or omissions in a series of related matters or transactions; and

(e)   all claims against one or more insured arising from one matter or transaction.[6]

Where there are a number of high value claims, each below the level of insurance for 'one claim' but collectively exceeding it, insurers will benefit from aggregation (treating a number of claims as one claim) in that their total exposure will be capped at the level for a single claim. Where there are a number of low level claims, collectively within the insured limit, the insured firm will benefit from aggregation, because there will then be only one deductible or excess, rather than a multiple.

In light of the decision in *Lloyds TSB General Insurance Holdings Ltd v Lloyds Bank Group Insurance Co Ltd*[7] and in response to market pressures by professional indemnity insurers, the Law Society amended clause 2.5 by adding sub-clauses (iii) and (iv), as set out above (at examples (c) and (d)).

The issue of aggregation is highly contentious and has been the subject of recent litigation in *AIG Europe Ltd v Woodman and others*.[8] The case concerned the interpretation of clause 2.5(a)(iv) of the MTC – ie what amounts to 'similar acts or omissions, in a series of related matters or transactions' in connection with the development of two holiday resorts.

At first instance, Teare J held that, although the claims arose out of 'similar acts or omissions', they were not part of 'a series of related matters or transactions' because they were not dependent on each other. The Court of Appeal rejected this 'inter-dependence' test. Instead, it concluded that the matters in question had to have an 'intrinsic relationship' with each other in order to be 'related'.

The Supreme Court allowed the insurers' appeal from that decision. It held that the 'intrinsic relationship' test was neither necessary nor satisfactory. Lord Toulson, giving the leading judgment observed that:

> 'Use of the word "related" implies that there must be some inter-connection between the matters or transactions, or in other words that they must in some way fit together, but the Law Society saw fit, after market negotiation, not to circumscribe the phrase "a series of related matters or transactions" by any particular criterion or set of criteria'.

Effectively, therefore, both the 'inter-dependency' and the 'intrinsic relationship' tests were jettisoned, and the Supreme Court considered that determining whether transactions are 'related' is an acutely fact-sensitive exercise, which should not be approached with any presumption as to the correct interpretation of the word.

As already mentioned, firms are free to negotiate the level of excess to be applied – meaning firms can elect to self-insure to a substantial extent without regard to the minimum terms.[9] Protection for the public is maintained as, if the insured fails to pay the amount of any excess to the claimant within 30 days, then following notification by the claimant, the insurer must make good the sum, reclaiming it from the insured as necessary.[10] The amount of any excess agreed between insurer and the insured does not reduce the total limit of liability;[11] however, if the insurer, upon being required to do so,[12] makes a payment to a claimant in default of an insured paying an excess, the insurer may stipulate that such payment (remedying the default) erodes the sum insured.[13] In contrast with previous rules, an excess may be applied to defence costs.[14] The insurance may provide for multiple claims to be treated as one claim for the purpose of calculating any excess, on terms that may be agreed between insurer and insured.[15]

The most important element of the minimum terms and conditions consists of the restrictions they impose on insurers for the purpose of ensuring that members of the public are not deprived of the benefits of compulsory professional indemnity insurance as a result of matters which, in other circumstances, might enable an insurer to disclaim or avoid liability. These are referred to in Annex 1 to SIIR 2019 as 'special conditions'.[16]

1   Clause 2.1 of Annex 1 to SIIR 2019. See **11.3** above for commentary on an expected change to the Glossary definition of recognised body.
2   Annex 1, clause 1.1.
3   Annex 1, clause 1.4.
4   Annex 1, clauses 1.2 and 2.2.
5   Annex 1, clause 2.3.
6   Annex 1, clause 2.5, the final example listed as 2.5(b).
7   [2003] 4 All ER 43, HL.
8   [2017] UKSC 18.

9   Annex 1, clause 3.1.
10 Annex 1, clause 3.4.
11 Annex 1, clause 3.2.
12 Annex 1, clause 3.4.
13 Annex 1, clause 3.4.
14 Annex 1, clause 3.3.
15 Annex 1, clause 3.5.
16 Annex 1, clause 4.

Restrictions on insurers – the 'special conditions'

11.6

Insurers are not entitled to avoid or repudiate insurance on any grounds whatsoever, including any breach of the duty to make a fair presentation of the risk or misrepresentation (fraudulent or otherwise). They are not entitled to reduce or deny their liability on any grounds whatsoever, including any breach of any term or condition of the insurance, other than if one of the specified exclusions applies (see further below). They are not entitled to cancel the insurance unless alternative qualifying insurance is in place (for example, in the event of a merger of firms), and cancellation must not affect rights and obligations that accrued prior to the cancellation. Insurers cannot set off any amounts due from the insured, such as any premium or reimbursement that may be due, against any amount payable to a claimant; they cannot reduce or exclude liability by reason of the existence or availability of other insurance (except other qualifying insurance in respect of an earlier period or cover by the SIF), although insurers are not prevented from seeking an appropriate contribution from that other insurer; and they cannot exclude or limit liability because relevant matters occurred before a specified date.

If there is a dispute as to whether a practice is a successor practice, all parties involved are required to take all reasonable steps to resolve it, including, if appropriate, referring the dispute to arbitration.

Insurers must meet defence costs (in so far as they are within the scope of insurance) as and when they are incurred unless and until the insured admits that he or she has committed or condoned dishonesty or a fraudulent act or omission, or a court or other judicial body finds that the insured was guilty of such dishonesty or fraudulent act or omission.[1]

The insurance must provide that its terms shall give effect to any variation in the SIIR (including the Glossary and MTC), to be implemented on the earliest of: renewal, replacement, or extension of the policy, or 18 months from the commencement of the policy period (although not if the 18-month period falls within the extended policy or cessation periods).[2]

Finally, the insurance is to be construed or rectified so as to comply with the requirements of the MTC (including any variation required to be implemented),[3] and any inconsistent provision must be severed or rectified to be compliant.[4]

1   Annex 1, clauses 4.1 to 4.9 of SIIR 2019.
2   Annex 1, clause 4.10.
3   Annex 1, clause 4.10.
4   Annex 1, clause 4.11.

Run-off and successor practices

11.7

Clause 5 of Annex 1 to SIIR 2019 deals with the extended indemnity period, the cessation period (see **11.4**), and run-off cover. Run-off cover must be for a minimum period of six years, and, subject to the rules on succession (see below), run from cessation, which may be during the policy, extended policy or cessation periods, or at the expiration of the policy or cessation periods. A practice shall be regarded as ceasing if and when it becomes a non-SRA firm, not authorised by another qualifying regulator – see **11.3**.

What is or is not a successor practice is a very material consideration, and not just in this respect, because the insurers of a successor practice will become liable for any claims against the former practice that have not already been discovered and notified. This term has its own definition in the Glossary for SIIR 2019 and is reproduced here for convenience.

successor practice

(a) means a *practice* identified in this definition as 'B', where:

  (i) 'A' is the *practice* to which B succeeds; and

  (ii) 'A's owner' is the owner of A immediately prior to transition; and

  (iii) 'B's owner' is the owner of B immediately following transition; and

  (iv) 'transition' means merger, acquisition, absorption or other transition which results in A no longer being carried on as a discrete legal *practice*.

(b) B is a successor practice to A where:

  (i) B is or was held out, expressly or by implication, by B's owner as being the successor of A or as incorporating A, whether such holding out is contained in notepaper, business cards, form of electronic communications, publications, promotional material or otherwise, or is contained in any statement or declaration by B's owner to any regulatory or taxation authority; and/or

  (ii) (where A's owner was a *sole practitioner* and the transition occurred on or before 31 August 2000) – the *sole practitioner* is a *principal* of B's owner; and/or

  (iii) (where A's owner was a *sole practitioner* and the transition occurred on or after 1 September 2000) – the *sole practitioner* is a *principal* or *employee* of B's owner; and/or

  (iv) (where A's owner was a *recognised body* or a *licensed body* (in respect of its *regulated activities*)) – that body is a *principal* of B's owner; and/or

  (v) (where A's owner was a *partnership*) – the majority of the *principals* of A's owner have become *principals* of B's owner; and/or

(vi) (where A's owner was a *partnership* and the majority of *principals* of A's owner did not become *principals* of the owner of another legal *practice* as a result of the transition) – one or more of the *principals* of A's owner have become *principals* of B's owner and:

(A) B is carried on under the same name as A or a name which substantially incorporates the name of A (or a substantial part of the name of A); and/or

(B) B is carried on from the same premises as A; and/or

(C) the owner of B acquired the goodwill and/or *assets* of A; and/or

(D) the owner of B assumed the liabilities of A; and/or

(E) the majority of staff employed by A's owner became *employees* of B's owner.

(c) notwithstanding the foregoing, B is not a successor practice to A under paragraph (b) (ii), (iii), (iv), (v) or (vi) if another *practice* is or was held out by the owner of that other *practice* as the successor of A or as incorporating A, provided that there is insurance complying with the *MTC* in relation to that other *practice*.

In brief, most circumstances involving the partners or other owners of a practice (or a majority of them) being absorbed into another firm – or even a minority in certain circumstances, or anything done or said which holds out expressly or impliedly that the second firm is succeeding to or incorporating the first firm – will result in the second firm being a successor practice. The definition focuses on people and ownership, rather than on cases and clients, so that if a firm does not hold itself out as a successor practice and acquires the clients and files of a firm that closes (for example) but does not take on its owners, either as principals or employees, it will not be a successor practice. Firms should be particularly careful when employing a solicitor who previously traded as a sole practitioner.

However, a firm which is about to close and to which there would be a successor practice for the purpose of SIIR 2019 has an option. It may allow that situation to occur, or it may, before the cessation of its business, elect to trigger its own run-off cover and pay the premium. In that event, there is no successor practice. If, prior to cessation, either the election is not made, or the run-off premium is not paid, the option is lost and the normal rules on succession will apply.[1] SIIR 2013 stipulated that notice must be given to the SRA by the insurer within seven days of receipt of notice of the election – this requirement is not replicated in SIIR 2019.

When a firm enters a run-off period but restarts practice (which might happen inadvertently), the insurer may cancel run-off cover provided that there is qualifying insurance in place, and it gives notice to the insured, and any other interested insurer, that it is providing qualifying insurance for the current indemnity period as a continuation of the insured firm's practice prior to cessation, and that it is liable for claims against the insured firm arising from circumstances which occurred prior to cessation.[2]

1   Clause 5.5 of Annex 1 to SIIR 2019.
2   Annex 1, clause 5.6.

Permitted exclusions

11.8

The minimum terms and conditions specify the permitted exclusions from liability in clause 6 of Annex 1 to SIIR 2019. They are:

- claims where cover is provided under insurance for a prior period;

- claims for death or bodily injury, except psychological injury and emotional distress arising from an insured breach of duty (that is, in the performance of or failure to perform legal work);

- claims for damage or loss to, or destruction of, property – unless it is property in the care of the insured in connection with the insured firm's practice, or where the damage or loss arises from an insured breach of duty;

- claims arising from partnership disputes within the firm or the like;

- claims in the nature of employment disputes about dismissal, harassment or discrimination and the like, including any training agreements;

- personal debts and trading liabilities (excluding HM Land Registry fees);

- claims in relation to guarantees, indemnities or undertakings in connection with the provision of financial or other benefits for the personal advantage of the insured;

- any fine or penalty or order for costs in relation to a professional conduct complaint; and

- punitive or exemplary damages awarded under US or Canadian law, other than in defamation.

Insurers may also exclude liability (and always do) for dishonesty or a fraudulent act or omission committed or condoned by an individual insured, but insurance must nonetheless cover each other insured and no dishonesty can be imputed to a body corporate unless it was committed or condoned by all directors of a company or members of a limited liability partnership.

Following the Supreme Court decision in *Ivey v Genting Casinos*, there should no longer be scope for significant disagreement on the test for dishonesty as there had been before that decision.[1]

Cover may also be excluded for company directors' or officers' liability, in that capacity (unless it arises from an insured breach of duty) and for claims arising from terrorism, war and other hostilities, and asbestos-related injury or damage (unless arising from an insured breach of duty).

1   *Ivey v Genting Casinos* [2017] UKSC 67. See **19.3**.

Definitions of 'claim' and 'defence costs'

11.9

A claim includes any civil claim for damages or compensation or an intimation of the same, and also includes an obligation on the insured to remedy any breach of the

SRA Accounts Rules, or any rules that replace them, even if no individual has made any claim or given any intimation of a claim in relation to such breach. At the time of writing, the proposed definition[1] of 'claim' refers only to 'the SRA Accounts Rules, or any rules which replace them'. The SRA Accounts Rules are the 2019 rules. Perhaps unintentionally, the proposed definition does not appear to cover, as it did in previous glossaries, either the Solicitors' Accounts Rules 1998 or SIIR 2013; this may be corrected or clarified prior to implementation. However, any breach of the earlier rules that has not been remedied is likely to constitute a breach of SIIR 2019, and thus if insurers are to be notified of such a breach in the indemnity year after implementation of the new definition, firms may be able to rely upon rule 6.1 of the SRA Accounts Rules.

Defence costs include legal costs and disbursements (including investigative and related expenses) reasonably and necessarily incurred with the consent of the insurer in:

- defending any proceedings relating to a claim;

- conducting any proceedings for indemnity, contribution or recovery relating to a claim;

- investigating, reducing, avoiding or compromising any actual or potential claim; and

- acting for any insured in connection with any investigation, inquiry or any disciplinary proceeding (save in respect of any disciplinary proceeding under the authority of the SRA or the Solicitors Disciplinary Tribunal).

Defence costs do not include any internal or overhead expenses of the insured firm or the insurer or the cost of the insured firm's time.

The costs of disciplinary proceedings were formerly required to be covered, with some limitations, but this obligatory aspect of cover was removed from 1 October 2010.

1   Currently set out in a separate Glossary for SRA Indemnity Insurance Rules (including the MTC) and SRA Compensation Fund Rules: the SRA intends to add the defined terms to the SRA Glossary 2019.

Other regulatory obligations

11.10

A firm must notify the SRA and its insurer as soon as reasonably practicable, and in any event within five business days, after entering the extended policy period, and after entering the cessation period, and must also notify both parties if qualifying insurance is obtained within either period, with the details of the participating insurer and policy.[1]

A firm, and any principal, is required to provide details of its qualifying insurance to any person who asserts a claim apparently covered by the policy, and to anyone who is insured under the policy, upon request.[2] The Provision of Services Regulations 2009[3] also obligate firms to provide contact details for the insurer and the territorial coverage,[4] which in the case of the minimum terms and conditions, is worldwide. The requirements can be met by a notice in the firm's reception area.

Whereas SIIR 2013 made reference to specific disciplinary offences (essentially, being two months in arrears of a premium or excess due, or taking on new instructions during a cessation period), SIIR 2019 do not. However, firms' overarching obligation to comply with the SRA's regulatory arrangements[5] will be sufficient for the SRA to take disciplinary action in the event of a breach of SIIR 2019, including, for example, if a firm were to accept new instructions during the cessation period.[6]

Additionally, whereas SIIR 2013 obligated the firm's insurer to bring to the attention of the SRA a variety of specified failures, SIIR 2019 do not. However, by and large the same obligations are typically set out in the participating insurers agreement entered into between the SRA and insurer. Therefore, while at the time of writing the participating insurers agreement for 2019 is not available,[7] firms can expect insurers to be obligated to report at least the following:

- the insurer becomes aware of any:

    – material inaccuracy in a proposal form;

    – matter or circumstances

    other than, in either case, where the insurer believes any relevant act or omission on the part of the firm to have been innocent; or

- the insurer suspects or becomes aware of dishonesty or fraud by any insured and as a result:

    – reserves its position as regards any part of a claim made by that firm; or

    – notifies that firm that it will not, or intends not to, indemnify that firm in full in respect of a claim made by that firm; or

    – seeks, or reserves its right to seek, reimbursement from any insured, of any amount paid out the policy;

- that the firm fails to pay any sum due to the insurer in respect of any policy, and the insurer has reasonable grounds for believing that such failure constitutes a wilful refusal to pay such sum.

1 Rule 8.1.
2 Rule 9.2.
3 SI 2009/2999.
4 Regulation 8(1)(n).
5 Paragraph 2.1 of the Code for Firms.
6 Rule 4.2 of SIIR 2019.
7 The 2018 agreement is available on the SRA website at www.sra.org.uk/documents/rules/participating-insurers-agreement-2018.pdf.

Non-SRA firms, freelance solicitors and non-commercial bodies

11.11

As described above, SIIR 2019 apply only to authorised bodies and their principals; thus they do not apply to solicitors providing unreserved legal services from bodies not authorised by the SRA ('non-SRA firms'), freelance solicitors or solicitors providing reserved legal services in non-commercial bodies.[1]

The SRA does not require non-SRA firms to carry professional indemnity insurance; thus, for example, the SRA permits solicitors practising in-house to provide unreserved legal services to members of the public without insurance. However, non-SRA firms may otherwise be obliged to carry such insurance, for example as may be required by another regulator.

Freelance solicitors that conduct reserved legal activities are obliged to 'take out and maintain indemnity insurance that provides adequate and appropriate cover in respect of the services that you provide or have provided, whether or not they comprise reserved legal activities, taking into account any alternative arrangements you or your clients may make'.[2]

Solicitors (and RELs) carrying on reserved legal activities in a non-commercial body must ensure that '(a) the body takes out and maintains indemnity insurance; and (b) this insurance provides adequate and appropriate cover in respect of the services that you provide or have provided, whether or not they comprise reserved legal activities, taking into account any alternative arrangements the body or its clients may make.'[3]

'Adequate and appropriate cover' is not defined, and at the time of writing, the SRA has not produced guidance.[4] If the SRA intended that adequate and appropriate cover should mean cover equivalent to the MTC, it would have imposed a duty upon freelance solicitors to procure such cover. In its application to the LSB, the SRA commented: 'only SRA authorised firms will be required to have insurance that meets our MTCs'.[5] Thus, adequate and appropriate cover may fall short of the MTC. One of the important protections of the MTC is that it cannot be avoided in the same way that commercial insurance can. Freelancers may need to take particular care when considering the terms of insurance including any avoidance provisions.

An amendment to the rules[6] obliges freelancers and solicitors providing reserved legal services in non-commercial bodes to address past practice, as authorised bodies are obliged to do.

As these categories of practitioner and practice are not subject to SIIR 2019, the obligations set out therein not to exclude liability below the minimum level of cover, and to procure run-off cover, are not applicable to them. Freelancers providing reserved legal services, and solicitors providing reserved legal services in non-commercial bodies, should proceed cautiously when seeking to exclude liability,[7] and have regard to general consumer laws, and the requirements upon them to provide adequate and appropriate cover, act in a client's best interests, not take unfair advantage of clients, and ensure that clients understand the impact of the limitation of liability. The SRA could potentially deem that adequate and appropriate cover would include run-off cover.

Freelancers are required to inform their clients, before engagement, that they are not subject to the requirement to purchase qualifying insurance on the SRA's MTC and, where applicable, that alternative arrangements are in place. The freelancer will also, upon request, need to provide information about the cover provided.[8]

---

1   As permitted by section 23(1) of the Legal Services Act (LSA) 2007 and as defined by section 23(2).
2   Regulation 10.2(b)(vi) of the SRA Authorisation of Individuals Regulations 2019 as amended by the SRA Regulatory Arrangements (Indemnity Insurance) (Amendment) Rules 2018.
3   Paragraph 5.6 of the Code for Individuals as amended by the SRA Regulatory Arrangements (Indemnity Insurance) (Amendment) Rules 2018.

4 In a letter of 1 April 2019 to the LSB, available on its website, the Law Society has provided an outline of what it considers would be required. In its decision notice of 31 May 2019, the LSB indicated that it had seen SRA produced 'draft guidance' and acknowledged that it will provide 'more clarity'.

5 Application 5 March 2019.

6 SRA Regulatory Arrangements (Indemnity Insurance) (Amendment) Rules 2018 approved by the LSB 31 May 2019.

7 In its Decision Notice of 31 May 2019, the LSB noted that SRA had confirmed that it will produce guidance on adequate and appropriate insurance for solicitors that will address any cap on liability.

8 Rule 4.3 of the SRA Transparency Rules 2018.

The Insurance Act 2015

11.12

The Insurance Act 2015, in force since 12 August 2016, imposes a duty on the insured to make a 'fair presentation of the risk' to insurers when taking out insurance (including renewals and variations) (section 3(1)). This requires disclosure of material circumstances that it knows of, those that it ought to know of and sufficient information to make further enquiries for the purpose of revealing those material circumstances.

Section 4(6) of the Act provides that

'… an insured ought to know what should reasonably have been revealed by a reasonable search of information available to the insured (whether the search is conducted by making enquiries or by any other means).'

It would be prudent for firms to err on the side of caution, to avoid allegations of a breach of this duty, which might lead to a claim for an increased premium, excess or reimbursement, as the policy may provide.

Other changes being considered

11.13

In June 2018 the SRA closed a consultation on proposed changes to SIIR 2013. Some of the proposals are not included in SIIR 2019, but are understood to remain under consideration. They include the following.

Reducing the compulsory layer of professional indemnity insurance

11.14

Excluding defence costs, the compulsory layer would be a minimum of £1 million for conveyancing claims, and a minimum of £500,000 for all other claims. Firms would need an endorsement to their policy to carry out conveyancing services. The existing imbalance in compulsory layers between sole practitioners and conventional partnerships[1] on the one hand, and LLPs and ABSs on the other would be removed.

Firms may find that they are forced to take out a higher level of cover in any event, to satisfy the conditions of panel membership, for example, mortgage lenders' panels, if not the requirement for 'adequate and appropriate cover'.

The SRA also planned to introduce a permitted exclusion for what it terms 'large commercial clients', which it defines as clients with a turnover exceeding £2 million in the most recent financial year. The exclusion would mean that firms catering only to such clients would not need qualifying insurance at all. However, firms providing services to such clients will still need to ensure that appropriate and adequate insurance cover is obtained. Turnover would be a defined term in the new Glossary, but firms may find that such data may not be readily available to determine whether the exclusion applies and when the evaluation should be made for the purposes of establishing whether qualifying insurance is needed. For example, if a firm advises a smaller business under the current rules, does it need to maintain qualifying insurance for a period of 14 years until limitation has fully expired? Does that obligation expire when the turnover of the business grows to exceed £2 million? What if a client falls just short of the £2 million figure in month 11 of its accounting year for an expected reason?

The SRA is motivated to reduce insurance premiums[2] and consequently, it hopes, the cost of legal services. Critics say the only significant consequence of the proposed rule change is a reduction in consumer protection.[3] There will be significant consequences too for solicitors exposed to claims without adequate insurance cover.

The SRA reasons that 98 per cent of claims over a ten-year research period settled for less than £500,000, and as such, most claims will continue to be protected.[4] Some insurers and brokers have commented that a significant reduction in premiums is unlikely, particularly as premiums are already set according to the risk, and thus have already factored in that most claims settle for less than £500,000.

A total of 442 claims, equivalent to 16.3 per cent of all claims included in the SRA's research data would have been at risk under the new rules, valued at £260 million. Of the 442 claims, 326 were consumer claims worth £189 million, 37 were claims relating to properties purchased for more than £1 million (at the time). Nevertheless, the SRA suggests that members of the public and small businesses are 'extremely unlikely to experience a claim that would be above the new minimum limits'. Therefore one assumes that the SRA research data reveals that the 16.3 per cent at risk relates almost exclusively to businesses with a turnover of more than £2 million. The data also reveals that 51 per cent of all claims related to conveyancing. Furthermore, the SRA only obtained claims records from insurers which had remained in the legal services market and thus its data collection is not complete.

In firms that elect to insure for the minimum, consumer protection will be lower, and solicitors' exposure to personal liability greater. Additionally, such reduced cover may increase the likelihood of an insurer deeming a claim uncommercial to litigate, notwithstanding any defence raised by the insured. The SRA has expressed that it wishes to create a climate where fewer claims are 'unnecessarily' defended. The SRA has not published data in support of this assertion; insurers would argue that claims are never unnecessarily defended, and some insureds complain that insurers are too willing to compromise claims for commercial reasons, even where a defence has reasonable merits.

Despite the reduction in consumer protection, the SRA has indicated that it expects to take stronger enforcement steps for non-payment of insurance premiums and misleading an insurer. Insurers will remain unable to exclude cover for a firm following such misconduct.

1   At the time of writing, SIIR 2019 impose the same compulsory layer for conventional firms as they do for LLPs and ABSs, however the SRA has indicated to the authors that this was unintended, and is expected to be corrected – see **11.3**.
2   The SRA believes that these changes will cause premiums to fall by between 9 per cent and 17 per cent for annual insurance, and even more for run-off insurance.
3   The SRA also planned to reduce the limit of a claim upon the SRA Compensation Fund to £500,000 and narrow eligibility requirements.
4   Note, however, that the claims data did not include data from insurers who had ceased operating in the market during that time.

Defence costs

11.15

Changes to the obligation to insure defence costs are also being considered.

In addition to the existing provision enabling insurers and insureds to agree an excess payable for each claim, the proposed MTCs will allow them to agree a limit on the cover provided for defence costs,. The SRA would look to introduce this flexibility with the aim of reducing insurance premiums, but also, by shifting the cost of defence to firms, the number of claims defended with the backing of insurers. Firms will need to assess their requirements carefully.

Run-off insurance

11.16

The requirement that policies provide six years' run-off cover would be retained, but capped at £3 million for firms that are insured for, or have provided, conveyancing services, or £1.5 million in all other cases. The SRA recognises that this may lead to partners, directors and members becoming liable for claims beyond these limits, and thus deems this to be an acceptable risk.

The SRA is motivated to reduce the cost of run-off insurance, with a view to making it easier for firms to close. It would remain to be seen whether run-off premiums would in fact fall, or whether firms would pay similar premiums for reduced cover. The SRA understandably considers that firms unable to close for want of the financial resources to pay for run-off cover represent a high regulatory risk. It believes that lower premiums from revised run-off requirements will lead to a reduction in the number of interventions.

Minor changes

11.17

In addition to the changes outlined above, other minor changes are proposed.

Where, upon the default of an insured, an insurer is required to pay the excess direct to a claimant, the insurer would no longer be permitted to set such payment off against the limit of its cover, but can still proceed otherwise to recover its loss from the insured.

If a dispute arises between insurer(s) and insured(s) as to whether a firm is a successor practice, which cannot be resolved by agreement, the rules would provide for resolution by Queen's Counsel.

Dealing with claims

11.18

Outcome 1.16 of the SRA Code of Conduct 2011 (namely that 'you inform current clients if you discover any act or omission which could give rise to a claim by them against you') is replaced by paragraph 3.5 of the Code for Firms: 'You are honest and open with clients if things go wrong and if a client suffers loss or harm as a result you put matters right (if possible) and explain fully and promptly what has happened and the likely impact …'.

Whereas compliance with the outgoing rule could be achieved simply by advising clients to seek independent legal advice, the new rule imposes a positive obligation to provide a full explanation of what has happened and the likely impact. Most professional indemnity insurance policies obligate an insured to not admit liability without the prior written consent of the insurer. Early contact with the firm's insurer will be key to ensuring that the full and prompt explanation does not prejudice the firm's insurance cover.

In a Tribunal judgment[1] on an application for an agreed outcome, pre-dating the introduction of the Code for Firms, a firm was found to have acted improperly in seeking to 'put matters right', in light of an own interest conflict. In light of paragraph 3.5 of the Code for Firms, firms should communicate with their insurers at an early stage to determine the appropriate steps to be taken.

1   *SRA v Howell Jones LLP*, 11846–2018.

CHAPTER 12

Registered European lawyers and registered foreign lawyers

12.1

A registered European lawyer (REL) is an individual registered with the Solicitors Regulation Authority (SRA) under regulation 17 of the European Communities (Lawyer's Practice) Regulations 2000[1] (the '2000 Regulations'): see **APPENDIX 8**.[2]

A registered foreign lawyer (RFL) is an individual registered with the SRA under section 89 of the Courts and Legal Services Act (CLSA) 1990: see **APPENDIX 19**.

By virtue of their registration, both RELs and RFLs become subject to regulation by the SRA and are subject to the same rules of professional conduct and the whole regulatory and disciplinary regime that is in place for solicitors, with very little modification or exception. Further, as a result of the move to entity-based regulation, RELs and RFLs are liable for compliance with all relevant professional rules, including the 2019 regulatory arrangements, as managers or employees of regulated practices (see **CHAPTER 2**).

1 SI 2000/1119.
2 At the time of writing, it is unclear whether recognition of professional qualifications across the European Union/European Economic Area will remain part of UK law following the UK's departure from the EU. In the event of a 'no deal' Brexit, current information is that the position of RELs registered before 'exit day' will be subject to transitional arrangements allowing RELs to continue in practice until 2020. There would be no entitlement to registration as an REL during the transitional period. RELs should ensure that they are fully informed as to the impact of Brexit on their professional status, both in the UK and in their home jurisdiction.

12.2

RELs may practise, for all practical purposes, as if they are solicitors, and subject to the same restrictions, in that they can practise on their own account (but only if they are authorised to as a recognised sole practice, as solicitors are required to be under the SRA Authorisation of Firms Rules 2019), or as employees or managers of authorised bodies in accordance with the SRA Authorisation of Firms Rules 2019.

There are some limitations on the practising rights of RELs set out in regulations 9.2 and 9.3 of the SRA Authorisation of Individuals Regulations 2019. These require:

(i)   that RELs conducting litigation before a court, preparing court documents or exercising rights of audience may only do so in conjunction with a solicitor or barrister authorised to do so;[1]

(ii) that RELs may only prepare and/or lodge instruments transferring or charging land for remuneration if they have a home title listed under regulation 12 of the European Communities (Lawyer's Practice) Regulations 2000;[2]

(iii)   that RELs may only carry on probate activities for remuneration if they have a home title listed under regulation 13 of the European Communities (Lawyer's Practice) Regulations 2000.[3]

The provisions permitting RELs to operate within England and Wales without necessarily needing to do so through an SRA-authorised body, by practising through an Exempt European Practice (EEP) as defined in the SRA Handbook Glossary 2012, have not been replicated in the 2019 regulatory arrangements. This is presumably because the SRA has instead advocated a revised approach permitting practice as a solicitor, REL or RFL in unregulated firms – provided that no reserved activities are provided to the public. This revised approach removes any need for the specific provisions of the EEP regime.

RELs working in unregulated firms, including firms which may have been EEPs, will still be required to comply with the SRA Code of Conduct for Solicitors, RELs and RFLs 2019.

1   Regulation 9.2.
2   Regulation 9.3(a)
3   Regulation 9.3(b).

12.3

RFLs, in contrast, are more restricted in the way they can practise. The main purpose of being registered as an RFL is to enable the individual to practise in a recognised body with a solicitor or solicitors, or an REL or RELs or a combination of the two – that is, as a manager, member or owner of a recognised body.[1] There is no requirement on a foreign lawyer to become an RFL for the purposes of being employed by a recognised body or a sole practitioner, or to be an owner, manager or employee of a licensed body. Registration does not permit an RFL to practise as a sole practitioner or an in-house RFL.[2]

Limitations on practising requirements for RFLs have largely been removed in the 2019 regulatory arrangements. The express requirements have been replaced by general information requirements in the SRA Code of Conduct for Solicitors, RELs and RFLs 2019, in particular at paragraph 8.10 (as discussed at **4.119**).

RFLs are not permitted to undertake reserved activities in the same way that solicitors and RELs are. Regulation 9.4 of the SRA Authorisation of Individuals Regulations 2019 provides that RFLs may only

'(a)   undertake advocacy in chambers in England and Wales under instructions given by a person who is authorised to do so;

(b)   under the direction and supervision of a person qualified to supervise:

   (i)   prepare *court* documents;

   (ii)   prepare instruments and the lodging of documents relating to the transfer or charge of land;

   (iii)   prepare papers on which to found or oppose a grant of probate, or a grant of letters of administration;

   (iv)   prepare trust deeds disposing of capital if you also are eligible to act as a *lawyer of England and Wales*;

(c)   in relation to *immigration work*:

(i)   undertake advocacy before immigration tribunals;

(ii) have conduct of, and prepare documents for, immigration tribunal proceedings.'

where immigration work may only be undertaken through an authorised body, an authorised non-SRA firm which is a qualified person for the purposes of the Immigration and Asylum Act 1999 or a body regulated by the Office of the Immigration Services Commissioner.[3]

RFLs are otherwise not permitted to undertake any reserved activities.

1   See rules 1.1(b) and 13.2 of the SRA Authorisation of Firms Rules 2019. RFLs are within the definition of 'legally qualified' pursuant to section 9A(6)(b) of the Administration of Justice Act 1985.
2   Rule 1.1(c) of the SRA Authorisation of Firms Rules 2019.
3   Regulation 9.5 of the SRA Authorisation of Individuals Regulations 2019.

12.4

Under Schedule 4 to the 2000 Regulations most of the statutory regime applying to solicitors through the Solicitors Act (SA) 1974 is extended to RELs, including provisions relating to:

- regulation through practising certificates (section 28 of SA 1974);

- all the rule-making powers in relation to professional conduct, accounts and insurance (sections 31, 32, 33A, 34 and 37 of SA 1974);

- the SRA's investigative and disciplinary powers (sections 44B, 44BA, 44BC, 44C and 44D of SA 1974);

- the control of the employment of disqualified persons, equally applicable to RELs as employers and employees (sections 41 to 44 of SA 1974);

- the powers of the Solicitors Disciplinary Tribunal and the High Court (sections 46 to 53 of SA 1974); and

- the powers of intervention (section 35 of and Schedule 1 to SA 1974).

This is not intended to be an exhaustive list.

The statutory regime governing RFLs is to be found in Schedule 14 to CLSA 1990 (see **APPENDIX 19**). This makes provision for applications for registration, registration subject to conditions, the renewal of registration, and for appeals to the High Court against a refusal to register, refusal to renew registration, and the imposition of conditions.

The Schedule also provides for contributions to the Compensation Fund (and this also is extended to RELs by the 2000 Regulations), imposes a requirement to provide accountants' reports, provides for the effect of bankruptcy and for the effect of disciplinary action leading to the RFL being dealt with in his or her home jurisdiction in a way that is equivalent to being struck off or suspended, and extends the jurisdiction of the Solicitors Disciplinary Tribunal to RFLs.

CHAPTER 13

Regulation by other approved regulators

13.1

As pointed out in **CHAPTER 2**, in any analysis of the regulation of solicitors it is no longer possible to consider only the rules and regulations promulgated by the Solicitors Regulation Authority (SRA). From 31 March 2009, a solicitor could be individually regulated by the SRA, but employed by or a manager of a business entity supplying legal services that is regulated by another approved regulator. In that situation, the solicitor, in his professional dealings, must comply with the rules of the business's regulator, because the Legal Services Act (LSA) 2007 specifies that if there is a conflict between the regulation of the entity and the regulation of the individual, the regulation of the entity takes precedence.[1]

Currently, there are no fewer than five approved regulators able to authorise and regulate entities in which solicitors could be employees or partners (or equivalent): the SRA, the Council for Licensed Conveyancers (CLC), the Bar Standards Board (BSB), the Institute of Chartered Accountants in England and Wales (ICAEW), and CILEx Regulation.

At present, the CLC (although a licensing authority for the purposes of LSA 2007) regulates only conveyancing, probate and will writing activity. As of April 2017, the BSB was authorised as a licensing authority for all reserved activities; however, its expressed focus is on litigation and advocacy before a court as it considers those matters to be reflective of its areas of expertise. CILEx Regulation's application for approval as a licensing authority was approved by the Legal Services Board in July 2018 and a statutory instrument giving effect to that decision came into force on 1 April 2019.

With the advent of changes to professional indemnity insurance requirements making it easier to change regulators, evidence is beginning to emerge of firms electing to move to other regulators, principally the CLC. On the information currently available, the CLC is the primary alternative regulator of choice, although this position may change as the possibility of an alternative regulator and the approach of individual regulators becomes more widely known. For the purposes of this edition, a brief consideration of the CLC rules is justified; however, this is not intended to be exhaustive.

---

1   Section 52(4) of LSA 2007.

Conduct rules

13.2

The Council for Licensed Conveyancers has its own 'Handbook' comprising principles, a Code of Conduct, and a series of supplementary codes dealing with accounts, anti-money laundering and combating terrorist financing, complaints, conflicts of interest, continuing professional development, dealing with non-authorised persons, disclosure of profits and advantages, equality, estimates and terms of engagement, management and supervision, notification requirements, professional indemnity insurance, transaction files, undertakings, acting as ancillary insurance intermediaries and acting for lenders and prevention and detection of mortgage fraud. There are also codes relating to the governance and operation of recognised bodies and licensed bodies.

The CLC has, like the SRA, embraced outcomes-focused regulation. It has its own six 'overriding principles' (compared with the SRA's seven (formerly ten)):

'1. Act with independence and integrity;

2. Maintain high standards of work;

3. Act in the best interests of your Clients;

4. Comply with your duty to the court;

5. Deal with regulators and ombudsmen in an open and co-operative way;

6. Promote equality of access and service.'

13.3

The whole of the CLC Code of Conduct is contained within some nine pages at **APPENDIX 10**.

Whereas the SRA Principles sit alongside the SRA Codes of Conduct, which deal with specific requirements, the CLC Code of Conduct is in six parts, each developing and expanding one of the six overriding principles by stating required outcomes, principles underlying the outcomes and specific requirements associated with the overriding principle. Stylistically, they are readily interpreted as rules, with little that is vague or uncertain.

Conflicts of interest – acting for buyer and seller

13.4

Perhaps the most stark variation between the approach of the CLC and the SRA is in this aspect of the regulation of conveyancing practice. It is notable that the attitude of the CLC to conflicts of interest in conveyancing is in vivid contrast to that of the SRA – in acting for buyer and seller the SRA considers that a conflict of interests is almost inevitable, and that solicitors should not generally act for both parties (although there is no longer any express requirement in the new Codes of Conduct to replicate indicative behaviour 3.3 of the SRA Code of Conduct 2011). The CLC's requirement is: 'Where the entity represents parties with different interests in any transaction each party is at all times represented by different Authorised Persons conducting themselves in the matter as though they were members of different entities'.[1]

Further guidance is given in the CLC's Conflicts of Interest Code:

'7. Before or when accepting instructions to act for a second Client you inform each Client in writing that the body has been asked to act for another Client in the same matter and you explain the relevant issues and risks to them.

8. You only act for both Clients if each Client has provided informed written consent that you may act for another Client in the matter.

9. You do not act, or do not continue to act, for a Client where your ability to give independent advice is in any way restricted. This may arise if:

   (a) you owe separate duties to act in the best interests of two or more clients in relation to the same or related matters, and those duties conflict, or there is a significant risk that those duties may conflict; or

   (b) your duty to act in the best interests of any client in relation to a matter conflicts, or there is a significant risk that it may conflict, with your own interests in relation to that or a related matter.

10. If a conflict arises which was or should have been foreseen, you do not charge either Client a fee for the work undertaken (other than for disbursements properly incurred).'[2]

1   CLC Code of Conduct, overriding principle 3 (client's best interests), specific requirement (n).
2   CLC Conflicts of Interest Code, specific requirements 7 to 10.

13.5

The CLC also expressly permits sole practitioners (or businesses where there is only one authorised person) to act for buyer and lender in the same transaction, if the lender is providing mortgages in the normal course of its business activities, without additional obligations.[1]

The guidance to the Conflicts of Interest Code includes references as to the nature and significance of transactions that are not at arm's length, and as to the need for additional caution when the selling client is a developer or builder, or a lessor granting a lease.[2]

1   CLC Conflicts of Interest Code, specific requirement 11.
2   CLC Conflicts of Interest Guidance.

Referrals and commission

13.6

The CLC's regulatory requirements in these areas are succinct and straightforward. Referral arrangements and fees are dealt with primarily within overriding principle 3 (the requirement to act in the client's best interests): that clients have the information they need to make informed decisions; clients are aware of any referral arrangements and that they are consistent with the practitioner's responsibilities both to them and to the CLC; and clients are informed promptly in writing of the existence and amount of any sum payable directly or indirectly as a result of receipt of the client's instructions.[1]

All referral arrangements between the CLC practice and a third party including any fee sharing arrangement must be in writing, and referral arrangements must be periodically reviewed to ensure that they deliver the appropriate outcomes to clients. Practitioners must inform clients in writing of the existence of the arrangement no later than when receiving instructions (or when introducing the client to another person). Clients should be advised that they have a choice of provider, and informed of the nature of the arrangement (including any payment made), with whom it is made, and any impact (including any legal costs they are charged).[2]

The CLC requirement in relation to payments received by the practitioner or business when the client is introduced to another party is found in principle 3 of the Code of Conduct, specific requirement (s): 'You promptly inform the Client in writing of the existence and amount of any sum payable (whether directly or indirectly) as a result of receipt of that Client's instructions.'

It may be noted that the requirement is to inform, not to account. However, as discussed at **4.87**, the obligation to account arises from the fiduciary relationship between the professional person and the client and is a matter of law independent of any professional rule. The CLC Code of Conduct, overriding principle 1: acting with independence and integrity, includes a compulsory outcome that clients receive an honest and lawful service,[3] and compliance with the law would require the client's informed consent if the sum is to be retained. However, it can be said that the CLC regulations follow the law, with no further complications, and the issue could be dealt with by standard terms and conditions of business if there is sufficient clarity.

Moreover, in relation to financial services, the CLC position also follows the law precisely. If commission is earned in relation to services regulated under the Financial Services and Markets Act (FSMA) 2000, there is an obligation to account to the client for any pecuniary award or other advantage received other than from the client.[4] See further at **8.5**.

1 CLC Code of Conduct, overriding principle 3, outcomes 3.3 and 3.4 and specific requirement (s).
2 CLC Disclosure of Profits and Advantages Code, specific requirements 12 to 16.
3 CLC Code of Conduct, overriding principle 1, outcome 1.2.
4 Section 327(3) of FSMA 2000 and specific requirement 36 of the CLC Acting as Insurance Intermediaries Code.

Accounts and financial services

13.7

Solicitors familiar (historically) with the Solicitors' Accounts Rules 1998 and the SRA Accounts Rules 2011 will not encounter any difficulties in complying with the CLC's Accounts Code and accompanying Guidance. The latter are a rather less complex set of rules but directed to the same ends.

The Accounts Code is in five parts, comprising basic rules on the treatment of client money, the obligation to maintain proper accounts, including the completion of bank reconciliations, provisions as to deposit interest, arrangements for monitoring by the CLC, and accountant's reports. There is separate guidance on aged balances.

All individuals and bodies regulated by the CLC must:

- comply with the Accounts Code, and not permit anyone else to act or fail to act in breach of the Code;

- ensure that partners, employees and directors (including partners, employees and directors who are not authorised persons) comply with the Code;

- use each client's money only for that client's matters;

- only pay money into, and withdraw money from the client account and office account for purposes related to the provision of services regulated by the CLC;

- establish and maintain proper accounting systems, procedures, processes and internal controls, to ensure compliance with the Code;

- ensure there is no debit balance on the client side of a client ledger account nor a credit balance on the office side of a client ledger account;

- remedy any breach of these requirements without delay (which means normally the same day or the next working day); and

- account to the client as soon as possible after completion of any transaction or after a retainer has been terminated.[1]

Money held on account of costs and disbursements must be withdrawn from client account within 28 days of the date on which a bill of costs is sent to a client, provided it is made clear to the client or the paying party either before or at the time the bill of costs is sent that such money will be applied towards or in payment of that bill of costs.[2] Undrawn costs or disbursements must not remain in client account, either in anticipation of future errors which could result in a shortage on that account or to make good any current shortage on that account, and are not available as a set-off against any general shortage on client account.[3] The CLC must be notified without delay (in normal circumstances, the same day or the next working day) upon discovery of any misappropriation of client money.[4]

When money is held for a client in a client account or if money should have been held in a client account but was not so held, the firm must account to the client for any interest earned or which should have been earned on that money. A client may apply to the CLC for a direction for the payment of interest, which must be paid within 15 days. If appropriate the CLC may require an interest calculation from the relevant bank or building society. There is no *de minimis* provision. There is a provision enabling contracting out which requires that clients are fully informed in writing and give informed consent in writing. This includes expressly drawing the client's attention to any contracting out provision which may be contained in terms of engagement.[5]

The guidance on aged balances is in two parts; the first part concentrates on mechanisms and systems designed to avoid the problem occurring. The CLC arrangements for withdrawing aged balances are in three bands depending on the amount: less than £20; £20 or more but less than £100, or £100 and over. In the first category the CLC may authorise payment to the office account subject to the provision of basic information about each balance and an undertaking from the firm to pay the amount due to a rightful recipient within 14 days of any request. The CLC may give permission for larger sums to be paid to the CLC's Compensation Fund, subject to being satisfied that all reasonable steps have been taken to trace the recipient. The difference in the 'banding' relates to the information the CLC needs before authority will be given.[6]

1   Preamble to and requirement 9 of the CLC Accounts Code.
2   Requirement 12.1.4.
3   Requirement 12.6.
4   Requirement 13.16.
5   Requirement 15.1 to 15.3.
6   CLC Accounts Guidance, Aged Balances Guidance.

13.8

The CLC has issued the Acting as Ancillary Insurance Intermediaries Code and accompanying Guidance to regulate the supply of services under Part XX of FSMA 2000 by bodies regulated by the CLC enabling firms to provide specified financial services that are incidental to conveyancing or other services regulated by the CLC.

The obligation to account for commission related to the supply of services regulated under FSMA 2000 has been mentioned above; see **13.6**. The CLC clarified the position with the Financial Services Authority (as it then was) and has offered further guidance, updated to reflect the replacement of the Financial Services Authority by the Financial Conduct Authority:

'The FCA considers that, in order for a Client to be accounted to for the purposes of s.327(3) FSMA, you must treat any commission or other pecuniary benefit received from third parties and which results from Regulated Activities carried on by the body, as held to the order of the Client. You will not be accounting to the Client simply by telling them that you receive commission. Unless the client agrees to you keeping it, the commission belongs to them and must be paid to them. There is no de minimis below which you may retain the sum. In the FCA's opinion, the condition would be satisfied if you pay over to the Client any third party payment received. Otherwise, it would be satisfied by informing the Client of the payment received and advising the Client that they have the right to require the body to pay them the sum concerned. This could then be used to offset fees due from the Client in respect of Professional Services provided or in recognition of other services provided. However, it does not permit retention of third party payments by seeking the Client's agreement through standard terms and conditions. Similarly, a mere notification to the Client that a particular sum has been received coupled with your request to retain it does not satisfy the condition.'[1]

1   Paragraph 9 of the CLC's Acting as Ancillary Insurance Intermediaries Guidance.

PART 4
The regulatory system in practice

CHAPTER 14

The Legal Ombudsman

14.1

The date 6 October 2010 was another major milestone on the road to the transformation of the regulation of legal services brought about by the Legal Services Act (LSA) 2007: the Legal Ombudsman opened for business. The Legal Ombudsman (LeO) is the brand adopted by the Office for Legal Complaints, a body corporate established by section 114 of LSA 2007.

All consumer complaints about the quality of service provided by any regulated legal professional (or 'authorised person' to use the terminology of LSA 2007) are now made to LeO. The previous fragmented system, whereby complaints about barristers went to the Bar Standards Board, those about solicitors went to the Legal Complaints Service (LCS) of the Law Society, and those about licensed conveyancers went to the Council for Licensed Conveyancers, has been replaced with a single complaints body. A typical consequence is that a litigation client who knows or believes that something has gone wrong, but does not know whether it is the fault of his solicitor or barrister, does not have to guess to whom he or she should complain, in the expectation of choosing the wrong one first. LeO has the task of establishing whether anything did go wrong and, if so, who should provide redress.

LeO started with a clean slate; it did not take over any complaints which were already in the hands of the former organisations.

The new approach

14.2

LSA 2007 does not contain any words which are the equivalent of 'inadequate professional services' as used in Schedule 1A to the Solicitors Act 1974. LeO has jurisdiction in relation to complaints made by clients (and limited other categories) about acts or omissions of authorised persons; the only threshold or test to be satisfied for an award or direction to be made is that it is fair and reasonable in all the circumstances of the case.[1]

LeO concentrates on what the client is actually complaining about, and in particular what would put it right (not, for example, what the client would like to happen to the solicitor). This may be as simple as an acknowledgement that something had gone wrong, and an apology or a modest amount of money to recognise non-economic or non-quantifiable loss for inconvenience, annoyance and distress, but may also be the equivalent of common law damages (in amount) for real financial loss.

The investigative approach is inquisitorial, not adversarial: a fact-gathering exercise. LeO examines what happened, and what if anything went wrong; to establish this it requests information and documents from the parties. The flow of information follows targeted requests, and the ping-pong of charge and counter-charge is avoided so far as possible. With that in mind there is no automatic exchange of documents containing complaints and explanations. LeO sends a summary of a complaint to the lawyer and will collect evidence *at the same time* from both complainants and lawyers. This is regarded as good investigative practice and meets the statutory test of dealing with matters quickly and with minimum formality. LeO considers carefully whether there is a need to share evidence before everything is gathered in from both parties and if that could adversely affect an investigation.

SRA regulated firms and individuals are obligated to cooperate with LeO's investigation.[2]

Bar Standards Board v Smith[3] involved a Bar disciplinary hearing, in which the barrister was acquitted of professional misconduct for failing to co-operate with LeO. The disciplinary tribunal held that although the barrister was in breach of the rules requiring him to co-operate, the breach did not amount to professional misconduct because he 'could be forgiven, if not justified in taking the stance that he did' in declining to co-operate when LeO refused to release material supplied by the complainant on which the LeO investigator intended to rely, until after she had reached her conclusion, albeit that her conclusion would not at that stage be binding. The tribunal added: 'A barrister could not reasonably or necessarily be expected to co-operate with the Ombudsman in that situation'. The consequence of the non-co-operation, however, was that the complaint to LeO by the client was inevitably upheld.

Following *Bar Standards Board v Smith*, LeO reviewed its evidence guidance and changed the reference to sharing evidence to make it clear how evidence would be shared, even if not asked for. The internal guidance for LeO investigators, extracts of which LeO has been kind enough to disclose to us, now states:

> 'We must ensure that any documentary evidence that we have relied upon to form a view or make a recommendation has been seen by both sides, and we should share it at the earliest appropriate opportunity. Ordinarily, this will be at the informal resolution stage as you can refer to the evidence to support the conclusions you have drawn and the recommendation you are making to resolve the complaint.
>
> However, it may be that sharing a piece of evidence early on in the investigation can help to facilitate a timely resolution if, for example, it proves or disproves an issue of complaint.'

The existence or otherwise of rule breaches is not a central consideration; after all, a clear, helpful and comprehensive client care letter may be followed by appalling service, and an excellent service might be provided despite muddled initial correspondence. Rule breaches are primarily matters for the regulator, not LeO.

Nor is the degree of fault the measure of compensation – a very bad error could have negligible consequences, and a small mistake could be very costly; redress will relate to the consequence of the failing, and is designed to put the complainant so far as possible in the position he or she should have been in; but it is not a penalty imposed on the professional for a more or less serious mistake.

Sometimes, in what they see as 'nuisance' complaints, solicitors are prepared to offer a small sum on an *ex gratia* and without prejudice basis to the disaffected client in order to retain goodwill and save the time and effort involved in dealing with complaints. We understand that LeO has no objection in principle to such proposals, and that if the offer is rejected, this will not be held against the solicitor who made it, or regarded as an admission. Any subsequent complaint would be dealt with on its merits. If such an offer were to be accepted, but the client nevertheless makes a complaint to LeO, the acceptance of the offer would be seen as an important factor in LeO's consideration of the case.

1   Section 137(1) of LSA 2007.
2   Paragraph 7.3 of the SRA Code of Conduct for Solicitors, RELs and RFLs 2019 (the 'Code for Individuals') and paragraph 3.2 of the SRA Code of Conduct for Firms 2019 (the 'Code for Firms').
3   PC 2013/0193.

Structure and process in outline

14.3

When it was set up, LeO expected to receive about 100,000 contacts a year, in the sense of enquiries and expressions of interest, of which about 20,000 would become legitimate complaints within LeO's jurisdiction. Experience of other ombudsman schemes suggests that only 10 per cent of that figure reaches the point of formal adjudication, the remainder being resolved by agreement or abandonment.

LeO's latest annual report, to 31 March 2019, reveals that it accepted 4,022 new cases within its legal jurisdiction in 2018–19 (compared with 7,527 in 2017–18 and 6,125 in 2016–17). In the same period, it resolved 6,125 cases. Of these, 36 per cent were resolved by agreed outcome, 41 per cent of cases were resolved by final decision and the remaining 23 per cent were closed by other means.

In contrast with previous years, when a final decision was required LeO found that in the majority of cases (54 per cent) the service provided was not reasonable.[1]

Analysis of the final decisions revealed that 42 per cent resulted in a financial or fee related remedy, 14 per cent in a non-financial remedy, and 44 per cent in no remedy. Residential conveyancing continues to produce the most complaints to LeO, followed by personal injury and family law.

1   2016–17: 46 per cent; 2017–18: 47 per cent.

14.4

LeO caseworkers first determine exactly what the complaint is about and what is sought by way of redress. Assuming that the complaint is not premature because the complainant has not used the solicitors' own complaints procedures, is not out of time and is not obviously without merit (more of which below), the caseworker investigates in the inquisitorial manner described above and, having given both parties the opportunity to make representations, comes to a provisional decision. However, LeO is committed to resolving complaints at the earliest possible stage, so that the process of investigation should not prevent an agreed resolution at any time.

Because LeO expects to look at complaints, in the ordinary course, only after the client has exhausted the firm's own complaints handling process, one of the first requests is likely to be for the firm's complaint file – its record of the handling of the complaint. Some firms are taken by surprise by this request, as opposed to a request for the client matter file or core extracts. But a key element of a LeO inquiry is to determine how the firm itself handled the matter. Firms have had to adjust to this, and to realise that it may be imprudent to exchange memoranda and emails with forthright expressions of opinion not originally intended for external consumption, but which are a part of the firm's investigation of the complaint, and thus disclosable to LeO.

Following the first stage of investigation a LeO investigator will make a 'preliminary decision' described as a 'case decision'. If both parties accept the preliminary decision, the matter is resolved on that basis; if either party demurs, the matter is referred to an ombudsman for final determination. Only information and documentation to be considered by the ombudsman will be disclosed to the parties, not necessarily everything gathered by the caseworker in the course of the investigation. The ombudsman may require further information and, for example, may conduct an oral hearing. However, it has always been envisaged that these will be exceedingly rare and only justified by compelling and exceptional circumstances (particularly in the case of solicitors whose actions are generally heavily documented).

If the ombudsman comes to a conclusion which is materially different from that of the investigator's preliminary decision, the ombudsman will issue a 'provisional decision' and provide an opportunity to both parties to make further representations.

It is open to the complainant (only) to accept or reject an ombudsman's determination (final decision). If it is accepted by the complainant, it is binding on all parties and final.[1] If it is rejected, the role of LeO is concluded and the complainant is free to pursue other remedies.

There is no appeal from an ombudsman's determination, so that judicial review is the only available mechanism for challenge. However, if it is clear that an obvious mistake has been made, an ombudsman might well be prepared voluntarily to reconsider the matter.

Despite LeO being threatened with judicial review on a fairly regular basis only five cases have yet reached a hearing. Four have been decided on a fact-sensitive basis (two in favour of LeO[2] and two against)[3] without developing any new body of law or changes in public law principles. The one clear point is the consistent acceptance that LeO has a wide discretion within a statutory framework which is itself drawn in very broad terms – what is fair and reasonable in all the circumstances of the case.[4] Two successful challenges have involved an obvious misinterpretation of the facts,[5] and a result influenced by the failure of LeO to file evidence which might have caused a different conclusion,[6] something that is unlikely to be repeated.

However in *Stenhouse v Legal Ombudsman*,[7] LeO was sharply criticised for exceeding its jurisdiction and acting in breach of natural justice. LeO had concluded that a barrister was open to criticism for issuing proceedings to recover his fees. Those proceedings were stayed pending LeO's determination and pending the result of the subsequent judicial review. The ombudsman decided that the barrister should pay compensation in the amount of costs incurred by the complainant in defending that claim to date, amounting to more than £2,000. Among the difficulties in this respect were that no complaint had been made as to this; the barrister had not known it was in issue until after the determination had been made; the criticisms of the barrister in relation to his commencement of the proceedings were irrational, and the award, relating to court proceedings, could not have been made by the court itself, as no part of the proceedings had been concluded. Although an award of compensation for distress arising from the aggressive and discourteous behaviour of the barrister was upheld (not without criticism of LeO for 'sloppy' drafting of key documents), that part of the determination relating to the complainant's costs was quashed.

Preliminary decisions and ombudsman determinations are narrative in form and seek to avoid the black and white concepts which involve 'upholding' the complaint or the opposite. It may be difficult or inappropriate to say whether a multiple complaint, of which one element was found to justify criticism, was 'upheld'. Rather, the decision recites what the caseworker or ombudsman has considered to have gone wrong and what the redress should be.

Compensation for non-financial loss (distress and inconvenience) is in modest amounts: a LeO guidance note indicates three bands, modest awards of between £50 and £250, significant awards of between £250 and £750, and exceptional awards of between £750 and £1,000.[8]

1   Section 140(4) of LSA 2007.
2   *Layard Horsfall Ltd v Legal Ombudsman* [2013] EWHC 4137 (QB) and *R (Rosemarine) v Office for Legal Complaints* [2014] EWHC 601 (Admin).
3   *R (Crawford) v Legal Ombudsman and anor* [2014] EWHC 182 (Admin) and *R (Hafiz & Haque Solicitors) v Legal Ombudsman* [2014] EWHC 1539 (Admin).
4   Section 137(1) of LSA 2007.
5   *Crawford* supra.
6   *Hafiz & Haque* supra.
7   [2016] EWHC 612 (Admin).
8   LeO, 'Our approach to putting things right', updated March 2019.

The overlap with negligence

14.5

The limit of compensation available through LeO is £50,000 (considered in more detail below), plus a reduction in costs in a theoretically unlimited amount, capped only by the amount of the costs that has been charged. This is sufficiently large to attract many cases which might otherwise have been pursued as negligence claims. A complaint to LeO involves no expense and no adverse costs risk for a complainant.

LeO does not reject complaints simply because they could be pursued as negligence claims. However, neither are they considered as if they were negligence claims. As in all matters, the question is whether it is fair and reasonable for redress to be provided in all the circumstances, in consequence of an act or omission by an authorised person. Awards may be made by LeO whether or not the complainant may have a cause of action against the authorised person in negligence.[1]

It must follow that there can be circumstances in which complainants might achieve a higher award of damages by court action than could be directed by LeO, and in accepting an award capped at £50,000, might lose what might have been available in another jurisdiction. If a LeO award is accepted and becomes binding, it is in full satisfaction; no further proceedings may be taken in relation to the subject matter (see **14.17**) and the potential for a higher award of damages will be lost. On the other hand, litigation is risky and expensive. It is essentially a choice for the complainant. In appropriate cases LeO may consider it prudent to remind the complainant of the options available where obviously high levels of loss are claimed to have been sustained, but the complaint will not be rejected; nor can it be expected that the complainant will, for example, be required to take advice before pursuing a complaint or accepting a determination.

Amounts paid or payable following a determination by LeO are insured under the SRA Minimum Terms and Conditions of Professional Indemnity Insurance[2] (except in respect of orders to refund fees) and thus a notification of a complaint to LeO should be reported by a firm to its insurer.

1   Section 137(5) of LSA 2007.
2   Clause 1.4, Annex to the SRA Indemnity Insurance Rules 2019.

Fee structure

14.6

No fee is payable by the complainant to LeO. A fee, called a case fee, is payable by the authorised person for every potential chargeable complaint[1] when it is closed, unless two conditions are satisfied: first, that the complaint is either (a) abandoned or withdrawn or (b) settled, resolved or determined in favour of the authorised person; and, second, that LeO is satisfied that the authorised person took all reasonable steps to try to resolve the complaint under his or her own complaints handling system.

In all other cases, the authorised person is liable to pay the case fee, currently £400 for each complaint.[2]

1   Defined at rule 6.1 of the LeO Scheme Rules, 1 April 2019.
2   Rules 6.1 to 6.3 of the LeO Scheme Rules.

Publicity

14.7

The extent to which decisions of LeO are published in a manner which will identify the lawyers involved has proved to be a vexed question. LeO conducted two full consultations on the subject. The Legal Services Board's Legal Services Consumer Panel, and others broadly representing consumer interests, favoured naming and shaming by the publication of awards and directions. Others are more cautious as to whether this is ultimately in the interests of consumers, if it discourages solicitors from taking on work associated with high levels of sometimes ill-informed complaint, such as immigration, or encourages the settlement of undeserving and unmeritorious complaints because of the perceived commercial consequences of publicity. Ultimately LeO is there to provide redress, not to impose penalties on lawyers, and publicity has a direct and effectively penal consequence. If there are 'season ticket holders' in terms of complaint generation, it may be a matter for the regulator, rather than LeO.

Anonymised case studies are published to give assistance in identifying trends and to offer guidance as to how typical cases are resolved. From the summer of 2011 anonymised summaries of all formal decisions by ombudsmen have been published.

Following the completion of the consultation process and the tracking of data the decision was finally made to publish the names of lawyers in two circumstances. First, there may be discretionary publication of cases where a pattern of complaints raises sufficient concerns that the public interest requires publication as a warning to consumers and potential consumers; this has so far been done in only one case, within its jurisdiction in respect of lawyers,[1] in December 2014 involving a barrister, where 25 complaints had been upheld in a two-year period involving total awards of over £8,000.

Second, on a quarterly basis all decisions made by ombudsmen are published, even where the decision is favourable to the lawyer and no action by LeO was necessary. The first list was published on 17 September 2012.

This is something of a compromise; cases which are resolved at an early stage, or where the parties accept a caseworker's recommendation, will not require an ombudsman's decision and so will not be published. On the other hand, if an aggrieved client insists on an ombudsman's decision, as is his or her right, the firm's name will appear on the list even though no fault may be found. So far, the information lacks a certain amount of context. Because LeO does not know how many clients a firm may have it cannot say whether the number of complaints is comparatively large or a tiny percentage of the firm's cases. This is a point that has been made in the FAQs part of LeO's website.

---

1   Prior to 1 April 2019 LeO had, in addition to its jurisdiction in respect of lawyers, power to hear complaints against claims management companies (CMCs), and has published decisions in respect of a CMC. By the Financial Guidance and Claims Act 2018, the regulation of CMCs transferred to the FCA, effective from 1 April 2019.

The Scheme Rules in more detail

Who can complain[1]

14.8

A complainant must be an individual, or any of the following:

- a small business: a micro-enterprise as defined in European Recommendation 2003/361/EC of 6 May 2003 (broadly, an enterprise with fewer than ten staff and a turnover or balance sheet value not exceeding €2 million);

- a charity with an annual income less than £1 million;

- a club, association or society with an annual income less than £1 million;

- a trustee of a trust with a net asset value less than £1 million;

- a personal representative or the beneficiary of an estate where a person with a complaint died before referring it to the ombudsman scheme.

If a complainant who has referred a complaint to LeO dies or is otherwise unable to act, the complaint may be continued by anyone authorised by law (for example, the executor of a complainant who has died or someone with a lasting power of attorney from a complainant who is incapable or the residuary beneficiaries of the estate of a complainant who has died).

A complainant must not have been, at the time of the act or omission to which the complaint relates, a public body (or acting for a public body) in relation to the services complained about, or an authorised person who procured the services complained about on behalf of someone else. For example, where the complaint is about a barrister who was instructed by a solicitor on behalf of a consumer, the consumer may complain but the solicitor may not.

A complainant may authorise someone else in writing (including an authorised person) to act on behalf of the complainant in pursuing a complaint, but LeO remains free to contact the complainant direct where it considers that to be appropriate.

1   See rules 2.1 to 2.5 of the LeO Scheme Rules.

What can be complained about[1]

14.9

There are no categories of complaint that are excluded. The complaint must relate to an act or omission by someone who was an authorised person at the relevant time. An act or omission by an employee is usually treated as an act or omission by the employer, whether or not the employer knew or approved. An act or omission by a partner is usually treated as an act or omission by the partnership, unless the complainant knew (at the time of the act or omission) that the partner had no authority to act for the partnership.[2]

The act or omission does not have to relate to a reserved legal activity, nor to have occurred after LSA 2007 came into force. The complaint must relate to services which the authorised person provided to the complainant or to another authorised person who procured them on behalf of the complainant, or to – or as – a personal representative or trustee where the complainant is a beneficiary of the estate or trust. However, a complaint may also be made about services which an authorised person offered or refused to provide to the complainant. This jurisdiction is not likely to be employed frequently. It would cover circumstances in which, for example, a lawyer refused to accept instructions for an unlawfully discriminatory reason, and would also be appropriate where a lawyer agrees to look at papers with a view to representing the complainant at a forthcoming court hearing, for example, but later decides not to accept instructions, leaving the complainant unrepresented with no adequate notice.

A complaint is not affected by any change in the composition of a partnership or other unincorporated body. Where a firm or business closes and another business succeeds to the whole of it, or substantially the whole of it, the successor body becomes responsible for the acts and omissions of and complaints against the original firm[3] unless an ombudsman decides that this is not fair and reasonable in all the circumstances.[4]

1   Rules 2.6 to 2.10 of the LeO Scheme Rules.
2   Section 131 of LSA 2007.
3   Section 132.
4   Rule 2.10 of the LeO Scheme Rules.

Jurisdiction and time limits

14.10

Ordinarily, a complainant cannot complain to LeO unless the complainant has first used the authorised person's complaints procedure.[1] However, this does not apply if the complaint has not been resolved to the complainant's satisfaction within eight weeks of being made to the authorised person, or if an ombudsman considers that there are exceptional reasons to consider the complaint sooner, or without it having been made first to the authorised person, or where in-house resolution is not possible due to irretrievable breakdown in the relationship between the lawyer and the person making the complaint. For example, an ombudsman may decide that the ombudsman service should consider the complaint where the authorised person has refused to consider it, or where delay would harm the complainant.[2]

Ordinarily, a complainant must refer a complaint to LeO within six months of the date of the authorised person's written response (within the firm's complaints handling system), but only if that written response prominently included an explanation that the LeO service was available if the complainant remained dissatisfied and full contact details for LeO were given, together with a warning that the complaint must be referred to LeO within six months.[3]

A complainant must also generally refer a complaint to LeO no later than six years from the act or omission complained of, or three years from the point at which the complainant should reasonably have known that there was cause for complaint.[4] Ordinarily the act or omission must also have occurred after 5 October 2010. In the case of a complaint made by a personal representative or beneficiary of the estate of a person who had not complained before he or she died, the period runs from the point at which the deceased should reasonably have known that there was cause for complaint.

If an ombudsman considers that there are exceptional circumstances (for example, a delay caused by illness), he or she may extend any of these time limits to the extent that he or she considers fair.[5] An ombudsman is likely to extend a time limit where the time limit had not expired when the complainant raised the complaint with the authorised person.[6]

1   Section 126 of LSA 2007.
2   Rules 4.1 to 4.3 and 5.3 of the LeO Scheme Rules.
3   Rule 4.4.
4   Rule 4.5.
5   Rules 4.7 and 4.8.
6   Rule 4.8(b).

Preliminary consideration and summary dismissal

14.11

If an ombudsman considers that all or part of the complaint is not within LeO's jurisdiction, or is out of time, or may be one that should be dismissed without considering its merits, the ombudsman will give the complainant an opportunity to make representations before deciding. If an authorised person challenges the complaint on the same grounds, the ombudsman will give all parties an opportunity to make representations. In either case, the ombudsman will then make a decision and give reasons.[1]

An ombudsman may (but does not have to) dismiss all or part of a complaint without considering its merits if, in his or her opinion:

- the complaint does not have any reasonable prospect of success, or is frivolous or vexatious;

- the complainant has not suffered (and is unlikely to suffer) financial loss, distress, inconvenience or other detriment;

- the authorised person has already offered fair and reasonable redress in relation to the circumstances alleged by the complainant and the offer is still open for acceptance;

- the complainant has previously complained about the same issue to LeO or a predecessor complaints scheme (unless the ombudsman considers that material new evidence, likely to affect the outcome, only became available to the complainant afterwards);

- a comparable independent complaints (or costs-assessment) scheme or a court has already dealt with the same issue;

- a comparable independent complaints (or costs-assessment) scheme or a court is dealing with the same issue, unless those proceedings are first stayed, by the agreement of all parties or by a court order, so that LeO can deal with the issue;

- it would be more suitable for the issue to be dealt with by a court, by arbitration or by another complaints (or costs-assessment) scheme;

- the issue concerns an authorised person's decision when exercising a discretion under a will or trust;

- the issue concerns an authorised person's failure to consult a beneficiary before exercising a discretion under a will or trust, where there is no legal obligation to consult;

- the issue involves someone else who has not complained and the ombudsman considers that it would not be appropriate to deal with the issue without that person's consent;

- it is not practicable to investigate the issue fairly because of the time which has elapsed since the act or omission;

- the issue concerns an act or omission outside England and Wales and the circumstances do not have a sufficient connection with England and Wales;

- the complaint is about an authorised person's refusal to provide a service and the complainant has not produced evidence that the refusal was for other than legitimate or reasonable reasons;

- there are other compelling reasons why it is inappropriate for the issue to be dealt with under the ombudsman scheme.[2]

Exceptionally, an ombudsman may refer a discrete legal question to a court if the resolution of the question is necessary to resolve the matter, but it is not more suitable for the court to deal with the whole dispute. The authorised person may request that a matter be considered as a test case by a court and an ombudsman may accommodate that request by dismissing the complaint to enable proceedings to be taken, but only on an undertaking that the authorised person will pay the complainant's costs and on such other terms as the ombudsman considers appropriate.[3]

An ombudsman may also refer the complaint to another complaints scheme in appropriate circumstances, and if the complainant agrees.[4]

1   Rules 5.4 to 5.6 of the LeO Scheme Rules.
2   Rule 5.7.
3   Rules 5.8 to 5.11.
4   Rule 5.12.

Procedure, evidence and hearings

14.12

LeO may request the assistance of others, including approved regulators, in the investigation and consideration of complaints.[1] LeO is not restricted by the terms of the complaint as to who is to be investigated. If appropriate LeO will investigate another authorised person as a joint respondent.[2]

Efforts will be made to resolve all complaints at the earliest possible stage by any appropriate means, including informal resolution.[3] If an investigation is necessary, after both parties have been given an opportunity to make representations, a caseworker will send the parties a preliminary decision (referred to in the Scheme Rules as a case decision) and will set a time limit for response. If no party disagrees within the specified time limit, the complaint may be treated as resolved by the preliminary decision. If any party disagrees, the matter is referred to an ombudsman for final decision.[4]

1   Rule 5.14 of the LeO Scheme Rules.
2   Rules 5.15 and 5.16.
3   Rule 5.17.
4   Rules 5.19 and 5.20.

14.13

An apology will not of itself be treated as an admission of liability. An ombudsman cannot require anyone to produce any information or document which that person could not be compelled to produce in High Court civil proceedings. Subject to this, an ombudsman may:

- give directions as to the issues on which evidence is required and the way in which evidence should be given;

- take into account evidence from approved regulators or the Legal Services Board (LSB) or from other third parties;

- treat any finding of fact in disciplinary proceedings against the authorised person as conclusive;

- include or exclude evidence that would be inadmissible or admissible in court;

- accept information in confidence where he or she considers that this is both necessary and fair;

- make a determination on the basis of what has been supplied;

- draw inferences from any party's failure to provide information requested; and

- dismiss a complaint if the complainant fails to provide information that has been requested.[1]

An ombudsman may require a party to attend to give evidence and produce documents at a specified time and place. An ombudsman may require a party to produce any information or document that the ombudsman considers necessary for the determination of a complaint; may specify the time within which this must be done; may specify the manner or form in which the information is to be provided; and may require the person producing the document to explain it. If the document is not produced, an ombudsman may require the relevant party to say, to the best of his or her knowledge and belief, where the document is.

If an authorised person fails to comply with a requirement to produce information or a document, the ombudsman will tell the relevant approved regulator and may require that approved regulator to tell the ombudsman what action it will take (and may report any failure by the approved regulator to the LSB). If any party fails to comply with a requirement to produce information or a document, the ombudsman may also enforce the requirement through the High Court.[2]

An ombudsman may fix (and may extend) a time limit for any stage of the investigation, consideration and determination of a complaint. If any party fails to comply with such a time limit, the ombudsman may proceed with the investigation, consideration and determination, and draw inferences from the failure. Where the failure is by the complainant, the ombudsman may dismiss the complaint; or where the failure is by the authorised person, the ombudsman may include compensation for any inconvenience caused to the complainant in any award.[3]

1   Rules 5.21 to 5.24 of the LeO Scheme Rules.
2   Sections 147 to 149 of LSA 2007; rules 5.25 to 5.30 of the LeO Scheme Rules.
3   Rules 5.31 and 5.32 of the LeO Scheme Rules.

14.14

An ombudsman will only hold an oral hearing where he or she considers that the complaint cannot be fairly determined without one. In deciding whether (and how) to hold a hearing, the ombudsman will take account of Article 6 of the European Convention on Human Rights. A party who wishes to request a hearing must do so in writing setting out the issues he or she wishes to raise and (if appropriate) any reasons why the hearing should be in private. The ombudsman will consider whether the issues are material, whether a hearing should take place and whether any hearing should be in public or private. A hearing may be held by any means the ombudsman considers appropriate in the circumstances, including (for example) by telephone.[1]

1   Rules 5.33 to 5.35 of the LeO Scheme Rules.

Determinations and awards

14.15

An ombudsman will determine a complaint by reference to what is, in his or her opinion, fair and reasonable in all the circumstances of the case. In determining what is fair and reasonable, the ombudsman will take into account (but is not bound by) what a court might decide, the relevant approved regulator's rules of conduct at the time of the act or omission, and what the ombudsman considers to have been good practice at the time.[1]

A LeO guidance note describes common factors which may influence its decision on what is fair and reasonable, including:

- the characteristics of the customer, for example, their vulnerability and level of experience;

- the expertise of the service provider/firm, for example the standard of service expected of a firm that holds itself out as an expert;

- promises, assurances and service level agreements and how circumstances might mean that a provider needs to go beyond their stated agreements; and

- reliance of the advice of others, and the expectation that service providers will use their own expertise to assess the work of others, for example the duty to consider any advice received from counsel.[2]

Awards and determinations may include any one or more of the following directions to the authorised person in favour of the complainant:

- to apologise;

- to pay compensation of a specified amount for loss suffered;

- to pay interest on that compensation from a specified time;

- to pay compensation of a specified amount for inconvenience or distress caused;

- to ensure (and pay for) putting right any specified error, omission or other deficiency;

- to take (and pay for) any specified action in the interests of the complainant;

- to pay a specified amount for costs incurred by the complainant in pursuing the complaint (however, as a complainant does not usually need assistance to pursue a complaint with LeO, awards of costs are likely to be rare);

- to limit the authorised person's fees to a specified amount.[3]

If the determination contains a direction to limit fees to a specified amount, it may also require the authorised person to ensure that: all or part of any amount paid is refunded; interest is paid on that refund from a specified time; all or part of the fees are remitted; the right to recover the fees is waived, wholly or to a specified extent; or any combination of these.[4]

An ombudsman may set a time limit for the authorised person to comply with a determination, and may set different time limits for different parts of a determination. Any interest payable under the determination will be at the rate specified in the determination or, if not specified, at the rate payable on High Court judgment debts.[5]

1   Section 137 of LSA 2007; rules 5.36 and 5.37 of the LeO Scheme Rules.
2   LeO, 'Our approach to determining complaints', January 2019.
3   Rules 5.38 and 5.39 of the LeO Scheme Rules.
4   Rule 5.40.
5   Rules 5.41 and 5.42.

14.16

There is a limit of £50,000 on the total value that can be awarded on the determination of a complaint in respect of the total of: compensation for loss suffered; compensation for inconvenience or distress caused; the reasonable cost of putting right any error, omission or other deficiency; and the reasonable cost of any specified action in the interests of the complainant. If (before or after the determination is issued) it appears that the total value will exceed £50,000, an ombudsman may direct which part or parts of the award are to take preference.[1]

The £50,000 limit does not apply to: an apology; interest on specified compensation for loss suffered; any specified amount for costs the complainant incurred in pursuing the complaint; the financial consequences of limiting fees to a specified amount; or interest on fees to be refunded.[2]

1   Section 138 of LSA 2007; rules 5.43 and 5.44 of the LeO Scheme Rules.
2   Rule 5.45 of the LeO Scheme Rules.

14.17

The determination is in writing, signed by the ombudsman. It must give reasons and require the complainant to notify the ombudsman, before a specified time, whether the complainant accepts or rejects the determination. The ombudsman may require any acceptance or rejection to be in writing, but will have regard to any reason why the complainant may be unable to communicate in writing. The ombudsman will send copies of the determination to the parties and the relevant approved regulator. If the complainant tells the ombudsman that he or she accepts the determination it is binding on the parties and final.[1]

Once a determination becomes binding and final, neither party may start or continue legal proceedings in respect of the subject matter of the complaint.[2]

If the complainant does not tell the ombudsman, before the specified time, that he or she accepts the determination, it is treated as rejected. But if the complainant later tells the ombudsman that he or she accepts the determination, and the complainant has not previously told the ombudsman that he or she rejects the determination, and if the ombudsman is satisfied that there are sufficient reasons why the complainant did not respond in time, the determination will be treated as accepted, final and binding. If the complainant does not respond before the specified time, the ombudsman will notify the parties and the relevant approved regulator of the outcome, describing the provisions concerning late acceptance. Whether the complainant accepts or rejects the determination, the ombudsman will notify the parties and the relevant approved regulator of the outcome.[3]

If a determination is rejected (or treated as rejected) by the complainant, it has no effect on the legal rights of any party.[4]

1   Section 140(1) to (4) of LSA 2007; rules 5.46 to 5.49 of the LeO Scheme Rules.
2   Section 140(11) of LSA 2007; rule 5.50 of the LeO Scheme Rules.
3   Rules 5.51 to 5.53 of the LeO Scheme Rules.
4   Rule 5.54.

Enforcement and misconduct

14.18

A binding and final determination can be enforced through the High Court or a county court by the complainant: in August 2011 the legal press reported that LeO had commenced proceedings in the Birmingham County Court against two firms in order to enforce awards. LeO may also enforce a determination through the courts if the complainant agrees and LeO considers it appropriate in all the circumstances. A court which makes an enforcement order must inform LeO and LeO will then inform the relevant approved regulator, may require the approved regulator to tell LeO what action it will take, and may report any failure by the approved regulator to the LSB.[1]

At any stage after LeO receives a complaint, if LeO considers that the complaint discloses any alleged misconduct about which the relevant approved regulator should consider action against the authorised person, or if LeO considers that an authorised person has failed to co-operate with LeO, LeO will tell the relevant approved regulator, may require the approved regulator to tell LeO what action it will take, and may report any failure by the approved regulator to the LSB. If an approved regulator is informed about a matter involving potential misconduct, LeO will tell the complainant that this has been done.[2] The duty to report potential misconduct is not affected by any withdrawal or abandonment of the complaint.

LeO will disclose to an approved regulator any information that the regulator requests to enable it to investigate alleged misconduct or to fulfil its regulatory functions, if LeO considers that the information is reasonably required, and the approved regulator has regard to any right of privacy of any complainant or third party involved.[3]

1   Sections 141 and 142 of LSA 2007; rules 5.56 to 5.58 of the LeO Scheme Rules.
2   Sections 143 and 146 of LSA 2007; rules 5.59 and 5.60 of the LeO Scheme Rules.
3   Rule 5.61 of the LeO Scheme Rules.

CHAPTER 15

SRA investigations

15.1

The rules which govern SRA investigations are the SRA Regulatory and Disciplinary Procedure Rules 2019 (the 'Disciplinary Rules 2019').

Investigations are undertaken through the 'Investigations and Supervision' function of the Solicitors Regulation Authority (SRA). A range of supervisory tools is employed. They include desk-based supervision, written or telephone contact, risk-based visits and relationship management. The intention is that the SRA will be able to respond to potential risk before its impact is felt upon clients or the wider public. Supervision may commission a forensic investigation, involving a visit by one or more investigating officers.

15.2

In the case of third party complaints the current practice is to treat the source of the complaint as an informant, rather than a complainant; that is, complaints are simply 'reports' for the SRA to consider. It is a matter for the supervisor or investigating officer to decide whether and to what extent the informant is kept advised and informed on the progress of the investigation. This will usually be done only where the informant can continue to contribute to the investigation by providing further information (for example) or where the informant has a legitimate personal interest in the outcome, as where the informant is complaining about non-compliance with an undertaking which is causing him prejudice.

In the overwhelming majority of cases complainants are advised that the SRA welcomes the information and will use it as an aid in assessing risks as a risk-based regulator, and that such action as is thought necessary will be taken, but the complainant will not be kept informed.

The Disciplinary Rules 2019 require the SRA, where practicable, to inform a complainant of a decision to close an investigation without further action and explain why.[1]

1   Rule 2.6 of the Disciplinary Rules 2019.

Forensic investigations

15.3

A forensic investigation is not pastoral in character: it can take weeks or months, with investigators staying for many days at a time. A forensic investigation is never random; the investigators will have specific concerns or specific reasons for their visit. Until relatively recently (2009/10) reasons were never given (although they could usually be deduced). Now some reason for the inquiry will usually be given, unless it is believed that this would amount to a breach of any duty of confidentiality; or would risk disclosure of a confidential source of information; or significantly increase the risk that someone under investigation might destroy evidence, influence a witness, default or abscond; or it would otherwise prejudice the investigation or other regulatory action.[1] Despite claims to transparency in relation to this process the reasons that are given are frequently opaque, such as 'concerns in respect of business management'.

Solicitors are under an obligation to co-operate with the SRA at all times.[2] They must promptly provide full and accurate explanations, information and documents in response to any SRA request or requirement, as well as ensure that relevant information held by them, or by third parties carrying out functions on their behalf which are critical to the delivery of their legal services, is available for inspection by the SRA. Firms are likely to be requested to provide consents and permissions necessary for investigators to seek verification from clients, staff, banks, building societies or other financial institutions, and to comply with requests for the supply of copies of documents or documents in electronic form.[3]

Refusal to co-operate either generally or in relation to specific requests is most unwise, at least in the absence of strong expert advice that the investigators are exceeding their powers or otherwise acting unlawfully. The SRA has the ultimate deterrent: if there is a failure to comply with any rule made by the SRA regulating, for example, professional practice, conduct, and accounts,[4] the powers of intervention will have arisen. No solicitor could prudently take that risk.

However, an obligation to provide information promptly is not an obligation to do so instantly, or without proper consideration or advice (if appropriate); nor is it unreasonable in a situation of complexity or apparent seriousness to obtain clarification of requests by seeking them in writing. Investigators are fully aware of this and should not object. In an exceptional case, however, where the facts appear clear and the investigators consider that such requests amount to evasion and prevarication, rather than proper caution, the request may be declined and the investigation concluded without further response from the person investigated.

1   SRA Guidance notes: On-site investigations.
2   Paragraph 7.3 of the SRA Code of Conduct for Solicitors, RELs and RFLs 2019 (the 'Code for Individuals') and paragraph 3.2 of the SRA Code of Conduct for Firms 2019 (the 'Code for Firms').
3   Paragraph 7.4(a) of the Code for Individuals and paragraph 3.3(a) of the Code for Firms.
4   Section 1(1)(c) of and Schedule 1 to the Solicitors Act (SA) 1974.

15.4

Many forensic investigations result in no action but, at the other extreme, when the SRA determines that the public interest requires, they can result in an intervention into the solicitor's practice without notice (as where apparent dishonesty is revealed).

Other than in the most extreme case of obvious dishonesty, when an urgent intervention will occur after a very brief inspection, forensic investigations will begin with an initial fact-finding exercise concerned with basic details about the practice and partners/managers (questionnaires are provided for completion in advance). Then will come investigations into accounts, office systems and business arrangements (such as agreements with introducers) and client files over a period of time, requests being made for further information and explanation as matters arise. The investigation concludes with a final interview at which the investigators summarise all matters identified as causing apparent concern, and on which they require a more formal response.

That interview is not under caution; there is no obligation to give a caution, as this is not a criminal investigation. However, it has some of the characteristics of a police interview in that it can be expected to be searching, challenging and potentially hostile in terms of the style of questioning. Admissions that rules have been broken may be expressly invited. The preferred option is to record the whole interview on a digital medium, although this can result in large and potentially unwieldy transcripts. While the historical position has been that individuals have not been compelled to have the interview recorded, it is more likely that investigators will insist, if this is what they want (it is not always necessary), which it will not be possible to resist as a consequence of the solicitor's obligation to co-operate. Further, there are additional powers under which the SRA can clearly compel such a process; see **15.10**.

The investigators are unlikely to be drawn on the question that virtually every solicitor will ask: 'What is going to happen?'. They will ordinarily say that they will submit a report that will be disclosed to you and you will be given an opportunity to comment, but are unlikely to be persuaded to go further. In the case of an urgent intervention the report will not be disclosed until after the intervention has occurred.

15.5

Following the conclusion of the on-site investigation the investigatory process may take any one of three routes. One has already been mentioned – if the situation is obviously serious enough to justify intervention, that may be the next event.

Otherwise there are two options: the investigator may continue the investigation him- or herself, in correspondence, or the matter may be passed back to the supervisor to follow up in the same way. The basis of the choice between the two methods is not clear on any published guidance.

A supervisor's investigation

15.6

Whether a matter arrives in a supervisor's or an investigation officer's[1] hands as a third party complaint/report, as a referral from elsewhere within the SRA (whether following a self-report or not), or as a result of a Forensic Investigations Report (an FI Report), the procedure that follows is the same. The process, which has largely been unchanged for a number of years, is now regulated by rules 1 and 2 of the Disciplinary Rules 2019. The Disciplinary Rules 2019 are drafted somewhat differently and more sparsely than the 2011 rules, but the investigation procedure is unchanged.

The supervisor, who may or may not be legally qualified, writes to the individual solicitor, the compliance officer for legal practice (COLP) or a senior manager (if a number of individuals, including any unadmitted individuals, are affected the request will be made that it be confirmed whether the response is on behalf of all, or whether separate responses will be made), requesting a formal explanation of the matters which the supervisor has identified as requiring an explanation. The letter may seek an explanation from the regulated entity itself, independently of any being sought from individuals.

The letter contains warnings that any reply may be used in disciplinary proceedings, and that a failure to provide a sufficient and satisfactory explanation may result in the imposition of practising certificate conditions.

The SRA's letter will usually require a reply within 14 days, being the minimum period the SRA is obliged to give. Some leeway is likely to be available, but it is wise to make progress as best you can, and then to explain that there are specific reasons why more time is needed, rather than to complain that the deadline is impossible and that you need (for example) a minimum of three months.

The SRA, as soon as reasonably practicable after commencing an investigation, will also inform the solicitor's employer, unless and to the extent that it considers that it would not be in the public interest to do so.[2]

1   Within the SRA, an investigation officer is of equivalent rank to a forensic investigation officer, in band S1, whereas supervisors may be graded in any of bands S1 to S3: both are authorised to make disciplinary decisions. As such, references to supervisors in this chapter should also be taken to include investigation officers (SRA Schedule of Delegations, March 2018).
2   Rule 2.2 of the Disciplinary Rules 2019.

15.7

There is no doubt that regulatory investigations can be exceptionally demanding and stressful, and may well interfere materially with your ability to carry on your practice. Specialist advice and assistance can assist, both in ensuring that efforts are appropriately targeted, and in ensuring balance and objectivity.

The process of interrogation by correspondence may continue with further requests for clarification or supplementary questions. The supervisor may consult with the forensic investigators or seek further information from any informant.

Firm or individual?

15.8

The shift to entity-based regulation (see **CHAPTER 2**) resulted in the entity being the main focus of any enquiry, with individuals targeted concurrently where appropriate. The SRA published guidance as to how it would approach this.

The opening words of the 2009 guidance were 'The primary responsibility for ensuring compliance with a firm's regulatory obligations rests with the firm itself'.

This was capable of being misconstrued. The firm's obligations are those of the business to comply with the SRA regulatory requirements. If a rogue employee or partner fails to act with integrity, it does not mean that the firm as a whole has done so. Entity regulation is not a means of imposing vicarious liability on the firm or the principals for everything that happens in it. Rather it is the responsibility of the firm to manage, in order to avoid regulatory risks as far as possible. The firm can be held to account for deficient management and systems, but there is no vicarious liability in conduct.[1]

In September 2011 the SRA reviewed this guidance. The opening was subtly altered: 'Firms are responsible for delivering outcomes and for all aspects of compliance within the firm. Action may be taken against the firm only, individuals or both'.

In 2019 the SRA introduced separate codes of conduct for firms and for solicitors. Thus the standards required of each are differentiated. Additionally, the SRA published a new Enforcement Strategy,[2] a link to which is provided in the introduction to the Disciplinary Rules 2019 which states that:

> 'We would take action against an individual where they were personally responsible ... However, we will usually take action against a firm alone, or in addition to taking action against an individual, where there is a breach of the code of conduct for firms or of our other requirements.'

The new Enforcement Strategy provides examples of when action will be taken against a firm:

- '● to mark the firm's responsibility and to hold it to account for the breach, especially where it is not possible or proportionate to establish individual responsibility.

- when the events demonstrate a failure which relates to the culture, systems, supervision arrangements or processes for which the firm, as a whole, should be held accountable.

- to encourage a culture of compliance and management of future risk.

- when firm-specific action is appropriate. This might include a fine to remove the benefit obtained from the wrongdoing, suspension or revocation of the firm's authorisation, or firm-based conditions or compliance plans. Examples of the latter might include: requirements relating to the firm's governance or oversight arrangements, mandatory remedial action such as establishing compliance systems or reporting to us of accounting records, or restrictions to prevent certain work being carried out or funds being held.'

Thus, if a breach of a principle or rule, by an individual or individuals, could or should have been prevented by adequate systems and controls, both the individual and the firm could face regulatory action. Whether regulatory action will be taken will depend on the perceived risk to the public interest.

Entity regulation has raised novel issues. If there is action against the firm but not the individual, is the partner or manager who was involved in any breach then free of any relevant history when he joins another firm? The SRA Enforcement Strategy states that, 'A finding against a firm is not a finding of personal misconduct against the partners or other managers.' However, enforcement action taken against the firm may well affect the firm's reputation as a whole, including the reputation of those persons who were not directly involved in any breach, particularly in smaller firms. In this respect, entity-based regulation in solicitors' firms may well have a very different impact from that of the similar approach adopted by the Financial Conduct Authority, where reputational issues are very much less personal and more manageable.

Managers, teams and their work can transfer from one firm to another with relative ease. There is a risk that if a public record hangs over the firm as a whole as a result of the enforcement action, the break-up of firms could follow, as partners or practice groups leave to avoid having to declare an entity sanction in their continuing client acquisition (tendering for example), or in relation to professional indemnity insurance. Where the SRA's focus in these circumstances is on supervision and advice rather than enforcement, sanction and publicity, there may be no problem, but any entity-based sanction and/or publicity could be disastrous to firms and wholly disproportionate. In this reputation-sensitive era, a publicised minor regulatory sanction of an individual can also be disastrous for that individual: for example, where they go on to seek employment with a firm concerned about reputational damage, or where the solicitor provides services to the public sector, and is required to disclose sanctions in a pass/fail tendering process. Thus, conflict can arise between the entity and the individual when responding to an SRA investigation.

A further issue is that a financial penalty could fall on a firm and all its partners despite a change in composition and the departure of the person or persons who caused the problem.

It is understood to be the official position of the SRA in terms of policy that firms could be guilty and liable to sanction for practically anything, that entity regulation should primarily involve 'supervision', with 'enforcement' being deployed only in two circumstances: (a) where there has been a serious failure of management – something fundamentally attributable to the way that the firm is being run; or (b) where on a problem being identified the firm is unwilling or unable to work with the SRA to put things right.

Current experience is that there has been some change in the way that the SRA communicates with the profession when something is perceived to have gone wrong. Increasingly, the entity is becoming an additional focus of enquiry, as well as the individual solicitor or solicitors, and entities are being joined as respondents to disciplinary proceedings.

1   *Akodu v SRA* [2009] EWHC 3588 (Admin).
2   7 February 2019. See www.sra.org.uk/sra/strategy-2017-2020/sub-strategies/sra-enforcement-strategy.

When will the SRA take action?

15.9

Historically, disciplinary action, particularly an application to the Solicitors Disciplinary Tribunal (the Tribunal or SDT), would follow where there was statutory misconduct, eg a breach of SA 1974, or non-statutory 'misconduct', typically described as 'professional misconduct' or 'conduct unbefitting a solicitor'. The steady change over the years to a principle and rule based system initially led to uncertainty regarding whether all rule breaches were matters that should result in disciplinary action. The SDT's view is that they are not.[1] In *SRA v Leigh Day and others*[2] the Administrative Court took the same view, when commenting as follows:

> '156As we have had cause to ask rhetorically before in this judgment: what was this particular allegation doing before the Tribunal if it was not a matter of professional misconduct? In truth, if such an allegation under Principle 5 is to be pursued before a tribunal then it ordinarily needs to have some inherent seriousness and culpability. It no doubt can be accepted that negligence may be capable of constituting a failure to

provide a proper standard of service to clients. But even so, questions of relative culpability and relative seriousness surely still come into the equation under this Principle if the matter is to be the subject of disciplinary proceedings before a tribunal. We do not, we emphasise, say that there is a set standard of seriousness or culpability for the purposes of assessing breaches of the core principles in tribunal proceedings. It is a question of fact and degree in each case. Whether the default in question is sufficiently serious and culpable thus will depend on the particular core principle in issue and on the evaluation of the circumstances of the particular case as applied to that principle. But an evaluation of seriousness remains a concomitant of such an allegation.

157. If authority be needed for such an approach, then it can be found not only in the observations of Jackson LJ (in the specific context of Principle 6) in Wingate and Evans (cited above) but also in the decision of the Court of Session in Sharp v The Law Society of Scotland [1984] SC 129. There, by reference to the applicable Scottish legislation and rules, it was among other things held that whether a breach of the rules should be treated as professional misconduct depended on whether it would be regarded as serious and reprehensible by competent and responsible solicitors and on the degree of culpability: see the opinion of the court delivered by the Lord President (Lord Emslie) at page 134.

158. We consider that, though the statutory schemes are by no means the same, the like approach is generally appropriate and required for the English legislative and regulatory regime in the treatment of alleged breaches of the core principles. We appreciate that there may be some breaches of some rules – for instance, accounts rules: see, for example, Holden v Solicitors Regulation Authority [2012] EWHC 2067 (Admin) – which can involve strict liability. But that cannot be said generally with regard to all alleged breaches of the core principles coming before the Tribunal; which in our view ordinarily will involve an evaluative judgment and an assessment of seriousness to be made. All that said, in the present case, we repeat that this debate under Principle 5 is particularly sterile, given that the evaluation of the majority was that AC had not even been proved to be personally negligent, let alone that the negligence was such that it constituted professional misconduct (paragraph 145.34).'

The SRA Handbook 2011 was a combination of high level principles, more detailed outcomes to be 'achieved' and very detailed rules. Despite the focus on 'outcomes' there were still many rules capable of being broken.

The 2019 Codes of Conduct introduce 'standards' rather than 'outcomes' and signal a different approach from the policies referred to above; they rely on a concept of 'seriousness'. The Code for Individuals contains this:

'You are personally accountable for compliance with this Code – and our other regulatory requirements that apply to you – and must always be prepared to justify your decisions and actions. A serious failure to meet our standards or a serious breach of our regulatory requirements may result in our taking regulatory action against you. A failure or breach may be serious either in isolation or because it comprises a persistent or concerning pattern of behaviour.'

While the Code for Firms contains:

'A serious failure to meet our standards or a serious breach of our regulatory requirements may lead to our taking regulatory action against the firm itself as an entity, or its managers or compliance officers, who each have responsibilities for ensuring that the standards and requirements are met. We may also take action against employees working within the firm for any breaches for which they are responsible. A failure or breach may be serious either in isolation or because it comprises a persistent or concerning pattern of behaviour.'

The addition of the phrase 'concerning pattern of behaviour', which was not included in the original draft of the proposed new rules, indicates that the SRA will consider a failure or breach to be serious, where it is neither an isolated event nor a persistent breach, but nevertheless is concerning.

Seriousness or the lack of it are highly subjective concepts, but the implication is that the SRA will only take 'action' as distinct, one infers, from giving advice and encouragement, if a breach is 'serious'.

When in 2017 the SRA consulted on a new Enforcement Strategy it indicated an intention to move to a principles-based, flexible approach to enforcement focusing on serious breaches of rules and making clear the rationale for its decisions.

The SRA's Enforcement Strategy indicates that the SRA is adopting a risk-based approach to taking regulatory action. It recognises that human and system errors are unavoidable and that a blanket response to non-compliance is counterproductive in that it inhibits the development of shared values, the exercise of judgement and a culture of openness which allows for learning from mistakes. The SRA also comments that the burden of regulation should not be open ended.

The 2019 Enforcement Strategy suggests that the SRA will focus its action on 'the most serious' issues and that it will not necessarily sanction all breaches, and in any event will impose sanctions only where they are required to protect and promote the public interest, having weighed the interests of the public against those of the individual or firm being investigated. In contrast to previous documented enforcement strategies, the Enforcement Strategy does not provide a convenient checklist of factors that it considers moves a breach of a principle or rule into the 'serious' category. Instead, the document contains reference to factors that are or might be relevant.[3] The examples given indicate that more or less any breach might in the given circumstances be considered serious.

1   See e g *Pabla and Pabla*, 10376–2009.
2   [2018] EWHC 2726 (Admin).
3   These include: abuse of trust; taking unfair advantage of clients; misuse of client money; intent/motivation; lack of knowledge/persistently poor levels of competence; concerning lack of judgement; systemic errors; deliberate or reckless disregard for obligations; lack of honesty or integrity; harm and impact; vulnerability; experience and seniority; repeated pattern of behaviour; time passed; insight and remedial action (the lack thereof); events in private life that damage public confidence; and criminal convictions.

Further investigatory powers

15.10

Where a firm fails to comply with an SRA request for documentation, information, or an explanation thereof, the SRA can use statutory powers to compel compliance, and use the powers of intervention to enforce that requirement.[1]

If there is a forensic investigation it is normal for investigators to come armed with notices under section 44B of SA 1974 to reinforce their requests for documents and information.

If a notice has been given under section 44B, the SRA may by notice under section 44BA require the person notified to attend at a specified time and place to provide an explanation of any information provided or document produced pursuant to the original notice. Because this also involves the use of intervention powers, non-compliance is a criminal offence and the costs of the process are a debt due from the individual to the SRA, unless the court orders otherwise.[2] It is a criminal offence deliberately to interfere in this investigation process, or deliberately or recklessly to give false or misleading information.[3]

This is a powerful and potentially oppressive weapon. A solicitor may be required to attend the SRA's offices at his own expense, to be subjected to interrogation while under an obligation to answer questions, with criminal sanctions for failing to co-operate or for providing inaccurate answers. The investigators are likely to be accompanied by their own legal adviser. While a solicitor (or other regulated person) is entitled to be accompanied by, for example, a specialist adviser, the latter may be excluded at the discretion of the SRA investigators if they conclude that the adviser's presence is obstructing the inquiry. And the solicitor may be required to pay the costs of the SRA (including its legal costs) incurred in the section 44BA investigation.

It is devoutly to be hoped that this process will be used sparingly and only in exceptional circumstances, which is understood to be the position to date.

Sections 44B and 44BA apply to solicitors, employees of solicitors, recognised bodies, employees and managers or a person having an interest in a recognised body. They do not apply to alternative business structures (ABSs), or to non-solicitor managers and employees of ABSs. For the parallel powers in relation to ABSs see **26.4**.

Section 44B in its current form (it was amended by the Legal Services Act (LSA) 2007) enables the SRA to require the production of documents and information from any individual or entity it regulates, whether or not that individual or entity is under investigation or suspected of any fault. If a client deposits papers with solicitors which the SRA considers to be relevant to any investigation it is undertaking against anyone, the SRA can take those papers, for its regulatory purposes, by putting solicitors in the position where they cannot refuse. If a customer deposits papers with a bank, an application would have to be made to the court.

The SRA may apply to the High Court for an order directing the provision of information and documents material to a regulatory investigation held by a person or body that is not regulated by the SRA.[4] For an example see *SRA v Charles Henry & Co.*[5]

1   Sections 44B and 44BA of SA 1974. See also 'limited intervention' at **17.26**. See also **APPENDIX 17** for the statutory provisions.
2   Section 44BA(3) and paras 9(3) and 13 of Schedule 1 to SA 1974.
3   Section 44BC.
4   Section 44BB.
5   [2015] EWHC 552 (QB).

15.11

The SRA may also in effect require solicitors and law firms to investigate themselves. By virtue of paragraphs 7.8 and 7.9 of the Code for Individuals and paragraphs 3.4 and 3.5 of the Code for Firms, if the SRA gives notice requiring such action to be taken in relation to a matter specified in the notice, you must:

- investigate whether anyone may have a claim against you;

- provide the SRA with a report on the outcome of your investigation;

- notify relevant persons that they may have such a claim; and

- act promptly to take any remedial action requested by the SRA.

This somewhat remarkable provision was designed, during the course of the Legal Services Bill through Parliament, to give the SRA additional powers to deal with firms caught up in the miners' compensation scheme in a manner thought to justify criticism. It enables the SRA to direct firms to act in a way which may result in an identified class of client being compensated *en masse*, although it would not be the SRA which imposes the obligation to provide the compensation. The SRA can only compel the firm to treat that class of client as if they had made a complaint. It cannot compel, even indirectly, the payment of compensation or redress, because of an express statutory provision.

Section 157 of LSA 2007 provides that 'The regulatory arrangements of an approved regulator must not include any provision relating to redress' – the clear legislative intent being that this is now exclusively a matter for the Legal Ombudsman.

The report stage

15.12

At the conclusion of the investigation process the supervisor has several options. He or she may decide that there are no grounds for disciplinary action, which will result in the file being closed. It is rare for the SRA to concede that the solicitor or firm is without fault. More usually it is said that the file is being closed, or no further action is being taken, but the SRA can review the position if new evidence is received and, sometimes, the SRA can also take the issues considered into account when deciding appropriate action if the SRA receives notification of any future issues or concerns.

Alternatively, the supervisor may decide that although there have been errors or rule breaches, no sanction is required. In this event a 'letter of advice' or 'warning regarding their future conduct' will be sent, which identifies the fault found and advises against repetition, but confirms that there is no sanction.[1] Such a result will, however, remain on the 'record' of the individuals affected in case it should ever be relevant in the future.

Items on a solicitor's record are never 'spent'; they remain forever, but can of course become irrelevant in practice due to lapse of time.

If the matter is to be considered for sanction, the supervisor will write with his or her findings, typically in the form of a report which usually includes a recommended sanction allowing a minimum period of 14 days for a response.[2]

The solicitor may agree with the recommendation, in which circumstances the SRA will either impose the recommended sanction or record the agreement in what is known as a regulatory settlement agreement.[3]

If agreement is not reached, and the SRA determines that it is not appropriate to use the fast track procedure and decides not to refer the matter for adjudication (see below), it will go on to make a decision applying the civil standard of proof.[4] Supervisors are authorised by the SRA to make disciplinary decisions.

Alternatively, the SRA has the option to refer consideration of the allegation to a single adjudicator or a panel of adjudicators. SRA adjudicators may have a legal or lay background. Their function forms part of the SRA decision-making process, it is not an independent review. The current Chief SRA Adjudicator has said that, generally speaking, the SRA refers decisions to adjudicators in complex cases.

Whether referred for adjudication or not, the supervisor's recommendations are not binding but give a clear indication to the solicitor as to what he or she faces so that focused representations can be made on the report. The solicitor might of course agree with the recommendations. Despite the fact that adjudicators can and do disagree with the recommendations and come to different conclusions there is a rather unfortunate practice of providing with the disclosed adjudication papers a 'draft decision' in the form of the recommended outcome, which gives the (misleading) impression that it awaits only the descent of the rubber stamp.

For adjudication powers and procedures see **CHAPTER 20**.

1 Rule 2.4 of the Disciplinary Rules 2019.
2 Rule 2.3 of the Disciplinary Rules 2019.
3 Rule 8.2 of the Disciplinary Rules 2019 expressly permits such agreements; for commentary on regulatory settlement agreements see **20.18**.
4 Rule 8.7 of the Disciplinary Rules 2019.

15.13

With effect from 1 June 2010, in respect of regulatory breaches occurring or continuing on or after that date, the SRA has powers to impose a statutory rebuke, to require the payment of a fine not exceeding £2,000 to be forfeit to the Crown, and to publicise such decisions (for commentary on sanctions see **CHAPTER 20**). For the much more extensive disciplinary powers of the SRA in relation to ABSs see **CHAPTER 26**.

Yet more seriously for the solicitor, the recommendation may be that he or she should be referred to the Tribunal, and/or that practising certificate conditions and/or intervention should be considered. The individual and/or firm will have 14 days to respond, with some leeway unless intervention is in contemplation.

The Disciplinary Rules 2019 empower the SRA to impose interim conditions on the practising certificate of a solicitor or the authorisation of a firm pending a final SRA decision or outcome of proceedings in the Tribunal.[1]

A supervisor can report direct to the SRA's legal department if it is considered appropriate to refer the matter to the Tribunal without further formality. The formal process of adjudication, involving disclosure of a report with recommendations, can be bypassed, with the result that a decision to refer the solicitor's conduct to the Tribunal can be made after a solicitor's explanation is received, but otherwise without notice and without any right of appeal.[2]

The decision may be taken by an SRA authorised decision-maker, if they are satisfied that evidential and public interest tests are satisfied. The Disciplinary Rules 2019 set the evidential test as 'a realistic prospect of the Tribunal making an order in respect of the allegation'.[3]

The more serious the allegation of misconduct, and the clearer the evidence, the more likely that this 'fast track' system will be employed. It is of course open to the SRA's legal department to advise the authorised decision-maker either that the decision is premature and that further questions need to be asked, or that the case is more suitable for consideration by an adjudicator. Many cases involve a fine judgement as to whether the matter requires referral to the Tribunal or can proportionately be dealt with by a rebuke and financial penalty. It would be most unfortunate if in any such case a solicitor was deprived of the opportunity to make submissions on that issue, on an informed basis that a referral to the Tribunal was clearly in prospect, if that was indeed the case.

At present, the dialogue between supervisor and the legal department involves an exchange of internal memoranda without disclosure to the regulated person or body. There is accordingly scope for human error, for example, in misunderstanding the facts or misinterpreting the explanations provided, without the solicitor having an opportunity to correct any such fault. On the assumption that this system is an SRA-preferred option in the interests of efficiency, it is to be hoped that solicitors will at least be given an opportunity to comment on the investigator's or supervisor's provisional conclusions so as to avoid the possibility of errors influencing the decision.

A solicitor finding him- or herself in this situation, with a belief that the decision is wrong, should not hesitate to make further representations voluntarily, in the hope that the SRA or any external advocate retained will review the evidence and give appropriate advice if necessary.

Less sensitively, this fast track system may also be employed to add further matters to a case to be considered by the Tribunal, after the conduct of a solicitor has already been the subject of a referral on other matters.[4]

1   Rule 3.2(a) of the Disciplinary Rules 2019.
2   Rules 2.5 and 3.1(g) of the Disciplinary Rules 2019.
3   Rule 6.1(a) of the Disciplinary Rules 2019.
4   Rule 2.5 of the Disciplinary Rules 2019.

Publicity during investigations

15.14

Generally, no publicity is given to investigations and matters remain confidential as between the solicitor and the SRA, but rule 9.1 of the Disciplinary Rules 2019 gives the SRA a discretion to publish information if it considers that it is in the public interest to do so, for example, where there is an investigation giving rise to significant public concern. The SRA may disclose how the investigation is progressing or that it has been concluded without an adverse finding against the solicitor.

Although matters of this nature are treated as confidential as between the SRA and the solicitor, nothing prevents the complainant, if informed, from disclosing the result.[1]

For publication of SRA-imposed fines and rebukes see **CHAPTER 20**.

1   *Napier and anor v Pressdram Ltd* [2009] EWCA Civ 443, [2010] 1 WLR 934.

CHAPTER 16

Practising certificate controls and removal of a solicitor's name from the roll

16.1

Every solicitor must at all times hold a valid practising certificate in order to practise as such.[1] Accordingly, the power to impose conditions on a solicitor's practising certificate represents a very powerful regulatory control in the hands of the Solicitors Regulation Authority (SRA).

1   Section 1 of the Solicitors Act (SA) 1974.

16.2

The SRA's powers to refuse to issue practising certificates, or to impose conditions on them, derive from statutory powers arising under Part 1 of SA 1974. Until 2009, the circumstances in which the powers could be exercised were prescribed by section 12 of SA 1974. The whole regulatory system in relation to practising certificates changed on 1 July 2009, when section 12 of SA 1974 and associated provisions were repealed and replaced by provisions that the powers could be exercised in circumstances prescribed by the SRA. In consequence, the control of practising certificates is now a rule-based system (subject to the overriding 'umbrella' of Part 1 of SA 1974). The rules are contained in the SRA Authorisation of Individuals Regulations 2019.

Although the circumstances in which the powers can be exercised are now prescribed by SRA regulations, rather than the old section 12, there have been no material changes in the processes of investigation and adjudication, or in the principles applied. Past decisions by the Master of the Rolls on practising certificate appeals under the former statutory regime have been accepted by the SRA to be relevant and binding.

Eligibility for practising certificates

16.3

An individual can apply for a practising certificate if the individual's name is on the roll and the individual has sufficient knowledge of written and spoken English or Welsh and has not been suspended from practice as a solicitor.[1]

1   Regulation 6.2 of the SRA Authorisation of Indivduals Regulations 2019.

Refusal of practising certificates

16.4

On an initial application for a practising certificate or on an application for its renewal, the SRA must refuse the application if it considers it to be in the public interest to do so.[1]

1 Regulation 7.1(a) of the SRA Authorisation of Individuals Regulations 2019. See also section 10(3) of SA 1974.

Imposition of conditions

16.5

The regulations governing the power to impose conditions, and the nature of the conditions, are contained in regulations 7.1 to 7.3 of the SRA Authorisation of Individuals Regulations 2019, and those are set out below.

7.1 If the *SRA* considers it to be in the public interest to do so, it must:

(a) refuse your application for a practising certificate, or your application for registration or renewal of registration, in the *register of European lawyers* or the *register of foreign lawyers*; or

(b) at any time, whether on grant of such an application or at the end of a period of suspension of a practising certificate or registration, or otherwise, impose such conditions on your certificate or registration as it thinks fit in accordance with regulations 7.2 and 7.3.

7.2 The *SRA* may impose conditions under regulation 7.1(b) if it is satisfied that you:

(a) are unsuitable to undertake certain activities or engage in certain business or practising arrangements;

(b) are putting, or are likely to put, at risk the interests of *clients*, third parties or the public;

(c) will not comply with the *SRA's regulatory arrangements* or require monitoring of compliance with the *SRA's regulatory arrangements*; or

(d) should take specified steps conducive to the *regulatory objectives*.

7.3 The conditions imposed by the *SRA* under regulation 7.1(b) may:

(a) specify certain requirements that must be met or steps that must be taken;

(b) restrict the carrying on of particular activities or holding of particular roles; or

(c) prohibit the taking of specified steps without its approval.

16.6

The purposes for which the SRA may impose conditions, either on renewal or on a current certificate, are spelled out in regulation 7.2, but it remains, as affirmed by the

Master of the Rolls (see **16.13**) a question as to what is necessarily and proportionately required for the protection of the public.

16.7

The SRA may also vary or revoke any conditions on a practising certificate.[1] The SRA Authorisation of Individuals Regulations 2019 do not specify that the power to vary is only exercisable if one or more of the circumstances set out in regulation 7.2 applies. Section 13A of SA 1974 (as amended by the Legal Services Act (LSA) 2007) provides that conditions may be imposed on a current practising certificate if it appears to the SRA that the case is of a 'prescribed description' and 'prescribed' means prescribed by the relevant regulations.[2] It is likely that the SRA Authorisation of Individuals Regulations 2019 are intended to be read so as to mean that the prescribed circumstances for the imposition of new varied conditions are those set out in regulation 7.2.

1   Regulation 7.4 of the SRA Authorisation of Individuals Regulations 2019.
2   Sections 13A and 28 of SA 1974.

16.8

If a condition is to be imposed or varied, the SRA must give 28 days' notice of its intention to do so, inviting representations regarding the issues giving rise to the proposed conditions. The SRA may shorten or dispense with the 28-day period where conditions are imposed on grant of a practising certificate, or otherwise if it is satisfied that it is in the public interest to do so.[1]

1   Regulations 7.5 and 7.6 of the SRA Authorisation of Individuals Regulations 2019.

Revocation of practising certificates

16.9

By regulation 8.4, the SRA may revoke a practising certificate at any time, if it is satisfied that it was granted or renewed as a result of error, misleading or inaccurate information or fraud; if the replacement or renewal date has passed and the SRA has not received an application for renewal of the certificate; or if a solicitor has failed to pay the prescribed fee.[1]

The SRA must revoke a practising certificate on the application of the person concerned unless the solicitor is subject to any proceedings, investigation or consideration of their conduct by the SRA or the Solicitors Disciplinary Tribunal (the Tribunal or SDT).[2] In those circumstances the SRA may refuse the application.[3]

If the SRA decides to revoke a practising certificate, it must give the person concerned 28 days' notice of its intention to do so, inviting representations regarding the issues giving rise to the proposed revocation.[4]

1   Regulation 8.4(a)–(c) of the SRA Authorisation of Individuals Regulations 2019. SA 1974 does not confer an express power on the SRA to revoke practising certificates on its own motion, and it is unclear whether the SRA has statutory jurisdiction to do so. For the statutory power to suspend a practising certificate under section 13B of SA 1974, see **16.10**.
2   Regulation 8.6 of the SRA Authorisation of Individuals Regulations 2019.
3   For rules on removal from the roll during pending proceedings before the Tribunal see **16.21** and **16.22**.
4   Regulation 8.5 of the SRA Authorisation of Individuals Regulations 2019.

Suspension of practising certificate

16.10

Under SA 1974, a practising certificate may be suspended with immediate effect in the following circumstances:

- where the solicitor has been convicted of an offence involving dishonesty or deception, or an indictable offence, *and* the SRA has made an application to the Tribunal with respect to him. The SRA may suspend his practising certificate for up to six months, and may renew that suspension once for a maximum of a further six months;[1]

- where an order has been made for the suspension of a solicitor from practice by a court or the Tribunal, or the court has made a bankruptcy order against a solicitor. These operate as an automatic suspension of the practising certificate[2] – from any date specified by the court or Tribunal in the case of a suspension from practice, and immediately on an adjudication of bankruptcy;

- where there is an intervention on the grounds of suspected dishonesty, or breaches of the SRA Accounts Rules, or breaches of any rules made under section 31 of SA 1974 (which include the SRA Codes of Conduct), or because the solicitor has been committed to prison in criminal or civil proceedings. This also automatically suspends the solicitor's practising certificate, unless the adjudicator or adjudication panel which resolves to intervene directs otherwise.[3] The additional provision relating to rules made under section 31 (the successive Practice Rules and Codes of Conduct, in addition to the Accounts Rules, made under section 32), which was effected by amendment of SA 1974 by LSA 2007, means that in practical terms the practising certificate can be expected to be suspended on every intervention unless the decision-maker directs otherwise.

1   Section 13B of SA 1974.
2   Section 15(1).
3   Section 15(1A) and (1B).

16.11

When a practising certificate is suspended on intervention or by reason of bankruptcy the solicitor may apply to the SRA to terminate the suspension.[1]

It is a common and erroneous belief that bankruptcy is the equivalent of being struck off. It is not; indeed, when a solicitor knows that he or she will be made bankrupt, or is very likely to be, it used to be possible to apply to the SRA in advance of the date on which the adjudication is expected for the inevitable and automatic suspension to be terminated either conditionally or unconditionally. At present, the SRA declines to do this and will not begin to process the application until a bankruptcy order is produced. The same principles as to necessity and proportionality apply as they do to any decision to impose conditions (see **16.13**).

For the situation that arises following interventions, see **17.10**.

1   Section 16(3) and (4) of SA 1974.

16.12

If a practising certificate is suspended, it expires on its replacement date, or if the replacement date has passed, 14 days after the suspension took effect.[1]

1   Regulation 8.7(e) of the SRA Authorisation of Individuals Regulations 2019; see also section 16(1) of SA 1974.

Common conditions on practising certificates – the test to apply

16.13

Practising certificate conditions are imposed solely to protect the public, primarily the solicitor's clients, by managing risk. The events listed in regulation 7.2 of the SRA Authorisation of Individuals Regulations 2019 are situations in which a solicitor may be regarded as representing an increased risk. Conditions are not imposed for the purposes of punishing solicitors, although conditions may be expensive for the solicitor, or even drive him or her out of business (for example, a condition of approved employment upon a sole practitioner who cannot or does not wish to find such employment).

The correct approach to the imposition of conditions is:

(1)   to identify the risk;

(2)   to identify a mechanism to manage and control the risk to minimise its consequences; and

(3)   to determine whether the proposed mechanism is necessary and proportionate to the risk. As conditions are not intended to be penal, the control mechanism should be no more than is necessary to manage the risk.

Thus in cases of accounts that have been badly kept, resulting in substantial accounting errors and breaches of the Accounts Rules, the imposition of a condition requiring the delivery of frequent accountants' reports (usually half-yearly) would be the obvious course. Where serious errors of judgement have occurred, and there is a risk of repetition, or where there have been serious administrative failings, a condition requiring a solicitor to practise only in approved partnership or, in extreme cases, approved employment, could be appropriate.

In *Razeen (No 15 of 2008)*[1] the Master of the Rolls stated:

> 'Mr Goodwin [for the SRA] submits that regulatory conditions are imposed either to protect the public interest or the reputation of the profession or both. It appears to me that the essential point is whether conditions are necessary and proportionate to protect the public interest. Reference to reputation of the profession is really an incident of the protection of the public interest … I am also unable, however, to accept what I think may be Mr Goodwin's submission, that the SRA does not have to identify a specific risk. Absent identification of the risk, it appears to me that the SRA cannot properly assess the reasonableness or proportionality of any conditions that it seeks to impose.'

1   *Razeen (No 15 of 2008)* [2008] EWCA Civ 1220 at [12] and [13]. See also *Lebow (No 13 of 2007)* [2008] EWCA Civ 411 at [23]: 'Conditions, however, if they are to be imposed, must be both necessary and proportionate'.

16.14

The precise content of conditions will depend upon the regulatory concerns of the SRA, and as to how the public can best be protected. For instance, the solicitor may be excluded from carrying out specified work of a particular kind, such as probate, or may be required to attend a particular type of training course on solicitors' accounting procedures or practice management. The SRA may take into account, when imposing conditions, that an application has been made against the solicitor to the Tribunal if the allegations are sufficiently serious, even though those allegations have not yet been adjudicated upon.[1]

Conditions, once imposed, are likely to be re-imposed from year to year, although it is open to the solicitor upon renewal to apply for a certificate free from conditions. If the condition was imposed by reason of a set of circumstances which by their nature continue (for example, the existence of judgment debts), the solicitor can expect the condition to continue until the underlying cause is removed (for example, by the discharge of those debts).[2]

If the cause of the condition was a particular event, such as the imposition of a penalty by the Tribunal, or a return to practice after suspension, conditions are likely to be imposed for at least three or four years. There is, however, no hard rule to this effect and it may well be possible for the solicitor to secure an unconditional certificate if it can clearly be demonstrated that the problem period is over, and there is no continuing cause for concern or the need for any additional safeguard.

1   *Burdett (No 8 of 2002)* [2002] EWCA Civ 1194; *Awan v Law Society* [2003] EWCA Civ 1969; *Walker (No 13 of 2001)* [2001] EWCA Civ 1596.
2   Comments by Lord Donaldson MR in *No 6 of 1990* (unreported).

Procedure

16.15

The procedure followed is similar to that used for adjudication on matters of conduct (see **15.12**), by the production of a supervisor's report which contains recommendations on which the solicitor has the opportunity to comment, usually within 14 days. If the solicitor does not oppose the recommended course or does not respond, the provisional decision becomes final (subject to appeal). To that extent the power to make decisions rests with the individual supervisor.

If the proposed course is not accepted and representations are made, the matter is adjudicated upon, but the level and seniority of the decision-maker can vary. The matter may be referred to an adjudicator, but increasingly decisions at first instance are being taken by supervisors or their managers.

Similar procedures are followed where, for example, there is an existing practising certificate condition requiring approval of any proposed partnership or employment, and application is made for approval.

Internal reviews

16.16

A solicitor has a right to an internal review of a decision to refuse an application for a practising certificate, impose conditions on or revoke the practising certificate.[1] The application for review must be made within 28 days of notice being given of the decision (or reasons for the decision if later) and must explain the grounds of review and provide reasons and any evidence in support. The review will be considered by an adjudicator or an adjudication panel on the papers.[2]

If an application is made for a review before expiry of the 28-day time period, the decision takes effect on determination of the review, unless the SRA directs that the decision is to take effect immediately. The SRA has a discretion to make such a direction if it considers it is necessary in the public interest to do so.[3]

1 Rule 3.2 of and Annex 1 to the SRA Application, Notice, Review and Appeal Rules 2019.
2 Rule 3.5 of the SRA Application, Notice, Review and Appeal Rules 2019.
3 Rules 6.1 and 6.2 of the SRA Application, Notice, Review and Appeal Rules 2019.

Appeals to the High Court

16.17

All the decisions of the SRA set out above can be contested by way of appeal to the High Court (rather than to the Master of the Rolls as was the case prior to LSA 2007).[1] Previous decisions of successive Masters of the Rolls will continue to be binding on the SRA, and highly persuasive in the High Court. In *Akodu v SRA*,[2] Moses LJ candidly accepted the inexperience of the High Court in dealing with such issues, and remitted the issue of practising certificate conditions to the adjudicator, stating:[3]

> 'I would, for my part, underline that which Mr Barton [for the SRA] urged, namely, that in the normal case, this court should deal with these questions rather than remitting them. No doubt, as the body of experience expands, confined as it will be to a number of nominated judges as we were told, it will not be necessary to adopt the course I have reluctantly decided should be adopted.'

Although the High Court has an unfettered discretion in hearing such appeals, appropriate weight will be accorded to the professional expertise of the SRA decision-makers who imposed the conditions.[4] The High Court has power to make such order as it thinks fit. On costs, the High Court applies traditional costs principles to practising certificate appeals, so that costs will ordinarily follow the event.

The SRA encourages solicitors to utilise its internal review procedure (see **16.16**) before exercising their statutory rights of appeal (historically the Master of the Rolls took the same view).

If and when the SRA makes rules to this effect, appeals may lie to the Tribunal rather than the High Court.[5] There is no sign that the SRA has any current intention of making such rules.

1   Sections 13, 13A(6), 13B(7) and 16(5) of SA 1974.
2   [2009] EWHC 3588 (Admin).
3   At [14].
4   See *Lebow (No 13 of 2007)* [2008] EWCA Civ 411 at [23]: 'This appeal is by way of re-hearing, although one of the factors which successive Masters of the Rolls and I myself have taken into account in the past is the importance of the judgment of the adjudicator and the appeal panel'. It may be noted, however, that the policy of the SRA is to have decisions made at the lowest practicable level of staff within the organisation and it remains to be seen whether this degree of confidence will continue to be held when most decisions are made by individuals employed full time by the SRA.
5   Section 49A of SA 1974.

SDT restriction orders

16.18

The Solicitors Disciplinary Tribunal has no specific power itself to impose conditions on a practising certificate when imposing a penalty upon a solicitor, but it can make recommendations to the SRA and, because it can make 'such order as it may think fit',[1] it can also make orders in the form of restrictions upon the way in which a solicitor continues to practise, either for a finite period or indefinitely with liberty to apply. The Divisional Court has first encouraged the Tribunal to use, and subsequently stated that the Tribunal should use, such a power, where it considers it to be in the public interest to do so, rather than to leave such future considerations to the SRA.[2] In *Olufeku (No 7 of 2007)* and *Brandon (No 12 of 2008)*,[3] the Master of the Rolls considered the overlapping jurisdictions of the SRA and Tribunal in such matters. The decisions of the Tribunal are punitive and disciplinary; those of the SRA are regulatory and not punitive.

Since the decision in *Ebhogiaye v Solicitors Regulation Authority*[4] the Tribunal has regularly made such orders, which it describes as 'restriction orders', and which can constitute the entirety of a sanction against a solicitor, or part thereof. Appeals against such orders would be made to the Administrative Court.

If the Tribunal makes a restriction order, the SRA may inform the solicitor that it intends to impose matching or more restrictive practising certificate conditions.

1   Section 47(2) of SA 1974.
2   *Camacho v Law Society* [2004] 33 LS Gaz R 37; *Taylor v Law Society* [2005] EWCA Civ 1473; *Ebhogiaye v Solicitors Regulation Authority* [2013] EWHC 2445 (Admin).
3   [2007] EWCA Civ 840 and [2008] EWCA Civ 967, respectively. Also see *Ebhogiaye v Solicitors Regulation Authority* [2013] EWHC 2445 (Admin).
4   [2013] EWHC 2445 (Admin).

Publicity

16.19

The SRA has published guidance on the publication of regulatory and disciplinary decisions, which states that it will publish controls on practising certificates when it considers it to be in the public interest to do so.[1] It appears that all or virtually all decisions to impose practising certificate conditions are being published when conditions are first imposed or materially varied. This is so even when the conditions have little relevance to members of the public (such as a condition requiring a solicitor to attend a course on a relevant subject). Decisions will not generally be published when they are the subject of an appeal (either internally or to the High

Court). Published information will usually be limited to a short statement as to the decision and the reasons for it. The current practice when a solicitor succeeds in obtaining a certificate free from conditions, having previously been subject to conditions, is not as one might expect to remove the reference to the former conditions from the SRA's website, but to publish the decision removing the conditions as well, and to retain the public record of the former conditions for three years.

The Master of the Rolls emphasised the importance of appeals to him being held in public save in exceptional circumstances.[2] Appeals to the High Court are heard in public in the usual way.

Under section 17(1) of SA 1974, the SRA must forthwith publish suspensions to practising certificates arising as a result of an order made by the High Court on appeal or a bankruptcy order.

1   'Publishing regulatory and disciplinary decisions', SRA guidance (see www.sra.org.uk/sra/decision-making/guidance/disciplinary-publishing-regulatory-disciplinary-decisions.page).
2   *L v Law Society (No 13 of 2008)* [2008] EWCA Civ 811. This appeal concerned the revocation of a student's membership on the grounds of fitness for admission to the roll, but considered the principles of public and private hearings generally.

Regulatory settlement agreements

16.20

The SRA may be prepared to enter into a regulatory settlement as an alternative to the imposition of practising certificate conditions (for regulatory settlements generally, see **20.18**). Such agreements may enable undertakings to be given, for example:

●   not to engage in a particular form of work, such as conveyancing, acting for lenders or in litigation;

●   to practise only as an employee after a specified date, pending the outcome of an investigation; or

●   to provide independent evidence that accounts are in compliance, or of a return to physical or mental good health.

The SRA usually requires that regulatory settlement agreements are publicised on its website.

The roll

16.21

A solicitor may keep his or her name on the roll without holding a practising certificate, but as explained above the circumstances in which a solicitor may practise or be held out as a solicitor without a practising certificate are now very few. A solicitor without a practising certificate may nevertheless be described as a 'solicitor – not practising'.

Until 2011, the SRA wrote every year during March or April to every solicitor whose name was on the roll but who did not have a practising certificate enquiring whether he or she wanted to remain on the roll. The process was changed and letters were written to all in this category in August 2011 with a requirement to register online. The current situation is that the SRA may enquire at intervals of its own choosing whether an individual wishes his or her name to remain on the roll: 'The SRA will write to you at the last notified version of your postal or email address to ask you whether you wish your name to remain on the roll at appropriate intervals as prescribed if you do not hold a practising certificate'.[1] Anyone who either replies asking to be removed from the roll, or who fails to reply and to pay the required fee within eight weeks, may have his or her name removed from the roll. A solicitor may also apply to have his or her name removed from the roll at any time.[2]

A person whose name has been removed from the roll in this way may apply to the SRA for it to be restored. On receipt of such an application, the SRA is entitled to assess the character and suitability of any applicant so the process is not automatic.[3] The SRA may refuse to restore the name of a solicitor to the roll if there are outstanding complaints, and may refuse to remove the solicitor from the roll in the same circumstances.[4]

The SRA will not remove a solicitor's name from the roll when there are disciplinary proceedings pending before the Tribunal or the court.[5]

There is a statutory right of appeal to the High Court for persons aggrieved by decisions of the SRA to refuse to restore a name to the roll. There is also a right to apply for an internal review of such a decision before appealing to the High Court.[6]

1   Regulation 5.4 of the SRA Authorisation of Individuals Regulations 2019.
2   Regulation 5.6(b) of the SRA Authorisation of Individuals Regulations 2019.
3   Regulation 5.9 of the SRA Authorisation of Individuals Regulations 2019. This does not, of course, apply if the solicitor has been struck off or the Tribunal has ordered that the solicitor may not be restored to the roll other than by order of the Tribunal.
4   Regulation 5.10 of the SRA Authorisation of Individuals Regulations 2019.
5   Regulation 5.10 of the SRA Authorisation of Individuals Regulations 2019.
6   Section 8(4) of SA 1974, and rule 3.2 of the SRA Application, Notice, Review and Appeal Rules 2019. Applications for internal review must be made within four weeks of the relevant decision. Rule 5.1 specifies a 28-day period for appeals to the High Court (which runs from the date of determination of the internal review, if the application for review is made in time), unless otherwise provided in rules of court. The relevant rules of court are CPR, Part 52 and the practice directions to CPR, Part 52.

Removal from the roll by consent

16.22

The SRA can, where it is in the interests of the public to do so, agree to the removal from the roll of a solicitor where the solicitor's conduct is under investigation, provided that there are no pending proceedings before the Solicitors Disciplinary Tribunal[1] (for the circumstances in which regulatory settlements may or may not be contemplated, see **20.18**).

Such an agreement can be expected to require a witness statement from the solicitor containing a statement of truth and which makes relevant admissions as to the facts, the allegations of misconduct and any previous relevant disciplinary history. It will record that a serious sanction from the Tribunal could be expected in the light of the admissions and will request removal from the roll to avoid costs, distress and further risk to the public. The statement will acknowledge that the statement itself and the agreement will be publicised by the SRA. Undertakings will be required not to apply to be restored to the roll, not to work in a solicitors' practice without the written permission of the SRA, and to make full and frank disclosure to any prospective employer of the agreement that had been reached.

1   Regulation 5.10 of the SRA Authorisation of Individuals Regulations 2019.

CHAPTER 17

Intervention and orderly closure

17.1

The intervention regime was introduced in the Solicitors Act 1941 as a necessary adjunct to the creation in the same statute of the Law Society Compensation Fund: if a solicitor's conduct might give rise to a claim on the Compensation Fund (which would then have to be met by the profession as a whole), it was felt that a power to intervene could operate to prevent or minimise such a claim. The Law Society has been described as the guardian not only of the profession, but also of the public in their dealings with the profession. The power to intervene provides the Solicitors Regulation Authority (SRA) with the opportunity to nip dishonesty in the bud, to preserve public confidence in the profession and to reduce claims on the Compensation Fund.[1]

Intervention represents the most powerful regulatory weapon available to the SRA, as it involves the effective destruction of a solicitor's practice (see **17.11** to **17.14**). In the many decades since the introduction of the intervention regime, there have been only a handful of successful statutory challenges to interventions,[2] and in those cases the Law Society did not oppose the withdrawal of the intervention. The claimant in *Sheikh v Law Society* succeeded in a contested challenge at first instance,[3] but the decision was reversed by the Court of Appeal.[4]

The statutory provisions are draconian. They have been described as such, and as potentially striking a mortal blow to the solicitor's practice.[5]

1 See *Buckley v Law Society (No 2)* [1984] 1 WLR 1101, ChD at 1105–6, per Sir Robert Megarry VC; *Sritharan v Law Society* [2005] EWCA Civ 476 at [17] and [18], [2005] 1 WLR 2708 at 2714A–D; and *Sheikh v Law Society* [2006] EWCA Civ 1577, [2007] 3 All ER 183.
2 See *Yogarajah v Law Society* (1982) 126 Sol Jo 430, *Patel v Law Society* [2008] EWHC 3564 (Ch) *Khan v SRA* (18 May 2012, unreported) and *Williams v SRA* [2015] EWHC 2302 (Ch), [2015] 1 WLR 4982. In each of these cases, the Law Society/SRA either consented to, or did not oppose, the setting aside of the intervention.
3 [2005] EWHC 1409 (Ch), [2005] 4 All ER 717.
4 [2006] EWCA Civ 1577, [2007] 3 All ER 183.
5 See *Buckley v Law Society (No 2)* [1984] 3 All ER 313, ChD; *Giles v Law Society* (1996) 8 Admin LR 105 at 116D–E, CA, per Ward LJ.

Grounds for action

17.2

The grounds upon which the SRA is entitled to intervene in a solicitor's practice are contained in Schedule 1 to the Solicitors Act (SA) 1974 as amended by the Legal Services Act (LSA) 2007.[1] Essentially, these are designed to permit intervention when a solicitor cannot run (through ill health, imprisonment, bankruptcy and the like), or alternatively cannot be trusted to run, a solicitor's practice so as to ensure that clients' monies are secure. The statutory grounds are the following:[2]

- The SRA has reason to suspect dishonesty on the part of the solicitor, an employee of the solicitor or the personal representatives of a deceased solicitor, in connection with that solicitor's practice or former practice, or in connection with any trust of which that solicitor is or formerly was a trustee or that employee is or was a trustee in his capacity as such an employee (para 1(1)(a) of Schedule 1).

- The SRA has reason to suspect dishonesty on the part of a solicitor in connection with (i) the business of any body of which the solicitor is or was a manager or (ii) any business carried on by the solicitor as a sole trader (para 1(1)(aa) of Schedule 1).

- The SRA considers that there has been undue delay on the part of the personal representatives of a deceased solicitor who immediately before his death was practising as a sole solicitor, in connection with that solicitor's practice or in connection with any trust (para 1(1)(b) of Schedule 1).

- The SRA is satisfied that the solicitor has failed to comply with rules made by virtue of sections 31, 32 or 37(2)(c) of SA 1974. Section 31 refers to rules of professional practice, conduct, fitness to practise and discipline of solicitors, section 32 to accounts rules and section 37 to rules in relation to professional indemnity insurance. In essence any breach of any part of the 2019 regulatory arrangements, or their statutory predecessors, will suffice.

- The solicitor has been made bankrupt or has made a composition or arrangement with his creditors (para 1(1)(d) of Schedule 1).

- The solicitor has been committed to prison in any civil or criminal proceedings (para 1(1)(e) of Schedule 1).

- The SRA is satisfied that a sole solicitor is incapacitated by illness, injury or accident to such an extent as to be unable to attend to his practice (para 1(1)(ee) of Schedule 1).

- The solicitor lacks capacity within the meaning of the Mental Capacity Act 2005 to act as a solicitor and powers under sections 15 to 20 or section 48 of that Act are exercisable in relation to him (para 1(1)(f)) of Schedule 1).

- The name of a solicitor has been removed from or struck off the roll or a solicitor has been suspended from practice (para 1(1)(g) of Schedule 1).

- The SRA is satisfied that a sole solicitor has abandoned his practice (para 1(1)(h) of Schedule 1).

- Any power conferred by Schedule 1 to SA 1974 has been exercised in relation to a sole solicitor by virtue of sub-paragraph (1)(a) (reason to suspect dishonesty) and he has acted as a sole solicitor within the period of 18 months beginning with the date on which it was so exercised (para 1(1)(j) of Schedule 1).[3]

- The SRA is satisfied that a person has acted as a solicitor at a time when he did not have a practising certificate which was in force (para 1(1)(k) of Schedule 1).

- The SRA is satisfied that the solicitor has failed to comply with any condition, subject to which his practising certificate was granted or otherwise has effect, to the effect that he may act as a solicitor only in employment which is approved by the SRA in connection with the imposition of that condition, or as a member of a partnership which is so approved, or as a manager of a body recognised by the SRA under section 9 of the Administration of Justice Act 1985 and so approved – or in any specified combination of those ways (para 1(1)(l) of Schedule 1). The word 'manager' has the same meaning as in LSA 2007 (see section 207 of LSA 2007).[4]

- The SRA is satisfied that it is necessary to exercise the powers of intervention, or any of them, to protect the interests of clients, or former or potential clients, of the solicitor or his firm, or the interests of the beneficiaries of any trust of which the solicitor is or was a trustee (para 1(1)(m) of Schedule 1).

1 Section 9(2)(f) of the Administration of Justice Act 1985 and paragraphs 32–35 of Schedule 2 thereto, as amended, provide for rules made under SA 1974, and the powers of intervention, to have effect in relation to recognised bodies and section 102 of and Schedule 14 to LSA 2007 confer similar powers in relation to alternative business structures (ABSs).
2 The statute refers to 'the Society' but in practice the powers are exercised by the SRA.
3 This is an anachronism – it has been superseded by the provision for the automatic suspension of the solicitor's practising certificate when an intervention occurs by reason of a suspicion of dishonesty. Before this power was acquired (by section 15(1A) of SA 1974, inserted by the Courts and Legal Services Act 1990) a solicitor who was the subject of an intervention could theoretically immediately set himself up in practice again and encourage all his clients to reinstruct him.
4 Paragraph 1(1A) of Schedule 1 to SA 1974.

17.3

It is arguable that the ground for intervention, paragraph 1(1)(m) of Schedule 1, introduced by LSA 2007, is so widely drawn that all other grounds are obsolete, but it is anticipated that reliance will continue to be placed on the traditional grounds, if only because there will be an obligation to explain why the SRA considered it 'necessary' to intervene.

Another ground added by LSA 2007 is paragraph 1(1)(aa) of Schedule 1, which envisages intervention when there is suspected dishonesty on the part of a solicitor in connection with a business that is not a solicitor's practice; that is, a business (not being a solicitor's practice or trust) of which the solicitor is the sole proprietor, or of which he or she is an employee or manager. This is intended to deal with the situation in which a solicitor has a legal practice but is also involved in another business, for example, one that provides financial services, where there is reason to suspect dishonesty in relation to that separate business. One could see that if the Financial Conduct Authority (using the same example) took action against such a business in circumstances where a suspicion of dishonesty arose, there could be a need to intervene in the solicitor's practice, as the same person could be seen to pose a risk to clients.

It was the case that the powers of intervention could only be exercised after specific notice had been given to the solicitor if they were to be exercised under sub-paragraph 1(c) – breaches of specified rules relating to professional practice, conduct and discipline of solicitors.[1] The solicitor had to be given notice in writing that he had failed to comply with the rules specified in the notice and also (at the same or any later time) notice that the powers of intervention were accordingly exercisable, but this provision was repealed by LSA 2007.

Intervention can therefore occur with no notice at all, and the solicitor may have no opportunity to make any representations on his or her own behalf before the decision to intervene is made.

1 Paragraph 1(2) of Schedule 1 to SA 1974 was repealed by para 77(2)(k) of Schedule 16 to LSA 2007.

The adjudication process

17.4

The resolution to intervene may be made by two adjudicators, including members of the adjudication panel and employed adjudicators, save that one adjudicator may so resolve in cases of 'severe and imminent risk to the public'.[1] Accordingly, an intervention into a solicitor's practice can be authorised by a single employee of the SRA. Typically the adjudicators will consider a Forensic Investigation Report, any representations the solicitor may have made in answer to that report, and the recommendations of a supervisor contained in his or her own report which will summarise the facts and issues. The recommendation of a supervisor is in no sense binding upon the panel; in *Sheikh v Law Society*,[2] the supervisor had recommended against intervention but the adjudication panel nevertheless resolved to intervene.

In cases of clear suspected dishonesty or where it is intended that the intervention should occur without notice, the supervisor's report will not be disclosed to the solicitor. Indeed, in the most serious cases, usually involving an obvious and substantial client account shortfall in circumstances amounting to theft, the procedure may involve a brief visit from an investigating officer, a report by way of a one-page memorandum and an intervention as soon as the necessary practical arrangements have been made.

1   SRA Schedule of Delegations, March 2018.
2   [2006] EWCA Civ 1577, [2007] 3 All ER 183.

Natural justice and Human Rights Act 1998 implications

17.5

Solicitors who are the subject of interventions have challenged the exercise of this powerful and terminally damaging regulatory weapon without any requirement for notice, on the grounds that it is in breach of the principles of natural justice and that it is incompatible with the rights protected by the Human Rights Act (HRA) 1998. All such challenges have failed. The natural justice arguments were rejected in *Giles v Law Society*,[1] and the HRA 1998 arguments failed in *Holder v Law Society*.[2] In the latter case, the Court of Appeal held that the statutory regime as a whole did not offend HRA 1998, although it remained open to a solicitor to assert that an intervention in a particular case breached the rights protected by the European Convention.

In *Neumans LLP v Law Society*[3] the Court of Appeal ruled that *Giles*[4] was binding authority that the common law rules of procedural fairness[5] are excluded by SA 1974. The appellant firm had argued that a lack of consultation and reasoning by the SRA amounted to procedural unfairness.

More compelling circumstances than were present in *Neumans* may yet lead to a relaxation of this approach, although the SRA's unbroken record of success over many decades must make this unlikely. In this regard, Singh LJ commented in *Neumans*:

'the [SRA] submits that the law should not impose a duty of procedural fairness in this context, where speed and sometimes secrecy are of the essence in order to protect the public interest. Yet, on the facts of this case, the [SRA] did afford the opportunity to make representations before intervention took place. That at least suggests that it is possible, depending on the facts of a particular case, to comply with the normal requirements of procedural fairness and so it may not be necessary to have an absolute rule that those requirements never apply before an intervention can take place. In other contexts public law has not shied away from imposing the duty of procedural fairness as a matter of principle, while recognising that (where appropriate, depending on the facts of the individual case) it may not be possible to comply with that duty in advance of a decision, for example because there is a need for speed or secrecy.'

1   (1996) 8 Admin LR 105, CA. See also *Neumans LLP v Law Society* (2018) EWCA Civ 325; *Yogarajah v Law Society* (1982) 126 Sol Jo 430; and *Buckley v Law Society* (9 October 1985, unreported).
2   [2003] EWCA Civ 39, [2003] 3 All ER 62, [2003] 1 WLR 1059.
3   [2018] EWCA Civ 325.
4   *Giles v Law Society* (1996) 8 Admin LR 105, CA.
5   Synonymous with the concept of natural justice.

The extent of the powers

17.6

The mechanism selected by Parliament to permit the Law Society to achieve intervention in a solicitor's practice is, in essence, to vest the solicitor's practice monies in the Society, and to require the solicitor to yield up the practice documents. These powers have been delegated to and are exercised by the SRA.

Money

17.7

The intervention resolution vests all sums of money held by or on behalf of a solicitor or his firm in connection with his practice, and the right to recover or receive those sums, in the SRA.[1] In short, the SRA takes control of office and client accounts. Where the intervention is solely by reason of the death of a sole practitioner, only client account is affected.[2]

The SRA holds the money on trust for the purposes of the intervention and 'subject thereto … upon trust for the persons beneficially entitled to them'.[3] What this means in practice is that the SRA holds client money on trust for the clients, and office money (if any) in circumstances where the solicitor is likely to be in substantial debt (a) to his clients in the event of any client account shortfall and (b) to the SRA in respect of the intervention costs (more of which below: see **17.13**). The SRA deals with the money in accordance with the SRA Statutory Trust Rules 2019. While the solicitor is 'beneficially entitled' to anything that might be left, it is unlikely that there will be anything. Sums recovered by the solicitor after the intervention in connection with his practice, such as payment of outstanding bills of costs, also vest in the SRA.[4]

Schedule 1 to SA 1974 provides the court with specific powers to assist the SRA in gaining control of the practice monies. The court may order that no payment shall be made without the leave of the court by any person (whether or not named in the order) of any money held by him (in whatever manner and whether it was received before or after the making of the order) on behalf of the solicitor or his firm.[5] The court may require a person suspected of holding money on behalf of the solicitor or his firm to provide information to the SRA as to such money and the accounts in which it is held.[6]

The SRA may also resolve to vest in itself the right to recover or receive debts due to the solicitor or his firm in connection with his practice or former practice.[7]

The extent of the statutory trust was considered in *Williams v SRA*,[8] in which the SRA had agreed to set aside an intervention. An issue later arose as to whether a sum of money which the SRA had received from the Legal Aid Agency, which the claimant said represented work carried out by him while an earlier partnership than the one that was the subject of the notice of intervention was still in being, was within the scope of the statutory trust. Sir William Blackburne held that:

- 'practice' for the purposes of paragraph 6(2) of Schedule 1 to SA 1974 meant the activities of a solicitor so far as carried out in that capacity, in contrast to the named organisation or structure though which the solicitor practised;

- the claimant's 'former practice' for the purposes of paragraph 6(2)(a) therefore included his practice while a partner of the earlier partnership, namely the activities he had carried on as a solicitor during that time, even though the earlier partnership had not been named in the intervention resolution; and

- accordingly, in so far as it derived from the solicitor's 'practice' while a member of the earlier partnership, the Legal Aid Agency payment fell within the scope of the statutory trust.

The extent of the statutory trust was considered again by the Court of Appeal in *Law Society of England and Wales v Pathania*.[9] Sir Geoffrey Vos, giving the leading judgment, reversed the decision of the High Court when it held that loans made by the solicitor from client account, in breach of trust/fiduciary duty, prior to the resolution to intervene, were not sums, 'held by or on behalf of the solicitor or his firm'.[10] This was so, as the funds the loans represented were, by their nature, not 'held' but had been paid away. The Law Society had not issued a resolution exercising the 'right to recover or receive debts due to the solicitor or his firm in connection with his practice or former practice'.[11]

The Court of Appeal held that while the solicitor 'is obliged to account to the client for the monies he has paid away on the footing of wilful default, and would be held liable to pay equitable compensation to the client for his breach of fiduciary duty' (at [72]), as the solicitor held no funds, the claims (against the debtors) arising from the money improperly paid away did not vest in the Law Society by virtue of the resolution made.[12]

Sir Geoffrey Vos held that historically,[13] the legislation[14] intended to cover monies actually held (bank deposits treated as being held despite the creditor/debtor relationship), or subsequently received, as well as monies held in a bare trust for the solicitor (eg where paid away to avoid the effects of an intervention). Thus he concluded (at [83]) that:

'paragraph 6(2)(a) does not cover monies wrongfully paid out of client account before the Intervention where there is no specific fund held by or on the solicitor's behalf to which the solicitor's obligation to replace the monies can directly attach. It is not enough that the borrower has an obligation to repay the monies under the terms of a loan agreement.'

Sir Geoffrey Vos also held that the solicitor was not required to account to the Law Society in respect of his past defaults; rather he was liable to account to his clients for his breaches. He added, however, that when the loans are repaid, they will be caught by the statutory trusts.

The court also commented (at [86]) that:

'the outcome is undesirable from the Law Society's point of view ... the Law Society has not historically made use of paragraph 6A. It may wish to do so in future ...'.

1   Paragraph 6 of Schedule 1 to SA 1974.
2   Paragraphs 2 and 6(2)(b) of Schedule 1.
3   Paragraph 6(1) of Schedule 1.
4   *Dooley v Law Society (No 2)* [2001] All ER (D) 362, *Times*, 16 January 2002, ChD.
5   Paragraph 5(1) of Schedule 1 to SA 1974.
6   Paragraph 8 of Schedule 1.
7   Paragraph 6A of Schedule 1. This was added by LSA 2007 and puts on an express statutory footing that which had been held in *Dooley* (above) to be the case as a matter of proper interpretation of the statute prior to its amendment.
8   *Williams v SRA* [2015] EWHC 2302 (Ch), [2015] 1 WLR 4982.
9   [2019] EWCA Civ 517.
10 Paragraph 6(2)(a) of Schedule 1.
11 Paragraph 6A of Schedule 1.
12 Resolution under paragraph 6(2)(a) of Schedule 1.
13 Prior to the introduction of paragraph 6A of Schedule 1.
14 Paragraph 6 of Schedule 1.

Practice documents

17.8

The intervention resolution results in a notice to the solicitor or his firm requiring the production or delivery to any person appointed by the SRA of all documents in the possession of the solicitor or his firm in connection with his practice.[1] Failure or refusal to comply with the notice is a criminal offence.[2] The High Court has power to order the production or delivery of documents by the solicitor and/or by any person suspected of being in possession of relevant documents.[3] Once possession has been taken of the documents, the SRA must serve on the solicitor a notice that possession has been taken by the person appointed on its behalf.[4]

1   Paragraph 9 of Schedule 1 to SA 1974.
2   Paragraph 9(3) of Schedule 1.
3   Paragraph 9(4) and (5) of Schedule 1.
4   Paragraph 9(7) of Schedule 1.

Other powers

17.9

The SRA's intervention costs, which can easily amount to £100,000 or more, are a debt due from the solicitor or his estate, unless the High Court orders otherwise.[1] The High Court may also make orders permitting forcible entry to premises to search for and seize documents,[2] for the redirection of mail, telephone and electronic communications[3] and for the appointment of a new trustee in substitution for the solicitor as trustee of any trust.[4]

The High Court may, on the application of the SRA, order a former partner of the solicitor to pay a specified proportion of the intervention costs otherwise payable by the solicitor if it is satisfied that the conduct of the solicitor that led to the intervention was carried on with the consent or connivance of, or attributable to any neglect on the part of, the former partner.[5]

The SRA's statutory powers in relation to money and documents take precedence over any lien or other right to possession in any other person.[6] These powers continue to be exercisable after a solicitor's death, or after his name has been removed from or struck off the roll.

1   Paragraph 13 of Schedule 1 to SA 1974.
2   Paragraph 9(6) of Schedule 1.
3   Paragraph 10 of Schedule 1.
4   Paragraph 11 of Schedule 1.
5   Paragraph 13A of Schedule 1.
6   Paragraph 12 of Schedule 1.

Practising certificate

17.10

Where an intervention is authorised because of a suspicion of dishonesty on the part of the solicitor, breaches of the SRA Accounts Rules 2019, breaches of any other rule or provision made under section 31 of SA 1974, including the SRA Codes of Conduct, or the solicitor's committal to prison, any practising certificate of the solicitor then in force is immediately suspended[1] – unless the adjudicator or adjudication panel authorising the intervention directs otherwise.[2]

The solicitor may (at any time before the certificate expires) apply to the SRA to terminate the suspension and the SRA may terminate the suspension conditionally or unconditionally or refuse the application.[3] If the SRA refuses the application, or the solicitor is aggrieved at the conditions imposed he or she may appeal to the High Court.[4]

In practice, the SRA is usually prepared to restore a solicitor's practising certificate subject to stringent conditions, commonly a requirement that the solicitor may only practise in employment approved by the SRA, and on condition that he or she has no access to clients' money.

1   Section 15(1A) of SA 1974, inserted by section 91(2) of the Courts and Legal Services Act 1990.
2   Section 15(1B) of SA 1974.
3   Section 16(3) and (4).
4   Section 16(5).

The practical reality

17.11

The legal department of the SRA, which manages interventions, appoints an intervening agent, a solicitor who is a member of the SRA's Intervention Panel practising in the relevant area, who will take direct responsibility for (in particular) client files. Provisional arrangements may be made in advance of the intervention resolution when it can reasonably be expected to occur. Notice of the intervention will not be given to the solicitor (even if the Panel has resolved on the intervention some days before) until the agents are ready to act and the solicitor's bank has received notice. The solicitor will therefore not know of the intervention until after his or her bank accounts are frozen. The first that a solicitor will typically hear of the decision will be by a cryptic telephone call from the SRA requesting him to expect an email or hand delivery. This is likely to be in the late afternoon when the agents and representative of the SRA are due to arrive at the firm's offices the following morning.

The intervening agents attend at the solicitor's address and take possession of the practice documents which in most cases are removed without delay. Matters which are urgent and require prompt action are identified and (hopefully, assuming the solicitor's co-operation) discussed. Practice monies are transferred to a bank account under the control of the intervening agents. The intervening agents attempt to bring the practice's accounting records into proper order.

Clients will receive a standard letter informing them that the SRA has been obliged to exercise its statutory powers and inviting them to nominate successor solicitors or, if appropriate, to accept delivery of the papers themselves.

If claims in professional negligence or breach of fiduciary duty are made against the solicitor, the solicitor's professional indemnity insurers may wish to see the files seized by the SRA to seek to discover grounds for declining indemnity cover. However, the SRA refuses to provide insurers with the files in those circumstances unless the lay client has provided consent, and this refusal was upheld by the Court of Appeal in *Quinn Direct Insurance Ltd v Law Society*[1] on the ground that privilege and confidentiality in the documents remain after intervention, and there is no room for implying into the statutory scheme any entitlement in insurers to see the documents.[2]

1   [2010] EWCA Civ 805.
2   At [29].

17.12

The intervening agents do not in any sense take over or run the practice. They seek to ensure that all clients are informed of the intervention and find alternative solicitors, and that the practice monies are distributed properly; they may have to seek directions from the court to achieve this. They are likely to have to take urgent and protective steps in circumstances where it is necessary to guard the interests of clients, but it is not their function to take over client matters in any other sense or for any other purpose.

The description of intervention as striking a mortal blow to the practice[1] is, if anything, an understatement. Quite apart from the automatic suspension of the practising certificate, the solicitor loses control of the practice's bank accounts and the practice's documentation. It instantly becomes impossible to service any bank overdraft. Unless the intervention is rapidly reversed by the court, the solicitor's practice is lost without any compensation, and the solicitor faces almost inevitable financial ruin.

1   *Giles v Law Society* (1996) 8 Admin LR 105, CA.

17.13

Many practices have little in the way of measurable assets – offices are rented, equipment and cars leased, and the office account is likely to be in substantial overdraft. Assets represented by goodwill and work in progress suddenly become worthless. In addition, as has been said, the solicitor is liable for the costs of intervention, recoverable as a debt due to the SRA.[1] As already indicated, these costs can be very substantial. Unless the solicitor has private wealth there will be nothing left. Intervention and subsequent bankruptcy commonly go hand in hand.

Although, in theory, a solicitor subject to an intervention is entitled to payment for work in progress at the time of the intervention, this entitlement is more apparent than real. The successor solicitor taking over an individual file will have to extract such payment from the client, and will often doubtless be met by an argument from the lay client that he or she should not be liable for two sets of fees in respect of the same legal work. The intervened solicitor has no means of compelling anyone to recover outstanding costs. The SRA is under no obligation to do so.[2] Any payments recovered in respect of work in progress will first be set off against the solicitor's liability for the intervention costs.[3] Further, the SRA may have vested in itself the right to recover debts due to the practice, including outstanding bills and the value of work in progress.

Ownership of the solicitor's other assets, such as office furniture, computer equipment and the like is not affected by the intervention. Only practice monies and documents are affected (save that the SRA may require possession of computer equipment necessary to access documents held only in electronic form).[4] Similarly, the solicitor's contractual obligations are unaffected – the intervention does not have the effect of dismissing employees or in itself making them redundant.[5]

1   Paragraph 13 of Schedule 1 to SA 1974. The solicitor may require the detailed assessment of the costs: *Pine v Law Society (No 2)* [2002] EWCA Civ 175, [2002] 2 All ER 658.
2   *Dooley v Law Society (No 2)* [2001] All ER (D) 362, *Times*, 16 January 2002. Under LSA 2007, the SRA acquired the right to recover sums due to the solicitor and may therefore elect to pursue outstanding costs and work in progress to meet client liabilities or intervention costs.
3   *Dooley v Law Society (No 2)* [2001] All ER (D) 362, *Times*, 16 January 2002.
4   Paragraph 9(5A) and (6)(b) of Schedule 1 to SA 1974.
5   *Rose v Dodd* [2005] EWCA Civ 957, [2006] 1 All ER 464.

17.14

Essentially, therefore, an intervention means the total destruction of a solicitor's practice. The solicitor is unable to sell that practice to a willing purchaser. The practice's clients have to find new solicitors. The practice's employees have to find new jobs. And the solicitor has to apply for the suspension of the practising certificate to be lifted if he or she is to resume any sort of practice as a solicitor. The solicitor will only be able to practise at all by finding a willing employer.

Ordinarily, at the time of making the resolution to intervene, the adjudication panel will also refer the solicitor's conduct to the Solicitors Disciplinary Tribunal.

Because all the statutory provisions refer to a solicitor, and a solicitor's practice, it is possible (and it does occur) that interventions are authorised into the practice of a solicitor who may be a partner in a firm, rather than a sole practitioner. In that event only the client funds, client documents and any practice funds and papers personal to that solicitor are subject to the intervention. Inevitably this has the potential to be highly disruptive for the remaining partners, but they are not directly affected by the exercise of the statutory powers.

Challenging an intervention[1]

17.15

The SRA must serve on the solicitor or his or her firm, and on any other person having possession of sums of money caught by the intervention, a certified copy of the intervention resolution and a notice prohibiting the payment out of any such sums of money.[2] Within eight days of the service of that notice, the solicitor, on giving not less than 48 hours' notice in writing to the SRA, may apply to the High Court for an order directing the SRA to withdraw the notice.[3]

Likewise, where the SRA has taken possession of practice documents, the solicitor may apply to the High Court (again, within eight days of the service of the notice) for an order directing the SRA to deliver the documents to such person as the solicitor claimant may require.[4]

If the court makes an order in favour of the solicitor, it shall have power also to make such other order as it may think fit.[5]

The eight-day time limit is mandatory, and cannot be extended by the court or by the consent of the parties.[6] The proceedings are assigned to the Chancery Division and are governed by CPR Part 8 and rule 67.4. If the proceedings are not litigated expeditiously by the solicitor, so that they eventually become academic as a result of the destruction of his practice, they may be struck out as an abuse of process.[7]

There is no power for the SRA to withdraw an intervention once it has been put in place. If it is rapidly concluded that the decision was lawful but not justified or was ill advised, the solution is a consent order of the High Court.[8]

1   This term is used as there is no 'appeal' against an intervention – the remedy is an application to the High Court for an order directing the withdrawal of the intervention.
2   Paragraph 6(3) of Schedule 1 to SA 1974.
3   Paragraph 6(4) of Schedule 1. The eight-day limitation period should be seen as a strict requirement: as to whether the courts may be able to apply any flexibility, see *Gadd v SRA* [2013] EWCA Civ 837.
4   Paragraph 9(8) and (9) of Schedule 1.
5   Paragraphs 6(5) and 9(11) of Schedule 1.
6   *Re a Solicitor* [1994] Ch 1994 B 4973.
7   *Virdi v Law Society* [1999] 29 LS Gaz R 29. Mr Virdi's appeal to the Court of Appeal was dismissed, but this is unreported.
8   *Patel v Law Society* [2008] EWHC 3564 (Ch). Norris J commented in approving a consent order that the parties were right to seek such an order as there was no power provided to the SRA by the statute to reverse its own decision.

17.16

As has been seen, it has proved to be almost impossible to challenge an intervention successfully. This is at least in part because of the financial consequences of an intervention described above. The solicitor is in a quandary – does he or she recognise the likely reality that the only way in which family and personal financial commitments can be met is if he or she finds a job with a willing employer? If so, the solicitor must recognise also that the original practice will not survive; the conditions on his or her practising certificate will prevent recovery of the remnants of that practice, even if the challenge is successful. There is the additional risk that the proceedings will be struck out as an abuse as they will no longer have any practical purpose.

Alternatively, does the solicitor fight on, without employment or other income, with mounting and unserviceable debts, probably without funds to pay for the needed specialist assistance, and with no prospect of obtaining public funding, against an opponent with unlimited resources?

If a solicitor believes that he or she is at risk of intervention, it is wise to take precautions (such as putting another solicitor in funds) to ensure that a rapid statutory challenge can be mounted if so advised. Once the intervention has commenced, it will be impossible to draw upon office account. Any attempt to put funds beyond the reach of the SRA after the intervention has commenced may well be taken into account against the solicitor at the High Court hearing.[1]

It is highly doubtful whether the courts have jurisdiction to provide interim relief by 'unscrambling' the intervention and/or reversing the suspension of the solicitor's practising certificate pending the full hearing. Where the solicitor challenges the intervention, the SRA will ordinarily be prepared to co-operate in slowing down the practical effect of the intervention (ie by not informing clients of the intervention unless the particular matter is urgent).

However, the problem will remain as to what is to be done for those clients whose matters are not particularly pressing but who cannot be ignored. The solicitor who is the subject of the intervention cannot continue to act; he or she has no practising certificate. It is possible, if there is a suitable and willing person and the solicitor can afford to remunerate him or her (allowing for the fact that money coming in to the practice will vest in the SRA), for the solicitor to appoint another solicitor with an unconditional practising certificate as practice manager; this might be an existing employee or someone brought in for the purpose. Such arrangements will in practice require the co-operation of the SRA but will provide a mechanism for maintaining the status quo where a challenge is credibly made and expeditiously pursued.

1   See *Sheikh v Law Society* [2006] EWCA Civ 1577, [2007] 3 All ER 183.

17.17

The solicitor mounting a statutory challenge will be well advised to make an early application for directions to ensure that the case is brought on speedily for trial, and that the essential issues are identified at the outset.

The statutory challenge provided for by paras 6 and 9 of Schedule 1 to SA 1974 is the only manner in which an intervention can be challenged.[1] Any issues under HRA 1998 can be considered within the statutory proceedings.

1   *Hedworth v Law Society* (1994, unreported); *Miller v Law Society* [2002] EWHC 1453 (Ch), [2002] 4 All ER 312.

The proceedings and the test to be applied

17.18

In providing an extremely short mandatory limitation period (see **17.15**), Parliament clearly envisaged a swift summary procedure. One reason for the lack of successful challenges to interventions may be that this laudable aim has become lost in the complexities of High Court litigation. The tortuous course of the proceedings in *Sheikh v Law Society*[1] indicated that the statutory remedy was not working efficiently. The claimant's application to set aside the intervention did not come on for hearing for four months, and occupied eight days of court time. The judgments at first instance and of the Court of Appeal each ran to 70 pages of single-spaced typescript.

In most cases, the reasons for intervention will be obvious to all. However, this is not invariably so, and unless the reasons are properly identified at an early stage, there is a danger that the solicitor will be denied the effective summary remedy that Parliament intended to provide.

The burden of proof to justify the continuation of the intervention rests on the SRA – the solicitor, though nominally the claimant, is in reality the defendant.[2] Accordingly, unless the parties agree otherwise, the SRA will present its case first.

The traditional approach to the statutory challenge was the 'two-stage test' propounded by Neuberger J in *Dooley v Law Society*[3] approved by the Court of Appeal in *Holder v Law Society*:[4]

> 'The court's decision is a two-stage process. First it must decide whether the grounds under paragraph 1 are made out; in this case, primarily, whether there are grounds for suspecting dishonesty. Secondly, if the court is so satisfied, then it must consider whether in the light of all the evidence before it the intervention should continue. In deciding the second question, the court must carry out a balancing exercise between the need in the public interest to protect the public from dishonest solicitors and the inevitably very serious consequences to the solicitor if the intervention continues.'

1   [2006] EWCA Civ 1577, [2007] 3 All ER 183.
2   See *Giles v Law Society* (1996) 8 Admin LR 105 at 114F–G, CA, per Nourse LJ.
3   (2000) HC Transcript 0002868.
4   [2003] EWCA Civ 39, [2003] 3 All ER 62.

17.19

That must now be considered in the light of the more subtle approach suggested by the Court of Appeal in *Sheikh v Law Society*.[1] The court may need to decide whether, at the time of the resolution to intervene, the statutory ground relied upon by the SRA actually existed – for example, whether there was, at that time, reason to suspect dishonesty on the basis of the information available to the SRA. It has not been conclusively decided whether, if no such ground existed, the solicitor is entitled to have the notices of intervention withdrawn for that reason alone, but it seems likely that in that event the resolution will have been fundamentally flawed and liable to be set aside. On the other hand, such a circumstance is likely to be very rare.

In *Neumans LLP v The Law Society*[2] the Administrative Court rejected the appellant's argument that the SRA may not intervene on the ground of suspected dishonesty, if the manager so suspected is no longer a manager at the date of intervention.[3]

If there is no challenge to the validity of the resolution or to the service of the intervention notices, the single issue for the court is whether the notices should be withdrawn. In considering this, the court is exercising its own judgement and is entitled to take into account material that was not available to the SRA when resolving to intervene, but which is available to the court. Moreover, the court will also take into account the views of the SRA as a relevant evidential factor, although it is unclear how these views are ascertained in practice – save through the mouths of the advocates representing the SRA at the hearing of the application to withdraw the intervention notices. This is an unsatisfactory 'evidential' basis upon which to ask a court to make decisions.

As noted above, the intervention regime is in principle compliant with the requirements of natural justice and HRA 1998, but is capable of being operated unfairly in an individual case.

1   [2006] EWCA Civ 1577, [2007] 3 All ER 183.
2   [2017] EWHC 2004 (Ch).
3   The appellant went on to appeal to the Court of Appeal on other grounds – which failed.

17.20

If the challenge is successful the statute envisages an order requiring the withdrawal of the paragraph 6(3) notice[1] so as to return control of practice monies to the solicitor, and an order directing the SRA to deliver the practice documents to such person as the solicitor claimant may require. In addition, the court probably has jurisdiction to restore the suspended practising certificate to the solicitor,[2] and in *Sheikh v Law Society*,[3] the judge at first instance imposed a condition on the successful claimant's practising certificate.

The statutory scheme set out in Schedule 1 to SA 1974 cannot be replaced by a judge-made scheme. There is no 'half-way house': the court must either direct or decline to direct withdrawal of the intervention[4] (although the court's power to make consequential orders should enable it to ensure that the SRA is able to exercise proper regulatory control over the solicitor in the light of the facts found by the court).

There is no statutory entitlement to damages at the suit of the successful solicitor if the challenge succeeds. Whether damages may be awarded at common law, under SA 1974 or under HRA 1998, has not been decided and may well depend upon the court's view as to whether the decision to intervene was justified at the time it was made.

1   *Holder v Law Society* [2003] EWCA Civ 39, [2003] 3 All ER 62; *Sritharan v Law Society* [2005] EWCA Civ 476, [2005] 4 All ER 1105.
2   *Sritharan v Law Society* [2005] EWCA Civ 476, [2005] 4 All ER 1105.
3   [2006] EWCA Civ 1577, [2007] 3 All ER 183.
4   *Sritharan v Law Society* [2005] EWCA Civ 476, [2005] 4 All ER 1105.

Alternatives to intervention

17.21

In recent years the Law Society increasingly sought to find alternatives to intervention, principally because the cost of intervention is high and recovery of this from the solicitor is uncertain. The SRA is more willing than hitherto to achieve tight regulatory control over a solicitor who would otherwise have been subject to an intervention by means of the imposition of stringent conditions on his practising certificate. Alternatively, the SRA may permit the orderly disposal of the practice. The SRA may be prepared to enter into a regulatory settlement whereby the solicitor agrees to close his firm within a set period, or to correct errors in the firm's accounts and provide independent evidence of the accounts being compliant, or to seek medical treatment and provide independent evidence, for example, as to an addiction being overcome (see **20.18** as to regulatory settlements generally).

Orderly closure

17.22

There are a number of instances when a practice may be required to close, for example:

- retirement;
- ill health or death of a sole practitioner (where there is no special executorship clause in a will);
- financial restructure;
- compulsory professional indemnity insurance cannot be obtained; or
- to avoid an intervention by the SRA because:
    - the practice is not financially viable; or
    - the practice is no longer authorised by the SRA, for example as a result of a decision to revoke authorisation or following restrictive practising certificate conditions.

It is prudent to consider the possibility of selling the practice rather than closing. It is often cheaper to do so, not least as a result of the impact of liability for run-off indemnity insurance; and it is less disruptive for staff and clients. However, the very same insurance factor will inhibit potential purchasers; if they become a successor practice (see **11.7**) the acquiring firm's insurers are liable for any possible negligence claims.

When closing a practice, the principals will normally wish to wind up the entity in an orderly manner (although there is nothing in practice to prevent the entity deregistering with the SRA and continuing in existence, without undertaking regulated legal activities). The procedure to be followed upon closure varies from practice to practice, reflecting factors such as the regulated entity's legal status (limited liability company, LLP or traditional partnership), the complexity of the structure of the practice, the practice's relationships with third parties and its obligations to clients. No two practices are the same and each closure will have its challenges.

Compliance plans

17.23

The SRA is now very likely to impose obligations on a closing firm in the form of a 'compliance plan', and can insist on its terms with a threat of intervention as an alternative. Although the circumstances in which this will occur will inevitably be fraught and pressured, it is extremely important that the terms of the required plan are considered with care. The terms are likely to incorporate undertakings, express or implied, as to the achievement of targets, for example to reduce the client account to a nil balance. A failure to achieve a target has been treated by the SRA as a breach of undertaking and potentially a disciplinary matter. It is important only to accept obligations which are achievable. If necessary it may be desirable to seek specialist advice. Indeed anyone facing pressure to close a solicitors' practice is likely to benefit from specialist advice.

The closure process

17.24

For regulatory and insurance purposes closure takes place when a regulated entity ceases to conduct work for clients. This is not the same as the winding up of the regulated entity. There is likely to be a lapse of time between the practice ceasing to engage in fee earning work and the winding up of the entity.

From the point of closure the practice cannot engage in fee earning work and its activities are restricted to recovery of fees and effecting a closure programme. Failure to adhere to the restriction on undertaking client work will revoke the practice's run-off insurance provision and imposes an obligation to obtain a new professional indemnity insurance policy. Therefore it is important to plan ahead for closure.

When a practice has set a date for closure it must inform the SRA. It is best practice to set out a closure programme, addressing procedures for dealing with current client matters, the client bank account, accounting requirements, relationships with third parties and the storage of archived files. The SRA may accept this but may also seek to impose its own terms, as above. If the programme is accepted (with or without amendments) the SRA will expect to receive regular reports on progress.

Clients must be contacted with information as to the proposed closure, and to make arrangements concerning the collection of their files and client funds or their transfer to another practice. Inevitably this is likely to be stressful for clients and the firm will have to determine how this is best done bearing in mind the nature of its clients, their degree of vulnerability and their chosen method of communication. A letter 'out of the blue' may not always be the best option. Clients must be advised that they are free to choose a solicitor of their choice although it is permissible to indicate that a client would be welcome to join principals or fee earners in any new practices they may have joined.

Client account balances need to be returned or transferred as instructed. If the practice has historical dormant balances any gradual process being followed to deal with such matters will have to be accelerated. Every effort should be made to reduce the client account to a nil balance, and this should receive priority as soon as a decision is made to close (as to dealing with dormant balances see **6.26**).

Archived files can be returned to clients, stored or, where permitted, destroyed. If files are stored then the SRA must be advised of their whereabouts. There have been situations where intervention has taken place in respect of archived files alone, which remain client property pending their destruction.

17.25

Upon closure the practice must accurately indicate its new status. The practice's letterhead, website, emails and all other material will need to be adapted. Incoming telephone calls should be greeted with a message indicating the closure and who can be contacted for guidance. A notice of closure should be advertised in the *London Gazette* and a local newspaper. All regulated persons should make necessary amendments to their 'MySRA' account.

When planning ahead for closure the practice will need to consider how best it can service its creditors at a time when the only income will be payment for work undertaken prior to closure. The advice of an insolvency practitioner may be required. It will be necessary to control overheads and manage redundancies, among other things. If the firm is a legal aid practice the Legal Aid Agency should become involved at an early stage, to manage both the transfer of cases and payments on account.

The practice must inform its professional indemnity insurer of the intended closure as closure triggers the run-off provisions in its contract of insurance. The practice must pay the contractual run-off premium as set out in the schedule of insurance. Whereas the SIIR 2013 obligated insurers to report certain policy default to the SRA, the SIIR 2019 do not. However, similar obligations are typically set out in the participating insurers agreement entered into between the SRA and insurer, and may be included in the participating insurers agreement for 2019, not available at the time of writing (see **11.10**). The practice's insurer is often the largest creditor in a solvent closure. If the practice is not in a financial position to make the payment, it is sometimes possible to negotiate a reduced premium. This is an area in which specialist advice can be sought.

The process of closure and the examination of all files in the practice not infrequently gives rise to the discovery of problems not previously identified which will need to be reported to insurers and possibly to the SRA by either the compliance officer for legal practice (COLP) or compliance officer for finance and administration (COFA), who will retain their responsibilities throughout (see **CHAPTER 7**). Some level of complaint from clients, including opportunistic complaints, should be anticipated. Principals may continue to be liable in respect of awards by the Legal Ombudsman despite closure of the practice (see **14.9**).

We are indebted to Andrew Blatt of Murdochs Solicitors for his contribution to this section.

Limited intervention

17.26

This form of intervention is of a very different character and for very different purposes and is almost entirely unrelated to the matters discussed above.

It is designed solely to recover from a solicitor a file or files relating to specific matters, either for the purposes of the file(s) being handed to clients or for the purposes of inspection by the SRA to assist in the investigation of complaints or regulatory concerns, respectively.

It may occur in two circumstances. The first is concerned exclusively with delay, and is somewhat convoluted. If the SRA is satisfied that there has been undue delay in connection with any matter in which the solicitor or his firm is or was acting on behalf of a client or with any trust, or by any employee of a solicitor in connection with a trust of which the employee is or was a trustee in his capacity as such an employee, and the solicitor has been invited to give an explanation in answer to the complaint within a specified period[1] and:

- the solicitor fails within that period to give an explanation which is regarded as satisfactory;

- notice has been given to the solicitor of the fact that he has failed to give a satisfactory explanation; and

- either then or later a notice is given that the powers of intervention are exercisable for those reasons,

the SRA may 'intervene' in the solicitor's practice for the limited purpose of recovering the file or files in question, and for that purpose only.[2] In this event the file(s) will be obtained and handed to the client or to successor solicitors appointed by the client, so that the problems encountered as a result of the unexplained delays are overcome.

The second circumstance arises if a decision is made to require the solicitor to produce a file or files for inspection by the SRA for the purposes of an investigation;[3] the powers of intervention can be employed to compel the delivery up of such file(s).[4] The documents required in these circumstances will be all the documents in the possession of the solicitor or his firm relevant to the matter under investigation.

In either event the procedure is the same: an agent of the SRA is appointed, usually a solicitor on the SRA's Intervention Panel or a member of the staff of the SRA. The solicitor is given notice of the time and date on which the agent will attend at his offices for the purposes of collecting the file or files, and the agent is instructed to collect the file or files accordingly. Such limited interventions generally occur only after an unsuccessful attempt has been made to persuade the solicitor to deliver up the file(s) voluntarily.

Because these powers are part of the intervention regime the statutory powers of the High Court are available and in the event of non-co-operation on the part of the solicitor an application could be made by the SRA for an order to compel delivery. One would naturally expect this to be an extremely rare occurrence, and it is understood only to have been necessary once.[5]

1   Paragraph 3 of Schedule 1 to SA 1974 requires not less than eight days' notice. In practice invariably 14 days' notice is given.
2   Paragraph 3 of Schedule 1 to SA 1974.
3   Section 44B(1) of SA 1974.
4   Section 44B(6).
5   *Stevenson*, 7814–1999, SDT.

CHAPTER 18

Control of solicitors' employees

18.1

Originally through the Solicitors Act (SA) 1974 and its predecessors, Parliament provided regulatory powers to the Law Society and the Solicitors Disciplinary Tribunal (the Tribunal or SDT) to enable the control of non-solicitors who work in solicitors' firms, and who may abuse their position. The rationale for the existence of these powers is the need to protect those who deal with solicitors, and to safeguard the reputation of the profession. The Legal Services Act (LSA) 2007 promotes the concept of firm- or business entity-based regulation so that all managers and employees of regulated practices are now subject to personal regulation by virtue of their employment, whether or not they are legally qualified. In consequence, regulation of solicitors' employees now takes three forms: (1) statutory restrictions on the employment of certain disqualified persons, for example, former solicitors who have been struck off (see **18.2** and **18.3**); (2) the making of orders that control the employment of non-solicitors guilty of material misconduct (see **18.4** to **18.7**); and (3) direct disciplinary control of employees of regulated practices (see **18.8** and **18.9**).

Restriction on employment of persons struck off or suspended

18.2

A solicitor may not, in connection with his practice as a solicitor, employ or remunerate persons who to his knowledge have been disqualified from acting as solicitors through being struck off or suspended from practice, save with the written permission of the Solicitors Regulation Authority (SRA). The SRA may grant permission for such period and subject to such conditions as it thinks fit.[1]

Until 31 March 2009, section 41(4) of SA 1974 provided a mandatory penalty of suspension or striking off for any solicitor found to have acted in breach of this prohibition. There were originally two offences attracting a mandatory penalty: acting as an agent for an unqualified person in court proceedings (section 39 of SA 1974 which was repealed in full in 1991, so removing the statutory offence as well as the mandatory penalty); and employing or remunerating a struck off or suspended solicitor without written permission. LSA 2007 retained the statutory offence but removed the mandatory penalty. In *Re a Solicitor (Rosen),*[2] the Divisional Court requested and was provided with a schedule of penalties imposed upon solicitors for breaches of section 41. There was a wide range, some suspensions being for a few days only, sometimes being timed to coincide with holidays already arranged by the solicitor concerned or (in the case of a number of partners all requiring to be sentenced) being staggered so as to minimise disruption to the practice concerned.[3] In these instances, the Tribunal had plainly felt that little or no moral blame attached to the solicitors in question, and would not have suspended them in the absence of the mandatory provision. At the other end of the spectrum were solicitors who had been struck off for deliberately flouting the statutory provisions. The removal of the mandatory penalty enables the Tribunal more effectively to tailor the penalty to the breach.

It is important to appreciate that a breach of section 41 is a strict liability offence. All that is required is (1) that the solicitor knows the true status of the employee, namely that he or she has been struck off or suspended; and (2) that, as a matter of fact, the written permission of the Law Society/SRA has not been obtained (or that conditions imposed on the grant of permission have not been met). It does not provide a defence, for example, to show that one partner had responsibility for making the employment arrangements and reassured all other partners that there was no compliance issue, and they reasonably relied on that reassurance.[4] It has even happened that a struck off solicitor has forged the permission; the employing solicitor was still guilty of the offence.[5] Indeed, this serves to reinforce the point that the employer, and not the proposed employee, must obtain the necessary SRA permission.

1 Section 41 of SA 1974.
2 [2004] EWHC 907 (Admin).
3 Cases in which this sort of leniency was shown include *McMillan*, 5740–1989, SDT; *Cunnew*, 6134–1992, SDT; and *Coxall*, 8401–2001, SDT.
4 *Coxall*, 8401–2001, SDT.
5 *Awoloye-Kio*, 8940–2003, SDT.

18.3

The Tribunal has also emphasised that an employer's wilful ignorance of the true status of the employee could lead to a breach of this provision:

> 'The Tribunal take the view that a solicitor can only claim not to have knowledge of a striking off order if he has first made appropriate enquiries. Total ignorance as a result of a total failure to make the enquiries which a prudent solicitor employer would make is not a state of knowledge but a state of deliberate ignorance.'[1]

As this is a statutory offence to be construed by reference to the precise words of the section this conclusion must be open to some doubt. Nevertheless, it is apparent that the Tribunal will strive to give a purposive construction to the section to meet the perceived mischief:

> 'The Tribunal accept that the mischief which section 41 seeks to avert is the handling of clients' affairs in a solicitors office by a struck off solicitor except in circumstances where he is subject to strict controls. It is clear that the constraints are imposed to protect the interests of the public and maintain the good name of the solicitors' profession.'[2]

The words 'employ or remunerate' have been construed widely, to include even the payment of expenses:

> 'The Tribunal consider that "employment" should be construed in the wider sense of "keeping busy" or "keeping occupied". It follows from that that payment of a wage is not essential to establish employment. The intention of section 41 is that struck off solicitors be kept out of solicitors offices save in exceptional and closely regulated cases. Although not argued

before them, the Tribunal believe it is useful to add that in its view the word "remunerate" should also be interpreted in its widest sense so that it not only means "to reward" or "to pay for services" but also "to provide recompense for". The payment of out of pocket expenses by the respondent was therefore remuneration.'[3]

Section 41 has been deployed by the SRA in one additional and highly unusual situation, against a former solicitor involved in a solicitors' practice, rather than against an employer. In *Law Society v Shah*[4] the defendant was a struck off former solicitor who continued to involve himself in solicitors' firms and there were non-conclusive indications that he continued to hold himself out as a solicitor. He was regarded as particularly dangerous, having allegedly misappropriated over £8 million in client funds and having served a term of imprisonment for mortgage fraud. The SRA sought an injunction on a *quia timet* basis to prevent him continuing to associate with solicitors' firms. It was held that section 41(4)(c) (which allowed the SDT or the High Court to 'make such other order in the matter as it thinks fit') was sufficiently widely drawn as to enable the court to grant the requested injunction.

1   *Cunnew,* 6134–1992, SDT.
2   *Cunnew,* 6134–1992, SDT.
3   *Cunnew,* 6134–1992, SDT.
4   [2014] EWHC 4382 (Ch).

Control of solicitors' employees and consultants

18.4

The SRA may act to prevent or control the employment in legal practice of those individuals whom it considers to be undesirable (section 43 orders).[1] Both the SRA and the Tribunal have the power to make the relevant order preventing all solicitors from employing or remunerating, in connection with their practice as solicitors, the individual in question (except in accordance with permission in writing granted by the SRA for such period and subject to such conditions as the SRA may think fit). The order can also prevent any employee of a solicitor from employing or remunerating the individual in relation to legal practice, and can prevent an individual being a manager of or having an interest in a legal practice. It seems that the SRA will consider it appropriate to make the order itself at the adjudication stage if there has been a conviction or there is no dispute as to the facts, and will make an application to the Tribunal for an order when there is likely to be a dispute of fact or other factor justifying an oral hearing, or when the employing solicitor also faces Tribunal proceedings arising from the same facts. In either event, an appeal lies to the Tribunal by way of review (see **18.10**).[2]

Such orders, whether made by the SRA or the Tribunal, are regulatory rather than disciplinary in nature.[3] In *Gregory*,[4] Treacy J stated that:

'Section 43 is not punitive in nature. It is there to protect the public, to provide safeguards and to exercise control over those who work for solicitors, in circumstances where there is necessity for such control shown by their past conduct. Its purpose is to maintain the good reputation of, and maintain confidence in, the solicitors' profession.'

1   Section 43 of SA 1974.
2   Section 43(3) of SA 1974.
3   *Gregory v The Law Society* [2007] EWHC 1724 (Admin), and *Solicitors Regulation Authority v Ali* [2013] EWHC 2584 (Admin).
4   *Gregory v The Law Society* [2007] EWHC 1724 (Admin) at [18].

The statutory grounds for an order

18.5

There are two statutory grounds for making a section 43 order: (a) criminal convictions, and (b) certain acts or defaults while working in a legal practice.

Criminal convictions

18.6

The order may be made when the person concerned has been convicted of a criminal offence which is such that, in the opinion of the SRA, it would be undesirable for him to be involved in legal practice.[1]

1   Section 43(1)(a) of SA 1974.

Acts or defaults while working in a legal practice

18.7

The order may also be made when the person concerned has 'occasioned or been a party to, with or without the connivance of a solicitor, an act or default in relation to a legal practice which involved conduct on his part of such a nature that in the opinion of the [SRA] it would be undesirable for him to be involved in a legal practice'.[1]

This somewhat convoluted subsection requires the SRA or the Tribunal to answer two essential questions:

(1)   Has the person concerned occasioned an act or default which involved conduct on his part of such a nature that it would be undesirable for him to be involved in a legal practice?

(2)   If so, was that act or default occasioned in relation to a legal practice?

The two subsections must be construed independently of each other. Section 43(1)(a) requires there to have been a criminal conviction, but subsection (b) does not require similar or equivalent conduct. An order under section 43(1)(b) can be founded upon foolishness, recklessness or errors of judgement if the consequence is that it is undesirable for the individual concerned to work in a legal practice.[2]

The statutory jurisdiction did not (as originally enacted) extend to or cover a situation in which the party alleged to be at fault remunerated himself, purporting to be an employee of a solicitor but in fact being his own employer in a sham arrangement;[3] however, the section as amended by LSA 2007 is probably sufficiently wide to overcome this difficulty.

The SRA and the Tribunal have, respectively, the power to make orders for costs when exercising this jurisdiction.[4]

1 Section 43(1)(b) of SA 1974.
2 See *Ojelade v Law Society* [2006] EWHC 2210 (Admin); and, particularly, *Gregory v Law Society* [2007] EWHC 1724 (Admin).
3 *Izegbu and Okoronkwo v Law Society* [2008] EWHC 1043 (Admin).
4 Section 43(2A) and (4) of SA 1974.

The procedure

18.8

The SRA may make an order under section 43 to control the person's activities in connection with legal practice or decide to make an application to the Tribunal for the allegation to be considered by the Tribunal.[1] The SRA also has power to apply a range of other disciplinary and regulatory sanctions against employees including rebukes, fines and disqualifications (see **18.11**).[2] The SRA may disclose or publish information relating to an investigation where the public interest outweighs other circumstances[3] and may impose a charge of up to £1,350 for the first 16 hours of its investigation, and further charges at the rate of £75 per hour thereafter for such further time rounded up or down to the nearest half-hour.[4]

Before deciding to apply to the Tribunal for an order in respect of an unadmitted employee (or indeed a solicitor), the SRA must determine whether there is a realistic prospect of the Tribunal making an order.[5] How the SRA makes the determination will depend upon the date it intends to file its application at the Tribunal. This is so as for applications made to the Tribunal on or after 25 November 2019 the Tribunal will apply the civil standard (see **18.9**), whereas for earlier applications made by the SRA (including those continuing after 25 November 2019), the Tribunal will apply the criminal standard.

1 Rule 3.1(d) and (g) of the SRA Regulatory and Disciplinary Procedure Rules 2019 (the 'Disciplinary Rules 2019').
2 Rule 3.1(a)–(c) of the Disciplinary Rules 2019.
3 Rules 9.1 and 9.2 of the Disciplinary Rules 2019.
4 Rule 10.1 of and Schedule 1 to the Disciplinary Rules 2019.
5 Rule 6.1 of the Disciplinary Rules 2019. It must also be in the public interest to make an application.

The standard of proof

18.9

The Disciplinary Rules provide that the SRA will apply the civil standard of proof[1] to the exercise of its powers under section 43 of SA 1974.[2] The SDT will also apply the civil standard in respect of all proceedings considered under its Rules,[3] that is, those in respect of applications made on or after 25 November 2019.[4] For applications made to the Tribunal prior to 25 November 2019, the civil standard applies to reviews of SRA-made section 43 orders,[5] whereas the criminal standard aopplies to applications to the Tribunal where the SRA has not made a section 43 order.[6]

In the past the Tribunal had held that the standard of proof should be the criminal standard, whoever makes the decision. That position was no longer sustainable in so far as it concerned decisions made by the SRA rather than the Tribunal, following *Solicitors Regulation Authority v Solicitors' Disciplinary Tribunal, Arslan Interested Party*,[7] when the SRA appealed to the High Court against decisions made by the SDT in respect of a Mr Arslan. An SRA adjudicator had made a section 43 order against, and imposed a fine upon, Mr Arslan: both decisions had been quashed on appeal by the SDT. Whereas the adjudicator had adopted the civil standard of proof in accordance with the SRA Disciplinary Procedure Rules 2011, the SDT had adopted the criminal standard of proof in accordance with its own long-standing practice, when dealing with the appeals.

On the further appeal to the High Court, the court held that it had been plainly appropriate for the SRA adjudicator to have adopted the civil standard in accordance with the 2011 Rules which had statutory effect, and that in carrying out a review on the appeal (which should not involve the finding of any facts by the Tribunal), the SDT was not entitled to apply its own, different, standard of proof. Although the court was invited by the SRA to give an opinion as to the standard of proof which the SDT should apply in cases in which it is the primary fact-finder, the court declined to do so. Both judges (Sir Brian Leveson P and Leggatt J) considered that the authorities which supported adoption of the criminal standard by the SDT when it sits in its fact-finding capacity were ripe for reconsideration.[8]

1   Rule 8.7 of the Disciplinary Rules 2019.
2   Rule 1.2(d) of the Disciplinary Rules 2019.
3   Rule 5 of the Solicitors (Disciplinary Proceedings) Rules 2019 (SI 2019/1185) (the '2019 Rules').
4   Rule 51 of the 2019 Rules.
5   Rule 3.1(d) of the Disciplinary Rules 2019.
6   Rule 3.1(g) of the Disciplinary Rules 2019.
7   [2016] EWHC 2862 (Admin).
8   See at [49] (Leggatt J) and [73] (Sir Brian Leveson P).

Appeals and reviews

18.10

The SRA and the Tribunal can revoke their own decision to make a section 43 order,[1] for example, because it is no longer required as the individual has been employed in the profession without further fault for a period of years. The Disciplinary Rules state that an application may be made to the SRA for a section 43 order to cease to apply 'where there has been a material change in circumstances'.[2]

If the order was made by the Tribunal any application for revocation is made to the Tribunal.[3] As indicated at **18.4**, a person aggrieved by an order made by the SRA can apply to the Tribunal for a review of that order and the Tribunal can quash it, vary it or confirm it.[4] An order made by the Tribunal can be appealed to the High Court.[5] The High Court has power to make such order on an appeal as it thinks fit. Any decision of the High Court is final and there is no further appeal.[6]

In *SRA v Ali*[7] a decision by the SDT to revoke an order was overturned because the Tribunal had wrongly focused its attention upon the individual's unsuccessful efforts to rehabilitate himself, whereas it ought to have asked itself whether the order remained necessary to safeguard the public and the reputation of the profession.

1   Section 43(3((b) of SA 1974.
2   Rule 7.1 of the Disciplinary Rules 2019.

3   Section 43(3) of SA 1974.
4   Section 43(3A).
5   Section 49(1).
6   Section 49(6).
7   [2013] EWHC 2584 (Admin), at [41].

Disciplinary control of employees

18.11

LSA 2007 amended SA 1974 by adding sections 34A and subsection 47(2E). Section 34A enables the SRA to provide that the rules of professional conduct: 'have effect in relation to employees of solicitors with such additions, omissions or other modifications as appear to the [SRA] to be necessary or expedient'. With effect from 31 March 2009 the SRA amended the Solicitors' Code of Conduct 2007 and other professional rules (including the Solicitors' Accounts Rules 1998) to make clear that it regulates not only solicitors but also the employees of solicitors, registered European lawyers and their employees, registered foreign lawyers, recognised bodies (including authorised sole practitioners) and their managers and employees. The 2011 SRA Handbook and the 2019 regulatory arrangements have maintained this position. Section 47(2E) of SA 1974 extends the Tribunal's jurisdiction to the employees of solicitors. LSA 2007 also amended Schedule 2 to the Administration of Justice Act (AJA) 1985 (which relates to incorporated practices or 'recognised bodies') to give the same powers to the Tribunal in relation to managers and employees of recognised bodies.

18.12

In relation to managers and employees, the Tribunal may:

- impose a fine, unlimited in amount, payable to the Treasury;[1]

- require the SRA to take such steps in relation to the relevant person as the Tribunal may specify;[2] and/or

- order the SRA to refer the conduct of the relevant person to an appropriate regulator,[3] as well as being able to make an order controlling the employment of the relevant person under section 43 of SA 1974.[4] An 'appropriate regulator' would be the relevant approved regulator authorised under LSA 2007 if the manager or employee is an authorised person in relation to a reserved legal activity (eg a barrister or licensed conveyancer) or any body which regulates the activities actually undertaken by the person concerned, if he or she was not an authorised person for LSA 2007 purposes.[5]

1   Section 47(2E)(a) of SA 1974; para 18A(2)(a) of Schedule 2 to AJA 1985.
2   Section 47(2E)(b) of SA 1974; para 18A(2)(b) of Schedule 2 to AJA 1985.
3   Section 47(2E)(d) of SA 1974; para 18A(2)(d) of Schedule 2 to AJA 1985.
4   Section 47(2E)(c) of SA 1974; para 18A(2)(c) of Schedule 2 to AJA 1985.
5   Section 47(2H) of SA 1974; para 18A(7) of Schedule 2 to AJA 1985.

18.13

There are mechanisms for the control of compliance officers for legal practice and compliance officers for finance and administration (COLPs and COFAs) including the power to disqualify, which could have the effect of rendering the individual unemployable in the legal services market. While COLPs and COFAs may be principals in the firm, partners, members or directors, they may also be employees. These powers are considered in detail in **CHAPTER 7**.

PART 5

The disciplinary system in practice

CHAPTER 19

Professional misconduct, its forms and formulation

19.1

Historically, there have been two types of professional misconduct by solicitors:

(1)   statutory misconduct, consisting of breaches of provisions of the Solicitors Act 1974 (for example, in relation to the obligation to deliver accountants' reports) or of rules made by virtue of that Act (such as, in their time, the Solicitors' Accounts Rules 1998 or the successive Solicitors' Practice Rules); and

(2)   non-statutory misconduct – what could be called the common law of conduct, which covered anything and everything that could bring the individual or the profession into sufficient disrepute so as to engage the risk of disciplinary sanction, but which was not covered by any specific rule.

In the Solicitors Disciplinary Tribunal (the Tribunal or SDT), any action, failing or course of conduct that offended the common law of conduct was alleged to be 'professional misconduct', until the late 1950s when the phrase 'conduct unbefitting a solicitor' was substituted. The latter formulation enabled the point to be made as necessary that misconduct outside a solicitor's professional practice, in his or her private life, could have disciplinary consequences.

On 1 July 2007 the Solicitors' Code of Conduct 2007 came into force. The 2007 Code was designed to be an all-embracing and codified system of professional regulation. Accordingly, prosecutors in the Tribunal started to allege a breach of a rule *simpliciter* (rather than conduct unbefitting) against solicitors whose conduct had been referred to the Tribunal. This presupposed that any breach of any rule could amount to a disciplinary offence – a controversial proposition which was rejected by the Tribunal in *Pabla and Pabla*.[1]

On 6 October 2011, the 2011 SRA Principles and Code came into force, based upon the principles of outcomes-focused regulation. Since then, the practice has been for prosecutors to allege breaches of either the Principles or the mandatory outcomes (or both), and allegations of conduct unbefitting a solicitor have fallen into disuse. Where prescriptive rules, such as the SRA Accounts Rules, are alleged to have been breached, the relevant allegation should make that clear.

1   10376–2009, SDT.

Dishonesty

19.2

For any solicitor to behave dishonestly strikes at the heart of the reputation of the profession, and will almost inevitably lead to an order striking that solicitor off the roll.[1] Until the autumn of 2017, the test for dishonesty was stated to be the mixed subjective/objective test, deriving from the criminal law (*R v Ghosh*[2]) and adopted in disciplinary proceedings against solicitors in *Bultitude v Law Society*[3] and *Bryant and Bench v Law Society*.[4] The twin test was expressed thus by Lord Hutton in *Twinsectra Ltd v Yardley*[5] (at [27]):

> 'before there can be a finding of dishonesty it must be established that the defendant's conduct was dishonest by the ordinary standards of reasonable and honest people and that he himself realised that by those standards his conduct was dishonest.'

1 See **CHAPTER 16**.
2 [1982] QB 1053.
3 [2004] EWCA Civ 1853.
4 [2009] 1 WLR 163.
5 [2002] UKHL 12.

19.3

This twin test created uncertainty, and was criticised in a line of cases concerned with the liability of accessories for breach of trust. On 25 October 2017, the Supreme Court handed down its judgment in *Ivey v Genting Casinos*,[1] and in doing so swept away 35 years of confusion about the correct test for dishonesty. In his judgment, Lord Hughes JSC laid bare the unnecessary difficulties which the *Ghosh/Twinsectra* twin test had created, among which was the unintended effect of the *Ghosh* decision that the more warped a defendant's standards of honesty, the less likely he was to be convicted of dishonest behaviour. Crucially, however, his Lordship pointed out that the twin test was not necessary to preserve the principle that dishonesty must depend upon the actual state of mind of the defendant. He made clear that the courts do not need to invent a two-stage test in order to ensure that an accused's state of mind is taken into account in assessing whether he has been dishonest. Two passages from his judgment set out what must now be seen as the correct test, although they are technically *obiter*:

> '60 It is plain that in Ghosh the court concluded that its compromise second leg test was necessary in order to preserve the principle that criminal responsibility for dishonesty must depend on the actual state of mind of the defendant. It asked the question whether "dishonestly", where that word appears in the Theft Act, was intended to characterise a course of conduct or to describe a state of mind. The court gave the following example, at p 1063, which was clearly central to its reasoning:
>
> "Take for example a man who comes from a country where public transport is free. On his first day here he travels on a bus. He gets off without paying. He never had any intention of paying. His mind is clearly honest; but his conduct, judged objectively by what he has done, is dishonest. It seems to us that in using the word 'dishonestly' in the Theft

Act 1968, Parliament cannot have intended to catch dishonest conduct in that sense, that is to say conduct to which no moral obloquy could possibly attach."

But the man in this example would inevitably escape conviction by the application of the (objective) first leg of the Ghosh test. That is because, in order to determine the honesty or otherwise of a person's conduct, one must ask what he knew or believed about the facts affecting the area of activity in which he was engaging. In order to decide whether this visitor was dishonest by the standards of ordinary people, it would be necessary to establish his own actual state of knowledge of how public transport works. Because he genuinely believes that public transport is free, there is nothing objectively dishonest about his not paying on the bus. The same would be true of a child who did not know the rules, or of a person who had innocently misread the bus pass sent to him and did not realise that it did not operate until after 10.00 in the morning. The answer to the court's question is that "dishonestly", where it appears, is indeed intended to characterise what the defendant did, but in characterising it one must first ascertain his actual state of mind as to the facts in which he did it. It was not correct to postulate that the conventional objective test of dishonesty involves judging only the actions and not the state of knowledge or belief as to the facts in which they were performed. What is objectively judged is the standard of behaviour, given any known actual state of mind of the actor as to the facts.'

The second passage from the judgment, at [74], also merits quotation:

'When dishonesty is in question the fact-finding tribunal must first ascertain (subjectively) the actual state of the individual's knowledge or belief as to the facts. The reasonableness or otherwise of his belief is a matter of evidence (often in practice determinative) going to whether he held the belief, but it is not an additional requirement that his belief must be reasonable; the question is whether it is genuinely held. When once his actual state of mind as to knowledge or belief as to facts is established, the question whether his conduct was honest or dishonest is to be determined by the fact-finder by applying the (objective) standards of ordinary decent people. There is no requirement that the defendant must appreciate that what he has done is, by those standards, dishonest.'

1   [2017] UKSC 67.

19.4

It should be noted that the 2019 Principles impose for the first time an explicit obligation upon a solicitor to act with honesty as well as with integrity.

Lack of integrity

19.5

It has long been required of solicitors by their professional rules that they behave with integrity. Rule 1 of the Solicitors' Practice Rules 1990 provided:

'(**Basic principles**) A solicitor shall not do anything in the course of practising as a solicitor, or permit another person to do anything on his or her behalf, which compromises or impairs or is likely to compromise or impair any of the following: (a) the solicitor's independence or integrity ...'

As noted above, the introduction of the 2007 Code (which set out in rule 1 a number of 'core duties' including at 1.02: Integrity, 'You must act with integrity') led to a change of practice. Henceforth, the SRA tended to charge breaches of specific core duties and rules, rather than the more general 'conduct unbefitting'. Prior to the adoption of the 2007 Code, the SRA and its predecessors had been content to charge 'conduct unbefitting', and to leave the SDT to determine the gravity of the conduct, if proved. 'Lack of integrity' was rarely, if ever, specifically charged. From 2007 onwards, however, it became common for disciplinary charges to make a specific allegation of lack of integrity. The 2011 Handbook reinforced this change of practice: Principle 2 requires that you must 'act with integrity', and for the first time reference was made to this requirement binding solicitors outside their practice in the notes to the Principles:

'5.   Application of the SRA Principles outside practice

      5.1   In relation to activities which fall outside practice, whether undertaken as a lawyer or in some other business or private capacity, Principles 1, 2 and 6 apply to you if you are a solicitor ...'

19.6

Just as had been the case with the meaning of dishonesty, the concept of lack of integrity gave rise to considerable judicial confusion and disagreement. The difficulties centred upon two issues: (a) what, if any, was the essential difference between honesty and integrity?; and (b) what is the relevance of the solicitor's state of mind to whether he or she had acted with a lack of integrity?

As for the first issue, the meaning of 'integrity' is somewhat elusive, and was explored in a series of cases arising out of the provision of financial services. The most frequently cited case was *Hoodless & Blackwell v FSA* (3 October 2003), in which the Financial Services and Markets Tribunal described it as such:

'In our view "integrity" connotes moral soundness, rectitude and steady adherence to an ethical code. A person lacks integrity if unable to appreciate the distinction between what is honest or dishonest by ordinary standards. (This presupposes, of course, circumstances where ordinary standards are clear. Where there are genuinely grey areas, a finding of lack of integrity would not be appropriate.)'

Attempts by the SRA to persuade the courts to expand upon the meaning of integrity were not initially successful. Like the proverbial elephant, it seems that integrity was easier to recognise than to define. In *SRA v Chan and others*,[1] Davis LJ said the following at [48]:

'As to want of "integrity", there have been a number of decisions commenting on the import of this word as used in various regulations. In my view, it serves no purpose to expatiate on its meaning. Want of integrity is capable of being identified as present or not, as the case may be, by an informed tribunal or court by reference to the facts of a particular case.'

1   [2015] EWHC 2659 (Admin).

19.7

As for the mental element involved in lack of integrity, the analysis which generally held sway before the Supreme Court decision in *Ivey* was that whereas dishonesty involved a twin subjective/objective test, the test for lack of integrity was objective only. Then in *SRA v Malins*[1] Mostyn J stated that honesty and integrity were synonymous and interchangeable concepts. He disagreed with the judgment of Holman J in *SRA v Wingate*[2] in which the judge had held that there was a clear distinction between the two concepts. But Mostyn J's view in turn was disapproved in *Williams v SRA*[3] by a strong Divisional Court (Sir Brian Leveson P and Carr J), who, for the first time, aligned the meaning of 'integrity' with adherence to high professional standards. Sir Brian Leveson observed at [130]:

'… in the absence of compelling justification, I would reject Mostyn J's description of the concept of want of integrity as second degree dishonesty. Honesty, i.e. a lack of dishonesty, is a base standard which society requires everyone to meet. Professional standards, however, rightly impose on those who aspire to them a higher obligation to demonstrate integrity in all of their work. There is a real difference between them.'

1   [2017] EWHC 835 (Admin).
2   [2016] EWHC 3455 (Admin).
3   [2017] EWHC 1478 (Admin).

19.8

In due course, in February 2018, the matter came before the Court of Appeal in the SRA's appeal against Mostyn J's judgment in *Malins* and the solicitors' appeal against Holman J's judgment in *Wingate*. In his judgment,[1] Rupert Jackson LJ upheld the traditional analysis that the concepts of honesty and integrity are distinct, and sought to provide some guidance as to the meaning of lack of integrity.

'96 Integrity is a more nebulous concept than honesty. Hence it is less easy to define, as a number of judges have noted.

97 In professional codes of conduct, the term "integrity" is a useful shorthand to express the higher standards which society expects from professional persons and which the professions expect from their own members. See the judgment of Sir Brian Leveson P in *Williams* at [130]. The underlying rationale is that the professions have a privileged and trusted role in society. In return they are required to live up to their own professional standards.

[…]

100 Integrity connotes adherence to the ethical standards of one's own profession. That involves more than mere honesty. To take one example, a solicitor conducting negotiations or a barrister making submissions to a judge or arbitrator will take particular care not to

mislead. Such a professional person is expected to be even more scrupulous about accuracy than a member of the general public in daily discourse.

101 The duty to act with integrity applies not only to what professional persons say, but also to what they do. It is possible to give many illustrations of what constitutes acting without integrity. For example, in the case of solicitors:

    (i)   A sole practice giving the appearance of being a partnership and deliberately flouting the conduct rules (*Emeana*);

    (ii)   Recklessly, but not dishonestly, allowing a court to be misled (*Brett*)

    (iii)   Subordinating the interests of the clients to the solicitors' own financial interests (*Chan*);

    (iv)   Making improper payments out of the client account (*Scott*);

    (v)   Allowing the firm to become involved in conveyancing transactions which bear the hallmarks mortgage fraud (*Newell-Austin*);

    (vi)   Making false representations on behalf of the client (*Williams*).

102 Obviously, neither courts nor professional tribunals must set unrealistically high standards, as was observed during argument. The duty of integrity does not require professional people to be paragons of virtue. In every instance, professional integrity is linked to the manner in which that particular profession professes to serve the public.'

1   [2018] EWCA Civ 366. See also *Zivancevic v SRA* [2019] EWHC 1950 (Admin).

19.9

The important question that the Court of Appeal left unanswered in *Wingate* is what differentiates 'ordinary' professional misconduct from professional misconduct which involves a lack of integrity. All proven or admitted instances of professional misconduct are serious, save those rare cases in which the SDT imposes no sanction, and therefore involve a departure from the high professional standards expected of solicitors. What then is the additional ingredient which merits the description 'lack of integrity'? Perhaps it is the scale of the departure from the standards imposed by the relevant rules, perhaps it is the mindset of the solicitor (intentional or reckless breaches of professional standards being more serious than inadvertent breaches), or perhaps it is both. In any event, even following the decision in *Wingate* it seems that lack of integrity, like an elephant, remains easier to recognise than to define.

Recklessness

19.10

The SRA sometimes alleges that breaches of principles or outcomes have been committed recklessly. This is plainly less serious professional misconduct than dishonesty, but is likely to be regarded as more serious than misconduct arising out of negligence/manifest incompetence. Recklessness is defined as a matter of law, and the definition has been applied by the SDT; see *Lawson*[1] and *Fuglers*[2] (undisturbed by the High Court on appeal). The following quotations, paraphrasing *R v G and another*,[3] were cited by the SDT in each of those cases:

> 'Recklessness means the taking of an unreasonable risk of which the risk-taker is aware: a person acts "recklessly" with respect to a circumstance when he is aware of a risk that did or would exist, and acts recklessly with respect to a consequence when he is aware of a risk that it will occur, and in either case, it is, in the circumstances known to him, unreasonable to take the risk.'

> '… it had to be shown that the defendant's state of mind was culpable in that he acted recklessly in respect of a circumstance if he was aware of a risk which did or would exist, or in respect of a result if he was aware of a risk that it would occur, and it was, in the circumstances known to him, unreasonable to take the risk.'

In the context of professional conduct, the concept of recklessness is best encapsulated by an assertion that the solicitor could not care less about the professional rules concerned. Although perhaps not breaching rules intentionally, the solicitor will have demonstrated a 'couldn't care less' attitude to the relevant ones, which renders the misconduct potentially very serious.

1   11048–2012, SDT.
2   10917–2012, SDT.
3   [2004] 1 AC 1034, HL.

Negligence and manifest incompetence

19.11

All lawyers make mistakes during the course of their professional careers. It has always been the case that solicitors were not penalised for making mistakes – 'generally the honest and genuine decision of a solicitor on a question of professional judgment does not give rise to a disciplinary offence'.[1] Equally, there is some professional negligence that is so serious that it calls into question a solicitor's fitness to practise, and needs to be marked with a sanction – not merely dealt with by way of a civil action leading to compensation. This is because the public is entitled to expect a basic level of competence from the lawyers whom they instruct, and because the reputation of the profession is bound to suffer where a solicitor exhibits an unacceptable level of professional competence.

In *Iqbal v Solicitors Regulation Authority*,[2] the appellant solicitor had incorrectly held out individuals as his partners who were not, in law, his partners (it was alleged that he had done this in order for his firm to be eligible for membership of mortgagee lenders' panels of solicitors, for which membership is not available for sole practitioners). Acquitted of dishonesty, he was nevertheless struck off the roll, and his appeal to the High Court failed. Sir John Thomas, President of the Queen's Bench Division at the time, said at [23]:

> 'It seems to me that trustworthiness also extends to those standards which the public are entitled to expect of a solicitor, including competence. If a solicitor exhibits manifest incompetence, as, in my judgment, the appellant did, then it is impossible to see how the public can have confidence in a

person who has exhibited such incompetence. It is difficult to see how a profession such as the medical profession would countenance retaining as a doctor someone who had showed himself to be incompetent. It seems to me that the same must be true of the solicitors' profession. If in a course of conduct a person manifests incompetence as, in my judgment, the appellant did, then he is not fit to be a solicitor. The only appropriate remedy is to remove him from the roll. It must be recalled that being a solicitor is not a right, but a privilege. The public is entitled not only to solicitors who behave with honesty and integrity, but solicitors in whom they can impose trust by reason of competence.'

1   *Connolly v Law Society* [2007] EWHC 1175 (Admin).
2   [2012] EWHC 3251 (Admin).

19.12

Where then is the line to be drawn between 'mere negligence' and manifest incompetence deserving of sanction? In *Re a Solicitor*[1] at [815] Lord Denning MR stated:

'In my opinion, negligence in a solicitor may amount to a professional misconduct if it is inexcusable and is such as to be regarded as deplorable by his fellows in the profession'.

In his judgment in *Wingate* (supra), Rupert Jackson LJ sounded a note of warning (at [106]):

'In applying Principle 6 it is important not to characterise run of the mill professional negligence as manifest incompetence. All professional people are human and will from time to time make slips which a court would characterise as negligent. Fortunately, no loss results from most such slips. But acts of manifest incompetence engaging the Principles of professional conduct are of a different order.'

1   [1972] 2 All ER 811, CA.

19.13

It is undesirable to attempt a comprehensive definition. The issue, as with all professional misconduct, is best decided on a case-by-case basis by the expert Tribunal charged by Parliament with the task of sitting in judgment upon solicitors:

'The suggestion was that the phrase "moral turpitude" is analogous to conduct unbefitting. My response to that is that it may be in some circumstances, but not in all. Allegations against professional men vary infinitely in gravity. What constitutes conduct unbefitting a solicitor is best judged, in my view, by his professional colleagues, applying their undoubted experience of what is to be properly expected of a solicitor in his practice, when they are sitting formally as part of a disciplinary tribunal in judgment of one of them. I should be most reluctant to attempt to provide any kind of definition of a term which is used, the words being slightly different here and there, in many professions, including the armed forces'.[1]

1   *Re a Solicitor* (1991, unreported), per Watkins LJ; cited with approval in *Re a Solicitor* (1995, unreported), per Lord Taylor CJ.

19.14

In *Wingate* one of the solicitors (Evans) had been acquitted by the SDT of professional misconduct: it had been alleged by the SRA that he ought to have checked a contract for the provision of finance which had been negotiated and signed by his partner. On the SRA's appeal to the Divisional Court, Holman J had reversed this acquittal, and found that the solicitor had been guilty of manifest incompetence. Evans appealed successfully to the Court of Appeal, Rupert Jackson LJ observing at [130]:

> 'The judge has held that Mr Evans' failure to obtain and read the funding agreement was manifest incompetence. I agree that Mr Evans was imprudent in that regard. But on the facts presented to Mr Evans, it was obviously advantageous to take a loan from Axiom and to repay the HBOS debt, which he had personally guaranteed. Mr Evans was hard pressed with other matters and he trusted Mr Wingate to deal with the finances. Mr Evans' failure to read the funding agreement and then to challenge his partner may be characterised as carelessness or negligence, but it did not amount to "manifest incompetence", engaging the Principles of professional conduct. In my view, the judge's decision in that regard is a bridge too far.'

Conduct not specifically outlawed in regulatory rules

19.15

No codified set of rules can possibly hope to capture each and every example of professional misconduct that can be committed. It has been argued that only instances of conduct specifically referred to and prohibited in *The Guide to the Professional Conduct of Solicitors* current at that time or specific rules are capable of being treated as conduct which is conduct unbefitting a solicitor. This was, unsurprisingly, rejected:

> 'The purpose of Professional Conduct Rules … is to identify in particular those areas of conduct in respect of which there should be specific prohibitions or requirements because they are likely to represent the most prevalent situations and the most prevalent conduct then in the profession. The fact that such a particular area of conduct is specifically dealt with does not mean that all other conduct is permissible or within the standards of the profession. It is thus ordinarily open to professional disciplinary tribunals to apply sanctions for professional misconduct generally, regardless of whether it is conduct singled out for mention in the rules. Were it otherwise, professional people might be permitted to conduct themselves in plainly deplorable ways without any disciplinary control.'[1]

1   *Henneberry v Law Society* (2000, unreported).

Trivial breaches of principles or rules

19.16

Occasionally, the SRA brings cases before the SDT which are felt by the Tribunal to have been too trivial to have merited prosecution. In such cases, the Tribunal may dismiss the allegation(s), or, alternatively, may impose no sanction. An example of the former was *Pabla and Pabla*,[1] in which the respondents were alleged to have contravened the provisions in the 2007 Code concerning referrals and introduction of business by third parties. Some of those breaches were admitted by the respondents, but the Tribunal nevertheless dismissed the case in its entirety.

1   10376–2009, SDT. See also *SRA v Day* [2018] EWHC 2726 (Admin) at [156]–[158]

Vicarious liability

19.17

In recent years there has been some confusion as to whether partners who have not known of or directly participated in a decision that breached a regulatory rule should face disciplinary action as a result. It was felt by the SRA that if, for instance, an equity partner benefited financially from a breach of the prohibition against referral fees, that partner should face disciplinary proceedings. It is submitted that the better view is that unless a disciplinary offence is truly one of strict liability (such as an Accounts Rules breach), a solicitor should only face disciplinary consequences if he or she is believed to be in some way culpable.

This had been the general approach of the Tribunal.[1] The concept of conduct unbefitting a solicitor, which was the method of charging before 2007, carried with it some degree of moral culpability: the Tribunal had held that partners should not be required to supervise or monitor the work of other partners, and that a partner was not guilty of professional misconduct merely because he is the partner of a solicitor who is guilty of professional misconduct.[2]

This general approach has been approved by the Divisional Court in *Akodu v SRA*[3] per Moses LJ (at [10]):

> 'there is no other reasonable conclusion that can be reached other than that the basis upon which he had been found guilty was merely on the basis that he was a partner of the firm. If that was the only basis, then there has been no argument advanced on behalf of the Law Society to suggest that that was a lawful basis upon which any solicitor can be found guilty of conduct unbefitting his profession. If authority is needed for the proposition, it can be found in *Cordery on Solicitors* at J 2225. Some degree of personal fault is required.'

1   See *Pabla and Pabla*, 10376–2009, SDT. See also *SRA v Day* [2018] EWHC 2726 (Admin) at [156]–[158].
2   *Ali and Shabir*, 9339–2005, SDT; *Aziz and Saunders*, 9032–2004, SDT; *Ross and others*, 10002–2008, SDT; and *Bagri and others*, 10229–2009, SDT.
3   [2009] EWHC 3588 (Admin).

19.18

For the same reason, the fact that something has gone seriously wrong in a regulated entity will not be enough to establish professional misconduct against a solicitor or the entity. It is not unknown for a rogue employee, or sometimes even a rogue partner, to engage in fraudulent activity under the noses of his or her colleagues, but without their knowledge. In order for individual solicitors in the firm (or the entity itself) to be liable in conduct in such circumstances, there must be some culpable failure by them, most typically a failure of supervision. However, in order to succeed with such a prosecution, the SRA must be able to point to something concrete that the respondent solicitor (or the entity) did that ought not to have been done, or failed to do that ought to have been done. If this cannot be proved to the criminal standard, the prosecution will fail.[1] Sadly, no system of oversight or supervision will always be proof against a determined and resourceful fraudster.

1   See *Bass and Ward v SRA* [2012] EWHC 2012 (Admin), especially at [24]; *Wilson and Carroll*, 10767–2011, SDT; and *Barber and Bagas*, 11631–2017, SDT.

Conduct away from work and criminal conduct

19.19

It may be no defence to an allegation of professional misconduct that the act took place away from work, and had nothing to do with the respondent's practice as a solicitor. The reputation of the profession can be damaged by a solicitor's conduct away from the workplace. The most obvious example is serious criminal conduct. Any conviction for an offence of dishonesty by a practising solicitor is likely to lead to the termination of the right to practise. Solicitors must also be careful in their use of social media. In *Mahmood*,[1] a solicitor was found to have posted anti-semitic comments on a Facebook page, and was severely dealt with by the Tribunal.[2]

1   11625–2017, SDT.
2   On 7 February 2019, the SRA issued a Topic Guide entitled 'Use of social media and offensive communications'.

CHAPTER 20

SRA-imposed sanctions

The statutory provisions

20.1

Until the summer of 2010 the only regulatory 'sanction' that the Solicitors Regulation Authority (SRA) could impose upon a solicitor was a reprimand or severe reprimand. This was generally kept confidential as between the solicitor and the SRA though if there was a third party complainant or informant involved that party would be informed, and was free to disclose it.[1] The Legal Services Act (LSA) 2007 introduced a new section 44D into the Solicitors Act (SA) 1974. This provided a statutory power for the SRA to impose fines of up to £2,000, or a written rebuke, upon solicitors. A parallel power in relation to recognised bodies, their managers and employees, was inserted in the Administration of Justice Act 1985 as paragraph 14B of Schedule 2. Parliament's intention was to remove the less serious cases from the Solicitors Disciplinary Tribunal (the Tribunal or SDT), and to allow the SRA to deal with them more speedily and cheaply instead. The worrying feature for solicitors is that the confidentiality of the process was removed. The SRA may itself publish details of any action it has taken under section 44D if it considers this to be in the public interest.

The new statutory powers could not be exercised until the SRA had made rules in accordance with the terms of section 44D, which also required consultation with the Tribunal about the content of the rules. There was considerable delay in the promulgation of the rules, caused largely by disagreement over the standard of proof to be adopted by the SRA in making disciplinary decisions. Eventually the SRA (which wanted to use the civil standard against the wishes of the Tribunal and the Master of the Rolls) prevailed, and the Legal Services Board (LSB) approved the SRA (Disciplinary Procedure) Rules 2010, which commenced on 1 June 2010. Those Rules were replaced on 6 October 2011 by the SRA Disciplinary Procedure Rules 2011 (the 'Disciplinary Rules 2011'). The Disciplinary Rules 2011 did not apply to any acts or omissions occurring wholly before 1 June 2010.[2] The Disciplinary Rules 2011 have now been replaced by the SRA Regulatory and Disciplinary Procedure Rules 2019 (the 'Disciplinary Rules 2019'). The Disciplinary Rules 2019 do not contain any transitional provisions, and it is submitted that they will therefore apply to all steps taken in disciplinary proceedings after they come into force.

1   *Napier and another v Pressdram Ltd* [2009] EWCA Civ 443, [2010] 1 WLR 934.
2   Rule 16.1 of the Disciplinary Rules 2011.

20.2

By section 44D(10) of SA 1974, the Lord Chancellor may by order increase the £2,000 limit to such other amount as may be specified in the order. The SRA is anxious to secure an increase, in part at least to reduce the disparity between its powers in relation to traditional law firms and those who work in them, and its powers in relation to alternative business structures (ABSs) and those who work in them: the SRA has a power to impose huge fines upon ABSs. For the more extensive powers of the SRA to take disciplinary action against ABSs see **CHAPTER 26**.

20.3

The issue of publicity is a vexed one. On the one hand, as a statutory regulator, regulating in the public interest, the SRA wishes to operate in an open and transparent manner. On the other, the effect of publicity for the individual solicitor may be wholly disproportionate to the regulatory breach that occurred. In the internet age, such information is easily obtained by a prospective client, and is bound to have a deterrent effect upon the prospective client's intention to instruct the solicitor in question.

20.4

Section 44E of SA 1974 confers a right of appeal upon a solicitor who is fined or rebuked under section 44D if, in the case of a rebuke, a decision has been made to publish the rebuke. The appeal lies to the Tribunal. For a consideration of this and other appellate jurisdictions of the Tribunal see **CHAPTER 23**.

Letters of advice and warnings

20.5

The SRA can close an investigation on terms that the solicitor is provided with a letter containing advice and a warning regarding future conduct and behaviour. Before issuing the letter the SRA must give the person under investigation notice of the allegations and facts in support and an opportunity to make representations in response.[1] The letter is used for minor regulatory breaches which are not sufficiently serious to justify a rebuke, fine or restriction on the ability to practise, and the decision to issue the letter can be taken by supervision staff.[2] The letter does not amount to a disciplinary finding against the solicitor, and need not ordinarily be reported to insurers unless an unusual term in the contract of insurance provides for this.

Breaches which are more serious are referred either to adjudication or directly to the Solicitors Disciplinary Tribunal.

1   Rule 2.4 of the Disciplinary Rules 2019. Similar provisions were contained in rules 5.1, 7.1 and 7.3 of the Disciplinary Rules 2011.
2   SRA Enforcement Strategy. See also the SRA Schedule of Delegations.

The powers of the adjudicator and adjudication panels

20.6

By rule 3.1 of the Disciplinary Rules 2019, an adjudicator or an adjudication panel can impose a rebuke or fine or refer a matter to the Solicitors Disciplinary Tribunal.[1]

1   Identical powers were set out in rule 3.1 of the Disciplinary Rules 2011.

20.7

A rebuke is a less serious sanction than a fine, and the SRA Enforcement Strategy states that the decision–maker will consider available sanctions and controls in turn, starting with the least restrictive.

The Disciplinary Rules 2019 do not specify the circumstances in which a rebuke is appropriate. The SRA Enforcement Strategy states that a rebuke is appropriate where the issues are only of moderate seriousness, and that the following factors favour a rebuke:

- no lasting significant harm to consumers or third parties;

- conduct or behaviour reckless as to risk of harm/regulatory obligations;

- breach rectified/remedial action taken, but persisted longer than reasonable/ only when prompted;

- low risk of repetition;

- some public sanction required to uphold public confidence in the delivery of legal services.[1]

1   Appendix A to the SRA Enforcement Strategy, February 2019.

20.8

By rule 4.1 of the Disciplinary Rules 2019, a fine can be imposed where it is appropriate to:

(a)   remove any financial or other benefit arising from the conduct;

(b)   maintain professional standards; or

(c)   uphold public confidence in the profession and in legal services provided by authorised persons.

The SRA Enforcement Strategy states that a fine is appropriate where there is a serious breach but protection of the public does not require suspension or striking off, and that the following factors favour a fine:

- conduct/behaviour caused/had potential to cause significant harm;

- direct control/responsibility for conduct/behaviour;

- conduct planned/premeditated;

- wilful or reckless disregard of risk of harm/regulatory obligations;

- breach rectified/remedial action taken, but persisted longer than reasonable/ only when prompted;

- fine appropriate to remove financial gain or other benefit as a consequence of the breach.[1]

1   Appendix A to the SRA Enforcement Strategy, February 2019.

20.9

The decision may be made by an adjudicator or an adjudication panel consisting of at least two members. Any evidence which the adjudicator or adjudication panel considers to be fair and relevant can be admitted whether or not the evidence would be admissible in court.[1] By rule 8.7 of the Disciplinary Rules 2019 the standard of proof adopted is the civil standard, and decisions of an adjudication panel are made by a simple majority.

Any decision may also be taken by agreement with the regulated person.

1   Rule 8.8 of the Disciplinary Rules 2019.

Setting the level of fine

20.10

The Disciplinary Rules 2019 do not specify the criteria which should be taken into account when deciding the level of the fine. The SRA Enforcement Strategy states that the factors which affect the SRA's view on seriousness include the nature of the misconduct, whether the conduct was deliberate or inadvertent, whether proper management systems were in place, whether any harm has been caused and if so the impact on the victim, whether an affected person is vulnerable, whether the regulated person had responsibility or control over the matters in question, whether there are patterns of repeated misconduct, whether there is remorse or insight or a poor regulatory history and whether any remedial action has been taken.

The SRA has stated that the Enforcement Strategy will be supported by indicative fining guidance. No new guidance has been published since the Disciplinary Rules 2019 were made.

The SRA issued a guidance note on 13 August 2013 which sets out a three-stage process for determining the level of a fine.[1] Subject to the limits to the SRA's fining powers, the level is decided by (1) identifying the appropriate base penalty having regard to the seriousness of the misconduct and, in the case of a regulated entity, the size of the turnover; (2) taking any mitigation into account; and (3) adjusting the level to eliminate any financial benefit obtained by the misconduct.

The two main criteria that are likely to affect the high levels of fines which can be imposed on ABSs (a maximum of £250 million for a licensed body and £50 million for a manager or employee; see **CHAPTER 26**) are the linking of the base penalty to turnover (under the 2013 guidance the base penalty can be up to 2.5 per cent of annual domestic turnover) and the adjustment of the base penalty to eliminate any financial gain obtained from the misconduct.

If a financial penalty is in contemplation the SRA may require a statement as to the financial means of the person or body, verified by a statement of truth, within a specified time.[2]

The SRA may suspend a fine, which may have the result of making it payable only if there is a further adverse finding within the period of the suspension.[3]

Any fine is payable to the Treasury, but is not payable until the time for appealing has expired.

1 'Guidance on the SRA's approach to financial penalties', SRA, 13 August 2013.
2 Rule 4.2 of the Disciplinary Rules 2019.
3 Rule 4.3(b) of the Disciplinary Rules 2019.

Publication of decisions

20.11

Rule 9.1 of the Disciplinary Rules 2019 states that the SRA may disclose or publish any information arising from or relating to an investigation where it considers it to be in the public interest to do so. In practice the SRA does not publicise investigations before a disciplinary decision is made and does not publish letters of advice or warnings.

Rule 9.2 of the Disciplinary Rules 2019 states that the SRA shall publish any decision to give a rebuke or impose fine unless it considers the particular circumstances outweigh the public interest in publication. That emphasis on publication is arguably wider than the statutory provision for publication, as section 44D(3) of SA 1974 states that the SRA may publish a decision to rebuke or fine if it considers it to be in the public interest to do so.

On 10 August 2016 the SRA issued a guidance note which states that representations against publication will be taken into account.[1] The guidance note emphasises transparency, states that the SRA generally expects rebukes and fines to be published, and lists a small number of factors which may lead to a decision not to publish. The main factor is 'in all the circumstances the impact of publication on the regulated person would be disproportionate'. In practice, it is difficult to persuade the SRA not to publish.

1 'Publishing regulatory and disciplinary decisions', SRA, 10 August 2016.

Oral hearings

20.12

Adjudication proceedings are normally conducted in private and decided on the papers. It is open to a solicitor to request an oral hearing. Rule 8.5 of the Disciplinary Rules 2019 states that an adjudication panel may decide to conduct a hearing, which could be held in public, if it considers it in the interests of justice to do so. That is a new rule, because there was no provision for oral hearings under the Disciplinary Rules 2011, and oral hearings were rarely if ever granted. It is too early to say whether the new rule will lead to many oral hearings.

By case law, in order to have any prospect of persuading the adjudicator to grant an oral hearing, the solicitor will have to demonstrate that fairness requires an oral hearing, and that the matter cannot be adequately considered on paper.[1] In order to have any prospect of success in judicial review proceedings based upon a failure to grant an oral hearing, it will be essential for the solicitor to have requested such a hearing; failure to have done so will be fatal to the application.[2]

The rarity of oral hearings may continue in relation to traditional (non-ABS) practices, where allegations of serious misconduct materially affecting reputation and the freedom to practise are referred to the Solicitors Disciplinary Tribunal. There will be stronger grounds for saying that fairness requires an oral hearing if the SRA pursues a disputed allegation of serious misconduct against an ABS via internal disciplinary proceedings, as the SRA has power to impose sanctions on ABSs that may have substantial consequences in financial and reputational terms.

1   See generally *Yussouf v SRA* [2018] EWHC 211 (Admin).
2   *R (Thompson) v Law Society* [2004] 1 WLR 2522, CA. See also *R (Smith) v Parole Board (No 2)* [2004] 1 WLR 421, CA.

Costs of the investigation

20.13

The SRA has a statutory power to make regulations requiring a solicitor to pay a charge for the costs of an investigation into possible professional misconduct by the solicitor, or a failure or apprehended failure by the solicitor to comply with any regulatory requirement.[1] Rule 10.1 of the Disciplinary Rules 2019 provides that a person who is subject to a rebuke or fine can be directed to pay a charge. The current practice is to charge on a time basis in bands. If an investigation takes less than two hours' work (which would be unusual), the costs are a fixed figure of £300. If the time spent is more than two but under eight hours, the charge is £600. Between eight and 16 hours' work results in a charge of £1,350 and longer investigations are charged at £1,350 plus £75 for each hour and £37.50 for every half-hour over the 16th hour, rounded up or down to the nearest half-hour.[2] There is a discretion to charge less if it would be just to do so.

1   Section 44C of SA 1974.
2   Schedule 1 to the Disciplinary Rules 2019.

Referrals to the Tribunal

20.14

The SRA can refer a regulated person to the Tribunal if satisfied that (a) there is a realistic prospect of the Tribunal making an order in respect of the allegation and (b) it is in the public interest to make the application.[1] The referral decision can be made by some categories of legal and supervision staff as well as adjudicators, heads of functions and directors of the SRA.

The Disciplinary Rules 2019 state that the SRA can publish the referral decision unless it considers that the particular circumstances of the case outweigh the public interest in publication.[2]

1   Rule 6.1 of the Disciplinary Rules 2019.
2   Rule 9.2 of the Disciplinary Rules 2019.

Internal reviews

20.15

The powers to rebuke, fine and publicise the sanction are subject to an internal right of review.[1] The application for review must be launched within 28 days, and it is important for the applicant to provide properly reasoned arguments in support of the review. The review is dealt with on paper and can be decided by an adjudicator or an adjudication panel. On the review, the decision-maker can uphold the decision, overturn all or part of the decision, make any other decision which could have been made by the original decision-maker or remit the matter for further investigation.

There is no right of review of a decision to refer a person or body to the Tribunal.[2]

The SRA can on its own initiative for any reason apply for a review of any regulatory decision made by an adjudicator or adjudication panel, apart from a decision made on a review. The regulated person must be given notice of the review and an opportunity to provide written representations.[3]

1   Rule 3.2 of and Annex 1 to the SRA Application, Notice, Review and Appeal Rules 2019.
2   Annex 1 to the SRA Application, Notice, Review and Appeal Rules 2019.
3   Rules 3.1 and 3.6 of the SRA Application, Notice, Review and Appeal Rules 2019.

Appeals to the Tribunal

20.16

In respect of regulatory breaches occurring after 1 June 2010, there is a free-standing right of appeal to the Tribunal against a fine, against any direction for publicity, and against a rebuke only if there is a direction to publicise.[1]

1   Section 44E of SA 1974. See **CHAPTER 23**.

Judicial review

20.17

Judicial review continues to be theoretically available in respect of decisions by an adjudicator or an adjudication panel to impose a rebuke without publication, or a finding or warning, as there is no statutory right of appeal to the Tribunal against such decisions.[1] Ordinary public law principles would apply to such applications. Judicial review is often seen as a disproportionate response in circumstances where the decision, even if challengeable, makes little difference to the solicitor in practice, and permission can be refused on that basis alone.

As for decisions in respect of which a statutory right of appeal to the Tribunal exists, these cannot be challenged in judicial review proceedings owing to the existence of this alternative remedy.

1   See section 44E(1) of SA 1974. Annex 2 to the SRA Application, Notice, Review and Appeal Rules 2019 states that any decision to give a written rebuke can be appealed to the Tribunal. It is submitted that is incorrect, as the appellate jurisdiction of the Tribunal under SA 1974 is determined by statute and not the SRA's internal rules.

Regulatory settlements

20.18

The SRA is prepared to enter into agreements to settle regulatory and disciplinary cases. The agreement may take two forms: a settlement agreement, which will resolve the whole matter, or an issue agreement, which will resolve a particular issue within an investigation without concluding the investigation.

There is no requirement or compulsion on the SRA to consider a regulatory settlement of either kind or to enter into negotiations. If negotiations are conducted they will be on a without prejudice basis, and will not be referred to in any investigations or proceedings unless the court or the Tribunal orders otherwise. Agreements may be rescinded if there proves to have been material misrepresentation.

In practice, the SRA will not enter into a regulatory settlement agreement if the solicitor's integrity is in issue, if the SRA believes the solicitor will not comply with the agreement, if there is a history of persistent non-compliance or if the sanction sought by the SRA is more severe than the sanctions which the SRA has the power to impose.

Agreements will be in writing, state the relevant facts, identify any failings admitted by the solicitor, identify the action the solicitor has taken or intends to take, identify any sanction imposed (such as a rebuke or fine), require the solicitor to pay investigation costs and will be published by the SRA unless expressly agreed otherwise.

Any agreed course of action will be supported by professional undertakings and a breach of the agreement will be considered to be misconduct.

The investigation will be reopened if the solicitor fails to comply with the agreement or acts inconsistently with it (for example, by denying misconduct that has been admitted for the purposes of the agreement).

CHAPTER 21

Proceedings before the SDT: (1) pre-trial

Membership and constitution of the Tribunal

21.1

Members of the Solicitors Disciplinary Tribunal (the Tribunal or SDT) are appointed by the Master of the Rolls. The Tribunal consists of solicitor members who are practising solicitors of not less than ten years' standing, and lay members, who are neither solicitors nor barristers. Lay members are paid a daily stipend by the Ministry of Justice; until 2009 solicitor members were unpaid but can now be paid from the Tribunal's annual budget met by the Law Society. The President of the Tribunal is elected to the post, and must be a solicitor member.[1] The members also appoint one solicitor member and one lay member to be vice-presidents. The Tribunal has been held to be an independent and impartial tribunal for the purposes of Article 6 of the European Convention on Human Rights.[2]

1 Rule 3 of the Solicitors (Disciplinary Proceedings) Rules 2007 (SI 2007/3588) and rule 7 of the Solicitors (Disciplinary Proceedings) Rules 2019 (SI 2019/1185) which come into force on 25 November: see **21.4**.
2 *Pine v Law Society* (2000) DC Transcript CO 1385/2000.

The Tribunal's statutory powers

21.2

On the hearing of an application, the Tribunal has the power, in relation to solicitors, to make such order as it thinks fit, and any such order may in particular include provision for any of the following matters:[1]

'(a) the striking off the roll of the name of the solicitor to whom the application or complaint relates;

(b) the suspension of that solicitor from practice indefinitely or for a specified period;

(c) the payment by that solicitor or former solicitor of a penalty, which shall be forfeit to Her Majesty;[2]

(d) in the circumstances referred to in subsection (2A) [of the Solicitors Act 1974], the exclusion of that solicitor from criminal legal aid work (either permanently or for a specified period);

(e) the termination of that solicitor's unspecified period of suspension from practice;

(f) the restoration to the roll of the name of a former solicitor whose name has been struck off the roll and to whom the application relates;

(g) in the case of a former solicitor whose name has been removed from the roll, a direction prohibiting the restoration of his name to the roll except by order of the Tribunal;

(h) in the case of an application under subsection (1)(f) [of the Solicitors Act 1974], the restoration of the applicant's name to the roll;

(i) the payment by any party of costs or a contribution towards costs of such amount as the Tribunal may consider reasonable.'

1 Section 47(2) of Solicitors Act (SA) 1974.
2 The former limit of £5,000 for each offence was removed by the Legal Services Act (LSA) 2007 with effect from 31 March 2009. Higher fines are now levied, particularly on recognised bodies in the context of firm-based regulation (see **CHAPTER 2**).

Other powers and jurisdictions

21.3

The Tribunal has jurisdiction over recognised bodies (incorporated practices registered with the Solicitors Regulation Authority (SRA)),[1] registered European lawyers,[2] registered foreign lawyers[3] and in respect of non-solicitors involved in legal practice.[4] The Tribunal also has jurisdiction to disqualify solicitors from undertaking legal aid work,[5] but so far as can be established the power has never been used.

The Tribunal has jurisdiction to consider the conduct of and to impose sanctions on an individual who was not a solicitor at the time of the actions complained of but who had since been admitted as a solicitor.[6]

The Tribunal has jurisdiction over former solicitors in respect of conduct while they were solicitors.[7]

Appeal lies to the Tribunal from the imposition of fines by the SRA under section 44D of SA 1974 and/or under paragraph 14B of Schedule 2 to the Administration of Justice Act (AJA) 1985 and in respect of written rebukes by the SRA (under the same provisions) if a decision is made that the rebuke should be published, and also against any decision to publish the details of any action taken by the SRA under section 44D of SA 1974.[8] On such an appeal the Tribunal may affirm or revoke the SRA's decision, vary the amount of any fine, and also may exercise its normal jurisdiction over the appellant (to strike off, suspend, revoke a sole solicitor endorsement, fine, and so forth) as if an application had been made against that person.[9] Appeal also lies to the Tribunal from licensing decisions of the SRA concerning alternative business structures (ABSs). For the appellate jurisdiction of the Tribunal see **CHAPTER 23**.

Section 47(3B) of SA 1974, inserted by LSA 2007, provides that the Tribunal is not permitted to make any order requiring redress to be made in respect of any act or omission of any person. An order, for example, that a solicitor compensate a client would therefore not be permitted. The parliamentary intention is clear: that redress is not a matter for either the SRA or the Tribunal, rather it is an issue for the Legal Ombudsman (see **CHAPTER 14**). This section came into force on 1 October 2011.

The SRA may also make rules, with the approval of the Tribunal, providing for appeals to the Tribunal from certain decisions of the SRA where appeal would otherwise lie to the High Court. These relate primarily to practising certificate conditions, and no such rules have yet been made.[10] It is understood that these are not in immediate contemplation.

1   Paragraphs 16 to 18A of Schedule 2 to AJA 1985.
2   Regulation 26 of the European Communities (Lawyer's Practice) Regulations 2000 (SI 2000/1119).
3   Paragraphs 15 to 17 of Schedule 14 to the Courts and Legal Services Act (CLSA) 1990.
4   Sections 43 and 47(2E) of SA 1974: see **18.4** to **18.13**.
5   Section 47(2A), (2B), (2C) and (2D) of SA 1974. These subsections were introduced by AJA 1985, granting the Tribunal the powers formerly vested in the Legal Aid (Complaints) Tribunal (established by the Legal Aid Act 1974, and which had dealt with two cases in its lifetime) and the Legal Aid in Criminal Cases (Complaints) Tribunal (established under the Criminal Justice Act 1967, which had dealt with one).
6   *Re a Solicitor (Ofosuhene)* (21 February 1997, unreported).
7   Section 47(1)(c) of SA 1974.
8   Section 44E(1) of SA 1974; para 14C of Schedule 2 to AJA 1985.
9   Section 44E(4) of SA 1974; para 14C of Schedule 2 to AJA 1985.
10   Section 49A of SA 1974. The matters which, subject to the rules if and when they are made, may be appealed to the Tribunal are: decisions as to restoring the name of a solicitor removed from the roll other than by order of the Tribunal (section 8(4) of SA 1974); the imposition of conditions on practising certificates or refusal to issue practising certificates or sole solicitor endorsements (sections 13A(6) and 28(3D)); decisions relating to the termination of the suspension of practising certificates (section 16(5)); decisions relating to the grant of permission to employ a struck off or suspended solicitor (section 41(3)); and decisions under the parallel jurisdiction in relation to conditions on the registration of foreign lawyers (para 14 of Schedule 14 to CLSA 1990).

The Tribunal's procedural rules, practice directions, guidance notes and application forms

21.4

The Tribunal has power to make its own rules about its procedure and practice. Any alterations to the procedural rules made after introduction of LSA 2007 are subject to the approval of the Legal Services Board (LSB), which also has the power to direct changes to the rules. The rules are made by way of statutory instrument.[1]

The Tribunal's procedures are governed by the Solicitors (Disciplinary Proceedings) Rules 2019 (the '2019 Rules'),[2] in force from 25 November 2019 onwards, and the Solicitors Disciplinary Tribunal (Appeals and Amendment) Rules 2011[3] which came into force on 1 October 2011 (the 'Appeal Rules').

The 2019 Rules are set out in full in **APPENDIX 14** and the chapters on the Tribunal in this edition of *The Solicitor's Handbook* contain commentary on the 2019 Rules.

The 2019 Rules replace the Solicitors (Disciplinary Proceedings) Rules 2007 (the '2007 Rules').[4] The 2007 Rules continue to apply after 25 November 2019 to applications made to the Tribunal before 25 November 2019, and commentary on the 2007 Rules can be found in *The Solicitor's Handbook 2017*.

By rule 6(3) of the 2019 Rules, the Tribunal has power to make practice directions. As at the date of writing of this edition, no practice directions have been made.[5]

The 2007 Rules were supplemented by a practice note on adjournments and six practice directions.

The Tribunal publishes guidance notes and policy documents. The main guidance note is a guidance note on sanctions. Other guidance notes relate to appeals to the Tribunal from SRA decisions, requests to give evidence by video link and special measures for vulnerable witnesses. The main policy documents are a policy note on adjournments, a judgment publication policy, and a policy on the supply of documents to a non-party from Tribunal records.

Under the 2019 Rules, there are prescribed forms for applications made by the SRA and lay persons against solicitors (rule 12), and applications for restoration and termination of indefinite suspensions (rule 17), for variation or removal of conditions on practice (rule 18), for review of section 43 orders made by the SRA (rule 19),[6] for procedural applications (rule 22) and for a re-hearing (rule 37). The Tribunal also publishes forms for certificates of readiness, applications for non party disclosure[7] and applications for special measures.[8]

1　Section 46(9)(b) and (12) of SA 1974; section 178 of LSA 2007.
2　SI 2019/1185.
3　SI 2011/2346.
4　SI 2007/3588.
5　The Tribunal made six practice directions under the 2007 Rules. Two related to service of documents and the other four related to disclosure, applications for a re-hearing, the inference to be drawn where the respondent does not give evidence and standard directions.
6　That is an order under section 43 of the Solicitors Act 1974 relating to an employee or consultant of a solicitors' firm.
7　That is an application to the Tribunal for the disclosure of Tribunal documents to a third party.
8　That is an application to the Tribunal for directions for facilitating the hearing of evidence by vulnerable witnesses.

The rule 12 statement and certification of a case to answer

21.5

When an adjudicator or adjudication panel or other authorised person of the SRA resolves to refer the conduct of a solicitor to the Tribunal, the case is allocated by the Legal Directorate of the SRA either to an in-house advocate in that department or to the solicitors instructed by the SRA to prosecute cases. The in-house advocate, or the solicitors, normally draft the originating process, which consists of an application notice under rule 12 of the 2019 Rules supported by a statement ('the rule 12 statement') which sets out the allegations and facts and matters in support and exhibits any documents relied on.[1] Occasionally counsel is instructed to draft the documents. The solicitor facing the allegations is described as the respondent.

1　Under the 2007 Rules regime it was the rule 5 statement.

Selecting the respondent(s)

21.6

In many cases, the identity of the appropriate respondent(s) will be obvious to the prosecutor: the proceedings will be commenced against those members of the firm who are felt to be culpable for what has occurred. Generally, the SDT will not be prepared to find a solicitor guilty of professional misconduct unless he or she can be said to be personally culpable. One obvious exception to this relates to the Accounts

Rules. The Tribunal regards liability for a breach of those Rules to be a matter of strict liability, as far as the principals of a practice are concerned, because the Accounts Rules require all the principals ('managers' in the terminology of the SRA Glossary) in a practice to ensure compliance with the Rules by themselves and by everyone else working in the practice;[1] this also applies to the firm's compliance officer for finance and administration (COFA) whether or not that individual is a manager. In Accounts Rules cases, the prosecutor must still decide how far to cast the net, ie how many 'principals' to join as respondents to the disciplinary proceedings. In this regard, partners in small firms may be less fortunate than their equivalents in the larger firms: the SRA may prosecute all of the partners in a small firm, whereas to do so in the case of a large firm would be regarded as absurd.

1   Rule 6 of the SRA Accounts Rules 2011 and rule 1.2 of the SRA Accounts Rules 2019.

Prosecuting 'innocent' partners

21.7

There has been confusion in recent years as to whether partners who have not known of or directly participated in a decision that breached a regulatory rule should face disciplinary action as a result. Please see the discussion of vicarious liability at **19.17**.

Prosecuting managers, COLPs and COFAs

21.8

In 2013 the SRA introduced a requirement for all firms to appoint a compliance officer for legal practice (COLP) and a compliance officer for finance and administration (COFA) with responsibilities for ensuring that the firm has systems and controls in place to enable the firm, its managers, owners and employees to comply with the Accounts Rules (in the case of the COFA) and with all other regulatory requirements (in the case of the COLP).[1] Although all managers (or partners) in a practice have similar obligations to ensure there are effective systems and controls in place,[2] the additional responsibilities placed on COLPs and COFAs, which cannot properly be delegated to others, has led to prosecutions against COLPs and COFAs rather than other managers when there are faults in a firm's management systems.

1   Rule 8.5 of the SRA Authorisation Rules 2011, the guidance notes to rule 8 of the SRA Authorisation Rules 2011 and paragraphs 9.1 and 9.2 of the SRA Code of Conduct for Firms 2019.
2   Chapter 7 of the SRA Code of Conduct 2011; paragraph 8.1 of the SRA Code of Conduct for Firms 2019.

Prosecuting entities

21.9

From the point at which it became possible to practise through a corporate structure as a recognised body in 1986,[1] the Law Society as regulator has been able to exercise direct control over the business entity. Disciplinary action could be taken against the recognised body by the revocation of recognition and applications could be made to the Tribunal for disciplinary sanctions, but in practice these powers were not used. Between 1986 and 31 March 2009, only two applications were made to the Tribunal against such a body as a respondent.[2] In both cases the company was a respondent to proceedings which were primarily directed at individuals, and in one of those two cases the Tribunal accepted a submission that any sanction on the company would simply be a second sanction against the individual who owned it, for the same offence, and declined to impose any separate sanction.[3]

The growth of entity regulation since 2009 suggested that there would be a marked increase in the number of entities (as opposed to individual solicitors) prosecuted before the Tribunal. However, that did not happen, and SRA prosecutions continued to focus upon individuals rather than entities. There was no published policy by the SRA as to when it considered it appropriate to prosecute an entity as well as, or instead of, individual solicitors, but it was understood to be the 'official position' of the SRA in terms of policy that entity regulation should primarily involve 'supervision', with 'enforcement' being deployed only in two circumstances: (a) where there is a serious failure of management – something fundamentally attributable to the way that the firm is being run; or (b) where on a problem being identified the firm is unwilling or unable to work with the SRA to put things right.[4] It is submitted that such an approach is sensible. In the last two or three years, the prosecution of entities has become rather more common than hitherto.

In 2019 the SRA separated the code of conduct into two separate codes for individual solicitors and firms. Prosecutions under the 2019 regulatory arrangements could take two years or more to reach the Tribunal, and it is too early to say whether the changes to the conduct rules in 2019 will lead to a change in approach.

1   Section 9 of and Schedule 2 to AJA 1985.
2   *Atikpakpa and others*, 8913–2004, SDT and *Le Moine and others*, 9048–2004, SDT.
3   *Le Moine and others*, 9048–2004, SDT.
4   See too SRA 'Criteria to determine the focus of an investigation', 10 May 2012.

Pleading the case against the respondent(s)

21.10

Great care is required in drafting the rule 12 statement. It is the entire basis of the prosecution case, containing not only the allegations which the respondent solicitor will have to face, but also the narrative supporting those allegations. If the narrative is unclear, or does not properly reflect the allegations, the Tribunal, or the High Court on appeal, is likely to be critical. One such instance was the case of *Thaker v SRA*,[1] in which the court was highly critical of the drafting of the relevant statement (at [17]):

> 'I regret to say that both the RAS [the re-amended statement of the SRA's case] and the schedule are chaotic documents. Although these documents are formidable at first sight, when one settles down to study them it is quite impossible to understand the case which Mr Thaker was being called upon to answer. The order in which matters are set out in the RAS is neither chronological nor logical. There are many cross references which are impossible to follow up, as the reader seeks to navigate a path through the hundreds of pages which form attachments to the RAS.'

Three further passages from reported cases should be borne in mind by any prosecutor. In his judgment in *Constantinides v Law Society*,[2] Lord Justice Moses said (at [35]):

'We should stress that we do not consider that the allegations of dishonesty were clearly and properly made in the Rule 4 statement. The Rule 4 statement, after alleging conduct unbefitting a solicitor, should have identified that conduct and stated with precision in relation to each aspect of the allegedly guilty conduct the respects in which it was said to be dishonest. It should have alleged that when the appellant acted, despite the conflict of interest, that that conduct was dishonest by the ordinary standards of honest behaviour and that he knew that he was transgressing the ordinary standards of honest behaviour.'[3]

Likewise in *Thaker v SRA*, Jackson LJ observed:

'[64] In order to have an effective re-trial, the SRA must serve a properly drafted Rule 4 statement in respect of any of the twelve allegations which it wishes to pursue. For the avoidance of doubt a properly drafted Rule 4 statement will set out a summary of the facts relied upon. It would be helpful if those facts are set out concisely and in chronological order ... It is the duty of the draftsman (not the reader) of a pleading or a Rule 4 statement to analyse the supporting evidence and to distil the relevant facts, discarding all irrelevancies.[4]

[65] If the Rule 4 statement alleges that Mr Thaker knew or ought to have known certain matters, the facts giving rise to that actual or constructive knowledge should also be set out. Once the Rule 4 statement has set out the primary facts asserted, it should then set out the allegations which are made on the basis of those primary facts. The person who drafts the Rule 4 statement should heed the guidance given by this court in *Constantinides* in relation to pleading dishonesty. In a complex case such as this the Solicitors' Disciplinary Tribunal needs to have a coherent and intelligible Rule 4 statement, in order to do justice between the parties.'

In *Connolly v Law Society*[5] Stanley Burnton J (with whom Laws LJ agreed) held (at [104]):

'the Law Society should avoid where possible formulating charges which include "and/or" allegations, such as charge (xl) in the present case, which comprised numerous alternatives. Where such a charge is laid, the Tribunal should make specific findings as to which allegation has been proved.'

These criticisms have to some extent fallen on deaf ears. 'And/or' allegations remain commonplace. In *SRA v Andersons and others*,[6] Treacy LJ observed, at [3]:

'During the course of the hearing we commented on the highly compli-cated structure of the charges, involving multiple allegations of breaches of rules, either cumulatively or in the alternative. Mr Dutton QC, for the SRA, acknowledged the force of this criticism. We would hope that in the future consideration would be given to a significantly clearer method of framing charges.'

1   [2011] EWHC 660 (Admin).
2   [2006] EWHC 725 (Admin).
3   The rule 4 statement was the originating process under rule 4 of the Solicitors (Disciplinary Proceedings) Rules 1994.
4   In *SRA v Manak and another* [2016] EWHC 1914 (Admin), Thirlwall J observed at [23] that paragraph 64 of the *Thaker* judgment should be part of the training manual for those who draft pleadings on behalf of the SRA.
5   [2007] EWHC 1175 (Admin).
6   [2013] EWHC 4021 (Admin).

Alleging breaches of the SRA Principles and the Codes of Conduct

21.11

Since 2011, the preferred method of charging disciplinary offences in matters which do not involve allegations of breaches of the Accounts Rules has been for the SRA to allege breaches of one or more of the SRA Principles, and, less universally, failure to achieve one or more of the outcomes in the SRA Code of Conduct 2011. This method of pleading has superseded allegations of conduct unbefitting a solicitor, which tended to be the norm prior to 2007.

The SRA Principles 2011 and the SRA Code of Conduct 2011 will continue to apply to breaches which occurred before introduction of the SRA Principles 2019 and the 2019 Codes of Conduct and pleadings alleging breaches of the 2011 rules will continue to be heard by the Tribunal for a number of years after introduction of the 2019 regulatory arrangements. If a course of conduct persists over a period of time, and leads to breaches of the 2011 rules as well as the 2019 regulatory arrangements, the pleadings are likely to include allegations of breaches of both sets of rules.

The Principles are deliberately couched in very wide terms. Not every breach of a principle will amount to professional misconduct. For instance, principle 5 of the SRA Principles 2011 requires solicitors to provide a proper standard of service to clients. Negligence can amount to professional misconduct, but only if it meets the test of being 'inexcusable and ... such as to be regarded as deplorable by his fellows in the profession'.[1] The same must apply to breaches of the mandatory outcomes in the 2011 Code: while such a breach may amount to professional misconduct, it must not necessarily do so.

1   *Re a Solicitor* [1972] 2 All ER 811, CA at 815 and see *Connolly v Law Society* [2007] EWHC 1175 (Admin) at [62]. See the general discussion of manifest incompetence in **19.11**.

Alleging dishonesty

21.12

If dishonesty is to be alleged against a solicitor, this must be pleaded with 'pitiless clarity'[1] and the allegation should be pleaded in the rule 12 statement.[2] None of the principles and outcomes in the 2011 rules expressly require a solicitor to act honestly and if the SRA considers that a solicitor's breach of any of the 2011 rules involves dishonesty, the SRA will allege a breach of the rule and add a separate allegation that the breach involved dishonesty. Principle 4 of the SRA Principles 2019 expressly requires a solicitor to act honestly, and an allegation of dishonesty relating to conduct occurring while the 2019 regulatory arrangements are in force will include an allegation that principle 4 has been breached.

Failure expressly to allege or particularise dishonesty in a document in advance of the Tribunal hearing is likely to amount to a serious procedural flaw, which may well result in any finding of dishonesty by the Tribunal being overturned.[3] In *Fish v GMC* Foskett J said:

> 'An allegation of dishonesty against a professional person … should not be made without good reason … no-one should be found to have been dishonest on a side wind or by some kind of default setting in the mechanism of the inquiry. It is an issue that must be articulated, addressed and adjudged head on.'[4]

It is not enough to make a free-standing allegation of dishonesty: such an allegation must make clear the acts or omissions that are said to be dishonest.[5]

The test for dishonesty is set out by Lord Hoffmann in *Barlow Clowes* as follows:

> 'Although a dishonest state of mind is a subjective mental state, the standard by which the law determines whether it is dishonest is objective. If by ordinary standards a defendant's mental state would be characterised as dishonest, it is irrelevant that the defendant judges by different standards.'[6]

In *Ivey* Lord Hughes confirmed that this is the test for dishonesty:

> 'The test of dishonesty is as set out by Lord Nicholls in *Royal Brunei Airlines Sdn Bhd v Tan* and by Lord Hoffmann in *Barlow Clowes* … When dishonesty is in question the fact-finding tribunal must first ascertain (subjectively) the actual state of the individual's knowledge or belief as to the facts. The reasonableness or otherwise of his belief is a matter of evidence (often in practice determinative) going to whether he held the belief, but it is not an additional requirement that his belief must be reasonable; the question is whether it is genuinely held. When once his actual state of mind as to knowledge or belief as to facts is established, the question whether his conduct was honest or dishonest is to be determined by the fact-finder by applying the (objective) standards of ordinary decent people. There is no requirement that the defendant must appreciate that what he has done is, by those standards, dishonest.'[7]

In *SRA v Wingate*, the Court of Appeal stressed that, although the test for dishonesty is an objective test, a defendant's state of mind is relevant. Jackson LJ said:

> 'As explained most recently in *Ivey*, the test for dishonesty is objective. Nevertheless, the Defendant's state of mind as well as their conduct are relevant to determining whether they have acted dishonestly.'[8]

The Tribunal is regularly called upon to consider whether the failings of a solicitor amount to dishonesty, with an understanding that if there is a finding of dishonesty, the solicitor will almost inevitably be struck off (see **22.18** and **22.19**).

1 This memorable phrase was used by Mostyn J in *Malins v SRA* [2017] EWHC 835 (Admin).
2 *SRA v Manak* [2016] EWHC 1914 (Admin) at [26].

3   *Singleton v Law Society* [2005] EWHC 2915 (Admin); *Constantinides v Law Society* [2006] EWHC 725 (Admin); *Onibudo v Law Society* [2002] EWHC 2030 (Admin).
4   *Fish v GMC* [2012] EWHC 1269 (Admin) at [68]–[70].
5   See *SRA v Manak* [2016] EWHC 1914 (Admin) at [26].
6   *Barlow Clowes International Ltd v Eurotrust International Ltd* [2006] 1 WLR 1476, PC at 1479–80. See too the discussion of dishonesty in **CHAPTER 19**.
7   *Ivey v Genting Casinos (UK) Ltd* [2017] UKSC 67 at [74].
8   *SRA v Wingate; SRA v Malins* [2018] EWCA Civ 366 at [94]. See also the two-stage approach on application of the test in *Zivancevic v SRA* [2019] EWHC 1950 (Admin) at [19].

Alleging lack of integrity

21.13

Principle 2 of the SRA Principles 2011 and principle 5 of the SRA Principles 2019 require solicitors to act with integrity. Allegations of lack of integrity have become popular with the SRA since 2011, as a means of alleging serious misconduct short of dishonesty.

The meaning of the phrase 'lack of integrity' has been explored in a series of cases relating to financial services and solicitors since 2003, and was considered by the Court of Appeal in *SRA v Wingate* in 2018.[1]

The first notable case was *Hoodless & Blackwell v FSA* in 2003, in which the Financial Services and Markets Tribunal said:

'In our view "integrity" connotes moral soundness, rectitude and steady adherence to an ethical code. A person lacks integrity if unable to appreciate the distinction between what is honest or dishonest by ordinary standards. (This presupposes, of course, circumstances where ordinary standards are clear. Where there are genuinely grey areas, a finding of lack of integrity would not be appropriate.)'[2]

In *Wingate* Jackson LJ said that the observations in *Hoodless* had met with general approbation between 2003 and 2018 but that it was not possible to formulate an all-purpose, comprehensive definition of integrity.[3]

As regards integrity in professional conduct cases, Jackson LJ said:

'In professional codes of conduct, the term "integrity" is a useful shorthand to express the higher standards which society expects from professional persons and which the professions expect from their own members … The underlying rationale is that the professions have a privileged and trusted role in society. In return they are required to live up to their own professional standards …

Integrity connotes adherence to the ethical standards of one's own profession. That involves more than mere honesty. To take one example, a solicitor conducting negotiations … will take particular care not to mislead. Such a professional person is expected to be even more scrupulous about accuracy than a member of the general public in daily discourse …

The duty to act with integrity applies not only to what professional persons say but also to what they do …

Obviously, neither Courts nor professional tribunals must set unrealistically high standards ... The duty of integrity does not require professional people to be paragons of virtue. In every instance, professional integrity is linked to the manner in which that particular profession professes to serve the public ...

A professional disciplinary tribunal has specialist knowledge of the profession to which the respondent belongs and of the ethical standards of that profession. Accordingly such a body is well placed to identify want of integrity ...'[4]

In *Wingate* the Court of Appeal did not expressly state that the test for lack of integrity is an objective test. That issue was considered by Morris J in *Newell-Austin v SRA*, who said that the test is an objective test, and that there is no requirement for the respondent to have an appreciation of the lack of integrity. However Morris J also said:

'The person's state of knowledge or intention in relation to the underlying conduct (said to demonstrate lack of integrity) is a relevant consideration in assessing whether, in carrying out such conduct, a person demonstrated a lack of integrity.'[5]

1   *SRA v Wingate; SRA v Malins* [2018] EWCA Civ 366 at [98] and [99]. See also *SRA v Chan* [2015] EWHC 2659 (Admin); *Scott v SRA* [2016] EWHC 1256 (Admin); *Newell-Austin v SRA* [2017] EWHC 411 (Admin) and *Williams v SRA* [2017] EWHC 1478 (Admin). See generally the discussion of lack of integrity in **CHAPTER 19**.
2   *Hoodless & Blackwell v FSA* [2003] FSMT 007.
3   *SRA v Wingate; SRA v Malins* [2018] EWCA Civ 366 at [98] and [99].
4   *SRA v Wingate; SRA v Malins* [2018] EWCA Civ 366 at [97]–[103].
5   *Newell-Austin v SRA* [2017] EWHC 411 (Admin) at [48]–[50]; see also *SRA v Wingate; SRA v Malins* [2018] EWCA Civ 366 at [85].

Alleging recklessness

21.14

An allegation of recklessness should be pleaded.[1] Recklessness is defined as a matter of law, and the definition has been applied by the SDT; see *Lawson*[2] and *Fuglers*[3] (undisturbed by the High Court on appeal). The following quotations, paraphrasing *R v G and another*,[4] are from *Lawson* and *Fuglers* respectively:

'Recklessness means the taking of an unreasonable risk of which the risk-taker is aware: a person acts "recklessly" with respect to a circumstance when he is aware of a risk that did or would exist, and acts recklessly with respect to a consequence when he is aware of a risk that it will occur, and in either case, it is, in the circumstances known to him, unreasonable to take the risk.'

'... it had to be shown that the defendant's state of mind was culpable in that he acted recklessly in respect of a circumstance if he was aware of a risk which did or would exist, or in respect of a result if he was aware of a risk that it would occur, and it was, in the circumstances known to him, unreasonable to take the risk.'

1   *Constantinides v Law Society* [2006] EWHC 725 (Admin) at [35]; *SRA v Manak* [2016] EWHC 1914 (Admin) at [26]. But see also *Keazor v Law Society* [2009] EWHC 267 (Admin) at [14].
2   11048–2012, SDT.
3   10917–2012, SDT.
4   [2004] 1 AC 1034, HL.

Certification of a case to answer

21.15

When the rule 12 statement and supporting documents are filed with the Tribunal, the papers are considered by a solicitor member of the Tribunal, who certifies whether a 'case to answer' is made out against the respondent.[1] If no such case is revealed, the papers are considered by a panel of three members, and, if all agree, the case can be dismissed without hearing any party. The respondent solicitor is not invited to make any representations as to why the Tribunal should not certify a prima facie case – indeed the solicitor will not even know that this process is taking place. If the case is dismissed the applicant must be given written reasons for the decision. If a decision is made to certify a case to answer, no reasons are given for the Tribunal's decision to certify, and indeed the affected solicitor is not even informed when and by whom this certification has been provided. It is believed that this somewhat unusual process results from the fact that any member of the public may commence disciplinary proceedings in the Tribunal against a solicitor, and that it is important to have a system by which hopeless cases can be weeded out at a very early stage. Occasionally, however, the Tribunal declines to certify a case when the proceedings have been initiated by the SRA. No statistics are available as to how often this happens.

After the case has been certified, the Tribunal serves the prescribed application form, the rule 12 statement and its exhibits on the respondent.[2]

1   See generally rule 13 of the 2019 Rules.
2   Rule 13(5) of the 2019 Rules.

The respondent's answer

21.16

Before October 2013, pre-trial procedures were governed by the 2007 Rules, and ad hoc arrangements made between the legal representatives for the parties. There were serious drawbacks in these procedures. In particular, there was no provision in the Rules for the defence case to be properly pleaded or set out for the benefit of the Tribunal unless the respondent chose to serve a defence case statement or detailed witness statement in answer to the allegations. There was no specific obligation to provide a defence case statement, and respondents often failed to serve a witness statement until the last moment or even at all.

In October 2013 the Tribunal introduced standard directions which require the respondent to serve an answer, and answers have been served as a matter of routine since then.

Rule 20(2) of the 2019 Rules states that the standard directions may specify the date by which the respondent must send to the Tribunal and serve on every party an answer to the allegations. Rule 20(4)(a) states that an answer 'sets out (a) which allegations in the Rule 12 statement are admitted and which are denied and (b) the reasons for denial. The answer does not need to deal with every matter in every paragraph of the rule 12 statement, and so does not resemble a defence in civil proceedings. It can set out the respondent's case succinctly, so that the Tribunal can understand from the pleadings alone what is asserted by each party in the case.

Standard Directions, Caselines, procedural applications and hearings

Standard Directions and Caselines

21.17

The Tribunal issues Standard Directions which are served on all parties at the same time as the rule 12 statement is served on the respondent.

Rule 20(2) of the 2019 Rules states that the Standard Directions may specify:

- the date fixed for the substantive hearing;

- the date by which a respondent must send to the Tribunal and serve on every other party an answer to the allegations;

- the date by which a respondent must send to the Tribunal and serve on every other party all documents on which the respondent intends to rely at the substantive hearing;

- the date by which all parties must send to the Tribunal and serve on every other party a list of witnesses upon whose evidence they intend to rely at the substantive hearing;

- the date by which the parties must notify the Tribunal of any intention to rely on expert evidence;

- the date on which any case management hearing will take place;

- the date by which the parties must send a statement of readiness to the Tribunal;

- the date by which hearing bundles must be sent to the Tribunal;

- any other Standard Directions which the Tribunal considers appropriate.

The other Standard Directions which the Tribunal may well make include directions for service of witness statements[1] and any civil evidence act notices,[2] a direction confirming the time by which any application for an agreed outcome should be made to the Tribunal[3] and directions specifying the time by which any statements of the respondent's means[4] or statements of costs should by served and sent to the Tribunal.

A 'statement of readiness' is a document confirming whether a party is ready for the substantive hearing, setting out what if any further directions are required and confirming the time estimate for the hearing. It is normally served and sent to the Tribunal four weeks before the substantive hearing.[5]

In April 2019 the Tribunal introduced Caselines, which is a digital court platform with a cloud based evidence management system. Under Caselines, the parties upload any documents for service onto a master bundle on the Tribunal's platform. The master bundle can be accessed by the parties via the internet. The hearings are conducted without paper files and by using laptops to provide access to the electronic master bundle.

The Tribunal does not in practice require hard copies of documents when Caselines is used. However, if a hard copy of a document does need to be presented to the Tribunal, four copies are normally required – one for each of the members and one for the clerk.

1   Rule 28(2) of the 2019 Rules.
2   By rule 29 of the 2019 Rules, the provisions of the Civil Evidence Act 1995 apply to Tribunal proceedings and any civil evidence act notices must be given no later than the date for service of the witness statements.
3   By rule 25(1) of the 2019 Rules the parties may submit any application for an agreed outcome to the tribunal up to 28 days before the substantive hearing, unless the Tribunal directs otherwise.
4   Rule 43(5) of the 2019 Rules.
5   Rule 20(4)(b) of the 2019 Rules.

Case management hearings

21.18

The standard directions served on the parties at the same time as the Tribunal's service of the rule 12 statement on the respondent will incude a direction for a case management hearing (CMH) in cases where (a) a clerk considers a CMH is justified by reason of the time estimate provided by the SRA or (b) the clerk who reviews the application on receipt identifies issues which in the opinion of the clerk justify the holding of a CMH.[1] The SRA is required to provide a time estimate for the substantive hearing when lodging the rule 12 statement with the Tribunal,[2] and in practice the Tribunal will hold a CMH if the time estimate is three days or more.

A CMH may also be fixed in any case at any other time before the substantive hearing by the Tribunal or a clerk.[3]

The parties are encouraged to agree directions for the management of the case going forward. The CMH can be held by telephone. Indeed in many cases, the parties will be able to agree appropriate directions in advance and obtain the Tribunal's consent to the directions on paper so that it is unnecessary for them to attend the CMH in person or by phone. General matters that may be dealt with at a CMH include:

- amending the rule 12 statement;

- ordering the SRA to provide 'further and better particulars of the rule 12 statement';

- variations to the standard directions.

In most cases, one CMH will suffice, but additional ones may prove necessary in the more complex cases. Other specific applications that may be made at the interlocutory stage are set out below.

1   See rule 21(1) of the 2019 Rules.

2   Rule 12(3)(b) of the 2019 Rules.
3   Rule 21(2) of the 2019 Rules.

Procedural applications generally

21.19

The Tribunal has a standard application form for procedural applications, which should be used on any interim application.[1] The application form should be sent to the Tribunal and every other party accompanied by any supporting documents. Minor applications, such as uncontroversial requests for extensions of time, are dealt with on paper by a clerk[2] or the Tribunal after the other parties have been invited to make representations on the application. Other applications are listed for hearing before the Tribunal, and in complex interim applications the Tribunal may give directions for service of evidence and exchange of skeleton arguments. The Tribunal issues written reasons for its decisions on interim applications.

There is no statutory appeal against an interim order of the Tribunal, and the only avenue of challenge is therefore an application for judicial review. In *Stokes v Law Society*,[3] Kennedy LJ observed that relief would be given only in exceptional circumstances 'and never where, as here, the error relied upon has been rectified'.

1   Rule 22(1) of the 2019 Rules.
2   For the powers of clerks on interim applications, see rule 8(6) of the 2019 Rules.
3   [2001] EWHC Admin 1101.

Applications for disclosure of documents

21.20

By rule 26(1), if an application is made for disclosure, the Tribunal may make an order for disclosure where it considers that the production of the material is necessary for proper consideration of the case, unless the Tribunal considers that there are compelling reasons in the public interest not to order disclosure.[1]

An order for disclosure will only apply to material which is in the possession or under the control of a party, and will not oblige the party to produce any material which they would be entitled to refuse to produce in court proceedings.[2]

A party to Tribunal proceedings is required to disclose only (a) the documents on which the party relies; (b) any documents which (i) adversely affect that party's own case, (ii) adversely affect another party's case, or (iii) support another party's case; and (c) any documents which a party is required to disclose by a relevant practice direction.[3]

In practice, applications by respondents to the Tribunal for disclosure of documents are unusual. Applications for disclosure made by the SRA against a respondent are even rarer, and there is considerable doubt as to whether the SRA is entitled to seek disclosure during disciplinary proceedings which it has brought. There is no obligation of disclosure upon defendants in criminal proceedings, to which disciplinary proceedings bear some relationship. Moreover, the SRA will have had an opportunity during its investigation to compel disclosure of documents by the regulated individual through use of its statutory powers under SA 1974.

1   Rule 26(1) of the 2019 Rules.
2   Rules 26(2) and (3) of the 2019 Rules
3   Rule 26(4) of the 2019 Rules. As at the date of writing, there are no relevant practice directions.

Applications for hearings to be held in private

21.21

Under the Tribunal's rules, any party to the disciplinary proceedings, or a third party who claims to be affected, may apply for all or part of the hearing to be conducted in private on the grounds of exceptional hardship or exceptional prejudice to a party, witness, or any person affected by the application.[1] Otherwise the presumption is that the case will be heard in public.[2]

The principle of open justice, and that legal proceedings should be conducted in public, is an important one.[3] The Tribunal will ordinarily depart from that to the least extent possible. As a result, in *Lee*,[4] rather than hearing the case in private, the Tribunal permitted (for the first time) a vulnerable female witness to give evidence from behind a screen about flirtatious texts sent to her by the respondent. Sometimes, however, the principle of open justice has to yield, and this will be particularly so in cases in which the lay client has not waived privilege, and to hear the case in public will necessarily involve identification of the client, and/or publication of confidential and privileged matters.[5]

The Tribunal is most unlikely to accede to any submission by or on behalf of the respondent that the case should be heard in private because of the emotional effect upon the respondent that a public hearing will have. Such an application would have to be supported by cogent and persuasive medical evidence in order to have any prospect of success, and even in such an event, the Tribunal may well feel that the desirability of open justice trumps any psychological effect upon the respondent. On the other hand, if there is compelling evidence that a public hearing might place the respondent or a witness in real physical danger, the Tribunal may be more sympathetic to an application for the case to be heard in private.

If a party or any other person wishes to apply for a hearing to be conducted in private, that person should consider whether to also apply for an order that the cause list be anonymised. Such an application should be made and served no later than 28 days before the hearing.[6] See **21.33**.

If the respondent is considering seeking a judicial review of an SRA decision to publish details of the allegations before the substantive hearing, the respondent will be well advised to apply to the Tribunal for any CMH to be heard in private, and/or that the respondent should not be identified on the Tribunal's lists for hearings.[7]

1   Rule 35(2) and (5) of the 2019 Rules.
2   Rule 35(1) of the 2019 Rules.
3   In *L v Law Society* [2008] EWCA Civ 811 at [41] (a case concerned with an appeal against a decision of the SRA to revoke student membership, but which canvassed wider issues concerning public and private hearings), the Master of the Rolls emphasised the importance of public hearings in the Tribunal in maintaining the confidence of the public in the disciplinary process. See too *Solicitors Regulation Authority v Spector* [2016] EWHC 37 (Admin), [2016] 4 WLR 16 at [19]–[21].
4   11398–2015, SDT.
5   One example of the entire proceedings being held in private is *Chapman and Abramson, News UK intervening*, 11164–2013, SDT. However, the decision that the whole proceedings should be in private

was based on the conclusion that there was a substantial risk of prejudice to the course of justice because of extant criminal proceedings, rather than the need to protect the client's privilege: see para 6.1.9 of the judgment.

6   Rule 34(3)(a) of the 2019 Rules.
7   See *Andersons v Solicitors Regulation Authority* [2012] EWHC 3659 (Admin).

Applications to strike out the rule 12 statement as an abuse of process, etc

21.22

The Tribunal may strike out proceedings if it considers that the prosecution amounts to an abuse of process. In the criminal courts, it has long been held that applications to stay proceedings for abuse of process should only rarely be granted, and that the threshold to be surmounted by the applicant is a high one.[1] The Tribunal takes a similar approach, and successful abuse of process applications are rare. A notable example was *Heer Manak and others*,[2] in which the Tribunal struck out the entire case at the close of the prosecution case on the ground that the rule 5 statement (2007 Rules) was so defective that the respondents (and the Tribunal) were unable to know the case that the respondents had to meet. The SRA's appeal against this decision in so far as it related to two of the six respondents was largely successful. Although critical of the way that the matter had been pleaded, Thirlwall J held that for the most part it was possible to understand what was alleged, and therefore it could not have been an abuse of process for the Tribunal to continue to hear it.[3]

One particular area in which such applications have succeeded is where there has been inordinate delay in bringing the case before the Tribunal.[4] This may amount to an abuse of process on a traditional common law analysis, or it may breach the 'reasonable time' requirement in article 6(1) of the European Convention on Human Rights. The Tribunal has held that time starts for this purpose when the decision to refer the solicitor to the Tribunal is made, and has struck out cases which have been inordinately delayed thereafter.[5]

The Tribunal has ruled that proceedings should generally be issued within three months of the decision to refer a respondent to the Tribunal, and that if necessary an application for further time (if needed before the matter was listed for hearing) could be considered by the Tribunal.[6] If a fair trial is possible despite delay in issuing the proceedings, it is open to the Tribunal to take the delay into account when deciding the penalty and costs.[7]

1   The leading cases are *Connelly v DPP* [1964] AC 1254, HL; *DPP v Humphrys* [1977] AC 1, HL; *R v Horseferry Road Magistrates' Court, ex p Bennett* [1994] 1 AC 42, HL; and *R v Maxwell* [2011] 1 WLR 1837, SC.
2   11165–2013, SDT.
3   *SRA v Manak and another* [2016] EWHC 1914 (Admin).
4   For the general approach of the courts, see *Attorney-General's Reference (No 2 of 2001)* [2004] 2 AC 72, HL; *Porter v Magill* [2002] 2 AC 357, HL; and *Dyer v Watson* [2004] 1 AC 379, PC.
5   See generally *Loomba and Loomba*, 9022–2004, SDT; *Davis*, 9017–2004, SDT; *Judge and Stanger*, 9028–2004, SDT; *Rutherford*, 9074–2004, SDT; *Fallon*, 9154–2004, SDT and *Sancheti and others*, 7976–2007, SDT.
6   *Nulty and Trotter*, 9871–2008, SDT – memorandum of preliminary hearing, 1 July 2008.
7   *SRA v Davis*, 9017–2014, SDT.

21.23

If the respondent considers that there is a fatal flaw in the applicant's case against him, the Tribunal may be willing to consider that as a preliminary issue with a view to saving time and expense. Accordingly, cases can be disposed of summarily at the start of the substantive hearing, and there would seem to be no reason in principle in an appropriate case why the respondent should not seek an early listing of the case to ascertain whether it can be summarily disposed of in this way.[1] It must be accepted that these situations are likely to be rare.

1   *Law Society v Adcock and Mocroft* [2006] EWHC 3212 (Admin) at [30].

Applications for adjournments

21.24

The Tribunal has published a practice note on the subject of adjournments. An application for an adjournment should be supported by documentary evidence of the need for the adjournment.[1]

The Tribunal is generally not prepared to adjourn the disciplinary proceedings pending completion of a criminal investigation or prosecution.[2] The same applies in relation to civil proceedings.[3] The only exception is where there is a risk of 'muddying the waters of justice' but in practice this is usually either an illusory or a manageable risk.

The Tribunal is sometimes faced with applications made at the last minute by respondents who claim to be unable properly to participate in the proceedings on grounds of psychiatric illness, psychological stress, or the like. Such applications are most unlikely to succeed unless supported by cogent medical evidence, and even then may be rejected. The Tribunal is well aware that facing a disciplinary tribunal hearing is a highly stressful experience for any individual, but once the case has been listed and arrangements have been made to hear it, it is plainly important that it should proceed if at all possible. That said, it would be unjust to proceed in the absence of the respondent if a last-minute application was made on the basis of medical evidence from a sufficiently qualified practitioner who had recently examined the respondent which clearly showed that the respondent's ability to participate properly in a hearing had been affected and impaired by a medical condition.[4]

1   Practice note on adjournment and rule 23 of the 2019 Rules.
2   *R v Solicitors Disciplinary Tribunal, ex p Gallagher* (1991, unreported).
3   *Lipman Bray v Hillhouse and Jacob* [1987] NLJR 171, CA.
4   *Rodriguez-Purcet v SRA* [2018] EWHC 2879 (Admin) at [42].

Applications relating to expert evidence

21.25

A party wishing to rely on expert evidence should make an application to the Tribunal for leave to adduce the evidence. No party can call an expert or rely on an expert's report at the substantive hearing without leave of the Tribunal.[1] The Tribunal may grant leave where it considers the expert evidence is necessary for the proper consideration of an issue or issues in the case.[2]

An expert's report must set out the expert's professional qualifications and the substance of the instructions provided for the report, and must contain a declaration that the expert is aware of the duty to assist the Tribunal and understands that this duty overrides any obligation to the party providing the instructions.[3]

1 Rule 30(1) of the 2019 Rules.
2 Rule 30(3) of the 2019 Rules.
3 Rule 30(6) of the 2019 Rules.

Applications by the SRA to withdraw allegations

21.26

Once proceedings have been issued, an allegation cannot be withdrawn without the consent of the Tribunal.[1] The Tribunal will often be resistant to giving that consent, because it has earlier certified a prima facie case on the papers: it has often enquired of the SRA advocate what has changed to justify withdrawal. Such an approach contrasts not only with the role of the court in criminal proceedings, but also with that of other courts or tribunals in proceedings that are similar to disciplinary proceedings: ordinarily, such courts and tribunals are discouraged from insisting that particular charges, allegations or issues be tried where the parties have agreed that they need not be tried (see e g *Secretary of State for Trade and Industry v Rogers*[2] in the context of directors' disqualification proceedings).

The origins and purposes of the principle are mentioned in the 1960 *Guide to the Professional Conduct and Etiquette of Solicitors* by Sir Thomas Lund:[3]

> '... an application made to the Disciplinary Committee cannot be with-drawn without the consent of the Committee. That is because it used to be a favourite dodge for clients to lodge an application against a solicitor alleging that moneys were unaccounted for and then, as soon as they were paid off, to withdraw the application, although probably Paul's money had been used for the benefit of Peter.'

So in historical context this provision was designed to ensure that lay applicants were not bought off, leaving a potential underlying issue disguised and undiscovered. It would appear to have no continuing relevance in the modern era when there is a statutory regulator involved.

1 Rule 24 of the 2019 Rules.
2 [1996] 1 WLR 1569, CA.
3 See page 116 and the second half of the middle paragraph.

Miscellaneous matters

Power of the Tribunal to regulate its own procedure

21.27

Rule 6(1) and (2) of the 2019 Rules confer the all-important powers on the Tribunal to regulate its own procedure subject to the Rules, and to dispense with any requirements of the Rules in respect of notices, statements, witnesses, service or time in any case where it appears to be just to do so. At the discretion of the Tribunal, the strict rules of evidence do not apply.[1]

1   Rules 38(2) of the 2019 Rules.

Witness statements and defence material

21.28

The 2019 Rules state that permission is needed for a witness to give evidence at the hearing unless a witness statement is provided to the Tribunal and the other parties on a date determined by the Tribunal which must be no less than 28 days before the hearing.[1] In practice the date determined by the Tribunal will be the date specified in the standard directions.

In the case of the respondent, it is standard practice in contested or complex cases to serve a witness statement as well as the answer (and the witness statement should be served within the time specified in the standard directions). In other cases, it has usually been accepted that the representations made to the SRA at the investigation stage can stand as the respondent's evidence.

The respondent has the option whether or not to give oral evidence, although it is unusual for him or her to elect not to do so in a contested case. In 2012 in *Iqbal v SRA* the High Court said that ordinarily the public would expect a professional man to give an account of his actions.[2] That is reflected in the 2019 Rules, which state that if a respondent fails to serve an answer, or give evidence at the substantive hearing or submit to cross-examination, the Tribunal can draw such adverse inferences as it considers appropriate.[3]

It is common to produce, without undue formality, bundles of testimonials as to the respondent's good character. This can be by way of pure mitigation but can also be directly relevant to issues of honesty and integrity. Such evidence is relevant and admissible where the disciplinary allegations brought against the solicitor impugn his or her honesty.[4]

1   Rule 28(2) and (5) of the 2019 Rule.
2   *Iqbal v SRA* [2012] EWHC 3251 (Admin) at [25].
3   Rule 33 of the 2019 Rules.
4   *Donkin v Law Society* [2007] EWHC 414 (Admin) and *Bryant and Bench v Law Society* [2007] EWHC 3043 (Admin).

Disputed facts and hearsay evidence

21.29

The nature of legal practice means that normally the case against the solicitor is largely or wholly documented. The primary evidence against the respondent in most cases is likely to be the content of his or her own accounts records and files. Serious disputes of fact relating to the underlying events in the prosecution case are comparatively rare, and often it is unnecessary for the applicant to call any oral evidence. The outcome of the case will usually depend upon the respondent's explanation for the accounts records and the documents in the files.

The applicant will normally serve a notice to admit the authenticity of the documents. Under rule 28(6) of the 2019 Rules, any party may (not later than 21 days before the date fixed for the hearing) request any other party to agree that any document may be admitted as evidence. In the absence of a counter-notice requiring authenticity to be proved, the recipient will be deemed to have admitted the document unless otherwise ordered by the Tribunal.[1]

Under rule 28(3) of the 2019 Rules each party must notify the other parties if they require any witnesses to attend for cross-examination, no later than seven days after service of witness statements. If no party requires the attendance of a witness, the Tribunal may accept the statement of the witness as evidence.[2]

As for hearsay evidence, the 2019 Rules import the hearsay provisions in the Civil Evidence Act 1995 into disciplinary proceedings before the Tribunal.[3]

Under rule 13(4) of the 2007 Rules, the applicant was entitled to serve a notice requiring the respondent to indicate within 14 days which of the facts set out in the rule 5 statement were in dispute. This was invariably done in a standard form letter at an early stage. There was no sanction for any failure to admit the facts (other than in costs). The 2019 rules do not include a similar procedure for service of a notice to admit facts: this is a welcome omission.

1   Rule 28(6)–(8) of the 2019 Rules.
2   Rule 28(1)–(3) of the 2019 Rules.
3   Rule 29 of the 2019 Rules. See also *R (Bonhoeffer) v General Medical Council* [2011] EWHC 1585 (Admin).

Witness summonses

21.30

Either party may compel the attendance of witnesses and the production by witnesses of documents by means of witness summonses.[1] Witness summonses are issued by the Administrative Court (not the Tribunal) under CPR rule 34.4 and the summons must be compliant with the Civil Procedure Rules 1998.

1   Section 46(11) of SA 1974 and rule 28(4) of the 2019 Rules.

Findings of another court or tribunal

21.31

Findings of fact by another court or tribunal are admissible as prima facie proof of those facts. Accordingly, civil judgments relevant to issues before the Tribunal can be admitted into evidence but may be rebutted. The Tribunal is free to depart from findings in civil proceedings and has done so in several cases,[1] although it will be slow to do so.[2] The situation in relation to criminal convictions is otherwise: it has been held that the Tribunal was right to refuse to hear evidence intended to show a wrongful conviction, as public policy required that, save in exceptional circumstances, a challenge to a criminal conviction should not be entertained by a disciplinary tribunal.[3] The 2019 Rules make explicit provision for these matters: findings of fact upon which a criminal conviction was based are admissible as conclusive proof of those facts save in exceptional circumstances, whereas a civil court judgment is admissible as proof but not conclusive proof of the findings of fact upon which the judgment was based.[4]

As for views formed by a judge in earlier proceedings, in *Constantinides v Law Society*,[5] Moses LJ stated at [28]–[33]:

> '[28] ... The judgment was admissible to prove background facts in the context of which the appellant's misconduct had to be considered. But that was the limit of its function, in the particular circumstances of this case. The judge's views as to the appellant's dishonesty and lack of integrity were not admissible to prove the Law Society's case against this appellant in these disciplinary proceedings ...
>
> [33] We ought, however, to record that we do not see why it was necessary to refer to the judgment at all. The background facts were not in dispute. Provided they were clearly set out within the Rule 4 statement there was no need to rely upon it save in so far as it emerged that the appellant disputed those primary facts. However, the Rule 4 statement was itself a mixture of assertion of fact and argument. We would suggest that had a simple account of the facts been set out with a reference to relevant paragraphs in the judgment there would have been no further need to refer to it.'

1 See *Gold*, 6050–1991, SDT; *Brebner*, 8805–2003, SDT; *Slater*, 9619–2006, SDT; and, for the general approach, *Choudry v Law Society* [2001] EWHC Admin 633.
2 See *General Medical Council v Spackman* [1943] AC 627, HL.
3 *Re a Solicitor*, *Times*, 18 March 1996.
4 Rule 32 of the 2019 Rules.
5 [2006] EWHC 725 (Admin).

Pre-trial publication of disciplinary allegations

21.32

The SRA's written guidance, 'Publishing regulatory and disciplinary decisions', states that there is a public interest in being transparent and that the SRA generally expects to publish its decisions to issue proceedings before the Tribunal once the Tribunal has certified there is a case to answer. The guidance states that a decision may be made not to publish if the publication would lead to disclosure of confidential or privileged information. In addition the SRA may decide not to publish if satisfied that:

> 'in all the circumstances the impact of publication on the regulated person would be disproportionate. In particular, we need to consider Article 8 of the European Convention on Human Rights and balance the right to a private life with the legitimate aim of publication.'[1]

The legality of an earlier SRA publication policy was challenged unsuccessfully in *Andersons v SRA*.[2]

1 Online guidance note 'Publishing regulatory and disciplinary decisions', SRA, 10 August 2016.
2 [2012] EWHC 3659 (Admin).

21.33

The Tribunal publishes a cause list of all interim and substantive hearings on its website, and a paper copy of the daily cause list is displayed in the Tribunal building. The Tribunal has a discretion to direct that a name on the cause list should be anonymised. The 2019 rules state that an application for anonymisation can be made on the grounds of exceptional hardship or exceptional prejudice to a party, a witness or any person affected by the proceedings. The application should be made no later than 28 days before the hearing.[1]

1 Rule 34 of the 2019 Rules.

Pre-trial procedure – what happens in practice

21.34

Following a decision to refer a solicitor to the Tribunal the solicitor will receive, after an interval, confirmation from the SRA that the papers have been referred to the SRA's external solicitors or to an in-house advocate. On the assumption that the Tribunal determines that there is a case to answer, the next development will be service of the papers. It is not unusual for there to be a delay of several months before proceedings are issued.

Service is arranged by the Tribunal by special delivery mail. It is possible to inform the applicant in advance that papers can be served on a nominated representative. The documents served will include the rule 12 statement and any documents annexed or exhibited to it, a full set of the current Solicitors (Disciplinary Proceedings) Rules, copies of the Tribunal's published practice directions, a list of those most regularly appearing in the Tribunal as advocates, and details of the Solicitors' Assistance Scheme.

21.35

The Tribunal generally sits between two and three days a week, in addition to any court time needed for multi-day cases, and has four courtrooms so that long cases can be accommodated in one court while routine matters occupy the other courts in greater numbers. A typical list of routine matters will have three to five applications listed for hearing. Because the Tribunal members pre-read the papers and most cases are well documented (see above), even quite substantial contests can be disposed of in less than a day.

The Tribunal expects the parties to have a sensible dialogue to refine issues and avoid unnecessary contention. The overwhelming majority of cases proceed on the basis of admissions and mitigation, or on the basis of admitted facts with argument limited to the proper interpretation of those facts and the inferences that it is proper to draw. In cases which are likely to last three days or more, there will be a case management hearing. Only infrequently, in very substantial or complex cases, is there any need to consider other interim applications. For example, even if there is a perceived need for the applicant to clarify the case the respondent has to meet, one would expect that clarification to be volunteered without the need for any formal intervention by the Tribunal.

Absence of the respondent from the substantive hearing

21.36

The Tribunal may proceed in the absence of the respondent upon proof of service of the notice of hearing.[1] This regularly occurs. Where a respondent is neither present nor represented, and the Tribunal decides the case in his absence, he may apply for a re-hearing within 14 days of the filing of the order (in practice therefore within 14 days of the hearing) – which the Tribunal may grant upon such terms as it thinks fit.[2] A solicitor who voluntarily absents himself from the hearing will ordinarily, however, receive little sympathy from the Tribunal, and is unlikely to obtain a re-hearing. In *R (Elliott) v Solicitors Disciplinary Tribunal*,[3] the applicant applied for an adjournment of the substantive hearing, and then walked out when the adjournment was refused. The Tribunal heard the remainder of the case in his absence, and subsequently refused an application for a re-hearing. It was held in judicial review proceedings that the rule (then rule 25 of the 1994 Rules) did not apply to such a situation.

1 Rule 36 of the 2019 Rules.
2 Rule 37(1) of the 2019 Rules.
3 [2004] EWHC 1176 (Admin). See also *Gurpinar v SRA* [2012] EWHC 192 (Admin).

CHAPTER 22

Proceedings before the SDT: (2) trial, sanctions, costs and appeals

The hearing

22.1

The Solicitors Disciplinary Tribunal (the Tribunal or SDT) sits in Gate House, at the south (Ludgate Circus) end of Farringdon Street, London EC4M 7LG. Hearings in the Tribunal are a mixture of the formal and informal; evidence is taken on oath but, as has been seen, the strict rules of evidence do not apply. The parties conduct their advocacy seated, and the hearings are recorded. No pleas to the allegations are formally taken. The applicant is expected to have established the position in this respect and will inform the Tribunal which allegations are admitted and which require to be resolved by the Tribunal. The respondent is required to do no more at this stage, hopefully, than give a monosyllabic confirmation.

The applicant will then open the case and call his or her evidence. As has been said, only rarely is it necessary for the applicant to rely on oral evidence, and usually the applicant's case can be presented entirely by reference to documents, including the written explanations and submissions of the respondent at the investigation stage. The one witness most frequently called by applicants will be the investigating officer of the Solicitors Regulation Authority (SRA)'s Forensic Investigation Unit who undertook the original investigation of, for example, the respondent's accounts.

Examination, cross-examination and re-examination of witnesses proceed as normal, following the pattern of the civil courts as to the use of any witness statement as primary evidence-in-chief.

Following the conclusion of the applicant's case the respondent may make a submission of no case to answer,[1] and then will open his or her case, give evidence and call witnesses, and may make a closing submission. In contested cases it tends to be assumed that the respondent will give evidence; in cases where the respondent is accused of and denies dishonesty it would be an exceptional course to fail to do so, and the Tribunal may draw an adverse inference from such a failure.[2] Once the evidence is completed, ordinarily the defence advocate will make a closing speech. It is not usual for the applicant (usually the SRA) to make a closing speech, but exceptionally and with the permission of the Tribunal he or she may do so in a lengthy or complex case where evidence can helpfully be summarised and commented upon. The applicant does not have a right of reply save in relation to points of law or to correct mistakes.[3]

---

1   The Tribunal has frequently demonstrated a reluctance to accede to such a submission. There is at this stage in a contested application an understandable interest in hearing what the respondent has to say. For an exceptional case in which the Tribunal acceded to such a submission see *Cohen and others*, 9942–2008, SDT.

2   See *Iqbal v SRA* [2012] EWHC 3251 (Admin) and rule 33 of the Solicitors (Disciplinary Proceedings) Rules 2019 (SI 2019/1185) (the '2019 Rules').

3   This should be taken to reflect current practice; there is no formal rule as to this.

Standard of proof

22.2

By rule 5 of the 2019 Rules the Tribunal applies the civil standard of proof.[1]

1 The 2007 Rules did not specfy the standard of proof and the Tribunal has applied the criminal standard to cases proceeding under the 2007 rules. The adoption of the criminal standard was supported by high authority. In *Campbell v Hamlet* [2005] UKPC 19, [2005] 3 All ER 1116, interpreting *Re a Solicitor* [1993] QB 69, it was held by the Privy Council that the standard of proof in deciding facts against a respondent solicitor in disciplinary proceedings should be the criminal standard, irrespective of whether dishonesty is alleged. In *Richards v Law Society* [2009] EWHC 2087 (Admin) the SRA sought to argue for the civil standard. The Divisional Court held that on the particular facts of the case, the issue was academic, but strongly implied that the Tribunal was bound to apply the criminal standard unless and until the Supreme Court ruled otherwise. See also *Law Society v Waddingham and others* [2012] EWHC 1519 (Admin), in which the SRA appealed against a finding by the Tribunal that it was not satisfied that dishonesty had been proved against two of the respondents: the High Court dismissed the appeal specifically on the basis that dishonesty had not been established to the criminal standard (at [60]). However, the regulatory tide generally was flowing in the direction of replacing the criminal standard with the civil standard in professional disciplinary proceedings, and in 2016 the High Court said the authorities were 'ripe for reconsideration': see *Solicitors Regulation Authority v Solicitors' Disciplinary Tribunal, ex p Arslan* [2016] EWHC 2862 (Admin) at [49] and [73]. In July 2018 the Tribunal issued a consultation paper on its new rules questioning whether the criminal standard should continue to apply, and a decision was made to apply the civil standard. The LSB approved the new rules adopting the civil standard on 25 July 2019. The statutory instrument for the new rules was made on 6 August 2019, with the new rules coming into force on 25 November 2019.

Decision, mitigation and penalty

22.3

The Tribunal invariably announces its findings, together with brief reasons, at the conclusion of the hearing. If it finds any of the allegations against the respondent substantiated, the Chairman asks the Tribunal clerk whether there have been previous findings against the respondent. The respondent is permitted to make a plea in mitigation (possibly at this stage adducing testimonials as to character) and the Tribunal then determines penalty.[1] If the Tribunal decides to suspend a solicitor, it may be prepared to delay the start of that suspension to enable the solicitor to make appropriate arrangements for running his practice during the period of suspension. The Tribunal is noticeably more reluctant to delay the effect of a striking-off order although this does occasionally happen.[2] Respondents seeking a stay pending appeal must, if the Tribunal does not grant a stay, appeal and apply to the Administrative Court for a stay pending a hearing of the substantive appeal. The appeal does not operate as a stay. For further guidance on appeals, see **22.42** to **22.50**.

1 This summary of the practice is enshrined in rule 41 of the 2019 Rules. Rule 40(1) of the 2019 Rules contains a provision that the Tribunal may reserve its decision for announcement at a later date, but in practice the decision is announced at the conclusion of the hearing.
2 *Aaronson*, 10099–2008, SDT.

The written judgment of the Tribunal

22.4

The written judgment of the Tribunal is ordinarily delivered some weeks after the hearing. In *Virdi v Law Society*[1] a full-scale attack was made on the Tribunal's process for production of the findings, on the basis that the clerk had a role in producing a first draft of the document based, inter alia, on the oral findings and reasons given by the Chairman at the conclusion of the hearing. Although the (exceptional) delay in producing the findings in that case was the subject of criticism, the process was held to be entirely proper by both the Divisional Court and the Court of Appeal.

By section 48 of the Solicitors Act (SA) 1974, a statement of the Tribunal's findings must be filed with the Law Society and the files are open to public inspection. The Tribunal also publishes its written judgments on the Tribunal website.

The Tribunal may make directions prohibiting publication of specified information relating to the proceedings including direction for anonymisation of the names of the respondents or any other persons.[2] In 2016 in *SRA v Spector*[3] the Tribunal anonymised the identities of the respondents who had been acquitted after the case was heard in public. On appeal, the Divisional Court held that there was no legal ground upon which the principle of open justice could be disapplied: the proceedings had been freely reportable, and the public had been able to attend the public hearing of the case. There was as much legitimate public interest in an acquittal as in a disciplinary 'conviction', and the importance of open justice was such that anonymisation of acquitted respondents was impermissible.

In October 2018 the Tribunal published a judgment publication policy stating that any application for restrictions on publication will be considered on its own merits. Factors supporting publication include the principle of open justice and the need to maintain public confidence in the profession. The fact that a case has been heard in private does not mean that the Tribunal must decide that the judgment should be anonymised. The policy also specifies the time periods for different categories of judgments to remain on the website.[4]

1   [2009] EWHC 918 (Admin) (Divisional Court); [2010] EWCA Civ 100 (Court of Appeal).
2   See rule 35(9) and (10) of the 2019 Rules and the Tribunal's 'Judgment Publication Policy' (updated October 2018, available on its website).
3   [2016] EWHC 37 (Admin), [2016] 4 WLR 16.
4   The Tribunal's 'Judgment Publication Policy', October 2018.

The range of penalties available to the Tribunal and Tribunal guidance

22.5

From the 'bottom' upwards, where allegations are proved or admitted, the Tribunal may:

- make no order – this course is followed when the Tribunal considers that it would be unfair or disproportionate to impose a sanction. It may nevertheless decide to make an order for costs against the respondent solicitor;

- impose a reprimand;

- impose an unlimited fine;

- impose a restriction order;

- suspend, either for a fixed period or indefinitely;

- strike off.

22.6

Until the summer of 2012, the Tribunal provided no published guidance to the profession or the public as to how it exercised its disciplinary powers. This was the subject of criticism by Nicola Davies J in *Hazelhurst v SRA*[1] in which she said (at [38]):

> 'It is of note that the SDT has not published Indicative Sanctions Guidance. Such guidance identifies the purpose, parameters and range of sanctions. It permits those who appear before it to better understand the proceedings and the thinking of the SDT. It assists the transparency of the proceedings. Such guidance has been used by other regulatory bodies for some years and is a valuable reference point both for the tribunal and for those who appear in front of it, as practitioners or advocates.'

Following that criticism, a Guidance Note on Sanctions was issued by the Tribunal in late August 2012 and has since been periodically updated. The current (sixth) edition came into force in December 2018. It is reproduced in full in **APPENDIX 16**. It sets out the Tribunal's principles, procedure and policies in imposing sanctions.

1   [2011] EWHC 462 (Admin).

The general approach – Bolton v Law Society

22.7

In *Bolton v Law Society*,[1] the Master of the Rolls, Sir Thomas Bingham, made a general and oft-cited statement of the rationale for and purpose of punishment by the Tribunal. It merits citation here, as it provides the logical cornerstone for much of what both the Tribunal and appellate courts decide:

> 'It is required of lawyers practising in this country that they should discharge their professional duties with integrity, probity and complete trustworthiness …
>
> Any solicitor who is shown to have discharged his professional duties with anything less than complete integrity, probity and trustworthiness must expect severe sanctions to be imposed upon him by the Solicitors Disciplinary Tribunal. Lapses from the required high standard may, of course, take different forms and be of varying degrees. The most serious involves proven dishonesty, whether or not leading to criminal proceedings and criminal penalties. In such cases the tribunal has almost invariably, no matter how strong the mitigation advanced for the solicitor, ordered that he be struck off the Roll of Solicitors … If a solicitor is not shown to have acted dishonestly, but is shown to have fallen below the required standards of integrity, probity and trustworthiness, his lapse is less serious but it remains very serious indeed in a member of a profession whose reputation depends upon trust. A striking off order will not necessarily follow in such a case, but it may well. The decision whether to strike off or to suspend will often involve a fine and difficult exercise of judgment, to be made by the tribunal as an informed and expert body on all the facts of the case. Only in

a very unusual and venial case of this kind would the tribunal be likely to regard as appropriate any order less severe than one of suspension.'

1   [1994] 1 WLR 512, CA.

Reprimands

22.8

Although it has no express statutory power to do so, the Tribunal frequently issues a reprimand to a solicitor. It has also censured a solicitor, stating that this was a more serious order than a reprimand and has directed a solicitor to pay counsels' fees (thereby making an unenforceable obligation enforceable as a High Court order).[1]

1   *Prince*, 6578–1994, SDT, unsuccessfully appealed as *Re a Solicitor*, CO 1324–1995. See also section 48(4) of SA 1974.

Fines

22.9

Since March 2009, there is no statutory limit on the amount of the fine (until then it was £5,000 per allegation). Fines are payable to the Treasury, which is responsible for enforcing payment.

The Guidance Note on Sanctions sets out five indicative fine bands ranging from fines of £2,000 or less for the lowest level of misconduct which justifies a fine rather than a reprimand (level 1) to fines over £50,000 for conduct assessed as significantly serious but falling short of conduct resulting in suspension or strike off (level 5).[1]

In practice, it is unusual for a fine against an individual to exceed £25,000, and the vast majority fall below that level. Fines against some entities are higher, but it is unusual for a fine against a firm to exceed £35,000.

A very small number of fines have been significantly higher, and the level of those high fines has increased over time. Up to 2014, the highest fine was £50,000 imposed in the case of *Fuglers v SRA*[2] upon the firm, with the two respondent partners being fined £20,000 and £5,000. In 2015 a fine of £305,000 was imposed on an individual in *Harvie*.[3] In July 2017 a fine of £250,000 was imposed on White & Case LLP under an agreed outcome,[4] and in November 2017 a fine of £500,000 was imposed on Locke Lord (UK) LLP under an agreed outcome.[5]

The general approach of the Tribunal to the level of fines was supported by the High Court in *SRA v Andersons and others*.[6] For the first time the SRA launched an appeal simply to obtain an increase in the fines imposed by the Tribunal. Although the High Court did order an increase in the fines (from £1,000 upon each of the individual respondents to £15,000 on one respondent and £5,000 in the others), these increases fell far below the figures contended for by the SRA. It would seem therefore, that the general approach of the Tribunal to individual solicitors is unlikely to change, unless, for instance, the Tribunal is satisfied that a solicitor has deliberately breached the rules in order to make a substantial profit. In such a case, it would be open to the Tribunal to impose a very substantial fine, as it did in *Harvie*. The position of large firms, with high turnovers, is different however, which explains some of the high six-figure fines that have been seen in recent times.

1   SDT Guidance Note on Sanctions, para 29.
2   [2014] EWHC 179 (Admin).
3   11257–2014, SDT.
4   11592–2016, SDT.
5   11592–2017, SDT.
6   [2013] EWHC 4021 (Admin).

22.10

As in the criminal courts, the financial circumstances of the respondent are highly relevant to the decision on the level of the fine. This was made clear in *D'Souza v Law Society*,[1] in which no apparent account had been taken of the admittedly parlous circumstances of Mr D'Souza, who had been ordered to pay a fine of £1,500 and costs in the order of £8,000. The total was reduced on appeal from £9,500 to £2,000: £500 by way of fine and £1,500 for costs.[2]

In imposing a financial penalty, the Tribunal should consider the respondent's overall financial liability for the fine and costs. In *Matthews v SRA*,[3] Collins J reduced a fine of £5,000 and costs of £16,000 to an overall liability of £5,000 on account of the appellant's limited means. The costs, which made up £4,500 of this sum, were not to be enforced without leave of the Tribunal.

Rule 43(5) of the 2019 Rules states that a respondent who wishes his means to be taken into account should provide a statement of means and supported by documentary evidence. The time for service of the statement is normally specified in the standard directions as 28 days before the substantive hearing.[4]

1   [2009] EWHC 2193 (Admin).
2   See also *Tinkler and others v SRA* [2012] EWHC 3645 (Admin) and the Guidance Note on Sanctions under the heading 'Level of Fine' at **APPENDIX 16**. The respondent's means may also be highly relevant to the correct costs order and this is discussed below at **22.37**.
3   [2013] EWHC 1525 (Admin).
4   Rule 43 of the 2019 Rules relates to costs, but the statement could be relied on in support of representations on the level of the fine. In practice it is rare for the Tribunal to take account of means when considering the level of the fine.

Restriction orders

22.11

The Tribunal has no power itself to impose conditions on a practising certificate when imposing a penalty upon a solicitor, but because it can make 'such order as it may think fit', it can also make orders requiring a solicitor not to practise in particular ways, for example as a sole practitioner.

In *Camacho v Law Society*,[1] the Tribunal had ordered the indefinite suspension of a solicitor. On the solicitor's appeal, the Divisional Court substituted a finite period of suspension but identified five conditions which it considered should be imposed in relation to the way in which the solicitor might practise. The court held that the terms of section 47(2) of SA 1974 were sufficiently wide to give the Tribunal itself power to impose restrictions on the manner in which a solicitor might practise, and that if the Tribunal considered that a period of complete suspension followed by a period of restricted practice was the appropriate sanction to protect the public, that was part of the decision it had made and – unless there were exceptional reasons – it should be for the Tribunal to make that order, rather than to make recommendations to the SRA as had been the former practice.

Where the Tribunal makes such an order for an indefinite period it should grant liberty to apply, as there is otherwise no mechanism for a solicitor subject to such an order to apply for it to be varied or reviewed.[2]

The Tribunal has on occasion refined this approach by imposing a suspension from practice for one year, but suspending that order for so long as the solicitor practised only (in substance) in employment expressly approved by the SRA without access to clients' money. The Tribunal gave guidance as to the circumstances in which an application might be made to the Tribunal to vary or revoke the terms of the restriction.[3]

Restriction orders are only made when considered necessary to protect the public or the reputation of the profession – they have no punitive function.[4] Inevitably, when the Tribunal makes such orders the SRA can be expected to impose matching or more restrictive practising certificate conditions.

1   [2004] EWHC 1675 (Admin), [2004] 1 WLR 3037. See too *Ebhogiaye v SRA* [2013] EWHC 2445 (Admin).
2   *Taylor v Law Society* [2005] EWCA Civ 1473. The formula substituted on appeal to the Master of the Rolls in *Taylor* was: 'In the future the petitioner may not practise as a sole practitioner but only in employment or partnership. When employed he must not operate a client account. The petitioner to have liberty to apply to the Tribunal to vary these conditions'.
3   *Bajela and Fonkwo*, 9543–2006, SDT.
4   See SDT Guidance Note on Sanctions, para 33.

Suspensions

22.12

Suspensions may be for a fixed term or for an indefinite period. The effect of a suspension for a solicitor will vary according to the size of the practice. For a middle-aged sole practitioner, suspension may in reality be equivalent to a striking off, as it may prove impossible for the solicitor to arrange cover during the period of the suspension, and/or the solicitor may face insurmountable practising certificate conditions when he or she returns to practice. For a solicitor working in a large firm, whose partners/employers have not dismissed him or her, the effect of a short suspension may be little more than an inconvenience.

Indefinite suspensions are usually imposed where there is a medical explanation for the solicitor's misconduct, or where there is truly exceptional personal mitigation. Such suspensions come within a whisker of a striking off, but the Tribunal may consider that there is a real prospect of successful rehabilitation, thus meriting an order which will not make it impossible for the solicitor to resume practice.[1]

Suspensions are normally imposed for one year or more. Where they are for a period of months (or less) it is important to note that the expiry of the suspension does not enable an automatic return to practice. The solicitor's practising certificate is not automatically restored; rather it remains suspended until the SRA terminates the suspension on the application of the solicitor (although an application may be made before the suspension expires, so minimising the consequences).[2] The termination of the suspension may be accompanied by the imposition of conditions on the practising certificate[3] and almost certainly will.

Suspensions may themselves be suspended, when accompanied by a restriction order.[4] An order of suspended suspension should make clear that the suspension will be activated if there is further misconduct during the period of suspension. As pointed out by Flaux LJ in *SRA v James, MacGregor and Naylor*[5] at [125]:

> 'There is a certain illogicality in the concept of suspension of a penalty that is itself a suspension. Suspension of striking off is easier to comprehend, since that is akin to a suspended sentence of imprisonment in criminal proceedings. However, suspended suspension is one of the range of possible sanctions available to the SDT.'

1   See para 47 of the SDT Guidance Note on Sanctions.
2   Section 16(3) of SA 1974.
3   Section 16(4).
4   See paras 41–44 of the SDT Guidance Note on Sanctions.
5   [2018] EWHC 3058 (Admin).

Striking off and restoration to the roll

22.13

A struck off solicitor can no longer describe him- or herself as a solicitor, and to do so may be a criminal offence under section 20 and/or section 21 of SA 1974. An unqualified person, as the struck off solicitor becomes, may not perform those activities which only a qualified solicitor may perform, in particular the reserved legal activities set out in the Legal Services Act (LSA) 2007. A struck off solicitor may not be employed by a solicitor without the prior consent of the SRA.[1]

1   See section 41 of SA 1974.

22.14

The Tribunal has a statutory power under section 47(1)(e) of SA 1974 to restore struck off solicitors to the roll. However, the guidance provided by the Court of Appeal in *Bolton v Law Society*[1] as to the purposes of imposing disciplinary sanctions and summarised at **22.7**, applies to applications to restore to the roll:

> 'the most fundamental [purpose] of all: to maintain the reputation of the solicitors' profession as one in which every member, of whatever standing, may be trusted to the ends of the earth. To maintain this reputation and sustain public confidence in the integrity of the profession it is often necessary that those guilty of serious lapses are not only expelled but denied re-admission.'

1   [1994] 1 WLR 512, CA at 518.

22.15

As a result, it has hitherto proved all but impossible for former solicitors who have been struck off for disciplinary offences involving dishonesty, to persuade the

Tribunal to permit restoration to the roll. The former Master of the Rolls, Lord Donaldson of Lymington said in one case:[1]

'however sympathetic one may be towards an individual member of either branch of the legal profession, if you fall very seriously below the standards of that profession and are expelled from it, there is a public interest in the profession itself in hardening its heart if any question arises of your rejoining it. Neither branch of the profession is short of people who have never fallen from grace. There is considerable public interest in the public as a whole being able to deal with members of those professions knowing that, save in the most exceptional circumstances, they can be sure that none of them have ever been guilty of any dishonesty at all.'

In his final decision as Master of the Rolls, Lord Donaldson went further, and wondered whether Parliament had ever contemplated that a solicitor who had been guilty of fraud could be restored to the roll, although he continued:[2]

'It may be that in a very exceptional case it did – something which really could be described as a momentary aberration under quite exceptional strain, the sort of strain which not everybody meets but some people do meet in the course of their everyday lives.'

To date in the modern era (that is for some three decades at least), only one solicitor who has been struck off for dishonesty has successfully applied for restoration to the roll.[3]

1   No 5 of 1987, unreported.
2   No 11 of 1990, unreported.
3   *Vane*, 8607–2002, SDT. For an example of a case in which the SRA appealed successfully against the SDT's decision to restore to the roll a solicitor who had been convicted of offences involving dishonesty, see *SRA v Kaberry* [2012] EWHC 3883 (Admin).

22.16

A former solicitor who has been struck off for less serious disciplinary offences, not involving dishonesty, may be more fortunate. In order to contemplate making an order of restoration, the Tribunal will need to be satisfied first that the former solicitor has demonstrated his or her complete rehabilitation, and secondly that restoration to the roll would not involve any damage to the reputation of the profession. Lord Donaldson encouraged the Tribunal to ask:[1]

'If this was the sort of case where, even if the back history was known (that is whatever explanation and mitigation was available to explain why the solicitor committed the original offence), and without the explanation as to what has happened subsequently, the members of the public would say "that does not shake my faith in solicitors as a whole".'

These hurdles, particularly the second, remain very difficult to surmount. Even if they are overcome, it is unlikely that the Tribunal, or the SRA, would contemplate permitting the solicitor, once restored to the roll, to practise without any form of restriction upon his or her practising certificate. Moreover, save in the most exceptional circumstances, an application for restoration to the roll within six years of the original striking off is likely to be regarded by the Tribunal as premature.

The Tribunal has published a guidance note which states that on an application for restoration the Tribunal will take account of the effect of restoration on public confidence in the profession, the period which has elapsed since the strike off, evidence of rehabilitation, the applicant's future employment intentions and the extent to which reparation has been made for any loss suffered by others as a result of the original misconduct.[2]

1   No 11 of 1990, unreported.
2   SDT Guidance Note on Other Powers of the Tribunal', December 2018, para 8.

Penalties – the approach in practice

22.17

Once again it is necessary to quote Sir Thomas Bingham in *Bolton*[1] in order to understand the rationale behind the sanctions imposed in disciplinary proceedings:

> 'It is important that there should be full understanding of the reasons why the tribunal makes orders which might otherwise seem harsh. There is, in some of these orders, a punitive element: a penalty may be visited on a solicitor who has fallen below the standards required of his profession in order to punish him for what he has done and to deter any other solicitor tempted to behave in the same way. Those are traditional objects of punishment. But often the order is not punitive in intention. Particularly is this so where a criminal penalty has been imposed and satisfied. The solicitor has paid his debt to society. There is no need, and it would be unjust, to punish him again. In most cases the order of the tribunal will be primarily directed to one or other or both of two other purposes. One is to be sure that the offender does not have the opportunity to repeat the offence. This purpose is achieved for a limited period by an order of suspension; plainly it is hoped that experience of suspension will make the offender meticulous in his future compliance with the required standards. The purpose is achieved for a longer period, and quite possibly indefinitely, by an order of striking off. The second purpose is the most fundamental of all: to maintain the reputation of the solicitors' profession as one in which every member, of whatever standing, may be trusted to the ends of the earth. To maintain this reputation and sustain public confidence in the integrity of the profession it is often necessary that those guilty of serious lapses are not only expelled but denied re-admission. If a member of the public sells his house, very often his largest asset, and entrusts the proceeds to his solicitor, pending re-investment in another house, he is ordinarily entitled to expect that the solicitor will be a person whose trustworthiness is not, and never has been, seriously in question. Otherwise, the whole profession, and the public as a whole, is injured. A profession's most valuable asset is its collective reputation and the confidence which that inspires.
>
> Because orders made by the tribunal are not primarily punitive, it follows that considerations which would ordinarily weigh in mitigation of punishment have less effect on the exercise of this jurisdiction than on the ordinary run of sentences imposed in criminal cases. It often happens that a solicitor appearing before the tribunal can adduce a wealth of glowing tributes from his professional brethren. He can often show that for him and

his family the consequences of striking off or suspension would be little short of tragic. Often he will say, convincingly, that he has learned his lesson and will not offend again. On applying for restoration after striking off, all these points may be made, and the former solicitor may also be able to point to real efforts made to re-establish himself and redeem his reputation. All these matters are relevant and should be considered. But none of them touches the essential issue, which is the need to maintain among members of the public a well-founded confidence that any solicitor whom they instruct will be a person of unquestionable integrity, probity and trust-worthiness. Thus it can never be an objection to an order of suspension in an appropriate case that the solicitor may be unable to re-establish his practice when the period of suspension is past. If that proves, or appears likely, to be so the consequence for the individual and his family may be deeply unfortunate and unintended. But it does not make suspension the wrong order if it is otherwise right. The reputation of the profession is more important than the fortunes of any individual member. Membership of a profession brings many benefits, but that is a part of the price.'

Cases before the Tribunal vary infinitely and no analytical consideration of particular facts, individual cases or individual penalties is of material assistance. There are, however, some general principles and typical classes of case that can usefully be considered.

The Tribunal adopts the procedure used in the criminal courts when the solicitor makes admissions but there is a dispute between the parties as to the facts upon which the admissions are based. In such cases, the Tribunal will hold a *Newton* hearing.[2] Often, the Tribunal does not differentiate between individual allegations when imposing a sanction. This is particularly the case with fines – the Tribunal may impose an overall fine without distinguishing between the allegations as to how the fine is calculated.[3] This may cause difficulties for the High Court on appeal where an appeal is partially successful and the court cannot know how much of the overall fine related to the allegations that have been quashed.

The SDT Guidance Note on Sanctions sets out details of how the Tribunal assesses seriousness, and what may be seen as aggravating and mitigating factors.

1 [1994] 1 WLR 512, CA at 518–19.
2 See *R v Newton* [1983] Crim LR 198, and paras 11–14 of the SDT Guidance Note on Sanctions. For an example of the events during a *Newton* hearing being considered on appeal, see *Slater v SRA* [2012] EWHC 3256 (Admin).
3 See paras 15 and 16 of the SDT Guidance Note on Sanctions.

Dishonesty in connection with client account

22.18

Such is the importance of the principle that clients' money must be held separately from a solicitor's own funds, that any dishonest misappropriation of clients' monies will lead inevitably to a striking-off order, whether or not the misappropriation also amounts to theft. This is now seen as all but automatic.[1] In *Bultitude v Law Society*,[2] the Law Society appealed against the reduction of a striking-off order to a suspension by the Divisional Court. The appeal was allowed by the Court of Appeal, and the court was informed that there was only one known instance of dishonesty in connection with client account that had not resulted in a striking off.

1   See *Bolton v Law Society* [1994] 1 WLR 512, CA; *Weston v Law Society, Times,* 15 July 1998.
2   [2004] EWCA Civ 1853.

Other forms of dishonesty

22.19

It is now well established that, save in exceptional circumstances, any solicitor who is found to have acted dishonestly will be struck off the roll. In *SRA v Sharma*[1] the Divisional Court allowed an appeal by the SRA against a three-year suspension imposed upon a solicitor who had forged documents, and sent them as 'duly signed' under cover of a letter written on his firm's notepaper. The court imposed a striking-off order in place of the suspension, and Coulson J stated (at [13]):

'(a) Save in exceptional circumstances, a finding of dishonesty will lead to the solicitor being struck off the roll, see *Bolton*[2] and *Salsbury*.[3] That is the normal and necessary penalty in cases of dishonesty: see *Bultitude*.[4]

(b)   There will be a small residual category where striking off will be a disproportionate sentence in all the circumstances: see *Salsbury*.

(c)   In deciding whether or not a particular case falls into that category, relevant factors will include the nature, scope and extent of the dishonesty itself; whether it was momentary, such as *Burrowes*,[5] or over a lengthy period of time, such as *Bultitude*; whether it was a benefit to the solicitor (*Burrowes*), and whether it had an adverse effect on others.'

And also (at [26]):

'The question for this court is whether in the light of the principles outlined above, the Tribunal's decision can be described as excessively lenient. If it can, then this court should substitute for the Tribunal's sentence, the sentence that it considers to be commensurate with these offences. If the sentence cannot be regarded as excessively lenient, even if it is not necessarily the sentence which this court would itself have imposed, the sentence should remain unchanged.'

1   [2010] EWHC 2022 (Admin).
2   *Bolton v Law Society* [1994] 1 WLR 512, CA.
3   *Law Society v Salsbury* [2008] EWCA Civ 1285.
4   *Bultitude v Law Society* [2004] EWCA Civ 1853.
5   *Burrowes v Law Society* [2002] EWHC 2900 (QB).

Exceptional circumstances

22.20

On a number of occasions, when the SDT has declined to strike off a solicitor who has been found to have acted dishonestly, the SRA has appealed. In every case save one (*SRA v Imram*;[1] see also *Burrowes v Law Society* and the cases referred to in the judgment[2] for earlier cases in which apparent dishonesty did not lead to a striking-off order), those appeals have succeeded and the High Court has substituted a striking-off order.[3] This pattern was followed in three appeals heard together in October 2018, *SRA v James, MacGregor and Naylor*.[4] All three solicitors had been found to have acted dishonestly in different cases at separate hearings, and on each occasion the SDT had declined to strike off, imposing instead a suspended suspension from practice. The SRA's appeals were successful, and striking-off orders were imposed by the High Court. In his judgment, Flaux LJ gave guidance as to what can and cannot constitute exceptional circumstances:[5]

'First, although it is well-established that what may amount to exceptional circumstances is in no sense prescribed and depends upon the various factors and circumstances of each individual case, it is clear from the decisions in *Sharma, Imran* and *Shaw*, that the most significant factor carrying most weight and which must therefore be the primary focus in the evaluation is the nature and extent of the dishonesty, in other words the exceptional circumstances must relate in some way to the dishonesty. This point was made very clearly by Dove J at [29] of *Imran*, where he said:

"… in my view it is not possible when assessing exceptional circumstances simply to pick off the individual features of the case. It is necessary, as the tribunal did, to record and stand back from all of those many factors, putting first and foremost in the assessment of whether or not there are exceptional circumstances the particular conclusions that had been reached about the act of dishonesty itself. The fact that many solicitors may be able to produce testimonials and may immediately confess the dishonest behaviour is certainly relevant to the determination of whether or not it is an exceptional case, but is not a factor that is likely to attract very substantial weight. Of far greater weight would be the extent of the dishonesty and the impact of that dishonesty both on the character of the particular solicitor concerned but, most importantly, on the wider reputation of the profession and how it impinges on the public's perception of the profession as a whole".'

1   [2015] EWHC 2572 (Admin).
2   [2002] EWHC 2900 (QB) at [6], [10]–[13], [17] and [20].
3   See *SRA v Tilsiter* [2009] EWHC 3787 (Admin); *SRA v Dennison* [2011] EWHC 291 (Admin) – the solicitor's appeal to the Court of Appeal failed: [2012] EWCA Civ 421; *SRA v Rahman* [2012] EWHC 1037 (Admin); and *SRA v Spence* [2012] EWHC 2977 (Admin).
4   [2018] EWHC 3058 (Admin).
5   At [101].

22.21

As for the relevance of the solicitor's mental health at the time of the dishonest act or omission, Flaux LJ observed at [103]:

'Inevitably, an assessment of the nature and extent of the dishonesty and the degree of culpability will involve an examination of what Ms Morris QC termed the "mind set" of the respondent, including whether the respondent is suffering from mental health issues and the workplace environment, as part of the overall balancing exercise. However, where the SDT has concluded that, notwithstanding any mental health issues or work or workplace related pressures, the respondent's misconduct was dishonest, the weight to be attached to those mental health and working environment issues in assessing the appropriate sanction will inevitably be less than is to be attached to other aspects of the dishonesty found, such as the length of time for which it was perpetrated, whether it was repeated and the harm which it caused, all of which must be of more significance. Certainly, it is difficult to see how in a case of dishonesty, as opposed to some lesser professional misconduct, the fact that the respondent suffered from stress and depression (whether alone or in combination with extreme pressure from the working environment) could without more amount to exceptional circumstances, a matter to which I return below.'

and, at [110]:

'… I do not consider that mental health issues, specifically stress and depression suffered by the solicitor as a consequence of work conditions or other matters can, without more, amount to "exceptional circumstances", justifying a lesser sanction than striking off where the SDT has found dishonesty.'

Non-dishonest serious misconduct and lack of integrity

22.22

It should be stressed that the absence of a finding of dishonesty does not protect a solicitor from a striking-off order. To return to what was said by Sir Thomas Bingham MR in *Bolton*:[1]

'… If a solicitor is not shown to have acted dishonestly, but is shown to have fallen below the required standards of integrity, probity and trustworthiness, his lapse is less serious but it remains very serious indeed in a member of a profession whose reputation depends upon trust. A striking off order will not necessarily follow in such a case, but it may well. The decision whether to strike off or to suspend will often involve a fine and difficult exercise of judgment, to be made by the tribunal as an informed and expert body on all the facts of the case. Only in a very unusual and venial case of this kind would the tribunal be likely to regard as appropriate any order less severe than one of suspension.'

Many solicitors have been struck off in such circumstances, and an appeal mounted on the principal basis that no finding of dishonesty has been made by the Tribunal is unlikely to attract much judicial sympathy. In *Moseley v SRA*,[2] Lewis J stated at [19]:

'In my judgment there is no requirement or presumption that, if the conduct is independent of the discharge of professional duties, then it must involve either dishonesty or a serious criminal offence, or that there be exceptional circumstances before striking off is appropriate. Rather, where the conduct complained of is found to involve a lack of integrity and diminishes public trust in the profession it may still, depending on the particular facts, be appropriate to impose the sanction of striking off the roll. Where conduct is dishonest or criminal, it is very likely that that would be the result. But even where conduct is not dishonest or criminal and even if it is unconnected the discharge of professional duties, it may justify striking off where it involves a lack of integrity or results in a diminution in the public trust in the profession.'

1   [1994] 1 WLR 512, CA at 518.
2   [2013] EWHC 2108 (Admin); see too *Afolabi v SRA* [2012] EWHC 3502 (Admin), *Law Society (SRA) v Emeana and others* [2013] EWHC 2130 (Admin) and *SRA v Good* [2019] EWHC 817 at [78]–[82].

22.23

The SRA has occasionally appealed against sanctions which it considers to have been too lenient in cases where dishonesty has not been established against the solicitor concerned. It was successful in *SRA v Uddin*[1] and *SRA v Chan and Ali*,[2] whereas it was unsuccessful in *SRA v Norman*.[3]

1   [2014] EWHC 4553 (Admin).
2   [2015] EWHC 2659 (Admin).
3   [2013] EWHC 3886 (Admin).

Breaches of the SRA Accounts Rules

22.24

Breaches of the Accounts Rules can range from the serious to the trivial. Improper transfers from client accounts to office accounts falling short of dishonesty may merit a striking-off order or suspension, as may a chaotic accounting system which creates risk to clients and to the public. The importance of regular reconciliations and accountants' reports cannot be overestimated, as these are the mechanisms by which problems can be detected at a relatively early stage. Other administrative failings and errors, including failure to carry out reconciliations timeously or to obtain accountants' reports at the correct time, if standing alone, are likely to be visited with a fine.

Solicitors providing banking facilities

22.25

Since 2011, the SRA has taken a vigorous approach to investigating and pursuing allegations that client accounts have been misused to provide banking facilities. There have been a number of cases in which solicitors who have provided banking facilities to clients have been fined by the Tribunal.[1]

Rule 14.5 of the SRA Accounts Rules 2011 provides:

> 'You must not provide banking facilities through a client account. Payments into, and transfers or withdrawals from, a client account must be in respect of instructions relating to an underlying transaction (and the funds arising therefrom) or to a service forming part of your normal regulated activities.'

The precise meaning of the 2011 rule has led to disputes on construction in the High Court: In *Patel v SRA*, Moore Bick LJ stated at [42]–[43]:

> '[Counsel for the Appellant] submitted that the word "or" is to be read disjunctively and that the existence of an underlying transaction of any kind which a solicitor can lawfully undertake, including one that does not form part of a solicitor's normal professional activities, is capable of supporting the use of a client account. The tribunal, he submitted, had erred in conflating the two limbs of rule 14.5 which had led it to hold that there must be an underlying transaction of a legal nature.
>
> In my view that argument states the position too broadly. The primary purpose of maintaining a client account is to segregate funds held for the

client from the solicitor's own funds in order to provide the client with a measure of protection. One would therefore expect it to be used to hold funds which have come into the solicitor's hands in relation to services carried out for the client, to be paid out in due course to the client or in accordance with his instructions. Rule 14.5 of the SRA Accounts Rules refers to instructions relating to an underlying transaction or a service forming part of the solicitor's normal regulated activities.'

The SRA issued a warning notice in December 2014, which contained guidance on the meaning of the banking facilities. The warning notice was updated in August 2018 and this is set out in **APPENDIX 9**.[2]

Rule 3.3 of the SRA Accounts Rules 2019 amended the rule on banking facilities. Rule 3.3 provides:

'You must not use a client account to provide banking facilities to clients or third parties. Payments into, and transfers or withdrawals from a client account must be in respect of the delivery by you of regulated services.'

The guidance on the prohibition of banking facilities in the August 2018 warning notice is as relevant to the SRA Accounts Rules 2019 as it is to the SRA Accounts Rules 2011.

1   See *Wood & Burdett*, 8669–2002, SDT; *Patel v SRA* [2012] EWHC 3373 (Admin); and *Fuglers v SRA* [2014] EWHC 179 (Admin).
2   The warning notice includes 'Case studies: improper use of client account as a banking facility', SRA, 6 August 2018.

Culpable or dishonest overcharging

22.26

There is potentially a wide spectrum of 'overcharging' by a solicitor. The reduction of a solicitor/own client bill at a detailed assessment is an everyday experience for solicitors and implies no professional misconduct of any sort. Where such a reduction is very substantial, however, the solicitor may be open to a charge of 'culpable overcharging'. As a rule of thumb, if a bill is reduced by more than 50 per cent on assessment, this may give cause for regulatory concern, and may lead to further investigation (and possible disciplinary proceedings).[1] The concept of culpable overcharging does not incorporate within it any implication or allegation of dishonesty.

At the most serious end of the spectrum is dishonest overcharging, where the solicitor has no honest belief that the sum charged is a reasonable sum for the work done. As with any form of dishonesty, a solicitor found guilty of dishonest overcharging can expect to be struck off.

Unsurprisingly, therefore, penalties imposed by the Tribunal on this subject vary considerably. Particular care may be required in probate cases, where a solicitor may be the sole executor of the estate and there may be no independent scrutiny of his or her charges.[2] In *Sheikh v Law Society*, Chadwick LJ observed that evidence from a costs draftsman with suitable experience as to what he would expect to see in such cases provides a useful starting point in evaluating the issue as to whether there has been not merely culpable but possibly dishonest overcharging, in the sense that significant deviation from the norm may require explanation.[3]

1   This is consistent with article 5(1) of the Solicitors' (Non-Contentious Business) Remuneration Order 1994 (SI 1994/2616), since repealed, which required any costs judge who reduces a solicitor/client non-contentious bill by more than half on detailed assessment to report the matter to the Law Society.
2   See e g *Sheikh v Law Society* [2006] EWCA Civ 1577, [2007] 3 All ER 183 at [45].
3   *Sheikh v Law Society* [2006] EWCA Civ 1577, [2007] 3 All ER 183 at [64].

Conflicts of interest

22.27

Actual or potential conflicts of interests may arise in a variety of ways and those of a relatively innocent nature, such as those due to an error of judgement, will merit no more than a fine.[1] Some conflicts are infinitely more serious and involve solicitors deliberately or recklessly preferring their own interests to those of their clients, for example, by obtaining unsecured loans from clients without ensuring that the clients receive independent advice. These are likely to be regarded very seriously and to result in the solicitor being struck off.[2]

1   For example *O'Brien*, 9574–2006, SDT (the 'Freshfields Two' case).
2   Unhappily, there have been very many cases in this category. Examples are *Predko*, 7099–1996, SDT, *Austin-Olsen*, 9361–2005, SDT and *Beller v Law Society* [2009] EWHC 2200 (Admin).

Payment of referral fees

22.28

As described above (at **4.45**), until 2004, there was an outright ban on the payment of referral fees by solicitors to introducers of work. This proved difficult to enforce, and there were concerns that it might offend competition law. In 2004 the ban was abolished. Instead, the Law Society required that solicitors be transparent about the fact and amount of referral fees in a new section 2A of the Solicitors' Introduction and Referral Code. This was substantially replicated by Chapter 9 of the SRA Code of Conduct 2011, and very similar provisions are now contained in paragraph 5 of the SRA Code of Conduct for Solicitors, RELs and RFLs 2019 and paragraph 7.1 of the SRA Code of Conduct for Firms 2019. The Tribunal recognised that regulation in this area had proved to be problematic and in the past dealt with such cases by way of a fine, save where there had been a deliberate and wholesale breach of the ban.[1]

It is likely that both the SRA and the Tribunal will take a less emollient view towards breaches of the referral fee ban in the Legal Aid, Sentencing and Punishment of Offenders Act (LASPO) 2012 than in the past. The ban is imposed by an Act of Parliament rather than a somewhat controversial professional rule. The Government will expect the ban to be enforced by the regulators, and part of that enforcement is likely to involve significant penalties being imposed upon those who transgress. However, at the time of writing there have been no prosecutions arising out of the LASPO 2012 ban.

1   For example, *Mendelson*, 9212–2005, SDT. In *Barber and others*, 9698–2007, SDT, two solicitors were suspended for deliberate and wholesale breach of the ban, in the context of the miners' compensation cases.

Misleading the court

22.29

Solicitors have a pivotal role in the administration of justice, and owe duties to the court which can sometimes override their duties to the lay client. The courts depend upon the legal profession to discharge its duties to them in order to ensure that cases can be efficiently determined. A useful summary of an advocate's duty is set out by Lord Steyn in *Arthur JS Hall v Simons:*[1]

> 'Lawyers conducting litigation owe a divided loyalty. They have a duty to their clients, but they may not win by whatever means. They also owe a duty to the court and the administration of justice. They may not mislead the court or allow the judge to take what they know to be a bad point in their favour. They must cite all relevant law, whether for or against their case. They may not make imputations of dishonesty unless they have been given the information to support them. They should not waste time on irrelevancies even if the client thinks that they are important. Sometimes the performance of these duties to the court may annoy the client. So, it was said, the possibility of a claim for negligence might inhibit the lawyer from acting in accordance with his overriding duty to the court. That would be prejudicial to the administration of justice.'

1   [2002] 1 AC 615, HL at 686.

22.30

As a result, any misleading of the court will be dealt with severely by the Tribunal. As stated by Lord Thomas CJ in *Brett v SRA:*[1]

> 'Every lawyer must be alive to the fact that circumstances can arise during the course of any lawyer's professional practice when matters come to his knowledge (or are obvious to him) which may have the effect of making his duty to the court his paramount duty and to act in the interests of justice. In many cases it will be clear what course the lawyer must take, either through the way in which the case is presented or by withdrawing from acting for the client. In others it may be more difficult. The lawyer may not be absolutely sure that his actions will discharge his duty to the court. In such a case, for reasons which I shall explain, a lawyer would be ill-advised if he did not put the matters before a person more senior within his firm or before independent counsel, making full and complete disclosure to such a person of all the relevant circumstances.
>
> The reason why that is so important is that misleading the court is regarded by the court and must be regarded by any disciplinary tribunal as one of the most serious offences that an advocate or litigator can commit. It is not simply a breach of a rule of a game, but a fundamental affront to a rule designed to safeguard the fairness and justice of proceedings. Such conduct will normally attract an exemplary and deterrent sentence. That is in part because our system for the administration of justice relies so heavily upon the integrity of the profession and the full discharge of the profession's duties and in part because the privilege of conducting litigation or appearing in court is granted on terms that the rules are observed not

merely in their letter but in their spirit. Indeed, the reputation of the system of the administration of justice in England and Wales and the standing of the profession depends particularly upon the discharge of the duties owed to the court.'

1   [2014] EWHC 2974 (Admin) at [110]–[111].

Improper use of litigation

22.31

In recent years there has been considerable concern expressed by the senior judiciary about the improper use of litigation by solicitors on behalf of clients about to be deported from the United Kingdom. This impropriety has tended to consist of last-minute applications in cases wholly lacking in merit, in which the solicitors have failed to make full and frank disclosure to the court in accordance with their professional duties. In *Ip v SRA*,[1] the appellant had been struck off in such circumstances. His appeal to the High Court failed, and Irwin LJ observed at [180]–[181]:

'The Courts well understand the vulnerability of many of those at risk of removal or deportation from the country. They can be desperate to remain. They are often prepared to grasp at straws. The Courts are also fully alive to the technicality and difficulty of immigration law, and of the Immigration Rules. These factors add to the difficulty of representing such clients. However, they also add to the responsibility of solicitors engaged for such clients.

It is critical that solicitors, and others, representing such clients, are scrupulous in observing professional standards. The cost of not doing so to the system is obvious and has been emphasised many times. Spurious, or merely hopeless, applications to courts and tribunals add greatly to the burden on the system of justice, and to the costs of government. However, it should not be forgotten that such applications also cost the applicants, both financially and in engendering prolonged and unjustified expectations. In addition, poor, and where it arises unscrupulous, representation must, to some degree at least, overshadow careful and expert immigration lawyers. The Solicitors Disciplinary Tribunal is entirely justified in taking very seriously cases such as this.'

1   [2018] EWHC 957 (Admin). See also *Malik v SRA* [2019] EWHC 37 for sanctions imposed on a COLP and co partner found to have ignored warnings that a co-partner was improperly conducting litigation.

Failure to reply to correspondence from clients and/or the SRA and the Legal Ombudsman

22.32

Failures to reply to correspondence are regarded seriously by the Tribunal, as they damage the reputation of the profession. Standing alone, such failures will merit a fine – even if the original complaint, to which the respondent failed to respond, was in fact without merit.

Tribunal's reasons for imposing sanctions

22.33

Whereas cases in which a solicitor has to be struck off or suspended will usually be fairly easy to identify, as will the misconduct that justifies such a sanction, the Tribunal nevertheless must reveal proper reasoning and explanation for selecting the sanction imposed. This was made clear by Nicola Davies J in *Hazelhurst v SRA*[1] in which she said (at [36]–[37]):

> '[36] … it is difficult to understand how the SDT decided that a monetary penalty was appropriate. No mention of other sanctions is made, no reason is given for the sum imposed nor how such sum is apportioned as between the three breaches so as to permit the respondents or indeed members of the public to understand what degree of seriousness should be attached to any given breach of the professional rules.
>
> [37] The absence of any or any adequate reasoning by the SDT as to why the sanction of the financial penalty was appropriate, the amount of that penalty and specifically in respect of any breach, how much of that penalty applied, renders it impossible for this court to determine whether the considerations of the SDT which led to the financial penalty were fair and/or reasonable.'

1   [2011] EWHC 462 (Admin) especially at [30] to [31]; see also *English v Emery Reinbold & Strick Ltd* [2002] 1 WLR 2409, CA.

Agreed outcomes[1]

22.34

An agreed outcome is a settlement agreement between the SRA and a respondent to Tribunal proceedings that has been approved by the Tribunal. An agreed outcome normally contains the following terms:

- a list of the allegations which are admitted by the respondent;

- a list of any allegations which are not admitted;

- an agreement as to whether the parties intend to dispose of any allegations which are not admitted by inviting the Tribunal to withdraw them or direct that they should lie on the file;

- a detailed statement of the agreed facts;

- a description of the mitigation upon which the respondent relies;

- a sanction which the parties agree to invite the Tribunal to impose by order;

- an explanation why the sanction is appropriate having regard to the Tribunal's Guidance Note on Sanctions;

- an agreement to pay the SRA's costs;

- a declaration signed by the parties confirming that the facts in the statement are true and that the parties agree to the outcome.

1   See also **20.18** on regulatory settlement agreements.

22.35

In practice the SRA is willing to negotiate agreed outcomes with most respondents unless dishonesty is alleged or there are other allegations which are so serious they are likely to lead to a strike-off if proved.[1] A respondent wishing to negotiate an agreed outcome should approach the SRA early in the proceedings, as negotiations with the SRA can take a long period of time and rule 25(1) of the 2019 Rules provides that any agreed outcome should be submitted to the Tribunal for approval not less than 28 days before the substantive hearing.

If an agreed outcome is submitted to the Tribunal for approval, the Tribunal will initially consider the matter on the papers, and may direct that there should be a case management hearing in private to consider submissions before making a decision. If there is more than one respondent, and the agreed outcome does not relate to all the respondents, the non-participating respondents are given an opportunity to comment before a decision is made. If the Tribunal does not approve the agreed outcome, it will give written reasons for its decision and the parties can then submit a revised proposal. If an agreed outcome is not ultimately approved the application will be treated as a without prejudice application and the substantive case will be heard before a different panel. If the agreed outcome is approved the Tribunal will make an order in the agreed terms and will announce its decision at a public hearing.[2]

1   In dishonesty cases, the SRA may exceptionally be willing to negotiate an agreed outcome if the dishonesty is admitted and the respondent agrees to a striking-off order.
2   The procedure is set out in rule 25 of the 2019 Rules.

Costs

Costs against the unsuccessful respondent

22.36

A very high percentage of applications against solicitors are successful in whole or in part and the respondent in those cases will ordinarily be ordered to pay the costs of the SRA.[1] Even if not all allegations are found proved it is the Tribunal's practice to award all the costs against the respondent if, on the facts, it was reasonable to make those allegations.[2] If there has been a substantial contest over part of the case in which the respondent has been successful, the order may be to pay a reduced percentage of the SRA's costs.

The normal order for costs in a case where there has been a forensic investigation is an order for the payment of costs 'of and incidental to the application and enquiry' to include the costs of the forensic investigation. These are usually considerable – several thousands of pounds – and can exceed the applicant's legal costs. Regrettably, there is little published material as to how these costs are calculated, and it is usually difficult or impossible for the respondent solicitor to make a meaningful challenge as to the quantum of those costs at a summary assessment by the Tribunal.

The Tribunal can endorse an agreement between the parties and make an order for fixed costs, can summarily assess the costs in appropriate circumstances, or can order that the costs be subject to detailed assessment if not agreed – with or without an interim payment of costs being directed. As orders made by the Tribunal are enforceable as orders of the High Court,[3] detailed assessment is dealt with by the Supreme Court Costs Office and the Civil Procedure Rules 1998 apply to that assessment in the usual way.

1   There is a section on costs in the SDT Guidance Note on Sanctions at paras 63–76.
2   See generally para 69 of the SDT Guidance Note on Sanctions. See also **22.40**.
3   Section 48(4) of SA 1974.

The relevance of the respondent's means

22.37

In imposing fines and making costs orders the Tribunal should take into account the means of the respondent. In particular, where a solicitor is suspended or struck off, enquiry as to the solicitor's means must be made before any decision is made.[1] These propositions were unsuccessfully attacked by the SRA in *SRA v Davis and McGlinchey*.[2] The SRA asserted that the respondent's means should be irrelevant to the making of an order for costs. This was rejected by Mitting J, who provided valuable guidance as to how the issue should be tackled in future (at [22]–[24]):

'[22]… where a solicitor admits the disciplinary charges brought against him, and who therefore anticipates the imposition of a sanction upon him, it should be incumbent upon him before the hearing to give advance notice to the SRA and to the Tribunal that he will contend either that no order for costs should be made against him, or that it should be limited in amount by reason of his own lack of means. He should also supply to the SRA and to the Tribunal, in advance of the hearing, the evidence upon which he relies to support that contention. In a case in which the solicitor disputes the charges brought against him, it would be burdensome to impose an advance obligation upon him of providing information about his means.

[23]… [But] once the Tribunal has found that the charges are proved, then the same obligations … will be imposed upon a solicitor arguing that he cannot meet an order for costs, or that one should be limited in amount.

[24] In either of the two sets of circumstances the SRA must be afforded a reasonable opportunity to test the evidence relied upon by the solicitor, and in an appropriate case to call evidence itself on the question of the solicitor's means and of course to make submissions about the matter to the Tribunal.'

The judge's recommendations in paragraph 22 of the judgment were acted upon by the SDT in promulgating the Standard Directions, which require proper disclosure of a respondent's means when the respondent wishes the Tribunal to take those means into account.

Where the respondent is shown to be impecunious, if the Tribunal is satisfied that there is a reasonable prospect that at some time in the future his or her ability to pay a costs order will improve, it may order the respondent to pay costs, but direct that such order is not to be enforced without further leave of the Tribunal.[3] However, a respondent must think carefully whether he or she wishes to plead poverty. While to do so may well reduce the amount of the fine or costs payable, there may be other regulatory repercussions for solicitors shown to be impecunious. Since the start of the 2008 recession, the SRA has devoted considerable resources to the issue of the financial stability of solicitors and entities, because of the potential damage to the reputation of the profession caused by the uncontrolled failures of law firms.

1   See *Merrick v Law Society* [2007] EWHC 2997 (Admin) at [60]–[66], in which an order for costs in the sum of £45,000 against a suspended solicitor, who did not have the means or ability to pay, was quashed on appeal. See also *Agyeman v SRA* [2012] EWHC 3472 (Admin) and *Sharma v SRA* [2012] EWHC 3176 (Admin) – in the latter case the Divisional Court observed that the solicitor must adduce evidence of inability to pay a costs order, including independent valuations of properties. In *Matthews v SRA* [2013] EWHC 1525 (Admin), Collins J held that in imposing a financial penalty, the Tribunal should consider the respondent's overall financial liability for the fine and costs, and reduced a fine of £5,000 and costs of £16,000 to an overall liability of £5,000 on account of the appellant's limited means.
2   [2011] EWHC 232 (Admin).
3   See para 68 of the SDT Guidance Note on Sanctions and eg *Ijomantu v SRA* [2013] EWHC 3905 (Admin).

Proportionality

22.38

Legal costs claimed by the SRA against unsuccessful respondents can be very high, as the regulator has frequently instructed barristers from commercial London Chambers. As for this, a word of warning was sounded by Lord Thomas CJ in *Brett v SRA*[1] in which he stated at [114]:

> 'It is now well established that the costs of proceedings which a person may be ordered to pay must be proportionate. It may well be that in a particular case, the regulatory authority bringing proceedings will wish to instruct a person or firm who in the current state of the legal market can command high fees which the regulatory authority may be prepared to pay. However the fact that the market enables such persons or firms to command such high fees does not mean that it is proportionate to make an order for costs by reference to the rates which the legal services market enables such persons or firms to command from the regulatory authority. A tribunal must assess what is proportionate, taking into account all the material circumstances.'

1   [2014] EWHC 2974 (Admin).

22.39

It regularly occurs that the SRA succeeds in large part against the respondent solicitor, but that some of the allegations are nevertheless dismissed by the Tribunal. In such circumstances, it may be appropriate for the Tribunal to take that into account when determining costs issues, and perhaps apply a discount to reflect the fact that the SRA failed in part.[1]

1   The authorities are not consistent. No discount was applied in *Baxendale-Walker v Law Society* [2007] EWCA Civ 233, [2007] 3 All ER 330, *Beresford v SRA* [2009] EWHC 3155 (Admin) and *Levy v SRA* [2011] EWHC 740 (Admin). See now though *Broomhead v SRA* [2014] EWHC 2772 (Admin), in which the High Court applied a discount and doubted *Levy*.

Costs against a successful respondent solicitor

22.40

Rule 22 of the 1994 Rules specifically provided that an order for costs may be made by the Tribunal against the respondent without finding any allegation proved – and even if no other order is made if, having regard to his or her conduct or to all the circumstances (or both), the Tribunal thinks it fit.[1] In *Rowe v Lindsay*, the Divisional Court indicated that this rule did not justify an order for costs against a successful respondent who had been acquitted of misconduct and whose conduct in relation to the questions before the Tribunal, and since the commencement of proceedings against him, had not in the event been criticised.[2]

If intending to impose a costs sanction (either an order against a successful respondent or an order depriving a successful respondent solicitor of his costs) by reason of any fault found against the solicitor, the Tribunal is bound to consider what impact the conduct of the solicitor, of which it is critical, has had on the costs incurred. The calculation need not be exact, but there must be a reasonable and just balance between the order made and what has occurred in the proceedings. There must be a causal connection between the fault found by the Tribunal and the incurring of costs.[3]

1   This provision was not carried into the 2007 Rules or the 2019 Rules. Rule 43(1) of the 2019 Rules give the Tribunal a wide discretion as to costs orders.
2   (2001) DC Transcript CO/4737/2000.
3   *Hayes v Law Society* [2004] EWHC 1165 (QB). In referring to depriving the successful respondent of his costs (as distinct from the possibility of an order against a successful respondent) this decision should now be considered to have been overruled by *Baxendale-Walker v Law Society* [2007] EWCA Civ 233, [2007] 3 All ER 330.

Costs orders against the Law Society/SRA

22.41

Until 2006, those appearing in the Tribunal could expect, and advise their clients to expect, that costs would probably follow the event. If a respondent were to be acquitted of all charges in the Tribunal, the successful solicitor could generally expect an order that his or her costs should be paid by the Law Society.

This state of affairs altered with the decision of the Divisional Court in *Baxendale-Walker v Law Society*,[1] which was upheld by the Court of Appeal.[2] The rationale is that the Law Society is a statutory regulator, exercising its powers in the public interest; when the Law Society/SRA is addressing the question whether there is sufficient evidence to justify an application to the Tribunal, the ambit of its responsibility is far greater than it would be for a litigant deciding whether to bring civil proceedings.

The normal approach to costs decisions in ordinary civil litigation, that costs should follow the event, accordingly has no direct application to disciplinary proceedings against solicitors. What will be considered just and reasonable will depend on all the relevant facts and circumstances. The Tribunal may consider it just that costs should follow the event, but need not think so in all cases. Where the regulatory authority has acted reasonably, properly and on grounds that reasonably appear to be sound in the exercise of its public duty, the Tribunal should consider – in addition to any other relevant fact or circumstance – the financial prejudice to the particular respondent if an order for costs is not made in his or her favour and the need to encourage public authorities to make and stand by honest, reasonable and apparently sound decisions made in the public interest without fear of exposure to undue financial prejudice if the decision is successfully challenged.

Success by a respondent is a factor in his or her favour, but is not decisive; it is not the starting point but simply one factor for consideration.

However, where for example disciplinary proceedings are held to amount to an abuse of process, have been inefficiently prosecuted or have been mounted upon inadequate evidence, the respondent solicitor will ordinarily have a powerful argument that costs should follow the event.

The principles set out in *Baxendale-Walker* do not apply to appeals from the Solicitors Disciplinary Tribunal to the High Court. On such appeals, the costs provisions of the Civil Procedure Rules are applied. An appellant who successfully challenges findings against him or her can ordinarily expect to be awarded the costs of the appeal.[3]

1   [2006] EWHC 643 (Admin), [2006] 3 All ER 675.
2   [2007] EWCA Civ 233, [2007] 3 All ER 330. See too *Murtagh v SRA* [2013] EWHC 2024 (Admin).
3   See *Bryant and Bench v Law Society* [2007] EWHC 3043 (Admin) at [251] and *Bass and Ward v SRA* (judgment on costs) [2012] EWHC 2457 (Admin).

Appeals from the Tribunal

Statutory provisions

22.42

Either party may appeal to the High Court without permission and such appeals are governed by CPR, Part 52.[1]

The time for appealing is now 21 days from the date on which the written judgment is sent to the appellant.[2]

The court has power to make such order on an appeal as it may think fit.[3] Appeals to the High Court are heard in the Administrative Court, usually by a single judge or on occasion by a two-judge Divisional Court.

1   Section 49 of SA 1974. The one exception, which will only be relevant when rules are made to permit appeals to the Tribunal from decisions of the SRA in relation to practising certificate and comparable issues, is that the decision of the Tribunal on such appeals will be final; see section 49A(3) of SA 1974. See footnote 10 to **21.3**.
2   CPR rule 52.12(2)(b) modified by Part 52 Practice Direction 52D, para 3.3A.
3   Section 49(4) of SA 1974.

Stay pending appeal

22.43

As has been said (see **22.3**), the Tribunal does not readily grant a stay pending appeal, or any other period of grace, in cases where an order for striking off is made, still less when there has been a finding of dishonesty, and an appeal does not in itself operate as a stay.[1] It is necessary to lodge an appeal and to apply within that appeal for interim relief. The test that will be applied is set out in *Re a Solicitor*:[2]

> 'For such a submission to succeed, it would be necessary to establish not only that the applicant's appeal against striking off would have a reasonable prospect of success, but, further, that this Court would be likely to impose in substitution for the order of the Tribunal a penalty no greater than suspension from practice for some three or four months [being the period within which the substantive appeal could be expected to be heard].'

In that case, in which the application was heard in November 1998, the appeal was expected to be heard in February 1999.

It will be seen that an application for a stay pending appeal would be more likely to succeed in a case of a suspension from practice where the suspension would substantially have been served by the time the appeal came to be heard. Successful applications for a stay pending appeal where the solicitor has been struck off can be expected to be rare.

1   CPR rule 52.16.
2   16 November 1998, unreported, transcript CO/4359/98, per Rose LJ.

Approach of the courts

22.44

Until the advent of the Human Rights Act 1998, the courts were reluctant to interfere with the decisions of the Tribunal as an expert professional disciplinary tribunal. It was stated that it would require a very strong case to interfere with sentence, because the Tribunal was best placed to weigh the seriousness of professional misconduct.[1] The modern approach of the courts in the light of the Human Rights Act 1998 has altered in this respect, and was first determined in *Langford v Law Society*.[2] The following extracts from Lord Millett's speech in *Ghosh v General Medical Council*[3] were cited by Rose LJ in *Langford*:

> 'their Lordships wish to emphasise that their powers are not as limited as may be suggested by some of the observations which have been made in the past ...
>
> ... the Board will accord an appropriate measure of respect to the judgment of the committee whether the practitioner's failings amount to serious professional misconduct and on the measures necessary to maintain professional standards and provide adequate protection to the public. But the Board will not defer to the committee's judgment more than is warranted by the circumstances. The council conceded, and their Lordships accept, that it is open to them to ... decide whether the sanction of erasure was appropriate and necessary in the public interest or was excessive and disproportionate; and in the latter event either to substitute some other penalty or to remit the case to the committee for reconsideration.'

1   See *McCoan v General Medical Council* [1964] 1 WLR 1107, PC; and *Bolton v Law Society* [1994] 1 WLR 512, CA.

2   [2002] EWHC 2802 (Admin); see particularly at [14] and [15].
3   [2001] 1 WLR 1915, PC.

22.45

The approach to an appeal against a disciplinary 'conviction' was summarised thus by Garnham J in *Barnett v SRA*:[1]

'(i)   The appeal proceeds by way of a review rather than a rehearing.

(ii)   The court will give appropriate weight to the fact that the Tribunal is a specialist tribunal which had the advantage of hearing the evidence first hand. It will therefore be slow to intervene with the Tribunal's findings unless they were "plainly wrong".

(iii)   The court may also interfere with the Tribunal's decision if it finds a serious procedural or other irregularity in the Tribunal proceedings.'

The approach of the courts to appeals against sanction from the Tribunal was comprehensively reviewed in *Law Society v Salsbury*:[2]

'The correct analysis is that the Solicitors Disciplinary Tribunal comprises an expert and informed tribunal, which is particularly well placed in any case to assess what measures are required to deal with defaulting solicitors and to protect the public interest. Absent any error of law, the High Court must pay considerable respect to the sentencing decisions of the tribunal. Nevertheless if the High Court, despite paying such respect, is satisfied that the sentencing decision was clearly inappropriate, then the court will interfere. It should also be noted that an appeal from the Solicitors Disciplinary Tribunal to the High Court normally proceeds by way of review; see CPR rule 52.11(1).'

1   [2016] EWHC 1160 (Admin) at [17]. See too a rather fuller formulation in *Bhatt v General Medical Council* [2011] EWHC 783 (Admin) at [9], per Langstaff J.
2   [2008] EWCA Civ 1285 at [30]. For a somewhat different approach, see the judgment of Mostyn J in *Obi v SRA* [2013] EWHC 3578 (Admin).

22.46

By CPR rule 52.21 the High Court will allow an appeal if the decision is 'wrong'. In *Re B(a child)* the Supreme Court considered the interface between convention rights and the appellate function in care proceedings where the appellant had to show the impugned decision was 'plainly wrong'. Lord Neuberger said:

'I do not agree with the view that the appellate court has to consider that [the] Judge's conclusion was "plainly wrong" on the issue of proportionality before it can be varied or reversed. ... Either "plainly" adds nothing, in which case it should be abandoned as it will cause confusion, or it means that an appellate court cannot vary or reverse a judge's conclusion on proportionality if it considers it to have been "merely" wrong. Whatever view the Strasbourg Court may take of such a notion, I cannot accept it, as it appears to me to undermine the role of judges in the field of human rights'.[1]

In *Obi v SRA* Mostyn J said the test in *Re B* should not be confined to care proceedings and that the court should decide an appeal against sentence in disciplinary proceedings by asking itself whether the Tribunal's decision was 'wrong'.[2]

1   *Re B (a child)* [2013] UKSC 33 at [91].
2   *Obi v SRA* [2013] EWHC 3578 (Admin).

22.47

These authorities now have to be considered against the judgment of a strong Court of Appeal in *Bawa-Garba v General Medical Council*[1] in which Lord Burnett CJ indicated that the courts may be less willing to intervene than hitherto, albeit in the context of medical, rather than legal, practitioners:

> '61   The decision of the Tribunal that suspension rather than erasure was an appropriate sanction for the failings of Dr Bawa-Garba, which led to her conviction for gross negligence manslaughter, was an evaluative decision based on many factors, a type of decision sometimes referred to as "a multi-factorial decision". This type of decision, a mixture of fact and law, has been described as "a kind of jury question" about which reasonable people may reasonably disagree: *Biogen Inc v Medeva Plc* [1997] RPC 1 at 45; *Pharmacia Corp v Merck & Co Inc* [2001] EWCA Civ 1610, [2002] RPC 41 at [153]; *Todd v Adams (t/a Trelawney Fishing Co) (The Maragetha Maria)* [2002] EWCA Civ 509, [2002] 2 Lloyd's Rep 293 at [129]; *Datec Electronics Holdings Ltd v United Parcels Service Ltd* [2007] UKHL 23, [2007] 1 WLR 1325 at [46]. It has been repeatedly stated in cases at the highest level that there is limited scope for an appellate court to overturn such a decision.
>
> [...]
>
> 67   That general caution applies with particular force in the case of a specialist adjudicative body, such as the Tribunal in the present case, which (depending on the matter in issue) usually has greater experience in the field in which it operates than the courts: see *Smech* at [30]; *Khan v General Pharmaceutical Council* [2016] UKSC 64, [2017] 1 WLR 169 at [36]; *Meadow* at [197]; and *Raschid v General Medical Council [2007] EWCA Civ 46, [2007] 1 WLR 1460* at [18]–[20]. An appeal court should only interfere with such an evaluative decision if (1) there was an error of principle in carrying out the evaluation, or (2) for any other reason, the evaluation was wrong, that is to say it was an evaluative decision which fell outside the bounds of what the adjudicative body could properly and reasonably decide: *Biogen* at 45; *Todd* at [129]; *Designers Guild Ltd v Russell Williams (Textiles) Ltd (trading as Washington DC)* [2001] FSR 11 (HL) at [29]; *Buchanan v Alba Diagnostics Ltd* [2004] UKHL 5, [2004] RPC 34 at [31]. As the authorities show, the addition of "plainly" or "clearly" to the word "wrong" adds nothing in this context.'

In *Gale v SRA* the High Court said that a decision of the Solicitors Disciplinary Tribunal is an evaluative decision that shoud be accorded respect and that the court should only interfere with its decision in the circumstances identified by the Court of Appeal in *Bawa-Gaba*.[2]

1   [2018] EWCA Civ 1879.
2   *Gale v SRA* [2019] EWHC 222 (Admin) at [24].

Fresh evidence

22.48

Solicitors may wish to adduce fresh evidence on appeal, often of the medical or financial variety. The *Ladd v Marshall* principles (which in any event do not hold sway to the extent that they did before the Woolf reforms) are not always applied with their full rigour in statutory appeals of this type, where the likelihood of prejudice to the regulator is minimal, and it is in the interests of both parties that the correct sanction is applied to the regulated individual.[1] Although the court may adopt a more flexible approach than in conventional civil litigation, this cannot be taken for granted.[2]

1   See *R (Adelakun) v SRA* [2014] EWHC 198 (Admin) and *R (Khan) v GMC* [2014] EWHC 404 (Admin).
2   See *Sohal v SRA* [2014] EWHC 1613 (Admin).

Costs

22.49

It has already been noted (see **22.41**) that costs in the High Court will ordinarily follow the event in accordance with CPR rule 44.2(2), and that *Baxendale-Walker* has no application to appeals from the SDT.[1] In the case of an impecunious unsuccessful appellant, the court may be prepared to order that its own costs order should not be enforced by the SRA without leave.[2]

1   See *Bryant and Bench v Law Society* [2007] EWHC 3043 (Admin) at [251] and *Bass and Ward v SRA (judgment on costs)* [2012] EWHC 2457 (Admin). See too *SRA v Wingate; SRA v Malins* [2018] EWCA Civ 366 at [133]–[136].
2   See *Webb v SRA* [2013] EWHC 2225 (Admin) and *R (Adelakun) v SRA* [2014] EWHC 198 (Admin).

Further appeal to the Court of Appeal

22.50

Further appeals require the permission of the Court of Appeal, as a second appeal governed by section 55(1) of the Administration of Justice Act 1985 and CPR rule 52.7, and are rarely mounted. To obtain permission, the appellant needs to show a real prospect of success and that either (a) the appeal would raise an important point of principle or practice or (b) there is some other compelling reason for the appeal. Since 1994 the Law Society has appealed to the Court of Appeal on only four occasions, in each case to establish important points of principle.[1]

1   *Bolton v Law Society* [1994] 1 WLR 512, CA; *Bultitude v Law Society* [2004] EWCA Civ 1853, *Times*, 14 January 2005; *Law Society v Salsbury* [2008] EWCA Civ 1285; and *SRA v Malins* [2018] EWCA Civ 366.

CHAPTER 23

Proceedings before the SDT: (3) appeals to the Tribunal

23.1

CHAPTER 20 dealt, among other things, with the Solicitors Regulation Authority (SRA)'s powers to impose fines on practices and practitioners, to impose rebukes, and to publish its decisions; see **20.1**. Those decisions are made, so far as they relate to individual solicitors and employees, under section 44D of the Solicitors Act (SA) 1974 (see **APPENDIX 17**); and so far as they relate to recognised bodies, their managers and employees, under paragraph 14B of Schedule 2 to the Administration of Justice Act (AJA) 1985 (see **APPENDIX 18**).

CHAPTER 2 considers the powers of the SRA in relation to the authorisation of alternative business structures (ABSs) or 'licensable bodies', including the power to refuse an application, to impose conditions and to revoke or suspend an authorisation, and the power to withhold approval of individuals as managers or compliance officers and to withdraw approval; see **2.9** to **2.15**. **CHAPTER 25** explains the process whereby ownership of ABSs is regulated. **CHAPTER 26** deals with the disciplinary powers of the SRA to fine ABSs and disqualify individuals. All of those decisions are made as a licensing authority under Part 5 of the Legal Services Act (LSA) 2007 (see **APPENDIX 20**) or licensing rules. For relevant purposes the 'licensing rules' comprise the SRA Handbook and most relevantly the SRA Authorisation of Firms Rules 2019.

Appeals lie to the Solicitors Disciplinary Tribunal (the Tribunal or SDT) against decisions of the SRA:

- to impose fines on individuals or recognised bodies;[1]
- to impose a rebuke on individuals or recognised bodies, if the SRA decides to publish the rebuke, but not otherwise;[2]
- to publish a rebuke or fine imposed by the SRA;[3]
- to disqualify a person from acting as Head of Legal Practice or Head of Finance and Administration or from being a manager or employee of a licensed body;
- to refuse to bring a disqualification to an end following a review;
- to impose fines on licensed bodies or managers or employees of licensed bodies;
- to refuse an application for authorisation as a licensed body;
- to impose a condition on the authorisation of a licensed body;
- to revoke or suspend a licensed body's authorisation;

- to extend, revoke or vary the terms and conditions of authorisation of a licensed body, or to refuse an application to do so;

- not to approve a person to be a manager or compliance officer of a licensed body;

- to approve a person to be a manager or compliance officer of a licensed body subject to conditions;

- to withdraw approval of a manager or compliance officer of a licensed body;

- not to approve a person being an owner of a licensed body;

- to impose conditions on the authorisation of a licensed body in connection with the approval of an owner;

- to withdraw approval of a person as an owner of a licensed body;

- to notify the Legal Services Board (LSB) that an owner has exceeded a share or voting limit;[4]

and against a failure of the SRA to make a decision on an application for authorisation within the required period.[5]

1   Section 44E of SA 1974 and para 14C of Schedule 2 to AJA 1985.
2   Section 44E of SA 1974 and para 14C of Schedule 2 to AJA 1985.
3   Section 44E of SA 1974 and para 14C of Schedule 2 to AJA 1985.
4   The appealable decisions relating to ownership are set out in further detail in **23.6**.
5   Legal Services Act 2007 (Appeals from Licensing Authority Decisions) (No 2) Order 2011 (SI 2011/2863).

23.2

In this chapter we consider only the procedural aspects of such appeals. The appeals are governed by the Solicitors Disciplinary Tribunal (Appeals and Amendment) Rules 2011[1] (the 'Appeal Rules'). The Appeal Rules came into force on 1 October 2011 to regulate appeals to the Tribunal under SA 1974 and AJA 1985. The Appeal Rules were amended by the Solicitors Disciplinary Tribunal (Appeals) (Amendment) Rules 2011[2] to cover appeals relating to licensed bodies under LSA 2007 with effect from 23 December 2011.

The Tribunal publishes a guidance note on appeals which summarises the categories of appeals that can be made to the Tribunal and the orders that can be made by the Tribunal.[3]

The number of appeals heard by the Tribunal is very small. At the time of writing, only one of the appeal decisions made by the Tribunal, *Arslan*,[4] has led to a second appeal to the High Court.

In **APPENDIX 15** we have included the Appeal Rules, including the ABS-specific provisions.

1   SI 2011/2346. See also **APPENDIX 15**.
2   SI 2011/3070.
3   SDT Guidance Note on Appeals, second edition, December 2018.
4   11356–2015, SDT; *SRA v SDT (re Arslan)* [2016] EWHC 2862 (Admin).

23.3

The Tribunal has jurisdiction to review orders made by the SRA under section 43(3) of SA 1974, relating to solicitors' employees. Applications to the Tribunal relating to section 43 orders are not regulated by the Appeal Rules.[1] For section 43 applications see **18.10**.

1   They are regulated by the Solicitors (Disciplinary Proceedings) Rules 2007 (SI 2007/3588) (the '2007 Rules') and the Solicitors (Disciplinary Proceedings) Rules 2019 (SI 2019/1185) (the '2019 Rules). See rule 1(2) of the Appeal Rules, rule 8(4) of the 2007 Rules and rule 2(a)(ii) of the 2019 Rules.

Constitution of appeal panels, delegation and general powers

23.4

The one certainty in relation to ABSs is that, however much informed opinion there may be, no one can predict reliably exactly how the market will develop, what forms the new businesses will take and what degree of complexity will be involved in licensing decisions, and therefore in appeals from licensing decisions. The Tribunal has sensibly created for itself a degree of flexibility. The 2019 Rules dealing with the historical and original jurisdiction of the Tribunal are rigid as to the constitution of the adjudicating panel; it consists of three and only three: a lay member and two solicitors.[1]

The Appeal Rules state that for the hearing of any appeal a panel will be 'at least three members of the Tribunal', and that 'Unless the President otherwise directs, the majority of the Panel members shall be solicitor members'.[2]

The lay members of the Tribunal have a wealth of expertise in a wide variety of subjects outside the law, including, for example, business management, and it could be foreseen that in appropriate cases an expanded appeal panel could draw on that experience.

1   Rule 9 of the 2019 Rules.
2   Rule 3 of the Appeal Rules.

23.5

A single solicitor member may make case management decisions and give directions under rule 9 of the Appeal Rules;[1] may waive or require a procedural failure to be remedied under rule 11; may make a direction adding, substituting or removing a party under rule 13; may deal with the prohibition of disclosure of documents under rule 14; may make orders about lead cases, rule 15, consent to the withdrawal of an appeal under rule 16, and give directions as to disclosure, evidence and submissions under rule 19(1).[2]

The Tribunal clerks have delegated authority to give case management directions under rules 9, 13 and 19(1), subject to the right of a party to apply, within 14 days, for the decision to be considered afresh by a panel or single solicitor member.[3]

The Tribunal (or a panel of Tribunal members consisting of no fewer than five members, of whom no fewer than two shall be lay members) may make general practice directions: notices or directions concerning the practices or procedures of the Tribunal, consistent with the Appeal Rules, which are to be promulgated under the authority of the President.[4]

Subject to the Appeal Rules themselves, the Tribunal may regulate its own procedure, and may dispense with any requirements of the Rules in respect of notices, statements or other documents, witnesses, service or time in any case where it appears to the Tribunal to be just so to do.[5] This does not extend, however, to the time limit for appeals from decisions of the SRA as a licensing authority relating to the ownership of ABSs; see **23.6**.

The Tribunal may consent to a witness giving, or require any witness to give, evidence on oath, and may administer an oath for that purpose.[6]

1   The detailed rules referred to in this paragraph are considered below at **23.9** and **23.10**.
2   Rule 5(4) of the Appeal Rules.
3   Rule 5(1) and (3).
4   Rule 10.
5   Rule 18.
6   Rule 19(3).

Preliminary steps

23.6

The time for appeal is in all cases 28 days from notification of the decision. In relation to some ABS appeals this is a statutory time limit fixed by rules made by the LSB under its powers in paragraph 8 of Schedule 13 to LSA 2007,[1] and may not be exceeded. Neither the Tribunal nor any other party has power to waive the limit or consent to its extension.

This statutory time limit applies to appeals by licensed bodies, their managers and employees against financial penalties[2] and to appeals concerning the following SRA licensing decisions as to ownership of a licensed body:

- to approve an investor's notified interest subject to conditions, on granting a licence;

- to object to an investor's notified interest;

- to approve an investor's notifiable interest subject to conditions, after a licence has been granted;

- to object to an investor's notifiable interest;

- to impose conditions or further conditions on an existing restricted interest;

- to object to an existing restricted interest; and

- to notify the LSB that an owner has exceeded a share or voting limit.[3]

1   Rule 5 of the LSB Rules on the Prescribed Period for the Making of Appeals against Decisions of a Licensing Authority Regarding Ownership of Licensed Bodies 2011.
2   Section 96(1) of LSA 2007. Particular care must be taken on the time for appealing financial penalties under LSA 2007. Section 96(8) of LSA 2007 states that the validity of a penalty is not to be questioned by any legal proceedings whatever, except those permitted by section 96(1). Section 96(1) permits an appeal before the end of the time period prescribed by the LSB rules. The LSB rules specify a 28-day period running from 'the date on which notice of the decision of the licensing

authority is given to the applicant'. If there is an internal SRA appeal, it is unclear whether time starts to run from the date of the original decision or the decision made on the internal appeal.

3   Respectively paras 17(1), 19(1), 28(1), 31(1), 33(1), 36(1) and 49(2) of Schedule 13 to LSA 2007.

23.7

There is no form for a notice of appeal, but under rule 6(4) of the Appeal Rules the notice of appeal must set out:

- the name and address of the appellant;

- the name and address of the appellant's representative (if any);

- an address where documents for the appellant may be sent or delivered;

- the basis on which the appellant has standing to start proceedings before the Tribunal;

- the name and address of the respondent;

- details of the decision or act to which the proceedings relate;

- the result the appellant is seeking;

- the grounds on which the appellant relies;

- any application for a stay, if the appellant is allowed to make such an application under the licensing rules;

- a statement as to whether the appellant would be content for the case to be dealt with without a hearing if the Tribunal considers it appropriate; and

- any further information or documents required by a practice direction.

A copy of any record of the decision which is the subject of the appeal, and any statement of reasons that the appellant has or can reasonably obtain, must be supplied. Three additional copies of the notice and all accompanying documents must be filed with the Tribunal. A copy of the notice of appeal and all accompanying documents must be served on the respondent at the same time that the appellant sends or delivers the notice of appeal to the Tribunal.[1]

1   Rule 6(5), (6) and (7) of the Appeal Rules.

23.8

The respondent's response to the notice of appeal must be sent or delivered to the Tribunal and the appellant within 28 days of receipt by the respondent of the notice of appeal. There is no set form but the response must include:

- the name and address of the respondent;

- the name and address of the respondent's representative (if any);

- an address where documents for the respondent may be sent or delivered;

- any further information or documents required by a practice direction or direction;

- a statement as to whether the respondent would be content for the case to be dealt with without a hearing if the Tribunal considers it appropriate; and

- a statement as to whether the respondent opposes the appellant's case and, if so, any grounds for such opposition which are not contained in another document sent or delivered with the response.

Documents relied on by the respondent in making the decision and any documents considered by the respondent to be relevant to the appeal should accompany the response, including any record of the decision under appeal or reasons if not provided by the appellant.[1]

The onus is thus placed initially on the respondent to produce all documents that are 'relevant' to the extent that they have not already been placed before the Tribunal by the appellant. This requires an exercise of judgement as the documents required are not limited simply to those upon which the respondent may wish to rely. The Tribunal's practice direction as to disclosure and discovery made under the 2007 Rules may be relevant by analogy.

Three copies of the respondent's material must be provided to the Tribunal and service must be effected contemporaneously. If the response is out of time a request for an extension of time and the reason for it must be included.

An appellant may file and serve a reply within 14 days from receipt of the respondent's response, and any additional documents intended to be relied upon. At the same time the appellant may elect to supply a list of documents intended to be relied upon that were not appended to the notice of appeal, and if requested by the respondent or the Tribunal must provide copies or make those documents available for inspection and/or copying within seven days.[2]

1   Rule 7 of the Appeal Rules.
2   Rule 8.

Case management

23.9

On the direction of the Tribunal parties may be added, substituted or removed as an appellant or a respondent.[1]

The Tribunal may give directions to:

- extend or shorten the time for complying with any rule, practice direction or direction, unless such extension or shortening would conflict with a provision of another enactment (or of any rule made under another enactment) containing a time limit;

- consolidate or hear together two or more sets of proceedings or parts of proceedings raising common issues, or treat a case as a lead case;

- hear any application for a stay;

- permit or require a party to amend a document;

- permit or require a party or another person to provide documents, information or submissions which are relevant to the proceedings to the Tribunal or a party;

- deal with an issue in the proceedings as a preliminary issue;

- hold a hearing to consider any matter, including a case management issue;

- decide the form of any hearing;

- adjourn or postpone a hearing;

- require a party to produce a bundle for a hearing;

- require a party to provide a skeleton argument;

- decide the place and time of any hearing;

- make requirements about documentation and inspection;

- stay proceedings;

- suspend the effect of its own decision pending the determination by the High Court of an application for permission to appeal against, and any appeal of, that decision.[2]

A clerk may appoint a time and place for the review of the progress of the matter and notify the parties.[3]

1   Rule 13 of the Appeal Rules.
2   Rule 9(1) and (2).
3   Rule 9(3).

23.10

Directions may also be given by the Tribunal as to:

- the exchange between parties of lists of documents which are relevant to the appeal, or relevant to particular issues, and the inspection of such documents;

- the provision by parties of statements of agreed matters;

- issues on which it requires evidence or submissions;

- the nature of the evidence or submissions it requires;

- whether the parties are permitted or required to provide expert evidence, and if so whether the parties must jointly appoint a single expert to provide such evidence;

- any limit on the number of witnesses whose evidence a party may put forward, whether in relation to a particular issue or generally;

- the manner in which any evidence or submissions are to be provided, which may include a direction for them to be given orally at a hearing or by written submissions or witness statement; and

- the time at which any evidence or submissions are to be sent or delivered.[1]

The Tribunal may admit evidence whether or not the evidence would be admissible in a civil trial in the United Kingdom; or the evidence was available to a previous decision-maker. It may also exclude evidence that would otherwise be admissible where the evidence was not provided within the time allowed by a direction or a practice direction; or where the evidence was otherwise provided in a manner that did not comply with a direction or a practice direction; or it would otherwise be unfair, disproportionate or unnecessary in the interests of justice to admit it.[2]

The Tribunal may in its discretion proceed on the basis of written evidence subject to provisions as to service, notice, and the entitlement of the other party to object. If a witness is to be called to give oral evidence a witness statement with a statement of truth must be filed and served at least ten days before the hearing date. Five copies must be provided to the Tribunal.

By rule 11 of the Appeal Rules a failure to comply with any provision of the Rules, a practice direction or a direction does not render void either the appeal or any step taken in the appeal. The Tribunal may waive the requirement; require the failure to be remedied; exercise its power to strike the whole or part of the appeal (see further below); bar or restrict a party's participation in the appeal, but an order barring or restricting a party's participation in the appeal may not be made without giving the party an opportunity to make representations.

Where two or more appeals give rise to common or related issues one or more lead cases may be selected and other affected appeals may be stayed.[3]

1   Rule 19(1) of the Appeal Rules.
2   Rule 19(2).
3   Rule 15.

Private and public hearings

23.11

All hearings, including interlocutory hearings, are heard in public unless the Tribunal is satisfied that exceptional hardship or exceptional prejudice will be caused to a party, a witness or any other person affected by the appeal, or if a hearing would prejudice the interests of justice.[1]

The Tribunal has the power to direct that someone be excluded from any hearing if he or she is likely to prove disruptive, or for comparable reasons.[2]

It may also, as it regularly does at present without an express power under the 2007 Rules, exclude a witness until he or she has given evidence.[3]

Under rule 14 of the Appeal Rules there is a power to prohibit the disclosure or publication of documents or other material likely to identify someone the Tribunal considers should not be identified (which is regularly if not invariably done to protect the identity of clients, by identifying them by initials alone).

Under the same rule there are more complex provisions enabling documents to be withheld from a party altogether if there is a likelihood of serious harm to someone and in the interests of justice, with appropriate safeguards. The use of such powers is likely to be highly exceptional.

1   Rule 23(1) to (4) of the Appeal Rules.
2   Rule 23(5).
3   Rule 23(6).

Listing, hearings and other methods of disposal

23.12

Appeals may be disposed of without a hearing if both parties consent and the Tribunal considers it can properly determine the issues in this way.[1] Otherwise, hearings are listed on the basis that at least 28 days' notice is given, unless all the parties agree and the Tribunal has ordered a shorter period.[2] Any party may appoint a representative, who need not be a legal representative.[3]

Appeals can be disposed of by consent if the Tribunal considers the agreement appropriate, and in this event there need not be a hearing.[4]

Either party may unilaterally withdraw – the appeal or opposition to it – but the withdrawal does not take effect until the Tribunal consents to it, which it may do on terms as to costs. A party may also apply to reinstate an appeal or opposition to an appeal. The application must be made in writing within 28 days of the withdrawal (whether that was on written notice or orally at a hearing).[5]

Under rule 12 the Tribunal may strike out the whole or part of an appeal if the appellant has failed to comply with a direction which stated that a failure to comply could lead to that result (if the appeal or part of it is struck out on this basis the appellant may apply to reinstate it, within 28 days). An appeal or part of it may also be struck out if the appellant has failed to co-operate to such an extent that the appeal cannot be dealt with fairly and justly, or if the Tribunal considers that there is no reasonable prospect of the appellant's case, or that part of it, succeeding.

The same provisions apply in relation to striking out a respondent's opposition to an appeal *mutatis mutandis*.[6]

If an appeal has been finally disposed of at a hearing at which a party neither attended in person nor was represented, that party may apply for a re-hearing. The application must be made within 14 days of receipt of the Tribunal's order. It can be expected that such applications will be dealt with in no different a manner from applications made in the same circumstances under the 2007 Rules; see **21.36**.

1 Rule 21 of the Appeal Rules.
2 Rule 22.
3 Rule 28.
4 Rule 17. For disposal of an appeal by consent which varied an adjudication order see *Heselton*, 11636–2017.
5 Rule 16.
6 Rule 12(6).

Review or rehearing

23.13

The Appeal Rules do not state whether an appeal should proceed by way of review or rehearing.

In *Arslan* the High Court accepted that an appeal in the Tribunal under section 44E should proceed by way of review and not a rehearing. Leggatt J said:

'It is not in dispute that the Tribunal was correct to hold that … the proper approach was to proceed by way of a review and not a rehearing. As for what such a review involves, the Tribunal accepted … that its function was analogous to that of a court dealing with an appeal from another court or from a tribunal and that it should apply by analogy the standard of review applicable to such appeals which is set out in rule 52.11 of the Civil Procedure Rules. Rule 52.11 makes it clear that a court or tribunal conducting a review should not generally receive new evidence that was not before the original decision-maker, although it may do so if justice requires it, and it should interfere with a decision under review only if satisfied that the decision was wrong or that the decision was unjust because of a serious procedural or other irregularity in the proceedings.

It follows that the Tribunal should not embark on an exercise of finding the relevant facts afresh. On matters of fact the proper starting point for the Tribunal in this case was the findings made by the adjudicator and the evidence before the adjudicator. The Tribunal had to consider whether, on that evidence, the adjudicator was justified in making the factual findings that he did.

More guidance on the proper approach to a review is given in the judgment of Clarke LJ in *Assicurazioni Generali SpA v Arab Insurance Group* [2003] 1 WLR 577 … In [the judgment] the point is made that the approach to any particular case will depend upon the nature of the issues under review. Where a challenge is made to conclusions of primary fact, the weight to be attached to the findings of the original decision-maker will depend upon the extent to which that decision-maker had an advantage over the reviewing body; the greater that advantage the more reluctant the reviewing body should be to interfere. Another important factor is the extent to which the original decision involved an evaluation of the facts on which there is room for reasonable disagreement. In such a case the reviewing body ought not generally to interfere unless it is satisfied that the conclusion reached lay outside the bounds within which reasonable disagreement is possible'.[1]

The Tribunal has adopted the principles set out in *Arslan* in subsequent appeals under section 44E in *Cannon*[2] and *White*.[3] Applications to introduce new evidence were made in both cases. In *White* the Tribunal admitted some additional documents and in *Cannon* the Tribunal admitted oral evidence from a witness limited to specific issues.

1   *SRA v SDT (re Arslan)* [2016] EWHC 2862 (Admin) at [38]–[40].
2   11547–2016.
3   11680–2017.

The burden of proof

23.14

The appellate jurisdiction of the Tribunal covers three areas: appeals against SRA in-house sanctions of rebukes and fines, imposed in relation to individual solicitors and traditional (non-ABS) practices; appeals against decisions of a disciplinary character involving ABSs to impose fines, revoke authorisations and disqualify individuals; and appeals against licensing decisions, such as to refuse to grant an ABS licence, to refuse to approve individual applicants in regulated positions, or to impose conditions. The first two areas relate to disciplinary matters and the third relates to licensing matters. At the time of writing there have been no known appeals to the Tribunal on licensing matters.

In *Arslan* the High Court accepted that disciplinary appeals under section 44E are analogous to appeals by way of review under CPR, Part 52.[1] That places the burden of proof on the appellant, and in subsequent disciplinary appeals the Tribunal has proceeded on the basis that the burden of proof falls on the appellant.[2]

1 *SRA v SDT (re Arslan)* [2016] EWHC 2862 (Admin) at [38]–[40].
2 *Cannon*, 11547–2016; *White*, 11680–2017.

23.15

As regards the burden of proof in licensing appeals, the closest analogy is that of those seeking to join the solicitors' profession, and about whom there is a question over character and fitness. The general principle is that no one has the right to become a solicitor, and the burden is on the applicant to demonstrate his or her fitness.[1]

1 See *Jideofo v Law Society, Evans v SRA* and *Begum v SRA*: respectively No 6 of 2006, No 1 of 2007 and No 11 of 2007, unreported.

The standard of proof

23.16

In *Arslan* the High Court said that the standard of proof to apply on an appeal under section 44E of SA 1974, is the civil standard:

> 'It follows from the nature of the Tribunal's role as a review body rather than a primary decision-maker that it was not for the Tribunal to apply its own standard of proof. In relation to the standard of proof the only relevant questions for the Tribunal were to ask, first, what standard the SRA as the primary fact-finder ought to have applied; and second, whether the SRA adjudicator had properly applied that standard.
>
> There can be no doubt that, in deciding whether to take action under section 44D, the SRA was correct to apply the civil standard ... It follows that the only question for the Tribunal when hearing an appeal under section 44E is whether the SRA properly applied the civil standard of proof. There is no scope for the Tribunal to apply the criminal standard.'[1]

Paragraph 8 of the Tribunal's Guidance Note on Appeals states that the only question relating to the standard of proof for decision by the Tribunal when hearing any appeal is whether the original decision-maker properly applied the civil standard of proof.[2]

1 *SRA v SDT (re Arslan)* [2016] EWHC 2862 (Admin) at [43]–[44].
2 SDT Guidance Note on Appeals, second edition, December 2018, para 8.

The Tribunal's order

23.17

The Tribunal's jurisdiction to hear appeals arises from three different statutes (SA 1974, AJA 1985 and LSA 2007) and the type of order which the Tribunal can make on appeal is dependent on the provisions of those statutes.

For appeals under SA 1974, the Tribunal can make such order as it thinks fit.[1] For appeals under AJA 1985 and LSA 2007, the Tribunal does not have a general power to make such order as it thinks fit. For appeals under AJA 1985, the Tribunal's powers are, in summary, aligned with the sanctions which can be imposed in respect of recognised bodies in first instance proceedings.[2] For appeals on financial penalties under LSA 2007, the Tribunal can quash the penalty, substitute a penalty of such lesser amount as it considers appropriate or, in the case of an appeal relating to the time for payment, substitute a different time or times.[3] For appeals relating to licensing matters under LSA 2007 the Tribunal in general terms has power to affirm or quash the decision in whole or in part, substitute another decision of the kind that could be made by the SRA or, in some circumstances, remit the matter back to the SRA.[4]

1   Section 44E of SA 1974.
2   See paras 14C, 18(2) and 18A(2)–(3) of Schedule 2 to AJA 1985.
3   Section 96(3) of LSA 2007. There is no express statutory power for the Tribunal to deal with any costs order made by the SRA at first instance.
4   See generally Schedule 13 to LSA 2007, and Legal Services Act 2007 (Appeals from Licensing Authority Decisions) (No 2) Order 2011 (SI 2011/2863).

Costs

23.18

By rule 29 of the Appeal Rules the Tribunal may make such order for costs as it thinks fit, at any stage of an appeal, including an order disallowing costs incurred unnecessarily; and may order that costs be paid by any party judged to be responsible for wasted or unnecessary costs.

The Tribunal may order that any party bear the whole or a part or a proportion of the costs, and the amount of costs may either be fixed by the Tribunal or be subject to detailed assessment by a costs judge. The Tribunal may also make an order for costs where an appeal is withdrawn or amended.

The costs regime in relation to the normal (original as opposed to appellate) jurisdiction of the Tribunal is very burdensome on successful respondents – see **22.36** and **22.41**. However, this would not seem to be relevant to an appellate jurisdiction. The same public interest considerations do not apply. Certainly, one can expect that those who appeal unsuccessfully to the Tribunal against a decision of the SRA will be ordered to pay the SRA's costs in the normal course of events, but if appellants are successful, unless there is some unusual circumstance, it will be on the basis that the SRA's decision will have been wrong.

One would expect successful appellants to be awarded their costs, and in *Hafiq and Haque*,[1] the successful appellants were awarded costs.[2] There are two analogies, situations where the SRA has historically made decisions which are open to challenge by appeal: the first relates to the imposition of practising certificate conditions and similar decisions; the second involves matters of character and fitness, and appeals by those seeking enrolment as students with the SRA or admission to the roll as solicitors. In both cases appeal lies to the High Court (to the Master of the Rolls before 2008). In both situations the normal considerations under the Civil Procedure Rules apply and the general position is that costs follow the event. If the SRA is held to be wrong to have imposed the practising certificate conditions or wrong to have refused enrolment or admission the starting point is that the appellant is entitled to his or her costs against the SRA. The same principles have been applied in relation to appeals from the Tribunal to the High Court, despite an attempt by the SRA to suggest that the principles of *Baxendale-Walker v Law Society*[3] apply not only to the original prosecution in the Tribunal but also to appeals from the Tribunal; see *Bryant and Bench v Law Society*.[4] On a purely pragmatic level, unless solicitors are to be awarded their costs if they appeal successfully, few if any are likely to avail themselves of the ability to appeal to the Tribunal, and in that way the intention of Parliament in providing this appeal route would be neutered.

1   11253–2014, SDT.
2   In contrast, the successful appellant in *Arslan v SRA*, 11356–2015, SDT was ordered to pay £20,000 towards the SRA's costs, but that was a decision upon its own unusual facts.
3   [2007] EWCA Civ 233, [2007] 3 All ER 330; for the principles see **22.41**.
4   [2007] EWHC 3043 (Admin) at [251]. See too *Bass and Ward v SRA (judgment on costs)* [2012] EWHC 2457 (Admin).

Further appeals

23.19

As in the case of the Tribunal's original (non-appellate) jurisdiction, appeal from the Tribunal lies to the High Court without permission,[1] save in relation to ABS appeals under LSA 2007. All appeals from decisions of the SRA as a licensing authority for ABSs, whether under Part 5 of LSA 2007 or the SRA's rules (and not only those made under Schedule 13 to LSA 2007 listed in **23.6**) are governed by the Legal Services Act 2007 (Appeals from Licensing Authority Decisions) (No 2) Order 2011.

In those cases appeal lies to the High Court only on a point of law arising from the decision of the Tribunal, and only with the permission of the High Court.[2] The time limit for appeals in that category is also a statutory limit set by the LSB and is 28 days from the date the party is given notice of the decision of the Tribunal.[3] If the Tribunal follows its normal practice of making an immediate decision but providing full written reasons on a later date it may therefore be necessary to lodge an appeal before the reasons are available.

1   Section 49 of SA 1974 and see **22.42**.
2   Article 5(3) of the Legal Services Act 2007 (Appeals from Licensing Authority Decisions) (No 2) Order 2011 (SI 2011/2863).
3   Rule 6 of the LSB Rules on the Prescribed Period for the Making of Appeals against Decisions of a Licensing Authority Regarding Ownership of Licensed Bodies 2011.

CHAPTER 24

Disciplinary jurisdiction of the High Court

24.1

Solicitors are officers of the Senior Courts: the court itself can discipline solicitors, and may order that a solicitor's name be struck off the roll of solicitors, rather than referring the matter to the Solicitors Regulation Authority (SRA). This power is available to the High Court, the Crown Court and the Court of Appeal, or any division or judge of those courts.[1] This jurisdiction is only rarely exercised, and the relevant principles as to its exercise were summarised by Hickinbottom J in *Coll v Floreat MB*[2] in the following terms at [45]:

'(i) The court's jurisdiction over solicitors is conceptually very wide, being curtailed only to the extent that legislation limits it.

(ii) However, although now maintained by section 50 of the Solicitors Act, the jurisdiction is one which the High Court has taken to itself as part of its inherent powers in pursuit of its duty to supervise the conduct of solicitors as officers of the court. The court has, in practice, imposed boundaries on the exercise of its own jurisdiction.

(iii) The jurisdiction has both punitive and compensatory elements. However, given that solicitors are now the subject of a comprehensive and sophisticated regulatory regime through the SRA, the jurisdiction will only usually be exercised where someone has lost out as a result of the solicitor's conduct and the court is the appropriate forum to require that loss to be put right on a summary basis. The jurisdiction is therefore primarily compensatory, although in a disciplinary context. However, whilst misconduct is necessary, simply because there has been misconduct is not sufficient for the jurisdiction to be exercised. Whether the court intervenes in a particular case is always a matter for the court's discretion.

(iv) Where another forum is more appropriate than the court for the investigation of misconduct by a solicitor and the subsequent imposition of a sanction, then the court will not exercise its discretion to act against that solicitor. The SRA is appointed by Parliament to investigate and deal with allegations of misconduct by solicitors: the court will not exercise its disciplinary function over solicitors if the alleged misconduct conduct can be as, or more, appropriately dealt with by the SRA.'

A claimant applying to the High Court to exercise this jurisdiction, rather than making an application to the Tribunal, would need to show that it was reasonable to follow this exceptional course. This has been done only once successfully in modern times.[3] The power has also been used in the course of other litigation, on the application of the Law Society.[4]

397

Applications of this kind made by litigants in person will not be entertained because the Solicitors Act (SA) 1974 preserves the court's inherent jurisdiction as it had been prior to the Supreme Court of Judicature Act 1873, and both before and after that Act it was settled law that the jurisdiction was limited in practice, in that an application could only be made if supported by counsel.[5]

Ordinarily, if a judge is concerned that a solicitor may have been guilty of professional misconduct, he will order that the matter be referred to the SRA, and a transcript made of the relevant part of the proceedings. Alternatively the judge may write to the SRA, setting out his or her concerns about the professional conduct of the solicitor in question.

1   Section 50 of the Solicitors Act 1974; the procedure is set out in section 51.
2   [2014] EWHC 1741 (QB) – see the discussion at [36]–[45].
3   *Parsons v Davies* (1983, CA, unreported).
4   *Penna v Law Society (No 3)* (1999, unreported); and *Law Society v Young* [2002] EWHC 2962 (Admin). In each case the solicitor had been the subject of an intervention on the grounds of a suspicion of dishonesty. In *Penna*, in the subsequent proceedings by which he sought to challenge the intervention the solicitor so misconducted himself in defiance of court orders that the court on the Law Society's application used its inherent powers to strike him off, taking the facts that led to the intervention and his subsequent conduct into account. In *Young* the solicitor continued to practise as a solicitor and to hold himself out as a solicitor in court proceedings, so that there was contempt as well as continuing misconduct.
5   *Re Solicitors, ex p Peasegood* [1994] 1 All ER 298, DC.

24.2

The court's inherent jurisdiction is exercisable only over solicitors, as officers of the court; barristers are not officers of the court, nor in the context of entity or firm-based regulation, are firms of solicitors, or other forms of law firm ('recognised bodies') including alternative business structures ('licensed bodies').

See *Assaubayev and others v Michael Wilson & Partners Ltd*:[1]

'A corporate body recognised under section 9 of the 1985 Act may provide legal services entirely lawfully. But it does not, on that account, become an officer of the Court and thereby subject to the supervisory jurisdiction. Noticeably neither the 1985 Act nor the LSA 2007 makes any provision for the exercise of the Court's jurisdiction in respect of solicitors to be extended to non-solicitors although section 14 (4) of the LSA 2007 does extend the contempt of court jurisdiction to those who offend against section 14 (1). Recognised legal bodies may, of course, have members who are solicitors, in respect of whom the court will have jurisdiction; but that will not apply to a body such as MWP – a BVI company – itself.'

It has been held that the jurisdiction extends to those who have pretended to be solicitors; see for example *Re Hurst & Middleton Ltd*.[2] The 'keystone of the success of such an application' was, as held by Kennedy LJ:

'that the man has, by virtue of his assumption of the position and privilege of a solicitor, either obtained something which he ought not to have obtained (I do not desire to limit it – there may be other cases, but broadly that would be generally the case), and therefore the restitution of which is just, or done some act for which there would be a remedy in the Court if it were an act done by an officer of the Court, and if the man has done the act or obtained the property by the assumption of the privilege and position of a solicitor. In such a case the Court will exercise the power which it would be right to exercise if the man were an officer of the Court; and in such a case the man cannot be allowed to say that he is free from the jurisdiction of the Court because he is not in fact, a solicitor, and therefore not an officer of the Court.'

1   [2014] EWCA Civ 1491 at [47].
2   [1912] 2 Ch 520, CA.

PART 6
The regulation of ABSs

CHAPTER 25

Alternative business structures: getting started

25.1

CHAPTER 2 deals with the authorisation of legal services bodies (traditional practices or recognised bodies – a recognised body is a legal services body that has become recognised and authorised by the Solicitors Regulation Authority (SRA)) and licensable bodies (alternative business structures (ABSs) or licensed bodies – in the same way, a licensed body is a licensable body that has become authorised).

The SRA approach to regulation is to apply the same authorisation system to all, regardless of size, label or structure. However, there are some ABS-specific considerations, principally concerned with ownership.

It is relevant to bear in mind that ABSs may vary enormously. The popular concept remains that of 'Tesco law' – in other words a large, possibly national or international, company taking control of one or more law firms or choosing to invest in them.

The main focus of the regulatory provisions of the Legal Services Act (LSA) 2007 in Part 5 and Schedules 11 to 14 is to ensure that the wrong kind of people do not end up controlling law firms, and to incorporate necessary checks and balances, including the requirement to have a lawyer as Head of Legal Practice.

But at the other end of the spectrum, any law firm which is currently a traditional practice of, say, four partners, which has chosen to appoint its non-lawyer financial director as one of the four, and is therefore designated as a legal disciplinary practice with a non-lawyer manager, is licensable as an ABS, and will have to have become authorised as such at some point. (The end of the transitional period, when existing recognised bodies of that kind will have to convert to ABSs, is to be set by the Legal Services Board (LSB) and has not yet been set. The LSB's 2018/19 business plan states that the transitional period will remain in place for the foreseeable future.)

An ABS, or in LSA 2007 terminology a licensable body, is a body that carries on (or wishes to carry on) reserved legal activities, and a non-authorised person[1] is a manager[2] of the body or has an interest[3] in it.[4] Alternatively, a body (B) is a licensable body if another body (A) is a manager of the body or has an interest in it and non-authorised persons are entitled to exercise, or control the exercise of, at least 10 per cent of the voting rights in A.[5] Accordingly, if a holding or parent company of a firm providing reserved legal activities is partly owned by a non-authorised person who holds less than 10 per cent of its voting rights then the firm would not need to be authorised as an ABS, but would still need to be regulated by an approved regulator in the provision of reserved legal activities.

Many firms who would not apply the 'Tesco law' label to themselves may have no option but to be regulated as ABSs.

1   The term 'person' includes a body of persons corporate or unincorporate (section 207 of LSA 2007). A non-authorised person is not defined in LSA 2007 but 'authorised person' is, and refers to a person who is authorised to provide reserved legal activities; see section 18.
2   The term 'manager' is defined in section 207. In summary, a manager will be a member of a limited liability partnership or similar organisation, director of a company, partner in a partnership or the member of a governing body of an unincorporated association.
3   Having an 'interest' is defined as either holding shares or being entitled to exercise, or control the exercise of, voting rights in the body – section 72(4).
4   Section 72(1) of LSA 2007.
5   Section 72(2).

25.2

There is a limited but expanding choice of regulator. The SRA, the Bar Standards Board (BSB) and the Council for Licensed Conveyancers (CLC) are licensing authorities approved by the LSB; in the case of CLC, limited to businesses undertaking conveyancing and probate; so is the Institute of Chartered Accountants in England and Wales (ICAEW), in relation to probate. CILEx Regulation has been approved as a licensing authority with effect from 1 April 2019. Currently the SRA regulates the supply of all reserved legal activities apart from notarial activities, and we will confine our commentary to regulation by the SRA.

Regulation of ownership

25.3

LSA 2007 regulates ownership of an ABS by a non-authorised person where that person controls a material interest in an ABS. Broadly, a material interest is one where the non-authorised person holds at least 10 per cent of the shares of the ABS (or equivalent) or at least 10 per cent of the shares of the parent of the ABS, or is able to exercise significant influence in the management of the ABS or its parent by virtue of the shareholding.[1] The licensing authority has to be satisfied that the non-authorised person holding a material interest in the ABS does not compromise the regulatory objectives set out in section 1 of LSA 2007 (see **1.4**). It must also not compromise the duty of regulated persons employed by the ABS to fulfil their duty to comply with regulatory requirements; and the person must be fit and proper to hold the interest.[2] In determining whether the licensing authority is satisfied as to the above matters, it must have regard to the non-authorised person's probity and financial position, whether he or she is disqualified from being a Head of Legal Practice, Head of Finance and Administration or as a manager or employee of a licensed body, under section 99 of LSA 2007, or included on the LSB's list of persons subject to objections and conditions (that is objections and conditions relating to ownership notified to the LSB by licensing authorities), and must also have regard to the person's associates.[3]

Where the ABS is owned by one or more non-authorised persons who have a less than 10 per cent interest in the ABS, these persons will not be subject to the same controls.

Where applicable, the SRA Assessment of Character and Suitability Rules 2019 will be applied to interest holders as they are to non-lawyer managers, which is essentially the same test as that which applies in relation to admission to the solicitors' profession. It is entirely logical that the character and suitability requirements for non-lawyers having a material interest in a regulated business should be identical to those applied to the lawyers. In some respects the test may need to be more onerous as LSA 2007 clearly contemplates consideration of the associates of the non-authorised owners and managers as part of the assessment process. These are widely defined to include family and other businesses related directly or indirectly to the non-authorised person.[4] There is no equivalent process for admission to one of the legal professions. The SRA Assessment of Character and Suitability Rules 2019 are less prescriptive than the SRA Suitability Test and place the onus of providing all relevant information squarely on the applicant. There is no full definition of 'relevant information' for the purposes of the Rules, the examples specified are expressly not intended to be exhaustive.[5]

1   Paragraph 3 of Schedule 13 to LSA 2007.
2   Paragraph 6(1) of Schedule 13.
3   Paragraph 6(3) of Schedule 13.
4   Paragraph 5 of Schedule 13.
5   See rules 6.1, 6.6 and 2.2, SRA Assessment of Character and Suitability Rules 2019.

25.4

There is a requirement to identify any non-authorised person who has or is expected to have a material interest in the ABS in the application for a licence.[1] There is also an obligation to inform the licensing authority when a non-authorised person acquires a material interest in an ABS.[2] It is a criminal offence to fail to comply with either of these requirements.[3] The licensing authority may impose conditions on the approval of the non-authorised person, either in the context of an application (a notified interest) or when notification is made of a new interest in an existing licensed body (a notifiable interest).[4] If it proposes to do so it must give a warning notice as to the proposed conditions and the reasons for imposing them, and permit representations to be made before a final decision is made. The licensing authority may also object altogether to the non-authorised person's interest in the ABS, with the same limitations.[5] Where a licence has already been granted and the objection or conditions relate to a new notifiable interest, notice and the opportunity for representations may be dispensed with if it is necessary or desirable to do so for the purpose of protecting any of the regulatory objectives.[6]

It is also possible to impose conditions or further conditions on an existing interest holder, or to raise an objection to an existing interest holder, with the same limitations and exceptions.[7]

There is a right of appeal to the Solicitors Disciplinary Tribunal (if the licensing authority is the SRA) against such decisions. See **CHAPTER 23** for appeals to the Tribunal.

There is, of course, no indication at present as to what conditions could sensibly be applied to an interest holder if in all respects he or she is suitable to hold the interest.

1   Paragraph 10 of Schedule 13 to LSA 2007.
2   Paragraph 21 of Schedule 13.
3   Paragraphs 11 and 22 of Schedule 13.
4   Paragraphs 17 and 28 of Schedule 13.
5   Paragraphs 17(3) to (5), 19(2) to (4), 28(3) to (5) and 31(2) to (5) of Schedule 13.
6   Paragraphs 28(4) and 31(3) of Schedule 13.
7   Paragraphs 33 and 36 of Schedule 13.

25.5

Paragraph 38 of Schedule 13 to LSA 2007 enables licensing rules to make general provision for the limitation of the level of the shareholding, control or voting rights of non-authorised persons. The SRA's rules do not expressly provide for this, but the same effect can be achieved by imposing conditions on a case-by-case basis. There is no restriction in LSA 2007 as to the number of ABSs in which a non-authorised person can take an interest.

25.6

If a non-authorised person continues to hold an interest in an ABS in breach of conditions or despite objection the licensing authority may apply to the High Court for an order that the person be divested of the interest; see **26.8**.

Other controls

25.7

All non-lawyer managers of ABSs must also be expressly approved, as must the Heads of Legal Practice and of Finance and Administration who, within the SRA Authorisation of Firms Rules 2019, become compliance officers for legal practice (COLPs) or for finance and administration (COFAs). No distinction is drawn by the SRA between the mechanisms for approval of COLPs and COFAs or non-lawyer managers by reference to whether the body is an ABS or a traditional law practice. As to authorisation generally see **CHAPTER 2**. As to COLPs and COFAs, see **CHAPTER 7**.

CHAPTER 26

Alternative business structures: discipline and enforcement

Disciplinary powers

26.1

In this chapter we will consider only alternative business structures (ABSs) licensed by the Solicitors Regulation Authority (SRA), which is overwhelmingly the largest regulator of licensable or licensed bodies. The Council for Licensed Conveyancers has licensed around 75 ABSs, whereas the SRA has licensed over 800. The Institute of Chartered Accountants in England and Wales may only license ABSs providing probate services (at present).

For law firms in their traditional form the relationship between their practices and their regulatory and disciplinary bodies had been unchanged for decades; indeed for a century. Discipline, in the sense of penalty, including the ultimate deterrent of being struck off the roll, was the province of the court (initially exclusively, but in modern times only through a surviving inherent jurisdiction rarely used – see **CHAPTER 24**), and the Solicitors Disciplinary Committee (from the nineteenth century until 1975), and the Solicitors Disciplinary Tribunal (the Tribunal or SDT) from 1975.

The Law Society, and latterly the SRA, had no disciplinary powers at all; it could exercise control through the training and admission process, and by means of practising certificate conditions, and by intervention, and it could elect to prosecute solicitors before the Tribunal, but in that respect it was not a decision-maker, it was a party in adversarial proceedings.

The practice which grew up of imposing what were first called rebukes, severe rebukes and chairman's rebukes (which involved the solicitor attending at the Law Society to be told off by the chairman of the relevant committee, warned that he (or much more rarely she) had come within a whisker of being referred to the Tribunal, and cautioned not to do it again),[1] and which later changed their name to reprimands and severe reprimands (for no discernible reason) had never had any statutory origin. They were developed as a mechanism by which a solicitor could be told that something had gone wrong in circumstances in which no further action was necessary.

1 These fell into disuse in the 1990s when solicitors became more argumentative.

26.2

It all changed as a result of the Legal Services Act (LSA) 2007 and another raft of changes to the much amended Solicitors Act (SA) 1974. After some wrangling over the required procedural rules the Law Society, in the guise of the SRA, became a disciplinary body in relation to solicitors in relation to acts and omissions occurring or continuing on or after 1 June 2010 (see **CHAPTER 20**).

Those powers however, in relation to solicitors in traditional law firms, remain modest. Formal statutory and potentially public rebukes have replaced informal non-statutory and largely private reprimands, and there is a power to impose a fine not exceeding £2,000. Importantly, this was only designed to reduce the caseload of the Tribunal and remove low level cases from its jurisdiction. The Tribunal remains the primary disciplinary body, although the SRA has, from a time shortly after it acquired the power, been seeking to increase the level of fines it can impose.

26.3

It may come as a shock to those solicitors who, instead of being partners or managers or employees of a traditional firm or recognised body, are partners or managers or employees of an ABS, to learn that their primary disciplinary body has become the SRA.

The structure of LSA 2007 is that the licensing authority is responsible for disciplinary as well as licensing decisions, with the Tribunal reverting to being an appeal body (see **CHAPTER 23**).

It is the SRA which has the power to fine the business, its managers and employees (not the Tribunal),[1] and the fine is not limited to £2,000, but extends to a maximum of £250 million, for the business, and £50 million, for an individual.[2]

Further the SRA has the power of disqualification – to disqualify any individual from being a Head of Legal Practice (HOLP) or Head of Finance and Administration (HOFA) (compliance officer for legal practice (COLP) or compliance officer for finance and administration (COFA) in SRA terminology) and from being a manager of an ABS, and from being even an employee of an ABS.[3]

A disqualification from being employed in one or more of those capacities could be as devastating in its consequences as being struck off as a solicitor.

However, although the consequences of an adverse result are infinitely more serious, the disciplinary powers in relation to ABSs and all individuals within ABSs are dealt with under the same rules and the same procedures as are applied to traditional practices (see **CHAPTERS 15** and **20**).

The SRA has not made clear whether and to what extent it will move from its present position of rarely if ever conducting oral hearings, although there is provision in the SRA Regulatory and Disciplinary Procedure Rules 2019 for public hearings in appropriate cases.[4] It is likely to be argued that an opportunity to appeal to the Tribunal and to obtain a discretionary stay would not be sufficient to provide a fair disciplinary system. It is understood that the SRA may well accept that oral hearings and a more formal and transparent approach to decision-making will be necessary for serious or contentious matters affecting ABSs, although the factors which may inform any such acceptance have yet to become apparent in practice.

For appeals to the Tribunal against the exercise of the SRA's disciplinary powers and licensing decisions see **CHAPTER 23**.

1   Section 95 of LSA 2007.

2   Legal Services Act 2007 (Licensing Authorities) (Maximum Penalty) Rules 2011 (SI 2011/1659).
3   Section 99 of LSA 2007.
4   See rule 8.5.

Investigatory powers

26.4

The SRA's investigatory powers under sections 44B and 44BA of SA 1974 are considered in **CHAPTER 15** (see **15.10**). These apply to solicitors subject to the regulation of the SRA whether they are employed in ABSs or traditional firms. They do not otherwise apply to ABSs. The parallel provisions in relation to non-solicitor managers or employees of ABSs are in sections 93 and 94 of LSA 2007.

The terms of section 93 are similar to sections 44B and 44BA combined, and extend the powers of the SRA, to require information to be provided and documents to be produced, to former managers and employees of the licensed body and any non-authorised person who has an interest or an indirect interest, or holds a material interest, in the licensed body. However, the powers are not backed by criminal sanctions and the remedy for non-compliance, provided by section 94, is an application by the licensing authority to the High Court for an order to comply with the notice.

The duty to co-operate fully with the SRA in relation to any investigation (paragraph 7.3 of the SRA Code of Conduct for Solicitors, RELs and RFLs 2019 (the 'Code for Individuals') and paragraph 3.2 of the SRA Code of Conduct for Firms 2019 (the 'Code for Firms')) continues to apply to every person and body regulated by the SRA, as do paragraph 7.4 of the Code for Individuals and paragraph 3.3 of the Code for Firms imposing an obligation to supply explanations, information and documents to the SRA in response to any requests or requirements.

Other quasi-disciplinary powers

26.5

The licence of an ABS may be suspended or revoked[1] in circumstances which are regulated by paragraph 24 of Schedule 11 to LSA 2007. These are replicated in rule 4.3 of the SRA Authorisation of Firms Rules 2019.[2] The SRA may revoke or suspend an authorised body's authorisation (that is, any practice that the SRA has authorised, ABS or non-ABS) where:

- authorisation was granted as a result of error, misleading or inaccurate information, or fraud;

- the body is or becomes ineligible to be authorised or the grounds for refusal of an application are met;

- the body has failed to provide any information the SRA has reasonably requested;

- the body has failed to pay any prescribed fee to the SRA;

- a relevant insolvency event has occurred in relation to the body or a sole principal;

- the body makes an application to the SRA for its authorisation to be revoked;

- the body is subject to any proceedings, investigation or consideration of their conduct or practice by the SRA or the Tribunal;

- the SRA has decided to exercise its intervention powers in relation to the body or a solicitor's practice within the body;

- the body has failed to comply with any obligations under the SRA's regulatory arrangements;

- in the case of a licensed body (applicable to ABSs alone) the body fails to comply with the prohibition on appointing disqualified managers; or in the case of any authorised body, the body fails to comply with the prohibition on employing disqualified persons (struck off solicitors and the like) if the manager or employee concerned was disqualified as a result of breach of the duties imposed upon the manager or employee by sections 176 or 90 of LSA 2007 (the general duties imposed to comply with all regulatory arrangements for ABSs); or

- for any other reason it is in the public interest.

In the case of a *licensed* body (applicable to ABSs alone), it may revoke or suspend a body's authorisation, where a non-authorised person holds an interest in the licensed body:

- as a result of the person taking a step in circumstances where that constitutes an offence under paragraph 24(1) of Schedule 13 to LSA 2007 (whether or not the person is charged with or convicted of an offence under that paragraph) – this is failing to give notice as to the proposed or actual acquisition of a material interest in an ABS;

- in breach of conditions imposed on the owners of material interests in the ABS; or

- the person's holding of which is subject to an objection by the licensing authority.

1   Section 101 of LSA 2007.
2   This subject is also dealt with in **CHAPTER 2** but is repeated here for convenience.

26.6

Before the SRA can revoke or suspend an authorisation it must first give the authorised body an opportunity to make representations to it on the issues that have led the SRA to consider this course, and it must also give at least 28 days' notice of its intention to make the decision to revoke or suspend.[1]

1   Rule 4.5 of the SRA Authorisation of Firms Rules 2019.

26.7

Where an interest holder holds a material interest in an ABS in breach of conditions imposed by a licensing authority the authority may apply to the High Court for an order to secure compliance with the conditions. The licensing authority may not make an application to the court unless it has given notice of its intention to do so and, at the end of the notice period, the interest holder is still in breach of the conditions. In other words, an opportunity must be given to the interest holder to regularise the position. The notice period is to be prescribed by the Legal Services Board (LSB) and has not yet been set.

No order may be made by the court until the end of any period for appeal against the imposition of conditions and, if there is an appeal, until the appeal is disposed of.[1]

1   Paragraph 46(5) of Schedule 13 to LSA 2007.

Divestiture

26.8

Part 5 of Schedule 13 to LSA 2007 contains provisions enabling the licensing authority to apply to the High Court for an order divesting an interest holder of an interest in an ABS where the interest consists of a shareholding in a company with a share capital, if the non-authorised person holds a material interest in the licensed body either in circumstances where notice has not been given of the acquisition or intended acquisition of the interest so that an offence has been committed under paragraph 24(1) of Schedule 13, or the interest is held in breach of conditions imposed by the licensing authority or in contravention of an objection by the authority.

The licensing authority may serve a 'restriction notice' which may provide that a transfer of shares or similar arrangement is void, that no voting rights may be exercised, that no further shares be issued to the holder and that no payment may be made by the company in relation to the shares (other than in a liquidation).[1]

On an application to the High Court the court may order the sale of the shares. The licensing authority may not make an application to the court for a divestiture order unless it has given notice of its intention to do so and, at the end of the notice period, the conditions for divestiture still apply. In other words, an opportunity must be given to the interest holder to regularise the position. The notice period is to be prescribed by the LSB and has not yet been set.

No order may be made by the court until the end of any period for appeal against the imposition of conditions or the objection and, if there is an appeal, until the appeal is disposed of.[2]

1   Paragraph 44 of Schedule 13 to LSA 2007.
2   Paragraph 45(5).

Intervention

26.9

Powers of intervention are available to the licensing authority which are broadly comparable to those applying to solicitors' practices under Schedule 1 to SA 1974. They are set out in Schedule 14 to LSA 2007.

An intervention may be authorised where a licence granted to a body has expired, and has not been renewed or replaced by the relevant licensing authority, or where one or more of the intervention conditions is satisfied.

The intervention conditions are:

'(a) that the licensing authority is satisfied that one or more of the terms of the licensed body's licence have not been complied with;

(b) that a person has been appointed receiver or manager of property of the licensed body;

(c) that a relevant insolvency event has occurred in relation to the licensed body;

(d) that the licensing authority has reason to suspect dishonesty on the part of any manager or employee of the licensed body in connection with—

    (i)   that body's business,

    (ii)   any trust of which that body is or was a trustee,

    (iii) any trust of which the manager or employee of the body is or was a trustee in that person's capacity as such a manager or employee, or

    (iv) the business of another body in which the manager or employee is or was a manager or employee, or the practice (or former practice) of the manager or employee;

(e) that the licensing authority is satisfied that there has been undue delay—

    (i)   on the part of the licensed body in connection with any matter in which it is or was acting for a client or with any trust of which it is or was a trustee, or

    (ii)   on the part of a person who is or was a manager or employee of the licensed body in connection with any trust of which that person is or was a trustee in that person's capacity as such a manager or employee,

and the notice conditions are satisfied;[1]

(f) that the licensing authority is satisfied that it is necessary to exercise the powers conferred by this Schedule (or any of them) in relation to a licensed body to protect:

    (i)   the interests of clients (or former or potential clients) of the licensed body,

    (ii)   the interests of the beneficiaries of any trust of which the licensed body is or was a trustee, or

    (iii) the interests of the beneficiaries of any trust of which a person who is or was a manager or employee of the licensed body is or was a trustee in that person's capacity as such a manager or employee.'

1   This only applies if the licensing authority has requested an explanation, that at least eight days have been given for a reply, and if notice has then been given that the licensing authority does not regard the response to be satisfactory and that the powers of intervention have arisen.

26.10

Essentially the same relief is available to challenge the intervention by application to the High Court as is available to solicitors' practices; see **CHAPTER 17**.

PART 7
Fraud and money laundering

CHAPTER 27

The risks of fraud

27.1

In this section it is intended to highlight certain danger areas which have resulted in guidance being given to the profession but which are not reflected in any specific rule.

There are three possible consequences of involvement in fraud. First, solicitors, even if innocent of any involvement in the fraud itself, may face regulatory or disciplinary action if they facilitate a fraud through a failure to be alert to warning signs or known red flags. Where an employee acts fraudulently, firms or managers may also be at risk of allegations of a failure to supervise or not having adequate systems in place.

Second, particularly in the context of identity fraud where funds are paid to a fraudster, solicitors may be immediately liable to replace the consequential shortage on client account. This may be true even where the fraudster is not the solicitor's own client.

Third, cyber fraud has become an enormous problem, by which criminals use technology to facilitate fraud, for example, by fooling solicitors into disclosing sensitive information and persuading them, for example, to pay client funds to the fraudster's bank account by masquerading as the client, using what appears to be the client's email address to communicate. Other forms of cybercrime such as ransom attacks are also increasing.

Mortgage fraud

27.2

The involvement, innocent or otherwise, of solicitors or licensed conveyancers is essential to all mortgage fraud, in the sense that they are required to enable the transaction to occur.

There have historically been four basic types of 'traditional' mortgage fraud, with a potentially endless selection of variations on the basic theme:

(1) exaggeration of the borrower's income to obtain a mortgage that would otherwise be declined;

(2) multiple purchases, where a fraudster uses false names or nominees to build up a portfolio of property through residential rather than commercial borrowing;

(3) identity theft, where money is borrowed in the name of the proprietor on a remortgage, and diverted to the fraudsters; and

(4) exaggeration of price or value, to obtain a higher mortgage than would properly be justified.

Of course, sometimes more than one element can feature in a fraudulent scheme.

More recently, identity theft as a mortgage fraud device has been extended to situations in which property is sold from under the genuine proprietor by a fraudster using the proprietor's name or situations where the fraudster sets up a bogus law firm or a bogus branch office of a legitimate firm.[1]

Solicitors will not generally expect to encounter false employers' references, for example, although there could well arise circumstances to put any reasonable solicitor on notice that the borrower client's means do not appear to match the lender's requirements for the amount being loaned. The extent to which a solicitor may be required to investigate the borrower client's financial position may well vary depending on the risk profile of the transaction.

The obligations under the Money Laundering, Terrorist Financing and Transfer of Funds (Information on the Payer) Regulations 2017[2] of due diligence and enhanced due diligence, and the obligation to monitor business relationships and transactions as they develop (considered in detail in **CHAPTER 28**) now have a direct relevance to these issues and should result in such patterns being detected.

Regrettably, there have been solicitors who have been prepared to provide false references for their own employees or even to indulge in this kind of fraud for their own benefit.[3]

Solicitors are well placed to detect and prevent frauds of the second and third kinds and in some cases their active complicity, or determinedly deliberate Nelsonian blindness, is essential to the success of the frauds.

1   See the Solicitors Regulation Authority (SRA)'s warning notice on bogus law firms and identity theft, and *Lloyds TSB Bank plc v Markandan & Uddin* [2012] 2 All ER 884; *Davisons Solicitors v Nationwide Building Society* [2012] EWCA Civ 1626; *Santander UK plc v RA Legal Solicitors* [2014] EWCA Civ 183; *Purrunsing v A'Court & Co* [2016] EWHC 789 (Ch).
2   SI 2017/692.
3   *Re a Solicitor (Maharaj)* (1999, unreported).

27.3

In a rising market fraud can frequently remain undetected as, if questions are asked or arrears develop, the property can be sold at a profit and the lender's concerns assuaged. It is when a sudden drop in prices occurs and there is no escape route that frauds become particularly apparent. It is for that reason that following the recession that started in about 1989 and continued into the 1990s the profession was caught up in one of its greatest scandals as the extent of widespread mortgage fraud became known, and the extent to which the negligence of solicitors, or worse, had contributed to it.

The continuing impact of the 2008 financial crisis and subsequent recession is having the same effect in disclosing mortgage fraud and, as expected, extensive fraudulent activities have been and are being uncovered. The adverse effects on the buy-to-let market caused by the economic downturn have provided opportunities for fraudsters in relation to the bulk refinancing/remortgaging of such borrowing. Lenders and the SRA, as well as other regulators, are becoming ever more proactive in policing and detecting trends and risks.

Multiple purchases

27.4

When it was the norm to meet your client in routine domestic conveyancing it was easier to spot warning signs. Now, despite the requirement for identity checks imposed by money laundering legislation, because of the development of commoditised conveyancing and online dealings, the conveyancing environment remains relatively friendly to frauds of this kind.

Individual buyers may be real people, but nominees. A common feature of this kind of fraud is a central figure through whom communications are required to be channelled. This could be a broker or a senior family member. All or most instructions are given by the key individual; solicitors may be encouraged to correspond with clients through that individual, and to send money and documents to that individual. Documents are sent to him or her to be signed by others and come back signed and witnessed. It all seems very efficient.

27.5

Solicitors should be alive to the fact that commercial pressures exist, and that fraudsters are highly attuned to the business community. They may be attracted to your practice, not because it has the best local reputation for efficient conveyancing, but because it is new or not apparently very wealthy, so that offers of substantial work might encourage the turning of a blind eye. Fraudsters will have their own intelligence network and will seek out those perceived to be vulnerable or susceptible to financial pressures, flattery, or occasionally coercion and blackmail. Coercion and blackmail sound like extreme scenarios, but you need to bear in mind that if a solicitor bends or breaks a rule as a 'favour' he also gives any person with knowledge of his wrongdoing power over him, including the person to whom he gave the favour ('We are now in this together ...').

A more sophisticated version of this fraud involves the fraudster instructing a panel of solicitors, without disclosing to any firm that he is using more than one. Multiple transactions become more difficult to detect. If you become aware that an individual has more than one firm acting for him in such circumstances or for unexplained reasons, be suspicious.

Mules

27.6

Experienced conveyancers are very familiar with the patterns of behaviour of purchaser clients. To most, buying a new home is a very substantial, serious and potentially stressful transaction; they will ask questions, be concerned about matters of detail, be anxious about dates and progress. If clients introduced by Mr X show a pattern of near indifference, and contact is limited and amounts to virtually no more than an exchange of documents, there are likely to be grounds for suspicion. If the attitude of Mr X appears to be that of a businessman asking questions that are consistent with a businessman's outlook, rather than the questions clients could be expected to ask, it is more likely that it is he who has the true interest in the transaction, rather than those he purports to represent.

Mules – nominees or people with false identification used as buyers of property to facilitate fraud – have none of the normal interest that buyers of property will display. They may sometimes be exposed by even casual questioning.

Identity theft

27.7

Fraudsters can steal the identity of property owners, either to remortgage the property or to sell it to a genuine buyer or a co-conspirator. Ensure you know with whom you are dealing. Be concerned if it is said that there are reasons why the seller cannot be contacted. Common features are:

- a central figure, usually a broker introducing multiple transactions to the practice. He will be the only point of contact and will deal with clients on your behalf. He will reassure you that all regulatory and professional obligations have already been attended to. You may rarely if ever meet or have direct dealings with the client;

- rushed transactions; there will be an explanation such as a family crisis or other reason for urgency;

- the only money changing hands being the mortgage advance;

- instructions to remit funds to the client account of a named firm of solicitors (possibly the funds are urgently needed for mother's nursing home fees). The destination account may involve a bogus firm of solicitors or a ghost branch office of a genuine firm.

In the examples given in footnote 1 to **27.2**, in *Lloyds TSB Bank plc v Markandan & Uddin*,[1] the true owners of the property were unaware of the transaction, the solicitors who purported to act for the vendors did not exist and the fraudsters took the money. In *Davisons Solicitors v Nationwide Building Society*,[2] an imposter had notified the Law Society and the SRA of a false business address for an existing sole practitioner. The sole practitioner had informed the Law Society and the SRA that the information was false but they had failed to remove it from their websites. The solicitors were relieved of liability for breach of trust as they had acted reasonably in making all necessary prudent enquiries.

In *Santander UK plc v RA Legal Solicitors*,[3] the fraud was perpetrated by a firm of solicitors which pretended to act for the seller, who had no contact with the firm at all. The signature on the transfer was forged. The buyer's solicitors were not relieved of liability as, among other things, they had released the purchase monies to the fraudulent firm before any contracts had been exchanged and without any undertakings being given.

In *Purrunsing v A'Court & Co*,[4] a fraudster purported to be the owner and seller of property which he did not own; neither the conveyancers acting for him nor the solicitors acting for the buyer had taken sufficient care and they were each held liable as to one-half of the loss.

It is not only the solicitor acting on behalf of the fraudster who faces potential liability for losses arising from a fraudulent sale. The question as to division of liability between a solicitor who has acted for a fraudster and a solicitor acting for an innocent purchaser has been considered by the Court of Appeal in the joined appeals in *P&P Property Ltd v (1) Owen White & Catlin LLP (2) Crownvent Ltd; Dreamvar (UK) Limited v Mishcon De Reya*.[5] Mishcon De Reya was found to be strictly liable for at least a portion of its innocent purchaser client's losses as a result of the release of the purchase monies to a person other than the true seller. Solicitors for the fraudster shared liability on the basis of a failure to properly identify their client. The Court of Appeal observed that failure to comply with money laundering requirements may be an important factor in establishing or apportioning civil liability on the part of solicitors in cases of identity fraud.[6]

1   [2012] 2 All ER 884.
2   [2012] EWCA Civ 1626.
3   [2014] EWCA Civ 183.
4   [2016] EWHC 789 (Ch).
5   [2018] EWCA Civ 1082.
6   Per Patten LJ at [31].

Exaggerated price or value

27.8

At its most basic this involves a friendly valuer putting too high a figure on the property and some private arrangement between buyer and seller, but in this type of fraud it is more often than not the case that the manipulation of the price is apparent to a watchful solicitor.

A solicitor should be alive to anything which could artificially inflate the price to be paid so that the amount of money that changes hands is less than the stated purchase price. Historically, this has been done by such things as mythical 'deposits paid direct' or an 'allowance on completion' operating as a substantial discount on the stated price.

Another mechanism is to introduce a third party into the chain so that the transaction proceeds as a sale and sub-sale, or a 'back-to-back' sale and resale – the first half of the transaction being at the correct price agreed to be paid to the seller and the second half involving a sale to the real buyer at the inflated price declared to the mortgagee.

The purpose is to achieve a situation in which the mortgagee lends more than 100 per cent of the true value or price so that the fraudulent buyer acquires the property and a cash bonus.

Another warning sign is a client instructing a solicitor geographically distant from the property for no good apparent reason; this limits the opportunities for personal dealing and avoids local knowledge of the housing market.

A flat property market offers limited opportunities for price leverage but sale and leaseback can be used for this purpose, for example where there is a distressed vendor (facing repossession), genuine or impersonated. A firm may be approached by a broker and offered a package of such transactions, all pre-agreed and pre-arranged.

27.9

Solicitors can become complicit by failing to identify the relevant features of the transaction for what they are, or occasionally by more active assistance. One solicitor, when faced with solicitors acting for the seller who refused to co-operate by agreeing, as requested, to an inflated contract price and an 'allowance on completion' amounting to more than 25 per cent of the true price, solved his fraudulent client's problem by acquiring an off the shelf Isle of Man company and arranging the sale to the company at the true price and immediate sale on by the company to his client at the inflated price declared to the mortgagee. He charged for both conveyancing transactions, and the services involved in arranging the company and its involvement.[1]

Solicitors will face not only civil claims from mortgagees if fraud has occurred, but also disciplinary proceedings with serious consequences – even if it is ultimately established that the solicitor was not actively complicit as a co-conspirator, but only insufficiently alert to the danger signs.

1   *Levinson,* 6942–1995, SDT. Mr Levinson explained to the Tribunal that this was not his own idea; he had copied it from his former partner, a Mr Nathan, who had in the meantime been struck off and sent to prison. Mr Levinson was struck off.

Fraud factories

27.10

Another development has involved the acquisition of law practices by fraudsters. Genuine firms facing difficulties or under financial pressure may be offered the opportunity of being taken over by a team which offers to introduce a portfolio of transactions, and conveyancing clerks to manage it. The purchaser may purport to be a solicitor, impersonating a genuine solicitor. Alternatively it may be a non-solicitor who makes the same offer, on the basis that he will become a financial controller or office manager. All such new arrivals, and their support teams, will be heavily resistant to supervision.

These arrangements are not designed to last for long, and the new owners have no interest in the success of the business; they are simply designed to obtain mortgage advances which are stolen. These 'fraud factories' may have a life of only three months, but those who control them can steal millions in that time.

A variation on the theme involves using the identity of an established firm by purporting to set up a branch office. The SRA publishes details of the misuse of solicitors' names on its website.

Solicitors as victims

27.11

Criminals, particularly international criminals, appear to have concluded that solicitors can be a soft touch by being too trusting. The Serious Organised Crime Agency (now the National Crime Agency) has issued a warning to solicitors, particularly litigation practices which, because they may undertake little or no transactional work and may not even be subject to the Money Laundering Regulations, may be less alive to the risks. Fraudsters are approaching British firms for assistance in relation to personal injury, debt and other claims. The firms shortly receive large cheques representing purported settlements. If the solicitors are incautious enough, under pressure, to release funds without waiting for the received cheques to clear, they find that the cheques are fraudulent or stolen, leaving the firm to bear the loss.

Firms are also vulnerable to social engineering attacks – attempts by fraudsters to dupe solicitors and accounts staff into disclosing bank login details. Such attacks are characterised by attempts on the part of the fraudster to build trust by revealing some knowledge of the account or transaction.

Investment fraud

27.12

Investment fraud is another serious issue for the profession because, in relation to the kinds of fraud that are discussed here, solicitors are essential to their success.

The broad nature of these frauds is that they offer to be highly profitable – to the point of absurdity – while being at the same time wholly secure. The justification for this investment paradox, which defies all normal rules, is that they are reserved to the few insiders who know about them. They are also targeted at those who can afford, or at least can find, large sums to invest – commonly US$1 million or more (the medium is usually US dollars) – so that the victim may think that it is his wealth that enables him to engage in business ventures unavailable to others.

The trap

27.13

These frauds are more successful than would otherwise be expected because of the involvement of solicitors. The necessity for the involvement of solicitors is explained by an understanding of the different attitudes of the three participants – fraudster, victim and solicitor – which the fraudster exploits.

The victim will think, 'This is new to me; I have not heard of this form of investment before, but I am sure that if it was not genuine no solicitor would permit himself to be involved'.

The solicitor's attitude is, 'I do not truly understand what is going on here, but I do not have to. All I am being asked to do is to confirm that this copy document is a true copy of an original, or that I have received a particular document or a document of a particular description, or that I have received a specific sum of money. I do not have to go beyond that and I am not required to'.

The fraudster's position is, 'If I can get a solicitor involved the victim will be reassured, and the scheme given a credibility that it would not otherwise have. I am prepared to pay substantial sums for that involvement; it will be money well spent'.

The solicitor may be offered generous fees for doing very little, or the opportunity to earn interest on very large sums of money that pass through his or her client account.

The test

27.14

It is not considered to be particularly helpful to attempt to describe the range of possible kinds of fraud or the (usually highly complex and turgid) details of those that have been attempted in the past. They change and become more sophisticated as time passes. The one thing they have in common is that if they are carefully considered they do not make sense. They were often referred to as 'Prime Bank Instrument' frauds, by reference to the kind of document that was used to perpetrate them; they have also been termed 'High Yield Investment Programmes'. They were described by Neuberger J in *Dooley v Law Society*[1] in these words:

> 'Bank instrument frauds are based on documents which are full of impressive phrases, which on analysis make little sense, and which promise returns which are fantastic in both senses in which that word is used, namely fictitious and enormous. They are used by unscrupulous rogues to encourage the badly advised, the ignorant, the gullible and the greedy to part with their money, tempted by promises of the fantastically high returns. Once these investors part with their money, they are lucky if they see any of it again. Generally speaking, a man may as well burn his money for all the good it would do him. At least it would remove the false hopes and subsequent agony that such so-called investments involve.'

1   2000, unreported.

27.15

The Tribunal has dealt with many such cases. The following comments made by the Tribunal help to identify the pattern, and particularly the kind of mistake, that solicitors make:

> 'Members of the solicitors' profession had been warned about the dangers of becoming involved in prime bank instrument fraud or money launder- ing. The matter in which the Respondent had become involved demon- strated many of the notified hallmarks of fraud; it was entirely clear that the Respondent himself had no understanding of the investment scheme and had simply done what he was told and allowed his client account to be a repository for a huge sum of money.
>
> The Tribunal has had cause in the past to make the observation which it again makes. A solicitor is not a bank. A solicitor can have no business simply in receiving and paying out money with no purpose attached to it. If a solicitor is not more knowledgeable about the subject matter of the cases of which he has conduct than his clients then he should not be handling such cases. A solicitor's stock-in-trade is his knowledge and expertise. If his clients are not utilising such knowledge and expertise it is likely that the solicitor is being involved in order that a spurious scheme be given a cloak of respectability.'[1]
>
> 'It is not for a client to explain the nature of a transaction to a solicitor but rather the solicitor's role is to explain the nature of a transaction to the client. It can be described as nothing other than crass stupidity to accept a role as, for example, an "escrow agent" when the solicitor cannot know

what that means as, indeed, that expression has no meaning in English law. It is, in any event, serious professional misconduct for a solicitor to accept instructions to undertake work in connection with which he has no knowledge, expertise or experience and where the only reason for his involvement is to add a "cloak of respectability" and thereby induce the victims of fraud to take part. The Respondent himself accepts that he should have known or suspected that the transactions in which he became involved were not viable commercial transactions.'[2]

'The Respondent had ensured that scurrilous transactions were given a cloak of respectability by allowing his firm's name to be used in connection with what was on its face a transaction of the type against which the Law Society had issued warnings. It is in the Tribunal's opinion perhaps the most important aspect of this case that the Respondent was prepared to write letters regarding a matter in which he played no part as a solicitor. He had no knowledge of the type of transactions involved, he had no relevant experience and he did not, and indeed could not, give anybody any advice as to the legal aspects. A solicitor becomes involved in acting for a client when the client needs the solicitor's advice and expertise in the relevant area of law. The Tribunal accepts that there are rogues and fraudsters who are extremely plausible. A solicitor is unlikely to be taken in by such a person if he asks himself the question "why am I invited to become involved in this matter?" If the answer is not "because the client seeks to rely upon my legal expertise, knowledge and experience", he should not be playing any part in the matter.'[3]

'The Respondent at the relevant time had been an experienced practitioner. He had stated that he had not seen the yellow warning card issued by the Law Society. The warning card had however not changed the then existing duties on solicitors but had provided clarificatory guidance. The Respondent had clearly been asked to become involved in something which was out of his ordinary line of business involving overseas countries and huge sums of money. The Respondent had put his name to unintelligible documents and to documents drafted by his client which he had not questioned. He had distributed funds received from third parties at the direction of his client and had produced no evidence of proper authority to do so. He had written letters of comfort to banks and solicitors. He had involved himself in the transactions over a period of time. The transactions had never completed. The Respondent had expected significant personal gain from his involvement.'[4]

'The Respondent himself had come to recognise that he should not have been involved in the dubious HYI [High Yield Investment] transactions details of which had been placed before the Tribunal. The attention of members of the profession had been drawn to the proliferation of fraudulent investment schemes purporting to produce extraordinarily high returns on investments. It was recognised that a number of fraudsters sought to deprive potential investors of large sums of money by the production of bizarre schemes, spurious documentation and promises of very high returns indeed, often with the added incentive to invest provided by an assurance that monies would be used for charitable causes or humanitarian projects. It ill behoves a solicitor to use phrases and expressions that have no meaning in English law. It beggars belief that a solicitor should employ such phrases in letters that he himself has written. The question has to be asked, "how can a solicitor offer advice to any client or third party upon a scheme which is so nonsensical that he himself cannot have any useful knowledge of it?" It is well recognised that the fraudsters customarily seek to involve a member of the solicitors' profession in order that a cloak of respectability may be achieved and those defrauded are encouraged to part with large sums of money because of the comfort they derive from the fact that a solicitor is involved in the transaction. In becoming involved in the fraudulent schemes, as the Respondent did, he falsely allowed his own status and the good reputation of the solicitors' profession to be used improperly to persuade potential "investors" to make substantial investment of money. The only proper way for a solicitor to behave when invited to participate in one of these schemes, in whatever capacity, is to refuse to do so and report the approach made to him to the appropriate authorities. For a solicitor to become involved in dubious and/or fraudulent transactions of this type was not compatible with his continued membership of the profession.'[5]

1   *Wayne*, 8189–2000, SDT.
2   *Wilson-Smith*, 8772–2003, SDT.
3   *Rose*, 9067–2004, SDT.
4   *Rosling*, 9242–2005, SDT.
5   *Heath*, 9502–2006, SDT.

27.16

It will have been noted that the single strand of logical concern that permeates these cases is that the client knows more about the subject matter than the solicitor: he is not seeking legal advice and assistance; he is directing the solicitor in what he is required to do and explaining matters to the solicitor, not seeking guidance. In fact, many such schemes are constructed purely for the purposes of money laundering between individuals with a common interest, serving only to move large amounts of money into and out of a solicitor's client account. Compliance with the Money Laundering, Terrorist Financing and Transfer of Funds (Information on the Payer) Regulations 2017[1] considered in **CHAPTER 28** is vital, and would be effective to prevent involvement in such schemes if faithfully followed.

Further, if solicitors ask themselves the questions identified by the Tribunal in *Rose* and *Heath* the precise nature of the fraudulent scheme will not matter. However much fraudsters change the language and apparent structure, and even if the consequence of such changes is that every 'common characteristic' or 'typical phrase' appearing in the Law Society's/SRA's warning card/notice[2] is avoided, it will be a straightforward matter for solicitors to identify dubious transactions and avoid involvement.

In *Bryant and Bench v Law Society*,[3] solicitors who had acted for clients in a series of 'dubious' transactions, even though not themselves dishonest, were both suspended. 'Dubious' in this context meant that the transactions bore the indicia of fraud or possible fraud, and that it was professional misconduct for the appellants to act or to continue to act in relation to them without carrying out sufficient enquiries to satisfy themselves that the transactions were not, in fact, fraudulent. The Divisional Court stated (at [199] and [239]):

'[199] In our view the appellants should have concluded that these transactions involving NIC and Mr Alonso were "dubious" in the sense described above at the very latest by the end of August 2003. But they never did so. They appeared to be naïve, uncommercial and unwilling to question matters; whereas we would have expected solicitors who had considerable experience of international clients and transactions to have developed a healthy scepticism.

[239] ... In the case of Mr Bryant, the incompetence displayed was considerable and continued for approximately a year. In the case of Mr Bench, his culpability was far less, but, on our findings, remains significant. We accept the submission on behalf of the Law Society that such incompetence threatens the reputation of the profession for prudence as well as competence and that it puts the public at risk.'

1   SI 2017/692.
2   See **APPENDIX 9**.
3   [2007] EWHC 3043 (Admin). See also *Yildiz*, 10997–2012 and the litigation which followed on the same facts: *Global Marine Drillships Ltd v La Bella and others* [2014] EWHC 2242 (Ch).

Land banking schemes

27.17

A further species of investment fraud, which also contains features of mortgage fraud, relates to so-called land banking schemes. These typically occur where agricultural, brownfield or other blighted land is acquired at low cost and divided into plots for sale to investors. Investors are informed that the land will soar in value once planning permission is obtained. However, as the land will usually be on a green belt or protected site, the land is unlikely to obtain planning permission or achieve the value intimated by the operator, resulting in the investor paying an inflated price for the land. Such schemes are often promoted on the basis that planning permission is imminent or that a well-known company is about to buy the land. Forged HM Land Registry letters and HM Land Registry estate plan approval letters have been used as evidence that planning permission is available when this is not the case. Also the obtaining of planning permission may be in the control of a management company which may have no intention of applying for planning permission. Operators of land banking schemes are often based overseas, making it difficult for an investor to recover funds invested in a scheme or for enforcement action to be taken against the operator. Operators may also attempt to conceal the original value of the land by inter-company transactions which inflate the original purchase price. In September 2012, the SRA issued a warning notice in respect of land banking schemes, and this is included in **APPENDIX 9**. The notice includes the following warning for solicitors acting for investors in these schemes:

'Please take extra care if it is envisaged that your retainer is to be limited in nature, for example it excludes providing advice to clients or is solely restricted to the registration of the properties. Before agreeing to act in these circumstances you should consider whether it is necessary to carry out due diligence in relation to the scheme in order to avoid unwittingly becoming involved in a fraudulent scheme.'

Cyber fraud

27.18

Criminals use a variety of ever-changing and increasingly sophisticated means, electronic and/or verbal, involving impersonation or infiltration, in an attempt to obtain confidential financial information and data with the aim of stealing money from bank accounts. A firm's client account can be targeted in this way. Banks and clients can also be targeted in an attempt to defraud the client account.

To make their fraud appear credible, the criminals may use tactics such as convincingly passing themselves off as calling from a bank or referring to the details of a genuine transaction which they have acquired dishonestly. Or they may use the names of law firms, solicitors, parties to a conveyancing transaction, beneficiaries of trusts and wills or persons linked directly or indirectly to a client account, to make their activity seem credible.

Fraud mechanisms are ever-changing and more sophisticated, but the following have been known to target law firms: variants on the 'CEO fraud'. Typically this occurs in commercial organisations with an email from a fraudster purporting to be a senior person in the organisation to a member of staff in an accounts or finance department, directing the urgent payment of money to a specified bank account for a credible reason. The money is sent to the fraudster's account and rapidly disappears. The email may have involved cloning a genuine email account or using an originating address which is very similar. Applied to law firms, this could involve the impersonation of a genuine CEO or equivalent, or of a client.

'Friday afternoon' frauds involve a late notification from someone pretending to be the client and likewise appearing to come from the client's email address, instructing the solicitor that there is a change of bank details to which to send the proceeds of sale. The new destination is the fraudster's bank account.

As technologies develop, the rise of malware (e g ransomware) is a risk against which solicitors need to be vigilant. Opening an infected attachment could lead to serious breaches of cyber security, potentially crippling a firm's systems or – perhaps more worryingly – enabling fraudsters to obtain detailed confidential information which could be used to facilitate more widespread frauds on clients and other firms.

CHAPTER 28

Money laundering

28.1

This chapter provides a brief introduction to this important and complex subject, specific guidance on the Money Laundering, Terrorist Financing and Transfer of Funds (Information on the Payer) Regulations 2017[1] (MLR 2017) and some commentary on the principal elements of the criminal law that are engaged. It does not provide an all-encompassing guide to the subject, which derives from the criminal law and is beyond the scope of this book. The focus in this chapter is on the regulation of practitioners and the warning signs.

1 SI 2017/692.

What is money laundering?

28.2

To quote the Financial Action Task Force of the Organisation for Economic Co-operation and Development:

> 'The goal of a large number of criminal acts is to generate a profit for the individual or group that carries out the act. Money laundering is the processing of these criminal proceeds to disguise their illegal origin. This process is of critical importance, as it enables the criminal to enjoy these profits without jeopardising their source.'

Money laundering is the process by which assets illegally obtained are 'cleaned' to give them apparent legitimacy to enable their subsequent use. It involves the purported legitimisation of *any asset* that is illegitimately obtained. An accumulation of small amounts obtained or retained by tax evasion would be criminal property for these purposes. Money laundering is designed to disguise the true origin of criminal proceeds. The process typically involves three stages – placement, layering and integration – but these are not clear cut distinctions and money laundering may become a seamless blend of all three.

Placement

28.3

The placement stage involves the placing in the financial/banking system of the proceeds of crime. The intention is to change the identity of the illegitimate asset. A solicitor's client account will serve this purpose.

Layering

28.4

The layering stage involves moving the asset through the financial system. The intention is to hide the origins of the illegitimate asset, making it difficult to trace and recover. Complex transactions may be used to disguise the source of funds. Sometimes the transactions may have no legitimate economic purpose, but simply result in money moving around (see the commentary on investment frauds at **27.12**).

Integration

28.5

The integration stage involves the translation of the laundered funds into a legitimate asset, such as the purchase of property through a conveyancing solicitor.

Solicitors as 'gatekeepers'

28.6

According to the Serious Organised Crime Agency (now the National Crime Agency):

> 'Serious organised criminals have a number of options when looking to realise the proceeds of their criminal activities. These include smuggling cash or assets out of the UK; laundering the money themselves; employing "gatekeepers", such as solicitors and accountants, with access to financial facilities; corrupting or coercing bank employees; or using professional launderers.'[1]

Professionals, including solicitors, may have a lack of awareness or lack of curiosity, so allowing themselves to be used by criminals to access the banking system and to enable the conversion of criminal funds into legitimate assets.

Solicitors may assist by becoming involved in normal transactions, such as a property purchase, but in circumstances where the client's true identity or status as nominee are disguised, and/or where the source of funds cannot be ascertained or is suspicious. Solicitors may also become involved in unusual transactions with no obvious logic where large amounts of money move about without any apparent aim. Investment frauds of the kind considered in **CHAPTER 27** invariably 'fail' in the sense that nothing comes of the 'investment' but it can be that all parties to the scheme are colluding and that the only real purpose is to move money in and out of a solicitor's client account.

A derivative of investment frauds is sham litigation. Here the fraudsters collude to litigate over an original scheme which, on close analysis, may make little sense. Signs to watch for will include clients with an unusual lack of interest in the risks of litigation, and who seem reluctant to engage in the detail. Another indicator is that one party to the litigation will suddenly capitulate, submitting to judgment for the full amount, without material effort to achieve a compromise solution. Note that the conduct of litigation does not necessarily fall within the scope of MLR 2017. Guidance issued by the Legal Services Affinity Group (LSAG) reports:

'HM Treasury has confirmed that the following would not generally be viewed as participation in a financial transaction:

- payment on account of costs to a legal professional or payment of a legal professional's bill

- provision of legal advice

- participation in litigation or a form of alternative dispute resolution

- will-writing, although you should consider whether any accompanying taxation advice is covered

- work funded by the Legal Services Commission

If you are uncertain whether the Regulations apply to your work, you should seek legal advice on the individual circumstances of your practice or simply take the broadest possible approach to compliance with the Regulations.'[2]

1   The Serious Organised Crime Agency, *United Kingdom Threat Assessment of Serious Organised Crime 2006/07*.
2   'Anti-Money Laundering: Guidance for the Legal Sector', LSAG, March 2018, at page 17.

Six key questions for solicitors

28.7

There is no substitute for understanding and following MLR 2017 (see **28.9**), but solicitors should always ask themselves:

- Am I confident I know who this person is and that I understand with whom I am really dealing?

- Am I confident that I know and understand the source of funds?

- Am I confident that I know and understand the transaction?

- Is there anything about the transaction which is unusual or financially illogical?

- Is the client showing an appropriate degree of interest in the transaction?

- Do I understand why this client has chosen to instruct me?

These are issues of which solicitors should be aware at the beginning of a business relationship or transaction, *and* which they should also continue to have in mind and to monitor as relationships and transactions develop.

Law Society guidance and assistance

28.8

Regulation 47(1) of MLR 2017 requires supervisory authorities (ie HM Treasury) to make up-to-date information available to those it supervises. A court must take into account any guidance approved by HM Treasury in determining whether certain offences under the Proceeds of Crime Act (POCA) 2002 and the Terrorism Act (TA) 2000 may have been committed. The guidance is also relevant to a number of obligations under MLR 2017.

HM Treasury has determined that there will only be one piece of Treasury-approved guidance across the whole legal sector. This, in its current form, is 'Anti-Money Laundering: Guidance for the Legal Sector' published by the Legal Services Affinity Group in March 2018 ('LSAG Guidance'). Solicitors should be familiar with the LSAG Guidance and the occasions on which they must have regard to it. See **28.9**.

The full guidance, which runs to 156 pages, can be found at www.law society.org.uk/policy-campaigns/documents/legal-sector-affinity-group-anti-money-laundering-guidance. In addition, the Law Society's Practice Advice Service will assist in understanding the LSAG Guidance and is available to talk through any problems (tel: 020 7320 5675). There is also a list[1] of solicitors with relevant expertise willing to give other solicitors 30 minutes' free advice on legal issues relating to money laundering.

The Law Society also produces a bi-monthly AML e-newsletter which provides useful information on developments in money laundering, including a section titled 'Launderers in the News', which summarises recent prosecutions.

1   See www.lawsociety.org.uk/Advice/Anti-money-laundering/AML-directory.

Money Laundering, Terrorist Financing and Transfer of Funds (Information on the Payer) Regulations 2017

28.9

MLR 2017[1] were implemented to ensure compliance with the Fourth Money Laundering Directive.[2] They came into force on 26 June 2017.

1   SI 2017/692.
2   Directive (EU) 2015/849 of the European Parliament and of the Council of 20 May 2015 on the prevention of the use of the financial system for the purposes of money laundering or terrorist financing, amending Regulation (EU) No 648/2012 of the European Parliament and of the Council, and repealing Directive 2005/60/EC of the European Parliament and of the Council and Commission Directive 2006/70/EC.

Relevant persons

28.10

MLR 2017 set administrative requirements for the anti-money laundering regime within the regulated sector and 'outline the scope of [customer due diligence]'.[1]

MLR 2017 aim to limit the use of professional services for money laundering by requiring professionals to know their clients and monitor the use of their services by clients.

Regulation 8 states that MLR 2017 apply to persons acting in the course of business carried on in the United Kingdom including independent legal professionals, which do not include solicitors employed by a public authority or working in-house.

MLR 2017 only apply to certain solicitors' activities where there is a high risk of money laundering occurring, as follows:

'(a) the buying and selling of real property or business entities;

(b) the managing of client money, securities or other assets;

(c) the opening or management of bank, savings or securities accounts;

(d) the organisation of contributions necessary for the creation, operation or management of companies; or

(e) the creation, operation or management of trusts, companies, foundations or similar structures,

and, for this purpose, a person participates in a transaction by assisting in the planning or execution of the transaction or otherwise acting for or on behalf of a client in the transaction.'[2]

The Treasury has confirmed that the following would not generally be viewed as participation in financial transactions, and therefore are not covered by MLR 2017:

- payment on account of costs to a solicitor or payment of a solicitor's bill;

- provision of legal advice;

- participation in litigation or a form of alternative dispute resolution;

- will-writing, although you should consider whether any accompanying taxation advice is covered;

- work funded by the Legal Aid Agency.

It is important therefore to identify whether a solicitor's work comes within the regulated sector; a firm conducting exclusively claimant litigation would not come within the regulated sector for example. The LSAG Guidance goes on to state:

'If you are uncertain whether the Regulations apply to your work, you should seek legal advice on the individual circumstances of your practice or simply take the broadest possible approach to compliance with the Regulations.'

1   LSAG Guidance, page 15.
2   Regulation 12(1).

Customer due diligence and ongoing monitoring

28.11

A solicitor must conduct customer due diligence (CDD) on clients who retain the solicitor for services regulated under MLR 2017. Regulation 27 requires that CDD be conducted when:

- establishing a business relationship;[1]

  (note that a relationship where the relevant person is asked to form a company for its customer is to be treated as a business relationship for the purpose of these Regulations, whether or not the formation of the company is the only transaction carried out for that customer[2]);

- carrying out an occasional transaction that amounts to a transfer of funds within the meaning of article 3.9 of the Funds Transfer Regulation[3] exceeding €1,000;

- the solicitor suspects money laundering or terrorist financing;[4] or

- the solicitor doubts the veracity or adequacy of documents or information previously obtained for the purposes of identification or verification.[5]

A relevant person must also apply customer due diligence measures 'at other appropriate times to existing customers on a risk based approach'[6] and when a solicitor 'becomes aware that the circumstances of an existing customer relevant to its risk assessment for that customer have changed'.[7]

Customer due diligence measures are covered by regulation 28 of MLR 2017 and require that a solicitor must:

- identify the customer and verify[8] the customer's identity unless the identity of the customer is already known to and has been verified by the solicitor;[9]

- assess and, where appropriate, obtain information on the purpose and intended nature of the business relationship or occasional transaction;[10]

- identify, where there is a beneficial owner who is not the customer, the beneficial owner and take reasonable measures to verify his identity so that the relevant person is satisfied that he knows who the beneficial owner is, including, in the case of a legal person, trust or similar legal arrangement, measures to understand the ownership and control structure of the person, trust or arrangement.[11]

Compliance with CDD requirements must reflect the risk assessment carried out by the relevant person under regulation 18(1)[12] and the assessment of the level of risk arising in any particular case; compliance may therefore vary from case to case.[13] The assessment of the level of risk in any particular case must take account of factors including: (a) the purpose of an account, transaction or business relationship; (b) the assets involved or the size of the transaction; and (c) the regularity and duration of the business relationship.[14]

A solicitor must 'be able to demonstrate to [his] supervisory authority that the extent of the measures … are appropriate in view of the risks of money laundering and terrorist financing' with regard to the risk assessments carried out under regulation 18(1) and information made available by the supervisory authority under regulations 17(9) and 47.[15] This is required as part of both customer due diligence measures, and ongoing monitoring. Where a relevant person has to apply customer due diligence in the case of a trust or similar arrangement and the beneficial owner consists of a class of persons, it may not be necessary to identify all members of the class.[16]

A relevant person must keep under review every business relationship and conduct 'ongoing monitoring'. This means:

> '(a) scrutiny of transactions undertaken throughout the course of the relationship (including, where necessary, the source of funds) to ensure that the transactions are consistent with the relevant person's knowledge of the customer, the customer's business and risk profile;

(b) undertaking reviews of existing records and keeping the documents or information obtained for the purpose of applying customer due diligence measures up-to-date.'[17]

1   'Business relationship' means a business, professional or commercial relationship between a relevant person and a customer, which: (a) arises out of the business of the relevant person; and (b) is expected by the relevant person, at the time when contact is established, to have an element of duration.
2   Regulation 4 of MLR 2017.
3   Regulation (EU) 2015/847 of the European Parliament and of the Council of 20 May 2015 on information accompanying transfers of funds and repealing Regulation (EC) No 1781/2006.
4   Regulation 27(1)(c).
5   Regulation 27(1)(d).
6   Regulation 27(8)(a).
7   Regulation 27(8)(b).
8   Where 'verify' means 'verify on the basis of documents or information … obtained from a reliable source which is independent', per regulation 28(18).
9   Regulation 28(2)(a) and (b).
10 Regulation 28(2)(c).
11 Regulation 28(4). Note that this does not apply where a customer is listed on a regulated market (see regulation 28(5)). Note also that it is not permissible to rely solely on the statement of significant control to comply with regulation 28(4) (per regulation 28(9)).
12 See **28.18**.
13 Regulation 28(12)(a) and (b).
14 Regulation 28(13).
15 Regulation 28(16).
16 Regulation 6(1) defines beneficial ownership as it relates to trusts and similar structures. Regulation 30(7) requires that, where CDD measures are required, they must be completed before a member of a class receives payment or exercises any vested rights under a trust, legal entity or legal arrangement.
17 Regulation 28(11).

28.12

It is important to note that, by requiring a risk-based assessment of the needs of due diligence and a full and proper understanding of transactions, the MLR 2017 impose obligations actively to monitor the way that business relationships and transactions develop, with an understanding of the aims of money laundering. This is not a box-ticking exercise so that, having obtained a copy passport and a utility bill (for example), a solicitor can consider the money laundering requirements to have been satisfied. There is an ongoing obligation for relevant persons in relation to all clients and all transactions. Many will involve minimal risk and commensurate monitoring, but the MLR 2017 require relevant persons to be watchful and thoughtful.

A client's identity must be verified before a business relationship is established or an occasional transaction is carried out[1] but the verification process may be completed during the establishment of a business relationship, if it is 'necessary not to interrupt the normal conduct of business' and 'there is little risk of money laundering or terrorist financing occurring' provided that the verification is completed as soon as practicable after contact is first established.[2]

A solicitor unable to establish a client's identity must not carry out any transaction with or for the client through a bank account; must not establish a business relationship or carry out an occasional transaction with the client; must terminate any existing business relationship with the client and must consider whether he or she is required to make a disclosure (under Part 7 of the Proceeds of Crime Act 2002 or Part III of the Terrorism Act 2000).[3]

There is an important exception in favour of a solicitor where he is 'in the course of establishing the legal position for his client or performing his task of defending or representing that client in, or concerning, legal proceedings, including advice on the institution or avoidance of proceedings'.[4]

This exception does not apply to transactional work so solicitors should be careful to distinguish between advice and litigation work, and transactional work.

1 Regulation 30(2).
2 Regulation 30(3).
3 Regulation 31.
4 Regulation 31(3).

Enhanced customer due diligence

28.13

There are requirements for 'enhanced customer due diligence and ongoing monitoring' to manage and mitigate the risks arising from, among other things:

- higher risks identified as a result of risk assessments under regulation 18(1) and/or information provided by the supervisory authority under regulations 17(9) and 47;[1]

- the client being established in a high risk country;[2]

- the client being a 'politically exposed person' (PEP) or a family member or known close associate of a PEP;[3]

- the client having provided false or stolen ID documents and the solicitor continuing to deal with the client;[4]

- unusually large and complex transactions, transactions forming an unusual pattern or transactions with no apparent economic or legal purpose;[5] or

- in any other situation which by its nature can present a higher risk of money laundering or terrorist financing.[6]

A politically exposed person is an individual who is or has at any time in the preceding year been entrusted with prominent public functions other than a middle-ranking or more junior official.[7]

Enhanced due diligence may be required in the case of clients who are not physically present for identification purposes, since non-face-to-face transactions are an increased risk factor pursuant to regulation 33(6). Enhanced due diligence in the case of politically exposed persons requires: senior management approval of the business relationship; measures to be taken to establish the source of wealth and source of funds involved in the proposed business relationship or occasional transaction; and enhanced ongoing monitoring.[8]

1 Regulation 33(1)(a).
2 Regulation 33(1)(b).
3 Regulation 33(1)(d).
4 Regulation 33(1)(e).
5 Regulation 33(1)(f).
6 Regulation 33(1)(g). Note the list of factors to be taken into account in assessing whether there is a higher risk set out in regulation 33(6).

7   Regulation 35(12).
8   Regulation 35(5).

Law Society guidance on customer due diligence

28.14

Chapter 4 of the LSAG Guidance contains comprehensive guidance on CDD. It provides detailed advice as to how to deal with the verification of UK residents; persons not resident in the United Kingdom; clients unable to produce standard documentation; other professionals; partnerships and LLPs; public companies listed in the United Kingdom; private and unlisted companies in the United Kingdom; public overseas companies; and private and unlisted overseas companies. It also explains how to approach money laundering issues concerning other legal or quasi-legal entities such as trusts, foundations, charities, deceased persons' estates, churches, schools, clubs and pension funds.

As for ongoing monitoring, the LSAG Guidance states (at paragraph 4.6):

'Regulation 28(11) requires that you conduct ongoing monitoring of a business relationship. Ongoing monitoring is defined as:

- scrutiny of transactions undertaken throughout the course of the relationship, (including where necessary, the source of funds), to ensure that the transactions are consistent with your knowledge of the client, their business and the risk profile

- undertaking reviews of existing records and keeping the documents, or information obtained for the purpose of applying CDD, up-to-date.

You must also be aware of obligations to keep clients' personal data updated under the Data Protection Act 1998 and the General Data Protection Regulation [...]

You are not required to:

- conduct the whole CDD process again every few years

- suspend or terminate a business relationship until you have updated information or documents, as long as you are still satisfied you know who your client is, and keep under review any request you have made for up to date information or documents

- use sophisticated computer analysis packages to review each new retainer for anomalies. Many practices operate a system of regular review and renewal of CDD as good practice.

[...]

Ongoing monitoring will normally be conducted by legal professionals handling the retainer, and involves staying alert to suspicious circumstances which may suggest money laundering, terrorist financing, or the provision of false CDD material. A high degree of professionalism and scrutiny is expected from legal professionals – see *R v Griffiths & Pattison* (2007) CA which confirmed that legal professionals are expected to fulfil these obligations "up to the hilt".'

Sanctions and counter-measures

28.15

Customer due diligence systems should be able to enable identification of persons subject to restrictions imposed by the UK Government. The Office of Financial Sanctions Implementation is responsible for publishing details of such restrictions.

Customer due diligence systems should also be able to enable identification of persons subject to financial sanctions following designation by the United Nations or the European Commission. The Office of Financial Sanctions publishes one consolidated list covering restrictions imposed by the UK, EU and UN. The full list can be accessed at www.gov.uk/government/publications/financial-sanctions-consolidated-list-of-targets.

Reliance on third parties and outsourcing

28.16

Solicitors may rely on a third party to conduct customer due diligence on their behalf, provided that the third party falls within specified categories;[1] and that the solicitor immediately obtains all necessary information and an arrangement is in place permitting the solicitor to obtain ID and verification data immediately upon request and ensuring that the third party keeps the records for five years.[2] The solicitor remains liable for any default by the person they relied upon.[3]

The reliance provisions are not required:

- for use of e-verification information to verify identity;

- for passporting clients between offices of the same legal practice;

- for receiving actual identity documents (including certified copied) to assist you with verification; or

- by financial institutions when applying the simplification provisions in regulation 37 to a solicitor's client account.

1   Listed in regulation 39(3); see also paragraphs 4.4.3–4.4.6 of the LSAG Guidance.
2   Regulation 39(2).
3   Regulation 39(1).

Record keeping

28.17

Relevant persons must keep records to demonstrate compliance with MLR 2017. In substance this requires you to keep evidence of identity and other file records of a relationship or transaction for five years from the completion of the transaction or the end of the relationship.[1] Note that this may have an impact on General Data Protection Regulation (GDPR)[2] and other data protection obligations in respect of the period for which personal data, and in particular special category data, may be retained.

1   Regulation 40.

2   Regulation (EU) 2016/679 of the European Parliament and of the Council of 27 April 2016 on the protection of natural persons with regard to the processing of personal data and on the free movement of such data, and repealing Directive 95/46/EC (General Data Protection Regulation).

Risk assessments

28.18

MLR 2017 introduce, for the first time, the requirement to undertake a practice-wide risk assessment.[1] The risk assessment must identify and assess the risk of money laundering and terrorist financing faced by a business. The LSAG Guidance contains detailed consideration of the assessment of a business's risk profile at paragraph 2.3. A risk assessment will need to take account of the nature of the business's work in the legal sector, the nature and location of its clients and their businesses and the geographic locations in which the business operates. Assessment of risk will vary between practices and it is essential to have a detailed understanding of both the generic risks facing the legal sector as a whole as discussed in the LSAG Guidance, and also the specific risks which are of more immediate relevance to the specific practice.

A comprehensive and well-documented risk assessment will assist businesses in ensuring consistency in decision-making, demonstrating appropriate systems and compliance and will help to justify any decisions to law enforcement agencies, the courts and interested regulators.

1   Regulation 18(1).

Systems and training

28.19

Relevant persons must establish and maintain appropriate risk-sensitive policies and procedures to prevent activities relating to money laundering or terrorist financing. These must address:

- customer due diligence measures and ongoing monitoring;
- reporting;
- reliance and record keeping;
- internal controls;
- risk assessment and management; and
- the monitoring and management of compliance with, and the internal communication of, such policies and procedures.[1]

Solicitors' firms must have a money laundering reporting officer (MLRO) – a 'nominated officer' for the purpose of MLR 2017 to receive and to make disclosures.[2]

Policies and procedures must include those which provide for the identification and scrutiny of:

- complex or unusually large transactions;

- unusual patterns of transactions which have no apparent economic or visible lawful purpose; and

- any other activity which the relevant person regards as particularly likely by its nature to be related to money laundering or terrorist financing.[3]

As mentioned above, the requirement to have a full and proper understanding of transactions is reinforced, and it will be seen that a responsible application of regulation 19 will avoid the involvement of solicitors in the kind of investment frauds considered in **CHAPTER 27**.

Relevant persons must take appropriate measures to ensure that 'all relevant employees' are 'made aware of the law relating to money laundering and terrorist financing', and are 'regularly given training in how to recognise and deal with transactions and other activities or situations which may be related to money laundering or terrorist financing'.[4]

For the guidance on training see paragraphs 3.7.2–3.7.3 of the LSAG Guidance. Paragraph 3.7.2 contains the following advice:

'When setting up a training and communication system you should consider:

- which staff require training

- what form the training will take

- how often training should take place

- how staff will be kept up-to-date with emerging risk factors for the practice.

Assessments of who should receive training should include who deals with clients in areas of practice within the regulated sector, handles funds or otherwise assists with compliance. Consider fee earners, reception staff, administration staff and finance staff, because they will each be differently involved in compliance and so have different training requirements.

Training can take many forms and may include:

- face-to-face training seminars

- completion of online training sessions

- attendance at AML/CTF conferences

- participation in dedicated AML/CTF forums

- review of publications on current AML/CTF issues

- practice or practice group meetings for discussion of AML/CTF issues and risk factors.

Providing an AML/CTF policy manual is useful to raise staff awareness and can be a continual reference source between training sessions.'

1   Regulation 19.
2   Regulation 21.
3   Regulation 19(4).
4   Regulation 24.

Compliance

28.20

The Law Society, through the SRA, is a supervisory authority with responsibility to monitor those it regulates and to take necessary measures for the purposes of securing compliance with MLR 2017.[1] A failure to comply with any of the requirements of MLR 2017 listed above is a criminal offence punishable by a term of imprisonment of up to two years.[2] No offence is committed if all reasonable steps were taken and all due diligence was exercised to avoid committing the offence.[3]

1   Regulation 7(1)(b) and Schedule 1.
2   Regulation 86(1).
3   Regulation 86(3).

Communications with clients

28.21

Although not required by MLR 2017, it may be regarded as good practice and good client relations to explain the statutory obligations to which solicitors are subject, in terms of customer due diligence and reporting, in client care material and/or terms of business.

The verification of identity will also, of necessity, require personal data to be processed. Where biometric data is included in identity documents, it will fall within the definition of special category data. Accordingly, solicitors should consider data protection obligations when communicating with clients and, in particular, should ensure that processing is carried out on grounds which do not bring data protection obligations into conflict with the requirements of MLR 2017 to verify identity and to retain appropriate records.

The criminal law – primary offences

28.22

The primary money laundering offences are currently found in Part 7 of POCA 2002. There are also separate offences aimed at preventing the laundering of and dealing with terrorist property in Part 3 of TA 2000.

The three primary money laundering offences are those contained in sections 327, 328 and 329 of POCA 2002. These are:

- transferring, converting, concealing, disguising or removing criminal property from the United Kingdom (section 327);

- arrangements involving criminal property (section 328); and

- acquiring, using or possessing criminal property (section 329).

A prohibited arrangement involving criminal property exists if a person 'enters into or becomes concerned in an arrangement which he knows or suspects facilitates (by whatever means) the acquisition, retention, use or control of criminal property by or on behalf of another person'.[1]

Knowledge or suspicion that the property is criminal property is required for an offence to be committed. The Crown must show that the offender knew or suspected that the arrangement was an arrangement which facilitated the acquisition, retention or control of criminal property. For property to be 'criminal property' the offender must be proved to have known or suspected that the property constituted a person's benefit from criminal conduct, or that it represented such a benefit (in whole or in part, directly or indirectly).[2]

There is no statutory definition of an arrangement; the courts have only been called upon to rule as to what 'arrangements' do *not* include. In *Bowman v Fels*,[3] the Court of Appeal held that an arrangement does not include action undertaken in the context of litigation:

> 'the issue or pursuit of ordinary legal proceedings with a view to obtaining the court's adjudication upon the parties' rights and duties is not to be regarded as an arrangement or a prohibited act within ss 327–9.'[4]

The Law Society's views as to whether and in what circumstances solicitors are involved in an 'arrangement' in the light of *Bowman v Fels* are set out in the LSAG Guidance at paragraph 6.4.3 in the following terms:

> '*Bowman v Fels* [2005] EWCA Civ 226 held that section 328 does not cover or affect the ordinary conduct of litigation by legal professionals, including any step taken in litigation from the issue of proceedings and the securing of injunctive relief or a freezing order up to its final disposal by judgment.
>
> Our view, supported by Counsel's opinion, is that dividing assets in accordance with the judgment, including the handling of the assets which are criminal property, is not an arrangement. Further, settlements, negotiations, out of court settlements, alternative dispute resolution and tribunal representation are not arrangements. However, the property will generally still remain criminal property and you may need to consider referring your client for specialist advice regarding possible offences they may commit once they come into possession of the property after completion of the settlement.
>
> The recovery of property by a victim of an acquisitive offence will not be committing an offence under either section 328 or section 329 of the Act.'

1   Section 328(1) of POCA 2002.
2   Section 340.
3   [2005] EWCA Civ 226, [2005] 1 WLR 3083, [2005] 4 All ER 609.
4   [2005] EWCA Civ 226, [2005] 1 WLR 3083, [2005] 4 All ER 609 at [95].

28.23

There are broadly comparable offences under TA 2000. Those most likely to be of concern to solicitors are contained in sections 17 and 18 of TA 2000. A person commits an offence if he 'enters into or becomes concerned in an arrangement as a result of which money or other property is made available or is to be made available to another', and he 'knows or has reasonable cause to suspect that it will or may be used for the purposes of terrorism';[1] and a person commits an offence if he 'enters into or becomes concerned in an arrangement which facilitates the retention or control by or on behalf of another person of terrorist property' by concealment, removal from the jurisdiction, transfer to nominees or in any other way.

It is a defence to prove that the person accused did not know and had no reasonable cause to suspect that the arrangement related to terrorist property.[2]

Although, as has been seen, MLR 2017 encourage and require a proportionate risk-based approach, this is not the test applied to the primary and secondary criminal offences, where the obligations not to engage in prohibited activities and to make disclosure when required are mandatory.

1   Section 17 of TA 2000.
2   Section 18.

Disclosure

28.24

The concept of 'disclosure' in relation to this area of the law is relevant in two respects.

The offence of non-disclosure

28.25

Section 330 of POCA 2002 applies to information received in the course of business in the regulated sector, and therefore applies to solicitors who are relevant persons for the purposes of MLR 2017. The corresponding non-disclosure offence in respect of terrorist funding is found in section 21A of TA 2000. It is a criminal offence for a person to fail to disclose information received in those circumstances where that person knows or suspects or has reasonable grounds to know or suspect that another person is involved in money laundering or terrorist funding, and is either able to identify the person concerned, or the whereabouts of any of the laundered property, or believes (or can reasonably be expected to believe) that the information will or may assist in identifying the person or the whereabouts of laundered property.

The information required to be disclosed is the identity of the person concerned if known, the whereabouts of the laundered property, so far as known, and any information leading to the identification of the person or location of the property.

Non-disclosure, tipping-off or otherwise prejudicing the course of an investigation (see further at **28.33** to **28.35**) are referred to as secondary offences.

It will have been noted that by introducing the concept of having 'reasonable grounds for knowing or suspecting', an objective test is applied. In the regulated sector you may be guilty of the offence under section 330 or section 331 if you should have known or suspected money laundering was taking place.

Where a solicitor has the relevant knowledge, suspicion or reasonable grounds to suspect, he or she should make a disclosure to their legal practice's nominated officer (often known as a MLRO) to avoid committing this offence.

Once the nominated officer receives such a disclosure, if he or she has the relevant knowledge, suspicion or reasonable grounds to suspect, the officer must make a disclosure to the National Crime Agency (NCA), in order to avoid committing an offence under section 331 of POCA 2002. This obligation is subject to considerations regarding privilege, see **28.30**.

If a nominated officer acting outside the regulated sector similarly has the relevant knowledge or suspicion, he or she too must make a disclosure to NCA, in order to avoid committing an offence under section 332 of POCA 2002. Again, this obligation is subject to considerations regarding privilege, see **28.30**.

Authorised disclosure – a defence

28.26

If a person is involved in an arrangement such as would be caught by section 328 of POCA 2002 (or would otherwise be dealing with criminal property contrary to section 327 or 329), it is a defence to make an authorised disclosure, and a solicitor in this position does not commit an offence of money laundering despite carrying through the transaction to completion if, having made proper disclosure, he or she is given 'appropriate consent' to continue to act. It is essential that all the statutory requirements are met. Such appropriate consent will not be a defence to any complicity in the underlying offence, such as fraud.

Timing

28.27

To constitute an authorised disclosure sufficient to amount to a defence for someone who has become involved in an activity prohibited by sections 327 to 329 of POCA 2002, disclosure must be made as soon as practicable after the information or other matter on which his or her knowledge or suspicion (or reasonable grounds for such knowledge or suspicion) was acquired.

Disclosure should be made *before* a prohibited act takes place.[1]

If disclosure is made *during* the prohibited act the solicitor must have had no relevant knowledge or suspicion when the act was started; the disclosure must be made as soon as practicable after relevant knowledge or suspicion was acquired; and the disclosure must be made on the solicitor's own initiative (that is, not for example prompted by the realisation of imminent discovery or the encouragement of another). The burden of proof will be on the accused to satisfy the court that these conditions are met, otherwise the disclosure is not an authorised disclosure and no defence is available.[2]

If disclosure is made *after* the prohibited act has taken place there must have been good reason why a disclosure was not made before the prohibited act was carried out; the disclosure must have been made as soon as practicable after the prohibited act has taken place; and the disclosure must have been made on the solicitor's own initiative. Again, the burden of proof will be on the accused to satisfy the court that these conditions are met, otherwise the disclosure is not an authorised disclosure and no defence is available.[3]

---

1   Section 338(2) of POCA 2002.

2   Section 338(2A).
3   Section 338(3).

Making the report

28.28

For individual solicitors an internal report may be made in any form and manner designed by the firm (there is no statutory requirement as to this) to the firm's nominated officer. Once such a report is made the reporting solicitor has no further responsibility and the onus is on the nominated officer to consider the information and, if required, to make disclosure to NCA. Because of the complicated considerations around privilege, the potential civil and criminal liability for continuing with a retainer even where consent has been given, and the need to manage different stakeholder expectations if consent is refused, it is best practice for the nominated officer or a designated deputy to make the report to NCA.

NCA has now removed the need to complete and post or fax paper-based forms or other existing certification processes and all reports are now made online to the NCA website which is self-explanatory and very user friendly.

Otherwise, the more onerous responsibilities falling on nominated officers are beyond the scope of this chapter.

'Appropriate consent' to further action

28.29

In general terms, once a disclosure has been made, the disclosing party can take no further action until consent is obtained. A nominated officer may give consent, but only if he or she has obtained consent from NCA or certain time limits have expired. In reality, in a firm of solicitors, further action is determined exclusively by the reaction of NCA.[1]

There are three possibilities:

(1)   NCA may give consent to the transaction continuing.

(2)   If NCA does not reply refusing consent within seven working days starting with the first working day after disclosure is made, this is treated as appropriate consent.

(3)   NCA may reply within the same period refusing consent. This imposes a moratorium on further action which lasts for 31 days starting with the day on which notice of refusal of consent is given. If the moratorium expires without any further action being taken by NCA this is treated as appropriate consent.

The delay could of course cause prejudice to clients, and although compliance with the statutory obligation would be a defence to any claim, solicitors may be required ultimately to justify the suspicion that prompted the report and caused the delay.[2]

1   Sections 335 and 336 of POCA 2002.
2   *Shah v HSBC Private Bank (UK) Ltd* [2010] EWCA Civ 31.

Disclosure, confidentiality and privilege

28.30

The disclosure offences under sections 330 to 332 of POCA 2002 and section 21A of TA 2000 specifically exclude any obligation to disclose information received in privileged circumstances.[1] The phrase 'privileged circumstances' is a term of art defined in section 330(10) of POCA 2002 and section 21A(8) of TA 2000 and is not identical with legal professional privilege. However, the two are closely linked concepts.

As noted above, the Court of Appeal held in *Bowman v Fels* that litigation did not involve an arrangement for the purposes of sections 327 to 329 of POCA 2002. It was also held that the giving of legal advice (other than where the crime/fraud exception applies) did not constitute an arrangement and did not itself give rise to any duty of disclosure.[2]

1   Section 330(6), (7B), (10) of POCA 2002; section 21A(5) of TA 2000.
2   *Bowman v Fels* [2005] EWCA Civ 226, [2005] 1 WLR 3083, [2005] 4 All ER 609 at [63].

28.31

Solicitors must keep the affairs of clients and former clients confidential except where disclosure is required or permitted by law,[1] but confidentiality and privilege are not synonymous, and confidentiality is overridden by the statutory duties of disclosure here being considered. The duties of disclosure are express duties imposed by statute and an authorised disclosure 'is not to be taken to breach any restriction on the disclosure of information (however imposed)'.[2]

Not all confidential information is covered by legal professional privilege, the ambit of which is quite narrow. Legal advice privilege covers all communications made in confidence between solicitors and their clients for the purpose of giving or obtaining legal advice. It does not matter whether the communication is directly between the client and his legal adviser or is made through an intermediate agent of either.[3]

Litigation privilege covers oral or written communications between a person or his lawyer (on the one hand) and third parties (on the other) or other documents created by or on behalf of the client or his lawyer, which came into existence once litigation is in contemplation or has commenced, and which came into existence for the dominant purpose of obtaining information or advice in connection with, or of conducting or aiding in the conduct of, such litigation (for example, obtaining evidence to be used in litigation or information which might lead to such evidence).[4]

A characteristic of litigation privilege is that it involves dealings between a lawyer and a third party (such as a potential witness). The characteristic of legal advice privilege is that it always relates to dealings between solicitor and client.

As has already been seen, litigation will not be likely to engage any of the primary offences.

Legal advice privilege is, expressly, limited to communications 'for the purposes of giving or obtaining legal advice'. Privilege does not attach to documents which are the products of legal advice. If one considers a typical property purchase (something that could readily engage money laundering concerns), the conveyancing documents and records of the financing of the transaction are not the subject of legal professional privilege, whereas correspondence between solicitor and client is privileged if directly related to the performance of the solicitor's professional duties as legal adviser.[5]

1   Paragraph 6.3 of the SRA Code of Conduct for Solicitors, RELs and RFLs 2019 and paragraph 6.3 of the SRA Code of Conduct for Firms 2019: see **4.86**.
2   Sections 337(4A) and 338(4) of POCA 2002; see also section 21B(1) of TA 2000.
3   *Three Rivers District Council and others v Governor and Company of the Bank of England (No 6)* [2005] 1 AC 610 at [50].
4   *Three Rivers District Council and others v Governor and Company of the Bank of England (No 6)* [2005] 1 AC 610 at [102].
5   *R v Inner London Crown Court, ex p Baines* [1988] 1 QB 579, [1988] 2 WLR 549, [1987] 3 All ER 1025; and see *Three Rivers District Council and others v Governor and Company of the Bank of England (No 6)* [2005] 1 AC 610 at [111].

Law Society guidance on disclosure

28.32

In short, legal professional privilege in both its limbs – litigation privilege and legal advice privilege – overrides the duty to disclose. The LSAG Guidance offers valuable further guidance at paragraph 7.4 in the following terms:

'**7.4.2 Advice privilege**

Principle

Communications between a legal professional, acting in his capacity as a legal professional, and a client, are privileged if they are both:

● confidential; and

● for the purpose of seeking legal advice from a legal professional or providing it to a client.

Scope

Communications are not privileged merely because a client is speaking or writing to you. The protection applies only to those communications which directly seek or provide advice or which are given in a legal context, that involve the legal professional using his legal skills and which are directly related to the performance of the legal professional's professional duties [*Passmore on Privilege* 2nd edition 2006].

Case law helps define what advice privilege covers.

Communications subject to advice privilege:

● a solicitor's bill of costs and statement of account [*Chant v Brown* (1852) 9 Hare 790];

● information imparted by prospective clients in advance of a retainer if the communications were made for the purpose of indicating the advice required [*Minster v Priest* [1930] AC 558 per Lord Atkin at 584].

Communications not subject to advice privilege:

- notes of open court proceedings [*Parry v News Group Newspapers* (1990) 140 New Law Journal 1719], as the content of the communication is not confidential;

- conversations, correspondence or meetings with opposing legal professionals [*Parry v News Group Newspapers* (1990) 140 New Law Journal 1719], as the content of the communication is not confidential;

- a client account ledger maintained in relation to the client's money [*Nationwide Building Society v Various Solicitors* [1999] PNLR 53];

- an appointments diary or time record on an attendance note, time sheet or fee record relating to a client [*R v Manchester Crown Court, ex p. Rogers* [1999] 1 W.L.R. 832];

- conveyancing documents as they are not communications [*R v Inner London Crown Court, ex p. Baines & Baines* [1988] QB 579].

Advice within a transaction

All communications between a legal professional and his or her client relating to a transaction in which the legal professional has been instructed for the purpose of obtaining legal advice are covered by advice privilege, notwithstanding that they do not contain advice on matters of law and construction, provided that they are directly related to the performance by the legal professional of his professional duty as legal adviser of his or her client [*Three Rivers District Council and others v the Bank of England* [2004] UKHL 48 at 111].

This will mean that where you are providing legal advice in a transactional matter (such as a conveyance) the advice privilege will cover all:

- communications with,

- instructions from, and

- advice given to

the client, including any working papers and drafts prepared, as long as they are directly related to your performance of your professional duties as a legal adviser.

7.4.3 Litigation privilege

Principle

This privilege, which is wider than advice privilege, protects confidential communications made after litigation has started, or is reasonably in prospect, between any of the following:

- a legal professional and a client;

- a legal professional and an agent, whether or not that agent is a legal professional; or

- a legal professional and a third party.

These communications must be for the sole or dominant purpose of litigation, for any of the following:

- for seeking or giving advice in relation to it;
- for obtaining evidence to be used in it; or
- for obtaining information leading to obtaining such evidence.

7.4.4 Important points to consider

An original document not brought into existence for these privileged purposes and so not already privileged, does not become privileged merely by being given to a legal professional for advice or other privileged purpose.

Further, where you have a corporate client, communication between you and the employees of a corporate client may not be protected by LPP if the employee cannot be considered to be "the client" for the purposes of the retainer. As such some employees will be clients, while others will not [*Three Rivers District Council v the Governor and Company of the Bank of England (No.5)* [2003] QB 1556].

It is not a breach of LPP to discuss a matter with your nominated officer for the purposes of receiving advice on whether to make a disclosure.

7.4.5 Crime/fraud exception

LPP protects advice you give to a client on avoiding committing a crime [*Bullivant v Att-Gen of Victoria* [1901] AC 196] or warning them that proposed actions could attract prosecution [*Butler v Board of Trade* [1971] Ch 680]. LPP does not extend to documents which themselves form part of a criminal or fraudulent act, or communications which take place in order to obtain advice with the intention of carrying out an offence [*R v Cox & Railton* (1884) 14 QBD 153]. It is irrelevant whether or not you are aware that you are being used for that purpose [*Banque Keyser Ullman v Skandia* [1986] 1 Lloyd's Rep 336].

Intention of furthering a criminal purpose

It is not just your client's intention which is relevant for the purpose of ascertaining whether information was communicated for the furtherance of a criminal purpose. It is also sufficient that a third party intends the legal professional/client communication to be made with that purpose (e.g. where the innocent client is being used by a third party) [*R v Central Criminal Court, ex p. Francis & Francis* [1989] 1 AC 346].

Knowing a transaction constitutes an offence

If you **know** the transaction you're working on is a principal offence, you risk committing an offence yourself. In these circumstances, communications relating to such a transaction are not privileged and should be disclosed.

Suspecting a transaction constitutes an offence

If you merely suspect a transaction might constitute a money laundering offence, the position is more complex. If the suspicions are correct, communications with the client are not privileged. If the suspicions are unfounded, the communications should remain privileged and are therefore non-disclosable.

Prima facie evidence

If you suspect you are unwittingly being involved by your client in a fraud, the courts require prima facie evidence before LPP can be displaced [*O'Rourke v Darbishire* [1920] AC 581]. The sufficiency of that evidence depends on the circumstances: it is easier to infer a prima facie case where there is substantial material available to support an inference of fraud. While you may decide yourself if prima facie evidence exists, you may also ask the court for directions [*Finers v Miro* [1991] 1 WLR 35].

The Crown Prosecution Service guidance for prosecutors indicates that if a legal professional forms a genuine, but mistaken, belief that the privileged circumstances exemption (...) applies (for example, the client misleads the legal professional and uses the advice received for a criminal purpose) the legal professional will be able to rely on the reasonable excuse defence. It is likely that a similar approach would be taken with respect to a genuine, but mistaken, belief that LPP applies.

We believe you should not make a disclosure unless you know of prima facie evidence that you are being used in the furtherance of a crime.'

Further, information obtained on disclosure of documents in litigation which gives rise to a relevant suspicion about the opposing party, but which is subject to the implied undertaking that the documents may not be used for any purpose other than the conduct of the litigation, is not subject to any duty of disclosure.[1]

But as privileged material is excluded from the duty of disclosure it is important to understand what is, and what is not, covered by legal professional privilege.

1   *Bowman v Fels* [2005] 4 All ER 609, [2005] EWCA Civ 226 at [89].

Other offences

28.33

Other secondary offences relevant to solicitors involve tipping-off or otherwise prejudicing the course of an investigation.

Tipping-off

28.34

It is an offence if a person discloses (other than in strictly limited circumstances) that a disclosure has been made under section 337 or 338 if it is likely to prejudice any investigation that might be conducted following the disclosure, and if the information came to the person in the course of business in the regulated sector.[1]

It is an offence if a person discloses that an investigation into allegations that an offence has been committed under Part 7 of POCA 2002 is being contemplated or carried out, if the disclosure is likely to prejudice that investigation and the information came to the person in the course of business in the regulated sector.[2]

It is *not* an offence if a professional legal adviser makes the disclosure to a client and it is made for the purposes of dissuading the client from committing an offence.[3] It is a defence if the person making the disclosure does not know or suspect that disclosure is likely to prejudice any investigation.[4]

1 Section 333A(1) and (2) of POCA 2002. The circumstances in which disclosure may be made are set out in sections 333B, 333C and 333D of POCA 2002 and relate, in summary, to disclosures within the same organisation; between financial organisations and legal professionals in relation to a client or transaction common to both parties, if the purpose is only to prevent an offence being committed; and to disclosures to the authorities with a view to the detection, investigation or prosecution of offences.
2 Section 333A(3) of POCA 2002.
3 Section 333D(2).
4 Section 333D(3) and (4).

Prejudicing an investigation

28.35

It is an offence if a person outside the regulated sector who knows or suspects that a relevant investigation[1] is being conducted or is about to be conducted makes a disclosure that is likely to prejudice an investigation, or if that person falsifies, conceals, destroys or otherwise disposes of documents that are relevant to any investigation, or causes any of the above to take place. An investigation for these purposes is a confiscation investigation, a civil recovery investigation or a money laundering investigation.[2]

It is a defence if a disclosure is made by a legal adviser to a client, or a client's representative, in connection with the giving of legal advice or to any person in connection with legal proceedings or contemplated legal proceedings. However, this defence will not apply if the disclosure is made with the intention of furthering a criminal purpose.

1 Section 342(1) of POCA 2002. The various kinds of investigations are defined in section 341.
2 Section 342(2)(a) and (b).

Law Society guidance on tipping-off and prejudicing an investigation

28.36

The LSAG Guidance contains helpful guidance at paragraphs 6.8.1 and 6.8.2:

'6.8.1 Offences

6.8.1.1 Tipping off – in the regulated sector

There are two tipping off offences in section 333A of POCA. They apply only to business in the regulated sector.

Section 333A(1) – disclosing a suspicious activity report (SAR)

It is an offence to disclose to a third person that a SAR has been made by any person to the police, HM Revenue and Customs, the NCA or a nominated officer, if that disclosure might prejudice any investigation that might be carried out as a result of the SAR. This offence can only be committed:

- **after** a disclosure to the NCA

- if you know or suspect that by disclosing this information, you are likely to prejudice any investigation related to that SAR

- the information upon which the disclosure is based came to you in the course of business in the regulated sector.

Section 333A(3) – disclosing an investigation

It is an offence to disclose the fact that an investigation into a money laundering offence is being contemplated or carried out if that disclosure is likely to prejudice that investigation. The offence can only be committed if the information on which the disclosure is based came to the person in the course of business in the regulated sector. The key point is that you can commit this offence, even when you are unaware that a SAR was submitted.

6.8.1.2 Prejudicing an investigation

Section 342(1) contains an offence to prejudice a confiscation, civil recovery or money laundering investigation, if the person making the disclosure knows or suspects that an investigation is being, or is about to be conducted. Section 342(1) was amended by paragraph 8 of the TACT and POCA Regulations 2007. It applies to those outside the regulated sector as well as those within the regulated sector.

You only commit this offence if you knew or suspected that the disclosure would, or would be likely to prejudice any investigation.

6.8.2 Defences

6.8.2.1 Tipping off

The following disclosures are permitted:

Section 333B – disclosures within an undertaking or group, including disclosures to a professional legal adviser or relevant professional adviser;

Section 333C – disclosures between institutions, including disclosures from a professional legal adviser to another professional legal adviser;

Section 333D – disclosures to your supervisory authority;

Section 333D(2) – disclosures made by professional legal advisers to their clients for the purpose of dissuading them from engaging in criminal conduct.

A person does not commit the main tipping off offence if he does not know or suspect that a disclosure is likely to prejudice an investigation.

Section 333B – disclosures within an undertaking or group etc

It is not an offence if an employee, officer or partner of a practice discloses that a SAR has been made if it is to an employee, officer or partner of the same undertaking.

A legal professional will not commit a tipping off offence if:

- the disclosure is to a professional legal adviser or a relevant professional adviser,

- both the person making the disclosure and the person to whom it is made carry on business in an EEA state or in a country or territory imposing equivalent money laundering requirements, and

- those persons perform their professional activities within different undertakings that share common ownership, management or control.

Section 333C – disclosures between institutions etc.

A legal professional will not commit a tipping off offence if **all** the following criteria are met:

- The disclosure is made to another legal professional in an EEA state, or one with an equivalent AML regime;

- The disclosure relates to a client or former client of both parties, or a transaction involving them both, or the provision of a service involving them both;

- The disclosure is made for the purpose of preventing a money laundering offence; and

- Both parties have equivalent professional duties of confidentiality and protection of personal data.

Section 333D(2) – limited exception for professional legal advisers.

A legal professional will not commit a tipping off offence if the disclosure is to a client and it is made for the purpose of dissuading the client from engaging in conduct amounting to an offence. This exception and the tipping off offence in section 333A apply to those carrying on activities in the regulated sector.

6.8.2.2 Prejudicing an investigation

Section 342(4) – professional legal adviser exemption.

It is a defence to a section 342(1) offence that a disclosure is made by a legal adviser to a client, or a client's representative, in connection with the giving of legal advice or to any person in connection with legal proceedings or contemplated legal proceedings.

Such a disclosure will not be exempt if it is made with the intention of furthering a criminal purpose (section 342(5)).'

CHAPTER 29

Data protection

29.1

This chapter provides a brief introduction to the important and complex subject of data protection, specific guidance on aspects of the Data Protection Act (DPA) 2018 as it relates to solicitors, and some commentary on the interaction between confidentiality, privilege and data protection. It does not provide an all-encompassing guide to the subject, which is beyond the scope of this book. The focus in this chapter is on the regulation of solicitors and key obligations arising under the General Data Protection (GDPR)[1] and DPA 2018. The GDPR came into force on 25 May 2018.

Solicitors should be aware of the modifications to the express wording of the GDPR contained within DPA 2018 and should be careful to consider both the GDPR and DPA 2018 as a collective whole, since modifications made by DPA 2018 are of particular importance in the provision of legal services.

The GDPR and DPA 2018 contain a number of criminal offences relating to the misuse of personal data and give the Information Commissioner's Office (ICO) the power to impose potentially significant penalties for data breaches.

---

1 Regulation (EU) 2016/679 of the European Parliament and of the Council of 27 April 2016 on the protection of natural persons with regard to the processing of personal data and on the free movement of such data, and repealing Directive 95/46/EC (General Data Protection Regulation).

Protected data

29.2

The essential purpose of the GDPR and DPA 2018 is to give individuals greater control of, and access to, the information organisations hold about them. Solicitors and other legal services providers hold significant amounts of personal data for various reasons. 'Personal data' as protected by the GDPR and DPA 2018 is defined in article 4 of the GDPR as:

> 'any information relating to an identified or identifiable natural person ("data subject"), an identifiable natural person is one who can be identified, directly or indirectly, in particular by reference to an identifier such as a name, an identification number, location data, an online identifier or to one or more factors specific to the physical, physiological, genetic, mental, economic, cultural or social identity of that natural person'

Solicitors will hold such information about a variety of individuals for various purposes – as employer, service provider, service user and regulated entity. The scope of the GDPR extends to all such information processed electronically in whole or in part and any such data processed other than by automated means which form or are intended to form part of a filing system.[1]

1   Article 2 of the GDPR.

Processing

29.3

Processing is defined as:

> 'any operation or set of operations which is performed on personal data or on sets of personal data, whether or not by automated means, such as collection, recording, organisation, structuring, storage, adaptation or alteration, retrieval, consultation, use, disclosure by transmission, dissemination or otherwise making available, alignment or combination, restriction, erasure or destruction'[1]

The definition of processing is intentionally wide. Simply the act of storing personal data amounts to processing and must be permissible within the ambit of the GDPR. Processing of personal data in accordance with the GDPR must be justifiable on one or more of the grounds set out in article 6 of the GDPR. These are:

(a)   the data subject has given consent to the processing of his or her personal data for one or more specific purposes;[2]

(b)   processing is necessary for the performance of a contract to which the data subject is party or in order to take steps at the request of the data subject prior to entering into a contract;

(c)   processing is necessary for compliance with a legal obligation to which the controller is subject;

(d)   processing is necessary in order to protect the vital interests of the data subject or of another natural person;

(e)   processing is necessary for the performance of a task carried out in the public interest or in the exercise of official authority vested in the controller;

(f)   processing is necessary for the purposes of the legitimate interests pursued by the controller or by a third party, except where such interests are overridden by the interests or fundamental rights and freedoms of the data subject which require protection of personal data, in particular where the data subject is a child.

1   Article 4 of the GDPR.
2   Article 6(1) of the GDPR. Note that consent must be freely given and affirmative (see article 4(11) of the GDPR). Consent must also be auditable and can be withdrawn at any time (see article 7 of the GDPR).

Special category data

29.4

Article 9 of the GDPR contains a prohibition on processing special category data, save in tightly defined specified circumstances. Special category data – broadly similar to the familiar concept of 'sensitive personal data' – is defined as:

> 'personal data revealing racial or ethnic origin, political opinions, religious or philosophical beliefs, or trade union membership, and the processing of genetic data, biometric data for the purpose of uniquely identifying a natural person, data concerning health or data concerning a natural person's sex life or sexual orientation.'[1]

Note that biometric data is included but data relating to criminal convictions is not.

Solicitors are likely to hold special category data about (at least) staff and clients. Firms should be able to demonstrate that processing of such data complies with one or more of the article 6 requirements discussed above *and* falls within the conditions of article 9(2) of the GDPR, as modified by Schedule 6 to DPA 2018. These conditions are that:

(a)   the data subject has given explicit consent to the processing of that personal data for one or more specified purposes;

(b)   processing is necessary for the purposes of carrying out the obligations and exercising specific rights of the controller or of the data subject in the field of employment and social security and social protection law in so far as it is authorised by domestic law (see section 10 of DPA 2018) or a collective agreement pursuant to member state law providing for appropriate safeguards for the fundamental rights and the interests of the data subject;

(c)   processing is necessary to protect the vital interests of the data subject or of another natural person where the data subject is physically or legally incapable of giving consent;

(d)   processing is carried out in the course of its legitimate activities with appropriate safeguards by a foundation, association or any other not-for-profit body with a political, philosophical, religious or trade union aim and on condition that the processing relates solely to the members or to former members of the body or to persons who have regular contact with it in connection with its purposes and that the personal data is not disclosed outside that body without the consent of the data subjects;

(e)   processing relates to personal data which is manifestly made public by the data subject;

(f)   processing is necessary for the establishment, exercise or defence of legal claims or whenever courts are acting in their judicial capacity;

(g)   processing is necessary for reasons of substantial public interest and is authorised by domestic law (see section 10 of DPA 2018);

(h)   processing is necessary for the purposes of preventive or occupational medicine, for the assessment of the working capacity of the employee, medical diagnosis, the provision of health or social care or treatment or the management of health or social care systems and services on the basis of domestic law (see section 10 of DPA 2018) or pursuant to contract with a health professional and subject to the conditions and safeguards referred to in article 9.3 of the GDPR;

(i)   processing is necessary for reasons of public interest in the area of public health, such as protecting against serious cross-border threats to health or ensuring high standards of quality and safety of health care and of medicinal products or medical devices, on the basis of domestic law (see section 10 of DPA 2018) which provides for suitable and specific measures to safeguard the rights and freedoms of the data subject, in particular professional secrecy

(j)   processing is necessary for archiving purposes in the public interest, scientific or historical research purposes or statistical purposes in accordance with article 89(1) of the GDPR (as supplemented by section 19 of DPA 2018) and is authorised by domestic law (see section 10 of DPA 2018).

In practice, the conditions most likely to be relevant to solicitors are: (a) explicit consent; (b) legal obligations relating to employment and social security; (e) public data; (f) pursuit of legal claims; and (g) substantial public interest.[2]

1   Article 9(1) of the GDPR.
2   Note that Part 2 of Schedule 1 to DPA 2018 contains additional requirements including that firms relying on this condition have appropriate policy documents in place.

Rights of the data subject

29.5

The GDPR extended the rights of data subjects and now provides for the following rights:

(1)   The right to be informed how and why data is processed and for how long it will be kept.[1]

(2)   The right of access – subject access requests must now be complied with within a month and at no cost to the data subject.[2]

(3)   The right to rectification.[3]

(4)   The right to erasure (the right to be forgotten): note that this is a qualified right and its availability will depend on the basis of processing.[4]

(5)   The right to restrict processing – this is also a qualified right and only available in certain circumstances.[5]

(6)   The right to data portability – this right only arises where processing is on the basis of consent or in performance of a contract and conducted electronically. It is, essentially, the right to receive a copy of the data in a usable electronic format.[6]

(7)   The right to object to processing – note that this is an absolute right as it relates to direct marketing and is otherwise qualified and capable of challenge. Data subjects should be given notice of their right to object to processing.[7]

(8)   Rights in relation to automated decision-making and profiling.[8]

1   Articles 13 and 14 of the GDPR.
2   See articles 12 and 15 and recitals 63 and 64 of the GDPR.

3   See articles 5, 12, 16 and 19 of the GDPR.
4   See article 17 of the GDPR.
5   See articles 18 and 19 of the GDPR.
6   See articles 13 and 20 of the GDPR.
7   See article 21 of the GDPR.
8   See article 22 of the GDPR.

Application to solicitors

29.6

As they relate to legal practices, the extent of the data subject's rights will depend on the nature of the data held and the purposes of the processing, since DPA 2018 contains a number of derogations from these rights. For example, data subjects may have restricted rights in relation to data collected for compliance with anti-money laundering legislation as it is likely to fall within a number of exemptions set out in Schedule 2 to DPA 2018, principally paragraphs 2(1) and 5(1).

More generally paragraph 19 of Schedule 2 to DPA 2018 contains potentially wide-ranging derogations in respect of information which is subject to legal professional privilege or in respect of which an obligation of confidence is owed to a client.

Further specific exemptions particularly relevant to solicitors are:

- paragraph 2: crime and taxation
- paragraph 5: processing required by law or in connection with legal proceedings
- paragraph 10: legal services regulation
- paragraph 19: legal professional privilege
- paragraph 20: self-incrimination
- paragraph 21: corporate finance
- paragraph 22: management forecasts
- paragraph 23: negotiations
- paragraph 24: confidential references.

29.7

Few of the derogations are absolute and solicitors will need to consider the extent to which a data subject's rights have been curtailed by a relevant derogation. Since the GDPR must be construed in line with EU law, any derogations must be narrowly construed as a matter of principle.

The rationale underpinning the numerous derogations and modifications in DPA 2018 is to ensure that rights of access to information are not used in order to circumvent proper regulation and business management or to derail proper legal processes and/or cause harm.

Solicitors need to be aware of the derogations, their applications and limitations in order to ensure that they do not, for example, inadvertently breach client confidentiality by complying with a subject access request which should have been rejected.

29.8

For the most part, firms are likely to be data controllers for the purposes of the GDPR and DPA 2018. Firms need to have appropriate policies in place to ensure compliance. It may assist firms to address compliance by reference to categories of data held, to ensure consistency of approach and to mitigate risk. The considerations that apply to personal data held on personnel files, for example, are likely different from those that apply to data held on client files and different again from those that apply to marketing databases.

Firms and individual solicitors will also need to be aware of the personal data entrusted to employees (for example, client contact data on personal mobile devices) and ensure that appropriate training is given and policies cover such issues.

Data protection and confidentiality

29.9

Confidentiality and data protection are not synonymous. Confidentiality is a much broader concept. While it may be possible for potential conflicts to arise between professional obligations of confidence and the transparency requirements of the GDPR, solicitors can take comfort in the derogations contained in paragraph 19 of Schedule 2 to DPA 2018, which, among other things, restrict data subjects' rights of access to information in respect of which solicitors owe a duty of confidentiality to their clients. This exemption is likely to attach to most information on client files, save for information already in the public domain or in respect of which confidentiality has been waived or lost.

This does not mean, of course, that solicitors are not obliged to comply with notice requirements and subject access requests which relate to information which is not confidential. It will be interesting to see, in due course, how the derogation in paragraph 19 is applied in practice. Construed literally, the derogation appears to provide that there is simply no right for any data subject – including a client – to request any confidential information held on a confidential client file, even his or her own.

This may seem a strange construction; however, clients are plainly entitled to the information on their files through other means and a subject access request would be a singularly inefficient way to obtain information available in any event.

In the absence of any binding guidance on the construction of this derogation, solicitors may need to consider carefully how to approach subject access requests from those against whom a claim of confidentiality could not be maintained. This may be of particular relevance where, for example, the client is a company and a subject access request is made by a director.

29.10

It is conceivable that solicitors could fall into error in a number of ways when considering competing confidentiality and data protection obligations. For example:

(a)   refusing a legitimate subject access request solely on the grounds of confidentiality without considering the proper extent of the statutory derogations from the GDPR or failing in some other way to uphold the rights of data subjects due to an unjustifiable over-reliance on confidentiality – this could lead to complaints being made to the ICO by a data subject;

(b)   permitting data subjects too much access to and/or control over personal data held by the firm as a result of failing to take proper account of derogations from the GDPR – this could lead to a complaint of breach of confidence if disclosure of information is not required or permitted by law;

(c)   where data is held pursuant to an express or implied undertaking or within a confidentiality ring where the obligation of confidence is not owed to the client but to a third party. Solicitors may need to be particularly astute to record the proper basis for processing personal data to avoid creating conflicts between any contractual or quasi-contractual duties of confidentiality imposed and compliance with the GDPR;

(d)   where clients – or other solicitors – provide material which contains unnecessary or excessive personal data, solicitors may need to consider whether they can properly accept it.

The starting point for solicitors is to understand the nature and extent of data protection obligations and to tie processing of personal data back to appropriate grounds. Embedding a culture of compliance and awareness through training should help to guard against problems arising.

Data protection and privilege

29.11

Solicitors can rely on the derogations in paragraph 19(a) of Schedule 2 to DPA 2018, in respect of subject access requests which impinge on legal professional privilege. Note that material attracting other forms of privilege such as litigation privilege appear to fall outside of the scope of this derogation.

In practice, the derogation under paragraph 19(b) relating to confidential information discussed above is likely to be of more use to solicitors, as it automatically includes material which may be subject to legal professional privilege.

Exporting data

29.12

Solicitors should be aware of how and where data is stored by suppliers and service providers. The GDPR imposes restrictions on the transfer of personal data outside the European Economic Area (EEA). The ICO has issued guidance confirming that putting personal data on a website or on a UK server which may then be accessed in a non-EEA country may be treated as a restricted transfer.

Solicitors wishing to transfer data to non-EEA countries will need to assess the basis of the transfer and consider the following questions:

(a)   Has there been an adequacy decision?

(b)   Is the restricted transfer covered by appropriate safeguards?

(c)   Is there an exception?

The ICO has issued guidance on how to approach each of these questions, including details of adequacy decisions made and detailed information on appropriate safeguards.

Data protection officers

29.13

Most law firms are unlikely to need to appoint a data protection officer (DPO). The GDPR requires a DPO to be appointed by (a) public bodies; (b) organisations whose core functions include large-scale regular and systematic monitoring of individuals; and (c) organisations whose core functions include large-scale processing of special category data and data relating to criminal convictions. Firms conducting criminal work and any work which requires access to medical records, biometric data and other special category data will need to assess whether they meet this requirement. The ICO publishes some guidance on what factors will need to be considered but the question is, to a certain extent, a matter of judgement.

If a decision is taken to appoint a DPO, the DPO must be independent, adequately resourced, an expert in data protection and report to the highest level of management. The role will involve acting as the main contact for data subjects and the ICO, and advising on and monitoring compliance.

Reporting data breaches

29.14

The ICO defines a personal data breach as:

> 'a breach of security leading to the accidental or unlawful destruction, loss, alteration, unauthorised disclosure of, or access to, personal data. This includes breaches that are the result of both accidental and deliberate causes. It also means that a breach is more than just about losing personal data.'

Some data breaches trigger an obligation to report to the ICO – within 72 hours where feasible – and to notify data subjects. In deciding whether a breach is reportable, solicitors will need to consider whether and to what extent there is a risk to the rights and freedoms of the data subject arising from the breach. The ICO highlights recital 85 of the GDPR as factors which must be borne in mind when assessing risk:

> 'A personal data breach may, if not addressed in an appropriate and timely manner, result in physical, material or non-material damage to natural persons such as loss of control over their personal data or limitation of their rights, discrimination, identity theft or fraud, financial loss, unauthorised reversal of pseudonymisation, damage to reputation, loss of confidentiality of personal data protected by professional secrecy or any other significant economic or social disadvantage to the natural person concerned.'

A record should be kept of all data breaches – whether reportable or not – as well as the reasons for deciding whether or not a breach is reportable. Solicitors will need to consider whether the data breach is also a breach of confidentiality or is otherwise reportable to the Solicitors Regulation Authority (SRA) as serious misconduct or a material failure to comply (in the terminology of the 2011 Handbook) or a serious breach of regulatory arrangements (in the terminology of the 2019 Standards and Regulations). In practice it is likely that any breach which is reportable to the ICO will also be reportable to the SRA.

PART 8
Appendices

SRA Principles 2019

[Law Society copyright. For the latest updates to the material, please see www.sra.org.uk.]

[Draft version as published February 2019]

SRA Principles 2019

Introduction

The SRA Principles comprise the fundamental tenets of ethical behaviour that we expect all those that we regulate to uphold. This includes all individuals we authorise to provide legal services (solicitors, RELs and RFLs), as well as authorised firms and their managers and employees. For licensed bodies, these apply to those individuals, and the part of the body (where applicable), involved in delivering the services we regulate in accordance with the terms of your licence.

Should the Principles come into conflict, those which safeguard the wider public interest (such as the rule of law, and public confidence in a trustworthy solicitors' profession and a safe and effective market for regulated legal services) take precedence over an individual client's interests. You should, where relevant, inform your client of the circumstances in which your duty to the Court and other professional obligations will outweigh your duty to them.

The Principles and Codes are underpinned by our Enforcement Strategy, which explains in more detail our approach to taking regulatory action in the public interest [Link].

Principles

The principles are as follows:

You act:

1. in a way that upholds the constitutional principle of the rule of law, and the proper administration of justice.

2. in a way that upholds public trust and confidence in the *solicitors'* profession and in legal services provided by *authorised persons.*

3. with independence.

4. with honesty.

5. with integrity.

6. in a way that encourages equality, diversity and inclusion.

7. in the best interests of each *client.*

Supplemental notes

Made by the SRA Board on 30 May 2018.

Made under section 31 of the Solicitors Act 1974, section 9 of the Administration of Justice Act 1985 and section 83 of the Legal Services Act 2007.

SRA Code of Conduct for Solicitors, RELs and RFLs [draft]

SRA Code of Conduct for Solicitors, RELs and RFLs [draft]

[Draft version published February 2019 as amended by the SRA Regulatory Arrangements (Reporting Concerns) (Amendment) Rules 2019, approved by the LSB on 9 May 2019.]

Introduction

The Code of Conduct describes the standards of professionalism that we, the SRA, and the public expect of individuals (solicitors, registered European lawyers and registered foreign lawyers) authorised by us to provide legal services.

They apply to conduct and behaviour relating to your practice, and comprise a framework for ethical and competent practice which applies irrespective of your role or the environment or organisation in which you work (subject to the Overseas Rules which apply to your practice overseas); although paragraphs 8.1 to 8.11 apply only when you are providing your services to the public or a section of the public.

You must exercise your judgement in applying these standards to the situations you are in and deciding on a course of action, bearing in mind your role and responsibilities, areas of practice, and the nature of your clients (which in an in house context will generally include your employer and may include other persons or groups within or outside your employer organisation).

You are personally accountable for compliance with this Code – and our other regulatory requirements that apply to you – and must always be prepared to justify your decisions and actions.

A serious failure to meet our standards or a serious breach of our regulatory requirements may result in our taking regulatory action against you. A failure or breach may be serious either in isolation or because it comprises a persistent or concerning pattern of behaviour. In addition to the regulatory requirements set by us in our Codes, Principles and our rules and regulations, we directly monitor and enforce the requirements relating to referral fees set out in section 56 of the Legal Aid, Sentencing and Punishment of Offenders Act 2012, and provisions relating to anti money laundering and counter terrorist financing, as set out in regulations made by the Treasury as in force from time to time [Link].

All these requirements are underpinned by our Enforcement Strategy. That strategy explains in more detail our views about the issues we consider to be serious, and our approach to taking regulatory action in the public interest.

Maintaining trust and acting fairly

1.1   You do not unfairly discriminate by allowing your personal views to affect your professional relationships and the way in which you provide your services.

1.2   You do not abuse your position by taking unfair advantage of *clients* or others.

1.3   You perform all *undertakings* given by you, and do so within an agreed timescale or if no timescale has been agreed then within a reasonable amount of time.

1.4   You do not mislead or attempt to mislead your *clients*, the *court* or others, either by your own acts or omissions or allowing or being complicit in the acts or omissions of others (including your *client*).

Dispute resolution and proceedings before courts, tribunals and inquiries

2.1   You do not misuse or tamper with evidence or attempt to do so.

2.2   You do not seek to influence the substance of evidence, including generating false evidence or persuading witnesses to change their evidence.

2.3   You do not provide or offer to provide any benefit to witnesses dependent upon the nature of their evidence or the outcome of the case.

2.4   You only make assertions or put forward statements, representations or submissions to the *court* or others which are properly arguable.

2.5   You do not place yourself in contempt of *court*, and you comply with *court* orders which place obligations on you.

2.6   You do not waste the *court's* time.

2.7   You draw the *court's* attention to relevant cases and statutory provisions, or procedural irregularities of which you are aware, and which are likely to have a material effect on the outcome of the proceedings.

Service and competence

3.1   You only act for *clients* on instructions from the *client*, or from someone properly authorised to provide instructions on their behalf. If you have reason to suspect that the instructions do not represent your *client's* wishes, you do not act unless you have satisfied yourself that they do. However, in circumstances where you have legal authority to act notwithstanding that it is not possible to obtain or ascertain the instructions of your *client*, then you are subject to the overriding obligation to protect your *client's* best interests.

3.2   You ensure that the service you provide to *clients* is competent and delivered in a timely manner.

3.3   You maintain your competence to carry out your role and keep your professional knowledge and skills up to date.

3.4   You consider and take account of your *client's* attributes, needs and circumstances.

3.5   Where you supervise or manage others providing legal services:

(a)   you remain accountable for the work carried out through them; and

(b)   you effectively supervise work being done for *clients*.

3.6   You ensure that the individuals you manage are competent to carry out their role, and keep their professional knowledge and skills, as well as understanding of their legal, ethical and regulatory obligations, up to date.

Client money and assets

4.1   You properly account to *clients* for any *financial benefit* you receive as a result of their instructions, except where they have agreed otherwise.

4.2   You safeguard money and *assets* entrusted to you by *clients* and others.

4.3   You do not personally hold *client money* save as permitted under regulation 10.2(b)(vii) of the Authorisation of Individuals Regulations, unless you work in an *authorised body*, or in an organisation of a kind *prescribed* under this rule on any terms that may be *prescribed* accordingly.

Business requirements

Referrals, introductions and separate businesses

5.1   In respect of any referral of a *client* by you to another *person*, or of any third party who introduces business to you or with whom you share your *fees*, you ensure that:

(a)   *clients* are informed of any financial or other interest which you or your business or employer has in referring the *client* to another *person* or which an *introducer* has in referring the *client* to you;

(b)   *clients* are informed of any fee sharing arrangement that is relevant to their matter;

(c)   the fee sharing agreement is in writing;

(d)   you do not receive payments relating to a referral or make payments to an *introducer* in respect of *clients* who are the subject of criminal proceedings; and

(e)   any *client* referred by an *introducer* has not been acquired in a way which would breach the *SRA's regulatory arrangements* if the *person* acquiring the *client* were regulated by the SRA.

5.2   Where it appears to the SRA that you have made or received a *referral fee*, the payment will be treated as a *referral fee* unless you show that the payment was not made as such.

5.3   You only:

(a)   refer, recommend or introduce a *client* to a *separate business*; or

(b)   divide, or allow to be divided, a *client's* matter between you and a *separate business*;

where the *client* has given informed consent to your doing so.

Other business requirements

5.4   You must not be a *manager, employee, member* or *interest holder* of a business that:

(a)   has a name which includes the word "solicitors"; or

(b)   describes its work in a way that suggests it is a *solicitors'* firm; unless it is an *authorised body*.

5.5   If you are a *solicitor* who holds a practising certificate, an *REL* or *RFL*, you must complete and deliver to the SRA an annual return in the *prescribed* form.

5.6   If you are a *solicitor* or an *REL* carrying on *reserved legal activities* in a non- *commercial body*, you must ensure that the body takes out and maintains indemnity insurance that provides adequate and appropriate cover in respect of the services that you provide, whether or not they comprise *reserved legal activities*.

Conflict, confidentiality and disclosure

Conflict of interests

6.1   You do not act if there is an *own interest conflict* or a significant risk of such a conflict.

6.2   You do not act in relation to a matter or particular aspect of it if you have a *conflict of interest* or a significant risk of such a conflict in relation to that matter or aspect of it, unless:

   (a)   the *clients* have a *substantially common interest* in relation to the matter or the aspect of it, as appropriate; or

   (b)   the *clients* are *competing for the same objective*, and the conditions below are met, namely that:

      (i)   all the *clients* have given informed consent, given or evidenced in writing, to you acting;

      (ii)   where appropriate, you put in place effective safeguards to protect your *clients'* confidential information; and

      (iii)   you are satisfied it is reasonable for you to act for all the *clients*.

Confidentiality and disclosure

6.3   You keep the affairs of current and former *clients* confidential unless disclosure is required or permitted by law or the *client* consents.

6.4   Where you are acting for a *client* on a matter, you make the *client* aware of all information material to the matter of which you have knowledge, except when:

   (a)   the disclosure of the information is prohibited by legal restrictions imposed in the interests of national security or the prevention of crime;

   (b)   your *client* gives informed consent, given or evidenced in writing, to the information not being disclosed to them;

   (c)   you have reason to believe that serious physical or mental injury will be caused to your *client* or another if the information is disclosed; or

   (d)   the information is contained in a privileged document that you have knowledge of only because it has been mistakenly disclosed.

6.5   You do not act for a *client* in a matter where that *client* has an interest adverse to the interest of another current or former *client* of you or your business or employer, for whom you or your business or employer holds confidential information which is material to that matter, unless:

   (a)   effective measures have been taken which result in there being no real risk of disclosure of the confidential information; or

   (b)   the current or former *client* whose information you or your business or employer holds has given informed consent, given or evidenced in writing, to you acting, including to any measures taken to protect their information.

Cooperation and accountability

7.1   You keep up to date with and follow the law and regulation governing the way you work.

7.2   You are able to justify your decisions and actions in order to demonstrate compliance with your obligations under the *SRA's regulatory arrangements*.

7.3 You cooperate with the SRA, other regulators, ombudsmen, and those bodies with a role overseeing and supervising the delivery of, or investigating concerns in relation to, legal services.

7.4 You respond promptly to the SRA and:·

(a) provide full and accurate explanations, information and documents in response to any request or requirement; and

(b) ensure that relevant information which is held by you, or by third parties carrying out functions on your behalf which are critical to the delivery of your legal services, is available for inspection by the SRA.

7.5 You do not attempt to prevent anyone from providing information to the SRA or any other body exercising regulatory, supervisory, investigatory or prosecutory functions in the public interest.

7.6 You notify the SRA promptly if:

(a) you are subject to any criminal charge, conviction or caution, subject to the Rehabilitation of Offenders Act 1974;

(b) a *relevant insolvency event* occurs in relation to you; or

(c) if you become aware:

(i) of any material changes to information previously provided to the SRA, by you or on your behalf, about you or your practice, including any change to information recorded in the *register*; and

(ii) that information provided to the SRA, by you or on your behalf, about you or your practice is or may be false, misleading, incomplete or inaccurate.

7.7 You report promptly to the SRA or another *approved regulator*, as appropriate, any facts or matters that you reasonably believe are capable of amounting to a serious breach of their regulatory arrangements by any *person* regulated by them (including you).

7.8 Notwithstanding paragraph 7.7, you inform the *SRA* promptly of any facts or matters that you reasonably believe should be brought to its attention in order that it may investigate whether a serious breach of its *regulatory arrangements* has occurred or otherwise exercise its regulatory powers.

7.9 You do not subject any *person* to detrimental treatment for making or proposing to make a report or providing or proposing to provide information based on a reasonably held belief under paragraph 7.7 or 7.8 above, or paragraph 3.9, 3.10, 9.1(d) or (e) or 9.2(b) or (c) of the SRA Code of Conduct for Firms, irrespective of whether the *SRA* or another *approved regulator* subsequently investigates or takes any action in relation to the facts or matters in question.

7.10 You act promptly to take any remedial action requested by the *SRA*. If requested to do so by the *SRA* you investigate whether there are any serious breaches that should be reported to the *SRA*.

7.11 You are honest and open with *clients* if things go wrong, and if a *client* suffers loss or harm as a result you put matters right (if possible) and explain fully and promptly what has happened and the likely impact. If requested to do so by the *SRA* you investigate whether anyone may have a claim against you, provide the *SRA* with a report on the outcome of your investigation, and notify relevant persons that they may have such a claim, accordingly.

7.12 Any obligation under this section or otherwise to notify, or provide information to, the *SRA* will be satisfied if you provide information to your firm's *COLP* or *COFA*, as and where appropriate, on the understanding that they will do so.

When you are providing services to the public or a section of the public

Client identification

8.1   You identify who you are acting for in relation to any matter.

Complaints handling

8.2   You ensure that, as appropriate in the circumstances, you either establish and maintain, or participate in, a procedure for handling complaints in relation to the legal services you provide.

8.3   You ensure that *clients* are informed in writing at the time of engagement about:

(a)   their right to complain to you about your services and your charges;

(b)   how a complaint can be made and to whom; and

(c)   any right they have to make a complaint to the *Legal Ombudsman* and when they can make any such complaint.

8.4   You ensure that when *clients* have made a complaint to you, if this has not been resolved to the *client's* satisfaction within 8 weeks following the making of a complaint they are informed, in writing:

(a)   of any right they have to complain to the *Legal Ombudsman*, the time frame for doing so and full details of how to contact the *Legal Ombudsman*; and

(b)   if a complaint has been brought and your complaints procedure has been exhausted:

(i)   that you cannot settle the complaint;

(ii)   of the name and website address of an alternative dispute resolution (ADR) approved body which would be competent to deal with the complaint; and

(iii)   whether you agree to use the scheme operated by that body.

8.5   You ensure that complaints are dealt with promptly, fairly, and free of charge.

Client information and publicity

8.6   You give *clients* information in a way they can understand. You ensure they are in a position to make informed decisions about the services they need, how their matter will be handled and the options available to them.

8.7   You ensure that *clients* receive the best possible information about how their matter will be priced and, both at the time of engagement and when appropriate as their matter progresses, about the likely overall cost of the matter and any *costs* incurred.

8.8   You ensure that any *publicity* in relation to your practice is accurate and not misleading, including that relating to your charges and the circumstances in which *interest* is payable by or to *clients*.

8.9   You do not make unsolicited approaches to members of the public, with the exception of current or former *clients*, in order to advertise legal services provided by you, or your business or employer.

8.10   You ensure that *clients* understand whether and how the services you provide are regulated. This includes:

(a)   explaining which activities will be carried out by you, as an *authorised person*;

(b)   explaining which services provided by you, your business or employer, and any *separate business* are regulated by an *approved regulator*; and

(c)   ensuring that you do not represent any business or employer which is not authorised by the SRA, including any *separate business*, as being regulated by the SRA.

8.11   You ensure that *clients* understand the regulatory protections available to them.

Supplemental notes

Made by the SRA Board on 30 May 2018.

Made under sections 31 and 32 of the Solicitors Act 1974, section 89 of, and paragraphs 2 and 3 of Schedule 14 to, the Courts and Legal Services Act 1990 and section 57(2) and (8) of the Legal Aid, Sentencing and Punishment of Offenders Act 2012.

SRA Code of Conduct for Firms [draft]

[Law Society copyright. For the latest updates to the material, please see www.sra.org.uk.]

SRA Code of Conduct for Firms [draft]

[Draft version published February 2019 as amended by the SRA Regulatory Arrangements (Reporting Concerns) (Amendment) Rules 2019, approved by the LSB on 9 May 2019.]

Introduction

This Code of Conduct describes the standards and business controls that we, the SRA, and the public expect of firms (including sole practices) authorised by us to provide legal services. These aim to create and maintain the right culture and environment for the delivery of competent and ethical legal services to clients. These apply in the context of your practice: the way you run your business and all your professional activities (subject, if you are a licensed body, to any terms of your licence).

Paragraphs 8.1 and 9.1 to 9.2 set out the requirements of managers and compliance officers in those firms, respectively.

A serious failure to meet our standards or a serious breach of our regulatory requirements may lead to our taking regulatory action against the firm itself as an entity, or its managers or compliance officers, who each have responsibilities for ensuring that the standards and requirements are met. We may also take action against employees working within the firm for any breaches for which they are responsible. A failure or breach may be serious either in isolation or because it comprises a persistent or concerning pattern of behaviour.

In addition to the regulatory requirements set by us in our Codes, Principles and our rules and regulations, we directly monitor and enforce the requirements relating to referral fees set out in section 56 of the Legal Aid, Sentencing and Punishment of Offenders Act 2012, and provisions relating to anti money laundering and counter terrorist financing, as set out in regulations made by the Treasury as in force from time to time [Link].

All of these requirements are underpinned by our Enforcement Strategy, which explains in more detail our views about the issues we consider to be serious, and our approach to taking regulatory action in the public interest.

Maintaining trust and acting fairly

1.1   You do not unfairly discriminate by allowing your personal views to affect your professional relationships and the way in which you provide your services.

1.2   You do not abuse your position by taking unfair advantage of *clients* or others.

1.3　You perform all *undertakings* given by you and do so within an agreed timescale or if no timescale has been agreed then within a reasonable amount of time.

1.4　You do not mislead or attempt to mislead your *clients*, the *court* or others, either by your own acts or omissions or allowing or being complicit in the acts or omissions of others (including your *client*).

1.5　You monitor, report and publish workforce diversity data, as *prescribed*.

Compliance and business systems

2.1　You have effective governance structures, arrangements, systems and controls in place that ensure:

(a)　you comply with all the *SRA's regulatory arrangements*, as well as with other regulatory and legislative requirements, which apply to you;

(b)　your *managers* and employees comply with the *SRA's regulatory arrangements* which apply to them;

(c)　your *managers* and *interest holders* and those you employ or contract with do not cause or substantially contribute to a breach of the *SRA's regulatory arrangements* by you or your *managers* or employees;

(d)　your *compliance officers* are able to discharge their duties under paragraphs 9.1 and 9.2 below.

2.2　You keep and maintain records to demonstrate compliance with your obligations under the *SRA's regulatory arrangements*.

2.3　You remain accountable for compliance with the *SRA's regulatory arrangements* where your work is carried out through others, including your *managers* and those you employ or contract with.

2.4　You actively monitor your financial stability and business viability. Once you are aware that you will cease to operate, you effect the orderly wind-down of your activities.

2.5　You identify, monitor and manage all material risks to your business, including those which may arise from your *connected practices*.

Cooperation and accountability

3.1　You keep up to date with and follow the law and regulation governing the way you work.

3.2　You cooperate with the SRA, other regulators, ombudsmen and those bodies with a role overseeing and supervising the delivery of, or investigating concerns in relation to, legal services.

3.3　You respond promptly to the SRA and:

(a)　provide full and accurate explanations, information and documentation in response to any requests or requirements;

(b)　ensure that relevant information which is held by you, or by third parties carrying out functions on your behalf which are critical to the delivery of your legal services, is available for inspection by the SRA.

3.4　You act promptly to take any remedial action requested by the SRA.

3.5　You are honest and open with *clients* if things go wrong, and if a *client* suffers loss or harm as a result you put matters right (if possible) and explain fully and promptly what has happened and the likely impact. If requested to do so by the SRA you investigate whether anyone may have a claim against you, provide the SRA with a report on the outcome of your investigation, and notify relevant persons that they may have such a claim, accordingly.

3.6 You notify the SRA promptly:

(a) of any indicators of serious financial difficulty relating to you;

(b) if a *relevant insolvency event* occurs in relation to you;

(c) if you intend to, or become aware that you will, cease operating as a legal business;

(d) of any change to information recorded in the *register*.

3.7 You provide to the SRA an information report on an annual basis or such other period as specified by the SRA in the *prescribed* form and by the *prescribed* date.

3.8 You notify the SRA promptly if you become aware:

(a) of any material changes to information previously provided to the SRA, by you or on your behalf, about you or your *managers*, *owners* or *compliance officers*; and

(b) that information provided to the SRA, by you or on your behalf, about you or your *managers*, *owners* or *compliance officers* is or may be false, misleading, incomplete or inaccurate.

3.9 You report promptly to the *SRA* or another *approved regulator*, as appropriate, any facts or matters that you reasonably believe are capable of amounting to a serious breach of their *regulatory arrangements* by any *person* regulated by them (including you). If requested to do so by the *SRA* you investigate whether there have been any serious breaches that should be reported to the *SRA*.

3.10 Notwithstanding paragraph 3.9, you inform the *SRA* promptly of any facts ot matters that you reasonably believe should be brought to its attention in order that it may investigate whether a serious breach of its *regulatory arrangements* has occurred or otherwise exercise its regulatory powers.

3.11 You do not attempt to prevent anyone from providing information to the *SRA* or any other body exercising regulatory, supervisory, investigatory or prosecutory functions in the public interest.

3.12 You do not subject any *person* to detrimental treatment for making or proposing to make a report or providing, or proposing to provide, information based on a reasonably held belief under paragraph 3.9 or 3.10 above or 9.1 (d) or (e) or 9.2 (b) or (c) below, or under paragraph 7.7 or 7.8 of the Code of Conduct for Solicitors, RFLs and RELs, irrespective of whether the *SRA* or another *approved regulator* subsequently investigates or takes any action in relation to the facts or matters in question.

Service and competence

4.1 You only act for *clients* on instructions from the *client*, or from someone properly authorised to provide instructions on their behalf. If you have reason to suspect that the instructions do not represent your *client's* wishes, you do not act unless you have satisfied yourself that they do. However, in circumstances where you have legal authority to act notwithstanding that it is not possible to obtain or ascertain the instructions of your *client*, then you are subject to the overriding obligation to protect your *client's* best interests.

4.2 You ensure that the service you provide to *clients* is competent and delivered in a timely manner, and takes account of your *client's* attributes, needs and circumstances.

4.3 You ensure that your *managers* and employees are competent to carry out their role, and keep their professional knowledge and skills, as well as understanding of their legal, ethical and regulatory obligations, up to date.

4.4 You have an effective system for supervising *clients'* matters.

Client money and assets

5.1   You properly account to *clients* for any *financial benefit* you receive as a result of their instructions, except where they have agreed otherwise.

5.2   You safeguard money and *assets* entrusted to you by *clients* and others.

Conflict, confidentiality and disclosure

Conflict of interests

6.1   You do not act if there is an *own interest conflict* or a significant risk of such a conflict.

6.2   You do not act in relation to a matter or a particular aspect of it if you have a *conflict of interest* or a significant risk of such a conflict in relation to that matter or aspect of it, unless:

(a)   the *clients* have a *substantially common interest* in relation to the matter or the aspect of it, as appropriate; or

(b)   the *clients* are *competing for the same objective*, and the conditions below are met, namely that:

(i)   all the *clients* have given informed consent, given or evidenced in writing, to you acting;

(ii)   where appropriate, you put in place effective safeguards to protect your *clients'* confidential information; and

(iii)   you are satisfied it is reasonable for you to act for all the *clients*.

Confidentiality and disclosure

6.3   You keep the affairs of current and former *clients* confidential unless disclosure is required or permitted by law or the *client* consents.

6.4   Any individual who is acting for a *client* on a matter makes the *client* aware of all information material to the matter of which the individual has knowledge except when:

(a)   the disclosure of the information is prohibited by legal restrictions imposed in the interests of national security or the prevention of crime;

(b)   the *client* gives informed consent, given or evidenced in writing, to the information not being disclosed to them;

(c)   the individual has reason to believe that serious physical or mental injury will be caused to the *client* or another if the information is disclosed; or

(d)   the information is contained in a privileged document that the individual has knowledge of only because it has been mistakenly disclosed.

6.5   You do not act for a *client* in a matter where that *client* has an interest adverse to the interest of another current or former *client* for whom you hold confidential information which is material to that matter, unless:

(a)   effective measures have been taken which result in there being no real risk of disclosure of the confidential information; or

(b)   the current or former *client* whose information you hold has given informed consent, given or evidenced in writing, to you acting, including to any measures taken to protect their information.

Applicable standards in the **SRA** Code of Conduct for Solicitors, RELs and RFLs

7.1 The following paragraphs in the SRA Code of Conduct for Solicitors, *RELs* and *RFLs* apply to you in their entirety as though references to "you" were references to you as a firm:

   (a) dispute resolution and proceedings before courts, tribunals and inquiries (2.1 to 2.7);

   (b) referrals, introductions and *separate businesses* (5.1 to 5.3); and

   (c) standards which apply when providing services to the public or a section of the public, namely client identification (8.1), complaints handling (8.2 to 8.5), and client information and publicity (8.6 to 8.11).

Managers in **SRA** authorised firms

8.1 If you are a *manager*, you are responsible for compliance by your firm with this Code. This responsibility is joint and several if you share management responsibility with other *managers* of the firm.

Compliance officers

9.1 If you are a *COLP* you must take all reasonable steps to:

   (a) ensure compliance with the terms and conditions of your firm's authorisation;

   (b) ensure compliance by your firm and its *managers*, employees or *interest holders* with the *SRA's regulatory arrangements* which apply to them;

   (c) ensure that your firm's *managers* and *interest holders* and those they employ or contract with do not cause or substantially contribute to a breach of the *SRA's regulatory arrangements*;

   (d) ensure that a prompt report is made to the *SRA* of any facts or matters that you reasonably believe are capable of amounting to a serious breach of the terms and conditions of your firm's authorisation, or the *SRA's regulatory arrangements* which apply to your firm, *managers* or employees;

   (e) notwithstanding paragraph (d), you ensure the SRA is informed promptly of any facts ot matters that you reasonably believe should be brought to its attention in order that it may investigate whether a serious breach of its *regulatory arrangements* has occurred or otherwise exercise its regulatory powers.

   save in relation to the matters which are the responsibility of the *COFA* as set out in paragraph 9.2 below.

9.2 If you are a *COFA* you must take all reasonable steps to:

   (a) ensure that your firm and its *managers* and employees comply with any obligations imposed upon them under the SRA Accounts Rules;

   (b) ensure that a prompt report is made to the *SRA* of any facts or matters that you reasonably believe are capable of amounting to a serious breach of the SRA Accounts Rules which apply to them;

   (c) notwithstanding paragraph (b), you ensure the *SRA* is informed promptly of any facts ot matters that you reasonably believe should be brought to its attention in order that it may investigate whether a serious breach of its *regulatory arrangements* has occurred or otherwise exercise its regulatory powers.

Supplemental notes

Made by the SRA Board on 30 May 2018.

Made under section 31 of the Solicitors Act 1974, section 9 of the Administration of Justice Act 1985, section 83 of the Legal Services Act 2007, and section 57(2) and (8) of the Legal Aid, Sentencing and Punishment of Offenders Act 2012.

SRA Accounts Rules [draft]

[Law Society copyright. For the latest updates to the material, please see www.sra.org.uk.]

[Draft version published February 2019.]

SRA Accounts Rules [draft]

[Draft version as published February 2019]

Introduction

These rules set out our requirements for when firms (including sole practices) authorised by us receive or deal with money belonging to clients, including trust money or money held on behalf of third parties. The rules apply to all firms we regulate, including all those who manage or work within such firms.

Firms will need to have systems and controls in place to ensure compliance with these rules and the nature of those systems must be appropriate to the nature and volumes of client transactions dealt with and the amount of client money held or received.

Part 1: General

Application section

1.1 These rules apply to *authorised bodies*, their *managers* and employees and references to "you" in these rules should be read accordingly.

1.2 The *authorised body's managers* are jointly and severally responsible for compliance by the *authorised body*, its *managers* and employees with these rules.

1.3 In relation to a *licensed body*, the rules apply only in respect of activities regulated by the SRA in accordance with the terms of its licence.

Part 2: Client money and client accounts

Client money

2.1 "*Client money*" is money held or received by you:

    (a) relating to *regulated services* delivered by you to a *client*;

    (b) on behalf of a third party in relation to *regulated services* delivered by you (such as money held as agent, stakeholder or held to the sender's order);

(c)   as a trustee or as the holder of a specified office or appointment, such as donee of a power of attorney, Court of Protection deputy or trustee of an occupational pension scheme;

(d)   in respect of your *fees* and any unpaid *disbursements* if held or received prior to delivery of a bill for the same.

2.2   In circumstances where the only *client money* you hold or receive falls within rule 2.1(d) above, and:

(a)   any money held for *disbursements* relates to costs or expenses incurred by you on behalf of your *client* and for which you are liable; and

(b)   you do not for any other reason maintain a *client account*;

you are not required to hold this money in a *client account* if you have informed your *client* in advance of where and how the money will be held. Rules 2.3, 2.4, 4.1, 7, 8.1(b) and (c) and 12 do not apply to *client money* held outside of a *client account* in accordance with this rule.

2.3   You ensure that *client money* is paid promptly into a *client account* unless:

(a)   in relation to money falling within 2.1(c), to do so would conflict with your obligations under rules or regulations relating to your specified office or appointment;

(b)   the *client money* represents payments received from the Legal Aid Agency for your *costs*; or

(c)   you agree in the individual circumstances an alternative arrangement in writing with the *client*, or the third party, for whom the money is held.

2.4   You ensure that *client money* is available on demand unless you agree an alternative arrangement in writing with the *client*, or the third party for whom the money is held.

2.5   You ensure that *client money* is returned promptly to the *client*, or the third party for whom the money is held, as soon as there is no longer any proper reason to hold those funds.

Client account

3.1   You only maintain a *client account* at a branch (or the head office) of a *bank* or a *building society* in England and Wales.

3.2   You ensure that the name of any *client account* includes:

(a)   the name of the *authorised body*; and

(b)   the word "client" to distinguish it from any other type of account held or operated by the *authorised body*.

3.3   You must not use a *client account* to provide banking facilities to *clients* or third parties. Payments into, and transfers or withdrawals from a *client account* must be in respect of the delivery by you of *regulated services*.

Client money must be kept separate

4.1   You keep *client money* separate from money belonging to the *authorised body*.

4.2   You ensure that you allocate promptly any funds from *mixed payments* you receive to the correct *client account* or business account.

4.3   Where you are holding *client money* and some or all of that money will be used to pay your *costs*:

(a)   you must give a bill of *costs*, or other written notification of the *costs* incurred, to the *client* or the paying party;

(b)   this must be done before you transfer any *client money* from a *client account* to make the payment; and

(c)   any such payment must be for the specific sum identified in the bill of *costs*, or other written notification of the *costs* incurred, and covered by the amount held for the particular *client* or third party.

Withdrawals from client account

5.1   You only withdraw *client money* from a *client account*:

(a)   for the purpose for which it is being held;

(b)   following receipt of instructions from the *client*, or the third party for whom the money is held; or

(c)   on the *SRA's* prior written authorisation or in *prescribed* circumstances.

5.2   You appropriately authorise and supervise all withdrawals made from a *client account*.

5.3   You only withdraw *client money* from a *client account* if sufficient funds are held on behalf of that specific *client* or third party to make the payment.

Duty to correct breaches upon discovery

6.1   You correct any breaches of these rules promptly upon discovery. Any money improperly withheld or withdrawn from a *client account* must be immediately paid into the account or replaced as appropriate.

Payment of interest

7.1   You account to *clients* or third parties for a fair sum of *interest* on any *client money* held by you on their behalf.

7.2   You may by a written agreement come to a different arrangement with the *client* or the third party for whom the money is held as to the payment of *interest*, but you must provide sufficient information to enable them to give informed consent.

Client accounting systems and controls

8.1   You keep and maintain accurate, contemporaneous, and chronological records to:

(a)   record in client ledgers identified by the *client's* name and an appropriate description of the matter to which they relate:

(i)   all receipts and payments which *client money* on the client side of the client ledger account;

(ii)   all receipts and payments which are not *client money* and bills of *costs* including transactions through the *authorised body's* accounts on the business side of the client ledger account;

(b)   maintain a list of all the balances shown by the client ledger accounts of the liabilities to *clients* (and third parties), with a running total of the balances; and

(c)   provide a cash book showing a running total of all transactions through *client accounts* held or operated by you.

8.2   You obtain, at least every five weeks, statements from *banks, building societies* and other financial institutions for all *client accounts* and business accounts held or operated by you.

8.3   You complete at least every five weeks, for all *client accounts* held or operated by you, a reconciliation of the *bank* or *building society* statement balance with the cash book balance and the client ledger total, a record of which must be signed off by the *COFA* or a *manager* of the firm. You should promptly investigate and resolve any differences shown by the reconciliation.

8.4   You keep readily accessible a central record of all bills or other written notifications of *costs* given by you.

Part 3: Dealings with other money belonging to clients or third parties

Operation of joint accounts

9.1   If, when acting in a *client's* matter, you hold or receive money jointly with the *client* or a third party, Part 2 of these rules does not apply save for:

(a)   rule 8.2 – statements from *banks*, *building societies* and other financial institutions;

(b)   rule 8.4 – bills and notifications of *costs*.

Operation of a client's own account

10.1   If, in the course of practice, you operate a *client's* own account as signatory, Part 2 of these rules does not apply save for:

(a)   rule 8.2 – statements from *banks*, *building societies* and other financial institutions;

(b)   rule 8.3 – reconciliations;

(c)   rule 8.4 – bills and notifications of *costs*.

Third party managed accounts

11.1   You may enter into arrangements with a *client* to use a *third party managed account* for the purpose of receiving payments from or on behalf of, or making payments to or on behalf of, the *client* in respect of *regulated services* delivered by you to the *client*, only if:

(a)   use of the account does not result in you receiving or holding the *client's* money; and

(b)   you take reasonable steps to ensure, before accepting instructions, that the *client* is informed of and understands:

(i)   the terms of the contractual arrangements relating to the use of the *third party managed account*, and in particular how any *fees* for use of the *third party managed account* will be paid and who will bear them; and

(ii)   the *client's* right to terminate the agreement and dispute payment requests made by you.

11.2   You obtain regular statements from the provider of the *third party managed account* and ensure that these accurately reflect all transactions on the account.

Part 4: Accountants' reports and storage and retention of accounting records

Obtaining and delivery of accountants' reports

12.1   If you have, at any time during an *accounting period*, held or received *client money*, or operated a joint account or a *client's* own account as signatory, you must:

(a)   obtain an accountant's report for that *accounting period* within six months of the end of the period; and

(b)   deliver it to the SRA within six months of the end of the *accounting period* if the accountant's report is qualified to show a failure to comply with these rules, such that money belonging to *clients* or third parties is, or has been, or is likely to be placed, at risk.

12.2   You are not required to obtain an accountant's report if:

(a)   all of the *client money* held or received during an *accounting period* is money received from the Legal Aid Agency; or

(b)   in the *accounting period*, the statement or passbook balance of *client money* you have held or received does not exceed:

    (i)   an average of £10,000; and

    (ii)   a maximum of £250,000,

or the equivalent in foreign currency.

12.3   In rule 12.2 above a "statement or passbook balance" is the total balance of:

(a)   all *client accounts* held or operated by you; and

(b)   any joint accounts and *clients'* own accounts operated by you, as shown by the statements obtained under rule 8.2.

12.4   The SRA may require you to obtain or deliver an accountant's report to the SRA on reasonable notice if you cease to operate as an *authorised body* and to hold or operate a *client account*, or the SRA considers that it is otherwise in the public interest to do so.

12.5   You ensure that any report obtained under this rule is prepared and signed by an accountant who is a member of one of the *chartered accountancy bodies* and who is, or works for, a registered auditor.

12.6   The SRA may disqualify an accountant from preparing a report for the purposes of this rule if:

(a)   the accountant has been found guilty by their professional body of professional misconduct or equivalent; or

(b)   the SRA is satisfied that the accountant has failed to exercise due care and skill in the preparation of a report under these rules.

12.7   The SRA may specify from time to time matters that you must ensure are incorporated into the terms on which an accountant is engaged.

12.8   You must provide to an accountant preparing a report under these rules:

(a)   details of all accounts held or operated by you in connection with your practice at any *bank*, *building society* or other financial institution at any time during the *accounting period* to which the report relates; and

(b)   all other information and documentation that the accountant requires to enable completion of their report.

12.9   The accountant must complete and sign their report in the *prescribed* form.

Storage and retention of accounting records

13.1   You must store all *accounting records* securely and retain these for at least six years.

Supplemental notes

Made by the SRA Board on 30 May 2018.

Made under sections 32, 33A, 34, 37 of the Solicitors Act 1974, section 9 of the Administration of Justice Act 1985, and section 83(5)(h) of, and paragraph 20 of Schedule 11 to, the Legal Services Act 2007.

SRA Transparency Rules 2018

[Law Society copyright. For the latest updates to the material, please see www.sra.org.uk.]

SRA Transparency Rules 2018

[Version as published 6 December 2018. Note: not all requirements of the SRA Transparency Rules 2018 are yet in force.]

Introduction

These rules set out the information authorised firms, and individuals providing services to the public from outside authorised firms, should make available to clients and potential clients.

The rules aim to ensure people have accurate and relevant information about a solicitor or firm when they are considering purchasing legal services and will help members of the public and small businesses make informed choices, improving competition in the legal market.

Costs information

1.1   An authorised body, [or an individual practising in the circumstances set out in regulation 10.2(b)(i) to (vii) of the SRA Authorisation of Individuals Regulations,] who publishes as part of its usual business the availability of any of the services set out at rule 1.3 to individuals or at rule 1.4 to businesses, must, in relation to those services, publish on its website cost information in accordance with rule 1.5 and 1.6.

1.2   Rule 1.1 does not apply to publicly funded work.

1.3   The services in relation to individuals are:

   (a)   The conveyance of residential real property or real estate which comprise:

      (i)   freehold or leasehold sales or purchases; or

      (ii)   mortgages or re-mortgages;

   (b)   the collection and distribution of *assets* belonging to a person following their death, where these are within the UK and the matters are not contested;

   (c)   the preparation and submission of immigration applications, excluding asylum applications;

   (d)   the provision of advice and representation at the First-tier Tribunal (Immigration and Asylum Chamber) in relation to appeals against Home Office visa or immigration decisions, excluding asylum appeals;

   (e)   the provision of advice and representation at the Magistrates Court in relation to summary only road traffic offences dealt with at a single hearing;

   (f)   the provision of advice and representation to employees in relation to the bringing of claims before the Employment Tribunal against an employer for unfair dismissal or wrongful dismissal.

1.4 The services in relation to businesses are:

    (a) the provision of advice and representation to employers in relation to defending claims before the Employment Tribunal brought by an employee for unfair dismissal or wrongful dismissal;

    (b) debt recovery up to the value of £100,000;

    (c) the provision of advice and assistance and representation in relation to licensing applications for business premises.

1.5 Costs information must include:

    (a) the total cost of the service or, where not practicable, the average cost or range of costs;

    (b) the basis for your charges, including any hourly rates or fixed fees;

    (c) the experience and qualifications of anyone carrying out the work, and of their supervisors;

    (d) a description of, and the cost of, any likely *disbursements*, and where the actual cost of a *disbursement* is not known, the average cost or range of costs;

    (e) whether any fees or *disbursements* attract VAT and if so the amount of VAT they attract;

    (f) details of what services are included in the price displayed, including the key stages of the matter and likely timescales for each stage, and details of any services that might reasonably be expected to be included in the price displayed but are not; and

    (g) if you use conditional fee or damages based agreements, the circumstances in which *clients* may have to make any payments themselves for your services (including from any damages).

1.6 Cost information published under this rule must be clear and accessible and in a prominent place on your website.

Complaints information

2.1 An *authorised body*, [or an individual practising in the circumstances set out in regulation 10.2(b)(i) to (vii) of the SRA Authorisation of Individuals Regulations,] must publish on its website details of its complaints handling procedure including, details about how and when a complaint can be made to the *Legal Ombudsman* and to the *SRA*.

Publication

3.1 An *authorised body*, [or an individual practising in the circumstances set out in regulation 10.2(b)(i) to (vii) of the SRA Authorisation of Individuals Regulations,] that does not have a website, must make the information set out in rules 1 to 2 available on request.

[Regulatory information

4.1 An *authorised body* must display in a prominent place on its website (or, in the case of a *licensed body*, the website relating to its legal services, if separate) its SRA number and the *SRA's* digital badge.

4.2 An *authorised body's* letterhead and e-mails must show its SRA authorisation number and the words "authorised and regulated by the Solicitors Regulation Authority".

4.3   A *solicitor*, an *REL* or *RFL* who is providing legal services to the public or a section of the public other than through a firm that is regulated by the *SRA*:

(a)   where they are not required to meet the *MTC*, must before engagement inform all *clients* of this fact and specify that alternative insurance arrangements are in place if this is the case (together with information about the cover this provides, if requested); and

(b)   where applicable, must inform all *clients* that they will not be eligible to apply for a grant from the SRA Compensation Fund.

4.4   Rule 4.3 does not apply to a *solicitor*, an *REL* or *RFL* that is working in an *authorised non-SRA firm* or a *non-commercial body*.]

Supplemental notes

Made by the SRA Board on 30 May 2018.

Made under section 31 of the Solicitors Act 1974, section 9 of the Administration of Justice Act 1985 and section 83 of, and Schedule 11 to, the Legal Services Act 2007.

CCBE Code of Conduct

[The Code is reproduced with the kind permission of the CCBE. For the latest updates to the material, please see www.ccbe.org.]

Code of Conduct for European Lawyers

This Code of Conduct for European Lawyers was originally adopted at the CCBE Plenary Session held on 28 October 1988, and subsequently amended during the CCBE Plenary Sessions on 28 November 1998, 6 December 2002 and 19 May 2006. The Code also takes into account amendments to the CCBE statutes formally approved at an Extraordinary Plenary Session on 20 August 2007.

Contents

EXPLANATORY MEMORANDUM

1. Preamble

1.1. The Function of the Lawyer in Society

In a society founded on respect for the rule of law the lawyer fulfils a special role. The lawyer's duties do not begin and end with the faithful performance of what he or she is instructed to do so far as the law permits. A lawyer must serve the interests of justice as well as those whose rights and liberties he or she is trusted to assert and defend and it is the lawyer's duty not only to plead the client's cause but to be the client's adviser. Respect for the lawyer's professional function is an essential condition for the rule of law and democracy in society.

A lawyer's function therefore lays on him or her a variety of legal and moral obligations (sometimes appearing to be in conflict with each other) towards:

–   the client;

–   the courts and other authorities before whom the lawyer pleads the client's cause or acts on the client's behalf;

–   the legal profession in general and each fellow member of it in particular;

–   the public for whom the existence of a free and independent profession, bound together by respect for rules made by the profession itself, is an essential means of safeguarding human rights in face of the power of the state and other interests in society.

1.2. The Nature of Rules of Professional Conduct

1.2.1. Rules of professional conduct are designed through their willing acceptance by those to whom they apply to ensure the proper performance by the lawyer of a function which is recognised as essential in all civilised societies. The failure of the lawyer to observe these rules may result in disciplinary sanctions.

1.2.2. The particular rules of each Bar or Law Society arise from its own traditions. They are adapted to the organisation and sphere of activity of the profession in the Member State concerned and to its judicial and administrative procedures and to its national legislation. It is neither possible nor desirable that they should be taken out of their context nor that an attempt should be made to give general application to rules which are inherently incapable of such application.

The particular rules of each Bar and Law Society nevertheless are based on the same values and in most cases demonstrate a common foundation.

1.3. The Purpose of the Code

1.3.1. The continued integration of the European Union and European Economic Area and the increasing frequency of the cross-border activities of lawyers within the European Economic Area have made necessary in the public interest the statement of common rules which apply to all lawyers from the European Economic Area whatever Bar or Law Society they belong to in relation to their cross-border practice. A particular purpose of the statement of those rules is to mitigate the difficulties which result from the application of "double deontology", notably as set out in Articles 4 and 7.2 of Directive 77/249/EEC and Articles 6 and 7 of Directive 98/5/EC.

1.3.2. The organisations representing the legal profession through the CCBE propose that the rules codified in the following articles:

– be recognised at the present time as the expression of a consensus of all the Bars and Law Societies of the European Union and European Economic Area;

– be adopted as enforceable rules as soon as possible in accordance with national or EEA procedures in relation to the cross-border activities of the lawyer in the European Union and European Economic Area;

– be taken into account in all revisions of national rules of deontology or professional practice with a view to their progressive harmonisation.

They further express the wish that the national rules of deontology or professional practice be interpreted and applied whenever possible in a way consistent with the rules in this Code.

After the rules in this Code have been adopted as enforceable rules in relation to a lawyer's cross-border activities the lawyer will remain bound to observe the rules of the Bar or Law Society to which he or she belongs to the extent that they are consistent with the rules in this Code.

1.4. Field of Application Ratione Personae

This Code shall apply to lawyers as they are defined by Directive 77/249/EEC and by Directive 98/5/EC and to lawyers of the Associate and Observer Members of the CCBE.

1.5. Field of Application Ratione Materiae

Without prejudice to the pursuit of a progressive harmonisation of rules of deontology or professional practice which apply only internally within a Member State, the following rules shall apply to the cross-border activities of the lawyer within the European Union and the European Economic Area. Cross-border activities shall mean:

(a)   all professional contacts with lawyers of Member States other than the lawyer's own;

(b)   the professional activities of the lawyer in a Member State other than his or her own, whether or not the lawyer is physically present in that Member State.

1.6. Definitions

In this Code:

"Member State" means a member state of the European Union or any other state whose legal profession is included in Article 1.4.

"Home Member State" means the Member State where the lawyer acquired the right to bear his or her professional title.

"Host Member State" means any other Member State where the lawyer carries on cross-border activities.

"Competent Authority" means the professional organisation(s) or authority(ies) of the Member State concerned responsible for the laying down of rules of professional conduct and the administration of discipline of lawyers.

"Directive 77/249/EEC" means Council Directive 77/249/EEC of 22 March 1977 to facilitate the effective exercise by lawyers of freedom to provide services.

"Directive 98/5/EC" means Directive 98/5/EC of the European Parliament and of the Council of 16 February 1998 to facilitate practice of the profession of lawyer on a permanent basis in a Member State other than that in which the qualification was obtained.

2. General Principles

2.1. Independence

2.1.1. The many duties to which a lawyer is subject require the lawyer's absolute independence, free from all other influence, especially such as may arise from his or her personal interests or external pressure. Such independence is as necessary to trust in the process of justice as the impartiality of the judge. A lawyer must therefore avoid any impairment of his or her independence and be careful not to compromise his or her professional standards in order to please the client, the court or third parties.

2.1.2. This independence is necessary in non-contentious matters as well as in litigation. Advice given by a lawyer to the client has no value if the lawyer gives it only to ingratiate him- or herself, to serve his or her personal interests or in response to outside pressure.

2.2. Trust and Personal Integrity

Relationships of trust can only exist if a lawyer's personal honour, honesty and integrity are beyond doubt. For the lawyer these traditional virtues are professional obligations.

2.3. Confidentiality

2.3.1. It is of the essence of a lawyer's function that the lawyer should be told by his or her client things which the client would not tell to others, and that the lawyer should be the recipient of other information on a basis of confidence. Without the certainty of confidentiality there cannot be trust. Confidentiality is therefore a primary and fundamental right and duty of the lawyer.

The lawyer's obligation of confidentiality serves the interest of the administration of justice as well as the interest of the client. It is therefore entitled to special protection by the State.

2.3.2. A lawyer shall respect the confidentiality of all information that becomes known to the lawyer in the course of his or her professional activity.

2.3.3. The obligation of confidentiality is not limited in time.

2.3.4. A lawyer shall require his or her associates and staff and anyone engaged by him or her in the course of providing professional services to observe the same obligation of confidentiality.

2.4. Respect for the Rules of Other Bars and Law Societies

When practising cross-border, a lawyer from another Member State may be bound to comply with the professional rules of the Host Member State. Lawyers have a duty to inform themselves as to the rules which will affect them in the performance of any particular activity.

Member organisations of the CCBE are obliged to deposit their codes of conduct at the Secretariat of the CCBE so that any lawyer can get hold of the copy of the current code from the Secretariat.

2.5. Incompatible Occupations

2.5.1. In order to perform his or her functions with due independence and in a manner which is consistent with his or her duty to participate in the administration of justice a lawyer may be prohibited from undertaking certain occupations.

2.5.2. A lawyer who acts in the representation or the defence of a client in legal proceedings or before any public authorities in a Host Member State shall there observe the rules regarding incompatible occupations as they are applied to lawyers of the Host Member State.

2.5.3. A lawyer established in a Host Member State in which he or she wishes to participate directly in commercial or other activities not connected with the practice of the law shall respect the rules regarding forbidden or incompatible occupations as they are applied to lawyers of that Member State.

2.6. Personal Publicity

2.6.1. A lawyer is entitled to inform the public about his or her services provided that the information is accurate and not misleading, and respectful of the obligation of confidentiality and other core values of the profession.

2.6.2. Personal publicity by a lawyer in any form of media such as by press, radio, television, by electronic commercial communications or otherwise is permitted to the extent it complies with the requirements of 2.6.1.

2.7. The Client's Interest

Subject to due observance of all rules of law and professional conduct, a lawyer must always act in the best interests of the client and must put those interests before the lawyer's own interests or those of fellow members of the legal profession.

2.8. Limitation of Lawyer's Liability towards the Client

To the extent permitted by the law of the Home Member State and the Host Member State, the lawyer may limit his or her liabilities towards the client in accordance with the professional rules to which the lawyer is subject.

3. Relations with Clients

3.1. Acceptance and Termination of Instructions

3.1.1. A lawyer shall not handle a case for a party except on that party's instructions. The lawyer may, however, act in a case in which he or she has been instructed by another lawyer acting for the party or where the case has been assigned to him or her by a competent body.

The lawyer should make reasonable efforts to ascertain the identity, competence and authority of the person or body who instructs him or her when the specific circumstances show that the identity, competence and authority are uncertain.

3.1.2. A lawyer shall advise and represent the client promptly, conscientiously and diligently. The lawyer shall undertake personal responsibility for the discharge of the client's instructions and shall keep the client informed as to the progress of the matter with which the lawyer has been entrusted.

A lawyer shall not handle a matter which the lawyer knows or ought to know he or she is not competent to handle, without co-operating with a lawyer who is competent to handle it.

3.1.3. A lawyer shall not accept instructions unless he or she can discharge those instructions promptly having regard to the pressure of other work.

3.1.4. A lawyer shall not be entitled to exercise his or her right to withdraw from a case in such a way or in such circumstances that the client may be unable to find other legal assistance in time to prevent prejudice being suffered by the client.

3.2. Conflict of Interest

3.2.1. A lawyer may not advise, represent or act on behalf of two or more clients in the same matter if there is a conflict, or a significant risk of a conflict, between the interests of those clients.

3.2.2. A lawyer must cease to act for both or all of the clients concerned when a conflict of interests arises between those clients and also whenever there is a risk of a breach of confidence or where the lawyer's independence may be impaired.

3.2.3. A lawyer must also refrain from acting for a new client if there is a risk of breach of a confidence entrusted to the lawyer by a former client or if the knowledge which the lawyer possesses of the affairs of the former client would give an undue advantage to the new client.

3.2.4. Where lawyers are practising in association, paragraphs 3.2.1 to 3.2.3 above shall apply to the association and all its members.

3.3. Pactum de Quota Litis

3.3.1. A lawyer shall not be entitled to make a *pactum de quota litis*.

3.3.2. By *"pactum de quota litis"* is meant an agreement between a lawyer and the client entered into prior to final conclusion of a matter to which the client is a party, by virtue of which the client undertakes to pay the lawyer a share of the result regardless of whether this is represented by a sum of money or by any other benefit achieved by the client upon the conclusion of the matter.

3.3.3. *"Pactum de quota litis"* does not include an agreement that fees be charged in proportion to the value of a matter handled by the lawyer if this is in accordance with an officially approved fee scale or under the control of the Competent Authority having jurisdiction over the lawyer.

3.4. Regulation of Fees

A fee charged by a lawyer shall be fully disclosed to the client, shall be fair and reasonable, and shall comply with the law and professional rules to which the lawyer is subject.

3.5. Payment on Account

If a lawyer requires a payment on account of his or her fees and/or disbursements such payment should not exceed a reasonable estimate of the fees and probable disbursements involved.

Failing such payment, a lawyer may withdraw from the case or refuse to handle it, but subject always to paragraph 3.1.4 above.

3.6. Fee Sharing with Non-Lawyers

3.6.1. A lawyer may not share his or her fees with a person who is not a lawyer except where an association between the lawyer and the other person is permitted by the laws and the professional rules to which the lawyer is subject.

3.6.2. The provisions of 3.6.1 above shall not preclude a lawyer from paying a fee, commission or other compensation to a deceased lawyer's heirs or to a retired lawyer in respect of taking over the deceased or retired lawyer's practice.

3.7. Cost of Litigation and Availability of Legal Aid

3.7.1. The lawyer should at all times strive to achieve the most cost effective resolution of the client's dispute and should advise the client at appropriate stages as to the desirability of attempting a settlement and/or a reference to alternative dispute resolution.

3.7.2. A lawyer shall inform the client of the availability of legal aid where applicable.

3.8. Client Funds

3.8.1. Lawyers who come into possession of funds on behalf of their clients or third parties (hereinafter called "client funds") have to deposit such money into an account of a bank or similar institution subject to supervision by a public authority (hereinafter called a "client account"). A client account shall be separate from any other account of the lawyer. All client funds received by a lawyer should be deposited into such an account unless the owner of such funds agrees that the funds should be dealt with otherwise.

3.8.2. The lawyer shall maintain full and accurate records showing all the lawyer's dealings with client funds and distinguishing client funds from other funds held by the lawyer. Records may have to be kept for a certain period of time according to national rules.

3.8.3. A client account cannot be in debit except in exceptional circumstances as expressly permitted in national rules or due to bank charges, which cannot be influenced by the lawyer. Such an account cannot be given as a guarantee or be used as a security for any reason. There shall not be any set-off or merger between a client account and any other bank account, nor shall the client funds in a client account be available to defray money owed by the lawyer to the bank.

3.8.4. Client funds shall be transferred to the owners of such funds in the shortest period of time or under such conditions as are authorised by them.

3.8.5. The lawyer cannot transfer funds from a client account into the lawyer's own account for payment of fees without informing the client in writing.

3.8.6. The Competent Authorities in Member States shall have the power to verify and examine any document regarding client funds, whilst respecting the confidentiality or legal professional privilege to which it may be subject.

3.9. Professional Indemnity Insurance

3.9.1. Lawyers shall be insured against civil legal liability arising out of their legal practice to an extent which is reasonable having regard to the nature and extent of the risks incurred by their professional activities.

3.9.2. Should this prove impossible, the lawyer must inform the client of this situation and its consequences.

4. Relations with the Courts

4.1. Rules of Conduct in Court

A lawyer who appears, or takes part in a case, before a court or tribunal must comply with the rules of conduct applied before that court or tribunal.

4.2. Fair Conduct of Proceedings

A lawyer must always have due regard for the fair conduct of proceedings.

4.3. Demeanour in Court

A lawyer shall while maintaining due respect and courtesy towards the court defend the interests of the client honourably and fearlessly without regard to the lawyer's own interests or to any consequences to him- or herself or to any other person.

4.4. False or Misleading Information

A lawyer shall never knowingly give false or misleading information to the court.

4.5. Extension to Arbitrators etc.

The rules governing a lawyer's relations with the courts apply also to the lawyer's relations with arbitrators and any other persons exercising judicial or quasi-judicial functions, even on an occasional basis.

5. Relations between Lawyers

5.1. Corporate Spirit of the Profession

5.1.1. The corporate spirit of the profession requires a relationship of trust and co-operation between lawyers for the benefit of their clients and in order to avoid unnecessary litigation and other behaviour harmful to the reputation of the profession. It can, however, never justify setting the interests of the profession against those of the client.

5.1.2. A lawyer should recognise all other lawyers of Member States as professional colleagues and act fairly and courteously towards them.

5.2. Co-operation among Lawyers of Different Member States

5.2.1. It is the duty of a lawyer who is approached by a colleague from another Member State not to accept instructions in a matter which the lawyer is not competent to undertake. The lawyer should in such case be prepared to help that colleague to obtain the information necessary to enable him or her to instruct a lawyer who is capable of providing the service asked for.

5.2.2. Where a lawyer of a Member State co-operates with a lawyer from another Member State, both have a general duty to take into account the differences which may exist between their respective legal systems and the professional organisations, competences and obligations of lawyers in the Member States concerned.

5.3. Correspondence between Lawyers

5.3.1. If a lawyer intends to send communications to a lawyer in another Member State, which the sender wishes to remain confidential or without prejudice he or she should clearly express this intention prior to communicating the first of the documents.

5.3.2. If the prospective recipient of the communications is unable to ensure their status as confidential or without prejudice he or she should inform the sender accordingly without delay.

5.4. Referral Fees

5.4.1. A lawyer may not demand or accept from another lawyer or any other person a fee, commission or any other compensation for referring or recommending the lawyer to a client.

5.4.2. A lawyer may not pay anyone a fee, commission or any other compensation as a consideration for referring a client to him- or herself.

5.5. Communication with Opposing Parties

A lawyer shall not communicate about a particular case or matter directly with any person whom he or she knows to be represented or advised in the case or matter by another lawyer, without the consent of that other lawyer (and shall keep the other lawyer informed of any such communications).

5.6.

(Deleted by decision of the Plenary Session in Dublin on 6 December 2002)

5.7. Responsibility for Fees

In professional relations between members of Bars of different Member States, where a lawyer does not confine him- or herself to recommending another lawyer or introducing that other lawyer to the client but instead him- or herself entrusts a correspondent with a particular matter or seeks the correspondent's advice, the instructing lawyer is personally bound, even if the client is insolvent, to pay the fees, costs and outlays which are due to the foreign correspondent. The lawyers concerned may, however, at the outset of the relationship between them make special arrangements on this matter. Further, the instructing lawyer may at any time limit his or her personal responsibility to the amount of the fees, costs and outlays incurred before intimation to the foreign lawyer of the instructing lawyer's disclaimer of responsibility for the future.

5.8. Continuing Professional Development

Lawyers should maintain and develop their professional knowledge and skills taking proper account of the European dimension of their profession.

5.9. Disputes amongst Lawyers in Different Member States

5.9.1. If a lawyer considers that a colleague in another Member State has acted in breach of a rule of professional conduct the lawyer shall draw the matter to the attention of that colleague.

5.9.2. If any personal dispute of a professional nature arises amongst lawyers in different Member States they should if possible first try to settle it in a friendly way.

5.9.3. A lawyer shall not commence any form of proceedings against a colleague in another Member State on matters referred to in 5.9.1 or 5.9.2 above without first informing the Bars or Law Societies to which they both belong for the purpose of allowing both Bars or Law Societies concerned an opportunity to assist in reaching a settlement.

Explanatory Memorandum

This Explanatory Memorandum was prepared at the request of the CCBE Standing Committee by the CCBE's deontology working party, who were responsible for drafting the first version of the Code of Conduct itself. It seeks to explain the origin of the provisions of the Code, to illustrate the problems which they are designed to resolve, particularly in relation to cross-border activities, and to provide assistance to the Competent Authorities in the Member States in the application of the Code. It is not intended to have any binding force in the interpretation of the Code. The Explanatory Memorandum was adopted on 28 October 1988 and updated on the occasion of the CCBE Plenary Session on 19 May 2006. The Explanatory Memorandum also takes into account amendments to the CCBE Statutes formally approved at an Extraordinary Plenary Session on 20 August 2007. The list of professions in the commentary on article 1.4 is subject to modification.

The original versions of the Code are in the French and English languages. Translations into other Community languages are prepared under the authority of the national delegations.

Commentary on Article 1.1 – The Function of the Lawyer in Society

The Declaration of Perugia, adopted by the CCBE in 1977, laid down the fundamental principles of professional conduct applicable to lawyers throughout the EC. The provisions of

Article 1.1 reaffirm the statement in the Declaration of Perugia of the function of the lawyer in society which forms the basis for the rules governing the performance of that function.

Commentary on Article 1.2 – The Nature of Rules of Professional Conduct

These provisions substantially restate the explanation in the Declaration of Perugia of the nature of rules of professional conduct and how particular rules depend on particular local circumstances but are nevertheless based on common values.

Commentary on Article 1.3 – The Purpose of the Code

These provisions introduce the development of the principles in the Declaration of Perugia into a specific Code of Conduct for lawyers throughout the EU the EEA and Swiss Confederation, and lawyers of the Associate and Observer Members of the CCBE, with particular reference to their cross-border activities (defined in Article 1.5). The provisions of Article 1.3.2 lay down the specific intentions of the CCBE with regard to the substantive provisions in the Code.

Commentary on Article 1.4 – Field of Application Ratione Personae

The rules are stated to apply to all lawyers as defined in the Lawyers Services Directive of 1977 and the Lawyers Establishment Directive of 1998, and lawyers of the Associate and Observer Members of the CCBE. This includes lawyers of the states which subsequently acceded to the Directives, whose names have been added by amendment to the Directives. The Code accordingly applies to all the lawyers represented on the CCBE, whether as full Members, Associate Members or as Observer Members, namely:

Albania	Avokat
Andorra	Advocat
Armenia	Pastaban
Austria	Rechtsanwalt
Belgium	Avocat / Advocaat / Rechtsanwalt
Bosnia and Herzegovina	Advokat / Odvjetnik
Bulgaria	Advokat
Croatia	Odvjetnik
Cyprus	Dikegóros
Czech Republic	Advokát
Denmark	Advokat
Estonia	Vandeadvokaat
Finland	Asianajaja / Advokat
FYROM	Advokat
France	Avocat
Georgia	Advokati / Advokatebi
Germany	Rechtsanwalt
Greece	Dikegóros

Hungary	Ügyvéd
Iceland	Lögmaður
Ireland	Barrister / Solicitor
Italy	Avvocato
Latvia	Zverinats advokats
Liechtenstein	Rechtsanwalt
Lithuania	Advokatas
Luxembourg	Avocat / Rechtsanwalt
Malta	Avukat / Prokuratur Legali
Montenegro	Advokat
Moldova	Avocat
Netherlands	Advocaat
Norway	Advokat
Poland	Adwokat / Radca prawny
Portugal	Advogado
Romania	Avocat
Serbia	Advokat
Slovak Republic	Advokát / Advokátka
Slovenia	Odvetnik / Odvetnica
Spain	Abogado / Advocat / Abokatu / Avogado
Sweden	Advokat
Switzerland	Rechtsanwalt / Anwalt / Fürsprech / Fürsprecher / Advocat / avocat / avvocato /advocat
Turkey	Avukat
Ukraine	Advokat
United Kingdom	Advocate / Barrister / Solicitor

It is also hoped that the Code will be acceptable to the legal professions of other non-member states in Europe and elsewhere so that it could also be applied by appropriate conventions between them and the Member States.

Commentary on Article 1.5 – Field of Application Ratione Materiae

The rules are here given direct application only to "cross-border activities", as defined, of lawyers within the EU, the EEA and Swiss Confederation and lawyers of the Associate and Observer Members of the CCBE – see above on Article 1.4, and the definition of "Member State" in Article 1.6. (See also above as to possible extensions in the future to lawyers of other states.) The definition of cross-border activities would, for example, include contacts in state A even on a matter of law internal to state A between a lawyer of state A and a lawyer of state B; it would exclude contacts between lawyers of state A in state A of a matter arising in state B, provided that none of their professional activities takes place in state B; it would include any activities of lawyers of state A in state B, even if only in the form of communications sent from state A to state B.

Commentary on Article 1.6 – Definitions

This provision defines a number of terms used in the Code, "Member State", "Home Member State", "Host Member State", "Competent Authority", "Directive 77/249/EEC" and "Directive 98/5/EC".

The reference to "where the lawyer carries on cross-border activities" should be interpreted in light of the definition of "cross-border activities" in Article 1.5.

Commentary on Article 2.1 – Independence

This provision substantially reaffirms the general statement of principle in the Declaration of Perugia.

Commentary on Article 2.2 – Trust and Personal Integrity

This provision also restates a general principle contained in the Declaration of Perugia.

Commentary on Article 2.3 – Confidentiality

This provision first restates, in Article 2.3.1, general principles laid down in the Declaration of Perugia and recognised by the ECJ in the *AM&S* case (157/79). It then, in Articles 2.3.2 to 4, develops them into a specific rule relating to the protection of confidentiality. Article 2.3.2 contains the basic rule requiring respect for confidentiality. Article 2.3.3 confirms that the obligation remains binding on the lawyer even if he or she ceases to act for the client in question. Article 2.3.4 confirms that the lawyer must not only respect the obligation of confidentiality him- or herself but must require all members and employees of his or her firm to do likewise.

Commentary on Article 2.4 – Respect for the Rules of Other Bars and Law Societies

Article 4 of the Lawyers Services Directive contains the provisions with regard to the rules to be observed by a lawyer from one Member State providing services on an occasional or temporary basis in another Member State by virtue of Article 49 of the consolidated EC treaty, as follows:

(a)   activities relating to the representation of a client in legal proceedings or before public authorities shall be pursued in each Host Member State under the conditions laid down for lawyers established in that state, with the exception of any conditions requiring residence, or registration with a professional organisation, in that state;

(b)   a lawyer pursuing these activities shall observe the rules of professional conduct of the Host Member State, without prejudice to the lawyer's obligations in the Member State from which he or she comes;

(c)   when these activities are pursued in the UK, "rules of professional conduct of the Host Member State" means the rules of professional conduct applicable to solicitors, where such activities are not reserved for barristers and advocates. Otherwise the rules of professional conduct applicable to the latter shall apply. However, barristers from Ireland shall always be subject to the rules of professional conduct applicable in the UK to barristers and advocates. When these activities are pursued in Ireland "rules of professional conduct of the Host Member State" means, in so far as they govern the oral presentation of a case in court, the rules of professional conduct applicable to barristers. In all other cases the rules of professional conduct applicable to solicitors shall apply. However, barristers and advocates from the UK shall always be subject to the rules of professional conduct applicable in Ireland to barristers; and

(d)   a lawyer pursuing activities other than those referred to in (a) above shall remain subject to the conditions and rules of professional conduct of the Member State from which he or she comes without prejudice to respect for the rules, whatever their source, which govern the profession in the Host Member State, especially those concerning the incompatibility of the exercise of the activities of a lawyer with the exercise of other activities in that state, professional secrecy, relations with other lawyers, the prohibition on the same lawyer acting for parties with mutually conflicting interests, and publicity. The latter rules are applicable only if they are capable of being observed by a lawyer who is not established in the Host Member State and to the extent to which their observance is objectively justified to ensure, in that state, the proper exercise of a lawyer's activities, the standing of the profession and respect for the rules concerning incompatibility.

The Lawyers Establishment Directive contains the provisions with regard to the rules to be observed by a lawyer from one Member State practising on a permanent basis in another Member State by virtue of Article 43 of the consolidated EC treaty, as follows:

(a)   irrespective of the rules of professional conduct to which he or she is subject in his or her Home Member State, a lawyer practising under his home-country professional title shall be subject to the same rules of professional conduct as lawyers practising under the relevant professional title of the Host Member State in respect of all the activities the lawyer pursues in its territory (Article 6.1);

(b)   the Host Member State may require a lawyer practising under his or her home-country professional title either to take out professional indemnity insurance or to become a member of a professional guarantee fund in accordance with the rules which that state lays down for professional activities pursued in its territory.

Nevertheless, a lawyer practising under his or her home-country professional title shall be exempted from that requirement if the lawyer can prove that he or she is covered by insurance taken out or a guarantee provided in accordance with the rules of the Home Member State, insofar as such insurance or guarantee is equivalent in terms of the conditions and extent of cover. Where the equivalence is only partial, the Competent Authority in the Host Member State may require that additional insurance or an additional guarantee be contracted to cover the elements which are not already covered by the insurance or guarantee contracted in accordance with the rules of the Home Member State (Article 6.3); and

(c)   a lawyer registered in a Host Member State under his or her home-country professional title may practise as a salaried lawyer in the employ of another lawyer, an association or firm of lawyers, or a public or private enterprise to the extent that the Host Member State so permits for lawyers registered under the professional title used in that state (Article 8).

In cases not covered by either of these Directives, or over and above the requirements of these Directives, the obligations of a lawyer under Community law to observe the rules of other Bars and Law Societies are a matter of interpretation of any relevant provision, such as the Directive on Electronic Commerce (2000/31/EC). A major purpose of the Code is to minimise, and if possible eliminate altogether, the problems which may arise from "double deontology", that is the application of more than one set of potentially conflicting national rules to a particular situation (see Article 1.3.1).

Commentary on Article 2.5 – Incompatible Occupations

There are differences both between and within Member States on the extent to which lawyers are permitted to engage in other occupations, for example in commercial activities. The general purpose of rules excluding a lawyer from other occupations is to protect the lawyer from influences which might impair the lawyer's independence or his or her role in the administration of justice. The variations in these rules reflect different local conditions, different perceptions of the proper function of lawyers and different techniques of rule-making. For instance in some cases there is a complete prohibition of engagement in certain named occupations, whereas in other cases engagement in other occupations is generally permitted, subject to observance of specific safeguards for the lawyer's independence.

Articles 2.5.2 and 3 make provision for different circumstances in which a lawyer of one Member State is engaging in cross-border activities (as defined in Article 1.5) in a Host Member State when he or she is not a member of the Host State legal profession.

Article 2.5.2 imposes full observation of Host State rules regarding incompatible occupations on the lawyer acting in national legal proceedings or before national public authorities in the Host State. This applies whether the lawyer is established in the Host State or not.

Article 2.5.3, on the other hand, imposes "respect" for the rules of the Host State regarding forbidden or incompatible occupations in other cases, but only where the lawyer who is established in the Host Member State wishes to participate directly in commercial or other activities not connected with the practice of the law.

Commentary on Article 2.6 – Personal Publicity

The term "personal publicity" covers publicity by firms of lawyers, as well as individual lawyers, as opposed to corporate publicity organised by Bars and Law Societies for their members as a whole. The rules governing personal publicity by lawyers vary considerably in the Member States. Article 2.6 makes it clear that there is no overriding objection to personal publicity in cross-border practice. However, lawyers are nevertheless subject to prohibitions or restrictions laid down by their home professional rules, and a lawyer will still be subject to prohibitions or restrictions laid down by Host State rules when these are binding on the lawyer by virtue of the Lawyers Services Directive or the Lawyers Establishment Directive.

Commentary on Article 2.7 – The Client's Interest

This provision emphasises the general principle that the lawyer must always place the client's interests before the lawyer's own interests or those of fellow members of the legal profession.

Commentary on Article 2.8 – Limitation of Lawyer's Liability towards the Client

This provision makes clear that there is no overriding objection to limiting a lawyer's liability towards his or her client in cross-border practice, whether by contract or by use of a limited company, limited partnership or limited liability partnership. However it points out that this can only be contemplated where the relevant law and the relevant rules of conduct permit – and in a number of jurisdictions the law or the professional rules prohibit or restrict such limitation of liability.

Commentary on Article 3.1 – Acceptance and Termination of Instructions

The provisions of Article 3.1.1 are designed to ensure that a relationship is maintained between lawyer and client and that the lawyer in fact receives instructions from the client, even though these may be transmitted through a duly authorised intermediary. It is the responsibility of the lawyer to satisfy him- or herself as to the authority of the intermediary and the wishes of the client.

Article 3.1.2 deals with the manner in which the lawyer should carry out his or her duties. The provision that the lawyer shall undertake personal responsibility for the discharge of the instructions given to him or her means that the lawyer cannot avoid responsibility by delegation to others. It does not prevent the lawyer from seeking to limit his or her legal liability to the extent that this is permitted by the relevant law or professional rules – see Article 2.8.

Article 3.1.3 states a principle which is of particular relevance in cross-border activities, for example when a lawyer is asked to handle a matter on behalf of a lawyer or client from another state who may be unfamiliar with the relevant law and practice, or when a lawyer is asked to handle a matter relating to the law of another state with which he or she is unfamiliar.

A lawyer generally has the right to refuse to accept instructions in the first place, but Article 3.1.4 states that, having once accepted them, the lawyer has an obligation not to withdraw without ensuring that the client's interests are safeguarded.

Commentary on Article 3.2 – Conflict of Interest

The provisions of Article 3.2.1 do not prevent a lawyer acting for two or more clients in the same matter provided that their interests are not in fact in conflict and that there is no significant risk of such a conflict arising. Where a lawyer is already acting for two or more clients in this way and subsequently there arises a conflict of interests between those clients or a risk of a breach of confidence or other circumstances where the lawyer's independence may be impaired, then the lawyer must cease to act for both or all of them.

There may, however, be circumstances in which differences arise between two or more clients for whom the same lawyer is acting where it may be appropriate for the lawyer to attempt to act as a mediator. It is for the lawyer in such cases to use his or her own judgement on whether or not there is such a conflict of interest between them as to require the lawyer to cease to act. If not, the lawyer may consider whether it would be appropriate to explain the position to the clients, obtain their agreement and attempt to act as mediator to resolve the difference between them, and only if this attempt to mediate should fail, to cease to act for them.

Article 3.2.4 applies the foregoing provisions of Article 3 to lawyers practising in association. For example a firm of lawyers should cease to act when there is a conflict of interest between two clients of the firm, even if different lawyers in the firm are acting for each client. On the other hand, exceptionally, in the "chambers" form of association used by English barristers, where each lawyer acts for clients individually, it is possible for different lawyers in the association to act for clients with opposing interests.

Commentary on Article 3.3 – Pactum de Quota Litis

These provisions reflect the common position in all Member States that an unregulated agreement for contingency fees (*pactum de quota litis*) is contrary to the proper administration of justice because it encourages speculative litigation and is liable to be abused. The provisions are not, however, intended to prevent the maintenance or introduction of arrangements under which lawyers are paid according to results or only if the action or matter is successful, provided that these arrangements are under sufficient regulation and control for the protection of the client and the proper administration of justice.

Commentary on Article 3.4 – Regulation of Fees

Article 3.4 lays down three requirements: a general standard of disclosure of a lawyer's fees to the client, a requirement that they should be fair and reasonable in amount, and a requirement to comply with the applicable law and professional rules.

In many Member States machinery exists for regulating lawyers' fees under national law or rules of conduct, whether by reference to a power of adjudication by the Bar authorities or otherwise. In situations governed by the Lawyers Establishment Directive, where the lawyer is subject to Host State rules as well as the rules of the Home State, the basis of charging may have to comply with both sets of rules.

Commentary on Article 3.5 – Payment on Account

Article 3.5 assumes that a lawyer may require a payment on account of the lawyer's fees and/or disbursements, but sets a limit by reference to a reasonable estimate of them. See also on Article 3.1.4 regarding the right to withdraw.

Commentary on Article 3.6 – Fee Sharing with Non-Lawyers

In some Member States lawyers are permitted to practise in association with members of certain other approved professions, whether legal professions or not. The provisions of Article 3.6.1 are not designed to prevent fee sharing within such an approved form of association. Nor are the provisions designed to prevent fee sharing by the lawyers to whom the Code applies (see on Article 1.4 above) with other "lawyers", for example lawyers from non-Member States or members of other legal professions in the Member States such as notaries.

Commentary on Article 3.7 – Cost of Litigation and Availability of Legal Aid

Article 3.7.1 stresses the importance of attempting to resolve disputes in a way which is cost-effective for the client, including advising on whether to attempt to negotiate a settlement, and whether to propose referring the dispute to some form of alternative dispute resolution.

Article 3.7.2 requires a lawyer to inform the client of the availability of legal aid where applicable. There are widely differing provisions in the Member States on the availability of legal aid. In cross-border activities a lawyer should have in mind the possibility that the legal aid provisions of a national law with which the lawyer is unfamiliar may be applicable.

Commentary on Article 3.8 – Client Funds

The provisions of Article 3.8 reflect the recommendation adopted by the CCBE in Brussels in November 1985 on the need for minimum regulations to be made and enforced governing the proper control and disposal of clients' funds held by lawyers within the Community. Article 3.8 lays down minimum standards to be observed, while not interfering with the details of national systems which provide fuller or more stringent protection for clients' funds.

The lawyer who holds clients' funds, even in the course of a cross-border activity, has to observe the rules of his or her home Bar. The lawyer needs to be aware of questions which arise where the rules of more than one Member State may be applicable, especially where the lawyer is established in a Host State under the Lawyers Establishment Directive.

Commentary on Article 3.9 – Professional Indemnity Insurance

Article 3.9.1 reflects a recommendation, also adopted by the CCBE in Brussels in November 1985, on the need for all lawyers in the Community to be insured against the risks arising from professional negligence claims against them.

Article 3.9.2 deals with the situation where insurance cannot be obtained on the basis set out in Article 3.9.1.

Commentary on Article 4.1 – Rules of Conduct in Court

This provision applies the principle that a lawyer is bound to comply with the rules of the court or tribunal before which the lawyer practises or appears.

Commentary on Article 4.2 – Fair Conduct of Proceedings

This provision applies the general principle that in adversarial proceedings a lawyer must not attempt to take unfair advantage of his or her opponent. The lawyer must not, for example, make contact with the judge without first informing the lawyer acting for the opposing party or submit exhibits, notes or documents to the judge without communicating them in good time to the lawyer on the other side unless such steps are permitted under the relevant rules of procedure. To the extent not prohibited by law a lawyer must not divulge or submit to the court any proposals for settlement of the case made by the other party or its lawyer without the express consent of the other party's lawyer. See also on Article 4.5 below.

Commentary on Article 4.3 – Demeanour in Court

This provision reflects the necessary balance between respect for the court and for the law on the one hand and the pursuit of the client's best interest on the other.

Commentary on Article 4.4 – False or Misleading Information

This provision applies the principle that the lawyer must never knowingly mislead the court. This is necessary if there is to be trust between the courts and the legal profession.

Commentary on Article 4.5 – Extension to Arbitrators etc.

This provision extends the preceding provisions relating to courts to other bodies exercising judicial or quasi-judicial functions.

Commentary on Article 5.1 – Corporate Spirit of the Profession

These provisions, which are based on statements in the Declaration of Perugia, emphasise that it is in the public interest for the legal profession to maintain a relationship of trust and cooperation between its members. However, this cannot be used to justify setting the interests of the profession against those of justice or of clients (see also on Article 2.7).

Commentary on Article 5.2 – Co-operation among Lawyers of Different Member States

This provision also develops a principle stated in the Declaration of Perugia with a view to avoiding misunderstandings in dealings between lawyers of different Member States.

Commentary on Article 5.3 – Correspondence between Lawyers

In certain Member States communications between lawyers (written or by word of mouth) are normally regarded as to be kept confidential as between the lawyers. This means that the content of these communications cannot be disclosed to others, cannot normally be passed to the lawyers' clients, and at any event cannot be produced in court. In other Member States, such consequences will not follow unless the correspondence is marked as "confidential".

In yet other Member States, the lawyer has to keep the client fully informed of all relevant communications from a professional colleague acting for another party, and marking a letter as "confidential" only means that it is a legal matter intended for the recipient lawyer and his or her client, and not to be misused by third parties.

In some states, if a lawyer wishes to indicate that a letter is sent in an attempt to settle a dispute, and is not to be produced in a court, the lawyer should mark the letter as "without prejudice".

These important national differences give rise to many misunderstandings. That is why lawyers must be very careful in conducting cross-border correspondence.

Whenever a lawyer wants to send a letter to a professional colleague in another Member State on the basis that it is to be kept confidential as between the lawyers, or that it is "without prejudice", the lawyer should ask in advance whether the letter can be accepted on that basis. A lawyer wishing that a communication should be accepted on such a basis must express that clearly in the communication or in a covering letter.

A lawyer who is the intended recipient of such a communication, but who is not in a position to respect, or to ensure respect for, the basis on which it is to be sent, must inform the sender immediately so that the communication is not sent. If the communication has already been received, the recipient must return it to the sender without revealing its contents or referring to it in any way; if the recipient's national law or rules prevent the recipient from complying with this requirement, he or she must inform the sender immediately.

Commentary on Article 5.4 – Referral Fees

This provision reflects the principle that a lawyer should not pay or receive payment purely for the reference of a client, which would risk impairing the client's free choice of lawyer or the client's interest in being referred to the best available service. It does not prevent fee-sharing arrangements between lawyers on a proper basis (see also on Article 3.6 above).

In some Member States lawyers are permitted to accept and retain commissions in certain cases provided: a) the client's best interests are served, b) there is full disclosure to the client and c) the client has consented to the retention of the commission. In such cases the retention of the commission by the lawyer represents part of the lawyer's remuneration for the service provided to the client and is not within the scope of the prohibition on referral fees which is designed to prevent lawyers making a secret profit.

Commentary on Article 5.5 – Communication with Opposing Parties

This provision reflects a generally accepted principle, and is designed both to promote the smooth conduct of business between lawyers and to prevent any attempt to take advantage of the client of another lawyer.

Commentary on Article 5.6 – Change of Lawyer

Article 5.6 dealt with change of lawyer. It was deleted from the Code on 6 December 2002.

Commentary on Article 5.7 – Responsibility for Fees

These provisions substantially reaffirm provisions contained in the Declaration of Perugia. Since misunderstandings about responsibility for unpaid fees are a common cause of difference between lawyers of different Member States, it is important that a lawyer who wishes to exclude or limit his or her personal obligation to be responsible for the fees of a foreign colleague should reach a clear agreement on this at the outset of the transaction.

Commentary on Article 5.8 – Continuing Professional Development

Keeping abreast of developments in the law is a professional obligation. In particular it is essential that lawyers are aware of the growing impact of European law on their field of practice.

Commentary on Article 5.9 – Disputes amongst Lawyers in Different Member States

A lawyer has the right to pursue any legal or other remedy to which he or she is entitled against a colleague in another Member State. Nevertheless it is desirable that, where a breach of a rule of professional conduct or a dispute of a professional nature is involved, the possibilities of friendly settlement should be exhausted, if necessary with the assistance of the Bars or Law Societies concerned, before such remedies are exercised.

The European Communities (Services of Lawyers) Order 1978

[With consolidated amendments to 25 July 2013.]

European Communities (Services of Lawyers) Order 1978

SI 1978/1910

Made 20th December 1978

Authority: European Communities Act 1972, s 2(2)

Citation and commencement

1

This Order may be cited as the European Communities (Services of Lawyers) Order 1978 and shall come into operation on 1st March 1979.

Interpretation

2

In this Order, unless the context otherwise requires—

"advocate", "barrister" and "solicitor" mean, in relation to any part of the United Kingdom, a person practising in that part as an advocate, barrister or solicitor as the case may be;

"country of origin", in relation to a European lawyer, means the country or countries in which he is established;

"the Directive" means the European Communities Council Directive No. 77/249/EEC to facilitate the effective exercise by lawyers of freedom to provide services;

"European lawyer" means a person entitled to pursue his professional activities in a state in column 1 under the designation referred to in column 2—

State	Designation(s)
Austria	Rechtsanwalt
Belgium	Avocat/Advocaat
Bulgaria	Адвокат [advokat]
Croatia	Odvjetnik/Odvjetnica
Cyprus	Δικηγόρος [dikhgoros]
Czech Republic	Advokát
Denmark	Advokat

State	Designation(s)
Estonia	Vandeadvokaat
Finland	Asianajaja/Advokat
France	Avocat
Germany	Rechtsanwalt
Hellenic Republic	Δικηγόρος [dikhgoros]
Hungary	Ügyvéd
Iceland	Lögmaður
Republic of Ireland	Barrister/solicitor
Italy	Avvocato
Latvia	Zverinâts advokâts
Liechtenstein	Rechtsanwalt
Lithuania	Advokatas
Luxembourg	Avocat-avoué
Malta	Avukat/Prokuratur Legali
Netherlands	Advocaat
Norway	Advokat
Poland	Adwokat/Radca prawny
Portugal	Advogado
Romania	Avocat
Slovakia	Advokát/Komercný právnik
Slovenia	Odvetnik/Odvetnica
Spain	Abogado/Advocat/Avogado/Abokatu
Sweden	Advokat
Switzerland	Avocat/Advokat/Rechtsanwalt/Anwalt/Fürsprecher/ Fürsprech/Avvocato

"own professional authority", in relation to a European lawyer, means an authority entitled to exercise disciplinary authority over him in his member State of origin.

3

(1)   The Interpretation Act 1978 shall apply to this Order as it applies to subordinate legislation made after the commencement of that Act.

(2)   Unless the context otherwise requires, any reference in this Order to a numbered article or to the Schedule is a reference to an article of, or the Schedule to, this Order.

Purpose of Order

4

The provisions of this Order shall have effect for the purpose of enabling a European lawyer to pursue his professional activities in any part of the United Kingdom by providing, under the conditions specified in or permitted by the Directive, services otherwise reserved to advocates, barristers and solicitors; and services which may be so provided are hereafter in this Order referred to as services.

Representation in legal proceedings

5

No enactment or rule of law or practice shall prevent a European lawyer from providing any service in relation to any proceedings, whether civil or criminal, before any court, tribunal or public authority (including appearing before and addressing the court, tribunal or public authority) by reason only that he is not an advocate, barrister or solicitor; provided that throughout he is instructed with, and acts in conjunction with, an advocate, barrister or solicitor who is entitled to practise before the court, tribunal or public authority concerned and who could properly provide the service in question.

6

Nothing in this Order shall enable a European lawyer:—

(a)   if he is established in practice as a barrister in the Republic of Ireland, to provide in the course of any proceedings any service which could not properly be provided by an advocate or barrister;

(b)   if he is instructed with and acts in conjunction with an advocate or barrister in any proceedings, to provide in the course of those proceedings, or of any related proceedings, any service which an advocate or barrister could not properly provide;

(c)   if he is instructed with and acts in conjunction with a solicitor in any proceedings, to provide in the course of those proceedings, or of any related proceedings, any service which a solicitor could not properly provide.

7

A European lawyer in salaried employment who is instructed with and acts in conjunction with an advocate or barrister in any proceedings may provide a service on behalf of his employer in those proceedings only in so far as an advocate or barrister in such employment could properly do so.

Drawing of documents, etc not related to legal proceedings

8

No enactment or rule of law or practice shall prevent a European lawyer from drawing or preparing for remuneration:—

(i)   in England, Wales or Northern Ireland, an instrument relating to personal estate, or

(ii)   in Scotland, a writ relating to moveable property,

by reason only that he is not an advocate, barrister or solicitor.

9

Nothing in this Order shall entitle a European lawyer to draw or prepare for remuneration any instrument, or in Scotland any writ:—

(i)   creating or transferring an interest in land; or

(ii)   for obtaining title to administer the estate of a deceased person.

Legal aid

10

Services may be provided by a European lawyer by way of legal advice and assistance or legal aid under the enactments specified in Part 1 of the Schedule; and references to counsel and solicitors in those and any other enactments relating to legal advice and assistance or legal aid shall be construed accordingly.

Title and description to be used by European lawyers

11

In providing any services, a European lawyer shall use the professional title and description applicable to him in his country of origin, expressed in the language or one of the languages of that country, together with the name of the professional organisation by which he is authorised to practise or the court of law before which he is entitled to practise in that country.

Power to require a European lawyer to verify his status

12

A competent authority may at any time request a person seeking to provide any services to verify his status as a European lawyer.

13

Where a request has been made under article 12, the person to whom it is made shall not, except to the extent (if any) allowed by the competent authority making the request, be entitled to provide services in the United Kingdom until he has verified his status as a European lawyer to the satisfaction of that authority.

14

For the purposes of articles 12 and 13, a competent authority is:—

    (a)   where the services which the person concerned seeks to provide are reserved to advocates or barristers, or in any case where the person concerned claims to be a barrister established in practice in the Republic of Ireland, the Senate of the Inns of Court and the Bar, the Faculty of Advocates, or the Benchers of the Inn of Court of Northern Ireland, according to the part of the United Kingdom concerned; or

    (b)   where sub-paragraph (a) does not apply, the Law Society, the Law Society of Scotland, or the Incorporated Law Society of Northern Ireland, according to the part of the United Kingdom concerned; or

    (c)   in any case, any court, tribunal or public authority before which the person concerned seeks to provide services.

Professional misconduct

15

(1)   A complaint may be made to a disciplinary authority that a European lawyer providing any services has failed to observe a condition or rule of professional conduct referred to in article 4 of the Directive and applicable to him.

(2)   Where a complaint is made under paragraph (1), the disciplinary authority concerned shall consider and adjudicate upon it in accordance with the same procedure, and subject to the same rights of appeal, as apply in relation to an advocate, barrister or solicitor (as the case may be) over whom that authority has jurisdiction.

(3)   For the purposes of this article and article 16, a disciplinary authority is:—

    (a)   where the services in question are reserved to advocates or barristers, or in any case where the person whose conduct is in question is established in practice as a barrister in the Republic of Ireland, an authority having disciplinary jurisdiction over advocates or barristers (as the case may be) in the part of the United Kingdom concerned;

(b)   where sub-paragraph (a) does not apply, an authority having disciplinary jurisdiction over solicitors in the part of the United Kingdom concerned.

16

(1)   Where a disciplinary authority finds that a European lawyer against whom a complaint has been made under article 15(1) has committed a breach of a condition or a rule of professional conduct mentioned in that article, that authority:—

(a)   shall report that finding to the European lawyer's own professional authority; and

(b)   may, if it thinks fit, direct him not to provide services in the United Kingdom, except to such extent and under such conditions (if any) as the disciplinary authority may specify in the direction.

(2)   A disciplinary authority may at any time, if it thinks fit, vary, cancel or suspend the operation of a direction given by it under paragraph (1)(b).

17

A European lawyer in respect of whom a direction is made under article 16(1)(b) shall not be entitled to provide services in the United Kingdom except as allowed by the direction.

Modification of enactments

18

(1)   Without prejudice to the generality of articles 5 and 8, the enactments specified in Part 2 of the Schedule (being enactments which reserve the provision of certain services to advocates, barristers, solicitors and other qualified persons) shall be construed subject to those articles.

(2)   Notwithstanding anything in the Solicitors (Scotland) Act 1980, the Solicitors Act 1974 or the Solicitors (Northern Ireland) Order 1976, references to unqualified persons, however expressed, in the enactments specified in Part 3 of the Schedule (being enactments relating to unqualified persons acting as solicitors) shall not include a European lawyer providing services within the meaning of this Order.

(3)   Nothing in section 33 of the Solicitors (Scotland) Act 1980 shall prevent a European lawyer from recovering any remuneration or expenses to which that section applies by reason only that he is not qualified as a solicitor.

SCHEDULE

Article 10

PART 1
ENACTMENTS RELATING TO THE PROVISION OF LEGAL ADVICE AND ASSISTANCE AND LEGAL AID

Legal Aid and Advice Act (Northern Ireland) 1965 (c. 8).

Legal Aid (Scotland) Act 1986 (c 47).

Legal Advice and Assistance Act 1972 (c. 50).

Legal Aid, Advice and Assistance (Northern Ireland) Order 1981 (SI No 228 (NI 8)).

Access to Justice Act 1999 (c 22).

Financial Services and Markets Act 2000 (c 8).

Legal Aid, Sentencing and Punishment of Offenders Act 2012 (c 10).

PART 2
ENACTMENTS RESERVING THE PROVISION OF SERVICES TO
ADVOCATES, BARRISTERS, SOLICITORS, ETC

Article 18(1)

Solicitors (Scotland) Act 1980 (c 46), section 32.

Magistrates' Courts (Northern Ireland) Order 1981, article 164(1).

County Courts (Northern Ireland) Order 1980, article 50.

Solicitors Act 1974 (c. 47), sections 20, 22 [and 23].

Solicitors (Northern Ireland) Order 1976 (SI No. 582 (NI 12)), articles 19, 23.

PART 3
ENACTMENTS RELATING TO UNQUALIFIED PERSONS ACTING
AS SOLICITORS

Article 18(2)

Solicitors (Scotland) Act 1980 (c 46), section 26.

Solicitors Act 1974 (c. 47), section 25(1).

Solicitors (Northern Ireland) Order 1976 (SI No. 582 (NI 12)), articles 25(1), 27.

The European Communities (Lawyer's Practice) Regulations 2000

[With consolidated amendments to 18 January 2016.]

European Communities (Lawyer's Practice) Regulations 2000

SI 2000/1119

Made 8th April 2000

Laid 19th April 2000

Coming into force in accordance with regulation 1

The Lord Chancellor, being a Minister designated for the purposes of section 2(2) of the European Communities Act 1972 in relation to matters relating to the practice of the profession of lawyer, in exercise of the powers conferred on him by that section, makes the following Regulations—

PART 1
INTRODUCTORY

1 Citation, commencement and transitional provisions

(1) These Regulations may be cited as the European Communities (Lawyer's Practice) Regulations 2000 and shall come into force on 22nd May 2000★, except for regulations 21 and 22, which shall come into force on 22nd November 2000★.

(2) Where, on 22nd May 2000, a European lawyer is practising professional activities under his home professional title on a permanent basis in England and Wales or Northern Ireland or commences such practice by 21st November 2000, he shall apply to be registered in accordance with regulation 16 by 21st November 2000 where he intends to continue to practise those activities on a permanent basis after that date.

(3) On or after 22nd November 2000, a European lawyer shall not practise as referred to in paragraph (2) without being registered in accordance with regulation 16, unless he was already practising before that date and has made an application for registration which has not been determined.

(4) In paragraphs (3) and (5), an application for registration shall, as at a particular date, be taken not to have been determined if as at that date the applicant—

(a) has not received a rejection of his application and the period for such a rejection or a deemed rejection has not yet expired; or

(b) is appealing against a rejection of the application (including a deemed rejection) and the appeal has not been determined.

(5) Regulations 21(1)(b) and 22 shall not apply to a European lawyer who satisfies all the following conditions—

(a)   immediately before 22nd November 2000 he was practising on a permanent basis in any part of the United Kingdom;

(b)   before 22nd November 2000 he applied for registration to any of the barristers' professional bodies or solicitors' professional bodies, or to the Faculty of Advocates or the Law Society of Scotland; and

(c)   as at the date in question his application for registration had not been determined.

[NOTES

*Modification

As from 16 September 2004 the Regulations were extended by SI 2004/1628 to cover Cyprus, the Czech Republic, Estonia, Hungary, Iceland, Latvia, Liechtenstein, Lithuania, Malta, Norway, Poland, Slovenia, Slovakia or Switzerland.

As from 11 February 2008 the Regulations were extended by SI 2008/81 to cover Bulgaria or Romania.

As from 25 July 2014 the Regulations were extended by SI 2013/1605 to cover Croatia.

2 Interpretation

(1) In these Regulations, unless the context otherwise requires—

"the 1974 Act" means the Solicitors Act 1974;

"appeal body" means the body or person specified in relation to that profession in Schedule 1;

"barrister" means, in relation to England and Wales or Northern Ireland, a person who is a barrister of England and Wales or Northern Ireland, as the case may be;

"barristers' professional bodies" means the Inns of Court and the General Council of the Bar of England and Wales and the Executive Council of the Inn of Court of Northern Ireland;

"competent authority", in relation to England and Wales and Northern Ireland, means any of the bodies designated as competent authorities by regulation 4 to undertake the activities required by the Directive set out in that regulation;

"the Directive" means the European Communities Parliament and Council Directive No 98/5/EC to facilitate practice of the profession of lawyer on a permanent basis in certain States other than the State in which the professional qualification was obtained;

"European lawyer" has the meaning given in paragraphs (2) and (3);

"home State" means the State in paragraph (4) in which a European lawyer acquired his authorisation to pursue professional activities and, if he is authorised in more than one of those States, it shall mean any of those States;

"home professional title" means, in relation to a European lawyer, the professional title or any of the professional titles specified in relation to his home State in paragraph (4) under which he is authorised in his home State to pursue professional activities;

"Irish barrister" means a European lawyer who is authorised in the Republic of Ireland to pursue professional activities under the professional title of barrister and whose home State is the Republic of Ireland;

"Irish solicitor" means a European lawyer who is authorised in the Republic of Ireland to pursue professional activities under the professional title of solicitor and whose home State is the Republic of Ireland;

"limited liability partnership" has the meaning given by section 1(2) of the Limited Liability Partnerships Act 2000;

"member of a limited liability partnership" shall be construed in accordance with section 4 of the Limited Liability Partnerships Act 2000;

"member of the professional body" means a practising solicitor or barrister, as the case may be;

"Qualification Regulations" means the European Union (Recognition of Professional Qualifications) Regulations 2015;

"registered European lawyer" means a European lawyer who is registered with a professional body in accordance with regulation 17 and whose registration has not been withdrawn or suspended;

"professional body" means, subject to regulation 16, any of the solicitors' professional bodies or the barristers' professional bodies;

"sole practitioner" means a registered European lawyer who is the sole principal in a practice (other than an incorporated practice);

"solicitor" means, in relation to England and Wales or Northern Ireland, a person who is a solicitor of England and Wales or Northern Ireland, as the case may be;

"solicitors' professional bodies" means the Law Society and the Law Society of Northern Ireland.

(2)   In these Regulations, "European lawyer" means a person who is—

(a)   a national of the United Kingdom or of a State listed in paragraph (4);

(b)   authorised in any of the States listed in paragraph (4) to pursue professional activities under any of the professional titles appearing in that paragraph; and

(c)   subject to paragraph (3), not a solicitor or barrister or, under the law of Scotland, a solicitor or advocate.

(3)   Where a person is a European lawyer registered with more than one of the following—

(a)   the solicitors' professional bodies or the barristers' professional bodies, or

(b)   the Law Society of Scotland or the Faculty of Advocates,

and subsequently acquires the title used by members of one of those bodies, then notwithstanding paragraph (2)(c), that person shall continue to fall within the definition of a European lawyer in relation to that other professional body for the period that he remains registered with that other professional body.

(4)   The States and professional titles referred to in the definition of European lawyer in paragraph (2) are as follows—

State	Professional title(s)
Belgium	Avocat/Advocaat/Rechtsanwalt
Denmark	Advokat
Germany	Rechtsanwalt
Greece	Δικηγόρος [dikegóros]
Spain	Abogado/Advocat/Avogado/Abokatu
France	Avocat
Republic of Ireland	Barrister/Solicitor

State	Professional title(s)
Italy	Avvocato
Luxembourg	Avocat
Netherlands	Advocaat
Austria	Rechtsanwalt
Portugal	Advogado
Finland	Asianajaja/Advokat
Sweden	Advokat
Switzerland	Avocat/Advokat/Rechtsanwalt/Anwalt/Fürsprecher/Fürsp
Iceland	Lögmaður
Liechtenstein	Rechtsanwalt
Norway	Advokat
Czech Republic	Advokát
Estonia	Vandeadvokaat
Cyprus	Δικηγόρος [dikhgóros]
Latvia	Zverinâts advokâts
Lithuania	Advokatas
Hungary	Ügyvéd
Malta	Avukat/Prokuratur Legali
Poland	Adwokat/Radca prawny
Slovenia	Odvetnik/Odvetnica
Slovakia	Advokát/Komercný právnik
Bulgaria	Адвокат [advokat]
Romania	Avocat
Croatia	Odvjetnik/Odvjetnica

(5) Unless the context otherwise requires, any reference in these Regulations to a numbered regulation, Part or Schedule is a reference to a regulation or Part of, or a Schedule to, these Regulations.

3 Purpose of Regulations

(1) The purpose of these Regulations is to implement the Directive in England and Wales and Northern Ireland.

(2) The provisions of these Regulations shall have effect for the purposes of facilitating the practice of the profession of lawyer on a permanent basis by a European lawyer in England and Wales and Northern Ireland.

(3) The provisions of these Regulations shall not affect the provision of services by lawyers within the meaning of the European Communities (Services of Lawyers) Order 1978.

4 Competent authorities

The bodies listed in column 2 of Schedule 2 shall be designated as the competent authorities for the purposes of—

(a) receiving applications for registration by European lawyers under Part III of these Regulations;

(b) receiving applications from registered European lawyers for entry into the profession of solicitor or barrister;

(c)   the regulation of registered European lawyers registered with them; and

(d)   the provision of certificates attesting to the registration of Solicitors or barristers registered with them.

5   Exchange of information

(1)   In order to facilitate the application of the Directive and to prevent its provisions from being misapplied, a professional body may supply to or receive from—

(a)   another professional body;

(b)   the Faculty of Advocates or the Law Society of Scotland; or

(c)   an authority in any of the States listed in regulation 2(4) which has been designated by that State under the Directive as a competent authority in that State,

any information relating to a European lawyer or to any person with whom he jointly practises.

(2)   Subject to paragraph (1), a professional body shall preserve the confidentiality of any information received in accordance with paragraph (1) relating to a European lawyer or to any person with whom he jointly practises.

(3)   A competent authority in England and Wales or Northern Ireland shall provide a certificate attesting to the registration of a solicitor or barrister registered with it and his authorisation to practise when requested to do so by that solicitor or barrister or by a competent authority in a State listed in regulation 2(4).

PART II
PRACTICE OF PROFESSIONAL ACTIVITIES BY A REGISTERED EUROPEAN LAWYER

6   Practice of professional activities

(1)   Subject to the provisions of these Regulations, a registered European lawyer shall be entitled to carry out under his home professional title any professional activity that may lawfully be carried out by a member of the professional body with which he is registered and any enactment or rule of law or practice with regard to the carrying out of professional activities by members of that professional body shall be interpreted and applied accordingly.

(2)   A registered European lawyer who is in salaried employment may carry out professional activities under his home professional title to the same extent that an employed member of the professional body with which he is registered may do so.

7   Title and description to be used by a registered European lawyer

(1)   Where a registered European lawyer is engaged in—

(a)   any professional activity authorised by the professional organisation in his home State which gave him the authorisation to practise; or

(b)   any professional activity that may be carried out by a member of the professional body with which he is registered,

he shall comply with the requirements set out in paragraph (2).

(2)   The requirements referred to in paragraph (1) are that a registered European lawyer shall—

(a)   use his home professional title expressed in an official language of his home State in a manner which avoids confusion with the title of solicitor, barrister or advocate;

(b)   indicate the professional organisation by which he is authorised to practise or the court of law before which he is entitled to practise in that State; and

(c)   indicate the professional body with which he is registered in the United Kingdom.

8 Joint practice

A registered European lawyer may carry out professional activities under his home professional title as part of a joint practice—

(a)   to the same extent and in the same manner as a member of the professional body with which he is registered may do so, with—

    (i)   a member of the professional body with which he is registered;

    (ii)   a registered European lawyer who is registered with the same professional body; or

    (iii)   any other person permitted by the professional body with which he is registered; or

(b)   with another European lawyer who is practising on a permanent basis under his home professional title in that registered European lawyer's home State.

9 Name of joint practice

(1) Subject to paragraph (2), where a registered European lawyer is a member of a joint practice in his home State, he may use the name of that practice with his home professional title when practising as a registered European lawyer.

(2) Rules of conduct of the professional body with which a registered European lawyer is registered may prohibit the use by him of the name of a joint practice to the extent that—

(a)   that name is also used by persons who are not European lawyers or solicitors of any part of the United Kingdom; and

(b)   those rules prohibit members of that professional body from using that name.

10 Notification of joint practice

(1) Where a European lawyer is a member of a joint practice in his home State, he shall inform the professional body with which he intends to register and provide it with the following information—

(a)   the name of the joint practice;

(b)   his place of business;

(c)   the name and place of business of any member of his joint practice;

(d)   any other information about the joint practice requested by the professional body.

(2) A European lawyer shall notify that professional body of any changes in the information whether before or after registration.

11 Representation in legal proceedings

(1) Subject to paragraph (2), no enactment or rule of law or practice shall prevent a registered European lawyer from pursuing professional activities relating to the representation of a client in any proceedings before any court, tribunal or public authority (including addressing the court, tribunal or public authority) only because he is not a solicitor or barrister.

(2) In proceedings referred to in paragraph (1), where the professional activities in question may (but for these Regulations) be lawfully provided only by a solicitor, barrister or other qualified person, a registered European lawyer shall act in conjunction with a solicitor or barrister who is entitled to practise before the court, tribunal or public authority concerned and who could lawfully provide those professional activities.

(3) The solicitor or barrister referred to in paragraph (2) shall, where necessary, be answerable to the court, tribunal or public authority concerned.

(4) Paragraph (2) does not apply to professional activities relating to the representation of a client in proceedings before the Asylum and Immigration Tribunal or the Asylum Support Tribunal, or any tribunal hearing an appeal from those tribunals.

12 Property transactions

A registered European lawyer is not entitled, by virtue of regulation 6(1), to prepare for remuneration any instrument creating or transferring an interest in land unless he has a home professional title obtained in Denmark, the Republic of Ireland, Finland, Sweden, Iceland, Liechtenstein, Norway, the Czech Republic, Cyprus, Hungary or Slovakia.

13 Probate

A registered European lawyer is not entitled, by virtue of regulation 6(1), to prepare for remuneration any instrument for obtaining title to administer the estate of a deceased person unless he has a home professional title obtained in Denmark, Germany, the Republic of Ireland, Austria, Finland, Sweden, Iceland, Liechtenstein, Norway, Cyprus or Slovakia.

14 Legal aid

A registered European lawyer may provide professional activities by way of legal advice and assistance or legal aid under the enactments specified in Part 1 of Schedule 3 and references to a solicitor, counsel or legal representative in those and any other enactments relating to legal advice and assistance or legal aid shall be interpreted accordingly.

PART III
REGISTRATION

15 Establishment and maintenance of registers of European lawyers

Each professional body shall establish and maintain a register of registered European lawyers.

16 Application to be entered on a register

(1) Subject to regulation 18, a European lawyer who wishes to pursue professional activities under his home professional title on a permanent basis in England and Wales or Northern Ireland shall apply to be entered on the register maintained by a professional body.

(2) A European lawyer who wishes to register with a professional body in accordance with paragraph (1) shall provide the professional body with a certificate confirming his registration with the competent authority in each home State under whose home professional title he intends to practise.

(3) A professional body may require that the certificate referred to in paragraph (2) shall not have been issued more than three months before the date of the application under this regulation.

(4) An application for registration under this regulation shall comply with any applicable regulations made by the relevant professional body and be accompanied by the appropriate fee.

(5) Subject to regulation 18, a European lawyer may apply to be entered on the registers maintained by more than one professional body.

(6) In this regulation, "professional body" includes the Law Society of Scotland and the Faculty of Advocates.

17 Registration by professional body

(1) Subject to regulation 18, a professional body shall enter on its register the name of a European lawyer who applies to it in accordance with regulation 16.

(2)   Where a professional body registers a European lawyer in accordance with paragraph (1), it shall inform the competent authority in the home State of the registration.

18   Restrictions on registration

(1)   A European lawyer shall not be registered at the same time both with one of the solicitors' professional bodies and with one of the barristers' professional bodies.

(2)   An Irish solicitor shall not be entered on a register maintained under regulation 15 by any of the barristers' professional bodies.

(3)   An Irish barrister shall not be entered on a register maintained under regulation 15 by any of the solicitors' professional bodies.

(4)   A European lawyer registered with the Law Society of Scotland shall not be entered on a register maintained under regulation 15 by any of the barristers' professional bodies.

(5)   A European lawyer registered with the Faculty of Advocates shall not be entered on a register maintained under regulation 15 by any of the solicitors' professional bodies.

19   Time limit for decision and notification by professional body

(1)   A professional body shall consider an application for registration under regulation 16 as soon as is reasonably practicable, and shall notify the European lawyer of its decision, and if the application is rejected or granted subject to conditions, the reasons upon which the rejection or the imposition of conditions is based, within four months of receipt of an application complying with regulation 16(2) and (4).

(2)   Where the professional body fails to take a decision and notify the European lawyer within four months in accordance with paragraph (1), it shall be deemed to have taken a decision to reject his application and to have notified it to him on the last day of that period.

(3)   Where a professional body withdraws or suspends a registration, it shall notify the European lawyer of its decision and of the reasons upon which the withdrawal or suspension is based.

20   Appeal by European lawyer

(1)   Within three months of the notification to him of the professional body's decision, or later with the permission of the appeal body, the European lawyer may appeal against the decision to the appeal body specified in Schedule 1.

(2)   An appeal body may, for the purpose of determining any appeal under this Part—

(a)   order the professional body to register the European lawyer;

(b)   refuse the appeal; or

(c)   remit the matter to the professional body with such directions as the appeal body sees fit.

(3)   The appeal body shall give reasons for its decision.

21   Offence of pretending to be a registered European lawyer

(1)   A person who is not registered as a European lawyer in any part of the United Kingdom (including a person whose registration has been suspended) and—

(a)   wilfully pretends to be a registered European lawyer or takes or uses any name, title, designation or description implying that he is a registered European lawyer; or

(b)   subject to paragraph (2), carries on professional activities under one of the professional titles listed in regulation 2(4) or under any name, designation or description implying that he is entitled to pursue those activities under one of those professional titles;

shall be guilty of an offence and liable on summary conviction to a fine not exceeding the fourth level on the standard scale.

(2) Paragraph (1)(b) shall not apply to a person who satisfies any of the following conditions—

(a) he is not a national of the United Kingdom or of any of the States listed in regulation 2(4);

(b) he is a solicitor or barrister or, under the law of Scotland, a solicitor or advocate; or

(c) he is providing services within the meaning of the European Communities (Services of Lawyers) Order 1978 at the time his activities fall within paragraph (1)(b).

22 Costs and fees of an unregistered European lawyer

Where a European lawyer is carrying on professional activities under his home professional title in England and Wales or Northern Ireland but is not registered as a European lawyer in any part of the United Kingdom (including a person whose registration has been suspended), any costs or fees in respect of those activities shall not be recoverable by him or any other person.

23 Evidence of registration

Any certificate purporting to be signed by an officer of a professional body and stating that a person—

(a) is, or is not, registered with that professional body; or

(b) was, or was not, registered with that professional body during a period specified in the certificate,

shall, unless the contrary is proved, be evidence of that fact and be taken to have been so signed.

24 Publication of names of registered European lawyers

(1) Where a professional body publishes the names of solicitors or barristers registered with it, it shall also publish the names of any European lawyers registered with it.

(2) In this regulation, "publishes" or "publish" includes the provision of information to a legal publisher.

PART IV
REGULATION AND DISCIPLINE

25 Rules of professional conduct applicable

Where a registered European lawyer is practising under his home professional title in the United Kingdom, he shall be subject to the same rules of professional conduct as a member of the professional body with which he is registered, and if he is registered with more than one, he shall be subject to the rules of professional conduct of all the professional bodies with which he is registered.

26 Disciplinary proceedings applicable

(1) Where a registered European lawyer fails to comply with the rules of professional conduct to which he is subject under regulation 25, he shall be subject to the same rules of procedure, penalties and remedies as a member of the professional body with which the European lawyer is registered and shall, if appropriate, be subject to disciplinary proceedings brought by an appropriate authority.

(2)   Any sanction against a registered European lawyer in relation to disciplinary proceedings may include withdrawal or suspension of his registration.

(3)   The appropriate authority shall give reasons for its decision.

(4)   In this regulation, an appropriate authority means—

(a)   where the registered European lawyer is registered with one of the solicitors' professional bodies, an authority having disciplinary jurisdiction over solicitors in England and Wales or Northern Ireland, as the case may be;

(b)   where the registered European lawyer is registered with one of the barristers' professional bodies, an authority having disciplinary jurisdiction over barristers in England and Wales or Northern Ireland, as the case may be;

(c)   where the registered European lawyer is registered with more than one of the solicitors' professional bodies or the barristers' professional bodies, an authority having disciplinary jurisdiction over solicitors or barristers, as the case may be, in England and Wales or Northern Ireland.

27   Disciplinary proceedings against a registered European lawyer

(1)   Where a professional body intends to begin disciplinary proceedings against a registered European lawyer, it shall—

(a)   inform the competent authority in his home State of the intention to begin those proceedings and furnish it with all the relevant details;

(b)   co-operate with that authority throughout those proceedings; and

(c)   inform that authority of the decision reached in those proceedings, including the decision in any appeal, as soon as practicable after the decision is given.

(2)   Subject to paragraph (3), where the competent authority in the registered European lawyer's home State withdraws his authorisation to practise under the home professional title either temporarily or permanently, his registration with the professional body shall be automatically withdrawn to the same extent.

(3)   Where a registered European lawyer is authorised to practise under a home professional title in two or more home States, his registration shall be withdrawn in accordance with paragraph (2) only if his authorisation to practise under a home professional title has been withdrawn in all those home States.

(4)   Where there is an appeal against a decision in disciplinary proceedings against a registered European lawyer, the body responsible for hearing the appeal shall afford the competent authority in the registered European lawyer's home State an opportunity to make representations in relation to that appeal.

28   Disciplinary proceedings against a solicitor or barrister

Where a professional body intends to begin disciplinary proceedings against a solicitor or barrister practising in a State listed in regulation 2(4), it shall inform the competent authority in that State of—

(a)   the intention to begin those proceedings and furnish it with all the relevant details; and

(b)   the decision reached in those proceedings, including the decision in any appeal, as soon as practicable after the decision is given.

PART V
ENTRY INTO THE PROFESSION OF SOLICITOR OR BARRISTER

29 Application by registered European lawyer

(1) Where a registered European lawyer applies to the professional body where he has been registered to become a solicitor or barrister, as the case may be, and that professional body requires him to pass an aptitude test under regulation 34(a) of the Qualification Regulations, he may apply to the professional body for an exemption from that requirement on the grounds that he falls within paragraph (2) or (3) of this regulation.

(2) A person falls within this paragraph if—

    (a)   he is a European lawyer and has been registered with that professional body for at least three years; and

    (b)   he has for a period of at least three years effectively and regularly pursued in England and Wales or Northern Ireland, professional activities under his home professional title in the law of England and Wales or Northern Ireland, as the case may be.

(3) A person falls within this paragraph if—

    (a)   he is a European lawyer and has been registered with that professional body for at least three years; and

    (b)   he has for a period of at least three years effectively and regularly pursued in England and Wales or Northern Ireland professional activities under his home professional title; and

    (c)   he has for a period of less than three years effectively and regularly pursued in England and Wales or Northern Ireland, professional activities under his home professional title in the law of England and Wales or Northern Ireland, as the case may be.

30 Decision by professional body

(1) Subject to paragraph (3), the professional body shall grant an exemption applied for under regulation 29 if it considers that the requirements under paragraph (2) or (3) of regulation 29 have been met.

(2) The registration of a registered European lawyer shall cease from the date he is granted entry into the profession of solicitor or barrister.

(3) The professional body may refuse to grant an exemption if it considers that the registered European lawyer would be unfit to practise as a solicitor or barrister.

31 Evidence in support of application for exemption under regulation 29(2)

(1) Where a registered European lawyer makes an application under paragraph (2) of regulation 29, he shall provide the professional body with any relevant information and documents which it may reasonably require.

(2) The professional body may verify the effective and regular nature of the professional activity pursued and may, if necessary, request the registered European lawyer to provide, orally or in writing, clarification of, or further details on, the information and documents referred to in paragraph (1).

32 Evidence in support of application for exemption under regulation 29(3)

(1) Where a registered European lawyer makes an application under paragraph (3) of regulation 29, he shall provide the professional body with any relevant information and documents it may reasonably require.

(2)   When deciding whether to grant an application under paragraph (3) of regulation 29, the professional body shall take into account the professional activities the registered European lawyer has pursued during the period he has been registered and any knowledge and professional experience he has gained of, and any training he has received in, the law of any part of the United Kingdom and the rules of professional conduct of the profession concerned.

(3)   Subject to paragraph (4), in the case of an application under paragraph (3) of regulation 29, the professional body shall assess and verify the registered European lawyer's effective and regular professional activity and his capacity to continue the activity he has pursued at an interview.

(4)   Where a professional body believes that an interview is unnecessary and intends to grant an application under paragraph (3) of regulation 29, it may dispense with that requirement.

33   Meaning of "effectively and regularly pursued"

For the purposes of regulations 29 to 32 activities shall be regarded as effectively and regularly pursued if they are actually exercised without any interruption other than those resulting from the events of everyday life.

34   Time limit for decision and notification by professional body

(1)   A professional body shall consider an application under regulation 29 as soon as is reasonably practicable, and shall notify the applicant of its decision and, if the application is rejected, the reasons for the rejection, within four months of receipt of all the relevant documents.

(2)   Where the professional body fails to take a decision and notify the registered European lawyer within four months in accordance with paragraph (1), it shall be deemed to have taken a decision to reject his application and to have notified it to him on the last day of that period.

35   Appeal by registered European lawyer

(1)   Within three months of the notification to him of the professional body's decision, or later with the permission of the appeal body, the registered European lawyer may appeal against the decision to the appeal body specified in Schedule 1.

(2)   An appeal body may, for the purpose of determining any appeal under this Part—

(a)   give the exemption and the authorisation to enter into the profession of solicitor or barrister, as the case may be;

(b)   refuse the appeal; or

(c)   remit the matter to the professional body with such directions as the appeal body sees fit.

(3)   The appeal body shall give reasons for its decision.

36   Practice under the title of solicitor or barrister

(1)   This regulation applies where a registered European lawyer ("the lawyer") is granted entry into the profession of solicitor or barrister.

(2)   Subject to paragraph (3), the lawyer shall be entitled to continue to practise in England and Wales or Northern Ireland, as the case may be, under his home professional title, and to use his home professional title, expressed in an official language of his home State, alongside the title of solicitor or barrister, provided that he continues to be authorised in his home State to pursue professional activities under that title.

(3)   For the purposes of rules of professional conduct, including those relating to disciplinary and complaints procedures, the lawyer's continuing practice in the United Kingdom under his

home professional title shall be deemed to form part of his practice as a solicitor or barrister, and those rules shall apply to his practice under his home professional title as they do to his practice as a solicitor or barrister.

(4)   Where this regulation applies, a lawyer's registration in accordance with regulation 17 with the professional body whose title he has acquired shall cease from the date he is entitled to use that title.

(5)   Paragraph (4) shall not affect any registration the lawyer may have in another part of the United Kingdom.

PART VI
SUPPLEMENTARY PROVISIONS

37   Modification of enactments

(1)   The enactments specified in Part 2 of Schedule 3 (being enactments which reserve certain activities to solicitors, barristers and other qualified persons) shall be interpreted subject to regulations 6, 11, 12 and 13.

(2)   References to unqualified persons, however expressed, in the enactments specified in Part 3 of Schedule 3 (being enactments relating to unqualified persons acting as solicitors) shall not include a registered European lawyer pursuing professional activities within the meaning of these Regulations.

(3)   Schedule 4 (extension of enactments (England and Wales)) shall apply in relation to the registration of European lawyers with the Law Society.

(4)   Schedule 5 (extension of enactments (Northern Ireland)) shall apply in relation to the registration of European lawyers with the Law Society of Northern Ireland.

Irvine of Lairg, C

Dated 8th April 2000

SCHEDULE 1
Appeals Concerning Registration as a European Lawyer, Exemption from Regulation 34(a) of the Qualification Regulations and Entry into the Profession of Solicitor or Barrister

Regulations 2, 20 and 35

Column 1 **Profession**	Column 2 **Appeal Body**
Solicitor (England and Wales)	The High Court
Solicitor (Northern Ireland)	The Lord Chief Justice of Northern Ireland
Barrister (England and Wales)	The High Court
Barrister (Northern Ireland)	The Executive Council of the Inn of Court of Northern Ireland

SCHEDULE 2
Competent Authorities

Regulation 4

Column 1 **Profession**	*Column 2* **Professional Body**
Solicitor (England and Wales)	The Law Society
Solicitor (Northern Ireland)	The Law Society of Northern Ireland
Barrister (England and Wales)	The Inns of Court and the General Council of the Bar of England and Wales
Barrister (Northern Ireland)	The Executive Council of the Inn of Court of Northern Ireland

SCHEDULE 3
Modification of Enactments

PART 1
ENACTMENTS RELATING TO THE PROVISION OF LEGAL ADVICE AND ASSISTANCE AND LEGAL AID

Regulation 14

Legal Aid, Advice and Assistance (Northern Ireland) Order 1981.

Legal Aid Act 1988.

Access to Justice Act 1999.

Financial Services and Markets Act 2000.

Legal Aid, Sentencing and Punishment of Offenders Act 2012.

PART 2
ENACTMENTS RESERVING CERTAIN ACTIVITIES TO SOLICITORS, BARRISTERS AND OTHER QUALIFIED PERSONS

Regulation 37(1)

Solicitors (Northern Ireland) Order 1976, articles 19, 23 and 24.

PART 3
ENACTMENTS RELATING TO UNQUALIFIED PERSONS ACTING AS SOLICITORS

Regulation 37(2)

Solicitors (Northern Ireland) Order 1976, articles 25(1) and 27.

SCHEDULE 4
Extension of Enactments in Relation to the Registration of European Lawyers with the
Law Society

Regulation 37(3)

1 (1) The power to make regulations under section 2 of the Solicitors Act 1974 shall also
be exercisable in relation to registered European lawyers.

(2) The power to make regulations under section 28(1)(c) to (d) of that Act shall also be
exercisable in relation to registered European lawyers as it is in relation to solicitors, subject to
the modifications specified in the Table and subject to paragraph 7(1A).

(2A) Section 28(3B) to (3G) of the 1974 Act has effect with respect to registered European
lawyers as it has effect with respect to solicitors, subject to the modifications specified in the
Table and subject to paragraph 7(1A).

(3) The power to make rules under—

(a) sections 31, 32, 33A, 34, 36 and 37 of the Solicitors Act 1974; and

(b) section 9 of the Administration of Justice Act 1985,

shall also be exercisable in relation to registered European lawyers.

(4) For the purpose of making rules under section 31 of the Solicitors Act 1974 and
section 9 of the Administration of Justice Act 1985 by virtue of sub-paragraph (3)—

(a) a reference to a sole solicitor is to be read as a reference to a sole practitioner; and

(b) a reference to a recognised sole solicitor's practice is to be read as a reference to a
recognised sole practitioner's practice (that is, to a sole practitioner's practice for the
time being recognised under section 9).

2 Any of the powers referred to in paragraph 1 may be exercised so as to make different
provision with respect to registered European lawyers.

3–6 [*repealed*]

7 (1) Subject to sub-paragraph (1A), the provisions of sections 9, 10, 10A, 11, 13, 13A,
13B, 15, 16, 17, 18 and 84 of the 1974 Act shall apply to registered European lawyers as they
apply to solicitors subject to the modifications specified in the Table.

(1A) An appeal by a European lawyer in respect of the following decisions of the Law
Society is to be made under regulation 20 and not under section 13 or 13B(7) of the 1974 Act
or under regulations made under section 28(3D) of the 1974 Act—

(a) refusal of initial registration;

(b) [*repealed*]

(c) grant of initial registration subject to a condition;

(d) refusal to renew a registration;

(e) failure to take a decision on an application for initial registration within the
statutory time limit;

(f) withdrawal or revocation of a registration;

(g) suspension of a registration.

(2) Sections 31(2), 32(3) and (4), 33, 33A, 34(6) and (9), 34A, 34B, 38, 40, 44B, 44BA,
44BC, 44C, 44D, 44E, 56(1)(f), (2) and (4) to (7), 57 to 75, 81, 81A and 83 of the 1974 Act
shall also apply to registered European lawyers as they apply to solicitors subject to the
modifications specified in the Table.

(2A)   The following provisions of the 1974 Act have effect as follows—

    (a)   in section 34(10) the reference to subsection (9) is to be read as including a reference to that subsection as it has effect by virtue of sub-paragraph (2);

    (b)   section 56(1)(a) to (e) to the extent necessary to give effect to section 56(1)(f) as it has effect by virtue of sub-paragraph (2).

(3)   Sections 41, 42, 43 and 44 of the 1974 Act shall apply to registered European lawyers as they apply to solicitors subject to the modifications specified in the Table.

(4)   Section 85 of the 1974 Act (bank accounts) shall apply to a registered European lawyer and to the partner of a registered European lawyer as it applies to a solicitor.

8   (1)   Subject to sub-paragraph (1A), sections 36 and 36A of the 1974 Act shall apply to registered European lawyers as they apply to solicitors.

(1A)   The Society may make different provision with respect to registered European lawyers, and European lawyers making an application for initial registration, from the provision made with respect to solicitors.

9   Section 35 of, and Schedule 1 to, the Solicitors Act 1974 shall apply to registered European lawyers as they apply to solicitors, and for that purpose—

    (aa)   reference to the roll is to be read as a reference to the register of European lawyers;.

    (ab)   reference to a solicitor suspended from practice is to be read as a reference to a European lawyer whose registration is suspended;

    (ac)   in paragraph 1(1)(k) of Schedule 1 to the 1974 Act, reference to a person acting as a solicitor when he did not have a practising certificate which was in force is to be read as a reference to a European lawyer or registered European lawyer who has committed an offence under regulation 21 of these Regulations;

    (b)   references to a solicitor's practising certificate shall be interpreted as references to a registered European lawyer's registration;

    (c)   reference to a sole solicitor is to be read as a reference to a sole practitioner.

10   Sections 46(10)(c), 47, 48, 49, 50(2), 50(3), 51, 52, 53 and 55 of the Solicitors Act 1974 shall apply to registered European lawyers as they apply to solicitors subject to the modifications specified in the Table.

11   Part XX of the Financial Services and Markets Act 2000, including the definition of "members" in section 325(2), has effect in relation to registered European lawyers as it has in relation to solicitors.

12   For the purposes of section 391 of the Insolvency Act 1986 and the Insolvency Practitioners (Recognised Professional Bodies) Order 1986, registered European lawyers and their partners shall be deemed to be—

    (a)   part of the solicitors' profession; and

    (b)   subject to the Law Society's rules in the practice of their profession.

13   Section 142 of the County Courts Act 1984 shall apply to registered European lawyers as it applies to solicitors.

14   (1)   Section 89 of the Courts and Legal Services Act 1990 shall be amended as follows.

(2)   In subsection (9), the following shall be substituted for the definition of "multi-national partnership"—

""multi-national partnership" means a partnership whose members consist of one or more registered foreign lawyers and one or more other lawyers as permitted by rules made under section 31 of the Solicitors Act 1974;"

15 *[repealed]*

16 *[repealed]*

17 In the Estate Agents Act 1979 the reference to a practising solicitor in section 1(2)(a) (which exempts solicitors from that Act) shall be interpreted as including a reference to a registered European lawyer and the partner of a registered European lawyer, providing professional services in accordance with rules made under section 31 of the Solicitors Act 1974 or section 9 of the Administration of Justice Act 1985.

18 *[repealed]*

19 In the Rehabilitation of Offenders Act 1974 (Exceptions) Order 1975 the reference to "solicitor" in Part I of Schedule 1 to the Order shall be interpreted as including reference to a registered European lawyer.

20 The Solicitors (Non-Contentious Business) Remuneration Order 1994 and any other order made under section 56 of the 1974 Act shall apply to registered European lawyers as it applies to solicitors.

21 Registered European lawyers shall be treated as if they were officers of the Supreme Court and shall be subject to the inherent jurisdiction of that court in like manner and to the same extent as if they were solicitors.

22 (1) References in the Charter to solicitors shall be deemed to include references to registered European lawyers.

(2) In this paragraph "the Charter" has the same meaning as it has in section 87(1) of the Solicitors Act 1974.

23 *[repealed]*

24 (1) The provisions of sections 9(2F) to (2H) and (5), 10A, 40 and 43 of the Administration of Justice Act 1985 apply to registered European lawyers as they apply to solicitors, and for this purpose

(a) the reference to a sole solicitor in sections 9 and 10A is to be read as a reference to a sole practitioner; and—

(b) the reference to a person's solicitor in section 40(1) is to be read as a reference to a registered European lawyer acting for a person.

(2) The provisions of Schedule 2 to that Act apply to registered European lawyers as they apply to solicitors, and for that purpose—

(a) reference to a sole solicitor is to be read as a reference to a sole practitioner;

(b) reference to a recognised sole solicitor's practice is to be read as a reference to a recognised sole practitioner's practice (that is, to a sole practitioner's practice for the time being recognised under section 9 of the 1985 Act);

(c) reference to the roll is to be read as a reference to the register of European lawyers, and accordingly—

(i) reference to a solicitor being suspended from practice is to be read as a reference to a European lawyer's registration being suspended; and

(ii) reference to a solicitor being struck off the roll is to be read as a reference to a European lawyer being struck off the register of European lawyers; and

(d) reference to a person who is not a solicitor is to be read as a reference to a person who is neither a solicitor nor a registered European lawyer.

Provision of the 1974 Act	Modification
Section 1B(1)(a)	Reference to a practising certificate in force is to be read as a reference to a European lawyer's registration.
Section 1B(1)(b)	Reference to a certificate is to be read as a reference to a European lawyer's registration.
	Reference to a sole solicitor endorsement is to be read as a reference to a sole practitioner endorsement.
Section 9(1)	Reference to a person whose name is on the roll is to be read as a reference to a European lawyer, as defined by regulation 2(1) to (4) of these Regulations.
	Reference to the issuing of a practising certificate is to be read as a reference to initial registration or renewal of registration in the register of European lawyers.
Section 9(4)(a)	Reference to a practising certificate is to be read as a reference to a European lawyer's registration.
Section 10(1) to (4)	Reference to the issuing of a practising certificate is to be read as a reference to initial registration or renewal of registration in the register of European lawyers.
	Reference to suspension from practice is to be read as a reference to suspension from the register of European lawyers.
Section 10(5)	Reference to a practising certificate is to be read as a reference to a European lawyer's registration.
Section 10A	Reference to solicitors who hold practising certificates is to be read as a reference to registered European lawyers.
Section 11(1)	Reference to the issuing of a practising certificate is to be read as a reference to initial registration or renewal of registration.
Section 11(3)	Reference to a practising certificate is to be read as a reference to a European lawyer's registration.
Section 11(3)(b)	Reference to a practising certificate not having been issued since the Society became aware of the failure is to be read as a reference to a registration in the register of European lawyers not having been entered or renewed since the Society became aware of the failure.
Section 13	Section 13 is to be read as if subsection (1)(a) were omitted.
Section 13(1)(c) and (4)(b) to (f)	Reference to the issuing of a practising certificate is to be read as a reference to renewal of registration.
	Reference to a practising certificate or certificate is to be read as a reference to a registration in the register of European lawyers.
Section 13(2)	Reference to a person who holds a practising certificate is to be read as a person who is registered in the register of European lawyers.

Provision of the 1974 Act	Modification
Section 13(3)	Reference to any application under section 9 is to be read as any application for renewal of registration in the register of European lawyers.
Section 13A(1), (2) and (7)(b)	Reference to a practising certificate being in force (a "current certificate") is to be read as a reference to a European lawyer's registration.
Section 13A(9)	Reference to a solicitor who holds a practising certificate is to be read as a European lawyer who is registered in the register of European lawyers.
Section 13B(1) and (8)(b)	References to a practising certificate or the appellant's certificate are to be read as references to a registered European lawyer's registration.
Section 13B(6)	Reference to a solicitor's suspension from practice is to be read as a reference to a European lawyer's suspension from the register of European lawyers.
Section 15	Reference to a practising certificate is to be read as a reference to a European lawyer's registration.
	Reference in subsection (1) to suspension from practice is to be read as a reference to a European lawyer's suspension from the register of European lawyers.
Section 16	Reference to a practising certificate or certificate is to be read as a reference to a registration in the register of European lawyers.
	Reference to a solicitor's suspension from practice or suspension is to be read as reference to the suspension of a European lawyer's registration.
	Reference in subsections (1) and (3) to expiry of a certificate is to be read as expiry of a European lawyer's registration.
Section 17	Reference to suspension of a solicitor's practising certificate is to be read as reference to the suspension of a European lawyer's registration.
	Reference to a note against a solicitor's name on the roll is to be read as reference to a note against a European lawyer's name on the register of European lawyers.
Section 18	References to the register kept under section 10A are to be read as a reference to the register of European lawyers.
	Subsection (1) is to be read as if reference to an extract from the roll were omitted.
	Section 18 is to be read as if subsection (2)(a) were omitted.
Section 28(1)(c) to (d)	Reference in subsection (1)(c) to a practising certificate is to be read as a reference to a European lawyer's registration.
	Reference in subsection (1)(d) to the register kept under section 10A is to be read as a reference to the register of European lawyers.

Provision of the 1974 Act	Modification
Section 28(3B) to (3G)	Reference to a practising certificate is to be read as a reference to a European lawyer's registration.
	Reference in subsection (3B)(d) and (e) to the issuing of a practising certificate is to be read as a reference to initial registration or renewal of registration.
	Subsection (3B)(i) is to be read as if reference to replacement were omitted.
	Reference in subsection (3B)(k) to solicitors who hold practising certificates is to be read as reference to registered European lawyers.
	Reference in subsection (3C) to the register under section 10A is to be read as a reference to the register of European lawyers.
Section 41	Reference to a solicitor is to be read as to include a reference to a registered European lawyer.
	Reference in subsections (1)(a) and (4)(a) to the roll is to be read as to include a reference to the register of European lawyers.
	Reference in subsections (1)(b) and (4)(b) to suspension from practising as a solicitor is to be read as to include a reference to suspension from the register of European lawyers.
	Reference in subsection (1)(c) to a practising certificate being suspended is to be read as to include a reference to a European lawyer's registration being suspended.
	Reference in subsection (1B) to the "employed solicitor" is not to be read as a reference to an employed European lawyer.
Section 42	In subsection (1) reference to a person who is disqualified from practising as a solicitor by reason of a fact mentioned in paragraphs (a) to (c) is to be read as to include a reference to a European lawyer whose name has been struck off the register of European lawyers or whose registration in that register is suspended.
Section 43	In section 43(1) reference to a person who is not a solicitor is to be read as a reference to a person who is neither a solicitor nor a registered European lawyer.
Section 44	Reference to section 43(2) is to be read as to include a reference to that section as it has effect by virtue of these Regulations.

Provision of the 1974 Act	Modification
Section 47	Reference to the roll is to be read as reference to the register of European lawyers.
	Reference in section 47(1)(d) and (2)(b) and (e) to suspension from practice is to be read as a reference to suspension from the register of European lawyers.
	Reference in section 47(2A)(a) to another solicitor is to be read as to include a reference to a solicitor or a registered European lawyer.
	Reference in section 47(2B) to a firm of solicitors is to be read as a reference to a firm of solicitors and/or registered European lawyers.
	Reference to an employee who is not a solicitor is to be read as a reference to an employee who is neither a solicitor nor a registered European lawyer
Section 51	Reference in section 51(1) and (3)(b) to the striking off of a name from the roll is to be read as reference to striking a European lawyer's name from the register of European lawyers.
Section 52	Reference to the striking off of a name from the roll is to be read as reference to striking a European lawyer's name from the register of European lawyers.
Section 53	Reference to the striking off of a name from the roll is to be read as reference to striking a European lawyer's name from the register of European lawyers.
	Reference to suspension from practice is to be read as a reference to suspension from the register of European lawyers.
	Reference to a note of the order on the roll is to be read as reference to a note on the register of European lawyers.
Section 55	Reference to the striking off of a name from the roll is to be read as reference to striking a European lawyer's name from the register of European lawyers.
Section 84	Reference to a solicitor who has in force, or who has applied for, a practising certificate is to be read as a reference to a European lawyer who is registered or who has applied for registration in the register of European lawyers.
	Reference in subsection (3) to a practising solicitor is to be read as a reference to a registered European lawyer.

SCHEDULE 5
Extension of Enactments in Relation to the Registration of European Lawyers with the Law Society of Northern Ireland

Regulation 37(4)

1 (1) The power to make rules and regulations under article 75 of the Solicitors (Northern Ireland) Order 1976 shall also be exercisable in relation to registered European lawyers.

(2) The power to make regulations under articles 6, 26, 26A, 33, 34, 35, 61 and 63 shall also be exercisable in relation to registered European lawyers.

2   The provisions of articles 7, 8, 10, 11, 13 and 14 to 18 of that Order shall apply to registered European lawyers as they apply to solicitors, except that—

(a)   references to a solicitor's practising certificate shall be interpreted as references to a registered European lawyer's registration; and

(b)   references to the roll shall be interpreted as references to the register of European lawyers.

3   Articles 27, 28, 29, 32, 36 to 60, 62, 64A to 71H, 72A, 77 and 78 of, and Schedules 1, 1A and 2 to, that Order shall apply to registered European lawyers as they apply to solicitors except that—

(a)   references to a solicitor's practising certificate shall be interpreted as references to a registered European lawyer's registration; and

(b)   references to the roll shall be interpreted as references to the register of European lawyers.

4   Article 51 of the County Courts (Northern Ireland) Order 1980 shall apply to registered European lawyers as it applies to solicitors.

5   In the Estate Agents Act 1979 the reference to a practising solicitor in section 1(2)(a) (which exempts solicitors from that Act) shall be interpreted as including a reference to a registered European lawyer, and the partner of a registered European lawyer providing professional services in accordance with article 26 of the Solicitors (Northern Ireland) Order 1976.

6   In the Rehabilitation of Offenders (Northern Ireland) Order 1978 the references to "solicitor" in the Order shall be interpreted as including reference to a registered European lawyer.

7   The Solicitors Remuneration Order (Northern Ireland) 1977 shall apply to registered European lawyers as it applies to solicitors.

8   Registered European lawyers shall be treated as if they were officers of the Supreme Court of Northern Ireland and shall be subject to the inherent jurisdiction of that court in like manner and to the same extent as if they were solicitors.

SRA warning notices

[Law Society copyright. Warning notices do not form part of the SRA Handbook, but we may have regard to them when exercising our regulatory functions.

Please note that warning notices written and issued before the introduction of the SRA Handbook on 6 October 2011 and may refer to regulatory material that is no longer in effect. For further information, please contact Professional Ethics.]

9.1   Bogus law firms and identity theft

9.2   Criminal legal aid and clients' best interests

9.3   Employed solicitors publicity and information provided to third parties

9.4   High-yield investment fraud

9.5   Holiday sickness claims

9.6   Improper use of client account as a banking facility

9.7   Investment schemes and client account

9.8   Investment schemes (including conveyancing

9.9   Land banking schemes

9.10 Money laundering and terrorist financing

9.11 Money laundering and terrorist financing – suspicious activity reports

9.12 Money missing from client account

9.13 Money missing from client account

9.14 Payment Protection Insurance (PPI) claims

9.15 Referral fees LASPO and SRA Principles

9.16 Risk factors in personal injury claims

9.17 Stamp duty land tax schemes

9.18 Tax avoidance – your duties

9.19 Use of non-disclosure agreements (NDAs)

9.1 Bogus law firms and identity theft

[Issued by the Solicitors Regulation Authority on 26 March 2012]

1.   There are serious and continuing risks to the public arising from the activities of criminals and criminal gangs who are setting up bogus law firms or bogus branch offices of genuine law firms with the intention, usually, of stealing mortgage loans. This warning notice provides information about the threat and advice about how to protect yourself and others from it.

2.   We are deploying our resources to mitigate the risk in various ways including rigorous

authorisation processes, use of intelligence, urgent investigation, removal of records from Find a solicitor and publication of warnings.

3. It is important to bear in mind, however, that we do not regulate the people who are perpetrating these frauds and our powers over them are relatively limited. However, in one case where sufficient evidence was available, we obtained a injunction against an individual preventing him from having anything to do with any law firm in the future. If we obtain sufficient evidence to take such steps in any case, then we will do so.

4. It is important to share some of the indicators of these frauds to maximise the chances of prevention.

5. If you become suspicious about a law firm for any reason, please contact our Red Alert Line (0345 850 0999 or email redalert@sra.org.uk) as a matter of extreme urgency since some frauds are carried out very quickly.

6. Bear in mind that you may come across these frauds in different contexts. Of course, you must keep an eye on any indication that your firm is being targeted or its name being used improperly. If you discover this, you should contact the SRA and your insurers, including consideration of legal action such as by way of injunction either to stop misleading statements or to freeze assets if money has gone missing. If there is any evidence of a crime having been committed, you should also inform the Police.

7. There are risks to you and your firm. For example, in *Lloyds TSB Bank PLC v Markandan and Uddin* [2012] EWCA Civ 65 the firm that was said to be the victim of the fraud was still held liable for breach of trust in paying away mortgage monies.

8. Some practical things you can do:

   a. Search your firm's name on the internet from time to time, since that might bring up a false office—it may be worth considering doing the same with the names of some of your partners or staff;

   b. Check your firm and individual details on the Law Society's Find a solicitor web page—in case someone has misused your name to set up a false office;

   c. Be alert to suspicious incidents such as transactions that others seem to think your firm is dealing with when you are not;

   d. Look out for alerts and warnings on the SRA website about bogus firms.

9. Law firms dealing with conveyancing transactions or other work also sometimes become suspicious of firms on the other side and again it is important that such suspicions are reported and acted upon immediately.

10. Some examples of **factors giving rise to suspicion** are[1]

   • errors in letterheading—in one case the bogus office had letterheading which misspelt the name of the town in which it was supposedly based;

   • no landline telephone number—note that numbers beginning with 07 are mobile telephone numbers;

   • inconsistent telephone or fax numbers with those usually used by the firm;

   • telephone calls being diverted to a call-back service;

   • a firm apparently based in serviced offices;

   • email addresses using generic email accounts—most law firms have addresses incorporating the name of their firm; if in doubt, check the genuine law firm's website to identify its contact email address. You may well notice a difference;

   • sudden appearance in your locality of a firm with no obvious connection to the area, probably not interacting with other local firms at all;

   • a firm appearing to open a branch office a considerable distance from its head office for no obvious reason;

- a firm based in one part of the country supposedly having a bank account in another part of the country—this is a strong indicator and has been seen several times;

- a client account apparently overseas—this is a breach of rule 13.4 of the SRA Accounts Rules and is a major red flag;

- a strange or suspicious bank account name—such as the account not being in the name of the law firm you are supposedly dealing with either at all or by some variation.

11. If you become concerned, you should consider checking some of the above points yourself. Because of the possibility of the theft of the identity of a genuine solicitor, it is worth trying to speak to the solicitor concerned. For example, if the solicitor is supposedly at one particular office but is also based at a head office of the firm, you could speak to the head office preferably after verifying its genuine nature, perhaps by contact with the senior partner.

12. You should check the Find a solicitor website since there are sometimes bogus law firms which have not sought registration with the SRA and will not appear there; but bear in mind also that the nature of identity theft is that fraudsters may have obtained some form of registration by fraudulent misstatement to the SRA and therefore an entry on Find a solicitor should not be taken as verification that the firm is genuine.

13. Do not assume that the SRA or the Police can take direct steps to protect your firm. We each will do what we can although we will be focused on fraud prevention and you must not exclude the possibility of urgently seeking an injunction particularly if you are in possession of the most direct evidence and indeed if action is required very urgently. In such circumstances, we will seek to assist as much as we properly can in light of the evidence and any order of the court.

NOTES

1. These do not necessarily individually establish a serious problem but are factors to be considered.

9.2 Criminal legal aid and clients' best interests

[Issued by the Solicitors Regulation Authority on 27 July 2015]

Status

Whilst this document does not form part of the SRA Handbook, the SRA may have regard to it when exercising its regulatory functions.

Who is this guidance relevant to?

Individual solicitors and firms undertaking criminal defence work.

Our concerns

We are concerned that solicitors and firms may not act in the best interests of each individual client, as required by the SRA Principles, should the protocol issued by the London Criminal Courts Solicitors Association (Protocol Phase 2 The Crown Court) be followed without fully considering the circumstances of each individual client.

It is a matter for each firm and individual solicitor to decide whether or not to represent clients in criminal cases. However, at all times, individuals and firms are bound to comply with regulatory requirements and the protocol issued by the LCCSA does not, in any way, modify these requirements.

Creating a limited pro bono retainer

Where you have a retainer with a client, whether it is pro bono or not, you have a duty to act in the client's best interests and to ensure the client is in a position to make an informed decision on their matter. Whilst it is open to you to limit a retainer, it is not clear why to do so would be in the best interests of a criminal defendant client. In order to achieve Outcome (1.12), you must inform the client of all his choices. It is likely to be in the client's best interests to instruct another firm able to act for him fully and to apply for legal aid. You should advise your client accordingly or as to any other options open to him.

Terminating a retainer

The Protocol also seeks to apply a policy described as 'no returns'. Where a firm is instructed in a criminal case where advocacy in court is required by the client, it is in the best interests of the client for the firm to use its best endeavours to secure advocacy for the client. This may include the use of appropriately qualified advocates employed by the firm as well as external advocates. Given this, it is not apparent that a firm following the approach of "if an instructed solicitor advocate is unable to cover a hearing the case will not revert to another member of the firm" would be compliant with existing regulatory obligations. It is the client's best interests that are paramount once instructions have been accepted. Such conduct is likely to undermine public confidence in the provision of legal services. It should be remembered that you can only terminate your retainer with good reason and on reasonable notice.

The SRA Principles

Principle 1 – upholding the rule of law and the proper administration of justice.

Principle 2 – act with integrity.

Principle 3 – not allow your independence to be compromised.

Principle 4 – act in the best interests of each client.

Principle 5 – provide a proper standard of service to your clients.

Principle 6 – behave in a way that maintains the trust the public places in you and in the provision of legal services.

Mandatory outcomes

You need to comply with the Solicitors Regulation Authority code of conduct and in particular the following outcomes:

- Outcome (1.1) you treat your clients fairly;

- Outcome (1.2) you provide services to your clients in a manner which protects their interests in their matter, subject to the proper administration of justice;

- Outcome (1.3) when deciding whether to act or terminate your instructions you comply with the law and the code;

- Outcome (1.5) the service you provide to clients is competent. Delivered in a timely manner and takes account of your clients needs and circumstances;

- Outcome (1.12) clients are in a position to make informed decisions about the services they need, how their matter will be handled and the options available to them.

Enforcement action

Failure to comply with this warning notice may lead to disciplinary action.

Further help

SRA Chief Executive Paul Philip on 4 August 2015 wrote to LCCSA Chair Jonathan Black setting out the SRA's position.

If you require further help in understanding your obligations under the Handbook, please contact the Professional Ethics team.

9.3 Employed solicitors publicity and information provided to third parties

[Issued by the Solicitors Regulation Authority on 8 July 2014]

Status

This warning notice does not form part of the Solicitors Regulation Authority (SRA) Handbook. However, the SRA will have regard to it when exercising its regulatory functions.

Who is this warning notice relevant to?

In-house/employed solicitors

Our concerns

There have been a number of complaints from the public regarding misleading information contained in letters and in letterheads, of some in-house solicitors. These complaints arise as a result of in-house solicitors giving the impression, through the wording contained in letters, through the use of business names by in-house solicitors, by the description of their regulatory status and by their contact details that they are an independent firm of solicitors or other legal services firm.

Overall, these approaches appear to be attempts to give the impression to a third party that an external agency or firm has been instructed to take legal action, up to and including, court proceedings.

These complaints have arisen most commonly in debt collection or enforcement matters where solicitors are employed in-house by the organisation seeking to recover the debt.

Further concern has been caused by complaints of solicitors having taken unfair advantage of a third party's lack of legal knowledge, particularly in debt collecting matters, where the third party is unrepresented.

The SRA Principles

The SRA Principles are mandatory and apply to all solicitors and to those acting under their supervision. The following SRA Principles are of particular relevance to this issue.

Principle 2 – You must act with integrity

Principle 6 – You must behave in a way that maintains the trust the public places in you and in the provision of legal services

SRA Mandatory Outcomes

The Outcomes in the SRA Code of Conduct 2011 are mandatory and describe what firms and individuals are expected to achieve in order to comply with the relevant SRA Principles. However, they are not an exhaustive list of the application of all the Principles.

The following Outcomes are of particular relevance to this issue.

O(8.1) – your publicity in relation to your firm or in house practice or for any other business is accurate and not misleading, and is not likely to diminish the trust the public places in you and in the provision of legal services.

O(8.4) – clients and the public have appropriate information about you, your firm and how you are regulated.

O(11.1) – you do not take unfair advantage of third parties in either your professional or personal capacity.

Regulatory action

Failure to comply with this warning notice will lead to regulatory action. Regulatory action may also be necessary because of misconduct that has already taken place.

Our expectations

All solicitors must act with integrity and maintain the trust the public places in them and in the provision of legal services. We expect that all publicity and information regarding your position, as an in house/employed solicitor, is compliant with the Principles and relevant Outcomes in the SRA Code of Conduct 2011.

We have reviewed a number of complaints and a range of letters sent by solicitors employed within financial (and similar) institutions to pursue debts or other outstanding sums of money. We consider that, through a range of approaches, attempts are being made to mislead third parties (invariably individual debtors) that their case has been referred by the organisation owed money to an independent law firm to pursue the debt, notably the "naming" of in-house legal teams in the style of independent law firms.

We consider that such approaches do not meet the requirements of Principles 2 and 6 and of Outcomes 8.1, 8.4 and 11.1.

Letterheads must be clear as to the organisation employing you and you must not give any impression that you are part of an independent law firm or firm of solicitors or an independent solicitor.

Any contact details should ensure the third party is aware who they are contacting whether you directly, the in-house legal department or other staff of your employer.

Any correspondence from you, or sent under your supervision, must indicate your individual status as a solicitor regulated by the SRA but must not seek to give any impression that the organisation which employs you is regulated by the SRA.

Overall, the obligation on you is to take positive steps to ensure that third parties are clear about your status and relationship with the organisation seeking recovery of the debt.

In considering any complaints or regulatory action the SRA will consider whether the Principles are being complied with and Outcomes being met. We will consider the overall impact on the third party of information provided in the letterhead, the body of the correspondence and in the references made to regulatory status. In particular we will consider whether the totality of the information provided makes the solicitor's status clear or whether it gives a false impression and may mislead.

Further help

If solicitors require further help, they can call or email the SRA Ethics helpline.

9.4 High-yield investment fraud

[Issued by the Solicitors Regulation Authority on 10 September 2013]

This warning notice is for anyone who is involved in, or is considering acting for clients involved in, the promotion or facilitation of financial arrangements that appear dubious.

Law firms have been targeted in the past by fraudsters promoting high-yield investment schemes which have proved to be ineffective and often fraudulent. Practitioners must not become involved in schemes that appear dubious or bear the hallmarks of possible fraud.

Economic pressures on law firms can lead to difficulty in obtaining work or finance and there is temptation to act in financial schemes either for fees or to make a promised profit. After a period of some years in which law firms were rarely involved in such schemes, the SRA is seeing a substantial increase in them again.

It is important always to bear in mind that a scheme that appears to be too good to be true is usually fraudulent. This notice sets out some factors that indicate there may be a fraud.

Whilst this notice does not form part of the SRA Handbook, the SRA may have regard to it when exercising its regulatory functions.

The Principles

It is your duty to ensure you do not become involved in potentially fraudulent financial arrangements. Failure to observe warnings from the SRA could lead to disciplinary action or criminal prosecution. Attempts to limit your involvement, particularly by a purportedly "limited retainer" are ineffective in protecting you if you simply should not become involved.

If you are, or are considering, becoming involved in any financial arrangement, you must consider whether you can comply with the Principles in the SRA Handbook. Whilst all the Principles may be relevant, some require particular attention:

• integrity

- independence
- best interests of the client
- behaving in a way that maintains the trust the public places in you and the provision of legal services.

What are high-yield investment frauds?

Frauds vary and fraudsters learn to avoid red flag phrases. Firms need to ensure that they understand the proposed scheme and that it makes logical and legal sense. Fraudsters use meaningless terminology but also use genuine terms to mask their frauds. It is important to assess the overall proposal and, if a genuine term is used, to check robustly whether it is being used in the correct context. Some common descriptions have included:

- High yield investment schemes
- Prime bank instrument schemes
- Private placement schemes.

Arrangements are formulated by fraudsters to prey upon vulnerable and sometimes wealthy people or companies. Those in need of money are often the most at risk. These schemes are often highly sophisticated confidence tricks, which involve lawyers facilitating what is essentially a fraud. Some schemes involve the movement of large sums of money and are a combination of a fraud—usually with the intention of stealing the "investment"—and the laundering of criminal proceeds by mixing them into other money transfers.

Common characteristics

It is your duty to ensure you comply with your professional obligations and exercise proper caution in considering any involvement in a scheme involving the "investment" of money or the transfer of funds that are presented to you. The following is a non-exhaustive list of common characteristics of fraudulent financial arrangements.

- Very high rate of return and disproportionate rewards, often within a short time frame—this is also a common characteristic in Ponzi schemes which involve payments to investors from subsequent investors rather than from any 'profit' earned by the individual or organisation running the fraudulent operation
- Very large sums of money said to be involved or required for "entry" to the "programme"
- Confusing and complex transactions with obscure descriptions
- Unusual currencies
- Prime Bank Guarantees (PBGs), Promissory Notes or Letters of Credit being offered or being the 'product' underpinning the finance
- Obscure "security" such as famous paintings or speculative international developments
- Opinions or letters from law firms or others that support the scheme but do not make sense or are empty of genuine content
- Security being offered to "investors" includes an undertaking from a law firm or that money will be held by a law firm—sometimes including reference to indemnity insurance or the Compensation Fund
- Security to be issued by an obscure or offshore bank that is difficult to contact—particularly if there is pressure not to contact the bank (or any other person) on (what are in fact spurious) confidentiality grounds

- Poorly drafted documentation

- Overwhelming amount of documents supposedly explaining the transaction; or a lack of any coherent explanation of the investment

- Suggestions that the scheme is supported by or operates under the auspices of a major international body (e.g. IMF, UN, Federal Reserve or Bank of England)

- Large projects that are difficult to verify e.g. financing of a project in distant jurisdiction where it hard to verify its genuineness

- The need for speed and great confidentiality to secure the deal – usually intended to prevent proper due diligence

- Unusual letters from genuine banks (that often turn out to be forged or provided by a rogue employee)—contact the bank's fraud prevention office for verification.

Promoters operating these scams engage the assistance of law firms for a number of reasons. The involvement of lawyers and their firms:

- Lends credibility to the scheme

- Enables promoters to offer a false sense of security based on the existence of compulsory insurance and the alleged safety net of the Compensation Fund

- Provides promoters with access to client accounts which can be utilised for the transfer of funds

- Enables promoters to make use of solicitors' undertakings as a means of appearing to give investors security

- Enables promoters to abuse legal professional privilege.

Types of legal services that promoters might request include:

- Moving monies through client account

- Advising on and drafting documents and/or contracts that have little genuine content

- Marketing and promoting the fraudulent scheme to attract investors

- Adding credibility to the fraudulent scheme by attending meetings, engaging in correspondence or providing undertakings

- Certifying or verifying documentation

- Use of the lawyer's office address and facilities.

Complying with the Principles

To comply with the Principles it is important that you and your firm are able to identify fraudulent or dubious financial arrangements and manage the associated risks.

The promoters of fraudulent arrangements will often want you or your firm to hold 'investor funds' in your client account (see Rule 14.5 of the SRA Accounts Rules 2011). You must not allow money to move through your accounts or an account you control unless you are doing so in the context of a genuine transaction about which you are providing legal services. Bear in mind also that the money may be the proceeds of the defrauding of the investors.

There are specific outcomes in chapter 11 of the SRA Code of Conduct 2011 in relation to undertakings.

If you are approached you must ensure that you comply with your obligations under the Money Laundering Regulations and related legislation.

Do not assume that because you are not acting for investors that you owe no duties as a matter of professional conduct. Not only must you avoid facilitating a fraud, monies sent by investors may well be subject to implied trust obligations particularly if the scheme is fraudulent.

Investors may be unrepresented or based overseas and may be unaware of the risks involved in financial arrangements or may have been induced in a scheme on the basis they will be protected because you or your firm is regulated. Whilst your client may be the promoter of the arrangement, you must not forget your public obligations as a lawyer and your overriding duty to act in the public interest.

How do I reduce the risk of fraud?

- Do not act if you have any doubts about the propriety of the transaction; or about how or why it is structured in a particular way.

- Never act if you do not fully understand the transaction, if it does not make sense or if you are essentially just providing a facility for the transfer of money.

- Do not be blinded by apparent involvement in high value international transactions sometimes including promises of or actual international travel or meetings since it is part of the psychological approach to fraud to impress the victim or professional who will facilitate the fraud.

- Always verify properly the identity of who you are dealing with.

- Bear in mind that Ponzi schemes involve the payment of "profits" at first—by using the funds of other investors—and so "evidence" that a scheme "works" is part of the fraud.

- Ensure that proper due diligence is performed before accepting any funds into your client account—be extremely wary of any scheme which requires the depositing of any substantial sums on money with you particularly if you are to be paid for doing very little. Do not hold money in your client account (or any other account) for clients you know little about or who you are not providing legal advice to in relation to the transaction for which you are expected to hold money.

- Why you? Be particularly careful if you are asked to act in an area outside of your usual expertise. A small firm asked to act in an international financial transaction is at severe risk.

- Use of documentation – beware of any scheme which requires you to send details of your bank, client account or blank letterheads. Such information may be used to make unauthorised payments from your client account.

- Undertakings – do not give any form of undertaking to guarantee a financial obligation unless you are acting in a transaction you fully understand and you are fully secure in having funds to meet the obligation.

SRA action

Whilst we are committed to working constructively with firms and practitioners, we will take enforcement action against those that fail to address the issues and risks associated with dubious financial arrangements.

We have seen a number of solicitors and firms who have become involved in fraudulent schemes, some as investors and some as participators of the fraud, each with the intention of gaining an extra funds for the firm that could be used to run the practice, whether that be through the payment of a success fee for participation in the fraud or through profits arising from the scheme.

A defence based on ignorance or lack of understanding of the transactions involved is considered weak. Turning a blind eye to the suspicious features of a scheme or failing to verify the promoter's true intentions can constitute dishonesty.

Further assistance

If you require further assistance with understanding your obligations in relation to high yield investment schemes please contact the Ethics Helpline.

If you have evidence of one of these schemes or are concerned that you have been approached or have become involved, please contact your SRA supervisor.

If you are already involved and become concerned, urgently contact the SRA Fraud and Confidential Intelligence Bureau: call 0345 850 0999 or email redalert@sra.org.uk.

9.5 Holiday sickness claims

[Issued by the Solicitors Regulation Authority on 6 September 2017/Updated on 9 August 2018]

Status

While this document does not form part of the SRA Handbook, we may have regard to it when exercising its regulatory functions.

Who is this warning notice relevant to?

This warning notice is relevant to all those we regulate who act in personal injury cases, particularly holiday sickness claims.

Our expectations

We expect that all those regulated by us comply with the Principles and Outcomes of the SRA Handbook 2011. We expect that law firms and solicitors do not conduct fraudulent or questionable cases and that all costs charged to a client are explained, agreed and set at a reasonable rate.

What misconduct we are seeing

According to the Association of British Travel Agents, there has been a 500 percent increase in compensation claims for holiday sickness since 2013. In matters reported to us we have seen some behaviours that give us cause for concern.

We have seen firms:

- taking on matters whilst lacking competence and skill in the area of law
- failing to ensure that they do not accept cases from introducers who are cold calling or failing to verify the source of the referral
- entering into improper referral arrangements and allowing their independence to be compromised by, for example favouring the interests of the referrer

- failing to properly identify clients and confirm client instructions including the verification of relevant documentation to support a claim

- bringing a claim without first investigating whether it is valid

- making unreasonable requests for disclosure from the defendant or their lawyers

- failing to objectively assess and investigate adverse evidence

- failing to properly advise clients about what will be expected of them when making a claim

- submitting false or dubious claims in the hope of a settlement without further investigation by the defendant

- seeking unreasonable costs – either from the client or the defendant

Firms who conduct cases which demonstrate one or more of these features may face regulatory action for breach of our Principles.

We are investigating firms involved in holiday claims, including potentially improper links with claims management companies and payment for referrals of holiday sickness claims. We are also seeing firms pursuing claims without the proper instructions of claimants.

Holiday claims exemplify our concern that some law firms fail to engage properly, or sometimes at all, with the merits of their clients' cases. This is of concern where there is evidence to suggest that the claim is false or dubious in some way. We are clear in our view that lawyers should not bring cases, or continue with them, where there is a serious concern about the honesty or reliability of the evidence

You should not pursue claims or continue with claims where you do not have the claimant's clear and express authority to do so. The extent to which law firms should verify their clients' cases is risk-specific. For example, there seems to be a serious risk that many holiday sickness claims are not genuine. Examples of risk factors in holiday sickness claims would include:

- The claim is made some time after the alleged incident

- There was no report of the claim to the hotel

- There was no extensive sickness amongst others in the same accommodation – see Wood v TUI Travel [2017] EWCA Civ 11

- The claim comes from or involves people that have actively sought out/farmed for claims in a resort

- The client's contemporaneous report of the holiday was positive

- The client drank or ate excessively before or after becoming ill

The difficulties of holiday sickness claims are clearly evident from the case of Wood v TUI Travel [2017] EWCA Civ 11 in which the Court of Appeal commented:

> … it will always be difficult (indeed, very difficult) to prove that an illness is a consequence of food or drink which was not of a satisfactory quality, unless there is cogent evidence that others have been similarly affected and alternative explanations would have to be excluded …

Solicitors must engage with this and properly assess all the evidence before submitting claims.

We have also seen failures to make sure that all documentary evidence is collated and analysed. We have seen highly improper advice to clients to delete evidence, for example, deleting social media updates or pictures.

In all litigation, firms must immediately inform clients of their duty to preserve evidence and require it all to be provided for the firm to review. This is a critical duty to the administration of justice, including to prevent or reduce the public cost of unmeritorious claims. Firms must of course also be rigorous in storing, retrieving, analysing and acting upon evidence they hold, including seeking disclosure where it is appropriate. Claims should not be submitted until the client has been properly advised on all relevant evidence and on the merits of their case – and when the client has given clear instructions and authority, on a fully informed basis, that the case should be pursued.

A narrow approach to this by the firm is liable to be treated as 'turning a blind eye' which of course can lead to dishonesty findings. In Barlow Clowes v Eurotrust [2005] UKPC 37 it was noted that a dishonest state of mind "may consist in suspicion combined with a conscious decision not to make inquiries which might result in knowledge".

These principles apply to all litigation. The impact of unmeritorious claims on the administration of justice and indeed on those who are subjected to such claims means that solicitors must not pursue them where there is evidence that they are false or clearly unmeritorious.

If there are allegations or concerns about a case, law firms must not turn a blind eye, but instead must engage with them and objectively assess whether the case can properly be pursued.

An example of this might be allegations that claims are being generated or co-ordinated by organised criminals, as we have seen in 'cash for crash' cases. Law firms cannot simply ignore such allegations, and nor can they simply assert that they consider them unproved or unfounded. They must engage properly with them and bear in mind their duty to the administration of justice.

Cold calling

There have been reports of introducers and people seeking out claims farmers approaching holiday makers to generate sickness claims. Outcome (8.3) requires that you do not make unsolicited approaches in person or by telephone to members of the public to publicise your firm or another business. Outcome (9.4) requires you to be satisfied that any client referred by an introducer has not been acquired because of marketing or other activities which, if done by you, would be contrary to the Principles or any requirements of the Code.

Referral arrangements

You should take steps to make sure that you verify the source of any referral.

You should terminate any arrangement with an introducer or fee-sharer which is causing you to breach the Principles or any requirements of the Code (IB (9.3)). Outcome (9.8) requires you not to pay a prohibited referral fee.

Please see our previously published guidance on the Legal Aid, Sentencing and Punishment of Offenders Act 2012 (LASPO).

Where you have a referral arrangement that is not in breach of LASPO, you still need to comply with the outcomes that are set out chapters 6 and 9 of the SRA Code of Conduct when making or receiving any referrals. Reports have been made that referrals are being made to a third party, for example a medical expert, when it is not in the client's best interests or likely to progress a claim as the referral is made after a significant time has passed.

Suspect or dubious claims

When taking instructions, you should make sure that you have clear details of the client's identity. You should analyse the evidence rigorously. No claim should be made unless there is a sound basis for the claim and you have valid instructions.

Dishonest claims

There are a number of reports of cases where claims have been dismissed as dishonest, leading to costs orders against claimants and even a criminal prosecution. Solicitors do not help clients by bringing claims that have not been rigorously investigated, including consideration of adverse evidence.

Taking unfair advantage

Outcome (11.1) provides that you must not take unfair advantage of third parties.

Acting in the following way may tend to show that you have not achieved outcomes and therefore complied with the principles.

IB (11.8) demanding anything for yourself or on behalf of your client that is not legally recoverable.

You should not demand anything from a third party, such as compensation for holiday sickness, where there is no legal right to recovery.

Seeking high costs from defendants that are not fair and reasonable, having regard to the complexities of the matter and work done, may also constitute an attempt to take unfair advantage. Submitting a claim for unfair and unreasonable costs might also involve you taking steps that could mislead the court, for example, about work you have not done.

Enforcement Action

Failure to have proper regard to this warning notice is likely to lead to disciplinary action.

Relevant SRA Principles

PRINCIPLE 1: UPHOLD THE RULE OF LAW AND THE PROPER ADMINISTRATION OF JUSTICE.

You have obligations not only to clients but also to the court and to third parties with whom you have dealings on your clients' behalf (Part 1 – SRA Principles para 2.5).

PRINCIPLE 2: ACT WITH INTEGRITY.

Personal integrity is central to your role as the client's trusted adviser and should characterise all your professional dealings with clients, the court, other lawyers and the public (Part 1 – SRA Principles para 2.6).

PRINCIPLE 4: YOU MUST ACT IN THE BEST INTERESTS OF EACH CLIENT.

You should always act in good faith and do your best for each of your clients (Part 1 – SRA Principles para 2.8).

PRINCIPLE 5: YOU MUST PROVIDE A PROPER STANDARD OF SERVICE TO YOUR CLIENTS.

You should provide a proper standard of client care and of work. This would include exercising competence, skill and diligence, and taking into account the individual needs and circumstances of each client (Part 1 – SRA Principles para 2.9).

PRINCIPLE 6: YOU MUST BEHAVE IN A WAY THAT MAINTAINS THE TRUST THE PUBLIC PLACES IN YOU AND IN THE PROVISION OF LEGAL SERVICES.

Members of the public should be able to place their trust in you. Any behaviour either within or outside your professional practice which undermines this trust damages not only you, but also the ability of the legal profession as a whole to serve society (Part 1 – SRA Principles para 2.11).

SRA Code of Conduct 2011 mandatory outcomes

You should also have regard to the specific outcomes in the SRA Code of Conduct 2011, that have been referred to in this warning notice.

Further assistance

For guidance on conduct issues, contact the Professional Ethics Team

9.6 Improper use of a client account as a banking facility

[Issued by the Solicitors Regulation Authority on 18 December 2014/Updated 6 August 2018]

Status

While this guidance does not form part of the SRA Handbook, we may have regard to it when exercising our regulatory functions.

Who is this guidance relevant to?

This guidance is relevant to all practitioners who have any involvement in holding or using money received for clients or others.

For a number of years, we have warned that solicitors must not provide banking facilities to clients or others. This warning notice is a reminder of some of the key issues and risks of which you should be aware. We have also set out some case studies to help you comply with your obligations.

Our rules and principles

Rule 14.5 of the SRA Accounts Rules 2011 provides that:

"You must not provide banking facilities through a client account. Payments into, and transfers or withdrawals from, a client account must be in respect of instructions relating to an underlying transaction (and the funds arising therefrom) or to a service forming part of your normal regulated activities."

The rule's guidance note states that:

"Rule 14.5 reflects decisions of the Solicitors Disciplinary Tribunal that it is not a proper part of a solicitor's everyday business or practice to operate a banking facility for third parties, whether they are clients of the firm or not. It should be noted that any exemption under the Financial Services and Markets Act 2000 is likely to be lost if a deposit is taken in circumstances which do not form part of your practice. It should also be borne in mind that there are criminal sanctions against assisting money launderers."

Concerns about the improper use of client account have been clearly and more broadly stated in case law. You should make sure that you are fully aware of the relevant case law including the Fuglers,[1] Patel,[2] and Zambia[3] cases.

The Principles

A breach of rule 14.5 is a serious matter in itself.

If you allow your firm's client account to be used improperly this may also result in a breach of the SRA Principles including:

- Principle 1: upholding the rule of law and the proper administration of justice;

- Principle 3: not allowing your independence to be compromised;

- Principle 6: behaving in a way that maintains the trust the public places in you and the provision of legal services; and

- Principle 8: running your business or carrying out your role in the business effectively and in accordance with proper governance and sound financial and risk management principles.

Our concerns

You or your firm should not be used to provide banking facilities to clients or third parties. You must also actively consider whether there are any risk factors suggesting that the transaction on which you are acting, even if it appears to be the normal work of a solicitor, is not genuine or is suspicious.

Some of the key issues you should be aware of include the following.

Providing banking facilities through a client account is objectionable in itself

The prohibition in rule 14.5 is simple and clear: "You must not provide banking facilities through a client account." The second sentence in the rule recognises that holding and moving money for clients may not be a breach where doing so is related to proper instructions regarding a transaction on which you are acting or in connection with the professional services you are providing.

The courts have confirmed that operating a banking facility for clients divorced from any legal or other professional work is in itself objectionable. You are not regulated as a bank to provide such facilities. If you do provide banking facilities for clients, you are trading on the trust and reputation from your status as a solicitor in doing so.[4]

You must therefore only receive funds into your client account where there is a proper connection between receipt of the funds and the legal services you are providing. It is not sufficient that there is simply an underlying transaction if you are not providing legal advice on the matter, or if the handling of money has no proper connection to that advice.

There must be a proper connection between the underlying legal transaction or advice and the payments you are asked to make or receive

The rule is not intended to prevent usual practice in traditional work undertaken by solicitors such as conveyancing, company acquisitions, the administration of estates or dealing with formal trusts. So, it does not affect your ability to make usual and proper payments from client account when they are related to the transaction (such as the payment of estate agents' fees in a conveyancing transaction).

Whether there is such a proper connection will depend on the facts of each case. The fact that you have a retainer with a client is insufficient to allow you to process funds freely through client account. You need to think carefully about whether there is any justification for money to pass through your client account when it could be simply paid directly between the clients.

Historically, some solicitors have held funds for clients to enable them to pay the client's routine outgoings. This has been mainly for the clients' convenience such as where they are long term private clients or based abroad. In view of technological change, such as the ease of internet and telephone banking, we consider that allowing client account to be used in this way is no longer justifiable and a breach of rule 14.5. Clients can now operate their bank accounts from their own homes or indeed from anywhere in the world. Allowing clients simply to hold money in a client account gives rise to significant risks and may evade sophisticated controls and risk analyses that banks apply to money held for their customers.

Factors you should bear in mind when considering such issues include:

- Throughout the retainer, you should question why you are being asked to receive funds and for what purpose. The further the details of the transaction are from the norm or from the usual services a solicitor provides, the higher the risk that you may breach rule 14.5.

- You should always ask why you are being asked to make a payment or why the client cannot make or receive the payment directly themselves. The client's convenience is not a legitimate reason, nor is not having access to a bank account in the UK. Risk factors could involve the payment of substantial sums to others, including family members, or to corporate entities, particularly overseas, if there is no reason why the client could not receive the money into their own account and transfer it from there.

- You have a separate obligation to return client money to the client promptly, as soon as there is no longer any proper reason for you to retain those funds (rule 14.3 of the SRA Accounts Rules). If you retain funds in client account after completion of a transaction, there is risk (depending on how long you hold the money) of breaching both rule 14.3 and 14.5.

Risk of insolvency

You should be aware that a client may ask you to hold or deal with money in client account to avoid their obligations under insolvency legislation. Banks commonly withdraw facilities when told that there has been a winding up petition.

If a law firm allows its client account to be used in an insolvency situation to receive and process money, the client will improperly obtain a banking service which would otherwise be unavailable to it. There are also risks that in making payments to order. You may improperly favour one creditor over another.

Finally, section 127 of the Insolvency Act 1986 may apply to require creditors to reimburse payments from the client account in a subsequent liquidation. A solicitor who knowingly makes or facilitates such payments may be subject to a personal liability, in addition to the liability of the payee to reimburse the amount transferred.

Rule 14.5 and the risk of money laundering

Allowing a client account to be used as a banking facility carries with it the additional risk that you may assist money laundering. Our rules specifically require you to comply with all relevant anti-money laundering legislation including the Money Laundering, Terrorist Financing and Transfer of Funds (information on the payer) Regulations 2017 (MLRs).

You should also be familiar with our warning notices on:

- Money laundering and terrorist financing

- Investment schemes (including conveyancing)

- Investment schemes and client account

You must remain alert to any unusual or suspicious factors such as concern about the source of funds or what you are asked to do with them. Your obligation to comply with rule 14.5 offers an important 'first line of defence' against clients or others who seek to use your client account to launder money. It also helps you to secure professional independence from your client in compliance with Principle 3.

We have also seen firms making multiple transfers of money between the ledgers of different clients or companies without evidence of the purpose or legal basis for the transfers (such as Board resolutions or contracts). Transfers in such circumstances will be a breach of rule 14.5, particularly if they are simply carried out on request. It is an important principle of anti-money laundering regulation that transactions are properly recorded and can be reconstructed.[5] Such conduct would be of significant concern to us as it makes the tracking of money difficult and may be aggravated by the number and the value of such transfers.

Although, allowing client account to be used as a banking facility can facilitate money laundering, rule 14.5 exists independently of the anti-money laundering legislation and a breach of rule 14.5 does not require there to be evidence of laundering. If there is such evidence, we would expect a prosecution under the Proceeds of Crime Act 2002.[6] It is no defence to, or mitigation, of a breach of rule 14.5 that there was no evidence of actual laundering. Indeed, such arguments indicate a lack of insight into the reasons for rule 14.5 and the risks it addresses. For example:

- Rule 14.5 and the MLRs are to a large extent preventative provisions, intended to make it more difficult for people to use regulated businesses for improper purposes but also to deter law firms from helping such people.

- Any impropriety may be distant from the movement of money through a client account. In a classic laundering process, the movement through a client account may be the third or fourth stage of laundering the proceeds of a distant crime. But every stage contributes to the effectiveness of the laundering process.

- There are many potential forms of impropriety as well as money laundering. The Fuglers[7] case is one example in an insolvency context but there are many others such as hiding assets improperly in commercial or matrimonial disputes. You should also be aware of the risks in allowing your client account to be used to add credibility to questionable investment schemes.

- Movement of money through client account is attractive to those with an improper purpose:

  - Attempts by law enforcement or opposing litigants to obtain information may be blocked by a claim to privilege, even though the claim to privilege may be unsustainable on proper analysis with access to the documents.

  - It largely circumvents the sophisticated risk systems used by banks.

  - Solicitors, particularly in smaller firms, with a close relationship to an important client may be vulnerable to pressure to avoid making suspicious activity reports.

Enforcement action

You should be prepared to justify to us any decision that you make that it was appropriate for you to hold or move client money. Failure to have proper regard to this warning notice is likely to lead to disciplinary action.

Further guidance

For guidance on conduct issues, contact the Professional Ethics Guidance Team.

NOTES

1. Fuglers LLP v SRA [2014] EWHC 179 (Admin).
2. Premji Naram Patel v Solicitors' Regulation Authority [2012] EWHC 3373 (Admin).
3. Attorney General of Zambia v Meer Care & Desai [2008] EWCA Civ 1007.
4. Cranston J at [34] SRA v Patel [2012] EWHC 3373 (Admin), Fuglers & Ors v SRA [2014] EWHC 179 (Admin) (QB).
5. See, for example, regulation 40(2)(b) of the Money Laundering, Terrorist Financing and Transfer of Funds (information on the payer) Regulations 2017.
6. See for example R v Khan (Shadab) [2010] EWCA Crim 2841 (four years' imprisonment).
7. Fuglers LLP v SRA [2014] EWHC 179 (Admin).

9.7 Investment schemes and client account

[Issued by the Solicitors Regulation Authority on 21 September 2016]

Status

While this document does not form part of the SRA Handbook, the SRA will have regard to it when exercising its regulatory functions.

Who is this warning notice relevant to?

This warning notice is for law firms that are involved or asked to become involved in investment schemes. Members of the public who are considering paying money into an investment scheme where a law firm or solicitor is involved might also find it helpful.

We are currently looking to highlight this risk more directly to the public and will produce additional information in the near future.

Our expectations

That all firms and individuals working within the legal services market and regulated by us comply with the Principles and Outcomes of the SRA Handbook 2011.

Our concerns

1. We are particularly concerned about the dangers of investment schemes where the involvement of a law firm is used to give an impression of credibility or security.

2. The involvement of a law firm that is acting for the promoters of the scheme, or is holding the investment money, does not mean that the scheme is definitely safe.

3. Some law firms are continuing to facilitate investment schemes which are dubious. Such firms improperly provide a banking service through their client account. In designing the schemes, law firms and the promoters of the scheme pay attention to red flags that we and other regulators warn about. They then deliberately create a scheme that avoids raising those red flags.

4. To evade rules preventing the improper movement of money, they also manufacture a process which they claim means that the firm is acting in a genuine underlying transaction. The reality is that they are simply allowing their client account to be used to commit what is very likely to be a fraud – and to launder the proceeds.

5. The facilitation of dubious investment schemes by law firms is not new. Over many years, we have closed down law firms and many solicitors have been disciplined as a result of their involvement in such schemes. Some have been prosecuted and imprisoned by others.

6. From at least 1997 onwards, we have warned about this problem and about the improper use of client account. This warning notice is being issued to:

    a. provide updated information

    b. alert the public and firms to the increasing number of these schemes and the losses being suffered

    c. warn that indemnity insurers may refuse to pay for losses

    d. warn that those who pay money into these schemes without taking extreme care might not receive any compensation

    e. remind the public and firms that fraudsters are designing schemes to avoid the red flag warnings that we and other regulators issue from time to time.

7. We are aware of clear consumer losses arising from these schemes. Our initial analysis of cases we are currently dealing with suggests these losses are significant – amounting to many millions of pounds.

8. The true figure is probably much higher than we are aware of because some cases are being dealt with by other regulators or the police. We are also aware that, in some schemes, many of the investors are from abroad and have not been in contact with us.

The schemes

9. We first warned about high-yield investment frauds or banking instrument frauds in October 1997 and our warning card is quoted in Constantinides v Law Society. Our latest warning was issued on 10 September 2013.

10. We have also warned for many years about the improper use of client accounts. One of our warning cards was discussed in detail in Attorney General for Zambia v Meer Care & Desai. Our latest warning on this subject is dated 18 December 2014.

11. We still see crude, high-yield investment schemes where "investors" are offered extraordinary returns which are clearly unrealistic. In the case of Wood-Atkins, in which the solicitor was struck off, the returns were said to be 40 percent per month. There is reference to secret banking or monetisation transactions through which high returns can be made. They are invariably nonsensical.

12. Our previous warnings on high-yield investment fraud remain important. The nature of these schemes is now so well known that any solicitor who becomes involved in them may face being closed down urgently and alleged to have acted dishonestly. Members of the public who "invest" in these schemes are very unlikely to be compensated because it is so dangerous and imprudent to become involved in them.

13. Fraudsters have paid attention to warnings and moulded their schemes. They will now usually avoid offering ridiculous profits but will still mention returns that are very high compared to conventional investments, such as 20 percent per year. The return is only one of the red flag indicators.

14. Fraudsters will claim that there is a lucrative market in a new or unusual investment, and will try to mimic genuine investments. Investment schemes we have seen carried out and which have failed with investors' money being lost include:

    a. Carbon credit trading – this was never a market that it was sensible or practicable for individuals to try to invest in.

    b. Diamond trading, fine wines, "rare earth minerals" (or metals) and graphene – products like this can of course be bought and sold but there is no special way to make substantial returns.

    c. Landbanking – buying a small strip of land which it is said will increase hugely in value if planning permission is obtained to develop it, but permission is never obtained and was never likely to be obtained.

    d. Hotel rooms – taking a lease of a hotel room. There is no obvious reason for someone wanting to invest in a hotel to take out a lease and pay for the conveyancing of one room. These arrangements may well be collective investment schemes.

    e. Overseas agricultural rights – we have seen schemes in Ukraine, Africa and elsewhere.

    f. Famous works of art being the "security" for an investment scheme.

    g. Property developments abroad – money being taken from numerous members of the public to pay for holiday homes before they are built, often in countries where verifying the development or recovering losses if things go wrong is difficult or impossible.

15. Unusual investments abroad are particularly problematic. They are difficult to verify. The chances of recovering money if things go wrong are very low. The legal system may be very different. For example, we have seen schemes where investors are assured that their money will be held "in trust", but the law in the country where the investment is taking place does not recognise the concept of a trust.

16. The involvement of a law firm or solicitor does not provide security or assurance. It may actually suggest a need for particular caution. This is because:

    a. The law firm will usually be acting for the promoters of the scheme (and not for the investors) and will not be looking after the investors' interests, although they may not realise that – investors must get advice from their own trusted professionals

    b. The law firm may itself know very little about the scheme, particularly if it involves overseas investments

c.   An honest or safe investment scheme does not need to involve a solicitor to give it credibility

d.   There is no good reason why money being paid to an investment scheme should pass through the client account of a law firm acting for the investment company – it could and should be paid direct to the investment company

e.   investment company and the law firm manufacture a process, sometimes involving "certification" or "verification" that something has happened to give the impression that they are doing some legal work when they are not. The law firm will be instructed or pressured by the investment company to release the money as soon as possible and will often have no independent knowledge of whether what the investment company is telling them is true or not.

The promoters might use the involvement of a law firm in their direct or indirect marketing, either in brochures, on websites or by briefings to trade and other journalists. An anonymised example from a case involving losses of more than £20m is: "You enter into an escrow agreement with [X & Co] Solicitors to manage and maintain the credibility of the account process. This gives full protection for you and us."

17.   Another brochure in the same case said: "The money is looked after by an English law firm which holds an insurance policy."

18.   In that case, the insurance company refused to pay claims. We also see cases where perhaps £50m passes through a law firm but it only has insurance cover of £3m.

Evasion of our rules

19.   We are particularly concerned that law firms and their clients are deliberately designing schemes to give the false impression that genuine legal services are being provided. There is no need for a law firm to be involved or for money to pass through its accounts.

20.   We see what we consider to be spurious attempts to create a legal context. This could include supposed "verification" or "certification" which is of no real benefit or relevance. We also see "anti money laundering checks" on investors when there is no requirement for such checks in the transaction in question. Even if there were a need for them, they should be carried out by the investment company and not a law firm.

The SRA Principles

21.   Law firms must ensure that they do not become involved in potentially-fraudulent financial schemes.

22.   Failure to observe warnings could lead to disciplinary action or criminal prosecution. Attempts to limit your involvement, particularly by a purportedly "limited retainer" are ineffective in protecting you if you simply should not become involved.

23.   If you are, or are considering, becoming involved in any financial arrangement, you must ensure you comply with the Principles in the SRA Handbook. While all Principles may be relevant, some require particular attention:

a.   Integrity (Principle 2)

b.   Independence (Principle 3)

c.   best interests of the client (Principle 4)

d.   behaving in a way that maintains the trust the public places in you and the provision of legal services.(Principle 6)

24.   You must also ensure you do not take unfair advantage of investors in any way.

25.   If you are likely to become involved in transactions involving large sums of money,

individually or cumulatively, you must ensure you have sufficient indemnity insurance. Outcome (7.13) is that "you assess and purchase the level of professional indemnity insurance cover that is appropriate for your current and past practice, taking into account potential levels of claim by your clients and others and any alternative arrangements you or your client may make." Your insurers might want to aggregate claims and you find that you have insufficient cover.

Practical tips

21. What should law firms do?

a. Do not become involved in investment schemes that you do not fully understand, or have not independently and rigorously verified

b. Do not allow your client account – or any account you control – to be used to receive investment money that could simply be sent by an investor to an investment company

c. Do not attempt to evade rule 14.5 of the SRA Accounts Rules 2011 by trying to manufacture a process of legal work or advice

d. Do not attempt to evade rule 14.5 by moving money through another account – you are still facilitating the scheme and might be helping launder the proceeds of crime

e. Do not assume that you can escape liability in law or in conduct by giving investors an obscure warning that you do not act for them

f. Bear in mind that even if you do not act for investors you have duties not to take unfair advantage of them and to act honestly and with integrity

g. Do not draft or facilitate the use of contracts that are unfair to the investors – promulgating a contract with unfair terms may be part of an overall case that you have taken unfair advantage, whether or not consumer protection legislation applies

h. Do not give undertakings as "security"

i. Do not allow your involvement to be used to promote the scheme in any way

j. Regularly check the internet to ensure your involvement is not being used to promote the scheme in any way and take action to stop or correct this – your name might not be mentioned, but if you are acting in some way and there is reference to the involvement of a law firm, you still need to stop it

k. Be particularly alert to any mention, directly or indirectly, of your insurance or the Compensation Fund

l. Research the investment company and any intermediaries fully by reference to official sources such as regulators and Companies House, also paying appropriate attention to media or other commentary

m. If you become aware that someone in your firm is involved in an investment scheme, ensure that you fully understand it and take urgent steps if necessary to cease involvement

n. Be particularly careful about acting for an investment company, ceasing to act and then acting for the investors – that gives rise to concern the firm is still looking after the interests of the investment company (particularly if someone who acted for the investment company leaves the firm to join the company or to be associated with it)

o. Bear in mind that in helping an investment company to carry out one of these schemes you might well be facilitating a fraud and laundering the proceeds.

Enforcement action

Failure to comply with this warning notice is likely to lead to disciplinary action.

Further assistance

If you require further assistance with understanding your obligations in relation to high yield investment schemes please contact the Professional Ethics Guidance Team.

If you have evidence of one of these schemes or are concerned that you have been approached or have become involved, please contact your SRA supervisor.

If you are already involved and become concerned, urgently contact the Red Alert line

9.8 Investment schemes (including conveyancing)

[Issued by the Solicitors Regulation Authority on 23 June 2017]

Status

While this document does not form part of the SRA Handbook, we will have regard to it when exercising its regulatory functions.

Who is this warning notice relevant to?

All law firms should read this warning notice because so-called "investment" schemes are being continually changed to avoid features that have been warned about previously. Practitioners in many fields of law may find that they are at risk of facilitating a dubious investment scheme.

This warning is also relevant to members of the public who are considering paying money into what is promoted as an "investment" scheme where a law firm or solicitor is involved. They also should also read this warning and other material we have published.

We will be issuing a further direct warning to the public and law firms should ensure that they are familiar with that and all previous warnings.

Our expectations

That all firms and individuals regulated by us comply with the Principles and Outcomes of the SRA Handbook 2011 and have had regard to our published warning notices.

Our concerns

1. We are particularly concerned about the dangers of schemes where the involvement of a law firm is used to give an impression of credibility or security. That is considered in our previous warnings.

2. Schemes are being devised to mislead and to try to evade rules and previous warnings.

3.   Dubious or risky schemes are being presented as routine conveyancing or investment in "land" when the reality is very different.

4.   Dubious schemes are being designed in particular to try to evade rule 14.5 of the SRA Accounts Rules 2011 by which law firms must not provide banking facilities.

This notice includes reference to schemes that are being presented as routine conveyancing when our view is that they involve consumer clients unwittingly financing high risk or fraudulent property development. Those designing these schemes will no doubt move into other types of transaction or even possibly fraudulent litigation in order to avoid the more obvious indicators of fraud or high risk "investments".

You must be very alert to the risks of becoming involved in a dubious transaction and ensure that you investigate the circumstances carefully.If there are concerns, you should refuse to act or consider ceasing to act .Any involvement in a dubious scheme is likely to constitute serious misconduct.

Conveyancing or purported investment in land

Financing a development

Schemes are being promoted as involving the routine buying of a property when in reality the buyers' money is being used to finance a development or refurbishment. This is of particular concern when in unusual developments such as the buying of individual hotel rooms, rooms in care homes, or self-storage units. Our concerns also apply to some extent to any "off-plan" purchases. These may not be investment frauds but they still involve higher risk than the simple purchase of a property.

High deposits" are used by property developers to finance their developments. Investors are not being advised, or properly advised, that this often presents a much higher risk than simply buying an existing house or apartment.

Where you are acting for the buyers in these types of transactions, you must advise clients fully about the transaction and how it significantly differs from the simple buying of an existing property, such as:

1.   Buying a property not yet built or completed i.e. off plan or subject to significant refurbishment, involves substantial risk that the developer or seller could fail and money will be lost

2.   Promises of substantial returns are often illusory – and standard warnings in publicity about the risk of capital loss are not enough to ensure that a law firm has properly advised a client upon the transaction (see outcomes (1.1),(1.2),(1.12) of the Code of Conduct)

3.   High "deposits" are being used to finance the development (see below).

We are seeing cases of solicitors simply processing transactions for buyers and adopting the language of conveyancing. The effect is to mask what is really happening. For example, investors provide money for a "deposit" which is released to the seller upon some (often spurious) condition. The investor's money is used to buy the property or finance its building or refurbishment. This carries substantial risks such as the money being misappropriated, the seller failing to complete the scheme or the seller becoming insolvent.

The usual deposit in a conveyancing transaction is 10 percent. It is paid to ensure that the buyer will complete the contract. In dubious schemes we have seen , the "deposit" has been 30 percent or even 80 percent. These are not market standard deposits but involve both pre-payment of the price and effectively the providing of finance to the developer. Referring to them as deposits is part of the psychology of presenting a risky "investment" as routine conveyancing. Clients are actually paying their money into often high-risk property development, and substantial losses have been suffered. You should ensure that clients fully understand the risks and it may well be necessary to strongly advise clients against entering into the transaction.

Taking a lease of a room, a storage unit etc

Schemes are being promoted by which investors take a lease of a supposed asset such as a hotel room, care home room, parking place or storage unit. This list is not exhaustive as fraudsters will continue to search for similar "assets".

Buyers pay a substantial amount for the asset and also pay conveyancing costs sometimes of several thousand pounds. There is no obvious reason for someone wanting to invest in a hotel to take out a lease and pay for the conveyancing of one room.

Investors may be inappropriately reassured by thinking that taking out a lease means that they have an interest in land or property when the reality is that their investment is dependent upon the business being well managed. In these circumstances there is no greater security than there would be in the more conventional method of buying shares in the hotel.

We also see no particular reason why such investments should provide high returns. and solicitors must – properly – advise their clients of this and of the risk

The Serious Fraud Office have announced an investigation into losses of up to £120m arising from self-storage schemes.[1]

Collective investment scheme – criminal liability

Many of these schemes are likely to be "collective investment schemes" under s235 of the Financial Services and Markets Act 2000.[2] If those involved in the schemes are not authorised by the FCA they will be committing a serious criminal offence and are likely to be imprisoned as was the group convicted in a land-banking case including a solicitor.[3]

In that case when sentencing the solicitor and others involved in the "landbanking" the judge commented:

"It was a subtle and cruel fraud because it involves the concept of owning land, a commodity that the public are bound to think has value and on which they cannot lose and on which they can easily be persuaded that they can make very substantial profits."[4]

Unfair terms

The documentation in dubious schemes is often, but not always, obscure It is frequently unfair to the consumer and any solicitor involved in drafting such documentation must pay close attention to the detail. The unfairness of the terms is often clear additional evidence that unfair advantage is being taken of the investor or buyer.

Evasion of rule 14.5 of the SRA Accounts Rules 2011

Fraudsters want to tell investors that a law firm is involved in a transaction because that gives credibility to their scheme.

We have warned about this several times and we brought in rule 14.5 to prevent law firms from providing both credibility and the facility simply to transfer investors' money through client account. This facilitates the fraud and provides a first form of layering of the proceeds. We are concerned that processes of apparent legal work or advice (such as unnecessary conveyancing) are being manufactured and designed both to evade rule 14.5 and to generate fees for the law firm that the client should not have to incur.

Insurance bonds

We have seen schemes promoted as being secured by insurance bonds which have proved worthless.

Where you are aware that the transaction is said to be secured by an insurance bond you should satisfy yourself about its validity or enforceability and advise the client properly and fully. Risk factors include:

1.   The issuer of the bond is not regulated.

2.   The issuer is based in a jurisdiction where it is likely to be very difficult to enforce the bond.

3.   Where there is any doubt about the propriety or financial soundness of the issuer.

4.   The bond is written in terms unfamiliar to a lawyer in England & Wales.

5.   Reputable insurers do not offer bonds for the particular type of investment.

Relationship with investors

In most dubious schemes, the law firm acts for the promoter and not for the investor.

However, we have also seen firms acting for both or sometimes for the investor only. If you are not acting for investors, you must make that absolutely clear and strongly advise them to take their own independent advice from professionals they choose themselves. You will be at risk under Outcome (11.1) and Indicative Behaviour (IB)11.7 if you do not.

Attempts to prevent or reduce the likelihood of investors obtaining their own legal advice may well be evidence of dishonesty.

Any attempt to prevent buyers or investors from obtaining objective and independent legal advice is a serious red flag indicator. This could involve, for example:

1.   Clear or subtle attempts to dissuade them from instructing their own solicitors – such as indications that they do not need legal advice or that the promoter and their solicitors will "deal with everything".

2.   A requirement, or pressure, to instruct a particular firm (which may have past links with the developer or be motivated not to advise about the risks of the transaction to maintain a flow of work).

3.   A refusal by the scheme promoter to accept any changes to standard "conveyancing" documentation – where the terms are in any way unusual such as requiring a high "deposit" or its release to finance the development.

We have seen evidence of conflicts of interest. Acting for both investor and developer is likely to be serious misconduct. Outcome (3.5) (see also IB 3.4)

We have seen solicitors supposedly acting for investors who appear more focused on ensuring the scheme continues than upon advising their investor clients properly.

Firms sometimes argue that they were not required to advise clients on a transaction because they had a "limited retainer". We have not seen a case where the retainer was limited at the client's (genuine) request. Limited retainers, particularly when dealing with consumers and small businesses, are in fact a red flag warning of serious misconduct. The law firm is aware that there is or might be a problem and is trying to avoid telling the client this.

The fact that a law firm acts only for the promoter does not mean that they owe no duties in conduct to buyers or investors. Solicitors must not facilitate dubious transactions. They must not take unfair advantage. They must act with integrity. Solicitors must rigorously assess the transaction and refuse or cease to act if, applying all warnings we have issued and considering past cases, there is any doubt about its propriety or whether buyers or investors are being misled in any way.

If you fail to make inquiries you will be at risk under the principles detailed below. In these circumstances the courts have warned that they "consider that by ordinary standards such a state of mind is dishonest."[5]

The SRA Principles

You must ensure that you do not become involved in potentially-fraudulent financial schemes. You must also ensure that you advise your clients fully, frankly and in good faith.

If you fail to observe our warnings this could lead to disciplinary action or criminal prosecution. Attempting to protect yourself by, for example, limiting your retainer will be ineffective if you simply should not become involved.

If you are, or are considering, becoming involved in any financial arrangement, you must ensure you comply with the Principles in the SRA Handbook. While all Principles may be relevant, some require particular attention:

a. Integrity (Principle 2)

b. Independence (Principle 3)

c. Best interests of the client (Principle 4)

d. Behaving in a way that maintains the trust the public places in you and the provision of legal services. (Principle 6)

You must also ensure you do not take unfair advantage of investors in any way either for your client or yourself.

Practical tips

a. Be familiar with all of our warnings.

b. Analyse the scheme or supposed transaction carefully and critically, with our warnings in mind.

c. Refuse to act or cease to act if you have concerns.

d. Look critically at documents to assess what they mean (if anything) and whether they are fair.

e. Apply the SRA Principles

f. Avoid rationalising suspicious factors – such as by thinking "the warnings do not mention the type of transaction I have been asked to deal with, so it must be safe".

g. Do not allow your client account – or any account you control – to be used to receive investment money that could simply be sent by an investor directly to an investment company.

h.   Do not attempt to evade rule 14.5 of the SRA Accounts Rules 2011 by trying to manufacture a process of legal work or advice.

Enforcement action

Failure to comply with this warning notice is likely to lead to disciplinary action.

Further assistance

If you require further assistance with understanding your obligations in relation to supposed investment schemes please contact the Professional Ethics Guidance team.

NOTES

1.   https://www.sfo.gov.uk/2017/05/22/sfo-seeks-information-from-investors-in-storage-pod-schemes/   See   also https://www.theguardian.com/money/2017/may/27/pensions-scam-self-storage-serious-fraud-office-warning
2.   See for example Financial Conduct Authority v Capital Alternatives Limited [2015] EWCA Civ 284.
3.   R v Crawley, Walker, Forsyth, Peters and Petrou, Southwark Crown Court, April 2015, see https:// www.fca.org.uk/news/press-releases/eight-convicted-role-unauthorised-collective-investment-scheme
4.   R v Crawley mentioned above.
5.   Barlow Clowes International Ltd & Anor v Eurotrust International Ltd & Ors (Isle of Man) [2005] UKPC 37.

9.9 Land banking schemes

[Issued by the Solicitors Regulation Authority on 14 September 2012]

This warning notice is for anyone who is involved or who is considering acting for clients involved in the promotion or facilitation of investment schemes which involve selling plots of land to investors on the basis of prospective planning permission.

Whilst this notice does not form part of the Solicitors Regulation Authority's (SRA) Handbook, the SRA may have regard to it when exercising its regulatory functions.

The issue

The SRA is aware that there are a number of fraudulent investment schemes. These are typically where agricultural, brownfield or other blighted land is acquired at low cost and divided into plots for sale to investors. Investors are informed that the land will soar in value once planning permission is obtained. However, as the land will usually be on a green belt or protected site, the land is unlikely to obtain planning permission or achieve the value intimated by the operator, resulting in the investor paying an inflated price for the land. This practice is sometimes known as "land banking".

In a recent case prosecuted by The Financial Services Authority (FSA), it was estimated that investors paid up to £32 million for land, when the actual value of the land was in the region of £3 million. The Financial Services Authority (FSA) estimate that the loss to investors through land banking schemes, is in the region of £200 million since 2006. Some schemes are run as 'collective investment schemes' and should be, but are rarely, authorised by the FSA.

The Principles

You should be aware that as a regulated individual or firm, you or your firm may be used by operators of land banking schemes to provide credibility to the scheme. You may also be asked to facilitate their operation by registering transfers of the individual plots and dealing with the proceeds of their sale. If you are involved or are considering becoming involved in a land banking scheme you should consider if you can comply with the Principles in the SRA Handbook and in particular:

Principle 2 – act with integrity;

Principle 3 – not allow your independence to be compromised;

Principle 4 – act in the best interests of each client;

Principle 6 – behave in a way that maintains the trust the public places in you and the provision of legal services;

Principle 8 – run your business or carry out you role in the business effectively and in accordance with proper governance and sound financial an risk management principles.

As land banking schemes may require you to deal with unrepresented investors, the outcomes in chapter 11 of the SRA Code of Conduct 2011 ("the Code") – relations with third parties – will also be relevant.

Complying with the Principles

To comply with the Principles it is important that you and your firm are able to identify land banking schemes and manage the risks associated with such schemes. Ensuring that you and everyone in your firm is aware of the following should assist with this:

FSA warnings: The FSA has released multiple warnings which detail how land banking schemes work and how you can protect yourself. You should consider these warnings and in particular the warning entitled Land banking 3 January 2007.

Misleading statements: Land banking schemes are often promoted on the basis that planning permission is imminent or that a well known company is about to buy the land. The SRA is aware that forged Land Registry letters and Land Registry estate plan approval letters have been used as evidence that planning permission is available when this is not the case. Also the obtaining of planning permission may be in the control of a management company which may have no intention of applying for planning permission.

If you are acting for the operator of a scheme you must ensure any information passed to third parties is not misleading. In such circumstances you must achieve O(11.1) – a requirement not to take unfair advantage of a third party.

Operators: Operators of land banking schemes are often based overseas, making it difficult for an investor to recover funds invested in a scheme or for enforcement action to be taken against the operator. Operators may also attempt to conceal the original value of the land by inter-company transactions which inflate the original purchase price.

Investors: Investors in land banking schemes may be unrepresented or based overseas and may be unaware of the risks involved in land banking schemes. Some investors may be investing their life savings in schemes or may have been induced into investing in a scheme on the basis they will be protected because you or your firm is regulated. In such circumstances, again, you must achieve O(11.1) (a requirement that you do not take unfair advantage of third parties on your client's behalf).

If you are acting for an investor in a landbanking scheme you must comply with Principle 4 (i.e. act in your client's best interests) and achieve the outcomes in Chapter 1 of the Code (you and your client). In particular, O(1.2) requires you to provide services to your in a manner which protects their interests in their matter, and O(1.5) makes it clear that the service you provide to clients must be competent, delivered in a timely manner and take account of your clients' needs and circumstances. This requires you to discuss with and advise clients of the risks and to ensure they understand all the relevant issues.

Please take extra care if it is envisaged that your retainer is to be limited in nature, for example it excludes providing advice to clients or is solely restricted to the registration of the properties. Before agreeing to act in these circumstances you should consider whether it is necessary to carry out due diligence in relation to the scheme in order to avoid unwittingly becoming involved in a fraudulent scheme. In particular Outcome 9.1 contains a requirement that your independence and your professional judgement are not prejudiced by virtue of any arrangement with another person. Outcome 9.2 makes it clear that you must ensure that your clients' interests are protected regardless of the interests of an introducer or fee sharer or your interest in receiving referrals. Outcome 9.3 makes it clear that you should ensure that; clients are in a position to make informed decisions about how to pursue their matter.

Collective investment schemes: Some land banking schemes are deliberately structured as 'collective investment schemes' (CIS) to prevent investors making their own enquiries and applications for planning permission. A CIS is an arrangement that enables a number of investors to pool their assets and have these professionally managed by an independent manager. Problems may be encountered because of the need for consent from all plot holders or the managing agent before an application for planning permission, which may never be given. A CIS must be authorised by the FSA. The definition of a CIS can be found in section 235 of the Financial Services and Markets Act 2000 and you should consider whether a scheme which has not been authorised by the FSA might fall within that definition.

Handling investor funds: The promoters of Land banking schemes will often require you or your firm to hold investor funds in your client account. There are specific outcomes in chapter 11 of the SRA Code of Conduct 2011 in relation to undertakings. They may also ask you to pay the proceeds of sale to unconnected third parties, who may be based off shore, or purchase high value assets on behalf of the company, its members or directors in which case consideration should also be given to compliance with Rule 14.5 of the SRA Accounts Rules 2011 (the prohibition on providing banking facilities through your client account) – and compliance with your obligations under the Money Laundering Regulations and related legislation.

Enforcement action

Whilst the SRA is committed to working constructively with firms, the SRA will take enforcement action against individuals or firms that fail to address the issues and risks associated with land banking schemes. The FSA are also investigating and prosecuting operators and those associated with land banking schemes.

The Solicitors Disciplinary Tribunal have recently prosecuted two cases involving solicitors in land banking schemes which were found to be collective investment schemes. These cases are Stephen Peter David Murrell who was struck off the roll and ordered to pay costs in the region of £42,000 and Ian David Campbell Smith who was fined £10,000 and ordered to pay costs in the sum of £25,000.

Further assistance

If you require further assistance with understanding your obligations in relation to land banking schemes please contact the Ethics Helpline [0370 606 25 77].

9.10 Money laundering and terrorist financing

[Issued by the Solicitors Regulation Authority 8 December 2014/Updated 2 March 2018]

Status

Whilst this document does not form part of the SRA Handbook, the SRA may have regard to it when exercising its regulatory functions.

Who is this warning notice relevant to?

This warning notice is relevant to all regulated persons who have a legal obligation to ensure that they:

- **do not** facilitate money laundering or terrorist financing

- **do report** any suspicious transactions.

This notice highlights warning signs which you should be aware of, and which may require you to take action in order to avoid committing a criminal offence or breaching your professional obligations under the Solicitors Regulation Authority (SRA) Handbook.

The Money Laundering, Terrorist Financing and Transfer of Funds (Information on the Payer) Regulations 2017 (MLR 2017) came into force on 26 June 2017 replacing the now repealed Money Laundering Regulations 2007. As a result law firms may need to make changes to their procedures and systems. [Read guidance on the key changes.]

The SRA mandatory outcomes

You should have regard to the specific outcomes under the SRA Code of Conduct 2011 Outcome 7.5 – to comply with your legal obligations under the Proceeds of Crime Act 2002, the Terrorism Act 2000 and the MLR 2017.

You must ensure that you do not facilitate money laundering, even when money does not pass through your firm's accounts. Your firm should have appropriate policies and procedures in place to protect it from being used for money laundering or terrorist financing Outcomes 7.2 and 7.3.

Our concerns

The SRA supervises those it regulates for compliance with money laundering legislation. Firms must move into compliance with the new regulation's. We are concerned that some firms have not made enough progress towards compliance by failing to have adequate systems and controls to prevent, detect and report money laundering.

The Financial Action Task Force (FATF), an independent inter-governmental body, issued a report in 2013 highlighting the vulnerabilities of legal professionals to money laundering and terrorist financing, in which it identified 42 'Red Flag Indicators'.

Being aware of these indicators or warning signs of money laundering and terrorist financing should assist you in applying a risk based approach to meeting your obligations under the

Money Laundering Regulations 2017 and other money laundering legislation. If red flag indicators are present in your dealings with a client, you should ask further questions and consider making a suspicious activity report to your firm's Money Laundering Reporting Officer (MLRO) or the National Crime Agency, as appropriate.

Our expectations

We expect all firms and individuals regulated by us to comply with money laundering legislation including taking appropriate steps to conduct customer due diligence when required to do so by the Money Laundering Regulations 2017. We expect firms and individuals to be aware of, and act properly upon, warning signs that a transaction may be suspicious.

The warning signs highlighted by FATF include:

If the client:

- Is secretive or evasive about who they are, the reason for the transaction, or the source of funds.
- Uses an intermediary, or does not appear to be directing the transaction, or appears to be disguising the real client.
- Avoids personal contact without good reason.
- Refuses to provide information or documentation or the documentation provided is suspicious.
- Has criminal associations.
- Has unusual level of knowledge about money laundering processes.
- Does not appear to have a business association with the other parties but appears to be connected to them.

If the source of funds is unusual, such as:

- Large cash payments.
- Unexplained payments from a third party.
- Large private funding that does not fit the business or personal profile of the payer.
- Loans from non-institutional lenders.
- Use of corporate assets to fund private expenditure of individuals.
- Use of multiple accounts or foreign accounts.

If the transaction has unusual features, such as:

- Size, nature, frequency or manner of execution.
- Early repayment of mortgages/loans.
- Short repayment periods for borrowing.
- An excessively high value is placed on assets/securities.
- It is potentially loss making.
- Involving unnecessarily complicated structures or steps in transaction.

- Repetitive instructions involving common features/parties or back to back transactions with assets rapidly changing value.

- The transaction is unusual for the client, type of business or age of the business.

- Unexplained urgency, requests for short cuts or changes to the transaction particularly at last minute.

- Use of a Power of Attorney in unusual circumstances.

- No obvious commercial purpose to the transaction.

- Instructions to retain documents or to hold money in your client account.

- Abandoning transaction and/or requests to make payments to third parties or back to source.

- Monies passing directly between the parties.

- Litigation which is settled too easily or quickly and with little involvement by you.

If the instructions are unusual for your business such as:

- Outside your or your firm's area of expertise or normal business, or if client is not local to you and there is no explanation as to why a firm in your locality has been chosen.

- Willingness of client to pay high fees.

- Unexplained changes to legal advisers.

- Your client appears unconcerned or lacks knowledge about the transaction.

If there are geographical concerns such as:

- Unexplained connections with and movement of monies between other jurisdictions.

- Connections with jurisdictions which are subject to sanctions or are suspect because drug production, terrorism or corruption is prevalent or there is a lack of money laundering regulation. Links to information about jurisdictions subject to sanctions or considered high risk.

Enforcement action

Failure to comply with this warning notice may lead to disciplinary action, criminal prosecution or both.

Further information

[Read full guidance on the 2017 Money Laundering Regulations.]

[Read resources and information about AML compliance.]

If you want technical advice about the questions, you can contact our Ethics Guidance helpline.

9.11 Money laundering and terrorist financing – suspicious activity reports

[Issued by the Solicitors Regulation Authority on 8 December 2014]

Status

Whilst this document does not form part of the SRA Handbook, the SRA may have regard to it when exercising its regulatory functions.

Who is this warning notice relevant to?

This warning notice is relevant to all regulated persons, especially Compliance Officers for Legal Practice (COLPs), Compliance Officers for Finance and Administration (COFAs) and firms' Money Laundering Reporting Officers.

Our concerns

The Solicitors Regulation Authority (SRA) supervises those it regulates for compliance with money laundering legislation. In the course of its business, the SRA has identified an increasing risk of firms failing to have adequate systems and controls to prevent, detect and report money laundering.

Recently, the National Crime Agency (NCA) produced an analysis of SARs it receives for consent to proceed with transactions ("consent SARs"). You will know that under the Proceeds of Crime Act (POCA) 2002 you are required to submit a SAR to the NCA if you know or suspect, or have reason to know or suspect, that an individual is engaged in money laundering and the information has come to you in the course of your business. There are similar obligations to submit SARs in relation to terrorist financing offences under the Terrorism Act (TACT) 2000.

The analysis conducted by the NCA concluded that a disproportionately high percentage of reports received from the legal sector were of poor quality because firms were providing inadequate information. The NCA has announced that, from 1 October 2014, consent SARs that do not contain reasons for suspicion, or a statement regarding criminal property, will be closed by the NCA upon receipt. The NCA has published detailed guidance on this new process.

The implications

Failure to make a disclosure to the NCA in appropriate circumstances can in itself be a criminal offence, and proceeding with a transaction in the absence of consent may result in the commission of a principal money laundering offence.

Our expectations

You should have regard to the SRA Principles; your specific obligations under Chapter 7 of the SRA Code of Conduct 2011, in particular Outcome 7.5 – to comply with the Money Laundering Regulations 2007; and generally with legislation such as your legal obligations under POCA 2002 and TACT 2000.

We expect all firms and individuals regulated by us to comply with the NCA guidance in relation to submitting consent SARs.

The NCA has stated that one of the causes behind delays in the turnaround of consent requests is the non inclusion of one or more of the elements required (where known in your course of business) of a submission, namely:

1.   The information or other matter that gives grounds for knowledge, suspicion or belief;

2.   A description of the property that is known, suspected or believed to be criminal property, terrorist property or derived from terrorist property;

3.   A description of the prohibited act for which consent is sought;

4.   If known, the identity of the person or persons known or suspected to be involved in money laundering or who committed or attempted to commit an offence under any of sections 15 to18 of TACT 2000;

5.   If known, the whereabouts of the property that is known or suspected to be criminal property, terrorist property or derived from terrorist property; and

If under (4) and (5) the identity of the person or persons and/or the whereabouts of the property is not known, then any information believed or reasonably believed that may assist in identifying (4) or (5) or both.

The SRA principles

You have a duty to ensure you comply with money laundering legislation. Failure to do so may result in you breaching one or more of the SRA Principles, including:

* Principle 1 – Uphold the rule of law and the proper administration of justice.

* Principle 4 – Act in the best interests of your client.

* Principle 6 – Behave in a way that maintains the trust the public places in you and in the provision of legal services.

* Principle 7 – Comply with your legal and regulatory obligations.

* Principle 8 – Run your business or carry out your role in the business effectively and in accordance with proper governance and sound financial and risk management principles.

The SRA mandatory outcomes

In order to achieve Outcome 7.2 and Outcome 7.3 of the SRA Code of Conduct 2011, we also expect firms to have systems and procedures in place which are adequate to prevent, detect and report money laundering; and that firms monitor the efficacy of such systems to ensure that any risks to compliance are identified and addressed. This includes ensuring that relevant staff are appropriately trained and regularly updated in respect of the relevant legislation and their professional obligations, including the NCA's requirements referred to above (see Outcome 7.6).

Enforcement action

Failure to comply with this enforcement notice may lead to disciplinary action, criminal prosecution or both.

Further guidance

From us

For guidance on warning signs that a transaction may be suspicious see our Warning notice: Money laundering and terrorist financing.

From others

NCA guidance on completing SARs; making consent requests; and the closure of inadequate consent SARs:

- The SARS regime
- Submitting a suspicious activity report (SAR) within the regulated sector

Further information and assistance on your reporting obligations can be found at Chapter 8 of the Law Society practice note and in the Law Society advice article Help! I'm a new MLRO: making a report.

9.12 Money missing from client account

[Issued by the Solicitors Regulation Authority on 12 June 2015]

Status

Whilst this document does not form part of the SRA Handbook, we may have regard to it when exercising our regulatory functions.

Who is this notice relevant to?

This warning notice is aimed at all those we regulate but is particularly relevant to you if you are a manager of a firm or a firm's COFA or COLP.

Any deficiency on client account exposes clients and others to a risk of financial loss and damage to public confidence. Missing money must be replaced with extreme urgency.

The Solicitors Regulation Authority's Principles

You have a duty to ensure that client money is safe. Operating a deficient client account may cause you to breach one or more of the SRA Principles, including:

- Principle 2 – acting with integrity
- Principle 5 – acting in the best interests of each client;
- Principle 6 – behaving in a way that maintains the trust the public places in you and in the provision of legal services;
- Principle 10 – protecting client money and assets.

The Solicitors Regulation Authority's mandatory outcomes

You should also have regard to the following mandatory Outcomes:

O(1.1) You treat your clients fairly;

O(1.2) You provide services to your clients in a manner which protects their interests in their matter, subject to the proper administration of justice;

O(1.12) Clients are in a position to make informed decisions about the services they need, how their matter will be handled and the options available to them;

O(1.16) You inform current clients if you discover any act or omission which could give rise to a claim by them against you.

O(4.2) Any individual who is advising a client makes that client aware of all information material to that retainer of which the individual has personal knowledge.

SRA Accounts Rules 2011

It is your duty to remedy breaches of the SRA Accounts Rules 2011. Specifically Rule 7 states:

7.1 Any breach of the rules must be remedied promptly upon discovery. This includes the replacement of any money improperly withheld or withdrawn from a client account.

7.2 In a private practice, the duty to remedy breaches rests not only on the person causing the breach, but also on all the principals in the firm. This duty extends to replacing missing client money from the principals' own resources, even if the money has been misappropriated by an employee or another principal, and whether or not a claim is subsequently made on the firm's insurance or the Compensation Fund.

The implications of missing money

It is important that all managers and employees of a firm fully understand the implications of money being missing from client account, including:

- There is a clear duty in the SRA Accounts Rules to replace a deficiency in a client account.

- In the general law, trustees in breach of trust also have a duty to replace a deficiency.

- In any event, operating a deficient client account is very likely to involve immediate and continuing breaches of trust – by paying some clients their full entitlement, the amount left for other clients reduces.

- Ultimately, a deficient trust account is likely to be distributed pro rata.

- You may well breach your duty to act in the best interests of clients if you pay client money into an already deficient account without fully informed consent – no properly advised client would pay funds into a deficient account with the risk of only receiving a proportion back. Failing to inform clients exposes them to a risk of loss (see O 4.2).

- Until missing money is replaced, you should not take costs from the client account – you cannot "properly" require payment of your fees from money held in a client account in such circumstances and so rules 17.2 and 17.3 of the SRA Accounts Rules 2011 will not apply. Nor is it in the best interests of clients for you to take costs from client account when there is insufficient in the account for you to pay them in full.

- If you or your insurers do not replace the money promptly, you are at serious risk of intervention by the SRA. Intervention may be necessary in any event if there is reason to suspect dishonesty or other grounds for intervention arise.

- Since it is unlikely that a deficient client account can be operated without further breach of trust, you may well need to apply to the court for directions as to how to distribute the remaining funds.

- Offences under the Fraud Act 2006 may be committed once you are on notice that money is missing if you do not act properly and honestly.

Complying with the Principles

It is critical that to protect your clients, you do not operate a deficient client account and that you keep client money safe.

If you are the firm's COFA, you must take all reasonable steps to ensure compliance with the SRA Accounts Rules 2011 and record any failure to comply. You also have an obligation to report material breaches to the SRA as soon as reasonably practicable.

If you are a manager, the COFA is not a substitute for you and your firm's responsibilities and obligations. Systems and actions that should aid compliance include:

- having appropriate accounting procedures for your business;
- having clear reporting lines to encourage appropriate reporting by all members of staff;
- ensuring that your systems only allow appropriate individuals to authorise payments from client account;
- immediately investigating and taking action against any member of staff who may have acted dishonestly or committed any financial impropriety whether in relation to client account or not;
- taking regular steps to monitor, review and manage risks.

Behaviours of concern that you should be alert to in your firm include:

- failure to deliver bills or provide written notification of costs;
- any suggestions of overcharging;
- borrowing from clients in the capacity of trustee or attorney, which is unsecured;
- borrowing that remains outstanding, in breach of any agreement to pay;
- delay or failure to account for monies due;
- any accumulation or pattern of one or more of the above.

If you identify that money is missing

If you identify that money is missing, you have a duty to take steps to ensure it is replaced, in full, immediately.

If you are a manager of the firm, you have a duty to replace missing client money from your own resources. It may be necessary for you to obtain a loan to do this. It is irrelevant that fault may not lie with you personally.

You may be able to make a claim on your professional indemnity insurance. The obligation to remedy a breach of the SRA Accounts Rules 2011 is treated as civil liability for the purposes of clause 1 of the Minimum Terms and Conditions.

Operating the client account when it is deficient may make you liable for breach of trust and failure to act in the best interests of your clients. If you cannot replace the missing money and your insurers do not do so very promptly, you may be unable lawfully to operate the account. You will have to consider the position as a matter of trust law including whether you need to apply to court for directions as trustee.

Enforcement action

Whilst we are committed to working constructively with you, we will take enforcement action if missing money is not replaced. Failure to replace missing money will usually lead to an intervention. It should not be assumed that replacing the money means that an intervention is not necessary since the conduct giving rise to the shortage may evidence dishonesty or other breaches giving rise to a need to intervene to protect clients and the public.

Further assistance

If you require further assistance with understanding your obligations in relation to anything please contact the Professional Ethics Guidance Team.

9.13 Offensive communications

[Issued by the Solicitors Regulation Authority on 24 August 2017]

Status

While this document does not form part of the SRA Handbook, we will have regard to it when exercising our regulatory functions.

Who is this warning notice relevant to?

This guidance is relevant to you if:

- you are a solicitor, a REL or an RFL and your communications fall short of the standards expected of the profession, whether in the course of private practice, in-house practice, or outside practice

- you work in an SRA-regulated practice as a manager, consultant, employee or trainee, whether as a lawyer or an unqualified person, in relation to communications made by you during the course of business

- you are an SRA-regulated law firm or the COLP in a SRA-regulated law firm

Our concerns

We have experienced a significant increase in the number of complaints we receive concerning inappropriate communications, specifically (but not limited to) in relation to emails and the use of social media, both inside and outside of practice.

Examples of the type of behaviour we have investigated, (and which we subsequently referred to the SDT), include:

- making offensive or pejorative comments relating to another person's race, sexual orientation or religion

- referring to women in derogatory terms and making sexually explicit comments

- making comments which harass or victimise the recipient

- using language intended to shock or threaten

- making offensive or abusive comments to another firm about that firm or its client, or to individuals who are unrepresented

The warning below focuses on social media (which in this context includes emails, texts and social media networks), but it is also relevant to communication by telephone or letter.

The SRA Principles and mandatory Outcomes

You must comply with the Principles and in particular:

- Uphold the rule of law and the proper administration of justice – Principle 1
- Act with integrity – Principle 2
- Behave in a way that maintains the trust the public places in you and in the provision of legal services – Principle 6
- Run your business or carry out your role in the business in a way that encourages equality of opportunity and respect for diversity – Principle 9

You must also have regard to the relevant Outcomes under the SRA Code of Conduct 2011, but in particular those referred to below.

Communications in the course of practice

Whether you are a manager, a consultant or an employee in a law firm, or you practise in-house, you must behave in a way that demonstrates integrity and maintains the trust the public places in you and in the provision of legal services.

In the context of letters, emails, texts or social media, this means ensuring that the communications you send to others or post online do not contain statements which are derogatory, harassing, hurtful, puerile, plainly inappropriate, or perceived to be threatening, causing the recipient alarm and distress.

In particular, you must achieve the following outcomes:

- O(2.1) – you do not discriminate unlawfully, or victimise or harass anyone, in the course of your professional dealings, and
- O(2.2) – you provide services to clients in a way which respects diversity

We treat any communications which are offensive seriously, whether on the grounds of any of the 'protected characteristics' under the Equality Act 2010 or otherwise. The protected characteristics are age, race, disability, religion or belief, pregnancy or maternity, sex or sexual orientation, gender reassignment and marriage or civil partnership. Depending on the circumstances, you may be at risk under all of the Principles referred to above.

You should also note that where a court or tribunal makes a finding that you have committed an unlawful act of discrimination in a communication sent or posted by you, we will treat that as prima facie evidence of misconduct which may give rise to disciplinary proceedings.

Bear in mind that sending an offensive, threatening or harassing communication may also amount to a criminal offence (eg under section 1 of the Malicious Communications Act 1988, section 127 of the Communications Act 2003 or the Protection from Harassment Act 1997). Depending on the circumstances, committing any of these offences or failing to comply with the Equality Act 2010, could leave you at risk under Principle 1.

Inter-office emails

The Principles and outcomes referred to above apply not only when communicating with third parties outside the firm, but also to emails addressed to colleagues within the firm. You are expected to act at all times with integrity and the fact that you intended such communications to be private will not excuse your conduct.

Bear in mind also that once sent, you have no control over what happens to your email. Moreover, by using the firm's email system, you run the risk that others may be able to access those emails.

Likewise, you cannot justify your conduct on the grounds that you did not intend to cause offence, or that the recipient(s) of your email was not offended. One of our key concerns as a regulator is to protect public confidence in the integrity and high standards of the profession; you should therefore bear in mind that you will be at risk of disciplinary action if you send an email which has the potential of causing offence and/or undermining public trust in the profession and that email subsequently comes to light.

Entering into an exchange with others which you perceive or intend to be humorous can pose a particular risk, especially when your humour is at the expense of others; what may seem to be light-hearted banter to you may be offensive to a third party. You should ensure that you do not inadvertently cross the line and become offensive in any of the ways referred to above.

Communications with clients

Most firms these days communicate with their clients by email or text rather than by letter. However, there are inherent risks in this. Such forms of communication by their nature are more 'instant' and tend to be less formal than letters.

This can lead to the blurring of the line between client and friend and the informality, together with the expectation of a quick reply, makes it easy to overlook the need to consider carefully what you are saying.

Whilst being on friendly terms with your client or using informal language is not of course a problem in itself, you must be careful to ensure that your communications remain professional, both in the tone and content, at all times. This is particularly so where it is foreseeable that the communication is likely to be disclosed to a wider audience at some point.

If a client makes derogatory, discriminatory or inappropriate references to others in their communications to you, you should not participate or endorse those comments. Nor should you pass the offensive comments on if it is not necessary to do so. Where your client's comments are potentially in breach of the law, you should draw this to your client's attention.

Communications with other law firms and litigants in person

It is not uncommon for emails between law firms in relation to a client's matter to be robust, particularly in litigation. However, you should ensure such communications do not cross the line by using inflammatory language or being gratuitously offensive, either to the other side or about their client.

Your role is to act in the client's best interests; antagonising the other side is unlikely to achieve this. You should remain objective and not allow the matter to become personal, regardless of the provocation or your client's instructions. You are not your client's 'hired gun' and you may be at risk under Principle 3 if you allow your independence to be compromised by being drawn into using offensive language or making offensive comments in order to meet your client's expectations.

It is equally important to remain professional when dealing with an individual who is representing him or herself, or has appointed a McKenzie Friend. In a recent decision, the SDT fined a solicitor for his heated and abusive exchange of emails with a litigant in person, calling this 'completely unacceptable'. The SDT said it was the solicitor's responsibility to maintain his professionalism regardless of what that person may have done.

Managers and supervisors

You will be at risk under the Principles referred to above if you are a sole practitioner or a manager of the firm and you become aware of such emails, but do not take appropriate steps to stop the behaviour and deal with the sender(s) (for example, in accordance with your disciplinary policy).

This also applies if you are not a manager, but you are responsible for supervising a colleague's work and do not take steps to stop the behaviour.

Bear in mind also that if the sender's comments amount to serious misconduct, you have an obligation (as indeed does anyone in your firm) to report the individual(s) to us under O(10.4) of the Code. To do this, please see How to report.

Conduct outside practice

Solicitors, RELs and RFLs

If you are a solicitor, a REL or an RFL, Principles 1 (administration of justice), 2 (integrity) and 6 (public trust) continue to apply to you outside your practice, whether in some other business capacity or in your personal life. It is in this sphere – namely outside of practice – that we are currently receiving the majority of complaints.

The risk referred to above – namely that social media by its nature tends to encourage instant communication without the necessary forethought – tends to be greater when you are outside a work context. You must at all times be aware of the content you are posting and the need for professionalism.

This is especially true if you are participating in online discussion (whether this be on Facebook, Twitter, other social media, forums, blogs, etc) and you have identified yourself as, or are known to be, a solicitor. You should bear in mind the possibility that users will re-share the content you have posted on their own social network, potentially leading to rapid sharing with a huge number of users. Similarly, you cannot rely on your own privacy settings to prevent the posting from being passed on by others.

Even if you do not identify yourself as a solicitor, anonymity is not guaranteed; material which you post under a pseudonym may still be traced back to you or you may be identified as a solicitor if you include a photograph of yourself.

You should also consider carefully before retweeting an offensive comment. Unless you refute the content, you will be at risk of being seen as implicitly endorsing it. If it comes to your attention that a third party has accessed your computer and posted an inappropriate comment in your name on a social media network, you should take immediate steps to go online to refute the comment. It is advisable in any event to regularly audit your site to remove any material which makes you uncomfortable.

Trainees and other managers or employees

If you do not fall into the category above, the Principles do not apply to you outside your role in an SRA-regulated firm.

However, that is not to say that there might not be serious consequences should you get it wrong (eg significant embarrassment and damage to your reputation should your comments end up in the public domain, as well as the risk of internal disciplinary proceedings).

In addition, if you are a trainee solicitor, your conduct may in some circumstances have an impact on your entry into the profession (for example, where you have made discriminatory comments). In order to be admitted, we will assess your character and suitability and in doing so, will have regard to the SRA Suitability Test.

Your systems and procedures

You should have regard to the following Outcomes if you are the COLP for your firm, or you are a sole practitioner, manager or the head of an in-house legal department:

* **O(7.2)** – you have effective systems and controls in place to achieve and comply with all the Principles, rules and outcomes and other requirements of the Handbook, where applicable

* **O(7.3)** – you identify, monitor and manage risks to compliance with all the Principles, rules and outcomes and other requirements of the Handbook, if applicable to you, and take steps to address issues identified

Where a member of your firm sends or posts an inappropriate or offensive communication, it not only puts you at risk under the Principles above, it also has the potential of causing significant damage to your firm, both in terms of reputation and financially; for example, if clients react by withdrawing their business or are deterred from instructing your firm. In some circumstances, you could also be liable for your employee's actions (eg if the communication amounts to victimising or harassing a third party).

To achieve O(7.3), you should assess the potential risks to your firm in light of the above, taking into account the nature and size of your firm to determine whether you need to put in place a social media policy or some other system or controls. It is likely to be easier to take disciplinary action against a staff member if you have a social media policy in place dealing with its improper use.

To be effective, you should ensure that members of your firm are conversant with any policy or system you put in place.

Remember: if a complaint is made against an individual in your firm, you may be asked to demonstrate how you have achieved the above Outcomes.

Enforcement action

Failure to have proper regard to this warning notice is likely to lead to disciplinary action.

Further guidance

For guidance on any of the above conduct matters, contact the Professional Ethics Guidance Team.

For advice on creating a social media policy for your firm, see the Law Society's practice note.

The Crown Prosecution Service has issued guidance on hate crime, which can include offensive communications.

9.14 Payment Protection Insurance (PPI) claims

[Issued by the Solicitors Regulation Authority on 29 August 2017/Updated 20 June 2018]

Status

While this document does not form part of the SRA Handbook, the SRA may have regard to it when exercising its regulatory functions.

This warning notice has been updated to reflect recent legislative changes and to remind regulated firms and individuals of their obligations.

Who is this warning notice relevant to?

This warning notice is relevant to all those we regulate acting in claims for mis-sold payment protection insurance (PPI).

Our concerns

Following our previously issued guidance and engagement with Government departments, lenders and others involved in the handling of PPI, we are concerned that firms are failing in their duties to act in accordance with the Principles and Outcomes of the Code by:

- acting in matters without first investigating whether there is a valid claim
- making claims without knowledge of the policyholder/consumer
- failing to properly identify clients and confirm client instructions
- submitting false claims in the hope of a settlement without further investigation by the defendant
- charging unreasonable costs for a limited amount of work contrary to their fiduciary and regulatory duties

Firms who conduct cases which demonstrate one or more of these features may face regulatory action for breach of our Principles. Further this may give us reason to suspect dishonesty by their principals or staff.

Our expectations

We expect that all those regulated by us comply with the Principles and Outcomes of the SRA Handbook 2011. That law firms and solicitors do not conduct fraudulent or questionable cases, and that all costs charged to a client are explained, agreed and set at a reasonable rate.

Previously issued guidance relating to PPI claims is still relevant and should be read alongside this notice.

The SRA Principles

Principle 1: Uphold the rule of law and the proper administration of justice.

You have obligations not only to clients but also to the court and to third parties with whom you have dealings on your clients' behalf (Part 1 – SRA Principles para 2.5).

Principle 2: Act with integrity.

Personal integrity is central to your role as the client's trusted adviser and should characterise all your professional dealings with clients, the court, other lawyers and the public (Part 1 – SRA Principles para 2.6).

Principle 4: You must act in the best interests of each client.

You should always act in good faith and do your best for each of your clients (Part 1 –SRA Principles para 2.8).

Principle 5: You must provide a proper standard of service to your clients.

You must provide a proper standard of service to your clients. You should provide a proper standard of client care and work. This would include exercising competence, skill and diligence, and taking into account the individual needs and circumstances of each client (Part 1 – SRA Principles para 2.9).

Principle 6: You must behave in a way that maintains the trust the public places in you and in the provision of legal services.

Members of the public should be able to place their trust in you. Any behaviour either within or outside your professional practice which undermines this trust damages not only you, but also the reputation of the legal profession and its ability to serve society SRA Principles para 2.11).

SRA Code of Conduct 2011 mandatory outcomes

You should have regard to the specific outcomes under the SRA Code of Conduct 2011, in particular those highlighted below.

O(1.1) you treat your clients fairly

O(1.6) you only enter into fee agreements with your clients that are legal, and which you consider are suitable for the client's needs and take account of the client's best interests

O(1.12) clients are in a position to make informed decisions about the services they need, how their matter will be handled and the options available to them

O(11.1) you do not take unfair advantage of third parties

Client interests and charges

You should always have regard to the SRA's Principles and Outcomes of the Code. You should make sure that you act in your client's best interests and with integrity, treat your clients fairly and uphold the rule of law.

Your retainer is with your client and you are responsible to your client both under the law and our regulatory requirements. To ensure that you can act in your clients' interests and deliver the required quality of service you should have clear instructions from your client and an agreed course of action. Your client should have all the necessary information to make informed decisions on how their matter should be dealt with. Unless you have regular contact with your client, you will be at risk of failing to achieve the required outcomes.

Unless instructions are confirmed with the client at each stage of the retainer, throughout the life cycle of a case including whether to accept an offer to settle a claim, you will be at risk of committing serious misconduct.

When agreeing your fees with a client you should make sure they are fair and reasonable (Solicitors (Non- Contentious Business) Remuneration Order 2009 Article 3) having regard to all the circumstances of the case.

Since issuing our previous notice the Financial Guidance and Claims Act 2018 ("the Act") received royal assent on 10 May 2018. The Act prohibits fees of more than 20 percent, excluding VAT, being charged for PPI claims and prevents you from charging a client where no award has been recovered.

The cap is effective from 10 July 2018.

We expect you to have informed your clients about the fee cap and its effect.

Read further information about the effect of fee cap and our expectations. The information is consistent with guidance that has been produced by the Claims Management Regulation Unit.

Although legislation sets a fee cap of 20 percent this does not allow for all clients to be charged at this rate. In our original warning notice we made clear that any fees charged that are greater than 15 percent of a client's damages are unreasonable, unless the work involved and the risk to the firm clearly demands a greater percentage of the damages.

Legal proceedings should not be issued to try to avoid or limit the impact of the fee cap. Proceedings should only be issued when it is in the client's interests. Attempts to avoid or limit the impact of the fee cap by issuing proceedings are likely to breach the SRA Principles 2011 and Outcomes in the SRA Code of Conduct 2011.It is unlikely that you would be acting in your clients' interests or treating them fairly if you have agreed to be paid a percentage of the client's damages that exceed fees that would have been payable had your usual hourly rate been charged.

In all circumstances, any fees you charge should be reasonable and proportionate to the work undertaken. This is particularly the case where the work carried out is limited, for example, to submitting a notice of claim and agreeing settlement. It is important that you do not exaggerate the time or effort involved in submitting a claim.

Claims Management Companies looking to engage with you and form an alternative business structure (ABS) firms will not avoid regulation as fees they charge will also be subject to the interim fee cap. All SRA licensed ABS's must comply with the SRA Principles and Code of Conduct and will be subject to regulatory action if issues of professional misconduct are identified.

Cold calling

You must make sure that clients do not come to you through cold calling by your firm or a third party. Some third parties obtain client details illegally and you may be at risk of infringing applicable data protection legislation by the unauthorised use or handling of data. You should ensure the introducer is aware of your duties and you check regularly that their methods of marketing and contact do not put you in breach of the code. You could, for example, ask clients how they were first contacted. If you fail to make the position clear you are at risk of non-compliance.

You should have regard to the following outcomes:

O(8.1) your publicity in relation to your firm is accurate and not misleading, and is not likely to diminish the trust the public places in you and in the provision of legal services

O(8.3) you do not make unsolicited approaches in person or by telephone to members of the public in order to publicise your firm Acting in the following way may tend to show you have not achieved the outcome and therefore complied with the principles

IB(8.6) allowing any other person to conduct publicity for your firm in a way that would breach the principles

Referral arrangements

All referral arrangements must comply with the required outcomes in Chapter 6 and/or 9 of the Code of Conduct. You must be satisfied and be able to evidence that the agreement or relationship with the referrer does not affect your ability to take proper and ongoing instructions from your client, or the way you deal with your client's information or manage your client's matter.

You have a duty to:

- make sure that contracts or other arrangements between your client and a referrer are fair, and

- cease dealing with a referrer whose contractual terms or other conduct are contrary to your clients' interests or to the rule of law.

You should have regard to the following outcomes:

O(9.1) your independence and your professional judgement are not prejudiced by virtue of any arrangement with another person

O(9.2) your clients' interests are protected regardless of the interests of an introducer or fee sharer, or your interest in receiving referrals

O(9.3) clients are in a position to make informed decisions about how to pursue their matter.

If you rely on an introducer, you should:

- only use the services of regulated claims management companies

- review your referral arrangements regularly, making sure this one referrer is not your sole source of work, and

- make sure that the arrangement or behaviour of the introducer does not put you in breach of your duties.

Fraudulent claims and taking unfair advantage

O(11.1) you do not take unfair advantage of third parties

Acting in the following way might tend to show that you have not achieved outcomes and therefore complied with the principles:

IB(11.8) demanding anything for yourself or on behalf of your client that is not legally recoverable

When taking instructions from a client, to make a claim against a third party, you should ensure you have correct details of the client's identity and claim. No claim should be made on behalf of a client unless you can evidence there is a sound basis for the claim and that you have valid instructions. You should not demand anything from a third party, such as compensation for mis-selling, where there is no legal right to recovery.

Where you issue a claim knowing it is not a valid one or not having investigated the validity of the claim, you will leave yourself open to disciplinary action for breach of:

- Principle 1, upholding the rule of law
- Principle 2, acting with integrity
- Principle 6, for behaving in a way that fails to maintain the trust the public places in you and in the provision of legal services

You may also leave yourself and your clients open to criminal action for fraudulent claims.

Enforcement action

Failure to have proper regard to this warning notice is likely to lead to disciplinary action.

Further guidance

Previously issued guidance on acting in PPI matters

For guidance on conduct issues, contact the Professional Ethics Guidance Team

Questions and answers relating to the interim fee cap

On 10 May 2018, the Financial Guidance and Claims Act 2018 ("the Act") received Royal Assent. The Act:

- prohibits fees of more than 20%, excluding VAT, being charged for PPI claims, and
- restricts SRA authorised firms and regulated individuals from charging a client where no award has been recovered.

The interim fee cap is effective from 10 July 2018 (two months from the date of Royal Assent).

These questions and answers form have been produced to help firms in understanding the effect of the interim fee cap and detail how we intend to monitor and enforce it. They should be read in conjunction with our warning notice.

Q1. Where is the interim fee cap set out in the Act?

Section 29 of the Act states:

"PPI claims and charges for claims management services: general

1. This section and sections 30 to 32 make provision for a fee cap to apply in certain circumstances to charges for regulated services provided in connection with a PPI claim.

2. The following provisions explain terms used in those sections.

3.   The fee cap applicable to the amount charged for regulated services provided in connection with a PPI claim is 20% of the amount recovered for the claimant in satisfaction of the claim.

Accordingly, where nothing is recovered (whether or not a claim has been made or concluded) the fee cap is zero."

Q2. When does the fee cap come into effect and who does it apply to?

The fee cap comes into effect on 10 July 2018 and applies to all SRA authorised firms and regulated individuals.

It also applies to Claims Management Companies (CMCs) and persons regulated by the General Council of the Bar or the Chartered Institute of Legal Executives.

Q3. Does the fee cap apply to retainers/fee agreements entered into before 10 July?

No. The fee cap applies only to fee agreements that are entered into with a client from 10 July 2018.

Agreements which include terms relating to fees that exceed the cap will be unenforceable and the client will be able to recover the excess amount paid from you.

Q4. If the PPI claim is referred from a claims management company or another third party, can all parties charge a fee that does not exceed 20%?

No.

Firms should make sure that, where the introducer has provided claims management services to the client or the client is referred to a third party to provide services relating to the PPI claim, that the collective fees to do not exceed the 20% fee cap.

Q5. Are there specific rules relating to the interim fee cap?

No. The fee cap is set out in primary legislation.

A firm that charges more than 20% of a client's redress will be in breach of the SRA Principles and likely to have breached Outcome 1.1 and 1.6 of the SRA Code of Conduct 2011.

Q6. Does the fee cap of 20% include VAT?

No.

The 20% cap is exclusive of VAT

Q7. Does the fee cap apply if hourly charging rates are applied?

Yes. If a client is charged fees at an hourly rate, firms will still be required to comply with the interim fee cap.

The total of fees that are charged on your hourly rate must therefore, not amount to more than 20% excluding VAT of the total amount of redress awarded.

Q8. Does this cap mean charging 20% in all cases is acceptable?

No.

All firms have a regulatory duty to act in their client's best interests, which means all charges must be justifiable and equate to the level of work undertaken. If we find evidence a firms' charges are unjustified, even if they are below the cap, we may still take potential action.

Since many PPI claims can be handled in a straightforward manner by members of the public themselves, without attracting a fee, we would also expect solicitors to always advise their clients accordingly in all such cases.

Q9. Does the interim fee cap apply to claims if legal proceedings have been issued?

"Regulated claims management services" do not include any reserved legal activities mentioned in section 12(1) (a) or (b) of the Legal Services Act 2007 (exercise of a right of audience or the conduct of litigation).

This means that the interim fee cap does not apply to charges for work carried out in taking formal steps in proceedings which have been issued.

The 'Conduct of litigation' however, does not include any steps taken prior to the commencement of litigation; i.e. before proceedings are issued or to work carried out after the issue of proceedings which are not formal steps. Therefore, the fee cap will apply to charges for work done prior to the commencement of proceedings and to work done after other than charges for steps taken in the actual proceedings such as filing court documents.

Attempts to avoid the fee cap by issuing proceedings are likely to breach the SRA Principles 2011 and the SRA Code of Conduct 2011. Firms should also have regard to Andrew & Ors v Barclays Bank plc [2012] EWHC B13 (Mercantile). Proceedings should only be issued if it is in the client's best interests.

Q10. How will the interim fee cap be enforced?

Decisions about what action we take are decided on a case by case basis and will depend on for example, intent, harm caused, patterns of behaviour and vulnerability of the client.

Firms have an obligation to make sure that all fees are fair and reasonable and to uphold the rule of law.

Q11. When does the interim fee cap come to an end?

Section 33 of the Act requires us to make rules which will prohibit SRA authorised firms and regulated individuals from charging fees above a specified amount in relation to all relevant claims management agreements, and services provided in connection with all relevant claims management activities, which concern claims in relation to financial products or services.

The interim fee cap will continue until those rules are made and come into force.

9.15 Referral fees, LASPO and the SRA Principles

[Issued by the Solicitors Regulation Authority on 11 October 2013]

Who is this guidance relevant to?

This warning notice is relevant to all practitioners who have referral arrangements for personal injury work. It reminds practitioners of the need, when entering into such arrangements, to consider not only whether they may be in breach of the ban in the Legal Aid, Sentencing and Punishment of Offenders Act 2012 (LASPO), but whether they are able to comply with their regulatory obligations, in particular the SRA Principles and the Outcomes in the SRA Code of Conduct 2011 ("the Code").

Whilst this notice does not form part of the SRA Handbook, the SRA may have regard to it when exercising its regulatory functions.

Our concerns

We know that the ban on referral fees has raised difficult issues in relation to its application and interpretation. We are also aware that, because of the wording of LASPO, it is possible for firms to have arrangements that involve the introduction of personal injury work without being in breach of LASPO. We are concerned, however, that in setting up arrangements in a way that does not breach LASPO, firms are failing to consider their wider duties to their clients and others, and in doing so may be breaching the Principles or failing to achieve the Outcomes. Examples include:

- agreeing with an introducer to deduct money from clients' damages;
- inappropriate outsourcing of work to introducers;
- referrals to other service providers which are not in the best interests of clients;
- failure to properly advise clients about the costs and how their claim should be funded; and
- lack of transparency about the arrangement.

The Principles

The most relevant Principles in relation to referral arrangements are that you must

1. uphold the rule of law and the proper administration of justice;
2. act with integrity;
3. not allow your independence to be compromised;
4. act in the best interests of each client;
5. provide a proper standard of service to your clients; and
6. behave in a way that maintains the trust the public places in you and in the provision of legal services.

The Outcomes

As well as the outcomes requiring practitioners to comply with LASPO (outcomes 6.4 and 9.8), chapters 6 and 9 of the Code include outcomes in connection with referrals to and by your firm, dealing with issues such as independence, transparency and the best interests of clients. These will apply in respect of any referral to or by your firm that is not prohibited by LASPO. You will also need to ensure that you achieve the outcomes relating to issues such as client care, conflict of interests, confidentiality and publicity.

Deductions from clients' damages

Some claims management companies ("CMCs") are seeking to charge clients a proportion of their damages in return for being referred to a suitable law firm and/or for other claims management services. In some cases firms are being asked, as part of their agreement with the CMC, to deduct these payments from the client's damages or even to forward the client's damages to the CMC. This type of arrangement can pose various risks to your ability to comply with the Principles.

Firstly, where the arrangement is not in the interests of your client, you will need to consider whether your ability to advise the client about the agreement they have entered into will be impaired by your relationship with the introducer. The Solicitors Disciplinary Tribunal has on a number of occasions criticised solicitors for failing to give such advice to their clients and for acting where their own commercial interests in a referral arrangement conflict with the interests of the client.

Money can only be deducted from a client's damages with the client's informed consent. Sending a client's damages to a third party introducer would also require the client's consent, but is unlikely ever to be in the client's interests.

In addition, this type of arrangement could place the introducer in breach of LASPO and you should not enter into any arrangement that would assist a third party to breach the legislation.

Outsourcing/paying for services

Some firms have arrangements that involve the introducer carrying out a certain amount of work on the client's matter and the firm paying the introducer for carrying out this work.

Provided the payment is for a genuine service and is reasonable in all the circumstances, such a payment may not breach LASPO. However, before entering into such an arrangement, you will need to consider carefully whether it is appropriate for the introducer to be carrying out such work. Failure to do so may compromise your ability to act in the best interests of your clients or to provide a proper standard of service. The work may, for example, include advising the client on the appropriate means of funding their matter, explaining and signing the client up to a conditional fee agreement or damages-based agreement. You have a duty to ensure that your clients receive sufficient information to make informed decisions about their matter and the way it will be handled. In our view, outsourcing this work, or relying on a third party to provide the necessary information to the client, represents a significant risk to your ability to achieve the relevant outcomes.

Inappropriate referrals

It has been suggested that some firms and introducers are arranging for clients to purchase insurance, medical reports or other products or services at inflated prices so that the firm or introducer will receive a higher commission. In some cases the firm may have an interest in the business providing the product or service. The receipt of such commissions, either by you or another person, may put you in breach of section 56(2) of LASPO. Also, where you refer your client to another service provider, the referral must be in the client's best interests and must not compromise your independence and you are required to account to the client for any financial benefit you receive as a result of their instructions. (See the outcomes in Chapters 1 and 6 of the Code.) Even if the client has been sold these products or service before instructing your firm you should be careful to ensure that you are not facilitating arrangements that are detrimental to clients' interests.

You should also consider whether any requirement by an introducer to use a particular provider compromises your independence or your ability to comply with the relevant outcomes (as well as whether your agreement to do so may amount to consideration and therefore a payment which breaches LASPO).

Funding and fee agreements

There have been suggestions that some firms are not discussing with clients the options for funding their claim and in particular that they are not exploring whether the client has insurance that would cover their legal costs, so that the firm can charge an uplift on their fees. It is important that clients are aware of, and understand, the options for funding their claim and any fee agreement they enter into with you. (See, for example, outcomes 1.1, 1.12 and 1.13 and indicative behaviours 1.13, 1.14, 1.15 and 1.17.)

Transparency

Clients need to be in a position to make informed decisions about any referral to a firm and about how their matter will be dealt with. Some introducers and firms have set up complex arrangements in order to ensure they do not breach LASPO, for example by ensuring it is the client, rather than the third party introducer, who provides information to the firm about a potential claim. If you are involved in such an arrangement, you need to be careful to ensure that the client is not misled about who they are dealing with and who is providing particular services. You will also need to achieve outcomes 9.3 and 9.4 and tell the client about any financial arrangement you have with the introducer.

Enforcement action

Whilst we are committed to working constructively with firms and practitioners, we will take enforcement action against those that fail to address the issues and risks associated with referral arrangements, particularly where those arrangements are detrimental to the interests of clients.

Further help

If you require further assistance in relation to your referral arrangements contact the Ethics Helpline.

9.16 Risk factors in personal injury claims

[First issued by the Solicitors Regulation Authority on 21 March 2016/Updated December 2017]

Status

While this document does not form part of the SRA Handbook, we will have regard to it when exercising our regulatory functions.

Who is this warning notice relevant to?

This warning notice is relevant to solicitors and all regulated persons who take personal injury referrals from third parties, work closely with them or act on their instructions.

Our concerns

We are concerned that firms are:

- failing in their duties to act in accordance with the Principles and Outcomes of the Code by allowing third parties to cold call potential clients

- entering into referral agreements that are in breach of the Legal Aid Sentencing and Punishment of Offenders Act 2012

- taking and acting on instructions from third parties without ensuring that the instructions originate from the client

- settling claims without a medical report

- paying damages or sending cheques to third parties without accounting properly to the client

- bringing personal injury claims without their clients' authority

- in some extreme cases, bringing claims without the knowledge of the named client claimant

- not training and supervising their staff adequately

Firms who conduct cases which demonstrate one or more of these features may face regulatory action for breach of our Principles or Code. Further this may give us reason to suspect dishonesty by their principals or staff.

Our expectations

That all firms and individuals regulated by us comply with the Principles and Outcomes of the SRA Handbook 2011. Law firms and solicitors conducting litigation are central to the administration of justice and must be alert to any risk that they are receiving or pursuing fraudulent or questionable cases and take action to remove that risk urgently.

The SRA Principles

You have a duty to:

Principle 1 – Uphold the rule of law and the proper administration of justice

Principle 2 – Act with integrity

Principle 3 – Not allow your independence to be compromised

Principle 4 – Act in the best interests of each client

Principle 5 – Provide a proper standard of service to your clients

Principle 6 – Behave in a way that maintains the trust the public places in you and in the provision of legal services

The SRA mandatory outcomes

You should have regard to the specific outcomes under the SRA Code of Conduct 2011, in particular those highlighted below.

Cold calling

You must ensure that clients do not come to you as a consequence of cold calling by your firm or a third party. Some third parties obtain client details illegally and you may be at risk of infringing the Data Protection Act by the unauthorised use or handling of data. You should ensure the introducer is aware of your duties and you check regularly that their methods of marketing and contact do not put you in breach of your code, for example, by asking clients how they were first contacted. If you fail to make the position clear you are at risk of non-compliance.

You should have particular regard to the following outcomes:

O(8.1) your publicity in relation to your firm is accurate and not misleading, and is not likely to diminish the trust the public places in you and in the provision of legal services.

O(8.3) you do not make unsolicited approaches in person or by telephone to members of the public in order to publicise your firm.

Acting in the following way may tend to show you have not achieved the outcome and therefore complied with the principles.

IB(8.6) allowing any other person to conduct publicity for your firm in a way that would breach the principles.

Referral arrangements

In personal injury matters, you should not enter into any arrangements contrary to the Legal Aid Sentencing and Punishment of Offenders Act 2012. In those cases where arrangements are permitted by law you must still comply with the required outcomes in Chapter 9 of the Code of Conduct. You must be satisfied and be able to evidence that the agreement or relationship with the referrer does not affect your ability to take proper and ongoing instructions from your client, or the way you deal with your client's information or manage your client's matter.

You have a duty to ensure that contracts or other arrangements between your client and a referrer are fair and to cease dealing with a referrer whose contractual terms or other conduct are adverse to your clients' interests or to the rule of law.

You should have regard to the following outcomes:

O(9.1) your independence and your professional judgement are not prejudiced by virtue of any arrangement with another person

O(9.2) your clients' interests are protected regardless of the interests of an introducer or fee sharer or your interest in receiving referrals

O(9.3) clients are in a position to make informed decisions about how to pursue their matter.

O(9.8) you do not pay a prohibited referral fee.

You should use the services of regulated claims management companies and review your referral arrangements regularly ensuring that they are not your sole source of work and that the arrangement or behaviour of the introducer does not put you in breach of your duties.

Third party instructions

The nature of personal injury litigation and the role of referral organisations in this sector mean that the risk to clients, defendants and the administration of justice are such that you must exercise extra caution to ensure that you are acting on valid instructions. This is likely to mean taking instructions—or checking them—direct with your client. This is an ongoing duty throughout the life of a case and will apply in particular to significant decisions such as whether to settle a claim and for how much.

The commercial interest of a referrer means that you cannot safely rely, without further scrutiny, on common practices such as instructions being given on behalf of another person by, for example, a trusted family member or one member of a couple or partnership.

Clients' interests

The Principles and Outcomes of the Code make clear that you must act in your clients' interests and with integrity. Your retainer is with your client and you are responsible to your client both under the law and our regulatory requirements. To ensure that you can act in your clients' interests and deliver the required quality of service you should have clear instructions from your client and an agreed course of action. Your client should have all the necessary information to make informed decisions on how their matter should be dealt with. Unless you have regular contact with your client, you will be at risk of failing to achieve the required outcomes.

Unless instructions are confirmed with the client at each stage of the retainer, throughout proceedings, you will be at risk of committing serious misconduct.

Before issuing proceedings, you must have proper authority to do so. You must be fully satisfied that the terms of the claim properly reflect client instructions. Instructions should be confirmed at each stage of the retainer and authority to make, accept or reject an offer must be separately obtained. Acting without client instructions may leave you open to wasted costs orders and negligence proceedings as well as disciplinary action.

In those cases where your client clearly wishes—and confirms to you directly—that you should act on instructions given by a third party, you will need to satisfy yourself that it is in your client's interests to take instructions in this way. You will need to explain to the client that taking third party instructions will mean the sharing of their confidential information and the implications and risks involved. e g inaccurate information being acted on, misuse of information by the third party.

Only if you are satisfied that the arrangement is in the best interests of the client and that there is no conflict between the interests of the client and the person giving instructions may you act in this way. You should be mindful of any arrangements which may incentivise the referrer to take a particular course of action in the case, for example an early settlement, without regard to the best outcome for the client.

In personal injury matters the best information on the facts and consequences of the injury are highly likely to rest with the client. Blanket forms of authority based on bulk or standard terms present a greater risk to the interests of clients and the administration of justice, and are highly unlikely to satisfy our requirements.

Even where you are satisfied it is in your client's interests to take third party instructions, you must be satisfied that your client has given free and informed consent to you doing so. Once again this is likely to require you to obtain this direct.

Identification

Because of the risks involved in bringing false claims, you must properly identify your client by obtaining and verifying proof of identity and address. Unusual or suspicious factors must be investigated fully. If any third party, including your agent, provides copy documentation such as a photocopy of a passport, you must ensure that the client confirms its authenticity directly to you.

Costs

Your client should be fully aware of the costs you are charging, the costs information you deliver should be transparent and clear. You have a duty to give clients' the best possible information both at the time of engagement and when appropriate as their matter progresses, about the likely overall cost of their matter; O(1.13).

When giving costs information you should consider the best way to deliver the information to that client. The information may be in writing or discussed with the client first and followed up in writing. Where you have vulnerable clients you should consider the matter very carefully to ensure the action you take delivers the outcomes required. See also IB(1.14) clearly explaining your fees and if and when they are likely to change.

Accounting

Damages must be paid to the client unless you have a valid reason and valid instructions direct from your client to make payments to a third party. Before making such payments you should familiarise yourself with our guidance on improper use of a client account. You should not make payments where there is any concern that the client may be avoiding liabilities eg bank overdraft, benefits claw back. Cheques made payable to the client must be given or sent to the client at their address. Failure to properly account to a client in this way may lead to regulatory action for failure to account for client money.

You should have regard to the following outcomes and rule:

O(1.1) You treat your clients fairly

O(1.2) you provide services to your clients in a manner which protects their interests in their matter, subject to the proper administration of justice

O(1.4) you have the resources, skills and procedures to carry out your clients' instructions

O(1.5) the service you provide to clients is competent, delivered in a timely manner and takes account of your clients' needs and circumstances

O(1.12) clients are in a position to make informed decisions about the services they need, how their matter will be handled and the options available to them

Acting in the following way(s) may tend to show that you have not achieved these outcomes and therefore not complied with the Principles:

IB(1.25) acting for a client when instructions are given by someone else, or by only one client when you act jointly for others unless you are satisfied that the person providing the instructions has the authority to do so on behalf of all of the clients

IB(1.28) acting for a client when there are reasonable grounds for believing that the instructions are affected by duress or undue influence without satisfying yourself that they represent the client's wishes

SRA Accounts Rules 14.3 (SAR)

Client money must be returned to the client (or other person on whose behalf the money is held) promptly as soon as there is no longer any proper reason to retain those funds. Should you delay in making payment you may find the client has moved on and you will then be required under Rule 20 SAR to make efforts to trace and pay the client. Costs incurred in finding the client are not recoverable and must be borne by you. Efficient and reliable systems of receipt and payment of damages will reduce the need to incur costs and time spent in pursuit of a client.

Misleading the court and other parties

If you fail to take proper steps to minimise risks or deal with issues that arise, you may face action for misleading the court and failing to comply with the SRA Principles and Code.

Your firm will be directly responsible for failures of all people working within it or for it, including partners, directors, members, employees, self-employed consultants and agents. You have a duty to ensure that those who refer cases to you or work on cases are acting properly at all times.

If proceedings are issued on behalf a client who has not given instructions to issue proceedings, you will be at serious risk of misleading the court or taking unfair advantage of other parties (for example, by attempting to negotiate a settlement) and will leave yourself open to accusations of fraud and possible legal action.

You should be aware that claims subject to the pre-action protocol that are submitted through the MoJ Claims Portal require the legal representative to confirm their clients' instructions to make a claim. Completing the submission when you do not have instructions from the claimant will also leave you at risk of legal and disciplinary action.

There are exceptional circumstances where a solicitor acts on third party instructions (eg when acting for a minor or on behalf of a client who does not have capacity), or on the implied authority of the client to issue proceedings. This may be where the client has given clear instructions to act, but for some justifiable reason may be out of contact just before issuing and you are unable to confirm instructions. This causes particular difficulty where the limitation period is about to expire. In such circumstances you should be able to justify and evidence your action and be aware of the risks inherent in issuing. In any cases of doubt you should seek guidance.

Before accepting a settlement on behalf of your client you should ensure you have all necessary information for an informed decision to be made by the client, this includes obtaining a medical report. Where you settle a matter, without first obtaining medical evidence, you run the risk of failing in your duty to your client. Without medical evidence you cannot be sure of your client's prognosis and the full extent of their injuries. You leave yourself open to complaints about inadequate compensation and disciplinary action for failing in your duties.

When you receive a medical report you should take care to fully understand the client's prognosis and be able to assess the information contained within the report.

If you are in any doubt as to the honesty or competence of an expert witness, such as a doctor preparing a medical report, you must cease using the expert, review all cases involving that expert, and check the underlying facts direct with your clients.

You should have regard to the following outcomes:

    O(5.1) you do not attempt to deceive or knowingly or recklessly mislead the court

    O(11.1) you do not take unfair advantage of third parties

Staff training and office systems

Before taking on a personal injury matter you should be sure that:

- you have well trained staff who are in a position to offer a proper standard of service to clients.

- systems in place to ensure that matters are triaged effectively by those who have experience in and an understanding of the litigation process.

- systems that allow for the diarising of limitation periods and court timetables.

- staff training that is reviewed regularly to ensure that skills and knowledge are updated.

- full and proper supervision of staff where work is overseen and support and further expertise is available to fee earners and case workers.

O(1.4) you have the resources, skills and procedures to carry out your clients' instructions;

O(1.5) the service you provide to clients is competent, delivered in a timely manner and takes account of your clients' needs and circumstances;

Taking on files from another firm

Before taking on cases from other firms you should carry out due diligence on the files you will be acquiring. Some files may be in a poor state, with imminent time limits, you should ensure you have the necessary time and resources to deal with the matters on an urgent basis.

You should not take on cases where you do not have the necessary skills and experience.

Enforcement action

Failure to have proper regard to this warning notice is likely to lead to disciplinary action.

Further guidance

For guidance on conduct issues, contact the Professional Ethics Guidance Team.

9.17 Stamp duty land tax schemes

[Issued by the Solicitors Regulation Authority on 16 February 2012]

We are concerned about the promotion or facilitation of stamp duty land tax schemes.

This warning notice is for anyone who is or is considering becoming involved in the promotion or facilitation of schemes the purpose of which is to avoid or reduce stamp duty land tax. We are particularly concerned with schemes involving residential properties, but this notice may be helpful in relation to schemes involving any type of property. This notice does not form part of the SRA Handbook, but the SRA may have regard to it when exercising its regulatory functions.

The Principles

If you are or are considering becoming involved in the implementation or promotion of a stamp duty land tax (SDLT) scheme, you should consider whether you can comply with the Principles in the SRA Handbook. Whilst all the Principles may be relevant, some require particular attention:

- integrity,
- independence,
- best interests of the client,
- behaving in a way that maintains the trust the public places in you and the provision of legal services.

What is a stamp duty land tax scheme?

A SDLT scheme is a scheme which is designed to reduce or eliminate the correct level of stamp duty payable on a property. Generally, buyers of residential property are required to pay stamp duty land tax when they spend more than £125,000 on a residential property. The tax is charged at between 1 per cent and 5 per cent of the value of the residential property.

Warnings by HM Revenue and Customs

HM Revenue and Customs (HMRC) has warned that "where HMRC find property sale arrangements that have been artificially structured to avoid paying the correct amount of SDLT these will be actively challenged, through the courts where appropriate". HMRC has also warned that, in general, these schemes do not genuinely provide the savings their promoters claim. *The Times* newspaper has reported that the loss to the HMRC "is conservatively estimated at £500 million but some tax specialists believe that the true figures could be more than £1 billion". If HMRC is successful in challenging an SDLT scheme, buyers could be liable to pay the whole of the SDLT plus interest and potentially a penalty.

Why are the Principles relevant?

Whilst buyers of property are free to use honest and proper tax planning to mitigate their tax liability, there are a number of risks and misconceptions surrounding SDLT schemes. If you are asked to promote or implement a SDLT scheme, buyers will place reliance on you to act with integrity, independently, and to consider whether an SDLT scheme is in their interests.

Even if a buyer is aware of the risks and would like to use an SDLT scheme, you should take care to act in a way that maintains the trust the public places in you and the provision of legal services. This is particularly important with SDLT schemes where significant fees can be made from the implementation of a scheme but which may, in view of the warnings by HMRC, result in financial loss to buyers and HMRC.

Enforcement action

In view of the level of concern on the part of HMRC and the fundamental importance of integrity in the provision of legal advice, we are likely to look very closely at the conduct of any firm that is actively involved in these schemes.

We are taking action in a number of cases. In a recent case that came before the Solicitors Disciplinary Tribunal (SDT), a solicitor was fined £15,000 and ordered to pay £30,000 costs. There was also a finding that there had been a lack of integrity. There are further cases due before the SDT which may result in more substantial penalties.

We are aware that a number of firms are taking corrective action such as ceasing to promote SDLT schemes, informing buyers that independent legal advice may be needed as well as ensuring lenders are aware of all the details of the SDLT scheme.

Factors to consider to help you decide if a SDLT scheme is in the interests of your clients

Below is a list of some of the factors which may be relevant in deciding if a SDLT scheme is in the interests of your client(s).

The SDLT scheme

- SDLT schemes are constantly changing and are usually very complex, bearing in mind what purchasers want to achieve. HMRC publish information on schemes which have been discredited;

- Be wary of claims by promoters of SDLT schemes that the scheme is backed by a "robust counsel's opinion". Based on what we have seen, we warn that you must check that the opinion

  - is genuine,

  - has not been tampered with,

  - is up to date, and

  - specifically covers the scheme which is being promoted.

- Bear in mind that reliance on counsel's opinion is not necessarily a defence to allegations of breaches of the Principles, and such a position is substantially weaker if the opinion has not been obtained by you for the particular client and the transaction in which you are acting;

- Be wary of claims that the SDLT scheme is approved by HMRC. Be aware that disclosure of the scheme to HMRC, and the issue of a scheme reference number by HMRC, is not confirmation the scheme is backed by HMRC;

- Be aware that HMRC can currently challenge SDLT schemes up to four years after the effective date of the transaction and this can be extended if there has been a careless or deliberate error in the submission of the SDLT return;

- Consider carrying out due diligence on the promoter of the SDLT scheme. If the promoter claims they will repay the fee charged for implementing the scheme, robustly check how realistic this is, bearing in mind that HMRC has four years to challenge the scheme. If the promoter is unable to repay the fee, the buyer may look to you to reimburse them;

- If the SDLT scheme is based on a supposed "no win no fee" basis said to be backed by insurance, robustly check that the policy is suitable and relevant to the purchasers circumstances.

The buyers

- Make sure that you have properly considered all the clients' interests and that no client will be disadvantaged by the scheme;

- Ensure that you account to the buyer for any benefit received by you, and disclose any referral arrangement connected to the scheme.

The lender

- If you act for a lender as well as the buyer, robust consideration needs to be given to whether the scheme could prejudice the interests of the lender. It is our view that it is likely to be very important to ensure that the lender is fully informed that the property is subject to an SDLT scheme with sufficient detail of how the scheme operates. Recent findings by the SDT would support this approach.

These schemes also carry significant risks for you. If you knowingly provide information in support of a tax return that is incorrect, HMRC could impose a penalty on you of £3,000 per submission.

For further advice on the application of the Principles in relation to stamp duty land tax avoidance schemes, please contact our Ethics helpline.

9.18 Tax avoidance – your duties

[Issued by the Solicitors Regulation Authority on 21 September 2017]

Status

While this warning notice does not form part of the SRA Handbook, we may have regard to it when exercising our regulatory functions.

Who is this guidance relevant to?

This guidance is relevant to all those we regulate. Solicitors and firms may be involved either directly in advising clients about tax, or handle client matters or transactions that involve them in the design, implementation, organisation or management of tax affairs, schemes or arrangements. It is therefore important that all are aware of it, particularly because the underlying approach of HM Revenue and Customs (HMRC) is changing rapidly

Background

In the House of Lords case of Ayrshire Pullman v CIR (1929) 14TC754, Lord Clyde said that "No man in this country is under the smallest obligation, moral or other, so as to arrange his legal relations to his business or to his property as to enable the Inland Revenue to put the largest possible shovel into his stores." That approach has been rejected by Parliament by bringing in the General Anti-Abuse Rule (GAAR) 2013 legislation. GAAR is clearly explained in HMRC guidance.

Similarly, the widespread assumption that "tax avoidance is legal" no longer applies and HMRC will take action against what it refers to as "abusive tax avoidance schemes". This is explained by HMRC: "The GAAR only comes into operation when the course of action taken by the taxpayer aims to achieve a favourable tax result that Parliament did not anticipate when it introduced the tax rules in question and, critically, where that course of action cannot reasonably be regarded as reasonable."

HMRC has also indicated it might challenge arrangements not caught by GAAR: "There may be tax avoidance arrangements that are challenged by HMRC using other parts of the tax code, but if they are not abusive they are not within the scope of the GAAR."

The Government has also legislated for other anti-avoidance reform including "follower notices" and "accelerated payments" and intends to bring in a new penalty that can be applied to professionals who enable tax avoidance which HMRC later defeats. A penalty regime is already in force for those who enable offshore tax evasion or non-compliance, under s162 and Schedule 20 of the Finance Act 2016.

Law firms and solicitors must be fully familiar with these changes to ensure they comply with the SRA Principles at all times, particularly the requirement to act with integrity.

Accountancy bodies have worked with HMRC to produce a statement of Professional Conduct in Relation to Taxation (PCRT). This is published on the websites of the accountancy bodies (and is liable to change). We welcomed this statement and said that: "These standards reflect our own principles, particularly that solicitors must be honest and act with integrity, and uphold the rule of law."

Tax practitioners should therefore also be familiar with the PCRT and adhere to its standards.

Our concerns

We have concerns about firms facilitating tax avoidance schemes that are aggressive in ways that go beyond the intentions of Parliament.

Solicitors and firms that we regulate are in a position of trust and not only owe duties to their client but also wider duties under the SRA Principles. They have a duty to act in clients' interests by giving sound and competent advice on the tax system while ensuring that the advice does not go beyond the proper arrangement of the clients' affairs.

The promotion or implementation of artificial arrangements will lead both client and adviser into difficulties with HMRC and leave the adviser open to disciplinary action. The most common schemes we have seen in recent years have related to avoiding Stamp Duty Land Tax (SDLT). We will continue to scrutinise any such schemes carefully.

The High Court decided that the following allegation was proved in relation to a scheme to save SDLT:

"They involved themselves in transactions and/or facilitated, permitted or acquiesced in the promotion and/or implementation of schemes to avoid the payment of Stamp Duty Land Tax ... in circumstances where the schemes were of a dubious nature and the respondents knew, or ought to have known concerns had been raised by both HMRC and counsel in relation to the nature of the transactions ..."

The High Court also commented more widely in the case:

"In my view, the evidence and the primary findings of fact of the tribunal – all eminently justified – compel a conclusion there was here a want of integrity and a failure to act with independence. They also compel a conclusion the respondents so acted as to diminish the trust the public would place in the respondents and the provision of legal services."

The tax system is a necessary part of our economic system, raising funds for public services and making for a healthy economy that serves society. Contributing to the tax system is a duty placed on members of society and solicitors and legal advisers play an important role in helping tax payers to comply with those legal obligations.

Law firms and practitioners must also act with integrity in their own dealings with HMRC. In the case of SRA v Scott it was noted by the High Court that the solicitor. "... admitted there had been financial mismanagement of his firm in breach of Principle 8 of the SRA Principles 2011, as evidenced by the firm's debt to HMRC of £232,317, which had led to the failure of the firm."

Also, a solicitor was struck off when allegations were found proved against him including: "he declared to ... HMRC ... that he (together with his wife) had bought a property for a price lower than that which he paid ... resulting in him paying too little in stamp duty land tax ..., and being subjected to a penalty by HMRC."

SRA Principles

Principle 1: You must uphold the rule of law and the proper administration of justice.

You have obligations not only to clients but also to the court and to third parties with whom you have dealings on your clients' behalf.

Principle 2: You must act with integrity.

Personal integrity is central to your role as the client's trusted adviser and should characterise all your professional dealings with clients, the court, other lawyers and the public.

Principle 4: You must act in the best interests of each client.

You should always act in good faith and do your best for each of your clients.

Principle 5: You must provide a proper standard of service to your clients.

You should provide a proper standard of client care and of work. This would include exercising competence, skill and diligence, and taking into account the individual needs and circumstances of each client.

Principle 6: You must behave in a way that maintains the trust the public places in you and in the provision of legal services.

Members of the public should be able to place their trust in you. Any behaviour either within or outside your professional practice which undermines this trust damages not only you, but also the ability of the legal profession as a whole to serve society.

Outcomes

All outcomes in Chapter 1 will apply to your dealings with clients. In particular O(1.4) you have the resources, skills and procedures to carry out your client's instructions, O(1.5) the service you provide is competent and O(1.12) clients are in a position to make informed decisions about the services they need.

O (11.1) will also be relevant and requires that you do not take unfair advantage of third parties. This, along with the Principle to act with integrity, would require that any dealings with HMRC are conducted on an open and honest basis and that you do not seek to rely on their lack of knowledge of your client's tax position.

When advising a client on avoidance of tax schemes you should make clear that any avoidance arrangements the client enters into might deliver tax outcomes that were never envisaged or intended by Parliament and may be challenged. You should be clear as to the legal implications, the costs and penalties of non compliance should the arrangement fail.

You should also consider your own position in advising or facilitating such an arrangement. It is likely that, should the arrangement fail, your conduct will be called into question. To be involved in such arrangements is likely to reflect badly on you and to damage public confidence in those delivering legal services. You will leave yourself open to the risk of disciplinary proceedings as well as committing a criminal offence. Where you believe, as a consequence of your client's instructions, you are at risk then you should advise your client you cannot comply with their instructions and unless they change instructions you should terminate your retainer.

You might have clients who are using avoidance schemes. As a consequence of the Finance Act 2016, the Serial Tax Avoidance Regime came into force on 15 September 2016 and affected users of avoidance schemes from 6 April 2017. Under the regime new sanctions and penalties are imposed on those using tax avoidance schemes. Anybody using an avoidance scheme is being advised to provide information of the scheme to HMRC. For further details, see https://www.gov.uk/guidance/serial-tax-avoidance

Enforcement action

It is for HMRC and the relevant courts and tribunals to adjudicate on the legality of tax avoidance schemes. However, where schemes are defeated and solicitors have advised on the efficacy of such schemes, we will investigate this as evidence of misconduct which may result in disciplinary action.

We will also take action where we see any lack of integrity in your dealings with HMRC, either on behalf of clients or directly.

Further assistance

If you require further assistance with understanding your obligations please contact the Professional Ethics Guidance Team.

9.19 Use of non-disclosure agreements (NDAs)

[Issued by the Solicitors Regulation Authority on 12 March 2018]

Our concerns

We recognise that NDAs, including with employees, can legitimately be used to protect commercial interests and confidentiality and in some circumstances, to protect reputation. Such agreements can operate to the mutual benefit of both parties. This warning notice, and the Handbook, should not be taken to prohibit the use of NDAs. However, we are concerned to ensure that you do not:

- use NDAs in circumstances in which the subject of the NDA may, as a result of the use of the NDA feel unable to notify the SRA or other regulators or law enforcement agencies of conduct which might otherwise be reportable

- fail to notify the SRA of misconduct, or a serious breach of our regulatory requirements, by any person or firm: including wrongdoing by the firm, or harassment or other misconduct towards others such as employees or clients

- use NDAs as a means of improperly threatening litigation or other adverse consequences, or otherwise exerting inappropriate influence over people not to make disclosures which are protected by statute, or reportable to regulators or law enforcement agencies.

This warning notice provides a reminder of some of the key issues and risks that you should be aware of.

Status

Whilst this guidance does not form part of the SRA Handbook, we may have regard to it when exercising our regulatory functions. This warning notice is additional to previous warning notices and does not replace them.

Who is this guidance relevant to?

This guidance is relevant to everyone we regulate, and in particular:

*   managers and employees of law firms
*   those responsible for managing human resources and complaints in law firms
*   practitioners advising clients on the use of NDAs.

This note highlights your obligations if your firm is considering an NDA with someone who has complained. It also sets out your obligations when advising clients on NDAs with individuals (usually the client's current or former partners or directors, employees or workers, collectively referred to in this note, for ease of reference, as "employee" or "employees").

The SRA Principles

Inappropriate use of NDAs, failure to report actual or suspected misconduct, or other wrongdoing or criminal conduct, by you or, when acting on behalf of a client, improperly proposing, or exerting inappropriate influence on a third party to enter into an NDA either in an inappropriate manner or with inappropriate content; or failure to report wrongdoing that is subject to an NDA may put you in breach of one or more of the SRA Principles 2011 set out below:

Principle 1: uphold the rule of law and the proper administration of justice

Principle 2: act with integrity

Principle 3: act independently

Principle 6: behave in a way that maintains the trust the public places in you and in the provision of legal services

Principle 7: comply with your legal and regulatory obligations and deal with your regulators and ombudsmen in an open, timely and co-operative manner

Principle 8: run your business or carry out your role in the business effectively and in accordance with proper governance and sound financial and risk management principles.

The SRA mandatory outcomes

You should have regard to specific outcomes under the SRA Code of Conduct 2011:

Outcome (10.3): you notify the SRA promptly of ...serious failure to comply with or achieve the Principles, rules, outcomes and other requirements of the Handbook

Outcome (10.4): you report to the SRA promptly, serious misconduct by any person or firm authorised by the SRA, or any employee, manager or owner of any such firm

Outcome (10.7): you do not attempt to prevent anyone from providing information to the SRA or the Legal Ombudsman

Outcome (11.1): you do not take unfair advantage of third parties in either your professional or personal capacity.

Our expectations

We consider that NDAs would be improperly used if you sought to:

- use an NDA as a means of preventing, or seeking to impede or deter, a person from:

  - reporting misconduct, or a serious breach of our regulatory requirements to us, or making an equivalent report to any other body responsible for supervising or regulating the matters in question

  - making a protected disclosure under the Public Interest Disclosure Act 1998

  - reporting an offence to a law enforcement agency

  - co-operating with a criminal investigation or prosecution.

- use an NDA to influence the substance of such a report, disclosure or co-operation

- use an NDA as a means of improperly threatening litigation against, or otherwise seeking improperly to influence, an individual in order to prevent or deter or influence a proper disclosure

- prevent someone who has entered into an NDA from keeping or receiving a copy.

NDAs or other settlement terms must not stipulate, and the person expected to agree the NDA must not be given the impression, that reporting or disclosure as set out above is prohibited. It may be appropriate for the NDA itself to be clear about what disclosures are not prohibited by the NDA.

Where you find, or have grounds to believe, that a member of your firm has or may have committed a serious breach of our requirements, we expect you to report such findings or concerns to us. We may wish to investigate and we have statutory powers that are not available to you. Failure to report may be a failure to achieve Outcomes 10.3 or 10.4 and of one or more SRA Principles.

Any attempt to prevent a person from complaining or providing information to us will be a failure to achieve Outcome 10.7. Indicative Behaviour (10.11) cites, by way of example, entering into an agreement which would attempt to preclude us from investigating any actual or potential complaint or allegation of professional misconduct. A practitioner who proposes or uses an NDA or behaves in some other way that is in breach of Outcome 10.7 is at risk of disciplinary action.

You may also be at risk if you use improper threats of litigation or improperly influence a party by reference to other adverse consequences of making such report or disclosure.

Inappropriate or disproportionate threats, including a threat of defamation proceedings where such a claim is known to be unsustainable,[1] may well involve serious breaches of the Principles or Code. These are likely to breach our requirements, including Principle 1 and 6 as well as Outcomes (10.7) and (11.1). Taking unfair advantage of an opposing party's lack of legal knowledge where they have not instructed a lawyer) is an aggravating feature of such conduct (see Indicative Behaviour 11.7).

Where the employee is not represented, your obligations will be heightened, to ensure that there is no abuse of position, or unfair advantage taken.

If the agreement is or forms part of a settlement agreement under the Employment Rights Act 1996, you should ensure that you are aware of the requirements governing those agreements, including for the employee to be in receipt of independent advice. You will also need to ensure that the NDA does not include clauses known to be unenforceable.

Enforcement action

Failure to comply with this warning notice may lead to disciplinary action.

Other sources of help

SRA Risk paper Walking The Line: The balancing of duties in litigation.

Law Society practice note The Use of non disclosure agreements.

Further help

For guidance on conduct issues, contact the Professional Ethics Guidance Team.

NOTES

1. Huda v Wells [2017] EWHC 2553 QB at paras 57 to 67 provides a recent analysis of the defence of absolute privilege as it applies to referrals to statutory regulatory bodies.

Council for Licensed Conveyancers Code of Conduct

[The Code is reproduced with the kind permission of the CLC. For the latest updates to the material, please see www.conveyancer.org.uk.]

Council for Licensed Conveyancers Code of Conduct

[6 October 2011]

Introduction

This *Code of Conduct* was made in accordance with s.20 of the *Administration of Justice Act 1985* and s.83 of the *Legal Services Act 2007*.

All individuals and bodies regulated by the *CLC* must comply with this Code and its associated *regulatory arrangements*. In this Code "you" refers to individuals and bodies (and the employees and managers within them) regulated by the *CLC*. You must not permit anyone else to act or fail to act in such a way as to amount to a breach of this Code. Your main driver should be the delivery of positive *client outcomes*. The Code comprises *principles* and *specific requirements*, which taken together deliver positive *Outcomes* for your *Clients* and, particularly in relation to *Overriding Principle* 6, for others you deal with.

To effectively secure the protection of, and the provision of choice for, the consumer of legal services, you must at all times comply with the following *Overriding Principles*:

1. Act with independence and integrity;

2. Maintain high standards of work;

3. Act in the best interests of your *Clients*;

4. Comply with your duty to the court;

5. Deal with regulators and ombudsmen in an open and co-operative way;

6. Promote equality of access and service.

These are underpinned by *principles* of behaviour which must be demonstrated and *specific requirements* which must be complied with in order that the *Overriding Principles* are supported.

Disciplinary proceedings may be taken against you if the *CLC* believes there has been a breach of this Code, meaning that *clients* do not receive the standard of legal services they should reasonably expect to receive. The *CLC's* response will be informed by the *CLC's* Regulatory and *Enforcement* Policies.

In exceptional circumstances the *CLC* may waive a provision, or provisions, of the *regulatory arrangements* for an individual, body or circumstance for a particular purpose, or purposes, and with the *conditions* specified in the waiver.

Overriding Principle 1. Act with independence and integrity

Outcomes – you must deliver the following *Outcomes*:

1.1   *Clients* receive good quality independent information, representation and advice;

1.2   *Clients* receive an honest and lawful service;

1.3   *Client money* is kept separately and safely.

Principles – delivery of these *Outcomes* requires you to act in a principled way:

(a)   You do not allow your independence to be compromised.

(b)   You act honestly, professionally and decently.

(c)   You do not conduct yourself in a manner which may result in a breach of the law nor in any other manner which may bring the legal profession into disrepute.

(d)   You *carry on Reserved Legal Activity* only through a person entitled to *carry on* that activity.

(e)   You do not give false or misleading information relating to the provision of *Regulated Services*.

(f)   You do not allow fee arrangements to prejudice your independence or professional judgement.

(g)   You do not conduct business under a misleading name.

(h)   You keep *Client money* safe.

(i)   You do not publicise your business through unsolicited communications in person or by telephone.

(j)   Your advertising is clear, accurate and fair.

(k)   You keep *Client money* entirely separate from your money or the money of the entity.

(l)   You do not take unfair advantage of any person, whether or not a *Client* of the business.

Specific Requirements – you must also comply with the following *specific requirements*:

(m)   You comply with *anti-money laundering and prevention of financing terrorism legislation*.

(n)   When acting as a *CLC* licensee, you accept instructions only to act in a matter which is regulated by the *CLC*.

(o)   All business *communications*, websites and office premises display information confirming the entity is regulated by the *CLC* and the names of the *Managers* (identifying those who are *Authorised Persons*).

Overriding Principle 2. Maintain high standards of work

Outcomes – you must deliver the following *Outcomes*:

2.1   *Clients* are provided with a high standard of legal services;

2.2   *Client* matters are dealt with using care, skill and diligence;

2.3   Appropriate *arrangements*, resources, procedures, skills and commitment are in place to ensure *Clients* always receive a high standard of service.

Principles – delivery of these *Outcomes* requires you to act in a principled way:

(a)   You provide the level of service appropriate for, and agreed with, the *Client*.

(b)   You keep your skills and legal knowledge up-to-date.

(c)   You ensure all individuals within the entity are competent to do their work.

(d)   You supervise and regularly check the quality of work in *Client* matters.

(e)   You comply fully with any undertaking given by you.

(f)   You *systematically* identify and mitigate risks to the business and to *Clients*.

(g)   You promote ethical practice and compliance with regulatory requirements.

(h)   You enable staff to raise concerns which are acted on appropriately.

(i)   You maintain proper governance, management, supervision, financial, and risk manage-
       ment *arrangements* and *controls*.

(j)   You administer oaths, affirmations and declarations properly.

(k)   You deliver services in accordance with timetables reasonably agreed with the *Client*.

Specific Requirements – you must also comply with the following *specific requirements*:

(l)   *Control* of an entity is from a permanent fixed address in England or Wales.

(m)   A *Manager* who is an *Authorised Person* is responsible for ensuring that all of the entity's
       employees are properly supervised.

(n)   You make provision for alternative supervision *arrangements* in case of illness, accident or
       other unforeseen event.

(o)   You maintain proper records to evidence your *arrangements* and *controls* and how they are
       applied.

Overriding Principle 3. Act in the best interests of your Clients

Outcomes – you must deliver the following *Outcomes*:

3.1   Each *Client's* best interests are served;

3.2   *Clients* receive advice appropriate to their circumstances;

3.3   *Clients* have the information they need to make informed decisions;

3.4   *Clients* are aware of any referral arrangements and that they are consistent with your
       responsibilities both to them and to the *CLC*;

3.5   *Clients* are aware of any limitation or any condition resulting from your relationship
       with another party;

3.6   *Clients'* affairs are treated confidentially (except as required or permitted by law or with
       the *Client's* consent).

Principles – delivery of these *Outcomes* requires you to act in a principled way:

(a)   You only accept instructions and act in relation to matters which are within your
       professional competence.

(b)   You keep the interests of the *Client* paramount (except as required by the law or the
       CLC's regulatory arrangements).

(c)   You do not act for a *Client* where you judge it is not in their best interests for you to do
       so.

(d)   You do not accept instructions from a person nor continue to act for a *Client* whose interests conflict directly with your own, the entity's, or another *Client*.

(e)   You disclose *client* information only as the *Client* has instructed (or as required by the *CLC's regulatory arrangements* or by law), keeping effective records of any disclosures you make.

(f)   You only recommend a particular person, business or product when it is in the best interests of the *Client*.

(g)   You cease acting in a matter if the *Client* so instructs or, in the absence of such instructions where it is reasonable to do so.

(h)   You provide the *Client* with information which is accurate, useful and appropriate to the particular *Client*.

(i)   You only provide *Regulated Services* whilst you have *CLC*-approved *professional indemnity insurance* in force.

(j)   You provide the *Client* with all relevant information relating to any fee arrangements or fee changes.

(k)   You advise *Clients* of the name and status of the person dealing with their matter and the name of the person responsible for overall supervision.

(l)   You consult *Clients* on key decisions in a timely way.

(m)   You *promptly* advise *Clients* of any significant changes to projected *costs*, timelines and strategies.

Specific Requirements – you must also comply with the following *specific requirements*:

(n)   Where the entity represents parties with different interests in any transaction each party is at all times represented by different *Authorised Persons* conducting themselves in the matter as though they were members of different entities.

(o)   You ensure there are adequate indemnity arrangements in respect of *claims* made against you for work carried out by you before you have ceased to practise by *purchasing professional indemnity insurance* for a minimum of 6 years from the expiry of the period of *professional indemnity insurance* stated in your evidence of insurance or policy document.

(p)   If you seek to exclude or limit liability, you do so only to the extent that such exclusion or limitation is above the minimum level of cover provided by *CLC*-approved *professional indemnity insurance*; you must obtain the written informed consent of the *Client* for such exclusion or limitation to be effective.

(q)   When offering and providing services which are not regulated by the *CLC*, you advise your *Client* of this and inform them in writing that the activity is not covered by *CLC*-approved *professional indemnity insurance* or the *CLC*-administered *Compensation Fund*.

(r)   Before or when accepting instructions, you inform *Clients* in writing of the terms on which the instructions are accepted, a complete, accurate estimate of fees and *disbursements* to be charged and if and when they are likely to change.

(s)   You *promptly* inform the *Client* in writing of the existence and amount of any sum payable (whether directly or indirectly) as a result of receipt of that *Client's* instructions.

(t)   With the exception of *disbursements*, you do not delay completion because fees are outstanding to you.

(u)   You discuss and agree with the *Client* how *costs* will be paid, whether directly by the *Client*, by public funding, through an insurance policy or otherwise.

Overriding Principle 4. Comply with your duty to the court

Note: this Principle will only be applicable if the *CLC's* application to regulate *advocacy* and *litigation* services is successful

Outcomes – you must deliver the following *Outcomes*:

4.1   You act in the interests of justice;

4.2   You act in good faith towards *Clients*.

Principles – delivery of these *Outcomes* requires you to act in a principled way:

(a)   You promote and protect the *client's* best interests.

(b)   You do not compromise your professional standards or independence.

(c)   You assist the court in the administration of justice.

(d)   You do not knowingly or recklessly mislead or deceive the court, or allow the court to be misled.

(e)   You ensure that the Court is informed of all relevant decisions and legislative provisions (whether this has a favourable or unfavourable effect on the case you are advancing).

(f)   You comply with any Court Order (unless an application for a stay is pending or the Order has been revoked by the Court).

(g)   You advise your *Client* to comply with Court Orders and of the consequences of failing to do so.

(h)   You properly protect sensitive evidence.

(i)   You safeguard the well being of children and other vulnerable persons.

Specific Requirement – you must also comply with the following specific requirement:

(j)   You ensure that the court is made aware of any relevant legal or factual matters which are likely to have a material effect on the outcome of the proceedings.

Overriding Principle 5. Deal with regulators and ombudsmen in an open and co-operative way

Outcome – you must deliver the following *Outcome*:

5.1   You act in accordance with your regulatory responsibilities.

Principles – delivery of these *Outcomes* requires you to act in a principled way:

(a)   You are open and honest in your dealings with us.

(b)   You comply with the *CLC Code of Conduct* and the *CLC's* other *regulatory arrangements*.

(c)   You comply *promptly* and fully with a *CLC* direction or request.

(d)   You comply with any *authorisation*, *permission* or *condition* endorsed on your *licence*, *Recognised Body Certificate* or *Licensed Body Licence*.

(e)   You co-operate with any *CLC* investigation.

(f)   You co-operate with any *Legal Ombudsman* investigation.

(g)   You comply *promptly* and fully with any *Legal Ombudsman* Order.

(h)   You co-operate with other regulators and ombudsmen.

Specific Requirements – you must also comply with the following *specific requirements*:

(i)   You make the *Compensation Fund* contribution determined by the *CLC*.

(j)   You *systematically* identify, monitor and manage risks to the delivery of this Code's *outcomes*.

(k)   You *promptly* notify insurers in writing of any facts or matters which may give rise to a *claim* under *CLC*-approved *professional indemnity insurance*.

(l)   You *promptly* notify the *CLC* in writing of any facts or matters which may give rise to a *claim* under its *Compensation Fund*.

(m)   As a *CLC* licensee operating in an entity regulated by another regulator you must comply with that regulator's regulations at all times in a way which is reasonably consistent with this Code.

(n)   You obtain permission from the *CLC* before offering *Reserved legal activities*:

   –   as a new business;

   –   in an entity regulated by another *Approved Regulator*; or

   –   through a entity with a *Manager* who is not a *Licensed Conveyancer*.

(o)   You notify the *CLC* of any material breach of this Code, whether by you, the entity or any other person.

(p)   You notify the *CLC* of a change as set out in the *CLC's* Notification Code.

Overriding Principle 6. Promote equality of access and service.

Outcomes – you must deliver the following *Outcomes*:

6.1   The service is accessible and responsive to the needs of individual *Clients*, including those who are vulnerable;[1]

6.2   No-one – *Client, employee*, colleague, job applicant, trainee or other party – you deal with feels discriminated[2] against (whether directly or indirectly), victimised or harassed;

6.3   You accept responsibility where the service you provide is not of the expected standard and provide appropriate redress for the *Client* where necessary;

6.4   Handling of *complaints* takes proper account of *Clients'* individual needs, including those who are vulnerable;

6.5   *Complaints* are dealt with impartially and comprehensively.

Principles – delivery of these *Outcomes* requires you to act in a principled way:

(a)   You comply with *Equalities legislation*.

(b)   You make reasonable adjustments to prevent persons with disabilities from being placed at a substantial disadvantage.

(c)   You provide equal opportunities for all partners, *employees* or applicants in employment and training.

(d)   You make all reasonable efforts to ensure your service is accessible and responsive to *Clients*, including those with vulnerabilities.

(e)   The *complaints* procedure is clear, well-publicised and free.

(f) You treat *complaints* seriously and provide appropriate redress options.

(g) You deal with *complaints* fairly and within 28 days.

(h) You identify and address systemic *Client Complaints* issues.

Specific Requirements – you must also comply with the following *specific requirements*:

(i) Any allegation of (direct or indirect) discrimination, victimisation and harassment is investigated thoroughly, resulting, where appropriate, in disciplinary action.

(j) From the outset you advise *Clients* in writing of their right to make a complaint, how to make it, to whom, and the timeframes involved.

(k) You advise *Clients* in writing of their right to have their *complaint* escalated to the *Legal Ombudsman* and provide them with contact details and timeframes of that body.

(l) You keep a record of *complaints* received and any action taken as a result.

Notes

1 A *Client* may be vulnerable because of a range of characteristics, including (but not limited to): basic skills: literacy and numeracy; complexity and confusion: difficulty of accessing and understanding large amounts of information; disability or other impairment; mental health issues; distress or sudden change in circumstances e.g. bereavement, divorce, illness or loss of employment; low income; age; caring responsibilities; limited knowledge of, or limited skills in, use of English; balance of power: lack of competition and or choice; or inexperience or lack of knowledge of a particular subject. Vulnerability can only be assessed on a case-by-case basis.

2 On the grounds of age, disability, gender reassignment, marital and civil partnership status, pregnancy and maternity, race, religion or faith, sex or sexual orientation.

SRA guidance on publishing regulatory and disciplinary decisions

[Law Society copyright. For the latest updates to the material, please see www.sra.org.uk.]

Publishing regulatory and disciplinary decisions

Introduction

Purpose and scope of this guidance

This document provides guidance for those considering whether to publish regulatory decisions on our website.

This guidance should be read in the context of decision making at the SRA and other guidance documents. It is a living document and will be reviewed and updated as appropriate. It reflects our approach to our regulatory role and any departure must be capable of justification on the individual facts of the case.

Decisions that may be published

We make a wide range of regulatory and disciplinary decisions. We have a statutory power to publish fines and rebukes. We also publish other information about our work and key decisions where we consider it is in the public interest for us to do so, such as the status of our ongoing investigations. And, for example, decisions to intervene have long been published as an essential part of informing clients that their law firm has been closed down. Similarly, cases before the Solicitors Disciplinary Tribunal (SDT) are generally heard in public.

Decisions that we publish include, but are not limited to:

- **fines and rebukes** – in accordance with the criteria set out in the SRA (Disciplinary Procedure) Rules

- **controls**, such as conditions on practising certificates or on the authorisation of firms which we regulate

- **issue of proceedings before the Solicitors Disciplinary Tribunal** (SDT) in general, once the SDT has certified there is a case to answer

- **Regulatory Settlement Agreements** – (Read RSA guidance)

- **intervention decisions**

- **revocation of a firm's authorisation**

- **approval of employment** of people who are subject to section 43 of the Solicitors Act 1974 or struck off or suspended solicitors, under s41 of the Solicitors Act 1974

- **refusal** to issue a practising certificate.

Generally we expect that these decisions will be published unless we consider that one or more of the factors below would make such publication inappropriate. Each decision to publish will be taken on its own merits and we will take into account all of the relevant circumstances, including any representations made by the person who is subject of the decision and, where appropriate, other relevant third parties.

Why do we publish?

We act in the public interest and this includes providing appropriate protection for consumers and supporting the administration of justice and the rule of law. There is a public interest in being transparent about the decisions we make and why we have made them, in order to:

- raise awareness amongst those we regulate about the action we have taken to improve understanding of our expectations, and deter them from action which would fall below standards or breach our requirements

- ensure consumers and others, including prospective employers are able to access appropriate information:
    - to inform them about the closure of a firm as a result of an intervention
    - to enable them to make informed choices about whom to instruct or to employ
    - to decide whether behaviour of concern should be reported to us for action

- ensure we are properly accountable to the public for the decisions we make and demonstrate that we are acting proportionately and consistently; and

- maintain public confidence by demonstrating appropriate action is taken when things go wrong.

Example I

We decide to intervene into a firm as we suspect dishonesty on the part of the managers. We publish the fact of the intervention on our website. The publication decision includes brief details for the reason for the intervention, as well as the contact details for the agents we have appointed so that clients can contact them to access their files or money.

When might publication not be appropriate?

We may decide not to publish a decision if we are satisfied that:

- we would be unable to do so without:
    - disclosing someone's confidential or legally privileged information
    - disclosing someone's confidential medical condition or treatment
    - prejudicing other investigations or legal proceedings

- in all the circumstances the impact of publication on the regulated person would be disproportionate. In particular, we need to consider Article 8 of the European Convention on Human Rights and balance the right to a private life with the legitimate aim of publication, as set out above.

These factors are not exhaustive and we will take into account all other factors that we consider to be relevant.

Example 2

We decide to fine a solicitor for a caution for a sexual offence, committed outside of practice. The solicitor has provided medical evidence which confirms that the stress of the publication of the fine will cause him to become a suicide risk. Taking these factors into account, we decide that publication is not in the public interest.

Other relevant issues

Nature of the publication

We will publish the decision on our website. We will usually publish a short statement of the decision with brief factual details, such as where the person is currently working or was previously working, and the reasons for the decision.

Regulatory Settlement Agreements will normally be published in full. The aim is to give the public sufficient information so they can understand the nature of and reason for the decision.

We will take reasonable steps to avoid the publication of information relating to other identifiable persons. Where it is necessary to refer to clients or colleagues their details will be appropriately anonymised.

Timing and length of publication

We will normally publish decisions promptly. In exceptional cases, we may publish the fact of a referral to the SDT prior to certification by the SDT if we consider it is in the public interest for us to do so.

Certain decisions we publish are appealable, such as fines and conditions. Generally, we will not publish such decisions during any appeal period and until any such appeal has been determined or withdrawn.

As it is important to let the clients of a firm we have intervened into know as soon as possible that that a firm has closed down, we will generally aim to publish such decisions immediately following the intervention. With the exception of intervention decisions, we will generally give the regulated person or firm the opportunity to comment in advance about whether the decision should be published. We will take their views in to account when making our decision whether to publish and will tell them what we have decided.

We may decide that it is not appropriate to publish the decision at the time it was made, for example, if this will risk prejudicing any ongoing proceedings, but we may then do so at a later date once those proceedings have concluded, or the risk is no longer material.

Generally, we will automatically remove decisions from our website three years after the date of publication, unless we consider that exceptionally it is not in the public interest for us to do so.

However, some publications such as section 43 orders or referrals to the SDT that result in a strike off or suspension of more than three years will remain on our website, until the period of the suspension has ended, or a successful application is made for the section 43 order, suspension or strike off to be lifted. This allows the public or other interested parties to find out important information on our website about individuals we regulate.

Example 3

We decide to issue proceedings against a solicitor at the SDT for allegations around significant misuse of client money and failure to comply with the Accounts Rules. After considering her representations, we decide that it is appropriate to publish the referral. We publish a brief summary of the allegations, making it clear on our website that the allegations have not yet been proven. At the subsequent SDT hearing, the solicitor is struck from the roll. We remove the allegations, confirming instead the sanction imposed by the SDT and including a link to the SDT's website should anyone require access to the full judgment (normally available six-eight weeks after the decision). We do not remove the decision after three years so that a member of the public searching for that solicitor's name on our website will be able to find out that they have been struck off by the SDT.

Review of publication

Decisions may be amended or removed from our website where we consider that publication is no longer necessary in the public interest, or to correct or update the information. We may decide to do this ourselves. For example, we will update the summary of allegations to be made at the SDT in a particular case when the SDT has agreed to make an amendment to those allegations and as a result the published summary is inaccurate.

If we are asked to remove a publication within the three year period because of new information or a change in circumstances, we will consider if this is appropriate. In doing so, we will have regard to all the circumstances and consider the request in line with the factors relating to the decision to publish set out above.

Regulators' Code

Regulators' Code

This Code was laid before Parliament in accordance with section 23 of the Legislative and Regulatory Reform Act 2006 ("the Act"). Regulators whose functions are specified by order under section 24(2) of the Act must have regard to the Code when developing policies and operational procedures that guide their regulatory activities. Regulators must equally have regard to the Code when setting standards or giving guidance which will guide the regulatory activities of other regulators. If a regulator concludes, on the basis of material evidence, that a specific provision of the Code is either not applicable or is outweighed by another relevant consideration, the regulator is not bound to follow that provision, but should record that decision and the reasons for it.

1. **Regulators should carry out their activities in a way that supports those they regulate to comply and grow**

1.1   Regulators should avoid imposing unnecessary regulatory burdens through their regulatory activities[1] and should assess whether similar social, environmental and economic outcomes could be achieved by less burdensome means. Regulators should choose proportionate approaches to those they regulate, based on relevant factors including, for example, business size and capacity.

1.2   When designing and reviewing policies, operational procedures and practices, regulators should consider how they might support or enable economic growth for compliant businesses and other regulated entities[2], for example, by considering how they can best:

  *   understand and minimise negative economic impacts of their regulatory activities;

  *   minimising the costs of compliance for those they regulate;

  *   improve confidence in compliance for those they regulate, by providing greater certainty; and

  *   encourage and promote compliance.

1.3   Regulators should ensure that their officers have the necessary knowledge and skills to support those they regulate, including having an understanding of those they regulate that enables them to choose proportionate and effective approaches.

1.4   Regulators should ensure that their officers understand the statutory principles of good regulation[3] and of this Code, and how the regulator delivers its activities in accordance with them.

2. **Regulators should provide simple and straightforward ways to engage with those they regulate and hear their views**

2.1   Regulators should have mechanisms in place to engage those they regulate, citizens and others to offer views and contribute to the development of their policies and service standards. Before changing policies, practices or service standards, regulators should consider the impact on business and engage with business representatives.

2.2　In responding to non-compliance that they identify, regulators should clearly explain what the non-compliant item or activity is, the advice being given, actions required or decisions taken, and the reasons for these. Regulators should provide an opportunity for dialogue in relation to the advice, requirements or decisions, with a view to ensuring that they are acting in a way that is proportionate and consistent.

This paragraph does not apply where the regulator can demonstrate that immediate enforcement action is required to prevent or respond to a serious breach or where providing such an opportunity would be likely to defeat the purpose of the proposed enforcement action.

2.3　Regulators should provide an impartial and clearly explained route to appeal against a regulatory decision or a failure to act in accordance with this Code. Individual officers of the regulator who took the decision or action against which the appeal is being made should not be involved in considering the appeal. This route to appeal should be publicised to those who are regulated.

2.4　Regulators should provide a timely explanation in writing of any right to representation or right to appeal. This explanation should be in plain language and include practical information on the process involved.

2.5　Regulators should make available to those they regulate, clearly explained complaints procedures, allowing them to easily make a complaint about the conduct of the regulator.

2.6　Regulators should have a range of mechanisms to enable and regularly invite, receive and take on board customer feedback, including, for example, through customer satisfaction surveys of those they regulate[4].

3.　Regulators should base their regulatory activities on risk

3.1　Regulators should take an evidence based approach to determining the priority risks in their area of responsibility, and should allocate resources where they would be most effective in addressing those priority risks.

3.2　Regulators should consider risk at every stage of their decision-making processes, including choosing the most appropriate type of intervention or way of working with those regulated; targeting checks on compliance; and when taking enforcement action.

3.3　Regulators designing a risk assessment framework[5], for their own use or for use by others, should have mechanisms in place to consult on the design with those affected, and to review it regularly.

3.4　Regulators, in making their assessment of risk, should recognise the compliance record of those they regulate, including using earned recognition approaches and should consider all available and relevant data on compliance, including evidence of relevant external verification.

3.5　Regulators should review the effectiveness of their chosen regulatory activities in delivering the desired outcomes and make any necessary adjustments accordingly.

4.　Regulators should share information about compliance and risk

4.1　Regulators should collectively follow the principle of "collect once, use many times" when requesting information from those they regulate.

4.2　When the law allows, regulators should agree secure mechanisms to share information with each other about businesses and other bodies they regulate, to help target resources and activities and minimise duplication.

5.　Regulators should ensure clear information, guidance and advice is available to help those they regulate meet their responsibilities to comply

5.1　Regulators should provide advice and guidance that is focused on assisting those they regulate to understand and meet their responsibilities. When providing advice and guidance, legal requirements should be distinguished from suggested good practice and the impact of the advice or guidance should be considered so that it does not impose unnecessary burdens in itself.

5.2 Regulators should publish guidance, and information in a clear, accessible, concise format, using media appropriate to the target audience and written in plain language for the audience.

5.3 Regulators should have mechanisms in place to consult those they regulate in relation to the guidance they produce to ensure that it meets their needs.

5.4 Regulators should seek to create an environment in which those they regulate have confidence in the advice they receive and feel able to seek advice without fear of triggering enforcement action.

5.5 In responding to requests for advice, a regulator's primary concerns should be to provide the advice necessary to support compliance, and to ensure that the advice can be relied on.

5.6 Regulators should have mechanisms to work collaboratively to assist those regulated by more than one regulator. Regulators should consider advice provided by other regulators and, where there is disagreement about the advice provided, this should be discussed with the other regulator to reach agreement.

6. Regulators should ensure that their approach to their regulatory activities is transparent

6.1 Regulators should publish a set of clear service standards, setting out what those they regulate should expect from them.

6.2 Regulators' published service standards should include clear information on:

a) how they communicate with those they regulate and how they can be contacted;

b) their approach to providing information, guidance and advice;

c) their approach to checks on compliance[6], including details of the risk assessment framework used to target those checks as well as protocols for their conduct, clearly setting out what those they regulate should expect;

d) their enforcement policy, explaining how they respond to non-compliance;

e) their fees and charges, if any. This information should clearly explain the basis on which these are calculated, and should include an explanation of whether compliance will affect fees and charges; and

f) how to comment or complain about the service provided and routes to appeal.

6.3 Information published to meet the provisions of this Code should be easily accessible, including being available at a single point[7] on the regulator's website that is clearly signposted, and it should be kept up to date.

6.4 Regulators should have mechanisms in place to ensure that their officers act in accordance with their published service standards, including their enforcement policy.

6.5 Regulators should publish, on a regular basis, details of their performance against their service standards, including feedback received from those they regulate, such as customer satisfaction surveys, and data relating to complaints about them and appeals against their decisions.

---

1 The term 'regulatory activities' refers to the whole range of regulatory options and interventions available to regulators.
2 The terms 'business or businesses' is used throughout this document to refer to businesses and other regulated entities.
3 The statutory principles of good regulation can be viewed in Part 2 (21) on page 12: http://www.legislation.gov.uk/ukpga/2006/51/pdfs/ukpga_20060051_en.pdf.
4 The Government will discuss with national regulators a common approach to surveys to support benchmarking of their performance.

5   The term 'risk assessment framework' encompasses any model, scheme, methodology or risk rating approach that is used to inform risk-based targeting of regulatory activities in relation to individual businesses or other regulated entities.

6   Including inspections, audit, monitoring and sampling visits, and test purchases.

7   This requirement may be satisfied by providing a single web page that includes links to information published elsewhere.

Legal Ombudsman Scheme Rules

[The Legal Ombudsman Scheme Rules are reproduced with the kind permission of the Legal Ombudsman. For the latest updates to the material, please see www.legalombudsman.org.uk.]

[Last updated 1 April 2019]

Legal Ombudsman Scheme Rules

1 Introduction and definitions

Contents

1.1   ●   These scheme rules are about *complaints* made from 6 October 2010 to *authorised persons* including legal practitioners and others, authorised in England and Wales.

      ●   They explain which *complaints* are covered by the *Legal Ombudsman* and how it will deal with them.

      ●   This version includes amendments that apply to complaints referred to the Legal Ombudsman from 28 January 2015.

1.2   Parliament, in the *Act*:

      ●   created the Legal Services Board (to oversee *Approved Regulators*) and the Office for Legal Complaints (to establish the *Legal Ombudsman*);

      ●   gave the Lord Chancellor power to make orders, including orders modifying who would be able to bring a *complaint* to the *Legal Ombudsman*;

      ●   gave the Legal Services Board power to set requirements for the rules of *Approved Regulators* about how *authorised persons* handle *complaints*[1] and cooperate with an *ombudsman*;[2] and

      ●   gave the Office for Legal Complaints power to make rules affecting which *complaints* can be handled by the *Legal Ombudsman* and how those *complaints* will be handled.

1.3   These scheme rules include:

      ●   a summary of relevant provisions in the *Act*, as modified by orders made by the Lord Chancellor (though it is the *Act* and the orders themselves that count);

      ●   a summary of requirements on complaint-handling made by the Legal Services Board under the powers given to it by the *Act*; and

      ●   rules made by the Office for Legal Complaints under the powers given to it by the *Act*.

The endnotes identify the section of the *Act* that is being summarised, or under which an order, requirement or rule has been made; and which are the rules made by the Office of Legal Complaints for the Legal Ombudsman.

1.4   This book also includes some general guidance. There are six chapters –

1:    Introduction and definitions:

  –   contents of this book;

  –   meaning of words that are underlined [italicised].

2:    Who can complain about what:

  –   who can complain;

  –   what they can complain about.

3:    What *authorised persons* must do:

  –   dealing with *complaints* themselves;

  –   cooperating with the *Legal Ombudsman*.

4:    When *complaints* can be referred to the *Legal Ombudsman*:

  –   after complaining to the *authorised person*;

  –   time limit from act/omission;

  –   *ombudsman* extending time limits.

5:    How the *Legal Ombudsman* deals with *complaints*:

  –   first contact;

  –   grounds for dismissal;

  –   referring a *complaint* to court;

  –   referring to another *complaints* scheme;

  –   related *complaints*;

  –   informal resolution and investigation;

  –   evidence;

  –   procedural time limits;

  –   hearings;

  –   determinations and awards by an *ombudsman*;

  –   acceptance/rejection of determinations;

  –   publication;

  –   enforcement.

6:    Case fees payable by *authorised persons*.

Meaning of words that are underlined [italicised]

1.5   The *Act* means the Legal Services Act 2007.

1.6   *Complaint* means an oral or written expression of dissatisfaction which:

  (a)   alleges that the complainant has suffered (or may suffer) financial loss, distress, inconvenience or other detriment; and

  (b)   is covered by chapter two (who can complain about what).[3]

1.7   *Authorised person* means:

  (a)   someone authorised, in England and Wales, to carry out a *reserved legal activity*[4] at the time of the relevant act/omission or covered under section 129 of the *Act*,[5] including:

   •   alternative business structures (licensed under part 5 of the *Act*);

628

- barristers;
- costs lawyers;
- chartered legal executives;
- licensed conveyancers;
- notaries;
- patent attorneys;
- probate practitioners;
- registered European lawyers;
- solicitors;
- trade mark attorneys; or

(b) (under section 131 of the *Act*):

- a business that is responsible for an act/omission of an employee; and
- a partnership that is responsible for an act/omission of a partner.[6]

1.8 *Approved Regulator* means:

(a) a regulator approved under schedule 4 of the *Act*, including:

- the Association of Chartered Certified Accountants (for reserved probate activities);
- the Association of Costs Lawyers, through the Costs Lawyer Standards Board;
- the Bar Council, through the Bar Standards Board (for barristers);
- the Chartered Institute of Patent Attorneys, through the Intellectual Property Regulation Board;
- the Council for Licensed Conveyancers;
- the Institute of Chartered Accountants in England and Wales (for reserved probate activities)
- the Institute of Chartered Accountants in Scotland (for reserved probate activities);
- CILEX Regulation, through the Chartered Institute of Legal Executives;
- the Chartered Institute of Trade Mark Attorneys, through the Intellectual Property Regulation Board;
- the Law Society, through the Solicitors Regulation Authority;
- the Master of the Faculties (for notaries); and
- the Legal Services Board (but only for any alternative business structures it licenses directly);

1.9 *Determination* means a final decision that is made by an ombudsman on a complaint.

1.10 *Legal Ombudsman* means the ombudsman scheme established by the Office for Legal Complaints.

1.11 *Ombudsman* means:

(a) any ombudsman from the *Legal Ombudsman;*[8] and

(b) any *Legal Ombudsman* staff member to whom an *ombudsman* has delegated the relevant functions (but an *ombudsman* cannot delegate the functions of determining a *complaint* or of dismissing or discontinuing it for any of the reasons under paragraph 5.7).[9]

1.12 *Party* includes:

    (a)   a complainant (covered by chapter two);

    (b)   an *authorised person* (covered by chapter two) against whom the *complaint* is made;

    (c)   an *authorised person* (covered by chapter five) whom an *ombudsman* treats as a joint respondent to a *complaint*.[10]

1.13 *Public body* means any government department, local authority or any other body constituted for the purposes of the public services, local government or the administration of justice.[11]

1.14 *Reserved legal activity* (as defined in schedule 2 of the *Act*) means:

    (a)   exercising a right of audience;

    (b)   conducting litigation;

    (c)   reserved instrument activities;

    (d)   probate activities;

    (e)   notarial activities;

    (f)   administration of oaths.

2 Who can complain about what

Who can complain

2.1 A complainant must be one of the following:[12]

    (a)   an individual;

    (b)   a business or enterprise that was a micro-enterprise (European Union definition) when it referred the complaint to the *authorised person*;[13]

    (c)   a charity that had an annual income net of tax of less than £1 million when it referred the complaint to the *authorised person*;

    (d)   a club/association/organisation, the affairs of which are managed by its members/a committee/a committee of its members, that had an annual income net of tax of less than £1 million when it referred the complaint to the *authorised person*;

    (e)   a trustee of a trust that had an asset value of less than £1 million when it referred the complaint to the *authorised person*; or;

    (f)   a personal representative or beneficiary of the estate of a person who, before he/she died, had not referred the complaint to the *Legal Ombudsman*.

For (e) and (f) the condition is that the services to which the complaint relates were provided by the respondent to a person –

    (a)   who has subsequently died; and

    (b)   who had not by his or her death referred the complaint to the ombudsman scheme.

2.2 If a complainant who has referred a *complaint* to the *Legal Ombudsman* dies or is otherwise unable to act, the *complaint* can be continued by:[14]

    (a)   anyone authorised by law (for example:

- the executor of a complainant who has died; or
- someone with a lasting power of attorney from a complainant who is incapable); or

(b) the residuary beneficiaries of the estate of a complainant who has died.[15]

2.3 A complainant must not have been, at the time of the act/omission to which the *complaint* relates:

(a) a *public body* (or acting for a *public body*) in relation to the services complained about; or

(b) an *authorised person* who procured the services complained about on behalf of someone else.[16] [17]

2.4 For example, where the *complaint* is about a barrister who was instructed by a solicitor on behalf of a consumer, the consumer can complain to the *ombudsman* but the solicitor cannot.

2.5 A complainant can authorise someone else in writing (including an *authorised person*) to act for the complainant in pursuing a *complaint*, but the *Legal Ombudsman* remains free to contact the complainant direct where it considers that appropriate.[18]

What they can complain about

2.6 The *complaint* must relate to an act/omission by someone who was an *authorised person* at that time[19] but:

(a) an act/omission by an employee is usually treated also as an act/omission by their employer, whether or not the employer knew or approved;[20] and

(b) an act/omission by a partner is usually treated also as an act/omission by the partnership, unless the complainant knew (at the time of the act/omission) that the partner had no authority to act for the partnership.[21]

2.7 The act/omission does not have to:

(a) relate to a *reserved legal activity*;[22] nor

(b) be after the *Act* came into force[23] (but see the time limits in chapter four).

2.8 The *complaint* must relate to services which the *authorised person*:

(a) provided to the complainant; or

(b) provided to another *authorised person* who procured them on behalf of the complainant; or

(c) provided to (or as) a personal representative/trustee where the complainant is a beneficiary of the estate/trust;[24] or

(d) offered, or refused to provide, to the complainant.[25]

2.9 A *complaint* is not affected by any change in the membership of a partnership or other unincorporated body.[26]

2.10 Where *authorised person* A ceases to exist and B succeeds to the whole (or substantially the whole) of A's business:

(a) acts/omissions by A become acts/omissions of B;[27] and

(b) *complaints* already outstanding against A become *complaints* against B[28]

unless an *Ombudsman* decides that this is, in his/her opinion, not fair and reasonable in all the circumstances of the case.

3 What authorised persons must do

Dealing with complaints themselves

3.1 *Authorised persons* including legal practitioners and others must comply with their *Approved Regulator's* rules on handling *complaints*, including any requirements specified by the Legal Services Board[29]

3.2 The Legal Services Board has required that:

(a) *authorised persons* tell all clients in writing at the time of engagement, or existing clients at the next appropriate opportunity that they can complain, how and to whom this can be done;

(b) this must include that they can complain to the *Legal Ombudsman* at the end of the *authorised person's* complaints process, the timeframe for doing so and full details of how to contact the *Legal Ombudsman*; and

(c) *authorised persons* tell all clients in writing at the end of the *authorised person's* complaints process that they can complain to the *Legal Ombudsman*, the timeframe for doing so and full details of how to contact the *Legal Ombudsman*.

3.3 The Legal Services Board expects that regulation of complaint-handling procedures by *Approved Regulators* will:

(a) give consumers confidence that:

- effective safeguards will be provided; and

- complaints will be dealt with comprehensively and swiftly, with appropriate redress where necessary;

(b) provide processes that are:

- convenient and easy to use (in particular for those that are vulnerable or have disabilities);

- transparent, clear, well-publicised, free and allow *complaints* to be made by any reasonable means;

- prompt and fair, with decisions based on sufficient investigation of the circumstances, and (where appropriate) offer a suitable remedy.

Cooperating with the Legal Ombudsman

3.4 *Authorised persons* must comply with their *Approved Regulator's* rules on cooperating with an *ombudsman*, including any requirements specified by the Legal Services Board.[30]

4 When complaints can be referred to the Legal Ombudsman

After complaining to the authorised person

4.1 Ordinarily, a complainant cannot use the *Legal Ombudsman* unless the complainant has first used the *authorised person's* complaints procedure (referred to in chapter three).[31]

Time limit from authorised person's final response

4.2 But a complainant can use the *Legal Ombudsman* if:[32]

(a)   the *complaint* has not been resolved to the complainant's satisfaction within eight weeks of being made to the *authorised person*; or

(b)   an *ombudsman* considers that there are exceptional reasons to consider the *complaint* sooner, or without it having been made first to the *authorised person*; or

(c)   where an *ombudsman* considers that in-house resolution is not possible due to irretrievable breakdown in the relationship between an *authorised person* and the person making the *complaint*.

4.3   For example, an *ombudsman* may decide that the *Legal Ombudsman* should consider the *complaint* where the authorised person has refused to consider it, or where delay would harm the complainant.

4.4   (a)   This time limit applies only if the *authorised person's* written response to a *complaint* included prominently:

- an explanation that the *Legal Ombudsman* was available if the complainant remained dissatisfied;

- full contact details for the *Legal Ombudsman*; and

- a warning that the *complaint* must be referred to the *Legal Ombudsman* within six months of the date of the written response;

(b)   If (but only if) the conditions in (a) are satisfied, a complainant must ordinarily refer the *complaint* to the *Legal Ombudsman* within six months of the date of that written response.

Time limit from act/omission

4.5   Ordinarily:

(a)   the act or omission, or when the complainant should reasonably have known there was cause for complaint, must have been after 5 October 2010; and

(b)   the complainant must refer the *complaint* to the *Legal Ombudsman* no later than:

    —   six years from the act/omission; or

    —   three years from when the complainant should reasonably have known there was cause for complaint.[33]

4.6   In relation to 4.5(b):

(a)   where a complaint is referred by a personal representative or beneficiary of the estate of a person who, before he/she died, had not referred the complaint to the *Legal Ombudsman*, the period runs from when the deceased should reasonably have known there was cause for complaint; and

(b)   when the complainant (or the deceased) should reasonably have known there was a cause for complaint will be assessed on the basis of the complainant's (or the deceased's) own knowledge, disregarding what the complainant (or the deceased) might have been told if he/she had sought advice.

Ombudsman extending time limits

4.7   If an *ombudsman* considers that there are exceptional circumstances, he/she may extend any of these time limits to the extent that he/she considers fair.[34]

4.8   For example, an *Ombudsman*:

(a)   might extend a time limit if the complainant was prevented from meeting the time limit as a result of serious illness; and

(b)   is likely to extend a time limit where the time limit had not expired when the complainant raised the *complaint* with the *authorised person*.

5 How the Legal Ombudsman will deal with complaints[35]

5.1 The *Legal Ombudsman* may require a complainant to complete its complaint form.[36]

5.2 In the case of a partnership (or former partnership), it is sufficient for the *Legal Ombudsman* to communicate with any partner (or former partner).[37]

First contact

5.3 Unless:

(a) the *authorised person* has already had eight weeks to consider the *complaint*; or

(b) the *authorised person* has already issued a written response to the *complaint*; or

(c) an *ombudsman* considers that there are exceptional reasons;

the *Legal Ombudsman* will:

(a) refer the *complaint* to the *authorised person*;

(b) notify the complainant; and

(c) explain why to both of them.[38]

5.4 If the *authorised person* claims that all or part of the *complaint*:

(a) is not covered by the Legal Ombudsman under chapter two; or

(b) is out-of-time under chapter four; or

(c) should be dismissed under paragraph 5.7;

an *ombudsman* will give all *parties* an opportunity to make representations before deciding.[39]

5.5 Otherwise, if an *ombudsman* considers that all or part of the *complaint*:

(a) may not be covered by the *Legal Ombudsman* under chapter two; or

(b) may be out-of-time under chapter four; or

(c) should be dismissed under paragraph 5.7;

the *ombudsman* will give the complainant an opportunity to make representations before deciding.[40]

5.6 The *ombudsman* will then give the complainant and the *authorised person* his/her decision and the reasons for it.[41]

Grounds for dismissing or discontinuing a complaint[42]

5.7 An *ombudsman* may (but does not have to) dismiss or discontinue all or part of a *complaint* if, in his/her opinion:

(a) it does not have any reasonable prospect of success, or is frivolous or vexatious; or

(b) the complainant has not suffered (and is unlikely to suffer) financial loss, distress, inconvenience or other detriment; or

(c) the *authorised person* has already offered fair and reasonable redress in relation to the circumstances alleged by the complainant and the offer is still open for acceptance; or

(d) the complainant has previously complained about the same issue to the *Legal Ombudsman* or a predecessor complaints scheme (unless the *ombudsman* considers that material new evidence, likely to affect the outcome, only became available to the complainant afterwards); or

(e)   a comparable independent complaints (or costs-assessment) scheme or a court has already dealt with the same issue; or

(f)   a comparable independent complaints (or costs-assessment) scheme or a court is dealing with the same issue, unless those proceedings are first stayed (by the agreement of all parties or by a court order) so that the *Legal Ombudsman* can deal with the issue; or

(g)   it would be more suitable for the issue to be dealt with by a court, by arbitration or by another complaints (or costs-assessment) scheme;[43] or

(h)   the issue concerns an *authorised person's* decision when exercising a discretion under a will or trust; or

(i)   the issue concerns an *authorised person's* failure to consult a beneficiary before exercising a discretion under a will or trust, where there is no legal obligation to consult;

(j)   the issue involves someone else who has not complained and the *ombudsman* considers that it would not be appropriate to deal with the issue without their consent; or

(k)   it is not practicable to investigate the issue fairly because of the time which has elapsed since the act/omission; or

(l)   the issue concerns an act/omission outside England and Wales and the circumstances do not have a sufficient connection with England and Wales;[44]

(m)   the *complaint* is about an *authorised person's* refusal to provide a service and the complainant has not produced evidence that the refusal was for other than legitimate or reasonable reasons; or

(n)   there are other compelling reasons why it is inappropriate for the issue to be dealt with by the *Legal Ombudsman*.

Referring a complaint to court

5.8   Exceptionally (at the instance of an *ombudsman*) where the *ombudsman* considers that:

(a)   resolution of a particular legal question is necessary in order to resolve a dispute; but

(b)   it is not more suitable for the whole dispute to be dealt with by a court;

the *ombudsman* may (but does not have to) refer that legal question to court.[45]

5.9   Exceptionally, (at the instance of an *authorised person*) where:

(a)   the *authorised person* requests, and also undertakes to pay the complainant's legal costs and disbursements on terms the *ombudsman* considers appropriate; and

(b)   an *ombudsman* considers that the whole dispute would be more suitably dealt with by a court as a test case between the complainant and the *authorised person*;

the *ombudsman* may (but does not have to) dismiss the *complaint*, so that a court may consider it as a test case.[46]

5.10   By way of example only, in relation to a test case (at the instance of an *authorised person*) the *ombudsman* might require an undertaking in favour of the complainant that, if the complainant or the *authorised person* starts court proceedings against the other in respect of the *complaint* in any court in England and Wales within six months of the *complaint* being dismissed, the *authorised person* will:

(a)   pay the complainant's reasonable costs and disbursements (to be assessed if not agreed on an indemnity basis);

(b)   pay these in connection with the proceedings at first instance and also any subsequent appeal made by the *authorised person*; and

(c) make interim payments on account if and to the extent that it appears reasonable to do so.

5.11 Factors the *ombudsman* may take into account in considering whether to refer a legal question to court, or to dismiss a *complaint* so that it may be the subject of a test case in court, include (but are not limited to):

(a) any representations made by the *authorised person* or the complainant;

(b) the stage already reached in consideration of the dispute.

(c) how far the legal question is central to the outcome of the dispute;

(d) how important or novel the legal question is in the context of the dispute;

(e) the remedies that a court could impose;

(f) the amount at stake; and

(g) the significance for the *authorised person* (or similar *authorised persons*) or their clients.[47]

Referring to another complaints scheme

5.12 An *ombudsman* may refer a *complaint* to another complaints scheme if:

(a) he/she considers it appropriate; and

(b) the complainant agrees.[48]

5.13 If an *ombudsman* refers a *complaint* to another complaints scheme, the *ombudsman* will give the complainant and the *authorised person* reasons for the referral.[49]

Arrangements for assistance

5.14 The *Legal Ombudsman* may make such arrangements as it considers appropriate (which may include paying fees) for *Approved Regulators* or others to provide assistance to an *ombudsman* in the investigation or consideration of a *complaint*.[50]

Related complaints

5.15 The *Legal Ombudsman* may:

(a) tell a complainant that a related *complaint* could have been brought against some other *authorised person*;[51] or

(b) treat someone else who was an *authorised person* at the time of the act/omission as a joint respondent to the *complaint*.[52]

5.16 Where two or more *complaints* against different *authorised persons* relate to connected circumstances:

(a) the *Legal Ombudsman* may investigate them together, but an *ombudsman* will make separate determinations;[53] and

(b) the determinations may require the *authorised persons* to contribute towards the overall redress in the proportions the *ombudsman* considers appropriate.[54]

Resolution

5.17 The *Legal Ombudsman* will try to resolve *complaints* at the earliest possible stage, by whatever agreed outcome is appropriate.[55]

5.18   If a *complaint* is settled, abandoned or withdrawn, an *ombudsman* will tell both the complainant and the *authorised person*.[56]

Investigation

5.19   If the *Legal Ombudsman* considers that an investigation is necessary, it will:

(a)   ensure both *parties* have been given an opportunity of making representations;

(b)   send the *parties* a case decision[57] (which the *Act* calls an 'assessment'), with a time limit for response; and

(c)   if any *party* indicates disagreement within that time limit, arrange for an *ombudsman* to issue a final decision (which the *Act* calls a 'determination').[58]

5.20   If neither *party* indicates disagreement within that time limit, the *Legal Ombudsman* may treat the *complaint* as resolved by the case decision.[59]

Evidence

5.21   An apology will not of itself be treated as an admission of liability.[60]

5.22   An *ombudsman* cannot require anyone to produce any information or document which that person could not be compelled to produce in High Court civil proceedings, and the following provisions are subject to this.[61]

5.23   An *ombudsman* may give directions on:

(a)   the issues on which evidence is required; and

(b)   the way in which evidence should be given.[62]

5.24   An *ombudsman* may:

(a)   take into account evidence from *Approved Regulators* or the Legal Services Board;

(b)   take into account evidence from other third parties;

(c)   treat any finding of fact in disciplinary proceedings against the *authorised person* as conclusive;

(d)   include/exclude evidence that would be inadmissible/admissible in court;

(e)   accept information in confidence where he/she considers that is both necessary and fair;[63]

(f)   make a determination on the basis of what has been supplied;

(g)   draw inferences from any *party's* failure to provide information requested; and

(h)   dismiss a *complaint* if the complainant fails to provide information requested.[64]

5.25   An *ombudsman* may require a *party* to attend to give evidence and produce documents at a time and place specified by the *ombudsman*.[65]

5.26   An *ombudsman* may require a *party* to produce any information or document that the *ombudsman* considers necessary for the determination of a *complaint*.[66]

5.27   An *ombudsman* may:

(a)   specify the time within which this must be done;

(b)   specify the manner or form in which the information is to be provided; and

(c)   require the person producing the document to explain it.[67]

5.28   If the document is not produced, an *ombudsman* may require the relevant *party* to say, to the best of his/her knowledge and belief, where the document is.[68]

5.29 If an *authorised person* fails to comply with a requirement to produce information or a document, the *ombudsman*:

(a) will tell the relevant *Approved Regulator*;

(b) may require that *Approved Regulator* to tell the *ombudsman* what action it will take; and

(c) may report any failure by that *Approved Regulator* to the Legal Services Board.[69]

5.30 Subject to this, if any *party* fails to comply with a requirement to produce information or a document, the *ombudsman* may enforce the requirement through the High Court.[70]

Procedural time limits

5.31 An *ombudsman* may fix (and may extend) a time limit for any stage of the investigation, consideration and determination of a *complaint*.[71]

5.32 If any *party* fails to comply with such a time limit, the *ombudsman* may:

(a) proceed with the investigation, consideration and determination;

(b) draw inferences from the failure;

(c) where the failure is by the complainant, dismiss the *complaint*; or

(d) where the failure is by the *authorised person*, include compensation for any inconvenience caused to the complainant in any award.[72]

Hearings

5.33 An *ombudsman* will only hold a hearing where he/she considers that the *complaint* cannot be fairly determined without one. In deciding whether (and how) to hold a hearing, the *ombudsman* will take account of article 6 in the European Convention on Human Rights.[73]

5.34 A *party* who wishes to request a hearing must do so in writing, setting out:

(a) the issues he/she wishes to raise; and

(b) (if appropriate) any reasons why the hearing should be in private;

so the *ombudsman* may consider whether:

(a) the issues are material;

(b) a hearing should take place; and

(c) any hearing should be in public or private.[74]

5.35 A hearing may be held by any means the *ombudsman* considers appropriate in the circumstances, including (for example) by phone.[75]

Determinations and awards by an ombudsman

5.36 An *ombudsman* will determine a *complaint* by reference to what is, in his/her opinion, fair and reasonable in all the circumstances of the case.[76]

5.37 In determining what is fair and reasonable, the *ombudsman* will take into account (but is not bound by):

(a) what decision a court might make;

(b) the relevant *Approved Regulator's* rules of conduct at the time of the act/omission; and

(c)   what the *ombudsman* considers to have been good practice at the time of the act/omission.[77]

5.38   The *ombudsman's* determination may contain one or more of the following directions to the *authorised person* in favour of the complainant:[78]

(a)   to apologise;

(b)   to pay compensation of a specified amount for loss suffered;

(c)   to pay interest on that compensation from a specified time;[79]

(d)   to pay compensation of a specified amount for inconvenience/distress caused;

(e)   to ensure (and pay for) putting right any specified error, omission or other deficiency;

(f)   to take (and pay for) any specified action in the interests of the complainant;

(g)   to pay a specified amount for costs the complainant incurred in pursuing the *complaint*;[80] [81]

(h)   to limit fees to a specified amount.

5.39   As a complainant does not usually need assistance to pursue a *complaint* with the *Legal Ombudsman*, awards of costs are likely to be rare.

5.40   If the determination contains a direction to limit fees to a specified amount, it may also require the *authorised person* to ensure that:[82]

(a)   all or part of any amount paid is refunded;

(b)   interest is paid on that refund from a specified time;[83]

(c)   all or part of the fees are remitted;

(d)   the right to recover the fees is waived, wholly or to a specified extent; or

(e)   any combination of these.

5.41   An *ombudsman* will set (and may extend) a time limit for the *authorised person* to comply with a determination (and may set different time limits for the *authorised person* to comply with different parts of a determination).[84]

5.42   Any interest payable under the determination will be at the rate:

(a)   specified in the determination; or

(b)   (if not specified) at the rate payable on High Court judgment debts.[85]

5.43   There is a limit of £50,000 on the total value that can be awarded by the determination of a *complaint* in respect of:[86]

(a)   compensation for loss suffered;

(b)   compensation for inconvenience/distress caused;

(c)   the reasonable cost of putting right any error, omission or other deficiency; and

(d)   the reasonable cost of any specified action in the interests of the complainant.

5.44   If (before or after the determination is issued) it appears that the total value will exceed £50,000, an *ombudsman* may direct which part or parts of the award are to take preference.[87]

5.45   That limit does not apply to:

(a)   an apology;

(b)   interest on specified compensation for loss suffered;[88]

(c)   a specified amount for costs the complainant incurred in pursuing the *complaint*;

(d)   limiting fees to a specified amount; or

(e)   interest on fees to be refunded.

Acceptance/rejection of determinations

5.46   The determination will:[89]

(a)   be in writing, signed by the *ombudsman*;

(b)   give reasons for the determination; and

(c)   require the complainant to notify the *ombudsman*, before a specified time, whether the complainant accepts or rejects the determination.

5.47   The *ombudsman* may require any acceptance or rejection to be in writing, but will have regard to any reason why the complainant may be unable to use writing.[90]

5.48   The *ombudsman* will send copies of the determination to the *parties* and the relevant *Approved Regulator*.[91]

5.49   If the complainant tells the *ombudsman* that he/she accepts the determination, it is binding on the *parties* and final.[92]

5.50   Once a determination becomes binding and final, neither *party* may start or continue legal proceedings in respect of the subject matter of the *complaint*.

5.51   If the complainant does not tell the *ombudsman* (before the specified time) that he/she accepts the determination, it is treated as rejected unless:

(a)   the complainant tells the *ombudsman* (after the specified time) that he/she accepts the determination; and

(b)   the complainant has not previously told the *ombudsman* that he/she rejects the determination; and

(c)   the *ombudsman* is satisfied that there are sufficient reasons why the complainant did not respond in time.[93]

5.52   If the complainant did not respond before the specified time, the *ombudsman* will notify the *parties* and the relevant *Approved Regulator* of the outcome, describing the provisions concerning late acceptance that are set out above.[94]

5.53   If the complainant accepts or rejects the determination, the *ombudsman* will notify the *parties* and the relevant *Approved Regulator* of the outcome.[95]

5.54   If a determination is rejected (or treated as rejected) by the complainant, it has no effect on the legal rights of any *party*.

Publication

5.55   The *Legal Ombudsman* may publish a report of its investigation, consideration and determination of a *complaint*. The report will not name (or otherwise identify) the complainant, unless the complainant agrees.[96]

Enforcement

5.56   A binding and final determination can be enforced through the High Court or a county court by the complainant.[97]

5.57   A binding and final determination can also be enforced through the High Court or a county court by an *ombudsman*, if:

(a)   the complainant agrees; and

(b) the *ombudsman* considers it appropriate in all the circumstances.[98]

5.58 A court which makes an enforcement order must tell the *Legal Ombudsman*, and then an *ombudsman*:

(a) will tell the relevant *Approved Regulator*;

(b) may require that *Approved Regulator* to tell the *ombudsman* what action it will take; and

(c) may report any failure by that *Approved Regulator* to the Legal Services Board.[99]

Misconduct

5.59 If (at any stage after the *Legal Ombudsman* receives a *complaint*) an *ombudsman* considers that the *complaint* discloses any alleged misconduct about which the relevant *Approved Regulator* should consider action against the *authorised person*, the *ombudsman*:

(a) will tell the relevant *Approved Regulator*;

(b) will tell the complainant that the *Approved Regulator* has been told;

(c) may require that *Approved Regulator* to tell the *ombudsman* what action it will take; and

(d) may report any failure by that *Approved Regulator* to the Legal Services Board.[100]

5.60 If an *ombudsman* considers that an authorised person has failed to cooperate with the *Legal Ombudsman*, the *ombudsman*:

(a) will tell the relevant *Approved Regulator*;

(b) may require that *Approved Regulator* to tell the *ombudsman* what action it will take; and

(c) may report any failure by that *Approved Regulator* to the Legal Services Board.[101]

5.61 An *ombudsman*, the *Legal Ombudsman* and members of its staff will disclose to an *Approved Regulator* any information that it requests in order to investigate alleged misconduct or to fulfil its regulatory functions, so far as an *ombudsman* considers that the information:

(a) is reasonably required by the *Approved Regulator*; and

(b) has regard to any right of privacy of any complainant or third party involved (including rights of confidentiality or rights under the Data Protection Act 1998 or the Human Rights Act 1998).[102]

6 Case fees payable by authorised persons

6.1 A *complaint* is potentially chargeable unless:

(a) it is out of jurisdiction; or

(b) it is dismissed or discontinued under paragraph 5.7.[103]

6.2 A case fee is payable by the business/partnership[104] or individual *authorised person* for every potentially chargeable *complaint* when it is closed unless:

(a) the *complaint* was:

- abandoned or withdrawn; or

- settled, resolved or determined in favour of the authorised person; and

(b) the *ombudsman* is satisfied that the *authorised person* took all reasonable steps, under his/her complaints procedures, to try to resolve the *complaint*.[105]

6.3 The case fee is £400 for all chargeable *complaints.*[106]

6.4 The remaining costs of running the *Legal Ombudsman* are covered by a levy on *Approved Regulators* by the Legal Services Board.[107]

6.5 There is no charge to complainants.

1. Section 112.
2. Section 145.
3. To distinguish complaints about service from those which relate solely to professional misconduct.
4. Sections 12 and 129.
5. This section covers the equivalent practitioners before the commencement of the Act.
6. [OLC rule] Sections 133(8) and 147(7).
7. Section 137.
8. Section 122(5).
9. Section 134.
10. [OLC rule]. Where it is apparent that another legal practitioner was also involved. Section 133(3)(c).
11. Section 128(7).
12. Individuals are covered under section 128(3). The others are covered under the Legal Services Act 2007 (Legal Complaints)(Parties) Order 2010 made by the Lord Chancellor.
13. Defined in European Commission Recommendation 2003/361/EC – broadly a business or enterprise with fewer than 10 employees and turnover or assets not exceeding €2 million.
14. [OLC rule] Section 132(4).
15. To save their having to take out a grant of representation if one is not otherwise required.
16. Section 128(5).
17. The Lord Chancellor can exclude others under section 130.
18. [OLC rule] Section 133(1).
19. Section 128(1).
20. Section 131(1).
21. Section 131(2) and (3).
22. Section 128(1).
23. Section 125(2).
24. Section 128(4).
25. The Lord Chancellor can include others under section 128. Note, Legal Services Act 2007 (Legal Complaints) (Parties) Order 2012.
26. Section 132(1).
27. [OLC rule] Section 132(2).
28. [OLC rule] Section 132(3).
29. Section 112(2)
30. Section 145.
31. Section 126(1).
32. [OLC rule] Section 126(3).
33. [OLC rule].
34. [OLC rule] Section 133(2)(b).
35. Section 133(1).
36. [OLC rule] This gives the Ombudsman service the right to require a complaint form, but does not oblige it to do so.
37. [OLC rule] To make it clear that the Ombudsman service does not have to communicate with each partner individually.
38. [OLC rule] Section 135.
39. [OLC rule] Section 135.
40. [OLC rule] Section 135.
41. Section 135.
42. [OLC rule] Section 133(3)(a).
43. Where a complaint is about professional negligence or judgement, the OLC will consider (on a case-by-case basis) whether the issue is one that the OLC can deal with or whether the issue would be better dealt with in court.
44. [OLC rule] For example, a French client wishes to complain about advice on French law given in France by a French lawyer who is also qualified in England and Wales.
45. [OLC rule].
46. Paragraph 5.9 only applies if the legal practitioner so requests. The idea is that, in suitable cases, the legal practitioner can go to court, provided the complainant's legal costs are met. In other circumstances, an Ombudsman cannot force a legal practitioner to pay the complainant's costs of going to court.
47. [OLC rule].
48. [OLC rule] Section 133(3)(b).
49. [OLC rule] Section 135.
50. Schedule 15, paragraph 18.
51. Where it is apparent that the complaint was made against the wrong legal practitioner.
52. [OLC rule] Where it is apparent that another legal practitioner was also involved. Section 133(3)(c).
53. There need to be separate determinations because of the £50,000 limit.
54. [OLC rule].
55. [OLC rule].
56. Section 135.

57. Previously referred to as a recommendation report or a preliminary decision
58. [OLC rule].
59. [OLC rule].
60. [OLC rule] To ensure legal practitioners are not discouraged from saying 'sorry'.
61. Sections 133(5) and 147(6).
62. [OLC rule].
63. Including, but not limited to, information which is "restricted information" under section 151.
64. [OLC rule].
65. [OLC rule] Section 133(3)(e).
66. Section 147(1) and (3).
67. Section 147(2) and (4).
68. Section 147(5).
69. Section 148.
70. Section 149.
71. [OLC rule].
72. [OLC rule].
73. [OLC rule].
74. [OLC rule].
75. [OLC rule]. The OLC has not exercised the power in section 133(3)(g) enabling it to make a rule about the OLC awarding expenses in connection with attending a hearing.
76. Section 137(1).
77. [OLC rule] Section 133(3)(f).
78. Section 137(2).
79. Section 137(4)(b).
80. [(g) is OLC rule] Section 133(3)(h).
81. The OLC has not exercised the power under section 133(3)(i) to make a rule requiring any party who has behaved unreasonably to pay costs to the Ombudsman service.
82. Section 137(2)(b)(ii).
83. Section 137(4)(b).
84. [OLC rule].
85. [OLC rule] Section 137(4).
86. Section 138(1) and (2). The Lord Chancellor can increase the limit under section 139. Note, Legal Services Act 2007 (Alteration of Limit) Order 2012.
87. [OLC rule].
88. Section 138(3).
89. Section 140(1) and (2).
90. [OLC rule].
91. Section 140(3).
92. Section 140(4).
93. [(c) is OLC rule] Section 140(5) and (6).
94. Section 140(7) and (8).
95. Section 140(7).
96. Section 150.
97. Section 141.
98. [OLC rule] Section 141(5).
99. Section 142.
100. Section 143.
101. Section 146.
102. [OLC rule] Section 144(1).
103. [OLC rule].
104. Note Section 131.
105. [OLC rule].
106. [OLC rule].
107. Sections 173 and 174.

The Solicitors (Disciplinary Proceedings) Rules 2019

[For the latest updates to the material, please see www.solicitorstribunal.org.uk.]

Solicitors (Disciplinary Proceedings) Rules 2019

SI 2019/1185

Made 14th December 2007

Coming into force 6th August 2019

The Solicitors Disciplinary Tribunal, in exercise of the powers conferred by section 46 of the Solicitors Act 1974, makes the following Rules:

The Legal Services Board has approved the Rules in accordance with section 178 of the Legal Services Act 2007.

PART 1
INTRODUCTORY

1 Citation and commencement

These Rules may be cited as the Solicitors (Disciplinary Proceedings) Rules 2019 and come into force on 25th November 2019.

2 Scope

These Rules apply to—

(a) any application made to the Tribunal under any enactment, including the following provisions of the 1974 Act—

    (i) section 43(1) (applications relating to the control of solicitors' employees and consultants);

    (ii) section 43(3) (applications for review of orders made in respect of applications under section 43(1));

    (iii) section 43(4) (applications for costs in relation to applications under section 43);

    (iv) section 47(1)(a) to (f) (applications in relation to solicitors and former solicitors);

(b) any complaint made to the Tribunal under any enactment, including the following—

    (i) section 43 of the Administration of Justice Act 1985 (legal aid complaints relating to solicitors);

    (ii) section 31(2) of the 1974 Act (complaints in respect of failure to comply with rules as to professional practice, conduct and discipline);

> (iii) section 32(3) of the 1974 Act (complaint in respect of failure to comply with accounts rules and trust accounts rules);
>
> (iv) section 34(6) of the 1974 Act (complaint in respect of failure by solicitor to comply with rules relating to accountants' reports);
>
> (v) section 34A(2) of the 1974 Act (complaint in respect of failure by employee of solicitor to comply with rules relating to professional practice, conduct and discipline);
>
> (vi) section 34A(3) of the 1974 Act (complaint in respect of failure by employee of solicitor to comply with rules relating to accountants' reports);
>
> (vii) section 37(4) of the 1974 Act (complaint in respect of failure by solicitor to comply with indemnity rules);
>
> (viii) section 44(2) of the 1974 Act (complaint in respect of contravention of order under section 43(2) in respect of solicitors' employees and consultants).

3 Interpretation

(1) In these Rules—

"the 1974 Act" means the Solicitors Act 1974;

"the 2007 Act" means the Legal Services Act 2007;

"applicant" means a person making an application;

"application" means an application or complaint to which these Rules apply and which is made in accordance with these Rules;

"prescribed form" means the appropriate form published by the Tribunal on its website;

"authorised body" means—

> (a) a body which holds a licence in force under Part 5 of the 2007 Act granted by the Solicitors Regulation Authority;
>
> (b) a recognised body under section 9 of the Administration of Justice Act 1985;
>
> (c) a sole solicitor's practice recognised under section 9 of the Administration of Justice Act 1985;

"business day" means any day except a Saturday or Sunday, Christmas Day, Good Friday or a bank holiday in England and Wales under section 1 of the Banking and Financial Dealings Act 1971;

"case to answer" means an arguable case;

"clerk" means any clerk appointed under rules 8(1) and (2);

"the Clerk to the Tribunal" means the Clerk to the Tribunal who is in office at the date these Rules come into force, or the Clerk to the Tribunal subsequently appointed under rule 8(1);

"a lay application" means an application other than one—

> (a) made by the Society; or
>
> (b) to which Chapter 2 of Part 3 of these Rules applies;

"panel" means a panel appointed under rule 9(1) for the hearing of an application or any matter connected with an application;

"party" means an applicant or respondent;

"practice direction" means a direction made under rule 6(3);

"practice notice" means a notice made under rule 6(3);

"the President" means the President of the Tribunal, elected under rule 7(2);

"respondent" means any party to an application other than the applicant;

"the Society" means the Law Society and includes any duly constituted committee of the Law Society or any body or person exercising delegated powers of the Law Society, including the Solicitors Regulation Authority;

"solicitor members" and "lay members" have the same meaning as in section 46 of the 1974 Act;

"Statement" means a written statement (including a witness statement) signed by the individual making the statement and containing a declaration of truth in the following form—

"I believe that the facts and matters stated in this statement are true";

"the Tribunal" means the Solicitors Disciplinary Tribunal and where a panel has been appointed for the hearing of an application or any matter connected with it, includes a panel;

"Vice President" means a Vice President of the Tribunal, elected under rule 7(3).

(2) References in these Rules to solicitors include, where appropriate, former solicitors.

(3) References in these Rules to registered foreign lawyers are references to lawyers whose names are entered in the register of foreign lawyers maintained under section 89 of the Courts and Legal Services Act 1990 and include, where appropriate, those who have ceased to be registered in that register or whose registration has been suspended.

(4) Subject to paragraph (5), references in these Rules to registered European lawyers are references to—

(a) those lawyers—

(i) whose names were entered in the register of registered European lawyers maintained by the Society under regulation 15 of the European Communities (Lawyer's Practice) Regulations 2000(b), as it had effect immediately before exit day, at a time before exit day, but

(ii) in relation to whom regulation 5 or 5A of the Services of Lawyers and Lawyer's Practice (Revocation etc.) (EU Exit) Regulations 2019 does not apply;

(b) those lawyers whose names are entered in the register of registered European lawyers maintained by the Society under regulation 15 of the European Communities (Lawyer's Practice) Regulations 2000, as that regulation has effect by virtue of regulation 5 or 5A of the Services of Lawyers and Lawyer's Practice (Revocation etc.) (EU Exit) Regulations 2019 and includes, where appropriate, those who have ceased to be registered in that register or whose registration has been suspended.

(5) During any period when these Rules are in force before exit day, references in these Rules to registered European lawyers are references to lawyers whose names are entered in the register of European lawyers maintained by the Society under regulation 15 of the European Communities (Lawyer's Practice) Regulations 2000 and include, where appropriate, those who have ceased to be registered in that register or whose registration has been suspended.

4 The overriding objective

(1) The overriding objective of these Rules is to enable the Tribunal to deal with cases justly and at proportionate cost.

(2) The Tribunal will seek to give effect to the overriding objective when it—

(a)   exercises any power under these Rules; or

(b)   interprets any rule or practice direction.

(3)   Dealing with a case justly and at proportionate cost includes, so far as is practicable—

(a)   ensuring that the parties are on an equal footing;

(b)   ensuring that the case is dealt with efficiently and expeditiously;

(c)   saving expense;

(d)   dealing with the case in ways which are proportionate to the nature, importance and complexity of the issues.

(4)   The parties are required to help the Tribunal to further the overriding objective set out above.

5   Standard of proof

The standard of proof that will be applied to proceedings considered under these Rules is the standard applicable in civil proceedings.

6   Regulation of procedure and practice directions

(1)   Subject to the provisions of the 1974 Act, these Rules and any other enactment, the Tribunal may regulate its own procedure.

(2)   The Tribunal may dispense with any requirements of these Rules in respect of notices, Statements, witnesses, service or time in any case where it appears to the Tribunal to be just so to do.

(3)   The Tribunal (or a panel of Tribunal members consisting of no fewer than five members of whom no fewer than two must be lay members) may give such notices or make such directions concerning the practices or procedures of the Tribunal as are consistent with these Rules and as the panel considers appropriate.

(4)   Practice notices and practice directions may be promulgated under the authority of the President.

PART 2
CONSTITUTION

7   President and Vice Presidents

(1)   The President holding office at the date these Rules come into force may not hold the office of President for a total period exceeding six years and will only be eligible for re-election as President if he or she has not previously been re-elected as President.

(2)   The Tribunal, by a simple majority, must elect a solicitor member to be its President to hold office for a term not exceeding three years and the member so elected may be re-elected for a further term not exceeding three years.

(3)   The Tribunal, by a simple majority, must elect one solicitor member and one lay member to be its Vice Presidents for a term not exceeding three years and the members so elected may be re- elected for a further term not exceeding three years. The Vice Presidents may exercise any functions as are exercisable under these Rules by the President, as the President may direct.

(4)   The Tribunal must meet at least once in each calendar year and must publish an annual report, a copy of which must be sent to the Master of the Rolls, the Society and the Legal Services Board.

8 The Clerk to the Tribunal and other clerks and staff

(1)   The Tribunal must appoint a Clerk to the Tribunal.

(2)   The Tribunal may appoint other clerks to assist the Clerk to the Tribunal.

(3)   The Clerk to the Tribunal is responsible to the Tribunal for the administration of the Tribunal in an efficient manner, including the general supervision of the other clerks and other administrative staff; maintaining records and collecting statistics required by the Tribunal.

(4)   The Clerk to the Tribunal or any other clerk appointed by the Tribunal under this Rule must be a solicitor or barrister of not less than ten years' standing.

(5)   The office of the Clerk to the Tribunal must be vacated if—

(a)   in the Tribunal's opinion, with which the Master of the Rolls agrees, the Clerk to the Tribunal is physically or mentally incapable of performing his or her duties; or

(b)   the Clerk to the Tribunal—

(i)   resigns; or

(ii)   retires; or

(iii)   is removed from office by a resolution of the Tribunal approved by the Master of the Rolls.

(6)   The Tribunal may prescribe the duties for which the clerks are to be responsible and those duties must include arrangements for—

(a)   the submission of applications for certification as to whether or not there is a case to answer (see rule 13);

(b)   making pre-listing arrangements;

(c)   variation of directions;

(d)   determining applications for adjournment of procedural or substantive hearings in accordance with rule 23(2);

(e)   considering parties' non-compliance with directions and orders (see rule 20(3));

(f)   securing a record of hearings (by electronic recording or other means) (see rule 39);

(g)   advising the Tribunal on matters of law or procedure;

(h)   preparing draft judgments for the consideration of the panel which heard an application (see rule 40);

(i)   determining applications in respect of substituted service (see rule 46);

(j)   drawing orders and findings and sending them to the Society.

9 Composition of panels

(1)   The Tribunal must appoint a panel of three members of the Tribunal for the hearing of any application. Two of the panel members must be solicitor members and one must be a lay member.

(2)   The President may appoint a member to be the chair of a panel.

(3)   If the President does not appoint a chair of a panel, a solicitor member must act as the chair.

10 Functions exercisable by a single solicitor member

A single solicitor member may exercise the functions set out in—

(a)   rule 8(6) (c) (d) and (i) (duties for which clerks are responsible);

(b)　rule 27(3) (directions relating to lodging of bundles);

(c)　rule 22 (4) (f) and (g) (determining procedural applications)

PART 3
APPLICATIONS

Chapter 1
Applications by the Law Society and lay applications

11　Application of Rules in Chapter 1

(1)　Rules 12, 13 and 14 apply to applications made by the Society and to lay applications.

(2)　Rule 15 applies to applications made by the Society.

(3)　Rule 16 applies to lay applications.

12　Method and form of application

(1)　An application to which this Rule applies must be sent to the Tribunal offices and must be made using the prescribed form.

(2)　The application must be supported by a Statement setting out the allegations, the facts and matters supporting the application and each allegation contained within it and exhibiting any documents relied upon by the applicant.

(3)　In the case of an application made by the Society, the application must be accompanied by—

(a)　sufficient copies of the application and supporting documents to enable the Tribunal to retain one complete set and to serve one complete set on each respondent;

(b)　a time estimate for the substantive hearing;

(c)　a schedule of the Society's costs incurred up to and including the date on which the application is made.

(4)　In the case of a lay application, the application must be accompanied by three copies of the application and supporting documents and one further copy for any second and each further respondent.

13　Certification of case to answer

(1)　An application made in accordance with rule 12 must initially be considered by a solicitor member ("the initial solicitor member") for consideration of the question of whether there is a case to answer in respect of the allegations made in the application.

(2)　If the initial solicitor member considers that there is a case to answer in respect of all the allegations made and is not of the opinion that the question is one of doubt or difficulty then the initial solicitor member must certify that there is a case to answer.

(3)　If the initial solicitor member is minded not to certify that there is a case to answer in respect of all or some of the allegations made or is of the opinion that the question is one of doubt or difficulty, the question must be considered by a panel of three members of the Tribunal, two of whom must be solicitor members and one of whom must be a lay member. The initial solicitor member may be a member of the panel. If the panel considers that there is a case to answer in respect of any of the allegations made then it must certify that there is a case to answer in respect of those allegations.

(4)　If the panel decides that there is no case to answer in respect of any of the allegations made, it may refuse or dismiss the application, or part of it, without requiring the respondent to answer the allegations and without hearing the applicant. The applicant must be provided with written reasons explaining the decision.

(5)   If a panel or solicitor member certifies that a case to answer is established in respect of all or any of the allegations made, a clerk must serve a copy of each of the documents referred to in rule 12(3) or (4), as the case may be, on each respondent.

14   Supplementary Statements

(1)   An applicant who has made an application to which this Rule applies may, subject to paragraph (4), send supplementary statements to the Tribunal containing additional facts or matters on which the applicant seeks to rely or further allegations in support of the application.

(2)   A supplementary statement must be supported by a Statement setting out any new allegations, facts and matters supporting the application and each allegation contained within it and exhibiting any new documents relied upon by the applicant.

(3)   In the case of an application made by the Society, when a supplementary statement is sent to the Tribunal, the Society must provide—

(a)   sufficient copies of the supplementary statement and supporting documents to enable the Tribunal to retain one complete set and to serve a complete set on each respondent;

(b)   a revised time estimate for the substantive hearing;

(c)   a revised schedule of the Society's costs incurred up to and including the date on which the supplementary statement is sent;

(d)   any proposed directions for the future progression of the case, including any proposals to vary any existing directions.

(4)   In the case of a lay application, when a supplementary statement is sent to the Tribunal, the applicant must provide sufficient copies of the supplementary statement and supporting documents to enable the Tribunal to retain one complete set and to serve a complete set on each respondent.

(5)   The applicant will not be permitted to send a supplementary statement without leave of the Tribunal—

(a)   more than 12 months from the date of the application under rule 12;

(b)   less than 30 days before the date fixed for the substantive hearing of the application.

(6)   Rule 13 applies in respect of any supplementary statement containing additional facts or matters on which the applicant seeks to rely or further allegations in support of the application as it applies to an application made in accordance with rule 12.

15   Applications in respect of solicitors' employees

In a case where an application is made for an order under section 43(2) of the 1974 Act, the solicitor, recognised body, registered European lawyer or registered foreign lawyer by or for whose benefit the respondent is employed or remunerated—

(a)   may also be named or joined as a respondent to the application; and

(b)   must be joined as a respondent to the application if the Tribunal so directs.

16   Adjournment of application pending Law Society investigation

(1)   The panel may adjourn the consideration of the question of whether to certify any application to which this Rule applies for an initial period of up to three months to enable the Society to carry out its own investigations and consider whether to—

(a)   initiate its own application; or

(b)   by agreement with the applicant, take over conduct of the application.

(2)   After the expiration of the initial adjournment period, the application may be referred to a panel on the first available date for further review and consideration, subject to the provisions of paragraph (3).

(3)   If at the expiration of the period specified by the Tribunal under paragraph (1) the Society has not made a decision as to whether to initiate or take over the conduct of an application, the Tribunal may adjourn the matter for a further period of up to three months, after which the application must be referred to a panel on the first available date for further review and consideration.

Chapter 2
Applications by solicitors, etc.

17   Applications for restoration and termination of indefinite suspension

(1)   This Rule applies to applications made to the Tribunal under section 47 of the Act by—

(a)   a former solicitor seeking restoration to the Roll of Solicitors kept by the Society under section 6 the 1974 Act;

(b)   a person seeking restoration to the register of European lawyers or the register of foreign lawyers if his name has been withdrawn or removed from either register by the Tribunal;

(c)   a solicitor, registered European lawyer or registered foreign lawyer seeking the termination of an indefinite period of suspension from practice imposed by the Tribunal.

(2)   An application to which this Rule applies must be sent to the Tribunal and must be made using the prescribed form.

(3)   The application must be supported by a Statement setting out the facts and matters supporting the application and exhibiting any documents relied upon by the applicant.

(4)   The Society must be a respondent to any application to which this Rule applies.

(5)   The applicant must serve on the Society-

(a)   a copy of the application; and

(b)   a Statement in support of the application.

(6)   Every application to which this Rule applies must be advertised by the applicant in the Law Society's Gazette and in a newspaper circulating in the area of the applicant's former practice (if available) and must also be advertised by the Tribunal on its website.

(7)   Any person may, no later than 21 days before the hearing date of an application to which this Rule applies, serve on the Tribunal and the parties to the application notice of that person's intention to oppose the allowing of the application and the Tribunal may allow the person to appear before it at the hearing of the application, call evidence and make representations upon which the Tribunal may allow the person to be cross-examined.

18   Application to vary or remove conditions on practice

(1)   This Rule applies to applications made to the Tribunal to vary or remove conditions on practice imposed by the Tribunal.

(2)   An application to which this Rule applies must be sent to the Tribunal and must be made using the prescribed form.

(3)   The application must be supported by a Statement setting out the facts and matters supporting the application and exhibiting any documents relied upon by the applicant.

(4)   The Society must be a respondent to any application to which this Rule applies.

19 Application for review of order relating to solicitors' employees and consultants

(1) An application for a review of an order made under section 43(3)(a) of the 1974 Act must be sent to the Tribunal and must be made using the prescribed form.

(2) The application must be supported by a Statement setting out the facts and matters supporting the application and exhibiting any documents relied upon by the applicant.

(3) An application under section 43(3)(a) of the 1974 Act must be served on the Society and the Society must, within 28 days of the service of the application, send a Statement to the Tribunal setting out the facts and matters on which it relied in making the order under section 43(2) of the 1974 Act.

PART 4
CASE MANAGEMENT

20 Standard Directions

(1) Following certification of a case to answer under rule 13, standard directions must be issued by a clerk and sent to the parties.

(2) The standard directions may specify—

  (a) the date fixed for the substantive hearing of the matter;

  (b) the date by which a respondent must send to the Tribunal and serve on every other party an Answer to the allegations contained in the Statement served under rules 12 and 14 and a reply to the application and Statement served under rules 17, 18 and 19;

  (c) the date by which the respondent must send to the Tribunal and serve on every other party all documents on which the respondent intends to rely at the substantive hearing;

  (d) the date by which the parties must send to the Tribunal and serve on every other party a list of witnesses upon whose evidence they intend to rely at the substantive hearing;

  (e) the date by which the parties must notify the Tribunal of any intention to rely on expert evidence;

  (f) the date on which any case management hearing will take place;

  (g) the date by which the parties must send a statement of readiness to the Tribunal;

  (h) the date by which hearing bundles (and the number of copies) must be sent to the Tribunal;

  (i) any other standard direction which the Tribunal considers appropriate to ensure the management of matters in accordance with the overriding objective of these Rules mentioned in rule 4.

(3) If a party fails to comply with the standard directions, any other direction or any of these Rules, the matter may be listed for a non-compliance hearing before a clerk, who will make appropriate directions, which may include listing the matter before the Tribunal which may direct that—

  (a) evidence which has not been sent or served as directed may not be relied upon without permission of the Tribunal;

  (b) an adverse costs order be made in default of compliance, which may be ordered to be paid immediately to any other party;

(c)   adverse inferences that the panel hearing the matter considers appropriate may be drawn at the substantive hearing from the failure to comply.

(4) In this rule—

(a)   an "Answer" is a document which sets out—

    (i)   which allegations in the Statement are admitted and which are denied; and

    (ii)   the reasons for denial;

(b)   a "statement of readiness" is a document—

    (i)   confirming that the parties are ready for the substantive hearing;

    (ii)   setting out what, if any, further directions are required by the parties; and

    (iii)   setting out whether the time estimate for the final hearing is the same as was anticipated when standard directions were issued or at any subsequent case management hearing, or otherwise providing a revised time estimate.

21 Case management hearings

(1) A case management hearing must be arranged by the Tribunal or a clerk in cases where—

(a)   a clerk considers that the holding of a case management hearing is justified by reason of the time estimate or revised time estimate provided by the Society under rule 12(3)(b) or 14(3)(b); or

(b)   the clerk who reviews the application on receipt identifies issues which in the opinion of the clerk justify the holding of a case management hearing.

(2) A case management hearing may be arranged by the Tribunal or a clerk at any other time before the hearing of an application.

(3) A case management hearing may be heard by the Tribunal or a clerk and may take place by telephone, in person, or by such electronic means as may be approved by the Tribunal.

(4) If the Tribunal notifies the parties in advance of a case management hearing that a further hearing is to be fixed or is likely to be fixed at the case management hearing, the parties must attend the case management hearing equipped with their dates to avoid and the dates to avoid of any witnesses.

(5) If on receipt of a list of witnesses (see rule 20(2)(d)) or a statement of readiness (see rule 20(2)(g)) a clerk considers that a further case management hearing is required, a further case management hearing date may be fixed so that any further directions can be made.

22 Procedural applications

(1) Any procedural application must be—

(a)   made using the prescribed form; and

(b)   sent to the Tribunal and served on every other party, together with any relevant supporting documentation.

(2) The Tribunal, single solicitor member or clerk must issue written reasons for its decisions on procedural applications.

(3) Any party aggrieved by a decision of a clerk under paragraph 8(6) may request that the application be re-determined by a panel or single solicitor member by notifying the Tribunal of this request within 14 days of receipt of the written reasons for the decision.

(4) In this rule, a "procedural application" means an application for—

(a)   a variation of directions;

(b)   an adjournment of the hearing of an application (see rule 23);

(c)   an amendment or withdrawal of an allegation (see rule 24);

(d)   disclosure and discovery (see rule 26);

(e)   leave to call or adduce expert evidence (see rule 30);

(f)   a direction that special measures may be provided or used to assist vulnerable witnesses or respondents;

(g)   a direction that a witness or respondent may give their evidence or otherwise participate in the proceedings by videolink or other electronic means;

(h)   any other procedural application, including an application for a stay of proceedings for abuse of process, and general applications to exclude or adduce evidence.

23   Adjournments

(1)   An application for an adjournment of the hearing of an application must be supported by documentary evidence of the need for the adjournment.

(2)   An application for an adjournment made more than 21 days before the hearing date will be considered by a clerk or a single solicitor member on the papers.

(3)   An application for an adjournment made 21 days or less before the hearing date will be considered by the panel listed to sit on the substantive hearing on the papers unless it is in the interests of justice for the matter to be dealt with at an oral hearing.

24   Amendment or withdrawal of allegations

No allegation made in an application may be amended or withdrawn without leave of the Tribunal.

25   Agreed Outcome Proposals

(1)   The parties may up to 28 days before the substantive hearing of an application (unless the Tribunal directs otherwise) submit to the Tribunal an Agreed Outcome Proposal for approval by the Tribunal.

(2)   An Agreed Outcome Proposal must—

(a)   contain a statement of the facts that are agreed between the relevant parties;

(b)   set out the agreed proposed penalty and an explanation as to why the penalty would be in accordance with any guidance published by the Tribunal on sanctions imposed by the Tribunal;

(c)   be signed by the relevant parties; and

(d)   comply with any relevant practice direction made by the Tribunal in respect of Agreed Outcome Proposals.

(3)   If the Tribunal approves the Agreed Outcome Proposal in the terms proposed it must make an Order in those terms. The case must be called into an open hearing and the Tribunal must announce its decision.

(4)   If the Tribunal wishes to hear from the parties before making its decision the Tribunal may direct that there be a case management hearing which the parties to the proposed Agreed Outcome Proposal must attend for the purpose of making submissions before a final decision is reached. The case management hearing must be heard in private.

(5)   Where the Tribunal is not satisfied that it is appropriate to make an Order in accordance with paragraph (3) it must provide reasons to the parties who may then submit a revised proposal. If the Tribunal is satisfied with the revised proposal, it must make an Order in accordance with it.

(6)   Some or all of the same members of the panel appointed in respect of the application may consider the initial Agreed Outcome Proposal, any submissions made at a case

management hearing and any revised proposal but may not subsequently participate in the panel for the substantive hearing (if there is one).

(7)   If on considering a submission under this rule the Tribunal decides not to make an Order in accordance with paragraph (3) it must make directions for the substantive disposal of the matter by a panel consisting of members who were not on the panel which considered the submission.

(8)   If on considering a submission under this rule the Tribunal decides not to make an Order and the Tribunal does not publish that decision or announce it in an open hearing, no information will be published or announced about the submission save that the Agreed Outcome Proposal was not approved.

26   Disclosure and discovery

(1)   If an application is made for the disclosure or discovery of material, the Tribunal may make an order that material be disclosed where it considers that the production of the material is necessary for the proper consideration of an issue in the case, unless the Tribunal considers that there are compelling reasons in the public interest not to order the disclosure.

(2)   Any order made by the Tribunal will only apply to material that is in the possession or under the control of a party.

(3)   An order made under paragraph (1) will not oblige the parties to produce any material which they would be entitled to refuse to produce in proceedings in any court in England and Wales.

(4)   A party to proceedings before the Tribunal is required to disclose only—

    (a)   the documents on which the party relies;

    (b)   any documents which –

        (i)   adversely affect that party's own case;

        (ii)   adversely affect another party's case; or

        (iii)   support another party's case; and

    (c)   any documents which the party is required to disclose by a relevant practice direction.

PART 5
EVIDENCE

27   Evidence generally and service and sending of Evidence and bundles

(1)   Without prejudice to the general powers in Parts 2 and 3 of these Rules the Tribunal may give directions in relation to an application relating to any of the following—

    (a)   the exchange between parties of lists of documents which are relevant to the application, or relevant to particular issues, and the inspection of such documents;

    (b)   the provision by parties of statements of agreed matters;

    (c)   issues on which the Tribunal requires evidence or submissions;

    (d)   the nature and manner of the evidence or submissions that the Tribunal requires;

    (e)   the time at which any evidence or submissions are to be sent;

    (f)   the time to be allowed during the hearing for the presentation of any evidence or submission.

(2)   The Tribunal may—

(a)   admit any evidence whether or not it would be admissible in a civil trial in England and Wales;

(b)   exclude evidence that would otherwise be admissible where—

    (i)   the evidence was not provided within the time allowed by a direction given under these Rules or a practice direction; or

    (ii)   the evidence was otherwise provided in a manner that did not comply with a direction given under these Rules or a practice direction; or

    (iii)   it would otherwise be unfair, disproportionate or contrary to the interests of justice to admit the evidence.

(3)   Unless otherwise directed by the Tribunal, in cases where the Society is the applicant, it must send five copies of a paginated hearing bundle to the Tribunal no later than 14 days before the date listed for the substantive hearing.

28   Written Evidence

(1)   If no party requires the attendance of a witness, the Tribunal may accept the Statement of that witness as evidence in respect of the whole case or of any particular fact or facts.

(2)   Every Statement upon which any party proposes to rely must be sent to the Tribunal by that party and served on every other party on a date determined by the Tribunal which must be no less than 28 days before the date fixed for the hearing of the application. The Statement must be accompanied by a notice, using the prescribed form.

(3)   Any party on whom a notice has been served under paragraph (2) and who requires the attendance of the witness in question at the hearing must, no later than seven days after service of the notice require, in writing, the party on whom the notice was served to produce the witness at the hearing.

(4)   Any application for a witness summons must be made to the High Court.

(5)   If a Statement has not been served in accordance with paragraph 28(2) in relation to a witness, a party must apply to the Tribunal for permission—

    (a)   to produce that Statement; and

    (b)   for the witness to give evidence at the hearing.

(6)   Any party to an application may, by written notice, not later than 21 days before the date fixed for the hearing, request any other party to agree that any document may be admitted as evidence.

(7)   If a party desires to challenge the authenticity of a document which is the subject of paragraph (6), that party must, within seven days of receipt of the notice served under that paragraph, give notice that he or she does not agree to the admission of the document and that he or she requires that its authenticity be proved at the hearing.

(8)   If the recipient of a notice given under paragraph (6) does not give a notice in response within the period mentioned in paragraph (7), that recipient is deemed to have admitted the document unless otherwise ordered by the Tribunal.

29   Civil Evidence Act notices

(1)   Subject to the following provisions of this Rule, the Civil Evidence Act 1995(a) apply in relation to proceedings before the Tribunal in the same manner as they apply in relation to civil proceedings.

(2)   Any notice given under the provisions of the Civil Evidence Act 1995 as so applied must be given no later than the latest date for the service of witness statements under rule 28.

30 Expert evidence

(1)   No party may call an expert or adduce in evidence an expert's report at the substantive hearing of an application without leave of the Tribunal.

(2)   An application under this rule must be determined by a panel.

(3)   The Tribunal may permit expert evidence to be adduced where it considers that such evidence is necessary for the proper consideration of an issue or issues in the case.

(4)   If two or more parties wish to submit expert evidence on a particular issue, the Tribunal may direct that the evidence on that issue is to be given by a single joint expert.

(5)   The Tribunal may, at any stage, direct that a discussion take place between experts for the purpose of requiring the experts to identify and agree the expert issues in the proceedings and provide a joint schedule setting out the matters that are agreed and not agreed. The Tribunal may specify the issues which the experts must discuss.

(6)   Any expert evidence must be in the form of a Statement and must set out—

    (a)   the expert's professional qualifications;

    (b)   the substance of all material instructions (including a general description of the documents provided), whether written or oral, on the basis of which the Statement was written;

    (c)   a declaration that the expert understands and has complied with the expert's duty to assist the Tribunal on matters within the expert's expertise and understands that this duty overrides any obligation to any party from whom the expert has received instructions or by whom they are paid.

31 Interpreters and Translators

(1)   If any witness or respondent requires the assistance of an interpreter to participate in a hearing the Tribunal must be notified of this fact by the party requiring the interpreter when sending the list of witnesses.

(2)   Where a witness statement has been translated from a language other than English it must be accompanied by a Statement confirming—

    (a)   the language in which the original witness statement was made; and

    (b)   that the translator has translated the witness statement into English to the best of the translator's skill and understanding.

32 Previous findings of record

(1)   A conviction for a criminal offence in the United Kingdom may be proved by the production of a certified copy of the certificate of conviction relating to the offence and proof of a conviction will constitute evidence that the person in question was guilty of the offence. The findings of fact upon which that conviction was based will be admissible as conclusive proof of those facts save in exceptional circumstances.

(2)   The judgment of any civil court, or any tribunal exercising a professional or disciplinary jurisdiction, in or outside England and Wales (other than the Tribunal) may be proved by producing a certified copy of the judgment and the findings of fact upon which that judgment was based is admissible as proof but not conclusive proof of those facts.

(3)   Where the Tribunal has made a finding based solely upon the certificate of conviction for a criminal offence which is subsequently quashed the Tribunal may, on the application of the Law Society or the respondent to the application in respect of which the finding arose, revoke its finding and make such order as to costs as appear to be just in the circumstances.

33 Adverse inferences

Where a respondent fails to—

(a)   send or serve an Answer in accordance with a direction under rule 20(2)(b); or

(b)   give evidence at a substantive hearing or submit themselves to cross-examination;

and regardless of the service by the respondent of a witness statement in the proceedings, the Tribunal is entitled to take into account the position that the respondent has chosen to adopt and to draw such adverse inferences from the respondent's failure as the Tribunal considers appropriate.

PART 6
HEARINGS AND COSTS

34   Publication of cause lists

(1)   A cause list will be published on the Tribunal's website before the case is due to be heard.

(2)   Any party or other person who claims to be affected by an application may apply to the Tribunal for the cause list to be anonymised on the grounds of—

(a)   exceptional hardship; or

(b)   exceptional prejudice

to a party, a witness or any person affected by the application.

(3)   Any person making an application under paragraph (2) must serve a copy of that application together with a Statement in support on all parties to the proceedings, and—

(a)   the application must be served no later than 28 days before the hearing in relation to which the application is made; and

(b)   must be made using the prescribed form.

(4)   The Tribunal may in its discretion consider the application on the papers or list it for an oral hearing.

(5)   If the Tribunal is satisfied that either of the grounds in paragraph (2) are met, the Tribunal must direct that the cause list be anonymised in such a way that appears to it to be just and proper.

35   Public or private hearings

(1)   Subject to paragraphs (2), (4), (5) and (6), every hearing of the Tribunal must take place in public.

(2)   Any person who claims to be affected by an application may apply to the Tribunal for the hearing of the application to be conducted in private on the grounds of—

(a)   exceptional hardship; or

(b)   exceptional prejudice

to a party, a witness or any person affected by the hearing.

(3)   Any person who makes an application under paragraph (2) must serve a copy of that application and a Statement in support on all parties to the proceedings. If there is no objection to the application from any of the parties, the Tribunal will consider the application on the papers unless it considers that it is in the interests of justice for the application to be considered at an oral hearing.

(4)   If the Tribunal decides that the application made under paragraph (2) is to be considered at an oral hearing, that hearing will take place in private unless the Tribunal directs otherwise.

(5)   The Tribunal may, before or during a hearing, direct without an application from any party that the hearing or part of it be held in private if—

    (a)   the Tribunal is satisfied that it would have granted an application under paragraph (2) had one been made; or

    (b)   the Tribunal considers that a hearing in public would prejudice the interests of justice.

(6)   The Tribunal may give a direction excluding from any hearing or part of it any person—

    (a)   whose conduct the Tribunal considers is disrupting or likely to disrupt the hearing;

    (b)   whose presence the Tribunal considers is likely to prevent another person from giving evidence or making submissions freely;

    (c)   whose attendance at the hearing would otherwise prejudice the overriding objective of these Rules.

(7)   Other than a party to the proceedings, a factual witness is excluded from the hearing until their evidence has been given, unless the parties agree or the Tribunal directs otherwise.

(8)   Save in exceptional circumstances, where the Tribunal disposes of proceedings following a hearing held in private, it must announce its decision in a public session.

(9)   The Tribunal may make a direction prohibiting the disclosure or publication of any matter likely to lead to the identification of any person whom the Tribunal considers should not be identified.

(10)   The Tribunal may give a direction prohibiting the disclosure of a document or information to a person if it is satisfied that—

    (a)   the disclosure would be likely to cause any person serious harm; and

    (b)   it is in the interests of justice to make such a direction.

36 Proceeding in absence

If a party fails to attend and is not represented at the hearing and the Tribunal is satisfied that notice of the hearing was served on the party in accordance with these Rules, the Tribunal may hear and determine any application and make findings, hand down sanctions, order the payment of costs and make orders as it considers appropriate notwithstanding that the party failed to attend and is not represented at the hearing.

37 Application for re-hearing

(1)   At any time before the Tribunal's Order is sent to the Society under rule 42(1) or within 14 days after it is sent, a party may apply to the Tribunal for a re-hearing of an application if—

    (a)   the party neither attended in person nor was represented at the hearing of the application; and

    (b)   the Tribunal determined the application in the party's absence.

(2)   An application for a re-hearing under this rule must be made using the prescribed form accompanied by a Statement setting out the facts upon which the applicant wishes to rely together with any supporting documentation.

(3)   If satisfied that it is just to do so, the Tribunal may grant the application upon such terms, including as to costs, as it thinks fit. The re-hearing must be held before a panel comprised of different members from those who determined the original application.

38 Evidence and submissions during the hearing

(1)   The Tribunal may consent to a witness giving, or require any witness to give, evidence on oath or affirmation and may administer an oath or affirmation for that purpose.

(2)   The Tribunal may, at any hearing, dispense with the strict rules of evidence.

(3) Without restriction on the general powers in Parts 2 and 3 of these Rules, the Tribunal may, pursuant to the overriding objective set out in rule 4(1), give directions in relation to—

(a) the provision by the parties of statements of agreed matters;

(b) issues on which it requires evidence to be given or submissions to be made and the nature and manner of the evidence or submissions it requires;

(c) the time at which any evidence or submissions are to be given or made;

(d) the time allowed during the hearing for the presentation of any evidence or submission;

(e) the time allowed for cross-examination of a witness.

39 Recording of the hearing

(1) All hearings of the Tribunal will be electronically audio-recorded.

(2) Where hearings of the Tribunal are held in public, a copy of the recording must be disclosed to any person on request, subject to any direction by the Tribunal in relation to the release of the recording.

(3) Where a hearing is held in private, a copy of the electronic recording may only be disclosed to the parties and only on the provision of an undertaking that the recording or any transcript of the hearing or any part of it will not be made public.

40 Decisions

(1) The Tribunal may announce its decision at the conclusion of the hearing or may reserve its decision for announcement at a later date. In either case the announcement must be made in public unless rule 35(8) applies.

(2) As soon as reasonably practicable after making a decision which finally disposes of all issues in the proceedings, the Tribunal must provide to each party a judgment containing written reasons for its decision, signed by a member of the Tribunal.

(3) As soon as reasonably practicable following a case management hearing, the Tribunal will provide to each party a memorandum containing written reasons for its decisions, signed by a member of the Tribunal.

(4) Decisions on applications made during the course of a substantive hearing will be announced in a public session and the written reasons will be contained in the judgment issued at the conclusion of the proceedings.

(5) The Tribunal or a clerk may, at any time, correct a clerical error or omission in a judgment or memorandum.

41 Sanction

(1) At the conclusion of the hearing, the Tribunal must make a finding as to whether any or all of the allegations in the application have been substantiated.

(2) If the Tribunal makes a finding that any or all of the allegations in the application have been substantiated, the Tribunal must ask—

(a) the clerk whether any allegations were found to have been substantiated against the respondent in any previous disciplinary proceedings before the Tribunal; and

(b) the Society (in those cases where the Society is the applicant) whether it has imposed any sanction against the respondent in respect of conduct which has not been the subject of any previous disciplinary proceedings before the Tribunal.

(3) The respondent will be entitled to make submissions by way of mitigation, including character references, in respect of the sanction, if any, to be imposed by the Tribunal.

(4)   The Tribunal will have regard to its guidance on sanctions in force at the time when determining the appropriate sanction.

42   The Order

(1)   The making of the Order that contains the Tribunal's decision must be announced by the Tribunal pursuant to Rule 40(1) and a copy of the Order signed by a member of the Tribunal must be sent by the Tribunal to the Society as soon as reasonably practicable following the hearing.

(2) An Order takes effect once it has been announced by the Tribunal in public session or in private where rule 35(8) applies.

43   Costs

(1)   At any stage of the proceedings, the Tribunal may make such order as to costs as it thinks fit, which may include an order for wasted costs.

(2)   The amount of costs to be paid may either be decided and fixed by the Tribunal following summary assessment or directed by the Tribunal to be subject to detailed assessment by a taxing Master of the Senior Courts.

(3)   Without prejudice to the generality of paragraph (1), the Tribunal may make an order as to costs in circumstances where—

(a)   any application, allegation or appeal is withdrawn or amended;

(b)   some or all of the allegations are not proved against a respondent;

(c)   an appeal or interim application is unsuccessful.

(4)   The Tribunal will first decide whether to make an order for costs and will identify the paying party. When deciding whether to make an order for costs, against which party, and for what amount, the Tribunal will consider all relevant matters including the following—

(a)   the conduct of the parties and whether any or all of the allegations were pursued or defended reasonably;

(b)   whether the Tribunal's directions and time limits imposed were complied with;

(c)   whether the amount of time spent on the matter was proportionate and reasonable;

(d)   whether any hourly rate and the amount of disbursements claimed is proportionate and reasonable;

(e)   the paying party's means.

(5)   If the respondent makes representations about the respondent's means, the representations must be supported by a Statement which includes details of the respondent's assets, income and expenditure (including but not limited to property, savings, income and outgoings) which must be supported by documentary evidence.

PART 7
MISCELLANEOUS

44   Sending and service of documents

(1)   Any document to be sent to the Tribunal or any other person or served on a party or any other person under these Rules, a practice direction or a direction given under these Rules must be—

(a)   sent by pre-paid first class post or by document exchange, or delivered by hand, to the Tribunal's or other person's office or as the case may be the address specified for the proceedings by the party (or if no such address has been specified to the last known place of business or place of residence of the person to be served); or

(b)   sent by email to the email address specified by the Tribunal or other person or specified for the proceedings by a party (or if no such address has been specified to the last known place of business or place of residence of the person to be served); or

(c)   sent or delivered by such other method as the Tribunal may direct.

(2)   Subject to paragraph (3), if a party specifies an email address for the electronic delivery of documents the Tribunal and other parties will be entitled to serve (and service will be deemed to be effective) documents by electronic means to that email address, unless the party states in writing that service should not be effected by those means.

(3)   If a party informs the Tribunal and every other party in writing that a particular form of communication, other than pre-paid post or delivery by hand, should not be used to send documents to that party, that form of communication must not be used.

(4)   Any recipient of a document sent by electronic means may request that the sender send a hard copy of the document to the recipient. The recipient must make such a request as soon as reasonably practicable after receiving the document electronically.

(5)   The Tribunal will proceed on the basis that the address, including an email address, provided by a party or its representative is and remains the address to which documents should be sent or delivered until receiving written notification to the contrary by that party or representative.

(6)   If a document submitted to the Tribunal is not written in English, it must be accompanied by an English translation and a Statement from the translator confirming that the translator carried out the translation and setting out the translator's qualifications.

45   Deemed Service

A document sent or served within the United Kingdom in accordance with these Rules or any relevant practice direction is deemed to be served on the day shown in the following table—

	Method of service	Deemed date of service
1.	First class post (or other service which provides for delivery on the next business day)	The second day after it was posted, left with, delivered to or collected by the relevant service provider provided that day is a business day; or if not, the next business day after that day.
2.	Document exchange	The second day after it was left with, delivered to or collected by the relevant service provider provided that day is a business day; or if not, the next business day after that day.
3.	Delivering the document by hand to or leaving it at an address	If it is delivered to or left at the address on a business day before 4.30p.m., on that day; or in any other case, on the next business day after that day.
4.	E-mail or other electronic method	If the e-mail or other electronic transmission is sent on a business day before 4.30p.m., on that day; or in any other case, on the next business day after the day on which it was sent.

5.	Fax	If the transmission of the fax is completed on a business day before 4.30p.m., on that day; or in any other case, on the next business day after the day on which it was transmitted.
6.	Personal service	If the document is served personally before 4.30p.m. on a business day, on that day; or in any other case, on the next business day after that day.

46 Substituted service by the applicant

(1) If the applicant believes that there is no reasonable prospect of being able to effect service on a respondent using the methods set out in rule 44 it may apply to the Tribunal for a direction for substituted service. This application must be made in writing and set out—

(a) the steps that have been taken to establish the address, place of business or email address of the respondent; and

(b) the proposed alternative method of service.

(2) The application may be determined by the Tribunal, a panel, a single solicitor member or a clerk, who may make a direction for substituted service if it is in the interests of justice to do so.

47 Calculating time

(1) Subject to rule 45 an act required by these Rules, a practice direction or a direction given under these Rules to be done on or by a particular day must be done by 4:30 p.m. on that day unless otherwise directed.

(2) If the time specified by these Rules, a practice direction or a direction given under these Rules for doing any act ends on a day other than a business day, the act is done in time if it is done on the next business day.

48 Representatives

(1) Any party may appoint a legal representative to represent that party in the proceedings.

(2) If a party appoints a legal representative, that party must send to the Tribunal and every other party written notice of the representative's name and address, together with a copy of the notice.

(3) Anything permitted or required to be done by a party under these Rules may be done by the legal representative of that party, except signing a witness statement.

(4) A party who receives due notice of the appointment of a legal representative—

(a) must send to the legal representative any document which, at any time after the appointment, is required to be sent to the represented party, and need not send that document to the represented party; and

(b) may proceed on the basis that the representative is and remains authorised as such until they receive written notification to the contrary from the representative or the represented party.

(5) At a hearing a party may be accompanied by another person whose name and address has not been notified under paragraph (2) but who, with the permission of the Tribunal, may assist the party in presenting the party's case at the hearing.

(6) Paragraphs (2) to (4) do not apply to a person who accompanies a party under paragraph (5).

(7)   In this rule "legal representative" means—

(a)   a solicitor;

(b)   a barrister;

(c)   a person who, for the purposes of the 2007 Act, is an authorised person in relation to an activity which constitutes the exercise of a right of audience or the conduct of litigation within the meanings given by Schedule 2 to that Act.

49   Amendments to the 2011 Appeals Rules

The Solicitors Disciplinary Tribunal (Appeals and Amendment) Rules 2011(a) are amended as follows—

(a)   In rule 2 (interpretation)—

(i)   for the definition of "the 2007 rules" substitute the following definition— ""the 2019 rules" means the Solicitors (Disciplinary Proceedings) Rules 2019";

(ii)   In the definition of "clerk", for "the 2007 rules" substitute "the 2019 rules";

(b)   In rule 5(1) for the words "listed in rule 3(11) of the 2007 Rules" substitute "listed in rule 8(6) of the Solicitors (Disciplinary Proceedings) Rules 2019";

(c)   In rule 5(2) for the words "rule 3(11) of the 2007 Rules" substitute "rule 8(6) of the Solicitors (Disciplinary Proceedings) Rules 2019";

(d)   In rule 27(1) for "5pm" substitute "4.30p.m.".

50   Revocation

The Solicitors (Disciplinary Proceedings) Rules 2007 are revoked.

51   Transitional provisions

These Rules do not apply to proceedings in respect of which an Application is made before the date on which these Rules come into force and those proceedings will be subject to the Solicitors (Disciplinary Proceedings) Rules 2007 as if they had not been revoked.

Signed by authority of the Solicitors Disciplinary Tribunal

Gate House, 1 Farringdon Street, London EC4M 7LG

6th August 2019

Edward Nally

President

Solicitors Disciplinary Tribunal

APPENDIX 15

The Solicitors Disciplinary Tribunal (Appeals and Amendment) Rules 2011

[With consolidated amendments, including correction slip issued 18 January 2013. For details see **www.solicitorstribunal.org.uk/constitution-and-procedures/appeals**]

Solicitors Disciplinary Tribunal (Appeals and Amendment) Rules 2011

SI 2011/2346

Made 22nd September 2011

Coming into force 1st October 2011

The Solicitors Disciplinary Tribunal in exercise of the powers conferred upon it by section 46 of the Solicitors Act 1974 as applied by paragraph 14C(2) of Schedule 2 to the Administration of Justice Act 1985 and section 44E(2) of the Solicitors Act 1974 and following the approval of the Legal Services Board makes the following Rules:

PART 1
INTRODUCTORY

1 Citation, commencement and application

(1) These Rules may be cited as the Solicitors Disciplinary Tribunal (Appeals and Amendment) Rules 2011 and shall come into force on 1st October 2011.

(2) These Rules (except rule 30) apply in relation to—

(a) appeals to the Tribunal under paragraph 14C of Schedule 2 to the Administration of Justice Act 1985;

(b) appeals to the Tribunal under section 44E of the 1974 Act (appeals against disciplinary action under section 44D); and

(c) appeals to the Tribunal in respect of decisions made by the Society which are appealable under Part 5 of the 2007 Act or the Society's licensing rules and which, by virtue of article 4(1) of the Legal Services Act 2007 (Appeals from Licensing Authority Decisions) (No.2) Order 2011 are appeals which may be heard and determined by the Tribunal.

2 Interpretation

In these Rules—

"the 1974 Act" means the Solicitors Act 1974;

"the 2007 Act" means the Legal Services Act 2007;

"the 2007 rules" means the Solicitors (Disciplinary Proceedings) Rules 2007;

"appeal" means a Schedule 2 appeal, a section 44E appeal or a licensing appeal;

"appellant" means—

> (a)   a person who makes an appeal to the Tribunal; or

> (b)   a person added or substituted as an appellant under rule 13(1);

"the Board" means the Legal Services Board;

"clerk" has the same meaning as in the 2007 rules;

a "licensing appeal" means an appeal of the type mentioned in rule 1(2)(c);

"Panel" means a panel appointed under rule 3 for the hearing of an appeal or any matter connected with an appeal;

"party" means the appellant or the respondent;

"practice direction" means a practice direction made under rule 10;

"the President" means the President of the Tribunal, appointed under rule 3 of the 2007 rules;

"respondent" means—

> (a)   the person who made the decision in respect of which an appeal is made; or

> (b)   a person added or substituted as a respondent under rule 13(1);

a "Schedule 2 appeal" means an appeal of the type mentioned in rule 1(2)(a);

a "section 44E appeal" means an appeal of the type mentioned in rule 1(2)(b);

"the Society" means the Law Society and includes any duly constituted committee of the Law Society or any body or person exercising delegated powers of the Law Society;

"the Society's licensing rules" means licensing rules made by the Society under section 83 of the 2007 Act (licensing rules);

"solicitor members" and "lay members" have the same meanings as in section 46 of the 1974 Act;

a "Stay" means a prohibition on the respondent implementing the decision in respect of which an appeal is made;

"the Tribunal" means the Solicitors Disciplinary Tribunal and where a Panel has been appointed for the hearing of an appeal or any matter connected with it, includes a Panel.

PART 2
CONSTITUTION OF APPEAL PANELS

3 Composition of panel

(1)   A Panel of at least three members of the Tribunal shall be appointed by the Tribunal for the hearing of any appeal.

(2)   Unless the President otherwise directs, the majority of the Panel members shall be solicitor members.

4 Appointment of chairman

The chairman of each Panel shall be appointed by the Tribunal and (unless the President determines otherwise) shall be a solicitor member.

5 Delegation

(1) The duties to be performed by the clerks shall, in addition to the duties listed in rule 3(11) of the 2007 rules, include—

    (a)   appointing panels under rule 3(1);

    (b)   appointing a chairman of a Panel under rule 4; and

    (c)   giving directions under rules 9, 13 and 19(1).

(2) Paragraph (1) is without prejudice to rule 3(11) of the 2007 rules.

(3) No later than the date on which expires the period of 14 days beginning with the date on which the Tribunal sends notice to a party of a decision made by a clerk in exercise of functions of a judicial nature under paragraph (1), that party may send an application in writing to the Tribunal for that decision to be considered afresh by a Panel or a single solicitor member.

(4) The following powers of the Tribunal may be exercised by a single solicitor member—

    (a)   giving directions under rules 9, 13,14(2), (4) and (5), 15 and 19(1);

    (b)   taking action under rule 11(2)(a) and (b);

    (c)   making a decision under rule 14(1);

    (d)   giving consent under rule 16(2).

PART 3
APPEAL PROCEDURE

6 Notice of appeal

(1) An appellant must start proceedings for an appeal by sending or delivering a notice of appeal to the Tribunal.

(2) In the case of a Schedule 2 appeal, the notice of appeal must be sent or delivered so that it is received by the Tribunal no later than the date on which expires the period of 28 days beginning with the date on which the appellant was notified in writing of the decision in question under paragraph 14B(4) of Schedule 2 to the Administration of Justice Act 1985.

(3) In the case of a section 44E appeal, the notice of appeal must be sent or delivered so that it is received by the Tribunal no later than the date on which expires the period of 28 days beginning with the date on which the appellant was notified in writing of the decision in question under section 44D(4) of the 1974 Act.

(4) The notice of appeal must set out—

    (a)   the name and address of the appellant;

    (b)   the name and address of the appellant's representative (if any);

    (c)   an address where documents for the appellant may be sent or delivered;

    (d)   the basis on which the appellant has standing to start proceedings before the Tribunal;

    (e)   the name and address of the respondent;

    (f)   details of the decision or act to which the proceedings relate;

    (g)   the result the appellant is seeking;

    (h)   the grounds on which the appellant relies;

(ha)   any application for an order for a Stay, if the appellant is allowed to make such an application under the Society's licensing rules;

(i)   whether the appellant would be content for the case to be dealt with without a hearing if the Tribunal considers it appropriate; and

(j)   any further information or documents required by a practice direction.

(4A)   In the case of a licensing appeal made under the Society's licensing rules, if no time limit for the making of an appeal is prescribed under those rules, the notice of appeal must be sent or delivered so that it is received by the Tribunal no later than the date on which expires the period of 28 days beginning with the date on which the appellant was notified in writing of the decision which is the subject of the appeal.

(5)   The appellant must send or deliver with the notice of appeal a copy of any written record of the decision in respect of which the appeal is made, and any statement of reasons for that decision that the appellant has or can reasonably obtain.

(6)   The appellant must send or deliver three additional copies of the notice of appeal and any accompanying documents to the Tribunal at the same time as the appellant sends or delivers the notice of appeal to the Tribunal.

(7)   The appellant must send or deliver a copy of the notice of appeal and any accompanying documents to the respondent at the same time as the appellant sends or delivers the notice of appeal to the Tribunal.

7   Response to notice of appeal

(1)   The respondent must send or deliver to the Tribunal a response to the notice of appeal so that it is received no later than the date on which expires the period of 28 days beginning with the date on which the respondent received the notice of appeal.

(2)   The response must set out at least—

(a)   the name and address of the respondent;

(b)   the name and address of the respondent's representative (if any);

(c)   an address where documents for the respondent may be sent or delivered;

(d)   any further information or documents required by a practice direction or a direction given under these Rules; and

(e)   whether the respondent would be content for the case to be dealt with without a hearing if the Tribunal considers it appropriate.

(3)   The response must include a statement as to whether the respondent opposes the appellant's case and, if so, any grounds for such opposition which are not contained in another document sent or delivered with the response.

(4)   The respondent must send or deliver with the response—

(a)   a copy of any written record of the decision, in respect of which the appeal is made, and any statement of reasons for that decision, that the appellant did not send or deliver with the notice of appeal and the respondent has or can reasonably obtain; and

(b)   any documents relied upon by the respondent in making the decision in respect of which the appeal is made and which the respondent considers are relevant to the appeal.

(5)   If the respondent sends or delivers the response to the Tribunal later than the time required by paragraph (1) or by any extension of time under rule 9(2)(a), the response must include a request for an extension of time and the reason why the response was not sent or delivered in time.

(6) The respondent must send or deliver three additional copies of the response and any accompanying documents to the Tribunal at the same time as the respondent sends or delivers the response to the Tribunal.

(7) The respondent must send or deliver a copy of the response and any accompanying documents to the appellant at the same time as it sends or delivers the response to the Tribunal.

8 Appellant's reply

(1) The appellant may send or deliver to the Tribunal—

    (a)   a reply to the respondent's response; and

    (b)   any additional documents relied upon by the appellant in the reply.

(2) Any reply and additional documents must be sent or delivered to the Tribunal so that they are received no later than the date on which expires the period of 14 days beginning with the date on which the appellant received the notice from the respondent.

(3) If the appellant sends or delivers a reply to the Tribunal later than the time required by paragraph (2) or by any extension of time under rule 9(2)(a) the reply must include a request for an extension of time and the reason why the reply was not sent or delivered in time.

(4) The appellant may send or deliver with the reply a list of documents on which the appellant relies in support of the appeal, and which the appellant did not send or deliver with the notice of appeal.

(5) The appellant must send or deliver three additional copies of the reply and any accompanying documents to the Tribunal at the same time as the appellant sends or delivers the reply to the Tribunal.

(6) The appellant must send or deliver a copy of any reply and any accompanying documents to the respondent at the same time as the appellant sends or delivers the reply to the Tribunal.

(7) If the appellant has sent or delivered a list of documents under paragraph (4), the appellant must within 7 days of receiving a request from the respondent or the Tribunal—

    (a)   send or deliver to the respondent or Tribunal a copy of any document specified in the list (and in the case of the Tribunal, any additional copies of the document requested by the Tribunal, up to a maximum of four in number); or

    (b)   make such document available to the respondent or Tribunal to read or copy.

9 Directions and case management

(1) The Tribunal may give a direction in relation to the conduct or disposal of appeal proceedings at any time, including a direction amending, suspending or setting aside an earlier direction.

(2) In particular, and without restricting the general powers in paragraph (1) and rule 18, the Tribunal may—

    (a)   extend or shorten the time for complying with any rule, practice direction or direction, unless such extension or shortening would conflict with a provision of another enactment (or of any rule made under another enactment) containing a time limit;

    (b)   consolidate or hear together two or more sets of proceedings or parts of proceedings raising common issues, or treat a case as a lead case (whether under rule 15 or otherwise);

    (ba)   hear any application for an Order for a Stay;

    (c)   permit or require a party to amend a document;

(d)   permit or require a party or another person to provide documents, information or submissions which are relevant to the proceedings to the Tribunal or a party;

(e)   deal with an issue in the proceedings as a preliminary issue;

(f)   hold a hearing to consider any matter, including a case management issue;

(g)   decide the form of any hearing;

(h)   adjourn or postpone a hearing;

(i)   require a party to produce a bundle for a hearing;

(j)   require a party to provide a skeleton argument;

(k)   decide the place and time of any hearing;

(l)   make requirements about documentation and inspection:

(m)   stay proceedings;

(n)   suspend the effect of its own decision pending the determination by the High Court of an application for permission to appeal against, and any appeal of, that decision.

(3)   A clerk may appoint a time and place for the review of the progress of the matter and shall notify the parties of the date, time and place of any such review.

(4)   A clerk may refer to the Tribunal any matter for a decision or directions and the Tribunal may itself or on the application of any party make a decision on such terms as to the Tribunal shall appear just—

(a)   to adjourn any hearing listed for directions or for a substantive hearing;

(b)   to agree to the amendment of any document or the correction of any matter;

(c)   to make any directions which shall appear necessary or appropriate to secure the timely hearing of the appeal.

(5)   Any hearing under this rule shall be held in public unless rule 23(2) or (3) applies.

10   Practice directions

(1)   The Tribunal (or a panel of Tribunal members consisting of not less than 5 members of whom no fewer than 2 shall be lay members) may give such notices or make such directions concerning the practices or procedures of the Tribunal as are consistent with these Rules and as shall seem appropriate.

(2)   The Tribunal shall promulgate notices or directions given or made under paragraph (1) under the authority of the President.

11   Failure to comply with rules, practice directions or tribunal directions

(1)   An irregularity resulting from a failure to comply with any provision of these Rules, a practice direction or a direction given under these Rules does not of itself render void the appeal or any step taken in the appeal.

(2)   If a party has failed to comply with a requirement in these Rules, a practice direction or a direction given under these Rules, the Tribunal may take such action as the Tribunal considers just, which may include—

(a)   waiving the requirement;

(b)   requiring the failure to be remedied;

(c)   exercising its power under rule 12;

(d)   otherwise barring or restricting a party's participation in the appeal.

(3) The Tribunal may not bar or restrict a party's participation in the appeal under paragraph (2)(d) without first giving the party an opportunity to make representations in relation to the proposed action.

12 Striking out a party's case

(1) The Tribunal must strike out the whole or a part of an appeal if the Tribunal does not have jurisdiction in relation to the appeal or that part of it.

(2) The Tribunal may strike out the whole or a part of an appeal if—

(a) the appellant has failed to comply with a direction given under these Rules which stated that failure by the appellant to comply with the direction could lead to the striking out of the appeal or part of it;

(b) the appellant has failed to co-operate with the Tribunal to such an extent that the Tribunal cannot deal with the appeal fairly and justly; or

(c) the Tribunal considers there is no reasonable prospect of the appellant's case, or part of it, succeeding.

(3) The Tribunal may not strike out the whole or a part of the appeal under paragraph (1) or (2)(b) or (c) without first giving the appellant an opportunity to make representations in relation to the proposed striking out.

(4) If the appeal, or part of it, has been struck out under paragraph (2)(a), the appellant may apply for the appeal, or part of it, to be reinstated.

(5) An application under paragraph (4) must be made in writing and received by the Tribunal no later than the date on which expires the period of 28 days beginning with the date on which the Tribunal sent notification of the striking out to the appellant.

(6) This rule applies to a respondent as it applies to an appellant except that—

(a) a reference to the striking out of the whole or a part of the appeal is to be read as a reference to the striking out of the whole or a part of the response to the appeal; and

(b) a reference to an application for the reinstatement of an appeal which has been struck out is to be read as a reference to an application for the reinstatement of a response to an appeal which has been struck out.

13 Addition, substitution and removal of parties

(1) The Tribunal may give a direction adding, substituting or removing a party as an appellant or a respondent.

(2) If the Tribunal gives a direction under paragraph (1) it may give such consequential directions as it considers appropriate.

(3) A person who is not a party may apply to the Tribunal to be added or substituted as a party.

(4) If a person who is entitled to be a party to an appeal by virtue of another enactment applies to be added as a party, and any conditions applicable to that entitlement have been satisfied, the Tribunal must give a direction adding that person as a respondent or, if appropriate, as an appellant.

14 Prevention of disclosure or publication of documents and information

(1) The Tribunal may make a decision prohibiting the disclosure or publication of—

(a) specified documents or information relating to any appeal proceedings; or

(b) any matter likely to lead members of the public to identify any person whom the Tribunal considers should not be identified.

(2) The Tribunal may give a direction prohibiting the disclosure of a document or information to a person if—

(a)   the Tribunal is satisfied that such disclosure would be likely to cause that person or some other person serious harm; and

(b)   the Tribunal is satisfied, having regard to the interests of justice, that it is proportionate to give such a direction.

(3) If a party ("the first party") considers that the Tribunal should give a direction under paragraph (2) prohibiting the disclosure of a document or information to another party ("the second party"), the first party must—

(a)   exclude the relevant document or information from any documents that will be sent or delivered to the second party; and

(b)   send or deliver to the Tribunal the excluded document or information, and the reason for its exclusion, so that the Tribunal may decide whether the document or information should be disclosed to the second party or should be the subject of a direction under paragraph (2).

(4) If the Tribunal gives a direction under paragraph (2) which prevents disclosure to a party who has appointed a representative, the Tribunal may give a direction that the documents or information be disclosed to that representative if the Tribunal is satisfied that—

(a)   disclosure to the representative would be in the interests of the party; and

(b)   the representative will act in accordance with paragraph (5).

(5) Documents or information disclosed to a representative in accordance with a direction under paragraph (4) must not be disclosed either directly or indirectly to any other person without the Tribunal's consent.

(6) The Tribunal may, on its own initiative or on the application of a party, give a direction that certain documents or information must or may be disclosed to the Tribunal on the basis that the Tribunal will not disclose such documents or information to other persons, or specified other persons.

(7) A party making an application for a direction under paragraph (6) may withhold the relevant documents or information from other parties until the Tribunal has granted or refused the application.

(8) Unless the Tribunal considers that there is good reason not to do so, the Tribunal must send notice that a party has made an application for a direction under paragraph (6) to each other party.

(9) The Tribunal must conduct proceedings and record its decision and reasons appropriately so as not to undermine the effect of a decision made under paragraph (1) or a direction given under paragraph (2) or (6).

15   Lead cases

(1)   This rule applies if—

(a)   two or more appeals have been started before the Tribunal;

(b)   in each such appeal the Tribunal has not made a decision finally disposing of all issues in the proceedings; and

(c)   the appeals give rise to common or related issues of fact or law.

(2)   The Tribunal may give a direction—

(a)   specifying one or more appeals falling under paragraph (1) as a lead case or lead cases; and

(b)   staying the other appeals falling under paragraph (1) ("the related cases").

(3)   When the Tribunal makes a decision in respect of the common or related issues—

    (a)   the Tribunal must send or deliver a copy of that decision to each party in each of the related appeals; and

    (b)   subject to paragraph (4), that decision shall be binding on each of those parties.

(4)   No later than the date on which expires the period of 28 days beginning with the date on which the Tribunal sent or delivered a copy of the decision to a party under paragraph (3)(a), that party may apply in writing for a direction that the decision does not apply to, and is not binding on the parties to, a particular related appeal.

(5)   The Tribunal must give directions in respect of appeals which are stayed under paragraph (2)(b), providing for the disposal of or further directions in those appeals.

(6)   If the lead case or cases lapse or are withdrawn before the Tribunal makes a decision in respect of the common or related issues, the Tribunal must give directions as to—

    (a)   whether another appeal or other appeals are to be specified as a lead case or lead cases; and

    (b)   whether any direction affecting the related appeals should be set aside or amended.

16 Withdrawal

(1) Subject to paragraph (2), an appellant may give notice of the withdrawal of its appeal, or any part of it, and the respondent may do likewise in respect of its case against the appeal—

    (a)   at any time before a hearing to consider the disposal of the appeal (or, if the Tribunal disposes of the appeal without a hearing, before that disposal), by sending or delivering to the Tribunal a written notice of withdrawal; or

    (b)   orally at a hearing.

(2) Notice of withdrawal will not take effect unless the Tribunal consents to the withdrawal, which may be given subject to such order relating to costs as the Tribunal shall think fit.

(3) A party which has withdrawn its appeal or case against the appeal may apply to the Tribunal for the appeal or case to be reinstated.

(4) An application under paragraph (3) must be made in writing and be received by the Tribunal no later than the date on which expires the period of 28 days beginning with—

    (a)   the date on which the Tribunal received the notice under paragraph (1)(a); or

    (b)   the date of the hearing at which the appeal or case was withdrawn orally under paragraph (1)(b).

(5) The Tribunal must notify each party in writing of a withdrawal under this rule.

17 Consent orders

(1) The Tribunal may, at the request of the parties and only if it considers it appropriate, make a consent order disposing of the appeal proceedings and making such other appropriate provision as the parties have agreed.

(2) Despite any other provision of these Rules, the Tribunal need not hold a hearing before making an order under paragraph (1), or provide reasons for the order.

18 General powers of Tribunal

(1) Subject to the provisions of these Rules, the Tribunal may regulate its own procedure.

(2) The Tribunal may dispense with any requirements of these Rules in respect of notices, statements or other documents, witnesses, service or time in any case where it appears to the Tribunal to be just so to do.

19 Disclosure, evidence and submissions

(1) Without restriction on the general powers in rule 9 and 18, the Tribunal may give directions in relation to an appeal as to—

(a) the exchange between parties of lists of documents which are relevant to the appeal, or relevant to particular issues, and the inspection of such documents;

(b) the provision by parties of statements of agreed matters;

(c) issues on which it requires evidence or submissions;

(d) the nature of the evidence or submissions it requires;

(e) whether the parties are permitted or required to provide expert evidence, and if so whether the parties must jointly appoint a single expert to provide such evidence;

(f) any limit on the number of witnesses whose evidence a party may put forward, whether in relation to a particular issue or generally;

(g) the manner in which any evidence or submissions are to be provided, which may include a direction for them to be given—

(i) orally at a hearing; or

(ii) by written submissions or witness statement; and

(h) the time at which any evidence or submissions are to be sent or delivered.

(2) The Tribunal may—

(a) admit evidence whether or not—

(i) the evidence would be admissible in a civil trial in the United Kingdom; or

(ii) the evidence was available to a previous decision maker; or

(b) exclude evidence that would otherwise be admissible where—

(i) the evidence was not provided within the time allowed by a direction given under these Rules or a practice direction;

(ii) the evidence was otherwise provided in a manner that did not comply with a direction given under these Rules or a practice direction; or

(iii) it would otherwise be unfair, disproportionate or unnecessary in the interests of justice to admit the evidence.

(3) The Tribunal may consent to a witness giving, or require any witness to give, evidence on oath, and may administer an oath for that purpose.

20 Written evidence

(1) The Tribunal may in its discretion, in respect of a whole case or of any particular fact or facts, proceed and act upon evidence given by Statement.

(2) Every Statement upon which any party proposes to rely shall be sent or delivered to the clerk and to all other parties no later than 21 days before the date fixed for the hearing of the appeal together with a notice in the form of Form 1 in the Schedule.

(3) Any party on whom a notice has been served under paragraph (2) and who requires the attendance, at the hearing, of the witness in question shall, no later than 9 days before the date of the hearing require, in writing, the other party to produce the witness at the hearing.

(4) If no party requires the attendance of a witness in accordance with the provisions of this rule, the Tribunal may accept the Statement in question in evidence.

(5)   If any party intends to call as a witness any person who has not produced a Statement, he must, no later than 10 days before the date fixed for the hearing, notify the clerk and any other party to the proceedings of his intention and forthwith send or deliver a copy of a written proof of evidence to the other party and lodge five copies of the proof with the clerk.

(6)   In this rule, "Statement" means a written statement (including a witness statement) containing a statement that the party putting forward or making the Statement believes the facts stated in the Statement are true.

21   Decision with or without a hearing

(1)   The Tribunal must hold a hearing before making a decision which disposes of proceedings unless—

(a)   each party has consented to the matter being determined without a hearing; and

(b)   the Tribunal is satisfied that it can properly determine the issues without a hearing.

(2)   Despite anything to the contrary in these Rules, if the Tribunal holds a hearing to consider a preliminary issue, and following the disposal of that preliminary issue no further issue remains to be determined, the Tribunal may dispose of the proceedings without holding any further hearing.

22   Listing of appeal hearing

(1)   Unless the Tribunal has made directions in respect of the hearing of an appeal, a clerk shall appoint a date for the hearing by the Tribunal and shall give notice of the date to the parties.

(2)   The hearing shall not, unless all the parties have agreed or the Tribunal has so ordered, take place sooner than the date on which expires the period of 28 days beginning with the date of service of the notice appointing the date of the hearing.

23   Public or private hearings

(1)   Subject to paragraphs (2) and (3) every appeal hearing shall take place in public.

(2)   Any party and any person who claims to be affected by an appeal may seek a decision from the Tribunal that the hearing or part of it be conducted in private on the grounds of—

(a)   exceptional hardship; or

(b)   exceptional prejudice,

to a party, a witness or any person affected by the appeal.

(3)   If it is satisfied that those grounds are met, the Tribunal shall conduct the hearing or part of it in private and make such decision as shall appear to it to be just and proper.

(4)   The Tribunal may, before or during a hearing, direct that the hearing or part of it be held in private if—

(a)   the Tribunal is satisfied that it would have granted an application under paragraph (2) had one been made; or

(b)   in the Tribunal's view a hearing in public would prejudice the interests of justice.

(5)   The Tribunal may give a direction excluding from any hearing, or part of it—

(a)   any person whose conduct the Tribunal considers is disrupting or is likely to disrupt the hearing;

(b)   any person whose presence the Tribunal considers is likely to prevent another person from giving evidence or making submissions freely;

(c)   any person who the Tribunal considers should be excluded in order to give effect to the requirement at rule 14(9); or

(d)   any person where the purpose of the hearing would be defeated by the attendance of that person.

(6)   The Tribunal may give a direction excluding a witness from a hearing until that witness gives evidence.

24   Decisions

(1)   The Tribunal may announce a decision orally at a hearing of or relating to an appeal or may reserve its decision for announcement at a later date. In either case the announcement shall be made in public.

(2)   Subject to rule 14(9), the Tribunal must provide to each party as soon as reasonably practicable after making a decision which finally disposes of all issues in the proceedings—

(a)   an order stating the Tribunal's decision;

(b)   written reasons for the decision; and

(c)   notification of any right of appeal against the decision and the time within which, and manner in which, such right of appeal may be exercised.

(3)   The Tribunal may provide written reasons for any decision to which paragraph (2) does not apply.

(4)   An order under paragraph (2)(a) shall be signed by a member of the Tribunal upon the announcement of the decision and shall, subject to paragraph (5), be filed forthwith with the Society.

(5)   The Tribunal may suspend the filing of an order under paragraph (2)(a) if it appears to the Tribunal that there is good reason to do so, in which event the decision shall not take effect until the order is filed with the Society.

(6)   Subject to rule 14(9), the Tribunal may publicise a decision in such manner as it thinks fit.

25   Re-hearing where a party neither appears nor is represented

(1)   At any time before the date on which expires the period of 14 days beginning with the date on which an order was provided to the party under rule 24(2), a party may apply to the Tribunal for a re-hearing of an appeal if—

(a)   he neither attended in person nor was represented at the hearing of the appeal in question; and

(b)   the Tribunal determined the appeal in his absence.

(2)   An application for a re-hearing under this rule shall be made in the form of Form 2 in the Schedule and shall be supported by a statement setting out the facts upon which the applicant wishes to rely.

(3)   If satisfied that it is just so to do, the Tribunal may grant the application upon such terms, including as to costs, as it thinks fit. The re-hearing shall be held before a Panel comprised of different members from those who heard the original appeal.

PART 4
MISCELLANEOUS

26   Sending and delivery of documents

(1)   Any document to be sent or delivered to the Tribunal or to a party under these Rules, a practice direction or a direction given under these Rules must be—

(a)   sent by pre-paid first class post or by document exchange, or delivered by hand, to the address specified for the proceedings;

(b)   sent by fax (in the case of documents to be sent or delivered to the Tribunal, to the number specified for the proceedings); or

(c)   sent or delivered by such other method as the Tribunal may permit or direct.

(2)   Subject to paragraph (3), if a party provides a fax number, email address or other details for the electronic transmission of documents to them, that party must accept delivery of documents by that method.

(3)   If a party informs the Tribunal and all other parties that a particular form of communication, other than pre-paid post or delivery by hand, should not be used to send or deliver documents to that party, that form of communication must not be so used.

(4)   If the Tribunal or a party sends a document to a party or the Tribunal by email or any other electronic means of communication, the recipient may request that the sender send or deliver a hard copy of the document to the recipient. The recipient must make such a request as soon as reasonably practicable after receiving the document electronically.

(5)   The Tribunal and each party may assume that the address provided by a party or its representative is and remains the address to which documents should be sent or delivered until receiving written notification to the contrary.

(6)   If a document submitted to the Tribunal is not written in English, it must be accompanied by an English translation.

27   Calculating time

(1)   An act required by these Rules, a practice direction or a direction given under these Rules to be done on or by a particular day must be done by 5pm on that day.

(2)   If the time specified by these Rules, a practice direction or a direction given under these Rules for doing any act ends on a day other than a working day, the act is done in time if it is done on the next working day.

(3)   In this rule "working day" means any day except a Saturday or Sunday, Christmas Day, Good Friday or a bank holiday under section 1 of the Banking and Financial Dealings Act 1971.

28   Representatives

(1)   A party may appoint a representative (whether a legal representative or not) to represent that party in the proceedings.

(2)   If a party appoints a representative, that party (or the representative if the representative is a legal representative) must send or deliver to the Tribunal written notice of the representative's name and address, together with a copy of the notice.

(3)   A party who sends or delivers a notice under paragraph (2) must, at the same time, send or deliver a copy of the notice to the other party.

(4)   Anything permitted or required to be done by a party under these Rules, a practice direction or a direction given under these Rules may be done by the representative of that party, except signing a witness statement.

(5)   A person who receives due notice of the appointment of a representative—

(a)   must send or deliver to the representative any document which, at any time after the appointment, is required to be sent or delivered to the represented party, and need not send or deliver that document to the represented party; and

(b)   may assume that the representative is and remains authorised as such until they receive written notification that this is not so from the representative or the represented party.

(6)   At a hearing a party may be accompanied by another person whose name and address has not been notified under paragraph (2) but who, with the permission of the Tribunal, may act as a representative or otherwise assist in presenting the party's case at the hearing.

(7)   Paragraphs (2) to (5) do not apply to a person who accompanies a party under paragraph (6).

(8)   In this rule "legal representative" means a person who, for the purposes of the 2007 Act, is an authorised person in relation to an activity which constitutes the exercise of a right of audience or the conduct of litigation within the meaning of that Act, an advocate or solicitor in Scotland or a barrister or solicitor in Northern Ireland.

29   Costs

(1)   The Tribunal may, at any stage of an appeal, make such order as to costs as the Tribunal shall think fit, including an order—

(a)   disallowing costs incurred unnecessarily; or

(b)   that costs be paid by any party judged to be responsible for wasted or unnecessary costs, whether arising through failure to comply with time limits or otherwise.

(2)   The Tribunal may order that any party bear the whole or a part or a proportion of the costs.

(3)   The amount of costs to be paid may either be fixed by the Tribunal or be subject to detailed assessment by a Costs Judge.

(4)   The Tribunal may also make an order as to costs under this rule where any appeal is withdrawn or amended.

30   Amendment of 2007 rules

(1)   The 2007 rules are amended as follows.

(2)   In Form 6 in the Schedule, for "21 days" substitute "9 days".

Signed by authority of the Solicitors Disciplinary Tribunal

Jeremy Barnecutt

President

Solicitors Disciplinary Tribunal

22nd September 2011

SCHEDULE
FORMS

Rules 20(2) and 25(2)

FORM 1

FORM of NOTICE to accompany Statement of Evidence

Number ....

IN THE MATTER OF the Solicitors Disciplinary Tribunal (Appeals and Amendment) Rules 2011

AND IN THE MATTER OF

....

TAKE NOTICE that the [appellant][respondent] proposes to rely upon the statement(s) listed below, copies of which are served herewith.

If you wish any person who has made one of these statements to be required to attend the hearing as a witness you must, not less than 9 days before the date set down for the hearing of the appeal, notify me and the Clerk to the Tribunal to that effect. In the event of your failure to do so the Tribunal may accept the statement in question in evidence.

LIST

Date of Statement   Name of Person who made the Statement

        1.

        2.

        3.

Date: ....

Signed: ....

Address: ....

FORM 2

FORM of APPLICATION for a Rehearing

Number ....

IN THE MATTER OF the Solicitors Disciplinary Tribunal (Appeals and Amendment) Rules 2011

AND IN THE MATTER OF

....

Number of Tribunal case in respect of which a rehearing is requested
....

I APPLY under Rule 25(1) of the Solicitors Disciplinary Tribunal (Appeals and Amendment) Rules 2011 that the above-mentioned case be reheard by the Tribunal. The facts upon which I rely in support of this application are set out below:

(set out here full details of the facts on which the applicant for a rehearing relies and include the reasons why the person applying for the rehearing did not appear or was not represented before the Tribunal at the earlier hearing and set out all matters which he wishes to place before the Tribunal in mitigation or otherwise).

Dated: ....

Signature: ....

Address: ....

APPENDIX 16

Solicitors Disciplinary Tribunal guidance notes on sanctions

[Reproduced with the kind permission of the Solicitors Disciplinary Tribunal. Issued by the SDT December 2018]

Guidance note on sanctions

[Sixth edition, December 2018]

Introduction

This Guidance Note consists of a distillation of current Solicitors Disciplinary Tribunal ("the Tribunal") sanctioning principles brought together in one document. Every case is fact-specific, and this Guidance Note consists of guidelines only; it is not intended in any way to fetter the discretion of the Tribunal when deciding sanction. The exercise of its powers and the imposition of sanctions are matters solely for determination by the Tribunal. The purpose of this Guidance Note is to assist the parties, the public and the legal profession in understanding the Tribunal's decision-making process.

The Tribunal is the statutory tribunal responsible for adjudicating upon applications and complaints made under the provisions of the Solicitors Act 1974 (as amended) ("the Act").

It is the function of the Tribunal to protect the public from harm, and to maintain public confidence in the reputation of the legal profession (and those that provide legal services) for honesty, probity, trustworthiness, independence and integrity. The public must be able to expect to receive a high standard of service from a competent and capable solicitor.

The Tribunal deals with an infinite variety of cases. Prescriptive, detailed guidelines for sanctions in individual cases are neither practicable nor appropriate. The Tribunal adopts broad guidance. Its focus is to establish the seriousness of the misconduct and, from that, to determine a fair and proportionate sanction.

The contents of the Guidance Note are reviewed at least annually.

Section A: Principles and procedure

Sanctions and orders available to the Tribunal

Solicitors

1.   The Tribunal's jurisdiction and powers on an application are set out in Section 47 of the Act and include:

- the imposition of a reprimand.

- the imposition of an unlimited financial penalty payable to HM Treasury.

- the imposition of restrictions upon the way in which a solicitor can practise (not explicitly listed in Section 47, but implied by the words "the Tribunal shall have power to make such order as it may think fit" in the preamble to that Section, and see *Camacho v The Law Society* [2004] EWHC 1675 (Admin)).

- suspension from practice indefinitely or for a specified period or a suspended suspension.

- striking off the Roll.

2. The Tribunal is not restricted as to the number or combination of sanctions which it may impose.

3. Other orders which the Tribunal can make in respect of solicitors or former solicitors include:

- no order.

- termination of a period of suspension (see separate "Guidance Note On Other Powers of the Tribunal").

- restoration to the Roll following strike off (see separate "Guidance Note On Other Powers of the Tribunal").

- costs.

Solicitors' non-lawyer employees and managers

4. By Section 43(1) and (1A) of the Act the Tribunal has jurisdiction to deal with misconduct by those who are not admitted but are employed or remunerated by solicitors and others. The powers which the Tribunal may exercise in respect of such individuals are:

- no order.

- to make an order prohibiting, save with the prior consent of the regulator, any solicitor and others from employing or remunerating the person to whom the order relates, or from being a manager or having an interest in a recognised body.

- to review or revoke a Section 43 Order (see separate Guidance Note on Other Powers of the Tribunal).

5. The Tribunal's powers in respect of complaints by the Solicitors Regulation Authority (SRA) concerning employees of solicitors and managers and employees of recognised bodies have been extended by Section 47(2E) of the Act and an amendment by the Legal Services Act 2007 to Schedule 2 to the Administration of Justice Act 1985 respectively. The Tribunal has the power to make one or more of the following:

- an order directing payment of an unlimited financial penalty payable to HM Treasury.

- an order requiring the SRA to consider taking such steps as the Tribunal may specify in relation to the individual.

- if the individual is not a solicitor, a Section 43(2) Order.

- an order requiring the SRA to refer to an appropriate regulator any matter relating to the conduct of that employee.

6. The Tribunal has the power to make one or more of the following in respect of complaints made to the Tribunal concerning a recognised body:

- an order revoking the recognition of the recognised body.

- an order requiring the payment of a penalty by the recognised body.

Purpose of sanctions

7. The case of *Bolton v The Law Society* [1994] 1 WLR 512 sets out the fundamental principle and purposes of the imposition of sanctions by the Tribunal:

   "Any solicitor who is shown to have discharged his professional duties with anything less than complete integrity, probity and trustworthiness must expect severe sanctions to be imposed upon him by the Solicitors Disciplinary Tribunal."

   "... a penalty may be visited on a solicitor ... in order to punish him for what he has done and to deter any other solicitor tempted to behave in the same way ..."

   "... to be sure that the offender does not have the opportunity to repeat the offence; and"

   "... the most fundamental of all: to maintain the reputation of the solicitors' profession as one in which every member, of whatever standing, may be trusted to the ends of the earth ... a member of the public ... is ordinarily entitled to expect that the solicitor will be a person whose trustworthiness is not, and never has been, seriously in question. Otherwise, the whole profession, and the public as a whole, is injured. A profession's most valuable asset is its collective reputation and the confidence which that inspires." (per Bingham, then Master of the Rolls)

Tribunal's approach to sanction

8. Guidance on the Tribunal's approach to sanction is set out in *Fuglers and Others v Solicitors Regulation Authority* [2014] EWHC 179 (per Popplewell J) as follows:

   "28. There are three stages to the approach ... The first stage is to assess the seriousness of the misconduct. The second stage is to keep in mind the purpose for which sanctions are imposed by such a tribunal. The third stage is to choose the sanction which most appropriately fulfils that purpose for the seriousness of the conduct in question."

Human rights, equality and diversity

9. The Tribunal is a "public authority" for the purposes of the Human Rights Act 1998, and it seeks to uphold and promote the principles of the European Convention on Human Rights in accordance with the Act. In deciding what sanction, if any, to impose the Tribunal should have regard to the principle of proportionality, weighing the interests of the public with those of the practitioner. The interference with the solicitor's right to practise must be no more than necessary to achieve the Tribunal's purpose in imposing sanctions. Reasons should be given for the sanction imposed, and the decision should usually be pronounced publicly.

10. The Tribunal is aware of and committed to the promotion of equality, diversity and inclusion in carrying out all its functions. It aims to ensure that its processes and procedures are fair, objective and transparent and free from unlawful discrimination. Promoting equality is also a requirement under current and emerging equality legislation, and in particular the Equality Act 2010. Tribunal Members and everyone acting for the Tribunal are expected to adhere to the spirit and letter of this legislation.

Common procedural issues affecting sanction

Admission, but dispute as to facts

11. A respondent may admit the alleged misconduct, but dispute particular details. The

Tribunal will hear from the parties to determine whether in its view the disputed evidence would materially affect its sanction. If not, the Tribunal will proceed to determine sanction on the respondent's version of events. Where the dispute is such that it would materially affect sanction the Tribunal shall decide, having heard all the evidence, the factual basis upon which sanction will be based.

12. The Tribunal adopts the principle established in *R v Newton* [1983] Crim LR 198, and will only impose sanction upon a respondent where the particular misconduct is either admitted by, or proved against the respondent.

13. If at a hearing to establish the facts on which sanction is to be based (a "Newton hearing"), the respondent fails to adduce evidence in support of facts exclusively within his knowledge, this will entitle the Tribunal to draw such inference from that failure as it might see fit – *R v Underwood* [2005] 1 Cr.App.R. 13.

14. Once the factual basis has been established, the respondent will have the opportunity to make representations as to the level of sanction to be imposed before the Tribunal makes its final decision.

Multiple/Alternative allegations

15. Multiple allegations involving essentially the same wrongdoing committed concurrently and drafted in the alternative, or numerous similar examples of wrongdoing committed over a period of time, sometimes come before the Tribunal. When some or all of such allegations are found proved, it may be disproportionate and unjust to impose a sanction for each matter. In such a situation the Tribunal may in respect of matters found proved:

- impose a sanction, determined by the totality of the misconduct, which is specified as being in respect of all those matters; or

- impose a sanction on the more serious allegation/s, and make no separate order (or sanction) in respect of other more minor matters.

Sanction for each separate and distinct allegation

16. Where distinct and separate allegations are either admitted or proved, the Tribunal may:

- impose a particular sanction (determined by the totality of the misconduct) specified as being in respect of all matters; or

- determine the individual seriousness of each separate and distinct proven allegation, and the appropriate sanction in respect of each. Sanctions imposed will be proportionate to the totality of the misconduct.

Section B: Determining sanction

The starting point in determining sanction is to establish the seriousness of the allegation proved. The Tribunal will determine which of the sanction thresholds have been crossed, working from the lowest sanction upwards.

In determining seriousness the Tribunal must consider the respondent's culpability for their conduct and the harm caused or the harm that was intended or might reasonably be foreseen to have been caused by their actions.

When the Tribunal has identified the starting point it can add to or reduce this to reflect any aggravating or mitigating features which impact on the culpability of the respondent and harm caused to reach a provisional sanction.

On reaching a provisional sanction the Tribunal should take appropriate account of personal mitigation of the respondent before coming to a final decision.

The following list of factors is not exhaustive. Each case must be determined on its own facts and merits. Where a factor is considered to reach a decision on seriousness, it should not be considered again in deciding aggravating factors.

Assessing seriousness

17. The Tribunal will assess the seriousness of the misconduct in order to determine which sanction to impose. Seriousness is determined by a combination of factors, including:

- the respondent's level of culpability for their misconduct.
- the harm caused by the respondent's misconduct.
- the existence of any aggravating factors.
- the existence of any mitigating factors.

Culpability

18. The level of culpability ("responsibility for fault or wrong") will be influenced by such factors as (but not limited to):

- the respondent's motivation for the misconduct.
- whether the misconduct arose from actions which were planned or spontaneous.
- the extent to which the respondent acted in breach of a position of trust.
- the extent to which the respondent had direct control of or responsibility for the circumstances giving rise to the misconduct.
- the respondent's level of experience.
- whether the respondent deliberately misled the regulator (*Solicitors Regulation Authority v Spence* [2012] EWHC 2977 (Admin)).

Harm

19. The Tribunal will determine the harm caused by the misconduct and in doing will assess:

- the impact of the respondent's misconduct upon those directly or indirectly affected by the misconduct, the public, and the reputation of the legal profession. The greater the extent of the respondent's departure from the "complete integrity, probity and trustworthiness" expected of a solicitor, the greater the harm to the legal profession's reputation.
- the extent of the harm that was intended or might reasonably have been foreseen to be caused by the respondent's misconduct.

Aggravating Factors

20. Factors that aggravate the seriousness of the misconduct include (but are not limited to):

- dishonesty, where alleged and proved.
- misconduct involving the commission of a criminal offence, not limited to dishonesty.
- misconduct which was deliberate and calculated or repeated.
- misconduct continuing over a period of time.

- taking advantage of a vulnerable person.

- concealment of wrongdoing.

- misconduct where the respondent knew or ought reasonably to have known that the conduct complained of was in material breach of obligations to protect the public and the reputation of the legal profession.

- previous disciplinary matter(s) before the Tribunal where allegations were found proved.

- the extent of the impact on those affected by the misconduct.

Mitigating Factors

21. Factors that mitigate the seriousness of the misconduct itself include (but are not limited to):

- misconduct resulting from deception or otherwise by a third party (including the client).

- the timing of and extent to which any loss arising from the misconduct is made good by the respondent.

- whether the respondent voluntarily notified the regulator of the facts and circumstances giving rise to misconduct.

- whether the misconduct was either a single episode, or one of very brief duration in a previously unblemished career.

- genuine insight, assessed by the Tribunal on the basis of facts found proved and the respondent's evidence.

- open and frank admissions at an early stage and/or degree of cooperation with the investigating body.

NOTE: Matters of purely personal mitigation are of no relevance in determining the seriousness of the misconduct. However, they will be considered by the Tribunal when determining the fair and proportionate sanction (see Section D, paragraphs 53 and 54).

Particular sanctions

22. Having determined the seriousness of the misconduct, the Tribunal will assess whether to make an order, and if so, which sanction to impose. The Tribunal, in making this assessment, will start from the least serious option.

No Order

23. The Tribunal may conclude that, having regard to all the circumstances, and where the Tribunal has concluded that the level of seriousness of the misconduct or culpability of the respondent is low, that it would be unfair or disproportionate to impose a sanction. In such circumstances, the Tribunal may decide not to impose a sanction, save for an order for costs.

Reprimand

24. A Reprimand will be imposed where the Tribunal has determined that the seriousness of the respondent's misconduct justifies a sanction at the lowest level and that the protection of the public and the reputation of the legal profession does not require a greater sanction.

25. Relevant factors may include:

- the respondent's culpability is low.

- there is no identifiable harm caused to any individual.

- the risk of any such harm is negligible.

- the likelihood of future misconduct of a similar nature or any misconduct is very low.

- evidence of genuine insight, assessed by the Tribunal on the basis of facts found proved and the respondent's evidence.

- minor breaches of regulation not dealt with under the SRA's own disciplinary jurisdiction.

Fine

26. A Fine will be imposed where the Tribunal has determined that the seriousness of the misconduct is such that a Reprimand will not be a sufficient sanction, but neither the protection of the public nor the protection of the reputation of the legal profession justifies Suspension or Strike Off.

Level of Fine

27. The Tribunal will consider the following guidance in determining the appropriate level of Fine or combination of Fines to be imposed upon an individual and/or an entity:

- there is no limit to the level of Fine the Tribunal may impose. In deciding the level of Fine, the Tribunal will consider all the circumstances of the case, including aggravating and mitigating factors. The Tribunal will fix the Fine at a level which reflects the seriousness of and is proportionate to the misconduct.

- the respondent shall be expected to adduce evidence that their ability to pay a Fine is limited by their means (please refer to Practice Direction No. 6, clause 13, and the terms of Standard Directions and/or specific Directions ordered by the Tribunal in the case).

- the factors to be considered include those outlined by Popplewell J at paragraph 35 of *Fuglers* (above), which may result in movement of the level of fine up or down the Indicative Fine Bands below. The Indicative Fine Bands provide broad starting points only. Factors to be considered include: (1) whether the seriousness of the misconduct, and giving effect to the purpose of the sanction, puts the case at or near the top, middle or bottom of the category (2) the level of fines imposed by other disciplinary tribunals or the High Court in analogous cases (3) the size or standing of the solicitor or firm in question (4) the means available to an individual or a firm. In considering means it is relevant to take into account the total financial detriment which is suffered, including any costs order, and any adverse financial impact of the decision itself.

28. In the absence of **evidence** of limited means, the Tribunal is entitled to assume that the respondent's means are such that they can pay the Fine which the Tribunal decides is appropriate.

29. Fines are payable to HM Treasury, which is responsible for enforcing payment, including the agreement of instalment terms.

Indicative Fine Bands (for individuals)

Fine Band	Overall Assessment of Seriousness of Conduct	Fine Range
Level 1	Lowest level for conduct assessed as sufficiently serious to justify a fine (rather than a reprimand)	£0–£2,000
Level 2	Conduct assessed as moderately serious	£2,001–£7,500
Level 3	Conduct assessed as more serious	£7,501–£15,000
Level 4	Conduct assessed as very serious	£15,001–£50,000
Level 5	Conduct assessed significantly serious but not so serious as to result in an order for suspension or strike off	£50,001 – unlimited

30. In determining the appropriate Fine for a firm the Tribunal will take into account the factors set out at paragraph 29 above. Any Fine imposed must be proportionate to the wrongdoing and be sufficient to meet the primary objectives of sanctions, including being a meaningful deterrent. The Tribunal will also take into consideration:

- the seriousness of the misconduct

- the size and financial resources of the firm and the effect of a Fine on its business. This assessment of resources should include considering the amount of revenue generated by the firm; the level of profitability per partner or registered individual and market share.

- the loss to clients

- the income generated by the misconduct

Restriction Order

31. A Restriction Order may be combined with any other sanction made by the Tribunal.

32. The Tribunal, in exercising its wide power to "make such order as it may think fit", may if it deems it necessary to protect the public, impose restrictions in the form of conditions upon the way in which a solicitor continues to practise. If the conditions are for an indefinite period it must be part of the order that the solicitor subject to the condition(s) has liberty to apply to the Tribunal to vary or discharge the conditions. Any breach of conditions imposed by the Tribunal would be a disciplinary offence which would generally merit a separate penalty. See in particular *Ebhogiaye v Solicitors Regulation Authority* [2013] EWHC 2445 (Admin).

33. Restricted practice will only be ordered if it is necessary to ensure the protection of the public and the reputation of the legal profession from future harm by the respondent.

34. A Restriction Order may be for either a finite or an indefinite period.

35. If the Tribunal makes an order for an indefinite period, it will specify as part of the order that the respondent may apply to the Tribunal to vary or rescind the restrictions either at any time or after the lapse of a defined period.

36. Examples of restrictions that may be imposed are as follows: The respondent may not:

- practise as a sole practitioner or sole manager or sole owner of an authorised or recognised body.

- be a partner or member of a Limited Liability Partnership (LLP), Legal Disciplinary Practice (LDP) or Alternative Business Structure (ABS) or other authorised or recognised body.

- be a Compliance Officer for Legal Practice or a Compliance Officer for Finance and Administration.

- hold client money.

- be a signatory on any client account.

- work as a solicitor other than in employment approved by the SRA.

37. In imposing any restriction the Tribunal must consider that restriction necessary and appropriate. The restrictions imposed should relate to the particular misconduct of the respondent.

Suspension

38. Suspension from the Roll will be the appropriate penalty where the Tribunal has determined that:

- the seriousness of the misconduct is such that neither a Restriction Order, Reprimand nor a Fine is a sufficient sanction or in all the circumstances appropriate.

- there is a need to protect both the public and the reputation of the legal profession from future harm from the respondent by removing their ability to practise, but

- neither the protection of the public nor the protection of the reputation of the legal profession justifies striking off the Roll.

- public confidence in the legal profession demands no lesser sanction.

- professional performance, including a lack of sufficient insight by the respondent (judged by the Tribunal on the basis of facts found proved and the respondent's evidence), is such as to call into question the continued ability to practise appropriately.

39. Suspension from the Roll, and thereby from practice, reflects serious misconduct.

40. Suspension can be for a fixed term or for an indefinite period. A term of suspension can itself be temporarily suspended.

Suspended Term of Suspension

41. Where the Tribunal concludes that the seriousness of the misconduct justifies suspension from the Roll, but it is satisfied that:

- by imposing a Restriction Order, the risk of harm to the public and the public's confidence in the reputation of the legal profession is proportionately constrained; and

- the combination of such an Order with a period of pending Suspension provides adequate protection and addresses the risk of harm to the public and the need to maintain the reputation of the profession

the Tribunal may suspend that period of suspension for so long as the Restriction Order remains in force.

42. If the Restriction Order referred to at paragraph 38 above is breached, activation by the Tribunal of the term of suspension may follow.

43. In accordance with the guidance set out in *Solicitors Regulation Authority v James et al* [2018] EWHC 3058 (Admin) if the Tribunal imposes a suspended suspension the Tribunal should make clear that the suspension will be activated if further misconduct is committed.

44. If the period under restriction is successfully completed and the Restriction Order lifted, the pending suspension will cease to have effect.

Fixed Term of Suspension

45. Having concluded that the respondent should be immediately removed from practice, but that the protection of the public and the protection of the reputation of the legal profession do not require that they be struck off the Roll, the Tribunal will fix a term of suspension of such length both to punish and deter whilst being proportionate to the seriousness of the misconduct.

46. The Tribunal can also impose a staged order with a fixed term of suspension followed by a period of restricted practice under a Restriction Order.

Indefinite Suspension

47. Indefinite Suspension marks the highest level of misconduct that can appropriately be dealt with short of striking off the Roll. In deciding that an indefinite period of suspension is the fair and proportionate sanction, the Tribunal will have formed the view that:

   • the seriousness of the misconduct is so high that striking off is the most appropriate sanction; but

   • the presence of truly compelling and exceptional personal mitigation makes that course of action unjust; and/or

   • there is a realistic prospect that the respondent will recover from, for example, illness, addiction, relevant medical condition etc. or respond to retraining so that they no longer represent a material risk of harm to the public or to the reputation of the profession.

Striking Off the Roll

48. Where the Tribunal has determined that:

   • the seriousness of the misconduct is at the highest level, such that a lesser sanction is inappropriate; and

   • the protection of the public and/or the protection of the reputation of the legal profession requires it

   the Tribunal will strike a solicitor's name off the Roll.

Sanction In Respect of a Registered European Lawyer (REL) or Registered Foreign Lawyer (RFL)

49. RELs and RFLs are individuals registered with the SRA under applicable legislation. They are subject to the same rules of professional conduct and regulatory and disciplinary regime as apply to solicitors. The powers of the Tribunal in relation to sanction apply to RELs and RFLs. It should be noted that the Tribunal's powers to sanction a REL include additionally the withdrawal or suspension of their registration (see Section 26(2), The European Communities (Lawyer's Practice) Regulations 2000).

50. The sanction of withdrawal of registration in respect of a REL "possesses a gravity that lies between the sanctions of suspension and/or strike-off in the case of an English solicitor" (per Laws LJ in *Giambrone v Solicitors Regulation Authority* [2014] EWHC 1421 (Admin) at paragraph 55, and see also paragraph 60 per Foskett J).

Section C: Dishonesty

51. The most serious misconduct involves dishonesty, whether or not leading to criminal

proceedings and criminal penalties. A finding that an allegation of dishonesty has been proved will almost invariably lead to striking off, save in exceptional circumstances (see *Solicitors Regulation Authority v Sharma* [2010] EWHC 2022 (Admin)).

Exceptional Circumstances

52. In considering what amounts to exceptional circumstances: relevant factors will include the nature, scope and extent of the dishonesty itself; whether it was momentary, or over a lengthy period of time; whether it was a benefit to the solicitor, and whether it had an adverse effect on others." (*Sharma* above). The exceptional circumstances must relate in some way to the dishonesty (James above)

53. The principal focus in determining whether exceptional circumstances exist is on the nature and extent of the dishonesty and the degree of culpability (*Sharma* and *R (Solicitors Regulation Authority) v Imran* [2015] EWHC 2572 (Admin)).

54. As a matter of principle nothing is excluded as being relevant to the evaluation, which could therefore include personal mitigation. In each case the Tribunal must when evaluating whether there are exceptional circumstances justifying a lesser sanction, focus on the critical questions of the nature and extent of the dishonesty and degree of culpability and engage in a balancing exercise as part of that evaluation between those critical questions on the one hand and matters such as personal mitigation, health issues and working conditions on the other. (*James* above).

55. Where dishonesty has been found mental health issues, specifically stress and depression suffered by the solicitor as a consequence of work conditions or other matters are unlikely without more to amount to exceptional circumstances:

"The SDT having concluded that, notwithstanding mental health issues, each of the respondents was dishonest, I consider that it was contrary to principle for it then to conclude that those mental health issues could amount to exceptional circumstances".

"... in my judgment, pressure of work or extreme working conditions whilst obviously relevant, by way of mitigation, to the assessment which the SDT has to make in determining the appropriate sanction, cannot either alone or in conjunction with stress or depression, amount to exceptional circumstances. Pressure of work or of working conditions cannot ever justify dishonesty by a solicitor ..." per Flaux LJ in *James* (above)

Absence of Dishonesty

56. Striking off can be appropriate in the absence of dishonesty where, amongst other things:

- the seriousness of the misconduct is itself very high; and

- the departure by the respondent from the required standards of integrity, probity and trustworthiness is very serious.

57. In such cases, the Tribunal will have regard to the overall facts of the misconduct, and in particular the effect that allowing the respondent's name to remain on the Roll will have upon the public's confidence in the reputation of the legal profession – see in particular *Solicitors Regulation Authority v Emeana, Ijewere and Ajanaku* [2013] EWHC 2130 (Admin).

Misappropriation of client money falling short of Dishonesty

58. The Tribunal regards the breach of the absolute obligation to safeguard client money, which is quite distinct from the solicitor's duty to act honestly, as extremely serious.

59.   The dishonest misappropriation of client money will invariably lead to strike off.

60.   Strike off can be appropriate in the absence of dishonesty. Where a respondent's failure properly to monitor client money leads to its misappropriation or misuse by others, such a serious breach of the obligation could warrant striking off.

"... the tribunal had been at pains to make the point, which was a good one, that the solicitors' accounts rules existed to afford the public maximum protection against the improper and unauthorised use of their money and that, because of the importance attached to affording that protection and assuring the public that such protection was afforded, an onerous obligation was placed on solicitors to ensure that those rules were observed" per Bingham LCJ in *Weston v Law Society* [1998] Times, 15th July.

Section D: Personal mitigation

61.   Before finalising sanction, consideration will be given to any particular personal mitigation advanced by or on behalf of the respondent. The Tribunal will have regard to the following principles:

"Because orders made by the tribunal are not primarily punitive, it follows that considerations which would ordinarily weigh in mitigation of punishment have less effect on the exercise of this jurisdiction than on the ordinary run of sentences imposed in criminal cases. It often happens that a solicitor appearing before the tribunal can adduce a wealth of glowing tributes from his professional brethren. He can often show that for him and his family the consequences of striking off or suspension would be little short of tragic. Often he will say, convincingly, that he has learned his lesson and will not offend again.

... All these matters are relevant and should be considered. But none of them touches the essential issue, which is the need to maintain among members of the public a well-founded confidence that any solicitor whom they instruct will be a person of unquestionable integrity, probity and trustworthiness. Thus it can never be an objection to an order of suspension in an appropriate case that the solicitor may be unable to re-establish his practice when the period of suspension is past. If that proves, or appears, likely to be so the consequence for the individual and his family may be deeply unfortunate and unintended. But it does not make suspension the wrong order if it is otherwise right. The reputation of the profession is more important than the fortunes of any individual member. Membership of a profession brings many benefits, but that is a part of the price." (*Bolton* above).

62.   Particular matters of personal mitigation that **may** be relevant and **may** serve to reduce the nature of the sanction, and/or its severity include that:

-   the misconduct arose at a time when the respondent was affected by physical or mental ill-health that affected his ability to conduct himself to the standards of the reasonable solicitor. Such mitigation must be supported by medical evidence from a suitably qualified practitioner.

-   the respondent was an inexperienced practitioner and was inadequately supervised by his employer.

-   the respondent made prompt admissions and demonstrated full cooperation with the regulator.

Section E: Costs

63.   The Tribunal has the power to make such order as to costs as it thinks fit, including the payment by any party of costs or a contribution towards costs of such amount (if any) as

the Tribunal may consider reasonable (Section 47 of the Act). Such costs are those arising from or ancillary to proceedings before the Tribunal.

64. The Tribunal may make an order for the payment of a fixed amount of costs. This will be the usual order of the Tribunal where the parties are in agreement as to the liability for, and the amount of, those costs. Otherwise, the Tribunal will determine liability for costs, and either summarily assess those costs itself or refer the case for detailed assessment by a Costs Judge.

Costs against Respondent: allegations admitted/proved

General considerations

65. The Tribunal, in considering the respondent's liability for the costs of the applicant, will have regard to the following principles, drawn from *R v Northallerton Magistrates Court, ex parte Dove* (1999) 163 JP 894:

- it is not the purpose of an order for costs to serve as an additional punishment for the respondent, but to compensate the applicant for the costs incurred by it in bringing the proceedings and

- any order imposed must never exceed the costs actually and reasonably incurred by the applicant.

66. Before making any order as to costs, the Tribunal will give the respondent the opportunity to adduce financial information and make submissions. A respondent is not entitled as of right to an adjournment to produce evidence of means and the granting of an adjournment, which is at the Tribunal's discretion, may increase the overall costs awarded against the respondent. Respondents should therefore strictly comply with Practice Direction No. 6 and case-specific directions regarding the provision of evidence of means:

"If a solicitor wishes to contend that he is impecunious and cannot meet an order for costs, or that its size should be confined, it will be up to him to put before the Tribunal sufficient information to persuade the Tribunal that he lacks the means to meet an order for costs in the sum at which they would otherwise arrive ... where a solicitor admits the disciplinary charges brought against him, and who therefore anticipates the imposition of a sanction upon him, it should be incumbent upon him before the hearing to give advance notice to the SRA and to the Tribunal that he will contend either that no order for costs should be made against him, or that it should be limited in amount by reason of his own lack of means. He should also supply to the SRA and to the Tribunal, in advance of the hearing, the evidence upon which he relies to support that contention" (*Solicitors Regulation Authority v Davis and McGlinchey* [2011] EWHC 232 (Admin) per Mitting J and *Agyeman v Solicitors Regulation Authority* [2012] EWHC 3472 (Admin)).

67. A respondent will be expected to adduce evidence that their ability to pay costs is limited by their means (please refer to Practice Direction No. 6, clause 13, and the terms of Standard Directions and/or specific Directions ordered by the Tribunal in the case).

68. Where the Tribunal decides that the respondent is, notwithstanding their limited means, properly liable for the applicant's costs (either in full or in part) and is satisfied that there is a reasonable prospect that, at some time in the future, their ability to pay those costs will improve, it may order the respondent to meet those costs but direct that such order is not to be enforced without leave of the Tribunal. Such orders will not be granted as a matter of course. A respondent must always provide evidence of means in support of an application for an order that any costs awarded by the Tribunal to the SRA should not be enforced without leave of the Tribunal. It should be noted that costs may be increased by an application by the SRA to enforce the same.

Costs against Respondent: some allegations not proved

69. Where the respondent is partially successful in defending the allegations pursued by the applicant, in considering the respondent's liability for costs the Tribunal will have regard to the following factors:

- the reasonableness of the applicant in pursuing an allegation on which it was unsuccessful.

- the manner in which the applicant pursued the allegation on which it was unsuccessful and its case generally.

- the reasonableness of the allegation, that is, was it reasonable for the applicant to pursue the allegation in all the circumstances.

- the extra costs in terms of preparation for trial, witness statements and documents and so on, taken up by pursuing the allegation upon which the applicant was unsuccessful.

- the extra Tribunal time taken in considering the unsuccessful allegation.

- the extent to which the allegation was inter-related in terms of evidence and argument with those allegations in respect of which the applicant was successful.

- the extra costs borne by the respondent in defending an allegation which was not found to be proved. (Please also refer to paragraph 65 below.)

70. The Tribunal may award costs against a respondent even if it makes *no* finding of misconduct, "if having regard to his conduct or to all the circumstances, or both, the Tribunal shall think fit" (Rule 18 of the Solicitors (Disciplinary Proceedings) Rules 2007).

Costs against Applicant

71. The starting point adopted by the Tribunal in considering whether costs should be awarded against the regulator (where that is the applicant in a particular case) is:

"In respect of costs, the exercise of its regulatory function placed the Law Society in a wholly different position from that of a party to ordinary civil litigation. Unless a complaint was improperly brought or, for example, had proceeded as a "shambles from start to finish", when the Law Society was discharging its responsibilities as a regulator of the profession, an order for costs should not ordinarily be made against it on the basis that costs followed the event." (per Laws LJ, *Baxendale-Walker v The Law Society* [2007] EWCA Civ 233).

72. Where a respondent seeks to pursue an application for costs against the regulator, the Tribunal will have regard to the following principles:

- an order that the applicant pay a successful respondent's costs on the grounds that costs follow the event should not ordinarily be made on that basis alone.

- there is no assumption that such an order will automatically follow.

- "to expose a regulator to the risk of an adverse costs order simply because it properly brought proceedings which were unsuccessful might have a chilling effect upon its regulatory function" (per *Baxendale-Walker*, above).

73. The Tribunal must also take into account the decision of *Broomhead v Solicitors Regulation Authority* [2014] EWHC 2772 (Admin), in which Mr Justice Nicol stated as follows:

"42. However, while the propriety of bringing charges is a good reason why the SRA should not have to pay the solicitor's costs, it does not follow that the solicitor who has successfully defended himself against those charges should have to pay the SRA's costs. Of course there may be something about the way the solicitor has conducted the proceedings or behaved in other ways which would justify a different conclusion. Even if the charges were properly brought it seems to me that in the normal case the SRA should have to shoulder its own costs where it has not been able to persuade the Tribunal that its case is made out. I do not see that this would constitute an unreasonable disincentive to take appropriate regulatory action."

74. The Tribunal may also take account of the decision in *Perinpanathan v Westminster Magistrates Court* [2010] EWCA Civ 40 which requires the Tribunal to examine the conduct of the Applicant so as to consider whether its conduct had been unreasonable or otherwise justified a costs order being made against it.

75. The Tribunal will consider the balance to be struck between:

- the financial prejudice to the successful respondent in the particular circumstances if an order for costs is not made in their favour; and

- "the need for a regulator to make and stand by honest, reasonable and apparently sound decisions made in the public interest without fear of exposure to undue financial prejudice if unsuccessful" (per Bingham LCJ, *Bradford MDC v Booth* (2000) 164 JP 485 DC).

76. The Tribunal will receive submissions from the parties at the substantive hearing, and will adjourn the hearing insofar as it relates to costs only for that purpose if necessary (but see paragraph 58 above).

Extracts from the Solicitors Act 1974

[With consolidated amendments to 6 April 2017]

Solicitors Act 1974

1974 CHAPTER 47

An Act to consolidate the Solicitors Acts 1957 to 1974 and certain other enactments relating to solicitors

[31st July 1974]

BE IT ENACTED by the Queen's most Excellent Majesty, by and with the advice and consent of the Lords Spiritual and Temporal, and Commons, in this present Parliament assembled, and by the authority of the same, as follows:—

PART I
RIGHT TO PRACTISE AS SOLICITOR

Qualifications and training

1   Qualifications for practising as solicitor

No person shall be qualified to act as a solicitor unless—

    (a)   he has been admitted as a solicitor, and

    (b)   his name is on the roll, and

    (c)   he has in force a certificate issued by the Society in accordance with the provisions of this Part authorising him to practise as a solicitor (in this Act referred to as a "practising certificate").

1A   Practising certificates: employed solicitors

A person who has been admitted as a solicitor and whose name is on the roll shall, if he would not otherwise be taken to be acting as a solicitor, be taken for the purposes of this Act to be so acting if he is employed in connection with the provision of any legal services—

    (a)   by any person who is qualified to act as a solicitor;

    (b)   by any partnership at least one member of which is so qualified;

    (c)   by a body recognised under section 9 of the Administration of Justice Act 1985 (incorporated practices); or

    (d)   by any other person who, for the purposes of the Legal Services Act 2007, is an authorised person in relation to an activity which is a reserved legal activity (within the meaning of that Act).

13   Appeals etc in connection with the issue of practising certificates

(1)   A person who makes an application under section 9 may appeal to the High Court against—

(a) a decision to refuse the application for a practising certificate,

(b) [...] or

(c) a decision to impose a condition on a practising certificate issued in consequence of the application.

(2) A person who holds a practising certificate subject to a condition within section 10(4)(b) may appeal to the High Court against any decision by the Society to refuse to approve the taking of any step for the purposes of that condition.

(3) The Society may make rules which provide, as respects any application under section 9 that is neither granted nor refused by the Society within such period as may be specified in the rules, for enabling an appeal to be brought under this section in relation to the application as if it had been refused by the Society.

(4) On an appeal under subsection (1), the High Court may—

(a) affirm the decision of the Society,

(b) [*repealed*]

(c) direct the Society to issue a certificate to the applicant free from conditions or subject to such conditions as the High Court may think fit,

(d) direct the Society not to issue a certificate,

(e) if a certificate has been issued, by order suspend it,

(f) [...] or

(g) make such other order as the High Court thinks fit.

(5) On an appeal under subsection (2), the High Court may—

(a) affirm the decision of the Society,

(b) direct the Society to approve the taking of one or more steps for the purposes of a condition within section 10(4)(b), or

(c) make such other order as the High Court thinks fit.

(6) In relation to an appeal under this section the High Court may make such order as it thinks fit as to payment of costs.

(7) The decision of the High Court on an appeal under subsection (1) or (2) shall be final.

13A Imposition of conditions while practising certificates are in force

(1) Subject to the provisions of this section, the Society may in the case of any solicitor direct that his practising certificate for the time being in force (his "current certificate") shall have effect subject to such conditions as the Society may think fit.

(2) The power conferred by subsection (1) is exercisable in relation to a solicitor at any time during the period for which the solicitor's current certificate is in force if—

(a) [*repealed*]

(b) it appears to the Society that the case is of a prescribed description.

(3) "Prescribed" means prescribed by regulations under section 28.

(6) A solicitor in whose case a direction is given under this section may appeal to the High Court against the decision of the Society.

(7) On an appeal under subsection (6), the High Court may—

(a) affirm the decision of the Society; or

(b)   direct that the appellant's current certificate shall have effect subject to such conditions as the High Court thinks fit; or

(c)   by order revoke the direction; or

(d)   make such other order as it thinks fit.

(7A)   The decision of the High Court on an appeal under subsection (6) shall be final.

(8) Subsections (4) and (5) of section 10 apply for the purposes of subsection (1) of this section as they apply for the purposes of that section.

(9) A solicitor who holds a practising certificate subject to a condition imposed under subsection (1) which prohibits that solicitor from taking any steps specified in the condition, except with the approval of the Society, may appeal to the High Court against any decision by the Society to refuse to approve the taking of any step for the purposes of that condition.

(10) On an appeal under subsection (9), the High Court may—

(a)   affirm the decision of the Society,

(b)   direct the Society to approve the taking of one or more steps for the purposes of the condition, or

(c)   make such other order as the High Court thinks fit.

(11) The decision of the High Court on an appeal under subsection (9) shall be final.

(12) In relation to an appeal under this section the High Court may make such order as it thinks fit as to payment of costs.

13B Suspension of practising certificates where solicitors convicted of fraud or serious crime

(1) Where—

(a)   a solicitor has been convicted of—

        (i)   an offence involving dishonesty or deception; or

        (ii)   an indictable offence; and

(b)   the Society has made an application to the Tribunal under section 47 with respect to him,

the Society may direct that any practising certificate of his which is for the time being in force be suspended.

(2) Any such suspension shall be for such period, not exceeding six months, as the Society shall specify in the direction.

(3) If, before the specified period expires—

(a)   the Tribunal determines the Society's application;

(b)   the conviction is quashed or set aside; or

(c)   the Society withdraws its application to the Tribunal,

the suspension shall cease to have effect.

(4) Where the specified period comes to an end without any of the events mentioned in subsection (3) having occurred, the Society may direct that the suspension be continued for such period, not exceeding six months, as it shall specify in the direction.

(5) A suspension under this section may only be extended once under subsection (4).

(6) Nothing in this section is to be taken as in any way affecting the Tribunal's power to suspend a solicitor from practice.

(7)   A solicitor in whose case a direction is given under subsection (1) or (4) may appeal to the High Court against the direction within one month of being notified of it.

(8)   In an appeal under subsection (7), the High Court may—

(a)   affirm the suspension;

(b)   direct that the appellant's certificate shall not be suspended, but shall have effect subject to such conditions as the High Court thinks fit;

(c)   by order revoke the direction; or

(d)   make such other order as it thinks fit.

(9)   In relation to an appeal under subsection (7) the High Court may make such order as it thinks fit as to payment of costs.

(10)   The decision of the High Court on an appeal under subsection (7) shall be final.

15   Suspension of practising certificates

(1)   The making by the Tribunal or by the court of an order suspending a solicitor from practice shall operate, and an adjudication in bankruptcy of a solicitor or the making of a debt relief order (under Part 7A of the Insolvency Act 1986) in respect of a solicitor shall operate immediately, to suspend any practising certificate of that solicitor for the time being in force.

(1A)   Where the power conferred by paragraph 6(1), 6A(1) or 9(1) of Schedule 1 has been exercised in relation to a solicitor by virtue of paragraph 1(1)(a)(i), (aa), (c) (so far as it applies to rules made by virtue of section 31 or 32) or (e) of that Schedule, the exercise of that power shall operate immediately to suspend any practising certificate of that solicitor for the time being in force.

(1B)   Subsection (1A) does not apply if, at the time when the power referred to there is exercised, the Society directs that subsection (1A) is not to apply in relation to the solicitor concerned.

(1C)   If, at the time when the power referred to in subsection (1A) is exercised, the Society gives a direction to that effect, the solicitor concerned may continue to act in relation to any matter specified in the direction as if his practising certificate had not been suspended by virtue of subsection (1A), but subject to such conditions (if any) as the Society sees fit to impose.

(2)   For the purposes of this Act, a practising certificate shall be deemed not to be in force at any time while it is suspended.

16   Duration of suspension of practising certificates

(1)   Where a practising certificate is suspended, it expires on such date as may be prescribed by regulations under section 28.

(2)   The suspension of a practising certificate by virtue of section 15(1) by reason of an adjudication in bankruptcy shall terminate if the adjudication is annulled and an office copy of the order annulling the adjudication is served on the Society.

(2A)   The suspension of a practising certificate by virtue of section 15(1) by reason of the making of a debt relief order shall terminate—

(a)   if the debt relief order is revoked on the ground mentioned in section 251L(2)(c) or (d) of the Insolvency Act 1986 and a copy of the notice provided to the debtor under Rule 9.18 of the Insolvency (England and Wales) Rules 2016 is served on the Society or the debt relief order is revoked by the court under section 251M(6)(e) of that Act and a copy of the court order is served on the Society;

(b)   if the debt relief order is revoked and a period of one year has elapsed beginning with the effective date of that order.

(3) Where a solicitor's practising certificate is suspended—

(a) by an order under section 13(4); or

(b) by virtue of section 15(1) by reason of his adjudication in bankruptcy or the making of a debt relief order (under Part 7A of the Insolvency Act 1986) in respect of him; or

(c) by virtue of section 15(1) by reason of his suspension from practice and the period of his suspension from practice expires before the date on which his certificate will expire,

(d) by virtue of section 15(1A)

the solicitor may at any time before the certificate expires (and, in the case of adjudication in bankruptcy, while the adjudication remains unannulled) apply to the Society to terminate the suspension.

(4) On an application under subsection (3), the Society may in its discretion—

(a) by order terminate the suspension either unconditionally or subject to such conditions as the Society may think fit; or

(b) refuse the application.

(5) If on an application by a solicitor under subsection (3) the Society refuses the application or terminates the suspension subject to conditions, the solicitor may appeal against the decision of the Society to the High Court, which may—

(a) affirm the decision; or

(b) terminate the suspension either unconditionally or subject to such conditions as it may think fit.

(6) In relation to an appeal under subsection (5) the High Court may make such order as it thinks fit as to payment of costs.

(7) The decision of the High Court on an appeal under subsection (5) shall be final.

17 Publicity in relation to suspension of practising certificates

(1) Where a solicitor's practising certificate is suspended by an order under section 13(4), or by virtue of section 15(1) by reason of his adjudication in bankruptcy, the Society shall forthwith cause notice of that suspension to be published and a note of it to be entered against the name of the solicitor on the roll.

(2) Where any such suspension of a practising certificate as is mentioned in subsection (1) is terminated under section 16(2), (4) or (5), the Society shall forthwith cause a note of that termination to be entered against the name of the solicitor on the roll and, if so requested in writing by the solicitor, a notice of it to be published.

Supplementary

28 Regulations

(1) The Society may make regulations about the following matters, namely—

(a) admission as a solicitor;

(b) the keeping of the roll;

(c) practising certificates;

(d) the keeping of the register under section 10A.

(2) [*repealed*]

(3) [*repealed*]

(3A) Regulations about the keeping of the roll may (among other things)—

(za) make provision about the form in which the roll is to be kept and the manner in which entries are to be made, altered and removed;

(a) provide for the Society, at such intervals as may be specified in the regulations, to enquire of solicitors of any class so specified whether they wish to have their names retained on the roll;

(b) require solicitors of any such class, at such intervals as aforesaid, to pay to the Society a fee in respect of the retention of their names on the roll of such amount as may be prescribed by the regulations;

(c) authorise the Society to remove from the roll the name of any solicitor who—

(i) fails to reply to any enquiry made in pursuance of paragraph (a) or to pay any fee payable by virtue of paragraph (b), or

(ii) replies to any such enquiry by indicating that he does not wish to have his name retained on the roll;

(d) authorise the Society to remove from the roll the name of any solicitor who has died;

(e) require the information on the roll to be made available to the public;

(f) specify the manner in which information is to be made so available and require it to be made so available during office hours and without charge.

(3B) Regulations about practising certificates may (among other things)—

(a) prescribe the form and manner in which applications for, or relating to, practising certificates are to be made;

(b) prescribe information which must be included in or accompany such applications;

(c) make provision about time limits for dealing with such applications, and confer on a person power to extend or bring forward such a time limit in prescribed circumstances;

(d) prescribe the requirements which applicants for practising certificates must satisfy before they may be issued with a practising certificate;

(e) prescribe descriptions of applicants, and conditions in relation to them, for the purposes of section 10(2) (circumstances in which practising certificates must be issued subject to prescribed conditions);

(f) [*repealed*];

(g) prescribe circumstances for the purposes of section 10(3) (circumstances in which application may be refused etc in the public interest);

(h) make provision about when conditions imposed on practising certificates take effect (including provision conferring power on the Society to direct that a condition is not to have effect until the conclusion of any appeal in relation to it);

(i) make provision for the commencement, duration, replacement, withdrawal and expiry of practising certificates;

(j) prescribe circumstances for the purposes of section 13A(2) (circumstances in which conditions can be imposed during period of practising certificate);

(k) require solicitors who hold practising certificates to notify the Society of such matters as may be prescribed, at such times, or in such circumstances as may be prescribed.

(3C)   Regulations about the keeping of the register under section 10A may (among other things)—

(a)   make provision about the form in which the register is to be kept and the manner in which entries are to be made, altered and removed;

(b)   require information of a specified kind to be included in entries in the register;

(c)   require information (or information of a specified description) on the register to be made available to the public;

(d)   specify the manner in which it is to be made so available and require it to be made so available during office hours and without charge.

(3D)   Regulations under this section may make provision for appeals to the High Court against decisions made by the Society under the regulations.

(3E)   In relation to an appeal under regulations made by virtue of subsection (3D), the High Court may make such order as it thinks fit as to payment of costs.

(3F)   The decision of the High Court on such an appeal shall be final.

(3G)   Regulations under this section may—

(a)   provide for a person to exercise a discretion in dealing with any matter;

(b)   include incidental, supplementary and consequential provision;

(c)   make transitory or transitional provision and savings;

(d)   make provision generally or only in relation to specified cases or subject to specified exceptions;

(e)   make different provision for different cases.

(4)   [*repealed*]

(5)   [*repealed*]

PART II
PROFESSIONAL PRACTICE, CONDUCT AND DISCIPLINE OF SOLICITORS AND CLERKS

Practice rules

31   Rules as to professional practice, conduct and discipline

(1)   Without prejudice to any other provision of this Part the Society may make rules for regulating in respect of any matter the professional practice, conduct, fitness to practise and discipline of solicitors and for empowering the Society to take such action as may be appropriate to enable the Society to ascertain whether or not the provisions of rules made, or of any code or guidance issued, by the Society are being, or have been, complied with.

(1A)   The powers conferred on the Society by subsection (1) include power to make, in relation to solicitors, provision of a kind which the Society would be prohibited from making but for section 157(5)(c) of the Legal Services Act 2007 (exception from prohibition on approved regulators making provision for redress).

(1B)   Rules under this section must provide that a solicitor may not practise as a sole solicitor unless there is in force in relation to that solicitor's practice a recognition under section 9 of the Administration of Justice Act 1985.

(1C)   Rules under this section may provide that, for the purposes of the rules, this Act and the Administration of Justice Act 1985, a solicitor is not to be regarded as practising as a sole solicitor in such circumstances as may be prescribed by the rules.

(2) If any solicitor fails to comply with rules made under this section, any person may make a complaint in respect of that failure to the Tribunal.

(3) [*repealed*]

(4) [*repealed*]

Accounts etc

32 Accounts rules and trust accounts rules

(1) The Society shall make rules—

(a) as to the opening and keeping by solicitors of accounts at banks or with building societies for money within subsection (1A);

(aa) as to the operation by solicitors of accounts kept by their clients or other persons at banks or with building societies or other financial institutions;

(b) as to the keeping by solicitors of accounts containing information as to money received, held or paid by them for or on account of their clients or other persons (including money received, held or paid under a trust); and

(c) empowering the Society to take such action as may be necessary to enable it to ascertain whether or not the rules are being, or have been, complied with.

(1A) The money referred to in subsection (1) is money (including money held on trust) which is received, held or dealt with for clients or other persons.

(2) [*repealed*]

(3) If any solicitor fails to comply with rules made under this section, any person may make a complaint in respect of that failure to the Tribunal.

(4) The Society shall be at liberty to disclose a report on or information about a solicitor's accounts obtained in the exercise of powers conferred by rules made under subsection (1) for use in investigating the possible commission of an offence by the solicitor or any of his employees and for use in connection with any prosecution of the solicitor or any of his employees consequent on the investigation.

(5) Rules under this section may specify circumstances in which solicitors or any class of solicitors are exempt from the rules or a part of the rules.

(6) [*repealed*]

33 Interest on clients' money

(1) Rules under section 32 may require a solicitor to pay interest, or sums in lieu of and equivalent to interest, to a client, any other person or any trust, for whom the solicitor holds money.

(2) The cases in which a solicitor may be required by the rules to act as mentioned in subsection (1) may be defined, among other things, by reference to the amount of any sum received or the period for which it is or is likely to be retained or both.

(3) Except as provided by the rules, a solicitor is not liable to account to any client, other person or trust for interest received by the solicitor on money held at a bank or building society in an account which is for money received or held for, or on account of—

(a) the solicitor's clients, other persons or trusts, generally, or

(b) that client, person or trust, separately.

(4) Rules under section 32 may—

(a)   prescribe the circumstances in which a solicitor may make arrangements to limit or exclude an obligation imposed on the solicitor by rules made by virtue of this section, and

(b)   prescribe the requirements to be met by and in relation to those arrangements.

33A Inspection of practice bank accounts etc

(1) The Society may make rules empowering the Society to require a solicitor to produce documents relating to any account kept by him at a bank or with a building society—

(a)   in connection with his practice; or

(b)   in connection with any trust of which he is or formerly was a trustee,

for inspection by a person appointed by the Society pursuant to the rules.

(2) The Society shall be at liberty to disclose information obtained in exercise of the powers conferred by rules made under subsection (1) for use in investigating the possible commission of an offence by the solicitor and for use in connection with any prosecution of the solicitor consequent on the investigation.

34 Accountants' reports

(1) The Society may make rules requiring solicitors to provide the Society with reports signed by an accountant (in this section referred to as an "accountant's report") at such times or in such circumstances as may be prescribed by the rules.

(2) The rules may specify requirements to be met by, or in relation to, an accountant's report (including requirements relating to the accountant who signs the report).

(6) If any solicitor fails to comply with the provisions of any rules made under this section, a complaint in respect of that failure may be made to the Tribunal by or on behalf of the Society.

(7) [*repealed*]

(8) [*repealed*]

(9) Where an accountant, during the course of preparing an accountant's report—

(a)   discovers evidence of fraud or theft in relation to money held by a solicitor for a client or any other person (including money held on trust) or money held in an account of a client of a solicitor, or an account of another person, which is operated by the solicitor, or

(b)   obtains information which the accountant has reasonable cause to believe is likely to be of material significance in determining whether a solicitor is a fit and proper person to hold money for clients or other persons (including money held on trust) or to operate an account of a client of the solicitor or an account of another person,

the accountant must immediately give a report of the matter to the Society.

(10) No duty to which an accountant is subject is to be regarded as contravened merely because of any information or opinion contained in a report under subsection (9).

Sole solicitors

34A Employees of solicitors

(1) Rules made by the Society may provide for any rules made under section 31, 32, 33A or 34 to have effect in relation to employees of solicitors with such additions, omissions or other modifications as appear to the Society to be necessary or expedient.

(2) If any employee of a solicitor fails to comply with rules made under section 31 or 32, as they have effect in relation to the employee by virtue of subsection (1), any person may make a complaint in respect of that failure to the Tribunal.

(3) If any employee of a solicitor fails to comply with rules made under section 34, as they have effect in relation to the employee by virtue of subsection (1), a complaint in respect of that failure may be made to the Tribunal by or on behalf of the Society.

34B Employees of solicitors: accounts rules etc

(1) Where rules made under section 32(1) have effect in relation to employees of solicitors by virtue of section 34A(1), section 85 applies in relation to an employee to whom the rules have effect who keeps an account with a bank or building society in pursuance of such rules as it applies in relation to a solicitor who keeps such an account in pursuance of rules under section 32.

(2) Subsection (3) applies where rules made under section 32—

(a)   contain any such provision as is referred to in section 33(1), and

(b)   have effect in relation to employees of solicitors by virtue of section 34A(1).

(3) Except as provided by the rules, an employee to whom the rules are applied is not liable to account to any client, other person or trust for interest received by the employee on money held at a bank or building society in an account which is for money received or held for, or on account of—

(a)   clients of the solicitor, other persons or trusts, generally, or

(b)   that client, person or trust, separately.

(4) Subsection (5) applies where rules made under section 33A(1) have effect in relation to employees of solicitors by virtue of section 34A(1).

(5) The Society may disclose a report on or information about the accounts of any employee of a solicitor obtained in pursuance of such rules for use—

(a)   in investigating the possible commission of an offence by the solicitor or any employees of the solicitor, and

(b)   in connection with any prosecution of the solicitor or any employees of the solicitor consequent on the investigation.

(6) Where rules made under section 34 have effect in relation to employees of solicitors by virtue of section 34A(1), section 34(9) and (10) apply in relation to such an employee as they apply in relation to a solicitor.

Intervention in solicitor's practice, Compensation Fund and professional indemnity

35 Intervention in solicitor's practice

The powers conferred by Part II of Schedule 1 shall be exercisable in the circumstances specified in Part I of that Schedule.

Restrictions on employment of certain persons

41 Employment by solicitor of person struck off or suspended

(1) No solicitor shall, except in accordance with a written permission granted under this section, employ or remunerate in connection with his practice as a solicitor any person who to his knowledge is disqualified from practising as a solicitor by reason of the fact that—

(a)   his name has been struck off the roll, or

(b)   he is suspended from practising as a solicitor, or

(c)   his practising certificate is suspended while he is an undischarged bankrupt.

(1A)   No solicitor shall, except in accordance with a written permission granted under this section, employ or remunerate in connection with his practice as a solicitor any person if, to his knowledge, there is a direction in force under section 47(2)(g) in relation to that person.

(1B)   Where—

(a)   a solicitor ("the employed solicitor") is employed by another solicitor in accordance with a written permission granted under this section, and

(b)   the employed solicitor is disqualified from practising as a solicitor by reason of a fact mentioned in subsection (1)(b) or (c),

section 20(1) does not apply in relation to anything done by the employed solicitor in the course of that employment.

(2)   The Society may grant a permission under this section for such period and subject to such conditions as the Society thinks fit.

(3)   A solicitor aggrieved by the refusal of the Society to grant a permission under subsection (2), or by any conditions attached by the Society to the grant of any such permission, may appeal to the High Court which may—

(a)   confirm the refusal or the conditions, as the case may be; or

(b)   grant a permission under this section for such period and subject to such conditions as it thinks fit.

(4)   If any solicitor acts in contravention of this section or of any conditions subject to which a permission has been granted under it, the Tribunal or, as the case may be, the High Court may—

(a)   order that his name be struck off the roll,

(b)   order that he be suspended from practice for such period as the Tribunal or court thinks fit, or

(c)   make such other order in the matter as it thinks fit.

(4A)   In relation to an appeal under subsection (3) the High Court may make such order as it thinks fit as to payment of costs.

(4B)   The decision of the High Court on an appeal under subsection (3) shall be final.

(5)   [*repealed*]

42   Failure to disclose fact of having been struck off or suspended

(1)   Any person who, while he is disqualified from practising as a solicitor by reason of the fact that—

(a)   his name has been struck off the roll, or

(b)   he is suspended from practising as a solicitor, or

(c)   his practising certificate is suspended while he is an undischarged bankrupt,

seeks or accepts employment by a solicitor in connection with that solicitor's practice without previously informing him that he is so disqualified shall be guilty of an offence and liable on summary conviction to a fine not exceeding level 3 on the standard scale.

(1A)   Any person—

(a)   with respect to whom a direction is in force under section 47(2)(g); and

(b)   who seeks or accepts employment by a solicitor in connection with that solicitor's practice without previously informing him of the direction, shall be guilty of an offence and liable on summary conviction to a fine not exceeding level three on the standard scale.

(2) Notwithstanding anything in the Magistrates' Courts Act 1980, proceedings under this section may be commenced at any time before the expiration of six months from the first discovery of the offence by the prosecutor, but no such proceedings shall be commenced except by, or with the consent of, the Attorney General.

43 Control of solicitors' employees and consultants

(1) Where a person who is or was involved in a legal practice but is not a solicitor—

(a) has been convicted of a criminal offence which is such that in the opinion of the Society it would be undesirable for the person to be involved in a legal practice in one or more of the ways mentioned in subsection (1A), or

(b) has, in the opinion of the Society, occasioned or been a party to, with or without the connivance of a solicitor, an act or default in relation to a legal practice which involved conduct on his part of such a nature that in the opinion of the Society it would be undesirable for him to be involved in a legal practice in one or more of the ways mentioned in subsection (1A),

the Society may either make, or make an application to the Tribunal for it to make, an order under subsection (2) with respect to that person.

(1A) A person is involved in a legal practice for the purposes of this section if the person—

(a) is employed or remunerated by a solicitor in connection with the solicitor's practice;

(b) is undertaking work in the name of, or under the direction or supervision of, a solicitor;

(c) is employed or remunerated by a recognised body;

(d) is employed or remunerated by a manager or employee of a recognised body in connection with that body's business;

(e) is a manager of a recognised body;

(f) has or intends to acquire an interest in such a body.

(2) An order made by the Society or the Tribunal under this subsection is an order which states one or more of the following—

(a) that as from the specified date—

(i) no solicitor shall employ or remunerate, in connection with his practice as a solicitor, the person with respect to whom the order is made,

(ii) no employee of a solicitor shall employ or remunerate, in connection with the solicitor's practice, the person with respect to whom the order is made,

(iii) no recognised body shall employ or remunerate that person, and

(iv) no manager or employee of a recognised body shall employ or remunerate that person in connection with the business of that body,

except in accordance with a Society permission;

(b) that as from the specified date no recognised body or manager or employee of such a body shall, except in accordance with a Society permission, permit the person with respect to whom the order is made to be a manager of the body;

(c) that as from the specified date no recognised body or manager or employee of such a body shall, except in accordance with a Society permission, permit the person with respect to whom the order is made to have an interest in the body.

(2A)   The Society may make regulations prescribing charges to be paid to the Society by persons who are the subject of an investigation by the Society as to whether there are grounds for the Society—

(a)   to make an order under subsection (2), or

(b)   to make an application to the Tribunal for it to make such an order.

(2B)   Regulations under subsection (2A) may—

(a)   make different provision for different cases or purposes;

(b)   provide for the whole or part of a charge payable under the regulations to be repaid in such circumstances as may be prescribed by the regulations.

(2C)   Any charge which a person is required to pay under regulations under subsection (2A) is recoverable by the Society as a debt due to the Society from the person.

(3)   Where an order has been made under subsection (2) with respect to a person by the Society or the Tribunal—

(a)   that person or the Society may make an application to the Tribunal for it to be reviewed, and

(b)   whichever of the Society and the Tribunal made it may at any time revoke it.

(3A)   On the review of an order under subsection (3) the Tribunal may order—

(a)   the quashing of the order;

(b)   the variation of the order; or

(c)   the confirmation of the order;

and where in the opinion of the Tribunal no prima facie case for quashing or varying the order is shown, the Tribunal may order its confirmation without hearing the applicant.

(4)   The Tribunal, on the hearing of any application under this section, may make an order as to the payment of costs by any party to the application.

(5)   Orders made under subsection (2) by the Society, or made, varied or confirmed under this section by the Tribunal and filed with the Society, may be inspected during office hours without payment.

(5A)   In this section—

"manager", in relation to a recognised body, has the same meaning as it has in relation to a body in the Legal Services Act 2007 (see section 207 of that Act);

"recognised body" means a body recognised under section 9 of the Administration of Justice Act 1985;

"specified date" means such date as may be specified in the order;

"Society permission" means permission in writing granted by the Society for such period and subject to such conditions as the Society may think fit to specify in the permission.

(5B)   A person has an interest in a recognised body for the purposes of this section if the person has an interest in that body within the meaning of Part 5 of the Legal Services Act 2007 (see sections 72 and 109 of that Act).

(6)   [*repealed*]

(7)   For the purposes of this section an order discharging a person absolutely or conditionally in respect of an offence shall, notwithstanding anything in section 14 of the Powers of Criminal Courts (Sentencing) Act 2000, be deemed to be a conviction of the offence for which the order was made.

44   Offences in connection with orders under section 43(2)

(1)   It is an offence for a person in respect of whom there is in force an order under section 43(2) which contains provision within section 43(2)(a)—

(a)   to seek or accept any employment or remuneration from a solicitor, or an employee of a solicitor, in connection with the practice carried on by that solicitor without previously informing the solicitor or employee of the order;

(b)   to seek or accept any employment or remuneration from a recognised body, or a manager or employee of a recognised body, in connection with that body's business, without previously informing the body, or manager or employee, of the order.

(1A)   It is an offence for a person in respect of whom there is in force an order under section 43(2) which contains provision within section 43(2)(b) to seek or accept a position as a manager of a recognised body, without previously informing that body of the order.

(1B)   It is an offence for a person in respect of whom there is in force an order under section 43(2) which contains provision within section 43(2)(c) to seek or accept an interest in a recognised body from any person, without previously informing that person and (if different) the recognised body of the order.

(1C)   A person guilty of an offence under subsection (1), (1A) or (1B) is liable on summary conviction to a fine not exceeding level 3 on the standard scale.

(2)   Where an order under section 43(2) is in force in respect of a person, then, if any solicitor knowingly acts in contravention of that order or of any conditions subject to which permission for the taking of any action has been granted under it, a complaint in respect of that contravention may be made to the Tribunal by or on behalf of the Society.

(3)   Any document purporting to be an order under section 43(2) and to be duly signed in accordance with section 48(1) shall be received in evidence in any proceedings under this section and be deemed to be such an order without further proof unless the contrary is shown.

(4)   Notwithstanding anything in the Magistrates' Courts Act 1980, proceedings under subsection (1) may be commenced at any time before the expiration of six months from the first discovery of the offence by the prosecutor, but no such proceedings shall be commenced, except with the consent of the Director of Public Prosecutions, by any person other than the Society or a person acting on behalf of the Society.

(5)   In this section—

"manager" has the same meaning as in section 43;

"recognised body" means a body recognised under section 9 of the Administration of Justice Act 1985;

and for the purposes of subsection (1B) a person seeks or accepts an interest in a recognised body if the person seeks or accepts an interest which if it were obtained by the person would result in the person having an interest in that body within the meaning of Part 5 of the Legal Services Act 2007 (see sections 72 and 109 of that Act).

44A

[*repealed*]

Examination of files

44B Provision of information and documents by solicitors etc

(1)   The Society may by notice require a person to whom this section applies—

    (a)   to provide information, or information of a description, specified in the notice, or

    (b)   produce documents, or documents of a description, specified in the notice.

(2)   This section applies to—

    (a)   a solicitor;

    (b)   an employee of a solicitor;

    (c)   a recognised body;

    (d)   an employee or manager of, or a person with an interest in, a recognised body.

(3)   The Society may give a notice under this section only if it is satisfied that it is necessary to do so for the purpose of investigating—

    (a)   whether there has been professional misconduct by a solicitor;

    (b)   whether a solicitor, or an employee of a solicitor, has failed to comply with any requirements imposed by or by virtue of this Act or any rules made by the Society;

    (c)   whether a recognised body, or any of its managers or employees has failed to comply with any requirement imposed by or by virtue of the Administration of Justice Act 1985 or any rules made by the Society and applicable to the body, manager or employee by virtue of section 9 of that Act;

    (d)   whether there are grounds for making, or making an application to the Tribunal for it to make, an order under section 43(2) with respect to a person who is or was involved in a legal practice (within the meaning of section 43(1A)).

(4)   A notice under this section—

    (a)   may specify the time and place at which, and manner and form in which, the information is to be provided or document is to be produced;

    (b)   must specify the period within which the information is to be provided or the document produced;

    (c)   may require the information to be provided or document to be produced to the Society or to a person specified in the notice.

(5)   The Society may pay to any person such reasonable costs as may be incurred by that person in connection with the provision of any information, or production of any document, by that person pursuant to a notice under this section.

(6)   Paragraphs 9(3) and (4) and 13, 15 and 16 of Schedule 1 apply in relation to the powers to obtain information conferred by this section, but for this purpose—

    (a)   paragraph 9 of that Schedule has effect as if—

        (i)   in sub-paragraph (3) for "such documents" there were substituted "information to which a notice given to him under section 44B applies",

        (ii)   in that sub-paragraph for "sub-paragraph (1)" there were substituted "the notice", and

        (iii)   in sub-paragraph (4) for "produce" (in the first place) to the end there were substituted "provide information pursuant to a notice under section 44B to provide the information to any person appointed by the Society at such time and place as may be specified in the order.", and

(b)   the reference to the solicitor or his personal representative in paragraph 13 of that Schedule is to be construed as a reference to the person to whom the notice was given under this section.

(7) Paragraphs 9 (other than sub-paragraphs (1) and (3)), 12, 13, 15 and 16 of Schedule 1 apply in relation to the powers to obtain documents conferred by this section as they apply in relation to the powers conferred by paragraph 9(1) of that Schedule, except that for this purpose—

(a)   any reference in paragraph 9 of that Schedule to a person appointed, or to a requirement, under sub-paragraph (1) of that paragraph is to be construed as a reference to a person appointed, or to a requirement to produce documents, under this section,

(b)   any reference in that paragraph to any such documents as are mentioned in paragraph 9(1) of that Schedule is to be construed as a reference to any documents to which a notice under this section applies,

(c)   the references to the solicitor or his firm in paragraph 9(5) and (6) of that Schedule, and the reference to the solicitor or personal representative in paragraph 9(7) of that Schedule, are to be construed as references to the person to whom the notice was given under this section, and

(d)   the reference in paragraph 9(12) of that Schedule to the Society is to be construed as including a reference to a person specified under subsection (4)(c).

(8) Where powers conferred by Part 2 of Schedule 1 to the 1974 Act are exercisable in relation to a person within paragraph (a), (b), (c) or (d) of subsection (2), they continue to be so exercisable after the person has ceased to be a person within the paragraph in question.

(9) In this section—

"manager" has the same meaning as in the Legal Services Act 2007 (see section 207 of that Act);

"recognised body" means a body recognised under section 9 of the Administration of Justice Act 1985;

and the reference to a person who has an interest in a recognised body is to be construed in accordance with sections 72 and 109 of the Legal Services Act 2007.

44BA Power to require explanation of document or information

(1) The Society may, by notice, require a person to whom a notice is given under section 44B (or a representative of the person) to attend at a time and place specified in the notice to provide an explanation of any information provided or document produced pursuant to the notice.

(2) The Society may pay to any person such reasonable costs as may be incurred by that person in connection with that person's compliance with a requirement imposed under subsection (1).

(3) Paragraphs 9(3) and (4) and 13, 15 and 16 of Schedule 1 apply in relation to a notice under this section, except that for this purpose—

(a)   paragraph 9 of that Schedule has effect as if—

(i)   in sub-paragraph (3) for "having" to "sub-paragraph (1)" there were substituted "refuses, neglects or otherwise fails to comply with a requirement under section 44BA(1)", and

(ii)   in sub-paragraph (4) for "produce" (in the first place) to the end there were substituted "provide an explanation of any information provided or document produced pursuant to a notice under section 44B (or a representative of

such a person) to attend at a time and place specified in the order to provide an explanation of any information so provided or document so produced.",
and

(b)   the reference to the solicitor or his personal representative in paragraph 13 of that Schedule is to be construed as a reference to the person to whom the notice was given under this section.

44BB Provision of information and documents by other persons

(1) The High Court, on the application of the Society, may order a person to whom section 44B does not apply—

(a)   to provide information, or information of a description, specified in the notice, or

(b)   to produce documents, or documents of a description, specified in the notice.

(2) The High Court may make an order under this section only if it is satisfied—

(a)   that it is likely that the information or document is in the possession or custody of, or under the control of, the person, and

(b)   that there is reasonable cause to believe that the information or document is likely to be of material significance to an investigation into any of the matters mentioned in section 44B(3)(a) to (d).

(3) An order under this section may direct the Society to pay to a person specified in the order such reasonable costs as may be incurred by that person in connection with the provision of any information, or production of any document, by that person pursuant to the order.

(4) Section 44B(4) applies in relation to an order under this section as it applies in relation to a notice under section 44B.

(5) Paragraphs 9(5A) and (7) to (12), 12, 13, 15 and 16 of Schedule 1 apply in relation to an order under this section as they apply in relation to an order under paragraph 9(4) of that Schedule, except that for this purpose—

(a)   the reference to the solicitor or personal representative in paragraph 9(7) of that Schedule is to be construed as a reference to the person in respect of whom the order under this section is made,

(b)   the reference in paragraph 9(12) of that Schedule to the Society is to be read as including a reference to a person specified under section 44B(4)(c) (as applied by subsection (4) of this section), and

(c)   the reference to the solicitor or his personal representative in paragraph 13 of that Schedule is to be construed as a reference to the person to whom the notice was given under this section.

44BC Information offences

(1) It is an offence for a person who knows or suspects an investigation into any of the matters mentioned in section 44B(3)(a) to (d) is being or is likely to be conducted—

(a)   to falsify, conceal, destroy or otherwise dispose of a document which the person knows or suspects is or would be relevant to the investigation, or

(b)   to cause or permit the falsification, concealment, destruction or disposal of such a document.

(2) In proceedings for an offence under subsection (1) it is a defence for the accused to show that the accused had no intention of concealing facts disclosed by the documents from the person conducting the investigation.

(3) It is an offence for a person, in purported compliance with a requirement imposed on the person under section 44B, 44BA or 44BB—

(a) to provide information which the person knows to be false or misleading in a material particular, or

(b) recklessly to provide information which is false or misleading in a material particular.

(4) A person who is guilty of an offence under subsection (1) or (3) is liable—

(a) on summary conviction, to imprisonment for a term not exceeding 12 months or a fine not exceeding the statutory maximum, or both;

(b) on conviction on indictment, to imprisonment for a term not exceeding 2 years or a fine, or both.

(5) In relation to an offence under subsection (1) or (3) committed before the commencement of section 154(1) of the Criminal Justice Act 2003 the reference in subsection (4)(a) to 12 months is to be read as a reference to 6 months.

Costs of investigations

44C Power to charge for costs of investigations

(1) The Society may make regulations prescribing charges to be paid to the Society by solicitors who are the subject of a discipline investigation.

(2) A "discipline investigation" is an investigation carried out by the Society into—

(a) possible professional misconduct by a solicitor, or

(b) a failure or apprehended failure by a solicitor to comply with any requirement imposed by or by virtue of this Act or any rules made by the Society.

(3) Regulations under this section may—

(a) make different provision for different cases or purposes;

(b) provide for the whole or part of a charge payable under the regulations to be repaid in such circumstances as may be prescribed by the regulations.

(4) Any charge which a solicitor is required to pay under regulations under this section is recoverable by the Society as a debt due to the Society from the solicitor.

(5) This section (other than subsection (2)(a)) applies in relation to an employee of a solicitor as it applies in relation to a solicitor.

Disciplinary powers of the Society

44D Disciplinary powers of the Society

(1) This section applies where the Society is satisfied—

(a) that a solicitor or an employee of a solicitor has failed to comply with a requirement imposed by or by virtue of this Act or any rules made by the Society, or

(b) that there has been professional misconduct by a solicitor.

(2) The Society may do one or both of the following—

(a) give the person a written rebuke;

(b) direct the person to pay a penalty not exceeding £2,000.

(3) The Society may publish details of any action it has taken under subsection (2)(a) or (b), if it considers it to be in the public interest to do so.

(4) Where the Society takes action against a person under subsection (2)(b), or decides to publish under subsection (3) details of any action taken under subsection (2)(a) or (b), it must notify the person in writing that it has done so.

(5) A penalty imposed under subsection (2)(b) does not become payable until—

(a) the end of the period during which an appeal against the decision to impose the penalty, or the amount of the penalty, may be made under section 44E, or

(b) if such an appeal is made, such time as it is determined or withdrawn.

(6) The Society may not publish under subsection (3) details of any action under subsection (2)(a) or (b)—

(a) during the period within which an appeal against—

(i) the decision to take the action,

(ii) in the case of action under subsection (2)(b), the amount of the penalty, or

(iii) the decision to publish the details,

may be made under section 44E, or

(b) if such an appeal has been made, until such time as it is determined or withdrawn.

(7) The Society must make rules—

(a) prescribing the circumstances in which the Society may decide to take action under subsection (2)(a) or (b);

(b) about the practice and procedure to be followed by the Society in relation to such action;

(c) governing the publication under subsection (3) of details of action taken under subsection (2)(a) or (b);

and the Society may make such other rules in connection with the exercise of its powers under this section as it considers appropriate.

(8) Before making rules under subsection (7), the Society must consult the Tribunal.

(9) A penalty payable under this section may be recovered as a debt due to the Society, and is to be forfeited to Her Majesty.

(10) The Lord Chancellor may, by order, amend paragraph (b) of subsection (2) so as to substitute for the amount for the time being specified in that paragraph such other amount as may be specified in the order.

(11) Before making an order under subsection (10), the Lord Chancellor must consult the Society.

(12) An order under subsection (10) is to be made by statutory instrument subject to annulment in pursuance of a resolution of either House of Parliament.

(13) This section is without prejudice to any power conferred on the Society or any other person to make an application or complaint to the Tribunal.

44E Appeals against disciplinary action under section 44D

(1) A person may appeal against—

(a) a decision by the Society to rebuke that person under section 44D(2)(a) if a decision is also made to publish details of the rebuke;

(b) a decision by the Society to impose a penalty on that person under section 44D(2)(b) or the amount of that penalty;

(c)   a decision by the Society to publish under section 44D(3) details of any action taken against that person under section 44D(2)(a) or (b).

(2)   Subsections (9)(b), (10)(a) and (b), (11) and (12) of section 46 (Tribunal rules about procedure for hearings etc) apply in relation to appeals under this section as they apply in relation to applications or complaints, except that subsection (11) of that section is to be read as if for "the applicant" to "application)" there were substituted "any party to the appeal".

(3)   Rules under section 46(9)(b) may, in particular, make provision about the period during which an appeal under this section may be made.

(4)   On an appeal under this section, the Tribunal has power to make such order as it thinks fit, and such an order may in particular—

(a)   affirm the decision of the Society;

(b)   revoke the decision of the Society;

(c)   in the case of a penalty imposed under section 44D(2)(b), vary the amount of the penalty;

(d)   in the case of a solicitor, contain provision for any of the matters mentioned in paragraphs (a) to (d) of section 47(2);

(e)   in the case of an employee of a solicitor, contain provision for any of the matters mentioned in section 47(2E);

(f)   make such provision as the Tribunal thinks fit as to payment of costs.

(5)   Where by virtue of subsection (4)(e) an order contains provision for any of the matters mentioned in section 47(2E)(c), section 47(2F) and (2G) apply as if the order had been made under section 47(2E)(c).

(6)   An appeal from the Tribunal shall lie to the High Court, at the instance of the Society or the person in respect of whom the order of the Tribunal was made.

(7)   The High Court shall have power to make such order on an appeal under this section as it may think fit.

(8)   Any decision of the High Court on an appeal under this section shall be final.

(9)   This section is without prejudice to any power conferred on the Tribunal in connection with an application or complaint made to it.

45

[repealed]

Disciplinary proceedings before Solicitors Disciplinary Tribunal

46   Solicitors Disciplinary Tribunal

(1)   Applications and complaints made by virtue of any provision of this Act shall be made, except so far as other provision is made by this Act or by any regulations under it, to the tribunal known as the "Solicitors Disciplinary Tribunal".

(2)   The Master of the Rolls shall appoint the members of the Tribunal.

(3)   The Tribunal shall consist—

(a)   of practising solicitors of not less than ten years' standing (in this section referred to as "solicitor members"); and

(b)   of persons who are neither solicitors nor barristers (in this section referred to as "lay members").

(4)   A member of the Tribunal shall hold and vacate his office in accordance with the terms of his appointment and shall, on ceasing to hold office, be eligible for re-appointment.

(5)   The Tribunal may pay its members such remuneration, fees or allowances as it may determine with the approval of the Legal Services Board.

(5A)   The Tribunal may do anything calculated to facilitate, or incidental or conducive to, the carrying out of any of its functions.

(6)   [*repealed*]

(7)   [*repealed*]

(8)   [*repealed*]

(9)   The Tribunal may make rules—

   (a)   empowering the Tribunal to elect a solicitor member to be its president; and

   (b)   about the procedure and practice to be followed in relation to the making, hearing and determination of applications and complaints (including provision about the composition of the Tribunal).

(10)   Without prejudice to the generality of subsection (9)(b), rules made by virtue of that paragraph may in particular—

   (a)   empower the president of the Tribunal to appoint a chairman for the hearing and determination of any application or complaint;

   (b)   provide that, if the president does not appoint a chairman, a solicitor member shall act as chairman; and

   (c)   provide, in relation to any application or complaint relating to a solicitor, that, where in the opinion of the Tribunal no prima facie case in favour of the applicant or complainant is shown in the application or complaint, the Tribunal may make an order refusing the application or dismissing the complaint without requiring the solicitor to whom it relates to answer the allegations and without hearing the applicant or complainant.

(11)   For the purposes of any application or complaint made to the Tribunal under this Act, the Tribunal may administer oaths, and the applicant or complainant and any person with respect to whom the application or complaint is made (or, in the case of an application under section 47(1)(b), any of the parties to the application) may issue writs of subpoena ad testificandum and duces tecum, but no person shall be compelled under any such writ to produce any document which he could not be compelled to produce on the trial of an action.

(12)   The power to make rules conferred by subsection (9) shall be exercisable by statutory instrument, and the Statutory Instruments Act 1946 shall apply to a statutory instrument containing such rules in like manner as if the rules had been made by a Minister of the Crown.

46A   Funding of the Tribunal

(1)   The Tribunal must submit to the Society in respect of each year a budget for the year approved by the Legal Services Board.

(2)   A budget for a year is a statement of the amount of money which the Tribunal estimates is required to enable it to meet all of its expenditure in that year (having regard to any amounts received but not spent in previous years).

(3)   Before approving a statement for the purposes of subsection (1) the Legal Services Board must consult the Society.

(4)   The budget for a year must be submitted to the Society under subsection (1) no later than the date in the preceding year specified by the Society for the purposes of this subsection.

(5) Before specifying a date for this purpose the Society must consult the Tribunal.

(6) The amount specified in a budget submitted under subsection (1) must be paid by the Society to the Tribunal—

(a)   in such instalments and at such times as may be agreed between the Society and the Tribunal, or

(b)   in the absence of such agreement, before the beginning of the year to which the budget relates.

(7) The Society may pay the Tribunal such other amounts as the Society considers appropriate.

(8) In this section "year" means a calendar year.

47 Jurisdiction and powers of Tribunal

(1)   Any application—

(a)   to strike the name of a solicitor off the roll;

(b)   to require a solicitor to answer allegations contained in an affidavit;

(c)   to require a former solicitor whose name has been removed from or struck off the roll to answer allegations contained in an affidavit relating to a time when he was a solicitor;

(d)   by a solicitor who has been suspended from practice for an unspecified period, by order of the Tribunal, for the termination of that suspension;

(e)   by a former solicitor whose name has been struck off the roll to have his name restored to the roll;

(f)   by a former solicitor in respect of whom a direction has been given under subsection (2)(g) to have his name restored to the roll,

shall be made to the Tribunal; but nothing in this subsection shall affect any jurisdiction over solicitors exercisable by the Master of the Rolls, or by any judge of the High Court, by virtue of section 50.

(2) Subject to subsections (2E) and (3) and to section 54, on the hearing of any application or complaint made to the Tribunal under this Act, other than an application under section 43, the Tribunal shall have power to make such order as it may think fit, and any such order may in particular include provision for any of the following matters—

(a)   the striking off the roll of the name of the solicitor to whom the application or complaint relates;

(b)   the suspension of that solicitor from practice indefinitely or for a specified period;

(c)   the payment by that solicitor or former solicitor of a penalty, which shall be forfeit to Her Majesty;

(d)   in the circumstances referred to in subsection (2A), the exclusion of that solicitor from criminal legal aid work (either permanently or for a specified period);

(e)   the termination of that solicitor's unspecified period of suspension from practice;

(f)   the restoration to the roll of the name of a former solicitor whose name has been struck off the roll and to whom the application relates;

(g)   in the case of a former solicitor whose name has been removed from the roll, a direction prohibiting the restoration of his name to the roll except by order of the Tribunal;

(h)   in the case of an application under subsection (1)(f), the restoration of the applicant's name to the roll;

(i)   the payment by any party of costs or a contribution towards costs of such amount as the Tribunal may consider reasonable.

(2A)   An order of the Tribunal may make provision for the exclusion of a solicitor from criminal legal aid work as mentioned in subsection (2)(d) where the Tribunal determines that there is good reason for doing so arising out of—

(a)   his conduct, including conduct in the capacity of agent for another solicitor, in connection with the provision for any person of services provided under arrangements made for the purposes of Part 1 of the Legal Aid, Sentencing and Punishment of Offenders Act 2012; or

(b)   his professional conduct generally.

(2B)   Where the Tribunal makes any such order as is referred to in subsection (2A) in the case of a solicitor who is a member of a firm of solicitors, the Tribunal may, if it thinks fit, order that any other person who is for the time being a member of the firm shall be excluded (either permanently or for a specified period) from criminal legal aid work.

(2C)   The Tribunal shall not make an order under subsection (2B) unless an opportunity is given to him to show cause why the order should not be made.

(2D)   Any person excluded from criminal legal aid work by an order under this section may make an application to the Tribunal for an order terminating his exclusion.

(2E)   On the hearing of any complaint made to the Tribunal by virtue of section 34A(2) or (3), the Tribunal shall have power to make one or more of the following—

(a)   an order directing the payment by the employee to whom the complaint relates of a penalty to be forfeited to Her Majesty;

(b)   an order requiring the Society to consider taking such steps as the Tribunal may specify in relation to that employee;

(c)   if that employee is not a solicitor, an order which states one or more of the matters mentioned in paragraphs (a) to (c) of section 43(2);

(d)   an order requiring the Society to refer to an appropriate regulator any matter relating to the conduct of that employee.

(2F)   Subsections (1) to (1C), (3) and (4) of section 44 apply in relation to an order under subsection (2E)(c) as they apply in relation to an order under section 43(2).

(2G)   Section 44(2), paragraph 16(1)(d) and (1A)(d) of Schedule 2 to the Administration of Justice Act 1985 and paragraph 15(3A) of Schedule 14 to the Courts and Legal Services Act 1990 apply in relation to an order under subsection (2E)(c) as they apply in relation to an order under section 43(2).

(2H)   For the purposes of subsection (2E)(d) an "appropriate regulator" in relation to an employee means—

(a)   if the employee is an authorised person in relation to a reserved legal activity (within the meaning of the Legal Services Act 2007), any relevant approved regulator (within the meaning of that Act) in relation to that employee, and

(b)   if the employee carries on activities which are not reserved legal activities (within the meaning of that Act), any body which regulates the carrying on of such activities by the employee.

(3)   On proof of the commission of an offence with respect to which express provision is made by any section of this Act, the Tribunal shall, without prejudice to its power of making an order as to costs, impose the punishment, or one of the punishments, specified in that section.

(3A)   Where, on the hearing of any application or complaint under this Act, the Tribunal is satisfied that more than one allegation is proved against the person to whom the application or complaint relates it may impose a separate penalty (by virtue of subsection (2)(c)) with respect to each such allegation.

(3B)   For the avoidance of doubt, nothing in this section permits the Tribunal to make an order requiring redress to be made in respect of any act or omission of any person.

(3C)   In this section "criminal legal aid work" means the provision under arrangements made for the purposes of Part 1 of the Legal Aid, Sentencing and Punishment of Offenders Act 2012 of—

(a)   advice or assistance described in section 13 or 15 of that Act, or

(b)   representation for the purposes of criminal proceedings.

(4)   [*repealed*]

(5)   [*repealed*]

(6)   [*repealed*]

47A

[*repealed*]

48   Orders of Tribunal

(1)   An order of the Tribunal shall be filed with the Society, and a statement of the Tribunal's findings, signed by the chairman or by some other member of the Tribunal authorised by him in that behalf, shall either be prefaced to the order or added to the file containing the order as soon as may be after the order has been made.

(2)   Where an order which has been filed includes provision for any of the matters referred to in paragraphs (a) to (i) of section 47(2), the Society—

(a)   shall cause a note of the effect of the order to be entered on the roll against the name of the solicitor or former solicitor with respect to whom the application or complaint was made; and

(b)   except where it only makes provision for matters referred to in paragraph (e), (ea), (f), (h) or (i) of section 47(2), shall forthwith upon filing the order cause a notice stating its effect to be published.

(3)   Any file kept by the Society under this section may be inspected during office hours without payment.

(4)   An order which has been filed shall be treated, for the purpose of enforcement, as if it had been made by the High Court.

(5)   In the case of orders of the Tribunal under section 44E, the reference in subsection (2)(a) to the application or complaint is to be read as a reference to the Tribunal's order.

49   Appeals from Tribunal

(1)   An appeal from the Tribunal shall lie to the High Court.

(2)   Subject to subsection (3) and to section 43(5) of the Administration of Justice Act 1985, an appeal shall lie at the instance of the applicant or complainant or of the person with respect to whom the application or complaint was made.

(3)   An appeal against an order under section 43(3A) shall lie only at the instance of the person with respect to whom the order was made, and an appeal against an order under section 47 excluding any person or persons from criminal legal aid work (as defined in that section) shall lie only at the instance of any person so excluded.

(4)   The High Court shall have power to make such order on an appeal under this section as it may think fit.

(5)   Subject to any rules of court, on an appeal against an order made by virtue of rules under section 46(10)(c) without hearing the applicant or complainant, the court—

(a)   shall not be obliged to hear the appellant, and

(b)   may remit the matter to the Tribunal instead of dismissing the appeal.

(6)   Any decision of the High Court—

(a)   on an application under section 43(3) or 47(1)(d), (e), (ea) or (f), or

(b)   against an order under section 43(3A),

shall be final.

(7)   [*repealed*]

49A   Appeals to the Tribunal instead of the High Court

(1)   The Society may, with the approval of the Tribunal, make rules which provide that in such circumstances as may be prescribed by the rules an appeal under any of the provisions listed in subsection (2) lies to the Tribunal and not to the High Court.

(2)   Those provisions are—

(a)   section 8(4);

(b)   section 13A(6);

(c)   section 16(5);

(d)   section 28(3D);

(e)   section 41(3);

(f)   paragraph 14 of Schedule 14 to the Courts and Legal Services Act 1990 (foreign lawyers: appeals against conditions or refusals).

(3)   Any decision of the Tribunal on an appeal by virtue of rules made under this section shall be final.

Disciplinary proceedings before Senior Courts

50   Jurisdiction of Senior Courts over solicitors

(1)   Any person duly admitted as a solicitor shall be an officer of the Senior Courts.

(2)   Subject to the provisions of this Act, the High Court, the Crown Court and the Court of Appeal respectively, or any division or judge of those courts, may exercise the same jurisdiction in respect of solicitors as any one of the superior courts of law or equity from which the Senior Courts were constituted might have exercised immediately before the passing of the Supreme Court of Judicature Act 1873 in respect of any solicitor, attorney or proctor admitted to practise there.

(3)   An appeal shall lie to the Court of Appeal from any order made against a solicitor by the High Court or the Crown Court in the exercise of its jurisdiction in respect of solicitors under subsection (2).

51 Procedure upon certain applications to High Court

(1)   Where an application to strike the name of a solicitor off the roll or to require a solicitor to answer allegations contained in an affidavit is made to the High Court, then, subject to section 54, the following provisions of this section shall have effect in relation to that application.

(2)   The court shall not entertain the application except on production of an affidavit proving that the applicant has served on the Society fourteen clear days' notice of his intention to make the application, together with copies of all affidavits intended to be used in support of the application.

(3)   The Society may appear by counsel on the hearing of the application and any other proceedings arising out of or in reference to the application, and may apply to the court—

(a)   to make absolute any order nisi which the court may have made on the application;

(b)   to make an order that the name of the solicitor be struck off the roll; or

(c)   to make such other order as the court may think fit.

(4)   The court may order the costs of the Society of or relating to any of the matters mentioned in subsections (2) and (3) to be paid by the solicitor against whom, or by the person by whom, the application was made, or was intended to be made, or partly by one and partly by the other of them.

Disciplinary proceedings—general

54 Restrictions on powers to strike names off roll

(1)   No solicitor shall be liable to have his name struck off the roll on account of any failure to comply with the requirements with respect to persons seeking admission as solicitors of any training regulations or on account of any defect in his admission and enrolment, unless—

(a)   the application to strike his name off the roll is made within twelve months of the date of his enrolment; or

(b)   fraud is proved to have been committed in connection with the failure or defect.

(2)   No solicitor shall be liable to have his name struck off the roll by reason only—

(a)   that a solicitor who undertook a training responsibility for him under training regulations neglected or omitted to take out a practising certificate; or

(b)   that the name of a solicitor who undertook such a responsibility for a period has been removed from or struck off the roll after the end of that period.

55 Applications to require solicitor to answer allegations

For the avoidance of doubt it is hereby declared that an application by any person to require a solicitor to answer allegations contained in an affidavit, whether that application is made to the Tribunal or to the High Court, may be treated as an application to strike the name of that solicitor off the roll on the grounds of the matters alleged.

SCHEDULE 1
Intervention in Solicitor's Practice

Section 35

PART I
CIRCUMSTANCES IN WHICH SOCIETY MAY INTERVENE

1 (1) Subject to sub-paragraph (2), the powers conferred by Part II of this Schedule shall be exercisable where—

(a) the Society has reason to suspect dishonesty on the part of—

    (i) a solicitor, or

    (ii) an employee of a solicitor, or

    (iii) the personal representatives of a deceased solicitor,

in connection with that solicitor's practice or former practice or in connection with any trust of which that solicitor is or formerly was a trustee or that employee is or was a trustee in his capacity as such an employee;

(aa) the Society has reason to suspect dishonesty on the part of a solicitor ("S") in connection with—

    (i) the business of any person of whom S is or was an employee, or of any body of which S is or was a manager, or

    (ii) any business which is or was carried on by S as a sole trader;

(b) the Society considers that there has been undue delay on the part of the personal representatives of a deceased solicitor who immediately before his death was practising as a sole solicitor in connection with that solicitor's practice or in connection with any trust;

(c) the Society is satisfied that a solicitor has failed to comply with rules made by virtue of section 31, 32 or 37(2)(c);

(d) a solicitor has been made bankrupt or has made a composition or arrangement with his creditors;

(e) a solicitor has been committed to prison in any civil or criminal proceedings;

(ee) the Society is satisfied that a sole solicitor is incapacitated by illness, injury or accident to such an extent as to be unable to attend to his practice;

(f) a solicitor lacks capacity (within the meaning of the Mental Capacity Act 2005) to act as a solicitor and powers under sections 15 to 20 or section 48 of that Act are exercisable in relation to him; or

(g) the name of a solicitor has been removed from or struck off the roll or a solicitor has been suspended from practice;

(h) the Society is satisfied that a solicitor has abandoned his practice;

(i) [*repealed*]

(j) any power conferred by this Schedule has been exercised in relation to a sole solicitor by virtue of sub-paragraph (1)(a) and he has acted as a sole solicitor within the period of eighteen months beginning with the date on which it was so exercised;

(k) the Society is satisfied that a person has acted as a solicitor at a time when he did not have a practising certificate which was in force;

(l) the Society is satisfied that a solicitor has failed to comply with any condition, subject to which his practising certificate was granted or otherwise has effect, to the effect that he may act as a solicitor only—

      (i)   in employment which is approved by the Society in connection with the imposition of that condition;

      (ii)   as a member of a partnership which is so approved;

      (iii) as a manager of a body recognised by the Society under section 9 of the Administration of Justice Act 1985 and so approved; or

      (iv) in any specified combination of those ways;

  (m)   the Society is satisfied that it is necessary to exercise the powers conferred by Part 2 of this Schedule (or any of them) in relation to a solicitor to protect—

      (i)   the interests of clients (or former or potential clients) of the solicitor or his firm, or

      (ii)   the interests of the beneficiaries of any trust of which the solicitor is or was a trustee.

(1A)   In sub-paragraph (1) "manager" has the same meaning as in the Legal Services Act 2007 (see section 207 of that Act).

(2)   [*repealed*]

2   On the death of a sole solicitor paragraphs 6 to 8 shall apply to the client accounts of his practice.

3   The powers conferred by Part II of this Schedule shall also be exercisable, subject to paragraphs 5(4) and 10(9), where—

  (a)   the Society is satisfied that there has been undue delay—

      (i)   on the part of a solicitor in connection with any matter in which the solicitor or his firm is or was acting on behalf of a client or with any trust, or

      (ii)   on the part of an employee of a solicitor in connection with any trust of which the employee is or was a trustee in his capacity as such an employee; and

  (b)   the Society by notice in writing invites the solicitor to give an explanation within a period of not less than 8 days specified in the notice; and

  (c)   the solicitor fails within that period to give an explanation which the Society regards as satisfactory; and

  (d)   the Society gives notice of the failure to the solicitor and (at the same or any later time) notice that the powers conferred by Part II of this Schedule are accordingly exercisable.

4   (1)   Where the powers conferred by Part II of this Schedule are exercisable in relation to a solicitor, they shall continue to be exercisable after his death or after his name has been removed from or struck off the roll.

(2)   The references to the solicitor or his firm in paragraphs 5(1), 6(2) and (3), 6A, 8, 9(1), (5) and (6) and 10(2) and (7) include, in any case where the solicitor has died, references to his personal representatives.

PART II
POWERS EXERCISABLE ON INTERVENTION

Money

5 (1) The High Court, on the application of the Society, may order that no payment shall be made without the leave of the court by any person (whether or not named in the order) of any money held by him (in whatever manner and whether it was received before or after the making of the order) on behalf of the solicitor or his firm.

(2) No order under this paragraph shall take effect in relation to any person to whom it applies unless the Society has served a copy of the order on him (whether or not he is named in it) and, in the case of a bank or other financial institution, has indicated at which of its branches the Society believes that the money to which the order relates is held.

(3) A person shall not be treated as having disobeyed an order under this paragraph by making a payment of money if he satisfies the court that he exercised due diligence to ascertain whether it was money to which the order related but nevertheless failed to ascertain that the order related to it.

(4) This paragraph does not apply where the powers conferred by this Part of this Schedule are exercisable by virtue of paragraph 3.

6 (1) Without prejudice to paragraph 5, if the Society passes a resolution to the effect that any sums of money to which this paragraph applies, and the right to recover or receive them, shall vest in the Society, all such sums shall vest accordingly (whether they were received by the person holding them before or after the Society's resolution) and shall be held by the Society on trust to exercise in relation to them the powers conferred by this Part of this Schedule and subject thereto and to rules under paragraph 6B upon trust for the persons beneficially entitled to them.

(2) This paragraph applies—

   (a) where the powers conferred by this paragraph are exercisable by virtue of paragraph 1, to all sums of money held by or on behalf of the solicitor or his firm in connection with:

      (i) his practice or former practice,

      (ii) any trust of which he is or formerly was a trustee, or

      (iii) any trust of which a person who is or was an employee of the solicitor is or was a trustee in the person's capacity as such an employee;

   (b) where they are exercisable by virtue of paragraph 2, to all sums of money in any client account; and

   (c) where they are exercisable by virtue of paragraph 3, to all sums of money held by or on behalf of the solicitor or his firm in connection with the trust or other matter in connection with which the Society is satisfied there has been undue delay as mentioned in sub-paragraph (a) of that paragraph.

(3) The Society shall serve on the solicitor or his firm and on any other person having possession of sums of money to which this paragraph applies a certified copy of the Council's resolution and a notice prohibiting the payment out of any such sums of money.

(4) Within 8 days of the service of a notice under sub-paragraph (3), the person on whom it was served, on giving not less than 48 hours' notice in writing to the Society and (if the notice gives the name of the solicitor instructed by the Society) to that solicitor, may apply to the High Court for an order directing the Society to withdraw the notice.

(5) If the court makes such an order, it shall have power also to make such other order with respect to the matter as it may think fit.

(6)   If any person on whom a notice has been served under sub-paragraph (3) pays out sums of money at a time when such payment is prohibited by the notice, he shall be guilty of an offence and liable on summary conviction to a fine not exceeding level 3 on the standard scale.

6A   (1)   Without prejudice to paragraph 5, if the Society passes a resolution to the effect that any rights to which this paragraph applies shall vest in the Society, those rights shall vest accordingly.

(2)   This paragraph applies to any right to recover or receive debts due to the solicitor or his firm in connection with his practice or former practice.

(3)   Any sums recovered by the Society by virtue of the exercise of rights vested under sub-paragraph (1) shall vest in the Society and shall be held by it on trust to exercise in relation to them the powers conferred by this Part of this Schedule and, subject to those powers and to rules under paragraph 6B, upon trust for the persons beneficially entitled to them.

(4)   The Society shall serve on the solicitor or his firm, and any person who owes a debt to which the order applies, a certified copy of the Society's resolution.

6B   (1)   The Society may make rules governing its treatment of sums vested in it under paragraph 6 or 6A(3).

(2)   The rules may in particular make provision in respect of cases where the Society, having taken such steps to do so as are reasonable in all the circumstances of the case, is unable to trace the person or persons beneficially entitled to any sum vested in the Society under paragraph 6 or 6A(3) (including provision which requires amounts to be paid into or out of compensation funds (within the meaning of section 36A)).

7   (1)   If the Society takes possession of any sum of money to which paragraph 6 or 6A(3) applies, the Society shall pay it into a special account in the name of the Society or of a person nominated on behalf of the Society, or into a client account of a solicitor nominated on behalf of the Society, and any such person or solicitor shall hold that sum on trust to permit the Society to exercise in relation to it the powers conferred by this Part of this Schedule and subject thereto and to rules under paragraph 6B on trust for the persons beneficially entitled to it.

(2)   A bank or other financial institution at which a special account is kept shall be under no obligation to ascertain whether it is being dealt with properly.

8   Without prejudice to paragraphs 5 to 7, if the High Court is satisfied, on an application by the Society, that there is reason to suspect that any person

(a)   holds money on behalf of the solicitor or his firm, or

(b)   has information which is relevant to identifying any money held by or on behalf of the solicitor or his firm,

the court may require that person to give the Society information as to any such money and the accounts in which it is held.

Documents

9   (1)   The Society may give notice to the solicitor or his firm requiring the production or delivery to any person appointed by the Society at a time and place to be fixed by the Society—

(a)   where the powers conferred by this Part of this Schedule are exercisable by virtue of paragraph 1, of all documents in the possession or under the control of the solicitor or his firm in connection with his practice or former practice or with any trust of which the solicitor is or was a trustee; and

(b)   where they are exercisable by virtue of paragraph 3, of all documents in the possession or under the control of the solicitor or his firm in connection with the trust or other matters of which the Society is satisfied (whether or not they relate also to other matters).

(2)   The person appointed by the Society may take possession of any such documents on behalf of the Society.

(3)   Except in a case where an application has been made to the High Court under sub-paragraph (4), if any person having possession or control of any such documents refuses, neglects or otherwise fails to comply with a requirement under sub-paragraph (1), he shall be guilty of an offence and liable on summary conviction to a fine not exceeding level 3 on the standard scale.

(4)   The High Court, on the application of the Society, may order a person required to produce or deliver documents under sub-paragraph (1) to produce or deliver them to any person appointed by the Society at such time and place as may be specified in the order, and authorise him to take possession of them on behalf of the Society.

(5)   If on an application by the Society the High Court is satisfied that there is reason to suspect that documents in relation to which the powers conferred by sub-paragraph (1) are exercisable have come into the possession or under the control of some person other than the solicitor or his firm, the court may order that person to produce or deliver the documents to any person appointed by the Society at such time and place as may be specified in the order and authorise him to take possession of them on behalf of the Society.

(5A)   In the case of a document which consists of information which is stored in electronic form, a requirement imposed by a notice under sub-paragraph (1) or an order under sub-paragraph (4) or (5), is a requirement to produce or deliver the information in a form in which it is legible or from which it can readily be produced in a legible form.

(6)   On making an order under this paragraph, or at any later time, the court, on the application of the Society, may authorise a person appointed by the Society to enter any premises (using such force as is reasonably necessary) to search for and take possession of—

(a)   any documents to which the order relates;

(b)   any property—

(i)   in the possession of or under the control of the solicitor or his firm, or

(ii)   in the case of an order under sub-paragraph (5), which was in the possession or under the control of such a person and has come into the possession or under the control of the person in respect of whom the order is made,

which the Society reasonably requires for the purpose of accessing information contained in such documents, and to use property obtained under paragraph (b) for that purpose.

(7)   The Society, on taking possession of any documents or other property under this paragraph, shall serve upon the solicitor or personal representatives and upon any other person from whom they were received on the Society's behalf or from whose premises they were taken a notice that possession has been taken on the date specified in the notice.

(8)   Subject to sub-paragraph (9) a person upon whom a notice under sub-paragraph (7) is served, on giving not less than 48 hours notice to the Society and (if the notice gives the name of the solicitor instructed by the Society) to that solicitor, may apply to the High Court for an order directing the Society to deliver the documents or other property to such person as the applicant may require.

(9)   A notice under sub-paragraph (8) shall be given within 8 days of the service of the Society's notice under sub-paragraph (7).

(10)   Without prejudice to the foregoing provisions of this Schedule, the Society may apply to the High Court for an order as to the disposal or destruction of any documents or other property in its possession by virtue of this paragraph or paragraph 10.

(11)   On an application under sub-paragraph (8) or (10), the Court may make such order as it thinks fit.

(12)   Except so far as its right to do so may be restricted by an order on an application under sub-paragraph (8) or (10), the Society may take copies of or extracts from any documents in its possession by virtue of this paragraph or paragraph 10 and require any person to whom it is proposed that such documents shall be delivered, as a condition precedent to delivery, to give a reasonable undertaking to supply copies or extracts to the Society.

Mail and other forms of communication

10   (1)   The High Court, on the application of the Society, may from time to time make a communications redirection order.

(2)   A communications redirection order is an order that specified communications to the solicitor or his firm are to be directed, in accordance with the order, to the Society or any person appointed by the Society.

(3)   For the purposes of this paragraph—

(a)   "specified communications" means communications of such description as are specified in the order;

(b)   the descriptions of communications which may be so specified include—

(i)   communications in the form of a postal packet;

(ii)   electronic communications;

(iii)   communications by telephone.

(4)   A communications redirection order has effect for such time not exceeding 18 months as is specified in the order.

(5)   Where a communications redirection order has effect, the Society or the person appointed by the Society may take possession or receipt of the communications redirected in accordance with the order.

(6)   Where a communications redirection order is made, the Society must pay to—

(a)   in the case of an order relating to postal packets, the postal operator concerned, and

(b)   in any other case, the person specified in the order,

the like charges (if any) as would have been payable for the redirection of the communications to which the order relates if the addressee had permanently ceased to occupy or use the premises or other destination of the communications and had applied to the postal operator or the specified person (as the case may be) to redirect the communications to him as mentioned in the order.

(7)   The High Court may, on the application of the Society, authorise the Society, or a person appointed by it, to take such steps as may be specified in the order in relation to any website purporting to be or have been maintained by or on behalf of the solicitor or his firm if the High Court is satisfied that the taking of those steps is necessary to protect the public interest or the interests of clients (or potential or former clients) of the solicitor or his firm.

(8)   In this paragraph "postal operator" and "postal packet" have the meaning given by section 27 of the Postal Services Act 2011.

(9)   This paragraph does not apply where the powers conferred by this Part of this Schedule are exercisable by virtue of paragraph 3.

Trusts

11 (1)   If the solicitor or his personal representative is a trustee of a trust, the Society may apply to the High Court for an order for the appointment of a new trustee in substitution for him.

(2)   The Trustee Act 1925 shall have effect in relation to an appointment of a new trustee under this paragraph as it has effect in relation to an appointment under section 41 of that Act.

General

12   The powers in relation to sums of money, documents and other property conferred by this Part of this Schedule shall be exercisable notwithstanding any lien on them or right to their possession.

13   Subject to any order for the payment of costs that may be made on an application to the court under this Schedule, any costs incurred by the Society for the purposes of this Schedule, including, without prejudice to the generality of this paragraph, the costs of any person exercising powers under this Part of this Schedule on behalf of the Society, shall be paid by the Solicitor or his personal representatives and shall be recoverable from him or them as a debt owing to the Society.

13A(1)   The High Court, on the application of the Society, may order a former partner of the solicitor to pay a specified proportion of the costs mentioned in paragraph 13.

(2)   The High Court may make an order under this paragraph only if it is satisfied that the conduct (or any part of the conduct) by reason of which the powers conferred by this Part were exercisable in relation to the solicitor was conduct carried on with the consent or connivance of, or was attributable to any neglect on the part of, the former partner.

(3)   In this paragraph "specified" means specified in the order made by the High Court.

14   Where an offence under this Schedule committed by a body corporate is proved to have been committed with the consent or connivance of, or to be attributable to any neglect on the part of, any director, manager, secretary or other similar officer of the body corporate or any person who was purporting to act in any such capacity, he, as well as the body corporate, shall be guilty of that offence and shall be liable to be proceeded against and punished accordingly.

15   Any application to the High Court under this Schedule may be disposed of in chambers.

16   The Society may do all things which are reasonably necessary for the purpose of facilitating the exercise of its powers under this Schedule.

Extracts from the Administration of Justice Act 1985

[With consolidated amendments to 6 April 2017]

Administration of Justice Act 1985

1985 CHAPTER 61

An Act to make further provision with respect to the administration of justice and matters connected therewith; to amend the Solicitors Act 1974; to regulate the provision of solicitors' services in the case of incorporated practices; to regulate the provision of conveyancing services by persons practising as licensed conveyancers; to make further provision with respect to complaints relating to the provision of legal aid services; to amend the law relating to time limits for actions for libel and slander; and to make further provision with respect to arbitrations and proceedings in connection with European patents

[30th October 1985]

BE IT ENACTED by the Queen's most Excellent Majesty, by and with the advice and consent of the Lords Spiritual and Temporal, and Commons, in this present Parliament assembled, and by the authority of the same, as follows:–

Legal services bodies and sole solicitors' practices

9 Recognition of legal services bodies and of sole solicitors' practices

(1) The Society may make rules—

(a) making provision as to the management and control of legal services bodies;

(b) prescribing the circumstances in which—

(i) legal services bodies may be recognised by the Society as being suitable bodies to undertake the provision of any solicitor services or other relevant legal services; and

(ii) sole solicitors' practices may be recognised by the Society as being suitable to undertake the provision of any such services;

(c) prescribing the requirements which (subject to any exceptions provided by the rules) must at all times be satisfied by bodies and sole solicitors' practices so recognised if they are to remain so recognised; and

(d) regulating the conduct of the affairs of such bodies and sole solicitors' practices.

(1A) Where the Society makes rules under subsection (1), it must by rules under subsection (1)(c) prescribe the requirement that (subject to any exceptions provided by the rules) recognised bodies and recognised sole solicitors' practices must not provide services other than—

(a) solicitor services, or

·(b) solicitor services and other relevant legal services.

(1B)   "Relevant legal services" means—

   (a)   solicitor services, and

   (b)   where authorised persons other than solicitors or registered European lawyers are managers or employees of, or have an interest in, a recognised body, or are employees in a recognised sole solicitor's practice, services of the kind provided by individuals practising as such authorised persons (whether or not those services involve the carrying on of reserved legal activities within the meaning of the Legal Services Act 2007).

(1C)   The Society may by rules under this section provide that services specified, or of a description specified, in the rules are not to be treated as solicitor services or other relevant legal services.

(2)   Rules made by the Society may also make provision—

   (a)   for the manner and form in which applications for recognition under this section, or for the renewal of such recognition, are to be made, and requiring such applications to be accompanied by a fee of such amount as the Society may from time to time determine;

   (aa)   for the manner and form in which other applications under the rules are to be made, and requiring such applications to be accompanied by a fee of such amount as the Society may from time to time determine;

   (ab)   requiring recognised bodies, recognised sole solicitors' practices or descriptions of such bodies or practices, to pay periodical fees of such amount as the Society may from time to time determine;

   (b)   for regulating the names that may be used by recognised bodies or recognised sole solicitors' practices;

   (c)   about the time when any recognition, or renewal of recognition, takes effect and the period for which it is (subject to the provisions made by or under this Part) to remain in force;

   (d)   for the suspension or revocation of any such recognition, on such grounds and in such circumstances as may be prescribed by the rules;

   (e)   about the effect on the recognition of a partnership or other unincorporated body ("the existing body") of any change in the membership of the existing body, including provision for the existing body's recognition to be transferred where the existing body ceases to exist and another body, or a sole solicitor's practice, succeeds to the whole or substantially the whole of its business;

   (eza)   about the effect on the recognition of a sole solicitor's practice where the sole solicitor ceases to practise as a sole principal and—

      (i)   another sole solicitor succeeds that sole solicitor as sole principal in the practice; or

      (ii)   a body or another sole solicitor succeeds to the whole or substantially the whole of the practice's business;

   (ea)   for the keeping by the Society of a register containing the names and places of business of all bodies and sole solicitors' practices which are for the time being recognised under this section, and such other information relating to them as may be specified in the rules;

   (eb)   for information (or information of a specified description) on such a register to be made available to the public, including provision about the manner in which, and times at which, information is to be made so available;

   (f)   for rules made under any provision of the 1974 Act to have effect in relation to recognised bodies or recognised sole solicitors' practices with such additions, omissions or other modifications as appear to the Society to be necessary or expedient;

(fa)   about the education and training requirements to be met by managers and employees of recognised bodies or employees in recognised sole solicitors' practices;

(fb)   for rules made under any provision of the 1974 Act to have effect in relation to managers and employees of recognised bodies or employees in recognised sole solicitors' practices with such additions, omissions or other modifications as appear to the Society to be necessary or expedient;

(fc)   requiring recognised bodies to appoint a person or persons to monitor compliance, by the recognised body, its managers and its employees, with requirements imposed on them by or by virtue of this Act or any rules applicable to them by virtue of this section;

(fd)   requiring the sole solicitor in a recognised sole solicitor's practice to appoint a person or persons to monitor compliance, by the sole solicitor and the employees in the practice, with requirements imposed on them by or by virtue of this Act, the 1974 Act or any rules applicable to them by virtue of this section or the 1974 Act;

(g)   [*repealed*]

(h)   for the manner of service on recognised bodies, or on sole solicitors in relation to recognised sole solicitors' practices, of documents authorised or required to be served under or by virtue of this Part.

(2ZA) Rules under subsection (2)(fd) may provide that the person appointed under that paragraph may be the sole solicitor.

(2A) If rules under this section provide for the recognition of legal services bodies which have one or more managers who are not legally qualified, the rules must make provision—

(a)   for the recognition of such bodies to be suspended or revoked, on such grounds and in such circumstances as may be prescribed by the rules;

(b)   as to the criteria and procedure for the Society's approving, as suitable to be a manager of a recognised body, an individual who is not legally qualified (and for the Society's withdrawing such approval).

(2B) Rules under this section may make provision for appeals to the High Court against decisions made by the Society under the rules—

(a)   to suspend or revoke the recognition of any body or sole solicitor's practice;

(b)   not to approve, as suitable to be the manager of a recognised body, an individual who is not legally qualified (or to withdraw such approval).

(2C) The rules may provide for appeals against decisions within subsection (2B)(b) to be brought by the individual to whom the decision relates (as well as the body).

(2D) In relation to an appeal under rules made by virtue of subsection (2B), the High Court may make such order as it thinks fit as to payment of costs.

(2E) The decision of the High Court on such an appeal shall be final.

(2F) Where the Society decides to recognise a body or a sole solicitor's practice under this section it must grant that recognition subject to one or more conditions if—

(a)   the case is of a kind prescribed for the purposes of this section by rules made by the Society, and

(b)   the Society considers that it is in the public interest to do so.

(2G) While a body or a sole solicitor's practice is recognised under this section, the Society—

    (a)   must direct that the recognition is to have effect subject to one or more conditions if—

        (i)   the case is of a prescribed kind, and

        (ii)   the Society considers that it is in the public interest to do so;

    (b)   may, in such circumstances as may be prescribed, direct that the recognition is to have effect subject to such conditions as the Society may think fit.

"Prescribed" means prescribed by rules made by the Society.

(2H) The conditions which may be imposed under subsection (2F) or (2G) include—

    (a)   conditions requiring the body or the sole solicitor to take specified steps that will, in the opinion of the Society, be conducive to the carrying on of an efficient business;

    (b)   conditions which prohibit the body or the sole solicitor from taking any specified steps except with the approval of the Society;

    (c)   if rules under this section provide for the recognition of legal services bodies which have one or more managers who are not legally qualified, a condition that all the managers of the body must be legally qualified.

"Specified" means specified in the condition.

(2I) Rules made by the Society may make provision about when conditions imposed under this section take effect (including provision conferring power on the Society to direct that a condition is not to have effect until the conclusion of any appeal in relation to it).

(2J) Section 86A of the 1974 Act applies to rules under this section as it applies to rules under that Act.

(2K) Rules under this section may contain such incidental, supplemental, transitional or transitory provisions or savings as the Society considers necessary or expedient.

(3) Despite section 24(2) of the 1974 Act, section 20 of that Act (prohibition on unqualified person acting as solicitor) does not apply to a recognised body; and nothing in section 24(1) of that Act applies in relation to such a body.

(4) [*repealed*]

(5) A certificate signed by an officer of the Society and stating that any body or sole solicitor's practice is or is not, or was or was not at any time, recognised under this section shall, unless the contrary is proved, be evidence of the facts stated in the certificate; and a certificate purporting to be so signed shall be taken to have been so signed unless the contrary is proved.

(6) Schedule 2 (which makes provision with respect to the application of provisions of the 1974 Act to recognised bodies, with respect to other matters relating to such bodies, and with respect to matters relating to recognised sole solicitors' practices) shall have effect.

(7) Subject to the provisions of that Schedule, the Lord Chancellor may by order made by statutory instrument subject to annulment in pursuance of a resolution of either House of Parliament provide for any enactment or instrument passed or made before or in the same session as the Legal Services Act 2007 was passed and having effect in relation to solicitors to have effect in relation to recognised bodies with such additions, omissions or other modifications as appear to the Lord Chancellor to be necessary or expedient.

(8) In this section—

"the 1974 Act" means the Solicitors Act 1974;

"authorised person" means an authorised person in relation to an activity which is a reserved legal activity (within the meaning of the Legal Services Act 2007);

references to employment in a recognised sole solicitor's practice are references to employment by a sole solicitor for the purposes of a practice recognised under this section;

"the Society" has the meaning given by section 87(1) of the 1974 Act;

"legally qualified" and "legal services body" have the meaning given by section 9A;

"manager", in relation to a body, has the same meaning as in the Legal Services Act 2007 (see section 207 of that Act);

"recognised body" means a body for the time being recognised under this section;

"recognised sole solicitor's practice" means a sole solicitor's practice for the time being recognised under this section;

"registered European lawyer" means a person who is registered with the Law Society under regulation 17 of the European Communities (Lawyer's Practice) Regulations 2000;

"sole solicitor" has the meaning given by section 87(1) of the 1974 Act;

"solicitor services" means professional services such as are provided by individuals practising as solicitors or lawyers of other jurisdictions;

and a person has an interest in a body if the person has an interest in the body within the meaning of Part 5 of the Legal Services Act 2007 (see sections 72 and 109 of that Act).

(9)   [*repealed*]

9A   Legal services bodies

(1)   For the purposes of section 9, a "legal services body" means a body (corporate or unincorporate) in respect of which—

   (a)   the management and control condition, and

   (b)   the relevant lawyer condition,

are satisfied.

(2)   The management and control condition is satisfied if—

   (a)   at least 75% of the body's managers are legally qualified,

   (b)   the proportion of shares in the body held by persons who are legally qualified is at least 75%,

   (c)   the proportion of voting rights in the body which persons who are legally qualified are entitled to exercise, or control the exercise of, is at least 75%,

   (d)   all the persons with an interest in the body who are not legally qualified are managers of the body, and

   (e)   all the managers of the body who are not legally qualified are individuals approved by the Society as suitable to be managers of a recognised body.

(3)   The Society may by rules under section 9 provide that, in relation to specified kinds of bodies, subsection (2) applies as if the references to 75% were to such greater percentage as may be specified (and different percentages may be specified for different kinds of bodies).

(4)   The relevant lawyer condition is satisfied in relation to a body if at least one manager of the body is—

   (a)   a solicitor,

(b)   a registered European lawyer, or

(c)   a qualifying body.

(5) For that purpose a qualifying body is a body in respect of which—

    (a)   the management and control condition is satisfied,

    (b)   the relevant lawyer condition is satisfied by virtue of subsection (4)(a) or (b), and

    (c)   the services condition is satisfied.

(6) For the purposes of this section the following are legally qualified—

    (a)   an authorised person who is an individual;

    (b)   a registered foreign lawyer (within the meaning of section 89 of the Courts and Legal Services Act 1990 (c 41));

    (c)   a person entitled to pursue professional activities under a professional title to which the Directive applies in a state to which the Directive applies (other than the title of barrister or solicitor in England and Wales);

    (d)   an authorised person which is a body in respect of which—

        (i)   the services condition is satisfied, and

        (ii)   the management and control condition would be satisfied if the references in subsection (2) to persons who are legally qualified were to persons who are legally qualified by virtue of paragraphs (a) to (c);

    (e)   a body which provides professional services such as are provided by individuals who are authorised persons or lawyers of other jurisdictions, and in respect of which the management and control condition would be satisfied if the references in subsection (2) to persons who are legally qualified were to persons who are legally qualified by virtue of paragraphs (a) to (c).

    (f)   a legal partnership which—

        (i)   was in existence immediately before the commencement of this paragraph,

        (ii)   since that time has continued to be a partnership of the kind mentioned in rule 12.01(1)(b), 12.02(1)(b) or 12.04(1)(c)(i) of the pre-commencement conduct rules (framework of practice), and

        (iii)   has not, since that time, had a body corporate (other than a body within paragraph (g)) as a member;

    (g)   a body corporate which—

        (i)   was recognised under section 9 immediately before the commencement of this paragraph, and

        (ii)   has since that time continued to satisfy the requirements of rule 14.03(1) and 14.04(1) to (3) or the requirements of rule 14.05(1) to (3) of the pre-commencement conduct rules (restrictions on directors, owners etc of incorporated practices);

    (h)   a body which—

        (i)   is an authorised person and satisfies the services condition, or

        (ii)   provides professional services such as are provided by individuals who are authorised persons or lawyers of other jurisdictions,

    and which satisfies the requirements of rules under subsection (6C).

(6A)   For the purposes of subsection (6)(f), a partnership is to be treated as the same partnership despite a change in membership, if any person who was a member before the change remains a member.

(6B)   For the purposes of subsection (6)(f) and (g), the references in the pre-commencement conduct rules to a recognised body are to be construed as references to a body which was recognised under section 9 immediately before the commencement of subsection (6)(f) and (g).

(6C)   The Society must make rules for the purposes of paragraph (h) of subsection (6) prescribing the requirements relating to management and control which must be satisfied by or in relation to a body for it to fall within that paragraph.

(7)   For the purposes of this section, the services condition is satisfied in relation to a body if the body provides only services which may be provided by a recognised body (having regard to rules under section 9(1A) and (1C)).

(8)   For the purposes of this section—

"authorised person" has the same meaning as in section 9;

"the Directive" means Directive 98/5/EC of the European Parliament and the Council, to facilitate practice of the profession of lawyer on a permanent basis in a Member State other than that in which the qualification was obtained;

"legal partnership" means a partnership in which a solicitor, a registered European lawyer or a recognised body is permitted to practise by virtue of rules made under section 31 of the Solicitors Act 1974 (c 47), as those rules had effect immediately before the commencement of subsection (6)(f);

"manager", in relation to a body, has the meaning given by section 9;

"pre-commencement conduct rules" means rules under Part 2 of the Solicitors Act 1974 or section 9 of this Act, known as the Solicitors' Code of Conduct 2007, as those rules had effect immediately before the commencement of subsection (6)(f) and (g);

"recognised body" has the same meaning as in section 9 (subject to subsection (6B) above);

"registered European lawyer" has the same meaning as in section 9;

"shares" has the same meaning as for the purposes of Part 5 of the Legal Services Act 2007 (see sections 72 and 109 of that Act);

"the Society" has the meaning given by section 87(1) of the Solicitors Act 1974;

"specified" means specified in rules made by the Society;

and a person has an interest in a body if the person has an interest in the body for the purposes of section 9.

10   Penalty for pretending to be a body recognised under s 9

(1)   A body shall not describe itself or hold itself out as a body for the time being recognised under section 9 unless it is so recognised.

(2)   Any body which contravenes subsection (1) shall be guilty of an offence and liable on summary conviction to a fine not exceeding the fourth level on the standard scale.

(3)   Where an offence under this section committed by a body corporate is proved to have been committed with the consent or connivance of or to be attributable to any neglect on the part of an officer of the body corporate, that officer (as well as the body corporate) is guilty of the offence and is liable to be proceeded against and punished accordingly.

(4)   Where the affairs of a body corporate are managed by its members, subsection (3) applies in relation to the acts and defaults of a member in connection with the member's functions of management as it applies to an officer of the body corporate.

(5) Proceedings for an offence under this section alleged to have been committed by an unincorporated body are to be brought in the name of that body (and not in that of any of its members) and, for the purposes of any such proceedings, any rules of court relating to the service of documents have effect as if that body were a corporation.

(6) A fine imposed on an unincorporated body on its conviction of an offence under this section is to be paid out of the funds of that body.

(7) If an unincorporated body is charged with an offence under this section, section 33 of the Criminal Justice Act 1925 (c 86) and Schedule 3 to the Magistrates' Courts Act 1980 (c 43) (procedure on charge of an offence against a corporation) have effect in like manner as in the case of a corporation so charged.

(8) Where an offence under this section committed by an unincorporated body (other than a partnership) is proved to have been committed with the consent or connivance of, or to be attributable to any neglect on the part of, any officer of the body or any member of its governing body, that officer or member as well as the unincorporated body is guilty of the offence and liable to be proceeded against and punished accordingly.

(9) Where an offence under this section committed by a partnership is proved to have been committed with the consent or connivance of, or to be attributable to any neglect on the part of, a partner, that partner as well as the partnership is guilty of the offence and liable to be proceeded against and punished accordingly.

(10) In this section "officer", in relation to a body corporate, means—

    (a)   any director, secretary or other similar officer of the body corporate, or

    (b)   any person who was purporting to act in any such capacity.

10A Penalty for sole solicitor pretending that practice is recognised

(1) A sole solicitor shall not describe or hold out the sole solicitor's practice as a practice for the time being recognised under section 9 unless it is so recognised.

(2) Any person who contravenes subsection (1) is guilty of an offence and liable on summary conviction to a fine not exceeding level 4 on the standard scale.

(3) In this section "sole solicitor" has the same meaning as in section 9.

SCHEDULE 2
Legal services practices: Supplementary Provisions

Section 9

Interpretation

1 (1) Subject to sub-paragraph (2), references in this Schedule to a recognised body or a recognised sole solicitor's practice are references to a body or sole solicitor's practice for the time being recognised under section 9 of this Act.

(2) References in this Schedule to a recognised body or a recognised sole solicitor's practice in relation to—

    (a)   a complaint (other than such a complaint as is mentioned in paragraph 16(1)(a));

    (b)   [*repealed*]

include references to a body or sole solicitor's practice that was recognised under section 9 of this Act at the time when the conduct to which the complaint relates took place.

(2A) References in this Schedule to a manager or employee of a recognised body, or to an employee in a recognised sole solicitor's practice, in relation to a complaint (other than such a complaint as is mentioned in paragraph 16(1A)(a)), include references to a person who was such a manager or employee at the time when the conduct to which the complaint relates took place.

(2B)   In this Schedule references to employment in a recognised sole solicitor's practice have the same meaning as in section 9.

(3)   [*repealed*]

(4)   In section 87(1) of the 1974 Act the definitions of "client", "contentious business" and "non-contentious business" shall apply for the purposes of this Schedule; and for the purposes of—

(a)   any provision of this Schedule in so far as it has effect in relation to a recognised body; and

(b)   any provision of the 1974 Act in so far as it has effect in relation to a recognised body by virtue of this Schedule,

they shall apply as if for any reference to a solicitor there were substituted a reference to a recognised body.

(5)   Subject to sub-paragraphs (4) and (6), any expression used in this Schedule which is also used in the 1974 Act has the same meaning as in that Act.

(6)   In this Schedule—

"manager", in relation to a body, has the same meaning as in the Legal Services Act 2007 (see section 207 of that Act);

"registered European lawyer" has the same meaning as in section 9A;

"the 1974 Act" means the Solicitors Act 1974.

Appeal against refusal of Society to grant recognition etc

2   (1)   A body may appeal to the High Court against—

(a)   a decision to refuse an application by the body for recognition under section 9;

(b)   a decision to impose a condition under subsection (2F) of that section on the body's recognition under that section;

(c)   a decision to impose a condition under subsection (2G) of that section on the body's recognition under that section.

(1A)   A sole solicitor may appeal to the High Court against—

(a)   a decision to refuse an application for recognition of the solicitor's practice under section 9;

(b)   a decision to impose a condition under subsection (2F) of that section on the recognition of the solicitor's practice under that section; and

(c)   a decision to impose a condition under subsection (2G) of that section on the recognition of the solicitor's practice under that section.

(2)   A recognised body whose recognition is subject to a condition within section 9(2H)(b) may appeal to the High Court against any decision by the Society to refuse to approve the taking of any step for the purposes of that condition.

(2A)   Where the recognition of a recognised sole solicitor's practice is subject to a condition within section 9(2H)(b), the sole solicitor may appeal to the High Court against any decision by the Society to refuse to approve the taking of any step for the purposes of that condition.

(3) Rules made by the Society may make provision, as respects any application for recognition that is neither granted nor refused by the Society within such period as may be specified in the rules, for enabling an appeal to be brought under this paragraph in relation to the application as if it had been refused by the Society.

(4) On an appeal under sub-paragraph (1)(a) or (b) or (1A)(a) or (b), the High Court may—

(a) affirm the decision of the Society,

(b) direct the Society to grant the body or sole solicitor's practice recognition under section 9 free from conditions or subject to such conditions as the High Court may think fit,

(c) direct the Society not to recognise the body or sole solicitor's practice,

(d) if the Society has recognised the body or sole solicitor's practice, by order suspend the recognition, or

(e) make such other order as the High Court thinks fit.

(5) On an appeal under sub-paragraph (1)(c) or (1A)(c), the High Court may—

(a) affirm the decision of the Society,

(b) direct that the recognition under section 9 is to have effect subject to such conditions as the High Court may think fit,

(c) by order revoke the direction given by the Society under section 9(2G), or

(d) make such other order as the High Court thinks fit.

(6) On an appeal under sub-paragraph (2) or (2A), the High Court may—

(a) affirm the decision of the Society,

(b) direct the Society to approve the taking of one or more steps for the purposes of a condition within section 9(2H)(b), or

(c) make such other order as the High Court thinks fit.

(7) In relation to an appeal under this paragraph, the High Court may make such order as it thinks fit as to payment of costs.

(8) The decision of the High Court on an appeal under this paragraph is final.

Accounts rules

3 (1) This paragraph applies where rules made under section 32(1) of the 1974 Act are applied—

(a) to recognised bodies in accordance with section 9(2)(f) of this Act, or

(b) to managers or employees of such bodies in accordance with section 9(2)(fb) of this Act.

(2) The Society may disclose a report on or information about the accounts of a recognised body, or a manager or employee of a recognised body, obtained in pursuance of such rules for use—

(a) in investigating the possible commission of an offence by the body or any of its managers or employees, and

(b) in connection with any prosecution of the body or any of its managers or employees consequent on the investigation.

Interest on clients' money

4 (1) Where rules made under section 32 of the 1974 Act and containing any such provision as is referred to in section 33(1) of that Act are applied to recognised bodies in accordance with section 9(2)(f) of this Act, then, except as provided by the rules, a recognised body is not liable to account to any client, other person or trust for interest received by the recognised body on money held at a bank or building society in an account which is for money received or held for, or on account of—

(a)   clients of the recognised body, other persons or trusts, generally, or

(b)   that client, person or trust separately.

(2) [*repealed*]

4ZA Where rules made under section 32 of the 1974 Act and containing any such provision as is referred to in section 33(1) of that Act are applied to managers or employees of recognised bodies in accordance with section 9(2)(fb), then, except as provided by the rules, a manager or employee to whom the rules are applied is not liable to account to any client, other person or trust for interest received by the manager or employee on money held at a bank or building society in an account which is for money received or held for, or on account of—

(a)   clients of the recognised body, other persons or trusts, generally, or

(b)   that client, person or trust, separately.

Inspection of bank accounts

4A (1) This paragraph applies where rules made under section 33A(1) of the 1974 Act are applied—

(a)   to recognised bodies in accordance with section 9(2)(f) of this Act, or

(b)   to managers or employees of such bodies in accordance with section 9(2)(fb) of this Act.

(2) The Society may disclose information about the accounts of a recognised body, or a manager or employee of a recognised body, obtained in pursuance of such rules for use—

(a)   in investigating the possible commission of an offence by the body or any of its managers or employees, and

(b)   in connection with any prosecution of the body or any of its managers or employees consequent on the investigation.

Accountants' reports

5   Where rules made under section 34 of the 1974 Act are applied to recognised bodies in accordance with section 9(2)(f), section 34(9) and (10) of that Act apply in relation to a recognised body as they apply in relation to a solicitor.

5A Where rules made under section 34 of the 1974 Act are applied to managers or employees of recognised bodies in accordance with section 9(2)(fb), section 34(9) and (10) of that Act apply in relation to a manager or employee to which the rules are applied as they apply in relation to a solicitor.

Compensation Fund

6 (1) Section 36 of the 1974 Act applies in relation to recognised bodies as if for paragraphs (a) and (b) of subsection (1) there were substituted—

"(a)   an act or omission of a recognised body or former recognised body;

(b)   an act or omission of a manager or employee, or former manager or employee, of a recognised body or former recognised body;".

(2)   Section 36A(2) and (3) of the 1974 Act applies in relation to recognised bodies as it applies in relation to solicitors.

Solicitor who is justice of the peace not to act in certain proceedings

7   In section 38 of the 1974 Act references to any partner of a solicitor shall be construed, in relation to a solicitor who is a manager of a recognised body, as references to any other solicitor who is a manager of that body.

8   [*repealed*]

Restriction on employment of person struck off roll or suspended

9   (1)   Section 41 of the 1974 Act (except subsection (4)) shall apply to a recognised body (and any manager or employee of it) and its business as such as it applies to a solicitor and his practice as such.

(2)   No recognised body (or manager or employee of such a body) may, except in accordance with a written permission granted by the Society under this paragraph, permit a person to whom sub-paragraph (3) applies to—

(a)   be a manager of the body, or

(b)   have an interest in the body;

and for this purpose a person has an interest in the body if he has an interest in the body within the meaning of Part 5 of the Legal Services Act 2007 (see sections 72 and 109 of that Act).

(3)   This sub-paragraph applies to a person who to the knowledge of the recognised body (or, as the case may be, the manager or employee) is a person—

(a)   who is disqualified from practising as a solicitor by reason of one of the facts mentioned in section 41(1)(a), (b) or (c) of the 1974 Act (name struck off the roll, suspension etc), or

(b)   in respect of whom there is a direction in force under section 47(2)(g) of that Act (prohibition on restoration to roll).

(4)   Permission granted for the purposes of sub-paragraph (2) may be granted for such period and subject to such conditions as the Society thinks fit.

(5)   A person aggrieved by the refusal of the Society to grant permission under sub-paragraph (4), or by any conditions attached by the Society to the grant of any such permission may appeal to the High Court which may—

(a)   confirm the refusal or the conditions, as the case may be, or

(b)   grant a permission under this paragraph for such period and subject to such conditions as it thinks fit.

(6)   In relation to an appeal under sub-paragraph (5) the High Court may make such order as it thinks fit as to payment of costs.

(7)   The decision of the High Court on an appeal under sub-paragraph (5) is final.

Failure to disclose fact of having been struck off or suspended

10   (1)   Section 42(1) and (1A) of the 1974 Act shall apply in relation to employment by a recognised body (or any manager or employee of such a body) in connection with its business as it applies in relation to employment by a solicitor in connection with his practice.

(2) It is an offence for a person ("P") to whom sub-paragraph (3) applies—

(a) to seek or accept from any person an interest in a recognised body, without previously informing that person (and, if different, the recognised body) that P is a person to whom that sub-paragraph applies, or

(b) to seek or accept a position as a manager of a recognised body, without previously informing that body that P is such a person.

(3) This sub-paragraph applies to a person—

(a) who is disqualified from practising as a solicitor by reason of one of the facts mentioned in section 41(1)(a), (b) or (c) of the 1974 Act (name struck off the roll, suspension etc), or

(b) in respect of whom there is a direction in force under section 47(2)(g) of that Act (prohibition on restoration to roll).

(4) A person guilty of an offence under sub-paragraph (2) is liable on summary conviction to a fine not exceeding level 3 on the standard scale.

(5) Subsection (2) of section 42 of the 1974 Act applies in relation to an offence under sub-paragraph (2) as it applies in relation to an offence under that section.

(6) For the purposes of sub-paragraph (2)(a) a person seeks or accepts an interest in a recognised body if the person seeks or accepts an interest which if it were obtained by the person would result in the person having an interest in that body within the meaning of Part 5 of the Legal Services Act 2007 (see sections 72 and 109 of that Act).

11 [*repealed*]

12 [*repealed*]

13 [*repealed*]

Information about suitability for recognition

14 (1) The Society may give a notice under this paragraph if it is satisfied that it is necessary to do so for the purpose of investigating whether—

(a) a recognised body continues to be suitable to be recognised under section 9, or

(b) a manager of a recognised body who is not legally qualified (within the meaning of section 9A) continues to be suitable to be a manager of a recognised body.

(2) A notice under this paragraph is a notice which requires a person within sub-paragraph (3)—

(a) to provide information, or information of a description, specified in the notice, or

(b) to produce documents, or documents of a description, specified in the notice.

(3) The persons are—

(a) the recognised body;

(b) an employee or manager of the recognised body;

(c) a person who has an interest in the recognised body (within the meaning of the Legal Services Act 2007 (see sections 72 and 109 of that Act)).

(4) For the purposes of this paragraph, section 44B(4) to (7) of the 1974 Act applies—

(a) in relation to a notice under this paragraph as if it were a notice under section 44B of that Act, and

    (b)   in relation to a person given a notice under this paragraph as if that person were a person given a notice under that section,

and references in subsections (6) and (7) of that section to powers conferred by that section are to be read as references to powers conferred by this paragraph.

(5)   Where powers conferred by Part 2 of Schedule 1 to the 1974 Act are exercisable in relation to a person within paragraph (a), (b) or (c) of sub-paragraph (3), they continue to be so exercisable after the person has ceased to be a person within the paragraph in question.

(6)   Section 44BA of the 1974 Act (power to require explanation of document or information) applies in relation to a notice under this paragraph and the person to whom such a notice is given as it applies in relation to a notice under section 44B of the 1974 Act and the person to whom such a notice is given.

(7)   Subsection (1) of section 44BC of that Act (falsification of documents etc) applies in relation to an investigation of the kind mentioned in sub-paragraph (1) as it applies in relation to the investigations mentioned in that subsection, and subsections (2), (4) and (5) of that section apply accordingly.

(8)   Subsection (3) of that section (provision of false information etc) applies in relation to a requirement imposed under this paragraph as it applies in relation to a requirement imposed by section 44B of that Act, and subsections (4) and (5) of that section apply accordingly.

14ZA) The Society may give a notice under this paragraph if it is satisfied that it is necessary to do so for the purpose of investigating whether a recognised sole solicitor's practice continues to be suitable to be recognised under section 9.

(2)   A notice under this paragraph is a notice which requires a person within sub-paragraph (3)—

    (a)   to provide information, or information of a description, specified in the notice, or

    (b)   to produce documents, or documents of a description, specified in the notice.

(3)   The persons are—

    (a)   the sole solicitor; and

    (b)   an employee in the recognised sole solicitor's practice.

(4)   For the purposes of this paragraph, section 44B(4) to (7) of the 1974 Act applies—

    (a)   in relation to a notice under this paragraph as if it were a notice under section 44B of that Act, and

    (b)   in relation to a person given a notice under this paragraph as if that person were a person given a notice under that section,

and references in subsections (6) and (7) of that section to powers conferred by that section are to be read as references to powers conferred by this paragraph.

(5)   Where powers conferred by Part 2 of Schedule 1 to the 1974 Act are exercisable in relation to a person within paragraph (a) or (b) of sub-paragraph (3), they continue to be so exercisable after the person has ceased to be a person within the paragraph in question.

(6)   Section 44BA of the 1974 Act (power to require explanation of document or information) applies in relation to a notice under this paragraph and the person to whom such a notice is given as it applies in relation to a notice under section 44B of the 1974 Act and the person to whom such a notice is given.

(7)   Subsection (1) of section 44BC of that Act (falsification of documents etc) applies in relation to an investigation of the kind mentioned in sub-paragraph (1) as it applies in relation to the investigations mentioned in that subsection, and subsections (2), (4) and (5) of that section apply accordingly.

(8)   Subsection (3) of that section (provision of false information etc) applies in relation to a requirement imposed under this paragraph as it applies in relation to a requirement imposed by section 44B of that Act, and subsections (4) and (5) of that section apply accordingly.

Power to charge for costs of investigation

14A(1)   The Society may make regulations prescribing charges to be paid to the Society by recognised bodies who are the subject of a discipline investigation or by the sole solicitor in a recognised sole solicitor's practice which is subject to a discipline investigation.

(2)   A discipline investigation is an investigation carried out by the Society into a failure or apprehended failure by a recognised body, or by a sole solicitor, or any employee, in a recognised sole solicitor's practice, to comply with any requirement imposed by or by virtue of this Act or any rules applicable to them by virtue of section 9.

(3)   Regulations under this paragraph may—

  (a)   make different provision for different cases or purposes;

  (b)   provide for the whole or part of a charge payable under the regulations to be repaid in such circumstances as may be prescribed by the regulations.

(4)   Any charge which a recognised body or a sole solicitor is required to pay under regulations under this paragraph is recoverable by the Society as a debt due to the Society from the recognised body or from that sole solicitor.

(5)   This paragraph applies in relation to a manager or employee of a recognised body as it applies in relation to a recognised body.

Disciplinary powers of the Society

14B(1)   This paragraph applies where the Society is satisfied that—

  (a)   a recognised body, or a manager or employee of a recognised body, or

  (b)   a sole solicitor, or any employee, in a recognised sole solicitor's practice,

has failed to comply with a requirement imposed by or by virtue of this Act or any rules applicable to that person by virtue of section 9 of this Act.

(2)   The Society may do one or both of the following—

  (a)   give the person a written rebuke;

  (b)   direct the person to pay a penalty not exceeding £2,000.

(3)   The Society may publish details of any action it has taken under sub-paragraph (2)(a) or (b), if it considers it to be in the public interest to do so.

(4)   Where the Society takes action against a person under sub-paragraph (2)(b), or decides to publish under sub-paragraph (3) details of such action under sub-paragraph (2)(a) or (b), it must notify the person in writing that it has done so.

(5)   A penalty imposed under sub-paragraph (2)(b) does not become payable until—

  (a)   the end of the period during which an appeal against the decision to impose the penalty, or the amount of the penalty, may be made under paragraph 14C, or

  (b)   if such an appeal is made, such time as it is determined or withdrawn.

(6)   The Society may not publish under sub-paragraph (3) details of any action under sub-paragraph (2)(a) or (b)—

  (a)   during the period within which an appeal against—

    (i)   the decision to take the action,

(ii)   in the case of action under sub-paragraph (2)(b), the amount of the penalty, or

(iii)   the decision to publish the details,

may be made under paragraph 14C, or

(b)   if such an appeal has been made, until such time as it is determined or withdrawn.

(7)   The Society must make rules—

(a)   prescribing the circumstances in which the Society may decide to take action under sub-paragraph (2)(a) or (b);

(b)   about the practice and procedure to be followed by the Society in relation to such action;

(c)   governing the publication under sub-paragraph (3) of details of action taken under sub-paragraph (2)(a) or (b);

and the Society may make such other rules in connection with the exercise of its powers under this paragraph as it considers appropriate.

(8)   Before making rules under sub-paragraph (7), the Society must consult the Tribunal.

(9)   A penalty under this paragraph may be recovered as a debt due to the Society, and is to be forfeited to Her Majesty.

(10)   The Lord Chancellor may, by order, amend paragraph (b) of sub-paragraph (2) so as to substitute for the amount for the time being specified in that paragraph such other amount as may be specified in the order.

(11)   Before making an order under sub-paragraph (10), the Lord Chancellor must consult the Society.

(12)   An order under sub-paragraph (10) is to be made by statutory instrument subject to annulment in pursuance of a resolution of either House of Parliament.

(13)   This paragraph is without prejudice to any power conferred on the Society, or any other person, to make an application or complaint to the Tribunal.

14C(1)   A person may appeal against—

(a)   a decision by the Society to rebuke that person under paragraph 14B(2)(a) if a decision is also made to publish details of the rebuke;

(b)   a decision by the Society to impose a penalty on that person under paragraph 14B(2)(b) or the amount of that penalty;

(c)   a decision by the Society to publish under paragraph 14B(3) details of any action taken against that person under paragraph 14B(2)(a) or (b).

(2)   Subsections (9)(b), (10)(a) and (b), (11) and (12) of section 46 of the 1974 Act (Tribunal rules about procedure for hearings etc) apply in relation to appeals under this paragraph as they apply in relation to applications or complaints, except that subsection (11) of that section is to be read as if for "the applicant" to "application)" there were substituted "any party to the appeal"

(3)   Rules under section 46(9)(b) of the 1974 Act may, in particular, make provision about the period during which an appeal under this paragraph may be made.

(4)   On an appeal under this paragraph, the Tribunal has power to make an order which—

(a)   affirms the decision of the Society;

(b)   revokes the decision of the Society;

(c)   in the case of a penalty imposed under paragraph 14B(2)(b), varies the amount of the penalty;

(d)   in the case of a recognised body, contains provision for any of the matters mentioned in paragraph 18(2);

(e)   in the case of a manager or employee of a recognised body, or in the case of a sole solicitor, or an employee, in a recognised sole solicitor's practice, contains provision for any of the matters mentioned in paragraph 18A(2);

(f)   makes such provision as the Tribunal thinks fit as to payment of costs.

(5)   Where, by virtue of sub-paragraph (4)(e), an order contains provision for any of the matters mentioned in sub-paragraph (2)(c) of paragraph 18A, sub-paragraphs (5) and (6) of that paragraph apply as if the order had been made under sub-paragraph (2)(c) of that paragraph.

(6)   An appeal from the Tribunal shall lie to the High Court, at the instance of the Society or the person in respect of whom the order of the Tribunal was made.

(7)   The High Court shall have power to make such order on an appeal under this paragraph as it may think fit.

(8)   Any decision of the High Court on an appeal under this section shall be final.

(9)   This paragraph is without prejudice to any power conferred on the Tribunal in connection with an application or complaint made to it.

15   [*repealed*]

Complaints to Tribunal with respect to recognised bodies and recognised sole solicitors' practices

16   (1)   The Tribunal shall have jurisdiction to hear and determine any of the following complaints made to it under this paragraph with respect to a recognised body, namely—

(a)   a complaint that the body has (while a recognised body) been convicted by any court of a criminal offence which renders it unsuitable to be recognised under section 9 of this Act;

(b)   a complaint that the body has failed to comply with any requirement imposed by or by virtue of this Act or with any rules applicable to it by virtue of section 9 of this Act;

(c)   a complaint that the body has acted in contravention of section 41 of the 1974 Act or paragraph 9(2) of this Schedule or of any conditions subject to which a permission has been granted under section 41 of that Act or that paragraph of this Schedule; or

(d)   a complaint that the body has knowingly acted in contravention of any such order as is mentioned in section 44(2) of the 1974 Act or of any conditions subject to which a permission has been granted under such an order.

(1A)   The Tribunal shall have jurisdiction to hear and determine any of the following complaints made to it under this paragraph with respect to a manager or employee of a recognised body ("the relevant person")—

(a)   a complaint that the relevant person has been convicted by any court of a criminal offence which renders that person unsuitable to be a manager or employee (or both) of a recognised body;

(b)   a complaint that the relevant person has failed to comply with any requirement imposed by or by virtue of this Act or any rules applicable to the relevant person by virtue of section 9 of this Act;

(c)   a complaint that the relevant person has acted in contravention of section 41 of the 1974 Act or paragraph 9(2) of this Schedule or of any conditions subject to which a permission has been granted under that section or for the purposes of paragraph 9(2) of this Schedule;

(d)   a complaint that the relevant person has knowingly acted in contravention of an order under section 43(2) of the 1974 Act or of any conditions subject to which a permission has been granted under such an order.

(1B)   The Tribunal has jurisdiction to hear and determine any of the following complaints made to it under this paragraph with respect to the sole solicitor, or an employee, in a recognised sole solicitor's practice ("the relevant person")—

(a)   a complaint that the relevant person has been convicted by any court of a criminal offence which renders that person unsuitable to be the sole solicitor, or an employee, in a recognised sole solicitor's practice (or both);

(b)   a complaint that the relevant person has failed to comply with any requirement imposed by or by virtue of this Act or any rules applicable to the relevant person by virtue of section 9 of this Act.

(2)   A complaint may be made to the Tribunal under this paragraph by any person.

Procedure on applications and complaints

17   In subsections (9) to (11) of section 46 of the 1974 Act—

(a)   any reference to an application or complaint shall be construed as including a reference to any such application as is mentioned in paragraph 21(1) or any such complaint as is mentioned in paragraph 16(1), 16(1A) or (1B);

(b)   any reference to an application or complaint made under that Act shall be construed as including a reference to any such application or complaint as aforesaid made under this Schedule; and

(c)   in the case of subsection (10)(c), any reference to a solicitor shall be construed as including a reference to a recognised body or, in the case of such a complaint as is mentioned in paragraph 16(1), (1A) or (1B), to a manager or employee of such a body or (as the case may be) to an employee in a recognised sole solicitor's practice.

Powers of Tribunal with respect to recognised bodies

18   (1)   Where on the hearing of any complaint made to it under this Schedule (other than paragraph 16(1A)) the Tribunal is satisfied that a recognised body—

(a)   has been convicted as mentioned in paragraph (a) of paragraph 16(1); or

(b)   has failed to comply with any requirement imposed by or by virtue of this Act or with any such rules as are mentioned in paragraph (b) of paragraph 16(1); or

(c)   has acted as mentioned in paragraph (c) or (d) of that provision;

(d)   [*repealed*]

the Tribunal may, if it thinks fit, make one or more of the orders referred to in sub-paragraph (2).

(2)   Those orders are—

(a)   an order revoking the recognition under section 9 of this Act of the body to which the complaint relates;

(b)   an order directing the payment by that body of a penalty, to be forfeited to Her Majesty;

(c) an order requiring that body to pay the costs incurred in bringing against it the proceedings before the Tribunal or a contribution towards those costs, being a contribution of such amount as the Tribunal considers reasonable.

(2A) Where, on the hearing of any application or complaint made to it under this Schedule, the Tribunal is satisfied that more than one allegation is proved against the recognised body to whom the application or complaint relates, it may impose a separate penalty (by virtue of sub-paragraph (2)(b)) with respect to each such allegation.

(3) [*repealed*]

(4) [*repealed*]

18A(1) Where, on the hearing of any complaint made to it under paragraph 16(1A) or (1B) of this Schedule, the Tribunal is satisfied that a manager or employee of a recognised body, or the sole solicitor, or an employee, in a recognised sole solicitor's practice—

(a) has been convicted as mentioned in paragraph (a) of paragraph 16(1A) or (as the case may be) paragraph (a) of paragraph 16(1B),

(b) has failed to comply with any requirement imposed by or by virtue of this Act or any rules applicable to the relevant person by virtue of section 9 of this Act, or

(c) (in the case of a manager or employee of a recognised body) has acted as mentioned in paragraph (c) or (d) of paragraph 16(1A),

the Tribunal may, if it thinks fit, make one or more of the orders referred to in sub-paragraph (2).

(2) Those orders are—

(za) in the case of a complaint relating to a sole solicitor, or an employee, in a recognised sole solicitor's practice, an order revoking the recognition under section 9 of this Act of the sole solicitor's practice;

(a) an order directing the payment by the relevant person of a penalty to be forfeited to Her Majesty;

(b) an order requiring the Society to consider taking such steps as the Tribunal may specify in relation to the relevant person;

(c) if the person is not a solicitor, an order which states one or more of the matters mentioned in sub-paragraph (3);

(d) an order requiring the Society to refer to an appropriate regulator any matter relating to the conduct of the relevant person.

(3) The matters referred to in sub-paragraph (2)(c) are—

(a) that as from the specified date—

(i) no solicitor or employee of a solicitor shall employ or remunerate, in connection with the practice carried on by that solicitor, the person with respect to whom the order is made, and

(ii) no recognised body, or manager or employee of such a body, shall employ or remunerate that person, in connection with the business of the recognised body,

except in accordance with a Society permission;

(b) that as from the specified date no recognised body or manager or employee of such a body shall, except in accordance with a Society permission, permit the person with respect to whom the order is made to be a manager of the body;

(c) that as from the specified date no recognised body or manager or employee of such a body shall, except in accordance with a Society permission, permit the person with respect to whom the order is made to have an interest in the body.

(4) For this purpose a person has an interest in a body if the person has an interest in the body within the meaning of Part 5 the Legal Services Act 2007 (see sections 72 and 109 of that Act).

(5) Subsections (1) to (1C), (3) and (4) of section 44 of the 1974 Act (offences in connection with orders under section 43(2) of that Act) apply in relation to an order under sub-paragraph (2)(c) as they apply in relation to an order under section 43(2) of that Act, except that references in those subsections to provision within section 43(2)(a), (b) or (c) of that Act are to be read as references to provision within sub-paragraph (3)(a), (b) or (c).

(6) Section 44(2) of the 1974 Act, paragraph 16(1)(d) and (1A)(d) of this Schedule and paragraph 15(3A) of Schedule 14 to the Courts and Legal Services Act 1990 apply in relation to an order under sub-paragraph (2)(c) as they apply in relation to an order under section 43(2) of the 1974 Act.

(7) For the purposes of sub-paragraph (2)(d) an "appropriate regulator" in relation to the relevant person means—

(a)   if the person is an authorised person in relation to a reserved legal activity for the purposes of the Legal Services Act 2007, any relevant approved regulator (within the meaning of that Act) in relation to that person, and

(b)   if the person carries on activities which are not reserved legal activities, any body which regulates the carrying on of such activities by the person.

19 [*repealed*]

Powers of Tribunal in respect of legal aid complaints

20 (1) Where the Tribunal makes any such order as is referred to in subsection (2A) of section 47 of the 1974 Act in the case of a solicitor who is a manager or employee of a recognised body, the Tribunal may, if it thinks fit, order that any solicitor who is for the time being a manager of that body shall be excluded (either permanently or for a specified period) from criminal legal aid work (as defined in that section).

(1A) Where the Tribunal makes any such order as is referred to in section 47(2A) of the 1974 Act in the case of a solicitor who is an employee in a recognised sole solicitor's practice, the Tribunal may, if it thinks fit, order that any solicitor who is for the time being the sole solicitor in that practice shall be excluded (either permanently or for a specified period) from criminal legal aid work (as defined in that section).

(2) [*repealed*]

Revocation of recognition by reason of default by director

21 (1) Where—

(a)   any order is made by the Tribunal under section 47 of the 1974 Act in the case of a manager of a recognised body or of the sole solicitor in a recognised sole solicitor's practice; or

(b)   an order is made by the High Court or the Court of Appeal that the name of a manager of a recognised body, or of the sole solicitor in a recognised sole solicitor's practice, be struck off the roll or that such a manager or sole solicitor be suspended from practice as a solicitor; or

(c)   any such order as is mentioned in paragraph (a) or (b) is made in the case of a person employed by a recognised body and the act or omission constituting the ground on which the order was made was instigated or connived at by a manager of the recognised body or, if the act or omission was a continuing act or omission, a manager of the body had or reasonably ought to have had knowledge of its continuance, or

(d)   any such order as is mentioned in paragraph (a) or (b) is made in the case of a person employed in a recognised sole solicitor's practice and the act or omission constituting the ground on which the order was made was instigated or connived at by the sole solicitor, or, if the act or omission was a continuing act or omission, the sole solicitor had or reasonably ought to have had knowledge of its continuance,

the Tribunal may, on an application made with respect to the recognised body or the recognised sole solicitor's practice by or on behalf of the Society, by order revoke its recognition under section 9 of this Act.

(2) The Tribunal shall not take a case into consideration during any period within which proceedings by way of appeal may be brought which may result in sub-paragraph (1) being rendered inapplicable in that case, or while any such proceedings are pending.

(3) Any reference to a manager of a recognised body, or to a sole solicitor in a recognised sole solicitor's practice, in any of paragraphs (a) to (c) of sub-paragraph (1) includes a reference to a person who was a manager of the body, or the sole solicitor in the practice, at the time of the conduct leading to the making of the order referred to in that paragraph.

(4) The reference in paragraph (c) of sub-paragraph (1) to a person employed by a recognised body, or in a sole solicitor's practice, includes a reference to a person who was so employed at the time of the conduct leading to the making of the order referred to in that paragraph.

Costs: general modification of provisions of Part III of 1974 Act

22 (1) In the provisions to which this paragraph applies—

(a)   any reference to a solicitor or to a client of a solicitor shall be construed as including a reference to a recognised body or to a client of such a body; and

(b)   any reference to a client's solicitor shall be construed as including a reference to any recognised body acting for a client.

(2) This paragraph applies to the following provisions of the 1974 Act (which relate to the remuneration of solicitors in respect of contentious and non-contentious business), namely—

section 56 (except subsections (1)(e) and (5));

sections 57 to 59;

section 60 (except subsection (5));

sections 61 and 62;

sections 64 and 65;

section 67;

section 69(1); and

sections 70 to 74.

Orders as to remuneration for non-contentious business

23 (1) In relation to an order under section 56 of the 1974 Act prescribing (by virtue of paragraph 22) general principles to be applied when determining the remuneration of recognised bodies in respect of non-contentious business, subsection (5) of that section shall have effect as if—

(a)   in paragraph (a), for "the solicitor" there were substituted "the recognised body"; and

(b)   in paragraph (d), the reference to the solicitor or any employee of the solicitor who is an authorised person were a reference to any manager or employee of the recognised body who is an authorised person.

(2)   In this paragraph "authorised person" means a person who is an authorised person in relation to an activity which is a reserved legal activity, within the meaning of the Legal Services Act 2007 (see section 18 of that Act).

Effect of contentious business agreements

24   (1)   This paragraph applies in relation to a contentious business agreement made between a recognised body and a client.

(2)   A provision in the agreement that the body shall not be liable for the negligence of any of its managers or employees shall be void if the client is a natural person who, in entering that agreement, is acting for purposes which are outside his trade, business or profession.

(3)   A provision in the agreement that the body shall be relieved from any responsibility to which it would otherwise be subject in the course of carrying on its business as a recognised body shall be void.

(4)   A provision in the agreement that any manager of the body shall be relieved from any responsibility to which the manager would otherwise be subject in the course of the carrying on by the body of its business as a recognised body shall be void.

Effect on contentious business agreement of supervening incapacity of recognised body to act for client

25   (1)   If, after some business has been done under a contentious business agreement made between a recognised body and a client but before the body has wholly performed it, the body ceases to be capable of wholly performing it by reason of one of the following events, namely—

(a)   the body ceases (for any reason) to be a recognised body;

(b)   a relevant insolvency event occurs in relation to the body; or

(c)   the client terminates the retainer or employment of the body in favour of another recognised body or a solicitor (as, notwithstanding the agreement, he shall be entitled to do),

any party to, or the representative of any party to, the agreement may apply to the court, and the court shall have the same jurisdiction as to enforcing the agreement so far as it has been performed, or setting it aside, as the court would have had if the recognised body were still capable of wholly performing it.

(2)   The court, notwithstanding that it is of the opinion that the agreement is in all respects fair and reasonable, may order the amount due in respect of business under the agreement to be ascertained by assessment, and in that case—

(a)   the costs officer, in ascertaining that amount, shall have regard so far as may be to the terms of the agreement; and

(b)   payment of the amount found by him to be due may be enforced in the same manner as if the agreement had been wholly performed.

(3)   If in such a case as is mentioned in sub-paragraph (1)(c) an order is made for the assessment of the amount due to the recognised body in respect of the business done under the agreement, the court shall direct the costs officer to have regard to the circumstances under which the termination of the body's retainer or employment has taken place, and the costs officer, unless he is of the opinion that there has been no default, negligence, improper delay or other conduct on the part of any manager or employee of the body affording the

client reasonable ground for terminating its retainer or employment, shall not allow to the body the full amount of the remuneration agreed to be paid to it.

(4)   For the purposes of this paragraph a relevant insolvency event occurs in relation to a recognised body if—

(a)   a resolution for a voluntary winding-up of the body is passed without a declaration of solvency under section 89 of the Insolvency Act 1986;

(b)   the body enters administration within the meaning of paragraph 1(2)(b) of Schedule B1 to that Act;

(c)   an administrative receiver within the meaning of section 251 of that Act is appointed;

(d)   winding up becomes a creditors' voluntary winding up under section 96 of that Act (conversion to creditors' voluntary winding up);

(e)   an order for the winding up of the body is made.

Assessments with respect to contentious business

26   (1)   Subject to the provisions of any rules of court, on every assessment of costs in respect of any contentious business done by a recognised body, the costs officer may—

(a)   allow interest at such rate and from such time as he thinks just on money disbursed by the body for the client, and on money of the client in the possession of, and improperly retained by, the body or any manager or employee of the body; and

(b)   in determining the remuneration of the body, have regard to the skill, labour and responsibility on the part of any authorised person, being a manager or employee of the body, which the business involved.

(2)   In this paragraph "authorised person" means an authorised person, in relation to an activity which is a reserved legal activity, within the meaning of the Legal Services Act 2007.

Power of court to order delivery of bill of costs, etc.

27   Any jurisdiction—

(a)   of the High Court to make any such orders as are referred to in subsection (1) of section 68 of the 1974 Act in relation to a solicitor (whether or not business has been done by him in the High Court); or

(b)   of the county court or the family court to make any such orders as are referred to in subsection (2) of that section in relation to a solicitor,

shall be exercisable in like manner in relation to a recognised body.

Power of court to order recognised body to pay over clients' money

28   Any jurisdiction of the High Court to make, in the case of a solicitor who is acting or has acted as such for a client, an order requiring the payment or delivery up of, or otherwise relating to, money or securities which the solicitor has in his possession or control on behalf of the client shall be exercisable in like manner in the case of a recognised body which is acting or has acted as such for a client or any manager or employee of such a body.

Actions to recover costs

29   (1)   Subsection (2A) of section 69 of the 1974 Act shall have effect in relation to a bill of costs delivered by a recognised body as if for paragraphs (a) and (b) there were substituted—

"(a)   signed on behalf of the recognised body by any manager or employee of the body authorised by it to do so, or

(b)   enclosed in, or accompanied by, a letter which is so signed and refers to the bill."

(2)   Subsection (2E) of that section shall have effect in relation to such a bill as if for "the solicitor" there were substituted "the recognised body".

Power of Society to inspect files relating to certain proceedings

30   Section 83 of the 1974 Act shall apply in relation to proceedings which have been brought with respect to a recognised body for any of the following purposes, namely—

(a)   for the winding-up of the body;

(b)   for the appointment of an administrative receiver within the meaning of section 251 of the Insolvency Act 1986; or

(c)   for the appointment of an administrator under Schedule B1 to the Insolvency Act 1986,

as it applies in relation to proceedings in bankruptcy which have been taken against a solicitor.

Bank accounts

31   Where rules made under section 32(1) of the 1974 Act are applied to recognised bodies in accordance with section 9(2)(f) of this Act, section 85 of the 1974 Act shall apply in relation to a recognised body which keeps an account with a bank or building society in pursuance of any such rules as it applies in relation to a solicitor who keeps such an account in pursuance of rules under section 32.

31A Where rules made under section 32(1) of the 1974 Act are applied to managers or employees in accordance with section 9(2)(fb) of this Act, section 85 of the 1974 Act shall apply in relation to a manager or employee to whom the rules are applied who keeps an account with a bank or building society in pursuance of any such rules as it applies in relation to a solicitor who keeps such an account in pursuance of rules under section 32.

Intervention by Society

32   (1)   Subject to sub-paragraph (2), where—

(a)   the Society is satisfied that a recognised body or a manager of such a body has failed to comply with any rules applicable to the body or manager by virtue of section 9 of this Act; or

(b)   a person has been appointed receiver or manager of property of a recognised body; or

(c)   a relevant insolvency event occurs in relation to a recognised body; or

(d)   the Society has reason to suspect dishonesty on the part of any manager or employee of a recognised body in connection with—

(i)   that body's business,

(ii)   any trust of which that body is or was a trustee,

(iii)   any trust of which the manager or employee is or was a trustee in his capacity as such a manager or employee, or

(iv)   the business of another body in which the manager or employee is or was a manager or employee or the practice (or former practice) of the manager or employee; or (da) the Society considers that there has been undue delay on the part of the personal representatives of a deceased solicitor who immediately before death was practising as the sole principal of a recognised body in connection with the recognised body's business or in connection with any trust; or

(db) the Society is satisfied that a solicitor practising as the sole principal of a recognised body is incapacitated by illness, injury or accident to such an extent as to be unable to attend to the solicitor's practice or to the recognised body's business; or

(e) the Society is satisfied that it is necessary to exercise the powers conferred by Part 2 of Schedule 1 to the 1974 Act (or any of them) in relation to a recognised body to protect—

  (i) the interests of clients (or former or potential clients) of the recognised body,

  (ii) the interests of the beneficiaries of any trust of which the recognised body is or was a trustee, or

  (iii) the interests of the beneficiaries of any trust of which a person who is or was a manager or employee of the recognised body is or was a trustee in that person's capacity as such a manager or employee;

the powers conferred by Part II of Schedule 1 to the 1974 Act shall be exercisable in relation to the recognised body and its business in like manner as they are exercisable in relation to a solicitor and his practice.

(1A) For the purposes of this paragraph a relevant insolvency event occurs in relation to a recognised body if—

(a) a resolution for a voluntary winding-up of the body is passed without a declaration of solvency under section 89 of the Insolvency Act 1986;

(b) the body enters administration within the meaning of paragraph 1(2)(b) of Schedule B1 to that Act;

(c) an administrative receiver within the meaning of section 251 of that Act is appointed;

(d) a meeting of creditors is held in relation to the body under section 95 of that Act (creditors' meeting which has the effect of converting a members' voluntary winding up into a creditors' voluntary winding up);

(e) an order for the winding up of the body is made.

(2) [*repealed*]

32A On the death of a solicitor practising as the sole principal of a recognised body, paragraphs 6 to 8 of Schedule 1 to the 1974 Act shall apply to the client accounts of the recognised body.

33 The powers conferred by Part II of Schedule 1 to the 1974 Act shall also be exercisable as mentioned in paragraph 32(1) of this Schedule where—

(a) the Society is satisfied that there has been undue delay—

  (i) on the part of a recognised body in connection with any matter in which it is or was acting on behalf of a client or with any trust of which it is or was a trustee, or

  (ii) on the part of a person who is or was a manager or employee of a recognised body in connection with any trust of which the manager or employee is or was a trustee in his capacity as such a manager or employee;

(b) the Society by notice in writing invites the body to give an explanation within such period following the giving of the notice as may be specified in it, being a period of not less than eight days; and

(c) the body fails within that period to give an explanation which the Society regards as satisfactory; and

(d) the Society gives notice of the failure to the body and (at the same or any later time) notice that the powers conferred by Part II of Schedule 1 to the 1974 Act are accordingly exercisable in its case by virtue of this paragraph.

34 (1) Where the recognition of a body under section 9 of this Act—

(a) has been revoked in accordance with rules under that section or by an order of the Tribunal under this Schedule; or

(b) has expired and no further recognition of that body has been granted under that section,

the powers conferred by Part II of Schedule 1 to the 1974 Act shall be exercisable in relation to the body and its former business as a recognised body as they are exercisable in relation to a solicitor and his practice.

(2) Where the powers conferred by Part II of Schedule 1 to the 1974 Act are exercisable in relation to a recognised body in accordance with paragraph 32 or 33 of this Schedule they shall continue to be so exercisable after that body's recognition under section 9 of this Act has been revoked or has otherwise ceased to be in force.

35 In connection with the application of Part II of Schedule 1 to the 1974 Act for the purposes of this Schedule, in that Part of that Schedule—

(a) any reference to the solicitor or to his practice shall be construed as including a reference to the body in relation to which the powers conferred by that Part of that Schedule are exercisable by virtue of paragraph 32, 32A, 33 or 34(1) of this Schedule or to its business (or former business) as a recognised body;

(b) any reference to paragraph 1 of that Schedule shall be construed as including a reference to paragraph 32 or 34(1) of this Schedule;

(ba) any reference to paragraph 2 of that Schedule shall be construed as including a reference to paragraph 32A of this Schedule;

(c) any reference to paragraph 3 of that Schedule shall be construed as including a reference to paragraph 33 of this Schedule;

(d) paragraph 6(2)(a) of that Schedule is to be construed as including a reference to sums of money held by or on behalf of the recognised body in connection with any trust of which a person who is or was a manager of the recognised body is or was a trustee in his capacity as such a manager;

(e) paragraph 9 of that Schedule is to be construed—

(i) as if sub-paragraph (1) included a reference to documents in the possession or under the control of the recognised body in connection with any trust of which a person who is or was a manager or employee of the recognised body is or was a trustee in his capacity as such a manager or employee, and

(ii) as applying to such a manager or employee and documents and property in his possession or under his control in connection with such a trust as it applies to a solicitor and documents and property in the possession or under the control of the solicitor;

(f) paragraph 11(1) of that Schedule is to be construed as including a power for the Society to apply to the High Court for an order for the appointment of a new trustee to a trust in substitution for a person who is a trustee, in his capacity as a manager or employee of the recognised body; and

(g) paragraph 13A of that Schedule is to be read as if the references to a former partner were references—

    (i) in the case of a recognised body which is a partnership, to a former partner in the partnership, and

    (ii) in any other case to a manager or former manager of the recognised body.

Privilege from disclosure etc.

36 (1) Where a recognised body acts as such for a client, any communication, document, material or information is privileged from disclosure in like manner as if the recognised body had at all material times been a solicitor acting for the client.

(2) Any enactment or instrument making special provision in relation to a solicitor or other legal representative as to the disclosure of information, or as to the production, seizure or removal of documents, with respect to which a claim to professional privilege could be maintained shall, with any necessary modifications, have effect in relation to a recognised body as it has effect in relation to a solicitor.

(3) In sections 748(4), 749 and 771(5) and (6) of the Income Tax Act 2007 and section 832(5) and (6) of the Corporation Tax Act 2010 any reference to a solicitor's client shall, in relation to a solicitor who is a manager or employee of a recognised body, be construed as a reference to a client of that body.

(4) This paragraph does not apply to a recognised body which holds a licence under Part 5 of the Legal Services Act 2007 (alternative business structures).

Modification of enactments relating to conveyancing etc.

37 In the following provisions, namely—

(a) sections 10(2), 48 and 182 of the Law of Property Act 1925;

(b) [*repealed*]

(c) section 12 of the Land Charges Act 1972;

(d) section 13 of the Local Land Charges Act 1975;

any reference to a solicitor shall be construed as including a reference to a recognised body, and any reference to a person's solicitor shall be construed as including a reference to a recognised body acting for that person.

Extracts from the Courts and Legal Services Act 1990

[With consolidated amendments to 1 January 2010 and prospective amendments in section 89.]

Courts and Legal Services Act 1990

1990 CHAPTER 41

An Act to make provision with respect to the procedure in, and allocation of business between, the High Court and other courts; to make provision with respect to legal services; to establish a body to be known as the Lord Chancellor's Advisory Committee on Legal Education and Conduct and a body to be known as the Authorised Conveyancing Practitioners Board; to provide for the appointment of a Legal Services Ombudsman; to make provision for the establishment of a Conveyancing Ombudsman Scheme; to provide for the establishment of Conveyancing Appeal Tribunals; to amend the law relating to judicial and related pensions and judicial and other appointments; to make provision with respect to certain officers of the Supreme Court; to amend the Solicitors Act 1974; to amend the Arbitration Act 1950; to make provision with respect to certain loans in respect of residential property; to make provision with respect to the jurisdiction of the Parliamentary Commissioner for Administration in connection with the functions of court staff; to amend the Children Act 1989 and make further provision in connection with that Act; and for connected purposes

[1st November 1990]

BE IT ENACTED by the Queen's most Excellent Majesty, by and with the advice and consent of the Lords Spiritual and Temporal, and Commons, in this present Parliament assembled, and by the authority of the same, as follows:–

...

PART IV
SOLICITORS

89 Foreign lawyers: recognised bodies and partnerships with solicitors

(1) The Law Society shall maintain a register of foreign lawyers for the purposes of this section.

(2) A foreign lawyer who wishes to be registered under this section must apply to the Society in accordance with the requirements of Part I of Schedule 14.

(3) The power to make rules under—

   (a) the following provisions of the Solicitors Act 1974—

      (i) section 31 (professional practice, conduct and discipline);

      (ii) section 32 (accounts and trust accounts);

      (iii) section 34 (accountants' reports);

(iv)   sections 36 and 36A (compensation grants); and

(v)   section 37 (professional indemnity); and

(b)   section 9 of the Administration of Justice Act 1985 (incorporated practices),

shall also be exercisable in relation to registered foreign lawyers.

(4)   Subject to the provisions of Schedule 14, any such power may be exercised so as to make different provision with respect to registered foreign lawyers to the provision made with respect to solicitors.

(5)   Subject to the provisions of Schedule 14, the Lord Chancellor may by order provide that any enactment or instrument—

(a)   passed or made before or in the same Session as the Legal Services Act 2007 was passed;

(b)   having effect in relation to solicitors; and

(c)   specified in the order,

shall have effect with respect to registered foreign lawyers as it has effect with respect to solicitors.

(6)   An order under subsection (5) may provide for an enactment or instrument to have effect with respect to registered foreign lawyers subject to such additions, omissions or other modifications as the Lord Chancellor sees fit to specify in the order.

(7)   Subject to the provisions of Schedule 14, the Lord Chancellor may by order provide that any enactment or instrument—

(a)   passed or made before or in the same Session as the Legal Services Act 2007 was passed;

(b)   having effect in relation to recognised bodies; and

(c)   specified in the order,

shall, in its application in relation to recognised bodies whose managers include one or more registered foreign lawyers, have effect with such additions, omissions or other modifications as the Lord Chancellor sees fit to specify in the order.

(8)   Schedule 14 shall have effect for the purposes of supplementing this section.

(8A)   Rules and regulations made by the Law Society under, or by virtue of, this section or Schedule 14 which are not regulatory arrangements within the meaning of the Legal Services Act 2007 are to be treated as such arrangements for the purposes of that Act.

(9)   In this section and in Schedule 14—

"foreign lawyer" means a person who is not a solicitor or barrister but who is a member, and entitled to practise as such, of a legal profession regulated within a jurisdiction outside England and Wales;

"manager", in relation to a body, has the same meaning as in the Legal Services Act 2007 (see section 207 of that Act);

"multi-national partnership" means a partnership whose members consist of one or more registered foreign lawyers and one or more other lawyers as permitted by rules made under section 31 of the Solicitors Act 1974;

"recognised body" has the same meaning as in section 9 of the Administration of Justice Act 1985 (management and control by solicitors of incorporated practices); and

"registered foreign lawyer" means a foreign lawyer who is registered under this section.

SCHEDULE 14
Foreign Lawyers: Partnerships and Recognised Bodies

Section 89

PART I
REGISTRATION

General

1 In this Schedule—

"the Act of 1974" means the Solicitors Act 1974;

"the register" means the register maintained by the Society under section 89;

"registration" means registration in that register;

"the Society" means the Law Society; and

"the Tribunal" means the Solicitors Disciplinary Tribunal.

Application for registration

2 (1) An application for registration or for renewal of registration—

(a) shall be made to the Society in such form as the Society may prescribe; and

(b) shall be accompanied by such fee as the Society may, with the concurrence of the Legal Services Board, prescribe.

(2) Where such an application is duly made by a foreign lawyer, the Society may register the applicant if it is satisfied that the legal profession of which the applicant is a member is one which is so regulated as to make it appropriate for members of that profession to be managers of recognised bodies.

(3) [*repealed*]

(4) The Society may make regulations, with the concurrence of the Legal Services Board, with respect to—

(a) the keeping of the register (including the form of the register and the manner in which entries are to be made, altered or removed); and

(b) applications for registration or renewal of registration; and

(c) the making available to the public of the information contained in the register (including the manner in which, and hours during which, the information is to be made so available and whether the information is to be made available free of charge).

(5) [*repealed*]

2A (1) The Society may direct that a foreign lawyer's registration is to have effect subject to such conditions as the Society thinks fit to impose.

(2) A direction under sub-paragraph (1) may be given in respect of a foreign lawyer

(a) at the time he is first registered, or

(b) at any time when the registration has effect.

Duration of registration

3   (1) Every registration shall have effect from the beginning of the day on which it is entered in the register.

(2) The Society may make regulations—

   (a)   prescribing the date ("the renewal date") by which each registered foreign lawyer must apply for his registration to be renewed; and

   (b)   requiring every entry in the register to specify the renewal date applicable to that registration.

(3) Any such regulations may—

   (a)   provide different renewal dates for different categories of registered foreign lawyer or different circumstances;

   (b)   provide for the Society to specify, in the case of individual registered foreign lawyers, different renewal dates to those prescribed by the regulations;

   (c)   make such transitional, incidental and supplemental provision in connection with any provision for different renewal dates as the Society considers expedient.

(4) Where a foreign lawyer is registered, the Society may cancel his registration if—

   (a)   the renewal date for his registration has passed but he has not applied for it to be renewed; or

   (b)   he has applied to the Society for it to be cancelled.

Evidence as to registration

4   Any certificate purporting to be signed by an officer of the Society and stating that a particular foreign lawyer—

   (a)   is, or is not, registered; or

   (b)   was registered during a period specified in the certificate,

shall, unless the contrary is proved, be evidence of that fact and be taken to have been so signed.

PART II
REGISTERED FOREIGN LAWYERS: SUPPLEMENTARY PROVISIONS

Intervention in practices

5   (1) In this paragraph "the intervention powers" means the powers conferred by Part II of Schedule 1 to the Act of 1974 (intervention in solicitors' practices) as modified by this Schedule or under section 89.

(2) Subject to sub-paragraphs (3) and (4), the intervention powers shall be exercisable in relation to a person who is or has been a registered foreign lawyer and the practice of the multi-national partnership of which he is or was a member as they are exercisable in relation to a solicitor and his practice.

(3) The intervention powers are only exercisable where—

   (a)   the Society has reason to suspect dishonesty on the part of the registered foreign lawyer, or on the part of an employee of the multi-national partnership, in connection with—

      (i)   the practice of that partnership; or

(ii)   any trust of which the registered foreign lawyer is or was a trustee;

(b)   in the case of a registered foreign lawyer who has died, the Society has reason to suspect dishonesty on the part of his personal representative, in connection with—

    (i)   the practice of the multi-national partnership; or

    (ii)   any trust of which the registered foreign lawyer was a trustee;

(ba)   the Society has reason to suspect dishonesty on the part of the registered foreign lawyer ("L") in connection with—

    (i)   the business of any person of whom L is or was an employee, or of any body of which L is or was a manager, or

    (ii)   any business which is or was carried on by L as a sole trader;

(c)   the Society is satisfied that the registered foreign lawyer has failed to comply with rules made under section 32 or 37(2)(c) of the Act of 1974;

(d)   a bankruptcy order (as defined in paragraph 10(3)) has been made against him or he has made a composition or arrangement with his creditors;

(e)   he has been committed to prison in any civil or criminal proceedings;

(ea)   the Society is satisfied that he has abandoned his practice;

(f)   he lacks capacity (within the meaning of the Mental Capacity Act 2005) to act as a registered foreign lawyer and powers under sections 15 to 20 or section 48 are exercisable in relation to him;

(g)   his name has been struck off the register or his registration has been suspended or cancelled;

(h)   he has purported to act as a member of a multi-national partnership at a time when he was not registered;

(i)   the Society is satisfied that he has failed to comply with any condition, subject to which he is registered, to the effect that—

    (i)   he may only be a member of a partnership which is approved by the Society; or

    (ii)   he may only be a manager of a recognised body which is so approved; or

    (iii)   he may only be such a member or such a manager

(j)   the Society is satisfied that it is necessary to exercise the intervention powers (or any of them) in relation to the registered foreign lawyer to protect—

    (i)   the interests of clients (or former or potential clients) of the registered foreign lawyer or the multi-national partnership, or

    (ii)   the interests of the beneficiaries of any trust of which the registered foreign lawyer is or was a trustee.

(4)   [*repealed*]

(5)   The intervention powers (other than those conferred by paragraphs 5 and 10 of Part II of Schedule 1 to the Act of 1974) shall also be exercisable where—

(a)   the Society is satisfied that there has been undue delay on the part of a registered foreign lawyer in connection with—

    (i)   any matter in which he, or the multi-national partnership of which he is or was a member, was instructed on behalf of a client; or

    (ii)   any trust;

(b)   the Society by notice invites the registered foreign lawyer to give an explanation within a period (of not less than 8 days) specified in the notice;

(c)   the registered foreign lawyer fails within that period to give an explanation which the Society regards as satisfactory; and

(d)   the Society gives notice of the failure to the registered foreign lawyer and notice that the intervention powers are accordingly exercisable.

(6)   Where the intervention powers are exercisable in relation to a registered foreign lawyer, they shall continue to be exercisable—

(a)   at any time when his registration is suspended;

(b)   after his name has been struck off the register or his registration has been cancelled; or

(c)   after his death.

(7)   Part II of Schedule 1 to the Act of 1974 shall have effect in relation to the intervention powers exercisable by virtue of this Schedule, subject to—

(a)   any express modifications made under section 89; and

(b)   any modifications necessary in the light of this paragraph.

(8)   For the purposes of this paragraph, Part II of Schedule 1 to the Act of 1974 shall be read with paragraph 4(2) of Part I of that Schedule.

(9)   The notices required to be given by this paragraph must be in writing but need not be given at the same time.

(10)   In this paragraph "manager", in relation to a recognised body, has the same meaning as in the Legal Services Act 2007 (see section 207 of that Act).

The Compensation Fund

6   Section 36 of the 1974 Act applies in relation to registered foreign lawyers as if for paragraphs (a) and (b) of subsection (1) there were substituted—

"(a)   an act or omission of a registered foreign lawyer or former registered foreign lawyer;

(b)   an act or omission of an employee or former employee of a registered foreign lawyer or former registered foreign lawyer;".

Contributions to the Fund

7   Section 36A(2) and (3) of the 1974 Act applies in relation to registered foreign lawyers as it applies in relation to solicitors.

Accountants' reports

8   Section 34 of the Act of 1974 applies in relation to registered foreign lawyers as it applies in relation to solicitors.

9   [*repealed*]

Effect of bankruptcy

10   (1)   The registration of any foreign lawyer against whom a bankruptcy order is made shall be suspended on the making of that order.

(2)   The suspension of any registration by reason of a bankruptcy order shall terminate if the order is annulled and an office copy of the order annulling it is served on the Society.

(3) In sub-paragraph (1), "bankruptcy order" includes any order which is not a bankruptcy order but which has the same, or a similar, effect under the law in force in any territory outside England and Wales.

Effect of disciplinary action

11 (1) Where a registered foreign lawyer is struck off, or suspended from practice, his registration shall be suspended.

(2) In sub-paragraph (1) "struck off" and "suspended from practice" mean—

(a) any action taken within the jurisdiction by reference to which the registered foreign lawyer is qualified to be registered; or

(b) where the registered foreign lawyer is qualified to be registered by reference to more than one jurisdiction, any action taken within any one of those jurisdictions,

which is the equivalent, respectively, of a solicitor being struck off the roll or suspended from practice under the Act of 1974.

Re-instatement of disciplined foreign lawyer

12 (1) Where a person's registration has been suspended by virtue of paragraph 11, it shall be revived—

(a) if his right to practise in the jurisdiction in question is restored; and

(b) a copy of the instrument restoring his right, certified to be a true copy by an officer of the appropriate court in the jurisdiction in question, or the professional body concerned, is served on the Society.

(2) Where a person whose registration is suspended by virtue of paragraph 11 applies to the Society for the suspension to be terminated, the Society may terminate it subject to such conditions, if any, as it thinks fit to impose.

Effective date of revived registration

13 Where a foreign lawyer's registration is revived (whether as the result of the termination of its suspension, restoration by order of the Tribunal or for any other reason), that revival shall take effect on such date, and subject to such conditions, as the Society may direct.

Appeal against conditions or refusals

14 (1) Any foreign lawyer may appeal to the High Court against—

(a) the refusal of the Society to register him or to renew his registration;

(b) the refusal of the Society to terminate the suspension of his registration on an application made by him under paragraph 12;

(c) the failure of the Society to deal with any application by him for registration, renewal of registration or the termination (under paragraph 12(2)) of a suspension within a reasonable time;

(d) any condition imposed by the Society under paragraph 2A, 12(2) or 13; or

(e) a decision of the Society to remove his name from the register.

(2) [*repealed*]

(3) On an appeal under this paragraph, the High Court may make such order as it thinks fit.

(4) In relation to an appeal under this paragraph the High Court may make such order as it thinks fit as to payment of costs.

(5)   The decision of the High Court on an appeal under this paragraph shall be final.

Jurisdiction and powers of Disciplinary Tribunal

15   (1)   Subject to paragraph 16, section 46 of the Act of 1974 (Solicitors Disciplinary Tribunal) shall apply, with the necessary modifications, in relation to applications and complaints made by virtue of any provision of this Schedule as it applies in relation to applications and complaints made by virtue of any provision of that Act.

(2)   Any application—

(a)   to strike the name of a foreign lawyer off the register;

(b)   to require a registered foreign lawyer to answer allegations in an affidavit;

(c)   to suspend the registration of a foreign lawyer for a specified or indefinite period;

(d)   by a foreign lawyer whose name has been struck off the register by order of the Tribunal to have his name restored to the register;

(e)   by a foreign lawyer whose registration has been suspended for an indefinite period by order of the Tribunal for the termination of that suspension,

shall be made to the Tribunal.

(3)   Any person who alleges that a registered foreign lawyer has failed to comply with any rule made under section 31, 32, 34, or 37 of the Act of 1974 may make a complaint to the Tribunal.

(3A)   Any person who alleges that a registered foreign lawyer has knowingly acted in contravention of any order under section 43(2) of the Act of 1974 or of any conditions subject to which a permission has been granted under such an order may make a complaint to the Tribunal.

(4)   On the hearing of any application or complaint made to the Tribunal with respect to a foreign lawyer, the Tribunal shall have power to make such order as it may think fit, and any such order may in particular include provision for any of the following matters—

(a)   the striking off the register of the name of the foreign lawyer to whom the application or complaint relates;

(b)   the suspension of that foreign lawyer's registration indefinitely or for a specified period;

(c)   the payment by that foreign lawyer of a penalty, which shall be forfeit to Her Majesty;

(d)   the termination of that foreign lawyer's unspecified period of suspension from registration;

(e)   the restoration to the register of the name of a foreign lawyer which has been struck off the register;

(f)   the payment by any party of costs or a contribution towards costs of such amount as the Tribunal may consider reasonable.

(5)   [*repealed*]

Foreign lawyers assisting the Tribunal

16   (1)   For the purposes of section 46 of the Act of 1974 (Solicitors Disciplinary Tribunal), the Tribunal may make rules providing for it to be assisted, in dealing with any application or complaint of a kind mentioned in paragraph 15, by a member of the legal profession in the jurisdiction by reference to which the foreign lawyer is or was qualified to be registered.

(2)   Rules under sub-paragraph (1) shall not be made without the concurrence of the Legal Services Board.

(3)   Subsection (12) of section 46 of the Act of 1974 (rules to be made by statutory instrument etc) shall apply to rules made under this paragraph as it applies to rules made under subsection (9) of that section.

Appeals from Tribunal

17   (1)   An Appeal from the Tribunal shall lie to the High Court.

(2)   The High Court shall have power to make such order on an appeal under this paragraph as it may think fit.

(3)   Any decision of the High Court on an appeal in the case of an order on an application under paragraph 15(2)(d) or (e), or the refusal of any such application, shall be final.

Extracts from the Legal Services Act 2007

[With consolidated amendments to 22 April 2014.]

Legal Services Act 2007

2007 CHAPTER 29

An Act to make provision for the establishment of the Legal Services Board and in respect of its functions; to make provision for, and in connection with, the regulation of persons who carry on certain legal activities; to make provision for the establishment of the Office for Legal Complaints and for a scheme to consider and determine legal complaints; to make provision about claims management services and about immigration advice and immigration services; to make provision in respect of legal representation provided free of charge; to make provision about the application of the Legal Profession and Legal Aid (Scotland) Act 2007; to make provision about the Scottish legal services ombudsman; and for connected purposes.

[30th October 2007]

Be it enacted by the Queen's most Excellent Majesty, by and with the advice and consent of the Lords Spiritual and Temporal, and Commons, in this present Parliament assembled, and by the authority of the same, as follows:—

PART 1
THE REGULATORY OBJECTIVES

1 The regulatory objectives

(1) In this Act a reference to "the regulatory objectives" is a reference to the objectives of—

(a)   protecting and promoting the public interest;

(b)   supporting the constitutional principle of the rule of law;

(c)   improving access to justice;

(d)   protecting and promoting the interests of consumers;

(e)   promoting competition in the provision of services within subsection (2);

(f)   encouraging an independent, strong, diverse and effective legal profession;

(g)   increasing public understanding of the citizen's legal rights and duties;

(h)   promoting and maintaining adherence to the professional principles.

(2)   The services within this subsection are services such as are provided by authorised persons (including services which do not involve the carrying on of activities which are reserved legal activities).

(3)   The "professional principles" are—

(a)   that authorised persons should act with independence and integrity,

(b)   that authorised persons should maintain proper standards of work,

(c)   that authorised persons should act in the best interests of their clients,

(d)   that persons who exercise before any court a right of audience, or conduct litigation in relation to proceedings in any court, by virtue of being authorised persons should comply with their duty to the court to act with independence in the interests of justice, and

(e)   that the affairs of clients should be kept confidential.

(4)   In this section "authorised persons" means authorised persons in relation to activities which are reserved legal activities.

PART 2
THE LEGAL SERVICES BOARD

Constitution

2   The Legal Services Board

(1)   There is to be a body corporate called the Legal Services Board ("the Board").

(2)   Schedule 1 is about the Board.

General functions

3   The Board's duty to promote the regulatory objectives etc

(1)   In discharging its functions the Board must comply with the requirements of this section.

(2)   The Board must, so far as is reasonably practicable, act in a way—

(a)   which is compatible with the regulatory objectives, and

(b)   which the Board considers most appropriate for the purpose of meeting those objectives.

(3)   The Board must have regard to—

(a)   the principles under which regulatory activities should be transparent, accountable, proportionate, consistent and targeted only at cases in which action is needed, and

(b)   any other principle appearing to it to represent the best regulatory practice.

4   Standards of regulation, education and training

The Board must assist in the maintenance and development of standards in relation to—

(a)   the regulation by approved regulators of persons authorised by them to carry on activities which are reserved legal activities, and

(b)   the education and training of persons so authorised.

5   Corporate governance

In managing its affairs, the Board must have regard to such generally accepted principles of good corporate governance as it is reasonable to regard as applicable to it.

6   Annual report

(1)   The Board must prepare a report ("the annual report") for each financial year.

(2)   The annual report must deal with—

(a)   the discharge of the Board's functions,

(b)   the extent to which, in the Board's opinion, the Board has met the regulatory objectives, and

(c)   such other matters as the Lord Chancellor may from time to time direct.

(3)   As soon as reasonably practicable after the end of each financial year, the Board must give the Lord Chancellor a copy of the annual report prepared for that year.

(4)   The Lord Chancellor must lay a copy of the annual report before Parliament.

(5)   In this section "financial year" means—

(a)   the period beginning with the day on which the Board is established and ending with the next following 31 March, and

(b)   each successive period of 12 months.

7 Supplementary powers

The Board may do anything calculated to facilitate, or incidental or conducive to, the carrying out of any of its functions.

8 The Consumer Panel

(1)   The Board must establish and maintain a panel of persons (to be known as "the Consumer Panel") to represent the interests of consumers.

(2)   The Consumer Panel is to consist of such consumers, or persons representing the interests of consumers, as the Board may appoint with the approval of the Lord Chancellor.

(3)   The Board must appoint one of the members of the Consumer Panel to be the chairman of the Panel.

(4)   The Board must secure that the membership of the Consumer Panel is such as to give a fair degree of representation to both—

(a)   those who are using (or are or may be contemplating using), in connection with businesses carried on by them, services provided by persons who are authorised persons in relation to activities which are reserved legal activities, and

(b)   those who are using (or are or may be contemplating using) such services otherwise than in connection with businesses carried on by them.

(5)   The Consumer Panel must not include any person who is—

(a)   a member of the Board or of its staff;

(b)   a member of the Office for Legal Complaints (see Part 6), an ombudsman appointed by it or a member of its staff appointed under paragraph 13 of Schedule 15;

(c)   a member of the governing body, or of the staff, of an approved regulator;

(d)   an authorised person in relation to an activity which is a reserved legal activity;

(e)   a person authorised, by a person designated under section 5(1) of the Compensation Act 2006 (c 29), to provide services which are regulated claims management services (within the meaning of that Act);

[(e)   an authorised person (within the meaning given in section 31 of the Financial Services and Markets Act 2000 (authorised persons)) in relation to regulated claims management activity (within the meaning given by section 417(1) of that Act (definitions));]

(f)   an advocate in Scotland;

(g)   a solicitor in Scotland;

(h)   a member of the Bar of Northern Ireland; or

(i)   a solicitor of the Court of Judicature of Northern Ireland.

(6)   The chairman and other members of the Consumer Panel are to be—

(a)   appointed for a fixed period, and on other terms and conditions, determined by the Board, and

(b)   paid by the Board in accordance with provision made by or under the terms of appointment.

(7)   But a person may be removed from office in accordance with those terms and conditions only with the approval of the Lord Chancellor.

(8)   A person who ceases to be chairman or another member of the Consumer Panel may be re-appointed.

9   Committees and the procedure of the Consumer Panel

(1)   The Consumer Panel may make such arrangements as it thinks fit for committees established by the Panel to give advice to the Panel about matters relating to the carrying out of the Panel's functions.

(2)   The Consumer Panel may make such other arrangements for regulating its own procedure, and for regulating the procedure of the committees established by it, as it thinks fit.

(3)   Those arrangements may include arrangements as to quorums and as to the making of decisions by a majority.

(4)   The committees established by the Consumer Panel may include committees the membership of which includes persons who are not members of the Panel.

(5)   The membership of every committee established by the Consumer Panel must contain at least one person who is a member of the Panel.

(6)   Where a person who is not a member of the Consumer Panel is a member of a committee established by it, the Board may pay to that person such remuneration and expenses as the Board may determine.

10   Representations by the Consumer Panel

(1)   The Board must consider any representations made to it by the Consumer Panel.

(2)   If the Board disagrees with a view expressed, or proposal made, in the representations, it must give the Consumer Panel a notice to that effect stating its reasons for disagreeing.

(3)   The Consumer Panel may publish such information as it thinks fit about any representations made by it to the Board.

(4)   Where the Consumer Panel publishes information about any representations made by it, the Board must publish any notice it gives under subsection (2) in respect of those representations.

11   Advice and research functions of the Consumer Panel

(1)   The Consumer Panel may, at the request of the Board—

(a)   carry out research for the Board;

(b)   give advice to the Board.

(2)   The Board must consider any advice given and the results of any research carried out under this section.

(3)   The Consumer Panel may publish such information as it thinks fit about advice it gives, and about the results of research carried out by it, under this section.

PART 3
RESERVED LEGAL ACTIVITIES

Reserved legal activities

12 Meaning of "reserved legal activity" and "legal activity"

(1) In this Act "reserved legal activity" means—

    (a)   the exercise of a right of audience;

    (b)   the conduct of litigation;

    (c)   reserved instrument activities;

    (d)   probate activities;

    (e)   notarial activities;

    (f)   the administration of oaths.

(2) Schedule 2 makes provision about what constitutes each of those activities.

(3) In this Act "legal activity" means—

    (a)   an activity which is a reserved legal activity within the meaning of this Act as originally enacted, and

    (b)   any other activity which consists of one or both of the following—

        (i)   the provision of legal advice or assistance in connection with the application of the law or with any form of resolution of legal disputes;

        (ii)   the provision of representation in connection with any matter concerning the application of the law or any form of resolution of legal disputes.

(4) But "legal activity" does not include any activity of a judicial or quasi-judicial nature (including acting as a mediator).

(5) For the purposes of subsection (3) "legal dispute" includes a dispute as to any matter of fact the resolution of which is relevant to determining the nature of any person's legal rights or liabilities.

(6) Section 24 makes provision for adding legal activities to the reserved legal activities.

Carrying on the activities

13 Entitlement to carry on a reserved legal activity

(1) The question whether a person is entitled to carry on an activity which is a reserved legal activity is to be determined solely in accordance with the provisions of this Act.

(2) A person is entitled to carry on an activity ("the relevant activity") which is a reserved legal activity where—

    (a)   the person is an authorised person in relation to the relevant activity, or

    (b)   the person is an exempt person in relation to that activity.

(3) Subsection (2) is subject to section 23 (transitional protection for non-commercial bodies).

(4) Nothing in this section or section 23 affects section 84 of the Immigration and Asylum Act 1999 (c 33) (which prohibits the provision of immigration advice and immigration services except by certain persons).

14 Offence to carry on a reserved legal activity if not entitled

(1) It is an offence for a person to carry on an activity ("the relevant activity") which is a reserved legal activity unless that person is entitled to carry on the relevant activity.

(2) In proceedings for an offence under subsection (1), it is a defence for the accused to show that the accused did not know, and could not reasonably have been expected to know, that the offence was being committed.

(3) A person who is guilty of an offence under subsection (1) is liable—

(a)   on summary conviction, to imprisonment for a term not exceeding 12 months or a fine not exceeding the statutory maximum (or both), and

(b)   on conviction on indictment, to imprisonment for a term not exceeding 2 years or a fine (or both).

(4) A person who is guilty of an offence under subsection (1) by reason of an act done in the purported exercise of a right of audience, or a right to conduct litigation, in relation to any proceedings or contemplated proceedings is also guilty of contempt of the court concerned and may be punished accordingly.

(5) In relation to an offence under subsection (1) committed before the commencement of section 154(1) of the Criminal Justice Act 2003 (c 44), the reference in subsection (3)(a) to 12 months is to be read as a reference to 6 months.

15 Carrying on of a reserved legal activity: employers and employees etc

(1) This section applies for the interpretation of references in this Act to a person carrying on an activity which is a reserved legal activity.

(2) References to a person carrying on an activity which is a reserved legal activity include a person ("E") who—

(a)   is an employee of a person ("P"), and

(b)   carries on the activity in E's capacity as such an employee.

(3) For the purposes of subsection (2), it is irrelevant whether P is entitled to carry on the activity.

(4) P does not carry on an activity ("the relevant activity") which is a reserved legal activity by virtue of E carrying it on in E's capacity as an employee of P, unless the provision of relevant services to the public or a section of the public (with or without a view to profit) is part of P's business.

(5) Relevant services are services which consist of or include the carrying on of the relevant activity by employees of P in their capacity as employees of P.

(6) Where P is an independent trade union, persons provided with relevant services do not constitute the public or a section of the public where—

(a)   the persons are provided with the relevant services by virtue of their membership or former membership of P or of another person's membership or former membership of P, and

(b)   the services are excepted membership services.

(7) Subject to subsection (8), "excepted membership services" means relevant services which relate to or have a connection with—

(a)   relevant activities of a member, or former member, of the independent trade union;

(b)   any other activities carried on for the purposes of or in connection with, or arising from, such relevant activities;

(c)   any event which has occurred (or is alleged to have occurred) in the course of or in connection with such relevant activities or activities within paragraph (b);

(d)   activities carried on by a person for the purposes of or in connection with, or arising from, the person's membership of the independent trade union;

and such other relevant services as the Lord Chancellor may by order specify.

(8)   The Lord Chancellor may by order make provision about the circumstances in which relevant services do or do not relate to, or have a connection with, the matters mentioned in paragraphs (a) to (d) of subsection (7).

(9)   Subject to that, the Lord Chancellor may by order make provision about—

(a)   what does or does not constitute a section of the public;

(b)   the circumstances in which the provision of relevant services to the public or a section of the public does or does not form part of P's business.

(10)   The Lord Chancellor may make an order under subsection (7), (8) or (9) only on the recommendation of the Board.

(11)   If P is a body, references to an employee of P include references to a manager of P.

(12)   In subsection (7), "relevant activities", in relation to a person who is or was a member of an independent trade union, means any employment (including self-employment), trade, occupation or other activity to which the person's membership of the trade union relates or related.

16   Offence to carry on reserved legal activity through person not entitled

(1)   Where subsection (2) applies it is an offence for a person ("P") to carry on an activity ("the relevant activity") which is a reserved legal activity, despite P being entitled to carry on the relevant activity.

(2)   This subsection applies if—

(a)   P carries on the relevant activity by virtue of an employee of P ("E") carrying it on in E's capacity as such an employee, and

(b)   in carrying on the relevant activity, E commits an offence under section 14.

(3)   If P is a body, references in subsection (2) to an employee of P include references to a manager of P.

(4)   In proceedings for an offence under subsection (1), it is a defence for the accused to show that the accused took all reasonable precautions and exercised all due diligence to avoid committing the offence.

(5)   A person who is guilty of an offence under subsection (1) is liable—

(a)   on summary conviction, to imprisonment for a term not exceeding 12 months or a fine not exceeding the statutory maximum (or both), and

(b)   on conviction on indictment, to imprisonment for a term not exceeding 2 years or a fine (or both).

(6)   A person who is guilty of an offence under subsection (1) by reason of an act done in the purported exercise of a right of audience, or a right to conduct litigation, in relation to any proceedings or contemplated proceedings is also guilty of contempt of the court concerned and may be punished accordingly.

(7)   In relation to an offence under subsection (1) committed before the commencement of section 154(1) of the Criminal Justice Act 2003 (c 44), the reference in subsection (5)(a) to 12 months is to be read as a reference to 6 months.

17 Offence to pretend to be entitled

(1) It is an offence for a person—

(a) wilfully to pretend to be entitled to carry on any activity which is a reserved legal activity when that person is not so entitled, or

(b) with the intention of implying falsely that that person is so entitled, to take or use any name, title or description.

(2) A person who is guilty of an offence under subsection (1) is liable—

(a) on summary conviction, to imprisonment for a term not exceeding 12 months or a fine not exceeding the statutory maximum (or both), and

(b) on conviction on indictment, to imprisonment for a term not exceeding 2 years or a fine (or both).

(3) In relation to an offence under subsection (1) committed before the commencement of section 154(1) of the Criminal Justice Act 2003 (c 44), the reference in subsection (2)(a) to 12 months is to be read as a reference to 6 months.

18 Authorised persons

(1) For the purposes of this Act "authorised person", in relation to an activity ("the relevant activity") which is a reserved legal activity, means—

(a) a person who is authorised to carry on the relevant activity by a relevant approved regulator in relation to the relevant activity (other than by virtue of a licence under Part 5), or

(b) a licensable body which, by virtue of such a licence, is authorised to carry on the relevant activity by a licensing authority in relation to the reserved legal activity.

(2) A licensable body may not be authorised to carry on the relevant activity as mentioned in subsection (1)(a).

(3) But where a body ("A") which is authorised as mentioned in subsection (1)(a) becomes a licensable body, the body is deemed by virtue of this subsection to continue to be so authorised from that time until the earliest of the following events—

(a) the end of the period of 90 days beginning with the day on which that time falls;

(b) the time from which the relevant approved regulator determines this subsection is to cease to apply to A;

(c) the time when A ceases to be a licensable body.

(4) Subsection (2) is subject to Part 2 of Schedule 5 (by virtue of which licensable bodies may be deemed to be authorised as mentioned in subsection (1)(a) in relation to certain activities during a transitional period).

(5) A person other than a licensable body may not be authorised to carry on the relevant activity as mentioned in subsection (1)(b).

(6) But where a body ("L") which is authorised as mentioned in subsection (1)(b) ceases to be a licensable body, the body is deemed by virtue of this subsection to continue to be so authorised from that time until the earliest of the following events—

(a) the end of the period of 90 days beginning with the day on which that time falls;

(b) the time from which the relevant licensing authority determines this subsection is to cease to apply to L;

(c) the time when L becomes a licensable body.

19 Exempt persons

In this Act, "exempt person", in relation to an activity ("the relevant activity") which is a reserved legal activity, means a person who, for the purposes of carrying on the relevant activity, is an exempt person by virtue of—

(a) Schedule 3 (exempt persons), or

(b) paragraph 13 or 18 of Schedule 5 (additional categories of exempt persons during transitional period).

20 Approved regulators and relevant approved regulators

(1) In this Act, the following expressions have the meaning given by this section—

"approved regulator";

"relevant approved regulator".

(2) "Approved regulator" means—

(a) a body which is designated as an approved regulator by Part 1 of Schedule 4 or under Part 2 of that Schedule (or both) and whose regulatory arrangements are approved for the purposes of this Act, and

(b) if an order under section 62(1)(a) has effect, the Board.

(3) An approved regulator is a "relevant approved regulator" in relation to an activity which is a reserved legal activity if—

(a) the approved regulator is designated by Part 1, or under Part 2, of Schedule 4 in relation to that reserved legal activity, or

(b) where the approved regulator is the Board, it is designated in relation to that reserved legal activity by an order under section 62(1)(a).

(4) An approved regulator is a "relevant approved regulator" in relation to a person if the person is authorised by the approved regulator to carry on an activity which is a reserved legal activity.

(5) Schedule 4 makes provision with respect to approved regulators other than the Board.

In that Schedule—

(a) Part 1 designates certain bodies as approved regulators in relation to certain reserved legal activities,

(b) Part 2 makes provision for bodies to be designated by order as approved regulators in relation to one or more reserved legal activities, and

(c) Part 3 makes provision relating to the approval of changes to an approved regulator's regulatory arrangements.

(6) An approved regulator may authorise persons to carry on any activity which is a reserved legal activity in respect of which it is a relevant approved regulator.

...

PART 4
REGULATION OF APPROVED REGULATORS

Introductory

27 Regulatory and representative functions of approved regulators

(1)   In this Act references to the "regulatory functions" of an approved regulator are to any functions the approved regulator has—

(a)   under or in relation to its regulatory arrangements, or

(b)   in connection with the making or alteration of those arrangements.

(2)   In this Act references to the "representative functions" of an approved regulator are to any functions the approved regulator has in connection with the representation, or promotion, of the interests of persons regulated by it.

General duties of approved regulators

28 Approved regulator's duty to promote the regulatory objectives etc

(1)   In discharging its regulatory functions (whether in connection with a reserved legal activity or otherwise) an approved regulator must comply with the requirements of this section.

(2)   The approved regulator must, so far as is reasonably practicable, act in a way—

(a)   which is compatible with the regulatory objectives, and

(b)   which the approved regulator considers most appropriate for the purpose of meeting those objectives.

(3)   The approved regulator must have regard to—

(a)   the principles under which regulatory activities should be transparent, accountable, proportionate, consistent and targeted only at cases in which action is needed, and

(b)   any other principle appearing to it to represent the best regulatory practice.

...

Regulatory conflict

52 Regulatory conflict with approved regulators

(1)   The regulatory arrangements of an approved regulator must make such provision as is reasonably practicable to prevent regulatory conflicts.

(2)   For the purposes of this section and section 53, a regulatory conflict is a conflict between—

(a)   a requirement of the approved regulator's regulatory arrangements, and

(b)   a requirement of the regulatory arrangements of another approved regulator.

(3)   Subsection (4) applies where a body is authorised by an approved regulator ("the entity regulator") to carry on an activity which is a reserved legal activity.

(4)   If a conflict arises between—

(a)   a requirement of the regulatory arrangements of the entity regulator, in relation to the body authorised by the entity regulator or an employee or manager of the body ("an entity requirement"), and

(b)   a requirement of the regulatory arrangements of another approved regulator in relation to an employee or manager of the body who is authorised by it to carry on a reserved legal activity ("an individual requirement"),

the entity requirement prevails over the individual requirement.

...

PART 5
ALTERNATIVE BUSINESS STRUCTURES

Introductory

71 Carrying on of activities by licensed bodies

(1) The provisions of this Part have effect for the purpose of regulating the carrying on of reserved legal activities and other activities by licensed bodies.

(2) In this Act "licensed body" means a body which holds a licence in force under this Part.

72 "Licensable body"

(1) A body ("B") is a licensable body if a non-authorised person—

(a) is a manager of B, or

(b) has an interest in B.

(2) A body ("B") is also a licensable body if—

(a) another body ("A") is a manager of B, or has an interest in B, and

(b) non-authorised persons are entitled to exercise, or control the exercise of, at least 10% of the voting rights in A.

(3) For the purposes of this Act, a person has an interest in a body if—

(a) the person holds shares in the body, or

(b) the person is entitled to exercise, or control the exercise of, voting rights in the body.

(4) A body may be licensable by virtue of both subsection (1) and subsection (2).

(5) For the purposes of this Act, a non-authorised person has an indirect interest in a licensable body if the body is licensable by virtue of subsection (2) and the non-authorised person is entitled to exercise, or control the exercise of, voting rights in A.

(6) In this Act "shares" means—

(a) in relation to a body with a share capital, allotted shares (within the meaning of the Companies Acts);

(b) in relation to a body with capital but no share capital, rights to share in the capital of the body;

(c) in relation to a body without capital, interests—

(i) conferring any right to share in the profits, or liability to contribute to the losses, of the body, or

(ii) giving rise to an obligation to contribute to the debts or expenses of the body in the event of a winding up;

and references to the holding of shares, or to a shareholding, are to be construed accordingly.

Licensing

84 Application for licence

(1) A licensing authority [other than the Board] must determine any application for a licence which is made to it.

(2) The Board (acting in its capacity as a licensing authority) may determine an application for a licence which is made to it only if the applicant is entitled to make the application by virtue of a decision of the Board (acting otherwise than in its capacity as a licensing authority) under Schedule 12.

(3) A licensing authority may not grant an application for a licence unless it is satisfied that if the licence is granted the applicant will comply with its licensing rules.

(4) If the licensing authority grants an application for a licence, it must issue the licence as soon as reasonably practicable.

(5) The licence has effect from the date on which it is issued.

(6) References in this section to an application for a licence are to an application for a licence which is—

(a) made to a licensing authority by a licensable body, in accordance with the authority's licensing rules, and

(b) accompanied by the required application fee (if any).

85 Terms of licence

(1) A licence issued under section 84 must specify—

(a) the activities which are reserved legal activities and which the licensed body is authorised to carry on by virtue of the licence, and

(b) any conditions subject to which the licence is granted.

(2) If an order under section 106 has been made in relation to the licensed body, the licence must also specify the terms of the order.

(3) In the case of a licensing authority other than the Board, the licence may authorise the licensed body to carry on activities which are reserved legal activities only if the licensing authority is designated in relation to the reserved legal activities in question.

(4) A licence must be granted subject to the condition that—

(a) any obligation which may from time to time be imposed on the licensed body or a person within subsection (5) by or under the licensing authority's licensing rules is complied with, and

(b) any other obligations imposed on the licensed body or a person within that subsection by or under this or any other enactment (whether passed before or after this Act) are complied with.

(5) The persons mentioned in subsection (4) are the managers and employees of a licensed body, and non-authorised persons having an interest or an indirect interest, or holding a material interest, in the licensed body (in their capacity as such).

(6) A licence may be granted subject to such other conditions as the licensing authority considers appropriate.

(7) Those conditions may include conditions as to the non-reserved activities which the licensed body may or may not carry on.

(8) In this Part references to the terms of the licence are to the matters listed in subsections (1) and (2).

86 Modification of licence

(1) A licensing authority may modify the terms of a licence granted by it—

    (a)   if the licensed body applies to the licensing authority, in accordance with its licensing rules, for it to do so;

    (b)   in such other circumstances as may be specified in its licensing rules.

(2) If a licensed body is a body to which section 106 applies, the licensing authority may modify the terms of its licence in accordance with sections 106 and 107.

(3) A licensing authority modifies the terms of a licensed body's licence by giving the licensed body notice in writing of the modifications; and the modifications have effect from the time the licensing authority gives the licensed body the notice or such later time as may be specified in the notice.

(4) The licensing authority's power under this section is subject to—

    (a)   section 85(3) and (4), and

    (b)   licensing rules made under paragraph 6 of Schedule 11.

...

Regulation of licensed bodies

...

93 Information

(1) The relevant licensing authority in relation to a licensed body may by notice require a person within subsection (2)—

    (a)   to provide information, or information of a description, specified in the notice, or

    (b)   produce documents, or documents of a description, specified in the notice,

for the purpose of enabling the licensing authority to ascertain whether the terms of the licensed body's licence are being, or have been, complied with.

(2) The persons are—

    (a)   the licensed body;

    (b)   any manager or employee (or former manager or employee) of the licensed body;

    (c)   any non-authorised person who has an interest or an indirect interest, or holds a material interest, in the licensed body.

(3) A notice under subsection (1)—

    (a)   may specify the manner and form in which any information is to be provided;

    (b)   must specify the period within which the information is to be provided or the document produced;

    (c)   may require the information to be provided, or the document to be produced, to the licensing authority or to a person specified in the notice.

(4) The licensing authority may, by notice, require a person within subsection (2) (or a representative of such a person) to attend at a time and place specified in the notice to provide an explanation of any information provided or document produced under this section.

(5) The licensing authority may pay to any person such reasonable costs as may be incurred by that person in connection with—

(a)   the provision of any information, or production of any document, by that person pursuant to a notice under subsection (1), or

(b)   that person's compliance with a requirement imposed under subsection (4).

(6)   The licensing authority, or a person specified under subsection (3)(c) in a notice, may take copies of or extracts from a document produced pursuant to a notice under subsection (1).

(7)   For the purposes of this section and section 94, references to a licensed body include a body which was, but is no longer, a licensed body.

94   Enforcement of notices under section 93

(1)   Where a person is unable to comply with a notice given to the person under section 93, the person must give the licensing authority a notice to that effect stating the reasons why the person cannot comply.

(2)   If a person refuses or otherwise fails to comply with a notice under section 93, the licensing authority may apply to the High Court for an order requiring the person to comply with the notice or with such directions for the like purpose as may be contained in the order.

95   Financial penalties

(1)   A licensing authority may, in accordance with its licensing rules, impose on a licensed body, or a manager or employee of a licensed body, a penalty of such amount as it considers appropriate.

(2)   The amount must not exceed the maximum amount prescribed under subsection (3).

(3)   The Board must make rules prescribing the maximum amount of a penalty which may be imposed under this section.

(4)   Rules may be made under subsection (3) only with the consent of the Lord Chancellor.

(5)   A penalty under this section is payable to the licensing authority.

(6)   For the purposes of this section—

(a)   references to a licensed body are to a body which was a licensed body at the time the act or omission in respect of which the penalty is imposed occurred, and

(b)   references to a manager or employee of a licensed body are to a person who was a manager or employee of a licensed body at that time,

(whether or not the body subsequently ceased to be a licensed body or the person subsequently ceased to be a manager or employee).

(7)   In sections 96 and 97 references to a "penalty" are to a penalty under this section.

96   Appeals against financial penalties

(1)   A person on whom a penalty is imposed under section 95 may, before the end of such period as may be prescribed by rules made by the Board, appeal to the relevant appellate body on one or more of the appeal grounds.

(2)   The appeal grounds are—

(a)   that the imposition of the penalty is unreasonable in all the circumstances of the case;

(b)   that the amount of the penalty is unreasonable;

(c)   that it is unreasonable of the licensing authority to require the penalty imposed or any portion of it to be paid by the time or times by which it was required to be paid.

(3)   On any such appeal, where the relevant appellate body considers it appropriate to do so in all the circumstances of the case and is satisfied of one or more of the appeal grounds, that body may—

(a)   quash the penalty,

(b)   substitute a penalty of such lesser amount as it considers appropriate, or

(c)   in the case of the appeal ground in subsection (2)(c), substitute for any time imposed by the licensing authority a different time or times.

(4)   Where the relevant appellate body substitutes a penalty of a lesser amount it may require the payment of interest on the substituted penalty at such rate, and from such time, as it considers just and equitable.

(5)   Where the relevant appellate body specifies as a time by which the penalty, or a portion of the penalty, is to be paid a time before the determination of the appeal under this section it may require the payment of interest on the penalty, or portion, from that time at such rate as it considers just and equitable.

(6)   A party to the appeal may appeal to the High Court on a point of law arising from the decision of the relevant appellate body, but only with the permission of the High Court.

(7)   The High Court may make such order as it thinks fit.

(8)   Except as provided by this section, the validity of a penalty is not to be questioned by any legal proceedings whatever.

97   Recovery of financial penalties

(1)   If the whole or any part of a penalty is not paid by the time by which, in accordance with licensing rules, it is required to be paid, the unpaid balance from time to time carries interest at the rate for the time being specified in section 17 of the Judgments Act 1838 (c. 110).

(2)   Where a penalty, or any portion of it, has not been paid by the time by which, in accordance with licensing rules, it is required to be paid and—

(a)   no appeal relating to the penalty has been made under section 96 during the period within which such an appeal can be made, or

(b)   an appeal has been made under that section and determined or withdrawn,

the licensing authority may recover from the person on whom the penalty was imposed, as a debt due to the licensing authority, any of the penalty and any interest which has not been paid.

(3)   A licensing authority must pay into the Consolidated Fund any sum received by it as a penalty (or as interest on a penalty).

98   Referral of employees etc to appropriate regulator

(1)   The relevant licensing authority may refer to an appropriate regulator any matter relating to the conduct of—

(a)   an employee or manager of a licensed body;

(b)   a person designated as a licensed body's Head of Legal Practice or Head of Finance and Administration.

(2)   The licensing authority may also refer any matter relating to the conduct of such a person to the Board.

(3)   Appropriate regulators are—

(a)   if the person is an authorised person in relation to a reserved legal activity, any relevant approved regulator in relation to that person, and

(b)   if the person carries on non-reserved activities, any person who exercises regulatory functions in relation to the carrying on of such activities by the person.

99   Disqualification

(1)   A licensing authority may in accordance with its licensing rules disqualify a person from one or more of the activities mentioned in subsection (2) if—

(a)   the disqualification condition is satisfied in relation to the person, and

(b)   the licensing authority is satisfied that it is undesirable for the person to engage in that activity or those activities.

(2)   The activities are—

(a)   acting as Head of Legal Practice of any licensed body,

(b)   acting as Head of Finance and Administration of any licensed body,

(c)   being a manager of any licensed body, or

(d)   being employed by any licensed body.

(3)   The disqualification condition is satisfied in relation to a person if, in relation to a licensed body licensed by the licensing authority, the person (intentionally or through neglect)—

(a)   breaches a relevant duty to which the person is subject, or

(b)   causes, or substantially contributes to, a significant breach of the terms of the licensed body's licence.

(4)   The relevant duties are—

(a)   the duties imposed on a Head of Legal Practice by section 91,

(b)   the duties imposed on a Head of Finance and Administration by section 92,

(c)   the duties imposed by section 176 on regulated persons (within the meaning of that section), and

(d)   the duty imposed on non-authorised persons by section 90.

...

PART 6
LEGAL COMPLAINTS

Complaints procedures of authorised persons

112   Complaints procedures of authorised persons

(1)   The regulatory arrangements of an approved regulator must make provision requiring each relevant authorised person—

(a)   to establish and maintain procedures for the resolution of relevant complaints, or

(b)   to participate in, or make arrangements to be subject to, such procedures established and maintained by another person,

and provision for the enforcement of that requirement.

(2)   The provision made for the purposes of subsection (1) must satisfy such requirements as the Board may, from time to time, specify for the purposes of that subsection.

(3)   In this section—

"relevant authorised person", in relation to an approved regulator, means a person in relation to whom the approved regulator is a relevant approved regulator;

"relevant complaint", in relation to a relevant authorised person, means a complaint which—

(a)   relates to an act or omission of that person, and

(b)   may be made under the scheme provided for by this Part

(4)   The Board must publish any requirements specified by it for the purposes of subsection (2).

(5)   This section applies in relation to the licensing rules of the Board as it applies in relation to the regulatory arrangements of an approved regulator except that subsection (3) has effect as if for the definition of "relevant authorised person" there were substituted—

"'relevant authorised person', in relation to the Board, means a person licensed by the Board under Part 5;".

Overview of the scheme

113   Overview of the scheme

(1)   This Part provides for a scheme under which complaints which—

(a)   relate to an act or omission of a person ("the respondent") in carrying on an activity, and

(b)   are within the jurisdiction of the scheme (see section 125),

may be resolved quickly and with minimum formality by an independent person.

(2)   Under the scheme—

(a)   redress may be provided to the complainant, but

(b)   no disciplinary action may be taken against the respondent.

(3)   Section 157 prevents provision relating to redress being included in the regulatory arrangements of an approved regulator, or licensing rules made by the Board in its capacity as a licensing authority.

(4)   But neither the scheme nor any provision made by this Part affects any power of an approved regulator, or the Board in its capacity as a licensing authority, to take disciplinary action.

(5)   "Disciplinary action" means the imposition of sanctions, in respect of a breach of conduct rules or discipline rules, on a person who is an authorised person in relation to an activity which is a reserved legal activity.

Jurisdiction and operation of the ombudsman scheme

125   Jurisdiction of the ombudsman scheme

(1)   A complaint which relates to an act or omission of a person ("the respondent") in carrying on an activity is within the jurisdiction of the ombudsman scheme if—

(a)   the complaint is not excluded from the jurisdiction of the scheme by section 126, or by scheme rules made under section 127,

(b)   the respondent is within section 128, and

(c)   the complainant is within section 128 and wishes to have the complaint dealt with under the scheme.

(2) In subsection (1) references to an act or omission include an act or omission which occurs before the coming into force of this section.

(3) The right of a person to make a complaint under the ombudsman scheme, and the jurisdiction of an ombudsman to investigate, consider and determine a complaint, may not be limited or excluded by any contract term or by notice.

126 Complaints excluded because respondent's complaints procedures not used

(1) A complaint is excluded from the jurisdiction of the ombudsman scheme if the complainant has not first used the respondent's complaints procedures in relation to the complaint.

(2) The respondent's complaints procedures are the procedures established by the respondent, or which the respondent participates in or is subject to, in accordance with regulatory arrangements (or licensing rules of the Board) made in accordance with section 112.

(3) Scheme rules may provide that subsection (1) does not apply in specified circumstances.

127 Complaints excluded by scheme rules

(1) Scheme rules may make provision excluding complaints of a description specified in the rules from the jurisdiction of the ombudsman scheme.

(2) But they may not make provision excluding a complaint from the jurisdiction of the ombudsman scheme on the ground that it relates to a matter which has been or could be dealt with under the disciplinary arrangements of the respondent's relevant authorising body.

128 Parties

(1) The respondent is within this section if, at the relevant time, the respondent was an authorised person in relation to an activity which was a reserved legal activity (whether or not the act or omission relates to a reserved legal activity).

(2) The complainant ("C") is within this section if C—

(a) meets the first and second conditions, and

(b) is not excluded by subsection (5).

(3) The first condition is that C is—

(a) an individual, or

(b) a person (other than an individual) of a description prescribed by order made by the Lord Chancellor in accordance with a recommendation made under section 130.

(4) The second condition is that—

(a) the services to which the complaint relates were provided by the respondent to C;

(b) the services to which the complaint relates were provided by the respondent to an authorised person who procured them on C's behalf;

(c) the services to which the complaint relates were provided by the respondent—

(i) in the respondent's capacity as a personal representative or trustee, or

(ii) to a person acting as a personal representative or trustee,

and C is a beneficiary of the estate or trust in question; or

(d) C satisfies such other conditions, in relation to the services to which the complaint relates, as may be prescribed by order made by the Lord Chancellor in accordance with a recommendation made under section 130.

(5) C is excluded if, at the relevant time—

(a)   C was an authorised person in relation to an activity which was a reserved legal activity and the services to which the complaint relates were procured by C on behalf of another person,

(b)   C was a public body or was acting on behalf of such a body in relation to the services to which the complaint relates, or

(c)   C was a person prescribed, or of a description prescribed, as excluded by order made by the Lord Chancellor in accordance with a recommendation made under section 130.

(6) In subsection (4)(b) "authorised person" means an authorised person in relation to any activity which is a reserved legal activity.

(7) In this section—

"public body" means any government department, local authority or other body constituted for purposes of the public services, local government or the administration of justice;

"relevant time", in relation to a complaint, means the time when the act or omission to which the complaint relates took place.

129 Pre-commencement acts and omissions

(1) For the purposes of section 128 a person is to be regarded as an authorised person in relation to an activity which is a reserved legal activity, at a time before section 125 comes into force, if the person was at that time—

(a)   a person of the kind mentioned in paragraph 2(4) of Schedule 15,

(b)   a body recognised under section 9 or 32 of the Administration of Justice Act 1985 (c. 61) (recognised bodies), or

(c)   a legal partnership, a conveyancing partnership, a patent attorney body or a trade mark attorney body.

(2) In this section—

"conveyancing partnership" has the meaning given by paragraph 11(5) of Schedule 5;

"legal partnership" has the meaning given by paragraph 7(4) of that Schedule;

"patent attorney body" has the meaning given by paragraph 14(7) of that Schedule;

"trade mark attorney body" has the meaning given by paragraph 16(7) of that Schedule.

130 Orders under section 128

(1) An interested body may, at any time, recommend to the Lord Chancellor that the Lord Chancellor make an order under section 128(3)(b), (4)(d) or (5)(c).

(2) An interested body must, if requested to do so by the Lord Chancellor, consider whether or not it is appropriate to make a recommendation under subsection (1).

(3) An interested body must, before making a recommendation under subsection (1)—

(a)   publish a draft of the proposed recommendation,

(b)   invite representations regarding the proposed recommendation, and

(c)   consider any such representations which are made.

(4) Where the Lord Chancellor receives a recommendation under subsection (1), the Lord Chancellor must consider whether to follow the recommendation.

(5)   If the Lord Chancellor decides not to follow the recommendation, the Lord Chancellor must publish a notice to that effect which includes the Lord Chancellor's reasons for the decision.

(6)   In this section "interested body" means—

    (a)   the OLC,

    (b)   the Board, or

    (c)   the Consumer Panel.

131   Acts and omissions by employees etc

(1)   For the purposes of this Part and the ombudsman scheme, any act or omission by a person in the course of the person's employment is to be treated as also an act or omission by the person's employer, whether or not it was done with the employer's knowledge or approval.

(2)   For the purposes of this Part and the ombudsman scheme, any act or omission by a partner in a partnership in the course of carrying on, in the usual way, business of the kind carried on by the partnership is to be treated as also an act or omission by the partnership.

(3)   But subsection (2) does not apply if the partner had no authority to act for the partnership and the person purporting to rely on that subsection knew, at the time of the act or omission, that the partner had no such authority.

132   Continuity of complaints

(1)   The ability of a person to make a complaint about an act or omission of a partnership or other unincorporated body is not affected by any change in the membership of the partnership or body.

(2)   Scheme rules must make provision determining the circumstances in which, for the purposes of the ombudsman scheme, an act or omission of a person ("A") is, where A ceases to exist and another person ("B") succeeds to the whole or substantially the whole of the business of A, to be treated as an act or omission of B.

(3)   Rules under subsection (2) must, in relation to cases where an act or omission of A is treated as an act or omission of B, make provision about the treatment of complaints under the ombudsman scheme which are outstanding against A at the time A ceases to exist.

(4)   Scheme rules must make provision permitting such persons as may be specified in the rules to continue a complaint made by a person who has died or is otherwise unable to act; and for that purpose may modify references to the complainant in this Part and in scheme rules.

133   Operation of the ombudsman scheme

(1)   Scheme rules must set out the procedure for—

    (a)   the making of complaints under the ombudsman scheme, and

    (b)   the investigation, consideration and determination of complaints by an ombudsman.

(2)   Scheme rules—

    (a)   must provide that a complaint is to be entertained under the ombudsman scheme only if the complainant has made the complaint under that scheme before the applicable time limit (determined in accordance with the scheme rules) has expired, and

    (b)   may provide that an ombudsman may extend that time limit in specified circumstances.

(3)   Scheme rules made under subsection (1) may (among other things) make provision—

(a)   for the whole or part of a complaint to be dismissed, in specified circumstances, without consideration of its merits;

(b)   for the reference of a complaint, in specified circumstances and with the consent of the complainant, to another body with a view to it being determined by that body instead of by an ombudsman;

(c)   for a person who, at the relevant time (within the meaning of section 128(7)) was an authorised person in relation to an activity to be treated in specified circumstances, for the purposes of the scheme and this Part, as if that person were a co-respondent in relation to a complaint;

(d)   about the evidence which may be required or admitted and the extent to which it should be oral or written;

(e)   for requiring parties to the complaint to attend to give evidence and produce documents, and for authorising the administration of oaths by ombudsmen;

(f)   about the matters which are to be taken into account in determining whether an act or omission was fair and reasonable;

(g)   for an ombudsman, in such circumstances as may be specified, to award expenses to persons in connection with attendance at a hearing before an ombudsman;

(h)   for an ombudsman to award costs against the respondent in favour of the complainant;

(i)   for an ombudsman to award costs against the complainant or the respondent in favour of the OLC for the purpose of providing a contribution to resources deployed in dealing with the complaint, if in the ombudsman's opinion that person acted so unreasonably in relation to the complaint that it is appropriate in all the circumstances of the case to make such an award;

(j)   for the purpose of facilitating the settlement of a complaint with the agreement of the parties to it;

(k)   for specified persons to be notified of complaints, determinations and directions under the ombudsman scheme.

(4)   The circumstances specified under subsection (3)(a) may include the following—

(a)   the ombudsman considers the complaint or part to be frivolous or vexatious or totally without merit;

(b)   the ombudsman considers that the complaint or part would be better dealt with under another ombudsman scheme, by arbitration or by other legal proceedings;

(c)   the ombudsman considers that there has been undue delay in the making of the complaint or part, or the provision of evidence to support it;

(d)   the ombudsman is satisfied that the matter which is the subject of the complaint or part has previously been dealt with under another ombudsman scheme, by arbitration or by other legal proceedings;

(e)   the ombudsman considers that there are other compelling reasons why it is inappropriate for the complaint or part to be dealt with under the ombudsman scheme.

(5)   No person may be required by scheme rules—

(a)   to provide any information or give any evidence which that person could not be compelled to provide or give in evidence in civil proceedings before the High Court, or

(b) to produce any document which that person could not be compelled to produce in such proceedings.

(6) Scheme rules may authorise an ombudsman making an award of costs in accordance with rules within subsection (3)(h) or (i) to order that the amount payable under the award bears interest, from a time specified in or determined in accordance with the order, at a rate specified in or determined in accordance with the rules.

(7) An amount due under an award made in favour of a person by virtue of provision made under subsection (3)(g), (h) or (i) is recoverable as a debt due to that person.

(8) In this section—

"party", in relation to a complaint, means—

(a) the complainant,

(b) the respondent, and

(c) any other person who in accordance with scheme rules is to be regarded as a party to the complaint;

"specified" means specified in scheme rules.

134 Delegation of an ombudsman's functions

(1) An ombudsman may delegate to a member of the OLC's staff appointed under paragraph 13 of Schedule 15—

(a) any function of the ombudsman in relation to the making, investigation or consideration of a complaint;

(b) any other function conferred on the ombudsman by or by virtue of this Part.

(2) Nothing in subsection (1) applies to the following functions—

(a) the function of determining a complaint;

(b) the function of deciding that a complaint should be dismissed by virtue of rules under section 133(3)(a);

(c) the Chief Ombudsman's power to consent to the appointment of an assistant ombudsman under section 122;

(d) the duties imposed on the Chief Ombudsman by section 123 (Chief Ombudsman's report).

135 Notification requirements

(1) This section applies where a complaint—

(a) is excluded from the jurisdiction of the ombudsman scheme under section 126, or by virtue of scheme rules made under section 127;

(b) is dismissed, or referred to another body, by virtue of scheme rules;

(c) is settled, withdrawn or abandoned (or treated as withdrawn or abandoned by virtue of scheme rules).

(2) The ombudsman must notify—

(a) the complainant;

(b) the respondent;

(c) any relevant authorising body, in relation to the respondent, notified of the complaint in accordance with rules within section 133(3)(k), and, in a case within subsection (1)(a) or (b), must give reasons for the exclusion, dismissal or referral.

136 Charges payable by respondents

(1)   Scheme rules must require respondents, in relation to complaints under the ombudsman scheme, to pay to the OLC such charges as may be specified in the rules.

(2)   The rules must provide for charges payable in relation to a complaint to be waived (or wholly refunded) where—

(a)   the complaint is determined or otherwise resolved in favour of the respondent, and

(b)   the ombudsman is satisfied that the respondent took all reasonable steps to try to resolve the complaint under the respondent's complaints procedures.

(3)   The rules may make provision as to—

(a)   the circumstances in which a complaint is to be treated as determined or otherwise resolved in favour of the respondent (which may include circumstances where a complaint is settled, withdrawn or abandoned (or treated as withdrawn or abandoned by virtue of scheme rules));

(b)   matters to be taken into account by the ombudsman for the purposes of subsection (2)(b).

(4)   The respondent's complaints procedures are the procedures established by the respondent, or which the respondent participates in or is subject to, in accordance with regulatory arrangements (or licensing rules of the Board) made in accordance with section 112.

(5)   The rules may, among other things—

(a)   provide for the OLC to reduce or waive a charge in such other circumstances as may be specified;

(b)   set different charges for different stages of the proceedings on a complaint;

(c)   provide for charges to be wholly or partly refunded in such other circumstances as may be specified;

(d)   provide that if the whole or any part of a charge is not paid by the time by which it is required to be paid under the rules, the unpaid balance from time to time carries interest at the rate specified in, or determined in accordance with, the rules.

(6)   Any charge which is owed to the OLC by virtue of rules made under this section may be recovered as a debt due to the OLC.

Determinations under the scheme

137 Determination of complaints

(1)   A complaint is to be determined under the ombudsman scheme by reference to what is, in the opinion of the ombudsman making the determination, fair and reasonable in all the circumstances of the case.

(2)   The determination may contain one or more of the following—

(a)   a direction that the respondent make an apology to the complainant;

(b)   a direction that—

(i)   the fees to which the respondent is entitled in respect of the services to which the complaint relates ("the fees") are limited to such amount as may be specified in the direction, and

(ii)   the respondent comply, or secure compliance, with such one or more of the permitted requirements as appear to the ombudsman to be necessary in order for effect to be given to the direction under sub-paragraph (i);

(c)   a direction that the respondent pay compensation to the complainant of such an amount as is specified in the direction in respect of any loss which has been suffered by, or any inconvenience or distress which has been caused to, the complainant as a result of any matter connected with the complaint;

(d)   a direction that the respondent secure the rectification, at the expense of the respondent, of any such error, omission or other deficiency arising in connection with the matter in question as the direction may specify;

(e)   a direction that the respondent take, at the expense of the respondent, such other action in the interests of the complainant as the direction may specify.

(3)   For the purposes of subsection (2)(b) "the permitted requirements" are—

(a)   that the whole or part of any amount already paid by or on behalf of the complainant in respect of the fees be refunded;

(b)   that the whole or part of the fees be remitted;

(c)   that the right to recover the fees be waived, whether wholly or to any specified extent.

(4)   Where—

(a)   a direction is made under subsection (2)(b) which requires that the whole or part of any amount already paid by or on behalf of the complainant in respect of the fees be refunded, or

(b)   a direction is made under subsection (2)(c),

the direction may also provide for the amount payable under the direction to carry interest from a time specified in or determined in accordance with the direction, at the rate specified in or determined in accordance with scheme rules.

(5)   The power of the ombudsman to make a direction under subsection (2) is not confined to cases where the complainant may have a cause of action against the respondent for negligence.

138 Limitation on value of directions under the ombudsman scheme

(1)   Where a determination is made under the ombudsman scheme in respect of a complaint, the total value of directions under section 137(2)(c) to (e) contained in the determination must not exceed £50,000.

(2)   For this purpose the total value of such directions is the aggregate of—

(a)   the amount of any compensation specified in a direction under subsection (2)(c) of section 137, and

(b)   the amount of any expenses reasonably incurred by the respondent when complying with a direction under subsection (2)(d) or (e) of that section.

(3)   For the purposes of determining that total value, any interest payable on an amount within subsection (2)(a) of this section, by virtue of section 137(4), is to be ignored.

139 Alteration of limit

(1)   The Lord Chancellor may by order amend section 138(1) in accordance with a recommendation made by an interested body under subsection (2).

(2)   An interested body may, at any time, recommend to the Lord Chancellor that section 138(1) should be amended so as to substitute the amount specified in the recommendation for the amount for the time being specified in that provision.

(3) An interested body must, if requested to do so by the Lord Chancellor, consider whether or not it is appropriate to make a recommendation under subsection (2).

(4) An interested body must, before making a recommendation under subsection (2)—

    (a)   publish a draft of the proposed recommendation,

    (b)   invite representations regarding the proposed recommendation, and

    (c)   consider any such representations which are made.

(5) Where the Lord Chancellor receives a recommendation under subsection (2), the Lord Chancellor must consider whether to follow the recommendation.

(6) If the Lord Chancellor decides not to follow the recommendation, the Lord Chancellor must publish a notice to that effect which includes the Lord Chancellor's reasons for the decision.

(7) In this section "interested body" means—

    (a)   the OLC,

    (b)   the Board, or

    (c)   the Consumer Panel.

140 Acceptance or rejection of determination

(1) When an ombudsman has determined a complaint the ombudsman must prepare a written statement of the determination.

(2) The statement must—

    (a)   give the ombudsman's reasons for the determination,

    (b)   be signed by the ombudsman, and

    (c)   require the complainant to notify the ombudsman, before a time specified in the statement ("the specified time"), whether the complainant accepts or rejects the determination.

(3) The ombudsman must give a copy of the statement to—

    (a)   the complainant,

    (b)   the respondent, and

    (c)   any relevant authorising body in relation to the respondent.

(4) If the complainant notifies the ombudsman that the determination is accepted by the complainant, it is binding on the respondent and the complainant and is final.

(5) If, by the specified time, the complainant has not notified the ombudsman of the complainant's acceptance or rejection of the determination, the complainant is to be treated as having rejected it.

(6) But if—

    (a)   the complainant notifies the ombudsman after the specified time that the determination is accepted by the complainant,

    (b)   the complainant has not previously notified the ombudsman of the complainant's rejection of the determination, and

    (c)   the ombudsman is satisfied that such conditions as may be prescribed by the scheme rules for the purposes of this subsection are satisfied,

the determination is treated as if it had never been rejected by virtue of subsection (5).

(7)   The ombudsman must give notice of the outcome to—

(a)   the complainant,

(b)   the respondent, and

(c)   any relevant authorising body in relation to the respondent.

(8)   Where a determination is rejected by virtue of subsection (5), that notice must contain a general description of the effect of subsection (6).

(9)   A copy of the determination on which appears a certificate signed by an ombudsman is evidence that the determination was made under the scheme.

(10)   Such a certificate purporting to be signed by an ombudsman is to be taken to have been duly signed unless the contrary is shown.

(11)   Neither the complainant nor the respondent, in relation to a complaint, may institute or continue legal proceedings in respect of a matter which was the subject of a complaint, after the time when a determination by an ombudsman of the complaint becomes binding and final in accordance with this section.

141   Enforcement by complainant of directions under section 137

(1)   This section applies where—

(a)   a determination is made in respect of a complaint under the ombudsman scheme,

(b)   one or more directions are made under section 137(2), and

(c)   the determination is final by virtue of section 140(4).

(2)   An amount payable in accordance with—

(a)   a direction under subsection (2)(b) of section 137 which requires that the whole or part of any amount already paid by or on behalf of the complainant in respect of the fees be refunded, or

(b)   a direction under subsection (2)(c) of that section,

including any interest payable by virtue of subsection (4) of that section, is recoverable, if a court so orders on the application of the complainant or an ombudsman, as if it were payable under an order of that court.

(3)   If the respondent fails to comply with any other direction under section 137(2), the complainant or an ombudsman may make an application to the court under this subsection.

(4)   If, on an application under subsection (3), the court decides that the respondent has failed to comply with the direction in question, it may order the respondent to take such steps as the court directs for securing that the direction is complied with.

(5)   An ombudsman may make an application under subsection (2) or (3) only in such circumstances as may be specified in scheme rules, and with the complainant's consent.

(6)   If the court makes an order under subsection (2) on the application of an ombudsman, the ombudsman may in such circumstances as may be specified in scheme rules and with the complainant's consent recover the amount mentioned in that subsection on behalf of the complainant.

(7)   In this section "court" means the High Court or the county court.

142   Reporting court orders made against authorised persons

(1)   Where a court makes an order under section 141, it must give the OLC notice to that effect.

(2)   Where the order is made against a person who is an authorised person in relation to any activity which is a reserved legal activity, the OLC must make arrangements to ensure that an ombudsman gives to each relevant authorising body, in relation to that person, a report which states that the order has been made.

(3)   A report under subsection (2) may require the relevant authorising body to report to the ombudsman the action which has been or is to be taken by it in response to the report under subsection (2) and the reasons for that action being taken.

(4)   If an ombudsman, having regard to any report produced by the relevant authorising body in compliance with a requirement imposed under subsection (3), or any failure to comply with such a requirement, considers—

(a)   that there has been a serious failure by the relevant authorising body to discharge its regulatory functions, or

(b)   if such a requirement has been imposed on the body on more than one occasion, that the relevant authorising body has persistently failed adequately to discharge its regulatory functions,

the ombudsman may make a report to that effect to the Board.

Reporting misconduct

143   Reporting possible misconduct to approved regulators

(1)   This section applies where—

(a)   an ombudsman is dealing, or has dealt, with a complaint under the ombudsman scheme, and

(b)   the ombudsman is of the opinion that the conduct of the respondent or any other person in relation to any matter connected with the complaint is such that a relevant authorising body in relation to that person should consider whether to take action against that person.

(2)   The ombudsman must give the relevant authorising body a report which—

(a)   states that the ombudsman is of that opinion, and

(b)   gives details of that conduct.

(3)   The ombudsman must give the complainant a notice stating that a report under subsection (2) has been given to the relevant authorising body.

(4)   A report under subsection (2) may require the relevant authorising body to report to the ombudsman the action which has been or is to be taken by it in response to the report and the reasons for that action being taken.

(5)   The duty imposed by subsection (2) is not affected by the withdrawal or abandonment of the complaint.

(6)   If an ombudsman, having regard to any report produced by the relevant authorising body in compliance with a requirement imposed under subsection (4), or any failure to comply with such a requirement, considers—

(a)   that there has been a serious failure by the relevant authorising body to discharge its regulatory functions, or

(b)   if such a requirement has been imposed on the body on more than one occasion, that the relevant authorising body has persistently failed adequately to discharge its regulatory functions,

the ombudsman may make a report to that effect to the Board.

Co-operation with investigations

144 Duties to share information

(1) Scheme rules must make provision requiring persons within subsection (3) to disclose to an approved regulator information of such description as may be specified in the rules, in such circumstances as may be so specified.

(2) The regulatory arrangements of an approved regulator must make provision requiring the approved regulator to disclose to persons within subsection (3) information of such description as may be specified in the arrangements, in such circumstances as may be so specified.

(3) The persons are—

   (a)   the OLC;

   (b)   an ombudsman;

   (c)   a member of the OLC's staff appointed under paragraph 13 of Schedule 15.

(4) Provision made under subsection (1) or (2) must satisfy such requirements as the Board may, from time to time, specify.

(5) In specifying requirements under subsection (4) the Board must have regard to the need to ensure that, so far as reasonably practicable—

   (a)   duplication of investigations is avoided;

   (b)   the OLC assists approved regulators to carry out their regulatory functions, and approved regulators assist with the investigation, consideration and determination of complaints under the ombudsman scheme.

(6) The Board must publish any requirements specified by it under subsection (4).

(7) The OLC must—

   (a)   before publishing under section 205(2) a draft of rules it proposes to make under subsection (1), consult each approved regulator to which the proposed rules apply, and

   (b)   when seeking the Board's consent to such rules under section 155, identify any objections made by an approved regulator to the rules and not withdrawn.

(8) An approved regulator must—

   (a)   consult the OLC before making provisions in its regulatory arrangements of the kind mentioned in subsection (2), and

   (b)   where an application is made for the Board's approval of such provisions, identify any objections made by the OLC to the provisions and not withdrawn.

(9) [*repealed*]

145 Duties of authorised persons to co-operate with investigations

(1) The regulatory arrangements of an approved regulator must make—

   (a)   provision requiring each relevant authorised person to give ombudsmen all such assistance requested by them, in connection with the investigation, consideration or determination of complaints under the ombudsman scheme, as that person is reasonably able to give, and

   (b)   provision for the enforcement of that requirement.

(2) The provision made for the purposes of subsection (1) must satisfy such requirements as the Board may, from time to time, specify for the purposes of that subsection.

(3)   The Board must publish any requirements specified by it under subsection (2).

(4)   In this section "relevant authorised person"—

(a)   in relation to an approved regulator, has the same meaning as in section 112, and

(b)   [*repealed*].

146   Reporting failures to co-operate with an investigation to approved regulators

(1)   This section applies where an ombudsman is of the opinion that an authorised person has failed to give an ombudsman all such assistance requested by the ombudsman, in connection with the investigation, consideration or determination of a complaint under the ombudsman scheme, as that person is reasonably able to give.

(2)   The ombudsman must give each relevant authorising body, in relation to that person, a report which—

(a)   states that the ombudsman is of that opinion, and

(b)   gives details of the failure.

(3)   A report under subsection (2) may require the relevant authorising body to report to the ombudsman the action which has been or is to be taken by it in response to the report under that subsection and the reasons for that action being taken.

(4)   The duty imposed by subsection (2) is not affected by the withdrawal or abandonment of the complaint.

(5)   If an ombudsman, having regard to any report produced by the relevant authorising body in compliance with a requirement imposed under subsection (3), or any failure to comply with such a requirement, considers—

(a)   that there has been a serious failure by the relevant authorising body to discharge its regulatory functions, or

(b)   if such a requirement has been imposed on the body on more than one occasion, that the relevant authorising body has persistently failed adequately to discharge its regulatory functions,

the ombudsman may make a report to that effect to the Board.

(6)   In this section "authorised person" means an authorised person in relation to any activity which is a reserved legal activity.

Information

147   Information and documents

(1)   An ombudsman may, by notice, require a party to a complaint under the ombudsman scheme—

(a)   to produce documents, or documents of a description, specified in the notice, or

(b)   to provide information, or information of a description, specified in the notice.

(2)   A notice under subsection (1) may require the information or documents to be provided or produced—

(a)   before the end of such reasonable period as may be specified in the notice, and

(b)   in the case of information, in such manner or form as may be so specified.

(3)   This section applies only to information and documents the provision or production of which the ombudsman considers necessary for the determination of the complaint.

(4) An ombudsman may—

(a) take copies of or extracts from a document produced under this section, and

(b) [*repealed*]

(5) If a person who is required under this section to produce a document fails to do so, an ombudsman may require that person to state, to the best of that person's knowledge and belief, where the document is.

(6) No person may be required under this section—

(a) to provide any information which that person could not be compelled to provide or give in evidence in civil proceedings before the High Court, or

(b) to produce any document which that person could not be compelled to produce in such proceedings.

(7) In this section "party", in relation to a complaint, means—

(a) the complainant;

(b) the respondent;

(c) any other person who in accordance with the scheme rules is to be regarded as a party to the complaint.

148 Reporting failures to provide information or produce documents

(1) This section applies where an ombudsman is of the opinion that an authorised person has failed to comply with a requirement imposed under section 147(1).

(2) The ombudsman must give each relevant authorising body, in relation to that person, a report which—

(a) states that the ombudsman is of that opinion, and

(b) gives details of the failure.

(3) A report under subsection (2) may require the relevant authorising body to report to the ombudsman the action which has been or is to be taken by it in response to the report under that subsection and the reasons for that action being taken.

(4) The duty imposed by subsection (2) is not affected by the withdrawal or abandonment of the complaint in relation to which the requirement was imposed under section 147(1).

(5) If an ombudsman, having regard to any report produced by the relevant authorising body in compliance with a requirement imposed under subsection (3), or any failure to comply with such a requirement, considers—

(a) that there has been a serious failure by the relevant authorising body to discharge its regulatory functions, or

(b) if such a requirement has been imposed on the body on more than one occasion, that the relevant authorising body has persistently failed adequately to discharge its regulatory functions,

the ombudsman may make a report to that effect to the Board.

(6) In this section "authorised person" means an authorised person in relation to any activity which is a reserved legal activity.

149 Enforcement of requirements to provide information or produce documents

(1) This section applies where an ombudsman is of the opinion that a person ("the defaulter") has failed to comply with a requirement imposed under section 147(1).

(2) The ombudsman may certify the defaulter's failure to comply with the requirement to the court.

(3) Where an ombudsman certifies a failure to the court under subsection (2), the court may enquire into the case.

(4) If the court is satisfied that the defaulter has failed without reasonable excuse to comply with the requirement, it may deal with—

(a)   the defaulter, and

(b)   in the case of a body, any manager of the body,

as if that person were in contempt.

(5) Subsection (6) applies in a case where the defaulter is an authorised person in relation to any activity which is a reserved legal activity.

(6) The ombudsman ("the enforcing ombudsman") may not certify the defaulter's failure to the court until a report by that or another ombudsman has been made as required by section 148(2) and the enforcing ombudsman is satisfied—

(a)   that each relevant authorising body to whom such a report was made has been given a reasonable opportunity to take action in respect of the defaulter's failure, and

(b)   that the defaulter has continued to fail to provide the information or produce the documents to which the requirement under section 147 related.

(7) In this section "court" means the High Court.

150   Reports of investigations

(1) The OLC may, if it considers it appropriate to do so in any particular case, publish a report of the investigation, consideration and determination of a complaint made under the ombudsman scheme.

(2) A report under subsection (1) must not (unless the complainant consents)—

(a)   mention the name of the complainant, or

(b)   include any particulars which, in the opinion of the OLC, are likely to identify the complainant.

151   Restricted information

(1) Except as provided by section 152, restricted information must not be disclosed—

(a)   by a restricted person, or

(b)   by any person who receives the information directly or indirectly from a restricted person.

(2) In this section and section 152—

"restricted information" means information (other than excluded information) which is obtained by a restricted person in the course of, or for the purposes of, an investigation into a complaint made under the ombudsman scheme (including information obtained for the purposes of deciding whether to begin such an investigation or in connection with the settlement of a complaint);

"restricted person" means—

(a)   the OLC,

(b)   an ombudsman, or

(c)   a person who exercises functions delegated under paragraph 22 of Schedule 15.

(3) For the purposes of subsection (2) "excluded information" means—

(a) information which is in the form of a summary or collection of information so framed as not to enable information relating to any particular person to be ascertained from it;

(b) information which at the time of the disclosure is or has already been made available to the public from other sources;

(c) information which was obtained more than 70 years before the date of the disclosure.

152 Disclosure of restricted information

(1) A restricted person may disclose restricted information to another restricted person.

(2) Restricted information may be disclosed for the purposes of the investigation in the course of which, or for the purposes of which, it was obtained.

(3) Section 151 also does not preclude the disclosure of restricted information—

(a) in a report made under—

(i) section 143(2) (report of possible misconduct to approved regulators),

(ii) section 146(2) (report of failure to co-operate with investigation),

(iii) section 148 (reporting failures to provide information or produce documents), or

(iv) section 150 (reports of investigations),

(b) for the purposes of enabling or assisting the Board to exercise any of its functions,

(c) to an approved regulator for the purposes of enabling or assisting the approved regulator to exercise any of its regulatory functions,

(d) with the consent of the person to whom it relates and (if different) the person from whom the restricted person obtained it,

(e) for the purposes of an inquiry with a view to the taking of any criminal proceedings or for the purposes of any such proceedings,

(f) where the disclosure is required by or by virtue of any provision made by or under this Act or any other enactment or other rule of law,

(g) to such persons (other than approved regulators) who exercise regulatory functions as may be prescribed by order made by the Lord Chancellor, for such purposes as may be so prescribed.

(4) Subsections (2) and (3) are subject to subsection (5).

(5) The Lord Chancellor may by order prevent the disclosure of restricted information by virtue of subsection (2) or (3) in such circumstances, or for such purposes, as may be prescribed in the order.

153 Data protection

In section 31 of the Data Protection Act 1998 (c. 29) (regulatory activity), after subsection (4B) (inserted by section 170) insert—

"(4C) Personal data processed for the purposes of the function of considering a complaint under the scheme established under Part 6 of the Legal Services Act 2007 (legal complaints) are exempt from the subject information provisions in any case to the extent to which the application of those provisions to the data would be likely to prejudice the proper discharge of the function."

Defamation

154 Protection from defamation claims

For the purposes of the law of defamation—

(a) proceedings in relation to a complaint under the ombudsman scheme are to be treated as if they were proceedings before a court, and

(b) the publication of any matter by the OLC under this Part is absolutely privileged.

PART 8
MISCELLANEOUS PROVISIONS ABOUT LAWYERS ETC

Duties of regulated persons

176 Duties of regulated persons

(1) A person who is a regulated person in relation to an approved regulator has a duty to comply with the regulatory arrangements of the approved regulator as they apply to that person.

(2) A person is a regulated person in relation to an approved regulator if the person—

(a) is authorised by the approved regulator to carry on an activity which is a reserved legal activity, or

(b) is not so authorised, but is a manager or employee of a person who is so authorised.

(3) This section applies in relation to the Board in its capacity as a licensing authority and its licensing rules, as it applies in relation to an approved regulator and its regulatory arrangements.

SCHEDULE 2
The reserved legal activities

Section 12

Introduction

1 This Schedule makes provision about the reserved legal activities.

2 In this Schedule "the appointed day" means the day appointed for the coming into force of section 13 (entitlement to carry on reserved legal activities).

Rights of audience

3 (1) A "right of audience" means the right to appear before and address a court, including the right to call and examine witnesses.

(2) But a "right of audience" does not include a right to appear before or address a court, or to call or examine witnesses, in relation to any particular court or in relation to particular proceedings, if immediately before the appointed day no restriction was placed on the persons entitled to exercise that right.

Conduct of litigation

4 (1) The "conduct of litigation" means—

(a) the issuing of proceedings before any court in England and Wales,

(b) the commencement, prosecution and defence of such proceedings, and

(c)   the performance of any ancillary functions in relation to such proceedings (such as entering appearances to actions).

(2)   But the "conduct of litigation" does not include any activity within paragraphs (a) to (c) of sub-paragraph (1), in relation to any particular court or in relation to any particular proceedings, if immediately before the appointed day no restriction was placed on the persons entitled to carry on that activity.

Reserved instrument activities

5 (1)   "Reserved instrument activities" means—

(a)   preparing any instrument of transfer or charge for the purposes of the Land Registration Act 2002 (c 9);

(b)   making an application or lodging a document for registration under that Act;

(c)   preparing any other instrument relating to real or personal estate for the purposes of the law of England and Wales or instrument relating to court proceedings in England and Wales.

(2)   But "reserved instrument activities" does not include the preparation of an instrument relating to any particular court proceedings if, immediately before the appointed day, no restriction was placed on the persons entitled to carry on that activity.

(3)   In this paragraph "instrument" includes a contract for the sale or other disposition of land (except a contract to grant a short lease), but does not include—

(a)   a will or other testamentary instrument,

(b)   an agreement not intended to be executed as a deed, other than a contract that is included by virtue of the preceding provisions of this sub-paragraph,

(c)   a letter or power of attorney, or

(d)   a transfer of stock containing no trust or limitation of the transfer.

(4)   In this paragraph a "short lease" means a lease such as is referred to in section 54(2) of the Law of Property Act 1925 (c 20) (short leases).

Probate activities

6 (1)   "Probate activities" means preparing any probate papers for the purposes of the law of England and Wales or in relation to any proceedings in England and Wales.

(2)   In this paragraph "probate papers" means papers on which to found or oppose—

(a)   a grant of probate, or

(b)   a grant of letters of administration.

Notarial activities

7 (1)   "Notarial activities" means activities which, immediately before the appointed day, were customarily carried on by virtue of enrolment as a notary in accordance with section 1 of the Public Notaries Act 1801 (c 79).

(2)   Sub-paragraph (1) does not include activities carried on—

(a)   by virtue of section 22 or 23 of the Solicitors Act 1974 (c 47) (reserved instrument activities and probate activities), or

(b)   by virtue of section 113 of the Courts and Legal Services Act 1990 (c 41) (administration of oaths).

Administration of oaths

8 The "administration of oaths" means the exercise of the powers conferred on a commissioner for oaths by—

    (a)   the Commissioners for Oaths Act 1889 (c 10);

    (b)   the Commissioners for Oaths Act 1891 (c 50);

    (c)   section 24 of the Stamp Duties Management Act 1891 (c 38).

SCHEDULE 3
Exempt persons

                                                  Section 19

Rights of audience

1 (1)   This paragraph applies to determine whether a person is an exempt person for the purpose of exercising a right of audience before a court in relation to any proceedings (subject to paragraph 7).

(2)   The person is exempt if the person—

    (a)   is not an authorised person in relation to that activity, but

    (b)   has a right of audience granted by that court in relation to those proceedings.

(3)   The person is exempt if the person—

    (a)   is not an authorised person in relation to that activity, but

    (b)   has a right of audience before that court in relation to those proceedings granted by or under any enactment.

(4)   The person is exempt if the person is the Attorney General or the Solicitor General and—

    (a)   the name of the person is on the roll kept by the Law Society under section 6 of the Solicitors Act 1974 (c 47), or

    (b)   the person has been called to the Bar by an Inn of Court.

(5)   The person is exempt if the person is the Advocate General for Scotland and is admitted—

    (a)   as a solicitor in Scotland under section 6 of the Solicitors (Scotland) Act 1980 (c 46), or

    (b)   to practise as an advocate before the courts of Scotland.

(6)   The person is exempt if the person—

    (a)   is a party to those proceedings, and

    (b)   would have a right of audience, in the person's capacity as such a party, if this Act had not been passed.

(7)   The person is exempt if—

    (a)   the person is an individual whose work includes assisting in the conduct of litigation,

    (b)   the person is assisting in the conduct of litigation—

        (i)   under instructions given (either generally or in relation to the proceedings) by an individual to whom sub-paragraph (8) applies, and

(ii) under the supervision of that individual, and

(c) the proceedings are not reserved family proceedings and are being heard in chambers—

(i) in the High Court or county court, or

(ii) in the family court by a judge who is not, or by two or more judges at least one of whom is not, within section 31C(1)(y) of the Matrimonial and Family Proceedings Act 1984 (lay justices)]

(8) This sub-paragraph applies to—

(a) any authorised person in relation to an activity which constitutes the conduct of litigation;

(b) any person who by virtue of section 193 is not required to be entitled to carry on such an activity.

(9) The person is an exempt person in relation to the exercise of a right of audience in proceedings on an appeal from the Comptroller-General of Patents, Designs and Trade Marks to the Patents Court under the Patents Act 1977 (c 37), if the person is a solicitor of the Court of Judicature of Northern Ireland.

(10) For the purposes of this paragraph—

"family proceedings" has the same meaning as in the Matrimonial and Family Proceedings Act 1984 (c 42) and also includes [any proceedings in the family court and] any other proceedings which are family proceedings for the purposes of the Children Act 1989 (c 41);

"reserved family proceedings" means such category of family proceedings as the Lord Chancellor may, after consulting the President of the Law Society and with the concurrence of the President of the Family Division, by order prescribe;

and any order made under section 27(9) of the Courts and Legal Services Act 1990 (c 41) before the day appointed for the coming into force of this paragraph is to have effect on and after that day as if it were an order made under this sub-paragraph.

Conduct of litigation

2 (1) This paragraph applies to determine whether a person is an exempt person for the purpose of carrying on any activity which constitutes the conduct of litigation in relation to any proceedings (subject to paragraph 7).

(2) The person is exempt if the person—

(a) is not an authorised person in relation to that activity, but

(b) has a right to conduct litigation granted by a court in relation to those proceedings.

(3) The person is exempt if the person—

(a) is not an authorised person in relation to that activity, but

(b) has a right to conduct litigation in relation to those proceedings granted by or under any enactment.

(4) The person is exempt if the person—

(a) is a party to those proceedings, and

(b) would have a right to conduct the litigation, in the person's capacity as such a party, if this Act had not been passed.

(5) The person is an exempt person in relation to any activity which is carried on in or in connection with proceedings on an appeal from the Comptroller-General of Patents, Designs

and Trade Marks to the Patents Court under the Patents Act 1977 (c 37), if the person is a solicitor of the Court of Judicature of Northern Ireland.

Reserved instrument activities

3 (1)   This paragraph applies to determine whether a person is an exempt person for the purpose of carrying on any activity which constitutes reserved instrument activities (subject to paragraph 7).

(2)   The person is exempt if the person prepares the instruments or applications in the course of the person's duty as a public officer.

(3)   The person ("E") is exempt if—

(a)   E is an individual,

(b)   E carries on the activity at the direction and under the supervision of another individual ("P"),

(c)   when E does so, P and E are connected, and

(d)   P is entitled to carry on the activity, otherwise than by virtue of sub-paragraph (10).

(4)   For the purposes of sub-paragraph (3), P and E are connected if—

(a)   P is E's employer,

(b)   P is a fellow employee of E,

(c)   P is a manager or employee of a body which is an authorised person in relation to the activity, and E is also a manager or employee of that body.

(5)   If the person is an accredited person, the person is exempt to the extent that the activity consists of the preparation of any instrument—

(a)   which creates, or which the person believes on reasonable grounds will create, a farm business tenancy (within the meaning of the Agricultural Tenancies Act 1995 (c 8)), or

(b)   which relates to an existing tenancy which is, or which the person believes on reasonable grounds to be, such a tenancy.

(6)   In sub-paragraph (5) "accredited person" means a person who is—

(a)   a Fellow of the Central Association of Agricultural Valuers, or

(b)   a Member or Fellow of the Royal Institution of Chartered Surveyors.

(7)   The person is exempt to the extent that the activity carried on by the person is also a reserved legal activity within sub-paragraph (8) and the person is—

(a)   authorised to carry on that activity (other than under Part 5) by a relevant approved regulator in relation to the activity,

(b)   authorised to carry on that activity by a licence under Part 5, or

(c)   an exempt person in relation to that activity by virtue of paragraph 1 or 2 of this Schedule.

(8)   The activities are—

(a)   the exercise of a right of audience;

(b)   the conduct of litigation.

(9)   The person is exempt if the person is employed merely to engross the instrument or application.

(10) The person is exempt if the person is an individual who carries on the activity otherwise than for, or in expectation of, any fee, gain or reward.

(11) The person is exempt if—

(a) the person is a person qualified to practise as a solicitor in Scotland in accordance with section 4 of the Solicitors (Scotland) Act 1980 (c 46), and

(b) the reserved instrument activities fall within paragraph 5(1)(c) of Schedule 2 (preparation of certain instruments relating to real or personal property or legal proceedings).

Probate activities

4 (1) This paragraph applies to determine whether a person is an exempt person for the purpose of carrying on any activity which constitutes probate activities (subject to paragraph 7).

(2) The person ("E") is an exempt person if—

(a) E is an individual,

(b) E provides the probate activities at the direction and under the supervision of another individual ("P"),

(c) when E does so, P and E are connected, and

(d) P is entitled to carry on the activity, otherwise than by virtue of sub-paragraph (4).

(3) For the purposes of sub-paragraph (2), P and E are connected if—

(a) P is E's employer,

(b) P is a fellow employee of E,

(c) P is a manager or employee of a body which is an authorised person in relation to the activity, and E is also a manager or employee of that body.

(4) The person is exempt if the person is an individual who carries on the activity otherwise than for, or in expectation of, any fee, gain or reward.

Notarial activities

5 (1) This paragraph applies to determine whether a person is an exempt person for the purpose of carrying on any activity which constitutes notarial activities (subject to paragraph 7).

(2) The person is exempt if the person is not an authorised person in relation to that activity under this Act, but is authorised to carry on that activity by or by virtue of any other enactment.

(3) The person is exempt if section 14 of the Public Notaries Act 1801 (c 79) applies to the person, and—

(a) where that section applies by virtue of the person holding or exercising an office or appointment, the person carries on the activity for ecclesiastical purposes;

(b) where that section applies by virtue of the person performing a public duty or service under government, the person carries on the activity in the course of performing that duty or service.

(4) The person is exempt if the person is an individual who carries on the notarial activities otherwise than for or in expectation of a fee, gain or reward.

Administration of oaths

6(1)   This paragraph applies to determine whether a person is an exempt person for the purpose of carrying on any activity which constitutes the administration of oaths (subject to paragraph 7).

(2)   The person is exempt if the person is not an authorised person in relation to that activity under this Act, but is authorised to carry on that activity by or by virtue of any other enactment.

(3)   The person is exempt if the person has a commission under section 1(1) of the Commissioners for Oaths Act 1889 (c 10).

European lawyers

7 A European lawyer (within the meaning of the European Communities (Services of Lawyers) Order 1978 (SI 1978/1910)) is an exempt person for the purposes of carrying on an activity which is a reserved legal activity and which the European lawyer is entitled to carry on by virtue of that order.

Employers etc acting through exempt person

8 (1)   This paragraph applies where—

(a)   a person ("P") carries on an activity ("the relevant activity") which is a reserved legal activity,

(b)   P carries on the relevant activity by virtue of an employee of P ("E") carrying it on in E's capacity as such an employee, and

(c)   E is an exempt person in relation to the relevant activity.

(2)   P is an exempt person in relation to the relevant activity to the extent that P carries on that activity by virtue of E so carrying it on.

(3)   This paragraph does not apply where E—

(a)   carries on the relevant activity at the direction and under the supervision of an authorised person in relation to that activity, and

(b)   is exempt in relation to that activity by virtue of paragraph 1(7), 3(3) or 4(2).

(4)   If P is a body, in this paragraph references to an employee of P include references to a manager of P.

Further exempt persons

9 (1)   The Lord Chancellor may, by order, amend this Schedule so as to provide—

(a)   for persons to be exempt persons in relation to any activity which is a reserved legal activity (including any activity which is a reserved legal activity by virtue of an order under section 24 (extension of reserved legal activities)),

(b)   for persons to cease to be such persons, or

(c)   for the amendment of any provision made in respect of an exempt person.

(2)   The Lord Chancellor may make an order under sub-paragraph (1) only on the recommendation of the Board.

SRA guidance on new regulatory arrangements

Guidance on the SRA Standards and Regulations and SRA Handbook

[See www.sra.org.uk/solicitors/guidance/guidance]

- Accountant's report and the exemption to obtain one (4 July 2019)
- Acting with integrity (23 July 2019)
- Can my business be authorised? (4 July 2019)
- Client care letters (23 July 2019)
- Do I need to operate a client account? (4 July 2019)
- Does my business need to be authorised? (4 July 2019)
- Firm authorisation (4 July 2019)
- Guidance on the SRA's approach to equality, diversity and inclusion (23 July 2019)
- Helping you keep accurate client accounting records (4 July 2019)
- Joint accounts and record keeping (4 July 2019)
- Not for profit sector – summary (23 July 2019)
- Planning for and completing an accountant's report (4 July 2019)
- Preparing to become a sole practitioner or an SRA-regulated freelance solicitor (4 July 2019)
- Registered Foreign Lawyers (23 July 2019)
- Third party managed accounts (4 July 2019)
- Unregulated organisations – Conflict and confidentiality (23 July 2019)
- Unregulated organisations – for employers of SRA-regulated lawyers (23 July 2019)
- Unregulated organsiations – giving information to clients (23 July 2019)
- When do I need a practising certificate? (4 July 2019)

Topic guides

[See www.sra.org.uk/sra/strategy-2017–2020/sub-strategies/enforcement-practice]

- Competence and standard of service (7 February 2019)
- Criminal offences outside of practice (7 February 2019)
- Driving with excess alcohol convictions (7 February 2019)
- SRA Transparency rules (February 2019)
- Use of social media and offensive communications (7 February 2019)

Examples of guidance

[See 'Application to the LSB for the approval of regulatory arrangements' at www.legalservicesboard.org.uk/Projects/statutory_decision_making/pdf/2018/ Annex_B_guidance.pdf]

- Businesses that are not authorised by a legal services regulator and that employ non sra regulated lawyers (August 2018)

- Giving information to clients that are not authorised by a legal services regulator (August 2018)

APPENDIX 22

Sources of help

[Law Society copyright. This material originally appeared as Chapter 19 in *The Solicitor's Handbook 2011*, Andrew Hopper and Gregory Treverton-Jones, published by the Law Society, 2011.]

What do you do when a letter arrives from the Solicitors Regulation Authority or Legal Ombudsman (LeO) with some kind of complaint, or if you are subject to a forensic investigation by the SRA, or if you face disciplinary proceedings? Where do you turn for assistance?

The first point to make is that doing nothing is not an option. Both the LeO and the SRA apply strict time limits; adjudications will be adverse if you do not provide your explanations – your side of the story – for the benefit of the adjudicator or ombudsman. Do not assume that you will be given extensions of time – any request for more time will have to be fully justified and will be considered on the premise that complying with the requirements of the regulator will be a matter of priority. At the other extreme, failing to appear at the Solicitors Disciplinary Tribunal in your own defence may be a terminal mistake.

Specialist assistance

In any matter of complexity or apparent seriousness it is desirable to obtain specialist assistance, and there are relatively few with the requisite expertise.

The ethics helpline formerly operated by the Law Society is now under the jurisdiction of the SRA. It is not known to what extent information received as a result of advice being sought will be treated as information about the person enquiring, for the purposes of regulatory action.

The **Solicitors' Assistance Scheme** is independent of the Law Society and SRA. Established over thirty years ago, it comprises around 80 volunteers from all over England and Wales, most of whom are practising solicitors with a high degree of skill and experience. The scheme members offer a minimum of one hour of pro bono advice and assistance. Any further advice and assistance will be offered at the discretion of the scheme member, or will be by way of a formal retainer.. They can be contacted via email at **help@thesas.org.uk** and via the website **www.thesas.org.uk**.

Professional indemnity insurance no longer provides cover for the costs of defending disciplinary or regulatory proceedings.

LawCare promotes and supports good mental health and wellbeing in the legal community. It provides information and support to anyone in the legal community experiencing mental health and wellbeing problems. The contact number for solicitors, law students and legal executives in England and Wales is 0800 279 6888. Their website is **www.lawcare.org.uk**.

The Law Society's **Practice Advice Service** is a dedicated support-line for solicitors, trainees and employees of law firms. It is staffed by a team of experienced solicitors who deal with enquiries using their own knowledge and a variety of information sources, as well as the experience of other specialists within the Law Society. They are able to assist with enquiries on legal practice in many areas including anti-money laundering; solicitors' costs; multi-party actions; conveyancing; conditional fee agreements; probate; and rights of audience in the Crown Court. Advice by the Practice Advice Service does not constitute legal advice and cannot be relied upon as such. The contact number is 020 7320 5675 and e-mail **practiceadvice@lawsociety.org.uk**.

Financial assistance

Less relevant to the regulatory context, but a potential source of financial assistance for those in need, is **SBA – The Solicitors' Charity**, formerly known as the Solicitors Benevolent Association, which is the principal nationwide charity for solicitors in England and Wales. SBA is run by solicitors, for solicitors and their families, SBA has been working at the heart of the legal profession for over 150 years. It is dedicated to helping solicitors past and present, and their families, in times of need. The Association's telephone number is 020 8675 6440, or see its website: **www.sba.org.uk**.

Index